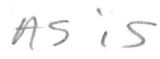

Weiss Ratings' Guide to HMOs and Health Insurers

A Quarterly Compilation of Health Insurance Company Ratings and Analyses

Winter 2003 - 04

Copyright ©2004 by Weiss Ratings, Inc.

P.O. Box 109665
Palm Beach Gardens, FL 33410
(561) 627-3300

www.WeissRatings.com

Our customer hotline is here to serve you.
Don't hesitate to call us at

(800) 289-9222

This line is open 8:30 am - 6:00 p.m. from Monday to Friday,
Eastern Standard Time.

All rights reserved. No portion of this publication may be
reproduced without written permission from the publishers
except by a reviewer or editor who may quote brief passages in
connection with a review or a news story.

ISSN: 1081-2318
ISBN: 1-58773-121-5

Edition No. 36, Winter 2003 - 04

Data Sources: Annual and quarterly statutory statements filed with state insurance commissioners and data provided by the insurance companies being rated. Medicare HMO complaint data were provided by the Centers for Medicare and Medicaid Services: The Center for Health Dispute Resolution, (formerly known as Health Care Financing Administration), and is reprinted here. The National Association of Insurance Commissioners has provided some of the raw data. Any analyses or conclusions are not provided or endorsed by the NAIC.

Date of data analyzed: See Section I

Contents

Introduction

    Welcome 3

    How to Use This Guide 7

    About the Weiss Safety Ratings 11

    Important Warnings and Cautions 21

Section I. Index of Companies 23

Section II. Analysis of Largest Companies 67

Section III. Weiss Recommended Companies 311

Section IV. Weiss Recommended Companies by State 319

Section V. Long-Term Care Insurers 375

Section VI. Medicare Supplement Insurers 381

Section VII. Analysis of Medicare HMO Complaints 389

Section VIII. Rating Upgrades and Downgrades 399

Appendix

    Risk-Adjusted Capital 409

    Long-Term Care Insurance Planner 419

    Recent Industry Failures 425

    State Contact Information 434

    Glossary 435

    Other Weiss Ratings Products 441

Terms and Conditions

This Document is prepared strictly for the confidential use of our customer(s) and those advising our customers. It has been provided to you at your specific request. This Document is not intended for the direct or indirect solicitation of business. Weiss Ratings, Inc. expressly disclaims any warranty of merchantability or fitness for any particular purpose that may exist with respect to this Document.

The information contained herein has been derived from data furnished by official sources that we deem reliable. However, Weiss Ratings, Inc. has not independently verified the data. The data and information contained herein are, therefore, provided "as is" without warranty of any kind. As such, Weiss Ratings, Inc. makes no warranty, express or implied, or representation as to the accuracy, adequacy or completeness of the information relied upon by it in preparing this Document.

Weiss Ratings, Inc. uses the most current information in its possession during the rating review process. However, in the interim, the institution may have disclosed other information which could have a bearing on the opinions expressed in this Document.

Weiss Ratings, Inc. disclaims any and all liability to any person or entity for any loss or damage caused, in whole or in part, by any error (negligent or otherwise) or other circumstances involved in, resulting from or relating to the procurement, compilation, analyses, interpretation, editing, transcribing, publishing and/or dissemination or transmittal of any information contained herein.

The ratings and other opinions contained in this Document must be construed solely as statements of opinion from Weiss Ratings, Inc., and not statements of fact. Each rating or opinion must be weighed solely as a factor in your choice of an institution and should not be construed as a recommendation to buy, sell or otherwise act with respect to the particular product or company involved.

This Document and the information contained herein is copyrighted by Weiss Ratings, Inc. Any copying, displaying, selling, distributing or otherwise delivering of this information or any part of this Document to any other person, without the express written consent of Weiss Ratings, Inc. except by a reviewer or editor who may quote brief passages in connection with a review or a news story, is prohibited.

Message To Insurers

All HMO data received on or before May 31, 2003 have been considered or incorporated into this edition of the Directory. If you have not yet completed our survey form, call Sandy Fenton at Weiss Ratings, Inc., (561) 627-3300. If there are particular circumstances which you believe could affect your rating, please use the survey sheets we have sent you or send a written request to bring it to our attention. If warranted, we will make every effort to incorporate the changes in our next edition.

Welcome to Weiss Ratings'
Guide to HMOs and Health Insurers

Most people automatically assume their insurance company will survive, year after year. However, prudent consumers and professionals realize that in this world of shifting risks, the solvency of insurance companies can't be taken for granted.

If you are looking for accurate, unbiased ratings and data to help you choose health insurance for yourself, your family, your company, or your clients, Weiss Ratings' *Guide to HMOs and Health Insurers* gives you precisely what you need.

In fact, it's the only source that currently provides ratings and analyses on over 1,200 health insurers, including all Blue Cross/Blue Shield plans and over 500 health maintenance organizations.

Weiss Ratings' Mission Statement

Weiss Ratings' mission is to empower consumers, business professionals, and institutions with high quality advisory information for selecting or monitoring a financial services company or financial investment.

In doing so, Weiss Ratings will adhere to the highest ethical standards by maintaining our independent, unbiased outlook and approach to advising our customers.

Why rely on Weiss?

For more than 30 years, Weiss Ratings, Inc. has been recognized as the insurance industry's leading consumer advocate. Our mission is to provide fair, objective ratings to help professionals and consumers alike make educated purchasing decisions.

At Weiss, integrity is number one. Weiss never takes a penny from insurance companies for its ratings. And, we publish the Weiss Safety Ratings without regard for insurers' preferences. However, other rating agencies like A.M. Best, Fitch, Moody's, and Standard & Poor's are paid by insurance companies for their ratings and may even suppress unfavorable ratings at an insurer's request.

Weiss' ratings are more frequently reviewed and updated than any other ratings. You can be sure that the information you receive is accurate and current – providing you with advance warning of financial vulnerability early enough to do something about it.

Other rating agencies focus primarily on a company's current claims paying ability and consider only mild economic adversity. Weiss also considers these issues, but in addition, our analysis covers a company's ability to deal with severe economic adversity and a sharp increase in claims.

Our use of more rigorous standards stems from the viewpoint that an insurance company's obligations to its policyholders should not depend on favorable business conditions. An insurer must be able to honor its policy commitments in bad times as well as good.

Weiss' rating scale, from A to F, is easy to understand. Only a few outstanding companies receive an A (Excellent) rating, although there are many to choose from within the B (Good) category. An even larger group falls into the broad average range which receives C (Fair) ratings. Companies that demonstrate marked vulnerabilities receive either D (Weak) or E (Very Weak) ratings.

The U.S. Government agrees — Weiss' ratings are the best

In a recent study, the United States General Accounting Office (GAO) concluded that Weiss was the most accurate of all five insurance rating agencies.

According to the GAO study, "only Weiss rated more than half of all life/health insurers." Weiss outperformed A.M. Best 3 to 1 in warning of coming financial troubles – with Weiss' warning coming an average of eight months earlier than Best's!

You can be confident that the same spirit of independence and consumer advocacy that has produced these excellent results will continue in the months and years ahead.

Thank you for your trust and purchase of this Guide. If you have any comments, or wish to review other products from Weiss Ratings, please call 1-800-289-9222, visit www.WeissRatings.com or send the order form at the back of this publication to Weiss Ratings, Inc., PO Box 109665, Palm Beach Gardens, FL 33410. We look forward to hearing from you.

How Others View Weiss Ratings

"The only agency to rate [most] insurers"

"Weiss was the only agency to rate more than half of all insurers....Weiss rated 1,449 – over 70 percent – of the universe we identified as compared to 795 rated by Best – about 40 percent. The other three raters covered 12 percent or less each."

U.S. General Accounting Office (GAO)

"The leader in identifying vulnerable insurance companies"

"Weiss ... was deemed (by the GAO) the leader in identifying vulnerable insurance companies. For example, on 23 occasions during the period studied ...Weiss was the first to spot problems, compared with just seven for Best, which has been in the rating business 100 years. On average, the GAO found, Weiss was 243 days ahead of Best in spotting financially weak insurers."

Barron's

"Free of any possible conflict of interest"

"Only a few organizations offer any financial ratings on healthcare companies, and most that do are actually paid fees as high as $35,000 by the companies themselves. In return, the companies usually acquire the right to prevent public dissemination of unfavorable ratings, which turns the process into something not unlike the issuance of corporate press releases."

Esquire

"One of the industry's few tough critics"

"Some industry experts [say]...the older ratings agencies are far too close to the companies they review and... Mr. Weiss is one of the industry's few tough critics."

The New York Times

"So good...[you] need look no further"

"Weiss' record of spotting weak insurers is so good compared with that of his competitors...insurance buyers need look no further."

Worth

How to Use This Guide

The purpose of the *Guide to HMOs and Health Insurers* is to provide policyholders and prospective policy purchasers with a reliable source of insurance company ratings and analyses on a timely basis. We realize that the financial safety of an insurer is an important factor to consider when making the decision to purchase a policy or change companies. The ratings and analyses in this Guide can make that evaluation easier when you are considering:

- medical reimbursement insurance
- managed health care (PPOs and HMOs)
- disability income
- long-term care (nursing home) insurance
- dental insurance

This Guide includes ratings for health insurers such as commercial for-profit insurers, mutual insurers, Blue Cross/Blue Shield plans, and for-profit and not-for-profit Health Maintenance Organizations (HMOs). This is the only source of ratings on many of these companies.

In addition, many companies that offer health insurance also offer life, property or liability insurance. If you are shopping for any of those types of coverage, please refer to either our *Guide to Life, Health & Annuity Insurers* or our *Guide to Property and Casualty Insurers.*

The rating for a particular company indicates our opinion regarding that company's ability to meet its commitments to the policyholder – not only under current economic conditions, but also during a declining economy or in the event of a sharp increase in claims. Such an increase in claims and related expenses may be triggered by any number of occurrences including rising medical costs, malpractice lawsuits, out-of-control administrative expenses, or the unexpected spread of a disease such as AIDS. The safest companies, however, should be prepared to deal with harsh and unforeseen circumstances.

To use this Guide most effectively, we recommend you follow the steps outlined below:

Step 1 To ensure you evaluate the correct company, verify the company's exact name and state of domicile as it was given to you or appears on your policy. Many companies have similar names but are not related to one another, so you want to make sure the company you look up is really the one you are interested in evaluating.

Step 2 Turn to Section I, the Index of Companies, and locate the company you are evaluating. This section contains all health insurance companies analyzed by Weiss including those that did not receive a Weiss Safety Rating. It is sorted alphabetically by the name of the company and shows the state of domicile following the name for additional verification.

Step 3 Once you have located your specific company, the first column after the state of domicile shows its Weiss Safety Rating. Turn to *About the Weiss Safety Ratings* on page 11 for information about what this rating means. If the rating has changed since the last issue of this Guide, a downgrade will be indicated with a down triangle ▼ to the left of the company name; an upgrade will be indicated with an up triangle ▲.

Step 4 Following the Weiss Safety Rating is some additional information about the company such as its type, size and capital level. You can turn to the Section I introduction beginning on page 25 to see what each of these factors measures.

How to Use This Guide

Step 5 Some insurers have a bullet • following the company type in Section I. This means that more detailed information about the company is available in Section II.

If the company you are evaluating is identified with a bullet, turn to Section II, the Analysis of Largest Companies, and locate it there (otherwise skip to step 9). Section II contains all HMOs and Blue Cross/Blue Shield plans plus the largest health insurers rated by Weiss, regardless of rating. It too is sorted alphabetically by the name of the company.

Step 6 Once you have identified your company in Section II, you will find its Weiss Safety Rating and a description of the rating immediately to the right of the company name. Then, below the company name is a description of the various rating factors that were considered in assigning the company's rating. These factors and the information below them are designed to give you a better feel for the company and its strengths and weaknesses. See the Section II introduction beginning on page 69 to get a better understanding of what each of these factors means.

Step 7 To the right, you will find a five-year summary of the company's Weiss Safety Rating, capitalization and income. Look for positive or negative trends in these data. Below the five-year summary, we have included a graphic illustration of the most crucial factor or factors impacting the company's rating. Again, the Section II introduction provides an overview of the content of each graph or table.

Step 8 If the company you are evaluating is a Medicare HMO, you can also look it up in Section VII to get some idea of the quality of service being offered. Here you can see the number of complaints against a company that have reached the federal review level based on the most recent data available.

Step 9 If you are interested in long-term care insurance, you can turn to Section V and get a listing of long-term care insurers. To compare long-term care policies see the Long-Term Care Insurance Planner on page 419 in the Appendix.

Step 10 If the company you are evaluating is not highly rated and you want to find an insurer with a higher rating, turn to the page in Section IV that has your state's name at the top. This section contains those Weiss Recommended Companies (rating of A+, A, A- or B+) that are licensed to underwrite health insurance in your state, sorted by rating. From here you can select a company and then refer back to Sections I and II to analyze it.

Step 11 If you decide that you would like to contact one of the Weiss Recommended Companies about obtaining a policy or for additional information, refer to Section III where you will find all of the Weiss recommended companies listed alphabetically by name. Following each company's name is its address and phone number to assist you in making contact.

Step 12 Many consumers have reported to us the difficulties they have encountered in finding a Weiss Recommended Company that offers the best pricing and benefits. Therefore, when considering medical reimbursement or managed care coverage, you may want to consider other companies that have received a good (B or B-) rating even though they did not make the Weiss Recommended List. However, for long-term policies such as nursing home care or disability income, we recommend sticking to companies with a rating of B+ or higher.

Step 13 In order to use the Weiss Safety Ratings most effectively, we strongly recommend you consult the Important Warnings and Cautions listed on page 21. These are more than just "standard disclaimers." They are very important factors you should be aware of before using this Guide. If you have any questions regarding the precise meaning of specific terms used in the Guide, refer to the Glossary beginning on page 435.

Step 14 Make sure you stay up to date with the latest information available since the publication of this Guide. For information on how to set up a rating change notification service, acquire follow-up reports, or receive a more in-depth analysis of an individual company, visit www.WeissRatings.com or call 1-800-289-9222.

About the Weiss Safety Ratings

The Weiss Safety Ratings represent a completely independent, unbiased opinion of an insurance company's financial safety – now, and in the future. The ratings are derived, for the most part, from annual and quarterly financial statements obtained from state insurance commissioners. These data are supplemented by information that we request from the insurance companies themselves. Although we seek to maintain an open line of communication with the companies being rated, we do not grant them the right to influence the ratings or stop their publication.

The Weiss Safety Ratings are assigned by our analysts based on a complex analysis of hundreds of factors that are synthesized into a series of indexes: risk-adjusted capital, capitalization (L&H and HMDI companies only), reserve adequacy (P&C companies only), profitability, investment safety (L&H and HMDI companies only), liquidity, and stability. These indexes are then used to arrive at a letter grade rating. A good rating requires consistency across all indexes. A weak score on any one index can result in a low rating, as insolvency can be caused by any one of a number of factors, such as inadequate capital, unpredictable claims experience, poor liquidity, speculative investments, or operating losses.

Following is an outline of the primary components of the Weiss Safety Rating.

Risk-Adjusted Capital Indexes gauge capital adequacy in terms of each insurer's risk profile under both *moderate* and *severe* loss scenarios. For more information please see Section I and page 409 in the Appendix.

Capitalization Index combines the two Risk-Adjusted Capital ratios with a leverage test that examines pricing risk.

Reserve Adequacy Index measures the adequacy of the company's reserves and its ability to accurately anticipate the level of claims it will receive.

Profitability Index measures the soundness of the company's operations and the contribution of profits to the company's financial strength.

Investment Safety Index measures the exposure of the company's investment portfolio to loss of principal and /or income due to default and market risks.

Liquidity Index values a company's ability to raise the necessary cash to settle claims. We model various cash flow scenarios, applying liquidity tests to determine how the company might fare in the event of an unexpected spike in claims and/or a run on policy surrenders.

Stability Index integrates a number of sub-factors that affect consistency (or lack thereof) in maintaining financial strength over time. These sub-factors will vary depending on the type of insurance company being evaluated but may include such things as 1) risk diversification in terms of company and group size, number of policies in force, patient and provider enrollment, use of reinsurance; 2) deterioration of operations as reported in critical asset, liability, income and expense items; 3) years in operation; 4) former problem areas where, despite recent improvement, the company has yet to establish a record of stable performance over a suitable period of time; 5) a substantial shift in the company's operations; 6) potential instabilities such as reinsurance quality, asset/liability matching, and source of capital; and 7) relationships with holding companies and affiliates.

Each of these indexes is measured according to the following range of values.

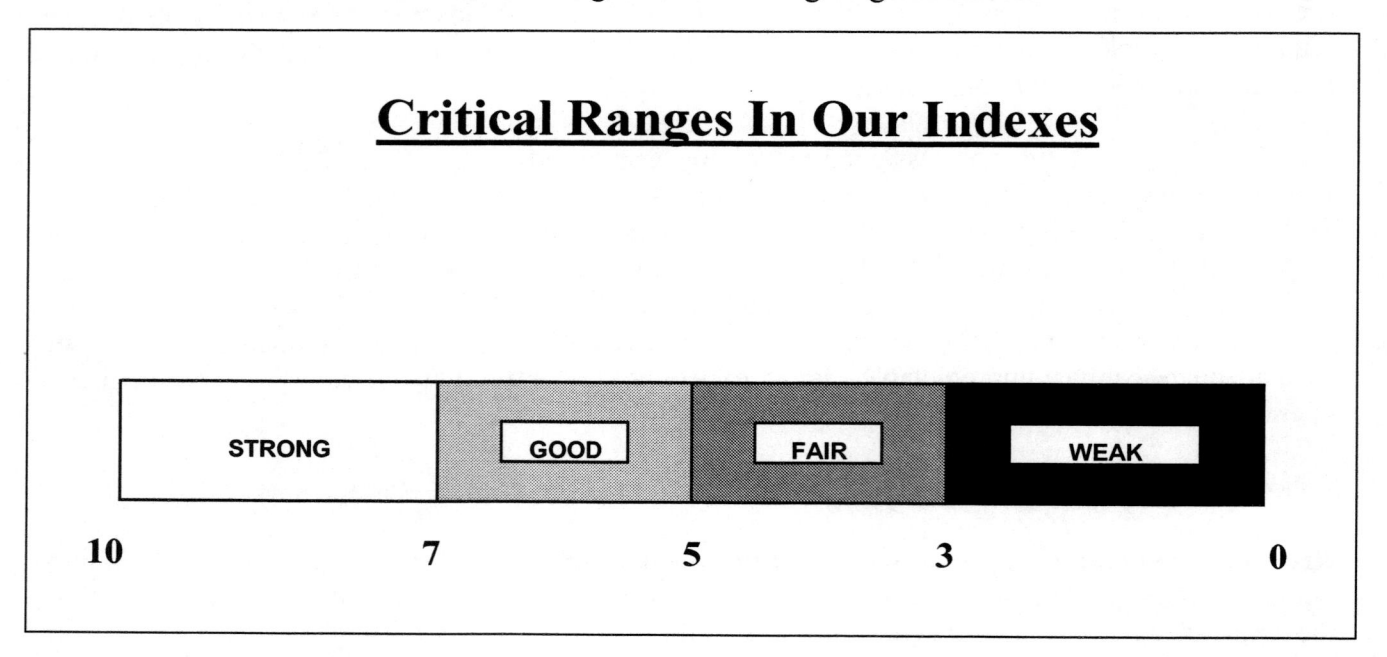

Critical Ranges In Our Indexes

STRONG	GOOD	FAIR	WEAK
10	7	5	3	0

What Our Ratings Mean

A   **Excellent.** The company offers excellent financial security. It has maintained a conservative stance in its investment strategies, business operations and underwriting commitments. While the financial position of any company is subject to change, we believe that this company has the resources necessary to deal with severe economic conditions.

B   **Good.** The company offers good financial security and has the resources to deal with a variety of adverse economic conditions. It comfortably exceeds the minimum levels for all of our rating criteria, and is likely to remain healthy for the near future. However, in the event of a *severe* recession or major financial crisis, we feel that this assessment should be reviewed to make sure that the firm is still maintaining adequate financial strength.

C   **Fair.** The company offers fair financial security and is currently stable. But during an economic downturn or other financial pressures, we feel it may encounter difficulties in maintaining its financial stability.

D   **Weak.** The company currently demonstrates what we consider to be significant weaknesses which could negatively impact policyholders. In an unfavorable economic environment, these weaknesses could be magnified.

E   **Very Weak.** The company currently demonstrates what we consider to be significant weaknesses and has also failed some of the basic tests that we use to identify fiscal stability. Therefore, even in a favorable economic environment, it is our opinion that policyholders could incur significant risks.

F   **Failed.** The company has failed and is either 1) under supervision of state insurance commissioners; 2) is in the process of liquidation; or 3) has voluntarily dissolved after disciplinary or other regulatory action by state insurance commissioners.

+   **The plus sign** is an indication that the company is at the upper end of the letter grade rating.

-   **The minus sign** is an indication that the company is at the lower end of the letter grade rating.

U   **Unrated Companies.** The company is unrated for one or more of the following reasons: 1) total assets are less than $1 million; 2) premium income for the current year is less than $100,000; 3) the company functions almost exclusively as a holding company rather than as an underwriter; or 4) we do not have enough information to reliably issue a rating.

How Our Ratings Differ From Those of Other Services

The Weiss Safety Ratings are conservative and consumer oriented. We use tougher standards than other rating agencies because our system is specifically designed to inform risk-averse consumers about the financial strength of HMOs and other health insurers.

Our rating scale (A to F) is easy to understand by the general public. Users can intuitively understand that an A+ rating is at the top of the scale rather than in the middle like some of the other rating agencies.

Weiss is currently the only rating agency to monitor the financial condition of the majority of HMOs in the U.S. This industry segment of managed care providers has grown into a major force in health insurance, and we feel that consumers need to be aware of the financial safety different HMOs offer.

Other rating agencies give top ratings more generously so that most companies receive excellent ratings.

More importantly, other rating agencies focus primarily on a company's *current* claims paying ability or consider only relatively mild economic adversity. We also consider these scenarios but extend our analysis to cover a company's ability to deal with severe economic adversity and potential liquidity problems. This stems from the viewpoint that an insurance company's obligations to its policyholders should not be contingent upon a healthy economy. The company must be capable of honoring its policy commitments in bad times as well.

Looking at the insurance industry as a whole, we note that several major rating firms have poor historical track records in identifying troubled companies. The 1980s saw a persistent decline in capital ratios, increased holdings of risky investments in the life and health industry as well as recurring long-term claims liabilities in the property and casualty industry. Despite these clear signs that insolvency risk was rising, other rating firms failed to downgrade at-risk insurance companies. Instead, they often rated companies by shades of excellence, understating the gravity of potential problems.

They have not issued clear warnings that the ordinary consumer can understand. Few, if any, companies receive "weak" or "poor" ratings. Surely, weak companies do exist. However, the other rating agencies apparently do not view themselves as consumer advocates with the responsibility of warning the public about the risks involved in doing business with such companies.

Additionally, these firms will at times agree *not* to issue a rating if a company denies them permission to do so. In short, too often insurance rating agencies work hand-in-glove with the companies they rate.

At Weiss Ratings, although we seek to maintain good relationships with the firms, we owe our primary obligation to the consumer, not the industry. We reserve the right to rate companies based on publicly-available data and make the necessary conservative assumptions when companies choose not to provide the additional data we request.

About the Weiss Safety Ratings

Weiss [a]	Best [a,b]	S&P [c]	Moody's	Fitch [d]
A+, A, A-	A++, A+	AAA	Aaa	AAA
B+, B, B-	A, A-	AA+, AA AA-	Aa1, Aa2, Aa3	AA+, AA, AA-
C+, C, C-	B++, B+,	A+, A, A-, BBB+, BBB, BBB-	A1, A2, A3, Baa1, Baa2, Baa3	A+, A, A-, BBB+, BBB, BBB-
D+, D, D-	B, B- C++, C+, C, C-	BB+, BB, BB-, B+, B, B-	Ba1, Ba2, Ba3, B1, B2, B3	BB+, BB, BB-, B+, B, B-
E+, E, E F	D E, F	CCC R	Caa, Ca, C	CCC+, CCC, CCC- DD

[a] Weiss and Best use additional symbols to designate that they recognize an insurer's existence but do not provide a rating. These symbols are not included in this table.

[b] Best added the A++, B++ and C++ ratings in 1992. In 1994, Best classified its ratings into "secure" and "vulnerable" categories, changed the definition of its "B" and "B-" ratings from "good" to "adequate" and assigned these ratings to the "vulnerable" category. This table contains GAO's assignment of Best's ratings to bands based on our interpretation of their rating descriptions prior to 1994.

[c] S&P discontinued CCC "+" and "-" signs, CC, C and D ratings and added the R rating in 1992.
Source: GAO.

[d] Duff & Phelps Credit Rating Co. merged with Fitch IBCA in 2000, and minor changes were made to the rating scale at that time. These changes were not reflected in the GAO's 1994 study, but *are* reflected in the chart.

Weiss Ratings Accuracy

The true yardstick for measuring a rating agency is "How often were they right?" Or more specifically for an insurance company solvency or claims paying ability rating, "How did they rate those companies that failed?" As you can see from the table below (updated through January 9, 2004), the track record for Weiss Ratings is the best you will find anywhere.

Weiss rates more companies than any other rating agency, and we make sure that only the safest companies receive our A (excellent) or B (good) ratings. Unlike the other rating agencies, Weiss does not allow the companies we rate to suppress their ratings. Instead, we publish all ratings, good or bad. That is how Weiss earned its reputation as the most accurate, reliable, and conservative rating agency around.

How Did Weiss and Best Rate the Insurance Companies that Failed?

Analyses of Insurance Company Failures from 1990 through 2003	At Date of Failure Weiss	At Date of Failure Best	12 Months Prior to Failure Weiss	12 Months Prior to Failure Best
Suppressed Publication of the Rating	0	17	0	14
Did Not Rate a Failed Insurer Rated by the Other	10	212	13	181
Assigned an Excellent* Rating	0	1	1	2
Assigned a Good* Rating	0	2	3	43

* "Excellent" and "Good" correspond to Weiss' A and B ratings, respectively. In keeping with the GAO study, "Excellent" corresponds to Best's A++ and A+ (superior) ratings, and "Good" relates to Best's A and A- (excellent) ratings.

Weiss Provides the Most Advance Warning of Trouble

Warnings don't do you any good if they come after it's too late to act. And as this next table of the largest insurance company failures shows (taken from page 26 of the GAO's *Insurance Ratings* study), Weiss issues its warnings well *before* a company fails or is taken over by regulators.

When Were "Vulnerable" Ratings Assigned to Large Insurers?

Number of Days Before or After Failure

	Weiss	Best
Mutual Benefit	40 days before	3 days after
Superior National Ins. Co	2276 days before	38 days after
Executive Life of CA	379 days before	6 days before
Monarch	162 days before	never
First Capital	617 days before	5 days after
Executive Life of NY	372 days before	1 day after
Fidelity Bankers	308 days before	2 days after
Kentucky Central	621 days before	3 days after
Fidelity Mutual	134 days before	5 days after
Investor's Equity	1,152 days before	4 days after
Electric Mutual Liability	671 days before	50 days after
Home Insurance Co	113 days before	375 days after

Source: GAO *Insurance Ratings* study; updated for more recent failures

Because most insurance policies represent significant commitments, you need to know about a company's deteriorating financial condition as soon as possible. At Weiss, we feel it's important to get the word out while you still have time to protect your investments. That way you can take steps to avoid the financial losses and headaches associated with doing business with a failed insurer.

Page 23 of the GAO's *Insurance Ratings* study says "Weiss was first (to identify financially-impaired insurers) in 23 cases, Best in 7 cases – about a three to one ratio." And looking at figures updated through January 9, 2004, Weiss' ratings predictability is still superior.

Weiss and Best: Who Assigned "Vulnerable" First?

Analyses of Financially Impaired Life Insurance Companies	In the GAO Study	Updated through 2003
Weiss was First to Downgrade to a "Vulnerable" Rating	23	102
A.M. Best was First to Downgrade to a "Vulnerable" Rating	7	34

Source: GAO *Insurance Ratings* study; updated for more recent failures
"Vulnerable" as defined by the GAO means:
  Weiss: rated D (weak); E (very weak); or, F (failed)
  Best: rated C++, C+ (Marginal); C, C- (Weak); D (Poor); E (State Supervision); F (In liquidation); Beginning in 1994, Best also considers B, B- (Fair) as vulnerable.

Rate of Insurance Company Failures

Weiss Ratings provides quarterly safety ratings for thousands of insurance companies each year. Weiss strives for fairness and objectivity in its ratings and analyses, ensuring that each company receives the rating that most accurately depicts its current financial status, and more importantly, its ability to deal with severe economic adversity and a sharp increase in claims. Weiss has every confidence that its financial safety ratings provide an accurate representation of a company's stability.

In order for these ratings to be of any true value, it is important that they prove accurate over time. One way to determine the accuracy of a rating is to examine those insurance companies that have failed, and their respective Weiss Safety Ratings. A high percentage of failed companies with "A" ratings would indicate that Weiss is not being conservative enough with its "secure" ratings, while conversely, a low percentage of failures with "vulnerable" ratings would show that Weiss is overly conservative.

Over the past 14 years (1989–2002) Weiss has rated 290 insurance companies that subsequently failed. The chart below shows the number of failed companies in each rating category, the average number of companies rated in each category per year, and the percentage of annual failures for each letter grade.

	Safety Rating	Number of Failed Companies	Average Number of Companies Rated per year	Percentage of Failed companies per year (by ratings category)*
Secure	A	0	133	0.00%
	B	0	970	0.00%
	C	45	1468	0.22%
Vulnerable	D	132	661	1.43%
	E	113	147	5.51%

A=Excellent, B=Good, C=Fair, D=Weak, E=Very Weak

Of the 2,571 companies receiving Secure ratings, less than quarter a percent of them failed over the 14 year period. On the other hand, almost seven percent of the 808 companies rated as Vulnerable failed annually.

When considering a Weiss safety rating, one can be sure that they are getting the most fair, objective, and accurate financial rating available anywhere.

*Percentage of Failed companies per year = (Number of Failed Companies) / [(Average Number of Companies Rated per year) x (years in study)]

What Does Average Mean?

At Weiss, we consider the words average and fair to mean just that – average and fair. So when we assign our ratings to insurers, a large percentage of companies receive an average C rating. That way, you can be sure that a company receiving Weiss' B or A rating is truly above average. Likewise, you can feel confident that companies with D or E ratings are truly below average.

Percentage of HMOs and Health Insurers in Each Rating Category

2003 Weiss Ratings Distribution

Rating	Description	Percentage
E	Very Weak	7.0%
D	Weak	15.3%
C	Fair	36.6%
B	Good	37.6%
A	Excellent	3.5%

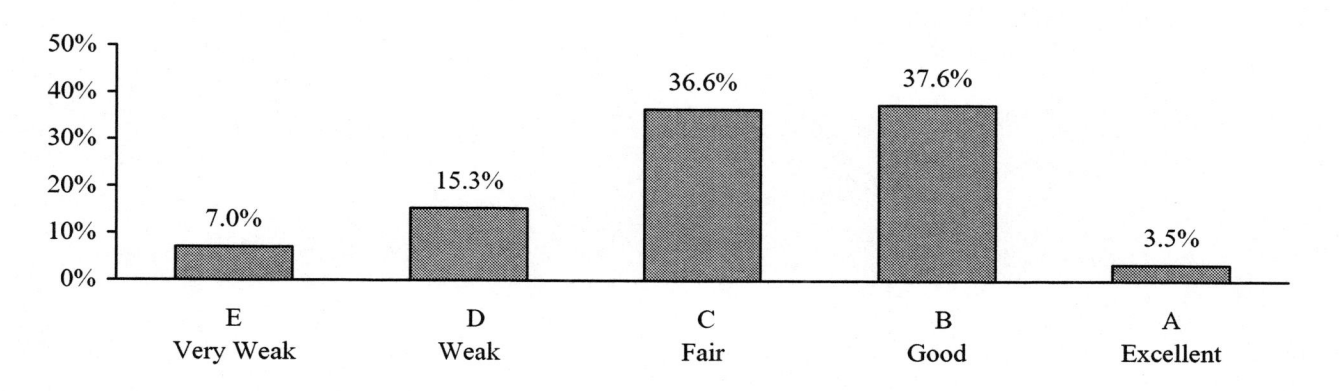

If you contrast the distribution of ratings assigned by Weiss to that of A.M. Best (see the chart below), it becomes apparent that Best considers over 50% of the insurance industry to be above average. Logically, this does not make sense. But more importantly, it does not allow you, the customer, to distinguish between those companies that are truly exceptional and those that are only mediocre.

Percentage of Insurers in Each Rating Category

2002 A.M. Best Ratings Distribution

Rating	Description	Percentage
D	Poor	0.9%
B, B-, C++, C+, C, C-	Fair to Weak	35.0%
B++, B+	Very Good	19.8%
A, A-	Excellent	42.8%
A++, A+	Superior	1.5%

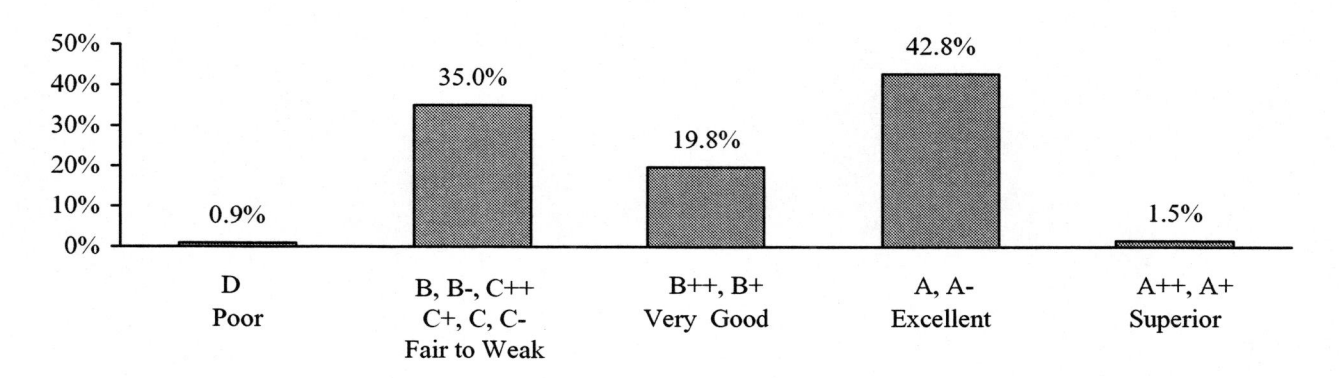

Comparison of ratings categories is based upon that established by the GAO with subsequent modifications by A.M. Best.

Important Warnings and Cautions

1. **A rating alone cannot tell the whole story.** Please read the explanatory information contained here, in the section introductions and in the appendix. It is provided in order to give you an understanding of our rating philosophy as well as to paint a more complete picture of how we arrive at our opinion of a company's strengths and weaknesses.

2. **Safety ratings shown in this directory were current as of the publication date.** In the meantime, the rating may have been updated based on more recent data. Weiss offers a notification service for ratings changes on companies that you specifiy. For more information call 1-800-289-9222, visit www.WeissRatings.com or see the last page of this publication for details.

3. **When deciding to buy or surrender a specific insurance policy, your decision must be based on a wide variety of factors in addition to the Weiss Safety Rating.** These include the cost and benefits of a policy, to what degree it meets your long-term planning needs, how the cost/benefits will change over the years, and what other choices are available to you, given your current age, health, and financial circumstances.

4. **The Weiss Safety Ratings represent our opinion of a company's insolvency risk.** As such, a high rating means we feel that the company has less chance of running into financial difficulties. A high rating is not a guarantee of solvency nor is a low rating a prediction of insolvency. The Weiss Safety Ratings are not deemed to be a recommendation concerning the purchase or sale of the securities of any insurance company that is publicly owned.

5. **All firms that have the same Weiss Safety Rating should be considered to be essentially equal in safety.** This is true regardless of any differences in the underlying numbers which might appear to indicate greater strengths. The Weiss Safety Rating already takes into account a number of lesser factors which, due to space limitations, cannot be included in this publication.

6. **A good rating requires consistency.** If a company is excellent on four indicators and fair on one, the company may receive a fair rating. This requirement is necessary due to the fact that fiscal problems can arise from any *one* of several causes including speculative investments, inadequate capital resources, or operating losses.

7. **Our rating standards are more conservative than those used by other agencies.** We believe that no one can predict with certainty the economic environment of the near or long-term future. Rather, we assume that various scenarios – from the extremes of double-digit inflation to a severe recession – are within the range of reasonable possibilities over the next one or two decades. To achieve a top rating according to our standards, a company must be adequately prepared for the worst-case reasonable scenario, without impairing its current operations.

8. **We are an independent rating agency and do not depend on the cooperation of the companies we rate**. Our data are derived, for the most part, from annual and quarterly financial statements that we obtain from state insurance commissioners. This is supplemented by information that we request from the insurance companies themselves. We also attempt to confirm the accuracy of any electronic data being used by sending a data verification sheet to the companies before assigning a rating. When a company fails to respond to our requests for additional data and data verification, we base our opinion on the unverified data as obtained from the state insurance commissioners. Although we seek to maintain an open line of

communication with the companies, we do not grant them the right to stop or influence publication of the ratings. This policy stems from the fact that this Guide is designed for the protection of the consumer.

9. **The ratios and indexes contained in this edition of the *Guide to HMOs and Health Insurers* reflect updates to previous editions.** Therefore, comparisons of indexes or ratios between this edition and previous editions may not be appropriate.

10. **This Guide covers some property and casualty companies that offer health insurance. In addition, it contains some companies which primarily sell life insurance or annuities, but which also market health policies.** Please consult Weiss Ratings' *Guide to Property & Casualty Insurers* for ratings and analyses on property and casualty insurers. For ratings on life insurers or annuity providers, please consult Weiss Ratings' *Guide to Life, Health and Annuity Insurers*.

11. **There are many companies with similar sounding names, despite no affiliation whatsoever.** Therefore, it is important that you have the exact name and state of domicile before you begin to research the company in this Guide.

12. **Affiliated companies do not automatically receive the same rating.** We recognize that a troubled company may expect financial support from its parent or affiliates. The Weiss Safety Ratings reflect our opinion of the measure of support that may become available to a subsidiary insurer, if the subsidiary were to experience serious financial difficulties. In the case of a strong parent and a weaker subsidiary, the affiliate relationship will generally result in a higher rating for the subsidiary than it would have on a stand-alone basis. Seldom, however, would the rating be brought up to the level of the parent.

    This treatment is appropriate because we do not assume the parent would have either the resources or the will to "bail out" a troubled subsidiary during a severe economic crisis. Even when there is a binding legal obligation for a parent corporation to honor the policy obligations of its subsidiary insurers, the possibility exists that the subsidiary could be sold and lose its parental support. Therefore, it is quite common for one affiliate to have a higher rating than another. This is another reason why it is especially important that you have the precise name of the company you are evaluating.

13. **This publication does not include Canadian companies.** Therefore, if the company you are evaluating is based in Canada, it may not be listed here, regardless of whether it is a strong or weak company. At the same time, do not be confused by a domestic insurer with a name which is the same as – or similar to – that of a Canada-based company. Even if there is an affiliation between the two, we have evaluated the U.S. insurer based on its own merits.

Section I

Index of Companies

An analysis of 1,772 rated and unrated

U.S. HMOs and Health Insurers

Companies are listed in alphabetical order.

Section I Contents

This section contains the information about company type, size and capital level for all rated and unrated health insurers analyzed by Weiss.

1. **Insurance Company Name** — The legally-registered name, which can sometimes differ from the name that the company uses for advertising. If you cannot find the company you are interested in, or if you have any doubts regarding the precise name, verify the information with the company before looking the name up in this Guide. Also, determine the domicile state for confirmation. (See column 2.)

2. **Domicile State** — The state which has primary regulatory responsibility for the company. It may differ from the location of the company's corporate headquarters. You do not have to be living in the domicile state to purchase insurance from this firm, provided it is licensed to do business in your state.

    Also use this column to confirm that you have located the correct company. It is possible for two unrelated companies to have the same name if they are domiciled in different states.

3. **Weiss Safety Rating** — Our rating is measured on a scale from A to F and considers a wide range of factors. Please see page 13 for specific descriptions of each letter grade. Also, refer to page 14 for information on how our ratings differ from those of other rating agencies. Most important, when using this rating, please be sure to consider the warnings beginning on page 21 regarding the ratings' limitations and the underlying assumptions.

4. **Company Type** — Regulatory designation under which the company files its financial statements. The only exception is HMOs which now file under the Health designation but for whom we chose to identify separately. L&H is Life and Health, P&C is Property and Casualty, HMO is Health Maintenance Organization and HLTH (Health) is the former HMDI (Hospital, Medical, Dental Indemnity). Preferred Provider Organizations (PPOs) are also noted here.

5. **Data Date** — The latest quarter-end for which we have received the company's financial statement.

6. **Total Assets** — All assets admitted by state insurance regulators in millions of dollars as of the most recent quarter end. This includes investments and current business assets such as receivables from agents, reinsurers and subscribers.

    The overall size is an important factor which affects the ability of a company to manage risk. Mortality, morbidity (sickness) and investment risks can be more effectively diversified by large companies. Because the insurance business is based on probability, the number of policies must be large enough so that actuarial statistics are valid. The larger the number of policyholders, the more reliable the actuarial projections will be. A large company with a correspondingly large policy base can spread its risk and minimize the effects of claims experience that exceeds actuarial expectations.

www.WeissRatings.com

7. **Total Premiums** The amount of insurance premiums received from policyholders as of the most recent year end. If the company issues life insurance or property insurance, those premiums are included in this figure as well.

Generally speaking, companies with large premium volume generally have more predictable claims experience.

8. **Health Premiums** The amount of insurance premiums received from policyholders for health policies only as of the most recent year end.

Compare this figure with Total Premiums in the previous column to see how much of the company's business relates to health coverage. For HMOs and HMDI companies, total premiums and health premiums are equal since these companies offer no other type of insurance.

9. **Capital and Surplus** The company's statutory net worth in millions of dollars as of the most recent quarter end. Consumers may wish to limit the size of any policy so that the policyholder's maximum benefits do not exceed approximately 1% of the company's capital and surplus. For example, when buying a policy from a company with capital and surplus of $10,000,000, the 1% limit would be $100,000. (When performing this calculation, do not forget that figures in this column are expressed in millions of dollars.)

Critical Ranges In Our Ratios

Indicators	Strong	Good	Fair	Weak
Risk-Adjusted Capital Ratio #1	—	1.0 or more	0.75 - 0.99	0.74 or less
Risk-Adjusted Capital Ratio #2	1.0 or more	0.75 - 0.99	0.5 - 0.74	0.49 or less

10. **Risk-Adjusted Capital Ratio #1** This ratio examines the adequacy of the company's capital base and whether the company has sufficient capital resources to cover potential losses which might occur in an average recession or other moderate loss scenario. Specifically, the figure cited in this column answers the question: For every dollar of capital that we feel would be needed, how many dollars in capital resources does the company actually have? (See the table above for the levels which we believe are critical.) You may find that some companies have unusually high levels of capital. This often reflects special circumstances related to the small size or unusual operations of the company.

11. **Risk-Adjusted Capital Ratio #2** This is similar to item 10. But in this case, the question relates to whether the company has enough capital cushion to withstand a *severe* recession or other severe loss scenario. For more details on risk-adjusted capital, see the Appendix on page 409.

Winter 2003 - 04
I. Index of Companies

INSURANCE COMPANY NAME	DOM. STATE	WEISS SAFETY RATING	COMPANY TYPE	DATA DATE	TOTAL ASSETS ($MIL)	TOTAL PREMIUMS ($MIL)	HEALTH PREMIUMS ($MIL)	CAPITAL & SURPLUS ($MIL)	RISK ADJUSTED CAPITAL RATIO 1	RATIO 2
AAA LIFE INS CO	MI	C	L&H	2q 2003	329.5	292.1	20.5	28.6	1.70	0.97
ACACIA LIFE INS CO	DC	B	L&H	2q 2003	1,035.6	66.0	0.1	160.9	2.39	1.53
ACADEMY LIFE INS CO	MO	B-	L&H	2q 2003	350.0	37.2	1.1	38.7	1.56	0.94
ACADIAN LIFE INS CO	LA	E+	L&H	4q 2001	21.8	8.7	0.0	1.5	0.39	0.23
ACCELERATION LIFE INS CO	OH	C	L&H	2q 2003	11.8	-1.1	0.0	11.7	5.95	5.35
ACCESS DENTAL PLAN	CA	U	HMO		--	--	--	--	--	--
ACCESS MANAGED HEALTH CARE	NY	U	HMO		--	--	--	--	--	--
ACCOUNTABLE HEALTH PLANS OF AMERICA	TX	U	HMO		--	--	--	--	--	--
ACE AMERICAN INS CO	PA	C	P&C	2q 2003	3,265.0	1,655.0	114.3	617.9	0.92	0.66
ACE FIRE UNDERWRITERS INS CO	PA	C-	P&C	2q 2003	102.1	94.9	1.9	49.3	7.16	6.44
ACE INS CO	PR	C-	P&C	1q 2003	79.2	78.6	9.4	14.7	0.20	0.15
ACE INS CO OF TEXAS	TX	C	P&C	2q 2003	137.4	135.5	13.2	89.0	5.12	3.52
ADAMS LIFE INS CO	AL	C-	L&H	1q 2003	3.6	0.6	0.1	2.6	2.35	2.11
ADMAR MED NETWORK	CA	U	HMO		--	--	--	--	--	--
ADVANCE INS CO	AZ	C+	L&H	2q 2003	28.6	17.5	9.4	21.7	2.77	2.01
ADVANTA LIFE INS CO	AZ	C-	L&H	2q 2003	10.5	0.0	0.0	9.5	3.94	3.55
ADVANTAGE CARE NETWORK INC	TX	U	HMO		--	--	--	--	--	--
ADVANTAGE DENTAL PLAN INC	OR	U	HMO		--	--	--	--	--	--
ADVANTAGE HEALTH SOLUTIONS INC	IN	U	HMO		--	--	--	--	--	--
ADVANTAGE HEALTHPLAN INC	DC	• C-	HMO	1q 2003	4.0	7.0	7.0	1.9	0.78	0.65
AECC TOTAL VISION HEALTH PLAN OF TX	TX	U	HMO		--	--	--	--	--	--
AEGIS SECURITY INS CO	PA	B-	P&C	2q 2003	60.9	72.4	4.3	29.1	1.66	1.24
AET HEALTH CARE PLAN INC	TX	• C	HMO	4q 2002	99.3	32.1	32.1	80.6	30.01	25.01
AETNA DENTAL INC (A PA CORP)	PA	U	HMO		--	--	--	--	--	--
AETNA DENTAL OF CALIFORNIA INC	CA	U	HMO		--	--	--	--	--	--
AETNA HEALTH INC (A COLORADO CORP)	CO	• C	HMO	1q 2003	66.1	188.4	188.4	48.4	4.21	3.51
AETNA HEALTH INC (A CT CORP)	CT	• C	HMO	1q 2003	54.8	106.5	106.5	31.4	5.84	4.87
AETNA HEALTH INC (A DE CORP)	DE	• C	HMO	1q 2003	14.7	33.2	33.2	10.0	3.65	3.04
AETNA HEALTH INC (A FLORIDA CORP)	FL	• C-	HMO	1q 2003	395.5	1,360.2	1,360.2	134.4	1.67	1.39
AETNA HEALTH INC (A GEORGIA CORP)	GA	• C+	HMO	1q 2003	106.8	323.9	323.9	57.4	3.73	3.11
AETNA HEALTH INC (A LOUISIANA CORP)	LA	• C	HMO	4q 2002	20.2	8.9	8.9	15.3	19.15	15.96
AETNA HEALTH INC (A MAINE CORP)	ME	• C	HMO	1q 2003	53.5	164.5	164.5	35.1	3.81	3.18
AETNA HEALTH INC (A MARYLAND CORP)	MD	• B-	HMO	1q 2003	202.6	748.4	748.4	116.2	4.28	3.56
AETNA HEALTH INC (A MICHIGAN CORP)	MI	• C+	HMO	1q 2003	18.6	27.7	27.7	8.5	3.18	2.65
AETNA HEALTH INC (A MISSOURI CORP)	MO	• C-	HMO	1q 2003	26.7	90.3	90.3	16.8	3.19	2.66
AETNA HEALTH INC (A NEW JERSEY CORP)	NJ	• B-	HMO	1q 2003	511.3	1,542.0	1,542.0	272.7	3.82	3.19
AETNA HEALTH INC (A NEW YORK CORP)	NY	• B-	HMO	1q 2003	703.9	1,617.0	1,617.0	350.8	4.45	3.71
AETNA HEALTH INC (A NH CORP)	NH	• C	HMO	4q 2002	10.2	14.2	14.2	8.7	6.39	5.33
AETNA HEALTH INC (A PA CORP)	PA	• B-	HMO	1q 2003	344.3	1,077.2	1,077.2	198.3	3.93	3.28
AETNA HEALTH INC (A TENNESSEE CORP)	TN	• C	HMO	1q 2003	44.0	86.3	86.3	31.8	6.61	5.51
AETNA HEALTH INC (A TEXAS CORP)	TX	• C-	HMO	1q 2003	262.2	1,292.9	1,292.9	111.6	1.52	1.27
AETNA HEALTH INC (A WASHINGTON CORP)	WA	• C-	HMO	1q 2003	45.6	85.7	85.7	26.5	4.06	3.39
AETNA HEALTH INC (AN ARIZONA CORP)	AZ	• C+	HMO	1q 2003	98.6	390.7	390.7	36.2	1.94	1.62
AETNA HEALTH INC (AN OHIO CORP)	OH	• C	HMO	1q 2003	135.9	472.7	472.7	77.6	3.22	2.68
AETNA HEALTH INC (AN OKLAHOMA CORP)	OK	• D+	HMO	1q 2003	30.9	151.0	151.0	13.3	1.48	1.23
AETNA HEALTH INS CO OF CT	CT	U	HMO		--	--	--	--	--	--
AETNA HEALTH INS CO OF NY	NY	• C+	HMO	1q 2003	46.4	28.4	28.4	31.6	11.37	9.47
AETNA HEALTH OF CALIFORNIA INC	CA	• C	HMO	1q 2003	373.4	1,423.4	1,423.4	116.5	2.11	1.30
AETNA HEALTH OF ILLINOIS INC	IL	• C	HMO	1q 2003	126.6	143.4	143.4	42.0	5.18	4.31
AETNA HEALTH OF THE CAROLINAS INC	NC	• C-	HMO	1q 2003	27.3	70.8	70.8	16.3	2.84	2.37
AETNA HEALTH OF WASHINGTON INC	WA	• C+	HLTH	1q 2003	16.8	25.6	25.6	11.3	5.55	4.62
AETNA INS CO OF CT	CT	• C	P&C	2q 2003	47.9	120.7	40.8	28.0	2.17	1.27

www.WeissRatings.com

Arrows denote recent upgrades ▲ or downgrades ▼   • Bullets denote a more detailed analysis is available in Section II.

I. Index of Companies

Winter 2003 - 04

INSURANCE COMPANY NAME	DOM. STATE	WEISS SAFETY RATING	COMPANY TYPE	DATA DATE	TOTAL ASSETS ($MIL)	TOTAL PREMIUMS ($MIL)	HEALTH PREMIUMS ($MIL)	CAPITAL & SURPLUS ($MIL)	RISK ADJUSTED CAPITAL RATIO 1	RATIO 2
AETNA LIFE INS CO	CT	• C+	L&H	2q 2003	25,565.8	4,393.4	3,110.0	1,798.0	2.15	1.32
AETNA U.S. HEALTHCARE (See AETNA HEALTH INC (A PA CORP))										
AETNA US HEALTHCARE DENTAL PLAN INC	TX	U	HMO		--	--	--	--	--	--
AETNA US HEALTHCARE INC (A MA CORP)	MA	• C-	HMO	2q 2002	47.8	176.7	176.7	16.3	0.84	0.69
AF&L INS CO	PA	D	P&C	2q 2003	95.1	59.9	59.9	10.4	0.89	0.71
AHC	WI	U	HMO		--	--	--	--	--	--
AHP PREFERRED PROVIDER NETWORK	PA	U	HMO		--	--	--	--	--	--
AIG CENTENNIAL INS CO	PA	B-	P&C	2q 2003	1,087.6	210.5	0.1	513.8	1.28	1.22
AIG HAWAII INS CO INC	HI	B	P&C	2q 2003	179.2	92.2	4.8	55.3	1.45	1.15
AIG LIFE INS CO	DE	• C+	L&H	2q 2003	13,650.1	1,248.3	318.1	517.1	1.42	0.67
AIG LIFE INS CO OF PR	PR	B	L&H	2q 2003	95.3	14.1	5.4	10.0	1.20	0.86
AIG PREMIER INS CO	PA	B	P&C	2q 2003	542.9	178.2	5.4	269.9	1.69	1.55
AIU INS CO	NY	• B	P&C	2q 2003	1,826.6	2,381.5	804.8	418.4	2.25	1.55
ALABAMA MEDICAL COALITION INC	AL	U	HMO		--	--	--	--	--	--
ALAMEDA ALLIANCE FOR HEALTH	CA	• B	HMO	3q 2002	67.3	97.3	97.3	46.5	3.86	2.37
ALFA LIFE INS CORP	AL	A-	L&H	2q 2003	821.5	103.1	0.1	130.4	2.72	1.60
ALFA MUTUAL INS CO	AL	A	P&C	2q 2003	1,151.8	520.1	0.4	729.0	2.43	2.03
ALIGNIS INC	GA	U	HMO		--	--	--	--	--	--
ALL FLORIDA PPO INC	FL	U	HMO		--	--	--	--	--	--
ALLIANCE FOR COMMUNITY HEALTH LLC	MO	• C	HMO	1q 2003	22.8	52.6	52.6	11.3	2.17	1.80
ALLIANCE HEALTH & LIFE INS CO	MI	B	L&H	2q 2003	26.1	50.1	50.1	13.0	1.61	1.34
ALLIANCE REGIONAL HEALTH NETWORK	TX	U	HMO		--	--	--	--	--	--
ALLIANT HEALTH PLANS INC	GA	• E+	HMO	1q 2003	5.6	32.7	32.7	1.4	0.25	0.21
ALLIANZ LIFE INS CO OF NORTH AMERICA	MN	B-	L&H	2q 2003	29,406.9	8,585.2	384.9	1,682.6	1.58	0.88
ALLIANZ LIFE INS CO OF NY	NY	B-	L&H	2q 2003	409.9	20.4	4.6	49.7	4.53	4.07
ALLIED NETWORK INC	TX	U	HMO		--	--	--	--	--	--
ALLMERICA FINANCIAL LIFE & ANNUITY	MA	D	L&H	2q 2003	12,368.8	2,827.2	25.2	483.8	1.84	1.33
ALLNATION INS CO	DE	U	HMO		--	--	--	--	--	--
ALLSTATE INS CO	IL	A-	P&C	2q 2003	40,978.7	13,842.6	23.1	14,795.2	2.13	1.68
ALLSTATE LIFE INS CO	IL	A-	L&H	2q 2003	60,033.7	2,488.9	106.1	3,421.8	1.65	0.97
ALLSTATE LIFE INS CO OF NEW YORK	NY	B+	L&H	2q 2003	4,816.0	910.2	9.6	284.5	2.11	1.06
ALOHACARE	HI	• B+	HMO	1q 2003	33.5	66.5	66.5	14.3	6.34	5.28
ALPHA DENTAL PROGRAMS INC	TX	U	HMO		--	--	--	--	--	--
ALTA HEALTH & LIFE INS CO	IN	• B	L&H	2q 2003	258.8	113.3	87.5	118.0	13.59	12.23
ALTIUS HEALTH PLANS	UT	• D+	HMO	1q 2003	36.3	223.7	223.7	9.5	0.35	0.29
ALTUS DENTAL INS CO INC	RI	U	HMO		--	--	--	--	--	--
ALTUS DENTAL INS CO INC	RI	U	HMO		--	--	--	--	--	--
ALTUS DENTAL INS CO INC	RI	C-	L&H	2q 2003	6.2	2.2	2.2	5.5	3.23	2.91
ALTUS DENTAL INS CO INC	RI	C-	L&H	2q 2003	6.2	2.2	2.2	5.5	3.23	2.91
AMALGAMATED LIFE & HEALTH INS CO	IL	D+	L&H	2q 2003	8.6	9.6	9.6	4.1	1.92	1.73
AMALGAMATED LIFE INS CO	NY	B-	L&H	2q 2003	39.5	28.0	3.3	17.8	2.88	2.26
AMCARE HEALTH PLANS OF LOUISIANA INC	LA	F	HMO	2q 2002	9.4	25.2	25.2	2.4	0.82	0.70
AMCARE HEALTH PLANS OF OKLAHOMA INC	OK	F	HMO	2q 2002	11.3	42.0	42.0	-17.3	0.33	0.28
AMCARE HEALTH PLANS OF TEXAS INC	TX	F	HMO	2q 2002	37.8	117.9	117.9	3.4	0.29	0.25
AMEDEX INS CO	FL	• C-	L&H	2q 2003	57.4	53.3	53.0	25.1	1.46	1.14
AMERICAN AUTOMOBILE INS CO	MO	C-	P&C	2q 2003	325.1	385.4	4.6	93.6	1.16	0.87
AMERICAN BANKERS INS CO OF FL	FL	• C	P&C	2q 2003	1,076.0	1,142.3	468.3	226.4	1.47	1.01
AMERICAN BANKERS LIFE ASR CO OF FL	FL	• B-	L&H	2q 2003	889.3	519.5	241.7	157.7	4.42	2.60
AMERICAN CAPITOL INS CO	TX	E+	L&H	2q 2003	72.5	15.0	8.5	4.7	0.58	0.40
AMERICAN CASUALTY CO OF READING	PA	C-	P&C	2q 2003	101.3	830.0	4.5	87.5	1.63	1.58
AMERICAN COMMUNITY MUT INS CO	MI	• C+	L&H	2q 2003	157.4	350.2	340.5	74.9	2.10	1.63
AMERICAN CREDITORS LIFE INS CO	DE	C-	L&H	2q 2003	15.8	0.3	0.1	10.0	3.25	2.93

Arrows denote recent upgrades ▲ or downgrades ▼   • Bullets denote a more detailed analysis is available in Section II.

Winter 2003 - 04   I. Index of Companies

INSURANCE COMPANY NAME	DOM. STATE	WEISS SAFETY RATING	COMPANY TYPE	DATA DATE	TOTAL ASSETS ($MIL)	TOTAL PREMIUMS ($MIL)	HEALTH PREMIUMS ($MIL)	CAPITAL & SURPLUS ($MIL)	RISK ADJUSTED CAPITAL RATIO 1	RATIO 2
AMERICAN DENTAL PLAN OF NC INC	NC	U	HMO	--	--	--	--	--	--	--
AMERICAN DENTAL PROVIDERS ARKANSAS	AR	U	HMO	--	--	--	--	--	--	--
AMERICAN EMPLOYERS INS CO	MA	C-	P&C	2q 2003	563.8	119.2	0.0	123.4	2.33	1.74
AMERICAN EXCHANGE LIFE INS CO	TX	• D+	L&H	2q 2003	110.4	5.8	5.6	109.0	0.89	0.79
AMERICAN FAMILY CARE OF UTAH (See MOLINA HEALTHCARE OF UTAH INC)										
AMERICAN FAMILY INS CO	OH	B	P&C	2q 2003	64.2	110.5	2.6	8.5	1.21	1.09
AMERICAN FAMILY LIFE ASR CO OF COLUM	NE	• B-	L&H	2q 2003	37,709.9	8,630.7	7,782.4	2,228.1	1.68	1.04
AMERICAN FAMILY LIFE ASR CO OF NY	NY	C	L&H	2q 2003	92.0	88.9	88.7	18.4	0.82	0.64
AMERICAN FAMILY MUT INS CO	WI	B	P&C	2q 2003	7,689.5	4,122.3	230.1	2,240.1	1.69	1.15
AMERICAN FEDERATED LIFE INS CO	MS	C-	L&H	2q 2003	14.5	5.5	2.5	9.1	3.08	2.77
AMERICAN FIDELITY ASR CO	OK	• A	L&H	2q 2003	2,382.6	669.7	462.1	141.2	1.63	0.99
AMERICAN FOUNDERS LIFE INS CO	TX	C-	L&H	2q 2003	634.6	42.7	0.7	31.5	1.42	0.73
AMERICAN GENERAL ASSURANCE CO	IL	• C+	L&H	2q 2003	1,370.4	215.6	116.2	153.0	1.69	1.16
AMERICAN GENERAL LIFE & ACC INS CO	TN	B-	L&H	2q 2003	8,602.0	904.4	81.6	487.7	1.59	0.85
AMERICAN GENERAL LIFE INS CO	TX	B+	L&H	2q 2003	24,549.9	2,020.3	26.0	3,331.5	1.42	1.07
AMERICAN HARDWARE MUTUAL INS CO	OH	B-	P&C	2q 2003	217.0	73.1	0.1	84.7	1.94	1.51
AMERICAN HEALTH & LIFE INS CO	TX	• B+	L&H	2q 2003	1,236.5	133.1	99.4	338.7	6.97	3.83
AMERICAN HEALTH NETWORK OF IN LLC	IN	U	HMO	--	--	--	--	--	--	--
AMERICAN HEALTHGUARD CORP	CA	U	HMO	--	--	--	--	--	--	--
AMERICAN HERITAGE LIFE INS CO	FL	• B	L&H	2q 2003	1,776.9	418.3	271.5	177.7	1.08	0.79
AMERICAN HOME ASR CO	NY	B	P&C	2q 2003	14,153.3	3,866.3	299.7	3,019.1	1.02	0.72
AMERICAN HOME LIFE INS CO	KS	C	L&H	2q 2003	115.4	13.8	0.0	11.6	1.48	1.33
AMERICAN INCOME LIFE INS CO	IN	B	L&H	2q 2003	1,119.0	342.4	52.1	146.2	2.21	1.34
AMERICAN INDEPENDENT NETWORK INS CO	NY	D	L&H	2q 2003	11.3	3.9	3.9	6.2	2.51	2.26
AMERICAN INDUSTRIES LIFE INS CO	TX	D	L&H	2q 2003	8.3	0.4	0.0	2.0	1.18	0.98
AMERICAN INS CO OF TEXAS	TX	D+	L&H	2q 2003	7.2	3.5	3.5	2.5	1.42	1.27
AMERICAN INTERNATL LIFE ASR CO OF NY	NY	B	L&H	2q 2003	8,150.7	1,258.5	37.4	446.4	1.54	0.76
AMERICAN INTL INS CO OF PR	PR	B	P&C	2q 2003	190.9	177.6	2.5	95.5	2.44	1.62
AMERICAN LIFE & ACC INS CO	TX	B	L&H	2q 2003	28.0	3.1	1.7	10.8	2.56	2.31
AMERICAN LIFE & HEALTH INS CO	MO	C-	L&H	2q 2003	19.9	7.5	7.4	14.0	4.13	3.72
AMERICAN LIFE INS CO	DE	B-	L&H	2q 2003	34,527.6	10,629.1	1,476.8	4,242.4	0.90	0.82
AMERICAN LIFE INS CO	IL	D+	L&H	2q 2003	4.4	0.3	0.2	3.5	2.64	2.38
AMERICAN LIFE INS CO OF NEW YORK	NY	D+	L&H	2q 2003	104.5	5.9	0.1	26.5	3.24	2.91
AMERICAN LIFECARE NETWORKS LLC	LA	U	HMO	--	--	--	--	--	--	--
AMERICAN MEDICAL & LIFE INS CO	NY	D+	L&H	2q 2003	11.2	12.1	10.5	8.4	2.87	2.11
AMERICAN MEDICAL HEALTHCARE (See AMERICAN MEDICAL SECURITY HEALTH PL)										
AMERICAN MEDICAL SECURITY HEALTH PL	FL	U	HMO	4q 2001	2.2	0.6	0.6	2.1	--	--
AMERICAN MEMORIAL LIFE INS CO	SD	C	L&H	2q 2003	1,149.5	291.7	0.0	103.8	2.27	1.30
AMERICAN MODERN LIFE INS CO	OH	B	L&H	2q 2003	54.8	44.4	19.5	16.5	2.58	2.32
AMERICAN NATIONAL INS CO	TX	B	L&H	2q 2003	9,548.4	1,307.0	162.7	1,553.6	1.59	1.22
AMERICAN NATIONAL LIFE INS CO OF TX	TX	• B-	L&H	2q 2003	157.3	118.2	113.4	54.2	1.93	1.56
AMERICAN NETWORK INS CO	PA	D	L&H	2q 2003	12.2	24.8	24.8	8.1	2.96	2.09
AMERICAN PHYSICIANS ASR CORP	MI	D	P&C	2q 2003	807.6	230.2	24.4	164.7	0.29	0.21
AMERICAN PIONEER LIFE INS CO	FL	C-	L&H	2q 2003	150.7	264.2	249.4	23.7	1.10	0.86
AMERICAN PREFERRED PROVIDER PLAN MID	DC	U	HMO	--	--	--	--	--	--	--
AMERICAN PROGRESSIVE L&H I C OF NY	NY	D+	L&H	2q 2003	131.8	88.7	72.6	9.2	0.73	0.51
AMERICAN PUBLIC LIFE INS CO	OK	B-	L&H	2q 2003	59.8	30.7	30.0	14.1	1.09	0.80
AMERICAN RE-INSURANCE CO	DE	C-	P&C	2q 2003	15,977.5	107.2	2.5	2,817.6	0.88	0.58
AMERICAN RELIABLE INS CO	AZ	C+	P&C	2q 2003	337.8	215.5	3.6	67.7	2.12	1.24
AMERICAN REPUBLIC INS CO	IA	• B	L&H	2q 2003	452.3	423.5	398.9	196.3	2.94	2.16
AMERICAN SECURITY INS CO	DE	• B	P&C	2q 2003	558.2	621.5	283.4	177.8	1.17	0.99
AMERICAN SENTINEL INS CO	PA	C-	P&C	2q 2003	18.9	1.6	1.6	8.7	1.87	1.36

www.WeissRatings.com

Arrows denote recent upgrades ▲ or downgrades ▼   • Bullets denote a more detailed analysis is available in Section II.

I. Index of Companies

Winter 2003 - 04

INSURANCE COMPANY NAME	DOM. STATE	WEISS SAFETY RATING	COMPANY TYPE	DATA DATE	TOTAL ASSETS ($MIL)	TOTAL PREMIUMS ($MIL)	HEALTH PREMIUMS ($MIL)	CAPITAL & SURPLUS ($MIL)	RISK ADJUSTED CAPITAL RATIO 1	RATIO 2
AMERICAN SPECIALTY HEALTH INS CO	IL	C	L&H	2q 2003	8.4	-5.2	0.0	8.1	3.86	3.47
AMERICAN SPECIALTY HEALTH PLANS INC	CA	U	HMO		--	--	--	--	--	--
AMERICAN STATES INS CO	IN	C	P&C	2q 2003	1,998.7	748.3	2.2	558.8	2.01	1.29
AMERICAN STATES LIFE INS CO	IN	B	L&H	2q 2003	560.2	57.9	1.6	84.0	2.61	1.38
AMERICAN TRAVELERS ASR CO	DC	D	L&H	2q 2003	13.6	25.2	25.2	5.0	0.62	0.51
AMERICAN UNDERWRITERS LIFE INS CO	AZ	D	L&H	2q 2003	33.2	4.3	1.9	12.6	1.49	1.09
AMERICAN UNITED LIFE INS CO	IN	B	L&H	2q 2003	9,809.2	1,576.6	172.9	622.5	2.89	1.56
AMERICAN ZURICH INS CO	IL	B-	P&C	2q 2003	98.9	427.2	0.5	98.8	3.21	2.96
AMERICAS HEALTH CHOICE MEDICAL PLANS	FL	● D	HMO	4q 2002	18.4	63.5	63.5	4.6	0.31	0.26
AMERICAS PPO	MN	U	HMO		--	--	--	--	--	--
AMERICHOICE OF NEW JERSEY INC	NJ	● B	HMO	1q 2003	85.9	376.6	376.6	31.6	1.22	1.02
AMERICHOICE OF NEW YORK INC	NY	● B+	HMO	1q 2003	83.0	147.0	147.0	44.2	6.63	5.53
AMERICHOICE OF PENNSYLVANIA INC	PA	● B	HMO	2q 2002	97.3	303.6	303.6	38.3	1.94	1.65
AMERICO FINANCIAL LIFE & ANNUITY INS	TX	C	L&H	2q 2003	1,931.9	336.2	0.2	132.7	1.94	1.00
AMERICOM LIFE & ANNUITY INS CO	TX	D-	L&H	2q 2003	198.1	113.9	0.1	9.7	1.17	0.68
AMERIGROUP FLORIDA INC	FL	● D+	HMO	1q 2002	61.7	256.5	256.5	14.0	0.35	0.30
AMERIGROUP ILLINOIS INC	IL	● C+	HMO	4q 2002	28.9	53.3	53.3	17.0	5.82	4.85
AMERIGROUP MARYLAND INC MANAGED CARE	DE	● C+	HMO	1q 2003	109.3	346.3	346.3	24.2	1.57	1.31
AMERIGROUP NEW JERSEY INC	NJ	● C-	HMO	1q 2003	43.2	194.2	194.2	10.7	0.98	0.82
AMERIGROUP TEXAS INC	TX	● D+	HMO	1q 2003	144.6	548.8	548.8	20.2	0.56	0.47
AMERIHEALTH HEALTH PLAN INC	NY	U	HMO	1q 2003	12.3	0.0	0.0	5.0	--	--
AMERIHEALTH HMO INC	PA	● B	HMO	1q 2003	534.6	645.3	645.3	401.9	2.16	1.80
AMERIHEALTH INSURANCE CO OF NJ	NJ	● C+	HMO	4q 2002	85.1	211.5	211.5	30.8	2.49	2.08
AMERITAS LIFE INS CORP	NE	● B+	L&H	2q 2003	2,417.9	398.9	312.1	601.9	4.02	2.49
AMERITAS MANAGED DENTAL PLAN INC	CA	U	HMO		--	--	--	--	--	--
AMERUS LIFE INS CO	IA	C+	L&H	2q 2003	5,718.4	828.9	0.1	245.0	1.27	0.71
AMEX ASSURANCE CO	IL	● B	P&C	2q 2003	344.3	442.7	129.4	208.5	3.22	2.01
AMIL INTERNATIONAL INS CO	TX	D	L&H	2q 2003	9.6	26.6	26.6	5.3	1.18	0.98
AMIL INTERNATIONAL TEXAS INC	TX	● D	HMO	1q 2003	14.2	65.8	65.8	5.0	0.50	0.42
ANTERO HEALTH PLANS INC	CO	● B-	HMO	1q 2003	12.3	21.9	21.9	10.4	5.14	4.28
ANTHEM ALLIANCE HEALTH INS CO	TX	● C+	L&H	2q 2003	102.1	0.9	0.6	74.9	9.01	8.11
ANTHEM BLUE CROSS BLUE SHIELD OF CONNECTICUT (See ANTHEM HEALTH PLANS INC)										
ANTHEM HEALTH & LIFE INS CO OF NY	NY	C	L&H	2q 2003	6.5	37.5	37.3	1.9	0.27	0.25
ANTHEM HEALTH NETWORK	NY	U	HMO		--	--	--	--	--	--
ANTHEM HEALTH PLANS INC	CT	● C+	HMO	1q 2003	786.0	2,167.2	2,167.2	304.5	2.67	2.23
▲ ANTHEM HEALTH PLANS OF KENTUCKY INC	KY	● B+	HMO	1q 2003	659.5	1,323.6	1,323.6	297.2	4.07	3.39
▲ ANTHEM HEALTH PLANS OF MAINE INC	ME	● B	HLTH	1q 2003	279.8	839.1	839.1	101.7	2.36	1.97
ANTHEM HEALTH PLANS OF NEW HAMPSHIRE	NH	● B	HLTH	1q 2003	247.6	215.4	215.4	128.8	3.51	2.92
ANTHEM HEALTH PLANS OF VIRGINIA	VA	● B+	L&H	2q 2003	1,621.3	2,420.7	2,420.7	615.6	2.27	1.80
ANTHEM INS COMPANIES INC	IN	● B-	P&C	2q 2003	3,657.3	1,805.5	1,805.5	2,202.3	1.43	1.31
ANTHEM LIFE INS CO	IN	● B-	L&H	2q 2003	249.4	117.8	36.7	69.1	3.26	2.28
ARAZ GREAT PLAINS	SD	U	HMO		--	--	--	--	--	--
ARBELLA LIFE & HEALTH INS CO INC	MA	C-	L&H	3q 2002	1.1	0.1	0.1	1.1	0.52	0.46
ARIZONA FOUNDATION FOR MEDICAL CARE	AZ	U	HMO		--	--	--	--	--	--
ARKANSAS BANKERS LIFE INS CO	AR	D	L&H	2q 2003	5.8	2.5	0.7	1.9	1.15	1.04
ARKANSAS BEHAVIORAL HEALTH LLC	AR	U	HMO		--	--	--	--	--	--
ARKANSAS BLUE CROSS AND BLUE SHIELD	AR	● B+	HMO	1q 2003	508.1	842.7	842.7	272.0	4.27	3.56
ARKANSAS FIRST SOURCE	AR	U	HMO		--	--	--	--	--	--
ARKANSAS PREFERRED PROVIDER ORG	AR	U	HMO		--	--	--	--	--	--
ARNETT HMO INC	IN	● C	HMO	4q 2002	19.0	112.8	112.8	7.7	0.79	0.66
ASSOCIATED AMERICAN MUTUAL L I C	UT	E+	L&H	2q 2003	29.4	2.4	1.1	1.6	0.48	0.43
ASSOCIATED MUTUAL HOSP SVC OF MI	MI	E+	L&H	2q 2003	6.0	12.4	11.8	3.5	1.24	1.02

Arrows denote recent upgrades ▲ or downgrades ▼   ● Bullets denote a more detailed analysis is available in Section II.

www.WeissRatings.com

Winter 2003 - 04

I. Index of Companies

INSURANCE COMPANY NAME	DOM. STATE	WEISS SAFETY RATING	COMPANY TYPE	DATA DATE	TOTAL ASSETS ($MIL)	TOTAL PREMIUMS ($MIL)	HEALTH PREMIUMS ($MIL)	CAPITAL & SURPLUS ($MIL)	RISK ADJUSTED CAPITAL RATIO 1	RATIO 2
ASSOCIATION CASUALTY	TX	C	P&C	2q 2003	58.3	37.2	0.2	17.1	1.04	0.62
ASSUMPTION MUTUAL LIFE INS CO	MA	C-	L&H	2q 2003	49.7	1.2	0.0	8.5	1.32	1.18
ASSURED INVESTORS LIFE CO	CA	U	L&H	4q 2002	9.2	0.1	0.1	8.9	--	--
ASSURITY LIFE INS CO	NE	• B-	L&H	2q 2003	188.5	53.9	41.6	29.6	2.29	1.46
ASURIS NORTHWEST HEALTH	WA	• C+	HLTH	1q 2003	22.3	53.6	53.6	7.8	2.16	1.80
ATHENS AREA HEALTH PLAN SELECT INC	GA	• D+	HMO	1q 2003	11.8	36.0	36.0	6.9	0.95	0.79
ATLANTA LIFE INS CO	GA	C	L&H	2q 2003	105.8	6.1	0.4	27.0	1.57	1.04
ATLANTIC COAST LIFE INS CO	SC	D+	L&H	2q 2003	47.3	4.5	0.5	6.9	1.28	0.80
ATLANTIC SOUTHERN INS CO	PR	D-	L&H	2q 2003	17.2	17.5	14.4	4.9	1.56	1.41
ATLANTICARE HEALTH PLANS INC	NJ	U	HMO	1q 2002	5.0	18.7	18.7	2.8	--	--
ATLANTIS HEALTH PLAN	NY	• E-	HMO	1q 2003	4.6	46.8	46.8	-6.6	0.00	0.00
ATRIUM HEALTH PLAN INC	WI	• B+	HMO	1q 2003	14.3	76.9	76.9	7.7	1.69	1.41
AULTCARE HMO	OH	• D+	HMO	1q 2003	6.5	9.9	9.9	2.0	0.82	0.68
AUTO CLUB LIFE INS CO	MI	C	L&H	2q 2003	372.5	25.0	2.5	25.2	0.98	0.61
AUTO-OWNERS INS CO	MI	A	P&C	2q 2003	6,582.7	1,961.8	0.0	2,989.3	2.17	1.64
AUTO-OWNERS LIFE INS CO	MI	A-	L&H	2q 2003	1,251.5	133.6	8.8	157.0	2.21	1.29
AVALON HEALTH LTD	PA	U	HMO		--	--	--	--	--	--
AVANTE BEHAVIORAL HEALTH PLAN	CA	U	HMO		--	--	--	--	--	--
AVANTE COMPLEMENTARY HEALTH PLAN	CA	U	HMO		--	--	--	--	--	--
AVEMCO INS CO	MD	• B+	P&C	2q 2003	191.7	203.1	155.1	116.1	4.77	3.59
AVERA HEALTH PLANS INC	SD	• D+	HMO	1q 2003	18.0	45.3	45.3	6.1	0.90	0.75
AVERA HEALTH PLANS OF MINNESOTA	MN	U	HMO		--	--	--	--	--	--
AVIVA LIFE INS CO	DE	B	L&H	2q 2003	4,291.3	814.5	0.3	251.6	1.60	0.86
AVMED INC	FL	• E	HMO	1q 2003	155.7	783.7	783.7	40.5	0.19	0.16
BALBOA INS CO	CA	B	P&C	2q 2003	772.1	329.9	2.4	321.3	1.63	1.08
BALBOA LIFE INS CO	CA	• B+	L&H	2q 2003	124.5	23.4	18.0	71.0	3.93	3.47
BALBOA LIFE INS CO OF NY	NY	B-	L&H	2q 2003	14.4	2.3	1.6	13.5	4.60	4.14
BALTIMORE LIFE INS CO	MD	• C	L&H	2q 2003	790.0	189.4	67.0	29.8	0.92	0.49
BANC ONE KENTUCKY INS CO	KY	C	L&H	2q 2003	17.0	0.7	0.2	14.9	4.69	4.22
BANKERS FIDELITY LIFE INS CO	GA	• C	L&H	2q 2003	109.5	60.3	44.8	26.5	1.58	1.10
BANKERS INDEPENDENT INS CO	MD	C-	P&C	2q 2003	27.9	26.3	0.2	4.3	0.59	0.41
BANKERS INS CO	FL	D	P&C	2q 2003	67.0	191.4	0.0	19.3	0.76	0.58
BANKERS LIFE & CAS CO	IL	• E	L&H	2q 2003	6,387.5	2,334.1	1,402.2	270.4	0.72	0.43
BANKERS LIFE INS CO	FL	D-	L&H	2q 2003	123.2	96.3	8.8	5.5	0.60	0.54
BANKERS LIFE INS CO OF IL	IL	U	L&H	4q 2002	296.8	0.0	0.0	273.0	--	--
BANKERS LIFE INS CO OF NY	NY	C+	L&H	2q 2003	490.2	110.3	1.7	32.0	1.76	0.91
BANKERS LIFE OF LOUISIANA	LA	C-	L&H	2q 2003	13.9	14.2	6.1	5.0	1.67	1.50
BANKERS MULTIPLE LINE INS CO	IL	D	P&C	2q 2003	8.1	0.2	0.2	7.4	22.72	20.45
BANKERS NATIONAL LIFE INS CO	TX	E	L&H	2q 2003	717.3	29.1	0.7	40.8	1.51	0.65
BANNER LIFE INS CO	MD	C+	L&H	2q 2003	1,004.4	312.2	0.0	265.7	1.63	1.34
BAPTIST HEALTH SERVICES GROUP	TN	U	HMO		--	--	--	--	--	--
BASIC CHIROPRACTIC HEALTH PLAN INC	CA	U	HMO		--	--	--	--	--	--
BAYCARE HEALTH NETWORK INC	FL	U	HMO		--	--	--	--	--	--
BAYOU STATE HEALTH PLAN INC	LA	U	HMO		--	--	--	--	--	--
BC LIFE & HEALTH INS CO	CA	• B	L&H	2q 2003	600.6	1,085.3	1,054.0	325.5	2.19	1.73
BCI HMO INC	IL	• B+	HMO	1q 2003	10.4	0.3	0.3	9.9	29.56	24.63
BCS INS CO	OH	• C	P&C	2q 2003	225.7	181.1	123.1	116.2	2.84	1.92
BCS LIFE INS CO	IL	• C	L&H	2q 2003	138.3	130.8	122.8	65.8	3.18	2.44
BEECH STREET CORP	CA	U	HMO		--	--	--	--	--	--
BENCHMARK INS CO	KS	C	P&C	2q 2003	66.4	105.4	66.5	19.7	2.06	1.12
BENEFICIAL LIFE INS CO	UT	B	L&H	2q 2003	2,461.3	309.0	1.3	182.7	1.86	0.94
BENICORP INS CO	IN	C	L&H	2q 2003	33.5	92.9	90.9	14.5	1.19	0.90

www.WeissRatings.com

Arrows denote recent upgrades ▲ or downgrades ▼   • Bullets denote a more detailed analysis is available in Section II.

I. Index of Companies

Winter 2003 - 04

INSURANCE COMPANY NAME	DOM. STATE	WEISS SAFETY RATING	COMPANY TYPE	DATA DATE	TOTAL ASSETS ($MIL)	TOTAL PREMIUMS ($MIL)	HEALTH PREMIUMS ($MIL)	CAPITAL & SURPLUS ($MIL)	RISK ADJUSTED CAPITAL RATIO 1	RATIO 2
BERKSHIRE HEALTH PLAN	PA	U	HMO	--	--	--	--	--	--	--
BERKSHIRE LIFE INS CO OF AMERICA	MA	● C	L&H	2q 2003	1,522.2	31.5	31.3	260.6	3.90	2.16
BEST CHOICE PLUS	FL	U	HMO	--	--	--	--	--	--	--
BEST LIFE & HEALTH INS CO	TX	D+	L&H	2q 2003	20.9	34.5	31.9	9.5	1.32	1.05
BEST MERIDIAN INS CO	FL	D	L&H	2q 2003	101.7	41.1	21.7	9.4	1.05	0.75
BETTER HEALTH PLANS INC	TN	U	HMO	4q 2002	11.6	38.3	38.3	3.5	--	--
BIG SKY COMMUNITY HEALTH PLAN INC	MT	U	HMO	--	--	--	--	--	--	--
BLOCK VISION OF TEXAS INC	TX	U	HMO	--	--	--	--	--	--	--
BLUE CARE INC (See GOOD HEALTH HMO INC)										
BLUE CARE NETWORK OF MICHIGAN	MI	● C+	HMO	1q 2003	457.0	1,285.8	1,285.8	92.0	1.58	1.32
BLUE CHOICE	NY	U	HMO	--	--	--	--	--	--	--
BLUE CROSS BLUE SHIELD HEALTHCARE GA	GA	● A	HMO	1q 2003	255.4	1,302.4	1,302.4	92.6	1.93	1.61
BLUE CROSS BLUE SHIELD OF ALABAMA	AL	● B	HLTH	1q 2003	1,263.5	2,320.0	2,320.0	457.4	3.37	2.81
BLUE CROSS BLUE SHIELD OF ARIZONA	AZ	● A	HLTH	1q 2003	409.0	737.1	737.1	228.5	5.11	4.26
BLUE CROSS BLUE SHIELD OF CENTRAL NEW YORK (See EXCELLUS HEALTH PLAN INC)										
BLUE CROSS BLUE SHIELD OF DELAWARE	DE	● B+	HLTH	1q 2003	206.6	234.4	234.4	99.3	7.22	6.01
BLUE CROSS BLUE SHIELD OF FLORIDA	FL	● B+	L&H	2q 2003	2,530.3	2,666.9	2,666.9	1,073.0	1.26	1.06
BLUE CROSS BLUE SHIELD OF GEORGIA	GA	● A	HLTH	1q 2003	798.7	1,499.5	1,499.5	344.0	5.26	4.39
BLUE CROSS BLUE SHIELD OF HAWAII (See HAWAII MEDICAL SERVICE ASSOCIATION)										
BLUE CROSS BLUE SHIELD OF INDIANA (See ANTHEM INS COMPANIES INC)										
BLUE CROSS BLUE SHIELD OF IOWA (See WELLMARK INC)										
BLUE CROSS BLUE SHIELD OF KANSAS INC	KS	● C+	L&H	2q 2003	675.6	1,061.8	1,061.8	252.9	1.39	1.11
▲ BLUE CROSS BLUE SHIELD OF KC	MO	● B+	HLTH	1q 2003	399.8	630.5	630.5	175.6	2.91	2.42
BLUE CROSS BLUE SHIELD OF LOUISIANA (See LA HEALTH SERVICE & INDEMNITY CO)										
BLUE CROSS BLUE SHIELD OF MA	MA	● A	HLTH	1q 2003	2,033.0	3,844.4	3,844.4	628.9	3.57	2.97
BLUE CROSS BLUE SHIELD OF MARYLAND (See CAREFIRST OF MARYLAND INC)										
BLUE CROSS BLUE SHIELD OF MICHIGAN	MI	● B	HLTH	1q 2003	3,804.0	5,287.3	5,287.3	1,596.6	3.68	3.06
BLUE CROSS BLUE SHIELD OF MINNESOTA	MN	● B+	HLTH	1q 2003	1,346.9	1,547.3	1,547.3	504.7	3.93	3.27
BLUE CROSS BLUE SHIELD OF MONTANA	MT	● C+	HLTH	2q 2002	160.2	286.0	286.0	53.4	1.37	1.04
BLUE CROSS BLUE SHIELD OF MS, MUTUAL	MS	● B-	L&H	4q 2002	346.9	778.7	778.7	179.5	2.21	1.79
BLUE CROSS BLUE SHIELD OF NC	NC	● B	HLTH	1q 2003	1,417.8	2,093.9	2,093.9	524.8	3.54	2.95
BLUE CROSS BLUE SHIELD OF NEBRASKA	NE	● B	HMO	1q 2003	508.5	606.1	606.1	299.8	9.24	7.70
BLUE CROSS BLUE SHIELD OF NEW HAMPSHIRE (See ANTHEM HEALTH PLANS OF NEW HAMPSHIRE)										
BLUE CROSS BLUE SHIELD OF NORTH DAKOTA (See NORIDIAN MUTUAL INS CO)										
BLUE CROSS BLUE SHIELD OF OHIO (See COMMUNITY INS CO)										
BLUE CROSS BLUE SHIELD OF OKLAHOMA	OK	● B	HLTH	1q 2003	390.7	762.3	762.3	102.7	1.90	1.58
BLUE CROSS BLUE SHIELD OF RI	RI	● B+	HLTH	1q 2003	458.3	892.6	892.6	221.3	2.16	1.80
BLUE CROSS BLUE SHIELD OF SC INC	SC	● B+	P&C	2q 2003	1,045.1	937.7	937.7	601.7	2.57	1.83
BLUE CROSS BLUE SHIELD OF VERMONT	VT	● B	HLTH	1q 2003	107.9	195.3	195.3	39.2	2.19	1.82
BLUE CROSS BLUE SHIELD OF VIRGINIA (See ANTHEM HEALTH PLANS OF VIRGINIA)										
BLUE CROSS BLUE SHIELD OF WASHINGTON & ALASKA (See PREMERA BLUE CROSS)										
BLUE CROSS BLUE SHIELD OF WYOMING	WY	● B+	HLTH	1q 2003	106.3	124.3	124.3	70.6	4.48	3.74
▲ BLUE CROSS BLUE SHIELD UNITED OF WI	WI	● B-	HLTH	1q 2003	328.2	623.0	623.0	159.5	1.91	1.59
BLUE CROSS OF CALIFORNIA	CA	● A	HMO	1q 2003	4,397.8	8,889.2	8,889.2	1,135.7	3.14	1.95
BLUE CROSS OF IDAHO HEALTH SERVICE	ID	● B+	L&H	2q 2003	177.2	455.8	455.8	84.6	1.57	1.16
BLUE CROSS OF NORTHEASTERN PENNSYLVANIA (See HOSPITAL SERV ASSN OF NORTH EAST PA)										
BLUE PLUS (See HMO MINNESOTA)										
BLUE RIDGE HEALTH NETWORK	PA	U	HMO	--	--	--	--	--	--	--
BLUE SHIELD OF CALIFORNIA (See CALIFORNIA PHYSICIANS SERVICE)										
BLUE SHIELD OF CALIFORNIA L&H INS CO	CA	● B	L&H	2q 2003	145.0	54.1	38.7	108.5	9.92	7.20
BLUEBONNET LIFE INS CO	MS	C	L&H	2q 2003	20.9	17.4	8.6	17.1	4.90	4.07
BLUECHIP (See COORDINATED HEALTH PARTNERS INC)										

Arrows denote recent upgrades ▲ or downgrades ▼   ● Bullets denote a more detailed analysis is available in Section II.

Winter 2003 - 04

I. Index of Companies

INSURANCE COMPANY NAME	DOM. STATE	WEISS SAFETY RATING	COMPANY TYPE	DATA DATE	TOTAL ASSETS ($MIL)	TOTAL PREMIUMS ($MIL)	HEALTH PREMIUMS ($MIL)	CAPITAL & SURPLUS ($MIL)	RISK ADJUSTED CAPITAL RATIO 1	RATIO 2
BLUECHOICE (See HMO MISSOURI INC)										
BLUECROSS BLUESHIELD OF TENNESSEE	TN	• B+	HLTH	1q 2003	1,093.8	1,446.4	1,446.4	628.4	5.53	4.61
▲ BLUEGRASS FAMILY HEALTH INC	KY	• B+	HMO	1q 2003	82.2	304.9	304.9	27.6	1.38	1.15
BLUELINCS HMO (See GHS HEALTH MAINTENANCE ORGANIZATION)										
BOOKER T WASHINGTON INS CO INC	AL	E+	L&H	2q 2003	53.8	6.7	0.1	3.8	0.38	0.30
BOSTON MUTUAL LIFE INS CO	MA	• B	L&H	2q 2003	683.9	265.3	103.4	65.1	1.52	1.00
BOTSFORD HEALTH PLAN CORP	MI	• B-	HMO	1q 2003	10.8	20.0	20.0	3.4	0.71	0.59
BOULDER VALLEY INDIV PRACTICE ASSN	CO	U	HMO		--	--	--	--	--	--
BPA HEALTH INC	ID	U	HMO		--	--	--	--	--	--
BRAZOS VALLEY HEALTH NETWORK	TX	U	HMO		--	--	--	--	--	--
BROKERS NATIONAL LIFE ASR CO	AR	C-	L&H	2q 2003	20.4	40.9	40.5	11.9	1.49	1.19
BROTHERHOOD MUTUAL INS CO	IN	B	P&C	2q 2003	189.9	151.3	6.5	53.3	1.40	1.13
BSH LIFE INS INC	HI	U	L&H	4q 2002	1.5	0.0	0.0	1.4	--	--
BUSINESS MEN'S ASSURANCE CO OF AMER	MO	C	L&H	2q 2003	2,035.0	288.4	27.8	76.8	0.63	0.39
CALFARM INS CO	CA	B	P&C	3q 2002	107.2	112.8	111.5	107.2	45.07	14.18
CALIFORNIA BENEFITS DENTAL PLAN	CA	U	HMO		--	--	--	--	--	--
CALIFORNIA PHYSICIANS SERVICE	CA	• A-	HMO	1q 2003	2,083.3	4,469.7	4,469.7	808.4	1.72	1.18
CALIFORNIA STATE AUTO ASN INTER-INS	CA	A-	P&C	2q 2003	4,180.2	1,802.0	3.6	1,955.0	3.82	2.61
CALOPTIMA (See ORANGE PREVENTION & TREATMENT INTEGR)										
CAMBRIDGE LIFE INS CO	MO	D+	L&H	2q 2003	7.4	0.4	0.4	6.2	3.28	2.95
CAMBRIDGE NETWORK PROVIDER SERV LLC	NY	U	HMO		--	--	--	--	--	--
CAMERON LIFE INS CO	MO	C-	L&H	1q 2003	5.9	1.1	0.0	1.8	1.10	0.99
CANADA LIFE ASSURANCE CO-US BRANCH	MI	• C	L&H	2q 2003	4,644.1	728.2	228.0	407.1	1.10	0.76
CANADA LIFE INS CO OF NEW YORK	NY	C+	L&H	2q 2003	302.9	37.7	0.0	19.4	1.77	0.88
CAPE HEALTH PLAN INC	MI	• D	HMO	1q 2003	26.4	101.4	101.4	7.0	0.31	0.26
▼ CAPITAL ADVANTAGE INS CO	PA	• C-	HMO	1q 2003	421.9	230.9	230.9	148.0	3.87	3.22
CAPITAL BLUE CROSS OF PENNSYLVANIA	PA	• B+	HLTH	1q 2003	982.4	1,029.1	1,029.1	485.6	5.27	4.39
CAPITAL COMMUNITY HEALTH PLAN	DC	U	HMO	2q 2002	23.9	46.6	46.6	10.3	--	--
CAPITAL DISTRICT PHYSICIANS HEALTH P	NY	• B+	HMO	1q 2003	246.1	707.9	707.9	96.5	1.70	1.42
CAPITAL HEALTH PLAN INC	FL	• B-	HMO	1q 2003	76.3	266.5	266.5	30.3	1.86	1.55
CAPITAL HEALTH PLANS INC	PA	• C	HLTH	1q 2003	2.6	6.0	6.0	1.2	0.97	0.81
CAPITALCARE INC	VA	U	HMO	1q 2003	3.9	5.1	5.1	2.5	--	--
CAPITOL INDEMNITY CORP	WI	C+	P&C	2q 2003	328.2	137.0	4.2	134.6	2.31	1.57
CAPITOL LIFE & ACCIDENT INS CO	AR	E+	L&H	2q 2003	1.8	1.4	0.2	0.3	0.60	0.54
CARE 1ST HEALTH PLAN	CA	U	HMO		--	--	--	--	--	--
CARE CHOICES HMO	IA	U	HMO		--	--	--	--	--	--
▲ CARE CHOICES HMO	MI	• C	HMO	1q 2003	55.8	286.4	286.4	24.8	0.91	0.76
CARE RESOURCES INC	CA	U	HMO		--	--	--	--	--	--
CAREAMERICA LIFE INS CO	CA	U	L&H	4q 2002	25.9	0.0	0.0	23.9	--	--
CAREFIRST BLUECHOICE INC	DC	• A-	HMO	1q 2003	261.2	607.5	607.5	128.7	3.26	2.72
CAREFIRST BLUECROSS BLUESHIELD (See GROUP HOSP & MEDICAL SERVICES INC)										
CAREFIRST OF MARYLAND INC	MD	• B+	HLTH	1q 2003	822.5	1,388.3	1,388.3	273.2	2.86	2.39
▲ CARELINK HEALTH PLANS INC	WV	• C	HMO	1q 2003	44.2	142.1	142.1	18.1	1.61	1.34
CAREMORE INSURANCE SERVICES INC	CA	U	HMO		--	--	--	--	--	--
CAREPLUS HEALTH PLANS INC	FL	• E	HMO	2q 2002	4.5	26.6	26.6	1.3	0.08	0.07
CARESOURCE (See DAYTON AREA HEALTH PLAN)										
CARESYS PREFERRED PROVIDER NETWORK	CT	U	HMO		--	--	--	--	--	--
CARIBBEAN AMERICAN LIFE ASR CO	PR	• B+	L&H	2q 2003	189.0	51.8	27.8	103.7	8.09	6.32
CARIBBEAN AMERICAN PROPERTY INS CO	PR	• C+	P&C	2q 2003	41.7	21.2	15.3	30.3	2.24	1.94
CARILION HEALTH PLANS INC	VA	• E+	HMO	1q 2003	14.0	23.1	23.1	5.1	0.53	0.44
CARITEN HEALTH PLAN INC	TN	• C-	HMO	1q 2003	41.3	102.8	102.8	11.8	0.91	0.76
CARITEN INS CO	TN	D-	L&H	4q 2001	32.5	64.6	64.6	12.9	1.24	1.02

www.WeissRatings.com

Arrows denote recent upgrades ▲ or downgrades ▼   • Bullets denote a more detailed analysis is available in Section II.

I. Index of Companies

Winter 2003 - 04

INSURANCE COMPANY NAME	DOM. STATE	WEISS SAFETY RATING	COMPANY TYPE	DATA DATE	TOTAL ASSETS ($MIL)	TOTAL PREMIUMS ($MIL)	HEALTH PREMIUMS ($MIL)	CAPITAL & SURPLUS ($MIL)	RISK ADJUSTED CAPITAL RATIO 1	RATIO 2
▲ CAROLINA CARE PLAN INC	SC	● B-	HMO	1q 2003	53.9	236.0	236.0	19.9	1.08	0.90
CAROLINA SUMMIT HEALTHCARE INC	NC	U	HMO	--	--	--	--	--	--	--
CASCADE EAST HEALTH PLANS INC	OR	● E	HLTH	1q 2003	3.1	9.7	9.7	1.3	0.38	0.32
CCN MANAGED CARE	CA	U	HMO	--	--	--	--	--	--	--
CDPHP UNIVERSAL BENEFITS INC	NY	● B-	HLTH	1q 2003	1.2	1.5	1.5	0.8	1.25	1.04
CEDARS-SINAI PROVIDER PLAN LLC	CA	U	HMO	3q 2002	4.2	0.0	0.0	4.2	--	--
CELTIC INS CO	IL	● B	L&H	2q 2003	113.0	204.4	204.0	46.5	2.42	1.94
CENTRAL BENEFITS MUTUAL INS CO	DC	● D+	L&H	2q 2003	61.9	12.1	12.1	41.3	1.89	1.58
CENTRAL BENEFITS NATL LIFE INS CO	OH	D+	L&H	2q 2003	13.1	10.6	9.7	9.0	3.60	3.24
CENTRAL COAST ALLIANCE FOR HEALTH (See SANTA CRUZ-MONTEREY MGD MED CARE)										
CENTRAL NATL LIFE INS CO OF OMAHA	DE	D	L&H	2q 2003	11.7	0.2	0.0	11.4	4.46	4.02
CENTRAL OREGON INDEPENDENT HEALTH SV	OR	● C+	HLTH	1q 2003	38.3	108.6	108.6	13.5	0.78	0.65
CENTRAL RESERVE LIFE INS CO	OH	● D	L&H	2q 2003	93.6	252.6	247.5	35.0	1.02	0.83
CENTRAL SECURITY LIFE INS CO	TX	C-	L&H	2q 2003	78.8	7.2	1.0	5.8	0.75	0.67
CENTRAL STATES H & L CO OF OMAHA	NE	● B-	L&H	2q 2003	344.1	183.0	116.2	74.5	3.71	2.65
CENTRAL STATES INDEMNITY CO OF OMAHA	NE	● A-	P&C	2q 2003	243.1	135.6	46.0	175.7	3.25	2.60
CENTRAL SUSQUEHANNA HC PROVIDERS	PA	U	HMO	--	--	--	--	--	--	--
CENTRAL UNITED LIFE INS CO	TX	● C	L&H	2q 2003	289.1	59.2	53.7	43.3	1.02	0.80
CENTRE INS CO	DE	● C	P&C	2q 2003	828.1	50.5	13.6	108.8	1.67	1.03
CENTRE LIFE INS CO	MA	● C	L&H	2q 2003	1,902.8	52.1	52.1	100.4	2.18	1.07
CENTRIS INS CO	IN	U	P&C	4q 2002	26.8	0.0	0.0	25.3	--	--
CENTURION CASUALTY CO	IA	B	P&C	2q 2003	275.7	9.6	0.0	228.4	35.35	31.82
CENTURION LIFE INS CO	MO	● A	L&H	2q 2003	1,024.0	36.0	20.3	810.4	37.72	21.99
CENTURY CREDIT LIFE INS CO	MS	D+	L&H	4q 2001	27.6	3.3	0.9	20.5	4.76	4.29
CENTURY DENTAL PLAN	CA	U	HMO	--	--	--	--	--	--	--
CENTURY HEALTH SOLUTIONS INC	KS	U	HMO	--	--	--	--	--	--	--
CENTURY LIFE ASR CO	OK	C	L&H	2q 2003	14.8	6.0	1.5	7.1	2.49	2.24
CHA HEALTH	KY	● C+	HMO	1q 2003	82.7	186.0	186.0	40.1	2.18	1.82
CHAMPIONS LIFE INS CO	TX	D+	L&H	2q 2003	33.8	0.9	0.2	4.8	0.31	0.25
CHASE LIFE & ANNUITY CO	DE	C	L&H	2q 2003	215.0	89.1	0.1	36.5	4.62	4.16
CHEROKEE INS CO	MI	C-	P&C	2q 2003	78.4	58.8	13.4	29.1	1.15	0.68
CHEROKEE NATIONAL LIFE INS CO	GA	C	L&H	2q 2003	36.2	28.0	9.5	7.0	1.44	0.90
CHESAPEAKE LIFE INS CO	OK	C	L&H	2q 2003	54.8	3.4	1.4	21.6	3.18	2.86
CHILDRENS MERCY FAMILY HEALTH PARTNR	MO	● E+	HMO	1q 2003	11.8	81.7	81.7	1.9	0.19	0.16
CHINESE COMMUNITY HEALTH PLAN	CA	● C+	HMO	1q 2003	7.9	38.2	38.2	4.7	1.18	0.75
CHIROPRACTIC SERVICE BUREAU INC	WA	U	HMO	--	--	--	--	--	--	--
CHIROSAVE INC	CA	U	HMO	3q 2001	0.1	0.4	0.4	-0.4	--	--
CHRISTIAN FIDELITY LIFE INS CO	TX	C-	L&H	2q 2003	79.1	55.3	54.7	19.1	1.17	0.84
CHRISTIANA CARE HEALTH PLANS	DE	● B-	HMO	1q 2003	69.8	192.8	192.8	38.2	1.75	1.46
CIGNA BEHAVIORAL HEALTH OF CA	CA	U	HMO	--	--	--	--	--	--	--
CIGNA DENTAL HEALTH OF CALIFORNIA	CA	U	HMO	--	--	--	--	--	--	--
CIGNA DENTAL HEALTH OF DE INC	DE	U	HMO	1q 2002	0.2	0.0	0.0	0.2	--	--
CIGNA DENTAL HEALTH OF NC	NC	U	HMO	2q 2002	1.6	4.1	4.1	1.2	--	--
CIGNA DENTAL HEALTH OF PENNSYLVANIA	PA	U	HMO	--	--	--	--	--	--	--
CIGNA DENTAL HEALTH OF TEXAS INC	TX	U	HMO	--	--	--	--	--	--	--
CIGNA HEALTHCARE MID-ATLANTIC INC	MD	● D+	HMO	1q 2003	29.1	74.4	74.4	15.0	0.00	0.00
CIGNA HEALTHCARE OF ARIZONA INC	AZ	● C+	HMO	1q 2003	204.8	842.9	842.9	51.2	1.25	1.04
CIGNA HEALTHCARE OF CALIFORNIA INC	CA	● C-	HMO	1q 2003	277.0	1,156.5	1,156.5	49.9	1.14	0.71
CIGNA HEALTHCARE OF COLORADO INC	CO	● C	HMO	1q 2003	52.5	234.2	234.2	15.8	1.18	0.99
CIGNA HEALTHCARE OF CONNECTICUT INC	CT	● C	HMO	1q 2003	19.3	52.9	52.9	11.8	4.03	3.36
CIGNA HEALTHCARE OF DELAWARE INC	DE	● D+	HMO	1q 2003	4.3	1.3	1.3	3.8	0.00	0.00
CIGNA HEALTHCARE OF FLORIDA INC	FL	● D	HMO	2q 2002	68.4	252.7	252.7	21.9	1.47	1.23

Arrows denote recent upgrades ▲ or downgrades ▼   ● Bullets denote a more detailed analysis is available in Section II.

Winter 2003 - 04

I. Index of Companies

INSURANCE COMPANY NAME	DOM. STATE	WEISS SAFETY RATING	COMPANY TYPE	DATA DATE	TOTAL ASSETS ($MIL)	TOTAL PREMIUMS ($MIL)	HEALTH PREMIUMS ($MIL)	CAPITAL & SURPLUS ($MIL)	RISK ADJUSTED CAPITAL RATIO 1	RATIO 2
CIGNA HEALTHCARE OF GEORGIA INC	GA	• C+	HMO	1q 2003	40.2	105.9	105.9	18.2	3.55	2.96
CIGNA HEALTHCARE OF ILLINOIS INC	IL	• D+	HMO	1q 2003	12.0	20.6	20.6	6.1	3.50	2.92
CIGNA HEALTHCARE OF INDIANA INC	IN	• C-	HMO	4q 2002	20.0	97.1	97.1	7.3	1.62	1.35
CIGNA HEALTHCARE OF KENTUCKY INC	KY	U	HMO	--	--	--	--	--	--	--
CIGNA HEALTHCARE OF LOUISIANA INC	LA	U	HMO	4q 2001	8.3	0.8	0.8	3.2	--	--
CIGNA HEALTHCARE OF MAINE INC	ME	• C	HMO	1q 2003	45.5	139.0	139.0	21.4	2.59	2.16
CIGNA HEALTHCARE OF MASSACHUSETTS	MA	• C	HMO	1q 2003	42.1	184.2	184.2	20.0	1.88	1.56
CIGNA HEALTHCARE OF NEW HAMPSHIRE	NH	• C+	HMO	1q 2003	101.4	343.1	343.1	60.4	3.62	3.02
CIGNA HEALTHCARE OF NEW JERSEY INC	NJ	• C	HMO	4q 2002	78.9	211.4	211.4	37.2	3.45	2.88
CIGNA HEALTHCARE OF NEW YORK	NY	• C	HMO	1q 2003	65.5	178.5	178.5	32.7	3.54	2.95
CIGNA HEALTHCARE OF NORTH CAROLINA	NC	• C-	HMO	1q 2003	89.8	475.2	475.2	31.2	1.38	1.15
CIGNA HEALTHCARE OF OHIO INC	OH	• D+	HMO	1q 2003	18.0	25.3	25.3	4.8	0.00	0.00
CIGNA HEALTHCARE OF PENNSYLVANIA INC	PA	• D+	HMO	1q 2003	5.0	8.0	8.0	1.4	0.90	0.75
CIGNA HEALTHCARE OF SOUTH CAROLINA	SC	• D+	HMO	1q 2003	35.7	137.9	137.9	13.4	1.56	1.30
CIGNA HEALTHCARE OF ST LOUIS	MO	• C	HMO	4q 2002	11.2	32.9	32.9	5.2	2.09	1.74
CIGNA HEALTHCARE OF TENNESSEE INC	TN	• C	HMO	1q 2003	45.9	171.7	171.7	19.6	2.39	1.99
CIGNA HEALTHCARE OF TEXAS INC	TX	• D-	HMO	1q 2003	90.6	456.9	456.9	13.9	0.66	0.55
CIGNA HEALTHCARE OF UTAH INC	UT	• D	HMO	1q 2003	4.5	13.2	13.2	1.7	0.82	0.69
CIGNA HEALTHCARE OF VIRGINIA INC	VA	• D+	HMO	1q 2003	34.0	84.6	84.6	15.0	2.67	2.22
CIGNA INS SERVICES CO	SC	• C+	HMO	1q 2003	11.7	2.2	2.2	10.5	8.22	6.85
CIGNA INSURANCE GROUP INC	NH	• C-	HMO	1q 2003	2.1	1.8	1.8	1.6	3.54	2.95
CIGNA LIFE INS CO OF NEW YORK	NY	• C-	L&H	2q 2003	310.0	942.4	933.4	63.4	3.73	2.33
CIGNA WORLDWIDE INS CO	DE	• C-	L&H	1q 2003	323.5	142.9	35.8	38.7	1.93	1.33
CIGNA WORLDWIDE INS CO	DE	C-	P&C	3q 2000	5.3	9.7	0.7	5.2	14.06	7.34
CIMARRON HEALTH PLAN INC	NM	• D	HMO	1q 2003	50.2	314.1	314.1	16.0	0.48	0.40
CINCINNATI CASUALTY CO	OH	B	P&C	2q 2003	306.6	190.1	0.0	241.4	4.79	2.79
CINCINNATI EQUITABLE LIFE INS CO	OH	C-	L&H	2q 2003	11.6	11.9	11.6	7.1	1.43	1.23
CINCINNATI INS CO	OH	A-	P&C	2q 2003	7,143.1	2,643.6	0.1	2,485.6	1.44	1.02
CINCINNATI LIFE INS CO	OH	B	L&H	2q 2003	1,940.1	243.9	5.2	366.9	2.53	1.41
CITICORP LIFE INS CO	AZ	• B+	L&H	2q 2003	1,058.7	2.3	0.8	772.5	2.73	2.55
CITIZENS FIDELITY INS CO	AR	C-	L&H	2q 2003	52.1	5.1	0.0	9.0	1.41	1.27
CITIZENS INS CO OF AMERICA	CO	D+	L&H	2q 2003	247.3	59.1	4.9	50.0	2.05	1.72
CITIZENS SECURITY LIFE INS CO	KY	D-	L&H	2q 2003	101.8	39.0	9.6	9.0	0.72	0.49
CLARENDON AMERICA INS CO	NJ	D+	P&C	2q 2003	394.3	330.6	5.6	154.7	0.78	0.68
CLARENDON NATIONAL INS CO	NJ	C	P&C	2q 2003	1,817.8	1,468.9	129.7	570.1	0.83	0.64
CLARICA LIFE INS CO	ND	C+	L&H	2q 2003	2,862.5	862.2	2.6	150.1	1.62	0.93
CLASSIC LIFE ASR CO	OH	D+	L&H	2q 2003	6.2	8.8	4.9	4.3	2.29	2.06
CLEAR CHOICE HEALTH PLANS (See CENTRAL OREGON INDEPENDENT HEALTH SV)										
CLEAR-CARE CORP	PA	U	HMO	--	--	--	--	--	--	--
CLOISTER MUTUAL CASUALTY INS CO	PA	U	P&C	4q 2002	3.7	0.0	0.0	3.7	--	--
CLUB INS CO	OH	C-	P&C	2q 2003	8.0	2.1	2.1	6.7	8.58	5.29
CNA GROUP LIFE ASR CO	IL	• C	L&H	2q 2003	3,177.3	13.0	9.9	346.8	1.71	1.08
CNA MANAGED CARE	IL	U	HMO		--	--	--	--	--	--
COASTAL HEALTHCARE ADMINISTRATORS	CA	U	HMO		--	--	--	--	--	--
COLONIAL AMERICAN LIFE INS CO	PA	C	L&H	2q 2003	17.4	2.0	1.8	6.4	2.05	1.84
COLONIAL LIFE & ACCIDENT INS CO	SC	• C-	L&H	2q 2003	1,262.3	716.3	576.9	186.1	1.68	1.07
COLONIAL LIFE INS CO OF TX	TX	D+	L&H	2q 2003	14.7	1.9	0.6	11.0	3.80	3.42
COLONIAL PENN LIFE INS CO	PA	E	L&H	2q 2003	819.8	146.1	16.0	37.4	1.38	0.71
COLORADO ACCESS	CO	• C	HMO	1q 2003	69.3	248.2	248.2	14.6	0.91	0.76
COLORADO BANKERS LIFE INS CO	CO	B+	L&H	2q 2003	113.3	35.6	3.3	21.3	2.38	2.09
COLORADO DENTAL SERVICE INC	CO	U	HMO		--	--	--	--	--	--
COLORADO VISION SERVICES INC	CO	U	HMO		--	--	--	--	--	--

www.WeissRatings.com

Arrows denote recent upgrades ▲ or downgrades ▼   • Bullets denote a more detailed analysis is available in Section II.

I. Index of Companies

Winter 2003 - 04

INSURANCE COMPANY NAME	DOM. STATE	WEISS SAFETY RATING	COMPANY TYPE	DATA DATE	TOTAL ASSETS ($MIL)	TOTAL PREMIUMS ($MIL)	HEALTH PREMIUMS ($MIL)	CAPITAL & SURPLUS ($MIL)	RISK ADJUSTED CAPITAL RATIO 1	RATIO 2
COLUMBIA CASUALTY CO	IL	C-	P&C	2q 2003	21.7	429.1	0.0	20.2	24.60	22.14
COLUMBIA DENTAL OF IDAHO INC	ID	U	HMO		--	--	--	--	--	--
COLUMBIA UNITED PROVIDERS INC	WA	•B+	HLTH	1q 2003	13.4	68.5	68.5	7.7	1.21	1.01
COLUMBIA UNIVERSAL LIFE INS CO	TX	C+	L&H	2q 2003	203.5	24.7	1.3	24.7	2.57	1.56
COLUMBIAN FAMILY LIFE INS CO	NY	C	L&H	2q 2003	23.4	3.0	0.0	10.1	2.58	2.32
COLUMBIAN LIFE INS CO	IL	C	L&H	2q 2003	203.3	97.8	31.6	23.9	2.52	1.79
COLUMBIAN MUTUAL LIFE INS CO	NY	C+	L&H	2q 2003	329.6	55.0	2.5	38.3	1.21	0.96
COLUMBUS LIFE INS CO	OH	B+	L&H	2q 2003	2,187.1	199.5	0.7	225.7	2.32	1.20
COMANCHE COUNTY HOSPITAL AUTHORITY	OK	•C	HMO	1q 2003	3.7	19.7	19.7	1.8	0.67	0.56
COMBINED INS CO OF AMERICA	IL	•C	L&H	2q 2003	2,408.5	1,257.0	1,150.3	594.3	1.74	1.34
COMBINED LIFE INS CO OF NEW YORK	NY	•C+	L&H	2q 2003	300.0	133.1	114.9	46.0	1.70	1.28
COMBINED UNDERWRITERS LIFE INS CO	TX	D+	L&H	2q 2003	14.7	13.9	11.8	2.5	2.32	1.79
COMMERCE NATIONAL INS CO	MS	C-	L&H	4q 2002	8.2	0.2	0.0	7.6	3.62	3.26
COMMERCIAL BANKERS LIFE INS CO	IN	E	L&H	2q 2003	1.4	2.0	1.1	0.6	1.06	0.95
COMMERCIAL TRAVELERS MUTUAL INS CO	NY	E	L&H	2q 2003	24.0	22.1	22.1	5.1	0.45	0.38
COMMONWEALTH DEALERS LIFE INS CO	VA	C-	L&H	2q 2003	32.5	8.2	4.1	7.2	1.55	1.39
COMMONWEALTH INS CO	MD	D-	P&C	2q 2003	1.8	2.4	0.8	0.6	0.26	0.24
COMMUNITY BLUE HMO OF BL CROSS W NY	NY	U	HMO		--	--	--	--	--	--
COMMUNITY CARE BEHAVIORAL HEALTH	PA	U	HMO	4q 2002	74.0	186.2	186.2	22.8	--	--
COMMUNITY CARE PLAN	MI	•C	HMO	2q 2002	13.4	43.8	43.8	5.9	0.83	0.70
COMMUNITY CAREPLUS (See ALLIANCE FOR COMMUNITY HEALTH LLC)										
COMMUNITY CHOICE MICHIGAN	MI	F	HMO	1q 2003	18.0	127.3	127.3	-1.9	0.02	0.02
COMMUNITY DENTAL SERVICES INC	CA	U	HMO		--	--	--	--	--	--
COMMUNITY FIRST GROUP HOSPITAL SERV	TX	U	HMO		--	--	--	--	--	--
▲ COMMUNITY FIRST HEALTH PLANS INC	TX	•C-	HMO	1q 2003	27.4	149.9	149.9	5.2	0.29	0.25
COMMUNITY HEALTH CHOICE INC	TX	•E+	HMO	1q 2003	23.5	53.7	53.7	4.9	0.40	0.34
COMMUNITY HEALTH GROUP	CA	•C+	HMO	1q 2003	49.0	103.8	103.8	21.7	1.87	1.15
COMMUNITY HEALTH PLAN	MO	•E	HMO	1q 2003	9.1	61.0	61.0	1.8	0.13	0.11
COMMUNITY HEALTH PLAN INC	NY	U	HMO		--	--	--	--	--	--
COMMUNITY HEALTH PLAN OF OHIO	OH	•E	HMO	4q 2002	4.3	7.6	7.6	1.9	0.26	0.22
COMMUNITY HEALTH PLAN OF THE ROCKIES	CO	F	HMO	1q 2003	14.1	81.4	81.4	0.2	0.02	0.02
COMMUNITY HEALTH PLAN OF WASHINGTON	WA	•A	HLTH	1q 2003	106.9	331.3	331.3	69.6	3.21	2.68
COMMUNITY INS CO	OH	•C	P&C	2q 2003	1,014.9	2,614.4	2,614.4	352.2	1.20	0.68
COMMUNITY PPO OF MIDDLE TENNESSEE	TN	U	HMO		--	--	--	--	--	--
COMMUNITYCARE HMO INC	OK	•C	HMO	1q 2003	56.1	286.3	286.3	14.0	0.87	0.72
COMMUNITYCARE LIFE AND HEALTH INS CO	OK	C-	L&H	2q 2003	5.2	4.6	4.6	3.8	2.34	2.10
COMPANION HEALTH CARE CORP	SC	•A-	HMO	1q 2003	73.7	199.6	199.6	44.0	3.09	2.57
COMPANION LIFE INS CO	NY	B	L&H	2q 2003	602.0	72.9	3.0	62.6	2.58	1.21
COMPANION LIFE INS CO	SC	•B+	L&H	2q 2003	75.6	156.1	130.7	44.0	2.87	2.10
COMPBENEFITS INS CO	TX	C	L&H	2q 2003	23.6	34.4	31.2	12.7	1.26	1.05
COMPCARE HEALTH SERVICES INS CORP	WI	•C-	HMO	1q 2003	160.3	383.3	383.3	79.8	1.86	1.55
COMPLEMENTARY HEALTHCARE INS INC	OR	U	HMO		--	--	--	--	--	--
CONCENTRAL MANAGED CARE INC	MA	U	HMO		--	--	--	--	--	--
CONCENTRATED CARE INC	CA	U	HMO		--	--	--	--	--	--
CONCERN: EMPLOYEE ASSISTANCE PROGRAM	CA	U	HMO		--	--	--	--	--	--
CONCERT HEALTH PLAN INS CO	IL	D-	L&H	2q 2003	10.3	13.5	13.5	4.9	0.88	0.74
CONCORD HERITAGE LIFE INS CO INC	NH	B	L&H	2q 2003	35.3	11.4	2.9	4.6	0.93	0.84
CONCORD NATIONAL LIFE INS CO	IN	C	L&H	2q 2003	4.1	3.8	2.3	4.0	2.65	2.39
CONGRESS LIFE INS CO	AZ	C	L&H	2q 2003	6.1	0.0	0.0	5.9	3.43	3.09
CONNECTICARE INC	CT	•B+	HMO	1q 2003	156.2	590.5	590.5	66.0	1.57	1.31
CONNECTICARE INS CO INC	CT	U	HMO		--	--	--	--	--	--
CONNECTICARE OF MASSACHUSETTS INC	MA	•B	HMO	1q 2003	6.3	14.6	14.6	2.3	1.11	0.92

Arrows denote recent upgrades ▲ or downgrades ▼   • Bullets denote a more detailed analysis is available in Section II.   www.WeissRatings.com

Winter 2003 - 04

I. Index of Companies

INSURANCE COMPANY NAME	DOM. STATE	WEISS SAFETY RATING	COMPANY TYPE	DATA DATE	TOTAL ASSETS ($MIL)	TOTAL PREMIUMS ($MIL)	HEALTH PREMIUMS ($MIL)	CAPITAL & SURPLUS ($MIL)	RISK ADJUSTED CAPITAL RATIO 1	RATIO 2
CONNECTICUT GENERAL LIFE INS CO	CT	• C-	L&H	2q 2003	68,525.6	5,691.4	4,027.4	2,380.3	2.09	1.16
CONNECTICUT INDEMNITY CO	CT	D	P&C	2q 2003	164.6	169.2	0.1	24.8	0.50	0.30
CONSECO ANNUITY ASSURANCE CO	IL	E	L&H	2q 2003	5,392.1	335.0	5.1	238.5	1.12	0.56
CONSECO HEALTH INS CO	AZ	• E	L&H	2q 2003	1,800.8	436.6	433.6	104.9	1.27	0.72
CONSECO LIFE INS CO	IN	E	L&H	2q 2003	4,203.7	464.4	5.9	146.3	0.73	0.39
CONSECO LIFE INS CO OF NY	NY	E	L&H	2q 2003	147.8	38.2	13.3	10.0	1.10	0.99
CONSECO SENIOR HEALTH INS CO	PA	• E	L&H	2q 2003	2,790.8	444.2	434.7	91.3	0.85	0.50
CONSOLIDATED HEALTHCARE MANAGEMENT	NJ	U	HMO	--	--	--	--	--	--	--
CONSOLIDATED INS ASN	TX	D	P&C	2q 2003	12.4	7.8	0.0	3.0	0.59	0.52
CONSTITUTION LIFE INS CO	TX	D	L&H	2q 2003	95.3	46.1	44.0	11.1	0.74	0.60
CONSUMER DENTAL CARE OF VA INC	VA	U	HMO	--	--	--	--	--	--	--
CONSUMER HEALTH NETWORK	NJ	U	HMO	--	--	--	--	--	--	--
CONSUMERHEALTH INC	CA	U	HMO	--	--	--	--	--	--	--
CONTINENTAL AMERICAN INS CO	SC	C+	L&H	2q 2003	41.3	13.5	11.9	12.3	1.98	1.47
CONTINENTAL ASSURANCE CO	IL	• C+	L&H	2q 2003	9,237.5	481.3	121.5	1,182.3	2.44	1.60
CONTINENTAL CASUALTY CO	IL	• C	P&C	2q 2003	27,424.2	4,381.5	1,316.0	5,431.3	1.09	0.85
CONTINENTAL GENERAL INS CO	NE	• D	L&H	2q 2003	418.3	407.2	389.6	55.5	0.72	0.57
CONTINENTAL INS CO	NH	C	P&C	2q 2003	2,952.7	994.9	0.3	714.6	1.35	0.82
CONTINENTAL LIFE INS CO	PA	D	L&H	2q 2003	19.2	4.1	0.2	2.0	0.61	0.55
CONTINENTAL LIFE INS CO OF BRENTWOOD	TN	• C	L&H	2q 2003	83.1	103.0	100.0	25.0	1.09	0.85
CONTINENTAL LIFE INS CO OF SC	SC	D	L&H	2q 2003	2.4	0.2	0.0	0.3	0.42	0.38
CONTRA COSTA HEALTH PLAN	CA	• C	HMO	2q 2002	26.7	72.9	72.9	5.5	0.46	0.28
COOK CHILDRENS HEALTH PLAN	TX	• C-	HMO	1q 2003	6.9	40.2	40.2	2.5	0.81	0.67
COOPERATIVA DE SEGUROS DE VIDA DE PR	PR	C	L&H	2q 2003	248.4	114.3	67.2	22.0	1.48	0.95
COOPERATIVE HEALTH NETWORK INC	OH	U	HMO	--	--	--	--	--	--	--
COORDINATED CARE CORP INDIANA INC	IN	• C+	HMO	1q 2003	40.0	131.8	131.8	11.6	1.28	1.07
COORDINATED CARE SOLUTIONS OF TEXAS	TX	U	HMO	2q 2002	3.0	22.0	22.0	-0.5	--	--
COORDINATED HEALTH PARTNERS INC	RI	• C	HMO	4q 2002	157.8	489.7	489.7	67.9	1.91	1.59
COPIC INS CO	CO	B	P&C	2q 2003	311.0	63.6	4.6	98.5	2.11	1.51
CORPORATE HEALTH INS CO	PA	• C+	L&H	2q 2003	67.9	178.5	178.5	43.7	1.22	1.01
COSMOPOLITAN LIFE INS CO	AR	E	L&H	2q 2003	1.8	0.5	0.4	1.1	0.91	0.74
COTTON STATES LIFE INS CO	GA	C	L&H	2q 2003	209.7	44.5	0.1	34.4	2.75	1.77
COUNTRY LIFE INS CO	IL	• A+	L&H	2q 2003	4,387.5	446.7	200.9	859.2	3.21	2.11
COUNTRYWAY INS CO	NY	C-	P&C	2q 2003	56.2	33.5	0.0	16.3	1.89	1.45
COVENTRY HEALTH & LIFE INS CO	DE	• C-	L&H	2q 2003	110.8	113.6	113.6	53.7	1.76	1.42
COVENTRY HEALTH CARE OF DELAWARE INC	DE	• B-	HMO	1q 2003	52.8	180.5	180.5	28.8	2.01	1.68
COVENTRY HEALTH CARE OF GEORGIA	GA	• B-	HMO	1q 2003	27.0	76.6	76.6	13.5	2.24	1.86
COVENTRY HEALTH CARE OF IOWA INC	IA	• B-	HMO	1q 2003	59.5	134.7	134.7	31.4	3.15	2.63
COVENTRY HEALTH CARE OF KANSAS INC	KS	• D+	HMO	1q 2003	139.1	678.3	678.3	56.5	1.28	1.07
COVENTRY HEALTH CARE OF LOUISIANA	LA	• C-	HMO	1q 2003	43.5	159.2	159.2	17.2	1.47	1.23
COVENTRY HEALTH CARE OF NEBRASKA INC	NE	• D+	HMO	1q 2003	22.8	63.6	63.6	11.4	2.12	1.77
COVENTRY HEALTH CARE OF PENNSYLVANIA	PA	U	HMO	1q 2003	2.0	0.0	0.0	2.0	--	--
COX HEALTH SYSTEMS HMO INC	MO	• E	HMO	1q 2003	6.4	43.7	43.7	2.2	0.34	0.29
COX HEALTH SYSTEMS INS CO	MO	D-	L&H	2q 2003	11.6	36.6	36.6	4.4	0.46	0.41
CREATIVE HEALTH PLANS INC	OH	U	HMO	--	--	--	--	--	--	--
CUMIS INS SOCIETY INC	WI	B+	P&C	2q 2003	826.9	350.4	8.8	296.3	2.45	1.66
CUNA MUTUAL INS SOCIETY	WI	• C	L&H	2q 2003	2,756.6	1,343.9	481.0	546.2	0.93	0.80
CUNA MUTUAL LIFE INS CO	IA	B-	L&H	2q 2003	6,318.6	1,311.9	4.5	228.6	2.03	1.10
DAILY UNDERWRITERS OF AMERICA	PA	C-	P&C	1q 2003	15.1	7.2	0.1	9.6	3.22	2.29
DAKOTACARE (See SD STATE MEDICAL HOLDING CO)										
DALLAS GENERAL LIFE INS CO	TX	E-	L&H	2q 2003	9.3	42.1	42.0	1.4	0.11	0.10
▲ DAYTON AREA HEALTH PLAN	OH	• B	HMO	1q 2003	85.9	373.1	373.1	37.6	1.02	0.85

www.WeissRatings.com

Arrows denote recent upgrades ▲ or downgrades ▼ • Bullets denote a more detailed analysis is available in Section II.

I. Index of Companies

Winter 2003 - 04

INSURANCE COMPANY NAME	DOM. STATE	WEISS SAFETY RATING	COMPANY TYPE	DATA DATE	TOTAL ASSETS ($MIL)	TOTAL PREMIUMS ($MIL)	HEALTH PREMIUMS ($MIL)	CAPITAL & SURPLUS ($MIL)	RISK ADJUSTED CAPITAL RATIO 1	RATIO 2
DC CHARTERED HEALTH PLAN INC	DC	• C	HMO	1q 2003	21.2	61.5	61.5	6.8	0.99	0.82
DEACONESS HEALTH PLANS	IN	U	HMO	--	--	--	--	--	--	--
DEAN HEALTH PLAN INC	WI	• B+	HMO	1q 2003	123.0	529.0	529.0	37.5	1.37	1.14
DEDICATED DENTAL SYSTEMS INC	CA	U	HMO	--	--	--	--	--	--	--
DELAWARE AMERICAN LIFE INS CO	DE	• B	L&H	2q 2003	102.5	23.1	12.6	35.6	4.22	3.28
DELMARVA HEALTH PLAN INC	MD	• B-	HMO	1q 2003	8.6	16.8	16.8	7.5	4.07	3.39
DELTA CARE DENTAL PLAN INC	NV	U	HMO	--	--	--	--	--	--	--
DELTA DENTAL INS CO	DE	• C	L&H	1q 2003	57.3	167.0	167.0	29.4	0.90	0.71
DELTA DENTAL OF NEW YORK	NY	U	HMO	--	--	--	--	--	--	--
DELTA DENTAL OF OHIO INC	OH	U	HMO	--	--	--	--	--	--	--
DELTA DENTAL OF RHODE ISLAND	RI	U	HMO	--	--	--	--	--	--	--
DELTA DENTAL PLAN OF ARIZONA INC	AZ	U	HMO	--	--	--	--	--	--	--
DELTA DENTAL PLAN OF ARKANSAS INC	AR	U	HMO	--	--	--	--	--	--	--
DELTA DENTAL PLAN OF CALIFORNIA	CA	U	HMO	--	--	--	--	--	--	--
DELTA DENTAL PLAN OF IDAHO INC	ID	U	HMO	--	--	--	--	--	--	--
DELTA DENTAL PLAN OF ILLINOIS	IL	U	HMO	--	--	--	--	--	--	--
DELTA DENTAL PLAN OF IOWA	IA	U	HMO	--	--	--	--	--	--	--
DELTA DENTAL PLAN OF KENTUCKY INC	KY	U	HMO	--	--	--	--	--	--	--
DELTA DENTAL PLAN OF MAINE	ME	U	HMO	--	--	--	--	--	--	--
DELTA DENTAL PLAN OF MASSACHUSETTS	MA	U	HMO	--	--	--	--	--	--	--
DELTA DENTAL PLAN OF MICHIGAN INC	MI	U	HMO	--	--	--	--	--	--	--
DELTA DENTAL PLAN OF MINNESOTA	MN	U	HMO	--	--	--	--	--	--	--
DELTA DENTAL PLAN OF N CAROLINA INC	NC	U	HMO	--	--	--	--	--	--	--
DELTA DENTAL PLAN OF OKLAHOMA	OK	U	HMO	--	--	--	--	--	--	--
DELTA DENTAL PLAN OF PUERTO RICO	PR	U	HMO	--	--	--	--	--	--	--
DELTA LIFE INS CO	GA	D+	L&H	2q 2003	80.7	13.5	1.7	25.4	1.33	0.83
DELTA LLOYDS INS CO OF HOUSTON	TX	D	P&C	2q 2003	10.8	17.8	0.0	7.2	3.05	1.88
DENTAL BENEFIT PROVIDERS OF CA INC	CA	U	HMO	--	--	--	--	--	--	--
DENTAL CONCERN INC	KY	U	HMO	--	--	--	--	--	--	--
DENTAL CONCERN LTD	IL	U	HMO	--	--	--	--	--	--	--
DENTAL HEALTH SERVICES	CA	U	HMO	--	--	--	--	--	--	--
DENTAL HEALTH SERVICES	WA	U	HMO	--	--	--	--	--	--	--
DENTAL INS CO OF AMERICA	NY	U	HMO	--	--	--	--	--	--	--
DENTAL SERVICE CORP OF NORTH DAKOTA	ND	U	HMO	--	--	--	--	--	--	--
DENTICARE INC	TX	U	HMO	--	--	--	--	--	--	--
DENTICARE INC (FLORIDA)	FL	U	HMO	--	--	--	--	--	--	--
DENTICARE OF ARKANSAS INC	AR	U	HMO	4q 2001	0.5	0.2	0.2	0.5	--	--
DENTICARE OF OKLAHOMA INC	OK	U	HMO	--	--	--	--	--	--	--
DENVER HEALTH MEDICAL PLAN INC	CO	• D+	HMO	1q 2003	5.0	16.6	16.6	2.4	0.85	0.71
DESERET MUTUAL INS CO	UT	B	L&H	2q 2003	41.4	17.4	15.5	7.4	1.76	1.49
DESTINY HEALTH INS CO	IL	D	L&H	2q 2003	22.7	21.4	21.4	11.4	1.66	1.25
DEVON HEALTH SERVICES INC	PA	U	HMO	--	--	--	--	--	--	--
DIRECTCARE AMERICA INC	OH	U	HMO	--	--	--	--	--	--	--
DMC CARE	MI	U	HMO	--	--	--	--	--	--	--
DOCTORS HEALTH PLAN	NC	U	HMO	1q 2003	5.6	13.0	13.0	1.1	--	--
DOMINION DENTAL SERVICES INC	VA	U	HMO	--	--	--	--	--	--	--
DRISCOLL CHILDRENS HEALTH PLAN	TX	• C+	HMO	1q 2003	13.2	22.2	22.2	10.2	3.39	2.82
EASTERN PENNSYLVANIA HEALTH NETWORK	PA	U	HMO	--	--	--	--	--	--	--
ECCA MANAGED VISION CARE INC	TX	U	HMO	--	--	--	--	--	--	--
EDUCATORS HEALTH CARE	UT	U	HMO	1q 2003	2.5	2.3	2.3	2.3	--	--
EDUCATORS HEALTH PARTNERS	PA	U	HMO	--	--	--	--	--	--	--
EDUCATORS MUTUAL INS ASN	UT	D	L&H	2q 2003	63.7	48.1	46.7	22.5	1.87	1.50

Arrows denote recent upgrades ▲ or downgrades ▼

• Bullets denote a more detailed analysis is available in Section II.

www.WeissRatings.com

Winter 2003 - 04 — I. Index of Companies

INSURANCE COMPANY NAME	DOM. STATE	WEISS SAFETY RATING	COMPANY TYPE	DATA DATE	TOTAL ASSETS ($MIL)	TOTAL PREMIUMS ($MIL)	HEALTH PREMIUMS ($MIL)	CAPITAL & SURPLUS ($MIL)	RISK ADJUSTED CAPITAL RATIO 1	RATIO 2
EDUCATORS MUTUAL LIFE INS CO	PA	• B	L&H	2q 2003	86.8	98.1	91.2	53.6	5.22	3.69
EL PASO FIRST HEALTH PLANS INC	TX	U	HMO		--	--	--	--	--	--
ELDER HEALTH HMO PENNSYLVANIA INC	PA	U	HMO	1q 2003	11.7	2.7	2.7	5.7	--	--
ELDER HEALTH MARYLAND HMO INC	MD	• C-	HMO	1q 2003	9.9	27.1	27.1	3.9	0.95	0.79
ELDERPLAN INC	NY	• E-	HMO	1q 2003	24.9	122.9	122.9	-1.8	0.00	0.00
EMC NATIONAL LIFE CO	IA	B	L&H	2q 2003	371.0	77.9	0.4	29.7	1.88	1.03
EMERALD HEALTH NETWORK	OH	U	HMO		--	--	--	--	--	--
EMPHESYS INS CO	TX	C-	L&H	2q 2003	3.9	2.8	2.7	3.6	2.15	1.94
EMPHESYS WISCONSIN INS CO	WI	U	HMO	4q 2001	29.6	33.0	33.0	15.3	--	--
EMPIRE BL CROSS BL SHIELD HEALTHNET	NY	U	HMO		--	--	--	--	--	--
EMPIRE BLUE CROSS BLUE SHIELD (See EMPIRE HEALTHCHOICE ASSURANCE INC)										
EMPIRE FIRE & MAR INS CO	NE	B-	P&C	2q 2003	223.4	599.3	24.9	121.2	15.82	14.24
EMPIRE GENERAL LIFE ASSURANCE CORP	TN	C+	L&H	2q 2003	161.1	187.0	1.7	37.0	2.93	1.69
EMPIRE HEALTHCHOICE ASSURANCE INC	NY	• A-	HLTH	1q 2003	1,762.8	3,999.1	3,999.1	853.8	3.35	2.79
EMPIRE HEALTHCHOICE HMO INC	NY	• B	HMO	1q 2003	331.3	561.8	561.8	111.3	3.74	3.12
EMPLOYEES LIFE CO MUTUAL	IL	D+	L&H	2q 2003	264.0	26.2	0.0	9.7	1.22	1.10
EMPLOYEES LIFE INS CO	TX	C	L&H	2q 2003	8.3	1.5	0.8	3.5	1.89	1.70
EMPLOYERS INS OF WAUSAU	WI	B-	P&C	2q 2003	3,864.8	795.9	1.8	718.2	1.12	0.75
EMPLOYERS LIFE INS CORP	SC	D	L&H	2q 2003	14.2	17.5	17.0	5.0	0.96	0.78
EMPLOYERS MUTUAL CAS CO	IA	B	P&C	2q 2003	1,603.7	695.4	0.0	475.3	1.53	1.13
EMPLOYERS REASSURANCE CORP	KS	• C	L&H	2q 2003	5,856.1	0.0	0.0	438.7	1.28	0.79
EMPLOYERS REINSURANCE CORP	MO	• C+	P&C	2q 2003	15,079.2	302.3	127.9	4,604.8	0.89	0.64
EMPLOYERS SECURITY INS CO	IN	E	P&C	2q 2003	16.5	5.7	0.5	2.7	0.54	0.30
ENCORE HEALTH NETWORK	IN	U	HMO		--	--	--	--	--	--
ENTERPRISE LIFE INS CO	TX	D+	L&H	2q 2003	36.4	33.5	17.3	13.2	2.48	2.23
EPIC LIFE INSURANCE CO	WI	C-	L&H	2q 2003	32.3	17.2	14.7	19.7	4.86	4.38
EQUITABLE LIFE & CASUALTY INS CO	UT	• C	L&H	2q 2003	135.1	110.5	100.4	30.8	1.41	1.06
EQUITABLE LIFE ASR SOC OF THE US	NY	B-	L&H	2q 2003	86,709.1	11,355.1	151.1	4,178.3	1.64	1.05
EQUITABLE LIFE INS CO OF IOWA	IA	B-	L&H	2q 2003	7,487.6	537.9	0.3	1,122.8	0.99	0.83
ERC LIFE REINSURANCE CORP	MO	• C	L&H	2q 2003	1,533.2	0.3	0.3	700.3	1.71	1.55
ERIE FAMILY LIFE INS CO	PA	B	L&H	2q 2003	1,363.0	236.2	0.4	89.3	1.63	0.88
ERLANGER HEALTH PLAN TRUST	TN	U	HMO		--	--	--	--	--	--
ESSENCE INC	MO	U	HMO		--	--	--	--	--	--
ESSEX INS CO	DE	C-	P&C	2q 2003	695.8	484.8	0.2	201.8	0.82	0.51
ETHIX SOUTHEAST INC	NC	U	HMO		--	--	--	--	--	--
EVERCARE OF TEXAS LLC	TX	• B-	HMO	1q 2003	35.9	121.6	121.6	6.4	8.37	6.98
EVERGREEN HEALTH PLAN INC	GA	• E+	HMO	2q 2002	4.0	19.9	19.9	1.0	0.29	0.24
EVERGREEN MEDICAL GROUP LLC	GA	U	HMO		--	--	--	--	--	--
EVOLUTIONS HEALTHCARE SYSTEMS INC	FL	U	HMO		--	--	--	--	--	--
EXCELLUS HEALTH PLAN INC	NY	• B+	HLTH	1q 2003	1,475.7	3,275.4	3,275.4	492.9	4.25	3.54
EXCLUSIVE HEALTHCARE INC	NE	• B	HMO	1q 2003	25.9	48.6	48.6	17.2	5.73	4.77
EYE CARE PLAN OF AMERICA-CALIFORNIA	CA	U	HMO		--	--	--	--	--	--
EYEMED INC	CA	U	HMO		--	--	--	--	--	--
FAIRFIELD INS CO	CT	B	P&C	2q 2003	53.1	119.0	51.9	24.0	2.30	1.37
FAIRMONT INS CO	CA	C	P&C	2q 2003	23.7	71.6	0.0	23.3	129.10	102.20
▲ FALLON COMMUNITY HEALTH PLAN	MA	• B	HMO	1q 2003	138.4	611.2	611.2	62.9	1.91	1.59
FALLON HEALTH & LIFE ASR CO	MA	C+	L&H	2q 2003	4.2	0.3	0.3	3.8	2.91	2.62
FAMILY BENEFIT LIFE INS CO	MO	C	L&H	2q 2003	55.6	4.3	0.0	6.4	0.94	0.84
FAMILY CHOICE HEALTH ALLIANCE	NJ	U	HMO		--	--	--	--	--	--
FAMILY FINANCIAL LIFE INS CO	IN	C+	L&H	2q 2003	6.2	6.8	0.6	4.9	2.63	2.19
FAMILY HEALTH CARE PLUS INC	MS	• D	HMO	1q 2002	3.2	6.9	6.9	1.5	0.78	0.67
FAMILY HEALTH PLAN INC	OH	• E	HMO	1q 2003	25.3	85.7	85.7	8.5	0.29	0.24

www.WeissRatings.com

Arrows denote recent upgrades ▲ or downgrades ▼   • Bullets denote a more detailed analysis is available in Section II.

I. Index of Companies

Winter 2003 - 04

INSURANCE COMPANY NAME	DOM. STATE	WEISS SAFETY RATING	COMPANY TYPE	DATA DATE	TOTAL ASSETS ($MIL)	TOTAL PREMIUMS ($MIL)	HEALTH PREMIUMS ($MIL)	CAPITAL & SURPLUS ($MIL)	RISK ADJUSTED CAPITAL RATIO 1	RATIO 2
FAMILY HERITAGE LIFE INS CO OF AMER	OH	C-	L&H	2q 2003	104.9	48.5	48.4	11.0	1.03	0.80
FAMILY LIFE INS CO	WA	C-	L&H	2q 2003	124.7	36.4	0.2	25.7	1.68	1.35
FAMILYCARE HEALTH PLANS INC	OR	U	HMO		--	--	--	--	--	--
FARA PPO NETWORK	LA	U	HMO		--	--	--	--	--	--
FARM BUREAU LIFE INS CO	IA	A-	L&H	2q 2003	4,695.3	501.3	16.2	414.7	1.77	1.08
FARM BUREAU LIFE INS CO OF MISSOURI	MO	A-	L&H	2q 2003	293.5	35.8	0.2	50.8	4.57	2.62
FARM BUREAU MUTUAL INS CO OF AR	AR	C	P&C	2q 2003	188.8	145.2	0.1	80.3	2.54	1.64
FARM BUREAU MUTUAL INS CO OF MI	MI	C+	P&C	2q 2003	433.5	116.1	0.1	140.4	2.73	1.86
FARM FAMILY LIFE INS CO	NY	B+	L&H	2q 2003	889.2	66.1	3.7	113.1	2.46	1.37
FARMERS & TRADERS LIFE INS CO	NY	C	L&H	2q 2003	474.4	57.8	0.0	31.5	2.45	1.33
FARMERS MUTUAL HAIL INS CO OF IA	IA	C+	P&C	2q 2003	284.3	101.7	0.0	121.5	2.45	1.60
FARMERS NEW WORLD LIFE INS CO	WA	B	L&H	2q 2003	6,467.4	859.3	9.1	1,096.4	3.57	1.95
FEDERAL HOME LIFE INS CO	VA	• B	L&H	2q 2003	2,199.3	45.1	24.4	969.0	1.12	1.03
FEDERAL INS CO	IN	B+	P&C	2q 2003	18,983.3	4,844.8	101.2	5,819.3	1.50	1.16
FEDERAL LIFE INS CO (MUTUAL)	IL	B	L&H	2q 2003	222.9	21.4	0.7	41.1	4.52	2.76
FEDERATED LIFE INS CO	MN	A-	L&H	2q 2003	864.3	129.0	15.3	178.9	4.20	2.34
FEDERATED MUTUAL INS CO	MN	• B+	P&C	2q 2003	3,013.6	1,169.4	308.1	1,091.3	2.33	1.69
FIDELIO INS CO	PA	D+	P&C	4q 2002	5.0	5.2	5.2	4.5	4.87	2.83
FIDELITY & GUARANTY LIFE INS CO	MD	C	L&H	2q 2003	8,050.3	3,875.5	0.0	480.8	1.45	0.72
FIDELITY SECURITY LIFE INS CO	MO	• B-	L&H	2q 2003	410.0	251.8	215.4	46.0	2.00	1.25
FIDUCIARY INS CO OF AMERICA	NY	U	L&H	4q 2002	0.4	-0.7	0.0	0.4	--	--
FINANCIAL AMERICAN LIFE INS CO	IL	C	L&H	2q 2003	22.1	18.0	10.6	9.7	2.77	2.49
FIREMANS FUND INS CO OF GA	GA	B-	P&C	2q 2003	6.4	0.5	0.0	6.4	372.60	335.30
FIRST ALLIANCE INS CO	KY	D+	L&H	2q 2003	26.5	8.2	0.4	4.1	1.16	1.04
FIRST ALLMERICA FINANCIAL LIFE INS	MA	D-	L&H	2q 2003	4,574.3	411.2	3.2	169.6	2.09	1.03
FIRST AMERITAS LIFE INS CO OF NY	NY	B	L&H	2q 2003	42.2	26.7	13.9	15.4	2.94	2.65
FIRST AMTENN LIFE INS CO	MS	C-	L&H	2q 2003	20.6	-0.1	0.0	17.0	4.70	4.23
FIRST ASR LIFE OF AMERICA	LA	C-	L&H	2q 2003	18.6	16.0	5.3	15.4	4.72	4.25
FIRST CENTRAL NATL LIC OF NEW YORK	NY	• B	L&H	2q 2003	48.4	6.1	3.0	32.4	5.02	4.52
FIRST CHOICE HEALTH PLAN INC	WA	• D	HLTH	1q 2003	15.4	41.4	41.4	6.0	0.90	0.75
FIRST CHOICE HEATLHPLAN OF MS	MS	U	HMO		--	--	--	--	--	--
FIRST CHOICE OF THE MIDWEST INC	SD	U	HMO		--	--	--	--	--	--
FIRST CITICORP LIFE INS CO	NY	C+	L&H	2q 2003	773.2	8.6	0.8	50.0	2.84	1.37
FIRST COLONY LIFE INS CO	VA	B	L&H	2q 2003	13,479.1	1,411.4	0.4	965.1	1.76	0.91
FIRST COMMONWEALTH HEALTH SERVICES	IL	U	HMO		--	--	--	--	--	--
FIRST COMMONWEALTH INS CO	IL	B	L&H	2q 2003	21.2	25.6	25.6	11.4	2.33	1.92
FIRST COMMONWEALTH LIMITED HEALTH	IL	U	HMO		--	--	--	--	--	--
FIRST COMMONWEALTH LIMITED HEALTH	WI	U	HMO		--	--	--	--	--	--
FIRST COMMUNITY HEALTH PLAN INC	AL	• C+	HMO	1q 2003	5.9	4.8	4.8	4.5	8.77	7.31
FIRST CONTINENTAL LIFE & ACC INS CO	UT	E	L&H	1q 2003	2.8	1.4	0.7	0.7	0.74	0.66
FIRST DAKOTA INDEMNITY CO	SD	D+	P&C	2q 2003	11.8	5.8	0.0	5.2	1.63	1.01
FIRST FORTIS LIFE INS CO	NY	• C+	L&H	2q 2003	229.0	118.8	82.2	69.0	4.86	3.25
FIRST GREAT WEST LIFE & ANNUITY INS	NY	• B	L&H	2q 2003	279.3	23.3	7.1	35.3	3.82	2.64
FIRST HEALTH GROUP CORP	IL	U	HMO		--	--	--	--	--	--
FIRST HEALTH LIFE & HEALTH INS CO	TX	C-	L&H	2q 2003	108.1	12.4	10.7	17.9	1.99	1.79
FIRST INS CO OF HI LTD	HI	C+	P&C	2q 2003	420.4	72.3	1.7	131.3	2.56	1.52
FIRST INVESTORS LIFE INS CO	NY	C+	L&H	2q 2003	1,035.0	107.0	0.0	71.0	4.45	2.73
FIRST MEDICAL HEALTH PLAN INC	PR	U	HMO	4q 2002	39.9	250.4	250.4	1.9	--	--
FIRST NATIONAL LIFE INS CO OF USA	NE	C	L&H	2q 2003	7.5	2.4	1.1	2.7	1.37	1.23
FIRST OPTION CORPORATION-NEBRASKA	NE	U	HMO		--	--	--	--	--	--
FIRST PENN-PACIFIC LIFE INS CO	IN	B	L&H	2q 2003	1,693.0	326.6	0.0	107.9	1.49	0.77
FIRST PLAN OF MINNESOTA	MN	• B+	HMO	4q 2002	19.3	52.9	52.9	6.9	1.14	0.95

Arrows denote recent upgrades ▲ or downgrades ▼ • Bullets denote a more detailed analysis is available in Section II.

www.WeissRatings.com

Winter 2003 - 04

I. Index of Companies

INSURANCE COMPANY NAME	DOM. STATE	WEISS SAFETY RATING	COMPANY TYPE	DATA DATE	TOTAL ASSETS ($MIL)	TOTAL PREMIUMS ($MIL)	HEALTH PREMIUMS ($MIL)	CAPITAL & SURPLUS ($MIL)	RISK ADJUSTED CAPITAL RATIO 1	RATIO 2
FIRST PRIORITY HEALTH (See HMO OF NORTHEASTERN PENNSYLVANIA INC)										
FIRST PROFESSIONALS INS CO INC	FL	C	P&C	2q 2003	535.1	229.7	0.0	117.3	1.65	1.28
FIRST PYRAMID LIFE INS CO OF AMERICA	AR	U	HMO	--	--	--	--	--	--	--
FIRST REHABILITATION INS CO OF AM	NY	• C+	L&H	2q 2003	70.7	62.7	62.4	40.5	4.73	3.54
FIRST RELIANCE STANDARD LIFE INS CO	NY	• C	L&H	2q 2003	86.0	34.5	17.4	26.9	3.05	2.21
FIRST SUNAMERICA LIFE INS CO	NY	B-	L&H	2q 2003	2,572.8	437.7	0.4	115.4	1.55	0.73
FIRST UNITED AMERICAN LIFE INS CO	NY	• B	L&H	2q 2003	82.9	49.4	37.8	25.5	1.83	1.26
FIRST UNUM LIFE INS CO	NY	• C-	L&H	2q 2003	1,172.9	387.9	321.2	107.1	1.35	0.81
FIRST VIRGINIA LIFE INS CO	VA	C-	L&H	2q 2003	16.0	0.0	0.0	5.9	1.87	1.68
FIRSTCARE (See SHA LLC)										
FIRSTCAROLINACARE INC	NC	• C	HMO	1q 2003	11.2	19.2	19.2	8.3	2.58	2.15
▲ FIRSTCHOICE HEALTHPLANS OF CT INC	CT	• D-	HMO	1q 2003	11.2	37.9	37.9	5.6	1.09	0.91
FIRSTGUARD HEALTH PLAN INC	MO	• C-	HMO	1q 2003	29.4	107.9	107.9	8.5	0.65	0.54
FIRSTGUARD HEALTH PLAN KANSAS INC	KS	U	HMO	--	--	--	--	--	--	--
FIVE STAR LIFE INS CO	LA	C	L&H	2q 2003	126.5	71.3	5.3	48.9	2.14	1.51
FLAGSHIP HEALTH SYSTEMS INC	NJ	U	HMO	--	--	--	--	--	--	--
FLORA HEALTH NETWORK	OH	U	HMO							
FLORIDA COMBINED LIFE INS CO INC	FL	• B	L&H	2q 2003	68.4	66.9	33.2	35.8	2.34	1.79
FLORIDA HEALTH CARE PLAN INC	FL	• B-	HMO	2q 2002	53.6	245.5	245.5	26.7	0.97	0.80
FOCUS HEALTHCARE MANAGEMENT	TN	U	HMO							
FOR EYES VISION PLAN INC	CA	U	HMO							
FORT DEARBORN LIFE INS CO	IL	B	L&H	2q 2003	1,309.3	415.4	42.1	300.3	1.56	1.28
FORT WAYNE HEALTH & CAS INS CO	IN	• C	P&C	2q 2003	474.3	224.1	224.3	172.2	1.64	1.13
FORTIS BENEFITS INS CO	MN	• B-	L&H	2q 2003	7,631.5	1,886.4	1,045.2	535.9	1.91	1.20
FORTIS INS CO	WI	• B-	L&H	2q 2003	687.7	1,122.6	1,040.9	166.4	2.06	1.45
FOUNDATION HEALTH PSYCHCARE SERVICES	CA	U	HMO							
FOUNDATION LIFE INS CO OF AR	AR	E	L&H	2q 2003	5.4	1.9	0.2	1.0	0.69	0.62
FREE STATE HEALTH PLAN INC	MD	• C+	HMO	2q 2002	95.1	374.1	374.1	39.8	2.15	1.74
FREEDOM LIFE INS CO OF AMERICA	TX	C-	L&H	2q 2003	35.2	57.2	57.0	7.5	0.97	0.74
FREMONT LIFE INS CO	CA	C-	L&H	2q 2003	18.2	0.8	0.7	4.3	1.26	1.13
GALAXY HEALTH NETWORK	TX	U	HMO							
GARDEN STATE LIFE INS CO	TX	C+	L&H	2q 2003	98.4	35.3	0.1	33.0	2.33	1.66
GATEWAY HEALTH PLAN INC	PA	• C	HMO	1q 2003	125.5	590.8	590.8	42.1	0.87	0.72
GE CAPITAL LIFE ASR CO OF NEW YORK	NY	B-	L&H	2q 2003	4,489.0	724.9	90.3	151.9	1.03	0.51
GE GROUP LIFE ASR CO	CT	• B-	L&H	2q 2003	832.0	638.1	536.5	200.3	2.24	1.53
GE LIFE & ANNUITY ASR CO	VA	B	L&H	2q 2003	19,138.4	3,177.8	74.7	557.6	1.62	0.76
GE REINSURANCE CORP	IL	• C	P&C	2q 2003	2,633.7	0.2	0.2	642.9	0.68	0.42
GEISINGER HEALTH PLAN	PA	• C	HMO	1q 2003	133.4	629.8	629.8	60.2	0.90	0.75
GEISINGER INDEMNITY INS CO	PA	E+	P&C	4q 2002	2.3	1.8	1.8	1.5	1.65	1.26
GENERAL AMERICAN LIFE INS CO	MO	B-	L&H	2q 2003	13,040.7	1,100.0	22.3	756.1	0.94	0.68
GENERAL ELECTRIC CAPITAL ASR CO	DE	C+	L&H	2q 2003	31,687.1	6,160.0	1,088.9	2,534.6	0.90	0.66
GENERAL FIDELITY LIFE INS CO	CA	C+	L&H	2q 2003	322.3	-0.3	0.0	201.6	18.61	11.08
GENERAL STAR INDEMNITY CO	CT	B	P&C	2q 2003	1,069.0	363.8	2.1	397.4	1.46	0.99
GENESIS HEALTH PLAN OF OHIO INC	OH	U	HMO							
GENESIS INS CO	CT	B	P&C	2q 2003	218.7	151.3	0.6	95.2	2.02	1.27
GEORGE WASHINGTON UNIVERSITY HEALTH	DC	U	HMO	4q 2001	27.3	148.9	148.9	4.9	--	--
GEORGIA FARM BUREAU MUTUAL INS CO	GA	A	P&C	2q 2003	642.5	371.8	0.2	328.1	4.80	3.58
GEORGIA HEALTH PLUS+	GA	U	HMO							
GERBER LIFE INS CO	NY	• B-	L&H	2q 2003	751.5	361.4	194.1	119.5	2.84	1.84
GERMANIA LIFE INS CO	TX	B	L&H	2q 2003	27.8	7.7	0.0	6.9	1.72	1.55
GHI HMO SELECT INC	NY	• C	HMO	1q 2003	20.2	72.7	72.7	5.6	0.34	0.28
GHS HEALTH MAINTENANCE ORGANIZATION	OK	• B-	HMO	1q 2003	29.0	64.9	64.9	14.4	2.86	2.38

www.WeissRatings.com

Arrows denote recent upgrades ▲ or downgrades ▼   • Bullets denote a more detailed analysis is available in Section II.

I. Index of Companies

Winter 2003 - 04

INSURANCE COMPANY NAME	DOM. STATE	WEISS SAFETY RATING	COMPANY TYPE	DATA DATE	TOTAL ASSETS ($MIL)	TOTAL PREMIUMS ($MIL)	HEALTH PREMIUMS ($MIL)	CAPITAL & SURPLUS ($MIL)	RISK ADJUSTED CAPITAL RATIO 1	RATIO 2
GHS PROPERTY & CASUALTY INS CO	OK	C+	P&C	2q 2003	10.0	9.6	1.2	2.2	0.62	0.43
GLOBE LIFE & ACCIDENT INS CO	DE	B	L&H	2q 2003	1,813.8	377.8	14.3	263.2	1.14	0.89
GMHP HEALTH INS LMTD	GU	D	L&H	2q 2002	3.2	0.2	0.2	2.6	1.93	1.68
GOLDEN CIRCLE LIFE INS CO	TN	D+	L&H	1q 2003	8.6	1.8	0.1	4.9	2.24	2.02
GOLDEN CROSS HMO HEALTH PLAN CORP	PR	U	HMO		--	--	--	--	--	--
GOLDEN RULE INS CO	IL	● B+	L&H	2q 2003	2,076.2	959.3	764.3	227.7	1.35	0.86
GOLDEN STATE MUTUAL LIFE INS CO	CA	D	L&H	2q 2003	120.1	13.6	0.9	7.5	0.89	0.77
GOLDEN WEST HEALTH PLAN INC	CA	U	HMO	2q 2002	5.4	24.5	24.5	1.4	--	--
GOOD HEALTH HMO INC	MO	● B	HMO	1q 2003	36.4	129.8	129.8	22.8	2.16	1.80
GOVERNMENT EMPLOYEES HOSP ASSOC	MO	U	HMO		--	--	--	--	--	--
GOVERNMENT EMPLOYEES INS CO	MD	A+	P&C	2q 2003	8,737.7	2,205.9	0.3	3,505.0	1.99	1.43
GOVERNMENT PERSONNEL MUTUAL L I C	TX	B	L&H	2q 2003	656.3	70.1	0.8	64.2	1.34	0.86
▲ GRAND VALLEY HEALTH PLAN INC	MI	● D-	HMO	1q 2003	8.0	40.8	40.8	2.6	0.47	0.39
GRANGE LIFE INS CO	OH	B+	L&H	2q 2003	159.8	40.7	0.6	18.4	1.89	1.20
GRANGE MUTUAL CAS CO	OH	A-	P&C	2q 2003	1,116.1	752.3	0.7	379.2	1.84	1.28
GRANT LIFE INS CO	IN	C-	L&H	2q 2003	6.7	0.2	0.1	5.7	3.17	2.85
GRAPHIC ARTS BENEFIT CORP	MD	● C	HMO	1q 2003	4.1	11.4	11.4	2.0	0.87	0.73
GREAT AMERICAN INS CO	OH	C	P&C	2q 2003	4,300.7	663.2	10.1	1,197.1	1.09	0.91
GREAT AMERICAN LIFE ASR CO OF PR	PR	C+	L&H	2q 2003	191.1	65.0	14.1	28.2	2.73	1.77
GREAT AMERICAN LIFE INS CO	OH	C	L&H	2q 2003	6,635.4	722.3	8.4	434.9	1.04	0.69
GREAT ATLANTIC LIFE INS CO	FL	D+	L&H	2q 2003	14.6	1.1	0.4	10.2	3.49	3.14
GREAT CENTRAL LIFE INS CO	LA	D	L&H	2q 2003	14.9	2.9	0.4	5.1	1.89	1.61
GREAT FIDELITY LIFE INS CO	IN	D+	L&H	2q 2003	3.5	0.8	0.8	2.3	2.21	1.99
GREAT LAKES DELTA INSURANCE CO	MI	C+	L&H	2q 2003	11.7	38.7	38.7	8.2	1.00	0.80
GREAT LAKES HEALTH PLAN INC	MI	● E-	HMO	1q 2003	14.4	163.2	163.2	-12.8	0.00	0.00
GREAT MIDWEST INS CO	MI	C	P&C	2q 2003	32.7	25.0	6.3	12.4	1.75	1.16
GREAT NORTHERN INS CO	MN	B+	P&C	2q 2003	1,088.5	941.0	0.2	216.3	1.36	0.91
GREAT REPUBLIC LIFE INS CO	WA	D-	L&H	2q 2003	18.3	3.7	3.6	3.1	0.97	0.87
GREAT RIVERS NETWORK	MO	U	HMO		--	--	--	--	--	--
GREAT SOUTHERN LIFE INS CO	TX	D	L&H	2q 2003	734.7	145.6	2.9	53.1	1.54	0.83
GREAT WEST LIFE ASR CO	MI	B	L&H	2q 2003	182.8	34.5	7.6	41.5	4.36	2.69
GREAT-WEST LIFE & ANNUITY INS CO	CO	B+	L&H	2q 2003	27,323.0	4,085.3	649.1	1,454.4	2.25	1.35
GREATER CALIFORNIA DENTAL PLAN	CA	U	HMO		--	--	--	--	--	--
GREATER GEORGIA LIFE INS CO	GA	B-	L&H	2q 2003	38.9	23.3	7.3	22.1	3.05	2.26
GREATER PACIFIC HMO INC	CA	F	HMO	4q 1998	2.7	0.0	0.0	0.5	0.57	0.43
GREENVILLE CASUALTY INS CO INC	SC	D-	P&C	2q 2003	4.7	0.5	0.1	3.9	4.51	3.62
GROUP DENTAL SERVICE OF MARYLAND INC	MD	U	HMO		--	--	--	--	--	--
GROUP HEALTH COOP OF EAU CLAIRE	WI	● D	HMO	1q 2003	30.0	98.2	98.2	6.1	0.61	0.51
GROUP HEALTH COOP OF S CENTRAL WI	WI	● A-	HMO	1q 2003	49.9	131.0	131.0	30.5	3.47	2.89
▲ GROUP HEALTH COOPERATIVE PUGET SOUND	WA	● B	HMO	1q 2003	683.3	1,609.7	1,609.7	208.9	2.07	1.73
GROUP HEALTH INCORPORATED	NY	● B+	HLTH	1q 2003	634.4	2,045.1	2,045.1	173.3	1.26	1.05
GROUP HEALTH OPTIONS INC	WA	● B-	HLTH	1q 2003	62.2	347.1	347.1	24.2	1.44	1.20
GROUP HEALTH PLAN INC	MN	● B	HMO	1q 2003	360.6	435.0	435.0	65.3	3.53	2.94
GROUP HEALTH PLAN INC	MO	● C+	HMO	1q 2003	136.2	452.0	452.0	43.5	1.70	1.41
▲ GROUP HOSP & MEDICAL SERVICES INC	DC	● A	HLTH	1q 2003	1,141.0	1,719.9	1,719.9	300.9	3.42	2.85
GROUP INS ADMINISTRATION INC	DC	U	HMO		--	--	--	--	--	--
GUARANTEE RESERVE LIFE INS CO	IN	C	L&H	2q 2003	293.7	147.8	19.9	21.5	2.08	1.18
GUARANTEE TRUST LIFE INS CO	IL	● C+	L&H	2q 2003	233.1	308.4	248.5	54.7	1.33	1.00
GUARANTY INCOME LIFE INS CO	LA	C-	L&H	2q 2003	365.4	100.4	2.3	14.7	1.56	0.99
GUARDIAN LIFE INS CO OF AMERICA	NY	● A	L&H	2q 2003	20,577.2	5,263.5	2,902.7	2,082.3	2.07	1.43
GUIDEONE LIFE INS CO	IA	B	L&H	2q 2003	327.0	58.4	4.2	18.2	1.59	0.92
GULF COAST REGIONAL PPO	AL	U	HMO		--	--	--	--	--	--

Arrows denote recent upgrades ▲ or downgrades ▼   ● Bullets denote a more detailed analysis is available in Section II.

I. Index of Companies

Winter 2003 - 04

INSURANCE COMPANY NAME	DOM. STATE	WEISS SAFETY RATING	COMPANY TYPE	DATA DATE	TOTAL ASSETS ($MIL)	TOTAL PREMIUMS ($MIL)	HEALTH PREMIUMS ($MIL)	CAPITAL & SURPLUS ($MIL)	RISK ADJUSTED CAPITAL RATIO 1	RATIO 2
GULF GUARANTY LIFE INS CO	MS	D+	L&H	2q 2003	20.3	7.5	3.6	11.1	1.59	1.16
GULF HEALTH PLANS PPO INC	AL	U	HMO	--	--	--	--	--	--	--
GULF INS CO	CT	B-	P&C	2q 2003	1,673.0	854.1	68.2	516.3	2.17	1.35
GULF STATES LIFE INS CO INC	LA	D-	L&H	2q 2003	2.1	1.1	0.4	1.6	2.34	2.10
GULF UNDERWRITERS INS CO	CT	C+	P&C	2q 2003	121.1	295.6	0.0	27.4	1.11	0.65
GULFCO LIFE INS CO	LA	C	L&H	2q 2003	11.8	10.3	6.8	6.9	2.68	2.41
GUNDERSEN LUTHERAN HEALTH PLAN INC	WI	• C-	HMO	1q 2003	20.9	110.6	110.6	7.0	0.79	0.66
HARLEYSVILLE LIFE INS CO	PA	B	L&H	2q 2003	294.1	75.6	14.2	22.9	1.53	0.97
▲ HARMONY HEALTH PLAN OF ILLINOIS INC	IL	• C+	HMO	1q 2003	36.8	97.9	97.9	9.9	0.93	0.77
HARRISON LIFE INS CO	MS	D+	L&H	2q 2003	8.2	1.7	0.5	6.9	3.32	2.99
HARTFORD FIRE INS CO	CT	B+	P&C	2q 2003	15,857.7	2,187.8	80.1	6,228.9	1.60	1.45
HARTFORD LIFE & ACCIDENT INS CO	CT	• B+	L&H	2q 2003	8,792.5	1,767.8	1,061.9	3,503.1	1.10	1.02
HARTFORD LIFE & ANNUITY INS CO	CT	B+	L&H	2q 2003	49,622.7	8,401.8	1.9	842.0	1.96	1.00
HARTFORD LIFE INS CO	CT	B+	L&H	2q 2003	97,564.5	9,221.7	415.0	2,755.6	1.73	1.12
HARVARD PILGRIM HC OF NEW ENGLAND	MA	• C-	HMO	4q 2002	14.3	92.3	92.3	10.5	1.18	0.98
HARVARD PILGRIM HEALTH CARE INC	MA	• C-	HMO	1q 2003	439.8	1,686.1	1,686.1	176.7	1.59	1.32
HAWAII MANAGEMENT ALLIANCE ASSOC	HI	• D	HLTH	2q 2002	12.2	40.0	40.0	3.6	0.33	0.28
HAWAII MEDICAL SERVICE ASSOCIATION	HI	• C	HLTH	1q 2003	706.1	1,283.6	1,283.6	409.9	4.20	3.50
HCC LIFE INS CO	IN	• B-	L&H	2q 2003	201.1	326.3	321.1	112.7	2.34	2.06
HCSC INS SERVICES CO	IL	C+	L&H	2q 2003	14.6	0.6	0.6	14.0	4.78	4.30
HEALTH & HUMAN RESOURCE CENTER INC	CA	U	HMO		--	--	--	--	--	--
HEALTH 123 INC	TN	U	HMO		--	--	--	--	--	--
HEALTH ADMINISTRATIVE SERVICES	TX	U	HMO		--	--	--	--	--	--
HEALTH ADVANTAGE (See HMO PARTNERS INC)										
HEALTH ALLIANCE MEDICAL PLANS	IL	• C+	L&H	2q 2003	114.8	52.4	52.4	38.4	2.15	1.63
HEALTH ALLIANCE PLAN OF MICHIGAN	MI	• A	HMO	1q 2003	316.7	1,291.0	1,291.0	153.8	1.82	1.52
HEALTH ALLIANCE-MIDWEST INC	IL	• C+	HMO	1q 2003	7.4	19.3	19.3	3.6	1.12	0.93
HEALTH CARE FOUNDATION OF SAN MATEO	CA	U	HMO		--	--	--	--	--	--
HEALTH CARE NETWORK OF WISCONSIN	WI	U	HMO		--	--	--	--	--	--
HEALTH CARE REVIEW	TX	U	HMO		--	--	--	--	--	--
HEALTH CARE SAVINGS INC	NC	U	HMO		--	--	--	--	--	--
HEALTH CARE SVC CORP A MUT LEG RES	IL	• B+	L&H	2q 2003	4,352.1	5,555.8	5,555.8	1,681.9	1.65	1.43
HEALTH CHOICE LLC	TN	U	HMO		--	--	--	--	--	--
HEALTH CHOICE OF ALABAMA	AL	U	HMO		--	--	--	--	--	--
HEALTH CHOICE OF CONNECTICUT INC	CT	U	HMO		--	--	--	--	--	--
HEALTH FIRST HEALTH PLANS	FL	• C+	HMO	1q 2003	32.2	179.5	179.5	12.1	0.78	0.65
HEALTH INSURANCE CORPORATION OF AL	AL	D	L&H	2q 2003	2.5	1.7	1.7	2.2	2.63	2.37
HEALTH INSURANCE PLAN OF GREATER NY	NY	• B+	HLTH	1q 2003	1,066.5	2,522.2	2,522.2	451.4	6.28	5.23
HEALTH LINK INC	MS	U	HMO		--	--	--	--	--	--
HEALTH MANAGEMENT ASSOCIATES INC	AZ	U	HMO		--	--	--	--	--	--
HEALTH MARKETING INC	IL	U	HMO		--	--	--	--	--	--
HEALTH MASTERS OF OREGON	OR	U	HMO		--	--	--	--	--	--
HEALTH NET	CA	• B+	HMO	1q 2003	1,245.5	5,180.9	5,180.9	482.4	1.51	0.93
HEALTH NET DENTAL INC	CA	U	HMO		--	--	--	--	--	--
HEALTH NET HEALTH PLAN OF OREGON INC	OR	• C+	HMO	1q 2003	55.6	171.2	171.2	26.9	2.38	1.98
HEALTH NET INS OF CONNECTICUT INC	CT	U	HMO		--	--	--	--	--	--
HEALTH NET INS OF NEW YORK INC	NY	• B	HMO	1q 2003	76.8	178.2	178.2	45.7	3.22	2.68
HEALTH NET LIFE INS CO	CA	• B-	L&H	2q 2003	284.1	425.3	422.6	146.7	2.14	1.77
HEALTH NET OF ARIZONA INC	AZ	• C-	HMO	1q 2003	154.2	462.6	462.6	69.4	2.33	1.94
HEALTH NET OF CONNECTICUT INC	CT	• B	HMO	1q 2003	265.2	1,234.6	1,234.6	112.0	1.55	1.30
HEALTH NET OF NEW JERSEY INC	NJ	• C	HMO	4q 2002	177.3	617.9	617.9	60.4	1.21	1.00
HEALTH NET OF NEW YORK INC	NY	• C-	HMO	1q 2003	169.1	416.2	416.2	42.9	1.77	1.48

www.WeissRatings.com

Arrows denote recent upgrades ▲ or downgrades ▼   • Bullets denote a more detailed analysis is available in Section II.

I. Index of Companies

Winter 2003 - 04

INSURANCE COMPANY NAME	DOM. STATE	WEISS SAFETY RATING	COMPANY TYPE	DATA DATE	TOTAL ASSETS ($MIL)	TOTAL PREMIUMS ($MIL)	HEALTH PREMIUMS ($MIL)	CAPITAL & SURPLUS ($MIL)	RISK ADJUSTED CAPITAL RATIO 1	RATIO 2
HEALTH NET OF PENNSYLVANIA INC	PA	U	HMO	1q 2003	29.4	131.5	131.5	9.7	--	--
HEALTH NET VISION INC	CA	U	HMO		--	--	--	--	--	--
HEALTH NETWORK OF COLORADO SPRINGS	CO	F	HMO	1q 2001	3.5	19.4	19.4	-0.6	0.00	0.00
HEALTH NEW ENGLAND INC	MA	• D+	HMO	1q 2003	41.8	184.7	184.7	10.6	0.54	0.45
HEALTH OPTIONS CONNECT INC	FL	U	HMO		--	--	--	--	--	--
HEALTH OPTIONS INC	FL	• B+	HMO	4q 2002	914.9	2,224.7	2,224.7	409.2	3.51	2.93
HEALTH PARTNERS OF KANSAS	KS	U	HMO		--	--	--	--	--	--
HEALTH PARTNERS OF PHILADELPHIA INC	PA	• C+	HMO	1q 2003	138.7	546.5	546.5	40.2	0.86	0.71
HEALTH PAYORS ORGANIZATION LTD	OH	U	HMO		--	--	--	--	--	--
HEALTH PLAN HAWAII	HI	U	HMO	4q 2001	20.1	158.3	158.3	1.7	--	--
HEALTH PLAN OF MICHIGAN	MI	• B-	HMO	1q 2003	19.2	64.7	64.7	9.0	1.26	1.05
HEALTH PLAN OF NEVADA INC	NV	• C	HMO	1q 2003	145.8	767.9	767.9	52.5	1.19	1.00
HEALTH PLAN OF SAN JOAQUIN	CA	• B+	HMO	3q 2002	50.2	61.9	61.9	32.5	6.22	3.89
HEALTH PLAN OF SAN MATEO (See SAN MATEO HEALTH COMMISSION)										
HEALTH PLAN OF THE REDWOODS	CA	F	HMO	3q 2002	56.8	187.7	187.7	-10.8	0.00	0.00
HEALTH PLAN OF THE UPPER OHIO VALLEY	WV	• B-	HMO	1q 2003	66.0	220.3	220.3	30.7	1.28	1.07
HEALTH PLANS OF PENNSYLVANIA	PA	U	HMO		--	--	--	--	--	--
HEALTH PLUS OF LOUISIANA INC	LA	• E	HMO	1q 2003	20.3	62.0	62.0	5.5	0.70	0.58
HEALTH RIGHT INC	DC	• C+	HMO	1q 2003	6.1	18.9	18.9	3.2	0.92	0.77
HEALTH TRADITION HEALTH PLAN	WI	• B-	HMO	1q 2003	13.7	66.9	66.9	6.2	1.32	1.10
HEALTH VENTURES NETWORK	MN	U	HMO	4q 2002	0.4	0.1	0.1	0.4	--	--
HEALTHAMERICA PENNSYLVANIA INC	PA	• C+	HMO	1q 2003	184.8	577.3	577.3	42.6	1.27	1.05
HEALTHASSURANCE PENNSYLVANIA INC	PA	• B-	HMO	1q 2003	134.9	478.1	478.1	35.7	1.16	0.97
HEALTHCARE DELAWARE INC	DE	U	HMO		--	--	--	--	--	--
HEALTHCARE INC	GA	• C+	HMO	1q 2003	11.4	44.7	44.7	5.8	1.75	1.46
HEALTHCARE NETWORKS OF AMERICA	AZ	U	HMO		--	--	--	--	--	--
HEALTHCARE OPTIONS INC (See ROCKY MOUNTAIN HEALTHCARE OPTIONS)										
HEALTHCARE USA OF MISSOURI LLC	MO	• B-	HMO	1q 2003	60.4	251.6	251.6	32.9	2.03	1.69
HEALTHCARE VALUE MANAGEMENT	MA	U	HMO		--	--	--	--	--	--
HEALTHCHOICE MANAGED SYSTEMS	FL	U	HMO		--	--	--	--	--	--
HEALTHDENT OF CALIFORNIA INC	CA	U	HMO		--	--	--	--	--	--
HEALTHEASE OF FLORIDA INC	FL	• D-	HMO	1q 2003	42.7	242.9	242.9	8.3	0.42	0.35
HEALTHFIRST PPO	OK	U	HMO		--	--	--	--	--	--
HEALTHGUARD OF LANCASTER INC	PA	• B	HMO	1q 2003	48.5	122.4	122.4	18.5	3.03	2.52
HEALTHKEEPERS INC	VA	• B+	HMO	1q 2003	178.7	474.7	474.7	93.0	3.83	3.19
HEALTHLINK HMO INC	MO	• B+	HMO	1q 2003	26.3	13.7	13.7	24.7	18.82	15.69
HEALTHMAX AMERICA	CA	U	HMO		--	--	--	--	--	--
HEALTHNOW NY INC	NY	• B	HLTH	1q 2003	463.3	1,520.1	1,520.1	137.2	1.10	0.92
HEALTHPARTNERS	MN	• B+	HMO	1q 2003	237.4	1,120.1	1,120.1	136.6	1.76	1.47
HEALTHPLAN OF TEXAS INC	TX	• C+	HMO	1q 2003	8.4	15.6	15.6	3.4	1.55	1.29
HEALTHPLEX INS CO	NY	U	HMO		--	--	--	--	--	--
HEALTHPLUS OF MICHIGAN	MI	• C+	HMO	1q 2003	79.0	401.9	401.9	26.6	0.71	0.60
HEALTHPLUS PARTNERS INC	MI	U	HMO		--	--	--	--	--	--
HEALTHREACH PPO INC	OH	U	HMO		--	--	--	--	--	--
HEALTHSMART PREFERRED CARE INC	TX	U	HMO		--	--	--	--	--	--
HEALTHSPAN INC	OH	U	HMO		--	--	--	--	--	--
HEALTHSPRING INC	TN	• D-	HMO	1q 2003	41.7	204.0	204.0	8.2	0.40	0.33
▲ HEALTHSPRING OF ALABAMA INC	AL	• E+	HMO	1q 2003	12.3	88.5	88.5	3.2	0.51	0.43
HEALTHSTAR INC	IL	U	HMO		--	--	--	--	--	--
HEALTHWISE	UT	• B	HMO	1q 2003	39.5	29.0	29.0	32.0	12.96	10.80
HEALTHY ALLIANCE LIFE INS CO	MO	• B	L&H	2q 2003	578.8	999.7	999.6	171.5	1.43	1.15
HEALTHY PALM BEACHES INC	FL	• A-	HMO	1q 2003	3.7	10.4	10.4	2.0	1.76	1.47

Arrows denote recent upgrades ▲ or downgrades ▼   • Bullets denote a more detailed analysis is available in Section II.

www.WeissRatings.com

Winter 2003 - 04

I. Index of Companies

INSURANCE COMPANY NAME	DOM. STATE	WEISS SAFETY RATING	COMPANY TYPE	DATA DATE	TOTAL ASSETS ($MIL)	TOTAL PREMIUMS ($MIL)	HEALTH PREMIUMS ($MIL)	CAPITAL & SURPLUS ($MIL)	RISK ADJUSTED CAPITAL RATIO 1	RATIO 2
HEART OF AMERICA HMO	ND	• D	HMO	1q 2003	1.2	4.9	4.9	0.6	0.45	0.38
HEARTLAND HEALTH PLAN OF OKLAHOMA	OK	• E-	HMO	1q 2003	22.8	226.1	226.1	-22.7	0.00	0.00
HERITAGE LIFE INS CO	AZ	B	L&H	2q 2003	64.7	-0.5	0.0	47.1	6.11	5.02
HERITAGE PROVIDER NETWORK INC	CA	• D	HMO	1q 2003	119.2	380.5	380.5	18.4	0.55	0.33
HFN INC	IL	U	HMO	--	--	--	--	--	--	--
HIGHMARK CASUALTY INS CO	PA	• C	P&C	2q 2003	80.2	75.6	44.5	30.3	0.42	0.28
HIGHMARK INC	PA	• B-	HLTH	1q 2003	3,377.7	3,615.5	3,615.5	1,862.7	3.56	2.97
HIGHMARK LIFE INS CO	CT	• C+	L&H	2q 2003	281.0	212.8	155.8	70.1	1.88	1.40
HIGHMARK LIFE INS CO OF NEW YORK	NY	B-	L&H	2q 2003	22.9	29.4	24.6	9.1	1.17	0.93
HIP INS CO OF NEW YORK	NY	• B	HMO	1q 2003	24.0	20.5	20.5	16.8	8.65	7.20
HMO BLUE	MA	U	HMO	--	--	--	--	--	--	--
▲ HMO COLORADO	CO	• C+	HMO	1q 2003	122.4	271.7	271.7	61.2	4.31	3.59
▲ HMO HEALTH PLANS INC	CO	• C+	HMO	1q 2003	5.3	12.2	12.2	2.7	0.98	0.81
HMO ILLINOIS	IL	U	HMO	--	--	--	--	--	--	--
HMO LOUISIANA INC	LA	• B-	HMO	1q 2003	95.2	213.4	213.4	52.2	3.31	2.76
HMO MINNESOTA	MN	• B+	HMO	1q 2003	216.9	570.3	570.3	74.7	1.84	1.53
HMO MISSOURI INC	MO	• C+	HMO	1q 2003	114.7	218.0	218.0	34.3	1.87	1.56
HMO MONTANA	MT	U	HMO	--	--	--	--	--	--	--
HMO NEW MEXICO INC	NM	• B+	HMO	1q 2003	28.6	65.2	65.2	12.6	3.02	2.52
HMO OF DELAWARE INC	DE	U	HMO	--	--	--	--	--	--	--
HMO OF MISSISSIPPI INC	MS	U	HMO	--	--	--	--	--	--	--
HMO OF NORTHEASTERN PENNSYLVANIA INC	PA	• B-	HMO	1q 2003	119.6	239.6	239.6	57.1	1.51	1.26
HMO PARTNERS INC	AR	• C	HMO	2q 2002	63.8	158.3	158.3	28.6	1.73	1.37
HOLMAN PROFESSIONAL COUNSELING CTRS	CA	U	HMO	--	--	--	--	--	--	--
HOME OWNERS LIFE INS CO	IL	B	L&H	2q 2003	33.3	-2.2	0.0	11.1	2.41	1.56
HOMESHIELD INS CO	OK	C-	L&H	2q 2003	33.9	0.2	0.1	16.1	3.40	3.06
HOMETOWN HEALTH PLAN	OH	• C-	HMO	1q 2003	20.6	105.3	105.3	7.8	0.74	0.62
HOMETOWN HEALTH PLAN INC	NV	• D+	HMO	1q 2003	25.4	111.5	111.5	7.8	1.16	0.97
HOMETOWN HEALTH PROVIDERS INS CO	NV	• C	HMO	1q 2003	16.2	31.4	31.4	6.4	1.41	1.18
HOMETOWN INS GROUP INC	OH	U	HMO	1q 2003	5.2	12.7	12.7	2.5	--	--
HOOSIER MOTOR MUTUAL INS CO	IN	C	P&C	2q 2003	18.0	0.7	0.7	17.3	11.66	5.86
HORACE MANN INS CO	IL	B-	P&C	2q 2003	411.5	265.7	0.0	109.8	1.53	0.97
HORACE MANN LIFE INS CO	IL	B	L&H	2q 2003	3,967.9	381.2	9.1	227.8	2.53	1.27
HORIZON BLUE CROSS BLUE SHIELD OF NEW JERSEY (See HORIZON HEALTHCARE SERVICES INC)										
HORIZON HEALTHCARE DENTAL INC	NJ	U	HMO	--	--	--	--	--	--	--
HORIZON HEALTHCARE INS CO OF NY	NY	• C	HMO	1q 2003	71.0	153.3	153.3	32.6	2.66	2.22
HORIZON HEALTHCARE INS CO OF PA	PA	U	HMO	--	--	--	--	--	--	--
HORIZON HEALTHCARE OF NEW JERSEY INC	NJ	• B+	HMO	1q 2003	595.7	1,445.0	1,445.0	216.5	2.81	2.34
HORIZON HEALTHCARE OF NEW YORK INC	NY	• C	HMO	1q 2003	2.0	1.1	1.1	1.1	2.38	1.99
HORIZON HEALTHCARE OF PENNSYLVANIA	PA	U	HMO	--	--	--	--	--	--	--
HORIZON HEALTHCARE SERVICES INC	NJ	• A	HLTH	1q 2003	1,684.0	2,812.5	2,812.5	741.5	3.40	2.83
HORIZON HMO (See HORIZON HEALTHCARE OF NEW JERSEY INC)										
HOSPITAL SERV ASSN OF NORTH EAST PA	PA	• B+	HLTH	1q 2003	588.5	298.0	298.0	367.7	5.08	4.23
HOUSEHOLD LIFE INS CO	MI	• C	L&H	2q 2003	1,262.8	183.9	103.4	415.9	4.82	3.51
HOUSTON CASUALTY CO	TX	B-	P&C	2q 2003	1,050.3	234.3	9.1	380.6	1.47	1.22
HPHC INS CO INC	MA	E+	P&C	4q 2002	9.5	3.2	3.2	8.6	4.01	3.41
HUMAN AFFAIRS INTERNATIONAL OF CA	CA	U	HMO	--	--	--	--	--	--	--
HUMANA EMPLOYERS HEALTH PLAN OF GA	GA	• C	HMO	1q 2003	32.2	43.5	43.5	15.4	4.23	3.52
HUMANA HEALTH INS CO OF FL INC	FL	• C-	HMO	1q 2003	115.0	239.9	239.9	72.7	4.92	4.10
HUMANA HEALTH PLAN INC	KY	• C	HMO	1q 2003	412.5	2,199.7	2,199.7	177.8	1.83	1.53
HUMANA HEALTH PLAN OF OHIO INC	OH	• C+	HMO	1q 2003	112.2	407.3	407.3	41.2	1.82	1.52
HUMANA HEALTH PLAN OF TEXAS INC	TX	• D+	HMO	1q 2003	173.5	646.2	646.2	44.3	1.29	1.07

Arrows denote recent upgrades ▲ or downgrades ▼   • Bullets denote a more detailed analysis is available in Section II.

I. Index of Companies

Winter 2003 - 04

INSURANCE COMPANY NAME	DOM. STATE	WEISS SAFETY RATING	COMPANY TYPE	DATA DATE	TOTAL ASSETS ($MIL)	TOTAL PREMIUMS ($MIL)	HEALTH PREMIUMS ($MIL)	CAPITAL & SURPLUS ($MIL)	RISK ADJUSTED CAPITAL RATIO 1	RATIO 2
HUMANA HEALTH PLANS OF PUERTO RICO	PR	U	HMO	--	--	--	--	--	--	--
HUMANA INS CO	WI	• C	L&H	2q 2003	835.0	2,464.2	2,418.1	384.4	1.29	1.04
HUMANA INS CO OF KENTUCKY	KY	• C	HMO	1q 2003	5.5	3.0	3.0	4.7	2.32	1.93
HUMANA INS CO OF PUERTO RICO INC	PR	C-	L&H	2q 2003	22.0	48.8	48.4	10.2	1.05	0.88
HUMANA MEDICAL PLAN INC	FL	• C+	HMO	1q 2003	361.4	2,218.2	2,218.2	139.7	1.62	1.35
HUMANA PRIME HEALTH	MO	U	HMO	--	--	--	--	--	--	--
HUMANA WISCONSIN HEALTH ORGANIZATION	WI	• C	HMO	1q 2003	74.7	246.3	246.3	23.9	1.61	1.34
HUMANADENTAL INS CO	WI	• C+	L&H	2q 2003	51.7	105.0	91.0	36.4	1.41	1.25
I B A HEALTH & LIFE ASR CO	MI	D-	L&H	2q 2003	25.7	46.2	45.4	13.9	1.50	1.24
IBA PHP HEALTH PLAN	MI	U	HMO	--	--	--	--	--	--	--
IDEAL DENTAL HEALTH PLAN INC	CA	U	HMO	--	--	--	--	--	--	--
IDEALIFE INS CO	CT	B	L&H	2q 2003	22.6	8.7	4.8	9.5	2.48	2.23
IDS LIFE INS CO	MN	B	L&H	2q 2003	46,324.3	5,731.8	341.4	2,487.8	1.65	1.06
IDS LIFE INS CO OF NEW YORK	NY	B+	L&H	2q 2003	2,757.9	368.9	21.9	218.5	3.50	1.78
IHC BENEFIT ASR CO INC	UT	• C	HMO	1q 2003	8.0	10.5	10.5	4.7	2.32	1.94
IHC HEALTH PLANS INC	UT	• B	HMO	1q 2003	157.7	680.9	680.9	73.3	1.33	1.11
ILLINOIS MUTUAL LIFE INS CO	IL	• B	L&H	2q 2003	1,011.4	173.2	55.0	104.0	1.65	0.95
INDEMNITY INS CO OF NORTH AMERICA	PA	C-	P&C	2q 2003	165.6	357.3	0.1	27.1	0.76	0.57
INDEPENDENCE AMERICAN INS CO	DE	• C	P&C	2q 2003	42.9	0.0	0.0	25.6	1.40	1.11
INDEPENDENCE BLUE CROSS	PA	• B-	HLTH	1q 2003	1,202.2	402.9	402.9	722.6	2.13	1.78
INDEPENDENT HEALTH ASSOC INC	NY	• B	HMO	1q 2003	240.1	754.1	754.1	103.1	3.08	2.56
INDEPENDENT HEALTH BENEFITS CORP	NY	• B-	HLTH	4q 2002	2.2	2.9	2.9	1.7	3.94	3.29
INDIANAPOLIS LIFE INS CO	IN	C	L&H	2q 2003	3,928.2	292.0	6.7	183.9	1.50	0.82
INDIVIDUAL ASR CO LIFE HEALTH & ACC	MO	C	L&H	2q 2003	49.2	45.4	11.8	16.4	1.87	1.28
ING LIFE INS & ANNUITY CO	CT	C+	L&H	2q 2003	47,882.8	7,246.1	2.0	1,152.4	1.42	0.80
ING LIFE INS CO OF AMERICA	CT	C	L&H	2q 2003	6,773.8	2,243.0	552.3	131.8	0.50	0.31
INITIAL GROUP INC	TN	U	HMO	--	--	--	--	--	--	--
INLAND EMPIRE HEALTH PLAN	CA	• C+	HMO	3q 2002	51.8	214.6	214.6	28.4	1.38	0.86
INS CO OF NORTH AMERICA	PA	D+	P&C	2q 2003	284.7	359.9	21.9	46.0	0.74	0.50
INS CO OF THE STATE OF PA	PA	B-	P&C	2q 2003	2,336.2	846.6	29.4	740.5	1.12	0.88
INTEGRATED HEALTH NETWORKS & SERVICE	OH	U	HMO	--	--	--	--	--	--	--
INTER-COUNTY HEALTH PLAN INC	PA	U	HMO	1q 2003	17.1	0.0	0.0	4.2	--	--
INTER-COUNTY HOSPITALIZATION PLAN	PA	U	HMO	1q 2003	37.8	0.0	0.0	9.9	--	--
INTERBORO MUTUAL INDEMNITY INS CO	NY	E	P&C	2q 2003	76.1	53.9	0.7	8.4	0.19	0.15
INTERGROUP OF ARIZONA (See HEALTH NET OF ARIZONA INC)										
INTERGROUP SERVICES CORP	PA	U	HMO	--	--	--	--	--	--	--
INTERNATIONAL HEALTHCARE SERVICES	NJ	U	HMO	--	--	--	--	--	--	--
INTERPLAN CORP	CA	U	HMO	--	--	--	--	--	--	--
INTERVALLEY HEALTH PLAN	CA	U	HMO	--	--	--	--	--	--	--
INTERWEST HEALTH	MT	U	HMO	--	--	--	--	--	--	--
INTRAMERICA LIFE INS CO	NY	B	L&H	2q 2003	57.3	3.8	0.0	19.8	2.85	2.56
INVESTORS CONSOLIDATED INS CO INC	NH	C	L&H	2q 2003	17.4	3.5	2.5	8.0	2.22	1.39
INVESTORS GUARANTY LIFE INS CO	CA	C+	L&H	2q 2003	10.4	1.3	0.0	10.2	4.20	3.78
INVESTORS HERITAGE LIFE INS CO	KY	C	L&H	2q 2003	317.6	71.7	4.3	14.4	1.26	0.73
INVESTORS INS CORP	DE	D	L&H	2q 2003	111.5	99.4	0.0	11.2	1.65	1.23
INVESTORS LIFE INS CO NORTH AMERICA	WA	C-	L&H	2q 2003	1,095.7	62.5	0.3	50.9	1.11	0.59
ISLAND CARE	HI	U	HMO	2q 2002	7.3	30.0	30.0	2.3	--	--
ISLAND GROUP ADMINISTRATION INC	NY	U	HMO	--	--	--	--	--	--	--
IU HEALTH PLAN INC	IN	• E	HMO	1q 2003	3.9	147.0	147.0	3.7	0.29	0.24
J M I C LIFE INS CO	FL	• C	L&H	2q 2003	281.9	77.6	39.4	65.1	2.99	2.06
JACKSONVILLE LIFE INS CO	TX	C	L&H	2q 2003	2.1	0.7	0.2	1.3	1.75	1.58
JAIMINI HEALTH INC	CA	U	HMO	--	--	--	--	--	--	--

Arrows denote recent upgrades ▲ or downgrades ▼

• Bullets denote a more detailed analysis is available in Section II.

www.WeissRatings.com

I. Index of Companies

Winter 2003 - 04

INSURANCE COMPANY NAME	DOM. STATE	WEISS SAFETY RATING	COMPANY TYPE	DATA DATE	TOTAL ASSETS ($MIL)	TOTAL PREMIUMS ($MIL)	HEALTH PREMIUMS ($MIL)	CAPITAL & SURPLUS ($MIL)	RISK ADJUSTED CAPITAL RATIO 1	RATIO 2
JEFFERSON NATIONAL LIFE INS CO	TX	D-	L&H	2q 2003	1,836.9	347.9	25.4	54.2	1.69	0.84
JEFFERSON PILOT FINANCIAL INS CO	NE	• B+	L&H	2q 2003	11,630.2	1,577.2	445.9	829.8	1.57	0.91
JEFFERSON PILOT LIFEAMERICA INS CO	NJ	B	L&H	2q 2003	1,303.6	168.7	1.7	115.8	2.56	1.27
JEFFERSON-PILOT LIFE INS CO	NC	A	L&H	2q 2003	13,405.5	2,009.8	15.4	848.1	2.39	1.15
JJ NEWMAN PREFERRED PROVIDER NETWORK	NY	U	HMO	--	--	--	--	--	--	--
JMH HEALTH PLAN	FL	• D	HMO	2q 2002	15.0	32.3	32.3	6.8	0.68	0.57
JOHN ALDEN LIFE INS CO	WI	• C	L&H	2q 2003	672.3	658.2	631.0	142.5	3.07	2.07
JOHN D KERNAN DMD PA	NJ	U	HMO	--	--	--	--	--	--	--
JOHN DEERE HEALTH PLAN INC	IL	• B	HMO	1q 2003	178.8	586.4	586.4	73.1	1.38	1.15
JOHN HANCOCK LIFE INS CO	MA	A-	L&H	2q 2003	73,183.9	7,520.5	673.2	3,676.6	2.03	1.07
JUSTDENTAL OF DELMARVA INC	MD	U	HMO	--	--	--	--	--	--	--
KAISER FOUNDATION HEALTH PLAN INC	CA	• B-	HMO	1q 2003	5,132.0	16,142.5	16,142.5	920.1	0.91	0.61
KAISER FOUNDATION HP INC HI	HI	U	HMO	--	--	--	--	--	--	--
KAISER FOUNDATION HP MID-ATL STATES	MD	• C-	HMO	1q 2003	434.3	1,291.5	1,291.5	103.7	1.58	1.31
KAISER FOUNDATION HP NORTHWEST	OR	• B	HMO	1q 2003	463.9	1,338.3	1,338.3	203.7	3.85	3.20
KAISER FOUNDATION HP OF CO	CO	• B	HMO	1q 2003	384.6	1,154.6	1,154.6	125.8	2.72	2.26
KAISER FOUNDATION HP OF CT	CT	U	HMO	--	--	--	--	--	--	--
KAISER FOUNDATION HP OF GA	GA	• B	HMO	1q 2003	171.5	675.0	675.0	64.7	2.10	1.75
KAISER FOUNDATION HP OF OH	OH	• B-	HMO	1q 2003	221.6	507.8	507.8	67.8	3.19	2.66
KAISER PERMANENTE HEALTH ALTERNATIVE	OR	• B	HLTH	1q 2003	4.0	5.2	5.2	3.7	5.65	4.71
KAISER PERMANENTE INS CO	CA	• B-	L&H	2q 2003	57.4	71.8	71.8	31.1	2.29	1.91
KANAWHA HEALTHCARE SOLUTIONS INC	SC	U	HMO	--	--	--	--	--	--	--
KANAWHA INS CO	SC	• B-	L&H	2q 2003	499.8	99.7	81.8	65.4	1.75	1.17
KANSAS CITY LIFE INS CO	MO	• B	L&H	2q 2003	2,740.8	181.9	53.5	220.8	1.28	0.88
KAPIOLANI HEALTHHAWAII	HI	U	HMO	4q 2002	2.5	19.2	19.2	2.2	--	--
KEMPER INVESTORS LIFE INS CO	IL	C+	L&H	2q 2003	18,373.0	2,233.2	0.0	364.3	1.61	0.95
KENTUCKY FARM BUREAU MUTUAL INS CO	KY	A	P&C	2q 2003	1,142.6	543.4	0.2	563.0	3.94	2.73
KENTUCKY HOME LIFE INS CO	KY	B	L&H	2q 2003	4.1	9.7	3.9	3.4	3.83	3.45
KEOKUK AREA HOSP ORG DELIVERY SYSTEM	IA	U	HMO	--	--	--	--	--	--	--
KERN HEALTH SYSTEMS	CA	• B	HMO	4q 2002	81.5	84.3	84.3	61.6	9.80	5.96
KEY LIFE INS CO INC	IN	E	L&H	2q 2003	46.2	1.8	0.0	2.4	0.24	0.22
KEYPORT LIFE INS CO	RI	B-	L&H	2q 2003	16,173.5	2,185.4	37.5	466.6	1.11	0.60
KEYSTONE HEALTH PLAN CENTRAL INC	PA	• B+	HMO	1q 2003	166.0	429.6	429.6	54.9	1.89	1.58
KEYSTONE HEALTH PLAN EAST INC	PA	• B+	HMO	1q 2003	1,026.1	3,665.0	3,665.0	352.4	2.67	2.23
KEYSTONE HEALTH PLAN WEST INC	PA	• B+	HMO	1q 2003	498.2	1,822.8	1,822.8	224.8	2.12	1.77
KEYSTONE INS CO	PA	C	P&C	2q 2003	330.3	73.1	7.7	79.4	1.40	1.09
KILPATRICK LIFE INS CO	LA	D+	L&H	2q 2003	124.4	18.0	0.1	8.5	1.07	0.72
KPHA HEALTH PLANS (See KAISER PERMANENTE HEALTH ALTERNATIVE)										
KPS HEALTH PLANS	WA	F	HLTH	1q 2003	22.3	110.0	110.0	1.6	0.03	0.03
LA CARE HEALTH PLAN (See LOCAL INITIATIVE HEALTH AUTH LA)										
LA HEALTH SERVICE & INDEMNITY CO	LA	• B	HMO	1q 2003	409.6	954.8	954.8	182.0	2.34	1.95
LAFAYETTE LIFE INS CO	IN	B-	L&H	2q 2003	1,561.7	403.8	17.5	83.0	1.85	0.94
LANDCAR LIFE INS CO	UT	C+	L&H	2q 2003	25.5	4.2	1.8	15.3	3.72	2.43
LANDMARK HEALTHPLAN OF CALIFORNIA	CA	U	HMO	--	--	--	--	--	--	--
LAPORTE HOSP-LAKELAND AREA HEALTH SV	IN	U	HMO	--	--	--	--	--	--	--
LEGACY HEALTH PLAN INC	TX	U	HMO	--	--	--	--	--	--	--
LEGAL SERVICE PLANS OF VIRGINIA INC	VA	U	HMO	--	--	--	--	--	--	--
LEON MEDICAL CENTERS HEALTH PLANS	FL	U	HMO	--	--	--	--	--	--	--
LEWER LIFE INS CO	MO	D	L&H	2q 2003	26.2	0.0	0.0	7.1	1.76	1.58
LIBERTY DENTAL PLAN OF CALIFORNIA	CA	U	HMO	--	--	--	--	--	--	--
LIBERTY HEALTH PLAN INC	NJ	U	HMO	--	--	--	--	--	--	--
LIBERTY LIFE ASR CO OF BOSTON	MA	• B-	L&H	2q 2003	7,190.9	807.2	249.5	125.3	1.06	0.51

www.WeissRatings.com

Arrows denote recent upgrades ▲ or downgrades ▼   • Bullets denote a more detailed analysis is available in Section II.

I. Index of Companies

Winter 2003 - 04

INSURANCE COMPANY NAME	DOM. STATE	WEISS SAFETY RATING	COMPANY TYPE	DATA DATE	TOTAL ASSETS ($MIL)	TOTAL PREMIUMS ($MIL)	HEALTH PREMIUMS ($MIL)	CAPITAL & SURPLUS ($MIL)	RISK ADJUSTED CAPITAL RATIO 1	RATIO 2
LIBERTY LIFE INS CO	SC	● B-	L&H	2q 2003	1,453.9	278.1	101.9	193.2	1.64	0.94
LIBERTY MUTUAL INS CO	MA	B	P&C	2q 2003	19,958.3	2,360.9	226.7	4,254.7	0.90	0.74
LIBERTY NATIONAL LIFE INS CO	AL	● B	L&H	2q 2003	3,997.3	581.8	158.6	381.3	1.53	1.01
LIBERTY SURPLUS INS CORP	NH	C	P&C	2q 2003	52.5	160.3	0.1	24.0	5.41	4.87
LIBERTY UNION LIFE ASR CO	MI	D	L&H	2q 2003	10.1	22.5	21.9	3.8	0.66	0.50
LIFE & HEALTH INS CO OF AMERICA	PA	E	L&H	2q 2003	47.9	19.0	11.6	2.1	0.32	0.28
LIFE ASSURANCE CO INC	OK	D-	L&H	2q 2003	8.0	5.6	1.5	1.8	0.85	0.77
LIFE INS CO OF AL	AL	D	L&H	2q 2003	58.5	30.6	26.8	7.9	0.68	0.48
LIFE INS CO OF BOSTON & NEW YORK	NY	B	L&H	2q 2003	39.7	20.3	7.8	6.3	1.22	0.96
LIFE INS CO OF GEORGIA	GA	B-	L&H	2q 2003	1,933.9	161.1	30.0	112.2	2.42	1.20
LIFE INS CO OF LOUISIANA	LA	D+	L&H	4q 2002	8.6	1.2	0.4	2.2	1.31	1.18
LIFE INS CO OF MISSISSIPPI	MS	C+	L&H	2q 2003	6.1	0.7	0.2	4.5	2.58	2.32
LIFE INS CO OF NORTH AMERICA	PA	● D	L&H	2q 2003	4,978.3	1,442.1	705.8	506.8	1.52	1.04
LIFE INS CO OF THE SOUTHWEST	TX	C+	L&H	2q 2003	3,142.0	438.9	0.1	137.4	1.30	0.63
LIFE INVESTORS INS CO OF AMERICA	IA	● B	L&H	2q 2003	11,110.0	1,121.1	542.2	742.8	1.36	0.70
LIFE OF AMERICA INS CO	TX	D-	L&H	2q 2003	7.1	2.4	2.3	4.0	1.06	0.97
LIFE OF MARYLAND INC	MD	C	L&H	2q 2003	6.1	12.2	0.5	6.1	5.97	5.38
LIFE OF THE SOUTH INS CO	GA	C-	L&H	2q 2003	44.5	52.2	28.1	12.2	0.76	0.63
LIFECARE MANAGEMENT SYSTEMS INC	NJ	U	HMO	--	--	--	--	--	--	--
LIFEGUARD HEALTH NETWORK	CA	U	HMO	--	--	--	--	--	--	--
LIFEGUARD INC	CA	F	HMO	2q 2002	85.2	439.5	439.5	6.8	0.23	0.15
LIFEGUARD LIFE INS CO	CA	F	L&H	4q 2002	25.1	84.0	84.0	10.5	0.70	0.58
LIFERE INS CO	TX	C	L&H	2q 2003	12.6	22.0	20.2	8.2	1.98	1.63
LIFEWISE ASR CO	WA	● B-	L&H	2q 2003	55.3	31.7	15.6	27.7	2.67	2.00
LIFEWISE HEALTH PLAN OF OREGON	OR	● B	HMO	1q 2003	127.4	337.7	337.7	49.1	2.08	1.73
LIFEWISE HEALTH PLAN OF WASHINGTON	WA	U	HLTH	1q 2003	26.2	41.7	41.7	5.4	--	--
LINCOLN BENEFIT LIFE CO	NE	B+	L&H	2q 2003	1,823.4	3,611.0	66.1	198.8	4.28	2.14
LINCOLN DIRECT LIFE INS CO	NE	B-	L&H	2q 2003	151.9	15.9	0.0	22.9	2.88	2.16
LINCOLN HERITAGE LIFE INS CO	IL	C	L&H	2q 2003	441.2	124.0	2.5	70.4	3.77	1.92
LINCOLN MUTUAL LIFE & CAS INS CO	ND	C	L&H	2q 2003	31.1	12.4	6.4	8.3	1.94	1.41
LINCOLN NATIONAL LIFE INS CO	IN	B-	L&H	2q 2003	72,330.1	8,473.2	49.9	2,675.0	1.25	0.74
LOCAL INITIATIVE HEALTH AUTH LA	CA	● C	HMO	4q 2002	247.0	930.2	930.2	67.3	1.22	0.74
LONDON LIFE REINSURANCE CO	PA	● B	L&H	2q 2003	730.4	2.5	2.5	65.7	3.98	2.53
LOUISIANA FARM BUREAU MUTUAL INS CO	LA	B	P&C	2q 2003	101.7	92.1	0.1	45.4	2.49	2.18
LOVELACE HEALTH SYSTEMS INC	NM	● C	HMO	1q 2003	153.6	497.4	497.4	60.6	1.74	1.45
LOYAL AMERICAN LIFE INS CO	OH	C	L&H	2q 2003	453.3	140.1	19.8	80.1	2.89	1.84
LUMBERMENS MUTUAL CAS CO	IL	E+	P&C	2q 2003	5,776.9	2,038.5	72.8	340.9	0.09	0.07
LUTHERAN PREFERRED	IN	U	HMO	--	--	--	--	--	--	--
LYNDON PROPERTY INS CO	MO	C+	P&C	2q 2003	425.5	136.2	0.2	144.6	2.93	2.31
M PLAN	IN	● C-	HMO	4q 2002	47.5	481.7	481.7	17.6	0.65	0.54
M-CARE	MI	● B-	HMO	1q 2003	123.2	488.7	488.7	43.3	1.23	1.03
MADISON NATIONAL LIFE INS CO INC	WI	● C	L&H	2q 2003	468.0	80.2	36.3	100.1	1.05	0.91
MAGELLAN BEHAVIORAL HEALTH OF IOWA	IA	U	HMO	2q 2002	29.4	96.6	96.6	8.1	--	--
MAGELLAN BEHAVIORAL HEALTH OF PA INC	PA	U	HMO	4q 2002	61.9	201.7	201.7	13.4	--	--
MAGNA INS CO	MS	C+	L&H	2q 2003	27.2	9.6	3.3	17.4	3.93	3.54
MAGNACARE	NY	U	HMO	--	--	--	--	--	--	--
MAGNAHEALTH OF NY INC	NY	● D+	HMO	2q 2002	3.1	0.7	0.7	2.1	7.37	6.52
MAGNET/MAGNACARE	NJ	U	HMO	--	--	--	--	--	--	--
MAINE PARTNERS HEALTH PLAN INC	ME	● C	HMO	1q 2003	42.7	107.4	107.4	13.9	2.26	1.88
MAMSI LIFE & HEALTH INS CO	MD	● B	HMO	1q 2003	337.7	660.4	660.4	187.9	3.94	3.28
MANAGED DENTAL CARE	CA	U	HMO	--	--	--	--	--	--	--
MANAGED DENTALGUARD INC	TX	U	HMO	--	--	--	--	--	--	--

Arrows denote recent upgrades ▲ or downgrades ▼   ● Bullets denote a more detailed analysis is available in Section II.

www.WeissRatings.com

Winter 2003 - 04 — I. Index of Companies

INSURANCE COMPANY NAME	DOM. STATE	WEISS SAFETY RATING	COMPANY TYPE	DATA DATE	TOTAL ASSETS ($MIL)	TOTAL PREMIUMS ($MIL)	HEALTH PREMIUMS ($MIL)	CAPITAL & SURPLUS ($MIL)	RISK ADJUSTED CAPITAL RATIO 1	RATIO 2
MANAGED HEALTH INC	NY	• E+	HMO	2q 2002	71.2	272.2	272.2	33.7	0.69	0.58
MANAGED HEALTH NETWORK	CA	U	HMO	--	--	--	--	--	--	--
MANAGED HEALTH SERVICES INS CORP	WI	• C	HMO	1q 2003	44.6	200.4	200.4	14.4	0.87	0.72
MANAGED HEALTHCARE NORTHWEST INC	OR	U	HMO	--	--	--	--	--	--	--
MANHATTAN NATIONAL LIFE INS CO	IL	C-	L&H	2q 2003	269.6	55.2	5.6	47.0	4.68	2.24
MANUFACTURERS LIFE INS CO USA	MI	B+	L&H	2q 2003	53,737.8	11,005.3	10.9	1,190.5	1.14	0.61
MARKEL INS CO	IL	D+	P&C	2q 2003	403.7	191.6	36.0	95.4	0.71	0.45
MARQUETTE GENERAL HOSPITAL	MI	U	HMO	--	--	--	--	--	--	--
MARQUETTE INDEMNITY & LIFE INS CO	AZ	C	L&H	2q 2003	11.0	1.3	0.9	6.3	2.51	2.26
MARYLAND CASUALTY CO	MD	C	P&C	2q 2003	339.6	1,051.4	0.0	334.9	1.76	1.52
MASSACHUSETTS MUTUAL LIFE INS CO	MA	A	L&H	2q 2003	80,322.1	10,426.0	377.9	6,514.6	3.29	1.76
MASTERCARE COMPANIES INC	NJ	U	HMO	--	--	--	--	--	--	--
MATTHEW THORNTON HEALTH PLAN	NH	• B+	HMO	1q 2003	210.3	570.6	570.6	99.7	3.33	2.78
MAYAN HEALTH PPO	NY	U	HMO	--	--	--	--	--	--	--
MAYO HEALTH PLAN ARIZONA	AZ	• C-	HMO	1q 2003	19.9	67.0	67.0	11.8	1.44	1.20
MCAID	MI	U	HMO	1q 2003	1.1	0.0	0.0	1.1	--	--
MCDONALD LIFE INS CO	TX	U	L&H	4q 2002	1.5	0.0	0.0	1.3	--	--
MCKINLEY LIFE INS CO	OH	D	L&H	4q 2002	24.6	75.5	75.5	6.7	0.50	0.42
MCLAREN HEALTH PLAN INC	MI	• C+	HMO	1q 2003	16.7	35.4	35.4	6.9	1.15	0.96
MCS HEALTH MANAGEMENT OPTIONS	PR	• C	HMO	4q 2002	91.6	367.8	367.8	25.7	0.97	0.81
MCS LIFE INS CO	PR	D	L&H	2q 2003	36.5	73.6	73.0	10.7	0.61	0.50
MD INDIVIDUAL PRACTICE ASSOC INC	MD	• B+	HMO	1q 2003	113.6	379.3	379.3	56.6	3.79	3.16
MDNY HEALTHCARE INC	NY	• E	HMO	2q 2002	42.8	146.6	146.6	6.7	0.20	0.17
MDNY PREFERRED NETWORK INC	NY	U	HMO	--	--	--	--	--	--	--
MEDAMERICA INS CO	PA	C-	L&H	2q 2003	233.9	21.1	21.1	19.5	1.75	1.18
MEDAMERICA INS CO OF NEW YORK	NY	D+	L&H	2q 2003	93.1	23.1	23.1	8.7	1.03	0.93
MEDCO CONTAINMENT INS CO OF NJ	NJ	U	HMO	1q 2003	17.1	3.3	3.3	11.7	--	--
MEDCO CONTAINMENT LIFE INS CO	PA	• C	L&H	2q 2003	40.9	2.3	2.3	35.5	6.95	6.26
MEDCOCAL INC	CA	U	HMO	--	--	--	--	--	--	--
MEDCORE HP	CA	U	HMO	--	--	--	--	--	--	--
MEDCOST LLC	NC	U	HMO	--	--	--	--	--	--	--
▲ MEDICA	MN	• A-	HMO	1q 2003	599.3	1,389.4	1,389.4	254.5	2.33	1.94
MEDICA HEALTH PLANS OF WI	WI	• C	HMO	1q 2003	3.6	10.5	10.5	2.1	0.62	0.51
MEDICA INS CO	MN	• B	HMO	1q 2003	103.2	279.9	279.9	55.7	2.51	2.09
MEDICAL ASR CO	AL	B-	P&C	2q 2003	1,050.3	267.2	0.0	194.6	0.90	0.70
MEDICAL ASSOC CLINIC HEALTH PLAN	WI	• C	HMO	1q 2003	1.9	17.2	17.2	1.5	0.85	0.71
▲ MEDICAL ASSOCIATES HEALTH PLAN INC	IA	• C+	HMO	1q 2003	12.8	64.6	64.6	6.1	0.99	0.83
MEDICAL BENEFITS MUTUAL LIFE INS CO	OH	C-	L&H	2q 2003	18.2	65.1	62.9	8.4	1.12	0.77
MEDICAL CARE REFERRAL GROUP	TX	U	HMO	--	--	--	--	--	--	--
MEDICAL CENTER HEALTH PLAN	MO	• E+	HMO	4q 2002	19.5	87.5	87.5	5.0	0.36	0.30
MEDICAL CONTROL NETWORK SOLUTIONS	TX	U	HMO	--	--	--	--	--	--	--
MEDICAL EYE SERVICES INC	CA	U	HMO	--	--	--	--	--	--	--
MEDICAL HEALTH INS CORP OF OHIO	OH	• C-	HMO	1q 2003	65.0	201.0	201.0	33.6	2.46	2.05
MEDICAL LIABILITY MUTUAL INS CO	NY	D+	P&C	2q 2003	5,094.9	606.2	0.2	1,028.9	0.63	0.51
MEDICAL LIFE INS CO	OH	• B	L&H	2q 2003	232.6	170.6	59.4	135.4	3.99	3.02
MEDICAL MUTUAL OF OHIO	OH	C-	P&C	4q 2002	646.9	1,435.8	1,435.8	231.5	1.65	0.97
MEDICAL RESOURCES NETWORK LLC	GA	U	HMO	--	--	--	--	--	--	--
MEDICAL SAVINGS INS CO	OK	C+	L&H	2q 2003	37.1	24.7	24.6	8.1	1.49	1.18
MEDICHOICE NETWORK INC	NJ	U	HMO	--	--	--	--	--	--	--
MEDICO LIFE INS CO	NE	D+	L&H	2q 2003	140.8	57.7	50.3	16.3	1.90	1.39
MEDPLUS INC	PR	U	HMO	--	--	--	--	--	--	--
MEGA LIFE & HEALTH INS CO	OK	• C+	L&H	2q 2003	989.5	947.9	928.3	236.1	1.41	1.05

Arrows denote recent upgrades ▲ or downgrades ▼ • Bullets denote a more detailed analysis is available in Section II.

I. Index of Companies

Winter 2003 - 04

INSURANCE COMPANY NAME	DOM. STATE	WEISS SAFETY RATING	COMPANY TYPE	DATA DATE	TOTAL ASSETS ($MIL)	TOTAL PREMIUMS ($MIL)	HEALTH PREMIUMS ($MIL)	CAPITAL & SURPLUS ($MIL)	RISK ADJUSTED CAPITAL RATIO 1	RATIO 2
MEMBER SERVICE LIFE INS CO	OK	B	L&H	2q 2003	35.5	28.0	20.6	24.5	3.99	2.98
MEMBERS LIFE INS CO	WI	C	L&H	2q 2003	718.5	8.4	0.2	44.4	1.76	0.86
MEMORIAL PROHEALTH INC	GA	• D	HMO	2q 2002	10.3	13.7	13.7	3.4	0.45	0.39
MEMPHIS MANAGED CARE CORP	TN	• E	HMO	1q 2003	13.2	117.0	117.0	9.6	0.13	0.11
MENNONITE GENERAL HOSPITAL INC	PR	U	HMO		--	--	--	--	--	--
MERCHANTS MUTUAL INS CO	NY	C	P&C	2q 2003	246.8	99.9	0.0	58.7	2.21	1.47
MERCY HEALTH PLANS OF MISSOURI INC	MO	• C-	HMO	2q 2002	70.3	402.6	402.6	18.2	0.91	0.78
MERCYCARE HEALTH PLAN INC	WI	U	HMO		--	--	--	--	--	--
MERCYCARE INS CO	WI	• D	HMO	1q 2003	14.3	67.2	67.2	6.9	0.48	0.40
MERIT BEHAVIORAL CARE OF CALIFORNIA	CA	U	HMO	3q 2002	6.3	0.0	0.0	1.3	--	--
MERIT HEALTH INS CO	IL	D	P&C	2q 2003	12.2	6.0	6.0	10.1	1.97	1.68
MERIT LIFE INS CO	IN	• B+	L&H	2q 2003	1,020.5	111.1	47.5	521.8	11.21	5.82
MERITER HEALTH INS CO	WI	U	HMO	1q 2003	5.1	2.9	2.9	4.4	--	--
METLIFE INVESTORS INS CO OF CA	CA	B-	L&H	2q 2003	521.7	124.3	0.0	15.3	1.32	0.84
METROPLUS HEALTH PLAN	NY	U	HMO		--	--	--	--	--	--
METROPOLITAN HEALTH PLAN	MN	• A-	HMO	1q 2003	40.9	99.9	99.9	23.5	1.98	1.65
METROPOLITAN INS & ANNUITY CO	DE	B	L&H	2q 2003	6,532.4	402.3	50.7	1,045.5	2.93	1.40
METROPOLITAN LIFE INS CO	NY	B+	L&H	2q 2003	220,093.6	24,150.6	2,746.8	7,811.4	1.62	0.98
METROPOLITAN PROPERTY & CAS INS CO	RI	B+	P&C	2q 2003	4,789.1	1,065.0	9.9	1,935.9	1.70	1.39
METROWEST HEALTH PLAN INC	TX	• B	HMO	1q 2003	6.2	15.8	15.8	4.0	1.39	1.16
MIC LIFE INS CORP	DE	C	L&H	2q 2003	17.7	0.6	0.6	11.7	3.63	3.26
MICHIGAN DENTAL PLAN INC	MI	U	HMO		--	--	--	--	--	--
MID AMERICA HEALTH NETWORK INC	MO	U	HMO		--	--	--	--	--	--
MID-SOUTH INS CO	NE	C	L&H	2q 2003	21.1	14.3	14.3	17.7	4.78	3.48
MID-WEST NATIONAL LIFE INS CO OF TN	TN	• C	L&H	2q 2003	372.5	305.8	281.7	89.5	1.69	1.22
MIDLAND NATIONAL LIFE INS CO	IA	A-	L&H	2q 2003	10,748.6	2,861.5	0.2	661.6	2.07	1.06
MIDLANDS CHOICE	NE	U	HMO		--	--	--	--	--	--
MIDWEST ASR CO	MN	C+	P&C	4q 2002	23.0	42.2	42.2	9.9	1.36	0.78
MIDWEST HEALTH PLAN INC	MI	• B	HMO	1q 2003	27.7	78.6	78.6	11.0	1.19	1.00
MIDWEST SECURITY LIFE INS CO	WI	• B+	L&H	2q 2003	132.8	207.0	200.6	51.9	1.88	1.42
MIDWESTERN UNITED LIFE INS CO	IN	B	L&H	2q 2003	252.8	6.1	0.1	76.8	7.85	3.65
MII LIFE INC	MN	• B	L&H	2q 2003	62.0	20.9	5.8	38.4	3.41	2.49
MINNESOTA LIFE INS CO	MN	A-	L&H	2q 2003	17,352.3	2,519.5	202.3	1,033.4	1.83	1.10
MISSISSIPPI PHYSICIANS CARE NETWORK	MS	U	HMO		--	--	--	--	--	--
MISSISSIPPI SELECT HEALTH CARE LLC	MS	U	HMO		--	--	--	--	--	--
▲ MISSOURI CARE HEALTH PLAN	MO	• D+	HMO	1q 2003	12.3	53.1	53.1	4.6	0.57	0.47
MISSOURI VALLEY LIFE AND HLTH INS CO	MO	B-	L&H	2q 2003	24.0	4.5	3.8	22.1	3.65	3.29
MMA INS CO	IN	D-	L&H	2q 2003	14.8	25.2	24.9	10.0	2.27	1.79
MMM HEALTHCARE INC	PR	U	HMO		--	--	--	--	--	--
MNM-1997 INC	TX	U	HMO		--	--	--	--	--	--
MOHR HEALTH SYSTEMS INC	IL	U	HMO		--	--	--	--	--	--
MOLINA HEALTHCARE OF CALIFORNIA	CA	• C+	HMO	1q 2003	85.7	314.1	314.1	30.0	0.98	0.62
MOLINA HEALTHCARE OF MICHIGAN INC	MI	• B-	HMO	1q 2003	20.8	52.4	52.4	5.7	0.88	0.74
MOLINA HEALTHCARE OF UTAH INC	UT	• C	HMO	1q 2003	29.1	63.3	63.3	4.9	1.21	1.01
MOLINA HEALTHCARE OF WASHINGTON INC	WA	• B	HMO	1q 2003	66.4	256.3	256.3	29.6	1.82	1.52
MONARCH LIFE INS CO	MA	F	L&H	4q 2002	1,026.0	49.1	44.7	10.4	0.59	0.30
MONITOR LIFE INS CO OF NEW YORK	NY	D-	L&H	2q 2003	29.2	5.4	0.0	3.6	0.84	0.76
MONTGOMERY WARD INS CO	IL	B-	P&C	2q 2003	38.5	19.0	0.1	19.2	5.95	5.14
MONUMENTAL GENERAL LIFE INS CO OF PR	PR	D-	L&H	2q 2003	6.0	19.4	6.6	0.8	0.38	0.34
MONUMENTAL LIFE INS CO	MD	B-	L&H	2q 2003	18,959.5	2,006.9	429.9	1,318.2	1.91	0.92
MONY LIFE INS CO	NY	C	L&H	2q 2003	11,222.2	810.8	67.6	871.7	1.31	0.89
MOTOR CLUB INS ASN	NE	C	P&C	2q 2003	30.2	20.1	0.4	11.2	1.97	1.51

Arrows denote recent upgrades ▲ or downgrades ▼

• Bullets denote a more detailed analysis is available in Section II.

www.WeissRatings.com

I. Index of Companies

INSURANCE COMPANY NAME	DOM. STATE	WEISS SAFETY RATING	COMPANY TYPE	DATA DATE	TOTAL ASSETS ($MIL)	TOTAL PREMIUMS ($MIL)	HEALTH PREMIUMS ($MIL)	CAPITAL & SURPLUS ($MIL)	RISK ADJUSTED CAPITAL RATIO 1	RATIO 2
MOTOR CLUB OF IOWA INS CO	IA	C	P&C	2q 2003	17.0	6.0	1.7	15.5	4.28	2.67
MOUNT CARMEL BEHAVIORAL HEALTHCARE	OH	U	HMO	--	--	--	--	--	--	--
MOUNT CARMEL HEALTH PLAN INC	OH	• D+	HMO	1q 2003	35.7	112.5	112.5	24.0	2.11	1.76
MOUNTAIN LIFE INS CO	TN	C-	L&H	2q 2003	13.5	15.2	4.3	3.2	1.13	1.01
MOUNTAIN MEDICAL AFFILIATES INC	CO	U	HMO	--	--	--	--	--	--	--
MOUNTAIN STATE BL CROSS BL SHIELD	WV	• B+	HLTH	1q 2003	156.0	391.2	391.2	44.7	2.07	1.72
MS LIFE INS CO	MS	C+	L&H	2q 2003	34.1	8.2	3.1	13.6	1.33	1.21
MTL INS CO	IL	B	L&H	2q 2003	1,088.4	149.2	0.7	83.0	2.13	1.08
MULTIPLAN INC	NY	U	HMO	--	--	--	--	--	--	--
MUNICIPAL INS CO OF AMERICA	IL	C-	L&H	2q 2003	21.5	1.2	1.2	5.2	2.99	1.79
MUTUAL ALLIANCE PLAN	MA	U	HMO	--	--	--	--	--	--	--
MUTUAL OF AMERICA LIFE INS CO	NY	B	L&H	2q 2003	10,389.6	1,013.8	8.3	557.6	1.95	0.95
MUTUAL OF DETROIT INS CO	MI	C+	L&H	2q 2003	63.7	8.6	0.1	16.9	2.35	2.11
MUTUAL OF OMAHA INS CO	NE	• A-	L&H	2q 2003	3,755.1	1,477.1	1,477.1	1,628.6	1.20	1.08
MUTUAL PROTECTIVE INS CO	NE	D+	P&C	1q 2003	223.1	206.6	206.6	21.3	0.79	0.55
MUTUAL SAVINGS LIFE INS CO	AL	D	L&H	2q 2003	419.7	50.4	8.8	23.6	1.35	0.78
MUTUAL SERVICE LIFE INS CO	MN	B-	L&H	2q 2003	377.9	39.1	4.9	40.1	2.45	1.23
MVP HEALTH INS CO	NY	• B-	HMO	1q 2003	18.4	12.5	12.5	4.5	2.67	2.23
MVP HEALTH PLAN INC	NY	• B+	HMO	1q 2003	264.0	857.1	857.1	76.2	1.26	1.05
MVP HEALTH SERVICES CORP	NY	• B	HLTH	1q 2003	5.7	3.4	3.4	4.0	6.31	5.26
MVPPO	FL	U	HMO	--	--	--	--	--	--	--
NATIONAL ASSOC PREFERRED PROVIDERS	TX	U	HMO	--	--	--	--	--	--	--
NATIONAL BENEFIT LIFE INS CO	NY	• B+	L&H	2q 2003	736.6	139.9	35.9	242.9	5.54	3.18
NATIONAL CAPITAL PPO	VA	U	HMO	--	--	--	--	--	--	--
NATIONAL CASUALTY CO	WI	B+	P&C	2q 2003	92.6	399.6	7.1	87.1	53.84	39.51
NATIONAL FAMILY CARE LIFE INS CO	TX	D+	L&H	2q 2003	16.0	10.3	8.8	6.6	2.12	1.79
NATIONAL FARMERS UNION LIFE INS CO	TX	C	L&H	2q 2003	315.7	14.3	0.0	33.7	2.61	1.43
NATIONAL FARMERS UNION PROP & CAS CO	CO	C+	P&C	2q 2003	261.4	211.4	0.0	84.6	2.04	1.44
NATIONAL FINANCIAL INS CO	TX	D-	L&H	2q 2003	16.5	11.1	11.1	2.1	0.56	0.46
NATIONAL FOUNDATION LIFE INS CO	TX	C+	L&H	2q 2003	46.3	41.0	40.7	7.2	0.48	0.37
NATIONAL GUARDIAN LIFE INS CO	WI	A-	L&H	2q 2003	947.4	62.0	2.3	112.5	1.14	0.81
NATIONAL HEALTH INS CO	TX	E	L&H	2q 2003	972.4	302.6	123.1	14.0	0.42	0.24
NATIONAL HEALTH PLAN CORP	NY	U	HMO	--	--	--	--	--	--	--
NATIONAL HEALTHCARE ALLIANCE INC	TX	U	HMO	--	--	--	--	--	--	--
NATIONAL HERITAGE INS CO	TX	• E	L&H	2q 2003	373.2	2,623.4	2,623.4	158.0	0.95	0.79
NATIONAL INCOME LIFE INS CO	NY	C-	L&H	3q 2002	11.4	1.4	0.2	10.5	5.40	4.86
NATIONAL INS CO OF WISCONSIN INC	WI	C	P&C	2q 2003	27.7	4.0	4.0	13.2	1.76	1.17
NATIONAL LIFE INS CO	VT	C+	L&H	2q 2003	7,006.2	749.6	48.7	430.5	1.16	0.74
NATIONAL LIFE INS CO	PR	B-	L&H	2q 2003	87.8	55.4	25.6	13.7	0.93	0.66
NATIONAL LLOYDS INS CO	TX	C+	P&C	2q 2003	108.9	61.1	0.0	36.9	2.08	1.52
NATIONAL MASONIC PROVIDENT ASN	OH	U	L&H	4q 2002	2.0	0.0	0.0	1.2	--	--
NATIONAL MED INC	CA	U	HMO	2q 2002	42.2	119.8	119.8	23.1	--	--
NATIONAL PACIFIC DENTAL INC	TX	U	HMO	--	--	--	--	--	--	--
NATIONAL PREFERRED PROVIDER NETWORK	NY	U	HMO	--	--	--	--	--	--	--
NATIONAL SAFETY LIFE INS CO	PA	C	L&H	2q 2003	5.1	1.2	1.1	3.8	2.47	2.22
NATIONAL SECURITY INS CO	AL	C	L&H	2q 2003	40.8	5.4	1.2	10.2	1.96	1.66
NATIONAL STATES INS CO	MO	D	L&H	2q 2003	106.4	111.7	75.0	15.4	0.84	0.61
NATIONAL TEACHERS ASSOCIATES L I C	TX	C+	L&H	2q 2003	72.4	35.0	33.3	12.4	1.12	0.85
NATIONAL UNION FIRE INS CO OF PITTSB	PA	B+	P&C	2q 2003	18,196.9	4,746.0	277.2	6,219.7	1.22	1.01
NATIONAL WESTERN LIFE INS CO	CO	C+	L&H	2q 2003	4,152.7	514.2	0.7	461.9	2.91	1.45
NATIONALCARE INS CO	OK	• B	L&H	2q 2003	120.6	7.5	7.5	118.0	1.43	1.40
NATIONSBANC INS CO INC	SC	B-	L&H	2q 2003	338.5	-18.6	0.0	134.7	10.21	6.13

I. Index of Companies

Winter 2003 - 04

INSURANCE COMPANY NAME	DOM. STATE	WEISS SAFETY RATING	COMPANY TYPE	DATA DATE	TOTAL ASSETS ($MIL)	TOTAL PREMIUMS ($MIL)	HEALTH PREMIUMS ($MIL)	CAPITAL & SURPLUS ($MIL)	RISK ADJUSTED CAPITAL RATIO 1	RATIO 2
NATIONWIDE HEALTH PLANS INC	OH	U	HMO	4q 2001	8.1	49.9	49.9	1.9	--	--
NATIONWIDE LIFE & ANNUITY CO AMERICA	DE	C+	L&H	2q 2003	1,086.0	86.2	0.0	36.8	1.58	0.78
NATIONWIDE LIFE INS CO	OH	B+	L&H	2q 2003	80,569.1	11,482.9	304.4	1,978.8	1.79	0.94
NATIONWIDE LIFE INS CO OF AMERICA	PA	B-	L&H	2q 2003	6,194.2	461.4	4.1	431.2	2.16	1.17
NATIONWIDE MUTUAL FIRE INS CO	OH	B+	P&C	2q 2003	3,610.4	2,920.1	0.0	1,225.2	2.89	2.03
NATIONWIDE MUTUAL INS CO	OH	C+	P&C	2q 2003	20,749.9	4,492.4	1.3	6,892.9	1.20	1.01
NEIGHBORHOOD HEALTH PARTNERSHIP INC	FL	● B-	HMO	1q 2003	120.1	671.0	671.0	20.6	0.80	0.67
NEIGHBORHOOD HEALTH PLAN	MA	● D-	HMO	1q 2003	52.4	394.3	394.3	16.7	0.51	0.43
NEIGHBORHOOD HEALTH PLAN OF RI INC	RI	● C-	HMO	1q 2003	38.5	130.3	130.3	7.1	0.45	0.37
NET PRO	IN	U	HMO		--	--	--	--	--	--
NETCARE LIFE & HEALTH INS CO	GU	E+	L&H	2q 2003	20.6	20.1	17.3	1.1	0.32	0.29
NETWORK HEALTH INS CORP	WI	U	HMO	1q 2003	4.1	3.9	3.9	3.7	--	--
NETWORK HEALTH PLAN OF WISCONSIN INC	WI	● D+	HMO	1q 2003	49.3	232.1	232.1	22.2	0.81	0.68
NEVADA PACIFIC DENTAL INC	NV	U	HMO	2q 2002	5.6	27.7	27.7	2.2	--	--
NEVADA PREFERRED PROFESSIONALS	NV	U	HMO		--	--	--	--	--	--
NEVADACARE INC	NV	● C	HMO	1q 2003	47.8	181.5	181.5	14.4	0.69	0.58
NEW ENGLAND LIFE INS CO	MA	B	L&H	2q 2003	7,480.9	2,054.8	118.6	395.3	2.46	1.60
NEW ERA LIFE INS CO	TX	D	L&H	2q 2003	130.1	66.3	58.8	20.1	0.54	0.44
NEW ERA LIFE INS CO OF THE MIDWEST	TX	D	L&H	2q 2003	28.9	7.0	6.6	8.8	1.68	1.11
NEW HAMPSHIRE INS CO	PA	B	P&C	2q 2003	2,237.3	1,463.2	67.7	664.7	1.25	0.96
NEW MEXICO TRIBAL HEALTHCARE ALLIANC	NM	U	HMO		--	--	--	--	--	--
NEW SOUTH LIFE INS CO	MS	D	L&H	2q 2003	6.4	0.6	0.2	5.8	3.23	2.91
NEW WEST HEALTH PLAN	MT	U	HMO		--	--	--	--	--	--
NEW YORK LIFE INS CO	NY	A	L&H	2q 2003	87,505.8	8,790.7	475.1	8,780.3	1.72	1.15
NGL AMERICAN LIFE INS CO	WI	B	L&H	2q 2003	122.7	25.1	0.7	25.2	3.00	2.70
NIAGARA FIRE INS CO	DE	● C-	P&C	2q 2003	124.2	1,151.2	1,151.3	72.0	4.52	2.66
NIPPON LIFE INS CO OF AMERICA	IA	● B-	L&H	2q 2003	147.5	210.5	195.5	97.4	3.41	2.64
NORIDIAN MUTUAL INS CO	ND	● B+	HLTH	1q 2003	298.8	574.1	574.1	140.2	2.38	1.98
NORTH ALABAMA MANAGED CARE INC	AL	U	HMO		--	--	--	--	--	--
NORTH AMERICAN CAPACITY INS CO	NH	C	P&C	2q 2003	89.3	107.5	4.5	37.6	5.50	4.95
NORTH AMERICAN CO FOR L&H INS OF NY	NY	C+	L&H	2q 2003	916.5	92.5	0.4	75.6	2.10	1.08
NORTH AMERICAN CO FOR LIFE & H INS	IL	C+	L&H	2q 2003	4,182.0	1,206.7	0.5	259.1	1.69	0.90
NORTH AMERICAN INS CO	WI	C-	L&H	2q 2003	26.2	32.4	23.0	11.1	2.51	1.77
NORTH CAROLINA FARM BU MUTUAL INS CO	NC	A-	P&C	2q 2003	1,007.2	550.0	0.3	492.9	4.80	3.65
NORTH CAROLINA MUTUAL LIFE INS CO	NC	D+	L&H	2q 2003	218.5	72.0	53.0	13.8	0.60	0.41
NORTH CENTRAL LIFE INS CO	IL	B-	L&H	2q 2003	124.7	28.1	14.6	17.5	2.00	1.65
NORTH COAST LIFE INS CO	WA	D-	L&H	2q 2003	95.4	9.2	0.0	5.5	0.71	0.48
NORTH DAKOTA VISION SERVICES INC	ND	U	HMO		--	--	--	--	--	--
NORTH POINTE INS CO	MI	C-	P&C	2q 2003	111.9	71.4	3.3	23.5	1.30	0.87
NORTH TEXAS HEALTHCARE NETWORK	TX	U	HMO		--	--	--	--	--	--
NORTHCARE	CO	U	HMO		--	--	--	--	--	--
NORTHEAST HEALTH DIRECT LLC	CT	U	HMO		--	--	--	--	--	--
NORTHERN ASR CO OF AMERICA	MA	C-	P&C	2q 2003	507.0	143.4	0.0	142.7	2.53	1.84
NORTHSTAR LIFE INS CO	NY	B	L&H	2q 2003	43.9	15.0	7.8	18.3	2.98	2.68
NORTHWESTERN LONG TERM CARE INS CO	WI	● B	L&H	2q 2003	81.7	31.1	31.1	54.5	4.65	2.95
NORTHWESTERN MUTUAL LIFE INS CO	WI	A	L&H	2q 2003	114,436.3	10,649.4	679.0	6,839.1	2.86	1.42
NORTHWESTERN NTL INS CO MILWAUKEE	WI	E	P&C	2q 2003	80.0	0.8	0.8	5.1	0.15	0.10
NOVA CASUALTY CO	NY	D-	P&C	2q 2003	64.2	52.6	0.0	14.9	0.42	0.28
NVAL VISIONCARE SYSTEMS OF CA INC	CA	U	HMO		--	--	--	--	--	--
NYLCARE DENTAL PLANS OF THE SW INC	TX	U	HMO		--	--	--	--	--	--
OCCIDENTAL LIFE INS CO OF NC	TX	C	L&H	2q 2003	307.9	34.3	11.7	21.1	1.50	0.82
OCHSNER HEALTH PLAN	LA	● D	HMO	4q 2002	154.3	683.9	683.9	33.7	0.50	0.42

Arrows denote recent upgrades ▲ or downgrades ▼   ● Bullets denote a more detailed analysis is available in Section II.

www.WeissRatings.com

I. Index of Companies

Winter 2003 - 04

INSURANCE COMPANY NAME	DOM. STATE	WEISS SAFETY RATING	COMPANY TYPE	DATA DATE	TOTAL ASSETS ($MIL)	TOTAL PREMIUMS ($MIL)	HEALTH PREMIUMS ($MIL)	CAPITAL & SURPLUS ($MIL)	RISK ADJUSTED CAPITAL RATIO 1	RATIO 2
ODS HEALTH PLAN INC	OR	• C+	HMO	1q 2003	77.3	107.9	107.9	27.9	1.63	1.36
OHIO CASUALTY INS CO	OH	C+	P&C	2q 2003	2,226.0	692.5	0.1	782.2	1.25	1.10
OHIO COMP NETWORK INC	OH	U	HMO	--	--	--	--	--	--	--
OHIO HEALTH CHOICE	OH	U	HMO	--	--	--	--	--	--	--
OHIO MOTORISTS LIFE INSURANCE CO	OH	C-	L&H	2q 2003	6.8	1.0	0.9	6.3	3.47	3.12
OHIO NATIONAL LIFE ASR CORP	OH	B	L&H	2q 2003	1,699.5	313.9	23.4	116.1	1.57	0.79
OHIO NATIONAL LIFE INS CO	OH	B	L&H	2q 2003	8,956.0	1,996.5	13.7	618.4	1.69	0.94
OHIO STATE LIFE INS CO	TX	C-	L&H	2q 2003	13.5	67.3	0.0	6.1	6.58	3.59
OKLAHOMA FARM BUREAU MUTUAL INS CO	OK	C+	P&C	2q 2003	206.0	195.4	0.1	70.2	1.57	1.08
OLD AMERICAN INS CO	MO	B-	L&H	2q 2003	261.3	77.6	4.1	16.6	1.81	0.94
OLD RELIANCE INS CO	AZ	E+	L&H	2q 2003	5.4	1.9	0.1	2.1	0.86	0.60
OLD REPUBLIC INS CO	PA	A-	P&C	2q 2003	1,644.5	592.5	41.8	572.4	2.26	1.25
OLD REPUBLIC LIFE INS CO	IL	• B	L&H	2q 2003	106.6	43.3	17.8	26.1	1.85	1.38
OLD SPARTAN LIFE INS CO INC	SC	C-	L&H	2q 2003	30.1	4.8	3.8	20.8	1.84	1.53
OLD SURETY LIFE INS CO	OK	D	L&H	2q 2003	14.9	12.2	11.9	4.9	1.11	0.82
OLD UNITED LIFE INS CO	AZ	C	L&H	2q 2003	60.2	18.8	10.0	24.7	4.01	3.20
OLYMPIA LIMITED HEALTH SERVICES ORG	IL	U	HMO	--	--	--	--	--	--	--
OMAHA LIFE INS CO	NE	B-	L&H	2q 2003	16.5	2.6	1.0	14.6	4.67	4.20
OMNICARE HEALTH PLAN	MI	F	HMO	1q 2003	8.9	173.0	173.0	-13.4	0.00	0.00
OMNICARE HEALTH PLAN INC	TN	• D	HMO	1q 2003	9.3	110.8	110.8	7.1	0.44	0.37
ON LOK SENIOR HEALTH SERVICES	CA	• B-	HMO	3q 2002	38.4	47.0	47.0	30.2	8.45	5.26
ONE HEALTH PLAN OF AZ INC	AZ	• B	HMO	1q 2003	9.1	5.8	5.8	5.1	13.85	11.54
ONE HEALTH PLAN OF CALIFORNIA INC	CA	• B-	HMO	1q 2003	52.2	109.4	109.4	18.0	5.55	3.50
ONE HEALTH PLAN OF COLORADO INC	CO	• B	HMO	1q 2003	20.8	19.5	19.5	8.6	7.99	6.66
ONE HEALTH PLAN OF FLORDIA INC	FL	• B-	HMO	1q 2003	8.9	12.5	12.5	4.6	3.17	2.64
ONE HEALTH PLAN OF GEORGIA INC	GA	• B	HMO	1q 2003	14.9	12.1	12.1	10.9	10.71	8.93
ONE HEALTH PLAN OF ILLINOIS INC	IL	• B-	HMO	1q 2003	13.3	10.2	10.2	3.5	5.36	4.47
ONE HEALTH PLAN OF IN INC	IN	• B	HMO	4q 2002	6.3	2.3	2.3	4.5	11.07	9.23
ONE HEALTH PLAN OF KANSAS/MISSOURI	KS	• B	HMO	1q 2003	4.3	3.6	3.6	3.7	9.02	7.52
ONE HEALTH PLAN OF MA INC	MA	• B	HMO	1q 2003	3.4	1.9	1.9	1.7	3.81	3.18
ONE HEALTH PLAN OF NEW JERSEY INC	NJ	• B-	HMO	1q 2003	5.6	1.9	1.9	4.7	12.97	10.81
ONE HEALTH PLAN OF NORTH CAROLINA	NC	• B-	HMO	1q 2003	4.9	0.9	0.9	3.9	9.69	8.07
ONE HEALTH PLAN OF OHIO INC	OH	• B-	HMO	1q 2003	7.8	3.1	3.1	5.4	12.56	10.46
ONE HEALTH PLAN OF OREGON INC	OR	• B-	HLTH	1q 2003	10.1	6.5	6.5	4.7	11.58	9.65
ONE HEALTH PLAN OF PENNSYLVANIA INC	PA	U	HMO	--	--	--	--	--	--	--
ONE HEALTH PLAN OF TENNESSEE	TN	• B	HMO	1q 2003	10.6	3.0	3.0	9.4	36.78	30.65
ONE HEALTH PLAN OF TEXAS INC	TX	• B	HMO	1q 2003	25.9	18.3	18.3	14.1	15.84	13.20
ONE HEALTH PLAN OF WASHINGTON INC	WA	• B	HLTH	1q 2003	11.2	4.1	4.1	8.3	19.76	16.47
ONEBEACON AMERICA INS CO	MA	C-	P&C	2q 2003	1,419.2	471.7	4.5	473.9	3.80	2.40
OPTIMA HEALTH INS CO	VA	U	HMO	--	--	--	--	--	--	--
OPTIMA HEALTH PLAN	VA	• B	HMO	1q 2003	122.4	489.7	489.7	53.3	1.59	1.32
OPTIMUM CHOICE INC	MD	• B	HMO	1q 2003	251.2	948.7	948.7	107.4	1.91	1.59
OPTIMUM CHOICE INC OF PENNSYLVANIA	PA	U	HMO	--	--	--	--	--	--	--
OPTIMUM CHOICE OF THE CAROLINAS INC	NC	• C	HMO	1q 2003	13.1	28.4	28.4	4.2	0.89	0.75
OPTIMUM HEALTH NETWORK	SC	U	HMO	--	--	--	--	--	--	--
ORANGE CTY FOUNDATION FOR MED CARE	CA	U	HMO	--	--	--	--	--	--	--
ORANGE PREVENTION & TREATMENT INTEGR	CA	• C	HMO	3q 2002	267.6	626.2	626.2	148.4	2.54	1.67
OREGON DENTAL SERVICE	OR	U	HMO	--	--	--	--	--	--	--
ORION LIFE INS CO	DE	D	L&H	2q 2003	5.7	2.0	2.0	3.8	2.42	2.18
ORISKA INS CO	NY	D	P&C	1q 2003	20.1	21.1	8.4	8.7	0.83	0.56
ORTHOPEDIC HEALTHCARE OF TX INC	TX	U	HMO	--	--	--	--	--	--	--
OSF HEALTH PLANS INC	IL	E+	L&H	2q 2003	36.0	3.0	3.0	9.5	1.65	1.48

www.WeissRatings.com

Arrows denote recent upgrades ▲ or downgrades ▼   • Bullets denote a more detailed analysis is available in Section II.

I. Index of Companies

Winter 2003 - 04

INSURANCE COMPANY NAME	DOM. STATE	WEISS SAFETY RATING	COMPANY TYPE	DATA DATE	TOTAL ASSETS ($MIL)	TOTAL PREMIUMS ($MIL)	HEALTH PREMIUMS ($MIL)	CAPITAL & SURPLUS ($MIL)	RISK ADJUSTED CAPITAL RATIO 1	RATIO 2
OXFORD HEALTH INS INC	NY	● B-	HMO	1q 2003	391.7	892.0	892.0	181.9	3.32	2.76
OXFORD HEALTH PLANS (CT) INC	CT	● B	HMO	1q 2003	109.1	203.7	203.7	49.4	4.28	3.57
OXFORD HEALTH PLANS (NH) INC	NH	U	HMO		--	--	--	--	--	--
OXFORD HEALTH PLANS (NJ) INC	NJ	● B	HMO	1q 2003	107.5	404.1	404.1	48.7	2.11	1.76
OXFORD HEALTH PLANS (NY) INC	NY	● B+	HMO	1q 2003	1,066.7	3,256.0	3,256.0	535.3	2.72	2.26
OXFORD LIFE INS CO	AZ	C-	L&H	2q 2003	798.0	179.0	35.7	51.2	0.70	0.44
OZARK NATIONAL LIFE INS CO	AR	E+	L&H	2q 2003	10.9	2.4	0.1	1.0	0.59	0.47
OZARK NATIONAL LIFE INS CO	MO	C+	L&H	2q 2003	448.3	100.3	0.5	59.1	2.97	1.73
PACIFIC CENTURY LIFE INS CORP	AZ	C	L&H	2q 2003	316.6	0.5	0.0	312.2	28.51	25.65
PACIFIC FOUNDATION FOR MEDICAL CARE	CA	U	HMO		--	--	--	--	--	--
PACIFIC GUARDIAN LIFE INS CO LTD	HI	● B+	L&H	2q 2003	431.5	71.7	20.0	71.0	3.30	1.92
PACIFIC HEALTH ALLIANCE	CA	U	HMO		--	--	--	--	--	--
PACIFIC HOSPITAL ASSOC	OR	● A-	HLTH	1q 2003	89.6	246.0	246.0	51.0	2.07	1.73
PACIFIC INDEMNITY CO	WI	B	P&C	2q 2003	3,704.6	484.7	0.2	769.0	1.18	0.80
PACIFIC LIFE & ACCIDENT INS CO	TX	U	L&H	4q 2002	8.8	0.0	0.0	5.3	--	--
PACIFIC LIFE & ANNUITY CO	AZ	● B	L&H	2q 2003	1,051.1	1,012.4	849.3	272.7	2.83	1.86
PACIFIC LIFE INS CO	CA	A-	L&H	2q 2003	54,639.9	7,025.4	62.3	1,891.1	2.26	1.15
PACIFIC UNION DENTAL	CA	U	HMO		--	--	--	--	--	--
PACIFIC VISIONCARE WASHINGTON INC	WA	U	HMO		--	--	--	--	--	--
PACIFICARE BEHAVIORAL HEALTH OF CA	CA	U	HMO		--	--	--	--	--	--
PACIFICARE DENTAL	CA	U	HMO		--	--	--	--	--	--
PACIFICARE HEALTH INS CO MICRONESIA	GU	D	L&H	1q 2002	20.5	79.2	79.2	7.8	0.56	0.48
PACIFICARE LIFE & HEALTH INS CO	IN	● C-	L&H	2q 2003	96.2	132.7	126.1	40.6	1.44	1.16
PACIFICARE LIFE ASR CO	CO	● C-	L&H	2q 2003	91.4	154.6	152.1	36.0	1.26	1.01
PACIFICARE OF ARIZONA INC	AZ	● B-	HMO	1q 2003	207.5	910.9	910.9	103.3	2.12	1.77
PACIFICARE OF CALIFORNIA INC	CA	● C-	HMO	1q 2003	1,045.3	6,089.3	6,089.3	337.6	0.82	0.51
PACIFICARE OF COLORADO INC	CO	● B-	HMO	1q 2003	207.7	842.8	842.8	102.7	2.14	1.78
PACIFICARE OF NEVADA INC	NV	● C-	HMO	1q 2003	63.7	238.0	238.0	34.8	3.04	2.53
PACIFICARE OF OKLAHOMA INC	OK	● C-	HMO	1q 2003	43.1	362.4	362.4	11.2	0.80	0.67
PACIFICARE OF OREGON	OR	● B-	HMO	1q 2003	85.0	373.4	373.4	43.4	2.29	1.91
▲ PACIFICARE OF TEXAS INC	TX	● D+	HMO	1q 2003	171.4	1,004.4	1,004.4	69.8	0.51	0.43
PACIFICARE OF WASHINGTON INC	WA	U	HMO		--	--	--	--	--	--
PACIFICARE OF WASHINGTON INC	WA	● C	HLTH	1q 2003	116.3	544.5	544.5	41.9	0.61	0.51
PACIFICSOURCE HEALTH PLANS (See PACIFIC HOSPITAL ASSOC)										
PAN AMERICAN INS CO	PR	B-	P&C	2q 2003	81.6	23.6	0.0	28.3	3.06	1.91
PAN-AMERICAN LIFE INS CO	LA	● C+	L&H	2q 2003	2,449.0	140.6	82.7	195.7	1.89	1.09
▲ PARAMOUNT CARE OF MI INC	MI	● C	HMO	1q 2003	4.7	13.3	13.3	2.3	1.37	1.14
PARAMOUNT HEALTH CARE	OH	● B-	HMO	1q 2003	104.6	452.9	452.9	43.9	1.39	1.16
PARKLAND COMMUNITY HEALTH PLAN INC	TX	● C-	HMO	1q 2003	29.5	142.1	142.1	3.5	0.28	0.23
PARTNERS NATIONAL HEALTH PLAN OF IN	IN	● E+	HMO	4q 2002	24.2	147.0	147.0	5.9	0.34	0.29
PARTNERS NATIONAL HEALTH PLANS OF NC	NC	● B	HMO	1q 2003	171.1	653.4	653.4	94.9	2.41	2.01
PASSPORT HEALTH PLAN (See UNIVERSITY HEALTH CARE INC)										
PAUL REVERE LIFE INS CO	MA	● C-	L&H	2q 2003	5,224.8	616.1	591.0	1,041.7	2.22	1.43
PEARLE MANAGED CARE HMO OF TX	TX	U	HMO	2q 2002	2.8	7.1	7.1	2.2	--	--
PEARLE VISIONCARE INC	CA	U	HMO		--	--	--	--	--	--
PEKIN LIFE INS CO	IL	● B+	L&H	2q 2003	653.8	194.4	109.0	84.3	1.99	1.27
PENINSULA HEALTH CARE INC	VA	● B+	HMO	1q 2003	56.2	106.8	106.8	35.6	6.59	5.49
PENINSULAR LIFE INS CO	FL	D+	L&H	2q 2003	5.8	0.1	0.0	5.8	3.42	3.08
PENN HIGHLANDS HEALTH PLAN	PA	U	HMO		--	--	--	--	--	--
PENN MUTUAL LIFE INS CO	PA	B	L&H	2q 2003	7,463.4	790.9	20.2	848.5	3.15	1.89
PENN TREATY NETWORK AMERICA INS CO	PA	● D	L&H	2q 2003	124.1	314.9	312.3	27.8	1.93	1.64
PENNSYLVANIA BLUE SHIELD (See HIGHMARK INC)										

Arrows denote recent upgrades ▲ or downgrades ▼

● Bullets denote a more detailed analysis is available in Section II.

I. Index of Companies

INSURANCE COMPANY NAME	DOM. STATE	WEISS SAFETY RATING	COMPANY TYPE	DATA DATE	TOTAL ASSETS ($MIL)	TOTAL PREMIUMS ($MIL)	HEALTH PREMIUMS ($MIL)	CAPITAL & SURPLUS ($MIL)	RISK ADJUSTED CAPITAL RATIO 1	RATIO 2
PENNSYLVANIA DENTAL SERVICE CORP	PA	U	HMO	--	--	--	--	--	--	--
PENNSYLVANIA LIFE INS CO	PA	• D+	L&H	2q 2003	455.9	114.8	69.8	51.3	1.52	0.93
PENNSYLVANIA MANUFACTURERS ASN INS	PA	C	P&C	2q 2003	683.5	353.0	20.4	191.8	1.58	1.18
PENSION LIFE INS CO OF AMERICA	NJ	B-	L&H	2q 2003	16.0	43.0	40.2	9.8	3.46	3.11
PEOPLES BENEFIT LIFE INS CO	IA	C+	L&H	2q 2003	13,012.0	1,035.5	103.1	442.8	1.72	0.87
PEOPLES HEALTH PLAN OF OHIO INC	OH	F	HMO	4q 2002	4.9	7.5	7.5	2.2	0.68	0.57
PERSONAL CARE PLAN OF NORTH CAROLINA	NC	U	HMO	--	--	--	--	--	--	--
PERSONAL SERVICE INS CO	OH	C+	P&C	2q 2003	26.4	21.7	0.0	7.8	1.05	0.71
PERSONALCARE INS OF ILLINOIS INC	IL	U	HMO	--	--	--	--	--	--	--
PERSONALCARE INS OF ILLINOIS INC	IL	E+	L&H	2q 2003	61.9	24.6	24.6	15.9	1.62	1.12
PHILADELPHIA AMERICAN LIFE INS CO	TX	D	L&H	2q 2003	45.6	74.8	72.1	11.1	1.48	1.12
PHILADELPHIA-UNITED LIFE INS CO	PA	C+	L&H	2q 2003	44.1	7.1	0.0	16.3	3.08	2.77
PHN-HMO INC	MD	• C	HMO	1q 2003	17.0	77.7	77.7	8.2	1.32	1.10
PHOEBE HEALTH PARTNERS INC	GA	U	HMO	--	--	--	--	--	--	--
PHOENIX LIFE INS CO	NY	C	L&H	2q 2003	16,409.4	1,569.0	3.2	798.0	1.25	0.79
PHOENIX NATIONAL INS CO	OH	C	L&H	2q 2003	13.4	2.1	0.0	12.8	4.85	4.36
PHOENIX PREFERRED PPO	CT	U	HMO	--	--	--	--	--	--	--
PHP HEALTH PLAN INC	OR	U	HMO	1q 2003	1.8	3.2	3.2	0.7	--	--
PHP INS PLAN INC	WI	• D+	HMO	1q 2003	16.9	63.9	63.9	4.3	0.80	0.67
PHP OF SOUTH MICHIGAN (See PHYSICIANS HEALTH PLAN OF S MICHIGAN)										
PHYSICIAN HEALTH PLAN OF SW MICHIGAN	MI	• C-	HMO	1q 2003	16.4	62.0	62.0	6.9	1.21	1.01
PHYSICIANS BENEFITS TRUST LIFE INS	IL	C-	L&H	2q 2003	19.0	32.5	32.5	7.5	1.20	0.97
PHYSICIANS CARE HMO INC	PA	F	HMO	2q 1999	1.6	0.0	0.0	1.6	5279.41	5279.41
PHYSICIANS CARE NETWORK	SC	U	HMO	--	--	--	--	--	--	--
PHYSICIANS GROUP INC	GA	U	HMO	--	--	--	--	--	--	--
PHYSICIANS HEALTH PLAN OF NO IN	IN	• B	HMO	1q 2003	38.4	135.7	135.7	16.8	1.03	0.86
PHYSICIANS HEALTH PLAN OF S MICHIGAN	MI	• C	HMO	1q 2003	27.1	67.3	67.3	10.6	1.44	1.20
PHYSICIANS HP MID-MICHIGAN FAMILY	MI	U	HMO	--	--	--	--	--	--	--
PHYSICIANS HP OF MID-MICHIGAN	MI	• C+	HMO	1q 2003	66.6	242.3	242.3	27.1	0.95	0.80
PHYSICIANS LIABILITY INS CO	OK	E+	P&C	1q 2003	120.7	75.1	33.6	11.7	0.20	0.18
PHYSICIANS LIFE INS CO	NE	B+	L&H	2q 2003	1,195.8	204.1	4.9	66.4	1.73	0.89
PHYSICIANS MUTUAL INS CO	NE	• A+	L&H	2q 2003	1,102.7	501.3	501.3	610.9	3.77	2.92
PHYSICIANS PLUS INS CORP	WI	• B-	HMO	1q 2003	49.4	233.7	233.7	27.5	1.82	1.52
PHYSICIANSPLUS BAPTIST & ST DOMINIC	MS	U	HMO	--	--	--	--	--	--	--
PIEDMONT COMMUNITY HEALTHCARE	VA	• D	HMO	1q 2003	11.2	27.2	27.2	3.2	0.41	0.34
PIEDMONT INS CO	SC	F	L&H	2q 2002	2.5	0.4	0.1	0.1	0.08	0.07
PIONEER HEALTH	MA	U	HMO	--	--	--	--	--	--	--
PIONEER HEALTH PLAN INC	NE	U	HMO	2q 2001	2.2	9.1	9.1	1.2	--	--
PIONEER MUTUAL LIFE INS CO	ND	B-	L&H	2q 2003	454.0	45.5	0.1	30.5	1.80	0.93
PL MEDICO SERV DE SALUD BELLA VISTA	PR	U	HMO	--	--	--	--	--	--	--
PLAN DE SALUD DE LA FEDERACION	PR	U	HMO	--	--	--	--	--	--	--
PLAN DE SALUD HOSP DE LA CONCEPCION	PR	U	HMO	--	--	--	--	--	--	--
PLAN DE SALUD UIA INC	PR	U	HMO	--	--	--	--	--	--	--
PLATEAU INS CO	TN	C	L&H	2q 2003	18.2	14.1	4.4	8.3	1.75	1.57
POMCO PLUS	NY	U	HMO	--	--	--	--	--	--	--
PPO OKLAHOMA	OK	U	HMO	--	--	--	--	--	--	--
PPOM	MI	U	HMO	--	--	--	--	--	--	--
PPONEXT - CALIFORNIA	CA	U	HMO	--	--	--	--	--	--	--
PREFERRED ASSURANCE CO	NY	U	HLTH	1q 2003	0.3	0.2	0.2	0.3	--	--
PREFERRED CARE (See ROCHESTER AREA HEALTH MAINTENANCE OR)										
PREFERRED CARE INC	PA	U	HMO	--	--	--	--	--	--	--
PREFERRED CARE PARTNERS INC	FL	U	HMO	1q 2003	3.7	4.3	4.3	1.2	--	--

Arrows denote recent upgrades ▲ or downgrades ▼   • Bullets denote a more detailed analysis is available in Section II.

I. Index of Companies

Winter 2003 - 04

INSURANCE COMPANY NAME	DOM. STATE	WEISS SAFETY RATING	COMPANY TYPE	DATA DATE	TOTAL ASSETS ($MIL)	TOTAL PREMIUMS ($MIL)	HEALTH PREMIUMS ($MIL)	CAPITAL & SURPLUS ($MIL)	RISK ADJUSTED CAPITAL RATIO 1	RATIO 2
PREFERRED COMMUNITYCHOICE PPO INC	OK	U	HMO	--	--	--	--	--	--	--
PREFERRED HEALTH	PR	U	HMO	--	--	--	--	--	--	--
PREFERRED HEALTH CARE	PA	U	HMO	--	--	--	--	--	--	--
PREFERRED HEALTH NORTHWEST INC	OR	U	HMO	--	--	--	--	--	--	--
PREFERRED HEALTH PARTNERSHIP TN	TN	• D+	HMO	1q 2003	72.5	110.0	110.0	12.8	1.27	1.06
PREFERRED HEALTH PLAN INC	KY	U	HMO							
PREFERRED HEALTH PROFESSIONALS	KS	U	HMO							
PREFERRED HEALTH SYSTEMS INC	SC	U	HMO	1q 2002	4.6	37.8	37.8	0.5	--	--
PREFERRED HEALTH SYSTEMS INS CO	KS	C-	L&H	2q 2003	32.9	122.4	122.3	12.9	0.62	0.55
PREFERRED HEALTHCARE SYSTEM INC	PA	U	HMO	--	--	--	--	--	--	--
PREFERRED MEDICAL PLAN INC	FL	• B	HMO	1q 2003	18.3	58.2	58.2	5.8	1.21	1.01
PREFERRED PLAN	GA	U	HMO	--	--	--	--	--	--	--
PREFERRED PLAN INC	IL	U	HMO	--	--	--	--	--	--	--
PREFERRED PLUS OF KANSAS INC	KS	• B-	HMO	1q 2003	42.4	206.9	206.9	15.3	0.88	0.73
PREFERREDONE COMMUNITY HEALTH PLAN	MN	• B	HMO	1q 2003	37.1	67.4	67.4	21.9	2.79	2.33
PREFERREDONE PREFERRED PROVIDER ORG	MN	U	HMO							
PREMERA BLUE CROSS	WA	• B	HLTH	1q 2003	896.3	2,147.8	2,147.8	319.1	1.95	1.62
PREMERA BLUE CROSS BLUE SHIELD AK	AK	U	HMO							
PREMIER ACCESS INS CO	CA	C+	L&H	2q 2003	15.6	37.9	37.9	8.7	1.07	0.89
PREMIER BEHAVIORAL SYSTEMS OF TN LLC	TN	U	HMO	1q 2003	35.4	273.1	273.1	1.5	--	--
PREMIER HEALTH INC	KS	U	HMO							
PREMIER HEALTH PLANS (See MERCY HEALTH PLANS OF MISSOURI INC)										
PREMIER HEALTH SYSTEMS	SC	U	HMO							
PREMIER MEDICAL INS GROUP INC	WI	• C+	HMO	1q 2003	42.0	0.9	0.9	40.9	1.39	1.16
PRESBYTERIAN HEALTH PLAN INC	NM	• C+	HMO	1q 2003	147.4	676.0	676.0	72.1	1.28	1.06
PRESBYTERIAN INS CO INC	NM	U	HMO	1q 2003	1.3	0.1	0.1	0.9	--	--
PRESIDENTIAL LIFE INS CO	NY	D	L&H	2q 2003	4,051.7	784.0	10.9	194.2	1.17	0.57
PRESIDENTIAL LIFE INS CO	TX	E	L&H	2q 2003	1.1	0.5	0.5	0.9	1.80	1.62
PRIMARY HEALTH NETWORK INC	ID	E+	L&H	2q 2003	3.0	23.4	23.4	2.4	0.87	0.77
PRIMARY HEALTH SERVICES INC	OH	U	HMO	--	--	--	--	--	--	--
PRIME ADVANTAGE HEALTH (See COMANCHE COUNTY HOSPITAL AUTHORITY)										
PRIMECARE MEDICAL NETWORK INC	CA	• D	HMO	4q 2002	43.7	255.8	255.8	13.6	0.75	0.47
PRIMEHEALTH INC	AL	U	HMO							
PRIMEHEALTH OF ALABAMA INC	AL	• E	HMO	1q 2003	3.7	19.9	19.9	1.2	0.29	0.24
PRIMERICA LIFE INS CO	MA	B+	L&H	2q 2003	5,073.8	1,315.7	1.7	1,614.0	2.96	2.18
PRIMETIME MEDICAL INS CO	OH	D+	P&C	4q 2002	28.6	115.0	115.0	7.7	0.23	0.13
PRINCIPAL LIFE INS CO	IA	• A-	L&H	2q 2003	83,957.6	5,262.2	2,307.9	3,739.8	2.67	1.34
PRIORITY HEALTH	MI	• B+	HMO	1q 2003	177.9	606.9	606.9	67.7	1.37	1.14
PRIORITY HEALTH CARE INC	VA	• B+	HMO	1q 2003	70.7	176.0	176.0	38.7	3.47	2.89
PRIORITY HEALTH GOVERNMENT PROGRAMS	MI	U	HMO	1q 2003	8.5	9.2	9.2	2.6	--	--
PRIVATE HEALTHCARE SYSTEMS	MA	U	HMO	--	--	--	--	--	--	--
PRIVATE MEDICAL-CARE INC	CA	U	HMO	3q 2001	52.1	140.9	140.9	17.8	--	--
PRIVATE MEDICAL-CARE OF ARIZONA INC	AZ	U	HMO							
PRIVATE MEDICAL-CARE OF NEW MEXICO	NM	U	HMO							
PROCARE HEALTH PLAN INC	MI	U	HMO	--	--	--	--	--	--	--
PROFESSIONAL INS CO	TX	C+	L&H	2q 2003	67.2	37.9	33.8	16.9	1.27	0.86
PROFESSIONAL LIFE & CAS CO	IL	D+	L&H	2q 2003	45.1	3.5	0.0	6.5	1.37	0.65
PROMED HEALTH CARE ADMINISTRATORS	CA	U	HMO	4q 2002	3.1	4.5	4.5	2.4	--	--
PROMEDICA LIFE INS CO	OH	U	HMO	1q 2003	3.9	0.3	0.3	3.0	--	--
PROMINA HEALTH PLAN INC	GA	U	HMO							
PRONET	TX	U	HMO							
PROTECTED HOME MUTUAL LIFE INS CO	PA	D+	L&H	2q 2003	207.8	26.8	4.2	8.4	0.91	0.50

Arrows denote recent upgrades ▲ or downgrades ▼

• Bullets denote a more detailed analysis is available in Section II.

www.WeissRatings.com

Winter 2003 - 04 — I. Index of Companies

INSURANCE COMPANY NAME	DOM. STATE	WEISS SAFETY RATING	COMPANY TYPE	DATA DATE	TOTAL ASSETS ($MIL)	TOTAL PREMIUMS ($MIL)	HEALTH PREMIUMS ($MIL)	CAPITAL & SURPLUS ($MIL)	RISK ADJUSTED CAPITAL RATIO 1	RATIO 2
PROTECTIVE INDUSTRIAL INS CO OF AL	AL	D-	L&H	2q 2003	18.7	3.3	0.1	5.3	0.75	0.65
PROTECTIVE INS CO	IN	A+	P&C	2q 2003	443.4	112.1	16.5	287.0	2.07	1.60
PROTECTIVE LIFE & ANNUITY INS CO	AL	B-	L&H	2q 2003	715.5	22.1	4.2	115.4	5.44	2.63
PROTECTIVE LIFE INS CO	TN	C+	L&H	2q 2003	14,856.9	2,483.9	291.2	881.1	1.21	0.83
PROTECTIVE LIFE INS CO OF KY	KY	C+	L&H	2q 2003	5.1	1.2	0.4	3.5	2.24	2.01
PROTECTIVE LIFE INS CO OF OH	OH	C+	L&H	2q 2003	3.8	11.5	6.5	3.4	3.11	2.80
PROVIDENCE HEALTH CARE	WA	U	HMO	--	--	--	--	--	--	--
PROVIDENCE HEALTH PLAN	OR	• C+	HMO	1q 2003	157.8	520.9	520.9	86.4	1.99	1.66
PROVIDENT AMER LIFE & HEALTH INS CO	OH	D	L&H	2q 2003	12.0	23.5	22.8	5.7	2.25	1.66
PROVIDENT AMERICAN INS CO	TX	E+	L&H	2q 2003	16.7	2.1	1.6	3.3	0.57	0.51
PROVIDENT INDEMNITY LIFE INS CO	PA	U	L&H	4q 2002	0.5	1.5	0.0	0.0	--	--
PROVIDENT LIFE & ACCIDENT INS CO	TN	• C-	L&H	2q 2003	8,875.7	1,561.0	1,096.1	1,100.9	2.43	1.21
PROVIDENT LIFE & CAS INS CO	TN	• C-	L&H	2q 2003	609.1	73.8	67.3	75.8	2.26	1.20
PROVIDERS DIRECT HEALTH PLAN OF GA	GA	F	HMO	2q 2002	4.9	1.8	1.8	0.1	3.56	3.24
PRUDENTIAL DENTAL MAINT ORGAN INC	TX	U	HMO	--	--	--	--	--	--	--
PRUDENTIAL INS CO OF AMERICA	NJ	B-	L&H	2q 2003	195,114.7	16,810.8	660.7	5,946.1	1.77	1.03
PSO HEALTH SERVICES LLC	TX	U	HMO	--	--	--	--	--	--	--
PUBLIC SERVICE MUTUAL INS CO	NY	C	P&C	2q 2003	528.1	132.1	0.0	155.2	1.66	1.01
PUERTO RICAN AMERICAN INS CO	PR	B	P&C	2q 2003	304.2	136.7	0.3	100.1	2.40	1.57
PUERTO RICAN-AMERICAN LIFE INS CO	PR	B-	L&H	2q 2003	35.2	18.0	6.0	9.0	1.71	1.22
PYRAMID LIFE INS CO	KS	C	L&H	2q 2003	112.3	104.4	95.4	23.2	1.28	0.95
QBE INS CORP	PA	C+	P&C	2q 2003	240.8	237.0	3.4	74.4	1.05	0.74
QCA HEALTH PLAN INC	AR	• E	HMO	1q 2003	25.4	81.3	81.3	5.3	0.26	0.22
QCC INS CO	PA	• C+	HMO	1q 2003	967.5	2,250.6	2,250.6	285.6	2.88	2.40
▲ QCC INS CO	PA	• C+	HMO	1q 2003	967.5	2,250.6	2,250.6	285.6	2.88	2.40
QUAL CHOICE HEALTH PLAN INC	OH	• D-	P&C	1q 2003	100.9	371.9	371.9	35.2	0.58	0.37
QUALCHOICE OF NORTH CAROLINA INC	NC	• D+	HMO	2q 2002	26.0	149.1	149.1	10.8	0.74	0.62
QUALITY HEALTH PLANS INC	FL	U	HMO	4q 2002	2.8	0.0	0.0	2.0	--	--
QUALITY HEALTHCARE PARTNERSHIP	GA	U	HMO	--	--	--	--	--	--	--
QUALMED PLANS FOR HEALTH WESTERN PA	PA	U	HMO	--	--	--	--	--	--	--
QUINCY HEALTH CARE MANAGEMENT INC	IL	U	HMO	--	--	--	--	--	--	--
REASSURE AMERICA LIFE INS CO	IL	C-	L&H	2q 2003	10,824.1	431.4	102.5	350.9	1.21	0.59
REGAL LIFE OF AMERICA INS CO	TX	D-	L&H	2q 2003	3.8	2.1	0.5	1.5	0.85	0.72
REGENCE BL CROSS BL SHIELD OREGON	OR	• B-	HLTH	1q 2003	544.7	1,343.8	1,343.8	230.2	2.09	1.75
REGENCE BLUE CROSS BLUE SHIELD OF UT	UT	• B-	HLTH	1q 2003	252.7	511.8	511.8	84.8	2.63	2.19
REGENCE BLUESHIELD	WA	• B	HLTH	1q 2003	796.9	1,505.9	1,505.9	349.7	3.71	3.10
REGENCE BLUESHIELD OF IDAHO INC	ID	• C	L&H	2q 2003	144.7	452.3	452.3	29.7	0.59	0.47
REGENCE HEALTH MAINTENANCE OF OREGON	OR	• B	HMO	1q 2003	27.6	28.7	28.7	17.9	6.97	5.81
REGENCE HMO OREGON	OR	• B-	HMO	1q 2003	238.3	549.6	549.6	103.2	2.52	2.10
REGENCE LIFE & HEALTH INS CO	OR	B	L&H	2q 2003	53.2	196.4	174.8	23.8	1.47	1.07
REGENCECARE	WA	• C+	HMO	1q 2003	32.1	85.5	85.5	20.9	3.32	2.76
RELIABLE LIFE INS CO	MO	B	L&H	2q 2003	662.6	110.9	4.2	62.1	1.83	1.24
RELIANCE LIFE INS CO	DE	E	L&H	2q 2003	9.2	-0.4	0.0	9.0	3.98	3.58
RELIANCE STANDARD LIFE INS CO	IL	• C	L&H	2q 2003	2,174.2	629.4	274.8	264.3	1.69	1.06
RELIANCE STANDARD LIFE INS CO OF TX	TX	U	L&H	4q 2002	359.0	0.4	0.2	237.2	--	--
RELIASTAR LIFE INS CO	MN	C+	L&H	2q 2003	18,554.7	1,936.3	357.1	1,354.6	1.43	0.93
RELIASTAR LIFE INS CO OF NEW YORK	NY	B	L&H	2q 2003	2,504.7	248.0	20.4	260.7	3.23	1.66
RENAISSANCE HEALTH PLAN	OH	F	HMO	2q 2002	8.3	102.5	102.5	-13.7	0.13	0.11
REPUBLIC AMERICAN LIFE INS CO	TX	D-	L&H	2q 2003	8.1	5.5	5.5	2.9	1.25	1.13
REPUBLIC WESTERN INS CO	AZ	F	P&C	4q 2002	513.5	150.9	2.9	165.6	1.91	1.06
RESERVE NATIONAL INS CO	OK	• B	L&H	2q 2003	143.4	115.4	114.6	81.9	3.91	2.95
RESOURCE LIFE INS CO	IL	• C+	L&H	2q 2003	113.5	113.6	64.0	32.7	4.54	3.34

I. Index of Companies

Winter 2003 - 04

INSURANCE COMPANY NAME	DOM. STATE	WEISS SAFETY RATING	COMPANY TYPE	DATA DATE	TOTAL ASSETS ($MIL)	TOTAL PREMIUMS ($MIL)	HEALTH PREMIUMS ($MIL)	CAPITAL & SURPLUS ($MIL)	RISK ADJUSTED CAPITAL RATIO 1	RATIO 2
RIGHTCHOICE INS CO	IL	D+	L&H	2q 2003	10.4	44.5	44.5	8.0	0.78	0.64
RIVERSIDE CTY FOUNDATION MED CARE	CA	U	HMO	--	--	--	--	--	--	--
ROCHESTER AREA HEALTH MAINTENANCE OR	NY	● B	HMO	4q 2002	120.7	499.0	499.0	55.7	2.05	1.71
ROCKFORD HEALTH PLANS INC	IL	D-	L&H	2q 2003	18.6	101.9	10.5	6.3	1.60	1.44
ROCKY MOUNTAIN HEALTH MAINT ORG	CO	● D+	HMO	2q 2002	61.6	296.7	296.7	14.4	0.49	0.43
ROCKY MOUNTAIN HEALTHCARE OPTIONS	CO	U	HMO	4q 2001	0.8	1.1	1.1	0.6	--	--
▲ ROCKY MOUNTAIN HOSPITAL & MEDICAL	CO	● C+	HMO	1q 2003	335.5	581.3	581.3	154.5	3.71	3.09
ROYAL INDEMNITY CO	DE	C-	P&C	2q 2003	2,474.4	1,131.2	1.0	558.9	1.08	0.66
ROYAL STATE NATIONAL INS CO LTD	HI	● C+	L&H	2q 2003	47.5	18.4	11.1	26.5	3.38	2.69
RURAL MUTUAL INS CO	WI	C	P&C	2q 2003	170.4	120.1	0.6	42.9	2.35	1.50
RUSHMORE NATIONAL LIFE INS CO	SD	C+	L&H	2q 2003	73.2	1.4	0.0	12.3	1.78	1.60
RYDER HEALTH PLAN INC	PR	U	HMO	--	--	--	--	--	--	--
S BAY IND PHYSICIANS MED GROUP INC	CA	U	HMO	--	--	--	--	--	--	--
SAFECO LIFE INS CO	WA	B	L&H	2q 2003	18,414.7	1,675.2	312.1	961.2	1.65	0.88
SAFEGUARD HEALTH PLANS INC	CA	U	HMO	--	--	--	--	--	--	--
SAFEGUARD HEALTH PLANS INC	TX	U	HMO	1q 2003	2.0	8.6	8.6	1.1	--	--
SAFEGUARD HEALTH PLANS INC A FL CORP	FL	U	HMO	--	--	--	--	--	--	--
SAFEGUARD HEALTH PLANS INC A NV CORP	NV	U	HMO	1q 2003	0.1	0.1	0.1	0.1	--	--
SAFEHEALTH LIFE INS CO	CA	C-	L&H	2q 2003	10.6	32.1	32.1	7.1	1.18	0.98
SAINT MARYS HEALTHFIRST	NV	● D-	HMO	1q 2003	26.0	73.1	73.1	7.0	2.37	1.98
SAINT MARYS PREFERRED HEALTH INS CO	NV	D-	L&H	3q 2002	2.3	1.0	1.0	1.6	1.58	1.42
SAN FRANCISCO HEALTH PLAN	CA	● B	HMO	3q 2002	25.1	44.4	44.4	12.1	2.52	1.56
SAN LUIS VALLEY HMO (See HMO HEALTH PLANS INC)										
SAN MATEO HEALTH COMMISSION	CA	● C-	HMO	1q 2003	53.8	108.3	108.3	16.0	1.66	1.01
SANTA BARBARA REGIONAL HEALTH AUTH	CA	U	HMO	3q 2002	43.9	0.0	0.0	12.8	--	--
SANTA CLARA COUNTY	CA	● D+	HMO	3q 2002	13.8	42.5	42.5	3.8	0.68	0.42
SANTA CLARA COUNTY HEALTH AUTHORITY	CA	● B	HMO	3q 2002	33.9	61.0	61.0	18.5	2.68	1.66
SANTA CRUZ-MONTEREY MGD MED CARE	CA	● C	HMO	1q 2003	78.3	203.5	203.5	37.3	1.89	1.18
SAVINGS BANK LIFE INS CO OF MA	MA	B+	L&H	2q 2003	1,548.3	174.0	0.1	165.4	3.54	2.15
SBLI USA MUT LIFE INS CO INC	NY	C-	L&H	2q 2003	1,411.1	126.7	0.4	112.7	1.91	1.05
▲ SCAN HEALTH PLAN	CA	● E	HMO	1q 2003	181.1	302.9	302.9	82.8	5.11	3.16
SCOR LIFE INS CO	TX	D+	L&H	2q 2003	576.1	3.0	1.2	17.3	1.33	0.68
SCOTT & WHITE GRP HOSPITAL SRV CORP	TX	U	L&H	4q 2002	0.2	0.0	0.0	0.2	--	--
SCOTT & WHITE HEALTH PLAN	TX	● B	HMO	1q 2003	79.5	409.6	409.6	33.3	1.68	1.40
SCRIPPS CLINIC HEALTH PLAN SERVICES	CA	● E	HMO	4q 2002	24.3	266.8	266.8	3.7	0.16	0.09
SD STATE MEDICAL HOLDING CO	SD	● D+	HMO	1q 2003	19.6	77.1	77.1	6.5	0.52	0.43
SEARS LIFE INS CO	IL	● C	L&H	2q 2003	56.2	77.7	54.2	47.6	7.15	6.43
SECURE HEALTH PLANS OF GEORGIA	GA	U	HMO	--	--	--	--	--	--	--
SECURECARE OF IOWA INC	IA	● C	HMO	1q 2003	18.9	53.1	53.1	7.7	1.04	0.87
SECURIAN LIFE INS CO	MN	B	L&H	2q 2003	17.8	2.4	0.5	12.5	3.90	3.51
SECURITAS LIFE INS CO	OK	D	L&H	2q 2003	2.2	0.0	0.0	2.1	2.64	2.37
SECURITY BENEFIT LIFE INS CO	KS	B-	L&H	2q 2003	7,841.1	1,122.2	4.0	426.4	1.82	1.10
SECURITY FINANCIAL LIFE INS CO	NE	B	L&H	2q 2003	693.6	78.4	4.4	67.3	2.44	1.33
SECURITY GENERAL LIFE INS CO	OK	B-	L&H	1q 2003	8.3	1.3	1.3	1.4	1.32	0.97
SECURITY HEALTH PLAN OF WI INC	WI	● B-	HMO	1q 2003	76.6	285.8	285.8	19.6	0.93	0.78
SECURITY INS CO OF HARTFORD	CT	D	P&C	2q 2003	866.8	540.7	7.2	155.7	0.64	0.40
SECURITY LIFE INS CO OF AMERICA	MN	D-	L&H	2q 2003	72.0	133.0	117.8	9.9	0.59	0.41
SECURITY LIFE OF DENVER INS CO	CO	B	L&H	2q 2003	18,344.0	1,561.0	0.0	848.6	1.20	0.64
SECURITY MUTUAL LIFE INS CO OF NY	NY	B-	L&H	2q 2003	1,713.7	305.4	31.7	97.4	1.49	0.86
SECURITY NATIONAL LIFE INS CO	UT	C-	L&H	2q 2003	194.3	10.1	0.2	13.2	0.76	0.54
SECURITY PLAN LIFE INS CO	LA	D	L&H	2q 2003	250.0	37.0	0.7	40.0	3.46	2.35
SEGUROS DE VIDA TRIPLE S INC	PR	C	L&H	2q 2003	50.6	21.3	11.0	20.7	2.27	1.59

Arrows denote recent upgrades ▲ or downgrades ▼   ● Bullets denote a more detailed analysis is available in Section II.   www.WeissRatings.com

Winter 2003 - 04 — I. Index of Companies

INSURANCE COMPANY NAME	DOM. STATE	WEISS SAFETY RATING	COMPANY TYPE	DATA DATE	TOTAL ASSETS ($MIL)	TOTAL PREMIUMS ($MIL)	HEALTH PREMIUMS ($MIL)	CAPITAL & SURPLUS ($MIL)	RISK ADJUSTED CAPITAL RATIO 1	RATIO 2
SELECT HEALTH OF SOUTH CAROLINA INC	SC	• D+	HMO	1q 2003	15.8	49.7	49.7	4.3	0.73	0.60
SELECT PROVIDERS INC	NY	U	HMO	--	--	--	--	--	--	--
SELECTCARE ACCESS CORP	PA	U	HMO	--	--	--	--	--	--	--
SELECTCARE OF TEXAS LLC	TX	U	HMO	1q 2003	17.4	77.8	77.8	1.6	--	--
SELECTIVE INS CO OF AMERICA	NJ	B	P&C	2q 2003	1,517.4	448.9	0.2	325.9	1.52	0.99
SELECTNET PLUS	WV	U	HMO	--	--	--	--	--	--	--
SENATE INS CO	AZ	F	L&H	4q 2002	1.5	0.0	0.0	1.5	2.23	2.21
SENIOR AMERICAN LIFE INS CO	PA	D	L&H	2q 2003	9.3	3.3	3.3	4.6	2.21	1.99
SENTARA HEALTH PLANS INC	VA	• C+	HMO	1q 2003	17.5	39.9	39.9	10.4	2.98	2.48
SENTRY INS A MUTUAL CO	WI	A	P&C	2q 2003	4,177.1	553.2	3.8	2,034.6	2.41	2.08
SENTRY LIFE INS CO	WI	A-	L&H	2q 2003	2,101.2	359.8	17.6	187.3	3.50	2.07
SENTRY LIFE INS CO OF NEW YORK	NY	B	L&H	2q 2003	45.8	8.4	0.5	10.4	1.71	1.54
SENTRY SELECT INS CO	WI	B	P&C	2q 2003	508.8	530.3	18.9	138.4	2.93	2.06
SERVCO LIFE INS CO	TX	C-	L&H	2q 2003	30.0	9.6	4.8	11.0	2.53	2.27
SERVICE LIFE & CAS INS CO	TX	• C	L&H	2q 2003	194.3	60.2	27.4	30.6	2.21	1.17
SERVICE LLOYDS INS CO	TX	C	P&C	2q 2003	170.4	118.8	9.0	57.2	1.31	0.81
SETON HEALTH PLAN INC	TX	• E	HMO	1q 2003	15.8	48.6	48.6	2.3	0.20	0.17
SETTLERS LIFE INS CO	VA	C+	L&H	2q 2003	232.9	21.9	0.7	20.3	2.15	1.37
SHA LLC	TX	• C-	HMO	1q 2003	31.9	181.2	181.2	7.0	0.64	0.54
SHARED HEALTH NETWORK	NY	U	HMO	--	--	--	--	--	--	--
▲ SHARP HEALTH PLAN	CA	• C-	HMO	4q 2002	26.2	146.5	146.5	5.0	18.38	11.24
SHELTER LIFE INS CO	MO	B+	L&H	2q 2003	811.0	106.8	16.2	139.7	3.87	2.40
SHENANDOAH LIFE INS CO	VA	B	L&H	2q 2003	1,194.2	316.0	54.0	90.3	1.71	1.01
SIDNEY HILLMAN HEALTH CENTRE	IL	U	HMO	1q 2003	0.4	2.5	2.5	0.3	--	--
SIERRA HEALTH AND LIFE INS CO INC	CA	C-	L&H	2q 2003	60.9	111.2	109.9	23.5	0.98	0.75
SIERRA HEALTHCARE OPTIONS INC	NV	U	HMO	--	--	--	--	--	--	--
SIERRA PACIFIC LIFE INS CO	CA	U	L&H	4q 2002	9.8	0.0	0.0	8.7	--	--
SIGNATURE DENTAL PLAN OF FLORIDA INC	FL	U	HMO	--	--	--	--	--	--	--
SIGNATURE HEALTH ALLIANCE	TN	U	HMO	--	--	--	--	--	--	--
▲ SIOUX VALLEY HEALTH PLAN	SD	• E+	HMO	1q 2003	15.6	64.1	64.1	6.0	0.37	0.31
SIOUX VALLEY HEALTH PLAN MINNESOTA	MN	• D-	HMO	1q 2003	2.3	7.5	7.5	1.2	0.85	0.71
SIRIUS AMERICA INS CO	DE	B+	P&C	2q 2003	216.8	204.9	25.9	79.3	1.74	1.18
SISTEMAS MEDICOS NACIONALES SA DE CV	CA	U	HMO	1q 2003	2.5	9.0	9.0	2.2	--	--
SOUTH CAROLINA FARM BU MUTUAL INS CO	SC	B	P&C	2q 2003	101.8	162.8	0.1	49.4	2.81	2.39
SOUTH CENTRAL PREFERRED	PA	U	HMO	--	--	--	--	--	--	--
SOUTHEASTERN INDIANA HEALTH OPER INC	IN	U	HMO	--	--	--	--	--	--	--
SOUTHEASTERN INDIANA HEALTH ORG INC	IN	U	HMO	--	--	--	--	--	--	--
SOUTHERN ARIZONA PHYSICIANS SERVICES	AZ	U	HMO	--	--	--	--	--	--	--
SOUTHERN FARM BUREAU LIFE INS CO	MS	A-	L&H	2q 2003	7,776.4	845.3	48.0	847.6	2.71	1.43
SOUTHERN FINANCIAL LIFE INS CO	KY	D+	L&H	2q 2003	5.6	17.1	5.9	3.8	1.82	1.64
SOUTHERN HEALTH SERVICES INC	VA	• C-	HMO	1q 2003	79.9	233.6	233.6	34.2	2.16	1.80
SOUTHERN HEALTH SYSTEMS INC	AL	F	HMO	1q 2001	2.4	11.2	11.2	0.6	0.37	0.32
SOUTHERN NATL LIFE INS CO INC	LA	B+	L&H	2q 2003	11.9	7.2	0.5	7.6	2.93	2.60
SOUTHERN PIONEER LIFE INS CO	AR	D	L&H	2q 2003	30.7	18.6	4.5	10.6	1.28	1.10
SOUTHERN SECURITY LIFE INS CO	FL	C-	L&H	2q 2003	56.7	8.4	0.1	8.9	1.27	1.14
SOUTHLAND LIFE INS CO	TX	B-	L&H	2q 2003	3,088.2	594.9	2.4	119.3	1.38	0.67
SOUTHLAND NATIONAL INS CORP	AL	C-	L&H	2q 2003	93.4	21.8	1.3	6.3	0.87	0.78
SOUTHWEST LIFE & HEALTH INS CO	TX	C-	L&H	2q 2003	11.0	35.0	34.8	4.6	0.67	0.56
SOUTHWEST MEDICAL PROVIDER NETWORK	TX	U	HMO	--	--	--	--	--	--	--
SOUTHWEST SERVICE LIFE INS CO	TX	E+	L&H	2q 2003	5.5	16.8	15.0	1.7	0.26	0.23
SOUTHWEST TEXAS HMO INC	TX	• C+	HMO	1q 2003	292.9	1,351.1	1,351.1	154.4	3.20	2.67
SOUTHWESTERN LIFE INS CO	TX	D+	L&H	2q 2003	1,778.3	140.7	5.1	113.6	1.70	0.85

Arrows denote recent upgrades ▲ or downgrades ▼   • Bullets denote a more detailed analysis is available in Section II.

I. Index of Companies

Winter 2003 - 04

INSURANCE COMPANY NAME	DOM. STATE	WEISS SAFETY RATING	COMPANY TYPE	DATA DATE	TOTAL ASSETS ($MIL)	TOTAL PREMIUMS ($MIL)	HEALTH PREMIUMS ($MIL)	CAPITAL & SURPLUS ($MIL)	RISK ADJUSTED CAPITAL RATIO 1	RATIO 2
SPARKS PREMIERCARE LLC	AR	U	HMO	--	--	--	--	--	--	--
SPECTERA EYECARE OF NORTH CAROLINA	NC	U	HMO	1q 2002	0.7	2.1	2.1	0.5	--	--
SPECTERA INS CO INC	TX	C+	L&H	2q 2003	11.5	27.6	27.6	10.0	2.08	1.73
SPECTERA VISION INC	VA	U	HMO	--	--	--	--	--	--	--
SPECTERA VISION SERVICES OF CA INC	CA	U	HMO	--	--	--	--	--	--	--
ST PAUL FIRE & MARINE INS CO	MN	B	P&C	2q 2003	17,027.9	3,891.1	0.0	4,916.8	1.25	1.00
STANDARD GUARANTY INS CO	DE	B-	P&C	2q 2003	90.8	66.4	9.5	28.5	1.58	1.26
STANDARD INS CO	OR	• B-	L&H	2q 2003	7,873.7	1,430.5	798.0	793.5	2.45	1.51
STANDARD LIFE & ACCIDENT INS CO	OK	• B	L&H	2q 2003	462.0	213.5	178.7	156.3	3.06	2.10
STANDARD LIFE & CAS INS CO	UT	C	L&H	2q 2003	19.7	3.3	2.8	3.4	1.01	0.89
STANDARD LIFE INS CO OF INDIANA	IN	D+	L&H	2q 2003	1,604.8	457.6	0.0	58.3	0.87	0.45
STANDARD LIFE INS CO OF NY	NY	D	L&H	2q 2003	11.4	2.6	2.5	7.9	3.09	2.78
STANDARD SECURITY LIFE INS CO OF NY	NY	• B	L&H	2q 2003	227.9	204.2	202.2	77.7	3.77	2.91
STAR INS CO	MI	C-	P&C	2q 2003	327.3	111.3	0.2	90.8	1.14	0.82
STARMOUNT LIFE INS CO	LA	C-	L&H	2q 2003	10.4	18.3	12.6	4.3	1.21	0.88
STATE AUTOMOBILE MUTUAL INS CO	OH	B+	P&C	2q 2003	1,299.8	521.0	0.0	912.2	1.81	1.58
STATE FARM FIRE & CAS CO	IL	B-	P&C	2q 2003	16,295.2	10,963.1	1.1	3,434.4	0.99	0.59
STATE FARM MUTUAL AUTOMOBILE INS CO	IL	B+	P&C	2q 2003	70,070.4	27,576.4	1,210.8	34,120.3	2.14	1.63
STATE LIFE INS CO	IN	B	L&H	2q 2003	386.5	71.4	15.7	44.3	3.22	1.67
STATE MUTUAL INS CO	GA	• C	L&H	2q 2003	341.7	164.4	118.6	26.0	1.83	1.04
STATES GENERAL LIFE INS CO	TX	D-	L&H	2q 2003	9.2	23.6	20.7	4.7	0.96	0.77
STEADFAST INS CO	DE	C	P&C	2q 2003	214.5	1,222.2	0.6	214.4	2.43	2.34
STERLING INVESTORS LIFE INS CO	FL	C-	L&H	2q 2003	27.6	6.3	0.1	11.7	2.59	2.28
STERLING LIFE INS CO	IL	C	L&H	2q 2003	57.0	214.6	214.6	17.5	0.46	0.36
STONEBRIDGE CASUALTY INS CO	OH	B-	P&C	2q 2003	26.2	39.6	2.4	10.8	1.96	1.18
STONEBRIDGE LIFE INS CO	VT	• B-	L&H	2q 2003	1,990.7	734.1	535.8	315.9	2.81	1.70
STRAUB HEALTH PLAN SERVICES INC	HI	U	HMO	--	--	--	--	--	--	--
▲ SUMMA INS CO	OH	• B-	HMO	1q 2003	29.3	21.0	21.0	22.3	1.80	1.50
▲ SUMMACARE INC	OH	• B-	HMO	1q 2003	43.6	257.6	257.6	18.2	1.01	0.84
SUMMIT INS CO	OH	D+	L&H	2q 2003	16.6	47.9	47.9	6.9	0.74	0.60
SUN HEALTH MEDISUN INC	AZ	• B-	HMO	1q 2003	10.4	91.6	91.6	4.8	0.97	0.81
SUN LIFE ASR CO OF CANADA	MI	• C+	L&H	2q 2003	9,562.8	1,478.9	371.4	436.5	0.96	0.61
SUN LIFE INS & ANNUITY CO OF NY	NY	B	L&H	2q 2003	2,423.6	608.7	8.9	173.8	2.54	1.30
SUNAMERICA LIFE INS CO	AZ	B-	L&H	2q 2003	44,856.5	191.0	0.2	3,762.4	1.40	0.88
SUNLAND LIFE INS CO	TX	U	L&H	4q 2002	5.1	0.0	0.0	4.7	--	--
SUNSET LIFE INS CO OF AMERICA	MO	B	L&H	2q 2003	469.1	36.7	0.0	29.1	2.33	1.10
SUPERIEN HEALTH NETWORK INC	OH	U	HMO	--	--	--	--	--	--	--
SUPERIOR CALIFORNIA PPO	CA	U	HMO	--	--	--	--	--	--	--
SUPERIOR HEALTHPLAN INC	TX	• D-	HMO	1q 2003	29.0	111.4	111.4	5.3	0.38	0.31
SURETY LIFE INS CO	NE	B+	L&H	2q 2003	50.3	71.5	0.2	25.9	4.00	2.59
SURETY MUTUAL LIFE & CAS CO	ND	E	L&H	2q 2003	2.2	0.5	0.5	0.1	0.19	0.17
SUSQUEHANNA HEALTH CARE INC	PA	U	HMO	--	--	--	--	--	--	--
SWISS RE LIFE & HEALTH AMER INC	CT	• C	L&H	2q 2003	10,038.8	1.2	1.2	1,809.7	1.34	1.06
TEACHERS INS & ANNUITY ASN OF AM	NY	A+	L&H	2q 2003	147,114.8	9,453.6	151.3	9,569.5	3.13	1.82
TEACHERS PROTV MUTUAL LIFE INS CO	PA	D+	L&H	2q 2003	37.7	22.5	21.3	6.7	1.07	0.78
TENET CHOICES INC	LA	• D-	HMO	1q 2003	10.8	204.8	204.8	2.8	0.26	0.22
TENNESSEE BEHAVIORAL HEALTH INC	TN	U	HMO	1q 2003	17.4	102.7	102.7	5.3	--	--
TENNESSEE COORDINATED CARE NETWORK	TN	F	HMO	2q 2001	36.1	582.4	582.4	-53.8	0.00	0.00
TENNESSEE HEALTH CARE NETWORK	TN	U	HMO	4q 2002	29.0	117.0	117.0	10.5	--	--
TEXAS CHILDRENS HEALTH PLAN INC	TX	• D+	HMO	1q 2003	52.3	95.8	95.8	19.6	1.98	1.65
TEXAS FARM BUREAU MUTUAL INS CO	TX	C+	P&C	2q 2003	183.4	20.6	0.5	77.1	2.83	2.37
TEXAS HEALTH CHOICE LC	TX	U	HMO	1q 2002	51.6	184.8	184.8	4.6	--	--

Arrows denote recent upgrades ▲ or downgrades ▼ · Bullets denote a more detailed analysis is available in Section II.

www.WeissRatings.com

I. Index of Companies

Winter 2003 - 04

INSURANCE COMPANY NAME	DOM. STATE	WEISS SAFETY RATING	COMPANY TYPE	DATA DATE	TOTAL ASSETS ($MIL)	TOTAL PREMIUMS ($MIL)	HEALTH PREMIUMS ($MIL)	CAPITAL & SURPLUS ($MIL)	RISK ADJUSTED CAPITAL RATIO 1	RATIO 2
TEXAS IMPERIAL LIFE INS CO	TX	D-	L&H	2q 2003	23.7	4.6	1.7	2.3	0.62	0.56
TEXAS LIFE INS CO	TX	B	L&H	2q 2003	829.2	64.0	0.0	31.8	1.10	0.59
TEXAS SAVINGS LIFE INS CO	TX	C-	L&H	2q 2003	2.5	0.1	0.0	0.9	1.03	0.93
TEXAS TRUE CHOICE	TX	U	HMO	--	--	--	--	--	--	--
TEXAS UNIVERSITIES HEALTH PLAN INC	TX	U	HMO	2q 2002	7.0	28.8	28.8	2.7	--	--
THE OATH	LA	F	HMO	3q 2001	79.5	209.7	209.7	3.1	0.00	0.00
THREE RIVERS HEALTH PLANS INC	PA	• B+	HMO	1q 2003	93.5	456.9	456.9	42.4	1.20	1.00
THRIVENT LIFE INS CO	MN	B	L&H	2q 2003	3,570.9	177.3	0.0	102.3	2.54	1.25
TIAA-CREF LIFE INS CO	NY	B	L&H	2q 2003	3,241.4	952.1	11.3	274.8	2.55	1.22
TIG INS CO	CA	D+	P&C	2q 2003	2,737.9	613.0	38.4	598.8	0.55	0.48
TIG INS CO OF MI	MI	C	P&C	2q 2003	21.6	11.2	0.0	21.4	355.50	319.90
TIG PREMIER INS CO	CA	C+	P&C	2q 2003	36.4	82.7	0.2	36.1	194.90	98.27
TIG SPECIALTY INS CO	CA	C	P&C	2q 2003	28.1	64.8	0.0	27.8	252.60	227.30
TOTAL HEALTH CARE INC	MD	U	HMO	--	--	--	--	--	--	--
TOTAL HEALTH CARE INC	MI	• D+	HMO	1q 2003	31.9	102.8	102.8	9.3	0.78	0.65
TOTAL HEALTH CHOICE	FL	• D+	HMO	1q 2003	11.5	37.9	37.9	3.1	0.75	0.63
TOUCHPOINT HEALTH PLAN INC	WI	• D-	HMO	1q 2003	65.8	303.1	303.1	16.6	0.36	0.30
TOUCHPOINT INS CO INC	WI	• D+	HMO	1q 2003	4.1	4.4	4.4	3.3	4.53	3.77
TOWER LIFE INS CO	TX	C+	L&H	2q 2003	80.9	3.1	0.4	37.0	4.64	4.18
TRANS CITY LIFE INS CO	AZ	C-	L&H	2q 2003	18.9	3.2	1.1	8.1	3.03	2.73
TRANS OCEANIC LIFE INS CO	PR	D+	L&H	2q 2003	14.7	15.3	13.4	4.5	0.84	0.60
TRANS-NATIONAL LIFE INS CO	TX	C-	L&H	2q 2003	43.2	-0.2	0.0	34.3	2.95	1.77
TRANSAMERICA ASR CO	MO	C	L&H	2q 2003	866.7	104.8	15.0	39.7	0.96	0.51
TRANSAMERICA FINANCIAL LIFE INS CO	NY	B-	L&H	2q 2003	14,613.6	1,608.1	32.4	642.8	2.30	1.12
TRANSAMERICA LIFE INS & ANNUITY CO	NC	B	L&H	2q 2003	24,359.7	4,207.6	0.3	1,026.3	1.60	0.79
TRANSAMERICA LIFE INS CO	IA	B-	L&H	2q 2003	36,275.7	9,036.5	171.5	1,549.3	1.28	0.63
TRANSAMERICA OCCIDENTAL L I C	IA	B	L&H	2q 2003	25,853.4	2,173.7	104.1	2,567.2	1.44	1.01
TRANSPORTATION INS CO	IL	C	P&C	2q 2003	76.9	859.6	0.0	73.2	56.55	50.90
TRAVELERS INDEMNITY CO	CT	B	P&C	2q 2003	13,676.4	1,567.6	0.0	4,163.1	1.27	1.05
TRAVELERS INS CO LIFE DEPT	CT	B+	L&H	2q 2003	58,317.0	4,094.4	277.5	7,254.6	2.18	1.56
TRAVELERS INS CO (ACCIDENT DEPT)	CT	B-	P&C	2q 2003	58,317.0	82.9	0.0	7,254.6	1.61	0.80
TRIANGLE LIFE INS CO	NC	C-	L&H	2q 2003	11.1	2.0	0.6	10.4	4.09	3.68
TRIGON HEALTH & LIFE INS CO	VA	U	L&H	4q 2002	14.8	0.0	0.0	13.0	--	--
TRINITY PHYSICIAN HOSPITAL ORG LTD	IL	U	HMO	--	--	--	--	--	--	--
TRIPLE S INC	PR	U	HMO	4q 2002	416.1	1,157.0	1,157.0	162.9	--	--
TRITON INS CO	MO	B	P&C	2q 2003	681.8	147.2	0.8	326.7	13.22	7.39
TRUSTMARK INS CO	IL	• B	L&H	2q 2003	981.0	1,102.0	986.5	184.7	1.32	1.03
TRUSTMARK LIFE INS CO	IL	• B-	L&H	2q 2003	667.0	26.9	26.5	67.2	1.32	0.89
TUFTS ASSOCIATED HEALTH MAINT ORG	MA	• B	HMO	1q 2003	520.9	2,306.7	2,306.7	190.3	1.19	0.99
TULANE REGIONAL HEALTH NETWORK	LA	U	HMO	--	--	--	--	--	--	--
TVHP-NC	NC	U	HMO	--	--	--	--	--	--	--
U S HEALTH & LIFE INS CO INC	MI	C-	L&H	2q 2003	10.0	28.9	28.7	6.5	1.59	1.10
UCARE MINNESOTA	MN	• B+	HMO	1q 2003	149.5	478.4	478.4	42.8	0.98	0.82
UCSD HEALTH PLAN	CA	• D-	HMO	3q 2002	4.1	23.3	23.3	1.5	0.73	0.47
UDC DENTAL CALIFORNIA INC	CA	U	HMO	--	--	--	--	--	--	--
UDC LIFE & HEALTH INSURANCE CO	OK	C+	L&H	2q 2003	4.6	4.1	4.1	4.4	3.17	2.86
UHP HEALTHCARE (See WATTS HEALTH FOUNDATION INC)										
ULICO CAS CO	DE	C-	P&C	1q 2003	130.3	77.2	4.3	58.7	1.14	0.90
ULTIMED HMO OF MICHIGAN INC	MI	• C-	HMO	1q 2003	6.6	19.4	19.4	2.2	2.73	2.27
UNDERWRITERS AT LLOYDS	KY	D	P&C	2q 2003	97.8	45.8	2.6	23.9	0.48	0.33
UNDERWRITERS AT LLOYDS LONDON	IL	D-	P&C	2q 2003	478.0	57.2	10.7	94.6	0.95	0.64
UNICARE HEALTH INS CO OF TX	TX	E+	L&H	3q 2002	6.4	15.2	15.2	2.9	0.33	0.23

www.WeissRatings.com

Arrows denote recent upgrades ▲ or downgrades ▼

• Bullets denote a more detailed analysis is available in Section II.

I. Index of Companies

Winter 2003 - 04

INSURANCE COMPANY NAME	DOM. STATE	WEISS SAFETY RATING	COMPANY TYPE	DATA DATE	TOTAL ASSETS ($MIL)	TOTAL PREMIUMS ($MIL)	HEALTH PREMIUMS ($MIL)	CAPITAL & SURPLUS ($MIL)	RISK ADJUSTED CAPITAL RATIO 1	RATIO 2
UNICARE HEALTH INS OF THE MIDWEST	IL	B	L&H	2q 2003	106.8	273.8	272.5	24.4	0.50	0.41
UNICARE HEALTH PLAN OF OKLAHOMA	OK	•B	HMO	1q 2003	21.8	69.6	69.6	4.5	1.29	1.07
UNICARE HEALTH PLAN OF VIRGINIA INC	VA	•B	HMO	1q 2003	18.7	80.1	80.1	8.4	1.72	1.43
UNICARE HEALTH PLANS OF TEXAS INC	TX	•C	HMO	1q 2003	45.4	125.1	125.1	26.4	3.08	2.57
UNICARE HEALTH PLANS OF THE MIDWEST	IL	•B+	HMO	1q 2003	151.4	333.5	333.5	36.6	2.71	2.26
UNICARE LIFE & HEALTH INS CO	DE	•B	L&H	2q 2003	1,463.5	1,390.5	1,135.6	283.0	1.75	1.32
UNIFIED LIFE INS CO	TX	C-	L&H	3q 2002	51.0	2.1	1.8	8.4	2.27	1.85
UNIMERICA INS CO	WI	B-	L&H	2q 2003	16.7	0.6	0.6	14.7	5.97	5.38
UNION BANKERS INS CO	TX	D+	L&H	2q 2003	90.7	65.1	61.7	8.0	1.30	1.17
UNION CENTRAL LIFE INS CO	OH	C+	L&H	2q 2003	6,089.6	1,054.6	80.0	286.3	1.57	0.77
UNION FIDELITY LIFE INS CO	IL	•C+	L&H	2q 2003	1,288.3	142.9	90.4	630.5	10.62	6.02
UNION HEALTH SERVICE INC	IL	•C	HMO	1q 2003	11.5	32.5	32.5	6.8	1.08	0.90
UNION LABOR LIFE INS CO	MD	D+	L&H	1q 2003	3,022.6	394.4	303.2	51.6	0.82	0.51
UNION NATIONAL LIFE INS CO	LA	A	L&H	2q 2003	377.5	82.2	7.2	84.4	1.90	1.42
UNION PACIFIC RR EMPLOYEES HEALTH	UT	U	HMO	--	--	--	--	--	--	--
UNION SAVINGS AMERICAN LIFE INS CO	MS	D	L&H	4q 2001	9.2	0.8	0.6	2.0	0.96	0.75
UNION SECURITY LIFE INS CO	DE	•B	L&H	2q 2003	166.3	203.5	110.2	52.9	3.66	2.24
UNION STANDARD OF AMERICA L I C	MD	C-	L&H	2q 2003	13.3	1.9	1.8	5.8	2.15	1.94
UNITED AMERICAN INS CO	DE	•B	L&H	2q 2003	969.0	824.9	742.1	136.2	1.06	0.75
UNITED BENEFIT LIFE INS CO	OH	E+	L&H	2q 2003	3.4	-0.2	0.0	3.0	2.30	2.07
UNITED CONCORDIA COMPANIES INC	PA	•D	L&H	2q 2003	210.2	308.3	308.3	76.5	0.42	0.38
UNITED CONCORDIA DENTAL PL MIDWEST	MI	U	HMO	--	--	--	--	--	--	--
UNITED CONCORDIA DENTAL PLANS INC	MD	U	HMO	--	--	--	--	--	--	--
UNITED CONCORDIA DENTAL PLANS OF AZ	AZ	U	HMO	--	--	--	--	--	--	--
UNITED CONCORDIA DENTAL PLANS OF CA	CA	U	HMO	--	--	--	--	--	--	--
UNITED CONCORDIA DENTAL PLANS OF CO	CO	U	HMO	--	--	--	--	--	--	--
UNITED CONCORDIA DENTAL PLANS OF DE	DE	U	HMO	--	--	--	--	--	--	--
UNITED CONCORDIA DENTAL PLANS OF FL	FL	U	HMO	--	--	--	--	--	--	--
UNITED CONCORDIA DENTAL PLANS OF IL	IL	U	HMO	--	--	--	--	--	--	--
UNITED CONCORDIA DENTAL PLANS OF KY	KY	U	HMO	--	--	--	--	--	--	--
UNITED CONCORDIA DENTAL PLANS OF OR	OR	U	HMO	--	--	--	--	--	--	--
UNITED CONCORDIA DENTAL PLANS OF PA	PA	U	HMO	--	--	--	--	--	--	--
UNITED CONCORDIA DENTAL PLANS OF TX	TX	U	HMO	--	--	--	--	--	--	--
UNITED CONCORDIA INS CO	AZ	•C+	L&H	2q 2003	50.6	142.6	142.6	29.9	1.91	1.40
UNITED CONCORDIA INS CO OF NY	NY	C	L&H	2q 2003	2.9	2.0	2.0	2.2	2.32	2.09
UNITED CONCORDIA LIFE & HEALTH INS	PA	•C+	L&H	2q 2003	134.2	188.8	188.8	79.3	1.02	0.89
UNITED DENTAL CARE INS CO	AZ	C	L&H	2q 2003	3.8	1.9	1.9	3.6	2.81	2.53
UNITED DENTAL CARE OF PENNSYLVANIA	PA	U	HMO	--	--	--	--	--	--	--
UNITED DENTAL CARE OF TX INC	TX	U	HMO	--	--	--	--	--	--	--
UNITED DENTAL CARE OF UT INC	UT	U	HMO	--	--	--	--	--	--	--
UNITED FAMILY LIFE INS CO	GA	C+	L&H	2q 2003	1,064.3	30.9	1.4	931.4	0.76	0.67
UNITED FARM FAMILY LIFE INS CO	IN	A	L&H	2q 2003	1,466.7	123.6	2.7	164.6	2.72	1.51
UNITED FIDELITY LIFE INS CO	TX	D	L&H	2q 2003	567.2	19.1	0.8	125.6	0.30	0.27
UNITED HEALTHCARE INS CO	CT	•B-	L&H	2q 2003	4,775.7	7,569.3	7,535.3	870.6	1.15	0.97
UNITED HEALTHCARE INS CO OF IL	IL	•C+	L&H	2q 2003	117.0	325.5	325.5	66.0	1.60	1.31
UNITED HEALTHCARE INS CO OF NY	NY	•B-	HMO	1q 2003	902.3	580.7	580.7	150.9	12.86	10.72
UNITED HEALTHCARE INS CO OF OH	OH	•C	L&H	2q 2003	90.3	324.1	324.1	36.2	0.64	0.53
UNITED HEALTHCARE OF ALABAMA INC	AL	•B+	HMO	1q 2003	122.0	361.3	361.3	72.1	4.11	3.42
UNITED HEALTHCARE OF ARIZONA INC	AZ	•C	HMO	1q 2003	136.4	328.6	328.6	92.6	4.13	3.44
UNITED HEALTHCARE OF ARKANSAS INC	AR	•B+	HMO	1q 2003	46.4	145.3	145.3	28.6	4.04	3.36
UNITED HEALTHCARE OF COLORADO INC	CO	•C-	HMO	1q 2003	64.7	233.6	233.6	28.3	1.37	1.14
UNITED HEALTHCARE OF FLORIDA INC	FL	•C-	HMO	1q 2003	483.2	2,168.3	2,168.3	93.0	0.88	0.73

Arrows denote recent upgrades ▲ or downgrades ▼ • Bullets denote a more detailed analysis is available in Section II.

Winter 2003 - 04

I. Index of Companies

INSURANCE COMPANY NAME	DOM. STATE	WEISS SAFETY RATING	COMPANY TYPE	DATA DATE	TOTAL ASSETS ($MIL)	TOTAL PREMIUMS ($MIL)	HEALTH PREMIUMS ($MIL)	CAPITAL & SURPLUS ($MIL)	RISK ADJUSTED CAPITAL RATIO 1	RATIO 2
UNITED HEALTHCARE OF GEORGIA INC	GA	• C+	HMO	1q 2003	61.4	199.4	199.4	35.1	3.18	2.65
UNITED HEALTHCARE OF ILLINOIS INC	IL	• C+	HMO	1q 2003	108.3	153.7	153.7	74.4	8.75	7.29
UNITED HEALTHCARE OF KENTUCKY	KY	• C+	HMO	1q 2003	65.6	221.1	221.1	29.9	2.43	2.02
UNITED HEALTHCARE OF LOUISIANA INC	LA	• C	HMO	1q 2003	70.7	230.4	230.4	29.4	2.21	1.84
UNITED HEALTHCARE OF MID-ATLANTIC	MD	• C	HMO	1q 2003	145.4	421.1	421.1	59.2	2.05	1.71
UNITED HEALTHCARE OF MISSISSIPPI INC	MS	• C	HMO	1q 2003	22.9	64.6	64.6	11.1	3.05	2.54
UNITED HEALTHCARE OF NC INC	NC	• B+	HMO	1q 2003	218.0	717.2	717.2	92.8	2.58	2.15
UNITED HEALTHCARE OF NEW ENGLAND INC	RI	• B	HMO	1q 2003	157.4	435.9	435.9	87.3	3.64	3.03
UNITED HEALTHCARE OF NEW JERSEY INC	NJ	• C+	HMO	1q 2003	51.1	192.2	192.2	18.2	1.53	1.27
UNITED HEALTHCARE OF NY INC	NY	• B	HMO	1q 2003	131.6	334.7	334.7	51.5	2.42	2.01
UNITED HEALTHCARE OF OHIO INC	OH	• B-	HMO	1q 2003	358.3	1,501.4	1,501.4	169.9	2.32	1.93
UNITED HEALTHCARE OF TENNESSEE INC	TN	• C+	HMO	1q 2003	42.7	165.1	165.1	19.5	2.18	1.82
UNITED HEALTHCARE OF THE MIDLANDS	NE	• B+	HMO	1q 2003	69.7	166.6	166.6	24.3	2.66	2.22
UNITED HEALTHCARE OF THE MIDWEST INC	MO	• B+	HMO	1q 2003	332.1	1,367.2	1,367.2	143.4	2.09	1.74
UNITED HEALTHCARE OF TX INC	TX	• D+	HMO	1q 2003	85.9	538.4	538.4	23.2	0.56	0.47
UNITED HEALTHCARE OF UTAH	UT	• C	HMO	1q 2003	41.1	138.6	138.6	24.8	3.17	2.64
UNITED HEALTHCARE OF WASHINGTON INC	WA	U	HLTH	1q 2002	5.6	2.5	2.5	5.5	--	--
UNITED HEALTHCARE OF WISCONSIN INC	WI	• B+	HMO	1q 2003	182.0	714.5	714.5	63.6	1.45	1.21
UNITED HEALTHCARE PLANS PUERTO RICO	PR	U	HMO		--	--	--	--	--	--
UNITED HEARTLAND LIFE INS CO	WI	C	L&H	2q 2003	44.7	0.1	0.0	13.8	1.20	0.93
UNITED HERITAGE LIFE INS CO	ID	B	L&H	2q 2003	368.8	64.6	1.2	29.2	2.16	1.15
UNITED HOME LIFE INS CO	IN	B-	L&H	2q 2003	48.2	3.5	0.1	10.2	1.43	1.28
UNITED INS CO OF AMERICA	IL	B+	L&H	2q 2003	2,064.3	259.2	24.8	335.0	0.75	0.64
UNITED LIBERTY LIFE INS CO	KY	D	L&H	2q 2003	32.1	0.8	0.1	1.9	0.47	0.42
UNITED LIFE & ANNUITY INS CO	IA	C	L&H	2q 2003	724.1	4.1	0.2	72.3	3.35	1.63
UNITED LIFE INS CO	IA	C+	L&H	2q 2003	1,335.1	257.9	6.7	100.1	1.69	0.80
UNITED MERCANTILE LIFE INS CO	TX	D	L&H	2q 2003	2.6	0.5	0.2	1.5	1.71	1.54
UNITED NATIONAL LIFE INS CO OF AM	IL	D+	L&H	2q 2003	7.4	2.6	0.5	2.3	1.18	1.07
UNITED OF OMAHA LIFE INS CO	NE	B+	L&H	2q 2003	12,298.3	1,803.7	398.6	974.7	1.84	0.93
UNITED OHIO INS CO	OH	B	P&C	2q 2003	150.9	108.2	0.2	52.0	2.31	1.76
UNITED PAYORS & UNITED PROVIDERS	MD	U	HMO		--	--	--	--	--	--
UNITED SECURITY ASSURANCE CO OF PA	PA	C	P&C	2q 2003	24.7	8.8	8.8	11.7	1.56	1.36
UNITED SECURITY LIFE INS CO OF IL	IL	E	L&H	2q 2003	22.3	43.1	39.3	5.4	0.48	0.39
UNITED STATES FIDELITY & GUARANTY CO	MD	C+	P&C	2q 2003	5,203.3	798.7	0.6	1,818.5	1.63	1.04
UNITED STATES LIFE INS CO IN NYC	NY	• B	L&H	2q 2003	3,422.9	943.5	398.6	313.5	2.43	1.20
UNITED TEACHER ASSOCIATES INS CO	TX	• C+	L&H	2q 2003	396.3	133.9	89.0	47.1	1.59	1.04
UNITED TRUST INS CO	AL	B-	L&H	2q 2003	4.0	0.3	0.3	3.9	3.15	2.84
UNITED WISCONSIN INS CO	WI	• C	P&C	2q 2003	104.8	107.0	57.4	51.9	1.88	1.07
UNITED WISCONSIN LIFE INS CO	WI	• C	L&H	2q 2003	329.7	777.0	743.8	167.6	1.89	1.52
UNITED WORLD LIFE INS CO	NE	B	L&H	2q 2003	61.1	4.2	0.8	17.0	2.43	2.19
UNITY FINANCIAL LIFE INS CO	PA	C-	L&H	2q 2003	20.5	12.4	0.0	5.5	1.62	1.46
UNITY HEALTH PLANS INS CORP	WI	• B	HMO	1q 2003	53.4	197.0	197.0	19.4	1.50	1.25
UNITY HEALTH SERVICES INC	NJ	U	HMO		--	--	--	--	--	--
UNITY MUTUAL LIFE INS CO	NY	C-	L&H	2q 2003	410.2	40.9	0.3	21.0	1.07	0.63
UNITY/PRECISION HEALTH PLANS	IN	U	HMO		--	--	--	--	--	--
UNIVERSAL CARE	CA	• D-	HMO	3q 2002	87.4	342.3	342.3	8.7	0.00	0.00
UNIVERSAL CARE OF TENNESSEE INC	TN	F	HMO	1q 2003	69.6	76.7	76.7	6.5	N/A	N/A
UNIVERSAL FIDELITY LIFE INS CO	OK	D-	L&H	2q 2003	3.3	27.7	26.5	2.1	1.96	1.76
UNIVERSAL GUARANTY LIFE INS CO	OH	D	L&H	2q 2003	234.3	17.3	0.0	15.7	0.78	0.57
UNIVERSAL HEALTH CARE INC	FL	U	HMO		--	--	--	--	--	--
UNIVERSAL HEALTH NETWORK	NV	U	HMO		--	--	--	--	--	--
UNIVERSAL LIFE INS CO	PR	E	L&H	2q 2003	15.6	18.6	11.9	4.5	1.52	1.14

www.WeissRatings.com

Arrows denote recent upgrades ▲ or downgrades ▼   • Bullets denote a more detailed analysis is available in Section II.

I. Index of Companies

Winter 2003 - 04

INSURANCE COMPANY NAME	DOM. STATE	WEISS SAFETY RATING	COMPANY TYPE	DATA DATE	TOTAL ASSETS ($MIL)	TOTAL PREMIUMS ($MIL)	HEALTH PREMIUMS ($MIL)	CAPITAL & SURPLUS ($MIL)	RISK ADJUSTED CAPITAL RATIO 1	RATIO 2
UNIVERSAL LIFE INS CO	AL	D	L&H	2q 2003	7.9	1.1	0.4	5.3	2.65	2.39
UNIVERSAL PREFRRED HEALTH NETWORK	OH	U	HMO	--	--	--	--	--	--	--
UNIVERSAL UNDERWRITERS LIFE INS CO	KS	● B	L&H	2q 2003	358.7	87.7	34.5	160.9	11.42	7.21
UNIVERSITY HEALTH CARE INC	KY	● C	HMO	1q 2003	81.8	395.7	395.7	23.0	0.76	0.63
UNIVERSITY HEALTH PLANS INC	NJ	● D+	HMO	1q 2003	25.5	133.0	133.0	7.3	0.57	0.48
UNUM LIFE INS CO OF AMERICA	ME	● C-	L&H	2q 2003	11,383.4	4,029.6	2,786.1	1,241.1	1.94	1.12
UPMC HEALTH BENEFITS	PA	E	P&C	4q 2002	15.7	43.9	43.9	3.4	0.12	0.08
UPMC HEALTH PLAN INC	PA	● C-	HMO	1q 2003	163.5	708.4	708.4	63.1	0.96	0.80
UPPER CHESAPEAKE HEALTH SYSTEMS	MD	U	HMO	--	--	--	--	--	--	--
UPPER PENINSULA HEALTH PLAN INC	MI	● C-	HMO	1q 2003	9.8	32.4	32.4	2.8	0.63	0.53
US BEHAVIORAL HEALTH PLAN CALIFORNIA	CA	U	HMO	--	--	--	--	--	--	--
US SPECIALTY INS CO	TX	B	P&C	2q 2003	289.2	143.4	27.4	110.6	4.58	2.76
USA MANAGED CARE ORGANIZATION	AZ	U	HMO	--	--	--	--	--	--	--
USAA LIFE INS CO	TX	A-	L&H	2q 2003	9,167.0	1,019.1	138.2	654.7	3.99	2.29
USABLE LIFE	AR	● C+	L&H	2q 2003	125.5	72.6	41.7	60.1	3.26	2.28
UTMB HEALTH PLANS INC	TX	U	HMO	--	--	--	--	--	--	--
VALLEY BAPTIST HEALTH PLAN INC	TX	● C-	HMO	1q 2003	9.5	30.0	30.0	4.9	0.92	0.76
VALLEY FORGE LIFE INS CO	PA	C	L&H	2q 2003	1,233.0	867.5	17.8	193.8	4.04	1.97
VALLEY GROUP HOSPITAL SERVICE CORP	TX	U	L&H	4q 2001	1.5	0.0	0.0	1.5	--	--
VALLEY HEALTH PLAN	WI	● B-	HMO	1q 2003	24.9	88.1	88.1	8.3	0.98	0.82
VALLEY HEALTH PLAN (See SANTA CLARA COUNTY)										
VALLEY PREFERRED	PA	U	HMO	--	--	--	--	--	--	--
VALUE BEHAVIORAL HEALTH OF PA	PA	U	HMO	--	--	--	--	--	--	--
VALUEOPTIONS OF CALIFORNIA INC	CA	U	HMO	--	--	--	--	--	--	--
VALUEOPTIONS OF TEXAS INC	TX	U	HMO	1q 2003	13.3	109.0	109.0	1.0	--	--
VANTAGE HEALTH PLAN INC	OH	● D-	HMO	1q 2003	4.1	13.3	13.3	0.8	0.29	0.24
VANTAGE HEALTH PLAN INC	LA	● B-	HMO	1q 2003	11.7	30.1	30.1	5.3	1.04	0.87
VANTISLIFE INS CO	CT	C	L&H	2q 2003	578.4	83.0	0.2	55.3	2.49	1.33
VENTURA COUNTY HEALTH CARE PLAN	CA	● D+	HMO	3q 2002	3.8	0.0	0.0	1.1	0.59	0.38
VERMONT HEALTH PLAN LLC	VT	● B-	HMO	1q 2003	36.6	76.0	76.0	12.5	1.69	1.41
VERSANT LIFE INS CO	MS	C-	L&H	2q 2003	3.3	1.1	0.3	2.1	1.57	1.51
VETERANS LIFE INS CO	IL	B-	L&H	2q 2003	306.2	101.9	10.8	53.0	4.09	1.71
VHP DENTAL INC	TX	U	HMO	--	--	--	--	--	--	--
VIAHEALTH PPO INC	NY	U	HMO	--	--	--	--	--	--	--
VICTORY HEALTH PLAN INC	TN	● D+	HMO	2q 2002	9.7	45.4	45.4	6.5	1.08	0.95
VIGILANT INS CO	NY	B	P&C	2q 2003	294.3	573.3	0.0	91.3	3.63	2.52
VIRGINIA FARM BUREAU MUTUAL INS CO	VA	C	P&C	2q 2003	193.8	141.4	0.1	67.6	2.05	1.51
VIRGINIA HEALTH NETWORK INC	VA	U	HMO	--	--	--	--	--	--	--
VIRGINIA PREMIER HEALTH PLAN INC	VA	● D	HMO	1q 2003	34.1	175.8	175.8	12.0	0.51	0.43
VIRGINIA SURETY CO INC	IL	B-	P&C	2q 2003	1,642.6	975.4	14.1	414.0	1.28	0.91
VISION BENEFITS OF AMERICA	PA	U	HMO	--	--	--	--	--	--	--
VISION CARE OF OREGON INC	OR	U	HMO	--	--	--	--	--	--	--
VISION FIRST EYE CARE INC	CA	U	HMO	--	--	--	--	--	--	--
VISION PLAN OF AMERICA	CA	U	HMO	--	--	--	--	--	--	--
VISION SERVICE PLAN	CA	U	HMO	--	--	--	--	--	--	--
VISION SERVICE PLAN	WA	U	HMO	4q 2001	30.8	26.4	26.4	27.1	--	--
VISION SERVICE PLAN - OHIO	OH	U	HMO	--	--	--	--	--	--	--
VISION SERVICE PLAN INS CO	CT	U	HMO	--	--	--	--	--	--	--
VISION SERVICE PLAN INS CO	MO	● C	P&C	2q 2003	38.7	43.8	43.8	32.8	6.65	3.56
VISION SERVICES PLAN INC OKLAHOMA	OK	U	HMO	--	--	--	--	--	--	--
VISIONCARE OF CALIFORNIA	CA	U	HMO	--	--	--	--	--	--	--
VISTA BEHAVIORAL HEALTH PLANS	CA	U	HMO	3q 2002	1.1	0.0	0.0	0.3	--	--

Arrows denote recent upgrades ▲ or downgrades ▼   ● Bullets denote a more detailed analysis is available in Section II.

Winter 2003 - 04

I. Index of Companies

INSURANCE COMPANY NAME	DOM. STATE	WEISS SAFETY RATING	COMPANY TYPE	DATA DATE	TOTAL ASSETS ($MIL)	TOTAL PREMIUMS ($MIL)	HEALTH PREMIUMS ($MIL)	CAPITAL & SURPLUS ($MIL)	RISK ADJUSTED CAPITAL RATIO 1	RATIO 2
VISTA HEALTH PLAN INC	PA	U	HMO		--	--	--	--	--	--
VISTA HEALTHPLAN	FL	• E	HMO	1q 2003	70.8	587.2	587.2	9.3	0.12	0.10
VISTA HEALTHPLAN OF SOUTH FLORIDA	FL	• E	HMO	1q 2003	65.1	412.2	412.2	7.7	0.14	0.12
VISTA HILL FOUNDATION	CA	U	HMO		--	--	--	--	--	--
VISTA INS PLAN	FL	D+	L&H	2q 2003	12.1	27.2	27.2	6.6	1.33	1.10
VIVA HEALTH INC	AL	• C	HMO	4q 2002	29.1	138.0	138.0	10.1	0.79	0.66
VOLUNTEER STATE HEALTH PLAN INC	TN	U	HMO	2q 2002	221.7	847.7	847.7	55.0	--	--
VOLUSIA HEALTH NETWORK	FL	U	HMO		--	--	--	--	--	--
VOYAGER LIFE & HEALTH INS CO	GA	C+	L&H	2q 2003	6.9	21.0	17.5	5.3	2.54	2.29
VOYAGER LIFE INS CO	GA	• C+	L&H	2q 2003	129.2	41.4	26.9	31.2	3.42	2.22
VOYAGER PROPERTY & CAS INS CO	SC	B-	P&C	2q 2003	71.5	130.9	0.3	32.7	1.09	0.97
VOYAGEURS INS CO	MN	C	P&C	2q 2003	9.7	0.8	0.8	9.6	5.63	3.39
VYTRA HEALTH PLANS LONG ISLAND INC	NY	• B	HMO	1q 2003	85.0	236.4	236.4	34.6	1.80	1.50
VYTRA HEALTH SERVICES INC	NY	• C	HLTH	1q 2003	16.3	76.0	76.0	2.3	0.14	0.12
WASATCH CREST INS CO	UT	E-	P&C	1q 2003	25.9	1.3	0.1	-8.4	-0.46	-0.27
WASATCH CREST MUTUAL INS CO	UT	F	P&C	1q 2003	23.7	3.3	1.4	9.3	0.32	0.20
WASHINGTON DENTAL SERVICE	WA	U	HMO		--	--	--	--	--	--
WASHINGTON NATIONAL INS CO	IL	• E	L&H	2q 2003	872.7	111.4	100.2	178.5	0.92	0.81
WATTS HEALTH FOUNDATION INC	CA	F	HMO	1q 2003	89.9	248.9	248.9	-13.2	0.00	0.00
WEA INS CORP	WI	• C-	L&H	2q 2003	347.2	648.1	648.1	134.6	1.52	1.18
WELBORN CLINIC/WELBORN HEALTH PLANS	IN	• E	HMO	4q 2002	23.5	107.1	107.1	4.8	0.24	0.20
WELL CARE HMO INC	FL	• D+	HMO	4q 2002	131.3	566.4	566.4	20.4	20.08	16.73
WELLCARE HEALTH PLANS OF TEXAS LLC	TX	U	HMO	4q 2001	0.2	0.4	0.4	-1.1	--	--
WELLCARE OF NEW YORK INC	NY	• E+	HMO	1q 2003	27.0	67.1	67.1	5.4	0.69	0.57
WELLCHOICE INS OF NEW JERSEY INC	NJ	U	HMO		--	--	--	--	--	--
WELLINGTON LIFE INS CO	AZ	C-	L&H	2q 2003	6.8	5.7	5.7	5.3	2.80	2.52
WELLMARK BLUE CROSS BLUE SHIELD OF SOUTH DAKOTA (See WELLMARK OF SOUTH DAKOTA INC)										
WELLMARK COMMUNITY INS INC	IA	B-	L&H	2q 2003	18.7	1.1	1.1	12.8	3.49	2.08
WELLMARK HEALTH PLAN OF IOWA	IA	• B-	HMO	1q 2003	49.8	130.7	130.7	21.5	2.17	1.81
WELLMARK HEALTHNETWORK INC	IL	U	HMO		--	--	--	--	--	--
WELLMARK INC	IA	• B-	L&H	2q 2003	1,015.0	1,503.0	1,503.0	447.8	1.30	0.97
WELLMARK OF SOUTH DAKOTA INC	SD	• B-	L&H	2q 2003	138.4	286.0	286.0	48.6	1.03	0.77
WELLNESS PLAN	MI	F	HMO	1q 2003	38.7	234.1	234.1	3.7	0.00	0.00
WELLPATH SELECT INC	NC	• C-	HMO	1q 2003	60.8	143.0	143.0	27.3	2.62	2.19
WESCO INS CO	DE	B-	P&C	2q 2003	336.8	78.0	0.2	182.0	14.74	8.27
WEST COAST LIFE INS CO	NE	C	L&H	2q 2003	2,166.2	483.5	0.3	103.7	1.45	0.72
WESTERN & SOUTHERN LIFE INS CO	OH	B+	L&H	2q 2003	7,850.2	292.2	35.6	2,486.1	1.96	1.45
WESTERN AMERICAN LIFE INS CO	TX	D+	L&H	2q 2003	27.1	3.7	0.1	1.3	0.32	0.29
WESTERN DENTAL SERVICES INC	CA	U	HMO		--	--	--	--	--	--
WESTERN HEALTH ADVANTAGE	CA	• E+	HMO	3q 2002	15.9	81.3	81.3	1.2	0.06	0.04
WESTERN MUTUAL INS CO	UT	D+	L&H	2q 2003	7.2	19.2	19.1	3.0	1.03	0.80
WESTFIELD INS CO	OH	B-	P&C	2q 2003	1,514.3	782.5	0.0	323.3	1.12	0.79
WESTPORT INS CORP	MO	C+	P&C	2q 2003	1,296.7	952.6	1.4	319.3	0.53	0.35
WESTWARD LIFE INS CO	AZ	• C	L&H	2q 2003	47.6	1.7	0.9	39.4	6.04	4.66
WICHITA NATIONAL LIFE INS CO	OK	C	L&H	2q 2003	21.2	7.9	1.4	6.7	1.87	1.68
WILLAMETTE DENTAL INS INC	OR	U	HMO		--	--	--	--	--	--
WILLAMETTE DENTAL OF WASHINGTON INC	WA	U	HMO		--	--	--	--	--	--
WILLAMETTE HEALTH SERVICE INC	OR	U	HMO		--	--	--	--	--	--
WILLIAM PENN LIFE INS CO OF NEW YORK	NY	B-	L&H	2q 2003	997.5	152.8	0.1	83.0	1.84	1.07
WILLIS-KNIGHTON HEALTH PLAN	LA	U	HMO		--	--	--	--	--	--
WINHEALTH PARTNERS	WY	• D+	HMO	1q 2003	7.7	22.7	22.7	2.8	0.51	0.42
WISCONSIN AUTO & TRUCK DEALERS INS	WI	D	L&H	3q 2002	8.7	9.7	9.7	4.6	1.28	0.96

www.WeissRatings.com

Arrows denote recent upgrades ▲ or downgrades ▼

• Bullets denote a more detailed analysis is available in Section II.

I. Index of Companies

Winter 2003 - 04

INSURANCE COMPANY NAME	DOM. STATE	WEISS SAFETY RATING	COMPANY TYPE	DATA DATE	TOTAL ASSETS ($MIL)	TOTAL PREMIUMS ($MIL)	HEALTH PREMIUMS ($MIL)	CAPITAL & SURPLUS ($MIL)	RISK ADJUSTED CAPITAL RATIO 1	RATIO 2
WISCONSIN PHYSICIANS SERVICE INS	WI	• C+	HLTH	1q 2003	177.1	294.9	294.9	82.8	2.86	2.39
WISCONSIN VISION SERVICE PLAN INC	WI	U	HMO	--	--	--	--	--	--	--
WORLD INS CO	NE	• C	L&H	2q 2003	215.9	189.7	182.5	73.7	1.29	1.04
WORLD SERVICE LIFE INS CO	CO	B-	L&H	2q 2003	40.5	6.6	0.0	19.3	3.39	3.05
WPPA INC	KS	U	HMO	--	--	--	--	--	--	--
XANTUS HEALTHPLAN OF TENNESSEE INC	TN	F	HMO	2q 2002	55.6	284.1	284.1	-77.2	0.00	0.00
XL LIFE INS & ANNUITY CO	IL	• C-	L&H	2q 2003	333.6	20.8	10.6	31.0	11.54	7.00
YALE PREFERRED HEALTH INC	CT	U	HMO	--	--	--	--	--	--	--
YELLOWSTONE COMMUNITY HEALTH PLAN	MT	U	HMO	--	--	--	--	--	--	--
YOSEMITE INS CO	IN	C	P&C	2q 2003	351.7	37.5	0.0	244.5	18.11	9.03
ZALE LIFE INS CO	AZ	C	L&H	2q 2003	12.7	2.3	0.8	8.9	3.48	3.13
ZURICH AMERICAN INS CO	NY	B-	P&C	2q 2003	16,698.7	3,833.8	226.0	3,126.5	0.94	0.65

Arrows denote recent upgrades ▲ or downgrades ▼   • Bullets denote a more detailed analysis is available in Section II.

www.WeissRatings.com

Section II

Analysis of Largest Companies

A summary analysis of all rated

U.S. HMOs and Blue Cross Blue Shield Plans

plus those other **U.S. Health Insurers**
with capital in excess of $25 million and health insurance
premiums equaling at least 25% of total premiums.

Companies are listed in alphabetical order.

Section II Contents

This section contains rating factors, historical data, and general information on all rated HMOs and Blue Cross/Blue Shield plans plus each of the largest health insurers. Health insurers with capital and surplus of less than $25 million and companies lacking year-end data do not appear in this section. You can find information on these firms in Section I.

1. **Weiss Safety Rating** The current Weiss rating appears to the right of the company name. Our ratings are designed to distinguish levels of insolvency risk and are measured on a scale from A (Excellent) to F (Failed). Highly rated companies are, in our opinion, less likely to experience financial difficulties than lower rated firms. See *About the Weiss Safety Ratings* on page 11 for more information.

2. **Major Rating Factors** A synopsis of the key indexes and sub-factors that have most influenced the rating of a particular insurer. Items are presented in the approximate order of their importance to the rating. There may be additional factors which have influenced the rating but do not appear due to space limitations or confidentiality agreements with insurers.

3. **Other Rating Factors** A summary of those Weiss indexes that were not included as Major Rating Factors, but nevertheless may have had some impact on the final grade.

4. **Principal Business** The major types of policies written by an insurer along with the percentages for each line in relation to the entire book of business, including direct premium, reinsurance assumed and deposit funds. Lines of business for HMOs include comprehensive medical, medical only, medicare supplemental, administrative service contracts, point of service, dental, vision, stop-loss, long-term care, disability, Federal Employee Health Benefits (FEHB), medicare, and medicaid.

5. **Member Physicians** The number of physicians who participated in the HMO's network of providers (shown for only HMOs) during the current and prior year.

6. **MLR (Medical Loss Ratio)** The percentage of total premium income paid out as benefits to HMO members.

7. **Administrative Expense Ratio** The percentage of total premium income paid out for administrative expenses.

8. **Enrollment** The total number of members (policyholders) as of the current quarter, current year end and prior year end (shown for only HMOs). The letter Q followed by a number represents the quarter (first, second, or third) from which the enrollment numbers were last available.

9. **Medical Expenses Per Member Per Month** The average dollar amount the HMO spends on each member per month based on average enrollment for the year.

10. Principal Investments	The major investments in an insurer's portfolio. These include nonCMO Bonds (debt obligations which are rated Class 1 through Class 6 based on risk of default), collateralized mortgage obligations (CMOs) and other structured securities, which consist primarily of mortgage-backed bonds, real estate, mortgages in good standing, nonperforming mortgages, common and preferred stocks, policy loans (which are loans given to policyholders), miscellaneous investments, and cash.
11. Provider Compensation	The total annual amount the HMO pays its providers (e.g., physicians, hospitals, etc.) and manner in which they are paid, including:

- fee-for-service (FFS) – amount paid for the services provided where the payment base is not fixed by contract
- contractual fees – amount paid for services whereby the amount is fixed by contract, e.g., hospital per diems, DRGs, etc.
- salary – amount paid providers who are direct employees of the HMO
- capitation – amount paid to providers on a per member basis as defined by contract
- other – amount paid under various contracts including bonus arrangements, stop-loss arrangements, etc.

12. Total Member Encounters	The number of contacts members of the HMO who are not confined to a health care facility have with the HMO's providers during the current year.
13. Investments in Affiliates	The percentage of bonds, common and preferred stocks, and other financial instruments an insurer has invested with affiliated companies. This is not a subcategory of "Principal Investments."
14. Group Affiliation	The name of the group of companies to which a particular insurer belongs.
15. Licensed in	List of the states in which an insurer is licensed to conduct business.
16. Address	The address of an insurer's corporate headquarters. This location may differ from the company's state of domicile.
17. Phone	The telephone number of an insurer's corporate headquarters.
18. Domicile State	The state that has primary regulatory responsibility for this company. You do not have to live in the domicile state to do business with this firm, provided it is registered to do business in your state.
19. Commenced Business	The month and year the insurer started its operations
20. NAIC Code	The identification number assigned to an insurer by the National Association of Insurance Commissioners (NAIC).

21. Historical Data   Five years of background data for the Weiss Safety Rating, risk-adjusted capital ratios (moderate and severe loss scenarios), total assets, capital (including capital stock and retained earnings), net premium, and net income. See the next page for more details on how to read the historical data table.

22. Customized Graph (or Table)   A graph or table depicting one of the company's major strengths or weaknesses. See page 73 for more details.

II. Analysis of Largest Companies

How to Read the Historical Data Table

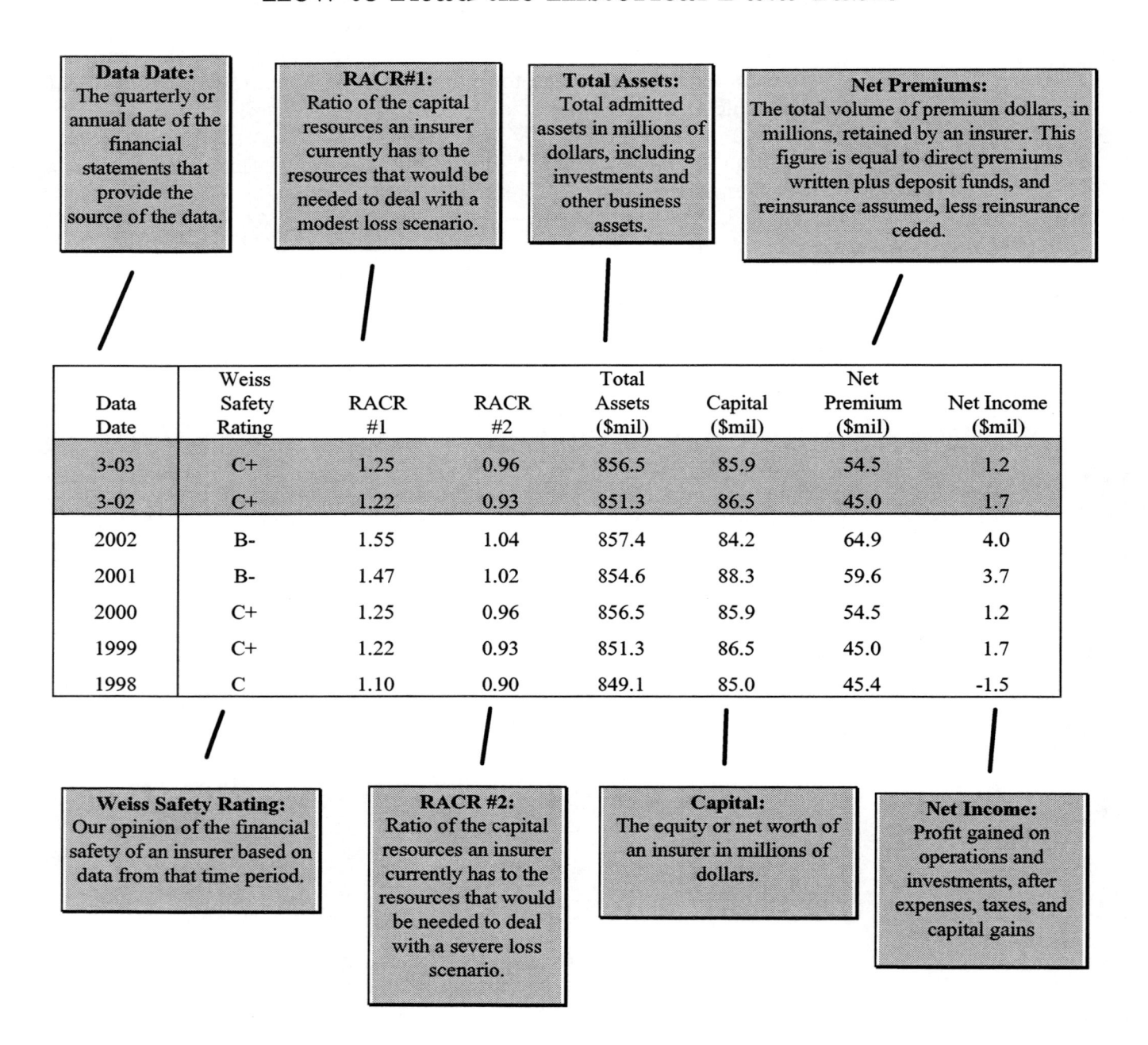

Data Date: The quarterly or annual date of the financial statements that provide the source of the data.

RACR#1: Ratio of the capital resources an insurer currently has to the resources that would be needed to deal with a modest loss scenario.

Total Assets: Total admitted assets in millions of dollars, including investments and other business assets.

Net Premiums: The total volume of premium dollars, in millions, retained by an insurer. This figure is equal to direct premiums written plus deposit funds, and reinsurance assumed, less reinsurance ceded.

Data Date	Weiss Safety Rating	RACR #1	RACR #2	Total Assets ($mil)	Capital ($mil)	Net Premium ($mil)	Net Income ($mil)
3-03	C+	1.25	0.96	856.5	85.9	54.5	1.2
3-02	C+	1.22	0.93	851.3	86.5	45.0	1.7
2002	B-	1.55	1.04	857.4	84.2	64.9	4.0
2001	B-	1.47	1.02	854.6	88.3	59.6	3.7
2000	C+	1.25	0.96	856.5	85.9	54.5	1.2
1999	C+	1.22	0.93	851.3	86.5	45.0	1.7
1998	C	1.10	0.90	849.1	85.0	45.4	-1.5

Weiss Safety Rating: Our opinion of the financial safety of an insurer based on data from that time period.

RACR #2: Ratio of the capital resources an insurer currently has to the resources that would be needed to deal with a severe loss scenario.

Capital: The equity or net worth of an insurer in millions of dollars.

Net Income: Profit gained on operations and investments, after expenses, taxes, and capital gains

Row Descriptions:

Row 1 contains the most recent quarterly data as filed with state regulators and is presented on a year-to-date basis. For example, the figure for third quarter premiums includes premiums received through the third quarter. **Row 2** consists of data from the same quarter of the prior year. Compare current quarterly results to those of a year ago.

Row 3 contains data from the most recent annual statutory filing. **Rows 4-7** includes data from year-end statements going back four years from the most recent annual filing. Compare current year-end results to those of the previous four years. With the exception of Total Assets and Capital, quarterly data are not comparable with annual data.

Customized Graphs

In the lower right-hand corner of each company section, a customized graph or text block highlights a key factor affecting that company's financial strength. One of 15 types of information is found, identified by one of the following headings:

# of Months of Claims and Expenses in Capital illustrates the number of months' worth of medical and administrative expenses the company could cover by drawing solely on its current capital position.

Adverse Trends in Operations lists changes in key balance sheet and income statement items which may be leading indicators of deteriorating business performance.

Allocation of Premium Income shows what portion of the company's premium income is being spent on medical benefits and administrative expenses. Any income left after the payment of these two types of expense, is used to pay taxes and extraordinary expenditures; the remainder is profit.

Capital History plots the company's reported capital and surplus in millions of dollars over the last five years. Volatile changes in capital levels may indicate unstable operations.

Detail of Risk-Adjusted Capital Ratio provides a percentage breakdown of target capital components based on lines of business and investments in a moderate or severe loss scenario. Target capital is our opinion of the level of capital the company should have, based on the risk it assumes. For example, if the percentage of target capital for individual life is 33%, this means that 33% of the company's target capital relates to individual life. C2 refers to the pricing risk element of the risk-adjusted capital formula. C3 refers to disintermediation (interest rate) risk.

Enrollment Trend charts an HMO's year-end membership levels over the last five years.

Exposure to Withdrawals Without Penalty answers the question: For each dollar of capital and surplus, how much does the company have in annuity and deposit funds that can be withdrawn by policyholders with minimal or no penalty? The figures do not include the effects of reinsurance or funds subject to withdrawals from cash value life insurance policies.

Group Ratings shows the group name, a composite Weiss Safety Rating for the group, and a list of the largest members with their ratings. The composite Weiss Safety Rating is made up of the weighted average, by assets, of the individual ratings of each company in the group (including life/health companies, property/casualty companies, or HMOs) plus a factor for the financial strength of the holding company, where applicable.

High Risk Assets as a % of Capital answers the question: For each dollar of capital and surplus, how much does the company have in junk bonds, nonperforming mortgages and repossessed real estate? Accumulations in the Asset Valuation Reserve or AVR, which provide some protection against investment losses, have not been included in the figure for capital. These figures are based on year-end data.

Income Trends shows underwriting and net income results over the last five years.

II. Analysis of Largest Companies

Investment Income Compared to Needs of Reserves answers the question: Is the company earning enough investment income to meet the expectations of actuaries when they priced their policies and set reserve levels? According to state insurance regulators, it would be "unusual" if an insurer were to have less than $1.25 in actual investment income for each dollar of investment income that it projected in its actuarial forecasts. This provides an excess margin of at least 25 cents on the dollar to cover any unexpected decline in income or increase in claims. This graph shows whether or not the company is maintaining the appropriate 25% margin and is based on year-end data.

Junk Bonds as a % of Capital answers the question: For each dollar of capital and surplus, how much does the company have in junk bonds? In addition, it shows a breakdown of the junk bond portfolio by bond rating – BB, B, CCC or in default. Accumulations in the Asset Valuation Reserve or AVR, which provide some protection against investment losses, have not been included in the figure for capital. These figures are based on year-end data.

Largest Net Exposure Per Risk shows the ratio of the largest net aggregate amount insured in any one risk (excluding workers' compensation) as a percent of capital.

Liquidity Index evaluates a company's ability to raise the cash necessary to pay claims. Various cash flow scenarios are modeled to determine how the company might fare in the event of an unexpected spike in claims costs.

Net Income History plots operating gains and losses over the most recent five-year period.

Nonperforming Mortgages (plus repossessed real estate) as a % of Capital answers the question: For each dollar of capital and surplus, how much does the company have in nonperforming mortgages and repossessed real estate? Nonperforming mortgages include those overdue more than 90 days and mortgages currently in process of foreclosure. Accumulations in the Asset Valuation Reserve or AVR, which provide some protection against investment losses, have not been included in the figure for capital. These figures are based on year-end data.

Policy Leverage answers the question: To what degree is this insurer capable of handling an unexpected spike in claims? Low leverage indicates low exposure; high leverage is high exposure.

Target leverage represents the maximum exposure we feel would be appropriate for a top-rated company.

Premium Growth History depicts the change in the insurer's net premiums written. Such changes may be the result of issuing more policies or changes in reinsurance arrangements. In either case, growth rates above 20% per year are considered excessive. "Standard" growth is under 20%; "shrinkage" refers to net declines.

Rating Indexes illustrate the score and range – strong, good, fair, or weak – on each of the Weiss rating indexes.

Reserve Deficiency shows whether the company has set aside sufficient funds to pay claims. A positive number indicates insufficient reserving and a negative number adequate reserving.

Reserves to Capital analyzes the relationship between loss and loss expense reserves to capital. Operating results and capital levels for companies with a high ratio are more susceptible to fluctuations than those with lower ratios.

Risk-Adjusted Capital Ratio #1 answers the question: In each of the past five years, does the insurer have sufficient capital to cover potential losses in its investments and business operations in a *moderate* loss scenario?

Risk-Adjusted Capital Ratio #2 answers the question: In each of the past five years, does the insurer have sufficient capital to cover potential losses in its investments and business operations in a *severe* loss scenario?

Risk-Adjusted Capital Ratios answers these questions for both a moderate loss scenario (RACR #1 shown by the dark bar), and a severe loss scenario (RACR #2, light bar).

II. Analysis of Largest Companies
Winter 2003 - 04

ADVANTAGE HEALTHPLAN INC   C-   Fair

Major Rating Factors: Fair capitalization (4.0 on a scale of 0 to 10) based on fair current risk-adjusted capital (moderate loss scenario) as results have slipped from the good range over the last year. Weak profitability index (1.5) with modest operating losses during 2000 and 2002. Average return on equity has been poor at -2%. Weak liquidity (2.5) as a spike in claims may stretch capacity.
Other Rating Factors: Good overall results on stability tests (5.8) despite fair risk-adjusted capital in prior years. High quality investment portfolio (8.8) containing little or no exposure to mortgages, junk bonds, or unaffiliated stocks.
Principal Business: Medicaid (98%), comp med (2%)
Mem Phys: 02: N/A **01:** N/A **02 MLR** 79% / **02 Admin Exp** 24%
Enroll(000): Q1 03: 4 **02:** 4 **01:** 3 **Med Exp PMPM:** $137
Principal Investments: Cash and equiv (25%), nonaffiliate common stock (4%), pref stock (1%), other (70%)
Provider Compensation ($000): Contr fee ($4,390), capitation ($1,020)
Total Member Encounters: Phys (4,413), non-phys (2,010)
Group Affiliation: None
Licensed in: DC
Address: 624 Ninth St NW Suite 222, Washington, DC 20001
Phone: (202) 783-8191 **Dom State:** DC **Commenced Bus:** November 1994

Data Date	Weiss Safety Rating	RACR #1	RACR #2	Total Assets ($mil)	Capital ($mil)	Net Premium ($mil)	Net Income ($mil)
3-03	C-	0.78	0.65	4.0	1.9	2.0	0.0
3-02	C	2.61	2.18	5.3	2.0	1.8	0.1
2002	C-	0.77	0.64	4.5	1.8	7.0	-0.1
2001	C	2.61	2.18	5.4	2.0	6.0	0.1
2000	C-	N/A	N/A	5.0	1.8	6.2	-0.2
1999	N/A	N/A	N/A	5.7	2.0	5.3	N/A
1998	N/A	N/A	N/A	5.7	2.5	3.9	N/A

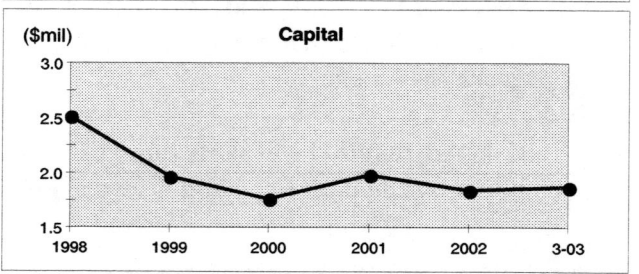

Capital ($mil) chart 1998–3-03

AET HEALTH CARE PLAN INC   C   Fair

Major Rating Factors: Weak profitability index (1.0 on a scale of 0 to 10) with operating losses during 1998, 1999, 2000 and 2001. Average return on equity has been poor at -46%. Weak overall results on stability tests (0.4) based on a significant 99% decrease in enrollment during the period, a decline in the number of member physicians during 2002 and a steep decline in capital during 2002. Rating is significantly influenced by the fair financial results of Aetna Inc. Strong capitalization (10.0) based on excellent current risk-adjusted capital (severe loss scenario) reflecting significant improvement over results in 1998.
Other Rating Factors: High quality investment portfolio (9.3) containing no exposure to mortgages, junk bonds, or unaffiliated stocks. Excellent liquidity (7.8) with ample operational cash flow and liquid investments.
Principal Business: Comp med (94%), FEHB (4%), Medicare (1%)
Mem Phys: 02: 1,423 **01:** 70,205 **02 MLR** 96% / **02 Admin Exp** -8%
Enroll(000): 02: 4 **01:** 392 **Med Exp PMPM:** $13
Principal Investments: Cash and equiv (11%), other (89%)
Provider Compensation ($000): Contr fee ($146,348), capitation ($4,313)
Total Member Encounters: Phys (101,006), non-phys (3,989)
Group Affiliation: Aetna Inc
Licensed in: AR, CO, DC, FL, IL, IN, KS, KY, MD, MS, MO, NJ, NC, OH, OK, PA, TN, TX, VA
Address: 2777 Stemmons Freeway, Dallas, TX 75207
Phone: (214) 200-8000 **Dom State:** TX **Commenced Bus:** October 1975

Data Date	Weiss Safety Rating	RACR #1	RACR #2	Total Assets ($mil)	Capital ($mil)	Net Premium ($mil)	Net Income ($mil)
2002	C	30.01	25.01	99.3	80.6	32.1	26.3
2001	C	3.93	3.03	395.3	214.2	986.7	-8.2
2000	C	1.18	0.99	654.2	172.7	2,866.6	-130.4
1999	C+	1.22	1.03	894.9	234.8	3,798.4	-211.6
1998	C+	0.58	0.49	697.8	107.8	3,575.1	-63.6

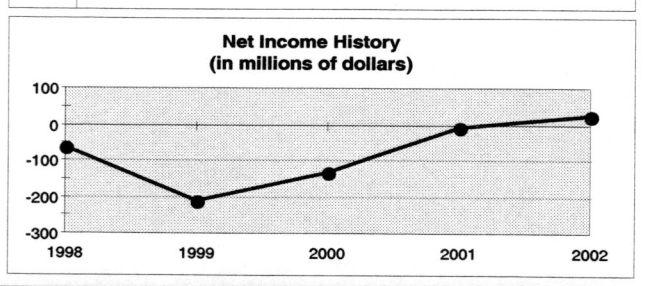

Net Income History (in millions of dollars) chart 1998–2002

AETNA HEALTH INC (A COLORADO CORP)   C   Fair

Major Rating Factors: Fair overall results on stability tests (4.0 on a scale of 0 to 10) based on rapid premium growth over the last five years, rapid enrollment growth during the past five years. Rating is significantly influenced by the fair financial results of Aetna Inc. Weak profitability index (1.9) with operating losses during 1998, 1999, 2000 and 2001. Average return on equity has been poor at -74%. Strong overall capitalization (10.0) based on excellent current risk-adjusted capital (severe loss scenario). Moreover, capital has steadily grown over the last five years.
Other Rating Factors: High quality investment portfolio (9.9) containing no exposure to mortgages, junk bonds, or unaffiliated stocks. Excellent liquidity (7.0) with ample operational cash flow and liquid investments.
Principal Business: Comp med (100%)
Mem Phys: 02: 5,757 **01:** 5,854 **02 MLR** 89% / **02 Admin Exp** 13%
Enroll(000): Q1 03: 37 **02:** 52 **01:** 181 **Med Exp PMPM:** $120
Principal Investments: Cash and equiv (61%), other (39%)
Provider Compensation ($000): Contr fee ($176,759), FFS ($11,598), capitation ($6,926)
Total Member Encounters: Phys (857,504)
Group Affiliation: Aetna Inc
Licensed in: CO
Address: 6430 S. Fiddler's Green Circle, Englewood, CO 80111
Phone: (800) 872-3862 **Dom State:** CO **Commenced Bus:** October 1995

Data Date	Weiss Safety Rating	RACR #1	RACR #2	Total Assets ($mil)	Capital ($mil)	Net Premium ($mil)	Net Income ($mil)
3-03	C	4.21	3.51	66.1	48.4	24.3	4.4
3-02	C	1.97	1.66	88.8	29.7	76.0	-6.9
2002	C	3.84	3.20	71.5	44.0	188.4	6.4
2001	C	1.96	1.66	100.0	38.2	353.2	-29.7
2000	C	1.55	1.31	62.0	21.0	220.1	-19.2
1999	C	1.72	1.46	29.3	9.5	90.7	-2.5
1998	C	1.85	1.57	10.3	3.1	18.5	-2.5

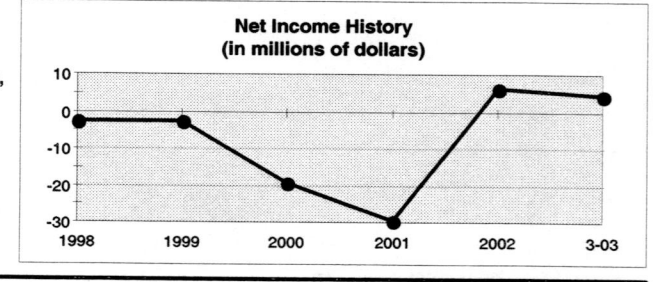

Net Income History (in millions of dollars) chart 1998–3-03

www.WeissRatings.com

Winter 2003 - 04 | II. Analysis of Largest Companies

AETNA HEALTH INC (A CT CORP) — C — Fair

Major Rating Factors: Fair overall results on stability tests (3.1 on a scale of 0 to 10) based on a steep decline in capital during 2002, a significant 64% decrease in enrollment during the period. Rating is significantly influenced by the fair financial results of Aetna Inc. Weak profitability index (1.3) with operating losses during 1998, 1999, 2000 and 2001. Average return on equity has been poor at -16%. Good liquidity (7.0) with sufficient resources (cash flows and marketable investments) to handle a spike in claims.

Other Rating Factors: Strong capitalization (10.0) based on excellent current risk-adjusted capital (severe loss scenario) reflecting significant improvement over results in 1999. High quality investment portfolio (9.5) containing little or no exposure to mortgages, junk bonds, or unaffiliated stocks.

Principal Business: Comp med (100%)
Mem Phys: 02: 6,693 **01:** 6,323 **02 MLR** 75% **/ 02 Admin Exp** 11%
Enroll(000): Q1 03: 31 **02:** 32 **01:** 90 **Med Exp PMPM:** $109
Principal Investments: Cash and equiv (20%), other (80%)
Provider Compensation ($000): Contr fee ($88,446), capitation ($6,533), FFS ($4,614)
Total Member Encounters: Phys (562,604)
Group Affiliation: Aetna Inc
Licensed in: CT
Address: 1000 Middle St, Middletown, CT 06457
Phone: (800) 872-3862 **Dom State:** CT **Commenced Bus:** June 1987

Data Date	Weiss Safety Rating	RACR #1	RACR #2	Total Assets ($mil)	Capital ($mil)	Net Premium ($mil)	Net Income ($mil)
3-03	C	5.84	4.87	54.8	31.4	24.8	2.7
3-02	C	3.41	2.75	73.7	40.7	31.9	2.7
2002	C	5.30	4.41	44.2	28.2	106.5	12.1
2001	C	3.40	2.74	74.5	38.6	209.3	-3.0
2000	C-	1.55	1.28	89.8	29.5	318.1	-13.6
1999	C-	0.73	0.60	79.9	9.9	221.9	-0.7
1998	C+	3.19	2.64	77.7	32.3	158.9	-10.8

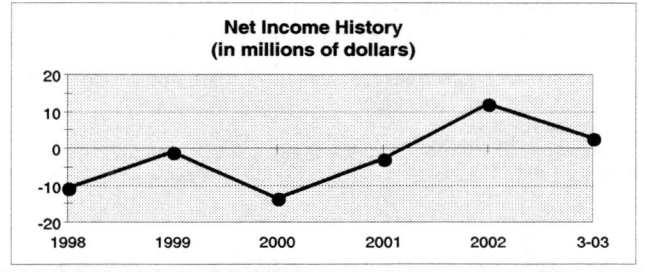

Net Income History (in millions of dollars) — chart spanning 1998 to 3-03

AETNA HEALTH INC (A DE CORP) — C — Fair

Major Rating Factors: Fair quality investment portfolio (3.7 on a scale of 0 to 10). Fair overall results on stability tests (3.1) based on a significant 64% decrease in enrollment during the period, a steep decline in premium revenue in 2002. Rating is significantly influenced by the fair financial results of Aetna Inc. Weak profitability index (0.9) with operating losses during 1998, 1999, 2000 and 2001. Average return on equity has been poor at -25%.

Other Rating Factors: Good liquidity (6.9) with sufficient resources (cash flows and marketable investments) to handle a spike in claims. Strong capitalization (10.0) based on excellent current risk-adjusted capital (severe loss scenario) reflecting improvement over results in 1999.

Principal Business: Comp med (100%)
Mem Phys: 02: 1,384 **01:** 1,332 **02 MLR** 85% **/ 02 Admin Exp** 13%
Enroll(000): Q1 03: 9 **02:** 9 **01:** 26 **Med Exp PMPM:** $131
Principal Investments: Cash and equiv (31%), other (69%)
Provider Compensation ($000): Contr fee ($28,274), capitation ($3,099), FFS ($2,830)
Total Member Encounters: Phys (120,025)
Group Affiliation: Aetna Inc
Licensed in: DC, DE, MD
Address: 980 Jolly Rd, Blue Bell, PA 19422
Phone: (800) 872-3862 **Dom State:** DE **Commenced Bus:** June 1987

Data Date	Weiss Safety Rating	RACR #1	RACR #2	Total Assets ($mil)	Capital ($mil)	Net Premium ($mil)	Net Income ($mil)
3-03	C	3.65	3.04	14.7	10.0	5.9	1.6
3-02	C	1.92	1.59	20.1	10.4	11.3	0.5
2002	C	3.38	2.82	15.7	9.2	33.2	0.3
2001	C	1.93	1.59	20.2	9.8	65.2	-5.4
2000	C	2.14	1.78	22.3	12.2	67.1	-3.9
1999	C	1.06	0.89	44.1	12.7	192.4	-1.0
1998	C	1.11	0.93	65.7	17.5	277.9	-4.8

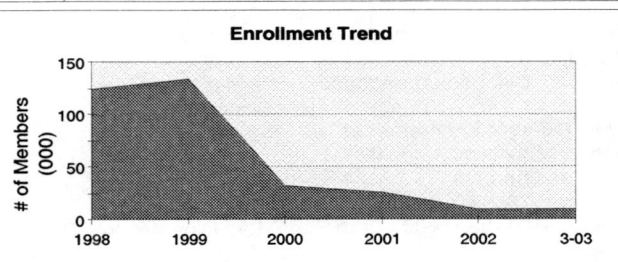

Enrollment Trend — chart of # of Members (000) from 1998 to 3-03

AETNA HEALTH INC (A FLORIDA CORP) — C- — Fair

Major Rating Factors: Fair liquidity (5.0 on a scale of 0 to 10) as cash resources may not be adequate to cover a spike in claims. Weak profitability index (0.9) with $60.4 million in losses in the last two years. Average return on equity has been poor at -57%. Good overall results on stability tests (6.7) based on consistent premium and capital growth in the last five years but a decline in enrollment during 2002. Rating is significantly influenced by the fair financial results of Aetna Inc.

Other Rating Factors: Strong capitalization (7.4) based on excellent current risk-adjusted capital (severe loss scenario) reflecting significant improvement over results in 2001. High quality investment portfolio (9.3) containing little or no exposure to mortgages, junk bonds, or unaffiliated stocks.

Principal Business: Comp med (100%)
Mem Phys: 02: 4,552 **01:** 4,178 **02 MLR** 91% **/ 02 Admin Exp** 10%
Enroll(000): Q1 03: 490 **02:** 537 **01:** 600 **Med Exp PMPM:** $182
Principal Investments: Cash and equiv (20%), other (80%)
Provider Compensation ($000): Contr fee ($1,062,946), FFS ($109,692), capitation ($41,679)
Total Member Encounters: Phys (7,179,767)
Group Affiliation: Aetna Inc
Licensed in: FL
Address: 5100 W Lemon Street, Ste 218, Tampa, FL 33609
Phone: (813) 261-9630 **Dom State:** FL **Commenced Bus:** July 1985

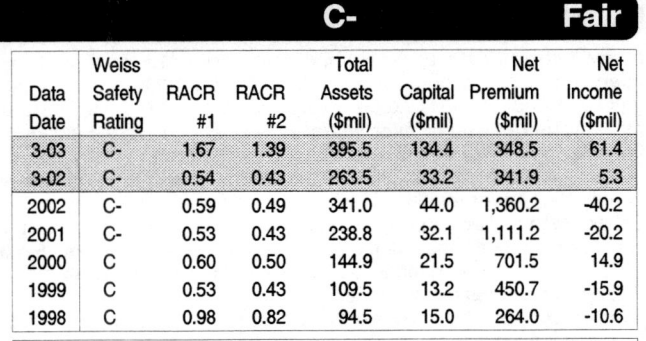

Data Date	Weiss Safety Rating	RACR #1	RACR #2	Total Assets ($mil)	Capital ($mil)	Net Premium ($mil)	Net Income ($mil)
3-03	C-	1.67	1.39	395.5	134.4	348.5	61.4
3-02	C-	0.54	0.43	263.5	33.2	341.9	5.3
2002	C-	0.59	0.49	341.0	44.0	1,360.2	-40.2
2001	C-	0.53	0.43	238.8	32.1	1,111.2	-20.2
2000	C	0.60	0.50	144.9	21.5	701.5	14.9
1999	C	0.53	0.43	109.5	13.2	450.7	-15.9
1998	C	0.98	0.82	94.5	15.0	264.0	-10.6

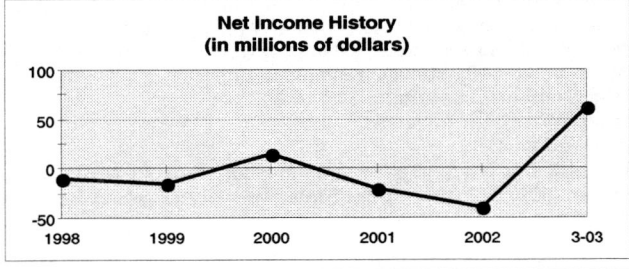

Net Income History (in millions of dollars) — chart spanning 1998 to 3-03

www.WeissRatings.com — * Denotes a Weiss Recommended Company

II. Analysis of Largest Companies

Winter 2003 - 04

AETNA HEALTH INC (A GEORGIA CORP)   C+   Fair

Major Rating Factors: Fair profitability index (4.1 on a scale of 0 to 10) with operating losses during 1998. Return on equity has been low, averaging 0%. Fair overall results on stability tests (4.4). Rating is significantly influenced by the fair financial results of Aetna Inc. Good liquidity (6.7) with sufficient resources (cash flows and marketable investments) to handle a spike in claims.
Other Rating Factors: Strong capitalization (10.0) based on excellent current risk-adjusted capital (severe loss scenario) reflecting improvement over results in 1999. High quality investment portfolio (9.7) containing no exposure to mortgages, junk bonds, or unaffiliated stocks.
Principal Business: Comp med (82%), FEHB (17%), dental (2%)
Mem Phys: 02: 1,788   **01:** 1,776   **02 MLR** 83% / **02 Admin Exp** 13%
Enroll(000): Q1 03: 174   **02:** 197   **01:** 205   **Med Exp PMPM:** $111
Principal Investments: Cash and equiv (25%), other (75%)
Provider Compensation ($000): Contr fee ($237,351), capitation ($29,370), FFS ($16,182)
Total Member Encounters: Phys (1,373,036), non-phys (4,194)
Group Affiliation: Aetna Inc
Licensed in: GA
Address: 11675 Great Oaks Way, Apharetta, GA 30022
Phone: (800) 872-3862   **Dom State:** GA   **Commenced Bus:** February 1986

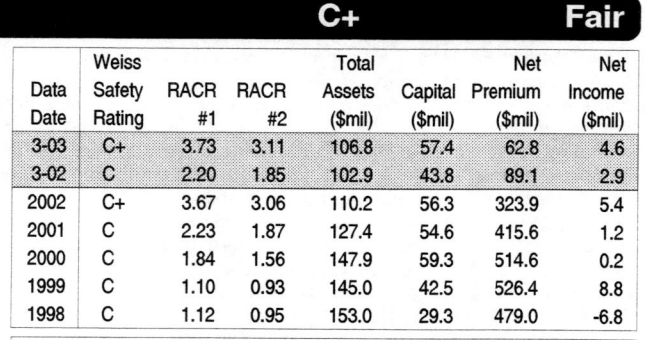

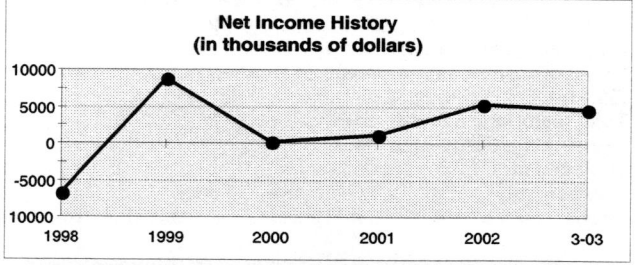

Data Date	Weiss Safety Rating	RACR #1	RACR #2	Total Assets ($mil)	Capital ($mil)	Net Premium ($mil)	Net Income ($mil)
3-03	C+	3.73	3.11	106.8	57.4	62.8	4.6
3-02	C	2.20	1.85	102.9	43.8	89.1	2.9
2002	C+	3.67	3.06	110.2	56.3	323.9	5.4
2001	C	2.23	1.87	127.4	54.6	415.6	1.2
2000	C	1.84	1.56	147.9	59.3	514.6	0.2
1999	C	1.10	0.93	145.0	42.5	526.4	8.8
1998	C	1.12	0.95	153.0	29.3	479.0	-6.8

Net Income History (in thousands of dollars) — chart showing values from 1998 (approx -7000) to 3-03.

AETNA HEALTH INC (A LOUISIANA CORP)   C   Fair

Major Rating Factors: Weak profitability index (0.9 on a scale of 0 to 10) with operating losses during 2000 and 2001. Average return on equity has been extremely poor. Weak overall results on stability tests (2.4) based on a significant 100% decrease in enrollment during the period, a steep decline in premium revenue in 2002 and excessive capital growth during 2002. Rating is significantly influenced by the fair financial results of Aetna Inc. Strong capitalization (10.0) based on excellent current risk-adjusted capital (severe loss scenario) reflecting significant improvement over results in 2001.
Other Rating Factors: High quality investment portfolio (9.7) containing no exposure to mortgages, junk bonds, or unaffiliated stocks. Excellent liquidity (9.1) with ample operational cash flow and liquid investments.
Principal Business: Comp med (91%), FEHB (9%)
Mem Phys: 02: N/A   **01:** 1,047   **02 MLR** 11% / **02 Admin Exp** 11%
Enroll(000):   **02:** 0   **01:** 55   **Med Exp PMPM:** $3
Principal Investments: Cash and equiv (49%), other (51%)
Provider Compensation ($000): Contr fee ($17,356), FFS ($2,662), capitation ($230)
Total Member Encounters: Phys (48,473)
Group Affiliation: Aetna Inc
Licensed in: LA
Address: 3838 N Causeway Blvd Ste 3350, Metairie, LA 70002-7283
Phone: (504) 830-5600   **Dom State:** LA   **Commenced Bus:** November 1987

Data Date	Weiss Safety Rating	RACR #1	RACR #2	Total Assets ($mil)	Capital ($mil)	Net Premium ($mil)	Net Income ($mil)
2002	C	19.15	15.96	20.2	15.3	8.9	11.0
2001	C	0.53	0.45	38.8	3.8	120.4	-15.0
2000	C	0.64	0.54	39.3	5.4	162.2	-11.3
1999	N/A	N/A	N/A	36.2	5.3	135.1	N/A
1998	C+	2.27	1.91	34.9	12.4	79.7	0.3

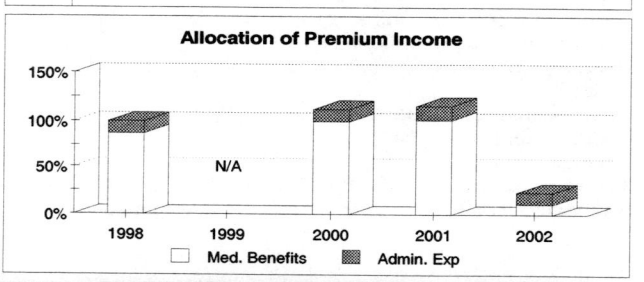

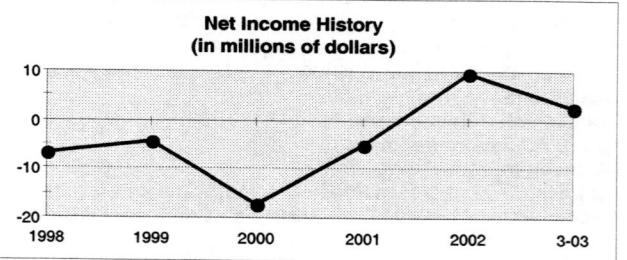

Allocation of Premium Income — bar chart 1998–2002 (1999 N/A) showing Med. Benefits and Admin. Exp.

AETNA HEALTH INC (A MAINE CORP)   C   Fair

Major Rating Factors: Weak profitability index (1.9 on a scale of 0 to 10) with operating losses during 1998, 1999, 2000 and 2001. Average return on equity has been poor at -65%. Good overall results on stability tests (5.6) despite fair risk-adjusted capital in prior years. Rating is significantly influenced by the fair financial results of Aetna Inc. Strong capitalization (10.0) based on excellent current risk-adjusted capital (severe loss scenario) reflecting significant improvement over results in 1998.
Other Rating Factors: High quality investment portfolio (9.9) containing no exposure to mortgages, junk bonds, or unaffiliated stocks. Excellent liquidity (7.2) with ample operational cash flow and liquid investments.
Principal Business: Comp med (100%)
Mem Phys: 02: 2,193   **01:** 2,172   **02 MLR** 79% / **02 Admin Exp** 12%
Enroll(000): Q1 03: 41   **02:** 41   **01:** 73   **Med Exp PMPM:** $192
Principal Investments: Cash and equiv (68%), other (32%)
Provider Compensation ($000): Contr fee ($130,852), FFS ($7,203), capitation ($2,313), bonus arrang ($1,016)
Total Member Encounters: Phys (660,714)
Group Affiliation: Aetna Inc
Licensed in: ME
Address: One Monument Square 4th Floor, Portland, ME 04101
Phone: (800) 872-3862   **Dom State:** ME   **Commenced Bus:** April 1996

Data Date	Weiss Safety Rating	RACR #1	RACR #2	Total Assets ($mil)	Capital ($mil)	Net Premium ($mil)	Net Income ($mil)
3-03	C	3.81	3.18	53.5	35.1	36.9	2.8
3-02	C	1.97	1.65	53.4	22.2	45.8	0.4
2002	C	3.55	2.96	66.2	32.6	164.5	9.6
2001	C	2.00	1.68	51.9	22.9	194.1	-4.8
2000	C	1.33	1.11	46.7	14.1	150.2	-17.1
1999	C	0.95	0.80	25.9	8.3	76.4	-4.2
1998	C	0.69	0.58	20.5	6.5	54.9	-6.8

Net Income History (in millions of dollars) — chart from 1998 to 3-03.

Winter 2003 - 04   II. Analysis of Largest Companies

AETNA HEALTH INC (A MARYLAND CORP) — B- Good

Major Rating Factors: Good overall profitability index (6.0 on a scale of 0 to 10) despite operating losses during 1998. Good overall results on stability tests (5.1) despite excessive capital growth during 2002, a decline in enrollment during 2002. Rating is significantly influenced by the fair financial results of Aetna Inc. Good liquidity (6.9) with sufficient resources (cash flows and marketable investments) to handle a spike in claims.
Other Rating Factors: Strong capitalization (10.0) based on excellent current risk-adjusted capital (severe loss scenario) reflecting improvement over results in 1998. High quality investment portfolio (9.9) containing little or no exposure to mortgages, junk bonds, or unaffiliated stocks.
Principal Business: Comp med (61%), FEHB (39%)
Mem Phys: 02: 15,939 01: 15,195 **02 MLR** 80% / **02 Admin Exp** 13%
Enroll(000): Q1 03: 252 02: 289 01: 405 **Med Exp PMPM:** $144
Principal Investments: Cash and equiv (32%), other (68%)
Provider Compensation ($000): Contr fee ($539,007), capitation ($53,030), FFS ($39,102)
Total Member Encounters: Phys (3,185,752)
Group Affiliation: Aetna Inc
Licensed in: DC, MD, VA
Address: 1301 McCormick Dr, Largo, MD 20774
Phone: (301) 636-0000 **Dom State:** MD **Commenced Bus:** January 1979

Data Date	Weiss Safety Rating	RACR #1	RACR #2	Total Assets ($mil)	Capital ($mil)	Net Premium ($mil)	Net Income ($mil)
3-03	B-	4.28	3.56	202.6	116.2	157.2	16.0
3-02	C+	2.39	1.94	201.4	76.3	195.5	10.5
2002	B-	3.77	3.14	204.0	101.3	748.4	47.7
2001	C+	2.37	1.93	214.4	82.9	857.3	21.0
2000	C+	1.14	0.95	165.0	39.3	786.7	3.7
1999	C+	1.40	1.11	174.9	45.6	733.3	16.1
1998	C	1.03	0.88	175.0	41.2	805.3	-23.2

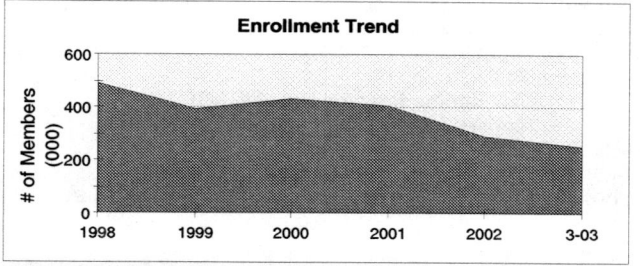

Enrollment Trend (1998–3-03)

AETNA HEALTH INC (A MICHIGAN CORP) — C+ Fair

Major Rating Factors: Fair overall results on stability tests (4.2 on a scale of 0 to 10) based on rapid premium growth over the last five years, a significant 63% decrease in enrollment during the period. Rating is significantly influenced by the fair financial results of Aetna Inc. Weak profitability index (0.9) with operating losses during 2001. Average return on equity has been poor at -11%. Strong capitalization index (9.3) based on excellent current risk-adjusted capital (severe loss scenario) despite some fluctuation in capital levels.
Other Rating Factors: High quality investment portfolio (9.9) containing no exposure to mortgages, junk bonds, or unaffiliated stocks. Excellent liquidity (7.1) with ample operational cash flow and liquid investments.
Principal Business: Comp med (100%)
Mem Phys: 02: 6,674 01: 5,921 **02 MLR** 92% / **02 Admin Exp** 12%
Enroll(000): Q1 03: 6 02: 8 01: 22 **Med Exp PMPM:** $142
Principal Investments: Cash and equiv (92%), other (8%)
Provider Compensation ($000): Contr fee ($24,160), FFS ($4,056), capitation ($768)
Total Member Encounters: Phys (148,271)
Group Affiliation: Aetna Inc
Licensed in: MI
Address: 26933 Northwestern Hwy Ste 100, Southfield, MI 43034-4728
Phone: (248) 208-8600 **Dom State:** MI **Commenced Bus:** April 1998

Data Date	Weiss Safety Rating	RACR #1	RACR #2	Total Assets ($mil)	Capital ($mil)	Net Premium ($mil)	Net Income ($mil)
3-03	C+	3.18	2.65	18.6	8.5	3.6	1.0
3-02	C+	1.63	1.38	26.6	4.9	8.5	0.1
2002	C+	2.64	2.20	14.5	7.0	27.7	0.7
2001	C+	1.64	1.38	15.3	4.7	31.6	-4.6
2000	B-	4.49	3.80	9.1	6.2	10.5	0.2
1999	B-	9.42	7.88	6.5	6.0	1.7	0.5
1998	B-	350.70	299.40	5.5	5.4	0.2	0.2

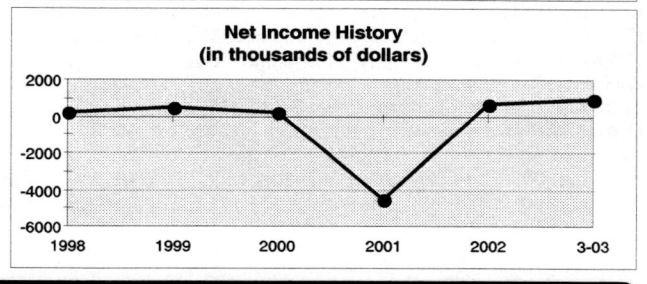

Net Income History (in thousands of dollars), 1998–3-03

AETNA HEALTH INC (A MISSOURI CORP) — C- Fair

Major Rating Factors: Fair overall results on stability tests (3.5 on a scale of 0 to 10) based on fair risk-adjusted capital in prior years, rapid premium growth over the last five years and rapid enrollment growth during the past five years. Rating is significantly influenced by the fair financial results of Aetna Inc. Weak profitability index (0.9) with operating losses during 1999, 2000 and 2001. Average return on equity has been poor at -63%. Strong capitalization (9.3) based on excellent current risk-adjusted capital (severe loss scenario) reflecting significant improvement over results in 2000.
Other Rating Factors: High quality investment portfolio (9.9) containing no exposure to mortgages, junk bonds, or unaffiliated stocks. Excellent liquidity (7.2) with ample operational cash flow and liquid investments.
Principal Business: Comp med (99%)
Mem Phys: 02: 7,624 01: 7,750 **02 MLR** 84% / **02 Admin Exp** 12%
Enroll(000): Q1 03: 26 02: 31 01: 88 **Med Exp PMPM:** $106
Principal Investments: Cash and equiv (98%), other (2%)
Provider Compensation ($000): Contr fee ($79,312), FFS ($8,027), capitation ($5,090)
Total Member Encounters: Phys (335,319), non-phys (68,679)
Group Affiliation: Aetna Inc
Licensed in: KS, MO
Address: Two City Place Dr., Ste 300, St. Louis, MO 63141
Phone: (314) 567-6660 **Dom State:** MO **Commenced Bus:** September 1998

Data Date	Weiss Safety Rating	RACR #1	RACR #2	Total Assets ($mil)	Capital ($mil)	Net Premium ($mil)	Net Income ($mil)
3-03	C-	3.19	2.66	26.7	16.8	16.4	2.2
3-02	C-	1.54	1.30	36.3	13.3	28.9	-0.6
2002	C-	2.85	2.38	27.0	14.8	90.3	1.5
2001	C-	1.54	1.31	43.2	14.3	150.6	-14.0
2000	C	0.71	0.60	21.4	3.6	65.4	-6.6
1999	C	4.31	3.65	8.2	5.0	12.3	-1.0
1998	N/A	N/A	N/A	5.6	5.4	0.3	0.2

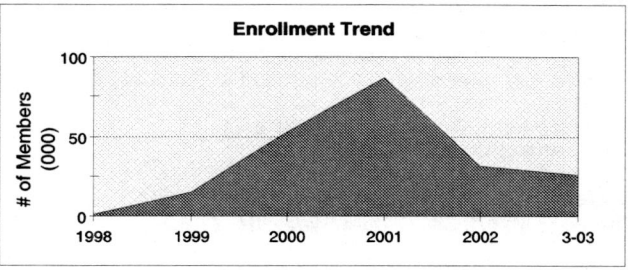

Enrollment Trend (1998–3-03)

www.WeissRatings.com   * Denotes a Weiss Recommended Company

II. Analysis of Largest Companies
Winter 2003 - 04

AETNA HEALTH INC (A NEW JERSEY CORP)   B-   Good

Major Rating Factors: Good overall results on stability tests (5.0 on a scale of 0 to 10) despite a decline in enrollment during 2002. Rating is significantly influenced by the fair financial results of Aetna Inc. Good liquidity (6.7) with sufficient resources (cash flows and marketable investments) to handle a spike in claims. Excellent profitability (8.3) with operating gains in each of the last five years.

Other Rating Factors: Strong capitalization (10.0) based on excellent current risk-adjusted capital (severe loss scenario) reflecting improvement over results in 1999. High quality investment portfolio (9.9) containing little or no exposure to mortgages, junk bonds, or unaffiliated stocks.

Principal Business: Comp med (76%), Medicare (18%), FEHB (6%)
Mem Phys: 02: 12,777   **01:** 12,187   **02 MLR** 80%   / **02 Admin Exp** 12%
Enroll(000): Q1 03: 520   **02:** 531   **01:** 726   **Med Exp PMPM:** $164
Principal Investments: Cash and equiv (5%), other (95%)
Provider Compensation ($000): Contr fee ($1,061,920), capitation ($161,347), FFS ($99,639)
Total Member Encounters: Phys (5,009,042)
Group Affiliation: Aetna Inc
Licensed in: NJ
Address: 55 Lane Rd, Fairfield, NJ 07004-1011
Phone: (800) 872-3862   **Dom State:** NJ   **Commenced Bus:** March 1983

Data Date	Weiss Safety Rating	RACR #1	RACR #2	Total Assets ($mil)	Capital ($mil)	Net Premium ($mil)	Net Income ($mil)
3-03	B-	3.82	3.19	511.3	272.7	382.5	33.7
3-02	B-	2.02	1.68	511.7	224.7	396.9	26.4
2002	B-	3.35	2.79	479.0	236.1	1,542.0	98.8
2001	B-	2.03	1.69	549.9	208.1	2,144.4	18.2
2000	B-	1.37	1.16	524.8	99.6	1,794.0	29.4
1999	B-	1.22	1.04	465.9	99.6	1,794.0	19.8
1998	B-	1.31	1.11	396.6	84.6	1,570.3	43.2

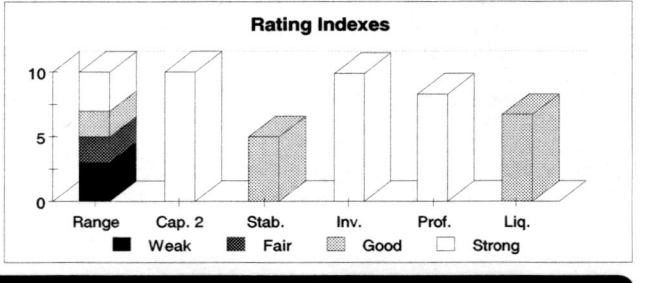

AETNA HEALTH INC (A NEW YORK CORP)   B-   Good

Major Rating Factors: Fair overall results on stability tests (4.7 on a scale of 0 to 10) based on excessive capital growth during 2002, a significant 36% decrease in enrollment during the period. Rating is significantly influenced by the fair financial results of Aetna Inc. Good liquidity (6.8) with sufficient resources (cash flows and marketable investments) to handle a spike in claims. Excellent profitability (7.5) with operating gains in each of the last five years.

Other Rating Factors: Strong capitalization (10.0) based on excellent current risk-adjusted capital (severe loss scenario) reflecting improvement over results in 1999. High quality investment portfolio (9.7) containing little or no exposure to mortgages, junk bonds, or unaffiliated stocks.

Principal Business: Comp med (81%), Medicare (12%), FEHB (7%)
Mem Phys: 02: 24,345   **01:** 22,279   **02 MLR** 80%   / **02 Admin Exp** 8%
Enroll(000): Q1 03: 416   **02:** 472   **01:** 735   **Med Exp PMPM:** $179
Principal Investments: Cash and equiv (21%), other (79%)
Provider Compensation ($000): Contr fee ($1,059,293), FFS ($152,196), capitation ($138,097)
Total Member Encounters: Phys (5,485,456)
Group Affiliation: Aetna Inc
Licensed in: NY
Address: 333 Earle Ovington Blvd #502, Uniondale, NY 11553-3645
Phone: (800) 872-3862   **Dom State:** NY   **Commenced Bus:** May 1986

Data Date	Weiss Safety Rating	RACR #1	RACR #2	Total Assets ($mil)	Capital ($mil)	Net Premium ($mil)	Net Income ($mil)
3-03	B-	4.45	3.71	703.9	350.8	334.7	63.7
3-02	C+	2.46	1.99	689.3	252.6	436.0	35.8
2002	B-	4.55	3.79	770.1	358.6	1,617.0	132.7
2001	C+	2.40	1.95	709.2	256.3	2,031.8	59.2
2000	C+	1.63	1.37	652.2	192.9	2,261.0	77.8
1999	C	1.04	0.86	497.8	110.0	1,847.1	3.3
1998	C+	1.90	1.61	461.9	136.0	1,557.5	23.9

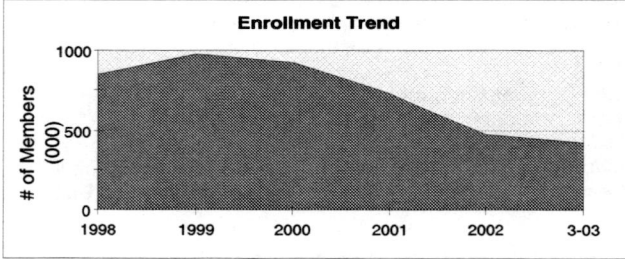

AETNA HEALTH INC (A NH CORP)   C   Fair

Major Rating Factors: Fair overall results on stability tests (4.1 on a scale of 0 to 10) based on a significant 89% decrease in enrollment during the period, a steep decline in premium revenue in 2002. Rating is significantly influenced by the fair financial results of Aetna Inc. Weak profitability index (0.8) with operating losses during 1998, 1999, 2000 and 2001. Average return on equity has been poor at -24%. Strong overall capitalization (10.0) based on excellent current risk-adjusted capital (severe loss scenario) despite some fluctuation in capital levels.

Other Rating Factors: High quality investment portfolio (9.9) containing no exposure to mortgages, junk bonds, or unaffiliated stocks. Excellent liquidity (7.7) with ample operational cash flow and liquid investments.

Principal Business: Comp med (100%)
Mem Phys: 02: 774   **01:** 735   **02 MLR** 90%   / **02 Admin Exp** 11%
Enroll(000):   **02:** 1   **01:** 13   **Med Exp PMPM:** $143
Principal Investments: Cash and equiv (83%), other (17%)
Provider Compensation ($000): Contr fee ($15,744), FFS ($1,903), capitation ($821)
Total Member Encounters: Phys (58,016)
Group Affiliation: Aetna Inc
Licensed in: NH
Address: 400-1 Totten Pond Rd, Waltham, MA 02451
Phone: (800) 872-3862   **Dom State:** NH   **Commenced Bus:** July 1991

Data Date	Weiss Safety Rating	RACR #1	RACR #2	Total Assets ($mil)	Capital ($mil)	Net Premium ($mil)	Net Income ($mil)
2002	C	6.39	5.33	10.2	8.7	14.2	2.1
2001	C	2.24	1.89	16.3	7.0	33.5	-6.3
2000	C+	3.18	2.63	13.6	8.2	24.0	-3.0
1999	C+	5.90	4.83	12.8	9.0	15.7	-1.4
1998	C+	6.65	5.62	18.5	14.3	22.0	-2.0

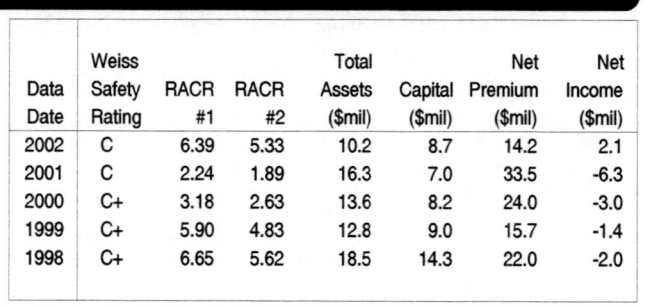

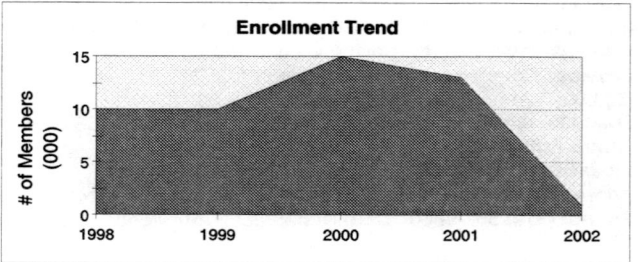

Winter 2003 - 04 II. Analysis of Largest Companies

AETNA HEALTH INC (A PA CORP) — B- Good

Major Rating Factors: Fair profitability index (4.7 on a scale of 0 to 10) with operating losses during 2001. Fair overall results on stability tests (4.5) based on a significant 33% decrease in enrollment during the period. Rating is significantly influenced by the fair financial results of Aetna Inc. Good quality investment portfolio (6.1) containing small junk bond exposure.
Other Rating Factors: Good liquidity (6.9) with sufficient resources (cash flows and marketable investments) to handle a spike in claims. Strong capitalization (10.0) based on excellent current risk-adjusted capital (severe loss scenario) reflecting improvement over results in 1999.
Principal Business: Comp med (68%), Medicare (24%), FEHB (8%)
Mem Phys: 02: 18,578   **01:** 18,471   **02 MLR** 79% / **02 Admin Exp** 12%
Enroll(000): Q1 03: 568   **02:** 583   **01:** 873   **Med Exp PMPM:** $97
Principal Investments: Cash and equiv (14%), other (86%)
Provider Compensation ($000): Contr fee ($812,063), capitation ($117,110), FFS ($44,362)
Total Member Encounters: Phys (3,440,717)
Group Affiliation: Aetna Inc
Licensed in: PA
Address: 980 Jolly Rd, Blue Bell, PA 19422
Phone: (800) 872-3862   **Dom State:** PA   **Commenced Bus:** September 1981

Data Date	Weiss Safety Rating	RACR #1	RACR #2	Total Assets ($mil)	Capital ($mil)	Net Premium ($mil)	Net Income ($mil)
3-03	B-	3.93	3.28	344.3	198.3	242.5	14.4
3-02	B-	1.94	1.61	452.1	204.3	297.4	15.3
2002	B-	4.03	3.36	365.8	203.3	1,077.2	68.4
2001	B-	1.91	1.60	501.3	195.5	1,949.8	-15.5
2000	B	1.24	1.01	487.0	132.7	2,029.3	0.8
1999	C+	1.06	0.87	444.0	102.3	1,929.8	6.1
1998	C+	1.10	0.94	419.0	87.8	1,859.3	22.0

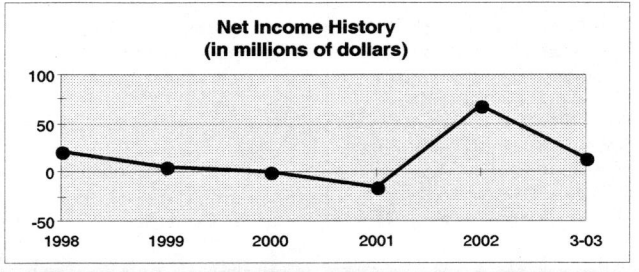

Net Income History (in millions of dollars)

AETNA HEALTH INC (A TENNESSEE CORP) — C Fair

Major Rating Factors: Fair overall results on stability tests (4.4 on a scale of 0 to 10) based on fair risk-adjusted capital in prior years, rapid premium growth over the last five years and rapid enrollment growth during the past five years. Rating is significantly influenced by the fair financial results of Aetna Inc. Weak profitability index (0.9) with operating losses during 1998, 1999, 2000 and 2001. Average return on equity has been poor at -56%. Strong capitalization (10.0) based on excellent current risk-adjusted capital (severe loss scenario) reflecting significant improvement over results in 2001.
Other Rating Factors: High quality investment portfolio (9.9) containing no exposure to mortgages, junk bonds, or unaffiliated stocks. Excellent liquidity (7.4) with ample operational cash flow and liquid investments.
Principal Business: Comp med (72%), FEHB (28%)
Mem Phys: 02: 665   **01:** 523   **02 MLR** 82% / **02 Admin Exp** 14%
Enroll(000): Q1 03: 33   **02:** 34   **01:** 23   **Med Exp PMPM:** $211
Principal Investments: Cash and equiv (85%), other (15%)
Provider Compensation ($000): Contr fee ($51,396), FFS ($11,481), capitation ($1,551)
Total Member Encounters: Phys (433,751)
Group Affiliation: Aetna Inc
Licensed in: TN
Address: 1801 West End Ave Suite 500, Nashville, TN 37207
Phone: (615) 322-1600   **Dom State:** TN   **Commenced Bus:** March 1988

Data Date	Weiss Safety Rating	RACR #1	RACR #2	Total Assets ($mil)	Capital ($mil)	Net Premium ($mil)	Net Income ($mil)
3-03	C	6.61	5.51	44.0	31.8	21.8	3.2
3-02	C	0.86	0.73	22.7	6.9	23.5	1.8
2002	C	1.79	1.49	48.1	8.2	86.3	2.0
2001	C	0.87	0.74	11.4	2.4	43.5	-3.1
2000	C	1.62	1.37	18.7	7.0	53.1	-5.6
1999	C	0.89	0.75	7.9	2.0	22.9	-3.0
1998	C+	2.93	2.49	8.1	3.5	17.0	-0.4

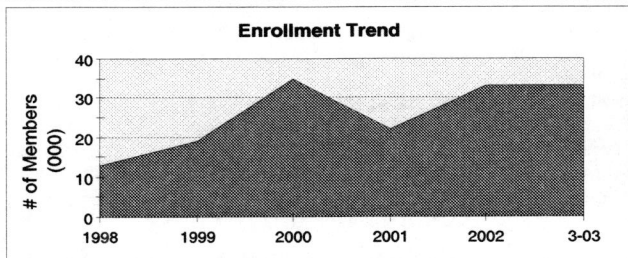

Enrollment Trend

AETNA HEALTH INC (A TEXAS CORP) — C- Fair

Major Rating Factors: Fair liquidity (4.8 on a scale of 0 to 10) as cash resources may not be adequate to cover a spike in claims. Weak profitability index (0.9) with operating losses during 1999, 2000 and 2001. Average return on equity has been poor at -39%. Good overall results on stability tests (5.1) despite a decline in enrollment during 2002, rapid premium growth over the last five years and excessive capital growth during 2002. Rating is significantly influenced by the fair financial results of Aetna Inc.
Other Rating Factors: Strong capitalization (7.2) based on excellent current risk-adjusted capital (severe loss scenario) reflecting significant improvement over results in 2000. High quality investment portfolio (9.9) containing little or no exposure to mortgages, junk bonds, or unaffiliated stocks.
Principal Business: Comp med (100%)
Mem Phys: 02: 21,423   **01:** 18,386   **02 MLR** 89% / **02 Admin Exp** 13%
Enroll(000): Q1 03: 355   **02:** 470   **01:** 848   **Med Exp PMPM:** $145
Principal Investments: Cash and equiv (14%), other (86%)
Provider Compensation ($000): Contr fee ($1,031,688), FFS ($143,416), capitation ($57,019)
Total Member Encounters: Phys (6,609,458)
Group Affiliation: Aetna Inc
Licensed in: TX
Address: 2777 Stemmons Freeway, Ste 400, Dallas, TX 75207
Phone: (713) 350-2844   **Dom State:** TX   **Commenced Bus:** November 1987

Data Date	Weiss Safety Rating	RACR #1	RACR #2	Total Assets ($mil)	Capital ($mil)	Net Premium ($mil)	Net Income ($mil)
3-03	C-	1.52	1.27	262.2	111.6	248.4	34.0
3-02	C-	0.77	0.64	185.7	36.8	202.8	6.4
2002	C-	1.17	0.97	291.1	84.6	1,292.9	15.7
2001	C-	0.78	0.65	346.3	67.1	1,612.6	-53.9
2000	C	0.57	0.48	140.1	18.1	757.8	-17.1
1999	C	0.77	0.66	81.8	18.4	401.4	-2.5
1998	C+	1.37	1.16	72.6	19.1	318.2	2.5

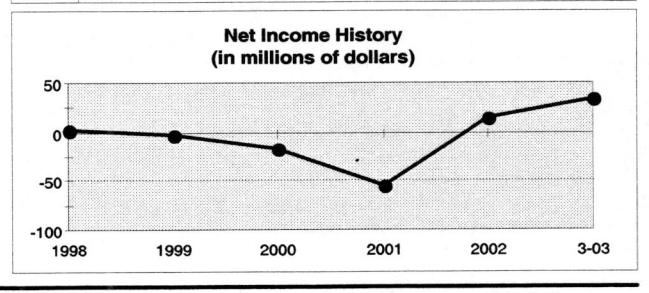

Net Income History (in millions of dollars)

www.WeissRatings.com   * Denotes a Weiss Recommended Company

II. Analysis of Largest Companies

Winter 2003 - 04

AETNA HEALTH INC (A WASHINGTON CORP) — C- Fair

Major Rating Factors: Fair overall results on stability tests (4.5 on a scale of 0 to 10) based on a significant 36% decrease in enrollment during the period, an inordinate decline in premium revenue in 2002. Rating is significantly influenced by the fair financial results of Aetna Inc. Weak profitability index (0.9) with $17.2 million in losses in the last two years. Average return on equity has been poor at -5%. Good liquidity (7.0) with sufficient resources (cash flows and marketable investments) to handle a spike in claims.

Other Rating Factors: Strong overall capitalization (10.0) based on excellent current risk-adjusted capital (severe loss scenario) despite some fluctuation in capital levels. High quality investment portfolio (9.9) containing no exposure to mortgages, junk bonds, or unaffiliated stocks.

Principal Business: Comp med (89%), FEHB (11%)
Mem Phys: 02: 9,376 **01:** 7,466 **02 MLR** 104% / **02 Admin Exp** 11%
Enroll(000): Q1 03: 21 **02:** 41 **01:** 64 **Med Exp PMPM:** $142
Principal Investments: Cash and equiv (84%), other (16%)
Provider Compensation ($000): Contr fee ($78,581), FFS ($10,332), capitation ($3,263)
Total Member Encounters: Phys (546,831)
Group Affiliation: Aetna Inc
Licensed in: WA
Address: 601 Union Square Suite 800, Seattle, WA 98101
Phone: (800) 872-3862 **Dom State:** WA **Commenced Bus:** December 1985

Data Date	Weiss Safety Rating	RACR #1	RACR #2	Total Assets ($mil)	Capital ($mil)	Net Premium ($mil)	Net Income ($mil)
3-03	C-	4.06	3.39	45.6	26.5	12.6	3.4
3-02	C+	2.40	2.02	43.3	19.7	27.8	-0.4
2002	C-	3.58	2.99	51.4	23.2	85.7	-10.5
2001	C+	2.41	2.03	40.6	15.3	105.8	-6.8
2000	B-	4.73	4.09	37.9	26.5	127.8	0.2
1999	C+	3.31	2.93	28.5	13.6	93.6	-1.2
1998	C+	6.23	5.43	26.1	16.0	62.3	6.1

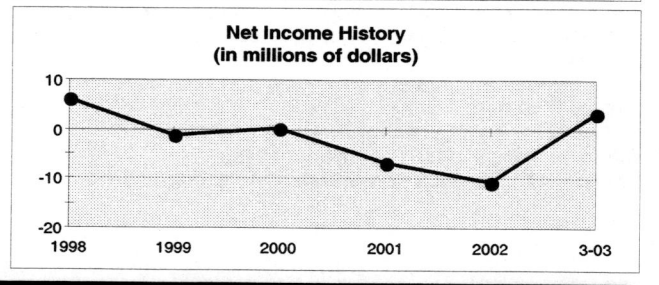

Net Income History (in millions of dollars)

AETNA HEALTH INC (AN ARIZONA CORP) — C+ Fair

Major Rating Factors: Good quality investment portfolio (6.7 on a scale of 0 to 10) containing small junk bond exposure. Good overall results on stability tests (5.3) despite rapid premium growth over the last five years, a decline in enrollment during 2002. Rating is significantly influenced by the fair financial results of Aetna Inc. Good liquidity (6.8) with sufficient resources (cash flows and marketable investments) to handle a spike in claims.

Other Rating Factors: Weak profitability index (2.0) with operating losses during 1999, 2000 and 2001. Strong overall capitalization (7.7) based on excellent current risk-adjusted capital (severe loss scenario) despite some fluctuation in capital levels.

Principal Business: Comp med (88%), FEHB (10%), dental (2%)
Mem Phys: 02: 7,534 **01:** 7,359 **02 MLR** 84% / **02 Admin Exp** 14%
Enroll(000): Q1 03: 210 **02:** 229 **01:** 243 **Med Exp PMPM:** $115
Principal Investments: Cash and equiv (50%), other (50%)
Provider Compensation ($000): Contr fee ($253,488), FFS ($45,540), capitation ($35,372)
Total Member Encounters: Phys (1,588,614)
Group Affiliation: Aetna Inc
Licensed in: AZ, NV
Address: 7720 N 16th St Ste 400, Phoenix, AZ 85020
Phone: (602) 427-2200 **Dom State:** AZ **Commenced Bus:** March 1994

Data Date	Weiss Safety Rating	RACR #1	RACR #2	Total Assets ($mil)	Capital ($mil)	Net Premium ($mil)	Net Income ($mil)
3-03	C+	1.94	1.62	98.6	36.2	89.6	7.2
3-02	C	1.30	1.09	119.6	38.3	101.2	14.4
2002	C+	1.53	1.28	99.5	27.8	390.7	10.8
2001	C	1.36	1.13	111.9	29.3	438.2	-10.5
2000	C	1.40	1.18	104.0	26.1	342.3	-15.3
1999	C+	1.37	1.16	44.2	11.8	169.1	-0.9
1998	C+	2.56	2.19	24.6	11.3	93.9	6.3

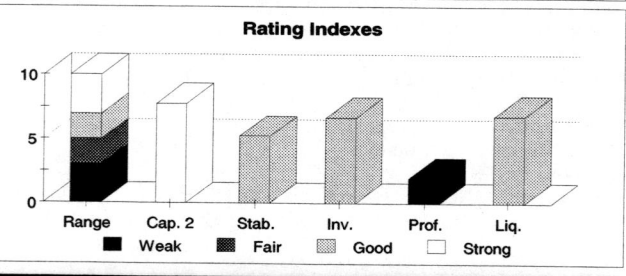

Rating Indexes: Range, Cap., Stab., Inv., Prof., Liq. — Weak / Fair / Good / Strong

AETNA HEALTH INC (AN OHIO CORP) — C Fair

Major Rating Factors: Fair overall results on stability tests (4.6 on a scale of 0 to 10) based on a significant 50% decrease in enrollment during the period, fair risk-adjusted capital in prior years. Rating is significantly influenced by the fair financial results of Aetna Inc. Weak profitability index (1.9) with operating losses during 1998, 1999, 2000 and 2001. Average return on equity has been poor at -40%. Good liquidity (6.9) with sufficient resources (cash flows and marketable investments) to handle a spike in claims.

Other Rating Factors: Strong capitalization (9.3) based on excellent current risk-adjusted capital (severe loss scenario) reflecting significant improvement over results in 1999. High quality investment portfolio (9.6) containing no exposure to mortgages, junk bonds, or unaffiliated stocks.

Principal Business: Comp med (92%), FEHB (8%)
Mem Phys: 02: 18,314 **01:** 18,344 **02 MLR** 83% / **02 Admin Exp** 12%
Enroll(000): Q1 03: 107 **02:** 149 **01:** 299 **Med Exp PMPM:** $147
Principal Investments: Cash and equiv (39%), other (61%)
Provider Compensation ($000): Contr fee ($382,447), FFS ($31,872), capitation ($17,481)
Total Member Encounters: Phys (2,296,639)
Group Affiliation: Aetna Inc
Licensed in: IN, KY, OH
Address: 4059 Kinross Lake Pkwy, Richfield, OH 44286
Phone: (330) 659-8000 **Dom State:** OH **Commenced Bus:** December 1983

Data Date	Weiss Safety Rating	RACR #1	RACR #2	Total Assets ($mil)	Capital ($mil)	Net Premium ($mil)	Net Income ($mil)
3-03	C	3.22	2.68	135.9	77.6	75.5	8.7
3-02	C	2.23	1.79	165.6	64.7	141.8	3.0
2002	C	2.91	2.42	148.8	69.5	472.7	22.9
2001	C	2.17	1.75	186.2	69.7	609.7	-19.1
2000	C	1.39	1.17	167.1	53.9	656.4	-33.4
1999	C	0.72	0.60	139.5	19.5	514.1	-21.6
1998	C	1.39	1.17	103.8	23.0	339.1	-1.5

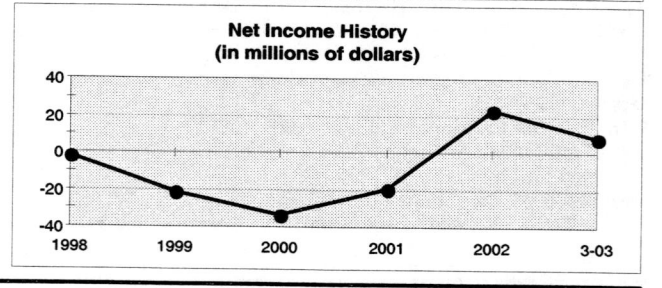

Net Income History (in millions of dollars)

Winter 2003 - 04   **II. Analysis of Largest Companies**

AETNA HEALTH INC (AN OKLAHOMA CORP)   D+   Weak

Major Rating Factors: Weak profitability index (0.9 on a scale of 0 to 10) with $12.6 million in losses in the last three years. Average return on equity has been poor at -57%. Fair overall results on stability tests (4.1) based on excessive capital growth during 2002, rapid premium growth over the last five years and an excessive 42% enrollment growth during the period. Rating is significantly influenced by the fair financial results of Aetna Inc. Good liquidity (6.8) with sufficient resources (cash flows and marketable investments) to handle a spike in claims.
Other Rating Factors: Strong capitalization (7.2) based on excellent current risk-adjusted capital (severe loss scenario) reflecting significant improvement over results in 2001. High quality investment portfolio (9.9) containing no exposure to mortgages, junk bonds, or unaffiliated stocks.
Principal Business: Comp med (100%)
Mem Phys: 02: 3,542 **01:** 3,097 **02 MLR** 89% **/ 02 Admin Exp** 15%
Enroll(000): Q1 03: 59 **02:** 72 **01:** 51 **Med Exp PMPM:** $184
Principal Investments: Cash and equiv (98%), other (2%)
Provider Compensation ($000): Contr fee ($107,277), capitation ($14,660), FFS ($8,451)
Total Member Encounters: Phys (688,420)
Group Affiliation: Aetna Inc
Licensed in: OK
Address: 7912 E 31st Ct Ste 300, Tulsa, OK 74145
Phone: (800) 872-3862 **Dom State:** OK **Commenced Bus:** April 1998

Data Date	Weiss Safety Rating	RACR #1	RACR #2	Total Assets ($mil)	Capital ($mil)	Net Premium ($mil)	Net Income ($mil)
3-03	D+	1.48	1.23	30.9	13.3	35.6	0.7
3-02	D	0.60	0.51	19.6	-3.1	36.0	-5.1
2002	D+	1.50	1.25	34.5	13.5	151.0	-4.6
2001	C-	0.60	0.51	17.8	2.8	66.1	-6.6
2000	C+	1.63	1.38	7.6	3.7	17.9	-1.4
1999	B-	6.11	5.12	6.9	5.5	4.2	0.1
1998	C+	163.40	140.00	5.7	5.5	0.4	0.2

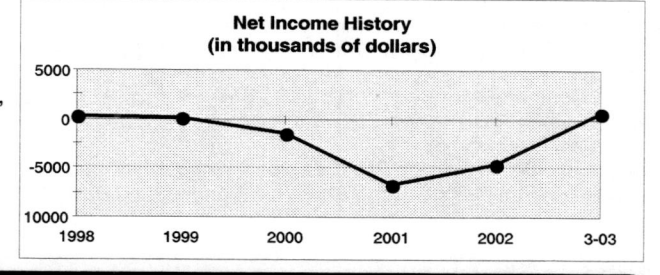

Net Income History (in thousands of dollars)

AETNA HEALTH INS CO OF NY   C+   Fair

Major Rating Factors: Good quality investment portfolio (5.5 on a scale of 0 to 10) containing small junk bond exposure. Excellent profitability (7.0). Strong capitalization (10.0) based on excellent current risk-adjusted capital (severe loss scenario) despite some fluctuation in capital levels.
Other Rating Factors: Excellent liquidity (7.6) with ample operational cash flow and liquid investments.
Principal Business: Comp med (100%)
Mem Phys: 02: 24,345 **01:** 22,279 **02 MLR** 85% **/ 02 Admin Exp** 27%
Enroll(000): Q1 03: 124 **02:** 130 **01:** 290 **Med Exp PMPM:** $9
Principal Investments: Cash and equiv (56%), other (44%)
Provider Compensation ($000): FFS ($34,348), contr fee ($3,521)
Total Member Encounters: N/A
Group Affiliation: Aetna Inc
Licensed in: NY
Address: 333 Earle Ovington Blvd, Uniondale, NY 11553
Phone: (516) 794-6565 **Dom State:** NY **Commenced Bus:** August 1986

Data Date	Weiss Safety Rating	RACR #1	RACR #2	Total Assets ($mil)	Capital ($mil)	Net Premium ($mil)	Net Income ($mil)
3-03	C+	11.37	9.47	46.4	31.6	11.8	3.4
3-02	N/A	N/A	N/A	N/A	N/A	N/A	N/A
2002	C+	10.18	8.48	58.0	27.9	28.4	0.4
2001	N/A	N/A	N/A	86.9	57.6	62.0	N/A
2000	U	3.52	2.63	79.5	53.9	78.9	11.6
1999	B-	4.10	3.10	175.0	127.3	254.2	118.1
1998	B-	3.79	3.04	102.9	84.8	171.9	73.6

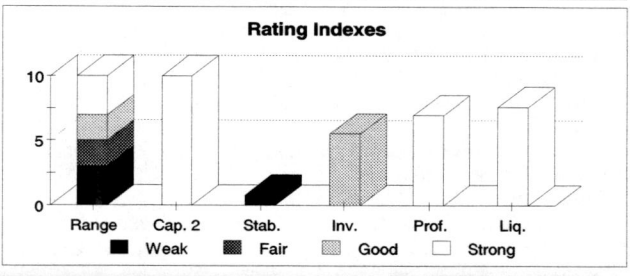

Rating Indexes (Range, Cap. 2, Stab., Inv., Prof., Liq.) — Weak, Fair, Good, Strong

AETNA HEALTH OF CALIFORNIA INC   C   Fair

Major Rating Factors: Fair overall results on stability tests (4.8 on a scale of 0 to 10). Rating is significantly influenced by the fair financial results of Aetna Inc. Weak profitability index (2.6) with operating losses during 2000 and 2001. Return on equity has been fair, averaging 5% over the last five years. Strong capitalization (7.3) based on excellent current risk-adjusted capital (severe loss scenario) reflecting significant improvement over results in 2000.
Other Rating Factors: Excellent liquidity (7.1) with ample operational cash flow and liquid investments.
Principal Business: Managed care (59%)
Mem Phys: 02: N/A **01:** N/A **02 MLR** 87% **/ 02 Admin Exp** 10%
Enroll(000): Q1 03: 400 **02:** 523 **01:** 839 **Med Exp PMPM:** $152
Principal Investments ($000): Cash and equiv ($330,126), bonds ($72,136), other ($7,987)
Provider Compensation ($000): None
Total Member Encounters: N/A
Group Affiliation: Aetna Inc
Licensed in: CA
Address: 2409 Camino Ramon, San Ramon, CA 94583
Phone: (925) 543-9000 **Dom State:** CA **Commenced Bus:** October 1981

Data Date	Weiss Safety Rating	RACR #1	RACR #2	Total Assets ($mil)	Capital ($mil)	Net Premium ($mil)	Net Income ($mil)
3-03	C	2.11	1.30	373.4	116.5	261.2	21.1
3-02	C	0.00	0.00	466.0	109.4	388.3	-11.9
2002	C	2.25	1.38	390.9	125.5	1,423.4	50.3
2001	C	1.01	0.61	423.7	73.0	1,673.0	-51.5
2000	C+	0.93	0.57	314.6	50.4	1,343.9	-3.0
1999	C+	1.22	0.75	239.5	50.6	1,106.5	5.1
1998	C+	1.41	0.87	239.6	48.4	1,018.5	21.0

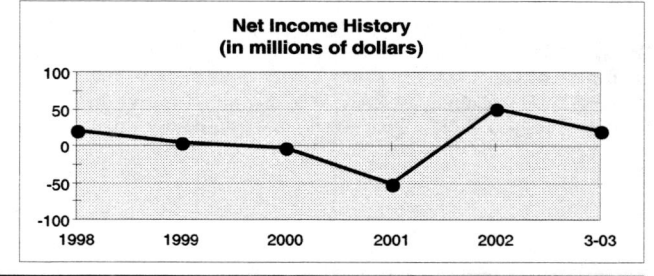

Net Income History (in millions of dollars)

II. Analysis of Largest Companies

AETNA HEALTH OF ILLINOIS INC — C Fair

Major Rating Factors: Fair overall results on stability tests (4.1 on a scale of 0 to 10) based on a significant 54% decrease in enrollment during the period. Rating is significantly influenced by the fair financial results of Aetna Inc. Weak profitability index (2.7) with operating losses during 2000 and 2001. Return on equity has been low, averaging 1%. Good liquidity (6.8) with sufficient resources (cash flows and marketable investments) to handle a spike in claims.
Other Rating Factors: Strong overall capitalization (10.0) based on excellent current risk-adjusted capital (severe loss scenario) despite some fluctuation in capital levels. High quality investment portfolio (9.0) containing little or no exposure to mortgages, junk bonds, or unaffiliated stocks.
Principal Business: Comp med (100%)
Mem Phys: 02: 10,252   01: 10,861   **02 MLR** 83% / **02 Admin Exp** 15%
Enroll(000): Q1 03: 44   02: 55   01: 119   **Med Exp PMPM:** $114
Principal Investments: Cash and equiv (14%), other (86%)
Provider Compensation ($000): Contr fee ($109,252), FFS ($19,088), capitation ($9,394)
Total Member Encounters: Phys (471,255)
Group Affiliation: Aetna Inc
Licensed in: IL, IN
Address: 100 N Riverside Plaza, FL 20, Chicago, IL 60606-1518
Phone: (312) 928-3000   **Dom State:** IL   **Commenced Bus:** September 1982

Data Date	Weiss Safety Rating	RACR #1	RACR #2	Total Assets ($mil)	Capital ($mil)	Net Premium ($mil)	Net Income ($mil)
3-03	C	5.18	4.31	126.6	42.0	27.5	6.1
3-02	C	2.31	1.64	107.0	32.5	41.8	2.3
2002	C	4.44	3.70	85.2	35.4	143.4	6.3
2001	C	2.31	1.64	103.8	32.3	238.0	-5.0
2000	C	1.62	1.33	95.2	23.1	275.0	-4.5
1999	C+	1.46	1.21	77.5	14.9	221.3	3.7
1998	C	2.17	1.86	69.5	16.2	173.2	0.8

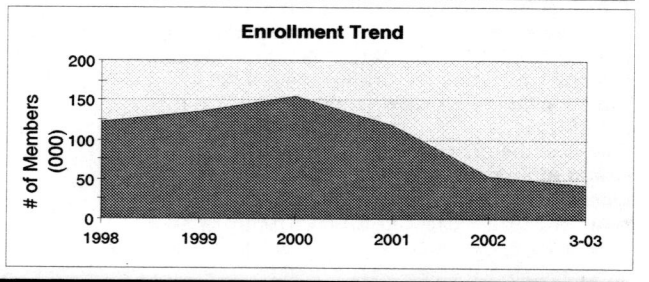

AETNA HEALTH OF THE CAROLINAS INC — C- Fair

Major Rating Factors: Fair overall results on stability tests (3.8 on a scale of 0 to 10) based on a significant 60% decrease in enrollment during the period, a steep decline in premium revenue in 2002 and weak risk-adjusted capital in prior years. Rating is significantly influenced by the fair financial results of Aetna Inc. Weak profitability index (0.7) with $40.5 million in losses in the last five years. Average return on equity over the last five years has been poor at -83%. Good liquidity (6.7) with sufficient resources (cash flows and marketable investments) to handle a spike in claims.
Other Rating Factors: Strong capitalization (8.9) based on excellent current risk-adjusted capital (severe loss scenario) reflecting significant improvement over results in 2000. High quality investment portfolio (9.9) containing no exposure to mortgages, junk bonds, or unaffiliated stocks.
Principal Business: Comp med (100%)
Mem Phys: 02: 1,703   01: 1,514   **02 MLR** 101% / **02 Admin Exp** 12%
Enroll(000): Q1 03: 18   02: 24   01: 59   **Med Exp PMPM:** $144
Principal Investments: Cash and equiv (77%), other (23%)
Provider Compensation ($000): Contr fee ($73,375), FFS ($9,485), capitation ($1,644)
Total Member Encounters: Phys (392,916)
Group Affiliation: Aetna Inc
Licensed in: NC, SC
Address: 128 S Tryon St Ste 2000, Charlotte, NC 28202
Phone: (800) 872-3862   **Dom State:** NC   **Commenced Bus:** September 1995

Data Date	Weiss Safety Rating	RACR #1	RACR #2	Total Assets ($mil)	Capital ($mil)	Net Premium ($mil)	Net Income ($mil)
3-03	C-	2.84	2.37	27.3	16.3	13.3	2.2
3-02	C	2.04	1.72	42.6	19.8	20.8	3.6
2002	C-	2.46	2.05	27.8	14.0	70.8	-3.9
2001	C	2.02	1.71	45.5	17.4	122.3	-9.0
2000	C	0.57	0.49	38.8	5.5	117.2	-16.6
1999	C	1.90	1.62	29.2	11.6	81.3	-7.7
1998	C	3.36	2.88	16.9	10.6	39.8	-3.4

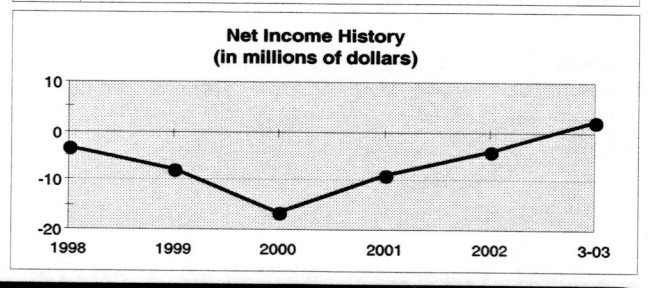

AETNA HEALTH OF WASHINGTON INC — C+ Fair

Major Rating Factors: Fair profitability index (5.0 on a scale of 0 to 10) due to a decline in earnings during 2002. Strong capitalization (10.0) based on excellent current risk-adjusted capital (severe loss scenario) reflecting significant improvement over results in 2000. High quality investment portfolio (9.9) containing no exposure to mortgages, junk bonds, or unaffiliated stocks.
Other Rating Factors: Excellent liquidity (7.4) with ample operational cash flow and liquid investments.
Principal Business: Comp med (51%), Medicaid (49%)
Mem Phys: 02: 9,376   01: 7,466   **02 MLR** 86% / **02 Admin Exp** 12%
Enroll(000): Q1 03: 2   02: 3   01: 20   **Med Exp PMPM:** $159
Principal Investments: Cash and equiv (88%), other (12%)
Provider Compensation ($000): FFS ($9,903), contr fee ($8,024), capitation ($4,190)
Total Member Encounters: Phys (92,461)
Group Affiliation: Aetna Inc
Licensed in: WA
Address: 600 University St Suite 1400, Seattle, WA 98101
Phone: (206) 447-0757   **Dom State:** WA   **Commenced Bus:** January 1995

Data Date	Weiss Safety Rating	RACR #1	RACR #2	Total Assets ($mil)	Capital ($mil)	Net Premium ($mil)	Net Income ($mil)
3-03	C+	5.55	4.62	16.8	11.3	1.5	1.8
3-02	C+	8.57	7.31	29.2	22.0	6.3	1.1
2002	C+	5.10	4.25	19.8	10.2	25.6	2.0
2001	C+	8.63	7.35	29.9	21.9	34.2	4.4
2000	C+	0.80	0.72	23.0	3.2	6.0	0.2
1999	C	2.24	1.89	31.6	6.4	9.6	0.6
1998	C	1.35	1.21	36.7	6.0	12.5	-1.5

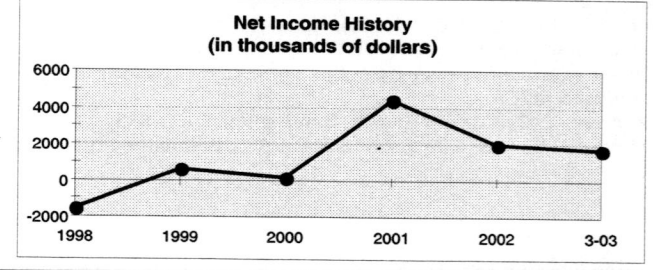

Winter 2003 - 04   II. Analysis of Largest Companies

AETNA INS CO OF CT   C   Fair

Major Rating Factors: Fair overall results on stability tests (3.7 on a scale of 0 to 10) including weak results on operational trends. Weak profitability index (2.7). Excellent expense controls. Return on equity has been fair, averaging 40.1% over the past five years.
Other Rating Factors: History of adequate reserve strength (6.0) as reserves have been consistently at an acceptable level. Good liquidity (6.5) with sufficient resources (cash flows and marketable investments) to handle a spike in claims. Strong long-term capitalization index (7.4) based on excellent current risk adjusted capital (severe and moderate loss scenarios), despite some fluctuation in capital levels.
Principal Business: Other liability (66%) and group accident & health (34%).
Principal Investments: Investment grade bonds (72%) and misc. investments (28%).
Investments in Affiliates: None
Group Affiliation: Aetna Inc
Licensed in: All states except HI, MO, NH, PR
Commenced Business: January 1990
Address: 151 Farmington Ave, Hartford, CT 06156
Phone: (203) 636-1612   **Domicile State:** CT   **NAIC Code:** 36153

Data Date	Weiss Safety Rating	RACR #1	RACR #2	Loss Ratio %	Total Assets ($mil)	Capital ($mil)	Net Premium ($mil)	Net Income ($mil)
6-03	C	2.17	1.27	N/A	47.9	28.0	51.5	2.4
6-02	C	2.60	1.52	N/A	52.7	36.5	50.4	4.1
2002	C	2.13	1.23	70.8	37.9	26.3	80.0	10.0
2001	C	2.32	1.36	66.5	50.0	32.6	79.8	14.5
2000	C+	6.45	3.36	62.5	47.1	38.1	67.2	13.5
1999	C+	6.71	3.52	52.5	47.5	38.4	62.9	18.9
1998	C+	11.29	5.84	44.1	60.6	51.0	54.4	22.7

Aetna Inc Composite Group Rating: C+ Largest Group Members	Assets ($mil)	Weiss Safety Rating
AETNA LIFE INS CO	25351	C+
AETNA HEALTH LIFE INS CO	1217	C
AETNA HEALTH INC (A NEW YORK CORP)	770	B-
AETNA HEALTH INC (A NEW JERSEY CORP)	479	B-
AETNA HEALTH OF CALIFORNIA INC	391	C

AETNA LIFE INSURANCE COMPANY   C+   Fair

Major Rating Factors: Fair overall results on stability tests (4.1 on a scale of 0 to 10). Good quality investment portfolio (6.0) despite mixed results such as: large holdings of BBB rated bonds but moderate junk bond exposure. Good overall profitability (6.1). Return on equity has been good over the last five years, averaging 13.2%.
Other Rating Factors: Strong capitalization (7.5) based on excellent risk adjusted capital (severe loss scenario). Excellent liquidity (7.1).
Principal Business: Group health insurance (68%), group life insurance (22%), group retirement contracts (5%), reinsurance (4%), and individual life insurance (1%).
Principal Investments: NonCMO investment grade bonds (54%), CMOs and structured securities (15%), mortgages in good standing (12%), noninv. grade bonds (5%), and misc. investments (15%).
Investments in Affiliates: 2%
Group Affiliation: Aetna Inc
Licensed in: All states, the District of Columbia and Puerto Rico
Commenced Business: December 1850
Address: 151 Farmington Ave, Hartford, CT 06156
Phone: (860) 273-0123   **Domicile State:** CT   **NAIC Code:** 60054

Data Date	Weiss Safety Rating	RACR #1	RACR #2	Total Assets ($mil)	Capital ($mil)	Net Premium ($mil)	Net Income ($mil)
6-03	C+	2.15	1.32	25,565.8	1,798.0	2,123.7	93.0
6-02	C+	1.70	1.10	25,821.9	1,627.7	2,147.5	16.3
2002	C+	1.87	1.19	25,351.2	1,669.3	4,260.8	84.5
2001	C+	1.71	1.11	26,728.1	1,710.8	4,965.3	126.4
2000	C+	1.86	1.16	30,515.5	1,966.8	6,238.6	437.2
1999	C+	1.80	1.10	32,609.2	1,862.7	5,443.9	388.9
1998	C+	1.69	1.12	34,686.4	1,697.0	4,745.8	269.5

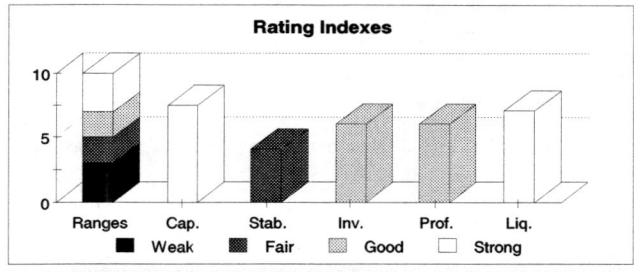

Rating Indexes (bar chart: Ranges, Cap., Stab., Inv., Prof., Liq.; legend: Weak, Fair, Good, Strong)

AETNA US HEALTHCARE INC (A MA CORP)   C-   Fair

Major Rating Factors: Fair capitalization (4.3 on a scale of 0 to 10) based on fair current risk-adjusted capital (moderate loss scenario) as results have slipped from the good range over the last year. Fair overall results on stability tests (4.2) based on weak risk-adjusted capital in prior years. Rating is significantly influenced by the fair financial results of Aetna Inc. Weak profitability index (0.8) with $26.2 million in losses in the last two years. Average return on equity has been extremely poor.
Other Rating Factors: Weak liquidity (0.3) as a spike in claims may stretch capacity. High quality investment portfolio (9.9) containing no exposure to mortgages, junk bonds, or unaffiliated stocks.
Principal Business: Comp med (93%), FEHB (7%).
Mem Phys: 01: 13,624 **00:** 11,869 **01 MLR** 99% **/ 01 Admin Exp** 13%
Enroll(000): Q2 02: 47 **01:** 81 **00:** 84 **Med Exp PMPM:** $177
Principal Investments: Cash and equiv (47%), other (53%).
Provider Compensation ($000): Contr fee ($147,127), capitation ($15,919), FFS ($9,884).
Total Member Encounters: N/A
Group Affiliation: Aetna Inc
Licensed in: MA, RI
Address: 400-1 Totten Pond Rd, Waltham, MA 02451
Phone: (800) 872-3862   **Dom State:** MA   **Commenced Bus:** January 1988

Data Date	Weiss Safety Rating	RACR #1	RACR #2	Total Assets ($mil)	Capital ($mil)	Net Premium ($mil)	Net Income ($mil)
6-02	C-	0.84	0.69	47.8	16.3	70.7	7.2
6-01	C	0.44	0.37	49.7	4.1	84.3	-21.7
2001	C-	0.82	0.67	48.2	9.2	176.7	-21.9
2000	C+	1.26	1.06	38.4	11.0	137.5	-4.3
1999	C+	0.52	0.44	25.6	3.5	107.5	0.7
1998	C+	1.13	0.95	61.4	14.8	203.5	-17.1
1997	N/A	N/A	N/A	55.1	1.8	193.8	N/A

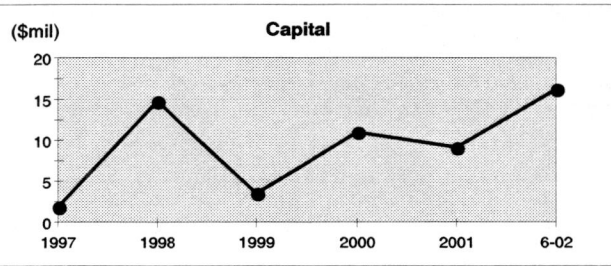

Capital ($mil) — line chart from 1997 to 6-02.

www.WeissRatings.com   85   * Denotes a Weiss Recommended Company

II. Analysis of Largest Companies

Winter 2003 - 04

AIG LIFE INSURANCE COMPANY — C+ Fair

Major Rating Factors: Fair overall results on stability tests (3.8 on a scale of 0 to 10) including fair risk adjusted capital in prior years. Good capitalization (5.6) based on good risk adjusted capital (moderate loss scenario). Good overall profitability (5.3). Return on equity has been fair, averaging 5.6%.
Other Rating Factors: Good liquidity (6.8). Low quality investment portfolio (2.8).
Principal Business: Individual annuities (37%), group health insurance (23%), group retirement contracts (17%), individual life insurance (14%), and other lines (8%).
Principal Investments: NonCMO investment grade bonds (72%), CMOs and structured securities (11%), noninv. grade bonds (9%), mortgages in good standing (4%), and policy loans (3%).
Investments in Affiliates: None
Group Affiliation: American International Group
Licensed in: All states except NY
Commenced Business: September 1962
Address: One ALICO Plaza, Wilmington, DE 19801
Phone: (302) 594-2000 **Domicile State:** DE **NAIC Code:** 66842

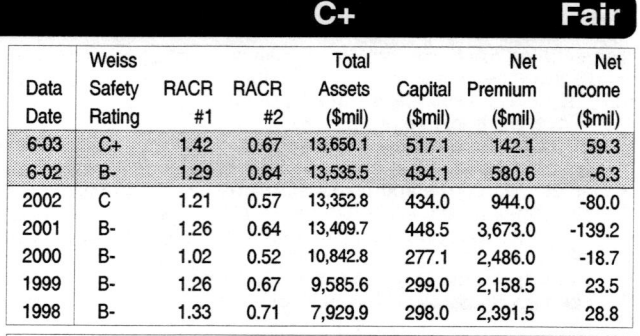

Data Date	Weiss Safety Rating	RACR #1	RACR #2	Total Assets ($mil)	Capital ($mil)	Net Premium ($mil)	Net Income ($mil)
6-03	C+	1.42	0.67	13,650.1	517.1	142.1	59.3
6-02	B-	1.29	0.64	13,535.5	434.1	580.6	-6.3
2002	C	1.21	0.57	13,352.8	434.0	944.0	-80.0
2001	B-	1.26	0.64	13,409.7	448.5	3,673.0	-139.2
2000	B-	1.02	0.52	10,842.8	277.1	2,486.0	-18.7
1999	B-	1.26	0.67	9,585.6	299.0	2,158.5	23.5
1998	B-	1.33	0.71	7,929.9	298.0	2,391.5	28.8

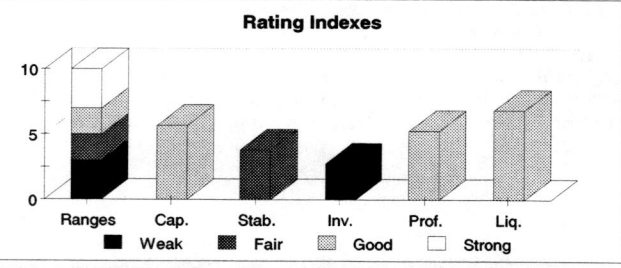

Rating Indexes chart: Ranges, Cap., Stab., Inv., Prof., Liq. — Weak / Fair / Good / Strong

AIU INS CO — B Good

Major Rating Factors: Good liquidity (6.8 on a scale of 0 to 10) with sufficient resources (cash flows and marketable investments) to handle a spike in claims. Fair profitability index (3.8) with operating losses during 2002. Return on equity has been fair, averaging 9.7% over the past five years.
Other Rating Factors: Fair overall results on stability tests (4.7) including weak results on operational trends. Strong long-term capitalization index (7.8) based on excellent current risk adjusted capital (severe and moderate loss scenarios), despite some fluctuation in capital levels. Ample reserve history (8.8) that helps to protect the company against sharp claims increases.
Principal Business: Other accident & health (34%), auto liability (32%), auto physical damage (12%), fire (8%), other liability (8%), inland marine (3%), and other lines (4%).
Principal Investments: Investment grade bonds (76%), misc. investments (18%), and cash (6%).
Investments in Affiliates: 5%
Group Affiliation: American International Group
Licensed in: All states except HI, WY, PR
Commenced Business: April 1851
Address: 70 Pine St, New York, NY 10270
Phone: (212) 770-7000 **Domicile State:** NY **NAIC Code:** 19399

Data Date	Weiss Safety Rating	RACR #1	RACR #2	Loss Ratio %	Total Assets ($mil)	Capital ($mil)	Net Premium ($mil)	Net Income ($mil)
6-03	B	2.25	1.55	N/A	1,826.6	418.4	1,240.8	32.8
6-02	B	2.94	2.05	N/A	1,734.0	448.6	1,022.3	18.8
2002	B	2.11	1.47	74.1	1,753.0	380.3	531.1	-51.2
2001	B	3.08	2.20	66.6	1,587.3	425.7	423.9	38.3
2000	B	2.45	1.74	69.9	1,789.5	385.4	451.1	47.7
1999	B	2.62	1.79	67.9	1,985.3	504.9	439.4	78.6
1998	B	3.20	2.21	69.3	1,840.5	445.6	382.8	97.2

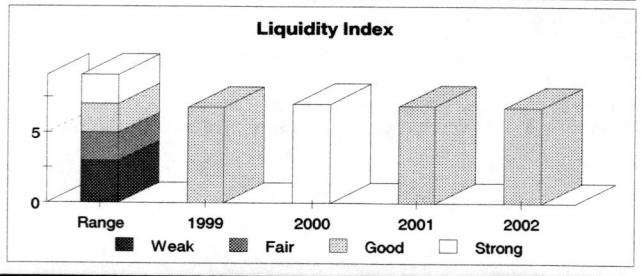

Liquidity Index chart: Range, 1999, 2000, 2001, 2002 — Weak / Fair / Good / Strong

ALAMEDA ALLIANCE FOR HEALTH — B Good

Major Rating Factors: Fair profitability index (4.6 on a scale of 0 to 10) with modest operating losses during 2001 and 2002. Fair overall results on stability tests (4.9). Strong overall capitalization (8.9) based on excellent current risk-adjusted capital (severe loss scenario) despite some fluctuation in capital levels.
Other Rating Factors: Excellent liquidity (7.3) with ample operational cash flow and liquid investments.
Principal Business: Managed care (5%)
Mem Phys: 02: N/A **01:** N/A **02 MLR** 95% **/ 02 Admin Exp** 8%
Enroll(000): Q1 03: 86 **02:** 85 **01:** 75 **Med Exp PMPM:** $110
Principal Investments ($000): Cash and equiv ($52,496), bonds ($40,187)
Provider Compensation ($000): None
Total Member Encounters: N/A
Group Affiliation: None
Licensed in: CA
Address: 1240 S Loop Rd, Alameda, CA 94502
Phone: (510) 895-4500 **Dom State:** CA **Commenced Bus:** January 1996

Data Date	Weiss Safety Rating	RACR #1	RACR #2	Total Assets ($mil)	Capital ($mil)	Net Premium ($mil)	Net Income ($mil)
3-03	B	3.86	2.37	67.3	46.5	31.2	1.4
3-02	B	0.00	0.00	66.1	46.9	25.5	1.6
2002	B	3.74	2.30	64.6	45.2	111.0	-0.2
2001	B	2.29	1.57	68.0	45.3	97.3	-4.9
2000	B	2.45	1.73	66.5	50.2	93.4	8.0
1999	C+	2.35	1.66	60.0	42.2	88.2	13.0
1998	C-	1.76	1.22	47.4	27.8	75.2	11.4

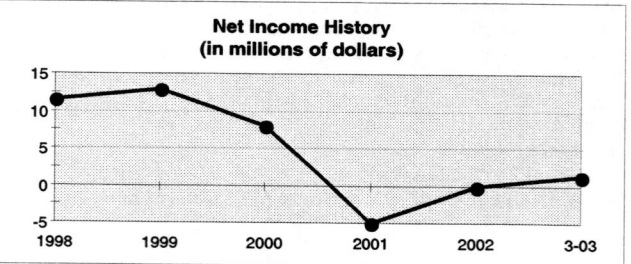

Net Income History (in millions of dollars) chart: 1998 through 3-03

86 www.WeissRatings.com

Winter 2003 - 04
II. Analysis of Largest Companies

ALLIANCE FOR COMMUNITY HEALTH LLC — C Fair

Major Rating Factors: Excellent profitability (9.8 on a scale of 0 to 10) despite a decline in earnings during 2002. Strong capitalization index (8.0) based on excellent current risk-adjusted capital (severe loss scenario). High quality investment portfolio (9.9) containing no exposure to mortgages, junk bonds, or unaffiliated stocks.
Other Rating Factors: Excellent overall results on stability tests (8.2) despite rapid enrollment growth during the past five years but consistent premium and capital growth in the last five years. Good financial strength from affiliates. Excellent liquidity (7.3) with ample operational cash flow and liquid investments.
Principal Business: Medicaid (100%)
Mem Phys: 02: 2,786 **01:** 2,548 **02 MLR** 80% **/ 02 Admin Exp** 12%
Enroll(000): Q1 03: 44 **02:** 35 **01:** 34 **Med Exp PMPM:** $102
Principal Investments: Cash and equiv (100%)
Provider Compensation ($000): Contr fee ($36,838), capitation ($7,486)
Total Member Encounters: Phys (111,975), non-phys (4,445)
Group Affiliation: Tenet Healthcare Corp
Licensed in: MO
Address: 5615 Pershing Suite 29, St Louis, MO 63112
Phone: (314) 454-0055 **Dom State:** MO **Commenced Bus:** August 1996

Data Date	Weiss Safety Rating	RACR #1	RACR #2	Total Assets ($mil)	Capital ($mil)	Net Premium ($mil)	Net Income ($mil)
3-03	C	2.17	1.80	22.8	11.3	17.2	0.5
3-02	D	0.00	0.00	21.1	8.4	13.0	0.4
2002	C	2.08	1.74	21.1	10.8	52.6	3.8
2001	D	0.00	0.00	18.9	7.9	45.0	4.3
2000	D	N/A	N/A	10.9	3.4	28.7	1.4
1999	D-	1.21	1.06	8.3	1.5	24.3	0.6
1998	E	0.18	0.16	9.5	0.9	24.7	0.2

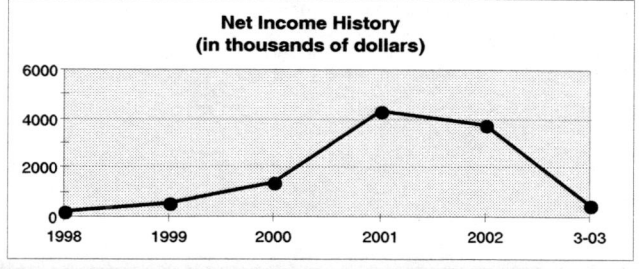

Net Income History (in thousands of dollars)

ALLIANT HEALTH PLANS INC — E+ Very Weak

Major Rating Factors: Weak profitability index (0.9 on a scale of 0 to 10) with operating losses during 1999, 2000, 2001 and 2002. Poor capitalization index (0.0) based on weak current risk-adjusted capital (severe loss scenario). Weak liquidity (0.0) as a spike in claims may stretch capacity.
Other Rating Factors: Fair overall results on stability tests (4.0) in spite of healthy premium and capital growth during 2002 but a significant 17% decrease in enrollment during the period. High quality investment portfolio (9.9) containing no exposure to mortgages, junk bonds, or unaffiliated stocks.
Principal Business: Comp med (100%)
Mem Phys: 02: 1,625 **01:** 1,641 **02 MLR** 91% **/ 02 Admin Exp** 15%
Enroll(000): Q1 03: 11 **02:** 11 **01:** 13 **Med Exp PMPM:** $208
Principal Investments: Cash and equiv (44%), other (56%)
Provider Compensation ($000): Contr fee ($30,908)
Total Member Encounters: Phys (5,938), non-phys (7,596)
Group Affiliation: Health One Alliance LLC
Licensed in: GA
Address: 401 S Wall St Ste 201, Calhoun, GA 30701
Phone: (706) 629-8848 **Dom State:** GA **Commenced Bus:** December 1998

Data Date	Weiss Safety Rating	RACR #1	RACR #2	Total Assets ($mil)	Capital ($mil)	Net Premium ($mil)	Net Income ($mil)
3-03	E+	0.25	0.21	5.6	1.4	8.2	0.1
3-02	E+	0.12	0.10	6.8	2.3	8.6	-0.3
2002	E+	0.23	0.19	7.0	1.3	32.7	-1.6
2001	E+	0.12	0.10	7.9	0.6	27.9	-5.2
2000	U	0.28	0.24	3.8	0.4	16.1	-1.6
1999	U	6.45	5.60	3.0	2.2	16.7	-0.5
1998	N/A	N/A	N/A	1.8	1.7	N/A	N/A

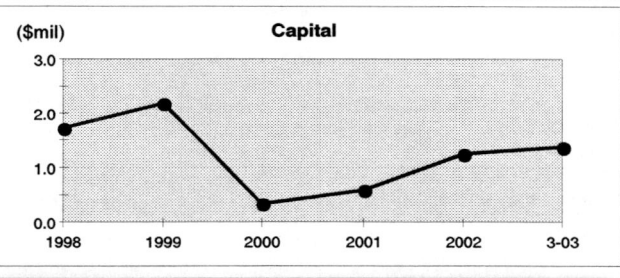

($mil) Capital

ALOHACARE * — B+ Good

Major Rating Factors: Good overall profitability index (6.8 on a scale of 0 to 10). Good overall results on stability tests (6.7) based on consistent premium and capital growth in the last five years but a decline in the number of member physicians during 2002. Strong capitalization (10.0) based on excellent current risk-adjusted capital (severe loss scenario) reflecting significant improvement over results in 1999.
Other Rating Factors: High quality investment portfolio (9.3) containing no exposure to mortgages, junk bonds, or unaffiliated stocks. Excellent liquidity (7.0) with ample operational cash flow and liquid investments.
Principal Business: Medicaid (100%)
Mem Phys: 02: 2,798 **01:** 3,158 **02 MLR** 83% **/ 02 Admin Exp** 10%
Enroll(000): Q1 03: 44 **02:** 43 **01:** 28 **Med Exp PMPM:** $130
Principal Investments: Cash and equiv (65%), other (35%)
Provider Compensation ($000): Contr fee ($44,309), capitation ($9,729)
Total Member Encounters: Phys (59,339), non-phys (14,027)
Group Affiliation: None
Licensed in: HI
Address: 1357 Kapiolani Blvd #1250, Honolulu, HI 96814
Phone: (808) 973-1650 **Dom State:** HI **Commenced Bus:** August 1994

Data Date	Weiss Safety Rating	RACR #1	RACR #2	Total Assets ($mil)	Capital ($mil)	Net Premium ($mil)	Net Income ($mil)
3-03	B+	6.34	5.28	33.5	14.3	21.3	1.7
3-02	B-	1.30	1.10	20.5	6.6	11.9	0.6
2002	B+	5.64	4.70	31.3	12.6	66.5	6.6
2001	B-	1.30	1.11	20.3	5.7	50.2	0.2
2000	C+	1.12	0.95	22.9	5.4	50.8	1.0
1999	C+	0.91	0.77	25.0	5.7	52.1	0.6
1998	N/A	N/A	N/A	23.0	5.0	52.4	N/A

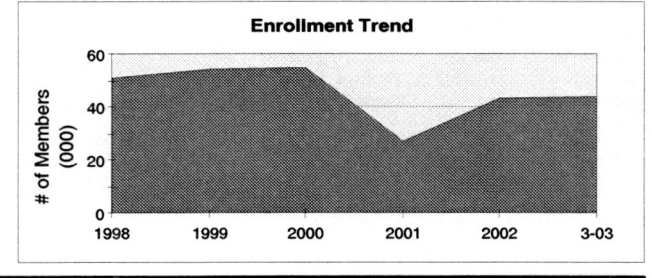

Enrollment Trend

www.WeissRatings.com * * Denotes a Weiss Recommended Company

II. Analysis of Largest Companies

Winter 2003 - 04

ALTA HEALTH & LIFE INSURANCE COMPANY — B — Good

Major Rating Factors: Fair profitability (4.1 on a scale of 0 to 10). Return on equity has been low, averaging -1.5%. Fair overall results on stability tests (4.0) including weak results on operational trends. Strong current capitalization (10.0) based on excellent risk adjusted capital (severe loss scenario) reflecting improvement over results in 1999.
Other Rating Factors: High quality investment portfolio (8.4). Excellent liquidity (9.9).
Principal Business: Group health insurance (77%) and group life insurance (22%).
Principal Investments: CMOs and structured securities (55%), nonCMO investment grade bonds (40%), cash (2%), and noninv. grade bonds (1%).
Investments in Affiliates: None
Group Affiliation: Great West Life Asr
Licensed in: All states except NY, PR
Commenced Business: February 1964
Address: 10401 N Meridian St Ste 350, Indianapolis, IN 46290
Phone: (303) 737-3000 **Domicile State:** IN **NAIC Code:** 67369

Data Date	Weiss Safety Rating	RACR #1	RACR #2	Total Assets ($mil)	Capital ($mil)	Net Premium ($mil)	Net Income ($mil)
6-03	B	13.59	12.23	258.8	118.0	42.2	12.3
6-02	B-	10.68	9.61	146.5	97.7	0.0	2.1
2002	B-	11.02	9.92	114.7	100.2	0.0	3.9
2001	B-	12.08	10.87	121.1	110.5	4.6	3.2
2000	B-	2.05	1.59	254.0	77.8	286.0	-8.3
1999	B-	1.11	0.87	321.9	68.2	412.9	2.2
1998	B-	1.11	0.87	305.6	68.5	428.8	-14.3

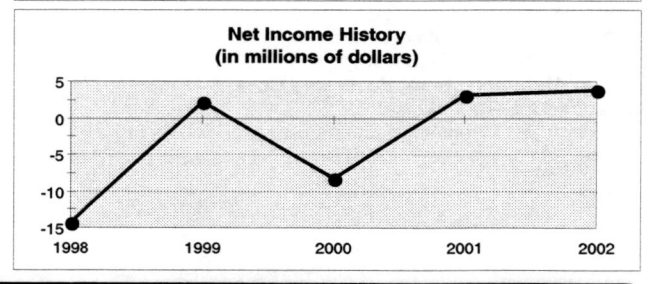

Net Income History (in millions of dollars) — chart 1998–2002

ALTIUS HEALTH PLANS — D+ — Weak

Major Rating Factors: Weak profitability index (0.9 on a scale of 0 to 10) with operating losses during 1998, 1999, 2000 and 2002. Average return on equity has been extremely poor. Poor capitalization index (0.5) based on weak current risk-adjusted capital (moderate loss scenario). Fair liquidity (4.6) as cash resources may not be adequate to cover a spike in claims.
Other Rating Factors: Good overall results on stability tests (5.6). Rating is significantly influenced by the fair financial results of Coventry Health Care Inc. High quality investment portfolio (9.9) containing little or no exposure to mortgages, junk bonds, or unaffiliated stocks.
Principal Business: Comp med (78%), FEHB (22%)
Mem Phys: 02: 3,256 **01:** 2,789 **02 MLR** 86% **/ 02 Admin Exp** 9%
Enroll(000): Q1 03: 137 **02:** 122 **01:** 103 **Med Exp PMPM:** $143
Principal Investments: Other (11%), affiliate common stock (1%), cash and equiv (89%)
Provider Compensation ($000): Contr fee ($138,091), FFS ($43,861), capitation ($10,105)
Total Member Encounters: Phys (716,080), non-phys (178,902)
Group Affiliation: Coventry Health Care Inc
Licensed in: UT
Address: 10421 S Jordan Gateway Ste 400, South Jordan, UT 84095
Phone: (801) 933-3500 **Dom State:** UT **Commenced Bus:** March 1976

Data Date	Weiss Safety Rating	RACR #1	RACR #2	Total Assets ($mil)	Capital ($mil)	Net Premium ($mil)	Net Income ($mil)
3-03	D+	0.35	0.29	36.3	9.5	68.7	2.0
3-02	E	0.10	0.08	27.6	4.3	53.3	0.2
2002	D+	0.28	0.23	30.5	7.5	223.7	-1.5
2001	E	0.09	0.08	24.6	3.8	166.4	4.8
2000	E-	0.00	0.00	18.5	-5.4	146.5	-7.3
1999	D	0.00	0.00	22.6	0.4	126.7	-12.1
1998	D+	0.26	0.23	25.4	5.0	193.6	-24.3

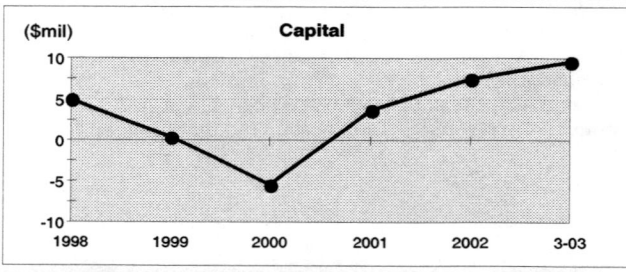

Capital ($mil) — chart 1998–3-03

AMEDEX INSURANCE COMPANY — C- — Fair

Major Rating Factors: Fair overall results on stability tests (3.3 on a scale of 0 to 10) including fair financial strength of affiliated Cincinnati Equitable Companies. Strong current capitalization (7.2) based on excellent risk adjusted capital (severe loss scenario) reflecting improvement over results in 1998. High quality investment portfolio (8.4).
Other Rating Factors: Excellent profitability (8.9) with operating gains in each of the last five years. Excellent liquidity (8.5).
Principal Business: Individual health insurance (90%), group health insurance (6%), and reinsurance (4%).
Principal Investments: NonCMO investment grade bonds (52%), cash (35%), CMOs and structured securities (6%), common & preferred stock (5%), and misc. investments (2%).
Investments in Affiliates: None
Group Affiliation: Cincinnati Equitable Companies
Licensed in: FL, PR
Commenced Business: July 1973
Address: 7001 S.W.97th Avenue, Miami, FL 33173
Phone: (305) 275-1400 **Domicile State:** FL **NAIC Code:** 81647

Data Date	Weiss Safety Rating	RACR #1	RACR #2	Total Assets ($mil)	Capital ($mil)	Net Premium ($mil)	Net Income ($mil)
6-03	C-	1.46	1.14	57.4	25.1	29.5	1.4
6-02	C-	N/A	N/A	N/A	N/A	N/A	N/A
2002	C-	1.44	1.12	54.8	23.4	53.2	3.5
2001	C-	1.34	1.03	47.8	19.7	46.7	2.3
2000	C-	1.37	1.03	43.2	17.2	37.1	2.8
1999	C-	1.15	0.85	42.4	15.4	37.6	2.3
1998	C-	1.00	0.75	41.7	12.1	36.5	5.6

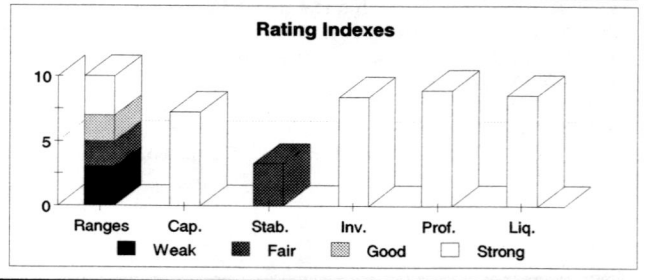

Rating Indexes — bar chart: Ranges, Cap., Stab., Inv., Prof., Liq. (Weak, Fair, Good, Strong)

Winter 2003 - 04 II. Analysis of Largest Companies

AMERICAN BANKERS INS CO OF FL C Fair

Major Rating Factors: Fair overall results on stability tests (3.6 on a scale of 0 to 10) including weak results on operational trends. Weak profitability index (2.2) with operating losses during 1999 and 2001. Return on equity has been low, averaging 3.6% over the past five years.
Other Rating Factors: Good liquidity (5.7) with sufficient resources (cash flows and marketable investments) to handle a spike in claims. Strong long-term capitalization (7.0) based on excellent current risk adjusted capital (severe and moderate loss scenarios) reflecting improvement over results in 1999. Ample reserve history (7.8) that can protect against increases in claims costs.
Principal Business: Credit accident & health (38%), inland marine (17%), aggregate write-ins for other lines of business (11%), homeowners multiple peril (9%), auto physical damage (9%), allied lines (6%), and other lines (9%).
Principal Investments: Investment grade bonds (75%), misc. investments (15%), non investment grade bonds (5%), cash (4%), and real estate (1%).
Investments in Affiliates: 1%
Group Affiliation: Fortis Inc
Licensed in: All states, the District of Columbia and Puerto Rico
Commenced Business: October 1947
Address: 11222 Quail Roost Dr, Miami, FL 33157
Phone: (305) 253-2244 **Domicile State:** FL **NAIC Code:** 10111

Data Date	Weiss Safety Rating	RACR #1	RACR #2	Loss Ratio %	Total Assets ($mil)	Capital ($mil)	Net Premium ($mil)	Net Income ($mil)
6-03	C	1.47	1.01	N/A	1,076.0	226.4	536.3	12.8
6-02	C	1.09	0.81	N/A	1,023.2	234.2	586.5	16.1
2002	C	1.50	1.04	45.2	1,081.5	212.9	496.2	16.0
2001	C	1.08	0.81	38.6	977.3	220.1	479.3	-27.7
2000	C+	1.39	1.02	29.3	820.3	245.7	464.7	12.9
1999	C+	1.17	0.91	34.4	766.2	261.6	433.8	-6.0
1998	C+	1.44	1.12	29.3	798.9	304.2	489.2	49.8

Fortis Inc Composite Group Rating: C+ Largest Group Members	Assets ($mil)	Weiss Safety Rating
FORTIS BENEFITS INS CO	7322	B-
AMERICAN BANKERS INS CO OF FL	1082	C
AMERICAN MEMORIAL LIFE INS CO	1075	C
UNITED FAMILY LIFE INS CO	997	C+
AMERICAN BANKERS LIFE ASR CO OF FL	925	B-

AMERICAN BANKERS LIFE ASSURANCE COMPANY OF FL B- Good

Major Rating Factors: Good quality investment portfolio (6.7 on a scale of 0 to 10) despite mixed results such as: substantial holdings of BBB bonds but moderate junk bond exposure. Fair overall results on stability tests (4.5) including fair financial strength of affiliated Fortis Inc and negative cash flow from operations for 2002. Fair profitability (4.4) with operating losses during the first six months of 2003.
Other Rating Factors: Strong capitalization (9.4) based on excellent risk adjusted capital (severe loss scenario). Excellent liquidity (7.2).
Principal Business: Credit life insurance (32%), credit health insurance (26%), group health insurance (14%), individual life insurance (12%), and other lines (16%).
Principal Investments: NonCMO investment grade bonds (63%), CMOs and structured securities (16%), noninv. grade bonds (6%), real estate (4%), and misc. investments (11%).
Investments in Affiliates: 1%
Group Affiliation: Fortis Inc
Licensed in: All states except NY
Commenced Business: April 1952
Address: 11222 Quail Roost Dr, Miami, FL 33157
Phone: (305) 253-2244 **Domicile State:** FL **NAIC Code:** 60275

Data Date	Weiss Safety Rating	RACR #1	RACR #2	Total Assets ($mil)	Capital ($mil)	Net Premium ($mil)	Net Income ($mil)
6-03	B-	4.42	2.60	889.3	157.7	111.9	-10.1
6-02	B-	4.97	2.83	900.6	164.5	111.1	15.3
2002	B-	4.54	2.66	924.7	161.2	211.5	8.1
2001	B-	4.26	2.41	895.6	148.3	234.7	-2.3
2000	B	3.93	2.31	847.5	147.9	186.1	7.8
1999	B	3.54	2.17	782.8	135.3	272.6	-19.9
1998	B	3.36	2.09	746.1	146.2	302.0	8.2

Fortis Inc Composite Group Rating: C+ Largest Group Members	Assets ($mil)	Weiss Safety Rating
FORTIS BENEFITS INS CO	7322	B-
AMERICAN BANKERS INS CO OF FL	1082	C
AMERICAN MEMORIAL LIFE INS CO	1075	C
UNITED FAMILY LIFE INS CO	997	C+
AMERICAN BANKERS LIFE ASR CO OF FL	925	B-

AMERICAN COMMUNITY MUTUAL INSURANCE COMPANY C+ Fair

Major Rating Factors: Fair profitability (4.5 on a scale of 0 to 10). Fair overall results on stability tests (3.0). Good liquidity (6.3) with sufficient resources to handle a spike in claims.
Other Rating Factors: Strong current capitalization (7.9) based on excellent risk adjusted capital (severe loss scenario) reflecting improvement over results in 2000. High quality investment portfolio (7.9).
Principal Business: Group health insurance (62%), individual health insurance (35%), group life insurance (2%), and individual life insurance (1%).
Principal Investments: CMOs and structured securities (50%), nonCMO investment grade bonds (34%), cash (5%), real estate (5%), and misc. investments (5%).
Investments in Affiliates: None
Group Affiliation: None
Licensed in: AZ, AR, CO, GA, IL, IN, IA, KS, KY, LA, MI, MO, NE, NC, OH, OK, PA, SC, SD, TN, UT, WI, WY
Commenced Business: December 1947
Address: 39201 W Seven Mile Rd, Livonia, MI 48152-1094
Phone: (734) 591-9000 **Domicile State:** MI **NAIC Code:** 60305

Data Date	Weiss Safety Rating	RACR #1	RACR #2	Total Assets ($mil)	Capital ($mil)	Net Premium ($mil)	Net Income ($mil)
6-03	C+	2.10	1.63	157.4	74.9	178.0	12.2
6-02	D	1.69	1.30	130.5	51.5	125.3	9.3
2002	C-	2.11	1.61	149.0	64.1	251.8	18.5
2001	D	1.63	1.24	125.9	40.1	166.2	18.5
2000	D	1.06	0.80	135.6	22.0	145.6	-25.2
1999	C	1.03	0.81	143.3	49.7	369.9	-9.1
1998	C	1.22	0.95	162.9	60.0	368.7	-10.8

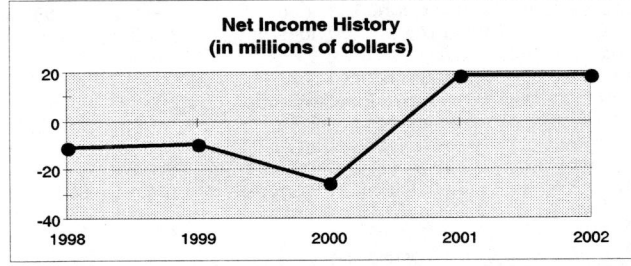

Net Income History (in millions of dollars)

www.WeissRatings.com * Denotes a Weiss Recommended Company

II. Analysis of Largest Companies

Winter 2003 - 04

AMERICAN EXCHANGE LIFE INSURANCE COMPANY — D+ — Weak

Major Rating Factors: Weak overall results on stability tests (2.8 on a scale of 0 to 10) including weak financial strength of affiliated Universal American Financial Corp. Low quality investment portfolio (1.3). Good current capitalization (5.3) based on good risk adjusted capital (severe loss scenario) reflecting some improvement over results in 2000.
Other Rating Factors: Good overall profitability (5.1). Excellent liquidity (9.3).
Principal Business: Individual health insurance (97%) and individual life insurance (3%).
Principal Investments: Common & preferred stock (92%), nonCMO investment grade bonds (6%), and cash (2%).
Investments in Affiliates: 92%
Group Affiliation: Universal American Financial Corp
Licensed in: LA, TX
Commenced Business: September 1965
Address: 80 E Campbell Rd Ste 345, Richardson, TX 75081-1889
Phone: (214) 520-1450 **Domicile State:** TX **NAIC Code:** 60372

Data Date	Weiss Safety Rating	RACR #1	RACR #2	Total Assets ($mil)	Capital ($mil)	Net Premium ($mil)	Net Income ($mil)
6-03	D+	0.89	0.79	110.4	109.0	0.6	2.3
6-02	U	N/A	N/A	78.7	76.7	0.8	3.2
2002	D+	0.86	0.76	110.6	105.7	1.4	4.3
2001	U	0.60	0.54	71.6	68.7	2.0	5.6
2000	D	0.59	0.53	60.2	57.1	3.1	-4.3
1999	D	0.58	0.52	66.9	62.4	3.6	0.0
1998	D	1.90	1.71	7.5	3.7	3.1	-0.4

Universal American Financial Corp
Composite Group Rating: D+

Largest Group Members	Assets ($mil)	Weiss Safety Rating
PENNSYLVANIA LIFE INS CO	429	D+
AMERICAN PIONEER LIFE INS CO	133	C-
AMERICAN PROGRESSIVE LH I C OF NY	115	D+
PYRAMID LIFE INS CO	114	C
AMERICAN EXCHANGE LIFE INS CO	111	D+

AMERICAN FAMILY LIFE ASSURANCE CO OF COLUMBUS — B- — Good

Major Rating Factors: Strong capitalization (6.5 on a scale of 0 to 10) based on excellent risk adjusted capital (severe loss scenario). Capital levels have been relatively consistent over the last five years. Good quality investment portfolio (5.7) despite mixed results such as: large holdings of BBB rated bonds but moderate junk bond exposure. Fair overall results on stability tests (4.9).
Other Rating Factors: Excellent profitability (7.9) with operating gains in each of the last five years. Excellent liquidity (7.8).
Principal Business: Individual health insurance (90%), individual life insurance (9%), and individual annuities (1%).
Principal Investments: NonCMO investment grade bonds (79%), common & preferred stock (13%), noninv. grade bonds (3%), cash (3%), and misc. investments (3%).
Investments in Affiliates: None
Group Affiliation: American Family Corp
Licensed in: All states except NY
Commenced Business: April 1956
Address: 1932 Wynnton Rd, Columbus, GA 31999
Phone: (706) 323-3431 **Domicile State:** NE **NAIC Code:** 60380

Data Date	Weiss Safety Rating	RACR #1	RACR #2	Total Assets ($mil)	Capital ($mil)	Net Premium ($mil)	Net Income ($mil)
6-03	B-	1.68	1.04	37,709.9	2,228.1	4,835.0	503.8
6-02	B-	1.67	1.06	34,081.7	1,963.4	4,128.2	186.5
2002	B-	1.66	1.02	36,287.1	2,112.7	8,625.0	505.5
2001	C	1.91	1.23	30,615.9	2,161.5	8,135.8	370.5
2000	C	1.55	1.01	30,308.0	1,672.8	8,207.3	208.8
1999	C	1.63	1.07	29,963.2	1,606.0	7,231.3	343.0
1998	C	2.03	1.33	24,720.6	1,648.3	5,915.2	229.0

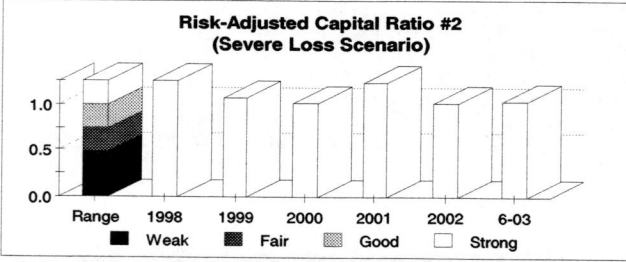

Risk-Adjusted Capital Ratio #2 (Severe Loss Scenario)
Range 1998 1999 2000 2001 2002 6-03
■ Weak ▨ Fair ▩ Good □ Strong

AMERICAN FIDELITY ASSURANCE COMPANY * — A — Excellent

Major Rating Factors: Good capitalization (6.9 on a scale of 0 to 10) based on good risk adjusted capital (severe loss scenario). Furthermore, this high level of risk adjusted capital has been consistently maintained over the last five years. Good quality investment portfolio (6.6) despite mixed results such as: no exposure to mortgages and substantial holdings of BBB bonds but minimal holdings in junk bonds. Good overall results on stability tests (6.9) excellent operational trends, excellent risk adjusted capital for prior years and excellent risk diversification.
Other Rating Factors: Excellent profitability (8.0) with operating gains in each of the last five years. Excellent liquidity (7.2).
Principal Business: Group health insurance (56%), individual life insurance (19%), individual health insurance (12%), individual annuities (10%), and other lines (4%).
Principal Investments: NonCMO investment grade bonds (55%), CMOs and structured securities (27%), mortgages in good standing (12%), cash (2%), and misc. investments (2%).
Investments in Affiliates: None
Group Affiliation: American Fidelity Group
Licensed in: All states except NY, PR
Commenced Business: December 1960
Address: 2000 N Classen Blvd, Oklahoma City, OK 73106
Phone: (405) 523-2000 **Domicile State:** OK **NAIC Code:** 60410

Data Date	Weiss Safety Rating	RACR #1	RACR #2	Total Assets ($mil)	Capital ($mil)	Net Premium ($mil)	Net Income ($mil)
6-03	A	1.63	0.99	2,382.6	141.2	206.3	6.3
6-02	A	1.81	1.08	2,070.7	141.2	176.2	7.5
2002	A	1.80	1.09	2,117.9	146.7	369.4	19.7
2001	A	1.88	1.13	2,018.6	142.8	311.3	15.7
2000	A	2.18	1.20	1,931.8	133.5	285.1	16.3
1999	A	2.27	1.37	1,499.9	132.2	264.5	13.9
1998	A	2.21	1.41	1,351.1	126.3	289.3	12.6

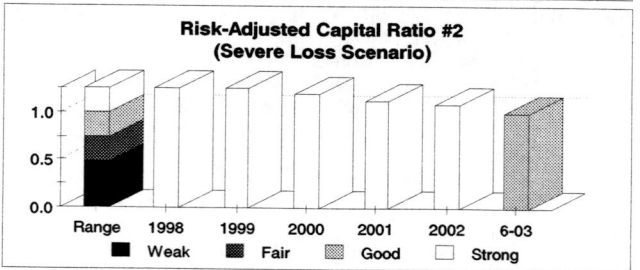

Risk-Adjusted Capital Ratio #2 (Severe Loss Scenario)
Range 1998 1999 2000 2001 2002 6-03
■ Weak ▨ Fair ▩ Good □ Strong

Winter 2003 - 04   II. Analysis of Largest Companies

AMERICAN GENERAL ASSURANCE COMPANY   C+   Fair

Major Rating Factors: Fair overall results on stability tests (4.7 on a scale of 0 to 10) including fair risk adjusted capital in prior years. Good current capitalization (6.3) based on excellent risk adjusted capital (severe loss scenario) reflecting significant improvement over results in 2001. Good quality investment portfolio (6.0).
Other Rating Factors: Good overall profitability (6.4). Excellent liquidity (7.0).
Principal Business: Reinsurance (71%), credit life insurance (12%), credit health insurance (9%), group health insurance (7%), and group life insurance (2%).
Principal Investments: NonCMO investment grade bonds (69%), CMOs and structured securities (20%), noninv. grade bonds (8%), and common & preferred stock (3%).
Investments in Affiliates: 2%
Group Affiliation: American International Group
Licensed in: All states except NY, PR
Commenced Business: February 1930
Address: 1000 Woodfield Lake, Schaumburg, IL 60173-4793
Phone: (847) 517-6000   **Domicile State:** IL   **NAIC Code:** 68373

Data Date	Weiss Safety Rating	RACR #1	RACR #2	Total Assets ($mil)	Capital ($mil)	Net Premium ($mil)	Net Income ($mil)
6-03	C+	1.69	1.16	1,370.4	153.0	321.1	18.6
6-02	C+	0.97	0.68	1,233.9	81.9	314.6	-1.3
2002	C+	1.20	0.82	1,294.3	138.6	686.4	11.8
2001	C+	0.85	0.61	1,160.1	86.0	588.9	16.2
2000	B-	0.95	0.69	1,147.5	106.2	659.5	-2.8
1999	B-	1.10	0.82	1,117.2	125.3	711.5	-1.7
1998	B-	1.04	0.75	975.7	83.5	311.2	6.5

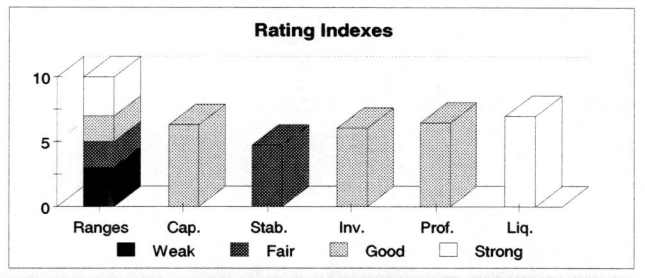

Rating Indexes (bar chart: Ranges, Cap., Stab., Inv., Prof., Liq. — Weak, Fair, Good, Strong)

AMERICAN HEALTH & LIFE INSURANCE COMPANY *   B+   Good

Major Rating Factors: Good overall results on stability tests (5.0 on a scale of 0 to 10). Stability strengths include excellent risk diversification. Strong capitalization (10.0) based on excellent risk adjusted capital (severe loss scenario). Capital levels have been relatively consistent over the last five years. High quality investment portfolio (7.0).
Other Rating Factors: Excellent profitability (9.0) with operating gains in each of the last five years. Excellent liquidity (9.1).
Principal Business: Credit health insurance (60%), reinsurance (19%), credit life insurance (19%), and individual life insurance (2%).
Principal Investments: CMOs and structured securities (51%), nonCMO investment grade bonds (38%), noninv. grade bonds (5%), common & preferred stock (3%), and policy loans (2%).
Investments in Affiliates: 4%
Group Affiliation: Citigroup Inc
Licensed in: All states except NY, PR
Commenced Business: June 1954
Address: 307 West 7th Street, Ste 400, Fort Worth, TX 76102
Phone: (817) 348-7500   **Domicile State:** TX   **NAIC Code:** 60518

Data Date	Weiss Safety Rating	RACR #1	RACR #2	Total Assets ($mil)	Capital ($mil)	Net Premium ($mil)	Net Income ($mil)
6-03	B+	6.97	3.83	1,236.5	338.7	19.9	78.4
6-02	B+	3.40	2.07	1,320.9	208.0	104.3	51.6
2002	B+	4.82	2.78	1,283.9	265.4	164.1	132.0
2001	B	2.64	1.65	1,340.3	182.5	332.5	47.9
2000	B	2.62	1.69	1,048.9	141.4	245.0	32.0
1999	B	3.34	2.18	963.6	156.3	232.5	30.9
1998	B-	5.07	3.27	827.4	174.0	164.1	39.0

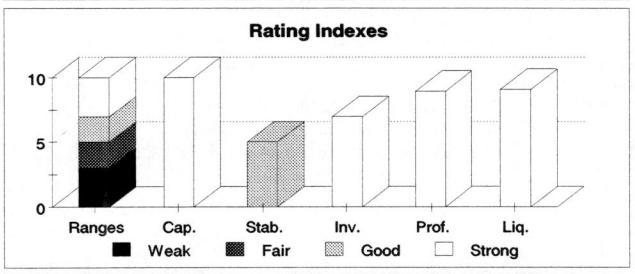

Rating Indexes (bar chart: Ranges, Cap., Stab., Inv., Prof., Liq. — Weak, Fair, Good, Strong)

AMERICAN HERITAGE LIFE INSURANCE COMPANY   B   Good

Major Rating Factors: Good current capitalization (5.3 on a scale of 0 to 10) based on good risk adjusted capital (severe loss scenario) reflecting some improvement over results in 2002. Good quality investment portfolio (6.0) despite mixed results such as: large holdings of BBB rated bonds but moderate junk bond exposure. Good liquidity (5.9).
Other Rating Factors: Good overall results on stability tests (5.1) despite fair risk adjusted capital in prior years good operational trends and excellent risk diversification. Weak profitability (2.7).
Principal Business: Reinsurance (29%), individual health insurance (28%), individual life insurance (14%), group health insurance (12%), and other lines (17%).
Principal Investments: NonCMO investment grade bonds (38%), policy loans (33%), CMOs and structured securities (10%), mortgages in good standing (8%), and misc. investments (10%).
Investments in Affiliates: 5%
Group Affiliation: Allstate Group
Licensed in: All states except NY
Commenced Business: December 1956
Address: 1776 American Heritage Life Dr, Jacksonville, FL 32224-6688
Phone: (904) 992-1776   **Domicile State:** FL   **NAIC Code:** 60534

Data Date	Weiss Safety Rating	RACR #1	RACR #2	Total Assets ($mil)	Capital ($mil)	Net Premium ($mil)	Net Income ($mil)
6-03	B	1.08	0.79	1,776.9	177.7	185.7	7.5
6-02	B+	1.04	0.75	1,679.3	140.5	191.5	4.3
2002	B	1.01	0.74	1,723.2	163.0	405.0	-13.0
2001	B+	1.11	0.79	1,671.1	155.8	362.3	-6.0
2000	B+	1.29	0.90	1,590.4	159.2	580.2	-33.0
1999	A-	1.40	1.01	1,251.0	153.8	292.9	12.7
1998	A-	1.32	0.96	1,273.8	150.7	269.9	26.0

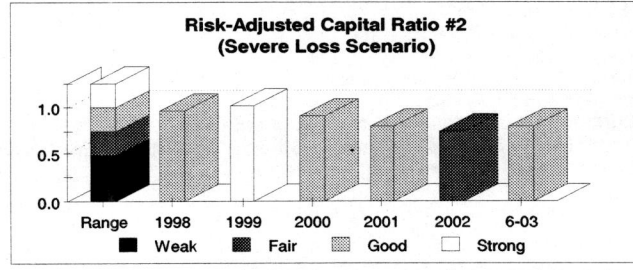

Risk-Adjusted Capital Ratio #2 (Severe Loss Scenario) (bar chart: Range, 1998, 1999, 2000, 2001, 2002, 6-03 — Weak, Fair, Good, Strong)

www.WeissRatings.com   * Denotes a Weiss Recommended Company

II. Analysis of Largest Companies

Winter 2003 - 04

AMERICAN NATIONAL LIFE INSURANCE COMPANY OF TEXAS — B- — Good

Major Rating Factors: Good quality investment portfolio (5.7 on a scale of 0 to 10) despite mixed results such as: no exposure to mortgages and large holdings of BBB rated bonds but small junk bond holdings. Good liquidity (6.7) with sufficient resources to handle a spike in claims. Good overall results on stability tests (5.2) excellent operational trends and excellent risk diversification.
Other Rating Factors: Fair profitability (3.5). Strong capitalization (7.8) based on excellent risk adjusted capital (severe loss scenario).
Principal Business: Group health insurance (43%), reinsurance (43%), individual health insurance (12%), and individual life insurance (2%).
Principal Investments: NonCMO investment grade bonds (82%), common & preferred stock (8%), noninv. grade bonds (8%), policy loans (2%), and CMOs and structured securities (1%).
Investments in Affiliates: 8%
Group Affiliation: American National Group Inc
Licensed in: All states except ME, NJ, NY, VT, PR
Commenced Business: December 1954
Address: One Moody Plaza, Galveston, TX 77550
Phone: (409) 763-4661 **Domicile State:** TX **NAIC Code:** 71773

Data Date	Weiss Safety Rating	RACR #1	RACR #2	Total Assets ($mil)	Capital ($mil)	Net Premium ($mil)	Net Income ($mil)
6-03	B-	1.93	1.56	157.3	54.2	49.2	1.2
6-02	B-	2.76	1.98	149.7	59.4	57.3	4.7
2002	B-	1.89	1.46	150.2	50.0	117.1	3.2
2001	B-	2.94	2.21	140.6	54.0	112.2	2.1
2000	B	2.73	2.07	135.3	51.7	119.6	-4.3
1999	B	2.79	2.16	138.5	59.9	141.1	-2.7
1998	B	3.77	2.85	150.8	63.1	111.6	-2.5

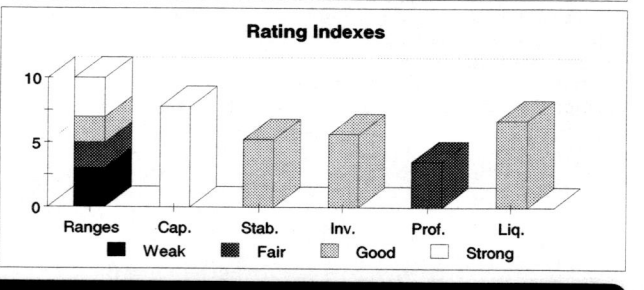

Rating Indexes (bar chart: Ranges, Cap., Stab., Inv., Prof., Liq.; legend: Weak, Fair, Good, Strong)

AMERICAN REPUBLIC INSURANCE COMPANY — B — Good

Major Rating Factors: Good liquidity (6.6 on a scale of 0 to 10) with sufficient resources to handle a spike in claims as well as a significant increase in policy surrenders. Good overall results on stability tests (5.2). Stability strengths include excellent operational trends and excellent risk diversification. Strong capitalization (8.7) based on excellent risk adjusted capital (severe loss scenario).
Other Rating Factors: High quality investment portfolio (7.3). Excellent profitability (7.7) despite modest operating losses during 2000.
Principal Business: Individual health insurance (76%), group health insurance (17%), individual life insurance (4%), credit life insurance (1%), and credit health insurance (1%).
Principal Investments: NonCMO investment grade bonds (71%), CMOs and structured securities (18%), noninv. grade bonds (4%), cash (2%), and misc. investments (3%).
Investments in Affiliates: None
Group Affiliation: American Republic Group
Licensed in: All states except NY, PR
Commenced Business: May 1929
Address: 601 Sixth Ave, Des Moines, IA 50309
Phone: (515) 245-2000 **Domicile State:** IA **NAIC Code:** 60836

Data Date	Weiss Safety Rating	RACR #1	RACR #2	Total Assets ($mil)	Capital ($mil)	Net Premium ($mil)	Net Income ($mil)
6-03	B	2.94	2.16	452.3	196.3	188.7	10.4
6-02	B	2.33	1.70	458.4	171.2	200.7	11.1
2002	B	2.77	2.03	456.0	187.9	394.1	31.0
2001	B	2.10	1.54	466.3	159.3	430.2	18.8
2000	B	1.83	1.35	454.5	131.6	412.3	-6.1
1999	B	2.08	1.52	451.8	134.0	374.9	10.4
1998	B	2.31	1.68	442.0	131.6	333.2	9.6

Adverse Trends in Operations

Decrease in premium volume from 2001 to 2002 (8%)
Decrease in asset base during 2002 (2%)
Decrease in capital during 2000 (2%)

AMERICAN SECURITY INS CO — B — Good

Major Rating Factors: Good overall long-term capitalization (6.4 on a scale of 0 to 10) based on good current risk adjusted capital (moderate loss scenario). However, capital levels have fluctuated during prior years. Fair overall results on stability tests (4.0) including weak results on operational trends. Strengths include potentially strong support from affiliation with Fortis Inc.
Other Rating Factors: Fair profitability index (4.1). Weak expense controls. Return on equity has been fair, averaging 17.4% over the past five years. Ample reserve history (7.4) that can protect against increases in claims costs. Vulnerable liquidity (2.7) as a spike in claims may stretch capacity.
Principal Business: Credit accident & health (45%), fire (35%), allied lines (12%), other liability (5%), inland marine (1%), auto physical damage (1%), and aggregate write-ins for other lines of business (1%).
Principal Investments: Investment grade bonds (71%), misc. investments (21%), real estate (6%), and non investment grade bonds (5%).
Investments in Affiliates: 19%
Group Affiliation: Fortis Inc
Licensed in: All states except NH
Commenced Business: September 1938
Address: 260 Interstate N Circle NW, Atlanta, GA 30339-2111
Phone: (770) 763-1000 **Domicile State:** DE **NAIC Code:** 42978

Data Date	Weiss Safety Rating	RACR #1	RACR #2	Loss Ratio %	Total Assets ($mil)	Capital ($mil)	Net Premium ($mil)	Net Income ($mil)
6-03	B	1.17	0.99	N/A	558.2	177.8	308.5	23.1
6-02	B	1.00	0.86	N/A	538.5	168.0	315.2	9.1
2002	B	1.18	1.02	27.6	537.5	176.9	327.2	30.8
2001	B	1.01	0.89	23.2	572.6	172.6	365.7	47.2
2000	B	0.90	0.82	18.5	487.5	194.0	318.3	32.6
1999	B	1.01	0.90	21.4	520.3	201.8	342.2	29.9
1998	B	1.02	0.91	20.9	422.0	179.1	266.7	10.9

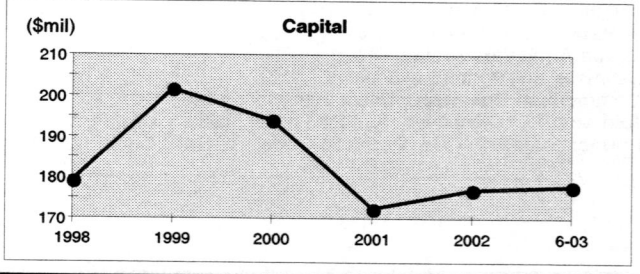

Capital ($mil) — line chart from 1998 to 6-03

www.WeissRatings.com

Winter 2003 - 04   II. Analysis of Largest Companies

AMERICAS HEALTH CHOICE MEDICAL PLANS   D   Weak

Major Rating Factors: Poor capitalization (0.1 on a scale of 0 to 10) based on weak current risk-adjusted capital (moderate loss scenario) as results have slipped from the good range over the last year. Fair overall results on stability tests (3.8) based on an excessive 47% enrollment growth during the period. Good liquidity (6.9) with sufficient resources (cash flows and marketable investments) to handle a spike in claims
Other Rating Factors: Excellent profitability (8.9). High quality investment portfolio (9.9) containing no exposure to mortgages, junk bonds, or unaffiliated stocks.
Principal Business: Medicare (100%)
Mem Phys: 02: 385   **01:** 325   **02 MLR** 57%   / **02 Admin Exp** 39%
Enroll(000): 02: 11   **01:** 8   **Med Exp PMPM:** $320
Principal Investments: Cash and equiv (98%), real estate (2%)
Provider Compensation ($000): FFS ($33,392), capitation ($3,940), other ($19,305)
Total Member Encounters: N/A
Group Affiliation: None
Licensed in: FL
Address: 1175 South US Highway 1, Vero Beach, FL 32962
Phone: (772) 794-0030   **Dom State:** FL   **Commenced Bus:** July 2000

Data Date	Weiss Safety Rating	RACR #1	RACR #2	Total Assets ($mil)	Capital ($mil)	Net Premium ($mil)	Net Income ($mil)
2002	D	0.31	0.26	18.4	4.6	63.5	2.1
2001	U	1.11	0.94	15.0	5.7	37.0	6.5
2000	N/A	N/A	N/A	5.6	2.3	7.5	1.7
1999	N/A	N/A	N/A	N/A	N/A	N/A	N/A
1998	N/A	N/A	N/A	N/A	N/A	N/A	N/A

Risk-Adjusted Capital Ratio #2 (Severe Loss Scenario)

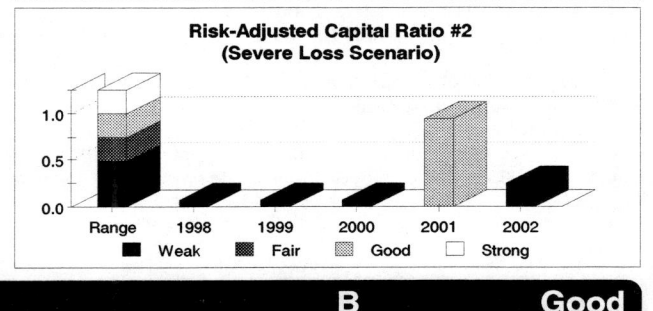

AMERICHOICE OF NEW JERSEY INC   B   Good

Major Rating Factors: Good overall profitability index (6.3 on a scale of 0 to 10) despite operating losses during 2002. Good capitalization (6.8) based on excellent current risk-adjusted capital (severe loss scenario) reflecting improvement over results in 2001. Good overall results on stability tests (6.3) despite good risk-adjusted capital in prior years, a decline in enrollment during 2002 but consistent premium and capital growth in the last five years. Rating is significantly influenced by the good financial results of UnitedHealth Group Inc.
Other Rating Factors: Good liquidity (5.7) with sufficient resources (cash flows and marketable investments) to handle a spike in claims. High quality investment portfolio (9.9) containing no exposure to mortgages, junk bonds, or unaffiliated stocks.
Principal Business: Medicaid (98%), Medicare (2%)
Mem Phys: 02: 5,132   **01:** 7,413   **02 MLR** 87%   / **02 Admin Exp** 13%
Enroll(000): Q1 03: 176   **02:** 179   **01:** 195   **Med Exp PMPM:** $147
Principal Investments: Cash and equiv (22%), other (78%)
Provider Compensation ($000): FFS ($295,092), capitation ($37,538)
Total Member Encounters: Phys (779,754), non-phys (373,837)
Group Affiliation: UnitedHealth Group Inc
Licensed in: NJ
Address: Two Gateway Center, Newark, NJ 07102
Phone: (973) 297-5500   **Dom State:** NJ   **Commenced Bus:** February 1996

Data Date	Weiss Safety Rating	RACR #1	RACR #2	Total Assets ($mil)	Capital ($mil)	Net Premium ($mil)	Net Income ($mil)
3-03	B	1.22	1.02	85.9	31.6	91.0	-0.2
3-02	B-	1.71	1.46	64.2	23.4	95.7	1.4
2002	B	1.21	1.01	77.8	31.3	376.6	-3.2
2001	B-	1.04	0.89	59.4	20.3	239.1	6.1
2000	C	1.20	1.03	31.5	11.5	112.2	2.9
1999	C	1.33	1.13	26.1	11.5	101.3	2.7
1998	C	1.57	1.33	20.3	7.8	59.3	1.2

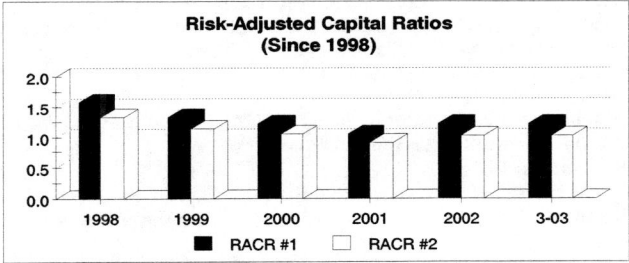

Risk-Adjusted Capital Ratios (Since 1998)

AMERICHOICE OF NEW YORK INC *   B+   Good

Major Rating Factors: Good overall results on stability tests (6.1 on a scale of 0 to 10) based on consistent premium and capital growth in the last five years but rapid enrollment growth during the past five years. Rating is significantly influenced by the good financial results of UnitedHealth Group Inc. Excellent profitability (9.0) despite a decline in earnings during 2002. Strong capitalization index (10.0) based on excellent current risk-adjusted capital (severe loss scenario).
Other Rating Factors: High quality investment portfolio (9.9) containing no exposure to mortgages, junk bonds, or unaffiliated stocks. Excellent liquidity (7.0) with ample operational cash flow and liquid investments.
Principal Business: Medicaid (85%), Medicare (13%), other (2%)
Mem Phys: 02: 4,960   **01:** 5,132   **02 MLR** 65%   / **02 Admin Exp** 21%
Enroll(000): Q1 03: 87   **02:** 81   **01:** 59   **Med Exp PMPM:** $114
Principal Investments: Cash and equiv (53%), other (47%)
Provider Compensation ($000): Contr fee ($62,242), capitation ($12,958), FFS ($10,419)
Total Member Encounters: Phys (295,716), non-phys (124,590)
Group Affiliation: UnitedHealth Group Inc
Licensed in: NY
Address: 7 Hanover Square, New York, NY 10004
Phone: (212) 509-5999   **Dom State:** NY   **Commenced Bus:** January 1994

Data Date	Weiss Safety Rating	RACR #1	RACR #2	Total Assets ($mil)	Capital ($mil)	Net Premium ($mil)	Net Income ($mil)
3-03	B+	6.63	5.53	83.0	44.2	45.8	6.2
3-02	B	5.04	4.31	48.4	26.8	32.0	2.2
2002	B+	5.44	4.53	72.7	35.9	147.0	11.8
2001	B	3.02	2.59	44.7	24.6	113.2	12.2
2000	D+	N/A	N/A	46.2	26.4	105.8	9.9
1999	D+	0.00	0.00	49.8	17.3	98.8	9.0
1998	D+	1.28	1.09	33.7	7.2	53.2	3.6

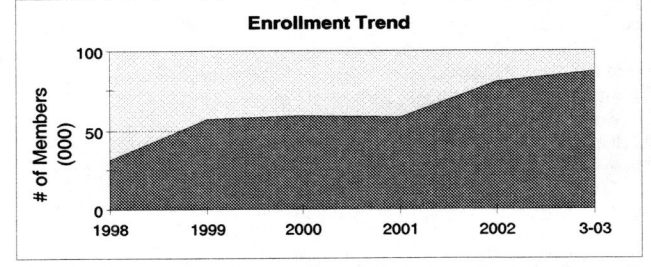

Enrollment Trend

www.WeissRatings.com   * Denotes a Weiss Recommended Company

II. Analysis of Largest Companies

Winter 2003 - 04

AMERICHOICE OF PENNSYLVANIA INC B Good

Major Rating Factors: Good overall results on stability tests (6.4 on a scale of 0 to 10). Rating is significantly influenced by the fair financial results of UnitedHealth Group Inc. Good liquidity (5.7) with sufficient resources (cash flows and marketable investments) to handle a spike in claims. Excellent profitability (7.5) despite operating losses during 1997.
Other Rating Factors: Strong capitalization (7.8) based on excellent current risk-adjusted capital (severe loss scenario) reflecting improvement over results in 1999. High quality investment portfolio (9.9) containing no exposure to mortgages, junk bonds, or unaffiliated stocks.
Principal Business: Medicaid (91%), Medicare (8%)
Mem Phys: 01: 6,357   **00:** 5,480   **01 MLR** 80% / **01 Admin Exp** 12%
Enroll(000): Q2 02: 114   **01:** 112   **00:** 71   **Med Exp PMPM:** $220
Principal Investments: Cash and equiv (24%), other (76%)
Provider Compensation ($000): Contr fee ($211,648), capitation ($14,929), other ($16,494)
Total Member Encounters: Phys (430,850), non-phys (350,834)
Group Affiliation: UnitedHealth Group Inc
Licensed in: PA
Address: 100 Penn Square E Ste 900, Philadelphia, PA 19107
Phone: (215) 832-4500   **Dom State:** PA   **Commenced Bus:** July 1989

Data Date	Weiss Safety Rating	RACR #1	RACR #2	Total Assets ($mil)	Capital ($mil)	Net Premium ($mil)	Net Income ($mil)
6-02	B	1.94	1.65	97.3	38.3	201.3	6.7
6-01	B-	2.02	1.71	84.0	36.4	124.2	6.0
2001	B	1.31	1.11	102.8	29.8	303.6	12.7
2000	B-	1.70	1.44	74.2	30.7	231.9	12.5
1999	C+	0.92	0.79	69.7	19.7	279.0	3.0
1998	C	0.97	0.84	65.0	17.2	238.2	4.0
1997	N/A	N/A	N/A	56.3	7.2	191.2	-4.4

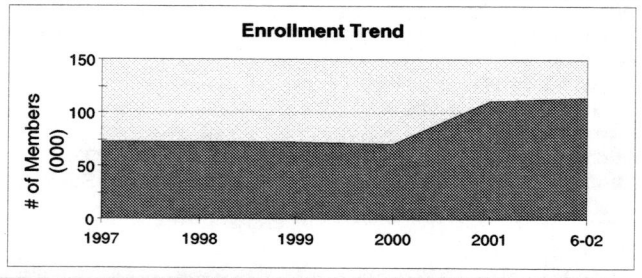

Enrollment Trend (1997–6-02)

AMERIGROUP FLORIDA INC D+ Weak

Major Rating Factors: Poor capitalization (0.6 on a scale of 0 to 10) based on weak current risk-adjusted capital (moderate loss scenario) as results have slipped from the fair range over the last two years. Fair overall results on stability tests (4.3) based on fair risk diversification due to the size of the company's affiliate group, an excessive 30% enrollment growth during the period. Good overall profitability index (6.3) despite operating losses during 1997.
Other Rating Factors: Good liquidity (7.0) with sufficient resources (cash flows and marketable investments) to handle a spike in claims. High quality investment portfolio (8.9) containing no exposure to mortgages, junk bonds, or unaffiliated stocks.
Principal Business: Medicaid (61%), Medicare (24%), comp med (15%)
Mem Phys: 01: N/A   **00:** N/A   **01 MLR** 77% / **01 Admin Exp** 16%
Enroll(000): Q1 02: 198   **01:** 167   **00:** 128   **Med Exp PMPM:** $112
Principal Investments: Cash and equiv (100%)
Provider Compensation ($000): FFS ($87,499), contr fee ($47,337), capitation ($30,832), other ($34,026)
Total Member Encounters: Phys (724,771), non-phys (298,733)
Group Affiliation: AMERIGROUP Corp
Licensed in: FL
Address: 1410 N Westshore Blvd Ste 200, Tampa, FL 33607
Phone: (813) 273-7474   **Dom State:** FL   **Commenced Bus:** October 1993

Data Date	Weiss Safety Rating	RACR #1	RACR #2	Total Assets ($mil)	Capital ($mil)	Net Premium ($mil)	Net Income ($mil)
3-02	D+	0.35	0.30	61.7	14.0	120.4	1.6
3-01	C+	0.27	0.23	40.3	6.6	57.4	0.7
2001	D+	0.35	0.30	52.6	11.4	256.5	10.5
2000	C-	0.80	0.68	46.7	13.0	219.7	6.8
1999	D+	0.87	0.74	38.8	11.8	159.6	4.2
1998	D-	0.46	0.39	33.0	7.0	131.8	2.9
1997	E	0.13	0.08	20.9	3.0	130.4	-2.3

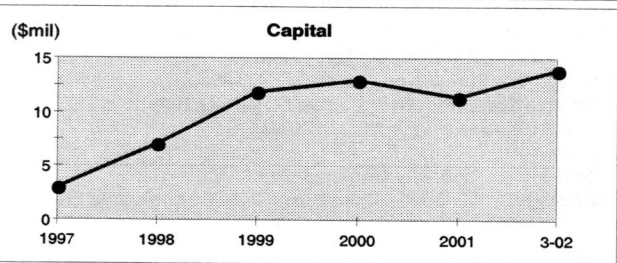

Capital ($mil) (1997–3-02)

AMERIGROUP ILLINOIS INC C+ Fair

Major Rating Factors: Good overall results on stability tests (7.0 on a scale of 0 to 10) based on consistent premium and capital growth in the last five years but a decline in enrollment during 2002. Poor financial strength from affiliates. Excellent profitability (7.6) despite a decline in earnings during 2002. Strong capitalization (10.0) based on excellent current risk-adjusted capital (severe loss scenario) reflecting significant improvement over results in 1998.
Other Rating Factors: High quality investment portfolio (9.9) containing no exposure to mortgages, junk bonds, or unaffiliated stocks. Excellent liquidity (7.3) with ample operational cash flow and liquid investments.
Principal Business: Medicaid (100%)
Mem Phys: 02: 1,445   **01:** 1,214   **02 MLR** 47% / **02 Admin Exp** 40%
Enroll(000): **02:** 34   **01:** 39   **Med Exp PMPM:** $57
Principal Investments: Cash and equiv (73%), other (27%)
Provider Compensation ($000): Capitation ($11,488), contr fee ($10,527), FFS ($3,573), bonus arrang ($976)
Total Member Encounters: Phys (286,144), non-phys (23,656)
Group Affiliation: AMERIGROUP Corp
Licensed in: IL
Address: 211 W Wacker Dr Ste 1350, Chicago, IL 60606
Phone: (757) 490-6900   **Dom State:** IL   **Commenced Bus:** April 1996

Data Date	Weiss Safety Rating	RACR #1	RACR #2	Total Assets ($mil)	Capital ($mil)	Net Premium ($mil)	Net Income ($mil)
2002	C+	5.82	4.85	28.9	17.0	53.3	4.4
2001	C-	2.72	2.39	28.1	12.9	56.1	8.4
2000	D	0.64	0.56	17.6	4.5	41.5	0.4
1999	D	0.75	0.65	9.7	3.5	22.9	1.1
1998	D	0.48	0.42	4.9	1.5	9.4	-1.9

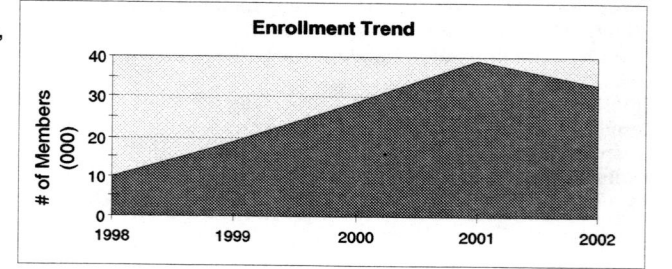

Enrollment Trend (1998–2002)

Winter 2003 - 04   II. Analysis of Largest Companies

AMERIGROUP MARYLAND INC MANAGED CARE   C+   Fair

Major Rating Factors: Good overall profitability index (5.6 on a scale of 0 to 10). Good liquidity (6.9) with sufficient resources (cash flows and marketable investments) to handle a spike in claims. Strong capitalization (7.3) based on excellent current risk-adjusted capital (severe loss scenario).
Other Rating Factors: High quality investment portfolio (9.9) containing no exposure to mortgages, junk bonds, or unaffiliated stocks.
Principal Business: Medicaid (100%)
Mem Phys: 02: 7,879   **01:** 7,273   **02 MLR** 78%   **/ 02 Admin Exp** 20%
Enroll(000): Q1 03: 163   **02:** 163   **01:** 131   **Med Exp PMPM:** $154
Principal Investments: Cash and equiv (73%), other (27%)
Provider Compensation ($000): Contr fee ($263,679), capitation ($7,465), FFS ($4,713)
Total Member Encounters: Phys (588,030), non-phys (274,297)
Group Affiliation: AMERIGROUP Corp
Licensed in: DC, MD
Address: 857 Elkridge landing Rd #300, Linthicum, MD 21090
Phone: (757) 490-6900   **Dom State:** DE   **Commenced Bus:** June 1999

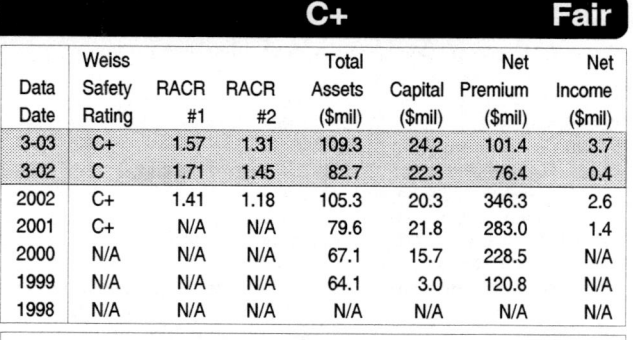

Data Date	Weiss Safety Rating	RACR #1	RACR #2	Total Assets ($mil)	Capital ($mil)	Net Premium ($mil)	Net Income ($mil)
3-03	C+	1.57	1.31	109.3	24.2	101.4	3.7
3-02	C	1.71	1.45	82.7	22.3	76.4	0.4
2002	C+	1.41	1.18	105.3	20.3	346.3	2.6
2001	C+	N/A	N/A	79.6	21.8	283.0	1.4
2000	N/A	N/A	N/A	67.1	15.7	228.5	N/A
1999	N/A	N/A	N/A	64.1	3.0	120.8	N/A
1998	N/A	N/A	N/A	N/A	N/A	N/A	N/A

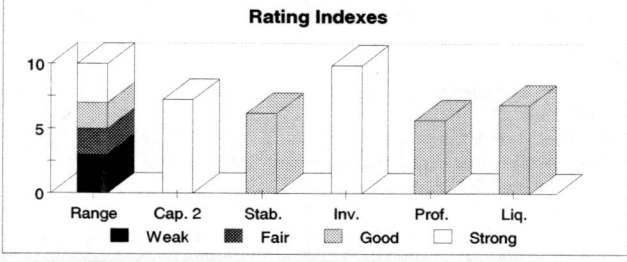

Rating Indexes chart: Range, Cap. 2, Stab., Inv., Prof., Liq. (Weak, Fair, Good, Strong)

AMERIGROUP NEW JERSEY INC   C-   Fair

Major Rating Factors: Fair overall results on stability tests (3.8 on a scale of 0 to 10) based on rapid premium growth over the last five years, rapid enrollment growth during the past five years. Weak profitability index (2.5) with operating losses during 2001 and 2002. Weak liquidity (1.1) as a spike in claims may stretch capacity.
Other Rating Factors: Good capitalization index (5.4) based on good current risk-adjusted capital (severe loss scenario). High quality investment portfolio (9.9) containing no exposure to mortgages, junk bonds, or unaffiliated stocks.
Principal Business: Medicaid (100%)
Mem Phys: 02: 6,091   **01:** 5,950   **02 MLR** 85%   **/ 02 Admin Exp** 18%
Enroll(000): Q1 03: 100   **02:** 99   **01:** 88   **Med Exp PMPM:** $148
Principal Investments: Cash and equiv (23%), other (77%)
Provider Compensation ($000): Contr fee ($158,298), capitation ($3,116), FFS ($2,587)
Total Member Encounters: Phys (879,475), non-phys (194,691)
Group Affiliation: AMERIGROUP Corp
Licensed in: NJ
Address: 399 Thomall St., 9th Floor, Edison, NJ 08818
Phone: (757) 490-6900   **Dom State:** NJ   **Commenced Bus:** February 1996

Data Date	Weiss Safety Rating	RACR #1	RACR #2	Total Assets ($mil)	Capital ($mil)	Net Premium ($mil)	Net Income ($mil)
3-03	C-	0.98	0.82	43.2	10.7	53.9	0.0
3-02	C-	1.48	1.26	41.2	12.9	45.8	0.2
2002	C-	0.94	0.78	39.1	10.3	194.2	-4.1
2001	C-	1.40	1.20	40.2	12.8	132.6	-2.3
2000	C-	1.86	1.57	36.2	12.7	84.3	2.8
1999	C-	1.59	1.33	39.6	9.6	71.8	3.3
1998	D-	1.49	1.27	23.8	7.3	40.6	4.4

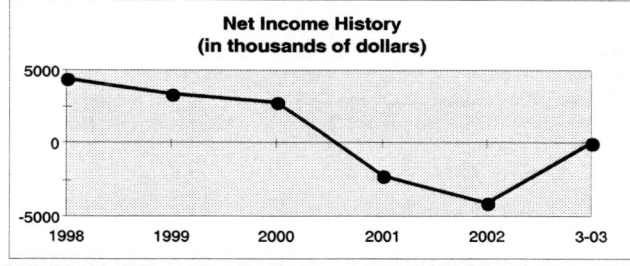

Net Income History (in thousands of dollars), 1998-3-03

AMERIGROUP TEXAS INC   D+   Weak

Major Rating Factors: Poor capitalization index (2.6 on a scale of 0 to 10) based on weak current risk-adjusted capital (moderate loss scenario). Fair overall results on stability tests (4.4) based on rapid premium growth over the last five years, rapid enrollment growth during the past five years. Good liquidity (5.7) with sufficient resources (cash flows and marketable investments) to handle a spike in claims.
Other Rating Factors: Excellent profitability (7.2) with operating gains in each of the last five years. High quality investment portfolio (9.9) containing no exposure to mortgages, junk bonds, or unaffiliated stocks.
Principal Business: Medicaid (92%), comp med (8%)
Mem Phys: 02: 5,526   **01:** 5,766   **02 MLR** 80%   **/ 02 Admin Exp** 18%
Enroll(000): Q1 03: 304   **02:** 295   **01:** 214   **Med Exp PMPM:** $144
Principal Investments: Cash and equiv (82%), other (18%)
Provider Compensation ($000): Contr fee ($374,051), FFS ($21,790), capitation ($20,997)
Total Member Encounters: Phys (2,593,589), non-phys (597,170)
Group Affiliation: AMERIGROUP Corp
Licensed in: TX
Address: 4425 Corporation Lane, Virginia Beach, VA 23462
Phone: (757) 490-6900   **Dom State:** TX   **Commenced Bus:** October 1996

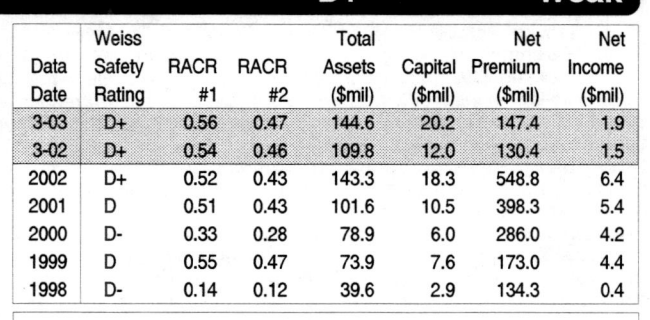

Data Date	Weiss Safety Rating	RACR #1	RACR #2	Total Assets ($mil)	Capital ($mil)	Net Premium ($mil)	Net Income ($mil)
3-03	D+	0.56	0.47	144.6	20.2	147.4	1.9
3-02	D+	0.54	0.46	109.8	12.0	130.4	1.5
2002	D+	0.52	0.43	143.3	18.3	548.8	6.4
2001	D	0.51	0.43	101.6	10.5	398.3	5.4
2000	D-	0.33	0.28	78.9	6.0	286.0	4.2
1999	D	0.55	0.47	73.9	7.6	173.0	4.4
1998	D-	0.14	0.12	39.6	2.9	134.3	0.4

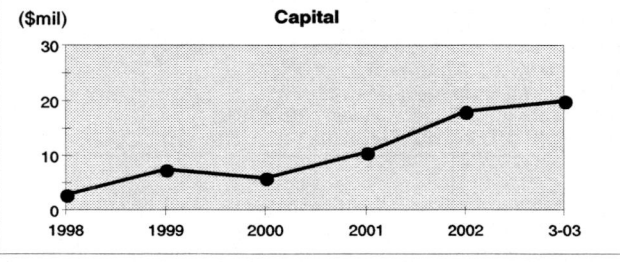

Capital ($mil) chart, 1998-3-03

www.WeissRatings.com   95   * Denotes a Weiss Recommended Company

II. Analysis of Largest Companies

AMERIHEALTH HMO INC — B Good

Major Rating Factors: Good overall profitability index (5.6 on a scale of 0 to 10) despite a decline in earnings during 2002. Good quality investment portfolio (6.8) containing little or no exposure to mortgages, junk bonds, or unaffiliated stocks. Good liquidity (6.6) with sufficient resources (cash flows and marketable investments) to handle a spike in claims.
Other Rating Factors: Strong capitalization index (8.0) based on excellent current risk-adjusted capital (severe loss scenario) despite some fluctuation in capital levels. Excellent overall results on stability tests (7.5) based on consistent premium and capital growth in the last five years. Good financial strength from affiliates.
Principal Business: Comp med (66%), Medicaid (25%), Medicare (5%), FEHB (4%).
Mem Phys: 02: 25,743 **01:** 24,698 **02 MLR** 89% **/ 02 Admin Exp** 10%
Enroll(000): Q1 03: 239 **02:** 252 **01:** 212 **Med Exp PMPM:** $207
Principal Investments: Affiliate common stock (75%), cash and equiv (1%), other (25%)
Provider Compensation ($000): Contr fee ($329,125), capitation ($198,423), FFS ($23,812)
Total Member Encounters: Phys (2,919,784), non-phys (1,023,101)
Group Affiliation: Independence Blue Cross Inc
Licensed in: DE, NJ, PA
Address: 1901 Market St, Philadelphia, PA 19103
Phone: (215) 241-2400 **Dom State:** PA **Commenced Bus:** April 1978

Data Date	Weiss Safety Rating	RACR #1	RACR #2	Total Assets ($mil)	Capital ($mil)	Net Premium ($mil)	Net Income ($mil)
3-03	B	2.16	1.80	534.6	401.9	170.6	0.6
3-02	B	0.00	0.00	498.0	396.3	146.8	1.6
2002	B	2.13	1.77	519.7	396.0	645.3	33.2
2001	B	2.47	2.29	480.1	391.7	499.4	42.9
2000	B	3.24	2.61	473.6	370.5	530.5	40.8
1999	B	3.38	2.74	478.5	357.0	491.6	16.7
1998	B	3.60	2.92	415.8	304.3	415.6	40.4

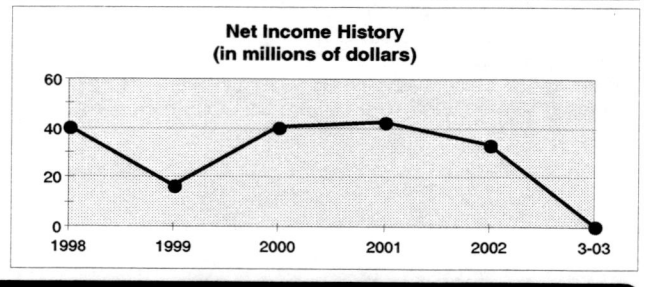

Net Income History (in millions of dollars) — 1998 through 3-03

AMERIHEALTH INSURANCE CO OF NJ — C+ Fair

Major Rating Factors: Fair quality investment portfolio (3.7 on a scale of 0 to 10). Good overall profitability index (6.7) despite a decline in earnings during 2002. Good liquidity (5.1) with sufficient resources (cash flows and marketable investments) to handle a spike in claims.
Other Rating Factors: Strong capitalization (8.4) based on excellent current risk-adjusted capital (severe loss scenario) reflecting significant improvement over results in 1999.
Principal Business: Comp med (100%)
Mem Phys: 02: 26,978 **01:** 26,952 **02 MLR** 85% **/ 02 Admin Exp** 14%
Enroll(000): 02: 64 **01:** 70 **Med Exp PMPM:** $224
Principal Investments: Other (1%), cash and equiv (99%)
Provider Compensation ($000): Contr fee ($146,731), FFS ($21,139), capitation ($498)
Total Member Encounters: Phys (370,050), non-phys (478,689)
Group Affiliation: Independence Blue Cross Inc
Licensed in: NJ
Address: 8000 Midlantic Dr Ste 333, Mount Laurel, NJ 08054-1560
Phone: (856) 778-6598 **Dom State:** NJ **Commenced Bus:** June 1995

Data Date	Weiss Safety Rating	RACR #1	RACR #2	Total Assets ($mil)	Capital ($mil)	Net Premium ($mil)	Net Income ($mil)
2002	C+	2.49	2.08	85.1	30.8	211.5	3.5
2001	U	0.84	0.67	75.8	27.1	201.5	4.9
2000	C	0.57	0.47	60.1	20.8	206.1	3.6
1999	C	0.56	0.46	59.6	18.5	193.0	2.0
1998	C+	0.56	0.47	51.1	17.1	170.3	-0.4

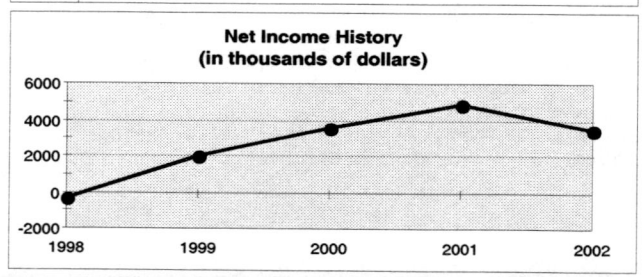

Net Income History (in thousands of dollars) — 1998 through 2002

AMERITAS LIFE INSURANCE CORPORATION * — B+ Good

Major Rating Factors: Good overall results on stability tests (5.2 on a scale of 0 to 10). Strengths include good financial strength of affiliated Ameritas Acacia Mutual Holding Co, good operational trends and excellent risk diversification. Good quality investment portfolio (5.0) despite mixed results such as: no exposure to mortgages and large holdings of BBB rated bonds but small junk bond holdings. Good liquidity (6.9).
Other Rating Factors: Strong capitalization (9.2) based on excellent risk adjusted capital (severe loss scenario). Excellent profitability (8.2) with operating gains in each of the last five years.
Principal Business: Group health insurance (64%), reinsurance (17%), individual life insurance (13%), and individual annuities (5%).
Principal Investments: NonCMO investment grade bonds (47%), mortgages in good standing (17%), common & preferred stock (10%), CMOs and structured securities (8%), and misc. investments (19%).
Investments in Affiliates: 5%
Group Affiliation: Ameritas Acacia Mutual Holding Co
Licensed in: All states except NY, PR
Commenced Business: May 1887
Address: 5900 O Street, Lincoln, NE 68510
Phone: (402) 467-1122 **Domicile State:** NE **NAIC Code:** 61301

Data Date	Weiss Safety Rating	RACR #1	RACR #2	Total Assets ($mil)	Capital ($mil)	Net Premium ($mil)	Net Income ($mil)
6-03	B+	4.02	2.49	2,417.9	601.9	236.1	6.5
6-02	A-	3.48	2.21	2,334.9	588.5	220.8	22.3
2002	B+	4.25	2.62	2,302.8	586.7	444.7	41.5
2001	A-	3.40	2.15	2,334.8	585.0	411.2	50.6
2000	A-	3.56	2.22	2,247.0	487.9	773.7	78.4
1999	A-	3.56	2.16	2,088.4	413.2	572.4	52.8
1998	A-	3.25	2.04	2,006.0	357.7	562.9	39.2

Ameritas Acacia Mutual Holding Co
Composite Group Rating: B
Largest Group Members

Largest Group Members	Assets ($mil)	Weiss Safety Rating
AMERITAS LIFE INS CORP	2303	B+
AMERITAS VARIABLE LIFE INS CO	2005	B
ACACIA LIFE INS CO	1033	B
ACACIA NATIONAL LIFE INS CO	598	B-
FIRST AMERITAS LIFE INS CO OF NY	36	B

AMEX ASSURANCE CO — B Good

Major Rating Factors: Good overall profitability index (5.5 on a scale of 0 to 10). Fair expense controls. Return on equity has been excellent over the last five years averaging 34.8%. Good liquidity (6.9) with sufficient resources (cash flows and marketable investments) to handle a spike in claims.
Other Rating Factors: Fair overall results on stability tests (4.0) including weak results on operational trends. Strengths include potentially strong support from affiliation with American Express Group. The largest net exposure for one risk is conservative at 1.6% of capital. Strong long-term capitalization index (8.0) based on excellent current risk adjusted capital (severe and moderate loss scenarios), despite some fluctuation in capital levels. Ample reserve history (9.3) that helps to protect the company against sharp claims increases.
Principal Business: Auto liability (29%), group accident & health (29%), auto physical damage (22%), inland marine (11%), homeowners multiple peril (6%), and other liability (2%).
Principal Investments: Investment grade bonds (99%) and cash (2%).
Investments in Affiliates: None
Group Affiliation: American Express Group
Licensed in: All states, the District of Columbia and Puerto Rico
Commenced Business: February 1973
Address: 227 W Monroe St Ste 3600, Chicago, IL 60606
Phone: (920) 330-5100   **Domicile State:** IL   **NAIC Code:** 27928

Data Date	Weiss Safety Rating	RACR #1	RACR #2	Loss Ratio %	Total Assets ($mil)	Capital ($mil)	Net Premium ($mil)	Net Income ($mil)
6-03	B	3.22	2.01	N/A	344.3	208.5	244.5	47.7
6-02	B	3.19	1.96	N/A	363.4	193.2	199.2	33.4
2002	B	2.57	1.62	28.7	348.1	176.4	197.1	57.7
2001	B	2.84	1.76	28.0	358.9	171.5	165.4	53.7
2000	B	2.95	1.83	26.7	378.4	180.7	138.2	62.9
1999	B	2.10	1.37	28.9	435.5	183.6	132.5	65.7
1998	B	1.74	1.18	34.5	452.1	177.1	125.6	59.7

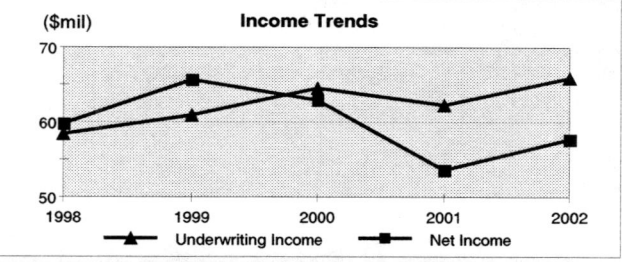

Income Trends chart ($mil): Underwriting Income and Net Income, 1998–2002.

AMIL INTERNATIONAL TEXAS INC — D Weak

Major Rating Factors: Weak profitability index (0.7 on a scale of 0 to 10) with operating losses during 1998, 1999 and 2002. Average return on equity has been poor at -31%. Poor capitalization (2.0) based on weak current risk-adjusted capital (moderate loss scenario) as results have slipped from the good range over the last two years. Weak overall results on stability tests (0.7) based on a decline in the number of member physicians during 2002, excessive premium growth during 2002.
Other Rating Factors: Good liquidity (6.4) with sufficient resources (cash flows and marketable investments) to handle a spike in claims. High quality investment portfolio (9.9) containing no exposure to mortgages, junk bonds, or unaffiliated stocks.
Principal Business: Comp med (100%)
Mem Phys: 02: 1,339   **01:** 2,100   **02 MLR** 96%   **/ 02 Admin Exp** 10%
Enroll(000): Q1 03: 24   **02:** 29   **01:** 24   **Med Exp PMPM:** $196
Principal Investments: Cash and equiv (97%), other (3%)
Provider Compensation ($000): FFS ($46,512), capitation ($13,364)
Total Member Encounters: Phys (5,180), non-phys (24,270)
Group Affiliation: Visions Group
Licensed in: TX
Address: 9229 Waterford Centre Blvd 500, Austin, TX 78758
Phone: (512) 349-4137   **Dom State:** TX   **Commenced Bus:** March 1997

Data Date	Weiss Safety Rating	RACR #1	RACR #2	Total Assets ($mil)	Capital ($mil)	Net Premium ($mil)	Net Income ($mil)
3-03	D	0.50	0.42	14.2	5.0	15.8	1.3
3-02	C-	1.09	0.92	14.8	6.2	15.7	0.1
2002	D	0.31	0.25	13.7	3.0	65.8	-3.3
2001	C-	1.09	0.93	14.1	6.2	44.8	0.1
2000	D	2.15	1.82	10.9	6.2	22.2	0.9
1999	D-	0.00	0.00	8.5	4.3	15.2	-0.2
1998	D	1.54	1.33	5.1	1.7	7.9	-2.1

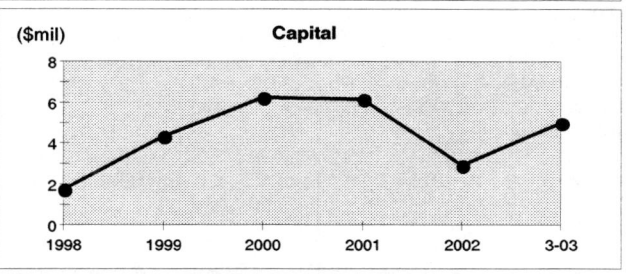

Capital chart ($mil), 1998 through 3-03.

ANTERO HEALTH PLANS INC — B- Good

Major Rating Factors: Fair overall results on stability tests (4.9 on a scale of 0 to 10). Rating is significantly influenced by the fair financial results of PacifiCare Health Systems. Excellent profitability (8.0). Strong capitalization index (10.0) based on excellent current risk-adjusted capital (severe loss scenario).
Other Rating Factors: High quality investment portfolio (9.9) containing no exposure to mortgages, junk bonds, or unaffiliated stocks. Excellent liquidity (8.3) with ample operational cash flow and liquid investments.
Principal Business: Comp med (100%)
Mem Phys: 02: 5,342   **01:** 4,863   **02 MLR** 70%   **/ 02 Admin Exp** 8%
Enroll(000): Q1 03: 6   **02:** 6   **01:** 7   **Med Exp PMPM:** $195
Principal Investments: Cash and equiv (91%), other (9%)
Provider Compensation ($000): Contr fee ($11,715), capitation ($2,867), FFS ($1,275)
Total Member Encounters: Phys (41,902), non-phys (23,116)
Group Affiliation: PacifiCare Health Systems
Licensed in: CO
Address: 6455 S Yosemite St, Greenwood Village, CO 80111
Phone: (303) 220-5800   **Dom State:** CO   **Commenced Bus:** April 1989

Data Date	Weiss Safety Rating	RACR #1	RACR #2	Total Assets ($mil)	Capital ($mil)	Net Premium ($mil)	Net Income ($mil)
3-03	B-	5.14	4.28	12.3	10.4	6.4	0.4
3-02	C	5.17	4.40	12.2	9.4	5.7	0.9
2002	B-	5.11	4.26	12.1	10.4	21.9	4.9
2001	C	5.16	4.39	13.8	8.9	15.7	2.0
2000	C	2.52	2.16	15.2	6.7	25.4	0.9
1999	B	0.00	0.00	17.4	1.2	22.1	-1.0
1998	B	1.00	0.87	N/A	N/A	N/A	-1.6

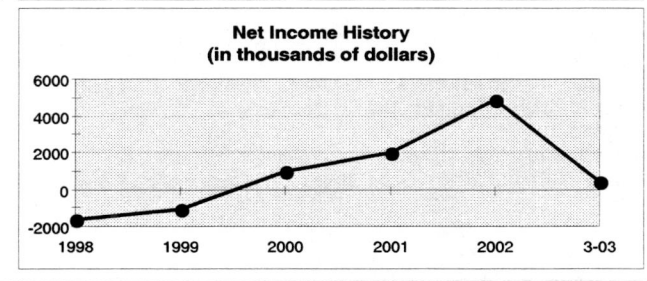

Net Income History chart (in thousands of dollars), 1998 through 3-03.

www.WeissRatings.com   * Denotes a Weiss Recommended Company

II. Analysis of Largest Companies

Winter 2003 - 04

ANTHEM ALLIANCE HEALTH INSURANCE COMPANY — C+ — Fair

Major Rating Factors: Fair overall results on stability tests (4.2 on a scale of 0 to 10) including negative cash flow from operations for 2002. Good overall profitability (6.8) despite operating losses during the first six months of 2003. Return on equity has been low, averaging 3.9%. Strong capitalization (8.0) based on excellent risk adjusted capital (severe loss scenario).
Other Rating Factors: High quality investment portfolio (8.7). Excellent liquidity (9.2).
Principal Business: Individual health insurance (47%), reinsurance (36%), individual life insurance (9%), and group life insurance (8%).
Principal Investments: NonCMO investment grade bonds (59%), CMOs and structured securities (39%), and cash (2%).
Investments in Affiliates: None
Group Affiliation: Anthem Ins Companies Inc
Licensed in: All states except NY, PR
Commenced Business: March 1975
Address: 5055 Keller Springs Rd, Dallas, TX 75248
Phone: (317) 577-1344 **Domicile State:** TX **NAIC Code:** 85286

Data Date	Weiss Safety Rating	RACR #1	RACR #2	Total Assets ($mil)	Capital ($mil)	Net Premium ($mil)	Net Income ($mil)
6-03	C+	9.01	8.11	102.1	74.9	28.3	-1.3
6-02	C+	5.51	4.30	94.0	77.0	0.0	1.9
2002	C+	10.84	9.76	87.8	76.3	0.0	1.2
2001	C+	3.28	2.64	112.0	75.1	192.3	26.9
2000	C+	6.45	4.99	240.8	62.4	83.8	3.7
1999	C+	7.20	6.48	252.4	59.2	28.5	5.0
1998	C+	6.53	5.88	212.1	49.9	41.2	14.2

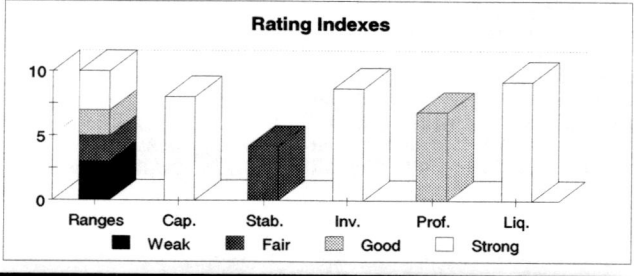

ANTHEM HEALTH PLANS INC — C+ — Fair

Major Rating Factors: Good overall profitability index (6.3 on a scale of 0 to 10) despite operating losses during 1999. Good liquidity (6.2) with sufficient resources (cash flows and marketable investments) to handle a spike in claims. Low quality investment portfolio (1.8).
Other Rating Factors: Strong capitalization (8.7) based on excellent current risk-adjusted capital (severe loss scenario) despite some fluctuation in capital levels.
Principal Business: Comp med (71%), Medicaid (12%), med supp (9%), FEHB (4%), dental (3%), stop loss (1%).
Mem Phys: 02: 18,180 **01:** 14,778 **02 MLR** 84% **/ 02 Admin Exp** 10%
Enroll(000): Q1 03: 767 **02:** 763 **01:** 691 **Med Exp PMPM:** $208
Principal Investments: Real estate (9%), nonaffiliate common stock (1%), other (93%).
Provider Compensation ($000): Contr fee ($1,389,933), FFS ($299,381), capitation ($111,713), bonus arrang ($109), other ($10,434)
Total Member Encounters: Phys (3,511,057), non-phys (3,938,063)
Group Affiliation: Anthem Ins Companies Inc
Licensed in: CT
Address: 370 Bassett Rd, North Haven, CT 06473
Phone: (203) 239-4911 **Dom State:** CT **Commenced Bus:** August 1977

Data Date	Weiss Safety Rating	RACR #1	RACR #2	Total Assets ($mil)	Capital ($mil)	Net Premium ($mil)	Net Income ($mil)
3-03	C+	2.67	2.23	786.0	304.5	571.9	27.7
3-02	C+	0.00	0.00	750.8	263.6	514.5	25.2
2002	C+	2.53	2.11	766.6	287.4	2,167.2	121.3
2001	N/A	N/A	N/A	744.8	229.4	1,884.2	N/A
2000	U	1.57	1.20	833.2	335.5	1,781.5	95.7
1999	C	1.63	1.25	689.0	273.1	1,452.7	-18.2
1998	C	2.23	1.68	661.3	336.1	1,114.1	42.6

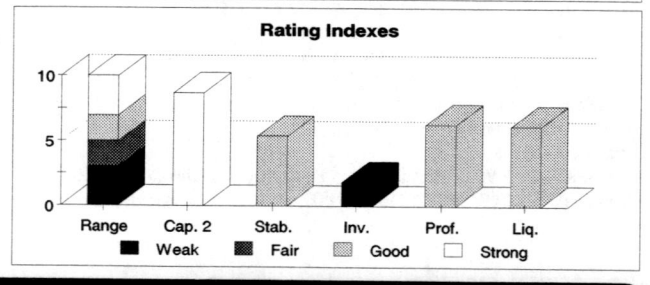

ANTHEM HEALTH PLANS OF KENTUCKY INC * — B+ — Good

Major Rating Factors: Good overall profitability index (5.4 on a scale of 0 to 10) despite operating losses during 1999. Good overall results on stability tests (6.3). Good financial strength from affiliates. Good liquidity (6.7) with sufficient resources (cash flows and marketable investments) to handle a spike in claims.
Other Rating Factors: Strong capitalization index (10.0) based on excellent current risk-adjusted capital (severe loss scenario) despite some fluctuation in capital levels. High quality investment portfolio (9.9) containing little or no exposure to mortgages, junk bonds, or unaffiliated stocks.
Principal Business: Comp med (85%), med supp (9%), Medicare (6%)
Mem Phys: 02: 6,821 **01:** 6,829 **02 MLR** 80% **/ 02 Admin Exp** 13%
Enroll(000): Q1 03: 555 **02:** 568 **01:** 529 **Med Exp PMPM:** $162
Principal Investments: Cash and equiv (9%), real estate (1%), nonaffiliate common stock (1%), other (89%).
Provider Compensation ($000): FFS ($532,939), contr fee ($464,812), bonus arrang ($57,321), capitation ($19,647)
Total Member Encounters: Phys (4,225,193), non-phys (2,660,824)
Group Affiliation: Anthem Ins Companies Inc
Licensed in: KY
Address: 9901 Linn Station Rd, Louisville, KY 40223
Phone: (502) 423-2011 **Dom State:** KY **Commenced Bus:** July 1993

Data Date	Weiss Safety Rating	RACR #1	RACR #2	Total Assets ($mil)	Capital ($mil)	Net Premium ($mil)	Net Income ($mil)
3-03	B+	4.07	3.39	659.5	297.2	336.5	17.0
3-02	B	3.99	2.75	602.2	224.8	323.8	17.1
2002	B	3.89	3.24	662.7	283.3	1,323.6	75.1
2001	B	3.95	2.73	637.9	284.1	1,148.3	15.6
2000	B-	4.96	3.94	549.9	283.4	1,027.4	39.7
1999	B-	4.11	3.26	478.7	225.7	903.1	-12.6
1998	B-	12.18	8.51	559.5	268.7	820.0	32.6

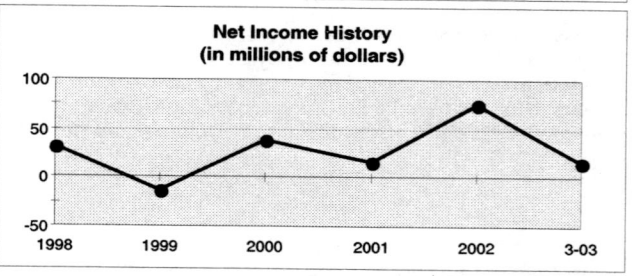

Winter 2003 - 04
II. Analysis of Largest Companies

ANTHEM HEALTH PLANS OF MAINE INC — B — Good

Major Rating Factors: Good liquidity (6.8 on a scale of 0 to 10) with sufficient resources (cash flows and marketable investments) to handle a spike in claims. Excellent profitability (8.8). Strong capitalization (8.3) based on excellent current risk-adjusted capital (severe loss scenario). Moreover, capital levels have been consistent in recent years.
Other Rating Factors: High quality investment portfolio (9.8) containing little or no exposure to mortgages, junk bonds, or unaffiliated stocks.
Principal Business: Comp med (81%), FEHB (10%), med supp (8%)
Mem Phys: 02: 2,558 **01:** 2,567 **02 MLR** 82% **/ 02 Admin Exp** 11%
Enroll(000): Q1 03: 303 **02:** 297 **01:** 307 **Med Exp PMPM:** $190
Principal Investments: Affiliate common stock (14%), real estate (10%), cash and equiv (7%), other (71%)
Provider Compensation ($000): Contr fee ($405,589), FFS ($223,490), capitation ($21,737)
Total Member Encounters: Phys (1,685,222), non-phys (1,725,624)
Group Affiliation: Anthem Ins Companies Inc
Licensed in: ME
Address: 2 Gannett Cr, S Portland, ME 04106-6911
Phone: (207) 822-7000 **Dom State:** ME **Commenced Bus:** June 2000

Data Date	Weiss Safety Rating	RACR #1	RACR #2	Total Assets ($mil)	Capital ($mil)	Net Premium ($mil)	Net Income ($mil)
3-03	B	2.36	1.97	279.8	101.7	225.5	8.7
3-02	C	2.17	1.68	222.3	51.9	206.3	7.1
2002	B-	2.16	1.80	268.2	92.1	839.1	44.8
2001	C	2.14	1.67	460.8	53.4	469.4	25.0
2000	B	N/A	N/A	184.8	25.4	173.1	7.7
1999	N/A	N/A	N/A	N/A	N/A	N/A	N/A
1998	N/A	N/A	N/A	N/A	N/A	N/A	N/A

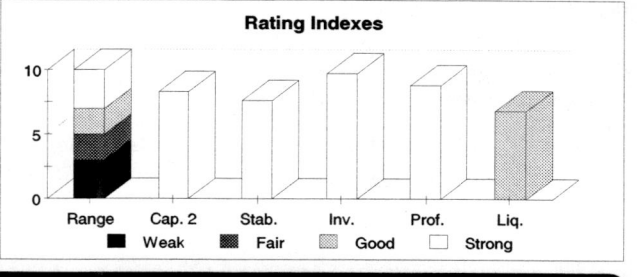

Rating Indexes: Range, Cap. 2, Stab., Inv., Prof., Liq. (Weak / Fair / Good / Strong)

ANTHEM HEALTH PLANS OF NEW HAMPSHIRE — B — Good

Major Rating Factors: Good overall profitability index (6.6 on a scale of 0 to 10). Good liquidity (6.7) with sufficient resources (cash flows and marketable investments) to handle a spike in claims. Strong capitalization (9.7) based on excellent current risk-adjusted capital (severe loss scenario) reflecting significant improvement over results in 2000.
Other Rating Factors: High quality investment portfolio (9.0) containing little or no exposure to mortgages, junk bonds, or unaffiliated stocks.
Principal Business: FEHB (42%), med supp (33%), comp med (25%)
Mem Phys: 02: 6,181 **01:** 4,191 **02 MLR** 85% **/ 02 Admin Exp** 14%
Enroll(000): Q1 03: 95 **02:** 89 **01:** 48 **Med Exp PMPM:** $226
Principal Investments: Affiliate common stock (57%), cash and equiv (10%), other (41%)
Provider Compensation ($000): Contr fee ($180,679)
Total Member Encounters: Phys (1,139,570), non-phys (239,618)
Group Affiliation: Anthem Ins Companies Inc
Licensed in: NH
Address: 3000 Goffs Falls Rd, Manchester, NH 03111-0001
Phone: (207) 822-7000 **Dom State:** NH **Commenced Bus:** October 1999

Data Date	Weiss Safety Rating	RACR #1	RACR #2	Total Assets ($mil)	Capital ($mil)	Net Premium ($mil)	Net Income ($mil)
3-03	B	3.51	2.92	247.6	128.8	65.2	3.8
3-02	B-	3.88	3.04	170.5	97.9	50.3	1.7
2002	B	3.15	2.62	258.5	115.7	215.4	3.8
2001	B-	3.92	3.07	171.1	89.9	191.7	7.8
2000	C	0.63	0.55	105.6	41.4	165.9	-0.2
1999	C	0.99	0.86	94.9	32.1	25.7	-1.0
1998	C-	0.91	0.81	N/A	N/A	N/A	-9.9

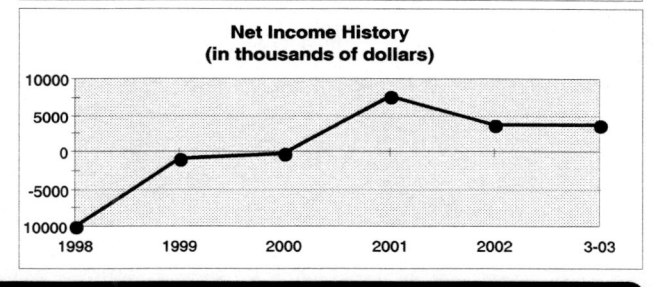

Net Income History (in thousands of dollars): 1998, 1999, 2000, 2001, 2002, 3-03

ANTHEM HEALTH PLANS OF VIRGINIA * — B+ — Good

Major Rating Factors: Good overall results on stability tests (6.1 on a scale of 0 to 10). Stability strengths include excellent operational trends, excellent risk adjusted capital for prior years and excellent risk diversification. Strong capitalization (5.9) based on excellent risk adjusted capital (severe loss scenario). Capital levels have been relatively consistent over the last five years. Good liquidity (6.2).
Other Rating Factors: High quality investment portfolio (8.3). Excellent profitability (8.8) with operating gains in each of the last five years.
Principal Business: Group health insurance (76%) and individual health insurance (24%).
Principal Investments: NonCMO investment grade bonds (57%), CMOs and structured securities (43%), and real estate (2%).
Investments in Affiliates: None
Group Affiliation: Anthem Ins Companies Inc
Licensed in: VA
Commenced Business: December 1935
Address: 2015 Staples Mill Rd, Richmond, VA 23230
Phone: (804) 354-7000 **Domicile State:** VA **NAIC Code:** 71835

Data Date	Weiss Safety Rating	RACR #1	RACR #2	Total Assets ($mil)	Capital ($mil)	Net Premium ($mil)	Net Income ($mil)
6-03	B+	2.27	1.80	1,621.3	615.6	1,324.1	94.6
6-02	B	1.76	1.31	1,183.5	501.1	1,172.4	40.3
2002	B+	1.87	1.49	1,476.4	560.4	2,424.7	135.2
2001	B	1.70	1.27	1,160.6	465.6	2,154.3	77.6
2000	B	2.14	1.58	1,152.6	490.0	1,852.0	88.5
1999	B	2.37	1.64	1,235.8	534.2	1,578.8	92.3
1998	B	2.50	1.77	1,108.0	489.0	1,435.4	93.1

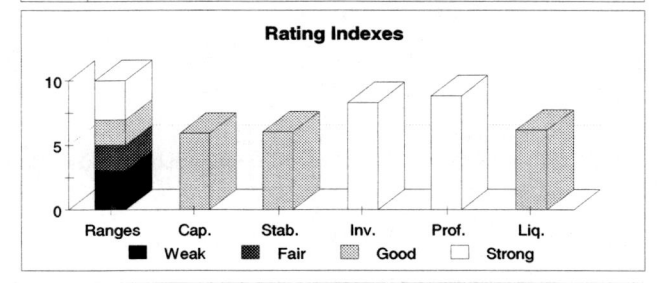

Rating Indexes: Ranges, Cap., Stab., Inv., Prof., Liq. (Weak / Fair / Good / Strong)

* Denotes a Weiss Recommended Company

II. Analysis of Largest Companies   Winter 2003 - 04

ANTHEM INS COMPANIES INC   B-   Good

Major Rating Factors: Fair overall results on stability tests (4.6 on a scale of 0 to 10) including weak results on operational trends. Strong long-term capitalization index (7.6) based on excellent current risk adjusted capital (severe and moderate loss scenarios), despite some fluctuation in capital levels.
Other Rating Factors: Ample reserve history (7.3) that can protect against increases in claims costs. Excellent profitability (7.0) with operating gains in each of the last five years. Excellent expense controls. Return on equity has been good over the last five years, averaging 10.3%. Excellent liquidity (7.5) with ample operational cash flow and liquid investments.
Principal Business: Group accident & health (86%) and other accident & health (14%).
Principal Investments: Misc. investments (58%) and investment grade bonds (45%).
Investments in Affiliates: 49%
Group Affiliation: Anthem Ins Companies Inc
Licensed in: AL, AZ, AR, CT, FL, GA, ID, IL, IN, IA, KS, KY, LA, MS, MO, MT, NE, NM, NC, ND, OH, OK, OR, SC, SD, TN, TX, UT, WA, WI, WY
Commenced Business: November 1944
Address: 120 Monument Circle, Indianapolis, IN 46204-4903
Phone: (317) 488-6484   **Domicile State:** IN   **NAIC Code:** 28207

Data Date	Weiss Safety Rating	RACR #1	RACR #2	Loss Ratio %	Total Assets ($mil)	Capital ($mil)	Net Premium ($mil)	Net Income ($mil)
6-03	B-	1.43	1.31	N/A	3,657.3	2,202.3	957.2	13.2
6-02	B-	1.51	1.41	N/A	3,352.5	2,090.4	863.7	119.9
2002	B-	1.56	1.47	88.0	3,614.6	2,260.7	1,806.2	347.1
2001	B-	1.72	1.62	90.4	3,515.5	2,338.7	1,753.2	406.9
2000	B-	1.40	1.31	89.8	2,856.9	1,907.5	1,509.2	91.7
1999	B-	1.17	1.11	90.9	2,541.2	1,444.2	1,109.3	201.7
1998	B-	1.43	1.36	91.4	2,618.8	1,729.6	904.7	80.6

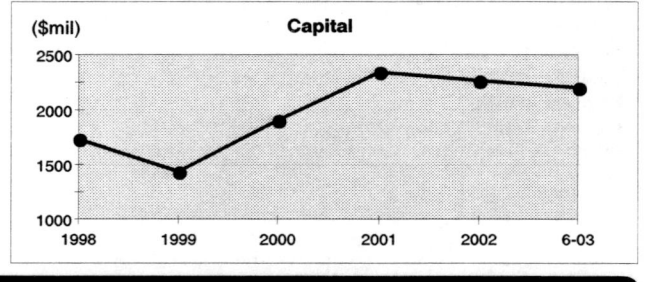

Capital ($mil) chart 1998-6-03

ANTHEM LIFE INSURANCE COMPANY   B-   Good

Major Rating Factors: Good overall results on stability tests (5.2 on a scale of 0 to 10). Stability strengths include excellent operational trends and excellent risk diversification. Strong capitalization (8.9) based on excellent risk adjusted capital (severe loss scenario). High quality investment portfolio (8.1).
Other Rating Factors: Excellent profitability (7.3) with operating gains in each of the last five years. Excellent liquidity (7.0).
Principal Business: Group life insurance (61%), group health insurance (23%), reinsurance (6%), individual health insurance (6%), and individual life insurance (4%).
Principal Investments: NonCMO investment grade bonds (51%), CMOs and structured securities (48%), and cash (1%).
Investments in Affiliates: None
Group Affiliation: Anthem Ins Companies Inc
Licensed in: All states except NY, RI, VT, PR
Commenced Business: September 1953
Address: 6740 N High St Suite 200, Worthington, OH 43085
Phone: (614) 438-3959   **Domicile State:** IN   **NAIC Code:** 61069

Data Date	Weiss Safety Rating	RACR #1	RACR #2	Total Assets ($mil)	Capital ($mil)	Net Premium ($mil)	Net Income ($mil)
6-03	B-	3.26	2.28	249.4	69.1	54.4	4.8
6-02	B-	3.72	2.57	257.9	72.8	49.7	5.7
2002	B-	2.87	2.01	244.8	64.3	97.5	12.3
2001	C+	3.02	2.09	239.5	66.5	92.9	12.8
2000	C+	2.64	1.86	252.3	65.1	112.5	13.8
1999	C+	2.86	1.99	111.5	33.0	45.8	8.1
1998	C+	2.53	1.78	101.1	30.1	49.8	5.3

Adverse Trends in Operations

Decrease in capital during 2002 (3%)
Decrease in asset base during 2001 (5%)
Decrease in premium volume from 2000 to 2001 (17%)
Decrease in premium volume from 1998 to 1999 (8%)
Increase in policy surrenders from 1998 to 1999 (110%)

ARKANSAS BLUE CROSS AND BLUE SHIELD *   B+   Good

Major Rating Factors: Excellent profitability (7.7 on a scale of 0 to 10). Strong capitalization (10.0) based on excellent current risk-adjusted capital (severe loss scenario). Moreover, capital levels have been consistent in recent years. High quality investment portfolio (8.7) containing little or no exposure to mortgages, junk bonds, or unaffiliated stocks.
Other Rating Factors: Excellent liquidity (7.0) with ample operational cash flow and liquid investments.
Principal Business: Comp med (64%), med supp (19%), FEHB (15%), dental (1%).
Mem Phys: 02: 9,881   01: 10,223   **02 MLR** 65%   / **02 Admin Exp** 12%
Enroll(000): Q1 03: 399   02: 394   01: 454   **Med Exp PMPM:** $109
Principal Investments: Affiliate common stock (22%), nonaffiliate common stock (10%), cash and equiv (9%), real estate (5%), other (54%).
Provider Compensation ($000): Contr fee ($562,313)
Total Member Encounters: Phys (36,112,667), non-phys (1,726,332)
Group Affiliation: Arkansas Bl Cross Bl Shield Group
Licensed in: AR
Address: 601 S Gaines, Little Rock, AR 72201
Phone: (501) 378-2000   **Dom State:** AR   **Commenced Bus:** November 1948

Data Date	Weiss Safety Rating	RACR #1	RACR #2	Total Assets ($mil)	Capital ($mil)	Net Premium ($mil)	Net Income ($mil)
3-03	B+	4.27	3.56	508.1	272.0	221.2	15.2
3-02	B+	0.00	0.00	468.4	226.2	208.1	19.5
2002	B+	4.08	3.40	495.9	259.6	842.7	48.2
2001	N/A	N/A	N/A	443.7	202.2	909.8	N/A
2000	U	1.60	1.20	367.2	158.4	770.8	11.2
1999	C	1.73	1.29	345.2	151.1	668.2	13.2
1998	C	1.83	1.37	293.0	140.0	576.2	6.3

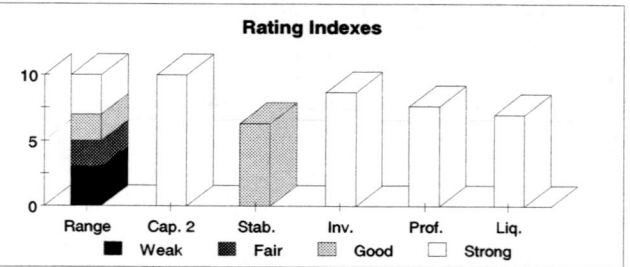

Rating Indexes chart: Range, Cap. 2, Stab., Inv., Prof., Liq. (Weak, Fair, Good, Strong)

100   www.WeissRatings.com

Winter 2003 - 04   II. Analysis of Largest Companies

ARNETT HMO INC   C   Fair

Major Rating Factors: Fair capitalization (4.1 on a scale of 0 to 10) based on fair current risk-adjusted capital (moderate loss scenario) reflecting improvement over results in 1999. Excellent profitability (9.3) with operating gains in each of the last five years. High quality investment portfolio (9.9) containing no exposure to mortgages, junk bonds, or unaffiliated stocks.
Other Rating Factors: Excellent overall results on stability tests (8.4) based on consistent premium and capital growth in the last five years. Excellent liquidity (7.0) with ample operational cash flow and liquid investments.
Principal Business: Comp med (77%), Medicare (18%), med only (4%), FEHB (1%)
Mem Phys: 02: 301   **01:** 291   **02 MLR** 85%   / **02 Admin Exp** 7%
Enroll(000):   **02:** 57   **01:** 53   **Med Exp PMPM:** $146
Principal Investments: Cash and equiv (100%)
Provider Compensation ($000): Capitation ($49,485), contr fee ($41,460), FFS ($3,501)
Total Member Encounters: Phys (214,741), non-phys (277,127)
Group Affiliation: Arnett Health Systems Inc
Licensed in: IN
Address: 415 N. 26th St., Ste 101, Lafayette, IN 47905
Phone: (765) 448-7400   **Dom State:** IN   **Commenced Bus:** June 1985

Data Date	Weiss Safety Rating	RACR #1	RACR #2	Total Assets ($mil)	Capital ($mil)	Net Premium ($mil)	Net Income ($mil)
2002	C	0.79	0.66	19.0	7.7	112.8	5.1
2001	C-	0.69	0.59	14.7	5.7	92.2	5.0
2000	D	0.57	0.49	13.0	4.4	77.8	2.3
1999	D	0.52	0.45	11.2	3.5	65.6	2.3
1998	D	0.52	0.46	7.2	2.4	56.5	0.4

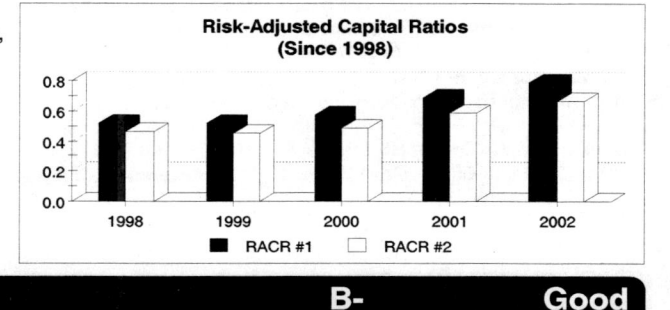

ASSURITY LIFE INSURANCE COMPANY   B-   Good

Major Rating Factors: Good overall results on stability tests (5.0 on a scale of 0 to 10). Stability strengths include good operational trends and good risk diversification. Good quality investment portfolio (6.1) despite mixed results such as: large holdings of BBB rated bonds but moderate junk bond exposure. Fair profitability (3.2). Return on equity has been low, averaging -2.4%.
Other Rating Factors: Strong capitalization (7.7) based on excellent risk adjusted capital (severe loss scenario). Excellent liquidity (7.6).
Principal Business: Group health insurance (29%), individual health insurance (28%), reinsurance (26%), individual annuities (13%), and individual life insurance (3%).
Principal Investments: NonCMO investment grade bonds (90%), noninv. grade bonds (6%), and mortgages in good standing (4%).
Investments in Affiliates: None
Group Affiliation: Lincoln Mutual Holding Co
Licensed in: All states except NY, PR
Commenced Business: March 1964
Address: 1526 K Street, Lincoln, NE 68508
Phone: (402) 476-6500   **Domicile State:** NE   **NAIC Code:** 71439

Data Date	Weiss Safety Rating	RACR #1	RACR #2	Total Assets ($mil)	Capital ($mil)	Net Premium ($mil)	Net Income ($mil)
6-03	B-	2.29	1.46	188.5	29.6	36.2	0.6
6-02	B-	2.56	1.66	166.3	29.2	19.5	2.6
2002	B-	2.83	1.72	174.0	30.8	46.4	3.3
2001	B-	2.18	1.45	159.8	28.1	56.1	-4.2
2000	B-	1.86	1.34	120.1	23.7	67.4	-7.0
1999	B-	4.28	3.85	74.6	33.0	9.7	2.0
1998	B-	4.30	3.87	73.2	33.0	7.7	0.8

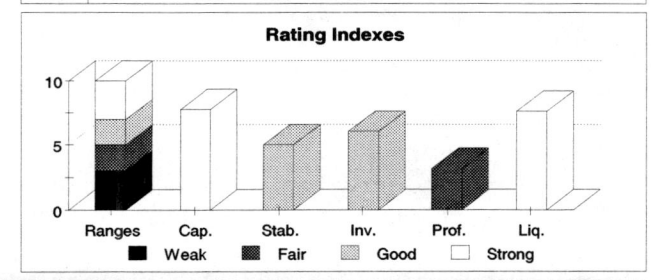

ASURIS NORTHWEST HEALTH   C+   Fair

Major Rating Factors: Good liquidity (6.9 on a scale of 0 to 10) with sufficient resources (cash flows and marketable investments) to handle a spike in claims. Weak profitability index (2.5) with operating losses during 1998, 1999, 2000 and 2001. Strong capitalization (8.0) based on excellent current risk-adjusted capital (severe loss scenario) reflecting significant improvement over results in 2000.
Other Rating Factors: High quality investment portfolio (9.9) containing no exposure to mortgages, junk bonds, or unaffiliated stocks.
Principal Business: Comp med (94%), med supp (5%), dental (2%)
Mem Phys: 02: 3,305   **01:** 2,484   **02 MLR** 81%   / **02 Admin Exp** 17%
Enroll(000): Q1 03: 36   **02:** 33   **01:** 26   **Med Exp PMPM:** $123
Principal Investments: Cash and equiv (63%), real estate (6%), other (31%)
Provider Compensation ($000): Contr fee ($43,601)
Total Member Encounters: Phys (112,406), non-phys (95,082)
Group Affiliation: Regence Group
Licensed in: WA
Address: 106 N 2nd, Walla Walla, WA 99362
Phone: (509) 525-5220   **Dom State:** WA   **Commenced Bus:** July 1933

Data Date	Weiss Safety Rating	RACR #1	RACR #2	Total Assets ($mil)	Capital ($mil)	Net Premium ($mil)	Net Income ($mil)
3-03	C+	2.16	1.80	22.3	7.8	17.8	-0.1
3-02	C+	2.09	1.76	18.2	6.5	11.7	0.4
2002	C+	2.21	1.84	20.7	8.0	53.6	1.1
2001	C+	2.09	1.76	20.9	6.8	43.2	-1.5
2000	C-	0.85	0.51	17.4	6.5	35.5	-1.4
1999	C-	0.86	0.66	14.2	5.3	27.3	-1.7
1998	C	1.05	0.59	16.6	3.1	9.8	-1.1

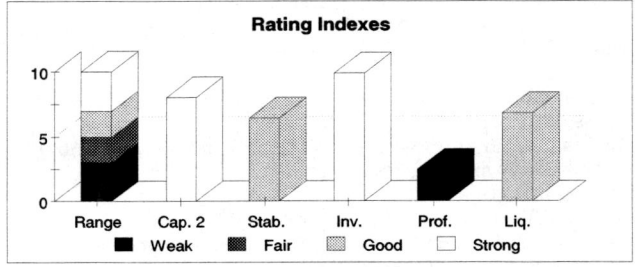

www.WeissRatings.com   * Denotes a Weiss Recommended Company

II. Analysis of Largest Companies

Winter 2003 - 04

ATHENS AREA HEALTH PLAN SELECT INC — D+ — Weak

Major Rating Factors: Weak profitability index (0.9 on a scale of 0 to 10) with $21.0 million in losses in the last five years. Good capitalization (5.1) based on good current risk-adjusted capital (severe loss scenario) reflecting some improvement over results in 2001. Good overall results on stability tests (5.1) despite fair risk-adjusted capital in prior years, rapid enrollment growth during the past five years.

Other Rating Factors: Good liquidity (6.8) with sufficient resources (cash flows and marketable investments) to handle a spike in claims. High quality investment portfolio (9.9) containing no exposure to mortgages, junk bonds, or unaffiliated stocks.

Principal Business: Comp med (100%)
Mem Phys: 02: 537 **01:** 523 **02 MLR** 97% **/ 02 Admin Exp** 17%
Enroll(000): Q1 03: 15 **02:** 17 **01:** 16 **Med Exp PMPM:** $178
Principal Investments: Cash and equiv (78%), other (22%)
Provider Compensation ($000): FFS ($33,913), capitation ($900)
Total Member Encounters: Phys (66,627), non-phys (52,523)
Group Affiliation: Athens Regional Health Services
Licensed in: GA
Address: 295 W Clayton St, Athens, GA 30601
Phone: (706) 549-0549 **Dom State:** GA **Commenced Bus:** October 1997

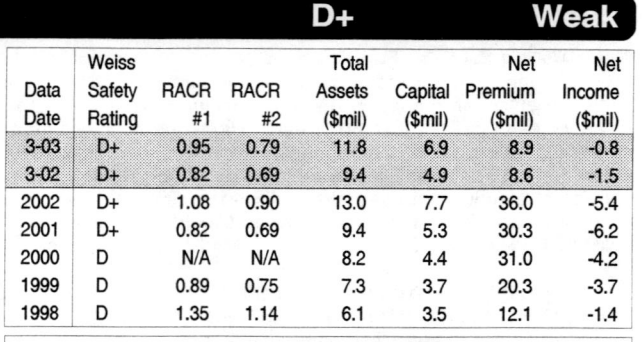

Data Date	Weiss Safety Rating	RACR #1	RACR #2	Total Assets ($mil)	Capital ($mil)	Net Premium ($mil)	Net Income ($mil)
3-03	D+	0.95	0.79	11.8	6.9	8.9	-0.8
3-02	D+	0.82	0.69	9.4	4.9	8.6	-1.5
2002	D+	1.08	0.90	13.0	7.7	36.0	-5.4
2001	D+	0.82	0.69	9.4	5.3	30.3	-6.2
2000	D	N/A	N/A	8.2	4.4	31.0	-4.2
1999	D	0.89	0.75	7.3	3.7	20.3	-3.7
1998	D	1.35	1.14	6.1	3.5	12.1	-1.4

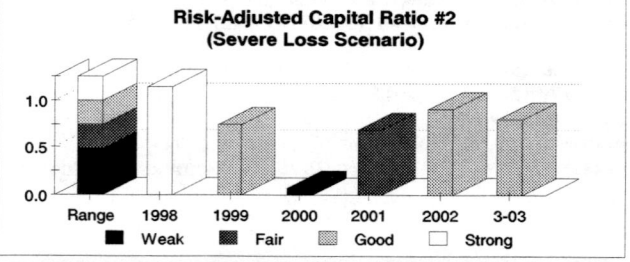

Risk-Adjusted Capital Ratio #2 (Severe Loss Scenario)

ATLANTIS HEALTH PLAN — E- — Very Weak

Major Rating Factors: Weak profitability index (0.0 on a scale of 0 to 10). Poor capitalization index (0.0) based on weak current risk-adjusted capital (severe loss scenario). Weak overall results on stability tests (0.0).

Other Rating Factors: Weak liquidity (0.1) as a spike in claims may stretch capacity. High quality investment portfolio (9.9) containing no exposure to mortgages, junk bonds, or unaffiliated stocks.

Principal Business: Comp med (100%)
Mem Phys: 02: 51,378 **01:** 1,929 **02 MLR** 83% **/ 02 Admin Exp** 24%
Enroll(000): Q1 03: 8 **02:** 11 **01:** 18 **Med Exp PMPM:** $221
Principal Investments: Cash and equiv (99%), other (1%)
Provider Compensation ($000): FFS ($33,157)
Total Member Encounters: Phys (223,142), non-phys (603,948)
Group Affiliation: Atlantis Health Systems Inc
Licensed in: NY
Address: 39 Broadway, Room 1240, New York, NY 10004
Phone: (212) 747-0877 **Dom State:** NY **Commenced Bus:** September 2000

Data Date	Weiss Safety Rating	RACR #1	RACR #2	Total Assets ($mil)	Capital ($mil)	Net Premium ($mil)	Net Income ($mil)
3-03	E-	0.00	0.00	4.6	-6.6	5.9	-0.1
3-02	U	0.00	0.00	15.6	0.1	14.3	0.0
2002	E-	0.00	0.00	7.8	-8.5	46.8	-2.6
2001	U	0.00	0.00	6.4	-1.7	13.5	-3.5
2000	E-	N/A	N/A	3.7	2.9	0.1	-2.6
1999	N/A	N/A	N/A	N/A	N/A	N/A	N/A
1998	N/A	N/A	N/A	N/A	N/A	N/A	N/A

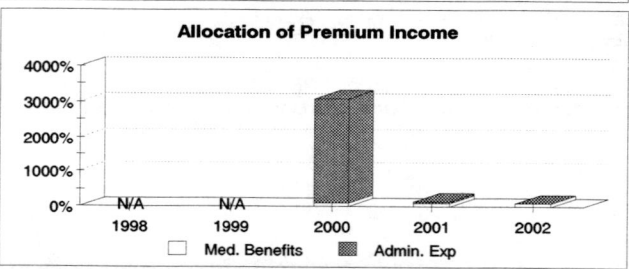

Allocation of Premium Income

ATRIUM HEALTH PLAN INC * — B+ — Good

Major Rating Factors: Good overall profitability index (6.4 on a scale of 0 to 10) despite a decline in earnings during 2002. Good overall results on stability tests (6.8) based on consistent premium and capital growth in the last five years but rapid enrollment growth during the past five years and a decline in the number of member physicians during 2002. Rating is significantly influenced by the fair financial results of Aware Integrated Inc. Good liquidity (5.8) with sufficient resources (cash flows and marketable investments) to handle a spike in claims.

Other Rating Factors: Strong capitalization (7.4) based on excellent current risk-adjusted capital (severe loss scenario) reflecting improvement over results in 1998. High quality investment portfolio (9.9) containing no exposure to mortgages, junk bonds, or unaffiliated stocks.

Principal Business: Medicaid (53%), comp med (45%), med supp (2%)
Mem Phys: 02: 4,619 **01:** 5,374 **02 MLR** 96% **/ 02 Admin Exp** 5%
Enroll(000): Q1 03: 44 **02:** 42 **01:** 36 **Med Exp PMPM:** $158
Principal Investments: Other (100%)
Provider Compensation ($000): Capitation ($40,290), contr fee ($23,031), FFS ($9,036), bonus arrang ($273)
Total Member Encounters: Phys (140,516), non-phys (23,501)
Group Affiliation: Aware Integrated Inc
Licensed in: WI
Address: 400 2nd St., Ste 270, Hudson, WI 54106
Phone: (715) 386-6886 **Dom State:** WI **Commenced Bus:** August 1984

Data Date	Weiss Safety Rating	RACR #1	RACR #2	Total Assets ($mil)	Capital ($mil)	Net Premium ($mil)	Net Income ($mil)
3-03	B+	1.69	1.41	14.3	7.7	22.7	0.6
3-02	B+	1.97	1.63	12.3	6.5	17.5	0.7
2002	B+	1.57	1.31	13.8	7.1	76.9	1.7
2001	B+	1.96	1.63	10.4	5.8	55.6	1.8
2000	B	1.61	1.35	7.1	3.9	34.9	0.3
1999	B-	1.50	1.26	7.0	3.6	25.6	0.5
1998	C+	1.13	0.95	7.6	3.1	27.6	-1.0

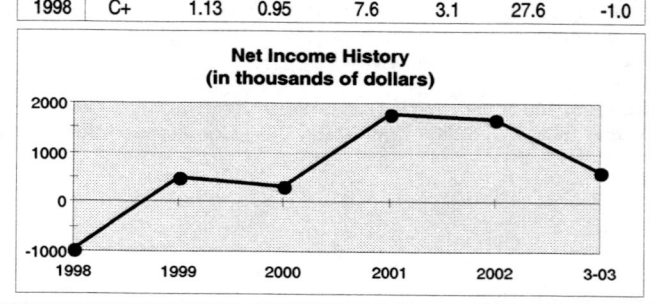

Net Income History (in thousands of dollars)

Winter 2003 - 04 | II. Analysis of Largest Companies

AULTCARE HMO — D+ Weak

Major Rating Factors: Weak profitability index (0.9 on a scale of 0 to 10) with modest operating losses during 2001 and 2002. Fair capitalization (4.2) based on fair current risk-adjusted capital (moderate loss scenario) as results have slipped from the good range over the last year. Fair overall results on stability tests (3.4).
Other Rating Factors: Good liquidity (6.7) with sufficient resources (cash flows and marketable investments) to handle a spike in claims. High quality investment portfolio (9.9) containing no exposure to mortgages, junk bonds, or unaffiliated stocks.
Principal Business: FEHB (61%), comp med (39%)
Mem Phys: 02: 893 **01:** 822 **02 MLR** 102% **/ 02 Admin Exp** 7%
Enroll(000): Q1 03: 5 **02:** 6 **01:** 5 **Med Exp PMPM:** $165
Principal Investments: Cash and equiv (16%), other (84%)
Provider Compensation ($000): Contr fee ($7,405), FFS ($1,581), capitation ($1,219)
Total Member Encounters: Phys (22,292), non-phys (35,592)
Group Affiliation: Aultman Health Foundation
Licensed in: OH
Address: 2600 Sixth St SW, Canton, OH 44710
Phone: (330) 438-6360 **Dom State:** OH **Commenced Bus:** March 1995

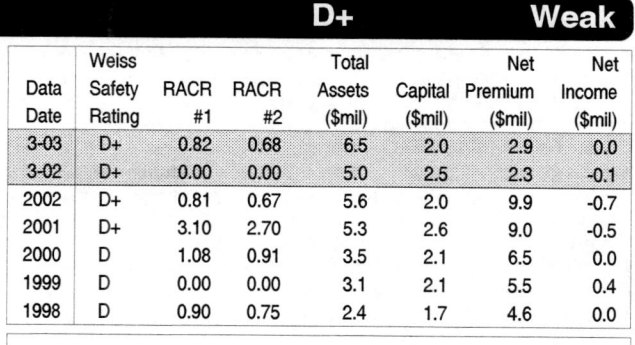

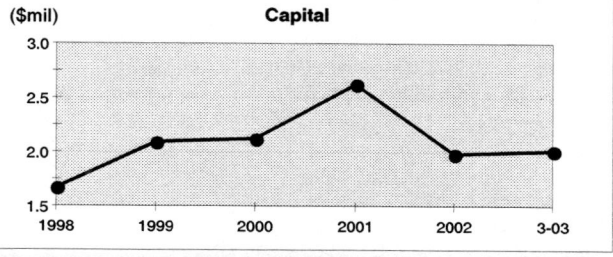

Data Date	Weiss Safety Rating	RACR #1	RACR #2	Total Assets ($mil)	Capital ($mil)	Net Premium ($mil)	Net Income ($mil)
3-03	D+	0.82	0.68	6.5	2.0	2.9	0.0
3-02	D+	0.00	0.00	5.0	2.5	2.3	-0.1
2002	D+	0.81	0.67	5.6	2.0	9.9	-0.7
2001	D+	3.10	2.70	5.3	2.6	9.0	-0.5
2000	D	1.08	0.91	3.5	2.1	6.5	0.0
1999	D	0.00	0.00	3.1	2.1	5.5	0.4
1998	D	0.90	0.75	2.4	1.7	4.6	0.0

AVEMCO INS CO * — B+ Good

Major Rating Factors: History of adequate reserve strength (5.7 on a scale of 0 to 10) as reserves have been consistently at an acceptable level. Good overall results on stability tests (5.0) despite weak results on operational trends. The largest net exposure for one risk is acceptable at 2.1% of capital.
Other Rating Factors: Strong long-term capitalization index (10.0) based on excellent current risk adjusted capital (severe and moderate loss scenarios), despite some fluctuation in capital levels. Excellent profitability (7.1) with operating gains in each of the last five years. Return on equity has been excellent over the last five years averaging 15.2%. Excellent liquidity (7.0) with ample operational cash flow and liquid investments.
Principal Business: Group accident & health (76%) and aircraft (23%).
Principal Investments: Investment grade bonds (69%), misc. investments (21%), cash (8%), and real estate (2%).
Investments in Affiliates: 12%
Group Affiliation: HCC Ins Holdings Inc
Licensed in: All states except PR
Commenced Business: September 1960
Address: 411 Aviation Way, Frederick, MD 21701
Phone: (301) 694-5700 **Domicile State:** MD **NAIC Code:** 10367

Data Date	Weiss Safety Rating	RACR #1	RACR #2	Loss Ratio %	Total Assets ($mil)	Capital ($mil)	Net Premium ($mil)	Net Income ($mil)
6-03	B+	4.77	3.59	N/A	191.7	116.1	91.6	6.7
6-02	B+	6.31	3.98	N/A	179.9	110.5	108.4	9.4
2002	B+	4.47	3.37	58.4	172.9	105.7	84.2	19.2
2001	B+	6.02	3.92	71.0	187.3	107.1	100.9	18.7
2000	B+	3.69	2.37	70.6	165.2	85.9	94.5	18.2
1999	B+	5.89	4.04	93.5	128.1	62.5	34.9	4.6
1998	A-	16.31	13.14	66.9	151.8	104.9	24.2	14.4

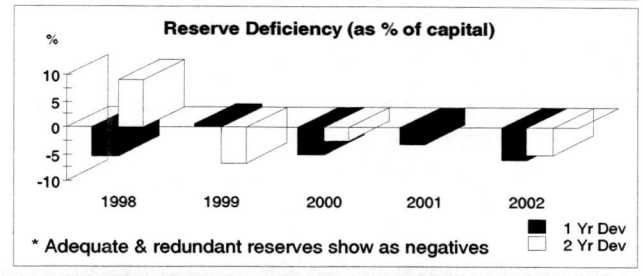

*Adequate & redundant reserves show as negatives

AVERA HEALTH PLANS INC — D+ Weak

Major Rating Factors: Weak profitability index (0.7 on a scale of 0 to 10). Fair overall capitalization (4.8) based on good current risk-adjusted capital (severe loss scenario) as results have slipped from the excellent range over the last year. Fair overall results on stability tests (4.2).
Other Rating Factors: Good liquidity (5.9) with sufficient resources (cash flows and marketable investments) to handle a spike in claims. High quality investment portfolio (9.9) containing no exposure to mortgages, junk bonds, or unaffiliated stocks.
Principal Business: Comp med (84%), med supp (18%)
Mem Phys: 02: 2,208 **01:** 1,828 **02 MLR** 86% **/ 02 Admin Exp** 18%
Enroll(000): Q1 03: 27 **02:** 25 **01:** N/A **Med Exp PMPM:** $259
Principal Investments: Cash and equiv (24%), other (76%)
Provider Compensation ($000): Contr fee ($35,991)
Total Member Encounters: Phys (40,453)
Group Affiliation: Avera Health
Licensed in: IA, SD
Address: 3900 W Avera Dr Suite 200, Sioux Falls, SD 57108
Phone: (605) 322-4500 **Dom State:** SD **Commenced Bus:** October 1999

Data Date	Weiss Safety Rating	RACR #1	RACR #2	Total Assets ($mil)	Capital ($mil)	Net Premium ($mil)	Net Income ($mil)
3-03	D+	0.90	0.75	18.0	6.1	15.4	-0.2
3-02	C-	1.97	1.67	15.2	9.7	8.4	-0.2
2002	D+	0.99	0.83	16.2	6.8	45.3	-1.0
2001	C-	1.97	1.66	12.9	8.1	24.8	-2.0
2000	U	1.14	0.96	N/A	N/A	N/A	-4.2
1999	N/A	N/A	N/A	N/A	N/A	N/A	-2.6
1998	N/A	N/A	N/A	N/A	N/A	N/A	N/A

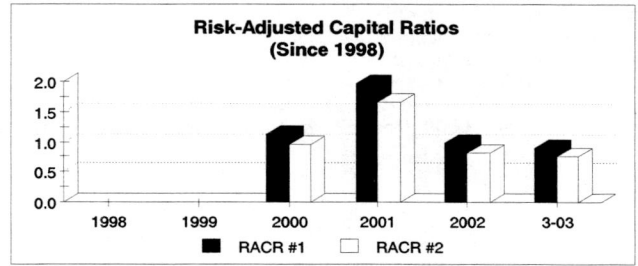

www.WeissRatings.com — * Denotes a Weiss Recommended Company

II. Analysis of Largest Companies

AVMED INC E Very Weak

Major Rating Factors: Weak profitability index (0.9 on a scale of 0 to 10) with $14.8 million in losses in the last two years. Poor capitalization index (0.0) based on weak current risk-adjusted capital (severe loss scenario). Weak liquidity (1.5) as a spike in claims may stretch capacity.
Other Rating Factors: Good overall results on stability tests (5.1) despite excessive capital growth during 2002. High quality investment portfolio (9.8) containing no exposure to mortgages, junk bonds, or unaffiliated stocks.
Principal Business: Comp med (66%), Medicare (28%), Medicaid (6%)
Mem Phys: 02: 15,366 **01:** 13,387 **02 MLR** 91% / **02 Admin Exp** 9%
Enroll(000): Q1 03: 248 **02:** 279 **01:** 253 **Med Exp PMPM:** $225
Principal Investments: Cash and equiv (27%), real estate (16%), other (57%)
Provider Compensation ($000): FFS ($667,898), capitation ($45,556)
Total Member Encounters: N/A
Group Affiliation: Health Improvement Inc
Licensed in: FL
Address: 4300 NW 89th Blvd., Gainesville, FL 32606
Phone: (352) 372-8400 **Dom State:** FL **Commenced Bus:** October 1977

Data Date	Weiss Safety Rating	RACR #1	RACR #2	Total Assets ($mil)	Capital ($mil)	Net Premium ($mil)	Net Income ($mil)
3-03	E	0.19	0.16	155.7	40.5	195.5	6.1
3-02	E+	0.14	0.11	146.4	25.7	193.5	5.4
2002	E	0.16	0.13	170.3	34.1	783.7	-6.2
2001	E+	0.14	0.11	150.2	20.5	690.7	-8.7
2000	D	N/A	N/A	136.8	15.8	763.5	2.5
1999	D	0.14	0.11	168.2	15.8	957.3	-32.0
1998	C	0.44	0.37	211.2	36.4	881.4	-25.5

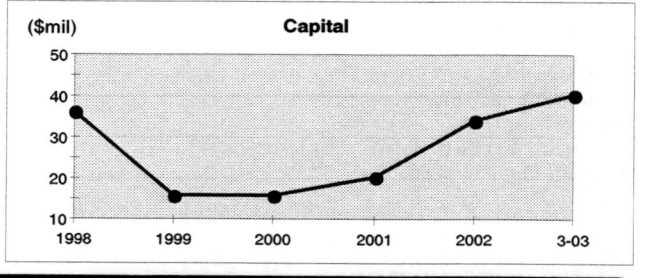

BALBOA LIFE INSURANCE COMPANY * B+ Good

Major Rating Factors: Good overall results on stability tests (5.0 on a scale of 0 to 10) despite negative cash flow from operations for 2002. Other stability subfactors include excellent risk diversification. Good overall profitability (5.6). Return on equity has been good over the last five years, averaging 13.7%. Strong capitalization (10.0) based on excellent risk adjusted capital (severe loss scenario).
Other Rating Factors: High quality investment portfolio (8.2). Excellent liquidity (7.6).
Principal Business: Credit health insurance (32%), group health insurance (30%), reinsurance (19%), credit life insurance (15%), and other lines (3%).
Principal Investments: CMOs and structured securities (58%), nonCMO investment grade bonds (31%), and common & preferred stock (11%).
Investments in Affiliates: 11%
Group Affiliation: Countrywide Credit Industries Inc
Licensed in: All states except PR
Commenced Business: January 1969
Address: 18581 Teller Avenue, Irvine, CA 92612-1627
Phone: (949) 553-0700 **Domicile State:** CA **NAIC Code:** 68160

Data Date	Weiss Safety Rating	RACR #1	RACR #2	Total Assets ($mil)	Capital ($mil)	Net Premium ($mil)	Net Income ($mil)
6-03	B+	3.93	3.47	124.5	71.0	11.1	1.8
6-02	B+	3.47	3.03	131.7	64.6	11.2	2.5
2002	B+	3.79	3.35	121.4	68.2	22.8	6.6
2001	B+	3.28	2.87	136.2	61.5	24.9	4.4
2000	B+	7.90	5.95	239.5	147.7	-5.0	18.2
1999	B+	12.53	7.99	277.4	130.4	-57.9	43.8
1998	B	3.58	2.37	377.5	74.9	118.8	8.3

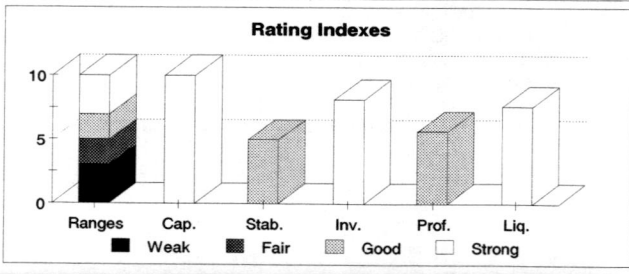

BALTIMORE LIFE INSURANCE COMPANY C Fair

Major Rating Factors: Fair overall capitalization (4.4 on a scale of 0 to 10) based on mixed results -- excessive policy leverage mitigated by fair risk adjusted capital (moderate loss scenario). Fair liquidity (4.9) due, in part, to cash value policies that are subject to withdrawals with minimal or no penalty. Low quality investment portfolio (2.1).
Other Rating Factors: Weak profitability (1.2). Weak overall results on stability tests (2.8) including weak risk adjusted capital in prior years.
Principal Business: Reinsurance (49%), individual life insurance (13%), individual annuities (11%), individual health insurance (9%), and other lines (18%).
Principal Investments: NonCMO investment grade bonds (68%), mortgages in good standing (11%), noninv. grade bonds (7%), CMOs and structured securities (5%), and misc. investments (10%).
Investments in Affiliates: None
Group Affiliation: Baltimore Life Group
Licensed in: All states except NY, PR
Commenced Business: March 1882
Address: 10075 Red Run Blvd, Owings Mills, MD 21117-6050
Phone: (410) 581-6600 **Domicile State:** MD **NAIC Code:** 61212

Data Date	Weiss Safety Rating	RACR #1	RACR #2	Total Assets ($mil)	Capital ($mil)	Net Premium ($mil)	Net Income ($mil)
6-03	C	0.92	0.49	790.0	29.8	43.8	1.9
6-02	C	0.71	0.51	548.9	40.5	44.4	-7.1
2002	C-	0.80	0.42	774.4	26.1	285.4	-24.7
2001	C+	0.83	0.60	545.3	45.4	84.0	-3.2
2000	B-	1.06	0.75	521.4	54.9	69.1	-5.1
1999	B-	1.22	0.86	510.1	60.5	70.3	2.4
1998	B-	1.50	1.06	502.1	69.7	73.8	3.1

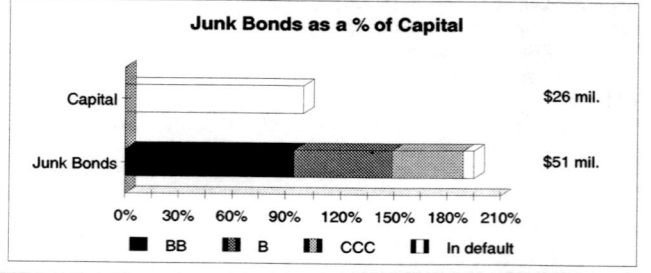

Winter 2003 - 04   **II. Analysis of Largest Companies**

BANKERS FIDELITY LIFE INSURANCE COMPANY   C   Fair

Major Rating Factors: Fair overall results on stability tests (3.9 on a scale of 0 to 10) including fair financial strength of affiliated Atlantic American Corp. Fair quality investment portfolio (4.8). Strong current capitalization (7.2) based on excellent risk adjusted capital (severe loss scenario) reflecting improvement over results in 2001.
Other Rating Factors: Excellent profitability (8.2) with operating gains in each of the last five years. Excellent liquidity (7.2).
Principal Business: Individual health insurance (74%), individual life insurance (25%), and reinsurance (1%).
Principal Investments: NonCMO investment grade bonds (55%), common & preferred stock (31%), cash (5%), mortgages in good standing (4%), and policy loans (2%).
Investments in Affiliates: None
Group Affiliation: Atlantic American Corp
Licensed in: All states except AK, CA, CT, HI, MN, NH, NJ, NY, RI, VT, PR
Commenced Business: November 1955
Address: 4370 Peachtree Rd NE, Atlanta, GA 30319
Phone: (404) 266-5500   **Domicile State:** GA   **NAIC Code:** 61239

Data Date	Weiss Safety Rating	RACR #1	RACR #2	Total Assets ($mil)	Capital ($mil)	Net Premium ($mil)	Net Income ($mil)
6-03	C	1.58	1.10	109.5	26.5	31.7	1.9
6-02	C-	1.46	1.01	94.8	23.0	30.1	1.3
2002	C-	1.61	1.13	97.5	25.9	60.8	4.0
2001	C-	1.40	0.97	88.9	22.7	55.5	2.9
2000	C-	1.51	1.02	85.6	23.7	47.9	2.5
1999	C-	1.78	1.19	87.1	26.5	41.8	2.9
1998	D+	1.58	1.05	81.7	26.0	31.8	2.0

Atlantic American Corp
Composite Group Rating: C
Largest Group Members

	Assets ($mil)	Weiss Safety Rating
BANKERS FIDELITY LIFE INS CO	98	C
AMERICAN SOUTHERN INS CO	95	C+
GEORGIA CASUALTY SURETY CO	89	C-
ASSOCIATION CASUALTY	57	C
AMERICAN SAFETY INS CO	22	C

BANKERS LIFE & CASUALTY COMPANY   E   Very Weak

Major Rating Factors: Weak overall results on stability tests (0.2 on a scale of 0 to 10) including weak financial strength of affiliated Conseco Group and weak risk adjusted capital in prior years. Poor current capitalization (2.8) based on excessive policy leverage and weak risk adjusted capital (moderate loss scenario), although results have slipped from the fair range during the last year. Fair quality investment portfolio (3.3).
Other Rating Factors: Good overall profitability (6.8) despite operating losses during the first six months of 2003. Excellent liquidity (7.2).
Principal Business: Individual health insurance (44%), individual annuities (32%), group health insurance (16%), individual life insurance (6%), and group life insurance (2%).
Principal Investments: NonCMO investment grade bonds (48%), CMOs and structured securities (35%), noninv. grade bonds (6%), common & preferred stock (5%), and misc. investments (7%).
Investments in Affiliates: 1%
Group Affiliation: Conseco Group
Licensed in: All states except NY, PR
Commenced Business: January 1879
Address: 222 Merchandise Mart Plaza, Chicago, IL 60654
Phone: (312) 396-6000   **Domicile State:** IL   **NAIC Code:** 61263

Data Date	Weiss Safety Rating	RACR #1	RACR #2	Total Assets ($mil)	Capital ($mil)	Net Premium ($mil)	Net Income ($mil)
6-03	E	0.72	0.43	6,387.5	270.4	1,277.5	-9.4
6-02	E	1.03	0.61	5,571.6	335.8	1,046.4	35.4
2002	E	0.82	0.49	5,865.3	281.1	2,253.7	-12.7
2001	E+	1.20	0.71	5,982.8	397.7	2,008.2	83.0
2000	C	1.32	0.75	4,960.1	402.3	1,844.8	79.3
1999	C	1.66	0.94	4,912.4	492.2	1,823.3	124.4
1998	C	1.31	0.76	4,253.5	356.0	1,609.6	110.9

Conseco Group
Composite Group Rating: E
Largest Group Members

	Assets ($mil)	Weiss Safety Rating
CONSECO ANNUITY ASSURANCE CO	5937	E
BANKERS LIFE CAS CO	5865	E
CONSECO LIFE INS CO	4253	E
CONSECO SENIOR HEALTH INS CO	2655	E
CONSECO HEALTH INS CO	1684	E

BC LIFE & HEALTH INSURANCE COMPANY   B   Good

Major Rating Factors: Strong capitalization (6.5 on a scale of 0 to 10) based on excellent risk adjusted capital (severe loss scenario). Moreover, capital has steadily grown over the last five years. Good quality investment portfolio (5.5) despite mixed results such as: no exposure to mortgages and substantial holdings of BBB bonds but small junk bond holdings. Good liquidity (6.9).
Other Rating Factors: Good overall results on stability tests (5.1) excellent operational trends, excellent risk adjusted capital for prior years and excellent risk diversification. Excellent profitability (9.5) with operating gains in each of the last five years.
Principal Business: Group health insurance (81%), individual health insurance (17%), and group life insurance (3%).
Principal Investments: NonCMO investment grade bonds (76%), CMOs and structured securities (12%), noninv. grade bonds (10%), and cash (2%).
Investments in Affiliates: None
Group Affiliation: WellPoint Health Networks Inc
Licensed in: CA
Commenced Business: August 1991
Address: 21555 Oxnard St, Woodland Hills, CA 91367
Phone: (818) 703-2345   **Domicile State:** CA   **NAIC Code:** 62825

Data Date	Weiss Safety Rating	RACR #1	RACR #2	Total Assets ($mil)	Capital ($mil)	Net Premium ($mil)	Net Income ($mil)
6-03	B	2.19	1.73	600.6	325.5	643.5	108.8
6-02	B	2.17	1.69	491.8	249.6	501.8	68.6
2002	B	1.99	1.57	514.6	272.3	1,072.1	140.3
2001	B	1.87	1.48	373.5	196.0	783.4	96.9
2000	B	1.72	1.37	319.3	153.4	680.1	85.7
1999	B	2.44	1.92	268.6	131.9	498.8	63.7
1998	B	1.97	1.54	207.3	110.7	389.2	42.9

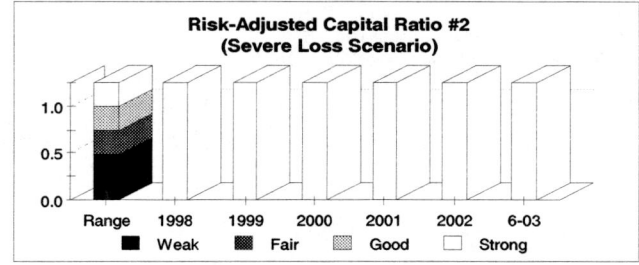

Risk-Adjusted Capital Ratio #2 (Severe Loss Scenario)

Range: 1998, 1999, 2000, 2001, 2002, 6-03
■ Weak   ▨ Fair   ▧ Good   ☐ Strong

www.WeissRatings.com   * Denotes a Weiss Recommended Company

II. Analysis of Largest Companies

Winter 2003 - 04

BCI HMO INC * — B+ — Good

Major Rating Factors: Good overall profitability index (5.5 on a scale of 0 to 10) despite modest operating losses during 1998. Strong overall capitalization (10.0) based on excellent current risk-adjusted capital (severe loss scenario) despite some fluctuation in capital levels. High quality investment portfolio (9.9) containing no exposure to mortgages, junk bonds, or unaffiliated stocks.

Other Rating Factors: Excellent liquidity (10.0) with ample operational cash flow and liquid investments. Fair overall results on stability tests (3.8) based on an overall decline in enrollment over the past five years. Rating is significantly influenced by the good financial results of HCSC Group.

Principal Business: Comp med (100%)
Mem Phys: 02: 9,499 **01:** 9,994 **02 MLR** 72% **/ 02 Admin Exp** 36%
Enroll(000): Q1 03: 0 **02:** 0 **01:** 0 **Med Exp PMPM:** $123
Principal Investments: Cash and equiv (26%), other (74%)
Provider Compensation ($000): Contr fee ($101), capitation ($89)
Total Member Encounters: Phys (394), non-phys (69)
Group Affiliation: HCSC Group
Licensed in: IL, IN
Address: 300 East Randolph Street, Chicago, IL 60601-5099
Phone: (312) 653-6600 **Dom State:** IL **Commenced Bus:** February 1984

Data Date	Weiss Safety Rating	RACR #1	RACR #2	Total Assets ($mil)	Capital ($mil)	Net Premium ($mil)	Net Income ($mil)
3-03	B+	29.56	24.63	10.4	9.9	0.1	0.0
3-02	B+	36.75	30.46	11.4	10.6	0.1	0.0
2002	B+	29.50	24.58	10.4	9.9	0.3	0.3
2001	B+	36.78	30.47	11.4	10.6	0.3	0.4
2000	B+	33.08	24.92	12.7	11.2	1.2	0.8
1999	B+	31.08	25.58	13.9	11.3	10.0	0.6
1998	B	32.40	25.82	15.0	11.8	9.5	0.0

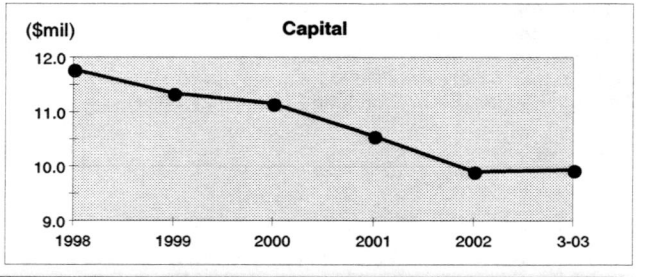

Capital chart 1998–3-03, declining from ~11.8 to ~9.9

BCS INS CO — C — Fair

Major Rating Factors: Fair overall results on stability tests (3.7 on a scale of 0 to 10) including weak results on operational trends. Good liquidity (6.8) with sufficient resources (cash flows and marketable investments) to handle a spike in claims.

Other Rating Factors: Strong long-term capitalization index (8.2) based on excellent current risk adjusted capital (severe and moderate loss scenarios). Moreover, capital levels have been consistent in recent years. Ample reserve history (9.3) that helps to protect the company against sharp claims increases. Excellent profitability (8.6) with operating gains in each of the last five years.

Principal Business: Group accident & health (68%), other liability (27%), inland marine (4%), and medical malpractice (1%).
Principal Investments: Investment grade bonds (95%), misc. investments (3%), and cash (2%).
Investments in Affiliates: 1%
Group Affiliation: BCS Ins Group
Licensed in: All states, the District of Columbia and Puerto Rico
Commenced Business: November 1952
Address: 676 N St Clair St 16th floor, Chicago, IL 60611
Phone: (312) 951-7700 **Domicile State:** OH **NAIC Code:** 38245

Data Date	Weiss Safety Rating	RACR #1	RACR #2	Loss Ratio %	Total Assets ($mil)	Capital ($mil)	Net Premium ($mil)	Net Income ($mil)
6-03	C	2.84	1.92	N/A	225.7	116.2	107.5	6.3
6-02	C+	4.20	2.70	N/A	201.8	103.2	92.2	2.3
2002	C	2.38	1.62	62.6	243.7	109.2	157.5	3.4
2001	C+	5.39	3.46	64.8	181.6	104.6	66.1	5.3
2000	C+	4.31	3.00	56.5	161.0	100.8	51.5	6.3
1999	C+	4.03	2.69	63.4	178.7	96.6	58.8	6.7
1998	C+	2.88	1.80	68.2	173.8	89.8	68.4	5.1

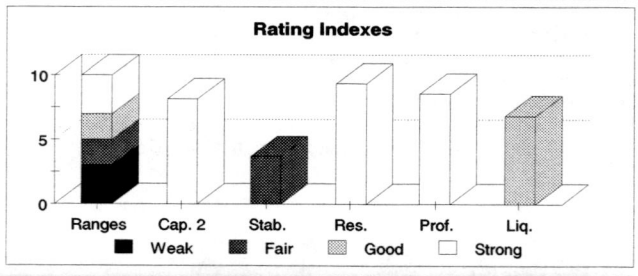

Rating Indexes: Ranges, Cap. 2, Stab., Res., Prof., Liq. (Weak/Fair/Good/Strong)

BCS LIFE INSURANCE COMPANY — C — Fair

Major Rating Factors: Fair overall results on stability tests (4.3 on a scale of 0 to 10) including fair financial strength of affiliated BCS Financial Corp. Good liquidity (6.9) with sufficient resources to handle a spike in claims as well as a significant increase in policy surrenders. Strong capitalization (9.2) based on excellent risk adjusted capital (severe loss scenario).

Other Rating Factors: High quality investment portfolio (7.6). Excellent profitability (8.6) with operating gains in each of the last five years.

Principal Business: Group health insurance (85%), reinsurance (10%), and group life insurance (5%).
Principal Investments: NonCMO investment grade bonds (54%), CMOs and structured securities (40%), noninv. grade bonds (3%), and common & preferred stock (3%).
Investments in Affiliates: None
Group Affiliation: BCS Financial Corp
Licensed in: All states except PR
Commenced Business: November 1949
Address: 676 North St Clair St, Chicago, IL 60611-2997
Phone: (312) 951-7700 **Domicile State:** IL **NAIC Code:** 80985

Data Date	Weiss Safety Rating	RACR #1	RACR #2	Total Assets ($mil)	Capital ($mil)	Net Premium ($mil)	Net Income ($mil)
6-03	C	3.18	2.44	138.3	65.8	85.6	2.6
6-02	C	3.73	2.69	108.7	62.2	58.6	1.1
2002	C	3.47	2.66	129.4	63.5	140.7	2.7
2001	C	4.09	2.93	106.7	59.5	89.5	2.7
2000	C	4.52	3.21	111.9	58.0	79.6	3.2
1999	C	4.40	3.10	111.1	56.7	75.4	3.0
1998	C	4.20	3.01	102.6	54.4	72.2	3.3

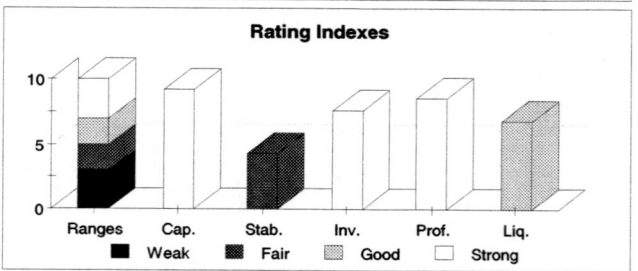

Rating Indexes: Ranges, Cap., Stab., Inv., Prof., Liq. (Weak/Fair/Good/Strong)

Winter 2003 - 04
II. Analysis of Largest Companies

BERKSHIRE LIFE INSURANCE COMPANY OF AMERICA — C — Fair

Major Rating Factors: Fair profitability (4.8 on a scale of 0 to 10) with operating losses during the first six months of 2003. Return on equity has been low, averaging 4.8%. Fair overall results on stability tests (3.7). Good quality investment portfolio (6.5) despite mixed results such as: large holdings of BBB rated bonds but moderate junk bond exposure.
Other Rating Factors: Strong capitalization (8.7) based on excellent risk adjusted capital (severe loss scenario). Excellent liquidity (8.2).
Principal Business: Reinsurance (85%) and individual health insurance (15%).
Principal Investments: NonCMO investment grade bonds (77%), mortgages in good standing (15%), noninv. grade bonds (5%), and CMOs and structured securities (2%).
Investments in Affiliates: None
Group Affiliation: Guardian Group
Licensed in: All states except PR
Commenced Business: May 1968
Address: 700 South St, Pittsfield, MA 01201
Phone: (413) 499-4321 **Domicile State:** MA **NAIC Code:** 71714

Data Date	Weiss Safety Rating	RACR #1	RACR #2	Total Assets ($mil)	Capital ($mil)	Net Premium ($mil)	Net Income ($mil)
6-03	C	3.90	2.16	1,522.2	260.6	149.1	-0.9
6-02	C+	4.39	2.52	1,493.8	259.4	137.1	-0.5
2002	C+	4.52	2.43	1,564.9	246.4	190.1	-16.0
2001	C-	7.41	3.84	1,452.8	264.1	77.5	-15.6
2000	U	11.38	10.24	8.5	8.0	-0.1	0.8
1999	U	10.16	9.15	14.1	12.6	0.0	1.1
1998	C	9.85	8.86	45.8	44.9	-20.0	5.3

Net Income History (in millions of dollars)

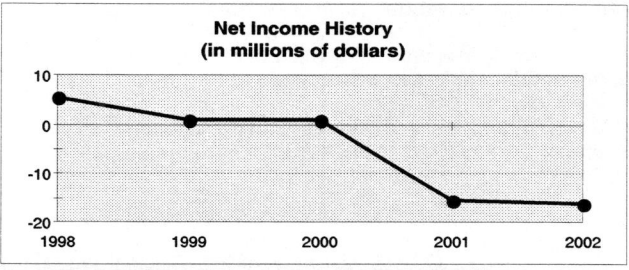

BLUE CARE NETWORK OF MICHIGAN — C+ — Fair

Major Rating Factors: Fair overall results on stability tests (4.9 on a scale of 0 to 10). Potentially strong support from affiliation with Bl Cross & Bl Shield of Michigan. Weak profitability index (1.6) with operating losses during 1998, 1999, 2000 and 2001. Average return on equity has been poor at -21%. Strong capitalization (7.3) based on excellent current risk-adjusted capital (severe loss scenario) reflecting improvement over results in 2000.
Other Rating Factors: High quality investment portfolio (9.9) containing little or no exposure to mortgages, junk bonds, or unaffiliated stocks. Excellent liquidity (7.0) with ample operational cash flow and liquid investments.
Principal Business: Comp med (92%), med supp (5%), FEHB (4%)
Mem Phys: 02: 9,696 **01:** 10,008 **02 MLR** 89% **/ 02 Admin Exp** 10%
Enroll(000): Q1 03: 505 **02:** 519 **01:** 572 **Med Exp PMPM:** $175
Principal Investments: Cash and equiv (83%), other (17%)
Provider Compensation ($000): Contr fee ($819,711), capitation ($275,727), salary ($67,698), bonus arrang ($20,780)
Total Member Encounters: Phys (1,644,336), non-phys (594,390)
Group Affiliation: Bl Cross & Bl Shield of Michigan
Licensed in: MI
Address: 25925 Telegraph, Southfield, MI 48086
Phone: (248) 354-7450 **Dom State:** MI **Commenced Bus:** May 1981

Data Date	Weiss Safety Rating	RACR #1	RACR #2	Total Assets ($mil)	Capital ($mil)	Net Premium ($mil)	Net Income ($mil)
3-03	C+	1.58	1.32	457.0	92.0	336.0	5.3
3-02	C+	1.35	1.14	448.3	73.1	317.9	-1.8
2002	C+	1.50	1.25	428.3	86.7	1,285.8	10.5
2001	C+	1.35	1.14	451.0	74.5	1,356.9	-5.7
2000	C	1.11	0.93	461.9	71.6	1,211.3	-27.0
1999	C	1.47	1.23	428.9	92.3	1,110.7	-33.2
1998	B-	1.68	1.41	427.5	98.2	985.2	-58.6

Net Income History (in millions of dollars)

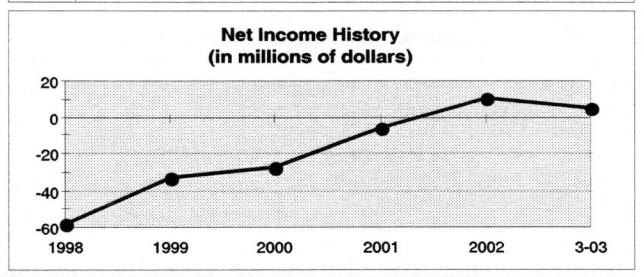

BLUE CROSS BLUE SHIELD HEALTHCARE GA * — A — Excellent

Major Rating Factors: Excellent profitability (8.4 on a scale of 0 to 10) despite a decline in earnings during 2002. Strong capitalization (7.7) based on excellent current risk-adjusted capital (severe loss scenario) reflecting significant improvement over results in 1998. High quality investment portfolio (9.9) containing no exposure to mortgages, junk bonds, or unaffiliated stocks.
Other Rating Factors: Excellent overall results on stability tests (8.2) based on consistent premium and capital growth in the last five years. Rating is significantly influenced by the good financial results of WellPoint Health Networks Inc. Good liquidity (5.8) with sufficient resources (cash flows and marketable investments) to handle a spike in claims.
Principal Business: Comp med (90%), Medicare (10%)
Mem Phys: 02: 8,136 **01:** 7,075 **02 MLR** 83% **/ 02 Admin Exp** 17%
Enroll(000): Q1 03: 662 **02:** 623 **01:** 550 **Med Exp PMPM:** $155
Principal Investments: Cash and equiv (15%), other (85%)
Provider Compensation ($000): Capitation ($783,350), contr fee ($316,136)
Total Member Encounters: Phys (2,717,593), non-phys (1,081,718)
Group Affiliation: WellPoint Health Networks Inc
Licensed in: GA
Address: 3350 Peachtree Rd NE, Atlanta, GA 30326
Phone: (404) 842-8400 **Dom State:** GA **Commenced Bus:** September 1986

Data Date	Weiss Safety Rating	RACR #1	RACR #2	Total Assets ($mil)	Capital ($mil)	Net Premium ($mil)	Net Income ($mil)
3-03	A	1.93	1.61	255.4	92.6	377.3	7.4
3-02	A-	1.69	1.48	229.8	75.7	309.1	10.3
2002	A	1.81	1.51	235.1	86.6	1,302.4	19.0
2001	A-	1.69	1.48	230.5	74.7	1,085.4	22.8
2000	B+	1.36	1.20	199.5	60.1	870.8	21.6
1999	B	1.11	0.98	151.8	45.5	665.0	14.4
1998	C+	0.81	0.71	125.8	26.0	509.5	11.4

Risk-Adjusted Capital Ratios (Since 1998)

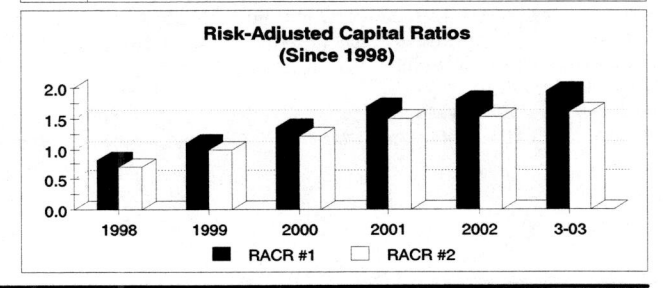

* Denotes a Weiss Recommended Company

II. Analysis of Largest Companies

Winter 2003 - 04

BLUE CROSS BLUE SHIELD OF ALABAMA — B — Good

Major Rating Factors: Good overall profitability index (5.4 on a scale of 0 to 10) despite a decline in earnings during 2002. Good liquidity (6.9) with sufficient resources (cash flows and marketable investments) to handle a spike in claims. Strong capitalization (9.5) based on excellent current risk-adjusted capital (severe loss scenario).
Other Rating Factors: High quality investment portfolio (9.9).
Principal Business: Comp med (72%), FEHB (16%), med supp (9%), dental (4%)
Mem Phys: 02: 17,337 **01:** 17,048   **02 MLR** 91%   **/ 02 Admin Exp** 7%
Enroll(000): Q1 03: 1,564 **02:** 1,428 **01:** 1,419   **Med Exp PMPM:** $124
Principal Investments: Cash and equiv (13%), real estate (13%), nonaffiliate common stock (8%), affiliate common stock (1%), other (65%).
Provider Compensation ($000): Contr fee ($2,058,585), capitation ($33,947), FFS ($18,361)
Total Member Encounters: Phys (12,063,162), non-phys (7,504,224)
Group Affiliation: Bl Cross & Bl Shield of AL Group
Licensed in: AL
Address: 450 Riverchase Parkway E, Birmingham, AL 35298
Phone: (205) 988-2100   **Dom State:** AL   **Commenced Bus:** January 1936

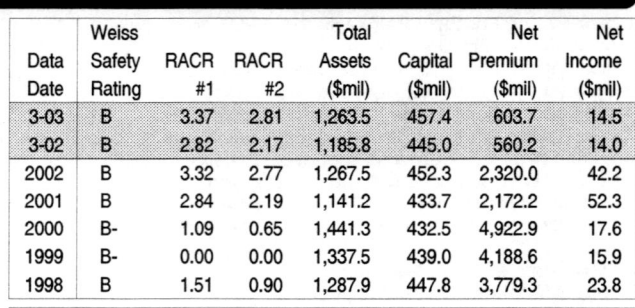

Data Date	Weiss Safety Rating	RACR #1	RACR #2	Total Assets ($mil)	Capital ($mil)	Net Premium ($mil)	Net Income ($mil)
3-03	B	3.37	2.81	1,263.5	457.4	603.7	14.5
3-02	B	2.82	2.17	1,185.8	445.0	560.2	14.0
2002	B	3.32	2.77	1,267.5	452.3	2,320.0	42.2
2001	B	2.84	2.19	1,141.2	433.7	2,172.2	52.3
2000	B-	1.09	0.65	1,441.3	432.5	4,922.9	17.6
1999	B-	0.00	0.00	1,337.5	439.0	4,188.6	15.9
1998	B	1.51	0.90	1,287.9	447.8	3,779.3	23.8

Net Income History (in millions of dollars)

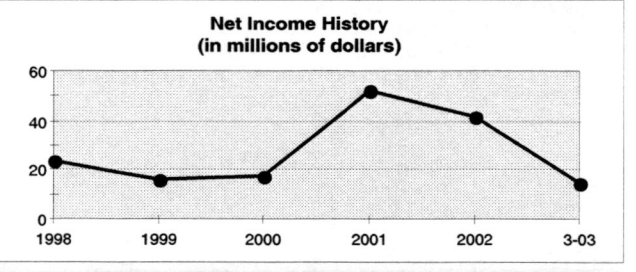

BLUE CROSS BLUE SHIELD OF ARIZONA * — A — Excellent

Major Rating Factors: Excellent profitability (9.0 on a scale of 0 to 10) with operating gains in each of the last five years. Strong capitalization (10.0) based on excellent current risk-adjusted capital (severe loss scenario) reflecting significant improvement over results in 1998. High quality investment portfolio (7.6).
Other Rating Factors: Excellent liquidity (7.0) with ample operational cash flow and liquid investments.
Principal Business: Comp med (73%), FEHB (22%), med supp (4%)
Mem Phys: 02: 9,549   **01:** 9,868   **02 MLR** 72%   **/ 02 Admin Exp** 16%
Enroll(000): Q1 03: 800   **02:** 770   **01:** 687   **Med Exp PMPM:** $61
Principal Investments: Nonaffiliate common stock (16%), cash and equiv (10%), affiliate common stock (7%), real estate (5%), pref stock (4%), other (58%)
Provider Compensation ($000): Contr fee ($409,389), FFS ($114,191), capitation ($9,300)
Total Member Encounters: Phys (3,115,984), non-phys (2,953,592)
Group Affiliation: None
Licensed in: AZ
Address: 2444 W Las Palmaritas Dr, Phoenix, AZ 85021
Phone: (602) 864-4100   **Dom State:** AZ   **Commenced Bus:** February 1939

Data Date	Weiss Safety Rating	RACR #1	RACR #2	Total Assets ($mil)	Capital ($mil)	Net Premium ($mil)	Net Income ($mil)
3-03	A	5.11	4.26	409.0	228.5	202.8	27.4
3-02	N/A	N/A	N/A	N/A	N/A	N/A	N/A
2002	A	4.76	3.97	393.9	213.7	737.1	69.7
2001	B+	2.80	2.08	310.3	159.9	626.8	39.1
2000	C+	1.67	1.03	254.9	121.8	569.3	24.6
1999	C	1.26	0.77	222.7	99.4	597.8	8.2
1998	C	1.20	0.71	211.2	91.6	563.4	13.0

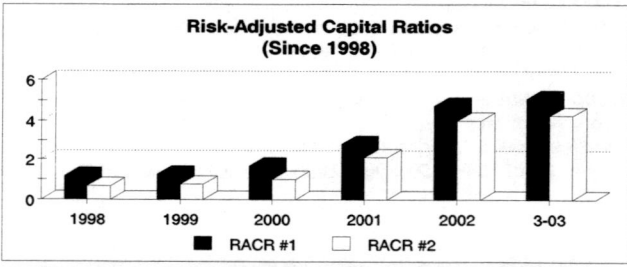

Risk-Adjusted Capital Ratios (Since 1998)

BLUE CROSS BLUE SHIELD OF DELAWARE * — B+ — Good

Major Rating Factors: Good overall profitability index (6.4 on a scale of 0 to 10) despite a decline in earnings during 2002. Good liquidity (6.9) with sufficient resources (cash flows and marketable investments) to handle a spike in claims. Strong capitalization (10.0) based on excellent current risk-adjusted capital (severe loss scenario).
Other Rating Factors: High quality investment portfolio (9.3).
Principal Business: Comp med (73%), FEHB (19%), med supp (6%), dental (2%)
Mem Phys: 02: N/A   **01:** N/A   **02 MLR** 83%   **/ 02 Admin Exp** 9%
Enroll(000): Q1 03: 332   **02:** 326   **01:** 282   **Med Exp PMPM:** $53
Principal Investments: Cash and equiv (24%), nonaffiliate common stock (10%), real estate (2%), other (63%)
Provider Compensation ($000): Contr fee ($187,368), capitation ($551)
Total Member Encounters: Phys (1,510,048), non-phys (211,398)
Group Affiliation: CareFirst Inc
Licensed in: DE
Address: One Brandywine Gateway, Wilmington, DE 19801
Phone: (302) 421-3000   **Dom State:** DE   **Commenced Bus:** September 1935

Data Date	Weiss Safety Rating	RACR #1	RACR #2	Total Assets ($mil)	Capital ($mil)	Net Premium ($mil)	Net Income ($mil)
3-03	B+	7.22	6.01	206.6	99.3	65.1	4.8
3-02	B	5.52	3.70	177.7	95.9	51.4	2.4
2002	B+	6.03	5.02	195.6	94.4	234.4	1.4
2001	B	5.50	3.69	193.0	93.6	205.5	10.0
2000	B+	3.90	2.46	197.2	79.7	171.3	-5.5
1999	B	0.00	0.00	185.0	89.1	159.3	4.6
1998	B	3.66	2.31	184.4	83.2	157.7	4.4

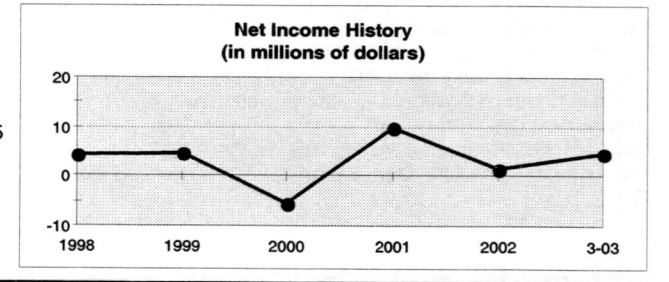

Net Income History (in millions of dollars)

BLUE CROSS BLUE SHIELD OF FLORIDA * — B+ Good

Major Rating Factors: Good liquidity (6.3 on a scale of 0 to 10) with sufficient resources to handle a spike in claims. Good overall results on stability tests (5.0). Stability strengths include excellent operational trends, good risk adjusted capital for prior years and excellent risk diversification. Fair quality investment portfolio (4.3).
Other Rating Factors: Strong capitalization (7.1) based on excellent risk adjusted capital (severe loss scenario). Excellent profitability (7.5) despite modest operating losses during 2000.
Principal Business: Group health insurance (74%) and individual health insurance (26%).
Principal Investments: Common & preferred stock (41%), nonCMO investment grade bonds (36%), CMOs and structured securities (11%), and real estate (9%).
Investments in Affiliates: 28%
Group Affiliation: Blue Cross Blue Shield Of Florida
Licensed in: FL
Commenced Business: January 1980
Address: 4800 Deerwood Campus Pkwy, Jacksonville, FL 32246
Phone: (800) 477-3736 **Domicile State:** FL **NAIC Code:** 98167

Data Date	Weiss Safety Rating	RACR #1	RACR #2	Total Assets ($mil)	Capital ($mil)	Net Premium ($mil)	Net Income ($mil)
6-03	B+	1.26	1.06	2,530.3	1,073.0	1,460.5	118.2
6-02	B	1.06	0.89	2,192.3	774.3	1,298.8	80.4
2002	B	1.12	0.96	2,265.0	846.6	2,661.9	166.4
2001	B-	1.00	0.84	2,013.6	665.3	2,396.7	69.4
2000	B-	1.03	0.87	1,782.0	526.3	2,107.3	-20.0
1999	B-	N/A	N/A	1,735.6	539.7	1,785.1	-0.6
1998	B-	1.21	0.98	1,588.2	564.2	1,601.1	46.5

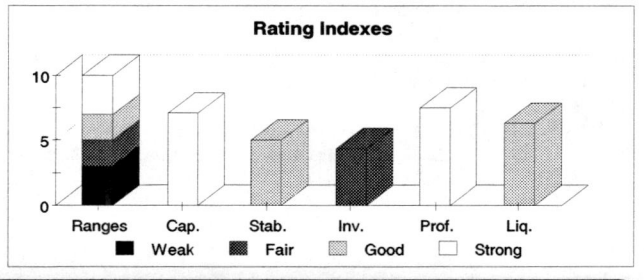

Rating Indexes chart: Ranges, Cap., Stab., Inv., Prof., Liq. — Weak, Fair, Good, Strong

BLUE CROSS BLUE SHIELD OF GEORGIA * — A Excellent

Major Rating Factors: Excellent profitability (7.9 on a scale of 0 to 10) with operating gains in each of the last five years. Strong capitalization (10.0) based on excellent current risk-adjusted capital (severe loss scenario) reflecting improvement over results in 1999. High quality investment portfolio (9.1).
Other Rating Factors: Good liquidity (6.1) with sufficient resources (cash flows and marketable investments) to handle a spike in claims.
Principal Business: Comp med (60%), FEHB (30%), med supp (6%), dental (4%).
Mem Phys: 02: 27,767 **01:** 26,889 **02 MLR** 82% / **02 Admin Exp** 12%
Enroll(000): Q1 03: 711 **02:** 676 **01:** 529   **Med Exp PMPM:** $171
Principal Investments: Nonaffiliate common stock (11%), affiliate common stock (5%), real estate (1%), cash and equiv (92%)
Provider Compensation ($000): Contr fee ($1,000,590), FFS ($213,991)
Total Member Encounters: N/A
Group Affiliation: WellPoint Health Networks Inc
Licensed in: GA
Address: 3350 Peachtree Rd NE, Atlanta, GA 30326
Phone: (404) 842-8000 **Dom State:** GA **Commenced Bus:** November 1937

Data Date	Weiss Safety Rating	RACR #1	RACR #2	Total Assets ($mil)	Capital ($mil)	Net Premium ($mil)	Net Income ($mil)
3-03	A	5.26	4.39	798.7	344.0	431.8	40.9
3-02	B+	3.96	3.14	642.3	260.1	337.6	31.6
2002	A	4.76	3.97	714.0	309.9	1,499.5	108.4
2001	B+	3.95	3.14	598.8	252.1	1,168.8	65.5
2000	B	1.57	0.98	508.0	173.1	967.1	44.0
1999	B	1.44	0.91	407.1	161.5	811.8	33.2
1998	B-	1.59	1.02	404.4	155.7	672.9	15.1

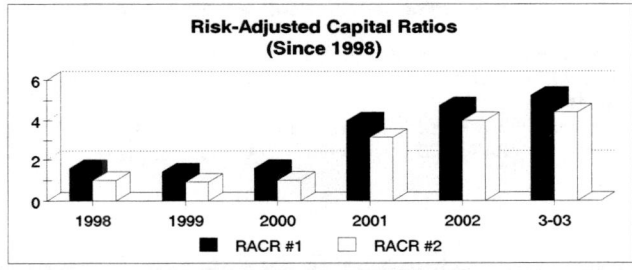

Risk-Adjusted Capital Ratios (Since 1998) chart: RACR #1 and RACR #2 from 1998 to 3-03

BLUE CROSS BLUE SHIELD OF KANSAS INCORPORATED — C+ Fair

Major Rating Factors: Fair profitability (3.4 on a scale of 0 to 10). Excellent expense controls. Fair liquidity (4.1) as cash from operations and sale of marketable assets may not be adequate to cover a spike in claims. Fair overall results on stability tests (4.7).
Other Rating Factors: Good overall capitalization (5.8) based on mixed results -- excessive policy leverage mitigated by excellent risk adjusted capital (severe loss scenario). Good quality investment portfolio (5.8).
Principal Business: Group health insurance (72%) and individual health insurance (28%).
Principal Investments: NonCMO investment grade bonds (48%), CMOs and structured securities (25%), common & preferred stock (24%), and real estate (5%).
Investments in Affiliates: 9%
Group Affiliation: Blue Cross Blue Shield Kansas
Licensed in: KS
Commenced Business: July 1942
Address: 1133 SW Topeka Blvd, Topeka, KS 66629-0001
Phone: (785) 291-7000 **Domicile State:** KS **NAIC Code:** 70729

Data Date	Weiss Safety Rating	RACR #1	RACR #2	Total Assets ($mil)	Capital ($mil)	Net Premium ($mil)	Net Income ($mil)
6-03	C+	1.39	1.11	675.6	252.9	543.6	22.4
6-02	C+	1.07	0.86	546.7	200.2	516.4	-7.0
2002	C+	1.31	1.05	575.6	227.6	1,059.0	12.9
2001	C+	1.18	0.94	619.4	212.0	913.5	-47.6
2000	C+	1.37	1.08	596.6	230.8	781.1	12.5
1999	C+	1.76	1.37	633.5	231.8	689.8	-21.7
1998	C+	1.76	1.34	609.4	284.4	624.6	34.4

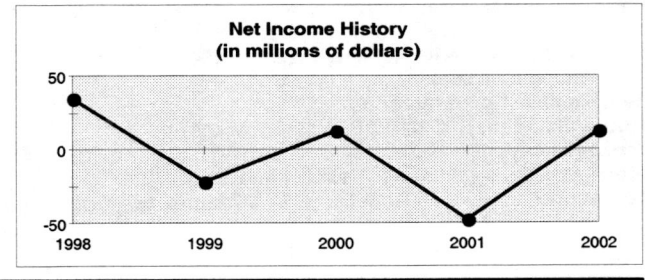

Net Income History (in millions of dollars) chart: 1998 to 2002

www.WeissRatings.com * * Denotes a Weiss Recommended Company

II. Analysis of Largest Companies
Winter 2003 - 04

BLUE CROSS BLUE SHIELD OF KC *   B+   Good

Major Rating Factors: Good overall profitability index (5.8 on a scale of 0 to 10) despite operating losses during 2000 and 2001. Good liquidity (6.9) with sufficient resources (cash flows and marketable investments) to handle a spike in claims. Strong capitalization (8.9) based on excellent current risk-adjusted capital (severe loss scenario) despite some fluctuation in capital levels.
Other Rating Factors: High quality investment portfolio (8.5).
Principal Business: Comp med (67%), FEHB (16%), Medicaid (10%), med supp (5%), dental (2%), stop loss (1%).
Mem Phys: 02: 4,021 **01:** 3,955 **02 MLR** 73% **/ 02 Admin Exp** 16%
Enroll(000): Q1 03: 353 **02:** 350 **01:** 284 **Med Exp PMPM:** $121
Principal Investments: Nonaffiliate common stock (24%), cash and equiv (16%), affiliate common stock (16%), other (44%).
Provider Compensation ($000): Contr fee ($286,805), FFS ($135,012), capitation ($45,338).
Total Member Encounters: Phys (1,437,075), non-phys (158,408)
Group Affiliation: RightCHOICE Managed Care Inc
Licensed in: KS, MO
Address: 2301 Main St, Kansas City, MO 64108-2428
Phone: (816) 395-2222 **Dom State:** MO **Commenced Bus:** May 1982

Data Date	Weiss Safety Rating	RACR #1	RACR #2	Total Assets ($mil)	Capital ($mil)	Net Premium ($mil)	Net Income ($mil)
3-03	B+	2.91	2.42	399.8	175.6	172.4	10.4
3-02	B-	2.15	1.54	369.8	158.1	150.1	4.3
2002	B	2.72	2.27	397.6	164.6	630.5	24.5
2001	B-	2.16	1.54	342.0	152.5	525.1	-7.7
2000	B-	1.59	1.06	328.5	152.3	415.1	-3.9
1999	B-	1.90	1.22	297.3	142.1	353.5	8.1
1998	B-	1.92	1.22	318.1	150.1	379.8	5.6

Net Income History (in millions of dollars)

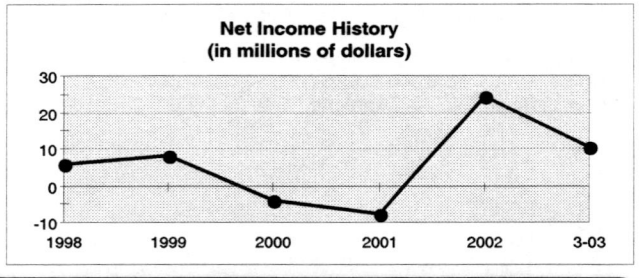

BLUE CROSS BLUE SHIELD OF MA *   A   Excellent

Major Rating Factors: Excellent profitability (8.8 on a scale of 0 to 10) despite a decline in earnings during 2002. Strong capitalization (9.8) based on excellent current risk-adjusted capital (severe loss scenario) reflecting significant improvement over results in 2000. High quality investment portfolio (7.7).
Other Rating Factors: Good liquidity (6.2) with sufficient resources (cash flows and marketable investments) to handle a spike in claims.
Principal Business: Comp med (79%), med supp (10%), Medicare (8%), dental (2%).
Mem Phys: 02: 16,194 **01:** 15,267 **02 MLR** 86% **/ 02 Admin Exp** 10%
Enroll(000): Q1 03: 2,455 **02:** 2,411 **01:** 2,392 **Med Exp PMPM:** $114
Principal Investments: Nonaffiliate common stock (33%), cash and equiv (7%), other (59%).
Provider Compensation ($000): Contr fee ($2,560,765), capitation ($607,329), bonus arrang ($122,912).
Total Member Encounters: Phys (22,470,717)
Group Affiliation: Bl Cross Bl Shield of Massachusetts
Licensed in: MA
Address: 401 Park Dr Landmark Center, Boston, MA 02215-3326
Phone: (617) 246-5000 **Dom State:** MA **Commenced Bus:** October 1937

Data Date	Weiss Safety Rating	RACR #1	RACR #2	Total Assets ($mil)	Capital ($mil)	Net Premium ($mil)	Net Income ($mil)
3-03	A	3.57	2.97	2,033.0	628.9	984.6	15.5
3-02	B+	1.61	1.13	2,037.5	533.8	951.3	12.4
2002	A	3.50	2.92	1,903.0	616.1	3,844.4	84.7
2001	B+	1.75	1.24	1,839.1	525.7	3,550.5	103.7
2000	B-	1.12	0.67	1,731.2	441.2	2,727.6	109.0
1999	C+	1.38	0.81	1,300.0	362.1	1,930.1	60.4
1998	C-	1.15	0.68	N/A	N/A	N/A	63.8

Risk-Adjusted Capital Ratios (Since 1998)

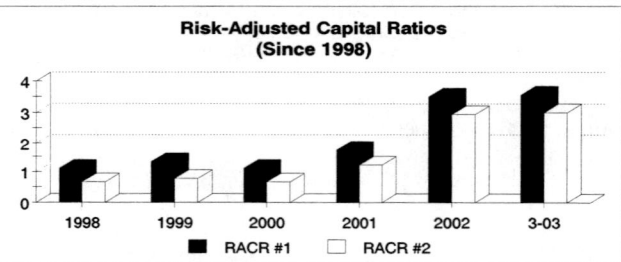

BLUE CROSS BLUE SHIELD OF MICHIGAN   B   Good

Major Rating Factors: Good overall profitability index (6.6 on a scale of 0 to 10) with operating gains in each of the last five years. Good liquidity (6.6) with sufficient resources (cash flows and marketable investments) to handle a spike in claims. Strong capitalization (10.0) based on excellent current risk-adjusted capital (severe loss scenario) reflecting significant improvement over results in 1999.
Other Rating Factors: High quality investment portfolio (7.6) containing little or no exposure to mortgages, junk bonds, or unaffiliated stocks.
Principal Business: Comp med (90%), med supp (4%), FEHB (3%), dental (2%), stop loss (1%).
Mem Phys: 02: 36,483 **01:** 35,373 **02 MLR** 87% **/ 02 Admin Exp** 12%
Enroll(000): Q1 03: 2,772 **02:** 2,660 **01:** 2,648 **Med Exp PMPM:** $144
Principal Investments: Affiliate common stock (23%), real estate (8%), cash and equiv (6%), nonaffiliate common stock (2%), other (62%).
Provider Compensation ($000): Contr fee ($4,630,682), capitation ($21,018), bonus arrang ($10,058).
Total Member Encounters: N/A
Group Affiliation: Bl Cross & Bl Shield of Michigan
Licensed in: MI
Address: 600 Lafayette East, Detroit, MI 48226
Phone: (313) 225-9000 **Dom State:** MI **Commenced Bus:** January 1975

Data Date	Weiss Safety Rating	RACR #1	RACR #2	Total Assets ($mil)	Capital ($mil)	Net Premium ($mil)	Net Income ($mil)
3-03	B	3.68	3.06	3,804.0	1,596.6	1,382.4	74.9
3-02	B-	3.22	2.52	3,395.0	1,318.8	1,317.0	53.2
2002	B	3.54	2.95	3,760.3	1,532.3	5,287.3	161.4
2001	C+	3.23	2.53	3,123.1	1,300.6	4,874.6	56.2
2000	C+	1.54	1.05	3,529.2	1,247.2	8,974.7	65.4
1999	C+	1.00	0.73	3,473.3	1,114.1	8,209.7	89.1
1998	B	1.41	1.01	3,214.2	1,111.8	7,240.2	83.4

Net Income History (in millions of dollars)

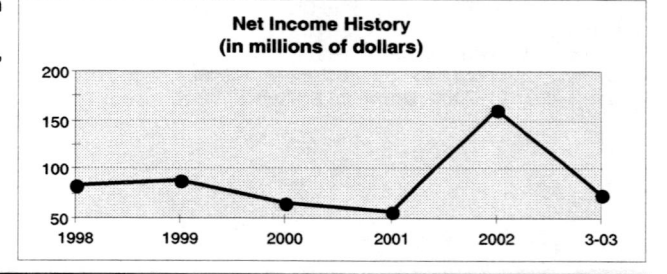

Winter 2003 - 04
II. Analysis of Largest Companies

BLUE CROSS BLUE SHIELD OF MINNESOTA * — B+ Good

Major Rating Factors: Strong capitalization (10.0 on a scale of 0 to 10) based on excellent current risk-adjusted capital (severe loss scenario) despite some fluctuation in capital levels. High quality investment portfolio (9.9). Excellent liquidity (7.2) with ample operational cash flow and liquid investments.
Other Rating Factors: Weak profitability index (2.7) with operating losses during 2001.
Principal Business: Comp med (62%), med supp (19%), FEHB (11%), stop loss (8%)
Mem Phys: 02: 13,418   **01:** 21,613   **02 MLR** 82%   / **02 Admin Exp** 12%
Enroll(000): Q1 03: 652   **02:** 633   **01:** 582   **Med Exp PMPM:** $174
Principal Investments: Cash and equiv (42%), nonaffiliate common stock (15%), real estate (7%), affiliate common stock (4%), other (32%)
Provider Compensation ($000): Contr fee ($667,773), bonus arrang ($473,918), FFS ($127,526)
Total Member Encounters: Phys (3,319,074), non-phys (903,671)
Group Affiliation: Aware Integrated Inc
Licensed in: MN
Address: 3535 Blue Cross Rd, St Paul, MN 55164
Phone: (651) 662-8000   **Dom State:** MN   **Commenced Bus:** June 1972

Data Date	Weiss Safety Rating	RACR #1	RACR #2	Total Assets ($mil)	Capital ($mil)	Net Premium ($mil)	Net Income ($mil)
3-03	B+	3.93	3.27	1,346.9	504.7	433.0	22.1
3-02	B+	2.63	1.88	1,342.2	407.6	371.2	10.2
2002	B+	3.84	3.20	1,320.9	494.8	1,547.3	47.7
2001	B+	2.63	1.88	1,315.0	403.5	1,392.6	-39.3
2000	B	1.70	1.03	1,212.5	421.1	1,221.3	42.1
1999	B	1.87	1.15	1,049.2	390.0	1,062.1	12.7
1998	B	1.73	1.06	942.3	309.3	75.2	247.6

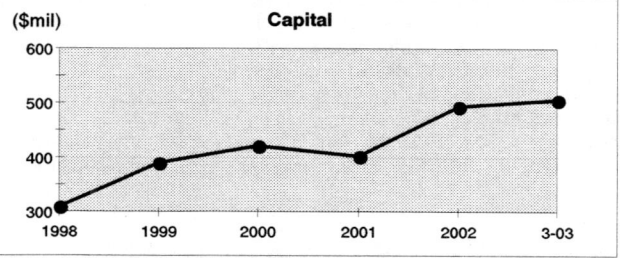

Capital chart (1998–3-03): ~310, ~385, ~415, ~395, ~490, ~500

BLUE CROSS BLUE SHIELD OF MISSISSIPPI, A MUTUAL — B- Good

Major Rating Factors: Good overall capitalization (5.9 on a scale of 0 to 10) based on mixed results -- excessive policy leverage mitigated by excellent risk adjusted capital (severe loss scenario). Moreover, capital has steadily grown over the last five years. Fair overall results on stability tests (4.6). Weak liquidity (2.6).
Other Rating Factors: High quality investment portfolio (7.6). Excellent profitability (9.2) with operating gains in each of the last five years.
Principal Business: Group health insurance (85%) and individual health insurance (15%).
Principal Investments: NonCMO investment grade bonds (54%), CMOs and structured securities (30%), common & preferred stock (7%), real estate (6%), and noninv. grade bonds (1%).
Investments in Affiliates: 6%
Group Affiliation: Bl Cross & Bl Shield of Mississippi
Licensed in: MS
Commenced Business: January 1948
Address: 3545 Lakeland Dr, Flowood, MS 39208
Phone: (601) 932-3704   **Domicile State:** MS   **NAIC Code:** 60111

Data Date	Weiss Safety Rating	RACR #1	RACR #2	Total Assets ($mil)	Capital ($mil)	Net Premium ($mil)	Net Income ($mil)
2002	B-	2.21	1.79	346.9	179.5	778.7	20.1
2001	B-	2.32	1.88	316.9	165.7	660.8	20.6
2000	B-	1.54	1.27	279.2	147.4	824.1	16.9
1999	B-	1.82	1.51	241.6	129.2	660.1	12.6

Policy Leverage: Target Leverage 100%, Actual Leverage 142%

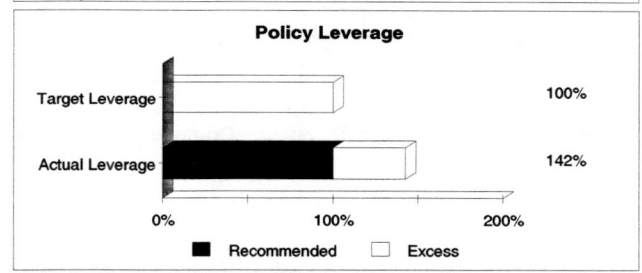

BLUE CROSS BLUE SHIELD OF MONTANA — C+ Fair

Major Rating Factors: Fair profitability index (3.7 on a scale of 0 to 10) with operating losses during 1999. Good capitalization (6.9) based on excellent current risk-adjusted capital (severe loss scenario) reflecting significant improvement over results in 2000. Good quality investment portfolio (5.1).
Other Rating Factors: Good liquidity (6.4) with sufficient resources (cash flows and marketable investments) to handle a spike in claims.
Principal Business: Comp med (73%), FEHB (15%), med supp (10%), dental (1%).
Mem Phys: 01: 3,963   **00:** 3,763   **01 MLR** 83%   / **01 Admin Exp** 16%
Enroll(000): Q2 02: 202   **01:** 170   **00:** N/A   **Med Exp PMPM:** $233
Principal Investments: Nonaffiliate common stock (20%), affiliate common stock (14%), real estate (9%), cash and equiv (4%), other (52%)
Provider Compensation ($000): FFS ($230,002), contr fee ($2,282), bonus arrang ($1,776), capitation ($1,722)
Total Member Encounters: N/A
Group Affiliation: Combined Benefits Group
Licensed in: MT
Address: 560 N Park Ave, Helena, MT 59601
Phone: (406) 444-8200   **Dom State:** MT   **Commenced Bus:** January 1946

Data Date	Weiss Safety Rating	RACR #1	RACR #2	Total Assets ($mil)	Capital ($mil)	Net Premium ($mil)	Net Income ($mil)
6-02	C+	1.37	1.04	160.2	53.4	157.8	0.3
6-01	C+	0.00	0.00	142.5	59.2	138.6	-0.2
2001	C+	1.37	1.04	150.2	54.1	286.0	6.2
2000	C+	1.08	0.69	156.0	56.0	245.9	1.3
1999	C+	1.27	0.80	148.7	65.5	219.4	-1.8
1998	C+	1.18	0.73	143.2	57.5	224.0	3.7
1997	C+	1.26	0.80	129.7	54.3	220.8	6.4

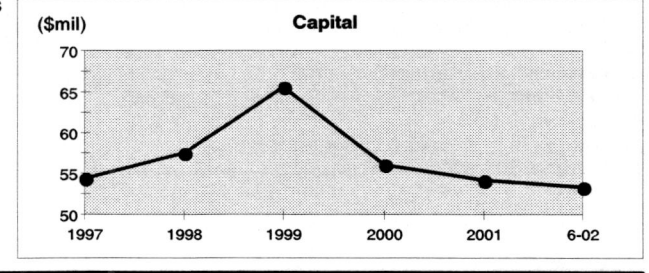

Capital chart (1997–6-02): ~54.5, ~57, ~65.5, ~56, ~54, ~53.5

www.WeissRatings.com   111   * Denotes a Weiss Recommended Company

II. Analysis of Largest Companies

Winter 2003 - 04

BLUE CROSS BLUE SHIELD OF NC — B — Good

Major Rating Factors: Good overall profitability index (5.7 on a scale of 0 to 10) despite a decline in earnings during 2002. Good liquidity (6.9) with sufficient resources (cash flows and marketable investments) to handle a spike in claims. Strong capitalization (9.7) based on excellent current risk-adjusted capital (severe loss scenario) despite some fluctuation in capital levels.
Other Rating Factors: High quality investment portfolio (9.2) containing little or no exposure to mortgages, junk bonds, or unaffiliated stocks.
Principal Business: Comp med (69%), FEHB (15%), med supp (14%), dental (2%)
Mem Phys: 02: 26,572 01: 27,883 **02 MLR** 80% / **02 Admin Exp** 17%
Enroll(000): Q1 03: 1,128 02: 1,118 01: 1,009 **Med Exp PMPM:** $131
Principal Investments: Cash and equiv (20%), nonaffiliate common stock (11%), affiliate common stock (9%), real estate (2%), other (58%)
Provider Compensation ($000): FFS ($975,748), contr fee ($650,498), capitation ($9,768), bonus arrang ($124)
Total Member Encounters: Phys (6,960,404)
Group Affiliation: Bl Cross & Bl Shield of N Carolina
Licensed in: NC
Address: 1830 US 15-501 North, Chapel Hill, NC 27514-2201
Phone: (919) 489-7431 **Dom State:** NC **Commenced Bus:** January 1968

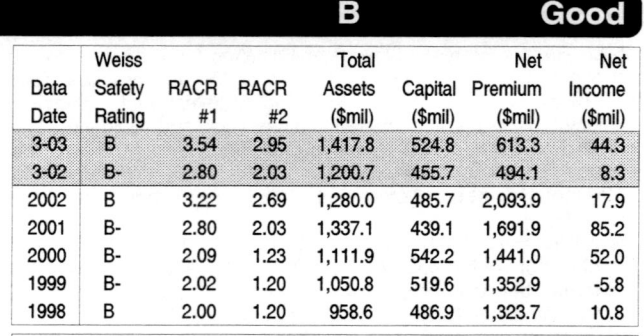

Data Date	Weiss Safety Rating	RACR #1	RACR #2	Total Assets ($mil)	Capital ($mil)	Net Premium ($mil)	Net Income ($mil)
3-03	B	3.54	2.95	1,417.8	524.8	613.3	44.3
3-02	B-	2.80	2.03	1,200.7	455.7	494.1	8.3
2002	B	3.22	2.69	1,280.0	485.7	2,093.9	17.9
2001	B-	2.80	2.03	1,337.1	439.1	1,691.9	85.2
2000	B-	2.09	1.23	1,111.9	542.2	1,441.0	52.0
1999	B-	2.02	1.20	1,050.8	519.6	1,352.9	-5.8
1998	B	2.00	1.20	958.6	486.9	1,323.7	10.8

Net Income History (in millions of dollars)

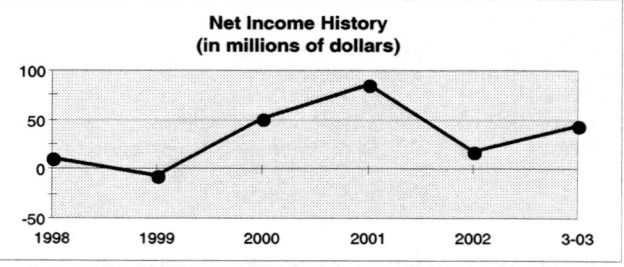

BLUE CROSS BLUE SHIELD OF NEBRASKA — B — Good

Major Rating Factors: Good liquidity (6.8 on a scale of 0 to 10) with sufficient resources (cash flows and marketable investments) to handle a spike in claims. Fair profitability index (4.4) due to a decline in earnings during 2002. Strong capitalization index (10.0) based on excellent current risk-adjusted capital (severe loss scenario) despite some fluctuation in capital levels.
Other Rating Factors: High quality investment portfolio (8.3).
Principal Business: Comp med (65%), med supp (17%), FEHB (15%), stop loss (3%)
Mem Phys: 02: 3,663 01: 3,670 **02 MLR** 84% / **02 Admin Exp** 11%
Enroll(000): Q1 03: 551 02: 580 01: 584 **Med Exp PMPM:** $73
Principal Investments: Nonaffiliate common stock (16%), real estate (9%), cash and equiv (8%), affiliate common stock (6%), other (63%)
Provider Compensation ($000): Contr fee ($516,745), other ($6,263)
Total Member Encounters: Phys (10,104,504), non-phys (215,822)
Group Affiliation: Bl Cross & Bl Shield of Nebraska
Licensed in: NE
Address: 7261 Mercy Rd, Omaha, NE 68124
Phone: (402) 390-1800 **Dom State:** NE **Commenced Bus:** January 1939

Data Date	Weiss Safety Rating	RACR #1	RACR #2	Total Assets ($mil)	Capital ($mil)	Net Premium ($mil)	Net Income ($mil)
3-03	B	9.24	7.70	508.5	299.8	165.5	5.6
3-02	N/A	N/A	N/A	N/A	N/A	N/A	N/A
2002	B	10.12	8.43	494.5	295.0	606.1	26.4
2001	U	2.07	1.57	469.6	286.1	643.4	29.8
2000	B-	2.17	1.62	433.2	266.9	552.3	18.2
1999	B-	2.17	1.61	417.0	263.0	529.7	38.8
1998	B-	2.01	1.52	458.5	229.6	454.2	-21.3

Rating Indexes (Range, Cap. 2, Stab., Inv., Prof., Liq.) — Weak / Fair / Good / Strong

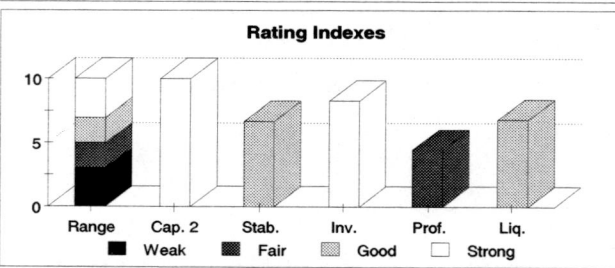

BLUE CROSS BLUE SHIELD OF OKLAHOMA — B — Good

Major Rating Factors: Fair liquidity (4.7 on a scale of 0 to 10) as cash resources may not be adequate to cover a spike in claims. Strong capitalization (7.7) based on excellent current risk-adjusted capital (severe loss scenario). High quality investment portfolio (8.4) containing little or no exposure to mortgages, junk bonds, or unaffiliated stocks.
Other Rating Factors: Weak profitability index (1.9) with operating losses during 2002.
Principal Business: Comp med (48%), FEHB (39%), med supp (11%), dental (2%)
Mem Phys: 02: 9,542 01: 9,760 **02 MLR** 88% / **02 Admin Exp** 16%
Enroll(000): Q1 03: 636 02: 675 01: 55 **Med Exp PMPM:** $153
Principal Investments: Affiliate common stock (30%), cash and equiv (23%), real estate (13%), nonaffiliate common stock (7%), other (27%)
Provider Compensation ($000): Contr fee ($548,780), FFS ($17,498), other ($67,609)
Total Member Encounters: Phys (937,324), non-phys (3,297,575)
Group Affiliation: Group Hospital Service of Oklahoma
Licensed in: OK
Address: 1215 S Boulder, Tulsa, OK 74119-2800
Phone: (918) 560-3500 **Dom State:** OK **Commenced Bus:** April 1940

Data Date	Weiss Safety Rating	RACR #1	RACR #2	Total Assets ($mil)	Capital ($mil)	Net Premium ($mil)	Net Income ($mil)
3-03	B	1.90	1.58	390.7	102.7	216.1	10.9
3-02	B	1.91	1.56	328.4	107.6	171.5	3.4
2002	B	0.00	0.00	379.8	91.6	762.3	-18.2
2001	B	1.91	1.57	319.9	102.7	583.1	12.4
2000	B-	0.99	0.67	278.5	76.9	544.8	6.7
1999	B-	1.07	0.74	230.7	76.7	465.1	3.6
1998	B-	1.12	0.74	226.1	73.3	437.6	0.6

Rating Indexes (Range, Cap. 2, Stab., Inv., Prof., Liq.) — Weak / Fair / Good / Strong

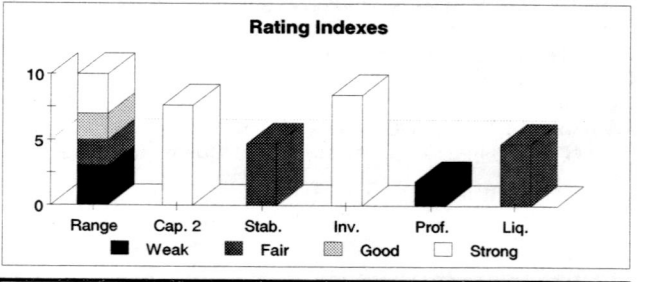

BLUE CROSS BLUE SHIELD OF RI *   B+   Good

Major Rating Factors: Good liquidity (6.6 on a scale of 0 to 10) with sufficient resources (cash flows and marketable investments) to handle a spike in claims. Excellent profitability (7.8) despite a decline in earnings during 2002. Strong capitalization (8.0) based on excellent current risk-adjusted capital (severe loss scenario) reflecting significant improvement over results in 1999.
Other Rating Factors: High quality investment portfolio (9.6) containing little or no exposure to mortgages, junk bonds, or unaffiliated stocks.
Principal Business: Comp med (86%), med supp (6%), FEHB (5%), dental (3%).
Mem Phys: 02: 3,483 **01:** 3,462 **02 MLR** 86% **/ 02 Admin Exp** 8%
Enroll(000): Q1 03: 367 **02:** 365 **01:** 434 **Med Exp PMPM:** $161
Principal Investments: Affiliate common stock (20%), real estate (8%), cash and equiv (4%), nonaffiliate common stock (1%), other (68%)
Provider Compensation ($000): Contr fee ($781,076)
Total Member Encounters: Phys (3,355,471), non-phys (572,701)
Group Affiliation: Bl Cross & Bl Shield of Rhode Island
Licensed in: RI
Address: 444 Westminster St, Providence, RI 02903-3279
Phone: (401) 459-1000 **Dom State:** RI **Commenced Bus:** September 1939

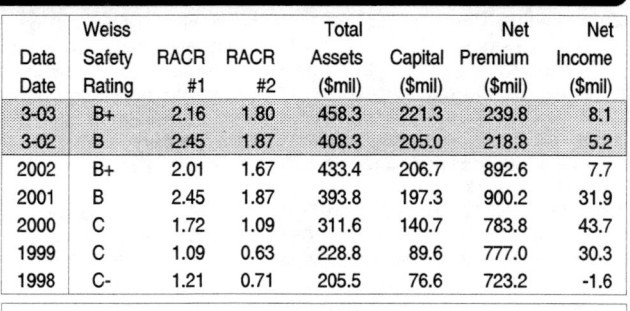

Data Date	Weiss Safety Rating	RACR #1	RACR #2	Total Assets ($mil)	Capital ($mil)	Net Premium ($mil)	Net Income ($mil)
3-03	B+	2.16	1.80	458.3	221.3	239.8	8.1
3-02	B	2.45	1.87	408.3	205.0	218.8	5.2
2002	B+	2.01	1.67	433.4	206.7	892.6	7.7
2001	B	2.45	1.87	393.8	197.3	900.2	31.9
2000	C	1.72	1.09	311.6	140.7	783.8	43.7
1999	C	1.09	0.63	228.8	89.6	777.0	30.3
1998	C-	1.21	0.71	205.5	76.6	723.2	-1.6

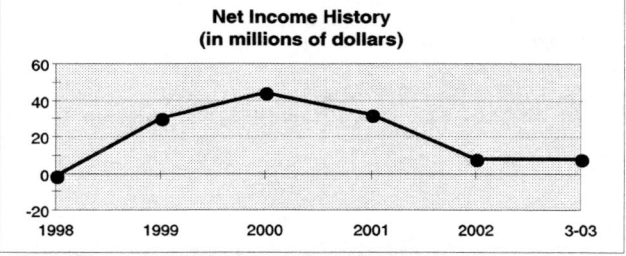

Net Income History (in millions of dollars)

BLUE CROSS BLUE SHIELD OF SC INC *   B+   Good

Major Rating Factors: Good liquidity (6.9 on a scale of 0 to 10) with sufficient resources (cash flows and marketable investments) to handle a spike in claims. Good overall results on stability tests (5.0) despite weak results on operational trends.
Other Rating Factors: Strong long-term capitalization index (8.0) based on excellent current risk adjusted capital (severe and moderate loss scenarios). Moreover, capital levels have been consistent in recent years. Ample reserve history (9.2) that helps to protect the company against sharp claims increases. Excellent profitability (9.1) with operating gains in each of the last five years. Excellent expense controls. Return on equity has been good over the last five years, averaging 14.5%.
Principal Business: Group accident & health (83%) and other accident & health (17%).
Principal Investments: Misc. investments (67%), investment grade bonds (27%), real estate (10%), and non investment grade bonds (1%).
Investments in Affiliates: 24%
Group Affiliation: Companion Ins Group
Licensed in: SC
Commenced Business: April 1947
Address: 2501 Faraway Dr, Columbia, SC 29219-0001
Phone: (803) 788-3860 **Domicile State:** SC **NAIC Code:** 38520

Data Date	Weiss Safety Rating	RACR #1	RACR #2	Loss Ratio %	Total Assets ($mil)	Capital ($mil)	Net Premium ($mil)	Net Income ($mil)
6-03	B+	2.57	1.83	N/A	1,045.1	601.7	524.1	48.7
6-02	B+	2.47	1.84	N/A	840.5	466.8	447.8	54.3
2002	B+	2.33	1.70	83.7	923.1	500.1	935.5	99.2
2001	B+	2.24	1.70	85.6	772.7	403.1	761.3	67.1
2000	B+	2.28	1.71	87.0	605.8	325.1	660.1	49.9
1999	B+	1.97	1.54	88.7	534.3	293.8	577.4	29.5
1998	B+	1.89	1.44	89.0	481.3	266.5	534.6	26.7

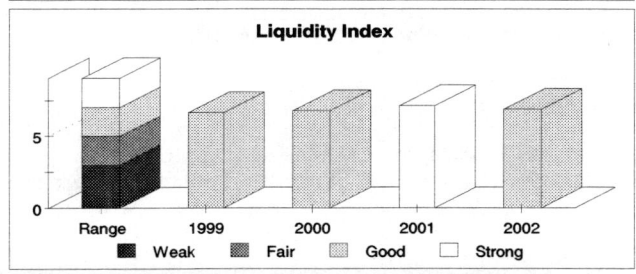

Liquidity Index

BLUE CROSS BLUE SHIELD OF VERMONT   B   Good

Major Rating Factors: Good liquidity (7.0 on a scale of 0 to 10) with sufficient resources (cash flows and marketable investments) to handle a spike in claims. Excellent profitability (7.5) despite operating losses during 1998. Strong capitalization (8.0) based on excellent current risk-adjusted capital (severe loss scenario) reflecting significant improvement over results in 1998.
Other Rating Factors: High quality investment portfolio (9.5) containing little or no exposure to mortgages, junk bonds, or unaffiliated stocks.
Principal Business: Comp med (76%), FEHB (12%), med supp (8%), stop loss (1%), other (2%)
Mem Phys: 02: 6,651 **01:** 6,692 **02 MLR** 84% **/ 02 Admin Exp** 12%
Enroll(000): Q1 03: 139 **02:** 137 **01:** 127 **Med Exp PMPM:** $103
Principal Investments: Cash and equiv (12%), real estate (11%), affiliate common stock (5%), nonaffiliate common stock (1%), other (70%)
Provider Compensation ($000): Contr fee ($140,994), FFS ($13,534), capitation ($7,053), other ($3,116)
Total Member Encounters: Phys (270,320), non-phys (180,036)
Group Affiliation: Blue Cross Blue Shield of Vermont
Licensed in: VT
Address: 445 Industrial Ln, Berlin, VT 05602
Phone: (802) 223-6131 **Dom State:** VT **Commenced Bus:** December 1980

Data Date	Weiss Safety Rating	RACR #1	RACR #2	Total Assets ($mil)	Capital ($mil)	Net Premium ($mil)	Net Income ($mil)
3-03	B	2.19	1.82	107.9	39.2	54.1	2.0
3-02	C+	1.60	1.34	98.3	29.8	47.1	2.0
2002	B	1.98	1.65	102.9	35.7	195.3	6.9
2001	C+	1.58	1.32	94.9	27.0	165.1	4.3
2000	C	0.83	0.62	86.6	24.3	164.6	4.6
1999	C-	0.79	0.61	80.3	20.1	258.8	0.9
1998	C-	0.78	0.56	78.0	19.6	238.8	-2.8

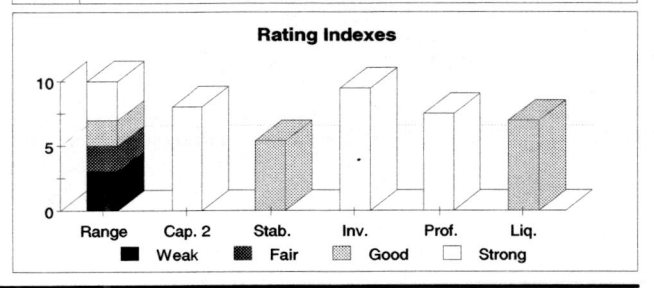

Rating Indexes

* Denotes a Weiss Recommended Company

II. Analysis of Largest Companies

Winter 2003 - 04

BLUE CROSS BLUE SHIELD OF WYOMING *   B+   Good

Major Rating Factors: Good overall profitability index (5.0 on a scale of 0 to 10) with operating gains in each of the last five years. Good liquidity (6.8) with sufficient resources (cash flows and marketable investments) to handle a spike in claims. Strong capitalization (10.0) based on excellent current risk-adjusted capital (severe loss scenario) despite some fluctuation in capital levels.
Other Rating Factors: High quality investment portfolio (7.1).
Principal Business: Comp med (67%), FEHB (22%), med supp (8%), dental (2%), stop loss (1%)
Mem Phys: 02: 2,259   **01:** 2,011   **02 MLR** 86%   **/ 02 Admin Exp** 12%
Enroll(000): Q1 03: 62   **02:** 63   **01:** 67   **Med Exp PMPM:** $138
Principal Investments: Nonaffiliate common stock (43%), cash and equiv (6%), real estate (2%), other (49%)
Provider Compensation ($000): FFS ($102,680), other ($625)
Total Member Encounters: Phys (623,216), non-phys (516,639)
Group Affiliation: None
Licensed in: WY
Address: 4000 House Ave, Cheyenne, WY 82001
Phone: (307) 634-1393   **Dom State:** WY   **Commenced Bus:** August 1976

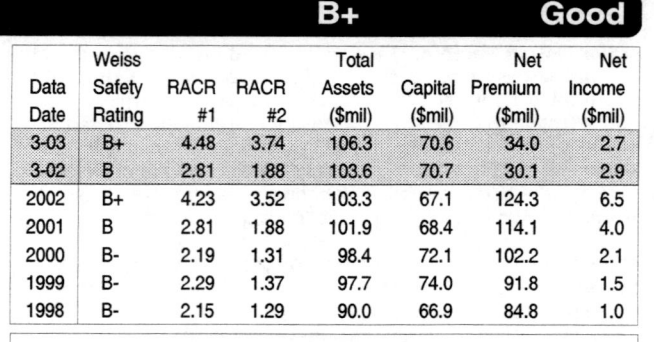

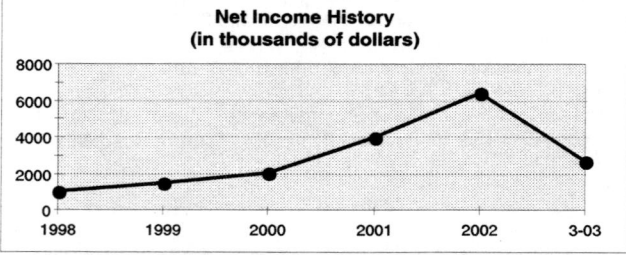

Data Date	Weiss Safety Rating	RACR #1	RACR #2	Total Assets ($mil)	Capital ($mil)	Net Premium ($mil)	Net Income ($mil)
3-03	B+	4.48	3.74	106.3	70.6	34.0	2.7
3-02	B	2.81	1.88	103.6	70.7	30.1	2.9
2002	B+	4.23	3.52	103.3	67.1	124.3	6.5
2001	B	2.81	1.88	101.9	68.4	114.1	4.0
2000	B-	2.19	1.31	98.4	72.1	102.2	2.1
1999	B-	2.29	1.37	97.7	74.0	91.8	1.5
1998	B-	2.15	1.29	90.0	66.9	84.8	1.0

Net Income History (in thousands of dollars)

BLUE CROSS BLUE SHIELD UNITED OF WI   B-   Good

Major Rating Factors: Good overall profitability index (5.1 on a scale of 0 to 10) despite operating losses during 1999, 2000 and 2001. Good quality investment portfolio (6.6) containing small junk bond exposure. Strong capitalization (7.7) based on excellent current risk-adjusted capital (severe loss scenario) reflecting significant improvement over results in 2000.
Other Rating Factors: Excellent liquidity (7.0) with ample operational cash flow and liquid investments.
Principal Business: Comp med (58%), FEHB (20%), med supp (17%), dental (4%)
Mem Phys: 02: 12,934   **01:** 11,612   **02 MLR** 79%   **/ 02 Admin Exp** 13%
Enroll(000): Q1 03: 341   **02:** 337   **01:** 294   **Med Exp PMPM:** $130
Principal Investments: Affiliate common stock (40%), nonaffiliate common stock (5%), real estate (2%), pref stock (1%), other (52%)
Provider Compensation ($000): Contr fee ($348,429), FFS ($158,990), capitation ($80)
Total Member Encounters: N/A
Group Affiliation: Cobalt Corp
Licensed in: WI
Address: 401 W Michigan St, Milwaukee, WI 53203
Phone: (414) 226-5823   **Dom State:** WI   **Commenced Bus:** October 1939

Data Date	Weiss Safety Rating	RACR #1	RACR #2	Total Assets ($mil)	Capital ($mil)	Net Premium ($mil)	Net Income ($mil)
3-03	B-	1.91	1.59	328.2	159.5	163.2	24.5
3-02	C-	1.60	1.32	228.0	93.3	148.3	29.6
2002	C+	1.79	1.49	303.7	150.2	623.0	116.4
2001	C-	1.59	1.32	246.7	88.0	597.0	-1.6
2000	C-	0.77	0.57	258.8	104.4	534.4	-28.2
1999	C-	1.18	0.90	274.8	142.4	416.2	-22.2
1998	C+	1.68	1.33	345.2	198.5	359.7	1.8

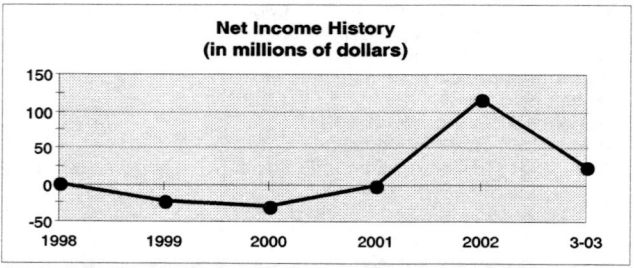

Net Income History (in millions of dollars)

BLUE CROSS OF CALIFORNIA *   A   Excellent

Major Rating Factors: Excellent profitability (9.1 on a scale of 0 to 10) with operating gains in each of the last five years. Strong overall capitalization (8.2) based on excellent current risk-adjusted capital (severe loss scenario). Furthermore, this high level of risk-adjusted capital has been consistently maintained in previous years. Excellent liquidity (7.3) with ample operational cash flow and liquid investments.
Other Rating Factors: Good overall results on stability tests (7.0).
Principal Business: Managed care (85%)
Mem Phys: 02: N/A   **01:** N/A   **02 MLR** 80%   **/ 02 Admin Exp** 13%
Enroll(000): Q1 03: 4,884   **02:** 4,837   **01:** 4,389   **Med Exp PMPM:** $129
Principal Investments ($000): Cash and equiv ($3,019,227), stocks ($256,062), bonds ($95,974), other ($407,450)
Provider Compensation ($000): None
Total Member Encounters: N/A
Group Affiliation: WellPoint Health Networks Inc
Licensed in: CA
Address: 4553 La Tienda Dr., T1-2C5, Thousand Oaks, CA 91362
Phone: (818) 234-2345   **Dom State:** CA   **Commenced Bus:** July 1982

Data Date	Weiss Safety Rating	RACR #1	RACR #2	Total Assets ($mil)	Capital ($mil)	Net Premium ($mil)	Net Income ($mil)
3-03	A	3.14	1.95	4,397.8	1,135.7	2,456.0	97.4
3-02	A	0.00	0.00	3,425.2	859.8	2,072.8	106.8
2002	A	2.93	1.82	4,270.8	1,042.9	8,889.2	434.6
2001	A	2.88	1.82	3,281.7	886.9	7,134.8	314.8
2000	A-	3.10	1.96	2,840.7	875.4	6,241.3	349.6
1999	A-	3.13	1.97	2,426.5	761.3	5,251.2	253.0
1998	A-	2.24	1.42	1,905.2	503.9	4,416.9	212.8

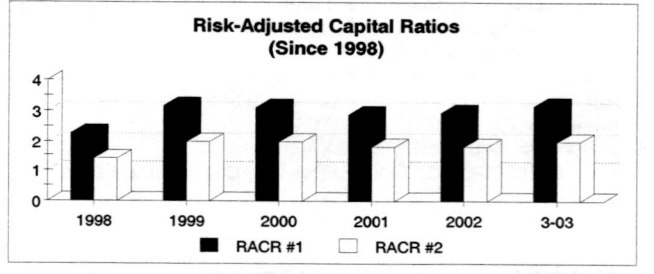

Risk-Adjusted Capital Ratios (Since 1998)

■ RACR #1   □ RACR #2

Winter 2003 - 04 — II. Analysis of Largest Companies

BLUE CROSS OF IDAHO HEALTH SERVICE INC *   B+   Good

Major Rating Factors: Strong capitalization (5.9 on a scale of 0 to 10) based on excellent risk adjusted capital (severe loss scenario). Good overall profitability (5.3). Excellent expense controls. Good overall results on stability tests (5.0) excellent operational trends, excellent risk adjusted capital for prior years and excellent risk diversification.
Other Rating Factors: Fair quality investment portfolio (4.6). Weak liquidity (1.5).
Principal Business: Group health insurance (75%) and individual health insurance (25%).
Principal Investments: NonCMO investment grade bonds (55%), CMOs and structured securities (23%), common & preferred stock (19%), real estate (5%), and noninv. grade bonds (1%).
Investments in Affiliates: None
Group Affiliation: Blue Cross of Idaho Group
Licensed in: ID
Commenced Business: January 1978
Address: 3000 Pine Ave, Meridian, ID 83642
Phone: (208) 345-4550 **Domicile State:** ID **NAIC Code:** 60095

Data Date	Weiss Safety Rating	RACR #1	RACR #2	Total Assets ($mil)	Capital ($mil)	Net Premium ($mil)	Net Income ($mil)
6-03	B+	1.57	1.16	177.2	84.6	256.6	8.7
6-02	B+	1.55	1.13	155.6	74.4	221.5	9.0
2002	B+	1.44	1.08	163.3	72.1	455.8	5.0
2001	B+	1.55	1.15	149.9	74.9	343.0	1.8
2000	B+	1.61	1.19	144.0	73.6	306.0	8.5
1999	B+	2.55	1.93	134.4	73.8	277.5	3.9
1998	B+	1.96	1.53	133.3	70.6	272.1	-4.9

Risk-Adjusted Capital Ratio #2 (Severe Loss Scenario)

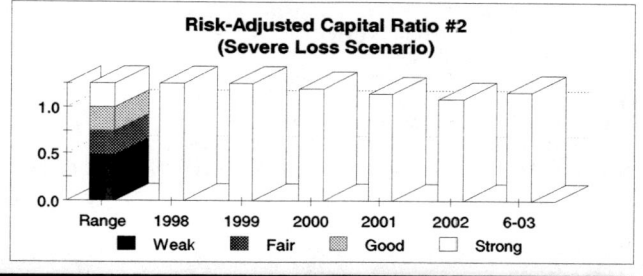

BLUECROSS BLUESHIELD OF TENNESSEE *   B+   Good

Major Rating Factors: Good overall profitability index (6.6 on a scale of 0 to 10) with operating gains in each of the last five years. Strong capitalization (10.0) based on excellent current risk-adjusted capital (severe loss scenario) despite some fluctuation in capital levels. High quality investment portfolio (9.9).
Other Rating Factors: Excellent liquidity (7.0) with ample operational cash flow and liquid investments.
Principal Business: Comp med (78%), FEHB (12%), med supp (7%), dental (2%).
Mem Phys: 02: 16,844 **01:** 16,632 **02 MLR** 82% **/ 02 Admin Exp** 10%
Enroll(000): Q1 03: 816 **02:** 824 **01:** 775 **Med Exp PMPM:** $124
Principal Investments: Cash and equiv (21%), nonaffiliate common stock (20%), real estate (6%), affiliate common stock (6%), other (48%)
Provider Compensation ($000): Contr fee ($1,183,095)
Total Member Encounters: Phys (787,870), non-phys (769,834)
Group Affiliation: Bl Cross & Bl Shield of Tennessee
Licensed in: TN
Address: 801 Pine St, Chattanooga, TN 37402
Phone: (423) 755-5600 **Dom State:** TN **Commenced Bus:** September 1945

Data Date	Weiss Safety Rating	RACR #1	RACR #2	Total Assets ($mil)	Capital ($mil)	Net Premium ($mil)	Net Income ($mil)
3-03	B+	5.53	4.61	1,093.8	628.4	396.3	33.8
3-02	B+	8.86	5.48	1,024.2	627.1	343.0	18.4
2002	B+	5.25	4.38	1,006.8	602.5	1,446.4	96.7
2001	B+	8.87	5.48	997.2	614.1	1,256.2	40.3
2000	B+	1.91	1.19	1,144.0	572.3	2,172.5	52.8
1999	B+	2.85	1.84	1,039.7	521.3	1,785.3	53.3
1998	B	2.86	1.87	1,026.4	469.7	1,603.6	38.1

Net Income History (in millions of dollars)

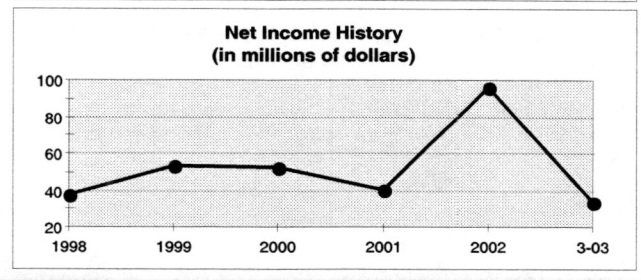

BLUEGRASS FAMILY HEALTH INC *   B+   Good

Major Rating Factors: Good liquidity (6.8 on a scale of 0 to 10) with sufficient resources (cash flows and marketable investments) to handle a spike in claims. Excellent profitability (7.1) despite operating losses during 1998. Strong capitalization index (7.0) based on excellent current risk-adjusted capital (severe loss scenario).
Other Rating Factors: High quality investment portfolio (9.9). Excellent overall results on stability tests (7.7) based on consistent premium and capital growth in the last five years but rapid enrollment growth during the past five years.
Principal Business: Comp med (100%)
Mem Phys: 02: 7,975 **01:** 6,644 **02 MLR** 88% **/ 02 Admin Exp** 7%
Enroll(000): Q1 03: 123 **02:** 123 **01:** 109 **Med Exp PMPM:** $193
Principal Investments: Cash and equiv (50%), nonaffiliate common stock (15%), other (35%)
Provider Compensation ($000): Contr fee ($243,881), FFS ($16,230), capitation ($7,082), bonus arrang ($742)
Total Member Encounters: Phys (851,170), non-phys (306,214)
Group Affiliation: Baptist Healthcare System Inc
Licensed in: KY
Address: 651 Perimeter Park, Ste 300, Lexington, KY 40517
Phone: (859) 269-4475 **Dom State:** KY **Commenced Bus:** April 1993

Data Date	Weiss Safety Rating	RACR #1	RACR #2	Total Assets ($mil)	Capital ($mil)	Net Premium ($mil)	Net Income ($mil)
3-03	B+	1.38	1.15	82.2	27.6	84.8	1.7
3-02	B	1.29	1.08	76.9	18.0	75.0	0.9
2002	B	1.33	1.11	80.3	26.5	304.9	10.0
2001	B	1.29	1.08	68.0	16.9	240.7	5.9
2000	D	0.89	0.75	48.0	9.6	180.3	4.8
1999	E	0.07	0.06	32.3	2.8	141.1	1.2
1998	E	0.09	0.08	15.6	1.7	62.9	-3.8

Net Income History (in thousands of dollars)

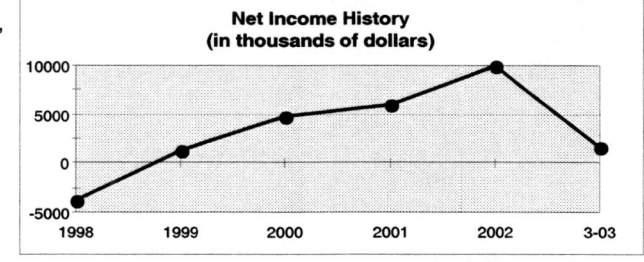

www.WeissRatings.com — * Denotes a Weiss Recommended Company

II. Analysis of Largest Companies

Winter 2003 - 04

BOSTON MUTUAL LIFE INSURANCE COMPANY — B — Good

Major Rating Factors: Good quality investment portfolio (6.6 on a scale of 0 to 10) despite mixed results such as: no exposure to mortgages and substantial holdings of BBB bonds but no exposure to junk bonds. Good liquidity (5.9) with sufficient resources to handle a spike in claims as well as a significant increase in policy surrenders. Good overall results on stability tests (5.2) excellent operational trends, good risk adjusted capital for prior years and excellent risk diversification.
Other Rating Factors: Strong capitalization (7.0) based on excellent risk adjusted capital (severe loss scenario). Excellent profitability (7.2) despite modest operating losses during 2002.
Principal Business: Individual life insurance (43%), group health insurance (38%), group life insurance (16%), and reinsurance (3%).
Principal Investments: NonCMO investment grade bonds (42%), CMOs and structured securities (27%), mortgages in good standing (19%), policy loans (8%), and misc. investments (5%).
Investments in Affiliates: 1%
Group Affiliation: Boston Mutual Group
Licensed in: All states except NY
Commenced Business: February 1892
Address: 120 Royall St, Canton, MA 02021-1098
Phone: (781) 828-7000 **Domicile State:** MA **NAIC Code:** 61476

Data Date	Weiss Safety Rating	RACR #1	RACR #2	Total Assets ($mil)	Capital ($mil)	Net Premium ($mil)	Net Income ($mil)
6-03	B	1.52	1.00	683.9	65.1	92.5	0.3
6-02	B-	1.32	0.88	645.0	54.2	93.8	0.6
2002	B	1.50	0.99	687.3	63.7	205.7	-2.2
2001	B-	1.42	0.95	606.2	55.0	191.1	2.0
2000	B-	1.65	1.01	556.1	50.8	171.1	4.7
1999	B-	1.83	1.12	515.3	51.4	158.9	4.0
1998	B-	1.66	1.07	487.1	49.7	162.6	4.4

Adverse Trends in Operations

Decrease in capital during 2000 (1%)
Decrease in premium volume from 1998 to 1999 (2%)

BOTSFORD HEALTH PLAN CORP — B- — Good

Major Rating Factors: Fair capitalization (3.5 on a scale of 0 to 10) based on weak current risk-adjusted capital (moderate loss scenario) as results have slipped from the good range over the last year. Good overall results on stability tests (6.9). Excellent profitability (8.9).
Other Rating Factors: High quality investment portfolio (9.9) containing no exposure to mortgages, junk bonds, or unaffiliated stocks. Excellent liquidity (7.3) with ample operational cash flow and liquid investments.
Principal Business: Medicaid (100%).
Mem Phys: 02: 189 **01:** 195 **02 MLR** 86% / **02 Admin Exp** 11%
Enroll(000): Q1 03: 10 **02:** 10 **01:** 7 **Med Exp PMPM:** $172
Principal Investments: Cash and equiv (100%)
Provider Compensation ($000): Contr fee ($9,525), bonus arrang ($2,353), capitation ($2,010)
Total Member Encounters: Phys (14,079), non-phys (21,007)
Group Affiliation: Zieger Health Care Corp
Licensed in: MI
Address: 28050 Grand River Ave, Farmington Hills, MI 48336
Phone: (248) 471-8157 **Dom State:** MI **Commenced Bus:** October 1996

Data Date	Weiss Safety Rating	RACR #1	RACR #2	Total Assets ($mil)	Capital ($mil)	Net Premium ($mil)	Net Income ($mil)
3-03	B-	0.71	0.59	10.8	3.4	5.7	0.2
3-02	U	1.26	1.07	7.4	3.9	4.5	0.9
2002	B-	0.71	0.59	10.2	3.4	20.0	0.7
2001	U	1.26	1.07	6.5	3.1	13.7	1.4
2000	U	1.03	0.87	4.5	1.7	9.3	0.9
1999	N/A	N/A	N/A	N/A	N/A	N/A	N/A
1998	N/A	N/A	N/A	N/A	N/A	N/A	N/A

Risk-Adjusted Capital Ratios (Since 1998)

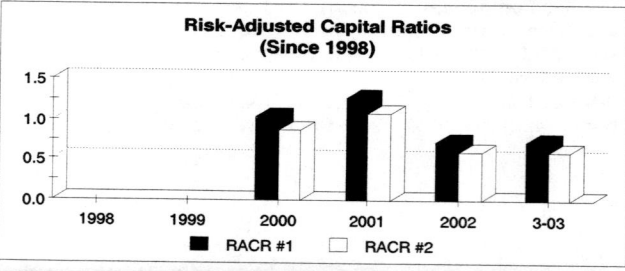

CALIFORNIA PHYSICIANS SERVICE * — A- — Excellent

Major Rating Factors: Excellent profitability (7.9 on a scale of 0 to 10) despite modest operating losses during 2000. Strong capitalization (7.1) based on excellent current risk-adjusted capital (severe loss scenario) reflecting improvement over results in 2000. Good overall results on stability tests (6.8).
Other Rating Factors: Good liquidity (6.6) with sufficient resources (cash flows and marketable investments) to handle a spike in claims.
Principal Business: Managed care (82%).
Mem Phys: 02: N/A **01:** N/A **02 MLR** 84% / **02 Admin Exp** 13%
Enroll(000): Q1 03: 2,642 **02:** 2,298 **01:** 2,276 **Med Exp PMPM:** $137
Principal Investments ($000): Cash and equiv ($223,102)
Provider Compensation ($000): None
Total Member Encounters: N/A
Group Affiliation: Blue Shield of California
Licensed in: CA
Address: Fifty Beale St, San Francisco, CA 94105
Phone: (415) 229-5821 **Dom State:** CA **Commenced Bus:** February 1939

Data Date	Weiss Safety Rating	RACR #1	RACR #2	Total Assets ($mil)	Capital ($mil)	Net Premium ($mil)	Net Income ($mil)
3-03	A-	1.72	1.18	2,083.3	808.4	1,449.7	76.0
3-02	A-	0.00	0.00	1,658.9	645.1	1,105.1	43.1
2002	A-	1.56	1.07	1,953.6	740.1	4,469.7	142.6
2001	A-	1.69	1.09	1,638.1	605.3	4,239.3	61.2
2000	A-	1.26	0.91	1,447.2	546.9	3,458.0	-4.1
1999	A-	1.68	1.11	1,310.8	546.7	2,891.6	16.9
1998	A	1.80	1.20	1,210.3	544.9	2,475.6	42.3

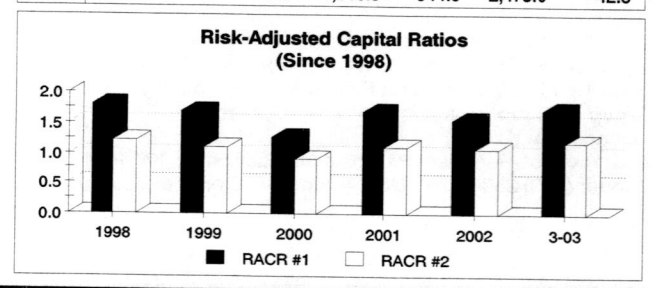

Risk-Adjusted Capital Ratios (Since 1998)

CANADA LIFE ASSURANCE CO-US BRANCH   C   Fair

Major Rating Factors: Fair overall results on stability tests (3.4 on a scale of 0 to 10) including fair risk adjusted capital in prior years. Good current capitalization (5.2) based on good risk adjusted capital (moderate loss scenario) reflecting some improvement over results in 2001. Good quality investment portfolio (5.2).
Other Rating Factors: Good liquidity (6.9). Weak profitability (2.5).
Principal Business: Reinsurance (25%), group health insurance (23%), individual life insurance (21%), group life insurance (17%), and other lines (14%).
Principal Investments: NonCMO investment grade bonds (49%), mortgages in good standing (26%), policy loans (8%), common & preferred stock (8%), and misc. investments (10%).
Investments in Affiliates: 4%
Group Affiliation: Canada Life Assurance Co
Licensed in: All states, the District of Columbia and Puerto Rico
Commenced Business: August 1847
Address: 330 University Ave, Toronto Ontario, CN M5G 1R8
Phone: (770) 953-1959   **Domicile State:** MI   **NAIC Code:** 80659

Data Date	Weiss Safety Rating	RACR #1	RACR #2	Total Assets ($mil)	Capital ($mil)	Net Premium ($mil)	Net Income ($mil)
6-03	C	1.10	0.76	4,644.1	407.1	309.0	17.6
6-02	C	0.80	0.54	4,392.0	288.7	386.4	14.2
2002	C	1.07	0.75	4,558.0	379.8	715.1	-31.5
2001	C	0.79	0.52	4,276.3	294.9	667.6	-74.6
2000	C	1.11	0.70	4,156.9	330.0	609.6	51.9
1999	U	1.08	0.71	4,036.5	296.4	649.3	-172.8
1998	N/A	N/A	N/A	2,471.3	275.1	425.6	34.0

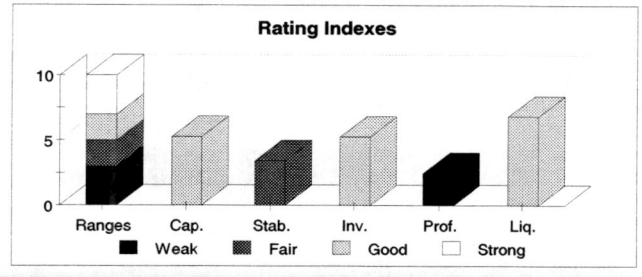

CAPE HEALTH PLAN INC   D   Weak

Major Rating Factors: Poor capitalization index (0.1 on a scale of 0 to 10) based on weak current risk-adjusted capital (moderate loss scenario). Weak liquidity (0.0) as a spike in claims may stretch capacity. Fair overall results on stability tests (4.3) based on rapid premium growth over the last five years, rapid enrollment growth during the past five years.
Other Rating Factors: Good overall profitability index (6.4) despite modest operating losses during 2002. High quality investment portfolio (9.9) containing no exposure to mortgages, junk bonds, or unaffiliated stocks.
Principal Business: Medicaid (100%)
Mem Phys: 02: 7,248   **01:** 7,050   **02 MLR** 90%   **/ 02 Admin Exp** 10%
Enroll(000): Q1 03: 57   **02:** 54   **01:** 44   **Med Exp PMPM:** $156
Principal Investments: Cash and equiv (96%), other (4%)
Provider Compensation ($000): Contr fee ($70,205), capitation ($18,820), other ($1,810)
Total Member Encounters: Phys (37,548), non-phys (18,535)
Group Affiliation: HCLB Inc
Licensed in: MI
Address: 26711 Northwestern Hwy Ste 300, Southfield, MI 48034
Phone: (248) 386-3000   **Dom State:** MI   **Commenced Bus:** April 1982

Data Date	Weiss Safety Rating	RACR #1	RACR #2	Total Assets ($mil)	Capital ($mil)	Net Premium ($mil)	Net Income ($mil)
3-03	D	0.31	0.26	26.4	7.0	27.1	0.2
3-02	C	0.00	0.00	22.5	8.0	23.2	0.4
2002	D	0.30	0.25	27.9	6.9	101.4	-0.1
2001	C	0.53	0.45	23.4	8.1	88.1	2.2
2000	C	1.68	1.43	25.7	9.7	68.4	12.5
1999	U	0.46	0.39	15.6	3.4	50.4	5.9
1998	C	1.05	0.87	7.7	4.0	31.9	4.5

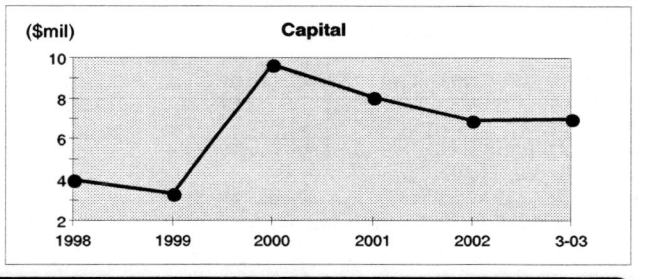

CAPITAL ADVANTAGE INS CO   C-   Fair

Major Rating Factors: Weak profitability index (0.9 on a scale of 0 to 10) with operating losses during 2002. Poor capitalization (2.9) based on good current risk-adjusted capital (moderate loss scenario). However, risk-adjusted capital has reached as low as the weak level during recent years. Good liquidity (6.8) with sufficient resources (cash flows and marketable investments) to handle a spike in claims.
Other Rating Factors: High quality investment portfolio (9.9) containing no exposure to mortgages, junk bonds, or unaffiliated stocks.
Principal Business: Comp med (80%), med only (10%), med supp (9%)
Mem Phys: 02: 12,423   **01:** N/A   **02 MLR** 100%   **/ 02 Admin Exp** 4%
Enroll(000): Q1 03: 586   **02:** 329   **01:** 0   **Med Exp PMPM:** $117
Principal Investments: Cash and equiv (62%), other (38%)
Provider Compensation ($000): FFS ($74,159), contr fee ($50,406)
Total Member Encounters: N/A
Group Affiliation: Capital Blue Cross Group
Licensed in: PA
Address: 2500 Elmerton Avenue, Harrisburg, PA 17110
Phone: (717) 541-7219   **Dom State:** PA   **Commenced Bus:** May 1982

Data Date	Weiss Safety Rating	RACR #1	RACR #2	Total Assets ($mil)	Capital ($mil)	Net Premium ($mil)	Net Income ($mil)
3-03	C-	3.87	3.22	421.9	148.0	212.3	-24.0
3-02	N/A	N/A	N/A	N/A	N/A	N/A	N/A
2002	C	4.60	3.83	353.3	172.1	230.9	-62.2
2001	C	23.19	20.87	10.2	9.3	0.3	1.7
2000	C	72.83	37.27	7.8	7.6	0.3	1.4
1999	C-	32.71	29.11	6.6	6.2	0.3	1.3
1998	D+	32.84	29.55	5.3	5.0	0.2	1.0

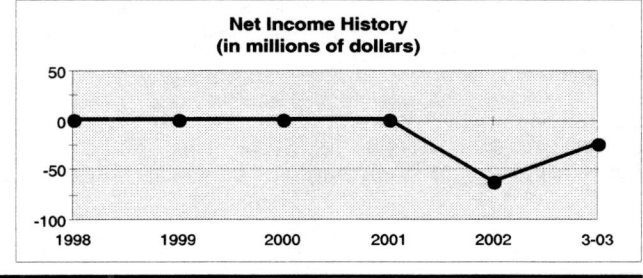

II. Analysis of Largest Companies — Winter 2003-04

CAPITAL BLUE CROSS OF PENNSYLVANIA * B+ Good

Major Rating Factors: Good liquidity (6.7 on a scale of 0 to 10) with sufficient resources (cash flows and marketable investments) to handle a spike in claims. Strong capitalization (10.0) based on excellent current risk-adjusted capital (severe loss scenario) despite some fluctuation in capital levels. High quality investment portfolio (7.8).
Other Rating Factors: Fair profitability index (4.4) with operating gains in each of the last five years.
Principal Business: Comp med (71%), med supp (10%), FEHB (5%), other (14%)
Mem Phys: 02: 488 **01:** 488 **02 MLR** 88% / **02 Admin Exp** 11%
Enroll(000): Q1 03: 210 **02:** 499 **01:** 928 **Med Exp PMPM:** $105
Principal Investments: Nonaffiliate common stock (14%), cash and equiv (10%), real estate (3%), affiliate common stock (3%), pref stock (1%), other (69%)
Provider Compensation ($000): Contr fee ($974,181), capitation ($4,720)
Total Member Encounters: Phys (4,953,304), non-phys (5,512,045)
Group Affiliation: Capital Blue Cross Group
Licensed in: PA
Address: 2500 Elmerton Ave, Harrisburg, PA 17110
Phone: (717) 541-7000 **Dom State:** PA **Commenced Bus:** March 1938

Data Date	Weiss Safety Rating	RACR #1	RACR #2	Total Assets ($mil)	Capital ($mil)	Net Premium ($mil)	Net Income ($mil)
3-03	B+	5.27	4.39	982.4	485.6	100.4	3.6
3-02	B+	5.00	3.67	1,174.0	607.2	306.9	-5.6
2002	B+	5.23	4.36	1,018.3	518.8	1,029.1	34.5
2001	B+	5.06	3.70	1,165.1	610.7	1,193.4	29.0
2000	B+	3.02	1.80	1,078.2	536.1	1,319.2	26.5
1999	B+	3.16	1.88	1,064.6	518.2	1,210.9	27.1
1998	B+	3.58	2.15	1,001.9	483.1	1,077.6	11.6

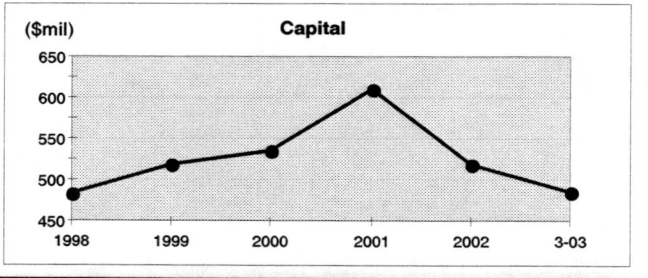

Capital chart (1998-3/03): rises from ~485 in 1998 to peak ~607 in 2001, then declines to ~485 at 3-03.

CAPITAL DISTRICT PHYSICIANS HEALTH P * B+ Good

Major Rating Factors: Good overall profitability index (5.5 on a scale of 0 to 10) despite a decline in earnings during 2002. Good overall results on stability tests (6.9) based on consistent premium and capital growth in the last five years. Good liquidity (6.9) with sufficient resources (cash flows and marketable investments) to handle a spike in claims.
Other Rating Factors: Strong capitalization (7.4) based on excellent current risk-adjusted capital (severe loss scenario) reflecting improvement over results in 2000. High quality investment portfolio (9.9) containing little or no exposure to mortgages, junk bonds, or unaffiliated stocks.
Principal Business: Comp med (78%), Medicaid (9%), Medicare (7%), FEHB (5%)
Mem Phys: 02: 8,066 **01:** 8,247 **02 MLR** 91% / **02 Admin Exp** 9%
Enroll(000): Q1 03: 319 **02:** 319 **01:** 302 **Med Exp PMPM:** $173
Principal Investments: Cash and equiv (54%), affiliate common stock (2%), other (44%)
Provider Compensation ($000): Contr fee ($328,504), bonus arrang ($256,646), capitation ($26,540), FFS ($11,941), other ($21,833)
Total Member Encounters: Phys (1,634,618), non-phys (479,152)
Group Affiliation: CDPHP Universal Benefits Inc
Licensed in: NY, VT
Address: 1223 Washington Ave, Albany, NY 12206-1057
Phone: (518) 641-3000 **Dom State:** NY **Commenced Bus:** July 1984

Data Date	Weiss Safety Rating	RACR #1	RACR #2	Total Assets ($mil)	Capital ($mil)	Net Premium ($mil)	Net Income ($mil)
3-03	B+	1.70	1.42	246.1	96.5	200.9	4.0
3-02	B+	1.91	1.60	236.0	85.5	173.9	1.1
2002	B+	1.62	1.35	220.0	92.0	707.9	4.9
2001	B+	1.91	1.60	212.8	85.9	626.7	30.8
2000	B	1.33	1.11	195.1	64.1	609.8	17.0
1999	B	1.49	1.24	126.0	47.1	364.3	-3.6
1998	B	1.88	1.56	113.8	50.7	316.5	2.8

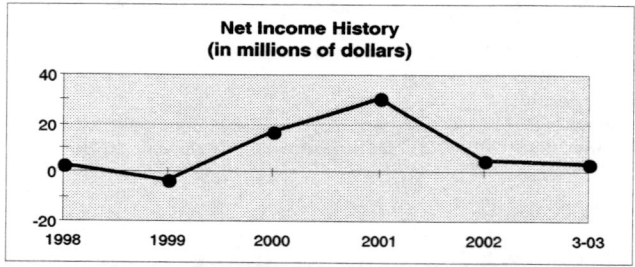

Net Income History (in millions of dollars), 1998-3/03: peaks ~30 in 2001.

CAPITAL HEALTH PLAN INC B- Good

Major Rating Factors: Fair profitability index (3.6 on a scale of 0 to 10) with operating losses during 1998 and 2000. Good overall results on stability tests (5.3). Rating is significantly influenced by the good financial results of Blue Cross Blue Shield Of Florida. Good liquidity (6.9) with sufficient resources (cash flows and marketable investments) to handle a spike in claims.
Other Rating Factors: Strong capitalization (7.6) based on excellent current risk-adjusted capital (severe loss scenario) reflecting improvement over results in 1999. High quality investment portfolio (9.8) containing no exposure to mortgages, junk bonds, or unaffiliated stocks.
Principal Business: Comp med (90%), Medicare (7%), FEHB (3%)
Mem Phys: 02: 351 **01:** 374 **02 MLR** 92% / **02 Admin Exp** 5%
Enroll(000): Q1 03: 109 **02:** 108 **01:** 108 **Med Exp PMPM:** $190
Principal Investments: Cash and equiv (52%), real estate (13%), other (35%)
Provider Compensation ($000): Contr fee ($193,617), capitation ($26,906), salary ($19,669), FFS ($2,299)
Total Member Encounters: Phys (686,502), non-phys (176,235)
Group Affiliation: Blue Cross Blue Shield Of Florida
Licensed in: FL
Address: 2140 Centerville Rd, Tallahassee, FL 32308
Phone: (850) 383-3333 **Dom State:** FL **Commenced Bus:** June 1982

Data Date	Weiss Safety Rating	RACR #1	RACR #2	Total Assets ($mil)	Capital ($mil)	Net Premium ($mil)	Net Income ($mil)
3-03	B-	1.86	1.55	76.3	30.3	77.3	2.3
3-02	B-	1.71	1.42	56.8	22.4	66.9	3.4
2002	B-	1.72	1.44	70.0	28.1	266.5	9.5
2001	B-	1.70	1.42	51.0	19.0	231.4	5.1
2000	B-	N/A	N/A	49.5	15.4	202.5	-6.7
1999	B-	1.10	0.91	52.9	21.8	184.1	1.7
1998	B-	1.31	1.07	47.4	19.8	146.6	-7.5

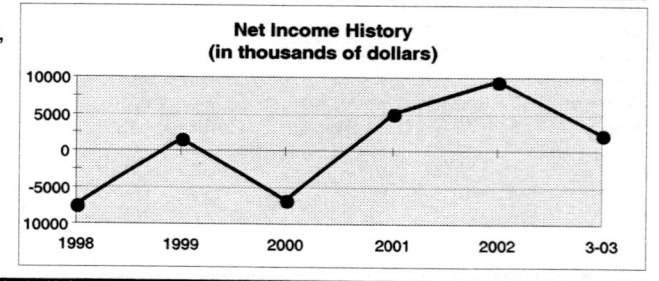

Net Income History (in thousands of dollars), 1998-3/03.

Winter 2003 - 04   II. Analysis of Largest Companies

CAPITAL HEALTH PLANS INC   C   Fair

Major Rating Factors: Weak profitability index (1.4 on a scale of 0 to 10) with modest operating losses during 2000 and 2002. Good capitalization (5.3) based on good current risk-adjusted capital (severe loss scenario). Good liquidity (7.0) with sufficient resources (cash flows and marketable investments) to handle a spike in claims.
Other Rating Factors: High quality investment portfolio (9.9) containing no exposure to mortgages, junk bonds, or unaffiliated stocks.
Principal Business: Comp med (100%)
Mem Phys: 02: 4,831   **01:** 5,134   **02 MLR** 107%   **/ 02 Admin Exp** 3%
Enroll(000): Q1 03: 3   **02:** 3   **01:** 3   **Med Exp PMPM:** $199
Principal Investments: Cash and equiv (100%)
Provider Compensation ($000): Bonus arrang ($3,773), FFS ($1,464), contr fee ($1,199)
Total Member Encounters: Phys (21,125), non-phys (8,554)
Group Affiliation: Managed Care of America Inc
Licensed in: PA
Address: 820 Parish St, Pittsburgh, PA 15220
Phone: (412) 922-2803   **Dom State:** PA   **Commenced Bus:** April 1996

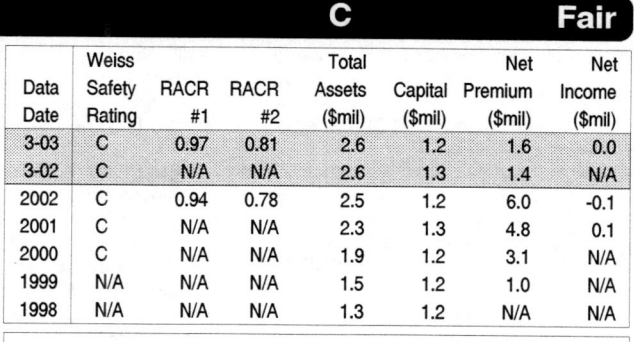

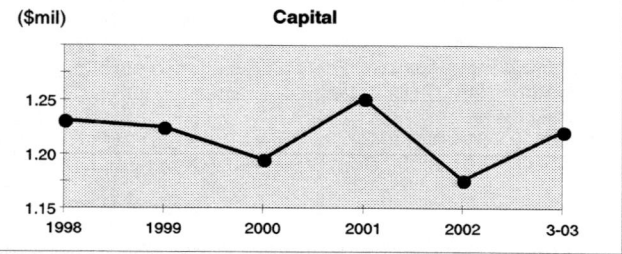

Data Date	Weiss Safety Rating	RACR #1	RACR #2	Total Assets ($mil)	Capital ($mil)	Net Premium ($mil)	Net Income ($mil)
3-03	C	0.97	0.81	2.6	1.2	1.6	0.0
3-02	C	N/A	N/A	2.6	1.3	1.4	N/A
2002	C	0.94	0.78	2.5	1.2	6.0	-0.1
2001	C	N/A	N/A	2.3	1.3	4.8	0.1
2000	C	N/A	N/A	1.9	1.2	3.1	N/A
1999	N/A	N/A	N/A	1.5	1.2	1.0	N/A
1998	N/A	N/A	N/A	1.3	1.2	N/A	N/A

CARE CHOICES HMO   C   Fair

Major Rating Factors: Fair capitalization (4.9 on a scale of 0 to 10) based on good current risk-adjusted capital (severe loss scenario) reflecting significant improvement over results in 2000. Weak profitability index (2.1) with operating losses during 1998, 2000 and 2001. Good overall results on stability tests (5.6) despite a decline in enrollment during 2002.
Other Rating Factors: Good liquidity (7.0) with sufficient resources (cash flows and marketable investments) to handle a spike in claims. High quality investment portfolio (9.9) containing no exposure to mortgages, junk bonds, or unaffiliated stocks.
Principal Business: Comp med (97%), Medicaid (3%)
Mem Phys: 02: 6,806   **01:** 4,436   **02 MLR** 86%   **/ 02 Admin Exp** 13%
Enroll(000): Q1 03: 102   **02:** 121   **01:** 130   **Med Exp PMPM:** $164
Principal Investments: Cash and equiv (95%), other (5%)
Provider Compensation ($000): Contr fee ($74,769), capitation ($59,562), FFS ($34,237), bonus arrang ($25,666)
Total Member Encounters: Phys (72,737), non-phys (123,395)
Group Affiliation: Trinity Health
Licensed in: MI
Address: 34605 Twelve Mile Rd, Farmington Hills, MI 48331
Phone: (248) 489-6321   **Dom State:** MI   **Commenced Bus:** January 1987

Data Date	Weiss Safety Rating	RACR #1	RACR #2	Total Assets ($mil)	Capital ($mil)	Net Premium ($mil)	Net Income ($mil)
3-03	C	0.91	0.76	55.8	24.8	63.7	1.5
3-02	D+	0.00	0.00	59.2	22.1	71.8	2.0
2002	C-	0.85	0.71	55.8	23.2	286.4	3.2
2001	D+	0.75	0.64	55.8	20.0	258.6	-2.8
2000	D	0.36	0.31	47.1	11.3	273.1	-3.4
1999	D	0.51	0.43	57.4	13.6	267.6	0.1
1998	D	0.38	0.32	59.6	9.1	274.4	-4.8

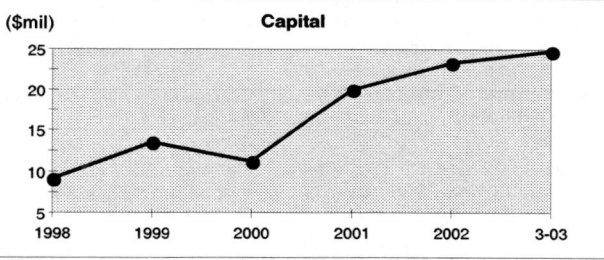

CAREFIRST BLUECHOICE INC *   A-   Excellent

Major Rating Factors: Strong overall capitalization (9.4 on a scale of 0 to 10) based on excellent current risk-adjusted capital (severe loss scenario) despite some fluctuation in capital levels. High quality investment portfolio (8.3) containing little or no exposure to mortgages, junk bonds, or unaffiliated stocks. Good overall profitability index (6.8) despite a decline in earnings during 2002.
Other Rating Factors: Good overall results on stability tests (5.8) despite rapid premium growth over the last five years, rapid enrollment growth during the past five years. Potential support from affiliation with CareFirst Inc. Good liquidity (6.1) with sufficient resources (cash flows and marketable investments) to handle a spike in claims.
Principal Business: Comp med (91%), FEHB (9%)
Mem Phys: 02: 17,255   **01:** 14,291   **02 MLR** 82%   **/ 02 Admin Exp** 16%
Enroll(000): Q1 03: 305   **02:** 310   **01:** 289   **Med Exp PMPM:** $140
Principal Investments: Affiliate common stock (10%), real estate (8%), nonaffiliate common stock (7%), cash and equiv (6%), pref stock (2%), other (66%)
Provider Compensation ($000): Contr fee ($465,572), bonus arrang ($16,126), capitation ($10,908)
Total Member Encounters: Phys (888,174)
Group Affiliation: CareFirst Inc
Licensed in: DC, MD, VA
Address: 550 12th St SW, Washington, DC 20065
Phone: (202) 479-8000   **Dom State:** DC   **Commenced Bus:** March 1985

Data Date	Weiss Safety Rating	RACR #1	RACR #2	Total Assets ($mil)	Capital ($mil)	Net Premium ($mil)	Net Income ($mil)
3-03	A-	3.26	2.72	261.2	128.7	179.8	6.1
3-02	B+	3.94	2.88	137.5	74.4	113.2	4.4
2002	A-	2.73	2.27	254.8	122.0	607.5	6.2
2001	B+	3.98	2.90	252.4	128.8	634.4	15.9
2000	B	3.57	2.91	81.2	54.0	189.4	16.9
1999	B	2.78	2.28	57.2	36.3	141.1	13.6
1998	C-	2.74	2.32	39.5	23.0	118.6	8.2

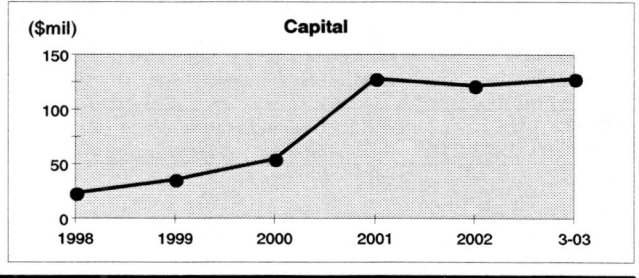

www.WeissRatings.com   * Denotes a Weiss Recommended Company

II. Analysis of Largest Companies

Winter 2003 - 04

CAREFIRST OF MARYLAND INC * B+ Good

Major Rating Factors: Good overall profitability index (5.5 on a scale of 0 to 10) despite a decline in earnings during 2002. Good liquidity (6.9) with sufficient resources (cash flows and marketable investments) to handle a spike in claims. Strong capitalization (8.9) based on excellent current risk-adjusted capital (severe loss scenario).
Other Rating Factors: High quality investment portfolio (8.5) containing little or no exposure to mortgages, junk bonds, or unaffiliated stocks.
Principal Business: Comp med (50%), FEHB (35%), med supp (8%), dental (3%), stop loss (1%), other (2%).
Mem Phys: 02: 30,890 **01:** 28,976 **02 MLR** 85% **/ 02 Admin Exp** 14%
Enroll(000): Q1 03: 492 **02:** 521 **01:** 563 **Med Exp PMPM:** $182
Principal Investments: Affiliate common stock (15%), cash and equiv (8%), nonaffiliate common stock (4%), pref stock (2%), other (71%).
Provider Compensation ($000): Contr fee ($970,342), FFS ($184,735), capitation ($10,442).
Total Member Encounters: Phys (646,857), non-phys (5,417,157)
Group Affiliation: CareFirst Inc
Licensed in: MD
Address: 10455 Mill Run Circle, Owings Mills, MD 21117
Phone: (410) 581-3000 **Dom State:** MD **Commenced Bus:** January 1985

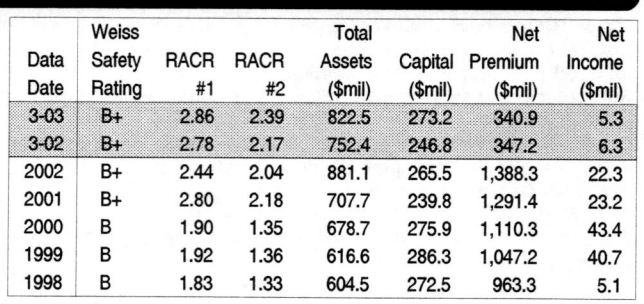

Data Date	Weiss Safety Rating	RACR #1	RACR #2	Total Assets ($mil)	Capital ($mil)	Net Premium ($mil)	Net Income ($mil)
3-03	B+	2.86	2.39	822.5	273.2	340.9	5.3
3-02	B+	2.78	2.17	752.4	246.8	347.2	6.3
2002	B+	2.44	2.04	881.1	265.5	1,388.3	22.3
2001	B+	2.80	2.18	707.7	239.8	1,291.4	23.2
2000	B	1.90	1.35	678.7	275.9	1,110.3	43.4
1999	B	1.92	1.36	616.6	286.3	1,047.2	40.7
1998	B	1.83	1.33	604.5	272.5	963.3	5.1

Net Income History (in millions of dollars)

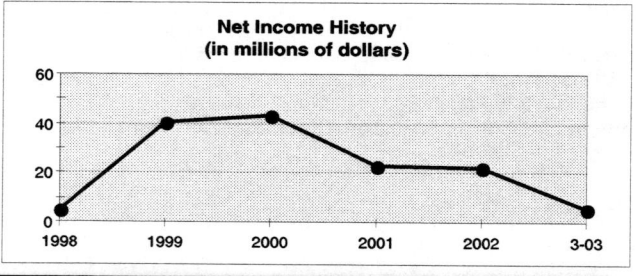

CARELINK HEALTH PLANS INC C Fair

Major Rating Factors: Weak profitability index (1.9 on a scale of 0 to 10) with operating losses during 1998, 1999 and 2000. Average return on equity has been poor at -45%. Good overall results on stability tests (5.2). Rating is significantly influenced by the fair financial results of Coventry Health Care Inc. Good liquidity (5.8) with sufficient resources (cash flows and marketable investments) to handle a spike in claims.
Other Rating Factors: Strong capitalization index (7.3) based on excellent current risk-adjusted capital (severe loss scenario). High quality investment portfolio (9.5) containing no exposure to mortgages, junk bonds, or unaffiliated stocks.
Principal Business: Comp med (74%), Medicaid (17%), Medicare (9%).
Mem Phys: 02: 2,868 **01:** 2,453 **02 MLR** 86% **/ 02 Admin Exp** 10%
Enroll(000): Q1 03: 56 **02:** 65 **01:** 66 **Med Exp PMPM:** $156
Principal Investments: Cash and equiv (8%), other (92%).
Provider Compensation ($000): Contr fee ($103,956), capitation ($14,017), FFS ($8,514), bonus arrang ($576).
Total Member Encounters: Phys (296,072), non-phys (88,044)
Group Affiliation: Coventry Health Care Inc
Licensed in: WV
Address: 500 Virginia St E Ste 400, Charleston, WV 25326
Phone: (304) 348-2900 **Dom State:** WV **Commenced Bus:** January 1995

Data Date	Weiss Safety Rating	RACR #1	RACR #2	Total Assets ($mil)	Capital ($mil)	Net Premium ($mil)	Net Income ($mil)
3-03	C	1.61	1.34	44.2	18.1	34.1	0.9
3-02	D	0.61	0.48	41.9	13.0	34.5	3.1
2002	C-	1.49	1.25	45.0	16.9	142.1	6.1
2001	D-	0.61	0.48	41.9	9.0	157.2	2.3
2000	E+	0.65	0.54	41.3	8.2	148.8	-6.3
1999	E+	0.80	0.68	36.3	9.9	137.0	-9.6
1998	E	0.16	0.14	35.7	9.5	130.4	-11.0

Net Income History (in millions of dollars)

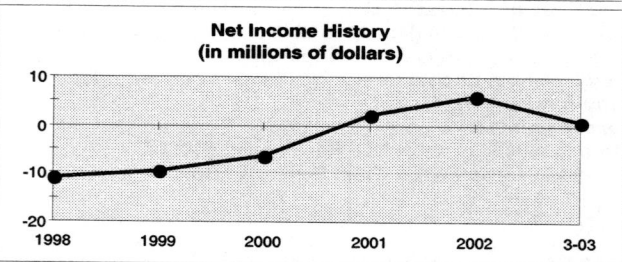

CAREPLUS HEALTH PLANS INC E Very Weak

Major Rating Factors: Weak profitability index (0.8 on a scale of 0 to 10) with operating losses during each of the last five years. Average return on equity over the last five years has been extremely poor. Poor capitalization index (0.0) based on weak current risk-adjusted capital (severe loss scenario). Weak overall results on stability tests (0.0).
Other Rating Factors: Weak liquidity (0.0) as a spike in claims may stretch capacity. High quality investment portfolio (9.9) containing no exposure to mortgages, junk bonds, or unaffiliated stocks.
Principal Business: Comp med (76%), Medicaid (24%).
Mem Phys: 01: 1,890 **00:** 1,877 **01 MLR** 103% **/ 01 Admin Exp** 7%
Enroll(000): Q2 02: 11 **01:** 12 **00:** 13 **Med Exp PMPM:** $187
Principal Investments: Cash and equiv (100%).
Provider Compensation ($000): Contr fee ($23,033), capitation ($4,838), FFS ($712).
Total Member Encounters: Phys (17,090), non-phys (303)
Group Affiliation: Mid-Florida Medical Services Inc
Licensed in: FL
Address: 3425 Lake Alfred Road, Winter Haven, FL 33881-1445
Phone: (863) 293-0785 **Dom State:** FL **Commenced Bus:** February 1986

Data Date	Weiss Safety Rating	RACR #1	RACR #2	Total Assets ($mil)	Capital ($mil)	Net Premium ($mil)	Net Income ($mil)
6-02	E	0.08	0.07	4.5	1.3	8.4	-0.7
6-01	E	0.36	0.31	5.9	1.6	11.6	0.0
2001	E	0.08	0.07	3.5	0.2	26.6	-1.3
2000	E	0.35	0.30	7.5	1.6	24.7	-0.9
1999	E-	0.29	0.25	7.0	0.7	21.5	-1.5
1998	N/A	N/A	N/A	6.6	-0.2	30.2	-3.0
1997	D	0.76	0.55	4.0	1.2	11.8	-2.2

Capital ($mil)

120 www.WeissRatings.com

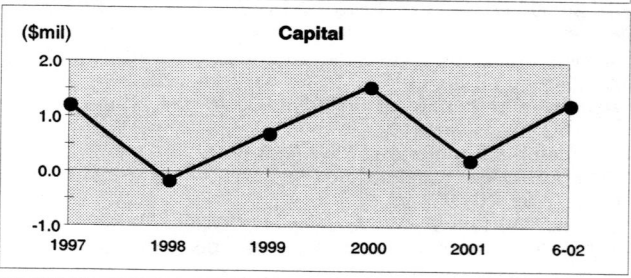

CARIBBEAN AMERICAN LIFE ASSURANCE COMPANY *   B+   Good

Major Rating Factors: Good overall results on stability tests (5.7 on a scale of 0 to 10) despite fair financial strength of affiliated Fortis Inc. Other stability subfactors include excellent operational trends and excellent risk diversification. Strong capitalization (10.0) based on excellent risk adjusted capital (severe loss scenario). Capital levels have been relatively consistent over the last five years. High quality investment portfolio (8.4).
Other Rating Factors: Excellent profitability (9.0) with operating gains in each of the last five years. Excellent liquidity (9.4).
Principal Business: Credit health insurance (47%), credit life insurance (42%), reinsurance (6%), group health insurance (3%), and group life insurance (2%).
Principal Investments: CMOs and structured securities (47%), nonCMO investment grade bonds (32%), cash (12%), common & preferred stock (8%), and noninv. grade bonds (1%).
Investments in Affiliates: 4%
Group Affiliation: Fortis Inc
Licensed in: PR
Commenced Business: December 1988
Address: 273 Ponce De Leon Ave Ste 350, Hato Rey, PR 00918
Phone: (787) 250-6470   **Domicile State:** PR   **NAIC Code:** 73156

Data Date	Weiss Safety Rating	RACR #1	RACR #2	Total Assets ($mil)	Capital ($mil)	Net Premium ($mil)	Net Income ($mil)
6-03	B+	8.09	6.32	189.0	103.7	19.3	5.9
6-02	B	7.30	5.71	166.4	90.3	16.4	7.0
2002	B	7.86	6.20	172.2	96.7	34.0	12.7
2001	B	6.69	5.24	162.2	83.7	36.3	14.4
2000	B	6.54	5.26	164.4	84.3	35.9	14.2
1999	B	7.77	6.06	153.1	69.9	52.6	12.7
1998	B	6.56	4.93	128.4	57.0	38.4	15.1

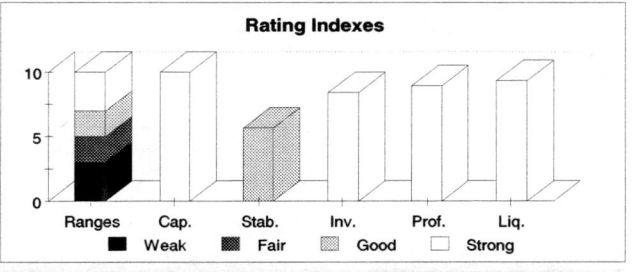

Rating Indexes chart: Ranges, Cap., Stab., Inv., Prof., Liq. (Weak, Fair, Good, Strong)

CARIBBEAN AMERICAN PROPERTY INS CO   C+   Fair

Major Rating Factors: Fair overall results on stability tests (3.7 on a scale of 0 to 10) including weak results on operational trends and excessive premium growth. Good liquidity (6.9) with sufficient resources (cash flows and marketable investments) to handle a spike in claims.
Other Rating Factors: Strong long-term capitalization index (8.4) based on excellent current risk adjusted capital (severe and moderate loss scenarios), despite some fluctuation in capital levels. Ample reserve history (8.8) that helps to protect the company against sharp claims increases. Excellent profitability (7.3) with operating gains in each of the last five years. Return on equity has been excellent over the last five years averaging 18.0%.
Principal Business: Credit accident & health (69%), inland marine (28%), and group accident & health (3%).
Principal Investments: Investment grade bonds (88%), misc. investments (8%), and cash (4%).
Investments in Affiliates: None
Group Affiliation: Fortis Inc
Licensed in: PR
Commenced Business: September 1992
Address: 273 Ponce de Leon Ave Ste 350, Hato Rey, PR 00918
Phone: (787) 250-6470   **Domicile State:** PR   **NAIC Code:** 30590

Data Date	Weiss Safety Rating	RACR #1	RACR #2	Loss Ratio %	Total Assets ($mil)	Capital ($mil)	Net Premium ($mil)	Net Income ($mil)
6-03	C+	2.24	1.94	N/A	41.7	30.3	12.3	2.0
6-02	C+	2.56	2.24	N/A	34.4	25.3	11.3	1.5
2002	C+	2.29	1.98	25.3	39.8	27.5	17.1	3.1
2001	C+	2.54	2.23	22.0	36.8	26.1	14.1	4.7
2000	C+	2.41	2.16	30.0	43.0	27.8	5.9	6.8
1999	C+	2.63	2.12	51.1	51.8	21.7	12.5	6.0
1998	C+	2.13	1.50	82.2	60.1	15.2	21.9	1.7

Fortis Inc Composite Group Rating: C+ Largest Group Members	Assets ($mil)	Weiss Safety Rating
FORTIS BENEFITS INS CO	7322	B-
AMERICAN BANKERS INS CO OF FL	1082	C
AMERICAN MEMORIAL LIFE INS CO	1075	C
UNITED FAMILY LIFE INS CO	997	C+
AMERICAN BANKERS LIFE ASR CO OF FL	925	B-

CARILION HEALTH PLANS INC   E+   Very Weak

Major Rating Factors: Weak profitability index (0.0 on a scale of 0 to 10) with $15.4 million in losses in the last five years. Average return on equity over the last five years has been poor at -86%. Poor capitalization index (2.3) based on weak current risk-adjusted capital (moderate loss scenario). Furthermore, this low level of risk-adjusted capital has been consistent in previous years. Fair overall results on stability tests (4.5) based on weak risk-adjusted capital in prior years, rapid premium growth over the last five years.
Other Rating Factors: High quality investment portfolio (9.9). Excellent liquidity (7.1) with ample operational cash flow and liquid investments.
Principal Business: Comp med (100%)
Mem Phys: 02: 940   **01:** 883   **02 MLR** 97%   / **02 Admin Exp** 10%
Enroll(000): Q1 03: 9   **02:** 12   **01:** 10   **Med Exp PMPM:** $171
Principal Investments: Cash and equiv (58%), nonaffiliate common stock (3%), other (38%)
Provider Compensation ($000): Bonus arrang ($14,728), FFS ($7,733)
Total Member Encounters: Phys (65,199), non-phys (13,937)
Group Affiliation: Carilion Health System
Licensed in: VA
Address: 110 Campbell Ave Suite 107, Roanoke, VA 24011
Phone: (540) 857-5200   **Dom State:** VA   **Commenced Bus:** May 1997

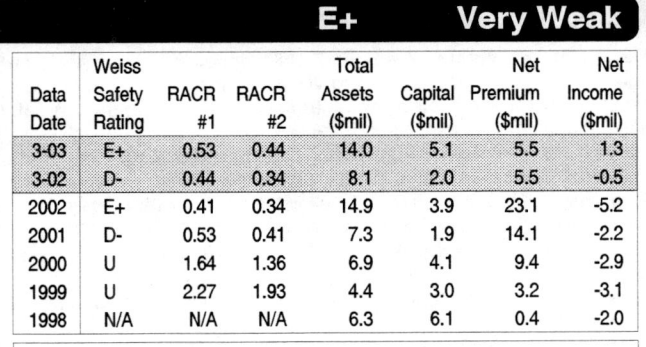

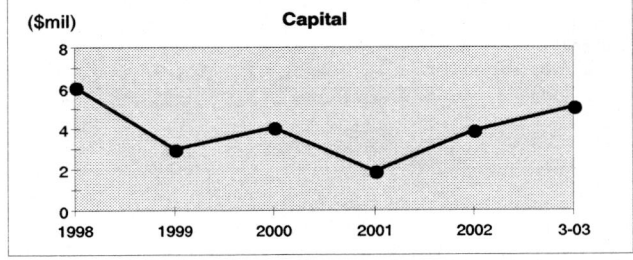

Data Date	Weiss Safety Rating	RACR #1	RACR #2	Total Assets ($mil)	Capital ($mil)	Net Premium ($mil)	Net Income ($mil)
3-03	E+	0.53	0.44	14.0	5.1	5.5	1.3
3-02	D-	0.44	0.34	8.1	2.0	5.5	-0.5
2002	E+	0.41	0.34	14.9	3.9	23.1	-5.2
2001	D-	0.53	0.41	7.3	1.9	14.1	-2.2
2000	U	1.64	1.36	6.9	4.1	9.4	-2.9
1999	U	2.27	1.93	4.4	3.0	3.2	-3.1
1998	N/A	N/A	N/A	6.3	6.1	0.4	-2.0

Capital chart ($mil): 1998: 6, 1999: 3, 2000: 4, 2001: 2, 2002: 4, 3-03: 5

* Denotes a Weiss Recommended Company

II. Analysis of Largest Companies

CARITEN HEALTH PLAN INC   C-   Fair

Major Rating Factors: Fair capitalization index (4.9 on a scale of 0 to 10) based on good current risk-adjusted capital (severe loss scenario) as results have slipped from the excellent range over the last year. Weak profitability index (0.8) due to a decline in earnings during 2002. Average return on equity has been extremely poor. Weak overall results on stability tests (2.6) based on rapid premium growth over the last five years.
Other Rating Factors: Weak liquidity (0.3) as a spike in claims may stretch capacity. High quality investment portfolio (9.9) containing no exposure to mortgages, junk bonds, or unaffiliated stocks.
Principal Business: Medicare (66%), comp med (34%)
Mem Phys: 02: 5,016   **01:** 4,486   **02 MLR** 89%   / **02 Admin Exp** 7%
Enroll(000): Q1 03: 30   **02:** 28   **01:** 23   **Med Exp PMPM:** $303
Principal Investments: Cash and equiv (13%), other (87%)
Provider Compensation ($000): FFS ($90,252), capitation ($543)
Total Member Encounters: Phys (295,205), non-phys (107,124)
Group Affiliation: PHP Companies Inc
Licensed in: TN
Address: 1420 Centerpoint Blvd, Knoxville, TN 37932
Phone: (865) 470-7599   **Dom State:** TN   **Commenced Bus:** December 1995

Data Date	Weiss Safety Rating	RACR #1	RACR #2	Total Assets ($mil)	Capital ($mil)	Net Premium ($mil)	Net Income ($mil)
3-03	C-	0.91	0.76	41.3	11.8	30.8	2.0
3-02	D+	2.18	1.83	43.1	17.3	24.0	1.3
2002	C-	1.29	1.07	49.4	17.1	102.8	5.1
2001	D+	2.18	1.83	46.5	17.5	75.0	7.8
2000	D	0.90	0.76	35.2	7.3	53.9	-0.8
1999	D-	0.00	0.00	19.7	2.2	31.4	-7.0
1998	D-	0.67	0.58	13.5	3.0	20.0	-8.4

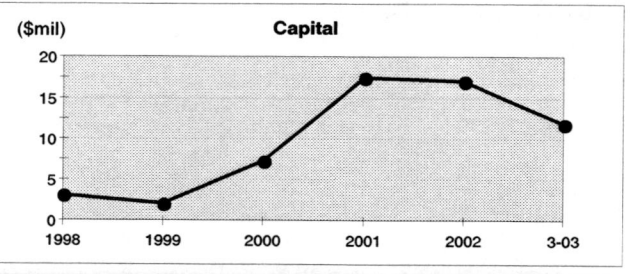

CAROLINA CARE PLAN INC   B-   Good

Major Rating Factors: Good overall profitability index (5.4 on a scale of 0 to 10) despite operating losses during 2000. Good capitalization (6.0) based on good current risk-adjusted capital (severe loss scenario) reflecting significant improvement over results in 2000. Good overall results on stability tests (5.4) despite a decline in enrollment during 2002, weak risk-adjusted capital in prior years.
Other Rating Factors: Good liquidity (7.0) with sufficient resources (cash flows and marketable investments) to handle a spike in claims. High quality investment portfolio (9.9) containing no exposure to mortgages, junk bonds, or unaffiliated stocks.
Principal Business: Comp med (100%)
Mem Phys: 02: 6,453   **01:** 6,309   **02 MLR** 81%   / **02 Admin Exp** 15%
Enroll(000): Q1 03: 81   **02:** 90   **01:** 104   **Med Exp PMPM:** $164
Principal Investments: Cash and equiv (92%), other (8%)
Provider Compensation ($000): Contr fee ($185,523), capitation ($5,438)
Total Member Encounters: Phys (207,387), non-phys (145,698)
Group Affiliation: None
Licensed in: SC
Address: 201 Executive Ctr Dr Ste 300, Columbia, SC 29210-8438
Phone: (803) 750-7400   **Dom State:** SC   **Commenced Bus:** March 1985

Data Date	Weiss Safety Rating	RACR #1	RACR #2	Total Assets ($mil)	Capital ($mil)	Net Premium ($mil)	Net Income ($mil)
3-03	B-	1.08	0.90	53.9	19.9	54.8	0.3
3-02	C	0.73	0.62	78.7	11.8	60.5	0.5
2002	C+	0.98	0.82	58.4	17.8	236.0	5.2
2001	C	0.73	0.62	51.6	10.9	222.8	4.5
2000	C	0.55	0.46	52.8	10.5	250.7	-2.4
1999	C	0.90	0.74	54.4	12.3	199.3	0.7
1998	C+	1.17	0.97	45.2	14.7	155.6	3.3

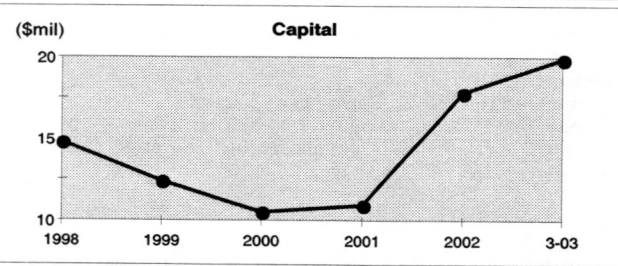

CASCADE EAST HEALTH PLANS INC   E   Very Weak

Major Rating Factors: Weak profitability index (0.9 on a scale of 0 to 10) with operating losses during 2001 and 2002. Poor capitalization index (0.8) based on weak current risk-adjusted capital (moderate loss scenario). Weak liquidity (0.0) as a spike in claims may stretch capacity.
Other Rating Factors: High quality investment portfolio (9.1).
Principal Business: Comp med (100%)
Mem Phys: 02: 1,086   **01:** 755   **02 MLR** 113%   / **02 Admin Exp** 13%
Enroll(000): Q1 03: 5   **02:** 4   **01:** 4   **Med Exp PMPM:** $223
Principal Investments: Nonaffiliate common stock (43%), cash and equiv (15%), other (41%)
Provider Compensation ($000): FFS ($10,444), capitation ($308), bonus arrang ($181)
Total Member Encounters: Phys (5,633), non-phys (6,722)
Group Affiliation: Good Shepherd Health Care System
Licensed in: OR
Address: 610 NW 11th St, Hermiston, OR 97838
Phone: (541) 567-5555   **Dom State:** OR   **Commenced Bus:** April 1998

Data Date	Weiss Safety Rating	RACR #1	RACR #2	Total Assets ($mil)	Capital ($mil)	Net Premium ($mil)	Net Income ($mil)
3-03	E	0.38	0.32	3.1	1.3	2.8	-0.3
3-02	E	0.26	0.20	3.0	1.0	2.5	-0.5
2002	E	0.39	0.33	3.2	1.4	9.7	-2.6
2001	E	0.26	0.20	2.7	0.8	6.8	-0.7
2000	D+	1.57	1.27	2.0	1.0	3.7	0.0
1999	U	1.86	1.67	0.8	0.4	0.7	0.1
1998	N/A	N/A	N/A	0.6	0.3	N/A	N/A

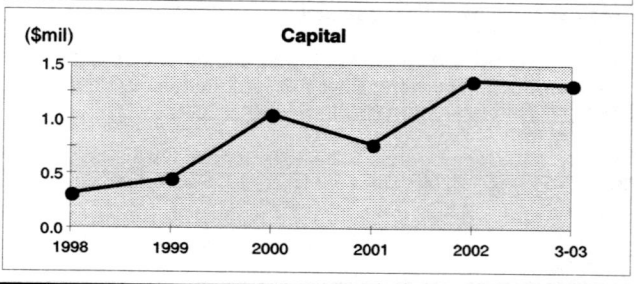

CDPHP UNIVERSAL BENEFITS INC   B-   Good

Major Rating Factors: High quality investment portfolio (9.9 on a scale of 0 to 10) containing no exposure to mortgages, junk bonds, or unaffiliated stocks. Excellent liquidity (7.3) with ample operational cash flow and liquid investments. Weak profitability index (1.4) with modest operating losses during 2002.
Other Rating Factors: Poor capitalization (2.9) based on good current risk-adjusted capital (moderate loss scenario). However, risk-adjusted capital has reached as low as the weak level during recent years.
Principal Business: Comp med (100%)
Mem Phys: 02: 5,987   01: N/A   02 MLR 94%   / 02 Admin Exp 42%
Enroll(000): Q1 03: 2   02: 2   01: 1   **Med Exp PMPM:** $74
Principal Investments: Cash and equiv (100%)
Provider Compensation ($000): Contr fee ($612), bonus arrang ($472), capitation ($72), other ($33)
Total Member Encounters: Phys (2,950), non-phys (829)
Group Affiliation: CDPHP Universal Benefits Inc
Licensed in: NY
Address: 1223 Wash Ave Patroon Creek, Albany, NY 12206-1057
Phone: (518) 641-3000   **Dom State:** NY   **Commenced Bus:** January 1998

Data Date	Weiss Safety Rating	RACR #1	RACR #2	Total Assets ($mil)	Capital ($mil)	Net Premium ($mil)	Net Income ($mil)
3-03	B-	1.25	1.04	1.2	0.8	0.7	-0.2
3-02	B-	3.27	2.75	1.6	1.4	0.2	-0.1
2002	B-	1.49	1.24	1.3	1.0	1.5	-0.5
2001	B-	3.30	2.76	1.6	1.5	0.2	0.4
2000	N/A	N/A	N/A	2.1	1.0	3.0	N/A
1999	N/A	N/A	N/A	1.7	1.3	0.8	N/A
1998	N/A	N/A	N/A	1.4	1.3	0.2	N/A

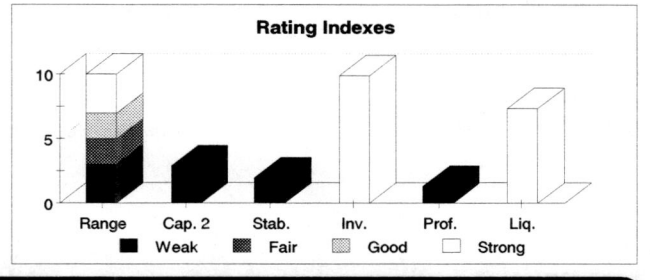

Rating Indexes chart: Range, Cap. 2, Stab., Inv., Prof., Liq. — Weak / Fair / Good / Strong

CELTIC INSURANCE COMPANY   B   Good

Major Rating Factors: Good overall profitability (5.3 on a scale of 0 to 10) despite operating losses during the first six months of 2003. Return on equity has been fair, averaging 6.8%. Good overall results on stability tests (5.2). Stability strengths include excellent operational trends and good risk diversification. Strong capitalization (8.4) based on excellent risk adjusted capital (severe loss scenario).
Other Rating Factors: High quality investment portfolio (8.7). Excellent liquidity (7.0).
Principal Business: Group health insurance (52%) and individual health insurance (47%).
Principal Investments: NonCMO investment grade bonds (65%) and CMOs and structured securities (37%).
Investments in Affiliates: None
Group Affiliation: Celtic Investment Group Inc
Licensed in: All states except NY, PR
Commenced Business: January 1950
Address: 233 S Wacker Dr Suite 700, Chicago, IL 60606-6393
Phone: (312) 332-5401   **Domicile State:** IL   **NAIC Code:** 80799

Data Date	Weiss Safety Rating	RACR #1	RACR #2	Total Assets ($mil)	Capital ($mil)	Net Premium ($mil)	Net Income ($mil)
6-03	B	2.42	1.94	113.0	46.5	78.7	-1.4
6-02	B	3.17	2.52	112.7	51.4	72.7	1.3
2002	B	2.70	2.16	114.7	49.7	151.4	3.1
2001	B	3.42	2.72	114.2	51.8	132.5	5.7
2000	B	3.82	3.04	113.1	52.3	109.0	5.4
1999	B	5.01	3.95	111.3	52.2	81.3	4.0
1998	B	4.81	3.78	110.5	51.2	80.4	2.8

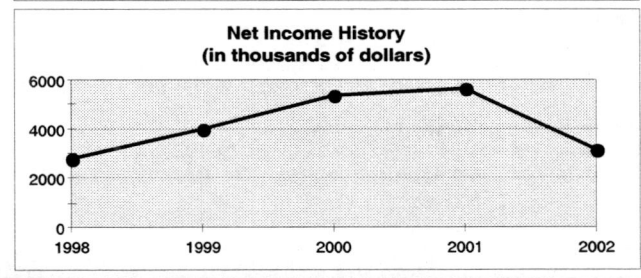

Net Income History (in thousands of dollars): 1998–2002

CENTRAL BENEFITS MUTUAL INS CO   D+   Weak

Major Rating Factors: Low quality investment portfolio (2.9 on a scale of 0 to 10). Weak profitability (1.9) with operating losses during the first six months of 2003. Weak overall results on stability tests (2.7) including negative cash flow from operations for 2002 and weak results on operational trends.
Other Rating Factors: Good liquidity (6.9). Strong capitalization (7.9) based on excellent risk adjusted capital (severe loss scenario).
Principal Business: Individual health insurance (67%), reinsurance (27%), and group health insurance (6%).
Principal Investments: Common & preferred stock (75%), nonCMO investment grade bonds (29%), CMOs and structured securities (11%), and real estate (6%).
Investments in Affiliates: 69%
Group Affiliation: Central Benefits Group
Licensed in: DC, IL, IN, OH, PA
Commenced Business: July 1986
Address: 255 E Main St, Columbus, OH 43215-5222
Phone: (614) 464-5711   **Domicile State:** DC   **NAIC Code:** 60255

Data Date	Weiss Safety Rating	RACR #1	RACR #2	Total Assets ($mil)	Capital ($mil)	Net Premium ($mil)	Net Income ($mil)
6-03	D+	1.89	1.58	61.9	41.3	8.5	-0.5
6-02	C-	2.15	1.80	59.3	44.8	8.1	0.4
2002	D+	1.21	1.12	61.8	43.6	16.6	-0.3
2001	C-	2.38	2.07	65.5	49.4	18.8	1.2
2000	C-	2.46	2.06	71.3	48.9	41.4	3.0
1999	D+	2.75	2.18	91.1	47.4	80.4	-18.6
1998	C-	5.94	4.67	113.1	80.0	85.8	-2.6

Adverse Trends in Operations

Change in asset mix during 2002 (12%)
Decrease in premium volume from 2000 to 2001 (55%)
Decrease in asset base during 2000 (22%)
Decrease in premium volume from 1999 to 2000 (49%)
Decrease in capital during 1999 (41%)

II. Analysis of Largest Companies

CENTRAL OREGON INDEPENDENT HEALTH SV — C+ — Fair

Major Rating Factors: Fair capitalization (4.0 on a scale of 0 to 10) based on fair current risk-adjusted capital (moderate loss scenario) reflecting improvement over results in 2000. Good liquidity (6.3) with sufficient resources (cash flows and marketable investments) to handle a spike in claims. Excellent profitability (8.9) despite a decline in earnings during 2002.
Other Rating Factors: High quality investment portfolio (9.9).
Principal Business: Medicare (50%), Medicaid (47%), comp med (3%)
Mem Phys: 02: 500 **01:** 500 **02 MLR** 91% **/ 02 Admin Exp** 7%
Enroll(000): Q1 03: 28 **02:** 34 **01:** 32 **Med Exp PMPM:** $254
Principal Investments: Cash and equiv (41%), nonaffiliate common stock (10%), real estate (2%), pref stock (2%), other (45%).
Provider Compensation ($000): Bonus arrang ($91,548), contr fee ($1,932), capitation ($1,712)
Total Member Encounters: Phys (441,471), non-phys (101,671)
Group Affiliation: None
Licensed in: OR
Address: 2650 NE Courtney Dr, Bend, OR 97701
Phone: (541) 382-5920 **Dom State:** OR **Commenced Bus:** October 1995

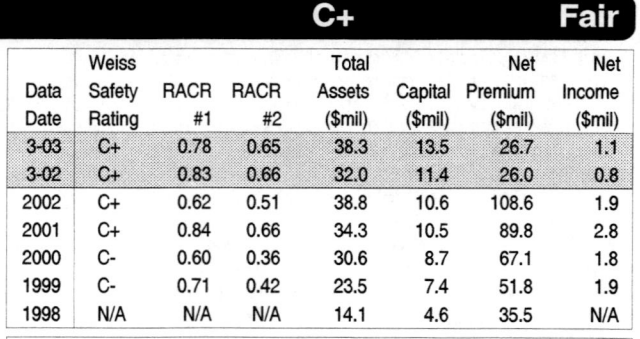

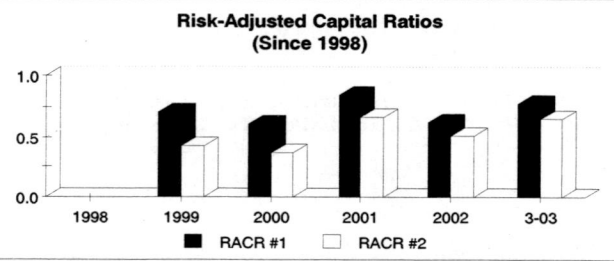

Data Date	Weiss Safety Rating	RACR #1	RACR #2	Total Assets ($mil)	Capital ($mil)	Net Premium ($mil)	Net Income ($mil)
3-03	C+	0.78	0.65	38.3	13.5	26.7	1.1
3-02	C+	0.83	0.66	32.0	11.4	26.0	0.8
2002	C+	0.62	0.51	38.8	10.6	108.6	1.9
2001	C+	0.84	0.66	34.3	10.5	89.8	2.8
2000	C-	0.60	0.36	30.6	8.7	67.1	1.8
1999	C-	0.71	0.42	23.5	7.4	51.8	1.9
1998	N/A	N/A	N/A	14.1	4.6	35.5	N/A

Risk-Adjusted Capital Ratios (Since 1998)

CENTRAL RESERVE LIFE INSURANCE COMPANY — D — Weak

Major Rating Factors: Weak overall results on stability tests (2.1 on a scale of 0 to 10) including potential financial drain due to affiliation with Ceres Group Inc, negative cash flow from operations for 2002 and weak risk adjusted capital in prior years. Weak profitability (2.9). Return on equity has been low, averaging -15.0%. Weak liquidity (1.3).
Other Rating Factors: Good overall capitalization (5.2) based on mixed results -- excessive policy leverage mitigated by good risk adjusted capital (severe loss scenario). High quality investment portfolio (7.1).
Principal Business: Group health insurance (93%), reinsurance (3%), individual health insurance (2%), and group life insurance (2%).
Principal Investments: NonCMO investment grade bonds (56%), CMOs and structured securities (37%), common & preferred stock (7%), and noninv. grade bonds (3%).
Investments in Affiliates: 7%
Group Affiliation: Ceres Group Inc
Licensed in: AL, AZ, AR, CO, DE, FL, GA, IL, IN, IA, KS, KY, LA, MA, MS, MO, MT, NE, NV, NM, NC, ND, OH, OK, OR, PA, SC, SD, TN, TX, UT, VA, WV, WI, WY
Commenced Business: May 1965
Address: 17800 Royalton Rd, Strongsville, OH 44136-5197
Phone: (440) 572-2400 **Domicile State:** OH **NAIC Code:** 61727

Data Date	Weiss Safety Rating	RACR #1	RACR #2	Total Assets ($mil)	Capital ($mil)	Net Premium ($mil)	Net Income ($mil)
6-03	D	1.02	0.83	93.6	35.0	82.3	3.2
6-02	D	0.70	0.58	97.6	24.9	102.2	0.1
2002	D	0.87	0.72	93.4	30.6	187.7	8.3
2001	D	0.72	0.59	118.6	27.4	245.3	-10.5
2000	D+	0.57	0.48	111.1	26.2	246.1	-1.0
1999	D+	0.76	0.64	110.3	23.1	170.5	-2.0
1998	D+	0.93	0.69	111.2	30.4	160.9	-21.2

Ceres Group Inc
Composite Group Rating: D
Largest Group Members	Assets ($mil)	Weiss Safety Rating
CONTINENTAL GENERAL INS CO	365	D
CENTRAL RESERVE LIFE INS CO	93	D
PROVIDENT AMER LIFE HEALTH INS CO	9	D
UNITED BENEFIT LIFE INS CO	4	E+

CENTRAL STATES HEALTH & LIFE COMPANY OF OMAHA — B- — Good

Major Rating Factors: Good quality investment portfolio (6.7 on a scale of 0 to 10) despite mixed results such as: no exposure to mortgages and substantial holdings of BBB bonds but small junk bond holdings. Good overall results on stability tests (5.1). Stability strengths include excellent operational trends and excellent risk diversification. Strong capitalization (9.5) based on excellent risk adjusted capital (severe loss scenario).
Other Rating Factors: Excellent profitability (7.8) despite operating losses during the first six months of 2003. Excellent liquidity (7.4).
Principal Business: Individual health insurance (39%), credit life insurance (34%), credit health insurance (21%), group health insurance (3%), and individual life insurance (3%).
Principal Investments: CMOs and structured securities (42%), nonCMO investment grade bonds (36%), common & preferred stock (12%), noninv. grade bonds (2%), and misc. investments (8%).
Investments in Affiliates: 4%
Group Affiliation: Central States Group
Licensed in: All states except NY, PR
Commenced Business: June 1932
Address: 1212 N 96th St, Omaha, NE 68114
Phone: (402) 397-1111 **Domicile State:** NE **NAIC Code:** 61751

Data Date	Weiss Safety Rating	RACR #1	RACR #2	Total Assets ($mil)	Capital ($mil)	Net Premium ($mil)	Net Income ($mil)
6-03	B-	3.71	2.65	344.1	74.5	66.4	-1.3
6-02	B-	4.63	3.09	320.0	76.7	69.2	0.3
2002	B-	3.66	2.57	350.5	77.6	138.7	2.0
2001	B-	4.61	3.08	316.3	77.1	134.1	4.1
2000	B-	4.64	3.18	295.9	75.4	134.3	8.7
1999	B-	4.54	3.17	281.2	68.6	127.8	7.1
1998	B-	3.50	2.63	271.4	62.6	161.6	5.7

Adverse Trends in Operations

Increase in policy surrenders from 1999 to 2000 (52%)
Decrease in premium volume from 1998 to 1999 (21%)

Winter 2003 - 04   II. Analysis of Largest Companies

CENTRAL STATES INDEMNITY CO OF OMAHA *   A-   Excellent

Major Rating Factors: Strong long-term capitalization index (9.2 on a scale of 0 to 10) based on excellent current risk adjusted capital (severe and moderate loss scenarios), despite some fluctuation in capital levels. Ample reserve history (8.0) that helps to protect the company against sharp claims increases.
Other Rating Factors: Good overall profitability index (5.6). Weak expense controls. Return on equity has been fair, averaging 6.3% over the past five years. Good liquidity (6.9) with sufficient resources (cash flows and marketable investments) to handle a spike in claims. Good overall results on stability tests (5.5) despite weak results on operational trends.
Principal Business: Aggregate write-ins for other lines of business (65%), credit accident & health (31%), group accident & health (3%), and inland marine (1%).
Principal Investments: Cash (44%), investment grade bonds (43%), and misc. investments (13%).
Investments in Affiliates: 5%
Group Affiliation: Berkshire-Hathaway
Licensed in: All states except PR
Commenced Business: June 1977
Address: 1212 N 96th St, Omaha, NE 68114
Phone: (402) 397-1111   **Domicile State:** NE   **NAIC Code:** 34274

Data Date	Weiss Safety Rating	RACR #1	RACR #2	Loss Ratio %	Total Assets ($mil)	Capital ($mil)	Net Premium ($mil)	Net Income ($mil)
6-03	A-	3.25	2.60	N/A	243.1	175.7	62.1	3.7
6-02	A-	3.14	2.53	N/A	235.0	165.6	69.3	2.6
2002	A-	3.17	2.57	22.1	241.4	169.1	74.8	12.0
2001	A-	2.98	2.44	19.8	231.2	161.2	81.0	7.7
2000	A	3.19	2.56	17.0	244.0	188.7	92.3	10.5
1999	A	3.21	2.54	15.8	233.9	177.1	84.2	8.5
1998	A	2.51	2.05	21.9	212.1	150.4	106.6	15.9

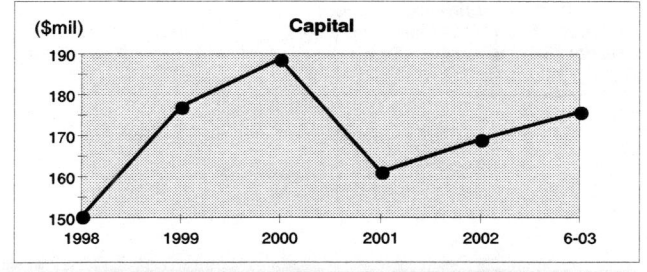

Capital ($mil) chart 1998–6-03

CENTRAL UNITED LIFE INSURANCE COMPANY   C   Fair

Major Rating Factors: Fair overall results on stability tests (3.6 on a scale of 0 to 10) including fair risk adjusted capital in prior years. Good current capitalization (5.4) based on good risk adjusted capital (severe loss scenario) reflecting some improvement over results in 2001. Good quality investment portfolio (5.9) with no exposure to mortgages and small junk bond holdings.
Other Rating Factors: Good liquidity (6.1). Excellent profitability (7.5) despite modest operating losses during 1999.
Principal Business: Individual health insurance (53%), reinsurance (36%), individual life insurance (6%), and group health insurance (5%).
Principal Investments: NonCMO investment grade bonds (77%), common & preferred stock (7%), real estate (5%), CMOs and structured securities (4%), and misc. investments (7%).
Investments in Affiliates: 7%
Group Affiliation: Central United Life Group
Licensed in: All states except AK, CT, DC, DE, HI, MI, NJ, NY, RI, VT, PR
Commenced Business: September 1963
Address: 2727 Allen Parkway, 6th Floor, Houston, TX 77019-2115
Phone: (713) 529-0045   **Domicile State:** TX   **NAIC Code:** 61883

Data Date	Weiss Safety Rating	RACR #1	RACR #2	Total Assets ($mil)	Capital ($mil)	Net Premium ($mil)	Net Income ($mil)
6-03	C	1.02	0.80	289.1	43.3	41.1	5.7
6-02	C	1.02	0.76	264.5	30.6	40.8	1.4
2002	C	0.92	0.71	279.0	32.0	79.5	7.6
2001	C	0.85	0.59	327.3	24.3	60.1	5.1
2000	C	0.94	0.70	188.4	17.4	36.2	2.6
1999	C	0.83	0.63	199.1	17.7	37.7	-3.5
1998	C	1.08	0.83	198.3	20.7	34.7	1.1

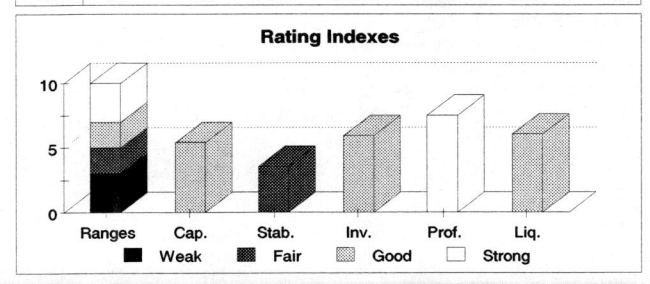

Rating Indexes chart: Ranges, Cap., Stab., Inv., Prof., Liq. — Weak, Fair, Good, Strong

CENTRE INS CO   C   Fair

Major Rating Factors: A history of deficient reserves (2.7 on a scale of 0 to 10) that places pressure on both capital and profits. In four of the last five years reserves (two year development) were between 18% and 31% deficient. Weak overall results on stability tests (2.7) including weak results on operational trends and negative cash flow from operations for 2002. The largest net exposure for one risk is excessive at 7.9% of capital.
Other Rating Factors: Good long-term capitalization (6.1) based on good current risk adjusted capital (moderate loss scenario) reflecting improvement over results in 2002. Good overall profitability index (5.3) despite operating losses during 1999. Return on equity has been good over the last five years, averaging 10.9%. Superior liquidity (9.8) with ample operational cash flow and liquid investments.
Principal Business: Homeowners multiple peril (71%), group accident & health (27%), and auto liability (2%).
Principal Investments: Investment grade bonds (100%) and cash (6%).
Investments in Affiliates: None
Group Affiliation: Zurich Financial Services Group
Licensed in: All states except PR
Commenced Business: January 1978
Address: 2711 Centerville Rd Ste 400, Wilmington, DE 19808-1645
Phone: (212) 898-5300   **Domicile State:** DE   **NAIC Code:** 34649

Data Date	Weiss Safety Rating	RACR #1	RACR #2	Loss Ratio %	Total Assets ($mil)	Capital ($mil)	Net Premium ($mil)	Net Income ($mil)
6-03	C	1.67	1.03	N/A	828.1	108.8	23.6	30.8
6-02	C	1.05	0.75	N/A	670.3	101.4	20.7	15.0
2002	C	1.21	0.75	96.1	811.7	84.2	76.7	6.1
2001	C	1.30	0.92	67.1	696.5	91.8	72.4	19.9
2000	C	3.98	1.60	85.4	366.0	70.5	32.9	11.0
1999	C	1.94	1.00	114.9	338.7	75.4	73.4	-13.2
1998	C	3.32	3.29	78.6	103.8	78.1	71.1	3.8

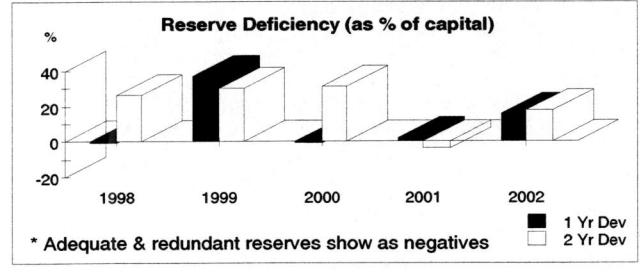

Reserve Deficiency (as % of capital) chart, 1998–2002. 1 Yr Dev / 2 Yr Dev.
* Adequate & redundant reserves show as negatives

www.WeissRatings.com   * Denotes a Weiss Recommended Company

II. Analysis of Largest Companies Winter 2003 - 04

CENTRE LIFE INSURANCE COMPANY   C   Fair

Major Rating Factors: Fair profitability (3.9 on a scale of 0 to 10) with operating losses during the first six months of 2003. Return on equity has been low, averaging -2.1%. Fair overall results on stability tests (4.2) including weak risk adjusted capital in prior years and negative cash flow from operations for 2002. Good quality investment portfolio (5.7).
Other Rating Factors: Strong capitalization (7.1) based on excellent risk adjusted capital (severe loss scenario). Excellent liquidity (9.1).
Principal Business: Reinsurance (61%) and individual health insurance (39%).
Principal Investments: NonCMO investment grade bonds (60%), CMOs and structured securities (36%), common & preferred stock (3%), and cash (1%).
Investments in Affiliates: None
Group Affiliation: Zurich Financial Services Group
Licensed in: All states except PR
Commenced Business: October 1927
Address: 1600 McConnor Parkway, Schaumburg, IL 60196-6801
Phone: (847) 874-7400 **Domicile State:** MA **NAIC Code:** 80896

Data Date	Weiss Safety Rating	RACR #1	RACR #2	Total Assets ($mil)	Capital ($mil)	Net Premium ($mil)	Net Income ($mil)
6-03	C	2.18	1.07	1,902.8	100.4	7.8	-21.2
6-02	C	2.00	0.99	1,841.9	107.6	6.2	-2.2
2002	C	2.70	1.34	1,881.9	120.6	12.2	14.7
2001	C-	1.87	0.93	1,861.7	102.2	14.1	-1.3
2000	C-	0.60	0.32	1,774.6	59.1	229.5	-2.5
1999	C-	2.12	1.91	261.2	33.9	0.0	-9.3
1998	C+	2.21	1.50	239.6	37.6	50.8	1.5

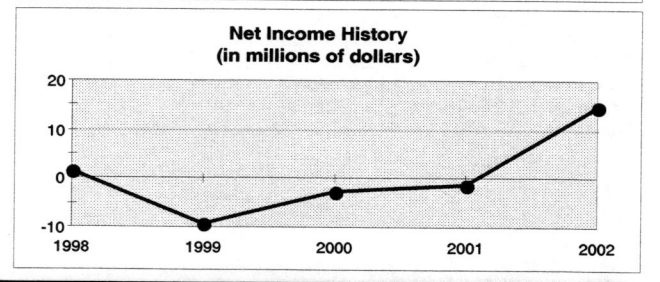

Net Income History (in millions of dollars) — 1998 through 2002

CENTURION LIFE INSURANCE COMPANY *   A   Excellent

Major Rating Factors: Good overall results on stability tests (6.7 on a scale of 0 to 10). Strengths that enhance stability include good operational trends and excellent risk diversification. Strong capitalization (10.0) based on excellent risk adjusted capital (severe loss scenario). Furthermore, this high level of risk adjusted capital has been consistently maintained over the last five years. High quality investment portfolio (8.4).
Other Rating Factors: Excellent profitability (9.6) with operating gains in each of the last five years. Excellent liquidity (9.3).
Principal Business: Credit health insurance (36%), reinsurance (36%), and credit life insurance (28%).
Principal Investments: NonCMO investment grade bonds (63%), CMOs and structured securities (33%), common & preferred stock (3%), and cash (1%).
Investments in Affiliates: 1%
Group Affiliation: Wells Fargo Group
Licensed in: All states except ME, VT, PR
Commenced Business: July 1956
Address: 206 Eighth Street, Des Moines, IA 50309
Phone: (515) 243-2131 **Domicile State:** MO **NAIC Code:** 62383

Data Date	Weiss Safety Rating	RACR #1	RACR #2	Total Assets ($mil)	Capital ($mil)	Net Premium ($mil)	Net Income ($mil)
6-03	A	37.72	21.99	1,024.0	810.4	17.0	22.7
6-02	A	25.40	14.97	970.1	743.4	28.7	8.2
2002	A-	34.91	20.63	975.3	766.7	53.3	30.0
2001	A	24.51	14.38	954.6	722.8	55.9	57.0
2000	A	20.63	12.47	889.1	678.1	67.7	56.2
1999	A	18.62	11.29	832.5	616.7	68.8	54.1
1998	A+	17.47	10.53	771.0	558.1	63.0	46.0

Adverse Trends in Operations
Decrease in premium volume from 2001 to 2002 (5%)
Decrease in premium volume from 2000 to 2001 (17%)
Decrease in premium volume from 1999 to 2000 (2%)

CHA HEALTH   C+   Fair

Major Rating Factors: Good overall results on stability tests (5.7 on a scale of 0 to 10). Weak profitability index (0.9) due to a decline in earnings during 2002. Average return on equity has been extremely poor. Strong capitalization index (8.0) based on excellent current risk-adjusted capital (severe loss scenario).
Other Rating Factors: High quality investment portfolio (9.9) containing no exposure to mortgages, junk bonds, or unaffiliated stocks. Excellent liquidity (7.4) with ample operational cash flow and liquid investments.
Principal Business: Comp med (100%)
Mem Phys: 02: 12,126 01: 10,068 02 MLR 85% / 02 Admin Exp 12%
Enroll(000): Q1 03: 117 02: 79 01: 79 **Med Exp PMPM:** $167
Principal Investments: Cash and equiv (100%)
Provider Compensation ($000): Bonus arrang ($74,528), contr fee ($51,729), FFS ($3,577), other ($29,915)
Total Member Encounters: Phys (624,169), non-phys (114,106)
Group Affiliation: CHA Service Company
Licensed in: KY
Address: 300 W Vine St, 16th Floor, Lexington, KY 40507
Phone: (859) 232-8686 **Dom State:** KY **Commenced Bus:** July 1995

Data Date	Weiss Safety Rating	RACR #1	RACR #2	Total Assets ($mil)	Capital ($mil)	Net Premium ($mil)	Net Income ($mil)
3-03	C+	2.18	1.82	82.7	40.1	77.3	1.2
3-02	C-	0.00	0.00	65.8	37.1	44.0	2.5
2002	C+	2.13	1.78	77.3	39.3	186.0	4.8
2001	C-	2.02	1.70	66.7	35.5	179.8	9.6
2000	D	0.76	0.64	59.0	24.0	270.3	11.3
1999	E	0.11	0.09	66.7	7.5	305.2	3.2
1998	E	0.02	0.02	51.4	1.5	275.5	-19.8

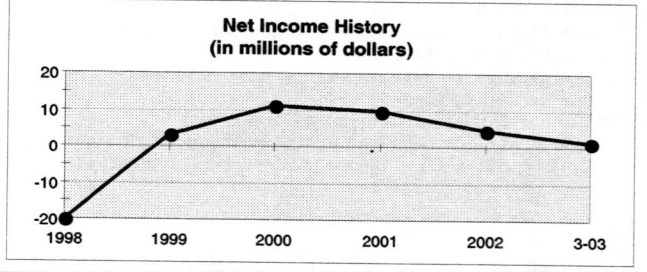

Net Income History (in millions of dollars) — 1998 through 3-03

CHILDRENS MERCY FAMILY HEALTH PARTNR — E+ Very Weak

Major Rating Factors: Weak profitability index (0.9 on a scale of 0 to 10) with modest operating losses during 1998, 1999, 2001 and 2002. Poor capitalization index (0.0) based on weak current risk-adjusted capital (severe loss scenario). Weak liquidity (2.8) as a spike in claims may stretch capacity.
Other Rating Factors: Fair overall results on stability tests (3.1). High quality investment portfolio (9.9) containing no exposure to mortgages, junk bonds, or unaffiliated stocks.
Principal Business: Medicaid (100%)
Mem Phys: 02: 1,905 **01:** 1,513 **02 MLR** 90% **/ 02 Admin Exp** 9%
Enroll(000): Q1 03: 47 **02:** 47 **01:** 46 **Med Exp PMPM:** $133
Principal Investments: Cash and equiv (69%), other (31%)
Provider Compensation ($000): Contr fee ($43,081), FFS ($23,815), capitation ($7,917)
Total Member Encounters: Phys (121,988), non-phys (18,099)
Group Affiliation: Childrens Mercy Hospital
Licensed in: KS, MO
Address: 215 W Pershing Rd Ste 600, Kansas City, MO 64108
Phone: (816) 855-1870 **Dom State:** MO **Commenced Bus:** April 1996

Data Date	Weiss Safety Rating	RACR #1	RACR #2	Total Assets ($mil)	Capital ($mil)	Net Premium ($mil)	Net Income ($mil)
3-03	E+	0.19	0.16	11.8	1.9	21.5	-0.1
3-02	D-	0.35	0.30	18.7	2.8	19.6	0.0
2002	E+	0.24	0.20	13.7	2.5	81.7	-0.4
2001	D-	0.35	0.30	17.1	2.6	71.9	-0.6
2000	D-	0.33	0.30	14.8	3.0	64.0	0.0
1999	D	0.40	0.35	15.9	2.4	52.3	0.0
1998	D	0.46	0.39	10.9	3.3	37.3	-0.3

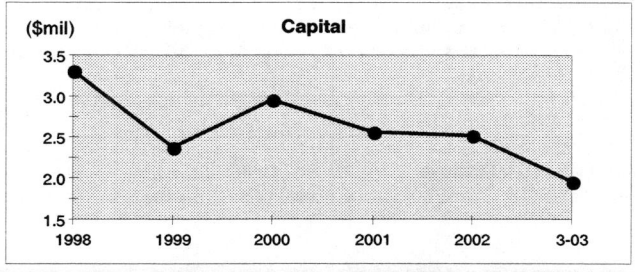

CHINESE COMMUNITY HEALTH PLAN — C+ Fair

Major Rating Factors: Fair overall results on stability tests (4.0 on a scale of 0 to 10) based on poor risk diversification due to the company's size, rapid enrollment growth during the past five years. Excellent profitability (7.9). Strong capitalization (7.1) based on good current risk-adjusted capital (moderate loss scenario). However, risk-adjusted capital has reached as low as the fair level during recent years.
Other Rating Factors: Excellent liquidity (7.0) with ample operational cash flow and liquid investments.
Principal Business: Managed care (27%)
Mem Phys: 02: N/A **01:** N/A **02 MLR** 86% **/ 02 Admin Exp** 12%
Enroll(000): Q1 03: 11 **02:** 11 **01:** 9 **Med Exp PMPM:** $283
Principal Investments ($000): Cash and equiv ($7,023), bonds ($1,003), other ($899)
Provider Compensation ($000): None
Total Member Encounters: N/A
Group Affiliation: Chinese Hospital Association
Licensed in: CA
Address: 170 Columbus Ave Ste 210, San Francisco, CA 94133
Phone: (415) 834-2128 **Dom State:** CA **Commenced Bus:** August 1987

Data Date	Weiss Safety Rating	RACR #1	RACR #2	Total Assets ($mil)	Capital ($mil)	Net Premium ($mil)	Net Income ($mil)
3-03	C+	1.18	0.75	7.9	4.7	11.4	0.3
3-02	C	0.00	0.00	6.2	3.8	8.9	0.2
2002	C+	1.10	0.70	10.6	4.4	38.2	0.8
2001	C	1.14	0.74	8.3	3.6	26.3	0.6
2000	C	1.31	0.86	6.5	3.0	16.4	0.2
1999	N/A	N/A	N/A	N/A	N/A	N/A	N/A
1998	D+	1.51	1.00	4.9	2.6	11.5	0.2

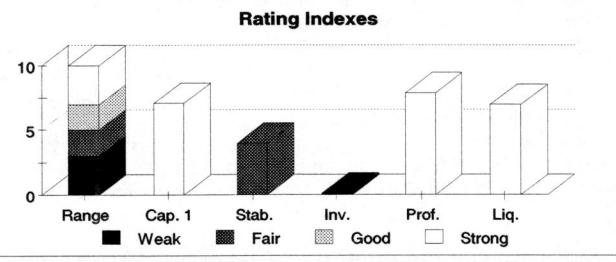

CHRISTIANA CARE HEALTH PLANS — B- Good

Major Rating Factors: Fair liquidity (3.8 on a scale of 0 to 10) as cash resources may not be adequate to cover a spike in claims. Good overall profitability index (5.5) despite a decline in earnings during 2002. Strong overall capitalization (7.5) based on excellent current risk-adjusted capital (severe loss scenario).
Other Rating Factors: High quality investment portfolio (9.9) containing no exposure to mortgages, junk bonds, or unaffiliated stocks.
Principal Business: Medicaid (82%), comp med (18%)
Mem Phys: 02: 2,735 **01:** 3,058 **02 MLR** 91% **/ 02 Admin Exp** 8%
Enroll(000): Q1 03: 103 **02:** 105 **01:** 55 **Med Exp PMPM:** $183
Principal Investments: Cash and equiv (34%), other (66%)
Provider Compensation ($000): Contr fee ($161,377), capitation ($7,776)
Total Member Encounters: Phys (41,596), non-phys (72,296)
Group Affiliation: Christiana Care Health System
Licensed in: DE
Address: 11 Reads Way, New Castle, DE 19720
Phone: (302) 327-7606 **Dom State:** DE **Commenced Bus:** January 1996

Data Date	Weiss Safety Rating	RACR #1	RACR #2	Total Assets ($mil)	Capital ($mil)	Net Premium ($mil)	Net Income ($mil)
3-03	B-	1.75	1.46	69.8	38.2	61.5	0.4
3-02	U	2.93	2.41	60.1	35.6	34.5	1.2
2002	B-	1.76	1.47	68.7	38.4	192.8	4.3
2001	B-	N/A	N/A	56.5	34.2	126.1	10.5
2000	N/A	N/A	N/A	56.5	22.2	116.6	N/A
1999	N/A	N/A	N/A	41.2	13.9	78.5	N/A
1998	N/A	N/A	N/A	25.1	5.8	62.6	N/A

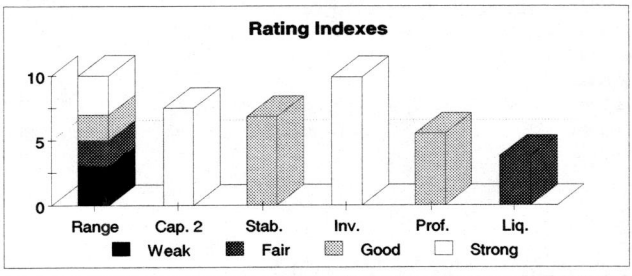

II. Analysis of Largest Companies
Winter 2003 - 04

CIGNA HEALTHCARE MID-ATLANTIC INC — D+ Weak

Major Rating Factors: Weak profitability index (1.9 on a scale of 0 to 10) with operating losses during 1998, 1999, 2000 and 2001. Average return on equity has been poor at -54%. Poor capitalization index (0.0) based on weak current risk-adjusted capital (severe loss scenario). Weak liquidity (0.0) as a spike in claims may stretch capacity.

Other Rating Factors: Good overall results on stability tests (5.0) despite an overall decline in enrollment over the past five years despite growth in 2000. Rating is significantly influenced by the fair financial results of CIGNA Corp. High quality investment portfolio (9.6) containing no exposure to mortgages, junk bonds, or unaffiliated stocks.

Principal Business: Comp med (100%)
Mem Phys: 02: 12,769 01: 11,854 **02 MLR** 80% / **02 Admin Exp** 15%
Enroll(000): Q1 03: 34 02: 32 01: 37 **Med Exp PMPM:** $143
Principal Investments: Cash and equiv (9%), other (91%)
Provider Compensation ($000): Contr fee ($46,105), capitation ($7,366), FFS ($7,336)
Total Member Encounters: Phys (67,499), non-phys (20,808)
Group Affiliation: CIGNA Corp
Licensed in: DC, MD, VA
Address: 9700 Patuxent Woods Dr., Columbia, MD 21046
Phone: (410) 720-5850 **Dom State:** MD **Commenced Bus:** December 1986

Data Date	Weiss Safety Rating	RACR #1	RACR #2	Total Assets ($mil)	Capital ($mil)	Net Premium ($mil)	Net Income ($mil)
3-03	D+	0.00	0.00	29.1	15.0	20.6	1.4
3-02	C	0.00	0.00	27.4	10.8	19.2	1.8
2002	D+	0.00	0.00	29.0	13.1	74.4	3.4
2001	C	0.00	0.00	31.0	10.1	72.0	-1.1
2000	C	1.50	1.26	34.4	11.1	110.6	-8.0
1999	C	0.75	0.63	30.6	4.1	76.3	-4.3
1998	C	0.61	0.53	20.4	2.5	84.5	-1.5

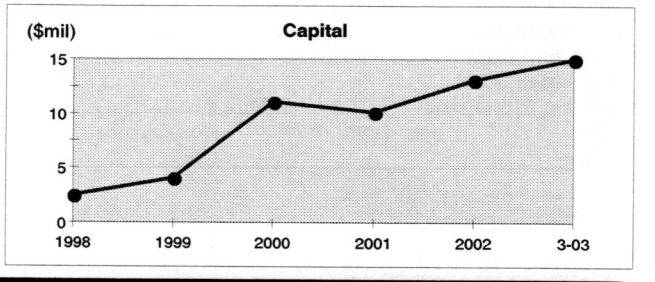

Capital chart 1998–3-03

CIGNA HEALTHCARE OF ARIZONA INC — C+ Fair

Major Rating Factors: Fair overall results on stability tests (4.1 on a scale of 0 to 10) based on fair risk-adjusted capital in prior years. Rating is significantly influenced by the fair financial results of CIGNA Corp. Good capitalization (6.9) based on excellent current risk-adjusted capital (severe loss scenario) reflecting significant improvement over results in 2000. Good liquidity (6.9) with sufficient resources (cash flows and marketable investments) to handle a spike in claims.

Other Rating Factors: Excellent profitability (7.7) despite a decline in earnings during 2002. High quality investment portfolio (8.7) containing little or no exposure to mortgages, junk bonds, or unaffiliated stocks.

Principal Business: Comp med (66%), Medicare (31%), other (3%)
Mem Phys: 02: 6,315 01: 5,508 **02 MLR** 85% / **02 Admin Exp** 13%
Enroll(000): Q1 03: 256 02: 268 01: 282 **Med Exp PMPM:** $217
Principal Investments: Cash and equiv (62%), real estate (17%), affiliate common stock (4%), other (16%)
Provider Compensation ($000): Contr fee ($458,219), salary ($104,962), capitation ($77,343), FFS ($57,891), bonus arrang ($52), other ($2,911)
Total Member Encounters: Phys (1,793,955), non-phys (387,031)
Group Affiliation: CIGNA Corp
Licensed in: AZ
Address: 11001 N Black Canyon Hwy, Phoenix, AZ 85029
Phone: (602) 371-2933 **Dom State:** AZ **Commenced Bus:** October 1977

Data Date	Weiss Safety Rating	RACR #1	RACR #2	Total Assets ($mil)	Capital ($mil)	Net Premium ($mil)	Net Income ($mil)
3-03	C+	1.25	1.04	204.8	51.2	219.1	3.9
3-02	B-	2.02	1.70	197.2	66.2	206.0	9.4
2002	C+	1.20	1.00	214.0	49.2	842.9	9.5
2001	B-	2.03	1.71	188.9	59.6	635.7	23.8
2000	C+	0.85	0.72	122.8	21.1	571.7	30.5
1999	C+	1.11	0.92	122.0	26.6	624.3	35.4
1998	B-	1.28	1.19	124.9	43.6	604.4	33.9

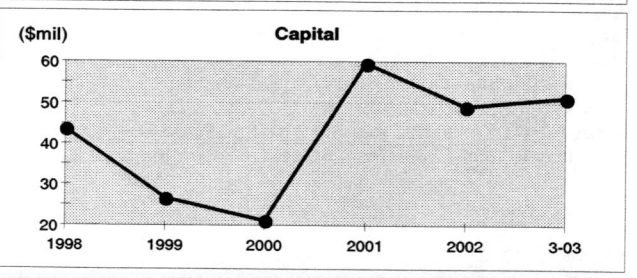

Capital chart 1998–3-03

CIGNA HEALTHCARE OF CALIFORNIA INC — C- Fair

Major Rating Factors: Fair profitability index (3.1 on a scale of 0 to 10) with operating losses during 2001 and 2002. Fair overall results on stability tests (4.3) based on fair risk-adjusted capital in prior years. Rating is significantly influenced by the fair financial results of CIGNA Corp. Good liquidity (6.9) with sufficient resources (cash flows and marketable investments) to handle a spike in claims.

Other Rating Factors: Strong capitalization index (7.0) based on good current risk-adjusted capital (moderate loss scenario).

Principal Business: Indemnity (63%), managed care (37%)
Mem Phys: 02: N/A 01: N/A **02 MLR** 94% / **02 Admin Exp** 17%
Enroll(000): Q1 03: 598 02: 635 01: 667 **Med Exp PMPM:** $139
Principal Investments ($000): Cash and equiv ($81,884), bonds ($64,964)
Provider Compensation ($000): None
Total Member Encounters: N/A
Group Affiliation: CIGNA Corp
Licensed in: CA
Address: 400 N Brand Blvd, Glendale, CA 91203
Phone: (818) 500-6284 **Dom State:** CA **Commenced Bus:** November 1978

Data Date	Weiss Safety Rating	RACR #1	RACR #2	Total Assets ($mil)	Capital ($mil)	Net Premium ($mil)	Net Income ($mil)
3-03	C-	1.14	0.71	277.0	49.9	318.4	-0.1
3-02	B-	0.00	0.00	212.7	45.0	284.4	1.2
2002	C-	1.02	0.64	240.9	43.5	1,156.5	-6.2
2001	B-	1.09	0.72	198.8	45.1	993.2	-2.7
2000	B	1.81	1.12	252.4	61.0	1,027.3	17.7
1999	B-	1.62	0.99	305.4	56.5	1,030.4	30.8
1998	B-	2.30	1.41	301.0	77.2	981.5	29.3

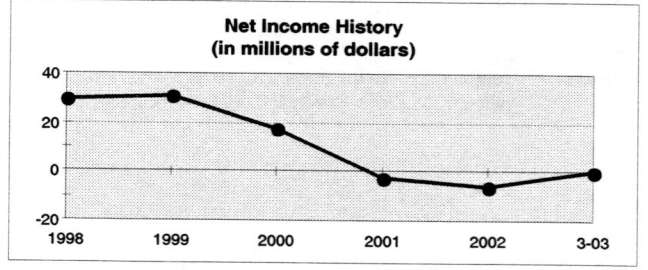

Net Income History (in millions of dollars), 1998–3-03

Winter 2003 - 04   II. Analysis of Largest Companies

CIGNA HEALTHCARE OF COLORADO INC — C Fair

Major Rating Factors: Fair profitability index (3.4 on a scale of 0 to 10) with operating losses during 2001. Return on equity has been fair, averaging 10% over the last five years. Good overall capitalization (6.7) based on good current risk-adjusted capital (severe loss scenario). Good overall results on stability tests (5.0) despite good risk-adjusted capital in prior years, rapid premium growth over the last five years and rapid enrollment growth during the past five years. Rating is significantly influenced by the fair financial results of CIGNA Corp.

Other Rating Factors: Good liquidity (6.4) with sufficient resources (cash flows and marketable investments) to handle a spike in claims. High quality investment portfolio (9.6) containing no exposure to mortgages, junk bonds, or unaffiliated stocks.

Principal Business: Comp med (100%)
Mem Phys: 02: 8,218 **01:** 9,067 **02 MLR** 89% / **02 Admin Exp** 12%
Enroll(000): Q1 03: 87 **02:** 102 **01:** 86 **Med Exp PMPM:** $186
Principal Investments: Cash and equiv (50%), other (50%)
Provider Compensation ($000): Contr fee ($167,096), FFS ($19,584), capitation ($9,764)
Total Member Encounters: Phys (428,091), non-phys (81,562)
Group Affiliation: CIGNA Corp
Licensed in: CO, KS, MO, OH
Address: 3900 E Mexico Ave Suite 1100, Denver, CO 80210
Phone: (303) 782-1500 **Dom State:** CO **Commenced Bus:** May 1986

Data Date	Weiss Safety Rating	RACR #1	RACR #2	Total Assets ($mil)	Capital ($mil)	Net Premium ($mil)	Net Income ($mil)
3-03	C	1.18	0.99	52.5	15.8	57.8	-1.9
3-02	C	1.37	1.16	45.8	13.3	54.4	1.8
2002	C	1.25	1.04	48.6	16.8	234.2	2.5
2001	B-	1.40	1.18	37.8	11.7	152.3	-4.6
2000	B-	1.31	1.10	23.3	6.9	90.8	1.1
1999	B-	1.74	1.46	24.6	7.0	71.4	2.6
1998	B-	1.40	1.21	24.1	7.1	67.5	1.7

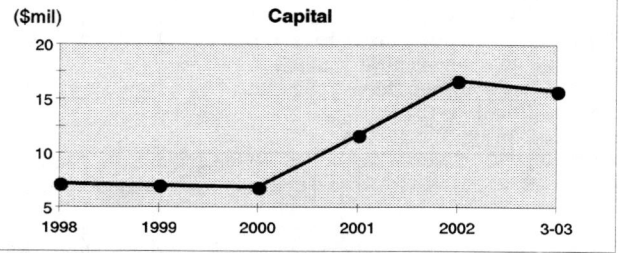

Capital chart ($mil), 1998–3-03

CIGNA HEALTHCARE OF CONNECTICUT INC — C Fair

Major Rating Factors: Weak overall results on stability tests (1.1 on a scale of 0 to 10) based on a steep decline in capital during 2002, a significant 28% decrease in enrollment during the period. Rating is significantly influenced by the fair financial results of CIGNA Corp. Good overall profitability index (5.8) despite a decline in earnings during 2002. Good liquidity (6.2) with sufficient resources (cash flows and marketable investments) to handle a spike in claims.

Other Rating Factors: Strong capitalization (10.0) based on excellent current risk-adjusted capital (severe loss scenario) reflecting significant improvement over results in 1999. High quality investment portfolio (8.9) containing no exposure to mortgages, junk bonds, or unaffiliated stocks.

Principal Business: Comp med (100%)
Mem Phys: 02: 10,867 **01:** 11,715 **02 MLR** 82% / **02 Admin Exp** 17%
Enroll(000): Q1 03: 21 **02:** 19 **01:** 26 **Med Exp PMPM:** $160
Principal Investments: Cash and equiv (4%), other (96%)
Provider Compensation ($000): Contr fee ($37,069), capitation ($7,188), FFS ($2,662)
Total Member Encounters: Phys (40,083), non-phys (36,224)
Group Affiliation: CIGNA Corp
Licensed in: CT
Address: 900 Cottage Grove Rd., B228, Hartford, CT 06152-1118
Phone: (860) 769-2300 **Dom State:** CT **Commenced Bus:** May 1986

Data Date	Weiss Safety Rating	RACR #1	RACR #2	Total Assets ($mil)	Capital ($mil)	Net Premium ($mil)	Net Income ($mil)
3-03	C	4.03	3.36	19.3	11.8	14.6	1.7
3-02	C	4.14	3.53	25.8	17.4	14.0	0.6
2002	C	3.16	2.63	16.6	8.7	52.9	1.4
2001	C+	4.13	3.53	27.2	16.5	69.9	4.3
2000	C+	2.20	1.86	45.6	15.5	142.1	7.6
1999	C	0.77	0.66	33.0	4.5	101.3	-1.6
1998	C+	1.72	1.55	22.2	8.3	77.9	4.7

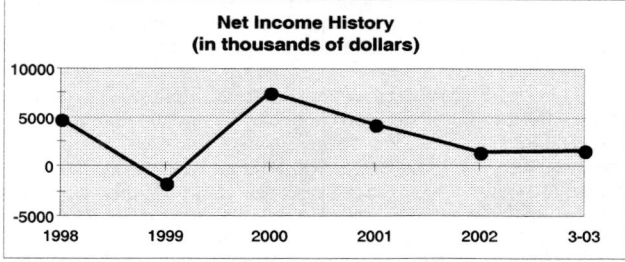

Net Income History (in thousands of dollars), 1998–3-03

CIGNA HEALTHCARE OF DELAWARE INC — D+ Weak

Major Rating Factors: Poor capitalization index (0.0 on a scale of 0 to 10) based on weak current risk-adjusted capital (severe loss scenario). Fair profitability index (3.5) with operating losses during 2000 and 2001. Return on equity has been fair, averaging 8% over the last five years. Fair overall results on stability tests (4.9) based on an excessive 59% enrollment growth during the period. Rating is significantly influenced by the fair financial results of CIGNA Corp.

Other Rating Factors: Good liquidity (6.2) with sufficient resources (cash flows and marketable investments) to handle a spike in claims. High quality investment portfolio (9.3) containing no exposure to mortgages, junk bonds, or unaffiliated stocks.

Principal Business: Comp med (97%), Medicare (3%)
Mem Phys: 02: 1,235 **01:** 1,087 **02 MLR** 56% / **02 Admin Exp** 39%
Enroll(000): Q1 03: 0 **02:** 1 **01:** 0 **Med Exp PMPM:** $122
Principal Investments: Cash and equiv (12%), other (88%)
Provider Compensation ($000): Contr fee ($812), FFS ($95), capitation ($50)
Total Member Encounters: Phys (1,610), non-phys (460)
Group Affiliation: CIGNA Corp
Licensed in: DE
Address: 590 Naamans Rd, Claymont, DE 19703
Phone: (302) 797-3700 **Dom State:** DE **Commenced Bus:** May 1985

Data Date	Weiss Safety Rating	RACR #1	RACR #2	Total Assets ($mil)	Capital ($mil)	Net Premium ($mil)	Net Income ($mil)
3-03	D+	0.00	0.00	4.3	3.8	0.3	-0.1
3-02	C+	0.00	0.00	6.0	3.7	0.3	0.1
2002	D+	0.00	0.00	4.3	3.9	1.3	0.4
2001	C+	0.00	0.00	6.2	3.5	1.6	-0.2
2000	C+	1.84	1.54	11.2	3.6	39.9	-0.1
1999	C+	1.08	0.91	11.1	1.7	34.6	0.3
1998	C+	3.44	3.03	5.0	1.5	13.7	0.3

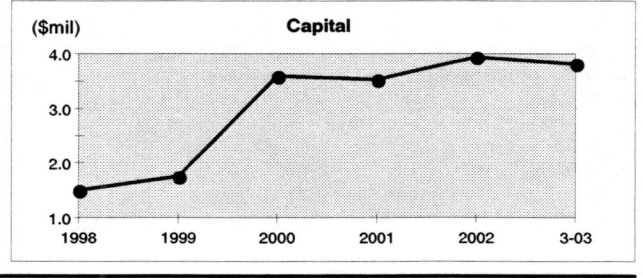

Capital chart ($mil), 1998–3-03

II. Analysis of Largest Companies

Winter 2003 - 04

CIGNA HEALTHCARE OF FLORIDA INC — D — Weak

Major Rating Factors: Weak profitability index (2.1 on a scale of 0 to 10) with operating losses during 2001. Average return on equity has been poor at -4%. Weak overall results on stability tests (2.6) based on a steep decline in premium revenue in 2001, a significant 80% decrease in enrollment during the period. Rating is significantly influenced by the fair financial results of CIGNA Corp. Weak liquidity (0.0) as a spike in claims may stretch capacity.
Other Rating Factors: Good quality investment portfolio (6.2) containing no exposure to mortgages, junk bonds, or unaffiliated stocks. Strong overall capitalization (7.2) based on excellent current risk-adjusted capital (severe loss scenario) despite some fluctuation in capital levels.
Principal Business: Comp med (98%), other (2%)
Mem Phys: 01: 13,818 00: 15,088   **01 MLR** 90% / **01 Admin Exp** 17%
Enroll(000): Q2 02: 122 01: 126 00: 613   **Med Exp PMPM:** $51
Principal Investments: Real estate (12%), cash and equiv (92%)
Provider Compensation ($000): Contr fee ($189,097), capitation ($25,642), FFS ($20,207), bonus arrang ($962)
Total Member Encounters: Phys (531,875), non-phys (185,611)
Group Affiliation: CIGNA Corp
Licensed in: FL
Address: 5404 Cypress Center Dr, ste 365, Tampa, FL 33609
Phone: (813) 281-1000   **Dom State:** FL   **Commenced Bus:** February 1981

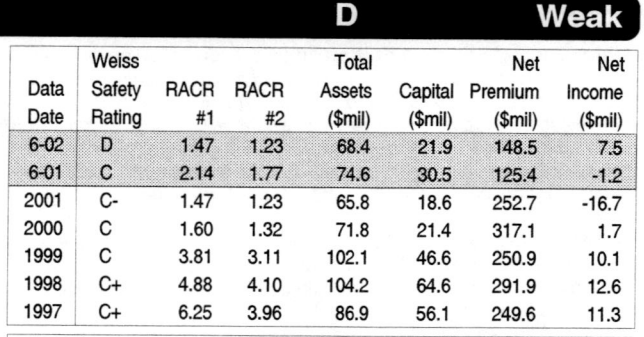

Data Date	Weiss Safety Rating	RACR #1	RACR #2	Total Assets ($mil)	Capital ($mil)	Net Premium ($mil)	Net Income ($mil)
6-02	D	1.47	1.23	68.4	21.9	148.5	7.5
6-01	C	2.14	1.77	74.6	30.5	125.4	-1.2
2001	C-	1.47	1.23	65.8	18.6	252.7	-16.7
2000	C	1.60	1.32	71.8	21.4	317.1	1.7
1999	C	3.81	3.11	102.1	46.6	250.9	10.1
1998	C+	4.88	4.10	104.2	64.6	291.9	12.6
1997	C+	6.25	3.96	86.9	56.1	249.6	11.3

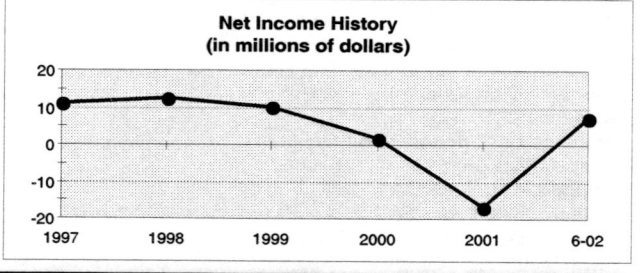

CIGNA HEALTHCARE OF GEORGIA INC — C+ — Fair

Major Rating Factors: Fair profitability index (4.5 on a scale of 0 to 10) due to a decline in earnings during 2002. Return on equity has been low, averaging 4%. Fair overall results on stability tests (4.5) based on a significant 16% decrease in enrollment during the period. Rating is significantly influenced by the fair financial results of CIGNA Corp. Good liquidity (6.9) with sufficient resources (cash flows and marketable investments) to handle a spike in claims.
Other Rating Factors: Strong overall capitalization (9.7) based on excellent current risk-adjusted capital (severe loss scenario) despite some fluctuation in capital levels. High quality investment portfolio (9.4) containing no exposure to mortgages, junk bonds, or unaffiliated stocks.
Principal Business: Comp med (100%)
Mem Phys: 02: 7,620 01: 6,510   **02 MLR** 85% / **02 Admin Exp** 16%
Enroll(000): Q1 03: 29 02: 46 01: 55   **Med Exp PMPM:** $148
Principal Investments: Cash and equiv (31%), other (69%)
Provider Compensation ($000): Contr fee ($64,021), capitation ($15,490), FFS ($10,352)
Total Member Encounters: Phys (160,352), non-phys (35,644)
Group Affiliation: CIGNA Corp
Licensed in: GA
Address: 100 Peachtree St Ste 800, Atlanta, GA 30503-1909
Phone: (404) 681-7000   **Dom State:** GA   **Commenced Bus:** December 1985

Data Date	Weiss Safety Rating	RACR #1	RACR #2	Total Assets ($mil)	Capital ($mil)	Net Premium ($mil)	Net Income ($mil)
3-03	C+	3.55	2.96	40.2	18.2	18.5	0.1
3-02	C+	3.66	3.13	53.3	19.4	26.9	0.4
2002	C+	3.39	2.83	44.8	17.2	105.9	3.7
2001	C+	3.63	3.10	58.2	18.7	115.6	5.0
2000	C+	1.42	1.21	56.1	12.6	174.7	-10.2
1999	B	3.06	2.58	75.7	23.4	153.2	0.5
1998	B	3.40	2.98	55.7	23.6	157.1	4.0

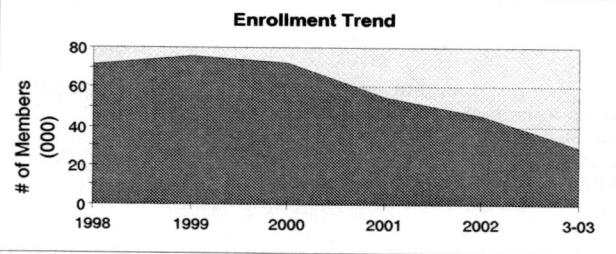

CIGNA HEALTHCARE OF ILLINOIS INC — D+ — Weak

Major Rating Factors: Weak profitability index (0.9 on a scale of 0 to 10) with operating losses during 2000 and 2001. Average return on equity has been poor at -33%. Weak overall results on stability tests (2.4) based on a steep decline in premium revenue in 2002, a decline in the number of member physicians during 2002 and a significant 45% decrease in enrollment during the period. Rating is significantly influenced by the fair financial results of CIGNA Corp. Strong overall capitalization (9.7) based on excellent current risk-adjusted capital (severe loss scenario) despite some fluctuation in capital levels.
Other Rating Factors: High quality investment portfolio (9.9) containing no exposure to mortgages, junk bonds, or unaffiliated stocks. Excellent liquidity (7.5) with ample operational cash flow and liquid investments.
Principal Business: Comp med (100%)
Mem Phys: 02: 7,324 01: 9,913   **02 MLR** 84% / **02 Admin Exp** 20%
Enroll(000): Q1 03: 6 02: 8 01: 14   **Med Exp PMPM:** $135
Principal Investments: Cash and equiv (88%), other (12%)
Provider Compensation ($000): Contr fee ($15,144), capitation ($1,448), FFS ($1,097)
Total Member Encounters: Phys (27,136), non-phys (11,349)
Group Affiliation: CIGNA Corp
Licensed in: IL, IN
Address: 525 West Monroe Ste 1800, Chicago, IL 60661
Phone: (312) 648-2460   **Dom State:** IL   **Commenced Bus:** July 1986

Data Date	Weiss Safety Rating	RACR #1	RACR #2	Total Assets ($mil)	Capital ($mil)	Net Premium ($mil)	Net Income ($mil)
3-03	D+	3.50	2.92	12.0	6.1	3.8	0.9
3-02	D+	1.75	1.50	11.7	3.3	5.7	-1.4
2002	D+	2.99	2.49	13.3	5.1	20.6	0.2
2001	C-	1.75	1.50	13.3	4.4	29.3	-6.1
2000	C	1.79	1.53	13.6	3.5	23.8	-2.2
1999	C	3.82	3.10	41.4	7.7	23.5	0.8
1998	C+	6.58	5.92	38.8	26.9	64.3	4.3

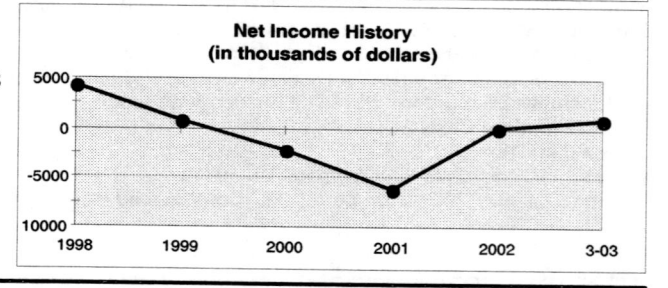

CIGNA HEALTHCARE OF INDIANA INC — C- Fair

Major Rating Factors: Fair overall results on stability tests (4.2 on a scale of 0 to 10) based on a significant 22% decrease in enrollment during the period. Rating is significantly influenced by the fair financial results of CIGNA Corp. Weak profitability index (2.2) with operating losses during 2001 and 2002. Good liquidity (6.9) with sufficient resources (cash flows and marketable investments) to handle a spike in claims.

Other Rating Factors: Strong overall capitalization (7.3) based on excellent current risk-adjusted capital (severe loss scenario) despite some fluctuation in capital levels. High quality investment portfolio (9.9) containing no exposure to mortgages, junk bonds, or unaffiliated stocks.

Principal Business: Comp med (100%)
Mem Phys: 02: 4,929 **01:** 5,283 **02 MLR** 89% **/ 02 Admin Exp** 14%
Enroll(000): 02: 34 **01:** 44 **Med Exp PMPM:** $185
Principal Investments: Cash and equiv (95%), other (5%)
Provider Compensation ($000): Contr fee ($61,477), capitation ($18,821), FFS ($6,625)
Total Member Encounters: Phys (120,897), non-phys (11,897)
Group Affiliation: CIGNA Corp
Licensed in: IN
Address: 429 N Pennsylvania St., Ste 301, Indianapolis, IN 43204
Phone: (317) 685-1133 **Dom State:** IN **Commenced Bus:** September 1986

Data Date	Weiss Safety Rating	RACR #1	RACR #2	Total Assets ($mil)	Capital ($mil)	Net Premium ($mil)	Net Income ($mil)
2002	C-	1.62	1.35	20.0	7.3	97.1	-1.3
2001	C	1.82	1.55	23.1	8.4	104.4	-1.8
2000	C	4.21	3.49	22.5	13.4	51.8	3.3
1999	C	3.38	2.90	14.9	7.7	37.7	0.4
1998	C	3.85	3.45	20.1	7.7	50.5	2.2

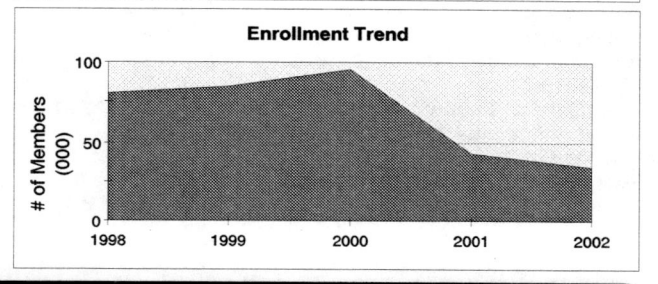

CIGNA HEALTHCARE OF MAINE INC — C Fair

Major Rating Factors: Fair profitability index (4.1 on a scale of 0 to 10) with operating losses during 1998 and 1999. Average return on equity has been poor at -1%. Good overall results on stability tests (5.1) despite fair risk-adjusted capital in prior years, a decline in enrollment during 2002. Rating is significantly influenced by the fair financial results of CIGNA Corp. Good liquidity (6.0) with sufficient resources (cash flows and marketable investments) to handle a spike in claims.

Other Rating Factors: Strong capitalization (8.5) based on excellent current risk-adjusted capital (severe loss scenario) reflecting significant improvement over results in 1998. High quality investment portfolio (9.5) containing no exposure to mortgages, junk bonds, or unaffiliated stocks.

Principal Business: Comp med (100%)
Mem Phys: 02: 3,361 **01:** 3,195 **02 MLR** 84% **/ 02 Admin Exp** 11%
Enroll(000): Q1 03: 38 **02:** 46 **01:** 65 **Med Exp PMPM:** $176
Principal Investments: Cash and equiv (38%), other (62%)
Provider Compensation ($000): Contr fee ($109,761), capitation ($6,717), FFS ($3,115)
Total Member Encounters: Phys (214,785), non-phys (86,805)
Group Affiliation: CIGNA Corp
Licensed in: ME
Address: 2 Stonewood Dr, Freeport, ME 04032-0447
Phone: (207) 865-5000 **Dom State:** ME **Commenced Bus:** April 1987

Data Date	Weiss Safety Rating	RACR #1	RACR #2	Total Assets ($mil)	Capital ($mil)	Net Premium ($mil)	Net Income ($mil)
3-03	C	2.59	2.16	45.5	21.4	31.8	0.7
3-02	C	1.69	1.42	52.4	20.9	35.5	0.4
2002	C	2.59	2.16	51.7	21.7	139.0	4.1
2001	C	1.69	1.43	53.2	19.7	158.3	1.2
2000	C+	1.63	1.36	42.1	16.7	163.7	3.2
1999	C+	1.08	0.91	44.6	14.7	173.7	-1.3
1998	C+	0.89	0.75	44.8	12.5	162.9	-4.3

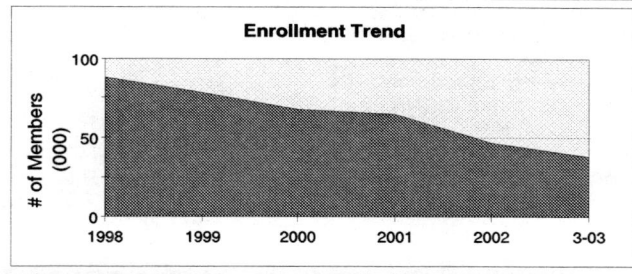

CIGNA HEALTHCARE OF MASSACHUSETTS — C Fair

Major Rating Factors: Good overall profitability index (6.7 on a scale of 0 to 10) despite a decline in earnings during 2002. Good overall results on stability tests (5.1) despite a decline in enrollment during 2002. Rating is significantly influenced by the fair financial results of CIGNA Corp. Good liquidity (6.7) with sufficient resources (cash flows and marketable investments) to handle a spike in claims.

Other Rating Factors: Strong capitalization (7.6) based on excellent current risk-adjusted capital (severe loss scenario) reflecting improvement over results in 1998. High quality investment portfolio (9.5) containing no exposure to mortgages, junk bonds, or unaffiliated stocks.

Principal Business: Comp med (100%)
Mem Phys: 02: 16,779 **01:** 15,372 **02 MLR** 87% **/ 02 Admin Exp** 14%
Enroll(000): Q1 03: 57 **02:** 61 **01:** 78 **Med Exp PMPM:** $193
Principal Investments: Cash and equiv (50%), other (50%)
Provider Compensation ($000): Contr fee ($134,299), FFS ($21,182), capitation ($13,005), bonus arrang ($1,360)
Total Member Encounters: Phys (289,252), non-phys (34,412)
Group Affiliation: CIGNA Corp
Licensed in: MA
Address: 100 Front St, 8th Floor, Worcester, MA 01608
Phone: (508) 849-8308 **Dom State:** MA **Commenced Bus:** February 1996

Data Date	Weiss Safety Rating	RACR #1	RACR #2	Total Assets ($mil)	Capital ($mil)	Net Premium ($mil)	Net Income ($mil)
3-03	C	1.88	1.56	42.1	20.0	40.2	0.6
3-02	C	1.72	1.45	53.1	18.6	51.0	-0.3
2002	C	1.83	1.52	44.2	19.5	184.2	1.2
2001	C+	1.73	1.46	54.0	19.1	206.9	1.7
2000	C	N/A	N/A	59.6	23.3	162.7	9.5
1999	C	2.37	1.97	38.8	14.8	116.3	3.7
1998	C	1.27	1.06	38.0	11.9	137.1	1.8

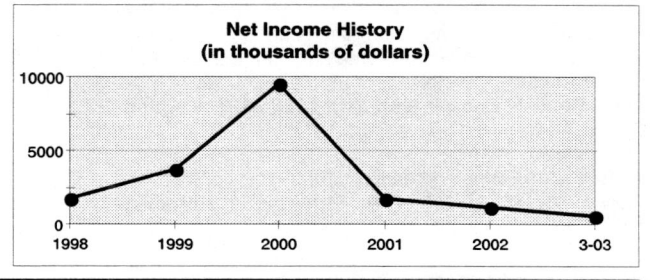

II. Analysis of Largest Companies

Winter 2003 - 04

CIGNA HEALTHCARE OF NEW HAMPSHIRE — C+ — Fair

Major Rating Factors: Fair overall results on stability tests (4.2 on a scale of 0 to 10) based on a significant 39% decrease in enrollment during the period. Rating is significantly influenced by the fair financial results of CIGNA Corp. Good overall profitability index (5.6) despite operating losses during 1998 and 1999. Good liquidity (6.9) with sufficient resources (cash flows and marketable investments) to handle a spike in claims.
Other Rating Factors: Strong overall capitalization (10.0) based on excellent current risk-adjusted capital (severe loss scenario) despite some fluctuation in capital levels. High quality investment portfolio (9.3) containing no exposure to mortgages, junk bonds, or unaffiliated stocks.
Principal Business: Comp med (100%)
Mem Phys: 02: 3,900   **01:** 4,327   **02 MLR** 79%   **/ 02 Admin Exp** 13%
Enroll(000): Q1 03: 83   **02:** 94   **01:** 154   **Med Exp PMPM:** $181
Principal Investments: Cash and equiv (28%), other (72%)
Provider Compensation ($000): Contr fee ($213,652), capitation ($38,599), FFS ($31,937)
Total Member Encounters: Phys (556,563), non-phys (273,176)
Group Affiliation: CIGNA Corp
Licensed in: MA, NH
Address: 2 College Park Dr, Hooksett, NH 03301
Phone: (603) 268-7000   **Dom State:** NH   **Commenced Bus:** June 1985

Data Date	Weiss Safety Rating	RACR #1	RACR #2	Total Assets ($mil)	Capital ($mil)	Net Premium ($mil)	Net Income ($mil)
3-03	C+	3.62	3.02	101.4	60.4	67.5	6.2
3-02	B-	3.01	2.55	135.4	67.1	100.6	5.8
2002	C+	3.35	2.79	105.7	55.4	343.1	19.4
2001	B-	3.01	2.55	125.8	61.0	419.0	13.6
2000	C+	1.90	1.59	89.7	39.9	399.2	3.9
1999	C+	1.45	1.21	93.0	31.8	392.3	-2.2
1998	C+	1.36	1.15	82.1	26.1	330.2	-11.8

Enrollment Trend

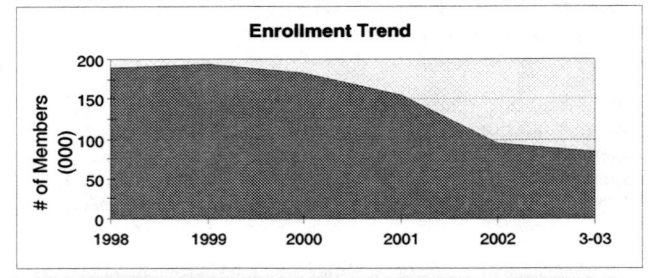

CIGNA HEALTHCARE OF NEW JERSEY INC — C — Fair

Major Rating Factors: Good overall results on stability tests (5.0 on a scale of 0 to 10). Rating is significantly influenced by the fair financial results of CIGNA Corp. Good liquidity (6.4) with sufficient resources (cash flows and marketable investments) to handle a spike in claims. Excellent profitability (7.5) despite a decline in earnings during 2002.
Other Rating Factors: Strong capitalization (9.6) based on excellent current risk-adjusted capital (severe loss scenario) reflecting improvement over results in 1998. High quality investment portfolio (9.2) containing no exposure to mortgages, junk bonds, or unaffiliated stocks.
Principal Business: Comp med (100%)
Mem Phys: 02: 17,188   **01:** 18,721   **02 MLR** 84%   **/ 02 Admin Exp** 17%
Enroll(000):   02: 87   **01:** 78   **Med Exp PMPM:** $179
Principal Investments: Cash and equiv (13%), other (87%)
Provider Compensation ($000): Contr fee ($133,564), capitation ($21,876), FFS ($17,039)
Total Member Encounters: N/A
Group Affiliation: CIGNA Corp
Licensed in: NJ
Address: 499 Washington Blvd 5th Floor, Jersey City, NJ 07310-1608
Phone: (201) 533-5001   **Dom State:** NJ   **Commenced Bus:** February 1988

Data Date	Weiss Safety Rating	RACR #1	RACR #2	Total Assets ($mil)	Capital ($mil)	Net Premium ($mil)	Net Income ($mil)
2002	C	3.45	2.88	78.9	37.2	211.4	1.2
2001	C+	3.68	3.12	82.9	35.5	200.3	6.4
2000	B-	2.49	2.07	91.8	24.7	255.4	12.5
1999	C+	1.42	1.19	92.8	16.3	239.8	1.0
1998	C	1.18	1.02	71.8	12.0	194.1	4.3

Rating Indexes (Range, Cap. 2, Stab., Inv., Prof., Liq.) — Weak / Fair / Good / Strong

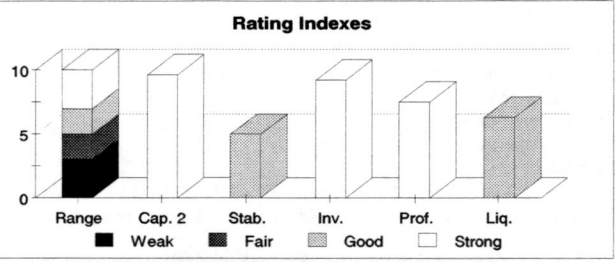

CIGNA HEALTHCARE OF NEW YORK — C — Fair

Major Rating Factors: Weak overall results on stability tests (1.7 on a scale of 0 to 10) based on excessive premium growth during 2002, an excessive 39% enrollment growth during the period. Rating is significantly influenced by the fair financial results of CIGNA Corp. Good overall profitability index (5.6) despite a decline in earnings during 2002. Good liquidity (6.3) with sufficient resources (cash flows and marketable investments) to handle a spike in claims.
Other Rating Factors: Strong capitalization (9.7) based on excellent current risk-adjusted capital (severe loss scenario) reflecting significant improvement over results in 1999. High quality investment portfolio (9.4) containing no exposure to mortgages, junk bonds, or unaffiliated stocks.
Principal Business: Comp med (100%)
Mem Phys: 02: 22,345   **01:** 23,808   **02 MLR** 83%   **/ 02 Admin Exp** 14%
Enroll(000): Q1 03: 72   **02:** 77   **01:** 56   **Med Exp PMPM:** $188
Principal Investments: Cash and equiv (28%), other (72%)
Provider Compensation ($000): Contr fee ($110,247), capitation ($18,904), FFS ($13,190)
Total Member Encounters: Phys (286,042), non-phys (23,268)
Group Affiliation: CIGNA Corp
Licensed in: NY
Address: 499 Washington Blvd.,5th Floor, Jersey City, NJ 07310
Phone: (201) 533-7000   **Dom State:** NY   **Commenced Bus:** October 1986

Data Date	Weiss Safety Rating	RACR #1	RACR #2	Total Assets ($mil)	Capital ($mil)	Net Premium ($mil)	Net Income ($mil)
3-03	C	3.54	2.95	65.5	32.7	51.7	4.4
3-02	C+	5.07	4.32	87.9	49.9	40.5	1.7
2002	C	3.18	2.65	72.4	29.0	178.5	0.5
2001	C+	4.98	4.26	80.4	48.8	136.3	2.5
2000	C+	3.22	2.68	78.8	47.9	188.7	14.2
1999	C	0.85	0.73	100.9	32.7	208.8	0.0
1998	C	1.30	1.15	85.4	31.4	221.0	6.5

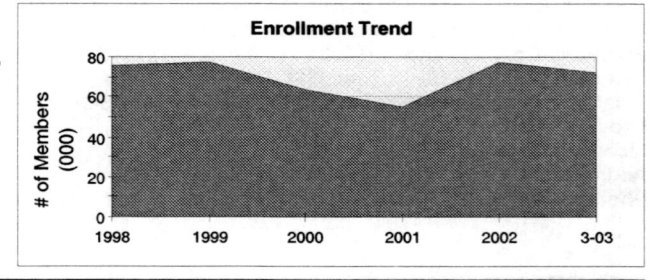

Enrollment Trend

www.WeissRatings.com

Winter 2003 - 04   II. Analysis of Largest Companies

CIGNA HEALTHCARE OF NORTH CAROLINA   C-   Fair

Major Rating Factors: Fair overall results on stability tests (3.2 on a scale of 0 to 10) based on a significant 15% decrease in enrollment during the period, a steep decline in capital during 2002 and a decline in the number of member physicians during 2002. Rating is significantly influenced by the fair financial results of CIGNA Corp. Fair liquidity (3.9) as cash resources may not be adequate to cover a spike in claims. Weak profitability index (2.3) with $17.0 million in losses in the last two years.
Other Rating Factors: Strong capitalization (7.0) based on excellent current risk-adjusted capital (severe loss scenario) reflecting improvement over results in 1998. High quality investment portfolio (9.2) containing no exposure to mortgages, junk bonds, or unaffiliated stocks.
Principal Business: Comp med (100%)
Mem Phys: 02: 7,364   **01:** 13,767   **02 MLR** 89%   **/ 02 Admin Exp** 14%
Enroll(000): Q1 03: 138   **02:** 195   **01:** 231   **Med Exp PMPM:** $165
Principal Investments: Cash and equiv (11%), other (89%)
Provider Compensation ($000): Contr fee ($349,409), FFS ($43,185), capitation ($26,842)
Total Member Encounters: Phys (784,164), non-phys (53,014)
Group Affiliation: CIGNA Corp
Licensed in: NC
Address: 701 Corporate Center Dr, Raleigh, NC 27607
Phone: (704) 556-5800   **Dom State:** NC   **Commenced Bus:** April 1986

Data Date	Weiss Safety Rating	RACR #1	RACR #2	Total Assets ($mil)	Capital ($mil)	Net Premium ($mil)	Net Income ($mil)
3-03	C-	1.38	1.15	89.8	31.2	92.9	-1.3
3-02	C+	2.17	1.84	111.3	48.7	121.2	7.1
2002	C-	1.51	1.26	100.9	35.1	475.2	-5.5
2001	C+	2.23	1.88	102.1	45.1	438.1	-11.5
2000	B-	3.35	2.78	100.4	48.0	321.8	12.6
1999	B-	2.32	1.93	110.5	44.9	319.0	22.5
1998	B-	1.09	0.91	112.7	28.9	418.8	1.5

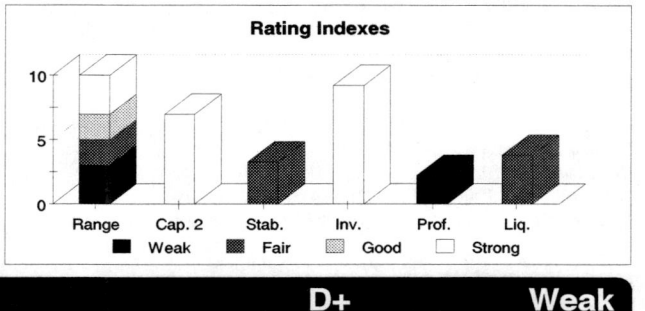

Rating Indexes (Range, Cap. 2, Stab., Inv., Prof., Liq.) — Weak / Fair / Good / Strong

CIGNA HEALTHCARE OF OHIO INC   D+   Weak

Major Rating Factors: Weak profitability index (0.9 on a scale of 0 to 10) with operating losses during 1999, 2001 and 2002. Average return on equity has been poor at -12%. Poor capitalization index (0.0) based on weak current risk-adjusted capital (severe loss scenario). Weak overall results on stability tests (1.8) based on a significant 43% decrease in enrollment during the period, a steep decline in capital during 2002. Rating is significantly influenced by the fair financial results of CIGNA Corp.
Other Rating Factors: Weak liquidity (0.0) as a spike in claims may stretch capacity. High quality investment portfolio (9.6) containing no exposure to mortgages, junk bonds, or unaffiliated stocks.
Principal Business: Comp med (100%)
Mem Phys: 02: 14,931   **01:** 15,205   **02 MLR** 97%   **/ 02 Admin Exp** 24%
Enroll(000): Q1 03: 7   **02:** 11   **01:** 19   **Med Exp PMPM:** $138
Principal Investments: Cash and equiv (52%), other (48%)
Provider Compensation ($000): Contr fee ($19,231), FFS ($3,561), capitation ($1,267)
Total Member Encounters: Phys (52,361), non-phys (18,165)
Group Affiliation: CIGNA Corp
Licensed in: KS, MO, OH
Address: 5005 Rockside Road #700, Independence, OH 44131
Phone: (216) 642-8969   **Dom State:** OH   **Commenced Bus:** May 1986

Data Date	Weiss Safety Rating	RACR #1	RACR #2	Total Assets ($mil)	Capital ($mil)	Net Premium ($mil)	Net Income ($mil)
3-03	D+	0.00	0.00	18.0	4.8	4.4	-0.5
3-02	C	0.00	0.00	19.5	7.4	6.9	-0.2
2002	D+	0.00	0.00	16.4	5.1	25.3	-2.1
2001	C	0.00	0.00	24.1	6.9	37.6	-1.8
2000	C	2.50	1.92	24.5	9.2	52.0	1.9
1999	C	0.54	0.43	42.9	3.2	100.7	-5.8
1998	C+	1.92	1.62	53.1	15.3	162.1	2.9

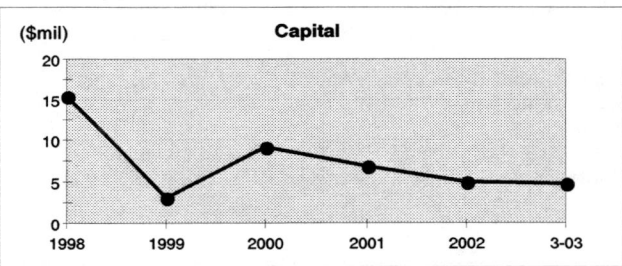

Capital ($mil) — 1998 through 3-03

CIGNA HEALTHCARE OF PENNSYLVANIA INC   D+   Weak

Major Rating Factors: Weak profitability index (0.8 on a scale of 0 to 10) with modest operating losses during 1998, 2000, 2001 and 2002. Average return on equity has been poor at -21%. Poor capitalization (2.9) based on fair current risk-adjusted capital (moderate loss scenario) as results have slipped from the good range over the last two years. Weak overall results on stability tests (2.5) based on a steep decline in capital during 2002. Rating is significantly influenced by the fair financial results of CIGNA Corp.
Other Rating Factors: High quality investment portfolio (9.9) containing no exposure to mortgages, junk bonds, or unaffiliated stocks. Excellent liquidity (7.1) with ample operational cash flow and liquid investments.
Principal Business: Comp med (100%)
Mem Phys: 02: 7,630   **01:** 6,905   **02 MLR** 103%   **/ 02 Admin Exp** 15%
Enroll(000): Q1 03: 3   **02:** 4   **01:** 3   **Med Exp PMPM:** $219
Principal Investments: Cash and equiv (98%), other (2%)
Provider Compensation ($000): Contr fee ($4,826), FFS ($1,352), capitation ($847)
Total Member Encounters: Phys (9,552), non-phys (2,822)
Group Affiliation: CIGNA Corp
Licensed in: PA
Address: 590 Naamans Rd, Claymont, DE 19703
Phone: (860) 226-6000   **Dom State:** PA   **Commenced Bus:** June 1987

Data Date	Weiss Safety Rating	RACR #1	RACR #2	Total Assets ($mil)	Capital ($mil)	Net Premium ($mil)	Net Income ($mil)
3-03	D+	0.90	0.75	5.0	1.4	2.0	-0.4
3-02	C	3.14	2.69	5.6	2.4	1.8	-0.5
2002	D+	1.19	0.99	5.5	1.9	8.0	-1.0
2001	C	3.16	2.70	5.3	2.9	5.9	-0.3
2000	C	3.77	3.26	4.9	3.4	4.6	-0.6
1999	C	2.54	2.16	5.2	2.0	4.4	0.4
1998	C	0.69	0.64	4.6	1.2	13.3	-0.9

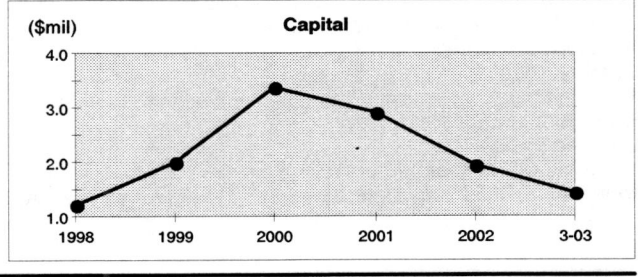

Capital ($mil) — 1998 through 3-03

II. Analysis of Largest Companies
Winter 2003 - 04

CIGNA HEALTHCARE OF SOUTH CAROLINA — D+ — Weak

Major Rating Factors: Weak profitability index (0.9 on a scale of 0 to 10) with operating losses during 2001. Average return on equity has been poor at -5%. Fair overall results on stability tests (3.1) based on a significant 37% decrease in enrollment during the period, a steep decline in premium revenue in 2002 and weak risk-adjusted capital in prior years. Rating is significantly influenced by the fair financial results of CIGNA Corp. Good liquidity (6.8) with sufficient resources (cash flows and marketable investments) to handle a spike in claims.
Other Rating Factors: Strong capitalization (7.3) based on excellent current risk-adjusted capital (severe loss scenario) reflecting significant improvement over results in 2001. High quality investment portfolio (9.6) containing no exposure to mortgages, junk bonds, or unaffiliated stocks.
Principal Business: Comp med (100%)
Mem Phys: 02: 5,535   **01:** 6,083   **02 MLR** 86%   **/ 02 Admin Exp** 14%
Enroll(000): Q1 03: 44   **02:** 55   **01:** 88   **Med Exp PMPM:** $138
Principal Investments: Cash and equiv (53%), other (47%)
Provider Compensation ($000): Bonus arrang ($103,839), FFS ($16,109), capitation ($5,370)
Total Member Encounters: Phys (163,970), non-phys (24,346)
Group Affiliation: CIGNA Corp
Licensed in: SC
Address: 146 Fairchild St, Charleston, SC 29492
Phone: (800) 962-8811   **Dom State:** SC   **Commenced Bus:** January 1987

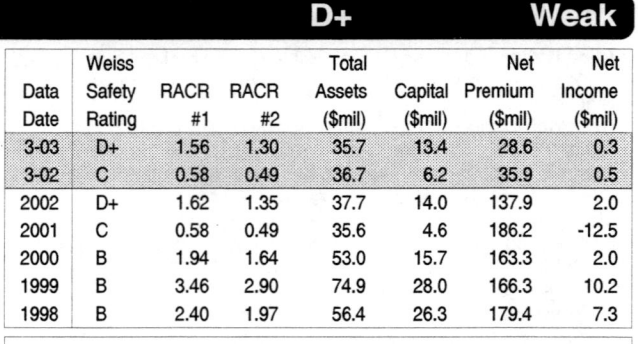

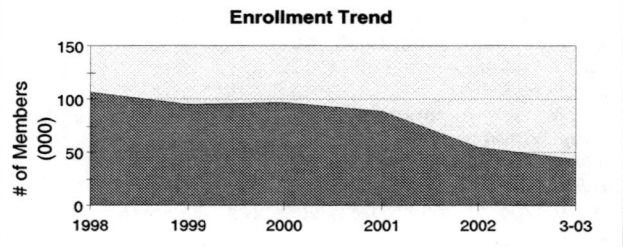

Data Date	Weiss Safety Rating	RACR #1	RACR #2	Total Assets ($mil)	Capital ($mil)	Net Premium ($mil)	Net Income ($mil)
3-03	D+	1.56	1.30	35.7	13.4	28.6	0.3
3-02	C	0.58	0.49	36.7	6.2	35.9	0.5
2002	D+	1.62	1.35	37.7	14.0	137.9	2.0
2001	C	0.58	0.49	35.6	4.6	186.2	-12.5
2000	B	1.94	1.64	53.0	15.7	163.3	2.0
1999	B	3.46	2.90	74.9	28.0	166.3	10.2
1998	B	2.40	1.97	56.4	26.3	179.4	7.3

Enrollment Trend (1998–3-03)

CIGNA HEALTHCARE OF ST LOUIS — C — Fair

Major Rating Factors: Fair overall results on stability tests (3.9 on a scale of 0 to 10). Rating is significantly influenced by the fair financial results of CIGNA Corp. Good overall profitability index (6.3) despite operating losses during 2000. Good liquidity (6.9) with sufficient resources (cash flows and marketable investments) to handle a spike in claims.
Other Rating Factors: Strong overall capitalization (7.9) based on excellent current risk-adjusted capital (severe loss scenario) despite some fluctuation in capital levels. High quality investment portfolio (9.4) containing no exposure to mortgages, junk bonds, or unaffiliated stocks.
Principal Business: Comp med (100%)
Mem Phys: 02: 3,074   **01:** 3,386   **02 MLR** 86%   **/ 02 Admin Exp** 7%
Enroll(000):   **02:** 11   **01:** 11   **Med Exp PMPM:** $214
Principal Investments: Cash and equiv (33%), other (67%)
Provider Compensation ($000): Contr fee ($23,534), FFS ($1,555), capitation ($1,011)
Total Member Encounters: Phys (75,936), non-phys (30,347)
Group Affiliation: CIGNA Corp
Licensed in: IL, MO
Address: 1 N Brentwood Suite 700, St Louis, MO 63105
Phone: (314) 726-7792   **Dom State:** MO   **Commenced Bus:** February 1986

Data Date	Weiss Safety Rating	RACR #1	RACR #2	Total Assets ($mil)	Capital ($mil)	Net Premium ($mil)	Net Income ($mil)
2002	C	2.09	1.74	11.2	5.2	32.9	1.8
2001	C	1.57	1.32	8.3	3.5	30.6	0.1
2000	C	2.13	1.79	8.1	2.8	17.4	-0.1
1999	C	3.01	2.52	9.3	3.2	13.0	0.5
1998	C+	2.56	2.30	8.4	4.2	26.4	1.9

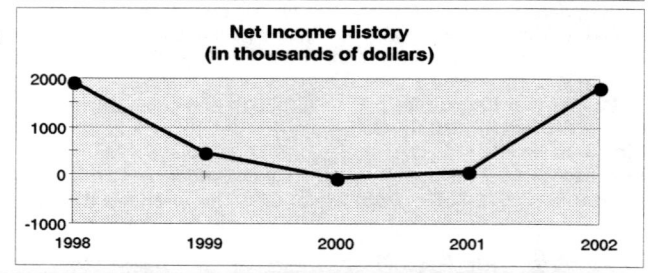

Net Income History (in thousands of dollars) (1998–2002)

CIGNA HEALTHCARE OF TENNESSEE INC — C — Fair

Major Rating Factors: Fair overall results on stability tests (4.5 on a scale of 0 to 10) based on an overall decline in enrollment over the past five years. Rating is significantly influenced by the fair financial results of CIGNA Corp. Good overall profitability index (5.3) despite operating losses during 2000 and 2001. Good liquidity (6.8) with sufficient resources (cash flows and marketable investments) to handle a spike in claims.
Other Rating Factors: Strong capitalization index (8.3) based on excellent current risk-adjusted capital (severe loss scenario) despite some fluctuation in capital levels. High quality investment portfolio (9.1) containing no exposure to mortgages, junk bonds, or unaffiliated stocks.
Principal Business: Comp med (100%)
Mem Phys: 02: 8,440   **01:** 7,400   **02 MLR** 79%   **/ 02 Admin Exp** 16%
Enroll(000): Q1 03: 78   **02:** 73   **01:** 85   **Med Exp PMPM:** $144
Principal Investments: Other (5%), cash and equiv (95%)
Provider Compensation ($000): Contr fee ($115,954), FFS ($12,072), capitation ($7,342)
Total Member Encounters: Phys (296,706), non-phys (45,767)
Group Affiliation: CIGNA Corp
Licensed in: TN
Address: 1000 Corporate Center Dr, Franklin, TN 37067
Phone: (615) 595-3000   **Dom State:** TN   **Commenced Bus:** November 1985

Data Date	Weiss Safety Rating	RACR #1	RACR #2	Total Assets ($mil)	Capital ($mil)	Net Premium ($mil)	Net Income ($mil)
3-03	C	2.39	1.99	45.9	19.6	52.1	2.7
3-02	C	2.26	1.91	50.7	20.0	40.5	2.8
2002	C	1.97	1.64	44.7	15.4	171.7	7.9
2001	C+	2.26	1.91	49.9	17.1	173.6	-0.1
2000	C+	1.49	1.27	55.1	13.7	209.4	-8.4
1999	B-	2.09	1.76	92.6	18.9	232.5	14.5
1998	C+	1.33	1.15	100.2	17.2	422.9	6.8

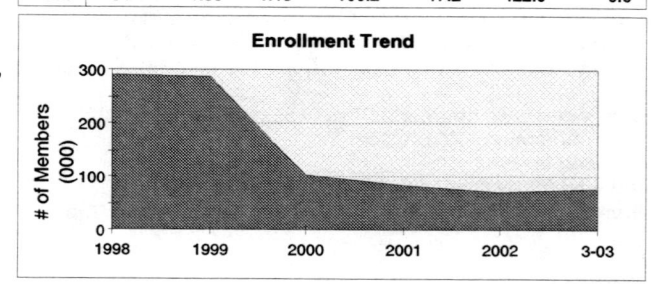

Enrollment Trend (1998–3-03)

Winter 2003 - 04   II. Analysis of Largest Companies

CIGNA HEALTHCARE OF TEXAS INC   D-   Weak

Major Rating Factors: Weak profitability index (0.8 on a scale of 0 to 10) with $30.9 million in losses in the last two years. Average return on equity has been poor at -50%. Fair capitalization (3.2) based on weak current risk-adjusted capital (moderate loss scenario) reflecting improvement over results in 1998. Fair overall results on stability tests (4.6) based on weak risk-adjusted capital in prior years. Rating is significantly influenced by the fair financial results of CIGNA Corp.
Other Rating Factors: Good liquidity (6.4) with sufficient resources (cash flows and marketable investments) to handle a spike in claims. High quality investment portfolio (9.9) containing no exposure to mortgages, junk bonds, or unaffiliated stocks.
Principal Business: Comp med (100%)
Mem Phys: 02: 15,764   **01:** 15,437   **02 MLR** 92%   **/ 02 Admin Exp** 15%
Enroll(000): Q1 03: 183   **02:** 198   **01:** 176   **Med Exp PMPM:** $187
Principal Investments: Cash and equiv (80%), other (20%)
Provider Compensation ($000): Contr fee ($286,823), capitation ($71,400), FFS ($41,122)
Total Member Encounters: Phys (633,938), non-phys (151,550)
Group Affiliation: CIGNA Corp
Licensed in: TX
Address: 6600 E Campus Circle Dr., Irving, TX 75063
Phone: (713) 552-7802   **Dom State:** TX   **Commenced Bus:** January 1996

Data Date	Weiss Safety Rating	RACR #1	RACR #2	Total Assets ($mil)	Capital ($mil)	Net Premium ($mil)	Net Income ($mil)
3-03	D-	0.66	0.55	90.6	13.9	122.5	-0.8
3-02	D	0.66	0.56	73.7	7.2	115.3	1.4
2002	D-	0.64	0.54	87.9	13.5	456.9	-13.5
2001	C-	0.66	0.56	78.9	7.8	319.9	-17.5
2000	C+	1.65	1.40	175.8	23.3	930.8	5.3
1999	C	2.27	1.96	147.2	22.1	730.7	0.4
1998	C	0.54	0.47	114.0	7.9	612.2	-2.9

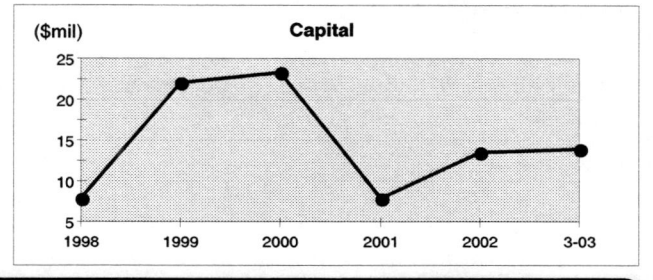

Capital chart 1998–3-03

CIGNA HEALTHCARE OF UTAH INC   D   Weak

Major Rating Factors: Weak profitability index (0.8 on a scale of 0 to 10) with operating losses during 1998 and 2001. Average return on equity has been poor at -8%. Poor capitalization (2.9) based on fair current risk-adjusted capital (moderate loss scenario). Fair overall results on stability tests (4.1) based on weak risk-adjusted capital in prior years, a significant 31% decrease in enrollment during the period. Rating is significantly influenced by the fair financial results of CIGNA Corp.
Other Rating Factors: Good liquidity (6.9) with sufficient resources (cash flows and marketable investments) to handle a spike in claims. High quality investment portfolio (9.9) containing no exposure to mortgages, junk bonds, or unaffiliated stocks.
Principal Business: Comp med (100%)
Mem Phys: 02: 1,989   **01:** 2,150   **02 MLR** 88%   **/ 02 Admin Exp** 13%
Enroll(000): Q1 03: 6   **02:** 7   **01:** 10   **Med Exp PMPM:** $117
Principal Investments: Cash and equiv (27%), other (73%)
Provider Compensation ($000): Contr fee ($9,168), FFS ($1,390), capitation ($1,183)
Total Member Encounters: Phys (15,389), non-phys (2,659)
Group Affiliation: CIGNA Corp
Licensed in: UT
Address: 5295 South 320 West Ste 280, Salt Lake City, UT 84107
Phone: (801) 265-2777   **Dom State:** UT   **Commenced Bus:** January 1986

Data Date	Weiss Safety Rating	RACR #1	RACR #2	Total Assets ($mil)	Capital ($mil)	Net Premium ($mil)	Net Income ($mil)
3-03	D	0.82	0.69	4.5	1.7	2.7	0.0
3-02	D	0.80	0.68	7.4	2.4	3.9	0.0
2002	D	0.83	0.69	5.4	1.7	13.2	0.1
2001	C-	0.77	0.66	7.7	1.5	12.2	-1.8
2000	C	6.10	4.95	6.1	4.6	5.9	0.8
1999	C	3.78	3.15	5.4	3.3	5.6	0.3
1998	C	1.29	1.16	5.5	2.1	6.5	-0.3

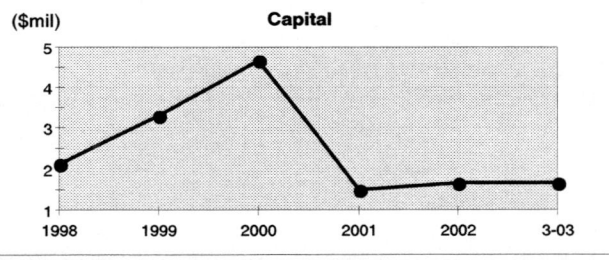

Capital chart 1998–3-03

CIGNA HEALTHCARE OF VIRGINIA INC   D+   Weak

Major Rating Factors: Weak profitability index (0.9 on a scale of 0 to 10) with operating losses during 2000 and 2001. Average return on equity has been poor at -4%. Fair overall results on stability tests (3.3) based on a steep decline in premium revenue in 2002, a significant 45% decrease in enrollment during the period. Rating is significantly influenced by the fair financial results of CIGNA Corp. Good liquidity (5.5) with sufficient resources (cash flows and marketable investments) to handle a spike in claims.
Other Rating Factors: Strong capitalization (8.6) based on excellent current risk-adjusted capital (severe loss scenario) reflecting improvement over results in 2000. High quality investment portfolio (9.2) containing no exposure to mortgages, junk bonds, or unaffiliated stocks.
Principal Business: Comp med (101%)
Mem Phys: 02: 6,673   **01:** 6,605   **02 MLR** 88%   **/ 02 Admin Exp** 12%
Enroll(000): Q1 03: 27   **02:** 38   **01:** 70   **Med Exp PMPM:** $115
Principal Investments: Cash and equiv (100%)
Provider Compensation ($000): FFS ($64,109), capitation ($12,327), contr fee ($2,468)
Total Member Encounters: Phys (91,046), non-phys (16,336)
Group Affiliation: CIGNA Corp
Licensed in: VA
Address: 7501 Boulders View Dr Ste 600, Richmond, VA 23225
Phone: (804) 267-5100   **Dom State:** VA   **Commenced Bus:** May 1984

Data Date	Weiss Safety Rating	RACR #1	RACR #2	Total Assets ($mil)	Capital ($mil)	Net Premium ($mil)	Net Income ($mil)
3-03	D+	2.67	2.22	34.0	15.0	15.0	0.3
3-02	C	1.72	1.45	46.9	9.1	23.3	1.2
2002	D+	2.38	1.98	25.7	13.2	84.6	1.3
2001	C	1.71	1.45	50.9	11.7	127.1	-6.0
2000	B-	1.31	1.08	48.8	13.9	189.5	-7.1
1999	B-	2.62	2.17	61.1	17.2	140.0	4.5
1998	B-	4.48	4.05	54.0	21.5	141.7	8.8

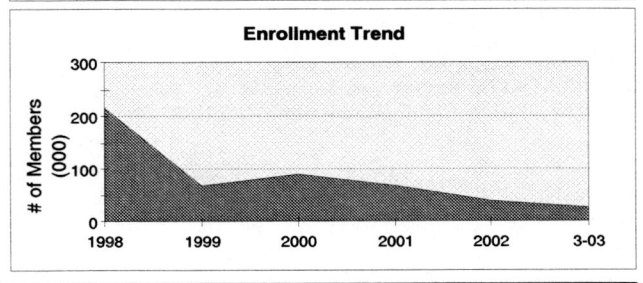

Enrollment Trend chart 1998–3-03

www.WeissRatings.com   * Denotes a Weiss Recommended Company

II. Analysis of Largest Companies — Winter 2003 - 04

CIGNA INS SERVICES CO — C+ Fair

Major Rating Factors: Good overall profitability index (7.0 on a scale of 0 to 10). Strong capitalization index (10.0) based on excellent current risk-adjusted capital (severe loss scenario). High quality investment portfolio (9.7) containing no exposure to mortgages, junk bonds, or unaffiliated stocks.
Other Rating Factors: Excellent liquidity (9.4) with ample operational cash flow and liquid investments.
Principal Business: Comp med (100%)
Mem Phys: 02: N/A **01:** N/A **02 MLR** 68% **/ 02 Admin Exp** -3%
Enroll(000): Q1 03: 19 **02:** 20 **01:** 30 **Med Exp PMPM:** $5
Principal Investments: Cash and equiv (40%), other (60%)
Provider Compensation ($000): FFS ($1,929), capitation ($11)
Total Member Encounters: Phys (4,424), non-phys (945)
Group Affiliation: CIGNA Corp
Licensed in: SC
Address: 146 Fairchild Street, Charleston, SC 29492
Phone: (800) 962-8811 **Dom State:** SC **Commenced Bus:** March 1992

Data Date	Weiss Safety Rating	RACR #1	RACR #2	Total Assets ($mil)	Capital ($mil)	Net Premium ($mil)	Net Income ($mil)
3-03	C+	8.22	6.85	11.7	10.5	0.3	0.0
3-02	N/A	N/A	N/A	N/A	N/A	N/A	N/A
2002	N/A	N/A	N/A	11.7	10.4	2.2	1.0
2001	N/A	N/A	N/A	10.9	9.3	3.4	N/A
2000	N/A	N/A	N/A	18.9	8.3	1.9	N/A
1999	C+	2.34	2.10	15.0	6.9	6.4	3.4
1998	C	2.50	2.25	6.7	4.6	5.2	2.3

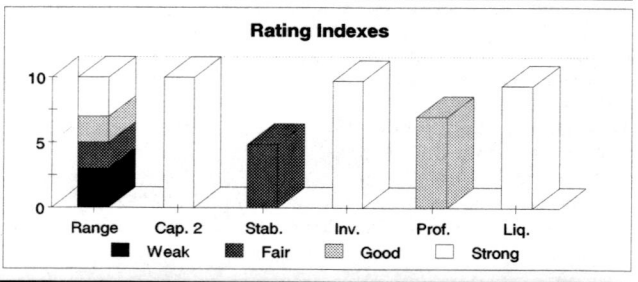

Rating Indexes (Range, Cap. 2, Stab., Inv., Prof., Liq.) — Weak / Fair / Good / Strong

CIGNA INSURANCE GROUP INC — C- Fair

Major Rating Factors: Weak profitability index (0.9 on a scale of 0 to 10) with operating losses during 1998 and 1999. Strong capitalization index (9.7) based on excellent current risk-adjusted capital (severe loss scenario). High quality investment portfolio (9.6) containing no exposure to mortgages, junk bonds, or unaffiliated stocks.
Other Rating Factors: Excellent liquidity (7.5) with ample operational cash flow and liquid investments.
Principal Business: Comp med (100%)
Mem Phys: 02: N/A **01:** N/A **02 MLR** 99% **/ 02 Admin Exp** 3%
Enroll(000): Q1 03: 8 **02:** 8 **01:** 17 **Med Exp PMPM:** $11
Principal Investments: Cash and equiv (48%), other (52%)
Provider Compensation ($000): FFS ($2,107)
Total Member Encounters: Phys (1,392), non-phys (1,579)
Group Affiliation: CIGNA Corp
Licensed in: NH
Address: 2 College Park Dr, Hooksett, NH 03106
Phone: (603) 225-5077 **Dom State:** NH **Commenced Bus:** July 1990

Data Date	Weiss Safety Rating	RACR #1	RACR #2	Total Assets ($mil)	Capital ($mil)	Net Premium ($mil)	Net Income ($mil)
3-03	C-	3.54	2.95	2.1	1.6	0.5	0.0
3-02	N/A	N/A	N/A	N/A	N/A	N/A	N/A
2002	N/A	N/A	N/A	2.2	1.6	1.8	0.1
2001	N/A	N/A	N/A	1.9	1.0	1.9	N/A
2000	U	2.25	1.99	2.3	1.6	3.6	0.3
1999	C	1.64	1.40	2.8	1.3	4.3	-1.0
1998	U	1.23	1.11	1.9	0.8	3.3	-0.6

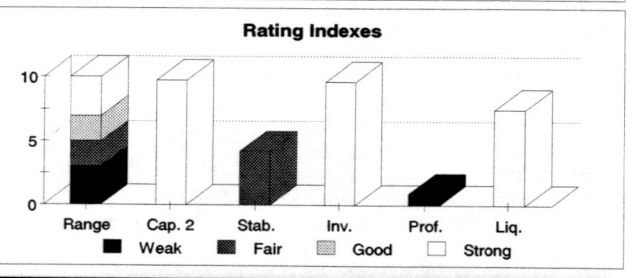

Rating Indexes (Range, Cap. 2, Stab., Inv., Prof., Liq.) — Weak / Fair / Good / Strong

CIGNA LIFE INSURANCE COMPANY OF NEW YORK — C- Fair

Major Rating Factors: Fair overall results on stability tests (3.2 on a scale of 0 to 10) including fair financial strength of affiliated CIGNA Group. Good quality investment portfolio (6.6) despite mixed results such as: large holdings of BBB rated bonds but moderate junk bond exposure. Good overall profitability (5.9). Despite its volitility, return on equity has been excellent over the last five years averaging 22.1%.
Other Rating Factors: Strong capitalization (9.0) based on excellent risk adjusted capital (severe loss scenario). Excellent liquidity (7.4).
Principal Business: Group health insurance (99%) and group life insurance (1%).
Principal Investments: NonCMO investment grade bonds (82%), noninv. grade bonds (7%), CMOs and structured securities (5%), and cash (5%).
Investments in Affiliates: None
Group Affiliation: CIGNA Group
Licensed in: AL, DC, MO, NY, PA, TN
Commenced Business: December 1965
Address: 499 Washington Blvd, Jersey City, NJ 07310-1995
Phone: (212) 618-5757 **Domicile State:** NY **NAIC Code:** 64548

Data Date	Weiss Safety Rating	RACR #1	RACR #2	Total Assets ($mil)	Capital ($mil)	Net Premium ($mil)	Net Income ($mil)
6-03	C-	3.73	2.33	310.0	63.4	40.0	6.9
6-02	C-	2.92	1.98	281.7	44.8	41.9	1.6
2002	C-	3.70	2.35	299.1	62.4	85.0	10.1
2001	C+	2.60	1.73	270.6	43.4	93.3	-1.8
2000	C+	3.73	2.54	267.2	62.5	89.1	21.1
1999	C+	2.91	1.83	403.1	53.0	78.2	16.5
1998	C+	2.95	1.85	403.3	52.4	72.0	15.1

CIGNA Group
Composite Group Rating: C-
Largest Group Members

	Assets ($mil)	Weiss Safety Rating
CONNECTICUT GENERAL LIFE INS CO	66798	C-
LIFE INS CO OF NORTH AMERICA	4814	D
CIGNA WORLDWIDE INS CO	313	C-
CIGNA LIFE INS CO OF NEW YORK	299	C-
CIGNA HEALTHCARE OF CALIFORNIA INC	199	C

Winter 2003 - 04
II. Analysis of Largest Companies

CIGNA WORLDWIDE INSURANCE COMPANY — C- Fair

Major Rating Factors: Fair overall results on stability tests (3.1 on a scale of 0 to 10) including potential financial drain due to affiliation with CIGNA Group and fair risk adjusted capital in prior years. Good quality investment portfolio (6.0) despite mixed results such as: no exposure to mortgages and substantial holdings of BBB bonds but no exposure to junk bonds. Good overall profitability (6.9).
Other Rating Factors: Strong capitalization (7.5) based on excellent risk adjusted capital (severe loss scenario). Excellent liquidity (8.0).
Principal Business: Individual life insurance (67%), group health insurance (15%), individual health insurance (9%), reinsurance (7%), and other lines (3%).
Principal Investments: NonCMO investment grade bonds (85%), cash (9%), common & preferred stock (3%), and noninv. grade bonds (2%).
Investments in Affiliates: 1%
Group Affiliation: CIGNA Group
Licensed in: DE
Commenced Business: May 1979
Address: One Beaver Valley Rd, Wilmington, DE 19803
Phone: (302) 479-6617 **Domicile State:** DE **NAIC Code:** 90859

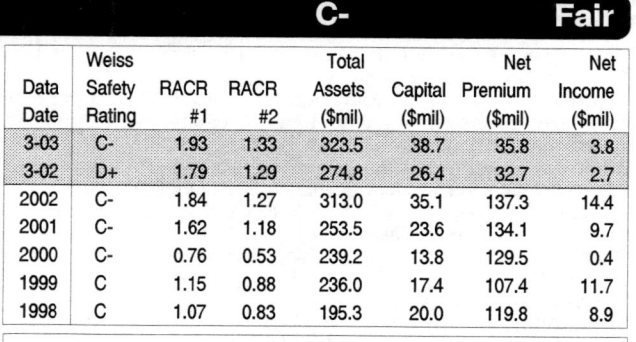

Data Date	Weiss Safety Rating	RACR #1	RACR #2	Total Assets ($mil)	Capital ($mil)	Net Premium ($mil)	Net Income ($mil)
3-03	C-	1.93	1.33	323.5	38.7	35.8	3.8
3-02	D+	1.79	1.29	274.8	26.4	32.7	2.7
2002	C-	1.84	1.27	313.0	35.1	137.3	14.4
2001	C-	1.62	1.18	253.5	23.6	134.1	9.7
2000	C-	0.76	0.53	239.2	13.8	129.5	0.4
1999	C	1.15	0.88	236.0	17.4	107.4	11.7
1998	C	1.07	0.83	195.3	20.0	119.8	8.9

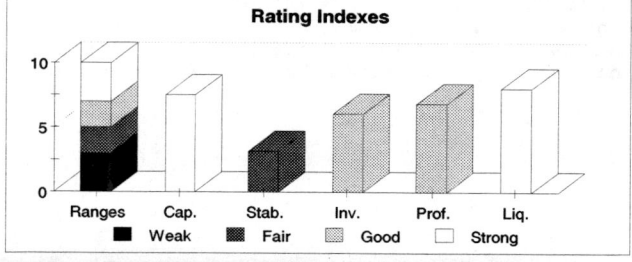

CIMARRON HEALTH PLAN INC — D Weak

Major Rating Factors: Weak profitability index (2.7 on a scale of 0 to 10) due to a decline in earnings during 2002. Return on equity has been fair, averaging 9% over the last five years. Poor capitalization index (1.8) based on weak current risk-adjusted capital (moderate loss scenario). Good overall results on stability tests (5.8) despite rapid enrollment growth during the past five years.
Other Rating Factors: Good liquidity (6.9) with sufficient resources (cash flows and marketable investments) to handle a spike in claims. High quality investment portfolio (9.5) containing no exposure to mortgages, junk bonds, or unaffiliated stocks.
Principal Business: Medicaid (66%), comp med (27%), FEHB (7%).
Mem Phys: 02: 7,546 **01:** 7,107 **02 MLR** 88% **/ 02 Admin Exp** 12%
Enroll(000): Q1 03: 109 **02:** 112 **01:** 111 **Med Exp PMPM:** $207
Principal Investments: Cash and equiv (99%), other (1%)
Provider Compensation ($000): Bonus arrang ($186,478), contr fee ($52,081), capitation ($33,103)
Total Member Encounters: Phys (602,223), non-phys (963,565)
Group Affiliation: Health Care Horizons
Licensed in: NM
Address: 7801 Academy NE Suite 205, Albuquerque, NM 87109
Phone: (505) 342-4660 **Dom State:** NM **Commenced Bus:** December 1993

Data Date	Weiss Safety Rating	RACR #1	RACR #2	Total Assets ($mil)	Capital ($mil)	Net Premium ($mil)	Net Income ($mil)
3-03	D	0.48	0.40	50.2	16.0	81.4	0.2
3-02	D-	0.45	0.38	44.0	12.9	72.9	0.0
2002	D	0.47	0.39	56.8	15.9	314.1	0.4
2001	D-	0.45	0.38	48.7	12.8	259.6	1.0
2000	D	0.45	0.38	37.6	8.8	198.7	-2.1
1999	D	0.22	0.19	23.2	3.2	134.8	-0.5
1998	D-	0.36	0.31	22.5	4.3	111.9	2.8

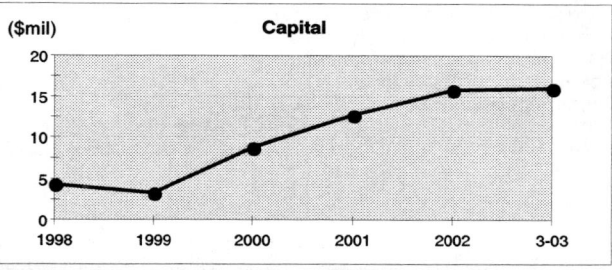

CITICORP LIFE INSURANCE COMPANY * — B+ Good

Major Rating Factors: Good overall results on stability tests (5.0 on a scale of 0 to 10). Stability strengths include excellent risk diversification. Good quality investment portfolio (6.4) with no exposure to mortgages and minimal holdings in junk bonds. Strong capitalization (9.3) based on excellent risk adjusted capital (severe loss scenario). Moreover, capital levels have been consistently high over the last five years.
Other Rating Factors: Excellent profitability (9.2) with operating gains in each of the last five years. Excellent liquidity (10.0).
Principal Business: Reinsurance (93%), individual annuities (3%), group health insurance (2%), credit life insurance (1%), and group life insurance (1%).
Principal Investments: NonCMO investment grade bonds (34%), CMOs and structured securities (33%), common & preferred stock (31%), and noninv. grade bonds (2%).
Investments in Affiliates: 31%
Group Affiliation: Citigroup Inc
Licensed in: All states except NY, PR
Commenced Business: February 1972
Address: 3225 North Central Avenue, Phoenix, AZ 85012
Phone: (860) 308-1000 **Domicile State:** AZ **NAIC Code:** 80322

Data Date	Weiss Safety Rating	RACR #1	RACR #2	Total Assets ($mil)	Capital ($mil)	Net Premium ($mil)	Net Income ($mil)
6-03	B+	2.73	2.55	1,058.7	772.5	12.0	14.1
6-02	B	2.84	2.59	1,023.1	703.4	14.9	6.0
2002	B	2.67	2.53	1,010.3	738.3	28.7	25.8
2001	B	2.79	2.58	999.0	676.0	37.3	37.1
2000	B	3.15	2.86	948.0	599.1	67.6	31.9
1999	B	3.73	3.32	895.7	525.6	107.8	30.2
1998	B	4.36	3.72	764.5	464.6	146.2	62.0

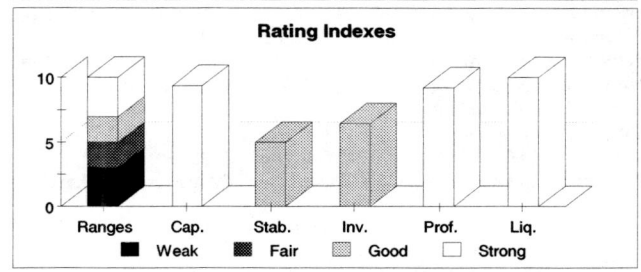

www.WeissRatings.com   * Denotes a Weiss Recommended Company

II. Analysis of Largest Companies

CNA GROUP LIFE ASSURANCE COMPANY   C   Fair

Major Rating Factors: Fair overall results on stability tests (4.1 on a scale of 0 to 10) including fair financial strength of affiliated CNA Financial Corp. Fair quality investment portfolio (4.2) with large holdings of BBB rated bonds in addition to junk bond exposure equal to 92% of capital. Weak profitability (2.0) with operating losses during the first six months of 2003.
Other Rating Factors: Strong capitalization (7.1) based on excellent risk adjusted capital (severe loss scenario). Excellent liquidity (7.6).
Principal Business: Reinsurance (99%) and group health insurance (1%).
Principal Investments: NonCMO investment grade bonds (71%), CMOs and structured securities (16%), noninv. grade bonds (12%), and common & preferred stock (1%).
Investments in Affiliates: None
Group Affiliation: CNA Financial Corp
Licensed in: All states except CA, NH, PR
Commenced Business: May 1960
Address: CNA Plaza, Chicago, IL 60685
Phone: (847) 940-7550   **Domicile State:** IL   **NAIC Code:** 74268

Data Date	Weiss Safety Rating	RACR #1	RACR #2	Total Assets ($mil)	Capital ($mil)	Net Premium ($mil)	Net Income ($mil)
6-03	C	1.71	1.08	3,177.3	346.8	673.7	-44.1
6-02	C	2.09	1.36	2,933.7	394.2	649.0	-8.5
2002	C	1.86	1.21	2,968.3	391.8	1,314.7	-44.7
2001	C	1.72	1.13	2,465.1	337.6	1,250.5	-73.6
2000	C	4.96	4.47	18.4	16.4	0.0	0.6
1999	C	3.55	3.20	29.1	15.8	12.0	-0.3
1998	C	3.76	3.01	27.2	16.0	11.6	0.5

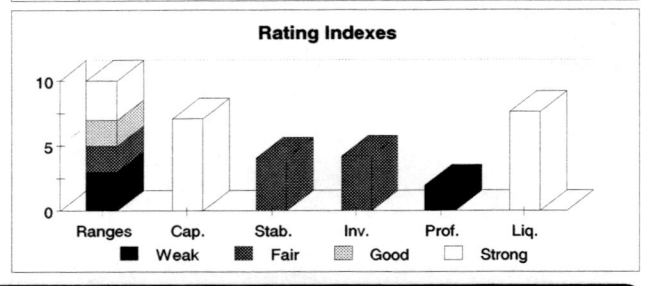

Rating Indexes

COLONIAL LIFE & ACCIDENT INSURANCE COMPANY   C-   Fair

Major Rating Factors: Fair overall results on stability tests (3.2 on a scale of 0 to 10) including fair financial strength of affiliated UnumProvident Corp and weak risk adjusted capital in prior years. Fair quality investment portfolio (4.7) with large holdings of BBB rated bonds in addition to junk bond exposure equal to 65% of capital. Good liquidity (6.9).
Other Rating Factors: Strong capitalization (7.1) based on excellent risk adjusted capital (severe loss scenario). Excellent profitability (8.1) with operating gains in each of the last five years.
Principal Business: Individual health insurance (75%), individual life insurance (18%), group health insurance (5%), group life insurance (1%), and reinsurance (1%).
Principal Investments: NonCMO investment grade bonds (63%), CMOs and structured securities (19%), noninv. grade bonds (11%), mortgages in good standing (4%), and policy loans (3%).
Investments in Affiliates: None
Group Affiliation: UnumProvident Corp
Licensed in: All states except NY
Commenced Business: September 1939
Address: 6335 S. East Street, Suite A, Indianapolis, IN 46227
Phone: (803) 798-7000   **Domicile State:** SC   **NAIC Code:** 62049

Data Date	Weiss Safety Rating	RACR #1	RACR #2	Total Assets ($mil)	Capital ($mil)	Net Premium ($mil)	Net Income ($mil)
6-03	C-	1.68	1.07	1,262.3	186.1	372.0	19.9
6-02	B-	1.44	0.90	1,115.8	154.8	328.0	-1.2
2002	C-	1.72	1.06	1,193.5	187.7	666.3	27.6
2001	B-	1.99	1.23	1,131.3	217.1	644.9	62.2
2000	B-	1.62	1.00	1,095.3	156.2	590.7	58.1
1999	B-	1.64	1.00	1,064.4	142.4	579.6	48.6
1998	C+	0.50	0.45	984.9	131.1	567.7	41.5

UnumProvident Corp Composite Group Rating: C- Largest Group Members	Assets ($mil)	Weiss Safety Rating
UNUM LIFE INS CO OF AMERICA	10982	C-
PROVIDENT LIFE ACCIDENT INS CO	8557	C-
PAUL REVERE LIFE INS CO	4976	C-
COLONIAL LIFE ACCIDENT INS CO	1194	C-
FIRST UNUM LIFE INS CO	1097	C-

COLORADO ACCESS   C   Fair

Major Rating Factors: Fair profitability index (4.9 on a scale of 0 to 10) with operating gains in each of the last five years. Fair capitalization (4.9) based on good current risk-adjusted capital (severe loss scenario) reflecting some improvement over results in 2001. Good overall results on stability tests (5.3) despite fair risk-adjusted capital in prior years, rapid enrollment growth during the past five years.
Other Rating Factors: Good liquidity (6.9) with sufficient resources (cash flows and marketable investments) to handle a spike in claims. High quality investment portfolio (9.9) containing no exposure to mortgages, junk bonds, or unaffiliated stocks.
Principal Business: Medicaid (100%)
Mem Phys: 02: 5,581   **01:** 4,755   **02 MLR** 88%   / **02 Admin Exp** 12%
Enroll(000): Q1 03: 211   **02:** 207   **01:** 182   **Med Exp PMPM:** $93
Principal Investments: Cash and equiv (99%), other (1%)
Provider Compensation ($000): Capitation ($138,380), contr fee ($68,397)
Total Member Encounters: Phys (245,642), non-phys (27,364)
Group Affiliation: None
Licensed in: CO
Address: 10065 E Harvard Ave, Denver, CO 80231
Phone: (720) 744-5100   **Dom State:** CO   **Commenced Bus:** January 1995

Data Date	Weiss Safety Rating	RACR #1	RACR #2	Total Assets ($mil)	Capital ($mil)	Net Premium ($mil)	Net Income ($mil)
3-03	C	0.91	0.76	69.3	14.6	62.1	0.0
3-02	C	0.72	0.63	56.3	10.9	57.8	0.1
2002	C	0.83	0.69	52.1	11.3	248.2	3.1
2001	C	0.72	0.63	45.2	10.1	209.6	1.2
2000	C+	1.10	1.00	55.5	9.6	184.7	1.1
1999	C+	1.22	1.04	48.5	13.2	143.8	2.4
1998	C+	1.21	1.04	36.9	1.0	98.7	4.6

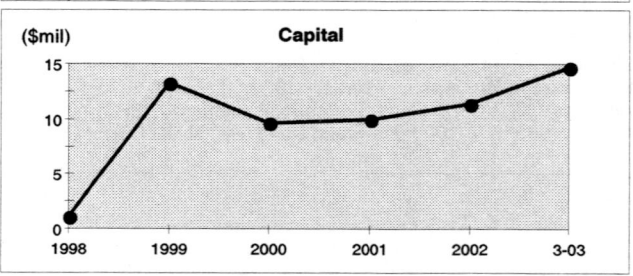

Capital

Winter 2003 - 04   II. Analysis of Largest Companies

COLUMBIA UNITED PROVIDERS INC *   B+   Good

Major Rating Factors: Good overall profitability index (6.5 on a scale of 0 to 10) despite a decline in earnings during 2002. Good capitalization (6.8) based on excellent current risk-adjusted capital (severe loss scenario) reflecting improvement over results in 1999. Good liquidity (6.9) with sufficient resources (cash flows and marketable investments) to handle a spike in claims.
Other Rating Factors: High quality investment portfolio (9.9) containing little or no exposure to mortgages, junk bonds, or unaffiliated stocks.
Principal Business: Medicaid (82%), comp med (18%).
Mem Phys: 02: 750 **01:** 700 **02 MLR** 90% **/ 02 Admin Exp** 11%
Enroll(000): Q1 03: 43 **02:** 42 **01:** 40 **Med Exp PMPM:** $124
Principal Investments: Cash and equiv (46%), nonaffiliate common stock (3%), other (51%).
Provider Compensation ($000): Capitation ($39,537), FFS ($15,586), contr fee ($5,832).
Total Member Encounters: Phys (144,844), non-phys (15,867)
Group Affiliation: HealthSystems Group
Licensed in: WA
Address: 19120 SE 34th Street #201, Vancouver, WA 98683
Phone: (360) 896-7093 **Dom State:** WA **Commenced Bus:** January 1994

Data Date	Weiss Safety Rating	RACR #1	RACR #2	Total Assets ($mil)	Capital ($mil)	Net Premium ($mil)	Net Income ($mil)
3-03	B+	1.21	1.01	13.4	7.7	18.7	0.2
3-02	B	1.30	1.10	13.5	7.8	17.1	0.4
2002	B+	1.20	1.00	18.4	7.6	68.5	0.2
2001	B	1.30	1.11	13.7	7.6	59.8	1.1
2000	C+	0.97	0.85	10.3	6.6	33.8	0.8
1999	C	1.31	0.79	10.2	6.3	26.2	1.6
1998	C	1.18	0.81	8.6	4.8	21.8	0.5

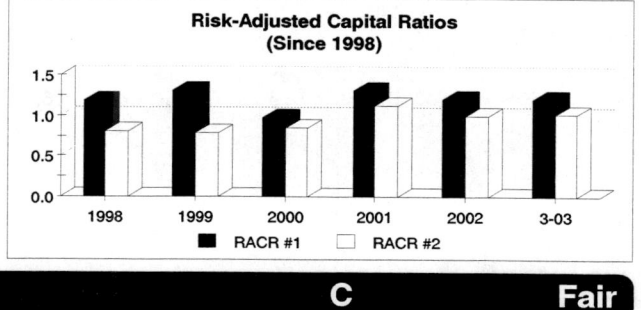

Risk-Adjusted Capital Ratios (Since 1998)

COMANCHE COUNTY HOSPITAL AUTHORITY   C   Fair

Major Rating Factors: Fair capitalization (3.3 on a scale of 0 to 10) based on weak current risk-adjusted capital (moderate loss scenario). Fair overall results on stability tests (4.7) based on weak risk-adjusted capital in prior years. Good overall profitability index (6.7) despite a decline in earnings during 2002
Other Rating Factors: High quality investment portfolio (9.9) containing no exposure to mortgages, junk bonds, or unaffiliated stocks. Excellent liquidity (7.0) with ample operational cash flow and liquid investments.
Principal Business: Medicaid (100%).
Mem Phys: 02: 594 **01:** 580 **02 MLR** 86% **/ 02 Admin Exp** 10%
Enroll(000): Q1 03: 8 **02:** 9 **01:** 10 **Med Exp PMPM:** $148
Principal Investments: Cash and equiv (91%), other (9%).
Provider Compensation ($000): FFS ($7,175), capitation ($5,802), contr fee ($4,345).
Total Member Encounters: Phys (51,549), non-phys (3,532)
Group Affiliation: None
Licensed in: OK
Address: 3401 NW Gore Blvd, Lawton, OK 73505
Phone: (580) 357-6684 **Dom State:** OK **Commenced Bus:** July 1996

Data Date	Weiss Safety Rating	RACR #1	RACR #2	Total Assets ($mil)	Capital ($mil)	Net Premium ($mil)	Net Income ($mil)
3-03	C	0.67	0.56	3.7	1.8	4.3	-0.3
3-02	C	0.79	0.67	5.2	2.6	5.1	0.2
2002	C	0.75	0.62	4.1	2.1	19.7	0.7
2001	C	0.79	0.67	4.5	2.3	19.5	1.5
2000	D-	0.84	0.72	4.1	1.8	16.3	0.8
1999	D-	0.48	0.41	4.2	1.0	15.5	-1.0
1998	D-	0.44	0.38	2.7	0.8	11.7	-0.7

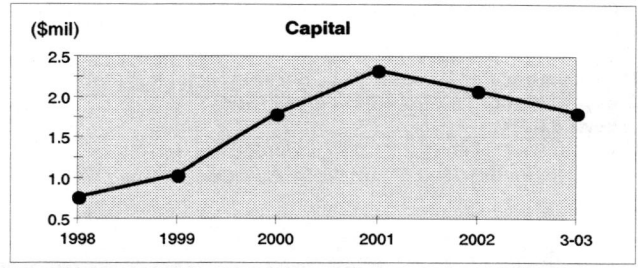

Capital ($mil)

COMBINED INSURANCE COMPANY OF AMERICA   C   Fair

Major Rating Factors: Fair overall results on stability tests (3.1 on a scale of 0 to 10). Good quality investment portfolio (6.2) despite mixed results such as: substantial holdings of BBB bonds but moderate junk bond exposure. Strong current capitalization (7.5) based on excellent risk adjusted capital (severe loss scenario) reflecting improvement over results in 2001.
Other Rating Factors: Excellent profitability (7.7). Excellent liquidity (7.7).
Principal Business: Individual health insurance (69%), reinsurance (15%), group health insurance (9%), individual life insurance (5%), and group life insurance (2%).
Principal Investments: NonCMO investment grade bonds (67%), common & preferred stock (13%), noninv. grade bonds (9%), CMOs and structured securities (5%), and misc. investments (6%).
Investments in Affiliates: 14%
Group Affiliation: Aon Corp
Licensed in: All states except NY
Commenced Business: December 1922
Address: 123 N Wacker Dr, Chicago, IL 60606
Phone: (312) 701-3000 **Domicile State:** IL **NAIC Code:** 62146

Data Date	Weiss Safety Rating	RACR #1	RACR #2	Total Assets ($mil)	Capital ($mil)	Net Premium ($mil)	Net Income ($mil)
6-03	C	1.74	1.34	2,408.5	594.3	570.3	28.4
6-02	C	1.11	0.87	2,703.6	445.2	631.6	-99.1
2002	C	1.45	1.12	2,260.9	501.5	1,231.7	-35.2
2001	C	1.15	0.89	2,989.9	454.8	1,069.5	18.4
2000	C	1.50	1.06	3,335.4	453.8	1,156.2	138.1
1999	C	1.38	0.99	3,469.0	453.4	1,362.6	113.1
1998	C+	1.76	1.21	3,502.2	593.6	1,246.7	239.4

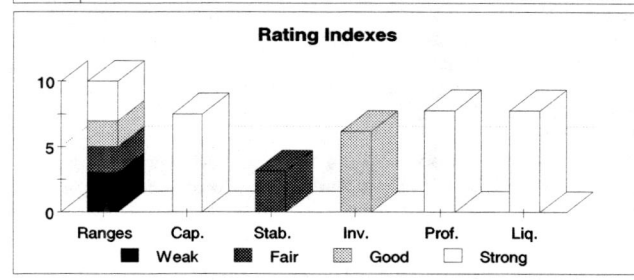

Rating Indexes

www.WeissRatings.com   139   * Denotes a Weiss Recommended Company

II. Analysis of Largest Companies

Winter 2003 - 04

COMBINED LIFE INSURANCE COMPANY OF NEW YORK — C+ — Fair

Major Rating Factors: Fair overall results on stability tests (3.1 on a scale of 0 to 10) including fair financial strength of affiliated Aon Corp. Good overall profitability (6.9). Excellent expense controls. Return on equity has been excellent over the last five years averaging 23.9%. Strong capitalization (7.4) based on excellent risk adjusted capital (severe loss scenario).
Other Rating Factors: High quality investment portfolio (8.6). Excellent liquidity (8.3).
Principal Business: Individual health insurance (68%), group health insurance (18%), and individual life insurance (14%).
Principal Investments: NonCMO investment grade bonds (91%), common & preferred stock (2%), policy loans (2%), noninv. grade bonds (2%), and misc. investments (3%).
Investments in Affiliates: None
Group Affiliation: Aon Corp
Licensed in: FL, IL, NY
Commenced Business: June 1971
Address: 11 British Anerican Blvd, Latham, NY 12110
Phone: (518) 220-9333 **Domicile State:** NY **NAIC Code:** 78697

Data Date	Weiss Safety Rating	RACR #1	RACR #2	Total Assets ($mil)	Capital ($mil)	Net Premium ($mil)	Net Income ($mil)
6-03	C+	1.70	1.28	300.0	46.0	65.5	6.1
6-02	B-	2.20	1.64	285.0	71.2	63.6	0.0
2002	B-	1.51	1.14	273.2	40.2	126.1	6.9
2001	B	2.66	1.95	268.0	68.8	75.6	13.7
2000	B	1.88	1.37	290.0	50.4	104.3	17.2
1999	B	2.26	1.62	297.5	60.6	100.0	11.8
1998	B	3.00	2.14	295.9	75.3	94.7	14.7

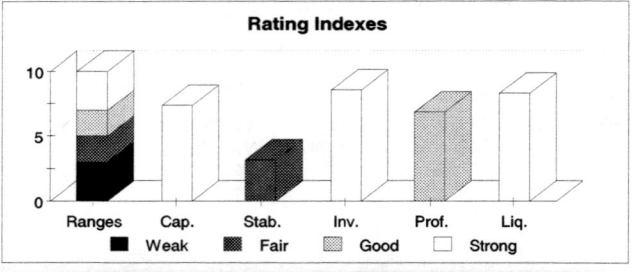

Rating Indexes (Ranges, Cap., Stab., Inv., Prof., Liq.) — Weak / Fair / Good / Strong

COMMUNITY CARE PLAN — C — Fair

Major Rating Factors: Fair capitalization (4.4 on a scale of 0 to 10) based on fair current risk-adjusted capital (moderate loss scenario) reflecting improvement over results in 2000. Excellent profitability (8.1). High quality investment portfolio (8.7) containing no exposure to mortgages, junk bonds, or unaffiliated stocks.
Other Rating Factors: Excellent overall results on stability tests (7.2) based on consistent premium and capital growth in the last five years but rapid enrollment growth during the past five years. Excellent liquidity (7.1) with ample operational cash flow and liquid investments.
Principal Business: Medicaid (100%).
Mem Phys: 01: 954 **00:** 810 **01 MLR** 89% **/ 01 Admin Exp** 8%
Enroll(000): Q2 02: 35 **01:** 31 **00:** 22 **Med Exp PMPM:** $123
Principal Investments: Cash and equiv (100%).
Provider Compensation ($000): Bonus arrang ($24,699), contr fee ($5,149), FFS ($3,841), capitation ($3,012).
Total Member Encounters: Phys (68,738), non-phys (3,075)
Group Affiliation: Metropolitan Health Corp
Licensed in: MI
Address: 2100 Ratbrook Dr SE, Grand Rapids, MI 49546
Phone: (616) 252-4500 **Dom State:** MI **Commenced Bus:** June 1996

Data Date	Weiss Safety Rating	RACR #1	RACR #2	Total Assets ($mil)	Capital ($mil)	Net Premium ($mil)	Net Income ($mil)
6-02	C	0.83	0.70	13.4	5.9	25.9	0.5
6-01	D	0.50	0.42	7.2	3.4	20.9	0.1
2001	C	0.82	0.69	11.7	5.3	43.8	2.0
2000	D	0.48	0.40	7.2	3.3	30.8	1.3
1999	N/A	N/A	N/A	5.2	2.1	21.7	N/A
1998	N/A	N/A	N/A	2.9	0.9	8.5	N/A
1997	N/A	N/A	N/A	1.5	0.8	4.5	N/A

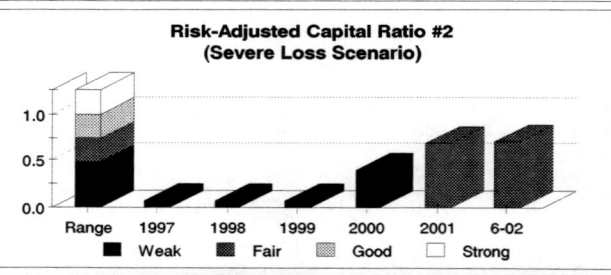

Risk-Adjusted Capital Ratio #2 (Severe Loss Scenario) — Range, 1997, 1998, 1999, 2000, 2001, 6-02 — Weak / Fair / Good / Strong

COMMUNITY FIRST HEALTH PLANS INC — C- — Fair

Major Rating Factors: Weak profitability index (1.8 on a scale of 0 to 10) with operating losses during 2002. Poor capitalization index (0.0) based on weak current risk-adjusted capital (severe loss scenario). Furthermore, this low level of risk-adjusted capital has been consistent in previous years. Weak liquidity (0.2) as a spike in claims may stretch capacity.
Other Rating Factors: Good overall results on stability tests (5.2) despite weak risk-adjusted capital in prior years, rapid premium growth over the last five years and rapid enrollment growth during the past five years. High quality investment portfolio (8.7) containing no exposure to mortgages, junk bonds, or unaffiliated stocks.
Principal Business: Comp med (62%), Medicaid (38%).
Mem Phys: 02: 3,336 **01:** 2,218 **02 MLR** 96% **/ 02 Admin Exp** 8%
Enroll(000): Q1 03: 97 **02:** 98 **01:** 81 **Med Exp PMPM:** $134
Principal Investments: Cash and equiv (32%), other (68%).
Provider Compensation ($000): Contr fee ($134,127), capitation ($3,805).
Total Member Encounters: Phys (567,184), non-phys (241,553)
Group Affiliation: Community First Group
Licensed in: TX
Address: 4801 NW Loop 410 Ste 1000, San Antonio, TX 78229
Phone: (210) 227-2347 **Dom State:** TX **Commenced Bus:** October 1995

Data Date	Weiss Safety Rating	RACR #1	RACR #2	Total Assets ($mil)	Capital ($mil)	Net Premium ($mil)	Net Income ($mil)
3-03	C-	0.29	0.25	27.4	5.2	40.6	0.1
3-02	D	0.43	0.37	27.0	5.9	35.3	0.6
2002	C-	0.32	0.27	29.0	5.7	149.9	-2.6
2001	D	0.43	0.37	23.7	5.3	106.6	0.7
2000	D+	0.65	0.55	15.6	4.5	66.3	1.1
1999	D	1.08	0.92	14.5	3.2	46.4	0.0
1998	C-	1.30	1.09	11.4	3.9	36.2	0.5

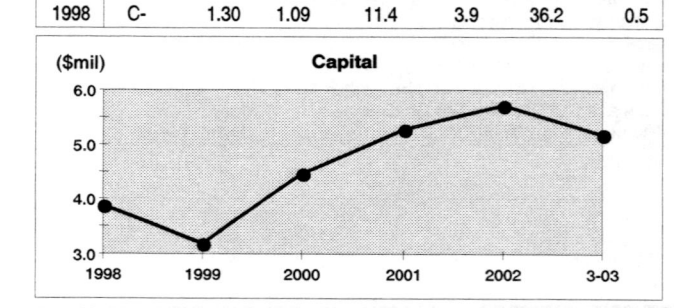

Capital ($mil) — 1998: ~3.9, 1999: ~3.2, 2000: ~4.5, 2001: ~5.3, 2002: ~5.7, 3-03: ~5.2

COMMUNITY HEALTH CHOICE INC — E+ Very Weak

Major Rating Factors: Weak profitability index (0.9 on a scale of 0 to 10) due to a decline in earnings during 2002. Poor capitalization index (1.1) based on weak current risk-adjusted capital (moderate loss scenario). Weak liquidity (0.0) as a spike in claims may stretch capacity.
Other Rating Factors: Fair overall results on stability tests (4.7) based on an excessive 203% enrollment growth during the period. High quality investment portfolio (9.9) containing no exposure to mortgages, junk bonds, or unaffiliated stocks.
Principal Business: Medicaid (100%)
Mem Phys: 02: 2,598 **01:** 2,536 **02 MLR** 89% **/ 02 Admin Exp** 11%
Enroll(000): Q1 03: 37 **02:** 33 **01:** 11 **Med Exp PMPM:** $180
Principal Investments: Cash and equiv (100%)
Provider Compensation ($000): Contr fee ($34,819), capitation ($1,507)
Total Member Encounters: Phys (169,837), non-phys (36,693)
Group Affiliation: Harris County Hospital District
Licensed in: TX
Address: 2636 South Loop West Ste 700, Houston, TX 77054
Phone: (713) 566-6994 **Dom State:** TX **Commenced Bus:** July 1997

Data Date	Weiss Safety Rating	RACR #1	RACR #2	Total Assets ($mil)	Capital ($mil)	Net Premium ($mil)	Net Income ($mil)
3-03	E+	0.40	0.34	23.5	4.9	22.5	0.5
3-02	E	0.29	0.25	11.1	4.0	8.6	0.2
2002	E	0.34	0.28	22.9	4.4	53.7	1.1
2001	E	0.29	0.25	9.5	3.7	23.4	1.3
2000	E-	0.00	0.00	9.1	2.5	27.8	1.1
1999	E-	0.00	0.00	9.5	-2.0	40.1	-1.9
1998	D-	0.49	0.33	14.2	-0.4	32.0	-0.7

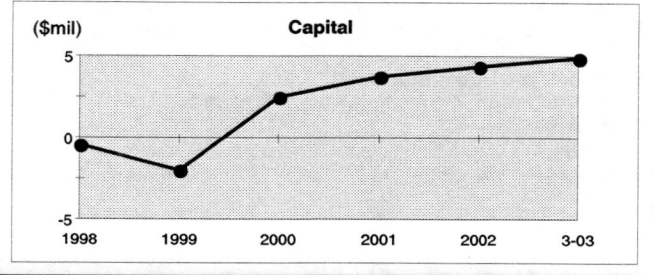

COMMUNITY HEALTH GROUP — C+ Fair

Major Rating Factors: Good overall profitability index (6.1 on a scale of 0 to 10) despite modest operating losses during 2002. Good overall results on stability tests (5.1). Strong capitalization index (7.0) based on excellent current risk-adjusted capital (severe loss scenario).
Other Rating Factors: Excellent liquidity (7.2) with ample operational cash flow and liquid investments.
Principal Business: Managed care (26%)
Mem Phys: 02: N/A **01:** N/A **02 MLR** 89% **/ 02 Admin Exp** 11%
Enroll(000): Q1 03: 96 **02:** 96 **01:** 90 **Med Exp PMPM:** $83
Principal Investments: Cash and equiv ($37,572), bonds ($2,525), stocks ($180), other ($13,528)
Provider Compensation ($000): None
Total Member Encounters: N/A
Group Affiliation: None
Licensed in: CA
Address: 740 Bay Blvd., Chula Vista, CA 91910
Phone: (619) 498-6484 **Dom State:** CA **Commenced Bus:** N/A

Data Date	Weiss Safety Rating	RACR #1	RACR #2	Total Assets ($mil)	Capital ($mil)	Net Premium ($mil)	Net Income ($mil)
3-03	C+	1.87	1.15	49.0	21.7	27.5	0.8
3-02	C+	0.00	0.00	41.1	21.6	24.6	0.3
2002	C+	1.79	1.11	45.5	20.9	103.8	-0.5
2001	C+	0.00	0.00	45.6	21.4	88.8	2.7
2000	N/A	N/A	N/A	N/A	N/A	N/A	N/A
1999	C	1.44	0.98	42.4	15.4	72.2	1.8
1998	N/A	N/A	N/A	31.8	13.6	54.1	0.4

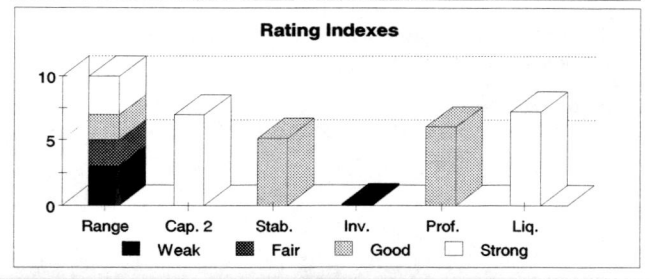

COMMUNITY HEALTH PLAN — E Very Weak

Major Rating Factors: Weak profitability index (0.9 on a scale of 0 to 10) with $18.9 million in losses in the last five years. Poor capitalization index (0.0) based on weak current risk-adjusted capital (severe loss scenario). Fair overall results on stability tests (5.0) based on a significant 29% decrease in enrollment during the period.
Other Rating Factors: Good liquidity (6.3) with sufficient resources (cash flows and marketable investments) to handle a spike in claims. High quality investment portfolio (9.9).
Principal Business: Comp med (100%)
Mem Phys: 02: 2,793 **01:** 2,823 **02 MLR** 85% **/ 02 Admin Exp** 17%
Enroll(000): Q1 03: 19 **02:** 20 **01:** 28 **Med Exp PMPM:** $178
Principal Investments: Cash and equiv (76%), nonaffiliate common stock (4%), other (20%)
Provider Compensation ($000): Contr fee ($43,237), FFS ($7,313), bonus arrang ($2,129), capitation ($556)
Total Member Encounters: Phys (158,900), non-phys (28,500)
Group Affiliation: Heartland Health System
Licensed in: KS, MO
Address: 137 N Belt, St Joseph, MO 64506
Phone: (816) 271-1247 **Dom State:** MO **Commenced Bus:** September 1994

Data Date	Weiss Safety Rating	RACR #1	RACR #2	Total Assets ($mil)	Capital ($mil)	Net Premium ($mil)	Net Income ($mil)
3-03	E	0.13	0.11	9.1	1.8	14.5	0.3
3-02	E	0.08	0.06	8.7	1.5	16.8	0.2
2002	E	0.11	0.10	8.6	1.6	61.0	-0.7
2001	E	0.08	0.06	9.7	1.4	65.2	-8.2
2000	E	0.09	0.08	10.6	1.6	59.8	-2.2
1999	E	0.11	0.09	11.1	1.9	50.2	0.0
1998	E	0.08	0.06	11.3	1.8	57.7	-7.8

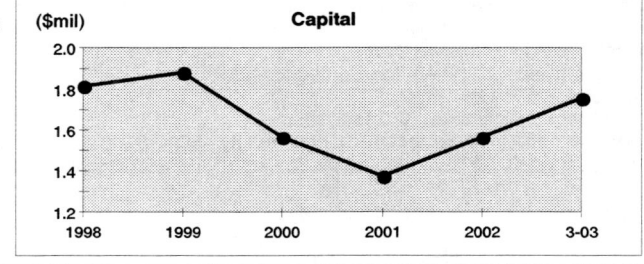

II. Analysis of Largest Companies
Winter 2003 - 04

COMMUNITY HEALTH PLAN OF OHIO — E Very Weak

Major Rating Factors: Weak profitability index (0.6 on a scale of 0 to 10) with operating losses during 2000 and 2002. Poor capitalization index (0.0) based on weak current risk-adjusted capital (severe loss scenario). Weak overall results on stability tests (1.6) based on a significant 72% decrease in enrollment during the period, a decline in the number of member physicians during 2002 and a steep decline in capital during 2002.

Other Rating Factors: Weak liquidity (0.0) as a spike in claims may stretch capacity. High quality investment portfolio (9.9) containing no exposure to mortgages, junk bonds, or unaffiliated stocks.

Principal Business: Comp med (100%)
Mem Phys: 02: 742 01: 852 **02 MLR** 135% / **02 Admin Exp** 14%
Enroll(000): 02: 4 01: 13 **Med Exp PMPM:** $104
Principal Investments: Cash and equiv (61%), other (39%)
Provider Compensation ($000): Contr fee ($10,380), capitation ($1,865), FFS ($96)
Total Member Encounters: N/A
Group Affiliation: Community Hospitals of Ohio
Licensed in: OH
Address: 715 South Taft Avenue, Fremont, OH 43420
Phone: (419) 334-6625 **Dom State:** OH **Commenced Bus:** November 1986

Data Date	Weiss Safety Rating	RACR #1	RACR #2	Total Assets ($mil)	Capital ($mil)	Net Premium ($mil)	Net Income ($mil)
2002	E	0.26	0.22	4.3	1.9	7.6	-3.2
2001	D-	0.35	0.30	9.8	3.2	35.7	0.1
2000	E+	N/A	N/A	11.5	2.5	60.0	-0.2
1999	E+	0.28	0.24	22.8	3.3	74.3	0.0
1998	E+	0.21	0.17	17.8	2.8	61.0	0.7

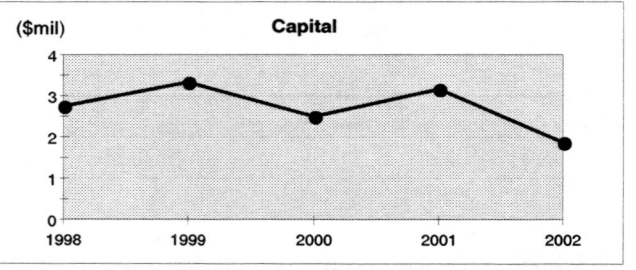

COMMUNITY HEALTH PLAN OF WASHINGTON * — A Excellent

Major Rating Factors: Excellent profitability (7.8 on a scale of 0 to 10) despite a decline in earnings during 2002. Strong capitalization (9.3) based on excellent current risk-adjusted capital (severe loss scenario) reflecting significant improvement over results in 2000. High quality investment portfolio (9.9).

Other Rating Factors: Excellent liquidity (7.0) with ample operational cash flow and liquid investments.

Principal Business: Medicaid (52%), comp med (48%)
Mem Phys: 02: 33,764 01: 31,716 **02 MLR** 88% / **02 Admin Exp** 11%
Enroll(000): Q1 03: 208 02: 208 01: 193 **Med Exp PMPM:** $121
Principal Investments: Cash and equiv (65%), nonaffiliate common stock (13%), other (22%)
Provider Compensation ($000): Capitation ($248,596), FFS ($9,813), other ($16,686)
Total Member Encounters: Phys (841,294), non-phys (488,142)
Group Affiliation: None
Licensed in: WA
Address: 720 Olive Way Ste 300, Seattle, WA 98101
Phone: (206) 521-8833 **Dom State:** WA **Commenced Bus:** July 1996

Data Date	Weiss Safety Rating	RACR #1	RACR #2	Total Assets ($mil)	Capital ($mil)	Net Premium ($mil)	Net Income ($mil)
3-03	A	3.21	2.68	106.9	69.6	90.7	4.1
3-02	B+	1.83	1.46	113.1	68.3	82.4	5.6
2002	A	2.96	2.47	131.4	65.1	331.3	6.5
2001	B+	1.84	1.46	95.0	62.8	310.6	15.3
2000	B-	0.95	0.67	70.1	38.2	241.0	6.2
1999	C+	0.91	0.81	41.5	20.3	143.2	2.3
1998	C	0.95	0.84	24.2	11.6	97.8	0.4

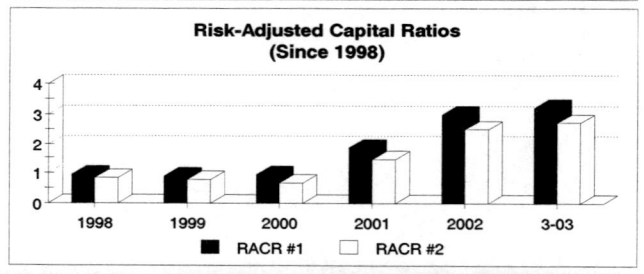

COMMUNITY INS CO — C Fair

Major Rating Factors: Good long-term capitalization index (5.1 on a scale of 0 to 10) based on fair current risk adjusted capital (severe loss scenario), although results have slipped from the good range over the last two years. Fair profitability index (3.0). Good expense controls. Return on equity has been fair, averaging 21.3% over the past five years.

Other Rating Factors: Fair overall results on stability tests (3.0) including weak results on operational trends and fair risk adjusted capital in prior years. The largest net exposure for one risk is excessive at 6.1% of capital. Good liquidity (5.4) with sufficient resources (cash flows and marketable investments) to handle a spike in claims. Ample reserve history (8.4) that helps to protect the company against sharp claims increases.

Principal Business: Group accident & health (77%) and other accident & health (23%).
Principal Investments: Investment grade bonds (100%), misc. investments (9%), and real estate (5%).
Investments in Affiliates: None
Group Affiliation: Anthem Ins Companies Inc
Licensed in: IN, OH
Commenced Business: October 1995
Address: 4361 Irwin Simpson Rd, Mason, OH 45040-9498
Phone: (513) 872-8100 **Domicile State:** OH **NAIC Code:** 10345

Data Date	Weiss Safety Rating	RACR #1	RACR #2	Loss Ratio %	Total Assets ($mil)	Capital ($mil)	Net Premium ($mil)	Net Income ($mil)
6-03	C	1.20	0.68	N/A	1,014.9	352.2	1,445.1	97.1
6-02	C	1.37	0.77	N/A	972.1	330.5	1,274.3	30.4
2002	C	0.96	0.55	87.5	970.0	257.3	2,615.1	89.8
2001	C	1.39	0.78	89.3	931.9	291.2	2,140.3	107.6
2000	C	1.76	0.98	88.9	849.9	334.5	1,905.9	11.0
1999	C	1.80	1.08	88.8	820.2	360.9	1,677.9	10.1
1998	C+	0.69	0.44	88.9	898.7	404.2	1,821.5	47.2

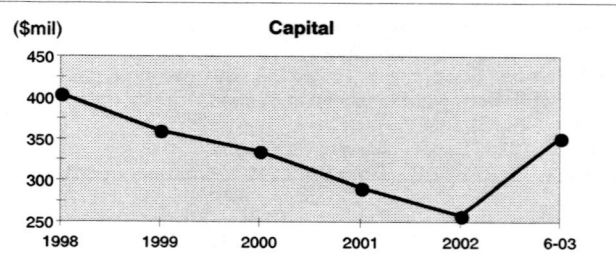

Winter 2003 - 04   II. Analysis of Largest Companies

COMMUNITYCARE HMO INC   C   Fair

Major Rating Factors: Fair capitalization index (4.6 on a scale of 0 to 10) based on fair current risk-adjusted capital (moderate loss scenario). Good overall profitability index (5.8) despite operating losses during 1998 and 2000. Good overall results on stability tests (6.1).
Other Rating Factors: High quality investment portfolio (9.9) containing no exposure to mortgages, junk bonds, or unaffiliated stocks. Excellent liquidity (7.0) with ample operational cash flow and liquid investments.
Principal Business: Comp med (45%), Medicare (40%), Medicaid (15%)
Mem Phys: 02: 2,903 **01:** 2,589 **02 MLR** 86% **/ 02 Admin Exp** 11%
Enroll(000): Q1 03: 113 **02:** 111 **01:** 119 **Med Exp PMPM:** $179
Principal Investments: Cash and equiv (99%), other (1%)
Provider Compensation ($000): Capitation ($145,177), contr fee ($92,510), FFS ($431)
Total Member Encounters: Phys (940,109), non-phys (24,034)
Group Affiliation: CommunityCare
Licensed in: OK
Address: 218 W. 6th Street, Tulsa, OK 74119
Phone: (918) 549-5200 **Dom State:** OK **Commenced Bus:** June 1994

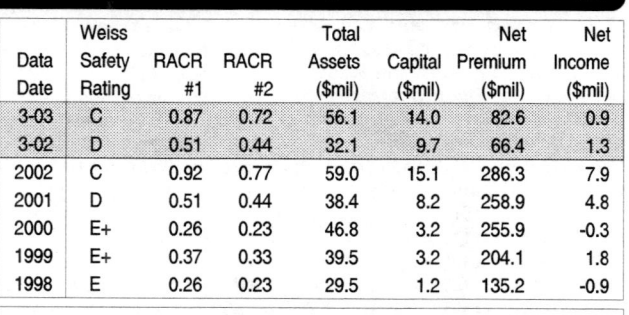

Data Date	Weiss Safety Rating	RACR #1	RACR #2	Total Assets ($mil)	Capital ($mil)	Net Premium ($mil)	Net Income ($mil)
3-03	C	0.87	0.72	56.1	14.0	82.6	0.9
3-02	D	0.51	0.44	32.1	9.7	66.4	1.3
2002	C	0.92	0.77	59.0	15.1	286.3	7.9
2001	D	0.51	0.44	38.4	8.2	258.9	4.8
2000	E+	0.26	0.23	46.8	3.2	255.9	-0.3
1999	E+	0.37	0.33	39.5	3.2	204.1	1.8
1998	E	0.26	0.23	29.5	1.2	135.2	-0.9

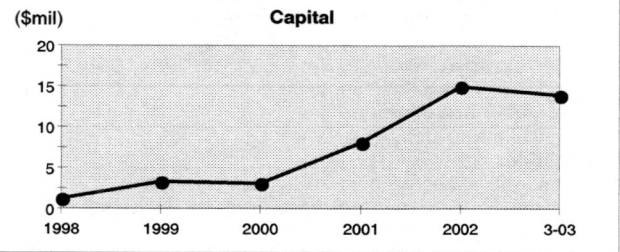

Capital ($mil) chart 1998–3-03.

COMPANION HEALTH CARE CORP *   A-   Excellent

Major Rating Factors: Excellent profitability (8.6 on a scale of 0 to 10) despite a decline in earnings during 2002. Strong overall capitalization (9.2) based on excellent current risk-adjusted capital (severe loss scenario). Furthermore, this high level of risk-adjusted capital has been consistently maintained in previous years. High quality investment portfolio (9.0) containing little or no exposure to mortgages, junk bonds, or unaffiliated stocks.
Other Rating Factors: Excellent overall results on stability tests (7.4) based on consistent premium and capital growth in the last five years. Good financial strength from affiliates. Good liquidity (6.7) with sufficient resources (cash flows and marketable investments) to handle a spike in claims.
Principal Business: Comp med (100%)
Mem Phys: 02: 7,208 **01:** 6,535 **02 MLR** 86% **/ 02 Admin Exp** 9%
Enroll(000): Q1 03: 68 **02:** 89 **01:** 88 **Med Exp PMPM:** $162
Principal Investments: Cash and equiv (10%), nonaffiliate common stock (6%), real estate (1%), affiliate common stock (1%), other (83%)
Provider Compensation ($000): Contr fee ($173,227), capitation ($2,554)
Total Member Encounters: Phys (610,178), non-phys (1,767)
Group Affiliation: Companion Ins Group
Licensed in: SC
Address: 4101 Percival Rd, Columbia, SC 29219
Phone: (803) 786-8466 **Dom State:** SC **Commenced Bus:** October 1984

Data Date	Weiss Safety Rating	RACR #1	RACR #2	Total Assets ($mil)	Capital ($mil)	Net Premium ($mil)	Net Income ($mil)
3-03	A-	3.09	2.57	73.7	44.0	42.2	3.0
3-02	A-	0.00	0.00	73.6	38.3	50.4	1.7
2002	A-	2.92	2.44	71.0	41.4	199.6	5.8
2001	A-	2.82	2.02	65.4	36.4	161.7	6.2
2000	B	2.08	1.77	54.6	29.6	134.5	4.0
1999	B	1.89	1.62	52.9	26.7	146.1	4.6
1998	B	1.77	1.53	47.4	21.3	118.2	4.4

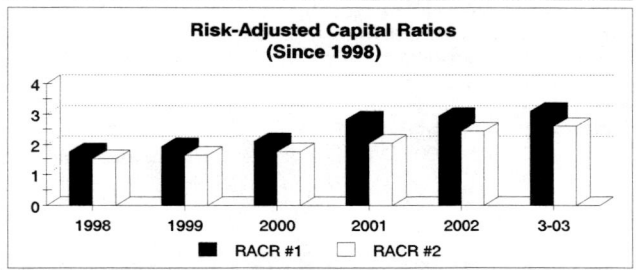

Risk-Adjusted Capital Ratios (Since 1998) chart — RACR #1, RACR #2.

COMPANION LIFE INSURANCE COMPANY *   B+   Good

Major Rating Factors: Good overall results on stability tests (6.7 on a scale of 0 to 10). Stability strengths include excellent operational trends and excellent risk diversification. Strong capitalization (8.7) based on excellent risk adjusted capital (severe loss scenario). Moreover, capital has steadily grown over the last five years. High quality investment portfolio (7.0).
Other Rating Factors: Excellent profitability (8.6) with operating gains in each of the last five years. Excellent liquidity (7.3).
Principal Business: Group health insurance (81%), group life insurance (16%), individual health insurance (2%), and reinsurance (1%).
Principal Investments: CMOs and structured securities (40%), nonCMO investment grade bonds (21%), common & preferred stock (21%), cash (15%), and noninv. grade bonds (3%).
Investments in Affiliates: 15%
Group Affiliation: Companion Ins Group
Licensed in: All states except CA, CT, HI, NJ, NY, PR
Commenced Business: July 1970
Address: 2501 Faraway Dr, Columbia, SC 29219
Phone: (800) 753-0404 **Domicile State:** SC **NAIC Code:** 77828

Data Date	Weiss Safety Rating	RACR #1	RACR #2	Total Assets ($mil)	Capital ($mil)	Net Premium ($mil)	Net Income ($mil)
6-03	B+	2.87	2.10	75.6	44.0	36.5	1.7
6-02	B	2.43	1.71	67.0	37.4	30.1	2.4
2002	B+	2.80	2.06	70.4	41.3	61.6	3.4
2001	B	2.40	1.69	63.7	35.7	50.3	4.4
2000	B	2.78	1.96	55.0	32.7	34.4	3.4
1999	B	3.14	2.19	54.2	30.8	28.7	2.0
1998	B	2.32	1.66	43.7	20.6	30.5	1.8

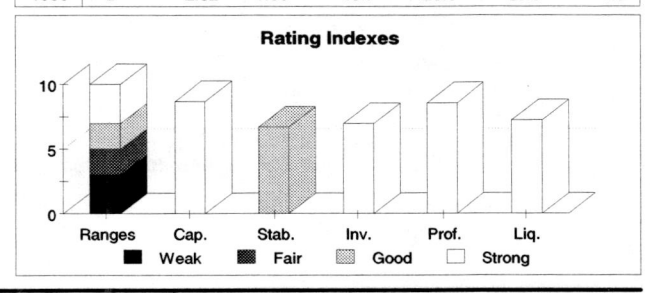

Rating Indexes chart: Ranges, Cap., Stab., Inv., Prof., Liq. — Weak, Fair, Good, Strong.

www.WeissRatings.com   143   * Denotes a Weiss Recommended Company

II. Analysis of Largest Companies

Winter 2003 - 04

COMPCARE HEALTH SERVICES INS CORP — C- — Fair

Major Rating Factors: Fair liquidity (4.7 on a scale of 0 to 10) as cash resources may not be adequate to cover a spike in claims. Weak profitability index (1.4) with operating losses during 1999, 2000 and 2001. Average return on equity has been poor at -28%. Good overall results on stability tests (5.2) despite excessive capital growth during 2002. Potentially strong support from affiliation with Cobalt Corp.
Other Rating Factors: Strong capitalization (7.6) based on excellent current risk-adjusted capital (severe loss scenario) reflecting significant improvement over results in 1999. High quality investment portfolio (8.1) containing little or no exposure to mortgages, junk bonds, or unaffiliated stocks.
Principal Business: Comp med (92%), dental (8%).
Mem Phys: 02: 6,488   **01:** 5,944   **02 MLR** 90%   **/ 02 Admin Exp** 13%
Enroll(000): Q1 03: 236   **02:** 250   **01:** 358   **Med Exp PMPM:** $94
Principal Investments: Affiliate common stock (36%), cash and equiv (11%), other (53%).
Provider Compensation ($000): FFS ($159,400), contr fee ($106,128), bonus arrang ($71,877), capitation ($33,057)
Total Member Encounters: N/A
Group Affiliation: Cobalt Corp
Licensed in: WI
Address: 401 W Michigan St, Milwaukee, WI 53203
Phone: (262) 785-7832   **Dom State:** WI   **Commenced Bus:** February 1976

Data Date	Weiss Safety Rating	RACR #1	RACR #2	Total Assets ($mil)	Capital ($mil)	Net Premium ($mil)	Net Income ($mil)
3-03	C-	1.86	1.55	160.3	79.8	96.2	2.4
3-02	D+	1.17	0.97	161.8	70.8	99.8	10.8
2002	C-	1.77	1.47	155.0	76.2	383.3	0.8
2001	D+	1.17	0.97	161.3	60.8	530.5	-16.5
2000	D+	1.06	0.87	143.1	48.9	387.1	-10.2
1999	D+	0.37	0.31	73.6	12.5	327.1	-24.3
1998	B	1.41	1.17	97.2	36.5	304.2	7.0

Net Income History (in millions of dollars)

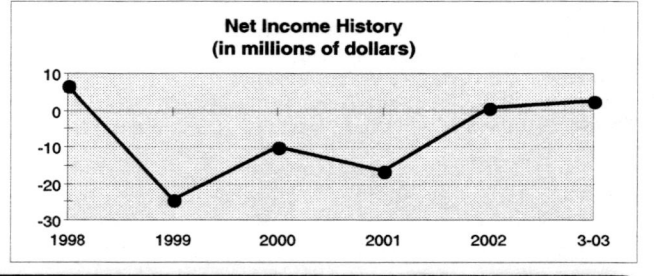

CONNECTICARE INC * — B+ — Good

Major Rating Factors: Good overall results on stability tests (6.7 on a scale of 0 to 10) despite a decline in enrollment during 2002. Good liquidity (6.8) with sufficient resources (cash flows and marketable investments) to handle a spike in claims. Excellent profitability (9.2).
Other Rating Factors: Strong capitalization index (7.3) based on excellent current risk-adjusted capital (severe loss scenario). High quality investment portfolio (9.4) containing little or no exposure to mortgages, junk bonds, or unaffiliated stocks.
Principal Business: Comp med (93%), FEHB (7%).
Mem Phys: 02: 10,472   **01:** 8,872   **02 MLR** 81%   **/ 02 Admin Exp** 15%
Enroll(000): Q1 03: 221   **02:** 224   **01:** 244   **Med Exp PMPM:** $171
Principal Investments: Cash and equiv (23%), pref stock (2%), other (75%)
Provider Compensation ($000): Contr fee ($275,052), bonus arrang ($189,382), capitation ($36,428), FFS ($6,092)
Total Member Encounters: Phys (894,698), non-phys (432,754)
Group Affiliation: ConnectiCare Group
Licensed in: CT
Address: 30 Batterson Park Rd, Farmington, CT 06032
Phone: (860) 674-5700   **Dom State:** CT   **Commenced Bus:** April 1982

Data Date	Weiss Safety Rating	RACR #1	RACR #2	Total Assets ($mil)	Capital ($mil)	Net Premium ($mil)	Net Income ($mil)
3-03	B+	1.57	1.31	156.2	66.0	163.3	5.0
3-02	B	1.20	0.96	141.0	57.1	141.9	4.0
2002	B+	1.49	1.24	139.7	62.7	590.5	22.1
2001	B	1.21	0.96	154.8	53.3	654.3	21.8
2000	C+	0.79	0.66	120.1	34.9	540.4	21.6
1999	D-	0.00	0.00	95.5	10.4	219.5	4.9
1998	D+	0.41	0.34	N/A	N/A	N/A	-7.0

Rating Indexes — Range, Cap. 2, Stab., Inv., Prof., Liq. — Weak / Fair / Good / Strong

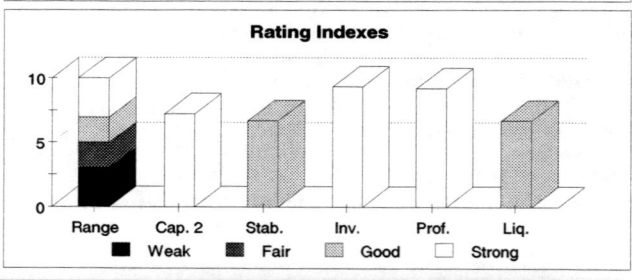

CONNECTICARE OF MASSACHUSETTS INC — B — Good

Major Rating Factors: Good overall capitalization (6.2 on a scale of 0 to 10) based on good current risk-adjusted capital (severe loss scenario). Good overall results on stability tests (6.9). Rating is significantly influenced by the good financial results of ConnectiCare Group. Good liquidity (6.5) with sufficient resources (cash flows and marketable investments) to handle a spike in claims.
Other Rating Factors: Excellent profitability (7.3). High quality investment portfolio (9.9) containing no exposure to mortgages, junk bonds, or unaffiliated stocks.
Principal Business: Comp med (100%).
Mem Phys: 02: 10,472   **01:** 8,872   **02 MLR** 87%   **/ 02 Admin Exp** 12%
Enroll(000): Q1 03: 8   **02:** 8   **01:** 4   **Med Exp PMPM:** $173
Principal Investments: Cash and equiv (27%), other (73%).
Provider Compensation ($000): Contr fee ($6,262), bonus arrang ($4,333), capitation ($752), FFS ($213)
Total Member Encounters: Phys (26,024), non-phys (6,743)
Group Affiliation: ConnectiCare Group
Licensed in: MA
Address: 260 Franklin St, Boston, MA 02110-3173
Phone: (860) 674-5700   **Dom State:** MA   **Commenced Bus:** July 1995

Data Date	Weiss Safety Rating	RACR #1	RACR #2	Total Assets ($mil)	Capital ($mil)	Net Premium ($mil)	Net Income ($mil)
3-03	B	1.11	0.92	6.3	2.3	5.4	0.0
3-02	B	2.05	1.73	3.9	2.1	2.5	0.2
2002	B	1.05	0.88	5.4	2.2	14.6	0.1
2001	B	2.05	1.73	4.1	2.1	6.7	0.5
2000	C	1.98	1.68	2.4	1.6	2.0	0.1
1999	D	1.59	1.34	N/A	N/A	N/A	0.1
1998	D	2.75	2.34	N/A	N/A	N/A	0.1

Risk-Adjusted Capital Ratios (Since 1998) — RACR #1 / RACR #2

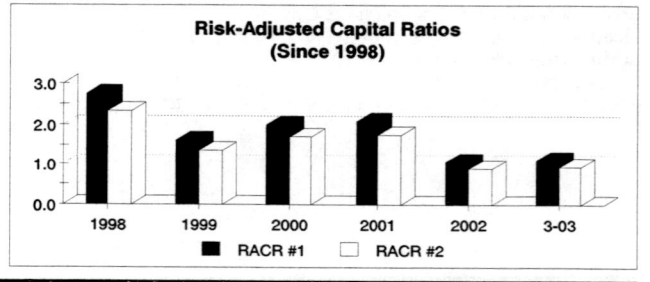

Winter 2003 - 04
II. Analysis of Largest Companies

CONNECTICUT GENERAL LIFE INSURANCE COMPANY — C- — Fair

Major Rating Factors: Fair overall results on stability tests (3.3 on a scale of 0 to 10). Good quality investment portfolio (5.9) despite mixed results such as: large holdings of BBB rated bonds but junk bond exposure equal to 52% of capital. Good overall profitability (6.9). Excellent expense controls. Despite its volitility, return on equity has been excellent over the last five years averaging 21.0%.
Other Rating Factors: Good liquidity (6.6). Strong capitalization (7.2) based on excellent risk adjusted capital (severe loss scenario).
Principal Business: Group health insurance (57%), reinsurance (19%), individual life insurance (13%), and group life insurance (10%).
Principal Investments: NonCMO investment grade bonds (44%), mortgages in good standing (24%), CMOs and structured securities (16%), policy loans (7%), and misc. investments (8%).
Investments in Affiliates: None
Group Affiliation: CIGNA Group
Licensed in: All states, the District of Columbia and Puerto Rico
Commenced Business: October 1865
Address: 900 Cottage Grove Rd,S-330, Bloomfield, CT 06002
Phone: (860) 726-7234 **Domicile State:** CT **NAIC Code:** 62308

Data Date	Weiss Safety Rating	RACR #1	RACR #2	Total Assets ($mil)	Capital ($mil)	Net Premium ($mil)	Net Income ($mil)
6-03	C-	2.09	1.16	68,525.6	2,380.3	3,267.6	305.7
6-02	C-	1.85	1.06	67,348.1	2,242.3	3,246.4	165.0
2002	C-	2.05	1.14	66,797.9	2,297.8	6,399.2	-444.9
2001	C+	1.82	1.03	69,511.0	2,140.9	5,846.7	357.7
2000	C+	1.81	0.97	69,004.5	2,058.8	15,613.4	684.5
1999	C+	1.89	1.05	69,727.3	1,980.9	13,623.8	747.2
1998	C+	1.66	0.96	69,212.9	1,789.1	12,704.8	824.3

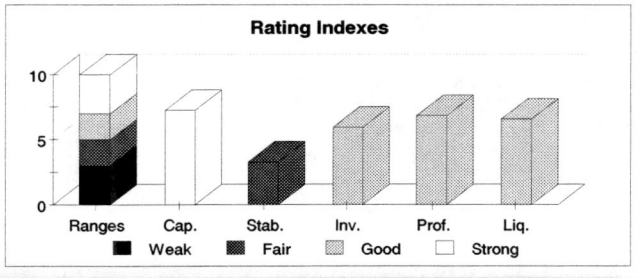

CONSECO HEALTH INSURANCE COMPANY — E — Very Weak

Major Rating Factors: Weak overall results on stability tests (0.2 on a scale of 0 to 10) including weak financial strength of affiliated Conseco Group. Fair quality investment portfolio (3.7) with large holdings of BBB rated bonds in addition to significant exposure to junk bonds. Good capitalization (5.4) based on good risk adjusted capital (moderate loss scenario).
Other Rating Factors: Good overall profitability (6.5). Excellent liquidity (8.2).
Principal Business: Individual health insurance (82%), group health insurance (17%), and individual life insurance (1%).
Principal Investments: NonCMO investment grade bonds (57%), CMOs and structured securities (26%), noninv. grade bonds (8%), common & preferred stock (4%), and mortgages in good standing (2%).
Investments in Affiliates: None
Group Affiliation: Conseco Group
Licensed in: All states except CT, MA, NY
Commenced Business: December 1970
Address: 11815 N Pennsylvania St, Carmel, IN 46032
Phone: (317) 817-3700 **Domicile State:** AZ **NAIC Code:** 78174

Data Date	Weiss Safety Rating	RACR #1	RACR #2	Total Assets ($mil)	Capital ($mil)	Net Premium ($mil)	Net Income ($mil)
6-03	E	1.27	0.72	1,800.8	104.9	176.2	11.0
6-02	E	1.23	0.68	1,627.3	103.3	169.6	-3.8
2002	E	1.20	0.68	1,683.7	100.3	354.1	-45.7
2001	E+	1.68	0.93	1,693.4	143.8	339.4	9.3
2000	C	1.38	0.81	1,391.3	106.2	303.1	21.9
1999	C	1.66	0.98	1,339.7	119.2	306.0	22.1
1998	C+	1.21	0.70	1,190.8	96.1	306.2	16.8

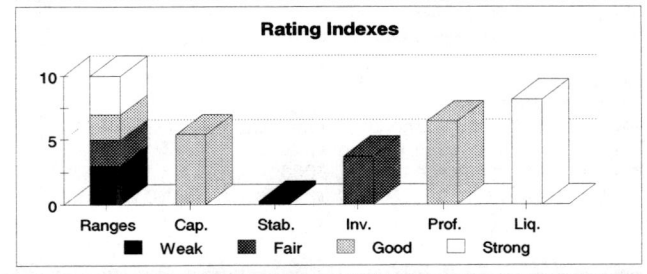

CONSECO SENIOR HEALTH INSURANCE COMPANY — E — Very Weak

Major Rating Factors: Weak overall results on stability tests (0.2 on a scale of 0 to 10) including weak financial strength of affiliated Conseco Group. Low quality investment portfolio (2.5) containing large holdings of BBB rated bonds in addition to significant exposure to junk bonds. Weak profitability (1.8) with operating losses during the first six months of 2003.
Other Rating Factors: Fair capitalization (3.8) based on fair risk adjusted capital (moderate loss scenario). Excellent liquidity (7.0).
Principal Business: Individual health insurance (92%), reinsurance (4%), individual life insurance (2%), and group health insurance (2%).
Principal Investments: NonCMO investment grade bonds (58%), CMOs and structured securities (26%), common & preferred stock (7%), noninv. grade bonds (5%), and misc. investments (3%).
Investments in Affiliates: None
Group Affiliation: Conseco Group
Licensed in: All states except CT, NY, RI, VT, PR
Commenced Business: February 1965
Address: 11815 N Pennsylvania St, Carmel, IN 46032
Phone: (317) 817-3700 **Domicile State:** PA **NAIC Code:** 76325

Data Date	Weiss Safety Rating	RACR #1	RACR #2	Total Assets ($mil)	Capital ($mil)	Net Premium ($mil)	Net Income ($mil)
6-03	E	0.85	0.50	2,790.8	91.3	216.1	-25.4
6-02	E	1.32	0.78	2,532.0	144.4	233.6	3.5
2002	E	1.21	0.72	2,654.5	136.6	454.7	-133.6
2001	E+	1.56	0.93	2,643.1	184.3	498.9	-12.3
2000	C-	1.84	1.01	2,317.6	202.1	501.2	-27.8
1999	C-	1.74	1.01	1,977.5	186.5	503.9	-38.5
1998	C-	1.09	0.71	1,660.0	125.8	513.7	-23.1

www.WeissRatings.com *Denotes a Weiss Recommended Company

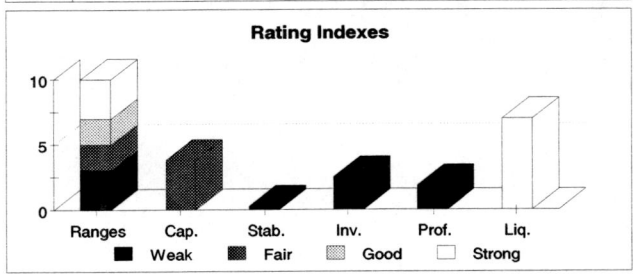

II. Analysis of Largest Companies

Winter 2003 - 04

CONTINENTAL ASSURANCE COMPANY — C+ — Fair

Major Rating Factors: Fair overall results on stability tests (4.5 on a scale of 0 to 10) including fair financial strength of affiliated CNA Financial Corp. Good quality investment portfolio (5.1) despite mixed results such as: large holdings of BBB rated bonds but junk bond exposure equal to 52% of capital. Good overall profitability (6.1) despite operating losses during the first six months of 2003.
Other Rating Factors: Good liquidity (6.7). Strong capitalization (7.9) based on excellent risk adjusted capital (severe loss scenario).
Principal Business: Reinsurance (52%), group life insurance (22%), group health insurance (12%), individual life insurance (8%), and individual annuities (6%).
Principal Investments: NonCMO investment grade bonds (45%), CMOs and structured securities (36%), noninv. grade bonds (11%), common & preferred stock (5%), and misc. investments (4%).
Investments in Affiliates: 4%
Group Affiliation: CNA Financial Corp
Licensed in: All states, the District of Columbia and Puerto Rico
Commenced Business: August 1911
Address: CNA Plaza, Chicago, IL 60685
Phone: (312) 822-5000 **Domicile State:** IL **NAIC Code:** 62413

Data Date	Weiss Safety Rating	RACR #1	RACR #2	Total Assets ($mil)	Capital ($mil)	Net Premium ($mil)	Net Income ($mil)
6-03	C+	2.44	1.60	9,237.5	1,182.3	275.4	-61.6
6-02	B-	2.84	1.93	9,150.8	1,456.4	267.6	-15.9
2002	C+	2.57	1.70	8,322.5	1,253.5	497.2	75.7
2001	B-	2.56	1.84	9,121.6	1,414.6	514.7	107.7
2000	B	1.77	1.32	10,011.2	1,273.7	2,854.4	-47.9
1999	B	1.70	1.26	11,537.6	1,222.5	3,762.8	68.4
1998	B	1.62	1.20	11,496.0	1,109.2	3,613.7	-48.6

CNA Financial Corp Composite Group Rating: C Largest Group Members	Assets ($mil)	Weiss Safety Rating
CONTINENTAL CASUALTY CO	25312	C
CONTINENTAL ASSURANCE CO	8322	C+
CNA GROUP LIFE ASR CO	2968	C
CONTINENTAL INS CO	2780	C
VALLEY FORGE LIFE INS CO	1251	C

CONTINENTAL CASUALTY CO — C — Fair

Major Rating Factors: Fair reserve development (3.2 on a scale of 0 to 10) as the level of reserves has at times been insufficient to cover claims. In 2001 and 2002 the two year reserve development was 18% and 24% deficient respectively. Fair overall results on stability tests (3.9) including weak results on operational trends and excessive premium growth.
Other Rating Factors: Weak profitability index (2.4) with operating losses during 2001 and the first six months of 2002. Return on equity has been fair, averaging 5.7% over the past five years. Good overall long-term capitalization (5.8) based on good current risk adjusted capital (moderate loss scenario). However, capital levels have fluctuated during prior years. Excellent liquidity (7.3) with ample operational cash flow and liquid investments.
Principal Business: Other liability (23%), group accident & health (20%), inland marine (11%), other accident & health (10%), workers compensation (8%), auto liability (6%), and other lines (23%).
Principal Investments: Investment grade bonds (65%), misc. investments (28%), and non investment grade bonds (8%).
Investments in Affiliates: 11%
Group Affiliation: CNA Financial Corp
Licensed in: All states, the District of Columbia and Puerto Rico
Commenced Business: December 1897
Address: CNA Plaza, Chicago, IL 60685
Phone: (312) 822-5000 **Domicile State:** IL **NAIC Code:** 20443

Data Date	Weiss Safety Rating	RACR #1	RACR #2	Loss Ratio %	Total Assets ($mil)	Capital ($mil)	Net Premium ($mil)	Net Income ($mil)
6-03	C	1.09	0.85	N/A	27,424.2	5,431.3	2,118.3	-24.2
6-02	C	0.92	0.75	N/A	22,581.3	4,755.2	1,851.1	-18.7
2002	C	1.08	0.85	76.3	25,312.1	5,115.9	7,073.3	1,667.5
2001	C	0.96	0.79	142.9	21,723.5	4,700.1	3,433.8	-881.5
2000	C+	1.37	1.13	78.7	22,973.7	6,342.3	4,848.3	972.6
1999	C+	1.41	1.12	92.3	23,412.8	6,709.5	5,170.8	72.9
1998	C+	1.31	1.07	81.6	23,148.6	5,944.5	5,544.4	88.3

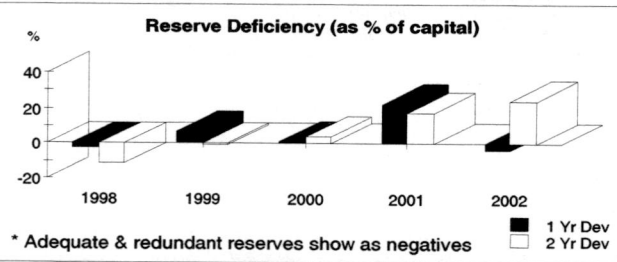

Reserve Deficiency (as % of capital) — 1998, 1999, 2000, 2001, 2002
* Adequate & redundant reserves show as negatives
(1 Yr Dev / 2 Yr Dev)

CONTINENTAL GENERAL INSURANCE COMPANY — D — Weak

Major Rating Factors: Weak profitability (2.1 on a scale of 0 to 10). Excellent expense controls. Return on equity has been low, averaging -10.1%. Weak overall results on stability tests (1.9) including weak risk adjusted capital in prior years. Fair overall capitalization (3.6) based on mixed results -- excessive policy leverage mitigated by fair risk adjusted capital (severe loss scenario).
Other Rating Factors: Fair quality investment portfolio (4.6). Good liquidity (5.7).
Principal Business: Individual health insurance (95%), individual life insurance (3%), and individual annuities (1%).
Principal Investments: NonCMO investment grade bonds (51%), CMOs and structured securities (33%), common & preferred stock (7%), noninv. grade bonds (4%), and misc. investments (4%).
Investments in Affiliates: 7%
Group Affiliation: Ceres Group Inc
Licensed in: All states except NY, PR
Commenced Business: July 1961
Address: 8901 Indian Hills Dr, Omaha, NE 68114
Phone: (402) 397-3200 **Domicile State:** NE **NAIC Code:** 71404

Data Date	Weiss Safety Rating	RACR #1	RACR #2	Total Assets ($mil)	Capital ($mil)	Net Premium ($mil)	Net Income ($mil)
6-03	D	0.72	0.57	418.3	55.5	181.6	30.7
6-02	D	0.56	0.44	334.2	34.0	124.8	-12.2
2002	D	0.46	0.37	365.4	33.8	291.7	-13.7
2001	D	0.77	0.62	369.8	48.1	230.0	-6.4
2000	C	0.72	0.58	313.8	42.5	197.8	-2.8
1999	C	1.21	0.84	263.8	33.5	-44.8	13.6
1998	C	0.93	0.66	432.0	37.0	213.1	-3.4

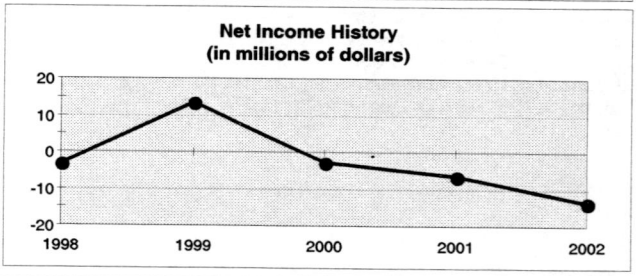

Net Income History (in millions of dollars) — 1998, 1999, 2000, 2001, 2002

Winter 2003 - 04   II. Analysis of Largest Companies

CONTINENTAL LIFE INSURANCE COMPANY OF BRENTWOOD   C   Fair

Major Rating Factors: Fair overall results on stability tests (3.7 on a scale of 0 to 10). Good current capitalization (5.8) based on good risk adjusted capital (severe loss scenario), although results have slipped from the excellent range during the last year. High quality investment portfolio (8.3) despite no exposure to mortgages and substantial holdings of BBB bonds but minimal holdings in junk bonds.
Other Rating Factors: Excellent profitability (8.7) despite operating losses during the first six months of 2003. Excellent liquidity (7.0).
Principal Business: Individual health insurance (97%), individual life insurance (3%), and group health insurance (1%).
Principal Investments: NonCMO investment grade bonds (74%), CMOs and structured securities (17%), cash (6%), and noninv. grade bonds (2%).
Investments in Affiliates: None
Group Affiliation: Continental Ins Service Inc
Licensed in: AZ, AR, CO, FL, GA, ID, IL, IN, KS, KY, LA, MI, MS, MO, MT, NE, NM, NC, ND, OH, OK, PA, SC, SD, TN, TX, UT, VA, WV, WI
Commenced Business: December 1983
Address: 101 Continental Plaza, Brentwood, TN 37027
Phone: (615) 377-1300 **Domicile State:** TN **NAIC Code:** 68500

Data Date	Weiss Safety Rating	RACR #1	RACR #2	Total Assets ($mil)	Capital ($mil)	Net Premium ($mil)	Net Income ($mil)
6-03	C	1.09	0.85	83.1	25.0	61.1	-0.2
6-02	C	1.01	0.78	67.7	21.8	49.2	-0.3
2002	C	1.31	1.02	77.5	27.4	102.2	3.6
2001	C	1.16	0.90	64.9	23.3	84.4	3.8
2000	C	1.06	0.84	54.3	18.7	65.8	1.1
1999	C	1.18	0.93	44.8	17.6	50.6	1.1
1998	C	1.26	1.00	40.0	16.6	45.1	1.1

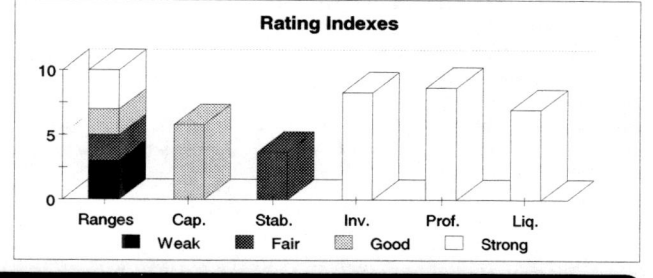

Rating Indexes

Ranges: Cap., Stab., Inv., Prof., Liq.
■ Weak   ▨ Fair   ▒ Good   □ Strong

CONTRA COSTA HEALTH PLAN   C   Fair

Major Rating Factors: Fair overall results on stability tests (4.1 on a scale of 0 to 10). Poor capitalization index (2.5) based on weak current risk-adjusted capital (moderate loss scenario). Good overall profitability index (5.8) despite a decline in earnings during 2002.
Other Rating Factors: Good liquidity (6.3) with sufficient resources (cash flows and marketable investments) to handle a spike in claims.
Principal Business: Managed care (34%)
Mem Phys: 02: N/A **01:** N/A **02 MLR** 122% **/ 02 Admin Exp** 10%
Enroll(000): 02: 59 **01:** 56 **Med Exp PMPM:** $151
Principal Investments ($000): Cash and equiv ($20,188)
Provider Compensation ($000): None
Total Member Encounters: N/A
Group Affiliation: None
Licensed in: CA
Address: 20 Allen St, Martinez, CA 94553
Phone: (925) 313-6000 **Dom State:** CA **Commenced Bus:** November 1973

Data Date	Weiss Safety Rating	RACR #1	RACR #2	Total Assets ($mil)	Capital ($mil)	Net Premium ($mil)	Net Income ($mil)
2002	C	0.46	0.28	26.7	5.5	84.7	0.1
2001	C	0.00	0.00	27.2	5.3	72.9	0.2
2000	D	N/A	N/A	36.2	5.0	64.7	0.2
1999	D	0.48	0.30	25.2	4.8	65.5	0.5
1998	D	0.47	0.29	26.9	4.3	59.1	0.7

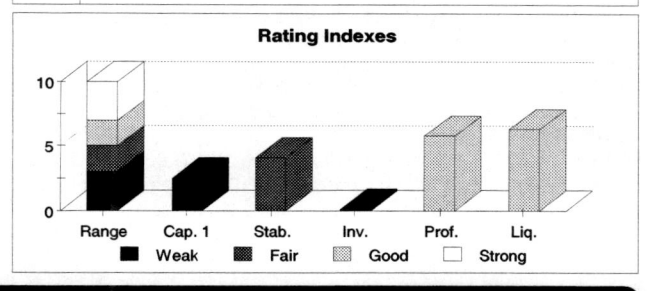

Rating Indexes

Range, Cap. 1, Stab., Inv., Prof., Liq.
■ Weak   ▨ Fair   ▒ Good   □ Strong

COOK CHILDRENS HEALTH PLAN   C-   Fair

Major Rating Factors: Fair profitability index (4.8 on a scale of 0 to 10). Fair capitalization (4.2) based on fair current risk-adjusted capital (moderate loss scenario) reflecting improvement over results in 2001. Fair overall results on stability tests (3.4).
Other Rating Factors: High quality investment portfolio (9.4) containing no exposure to mortgages, junk bonds, or unaffiliated stocks. Excellent liquidity (7.1) with ample operational cash flow and liquid investments.
Principal Business: Comp med (100%)
Mem Phys: 02: N/A **01:** 972 **02 MLR** 78% **/ 02 Admin Exp** 12%
Enroll(000): Q1 03: 41 **02:** 39 **01:** 35 **Med Exp PMPM:** $70
Principal Investments: Cash and equiv (82%), real estate (2%), other (16%)
Provider Compensation ($000): FFS ($22,708), capitation ($2,671)
Total Member Encounters: Phys (231,207), non-phys (65,498)
Group Affiliation: Cook Childrens Health Care System
Licensed in: TX
Address: 801 Seventh Ave, Fort Worth, TX 76104
Phone: (817) 334-2247 **Dom State:** TX **Commenced Bus:** April 1999

Data Date	Weiss Safety Rating	RACR #1	RACR #2	Total Assets ($mil)	Capital ($mil)	Net Premium ($mil)	Net Income ($mil)
3-03	C-	0.81	0.67	6.9	2.5	10.1	0.7
3-02	D-	0.38	0.32	6.3	2.5	10.4	1.0
2002	C-	0.81	0.67	7.6	2.5	40.2	3.9
2001	D-	0.36	0.30	7.7	2.5	34.9	-3.2
2000	U	2.34	1.97	7.4	3.6	7.9	-0.6
1999	U	5.30	4.42	2.8	2.6	0.3	0.0
1998	N/A	N/A	N/A	N/A	N/A	N/A	N/A

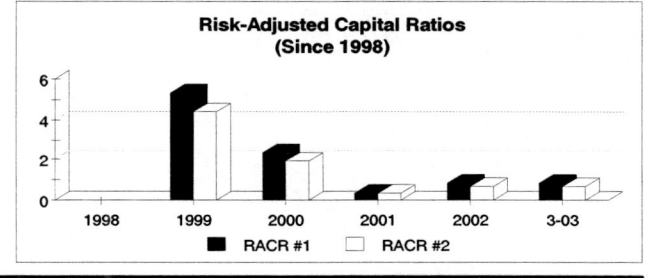

Risk-Adjusted Capital Ratios (Since 1998)

1998, 1999, 2000, 2001, 2002, 3-03
■ RACR #1   □ RACR #2

www.WeissRatings.com   147   * Denotes a Weiss Recommended Company

II. Analysis of Largest Companies

Winter 2003 - 04

COORDINATED CARE CORP INDIANA INC — C+ — Fair

Major Rating Factors: Good capitalization index (6.9 on a scale of 0 to 10) based on excellent current risk-adjusted capital (severe loss scenario). Good overall results on stability tests (5.9). Fair financial strength from affiliates. Good liquidity (6.8) with sufficient resources (cash flows and marketable investments) to handle a spike in claims.
Other Rating Factors: Excellent profitability (8.3) despite a decline in earnings during 2002. High quality investment portfolio (9.7) containing no exposure to mortgages, junk bonds, or unaffiliated stocks.
Principal Business: Medicaid (100%)
Mem Phys: 02: 921 **01:** 594 **02 MLR** 81% **/ 02 Admin Exp** 13%
Enroll(000): Q1 03: 105 **02:** 106 **01:** 66 **Med Exp PMPM:** $104
Principal Investments: Cash and equiv (58%), other (42%)
Provider Compensation ($000): Contr fee ($64,355), capitation ($32,633), bonus arrang ($3,405)
Total Member Encounters: Phys (102,986), non-phys (303,880)
Group Affiliation: Centene Corp
Licensed in: IN
Address: 1099 N Meridian St Ste 400, Indianapolis, IN 46204
Phone: (314) 725-4477   **Dom State:** IN   **Commenced Bus:** August 1996

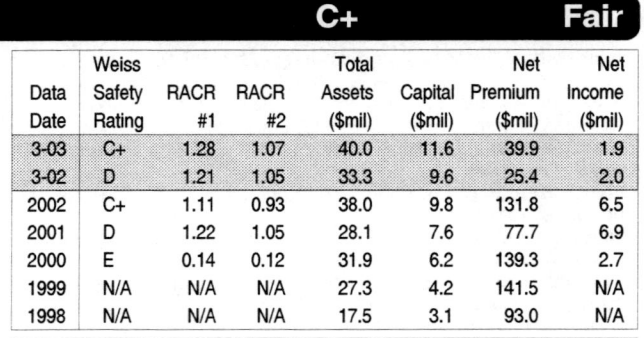

Data Date	Weiss Safety Rating	RACR #1	RACR #2	Total Assets ($mil)	Capital ($mil)	Net Premium ($mil)	Net Income ($mil)
3-03	C+	1.28	1.07	40.0	11.6	39.9	1.9
3-02	D	1.21	1.05	33.3	9.6	25.4	2.0
2002	C+	1.11	0.93	38.0	9.8	131.8	6.5
2001	D	1.22	1.05	28.1	7.6	77.7	6.9
2000	E	0.14	0.12	31.9	6.2	139.3	2.7
1999	N/A	N/A	N/A	27.3	4.2	141.5	N/A
1998	N/A	N/A	N/A	17.5	3.1	93.0	N/A

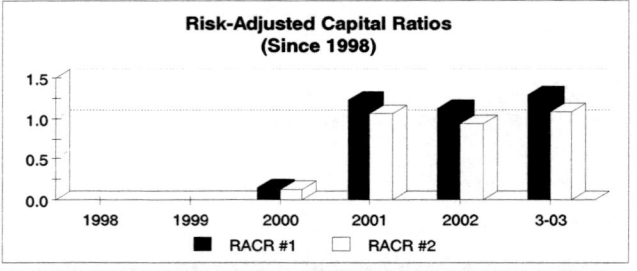

Risk-Adjusted Capital Ratios (Since 1998)

COORDINATED HEALTH PARTNERS INC — C — Fair

Major Rating Factors: Weak profitability index (0.9 on a scale of 0 to 10) due to a decline in earnings during 2002. Average return on equity has been extremely poor. Good liquidity (6.8) with sufficient resources (cash flows and marketable investments) to handle a spike in claims. Strong capitalization index (7.7) based on excellent current risk-adjusted capital (severe loss scenario).
Other Rating Factors: High quality investment portfolio (9.9) containing no exposure to mortgages, junk bonds, or unaffiliated stocks. Excellent overall results on stability tests (8.2) based on consistent premium and capital growth in the last five years.
Principal Business: Medicare (61%), comp med (31%), FEHB (5%), Medicaid (3%)
Mem Phys: 02: 3,198 **01:** 3,038 **02 MLR** 88% **/ 02 Admin Exp** 9%
Enroll(000): 02: 124 **01:** 117 **Med Exp PMPM:** $299
Principal Investments: Cash and equiv (17%), other (83%)
Provider Compensation ($000): Contr fee ($407,652), capitation ($26,148)
Total Member Encounters: Phys (1,098,085), non-phys (2,370,063)
Group Affiliation: Bl Cross & Bl Shield of Rhode Island
Licensed in: MA, RI
Address: 15 LaSalle Square, Providence, RI 02903
Phone: (401) 459-5500   **Dom State:** RI   **Commenced Bus:** October 1986

Data Date	Weiss Safety Rating	RACR #1	RACR #2	Total Assets ($mil)	Capital ($mil)	Net Premium ($mil)	Net Income ($mil)
2002	C	1.91	1.59	157.8	67.9	489.7	14.0
2001	C	1.86	1.44	139.9	55.2	430.2	22.2
2000	D+	1.00	0.85	121.6	30.3	369.4	12.1
1999	D+	0.61	0.52	85.3	15.6	253.3	-19.9
1998	D	0.20	0.17	59.2	3.9	138.5	-23.2

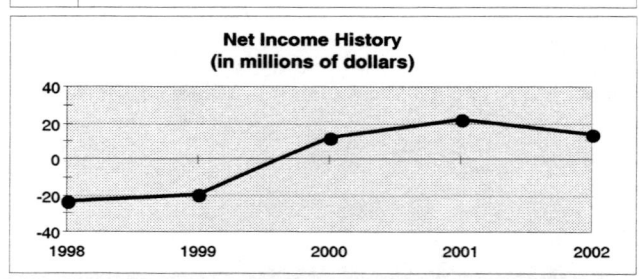

Net Income History (in millions of dollars)

CORPORATE HEALTH INSURANCE COMPANY — C+ — Fair

Major Rating Factors: Fair overall results on stability tests (3.1 on a scale of 0 to 10) including fair financial strength of affiliated Aetna Inc and weak risk adjusted capital in prior years. Good current capitalization (5.5) based on mixed results -- excessive policy leverage mitigated by excellent risk adjusted capital (severe loss scenario) reflecting significant improvement over results in 2000. Good quality investment portfolio (6.8).
Other Rating Factors: Good overall profitability (5.6). Excellent liquidity (7.7).
Principal Business: Group health insurance (77%) and reinsurance (23%).
Principal Investments: Cash (52%), nonCMO investment grade bonds (33%), CMOs and structured securities (11%), and noninv. grade bonds (5%).
Investments in Affiliates: None
Group Affiliation: Aetna Inc
Licensed in: All states except CA, CT, MS, NY, PR
Commenced Business: December 1956
Address: 980 Jolly Rd, Blue Bell, PA 19422
Phone: (215) 628-4800   **Domicile State:** PA   **NAIC Code:** 72052

Data Date	Weiss Safety Rating	RACR #1	RACR #2	Total Assets ($mil)	Capital ($mil)	Net Premium ($mil)	Net Income ($mil)
6-03	C+	1.22	1.01	67.9	43.7	85.0	22.2
6-02	B-	2.05	1.65	97.5	68.1	126.2	38.5
2002	B-	1.04	0.86	68.1	43.3	232.7	66.7
2001	B-	2.10	1.67	148.8	85.0	326.5	109.8
2000	B-	0.53	0.43	263.2	86.4	1,340.3	38.9
1999	B-	2.70	2.07	144.3	90.8	282.3	106.0
1998	B-	2.29	1.82	109.5	60.7	223.8	66.5

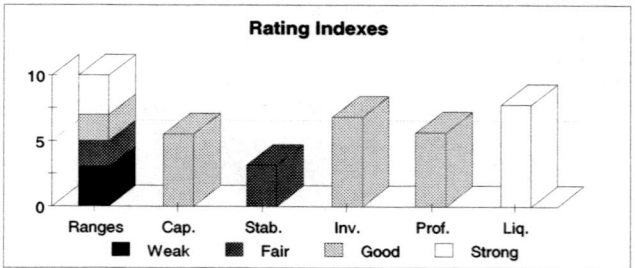

Rating Indexes

Winter 2003 - 04   II. Analysis of Largest Companies

COUNTRY LIFE INSURANCE COMPANY *   A+   Excellent

Major Rating Factors: Good quality investment portfolio (6.2 on a scale of 0 to 10) despite mixed results such as: no exposure to mortgages and substantial holdings of BBB bonds but small junk bond holdings. Good liquidity (6.8) with sufficient resources to handle a spike in claims as well as a significant increase in policy surrenders. Strong capitalization (8.7) based on excellent risk adjusted capital (severe loss scenario).
Other Rating Factors: Excellent profitability (8.5) with operating gains in each of the last five years. Excellent overall results on stability tests (8.3) excellent operational trends and excellent risk diversification.
Principal Business: Individual life insurance (54%), individual health insurance (25%), group health insurance (19%), group life insurance (1%), and reinsurance (1%).
Principal Investments: NonCMO investment grade bonds (48%), CMOs and structured securities (22%), common & preferred stock (9%), mortgages in good standing (9%), and misc. investments (12%).
Investments in Affiliates: 4%
Group Affiliation: Country Companies
Licensed in: AK, AZ, AR, CO, CT, DE, ID, IL, IN, IA, KS, KY, ME, MD, MA, MI, MN, MO, MT, NE, NV, NM, ND, OH, OK, OR, PA, RI, SD, TN, TX, UT, WA, WV, WI, WY
Commenced Business: December 1928
Address: 1701 Towanda Ave, Bloomington, IL 61701
Phone: (309) 821-3000   **Domicile State:** IL   **NAIC Code:** 62553

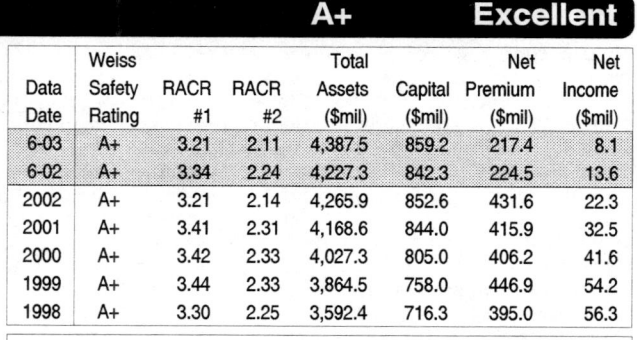

Data Date	Weiss Safety Rating	RACR #1	RACR #2	Total Assets ($mil)	Capital ($mil)	Net Premium ($mil)	Net Income ($mil)
6-03	A+	3.21	2.11	4,387.5	859.2	217.4	8.1
6-02	A+	3.34	2.24	4,227.3	842.3	224.5	13.6
2002	A+	3.21	2.14	4,265.9	852.6	431.6	22.3
2001	A+	3.41	2.31	4,168.6	844.0	415.9	32.5
2000	A+	3.42	2.33	4,027.3	805.0	406.2	41.6
1999	A+	3.44	2.33	3,864.5	758.0	446.9	54.2
1998	A+	3.30	2.25	3,592.4	716.3	395.0	56.3

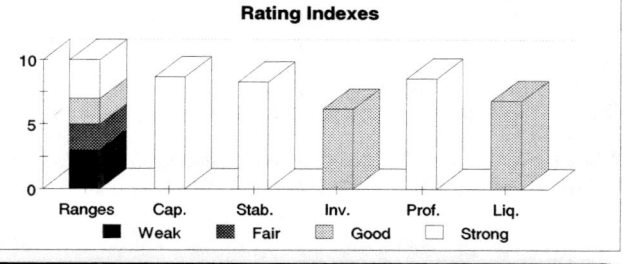

COVENTRY HEALTH & LIFE INSURANCE COMPANY   C-   Fair

Major Rating Factors: Weak overall results on stability tests (2.8 on a scale of 0 to 10) including weak results on operational trends. Good current capitalization (5.8) based on mixed results -- excessive policy leverage mitigated by excellent risk adjusted capital (severe loss scenario) reflecting significant improvement over results in 2001. Good overall profitability (6.6). Excellent expense controls.
Other Rating Factors: Good liquidity (6.8). High quality investment portfolio (8.5).
Principal Business: Group health insurance (63%) and reinsurance (37%).
Principal Investments: NonCMO investment grade bonds (60%), CMOs and structured securities (26%), and cash (12%).
Investments in Affiliates: None
Group Affiliation: Coventry Health Care Inc
Licensed in: AL, AK, AZ, AR, CO, DC, DE, GA, IL, IA, KS, KY, LA, MD, MA, MI, MS, MO, NE, NV, NC, ND, OH, OK, PA, SC, SD, TN, TX, UT, VA, WA, WV, WI, WY
Commenced Business: May 1969
Address: 200 Bailey Ave, Ft Worth, TX 76107
Phone: (615) 391-2440   **Domicile State:** DE   **NAIC Code:** 81973

Data Date	Weiss Safety Rating	RACR #1	RACR #2	Total Assets ($mil)	Capital ($mil)	Net Premium ($mil)	Net Income ($mil)
6-03	C-	1.76	1.42	110.8	53.7	120.2	12.6
6-02	D	0.92	0.76	83.2	32.9	83.6	4.4
2002	D+	1.57	1.27	94.4	40.6	180.6	12.1
2001	D	0.64	0.53	81.1	28.6	287.0	9.4
2000	D+	0.80	0.65	102.8	39.6	365.9	4.6
1999	D+	0.81	0.66	83.4	33.2	300.9	12.0
1998	D+	0.75	0.61	90.6	33.1	269.1	-6.9

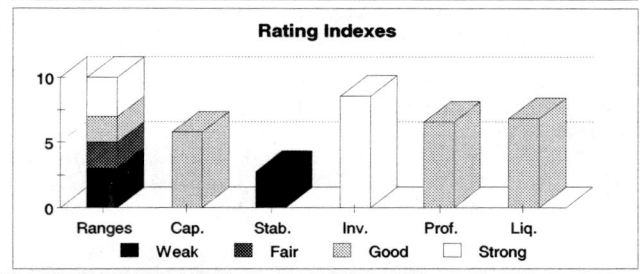

COVENTRY HEALTH CARE OF DELAWARE INC   B-   Good

Major Rating Factors: Good overall results on stability tests (5.8 on a scale of 0 to 10) despite a decline in enrollment during 2002. Rating is significantly influenced by the fair financial results of Coventry Health Care Inc. Good liquidity (6.5) with sufficient resources (cash flows and marketable investments) to handle a spike in claims. Excellent profitability (8.2) with operating gains in each of the last five years.
Other Rating Factors: Strong overall capitalization (7.8) based on excellent current risk-adjusted capital (severe loss scenario) despite some fluctuation in capital levels. High quality investment portfolio (9.0) containing little or no exposure to mortgages, junk bonds, or unaffiliated stocks.
Principal Business: Comp med (68%), Medicaid (30%), Medicare (2%)
Mem Phys: 02: 16,052   **01:** 11,173   **02 MLR** 80%   **/ 02 Admin Exp** 14%
Enroll(000): Q1 03: 49   **02:** 51   **01:** 98   **Med Exp PMPM:** $161
Principal Investments: Cash and equiv (5%), other (95%)
Provider Compensation ($000): FFS ($131,197), contr fee ($20,225), capitation ($7,292)
Total Member Encounters: Phys (426,745), non-phys (223,788)
Group Affiliation: Coventry Health Care Inc
Licensed in: DE, MD, NJ
Address: 2751 Centerville Rd., Ste 400, Wilmington, DE 19808-1627
Phone: (302) 995-6100   **Dom State:** DE   **Commenced Bus:** December 1986

Data Date	Weiss Safety Rating	RACR #1	RACR #2	Total Assets ($mil)	Capital ($mil)	Net Premium ($mil)	Net Income ($mil)
3-03	B-	2.01	1.68	52.8	28.8	32.4	-1.3
3-02	C+	1.98	1.50	75.9	30.4	59.5	4.6
2002	B-	2.04	1.70	60.7	29.8	180.5	10.4
2001	C+	1.98	1.50	71.8	25.2	189.5	6.7
2000	C	1.45	1.18	58.9	16.3	167.7	3.4
1999	C	2.09	1.74	46.7	16.7	120.2	4.5
1998	C	1.90	1.62	45.2	13.5	108.3	2.0

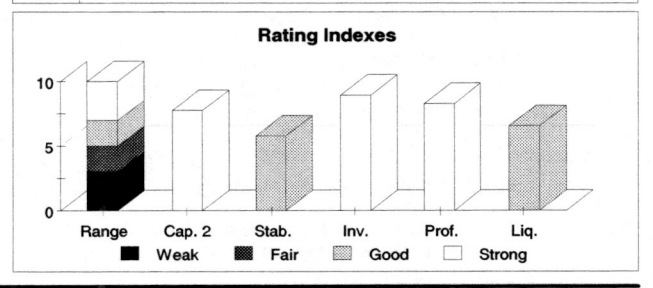

www.WeissRatings.com   * Denotes a Weiss Recommended Company

II. Analysis of Largest Companies

Winter 2003 - 04

COVENTRY HEALTH CARE OF GEORGIA — B- Good

Major Rating Factors: Good liquidity (6.8 on a scale of 0 to 10) with sufficient resources (cash flows and marketable investments) to handle a spike in claims. Excellent profitability (8.1) despite operating losses during 1998. Strong capitalization (8.1) based on excellent current risk-adjusted capital (severe loss scenario) reflecting improvement over results in 1998.

Other Rating Factors: High quality investment portfolio (9.9) containing no exposure to mortgages, junk bonds, or unaffiliated stocks. Excellent overall results on stability tests (7.8) based on consistent premium and capital growth in the last five years but a decline in enrollment during 2002. Rating is significantly influenced by the fair financial results of Coventry Health Care Inc.

Principal Business: Comp med (100%)
Mem Phys: 02: 4,713 01: 4,446 **02 MLR** 84% / **02 Admin Exp** 12%
Enroll(000): Q1 03: 40 02: 38 01: 41 **Med Exp PMPM:** $136
Principal Investments: Cash and equiv (21%), other (79%)
Provider Compensation ($000): Contr fee ($42,298), capitation ($12,655), FFS ($7,466)
Total Member Encounters: Phys (551,690), non-phys (49,085)
Group Affiliation: Coventry Health Care Inc
Licensed in: GA
Address: 1100 Circle 75 Pkwy Ste 1400, Atlanta, GA 30339
Phone: (404) 231-9911 **Dom State:** GA **Commenced Bus:** January 1994

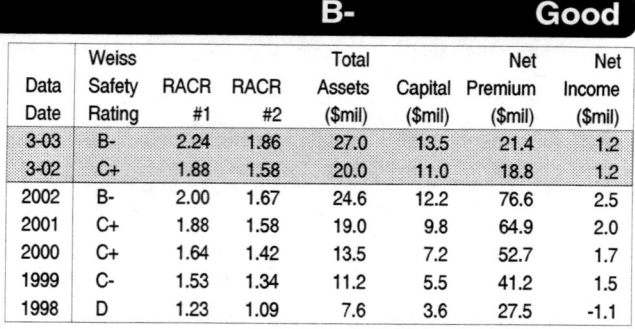

Data Date	Weiss Safety Rating	RACR #1	RACR #2	Total Assets ($mil)	Capital ($mil)	Net Premium ($mil)	Net Income ($mil)
3-03	B-	2.24	1.86	27.0	13.5	21.4	1.2
3-02	C+	1.88	1.58	20.0	11.0	18.8	1.2
2002	B-	2.00	1.67	24.6	12.2	76.6	2.5
2001	C+	1.88	1.58	19.0	9.8	64.9	2.0
2000	C+	1.64	1.42	13.5	7.2	52.7	1.7
1999	C-	1.53	1.34	11.2	5.5	41.2	1.5
1998	D	1.23	1.09	7.6	3.6	27.5	-1.1

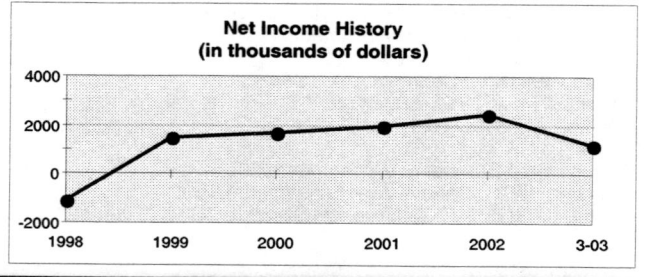

Net Income History (in thousands of dollars)

COVENTRY HEALTH CARE OF IOWA INC — B- Good

Major Rating Factors: Good overall results on stability tests (5.8 on a scale of 0 to 10). Rating is significantly influenced by the fair financial results of Coventry Health Care Inc. Good liquidity (6.8) with sufficient resources (cash flows and marketable investments) to handle a spike in claims. Excellent profitability (7.2) despite operating losses during 2000.

Other Rating Factors: Strong overall capitalization (9.3) based on excellent current risk-adjusted capital (severe loss scenario) despite some fluctuation in capital levels. High quality investment portfolio (9.9) containing little or no exposure to mortgages, junk bonds, or unaffiliated stocks.

Principal Business: Comp med (97%), Medicaid (3%)
Mem Phys: 02: 2,627 01: 2,378 **02 MLR** 81% / **02 Admin Exp** 12%
Enroll(000): Q1 03: 82 02: 80 01: 85 **Med Exp PMPM:** $110
Principal Investments: Cash and equiv (14%), other (86%)
Provider Compensation ($000): FFS ($93,067), bonus arrang ($12,712), capitation ($6,618)
Total Member Encounters: Phys (584,256), non-phys (98,266)
Group Affiliation: Coventry Health Care Inc
Licensed in: IA
Address: 4600 Westown Pkwy, Suite 200, W Des Moines, IA 50266-1099
Phone: (515) 225-1234 **Dom State:** IA **Commenced Bus:** January 1986

Data Date	Weiss Safety Rating	RACR #1	RACR #2	Total Assets ($mil)	Capital ($mil)	Net Premium ($mil)	Net Income ($mil)
3-03	B-	3.15	2.63	59.5	31.4	36.9	2.9
3-02	C+	2.22	1.67	53.9	25.6	34.1	2.7
2002	B-	2.84	2.37	55.6	28.4	134.7	9.7
2001	C+	2.22	1.67	52.2	22.8	125.4	4.4
2000	C+	N/A	N/A	45.4	18.3	120.2	-1.2
1999	C	2.65	2.21	48.7	22.1	117.6	0.4
1998	C	2.75	2.32	51.0	23.7	120.1	1.9

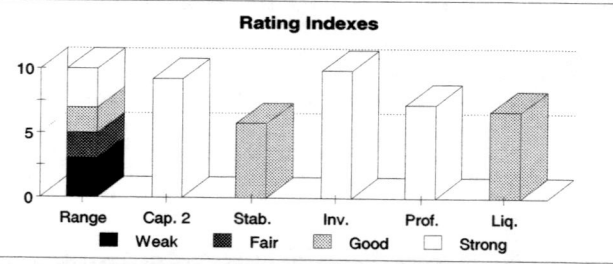

Rating Indexes

COVENTRY HEALTH CARE OF KANSAS INC — D+ Weak

Major Rating Factors: Weak profitability index (0.9 on a scale of 0 to 10) with $17.6 million in losses in the last three years. Average return on equity has been poor at -8%. Good capitalization (6.9) based on excellent current risk-adjusted capital (severe loss scenario) reflecting improvement over results in 2001. Good overall results on stability tests (5.5) despite good risk-adjusted capital in prior years, a decline in enrollment during 2002 but consistent premium and capital growth in the last five years. Potentially strong support from affiliation with Coventry Health Care Inc.

Other Rating Factors: Good liquidity (5.3) with sufficient resources (cash flows and marketable investments) to handle a spike in claims. High quality investment portfolio (9.9) containing no exposure to mortgages, junk bonds, or unaffiliated stocks.

Principal Business: Comp med (58%), Medicare (36%), FEHB (5%)
Mem Phys: 02: 2,494 01: 11,991 **02 MLR** 93% / **02 Admin Exp** 11%
Enroll(000): Q1 03: 202 02: 259 01: 283 **Med Exp PMPM:** $194
Principal Investments: Cash and equiv (27%), other (73%)
Provider Compensation ($000): Contr fee ($494,749), FFS ($65,891), capitation ($57,700)
Total Member Encounters: Phys (1,155,341), non-phys (140,555)
Group Affiliation: Coventry Health Care Inc
Licensed in: KS, MO
Address: 8301 E 21st St N Ste 300, Wichita, KS 67206
Phone: (816) 221-8400 **Dom State:** KS **Commenced Bus:** October 1981

Data Date	Weiss Safety Rating	RACR #1	RACR #2	Total Assets ($mil)	Capital ($mil)	Net Premium ($mil)	Net Income ($mil)
3-03	D+	1.28	1.07	139.1	56.5	132.3	10.1
3-02	C-	0.98	0.79	101.5	23.6	101.2	-3.3
2002	D+	1.08	0.90	159.6	47.6	678.3	-8.6
2001	C	0.98	0.79	154.9	42.1	610.1	-7.3
2000	C	1.05	0.87	50.8	15.5	216.6	-1.8
1999	C	1.51	1.27	42.0	17.1	161.5	2.6
1998	D+	1.53	1.30	34.0	14.1	125.7	0.2

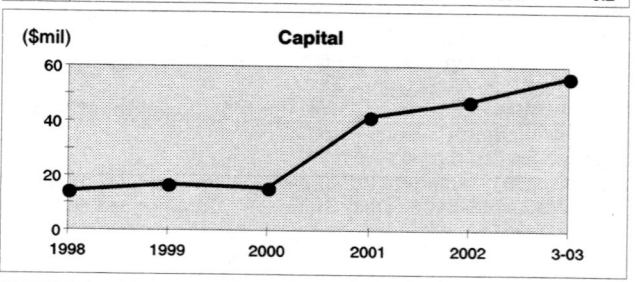

Capital ($mil)

www.WeissRatings.com

Winter 2003 - 04
II. Analysis of Largest Companies

COVENTRY HEALTH CARE OF LOUISIANA C- Fair

Major Rating Factors: Weak profitability index (0.9 on a scale of 0 to 10) with operating losses during 1998, 1999, 2000 and 2001. Average return on equity has been poor at -47%. Good overall results on stability tests (5.9) despite weak risk-adjusted capital in prior years. Rating is significantly influenced by the fair financial results of Coventry Health Care Inc. Good liquidity (6.7) with sufficient resources (cash flows and marketable investments) to handle a spike in claims.
Other Rating Factors: Strong capitalization (7.2) based on excellent current risk-adjusted capital (severe loss scenario) reflecting significant improvement over results in 2000. High quality investment portfolio (9.9) containing no exposure to mortgages, junk bonds, or unaffiliated stocks.
Principal Business: Comp med (93%), FEHB (7%)
Mem Phys: 02: 3,135 **01:** 3,015   **02 MLR** 85% **/ 02 Admin Exp** 12%
Enroll(000): Q1 03: 71 **02:** 70 **01:** 60   **Med Exp PMPM:** $174
Principal Investments: Cash and equiv (37%), other (63%)
Provider Compensation ($000): Contr fee ($119,944), FFS ($10,411), capitation ($3,452)
Total Member Encounters: Phys (859,277), non-phys (42,812)
Group Affiliation: Coventry Health Care Inc
Licensed in: LA
Address: 2424 Edenborn Ave, Ste 350, Metairie, LA 70001
Phone: (504) 834-0840 **Dom State:** LA **Commenced Bus:** July 1985

Data Date	Weiss Safety Rating	RACR #1	RACR #2	Total Assets ($mil)	Capital ($mil)	Net Premium ($mil)	Net Income ($mil)
3-03	C-	1.47	1.23	43.5	17.2	45.6	2.2
3-02	D+	0.53	0.44	27.2	4.9	38.1	1.2
2002	C-	1.21	1.01	39.5	14.3	159.2	0.8
2001	D+	0.53	0.44	26.5	4.4	118.1	-1.2
2000	D+	0.46	0.39	25.0	3.1	107.3	-4.4
1999	D+	0.61	0.51	25.0	6.9	90.2	-4.9
1998	D+	0.52	0.44	19.3	7.5	87.3	-5.1

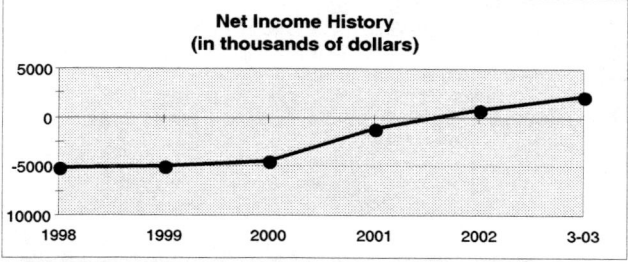

Net Income History (in thousands of dollars)

COVENTRY HEALTH CARE OF NEBRASKA INC D+ Weak

Major Rating Factors: Weak profitability index (0.9 on a scale of 0 to 10) with operating losses during 1998, 1999, 2000 and 2001. Average return on equity has been poor at -67%. Good liquidity (6.5) with sufficient resources (cash flows and marketable investments) to handle a spike in claims. Strong capitalization (8.0) based on excellent current risk-adjusted capital (severe loss scenario) reflecting significant improvement over results in 1998.
Other Rating Factors: High quality investment portfolio (9.9) containing little or no exposure to mortgages, junk bonds, or unaffiliated stocks. Excellent overall results on stability tests (7.0) despite fair risk-adjusted capital in prior years. Rating is significantly influenced by the fair financial results of Coventry Health Care Inc.
Principal Business: Comp med (100%)
Mem Phys: 02: 2,543 **01:** 2,369 **02 MLR** 85% **/ 02 Admin Exp** 12%
Enroll(000): Q1 03: 43 **02:** 32 **01:** 38   **Med Exp PMPM:** $128
Principal Investments: Cash and equiv (11%), other (89%)
Provider Compensation ($000): Contr fee ($55,361), FFS ($2,412), capitation ($1,330)
Total Member Encounters: Phys (100,280), non-phys (24,836)
Group Affiliation: Coventry Health Care Inc
Licensed in: IA, NE
Address: 13305 Birch St Ste 100, Omaha, NE 68154
Phone: (402) 498-9030 **Dom State:** NE **Commenced Bus:** October 1987

Data Date	Weiss Safety Rating	RACR #1	RACR #2	Total Assets ($mil)	Capital ($mil)	Net Premium ($mil)	Net Income ($mil)
3-03	D+	2.12	1.77	22.8	11.4	20.8	0.6
3-02	D	1.14	0.93	22.5	8.4	15.7	0.5
2002	D+	2.02	1.68	19.5	11.0	63.6	3.5
2001	D	1.13	0.92	23.7	7.2	66.6	-7.1
2000	D	0.98	0.82	13.8	4.3	43.1	-3.5
1999	D	1.15	0.97	12.2	4.4	36.4	-3.0
1998	D	0.72	0.61	13.4	2.3	43.4	-2.1

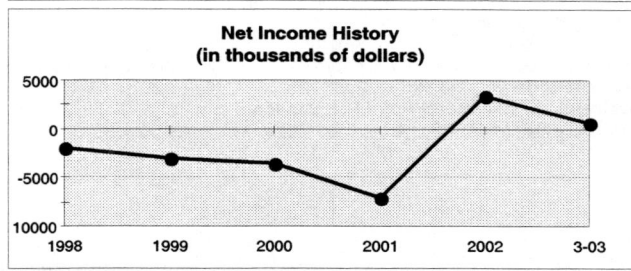

Net Income History (in thousands of dollars)

COX HEALTH SYSTEMS HMO INC E Very Weak

Major Rating Factors: Weak profitability index (0.9 on a scale of 0 to 10) with operating losses during each of the last five years. Average return on equity over the last five years has been extremely poor. Poor capitalization index (0.5) based on weak current risk-adjusted capital (moderate loss scenario). Good liquidity (6.8) with sufficient resources (cash flows and marketable investments) to handle a spike in claims.
Other Rating Factors: High quality investment portfolio (9.9) containing no exposure to mortgages, junk bonds, or unaffiliated stocks. Excellent overall results on stability tests (7.9) based on consistent premium and capital growth in the last five years.
Principal Business: Comp med (100%)
Mem Phys: 02: 720 **01:** 705 **02 MLR** 92% **/ 02 Admin Exp** 12%
Enroll(000): Q1 03: 17 **02:** 18 **01:** 18   **Med Exp PMPM:** $184
Principal Investments: Cash and equiv (100%)
Provider Compensation ($000): Contr fee ($37,405), FFS ($3,033), other ($20)
Total Member Encounters: Phys (77,637), non-phys (8,026)
Group Affiliation: Cox Health Systems
Licensed in: MO
Address: 1443 N Roberson Ste 700, Springfield, MO 65802
Phone: (417) 269-2990 **Dom State:** MO **Commenced Bus:** January 1997

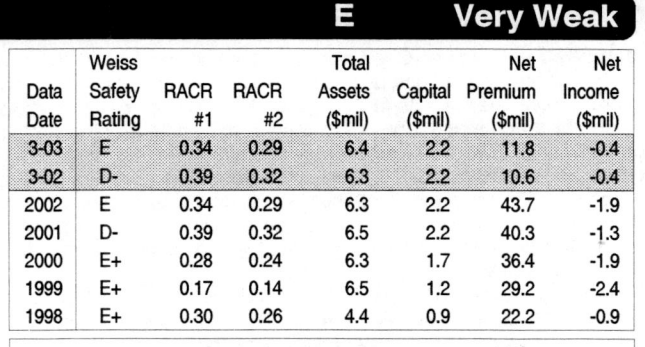

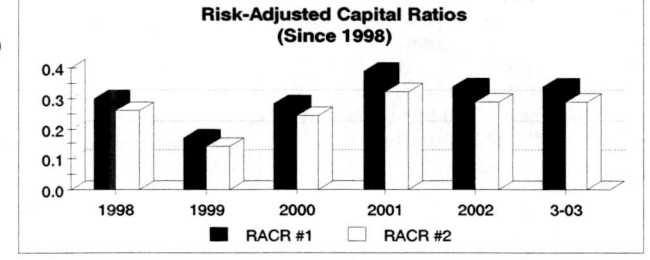

Data Date	Weiss Safety Rating	RACR #1	RACR #2	Total Assets ($mil)	Capital ($mil)	Net Premium ($mil)	Net Income ($mil)
3-03	E	0.34	0.29	6.4	2.2	11.8	-0.4
3-02	D-	0.39	0.32	6.3	2.2	10.6	-0.4
2002	E	0.34	0.29	6.3	2.2	43.7	-1.9
2001	D-	0.39	0.32	6.5	2.2	40.3	-1.3
2000	E+	0.28	0.24	6.3	1.7	36.4	-1.9
1999	E+	0.17	0.14	6.5	1.2	29.2	-2.4
1998	E+	0.30	0.26	4.4	0.9	22.2	-0.9

Risk-Adjusted Capital Ratios (Since 1998) ■ RACR #1 □ RACR #2

II. Analysis of Largest Companies

Winter 2003 - 04

CPIC LIFE INSURANCE COMPANY — B — Good

Major Rating Factors: Good overall results on stability tests (5.3 on a scale of 0 to 10). Strengths include good financial support from affiliation with Blue Shield of California, excellent operational trends and excellent risk diversification. Strong capitalization (10.0) based on excellent risk adjusted capital (severe loss scenario). Moreover, capital levels have been consistently high over the last five years. High quality investment portfolio (8.6).
Other Rating Factors: Excellent profitability (9.3) with operating gains in each of the last five years. Excellent liquidity (8.3).
Principal Business: Individual health insurance (35%), group health insurance (34%), group life insurance (25%), reinsurance (3%), and individual life insurance (2%).
Principal Investments: NonCMO investment grade bonds (50%), CMOs and structured securities (39%), and cash (11%).
Investments in Affiliates: None
Group Affiliation: Blue Shield of California
Licensed in: AZ, CA, CO, ID, MT, NV, NM, ND, OR, UT, WA
Commenced Business: July 1954
Address: 50 Beach St, San Francisco, CA 94105
Phone: (800) 642-5599 **Domicile State:** CA **NAIC Code:** 61557

Data Date	Weiss Safety Rating	RACR #1	RACR #2	Total Assets ($mil)	Capital ($mil)	Net Premium ($mil)	Net Income ($mil)
6-03	B	9.92	7.20	145.0	108.5	27.4	4.2
6-02	B-	9.43	6.83	124.2	98.1	26.9	5.0
2002	B-	9.59	7.00	130.3	104.2	55.0	11.7
2001	B-	9.19	6.69	120.3	92.8	50.0	13.1
2000	B-	8.37	5.96	102.8	79.1	42.5	10.4
1999	B-	7.28	5.36	90.3	68.7	39.2	9.3
1998	B-	6.81	5.00	81.7	59.4	35.7	10.0

Blue Shield of California
Composite Group Rating: B+
Largest Group Members

	Assets ($mil)	Weiss Safety Rating
CALIFORNIA PHYSICIANS SERVICE	1638	A-
CPIC LIFE INS CO	130	B

CUNA MUTUAL INSURANCE SOCIETY — C — Fair

Major Rating Factors: Fair overall results on stability tests (3.6 on a scale of 0 to 10) including fair risk adjusted capital in prior years. Good current capitalization (5.4) based on good risk adjusted capital (severe loss scenario) reflecting some improvement over results in 1999. Good quality investment portfolio (5.3) despite mixed results such as: no exposure to mortgages and substantial holdings of BBB bonds but small junk bond holdings.
Other Rating Factors: Excellent profitability (7.3). Excellent liquidity (7.2).
Principal Business: Group retirement contracts (26%), credit health insurance (26%), credit life insurance (16%), group life insurance (15%), and other lines (17%).
Principal Investments: NonCMO investment grade bonds (46%), common & preferred stock (23%), CMOs and structured securities (14%), noninv. grade bonds (3%), and misc. investments (14%).
Investments in Affiliates: 28%
Group Affiliation: CUNA Mutual Ins Group
Licensed in: All states, the District of Columbia and Puerto Rico
Commenced Business: August 1935
Address: 5910 Mineral Point Rd, Madison, WI 53705
Phone: (608) 238-5851 **Domicile State:** WI **NAIC Code:** 62626

Data Date	Weiss Safety Rating	RACR #1	RACR #2	Total Assets ($mil)	Capital ($mil)	Net Premium ($mil)	Net Income ($mil)
6-03	C	0.93	0.80	2,756.6	546.2	676.1	13.7
6-02	C+	0.87	0.76	2,463.7	504.1	650.1	7.5
2002	C	0.83	0.72	2,594.1	496.2	1,294.0	9.7
2001	C+	0.87	0.77	2,390.5	506.3	1,163.4	13.4
2000	C+	1.00	0.87	2,284.9	574.6	1,194.6	203.5
1999	C+	0.79	0.71	2,220.4	423.2	1,179.3	4.3
1998	C+	0.79	0.71	2,130.6	390.8	1,075.2	38.8

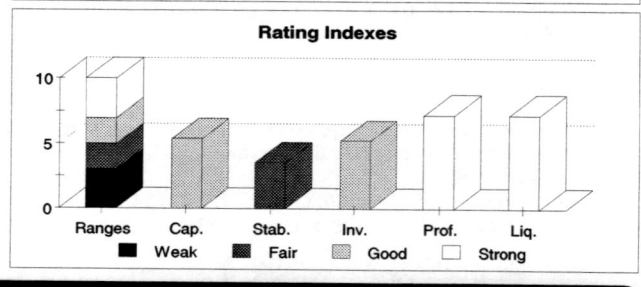

Rating Indexes (Ranges, Cap., Stab., Inv., Prof., Liq. — Weak, Fair, Good, Strong)

DAYTON AREA HEALTH PLAN — B — Good

Major Rating Factors: Good capitalization (5.6 on a scale of 0 to 10) based on good current risk-adjusted capital (severe loss scenario) reflecting some improvement over results in 2000. Good liquidity (6.9) with sufficient resources (cash flows and marketable investments) to handle a spike in claims. Excellent profitability (8.3) with operating gains in each of the last five years.
Other Rating Factors: High quality investment portfolio (9.9) containing no exposure to mortgages, junk bonds, or unaffiliated stocks. Excellent overall results on stability tests (7.2) based on consistent premium and capital growth in the last five years but rapid enrollment growth during the past five years.
Principal Business: Medicaid (100%).
Mem Phys: 02: 6,500 01: 6,201 **02 MLR** 89% / **02 Admin Exp** 5%
Enroll(000): Q1 03: 268 02: 246 01: 172 **Med Exp PMPM:** $133
Principal Investments: Cash and equiv (42%), other (58%).
Provider Compensation ($000): Contr fee ($287,463), capitation ($33,955)
Total Member Encounters: N/A
Group Affiliation: CareSource USA
Licensed in: OH
Address: One South Main St, Ste 440, Dayton, OH 45402
Phone: (937) 224-3300 **Dom State:** OH **Commenced Bus:** June 1988

Data Date	Weiss Safety Rating	RACR #1	RACR #2	Total Assets ($mil)	Capital ($mil)	Net Premium ($mil)	Net Income ($mil)
3-03	B	1.02	0.85	85.9	37.6	116.1	3.5
3-02	B-	0.89	0.75	77.7	20.5	80.9	4.6
2002	B-	0.91	0.76	111.6	34.0	373.1	18.5
2001	B-	0.90	0.76	65.8	15.9	194.9	5.7
2000	C-	0.87	0.74	29.1	10.6	94.6	1.5
1999	C-	1.09	0.92	24.8	9.1	86.8	0.7
1998	C-	1.02	0.86	26.3	8.3	84.9	1.4

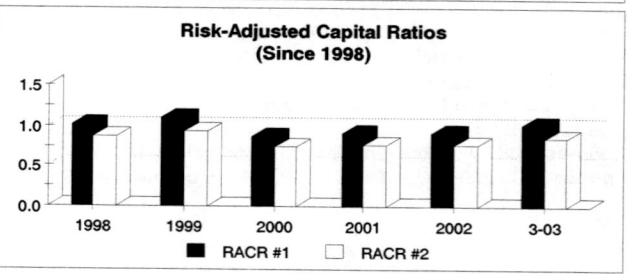

Risk-Adjusted Capital Ratios (Since 1998) — RACR #1, RACR #2 for years 1998–3-03

Winter 2003 - 04   II. Analysis of Largest Companies

DC CHARTERED HEALTH PLAN INC   C   Fair

Major Rating Factors: Fair quality investment portfolio (3.8 on a scale of 0 to 10). Good overall profitability index (5.2) despite a decline in earnings during 2002. Good capitalization (5.4) based on good current risk-adjusted capital (severe loss scenario) reflecting significant improvement over results in 2001.
Other Rating Factors: Good overall results on stability tests (5.7) despite weak risk-adjusted capital in prior years. Good liquidity (6.8) with sufficient resources (cash flows and marketable investments) to handle a spike in claims.
Principal Business: Medicaid (100%)
Mem Phys: 02: 1,353   **01:** 1,348   **02 MLR** 80%   / **02 Admin Exp** 19%
Enroll(000): Q1 03: 35   **02:** 34   **01:** 27   **Med Exp PMPM:** $134
Principal Investments: Cash and equiv (66%), other (34%)
Provider Compensation ($000): Contr fee ($22,844), capitation ($15,103), FFS ($4,800), other ($5,036)
Total Member Encounters: Phys (99,642), non-phys (37,103)
Group Affiliation: DC Healthcare Systems Inc
Licensed in: DC
Address: 820 First St NE Suite LI100, Washington, DC 20002-4205
Phone: (202) 408-3965   **Dom State:** DC   **Commenced Bus:** September 1986

Data Date	Weiss Safety Rating	RACR #1	RACR #2	Total Assets ($mil)	Capital ($mil)	Net Premium ($mil)	Net Income ($mil)
3-03	C	0.99	0.82	21.2	6.8	19.5	0.7
3-02	D+	0.50	0.43	16.7	5.3	12.8	1.4
2002	C	0.95	0.79	17.6	6.6	61.5	0.9
2001	D+	0.50	0.43	12.6	4.1	48.5	1.3
2000	D+	0.66	0.55	10.8	4.0	45.1	1.2
1999	N/A	N/A	N/A	9.3	3.7	41.3	N/A
1998	D+	1.14	0.95	21.6	12.5	36.2	-4.2

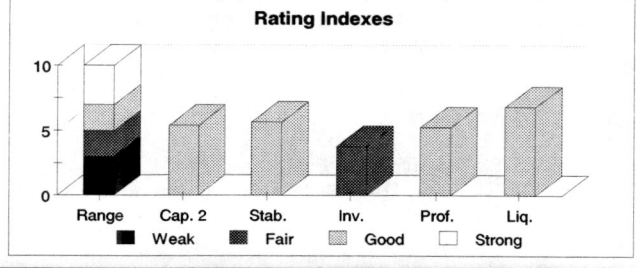

Rating Indexes (bar chart: Range, Cap. 2, Stab., Inv., Prof., Liq.; legend: Weak, Fair, Good, Strong)

DEAN HEALTH PLAN INC *   B+   Good

Major Rating Factors: Good overall results on stability tests (6.4 on a scale of 0 to 10) based on steady enrollment growth, averaging 4% over the past five years. Strong capitalization (7.0) based on excellent current risk-adjusted capital (severe loss scenario) reflecting improvement over results in 2001. High quality investment portfolio (9.7).
Other Rating Factors: Excellent liquidity (7.0) with ample operational cash flow and liquid investments. Fair profitability index (4.6) with operating gains in each of the last five years. Return on equity has been low, averaging 4% over the last five years.
Principal Business: Comp med (87%), FEHB (5%), Medicaid (3%), med supp (3%), Medicare (2%)
Mem Phys: 02: 1,802   **01:** 1,726   **02 MLR** 93%   / **02 Admin Exp** 6%
Enroll(000): Q1 03: 216   **02:** 212   **01:** 200   **Med Exp PMPM:** $199
Principal Investments: Cash and equiv (36%), real estate (16%), nonaffiliate common stock (13%), affiliate common stock (1%), other (35%)
Provider Compensation ($000): Capitation ($491,897)
Total Member Encounters: Phys (726,653), non-phys (196,319)
Group Affiliation: Dean Health Group
Licensed in: WI
Address: 1277 Deming Way, Madison, WI 53562
Phone: (608) 836-1400   **Dom State:** WI   **Commenced Bus:** January 1984

Data Date	Weiss Safety Rating	RACR #1	RACR #2	Total Assets ($mil)	Capital ($mil)	Net Premium ($mil)	Net Income ($mil)
3-03	B+	1.37	1.14	123.0	37.5	148.0	0.5
3-02	B+	1.14	0.94	114.9	38.8	127.6	0.9
2002	B+	1.44	1.20	99.4	39.1	529.0	2.2
2001	B+	1.15	0.95	89.3	36.4	456.0	1.9
2000	B+	1.26	1.06	85.9	38.1	376.4	1.3
1999	B+	1.58	1.35	74.7	38.7	330.4	0.4
1998	B+	1.58	1.35	70.7	38.4	317.3	1.5

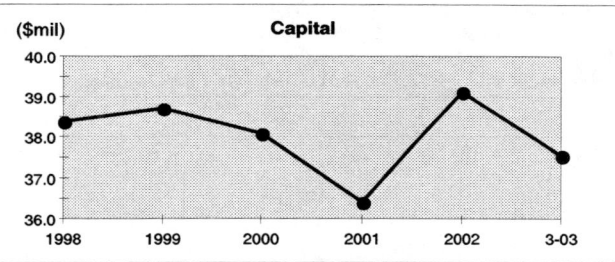

Capital ($mil) line chart from 1998 to 3-03, ranging approximately 36.0 to 40.0.

DELAWARE AMERICAN LIFE INSURANCE COMPANY   B   Good

Major Rating Factors: Good overall results on stability tests (6.3 on a scale of 0 to 10). Stability strengths include excellent operational trends and excellent risk diversification. Good quality investment portfolio (6.2) despite mixed results such as: no exposure to mortgages and large holdings of BBB rated bonds but small junk bond holdings. Strong capitalization (10.0) based on excellent risk adjusted capital (severe loss scenario).
Other Rating Factors: Excellent profitability (7.8) with operating gains in each of the last five years. Excellent liquidity (7.5).
Principal Business: Group health insurance (47%), individual life insurance (21%), group life insurance (17%), and reinsurance (14%).
Principal Investments: NonCMO investment grade bonds (90%), noninv. grade bonds (4%), policy loans (4%), and common & preferred stock (1%).
Investments in Affiliates: None
Group Affiliation: American International Group
Licensed in: All states except MN, MO, NH, NY, NC, PR
Commenced Business: August 1966
Address: One ALICO Plaza, Wilmington, DE 19801
Phone: (302) 594-2000   **Domicile State:** DE   **NAIC Code:** 62634

Data Date	Weiss Safety Rating	RACR #1	RACR #2	Total Assets ($mil)	Capital ($mil)	Net Premium ($mil)	Net Income ($mil)
6-03	B	4.22	3.28	102.5	35.6	7.6	2.2
6-02	B	3.37	2.35	94.2	27.4	10.6	1.0
2002	B	4.12	3.39	98.3	33.6	18.8	7.5
2001	B	3.45	2.51	92.9	26.6	19.7	4.1
2000	B	2.99	2.45	91.7	22.6	18.2	4.1
1999	B	2.55	1.89	87.7	18.2	20.3	3.6
1998	B	3.39	2.72	97.7	26.9	20.2	6.3

Adverse Trends in Operations

Increase in policy surrenders from 1999 to 2000 (28%)
Decrease in premium volume from 1999 to 2000 (10%)
Increase in policy surrenders from 1998 to 1999 (60%)
Decrease in asset base during 1999 (10%)
Decrease in capital during 1999 (32%)

www.WeissRatings.com   * Denotes a Weiss Recommended Company

II. Analysis of Largest Companies

Winter 2003 - 04

DELMARVA HEALTH PLAN INC   B-   Good

Major Rating Factors: Fair overall results on stability tests (3.4 on a scale of 0 to 10) based on fair risk-adjusted capital in prior years, a steep decline in premium revenue in 2002 and a significant 90% decrease in enrollment during the period. Rating is significantly influenced by the good financial results of CareFirst Inc. Good overall profitability index (5.5) despite operating losses during 2001. Good liquidity (6.9) with sufficient resources (cash flows and marketable investments) to handle a spike in claims.
Other Rating Factors: Strong capitalization (10.0) based on excellent current risk-adjusted capital (severe loss scenario) reflecting significant improvement over results in 1999. High quality investment portfolio (9.9) containing little or no exposure to mortgages, junk bonds, or unaffiliated stocks.
Principal Business: Comp med (100%)
Mem Phys: 02: 1,183   **01:** 1,155   **02 MLR** 93%   / **02 Admin Exp** 4%
Enroll(000): Q1 03: 0   **02:** 1   **01:** 13   **Med Exp PMPM:** $188
Principal Investments: Cash and equiv (10%), other (90%)
Provider Compensation ($000): Contr fee ($19,401), capitation ($1,105)
Total Member Encounters: Phys (42,951), non-phys (7,908)
Group Affiliation: CareFirst Inc
Licensed in: DE, MD
Address: 301 Bay St Suite 401, Easton, MD 21601
Phone: (410) 822-7223   **Dom State:** MD   **Commenced Bus:** March 1982

Data Date	Weiss Safety Rating	RACR #1	RACR #2	Total Assets ($mil)	Capital ($mil)	Net Premium ($mil)	Net Income ($mil)
3-03	B-	4.07	3.39	8.6	7.5	0.1	-0.2
3-02	B-	1.85	1.49	14.6	6.8	6.2	-0.2
2002	B-	3.65	3.04	10.1	7.7	16.8	1.0
2001	B-	2.36	1.90	18.1	9.0	61.9	-0.3
2000	C+	1.00	0.83	22.2	9.1	83.0	3.9
1999	C+	0.70	0.59	23.9	5.2	91.6	0.1
1998	C+	0.91	0.77	19.3	5.1	82.6	0.1

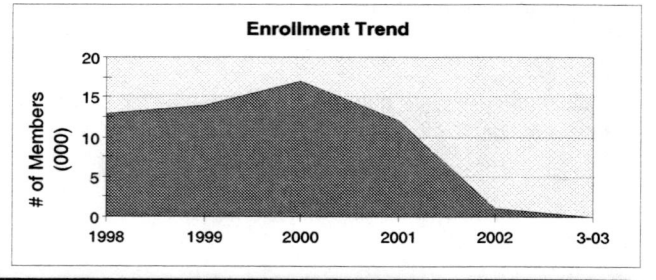

Enrollment Trend

DELTA DENTAL INSURANCE COMPANY   C   Fair

Major Rating Factors: Fair current capitalization (4.7 on a scale of 0 to 10) based on mixed results -- excessive policy leverage mitigated by fair risk adjusted capital (moderate loss scenario), although results have slipped from the good range over the last two years. Fair overall results on stability tests (4.0) including fair risk adjusted capital in prior years. Weak liquidity (2.0).
Other Rating Factors: High quality investment portfolio (8.7). Excellent profitability (7.7) with operating gains in each of the last five years.
Principal Business: Group health insurance (96%) and reinsurance (4%).
Principal Investments: NonCMO investment grade bonds (86%), cash (11%), and common & preferred stock (3%).
Investments in Affiliates: None
Group Affiliation: Dentegra Group
Licensed in: AL, AK, AZ, CA, CT, DC, DE, FL, GA, HI, IL, IN, KS, KY, LA, ME, MD, MS, MO, MT, NE, NV, NM, NY, NC, ND, OR, SC, TN, TX, UT, WV
Commenced Business: October 1970
Address: 100 First St, San Francisco, CA 94105
Phone: (415) 972-8400   **Domicile State:** DE   **NAIC Code:** 81396

Data Date	Weiss Safety Rating	RACR #1	RACR #2	Total Assets ($mil)	Capital ($mil)	Net Premium ($mil)	Net Income ($mil)
3-03	C	0.90	0.71	57.3	29.4	36.5	0.2
3-02	C	0.90	0.71	50.5	23.0	33.2	0.1
2002	C	0.91	0.71	56.0	29.0	137.5	0.2
2001	C	1.01	0.79	48.3	24.2	111.3	0.4
2000	C	1.04	0.83	40.6	19.1	96.2	0.1
1999	C	1.17	0.91	38.5	18.6	81.8	0.2
1998	E+	1.37	1.08	35.8	18.5	67.0	0.1

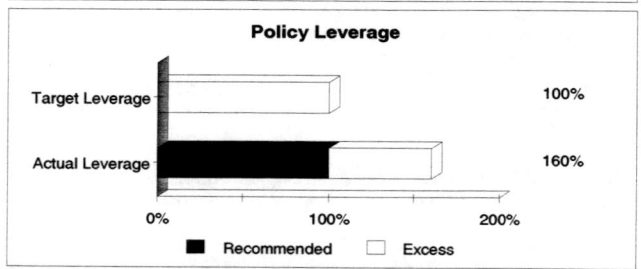

Policy Leverage
Target Leverage 100%
Actual Leverage 160%

DENVER HEALTH MEDICAL PLAN INC   D+   Weak

Major Rating Factors: Weak profitability index (1.1 on a scale of 0 to 10) with operating losses during 2001. Fair capitalization (4.5) based on fair current risk-adjusted capital (moderate loss scenario) reflecting improvement over results in 2001. Good overall results on stability tests (5.0) despite weak risk-adjusted capital in prior years, rapid premium growth over the last five years and rapid enrollment growth during the past five years.
Other Rating Factors: Good liquidity (6.9) with sufficient resources (cash flows and marketable investments) to handle a spike in claims. High quality investment portfolio (9.9) containing no exposure to mortgages, junk bonds, or unaffiliated stocks.
Principal Business: Comp med (84%), other (16%)
Mem Phys: 02: 1,753   **01:** 1,245   **02 MLR** 90%   / **02 Admin Exp** 10%
Enroll(000): Q1 03: 11   **02:** 11   **01:** 10   **Med Exp PMPM:** $120
Principal Investments: Cash and equiv (82%), other (18%)
Provider Compensation ($000): FFS ($7,988), capitation ($5,729), contr fee ($979)
Total Member Encounters: Phys (45,193), non-phys (862)
Group Affiliation: Denver Health & Hospital Authority
Licensed in: CO
Address: 777 Bannock St, Denver, CO 80204
Phone: (303) 436-7253   **Dom State:** CO   **Commenced Bus:** January 1997

Data Date	Weiss Safety Rating	RACR #1	RACR #2	Total Assets ($mil)	Capital ($mil)	Net Premium ($mil)	Net Income ($mil)
3-03	D+	0.85	0.71	5.0	2.4	5.5	0.8
3-02	D+	0.47	0.40	3.3	1.6	4.0	0.6
2002	D+	0.58	0.49	3.6	1.6	16.6	0.1
2001	D+	0.47	0.40	3.0	1.0	13.9	-0.9
2000	C-	1.15	0.98	3.9	1.9	11.2	0.4
1999	C-	1.69	1.42	3.7	2.1	8.0	0.3
1998	D+	1.12	0.99	2.5	1.8	5.1	0.1

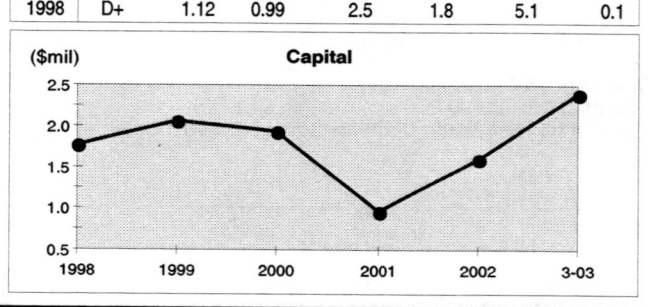

Capital ($mil)

Winter 2003 - 04   II. Analysis of Largest Companies

DRISCOLL CHILDRENS HEALTH PLAN   C+   Fair

Major Rating Factors: Fair profitability index (3.3 on a scale of 0 to 10) with operating losses during 1998, 1999, 2000 and 2001. Good overall results on stability tests (6.9) based on healthy premium and capital growth during 2002 but a decline in enrollment during 2002. Strong overall capitalization (9.5) based on excellent current risk-adjusted capital (severe loss scenario) despite some fluctuation in capital levels.
Other Rating Factors: High quality investment portfolio (9.9) containing no exposure to mortgages, junk bonds, or unaffiliated stocks. Excellent liquidity (7.7) with ample operational cash flow and liquid investments.
Principal Business: Other (100%)
Mem Phys: 02: 564   **01:** 355   **02 MLR** 68%   / **02 Admin Exp** 17%
Enroll(000): Q1 03: 19   **02:** 19   **01:** 21   **Med Exp PMPM:** $62
Principal Investments: Cash and equiv (62%), other (38%)
Provider Compensation ($000): Contr fee ($10,423), capitation ($2,750), FFS ($1,868), bonus arrang ($560)
Total Member Encounters: Phys (66,264), non-phys (5,142)
Group Affiliation: None
Licensed in: TX
Address: 3455 S Alameda, Corpus Christi, TX 78411
Phone: (361) 694-6750   **Dom State:** TX   **Commenced Bus:** April 1997

Data Date	Weiss Safety Rating	RACR #1	RACR #2	Total Assets ($mil)	Capital ($mil)	Net Premium ($mil)	Net Income ($mil)
3-03	C+	3.39	2.82	13.2	10.2	4.6	0.4
3-02	U	2.84	2.33	9.8	6.2	5.5	-0.2
2002	C+	3.23	2.69	12.5	9.8	22.2	3.5
2001	U	2.85	2.34	8.8	6.5	15.0	-1.2
2000	U	6.14	5.28	5.5	4.3	2.6	-1.2
1999	N/A	N/A	N/A	4.3	4.1	N/A	-0.5
1998	N/A	N/A	N/A	4.1	4.1	N/A	-0.9

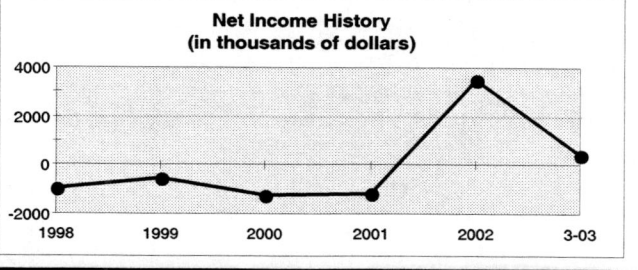

Net Income History (in thousands of dollars)

EDUCATORS MUTUAL LIFE INSURANCE COMPANY   B   Good

Major Rating Factors: Good liquidity (6.6 on a scale of 0 to 10) with sufficient resources to handle a spike in claims. Fair profitability (4.2). Fair overall results on stability tests (4.3) including negative cash flow from operations for 2002.
Other Rating Factors: Strong capitalization (10.0) based on excellent risk adjusted capital (severe loss scenario). High quality investment portfolio (7.2).
Principal Business: Group health insurance (93%) and group life insurance (7%).
Principal Investments: NonCMO investment grade bonds (87%), noninv. grade bonds (5%), mortgages in good standing (2%), and , and misc. investments (6%).
Investments in Affiliates: 9%
Group Affiliation: EML Ins Group
Licensed in: AL, AZ, AR, CT, DC, DE, FL, GA, ID, IL, IN, KS, KY, MD, MI, MT, NE, NV, NJ, NC, ND, OH, OK, OR, PA, RI, SC, TN, TX, VT, VA, WA, WV
Commenced Business: March 1940
Address: 202 North Prince St, Lancaster, PA 17604
Phone: (800) 233-0307   **Domicile State:** PA   **NAIC Code:** 62804

Data Date	Weiss Safety Rating	RACR #1	RACR #2	Total Assets ($mil)	Capital ($mil)	Net Premium ($mil)	Net Income ($mil)
6-03	B	5.22	3.69	86.8	53.6	23.2	1.3
6-02	B	4.09	2.96	100.4	54.6	52.8	0.3
2002	B	4.22	3.07	91.5	53.1	94.8	-2.5
2001	B	4.05	2.96	104.7	54.3	106.5	1.6
2000	B	4.06	3.05	105.7	57.0	102.3	3.9
1999	B	5.17	3.87	105.5	57.7	72.7	4.4
1998	B	3.68	2.81	129.7	53.7	105.1	-4.9

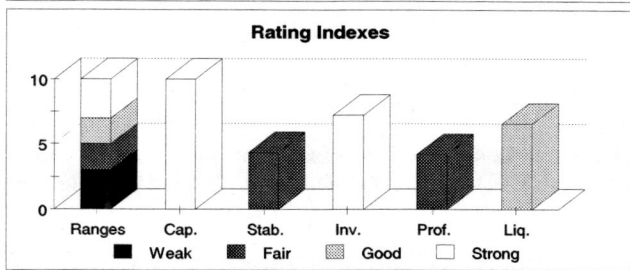

Rating Indexes — Ranges, Cap., Stab., Inv., Prof., Liq. — Weak, Fair, Good, Strong

ELDER HEALTH MARYLAND HMO INC   C-   Fair

Major Rating Factors: Weak profitability index (0.9 on a scale of 0 to 10). Good capitalization (5.1) based on good current risk-adjusted capital (severe loss scenario) reflecting some improvement over results in 2001. High quality investment portfolio (9.9) containing no exposure to mortgages, junk bonds, or unaffiliated stocks.
Other Rating Factors: Excellent overall results on stability tests (7.8) based on healthy premium and capital growth during 2002. Excellent liquidity (7.2) with ample operational cash flow and liquid investments.
Principal Business: Medicare (100%)
Mem Phys: 02: 321   **01:** 345   **02 MLR** 78%   / **02 Admin Exp** 19%
Enroll(000): Q1 03: 3   **02:** 2   **01:** 2   **Med Exp PMPM:** $754
Principal Investments: Cash and equiv (100%)
Provider Compensation ($000): FFS ($12,545), contr fee ($5,225), salary ($1,221), capitation ($912)
Total Member Encounters: Phys (29,309), non-phys (23,860)
Group Affiliation: Elder Health Inc
Licensed in: MD
Address: 1001 W Pratt St, Baltimore, MD 21223
Phone: (410) 864-4400   **Dom State:** MD   **Commenced Bus:** January 2001

Data Date	Weiss Safety Rating	RACR #1	RACR #2	Total Assets ($mil)	Capital ($mil)	Net Premium ($mil)	Net Income ($mil)
3-03	C-	0.95	0.79	9.9	3.9	7.5	0.2
3-02	U	0.70	0.60	10.5	2.6	6.7	-0.2
2002	C-	0.89	0.74	11.9	3.7	27.1	0.9
2001	U	0.68	0.58	9.8	2.8	22.3	-1.6
2000	N/A	N/A	N/A	1.6	1.6	N/A	N/A
1999	N/A	N/A	N/A	N/A	N/A	N/A	N/A
1998	N/A	N/A	N/A	N/A	N/A	N/A	N/A

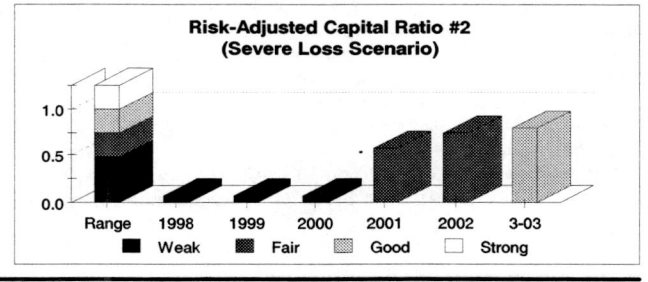

Risk-Adjusted Capital Ratio #2 (Severe Loss Scenario) — Weak, Fair, Good, Strong

www.WeissRatings.com   155   * Denotes a Weiss Recommended Company

II. Analysis of Largest Companies
Winter 2003 - 04

ELDERPLAN INC — E- Very Weak

Major Rating Factors: Weak profitability index (0.7 on a scale of 0 to 10) with operating losses during 1998, 1999, 2000 and 2002. Poor capitalization index (0.0) based on weak current risk-adjusted capital (severe loss scenario). Weak overall results on stability tests (0.0).
Other Rating Factors: Weak liquidity (0.1) as a spike in claims may stretch capacity. High quality investment portfolio (9.9).
Principal Business: Medicare (100%)
Mem Phys: 02: 3,834 **01:** 2,000 **02 MLR** 82% **/ 02 Admin Exp** 23%
Enroll(000): Q1 03: 11 **02:** 11 **01:** 10 **Med Exp PMPM:** $828
Principal Investments: Cash and equiv (37%), nonaffiliate common stock (8%), other (55%)
Provider Compensation ($000): Contr fee ($34,265), capitation ($14,645), FFS ($9,622), other ($39,070)
Total Member Encounters: N/A
Group Affiliation: None
Licensed in: NY
Address: 6323 7th Ave, Brooklyn, NY 11220
Phone: (718) 921-7990 **Dom State:** NY **Commenced Bus:** March 1985

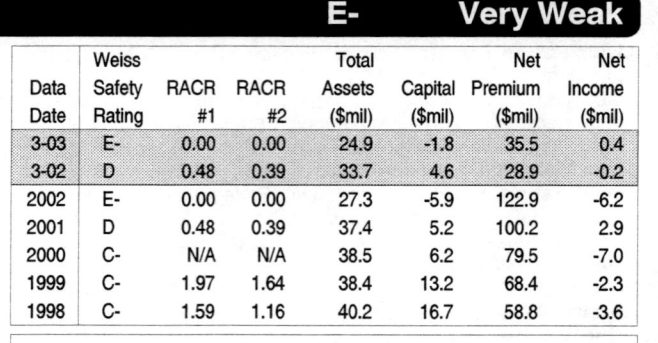

Data Date	Weiss Safety Rating	RACR #1	RACR #2	Total Assets ($mil)	Capital ($mil)	Net Premium ($mil)	Net Income ($mil)
3-03	E-	0.00	0.00	24.9	-1.8	35.5	0.4
3-02	D	0.48	0.39	33.7	4.6	28.9	-0.2
2002	E-	0.00	0.00	27.3	-5.9	122.9	-6.2
2001	D	0.48	0.39	37.4	5.2	100.2	2.9
2000	C-	N/A	N/A	38.5	6.2	79.5	-7.0
1999	C-	1.97	1.64	38.4	13.2	68.4	-2.3
1998	C-	1.59	1.16	40.2	16.7	58.8	-3.6

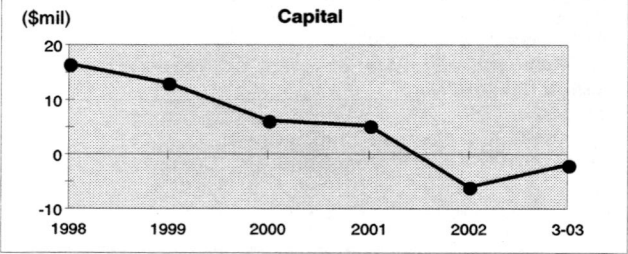

Capital ($mil) chart 1998–3-03

EMPIRE HEALTHCHOICE ASSURANCE INC * — A- Excellent

Major Rating Factors: Excellent profitability (7.1 on a scale of 0 to 10) with operating gains in each of the last five years. Strong capitalization (9.5) based on excellent current risk-adjusted capital (severe loss scenario) reflecting improvement over results in 1998. High quality investment portfolio (9.8) containing little or no exposure to mortgages, junk bonds, or unaffiliated stocks.
Other Rating Factors: Good liquidity (7.0) with sufficient resources (cash flows and marketable investments) to handle a spike in claims.
Principal Business: Comp med (80%), Medicare (10%), med supp (6%), FEHB (4%)
Mem Phys: 02: 50,174 **01:** 63,717 **02 MLR** 86% **/ 02 Admin Exp** 11%
Enroll(000): Q1 03: 2,720 **02:** 2,704 **01:** 3,143 **Med Exp PMPM:** $97
Principal Investments: Cash and equiv (23%), affiliate common stock (9%), other (68%)
Provider Compensation ($000): Contr fee ($2,943,945), FFS ($615,902), capitation ($65,258)
Total Member Encounters: Phys (9,698,528), non-phys (3,095,330)
Group Affiliation: WellChoice Inc
Licensed in: NY
Address: 11 W 42nd St, New York, NY 10036
Phone: (212) 476-7470 **Dom State:** NY **Commenced Bus:** June 1974

Data Date	Weiss Safety Rating	RACR #1	RACR #2	Total Assets ($mil)	Capital ($mil)	Net Premium ($mil)	Net Income ($mil)
3-03	A-	3.35	2.79	1,762.8	853.8	802.3	38.4
3-02	B+	0.00	0.00	1,919.3	668.5	1,078.4	62.5
2002	A-	3.17	2.64	1,687.5	819.8	3,999.1	248.6
2001	B+	2.54	2.06	1,925.9	610.8	4,155.3	98.4
2000	C+	2.54	1.58	1,828.7	532.1	3,836.6	106.7
1999	C-	1.78	1.09	1,769.2	538.3	3,355.2	110.6
1998	D+	1.42	0.87	1,738.5	404.1	3,062.5	34.5

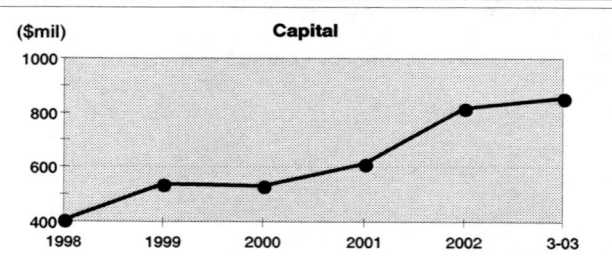

Capital ($mil) chart 1998–3-03

EMPIRE HEALTHCHOICE HMO INC — B Good

Major Rating Factors: Fair profitability index (4.8 on a scale of 0 to 10) with operating losses during 1999, 2000 and 2001. Return on equity has been low, averaging 3%. Fair overall results on stability tests (3.5) based on rapid premium growth over the last five years, a decline in the number of member physicians during 2002 and an excessive 2218% enrollment growth during the period. Potentially strong support from affiliation with WellChoice Inc. Strong capitalization index (10.0) based on excellent current risk-adjusted capital (severe loss scenario).
Other Rating Factors: High quality investment portfolio (9.9) containing no exposure to mortgages, junk bonds, or unaffiliated stocks. Excellent liquidity (7.2) with ample operational cash flow and liquid investments.
Principal Business: Comp med (87%), Medicare (13%)
Mem Phys: 02: 37,037 **01:** 72,324 **02 MLR** 78% **/ 02 Admin Exp** 13%
Enroll(000): Q1 03: 403 **02:** 404 **01:** 17 **Med Exp PMPM:** $174
Principal Investments: Cash and equiv (96%), other (4%)
Provider Compensation ($000): Contr fee ($299,511), capitation ($26,894)
Total Member Encounters: Phys (1,111,483), non-phys (266,459)
Group Affiliation: WellChoice Inc
Licensed in: NJ, NY
Address: 11 W 42nd St, New York, NY 10036
Phone: (212) 476-1000 **Dom State:** NY **Commenced Bus:** March 1996

Data Date	Weiss Safety Rating	RACR #1	RACR #2	Total Assets ($mil)	Capital ($mil)	Net Premium ($mil)	Net Income ($mil)
3-03	B	3.74	3.12	331.3	111.3	351.8	20.0
3-02	C	0.00	0.00	23.4	15.4	9.4	0.7
2002	B	3.17	2.64	295.0	95.7	561.8	32.0
2001	C	0.00	0.00	21.3	14.9	29.5	-1.4
2000	U	6.21	5.46	18.4	14.3	14.7	-4.1
1999	U	26.53	24.25	21.6	18.5	3.2	-1.3
1998	N/A	N/A	N/A	20.6	19.9	1.0	0.1

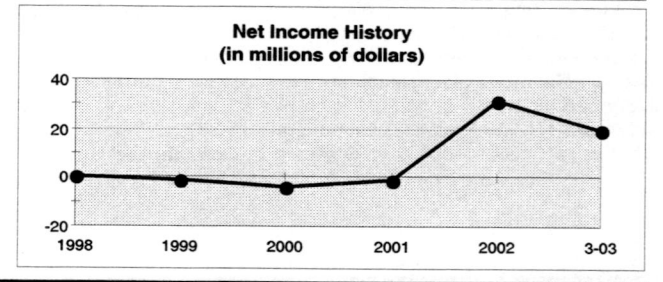

Net Income History (in millions of dollars) chart 1998–3-03

EMPLOYERS REASSURANCE CORPORATION   C   Fair

Major Rating Factors: Good overall capitalization (5.4 on a scale of 0 to 10) based on good risk adjusted capital (moderate loss scenario). Nevertheless, capital levels have fluctuated during prior years. Good quality investment portfolio (6.3) despite mixed results such as: substantial holdings of BBB bonds but moderate junk bond exposure. Weak profitability (2.1) with operating losses during the first six months of 2003.
Other Rating Factors: Weak overall results on stability tests (2.8) including weak results on operational trends. Excellent liquidity (7.0).
Principal Business: Reinsurance (100%).
Principal Investments: NonCMO investment grade bonds (65%), CMOs and structured securities (26%), policy loans (3%), noninv. grade bonds (2%), and misc. investments (5%).
Investments in Affiliates: None
Group Affiliation: General Electric Corp Group
Licensed in: All states except NY
Commenced Business: November 1907
Address: 5200 Metcalf Ave, Overland Park, KS 66201
Phone: (913) 676-5724 **Domicile State:** KS **NAIC Code:** 68276

Data Date	Weiss Safety Rating	RACR #1	RACR #2	Total Assets ($mil)	Capital ($mil)	Net Premium ($mil)	Net Income ($mil)
6-03	C	1.28	0.79	5,856.1	438.7	705.2	-64.9
6-02	B-	2.25	1.34	5,345.3	605.9	342.1	-17.6
2002	C+	1.40	0.87	5,653.2	472.1	999.9	-151.6
2001	B-	2.26	1.35	5,352.3	637.6	1,699.3	53.0
2000	B-	2.75	1.65	4,201.9	617.7	741.8	451.3
1999	B-	2.09	1.24	4,128.3	480.7	660.6	-274.9
1998	B	2.19	1.28	3,858.8	434.7	929.5	30.3

Risk-Adjusted Capital Ratio #1 (Moderate Loss Scenario)

EMPLOYERS REINSURANCE CORP   C+   Fair

Major Rating Factors: Fair overall results on stability tests (3.0 on a scale of 0 to 10) including weak results on operational trends and fair risk adjusted capital in prior years. The largest net exposure for one risk is excessive at 5.9% of capital. Strengths include potentially strong support from affiliation with General Electric Corp Group. Fair long-term capitalization index (4.3) based on fair current risk adjusted capital (severe loss scenario), although results have slipped from the excellent range over the last two years.
Other Rating Factors: Fair profitability index (4.0) with small operating losses during 2001. Return on equity has been fair, averaging 9.2% over the past five years. A history of deficient reserves (2.6) that places pressure on both capital and profits. In 2002, the two year reserve development was 47% deficient. Excellent liquidity (7.9) with ample operational cash flow and liquid investments.
Principal Business: Group accident & health (42%), aggregate write-ins for other lines of business (32%), other liability (17%), fire (4%), allied lines (3%), and earthquake (1%).
Principal Investments: Investment grade bonds (69%), misc. investments (30%), and non investment grade bonds (1%).
Investments in Affiliates: 27%
Group Affiliation: General Electric Corp Group
Licensed in: All states, the District of Columbia and Puerto Rico
Commenced Business: September 1981
Address: 5200 Metcalf, Overland Park, KS 66201
Phone: (913) 676-5200 **Domicile State:** MO **NAIC Code:** 39845

Data Date	Weiss Safety Rating	RACR #1	RACR #2	Loss Ratio %	Total Assets ($mil)	Capital ($mil)	Net Premium ($mil)	Net Income ($mil)
6-03	C+	0.89	0.64	N/A	15,079.2	4,604.8	171.1	225.9
6-02	B-	1.29	1.05	N/A	12,768.9	4,463.1	132.2	-21.6
2002	C+	0.93	0.67	145.1	15,568.8	4,876.1	2,853.2	744.0
2001	B-	1.42	1.16	116.0	12,740.3	4,857.9	1,920.3	-40.4
2000	B-	1.13	0.94	82.3	10,262.1	4,050.1	2,227.1	262.9
1999	B-	1.21	1.01	79.7	10,463.6	4,269.7	1,888.6	349.1
1998	B-	1.13	0.96	70.7	10,712.0	4,098.6	1,862.2	671.4

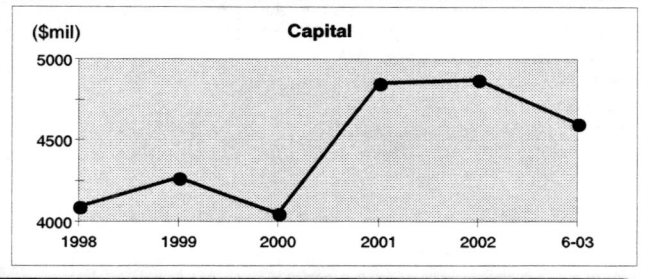

Capital

EQUITABLE LIFE & CASUALTY INSURANCE COMPANY   C   Fair

Major Rating Factors: Fair overall results on stability tests (4.1 on a scale of 0 to 10). Good quality investment portfolio (6.2) with no exposure to mortgages and minimal holdings in junk bonds. Strong current capitalization (7.1) based on excellent risk adjusted capital (severe loss scenario) reflecting improvement over results in 1998.
Other Rating Factors: Excellent profitability (7.8) with operating gains in each of the last five years. Excellent liquidity (7.2).
Principal Business: Individual health insurance (91%) and individual life insurance (9%).
Principal Investments: NonCMO investment grade bonds (68%), CMOs and structured securities (17%), mortgages in good standing (8%), cash (4%), and misc. investments (2%).
Investments in Affiliates: None
Group Affiliation: Insurance Investment Co
Licensed in: AL, AK, AZ, AR, CO, DC, DE, HI, ID, IL, IN, IA, KS, KY, LA, MI, MS, MO, MT, NE, NV, NH, NM, NC, ND, OH, OK, OR, PA, RI, SC, SD, TN, TX, UT, VT, VA, WA, WV, WY
Commenced Business: June 1935
Address: 3 Triad Center Suite 200, Salt Lake City, UT 84180
Phone: (801) 579-3400 **Domicile State:** UT **NAIC Code:** 62952

Data Date	Weiss Safety Rating	RACR #1	RACR #2	Total Assets ($mil)	Capital ($mil)	Net Premium ($mil)	Net Income ($mil)
6-03	C	1.41	1.06	135.1	30.8	53.6	1.1
6-02	C	1.32	0.99	121.5	27.5	49.2	-1.3
2002	C	1.39	1.06	127.3	30.0	100.9	1.3
2001	C	1.52	1.14	116.3	29.2	90.2	1.0
2000	C	1.58	1.11	108.0	29.6	85.7	2.4
1999	C	1.41	1.08	101.2	28.7	83.9	3.8
1998	C	1.21	0.93	94.6	26.9	78.7	3.4

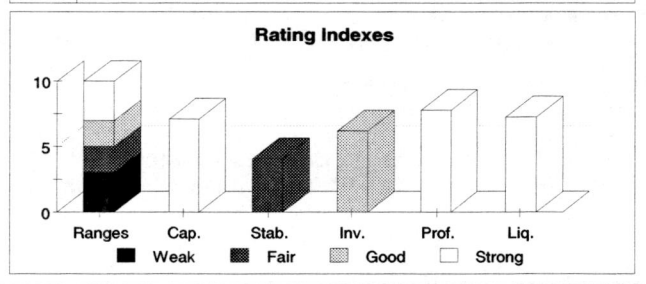

Rating Indexes

II. Analysis of Largest Companies

ERC LIFE REINSURANCE CORP   C   Fair

Major Rating Factors: Good overall profitability (5.9 on a scale of 0 to 10). Excellent expense controls. Return on equity has been fair, averaging 8.6%. Weak overall results on stability tests (2.9) including weak results on operational trends. Strong overall capitalization (7.8) based on excellent risk adjusted capital (severe loss scenario). Nevertheless, capital levels have fluctuated during prior years.
Other Rating Factors: High quality investment portfolio (7.1). Excellent liquidity (8.4).
Principal Business: Reinsurance (100%).
Principal Investments: NonCMO investment grade bonds (46%), common & preferred stock (39%), CMOs and structured securities (8%), policy loans (1%), and cash (1%).
Investments in Affiliates: 39%
Group Affiliation: Scottish Annuity & Life Holdings Ltd
Licensed in: All states except AL, HI, NC, ND, RI, PR
Commenced Business: October 1979
Address: 2405 Grand Ave Suite 900, Kansas City, MO 64108-2554
Phone: (913) 676-3014   **Domicile State:** MO   **NAIC Code:** 90670

Data Date	Weiss Safety Rating	RACR #1	RACR #2	Total Assets ($mil)	Capital ($mil)	Net Premium ($mil)	Net Income ($mil)
6-03	C	1.71	1.55	1,533.2	700.3	81.5	2.5
6-02	B	6.23	5.31	2,786.6	1,867.8	57.8	59.0
2002	C+	1.68	1.54	1,543.2	697.8	312.1	-58.9
2001	B	6.42	5.47	2,852.8	1,930.4	177.8	216.9
2000	B	6.22	5.36	2,891.2	1,845.0	218.3	213.3
1999	B	3.04	2.81	3,525.5	2,073.0	516.5	265.8
1998	B	2.59	2.41	2,676.0	1,778.3	378.9	137.8

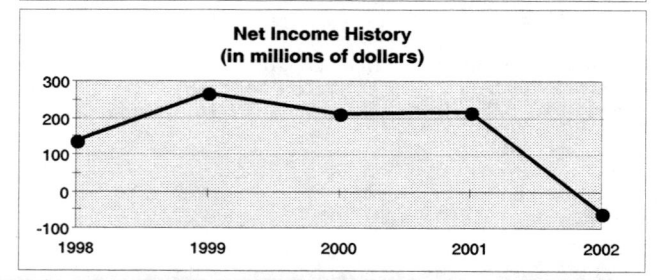

Net Income History (in millions of dollars)

EVERCARE OF TEXAS LLC   B-   Good

Major Rating Factors: Good overall results on stability tests (6.9 on a scale of 0 to 10). Rating is significantly influenced by the good financial results of UnitedHealth Group Inc. Good liquidity (6.9) with sufficient resources (cash flows and marketable investments) to handle a spike in claims. Excellent profitability (7.8).
Other Rating Factors: Strong overall capitalization (10.0) based on excellent current risk-adjusted capital (severe loss scenario). High quality investment portfolio (9.9) containing no exposure to mortgages, junk bonds, or unaffiliated stocks.
Principal Business: Other (100%)
Mem Phys: 02: N/A   **01:** N/A   **02 MLR** 84%   **/ 02 Admin Exp** 13%
Enroll(000): Q1 03: 29   **02:** 87   **01:** N/A   **Med Exp PMPM:** $197
Principal Investments: Cash and equiv (97%), other (3%)
Provider Compensation ($000): FFS ($98,956), capitation ($4,271)
Total Member Encounters: N/A
Group Affiliation: UnitedHealth Group Inc
Licensed in: TX
Address: 9700 Bissonnet, Ste 2225, Houston, TX 77036
Phone: (602) 331-5100   **Dom State:** TX   **Commenced Bus:** August 2001

Data Date	Weiss Safety Rating	RACR #1	RACR #2	Total Assets ($mil)	Capital ($mil)	Net Premium ($mil)	Net Income ($mil)
3-03	B-	8.37	6.98	35.9	6.4	33.4	0.6
3-02	N/A	N/A	N/A	N/A	N/A	N/A	N/A
2002	B-	8.08	6.73	35.3	5.8	121.6	2.4
2001	N/A	N/A	N/A	3.1	3.1	N/A	N/A
2000	N/A	N/A	N/A	0.1	0.1	N/A	N/A
1999	N/A	N/A	N/A	N/A	N/A	N/A	N/A
1998	N/A	N/A	N/A	N/A	N/A	N/A	N/A

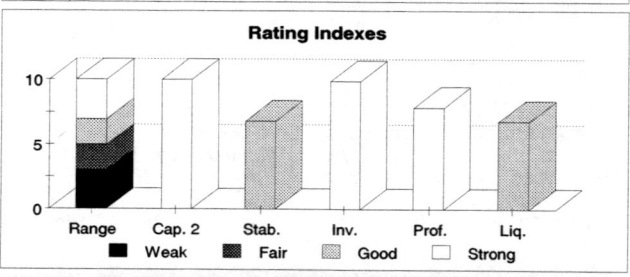

Rating Indexes

EVERGREEN HEALTH PLAN INC   E+   Very Weak

Major Rating Factors: Weak profitability index (0.4 on a scale of 0 to 10) with operating losses during 1998, 1999 and 2001. Poor capitalization index (0.0) based on weak current risk-adjusted capital (severe loss scenario). Fair overall results on stability tests (4.4) based on rapid premium growth over the last five years.
Other Rating Factors: Good liquidity (5.5) with sufficient resources (cash flows and marketable investments) to handle a spike in claims. High quality investment portfolio (9.6) containing no exposure to mortgages, junk bonds, or unaffiliated stocks.
Principal Business: Comp med (85%), other (15%)
Mem Phys: 01: 262   **00:** 267   **01 MLR** 99%   **/ 01 Admin Exp** 7%
Enroll(000): Q2 02: 12   **01:** 11   **00:** 12   **Med Exp PMPM:** $145
Principal Investments: Cash and equiv (100%)
Provider Compensation ($000): Contr fee ($18,104), FFS ($1,420), capitation ($279)
Total Member Encounters: N/A
Group Affiliation: Evergreen Medical Group, LLC
Licensed in: GA
Address: 707 Center St Ste 110, Columbus, GA 31901
Phone: (706) 660-6175   **Dom State:** GA   **Commenced Bus:** June 1998

Data Date	Weiss Safety Rating	RACR #1	RACR #2	Total Assets ($mil)	Capital ($mil)	Net Premium ($mil)	Net Income ($mil)
6-02	E+	0.29	0.24	4.0	1.0	11.1	-0.1
6-01	U	N/A	N/A	2.7	1.5	9.7	0.3
2001	E+	0.29	0.24	4.6	1.1	19.9	-1.2
2000	N/A	N/A	N/A	4.6	1.3	19.1	N/A
1999	U	0.72	0.60	3.2	1.4	10.7	-0.2
1998	N/A	N/A	N/A	2.5	1.0	4.0	-0.2
1997	N/A	N/A	N/A	1.3	1.3	N/A	N/A

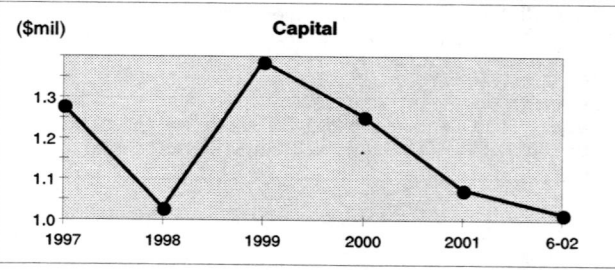

Capital ($mil)

Winter 2003 - 04
II. Analysis of Largest Companies

EXCELLUS HEALTH PLAN INC *   B+   Good

Major Rating Factors: Good liquidity (6.5 on a scale of 0 to 10) with sufficient resources (cash flows and marketable investments) to handle a spike in claims. Excellent profitability (7.5) despite operating losses during 1998. Strong capitalization (10.0) based on excellent current risk-adjusted capital (severe loss scenario) reflecting significant improvement over results in 2000.
Other Rating Factors: High quality investment portfolio (9.4) containing little or no exposure to mortgages, junk bonds, or unaffiliated stocks.
Principal Business: Comp med (79%), Medicare (10%), med supp (5%), Medicaid (2%), dental (2%), FEHB (2%)
Mem Phys: 02: N/A **01:** 18,356 **02 MLR** 89% / **02 Admin Exp** 7%
Enroll(000): Q1 03: 1,646 **02:** 1,720 **01:** 1,893 **Med Exp PMPM:** $134
Principal Investments: Cash and equiv (15%), affiliate common stock (8%), nonaffiliate common stock (6%), real estate (6%), other (65%)
Provider Compensation ($000): Contr fee ($2,290,633), capitation ($500,780), FFS ($74,645), bonus arrang ($1,413)
Total Member Encounters: Phys (14,850,812), non-phys (3,319,482)
Group Affiliation: Bl Cross & Bl Shield of Central NY
Licensed in: NY
Address: 165 Court St, Rochester, NY 14647
Phone: (716) 238-4506 **Dom State:** NY **Commenced Bus:** January 1936

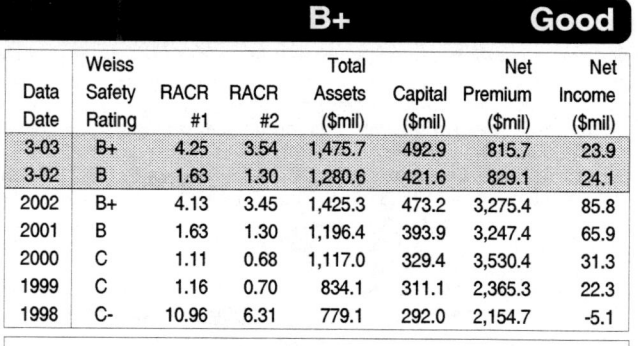

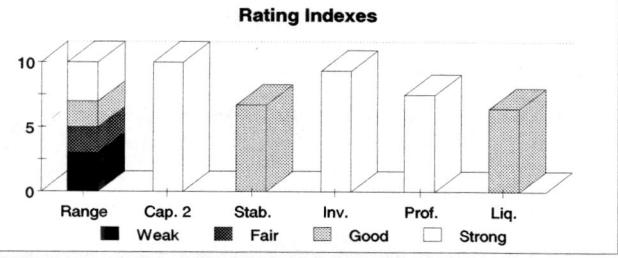

Data Date	Weiss Safety Rating	RACR #1	RACR #2	Total Assets ($mil)	Capital ($mil)	Net Premium ($mil)	Net Income ($mil)
3-03	B+	4.25	3.54	1,475.7	492.9	815.7	23.9
3-02	B	1.63	1.30	1,280.6	421.6	829.1	24.1
2002	B+	4.13	3.45	1,425.3	473.2	3,275.4	85.8
2001	B	1.63	1.30	1,196.4	393.9	3,247.4	65.9
2000	C	1.11	0.68	1,117.0	329.4	3,530.4	31.3
1999	C	1.16	0.70	834.1	311.1	2,365.3	22.3
1998	C-	10.96	6.31	779.1	292.0	2,154.7	-5.1

EXCLUSIVE HEALTHCARE INC   B   Good

Major Rating Factors: Fair overall results on stability tests (3.4 on a scale of 0 to 10) based on a steep decline in premium revenue in 2002, an overall decline in enrollment over the past five years. Rating is significantly influenced by the good financial results of Mutual of Omaha Ins Co. Strong overall capitalization (10.0) based on excellent current risk-adjusted capital (severe loss scenario) despite some fluctuation in capital levels. High quality investment portfolio (8.9) containing no exposure to mortgages, junk bonds, or unaffiliated stocks.
Other Rating Factors: Excellent liquidity (7.1) with ample operational cash flow and liquid investments. Weak profitability index (1.0) with operating losses during 1998, 2000 and 2001. Average return on equity has been poor at -55%.
Principal Business: Comp med (100%)
Mem Phys: 02: 4,117 **01:** 3,815 **02 MLR** 84% / **02 Admin Exp** 16%
Enroll(000): Q1 03: 14 **02:** 19 **01:** 22 **Med Exp PMPM:** $167
Principal Investments: Cash and equiv (40%), other (60%)
Provider Compensation ($000): Bonus arrang ($21,567), contr fee ($18,443), FFS ($2,116)
Total Member Encounters: Phys (136,724), non-phys (33,910)
Group Affiliation: Mutual of Omaha Ins Co
Licensed in: IA, NE
Address: Mutual Of Omaha Plaza, Omaha, NE 68175
Phone: (402) 342-7600 **Dom State:** NE **Commenced Bus:** May 1988

Data Date	Weiss Safety Rating	RACR #1	RACR #2	Total Assets ($mil)	Capital ($mil)	Net Premium ($mil)	Net Income ($mil)
3-03	B	5.73	4.77	25.9	17.2	9.9	2.1
3-02	B-	3.17	2.66	24.6	13.9	12.7	0.6
2002	B	5.15	4.29	24.5	15.2	48.6	1.8
2001	B-	3.19	2.67	24.2	13.3	61.0	-2.8
2000	B	2.56	2.14	42.9	16.2	94.8	-12.9
1999	B	1.77	1.57	58.9	23.7	151.5	0.4
1998	B	1.84	1.57	75.3	23.6	140.9	-37.3

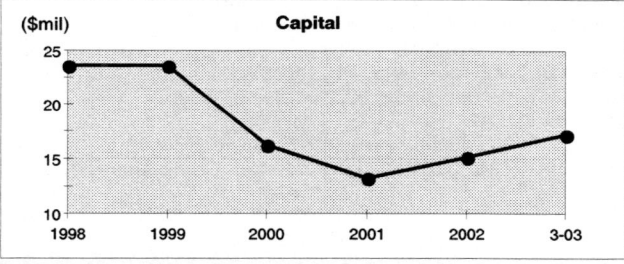

FALLON COMMUNITY HEALTH PLAN   B   Good

Major Rating Factors: Good overall results on stability tests (5.7 on a scale of 0 to 10) despite fair risk-adjusted capital in prior years. Good liquidity (7.0) with sufficient resources (cash flows and marketable investments) to handle a spike in claims. Fair profitability index (4.1) due to a decline in earnings during 2002.
Other Rating Factors: Strong capitalization (7.7) based on excellent current risk-adjusted capital (severe loss scenario) reflecting significant improvement over results in 1999. High quality investment portfolio (9.5).
Principal Business: Comp med (48%), Medicare (42%), FEHB (6%), Medicaid (5%)
Mem Phys: 02: 6,111 **01:** 5,007 **02 MLR** 90% / **02 Admin Exp** 9%
Enroll(000): Q1 03: 181 **02:** 186 **01:** 187 **Med Exp PMPM:** $247
Principal Investments: Cash and equiv (48%), nonaffiliate common stock (11%), affiliate common stock (3%), other (38%)
Provider Compensation ($000): Capitation ($471,199), contr fee ($76,207)
Total Member Encounters: Phys (1,313,651), non-phys (209,244)
Group Affiliation: Fallon Foundation
Licensed in: MA
Address: 10 Chestnut St, Worcester, MA 01608-2810
Phone: (508) 799-2100 **Dom State:** MA **Commenced Bus:** February 1977

Data Date	Weiss Safety Rating	RACR #1	RACR #2	Total Assets ($mil)	Capital ($mil)	Net Premium ($mil)	Net Income ($mil)
3-03	B	1.91	1.59	138.4	62.9	163.9	1.8
3-02	C+	1.67	1.31	113.1	67.6	150.0	2.8
2002	B-	1.82	1.51	141.9	60.2	611.2	6.8
2001	C+	1.67	1.31	125.0	64.4	585.9	26.7
2000	C	0.92	0.79	117.5	38.5	585.1	6.7
1999	C	0.62	0.53	102.6	32.3	544.3	-12.8
1998	B+	3.50	2.94	100.2	43.9	486.9	-21.0

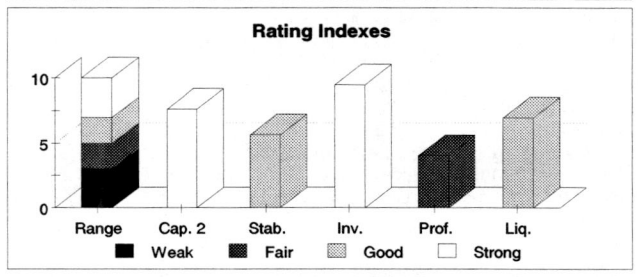

www.WeissRatings.com   * Denotes a Weiss Recommended Company

II. Analysis of Largest Companies

Winter 2003 - 04

FAMILY HEALTH CARE PLUS INC   D   Weak

Major Rating Factors: Weak overall results on stability tests (2.5 on a scale of 0 to 10) in spite of healthy premium and capital growth during 2001 but poor risk diversification due to the company's size. Weak liquidity (0.0) as a spike in claims may stretch capacity. Fair profitability index (3.2) with operating losses during 2000.
Other Rating Factors: Fair capitalization (4.2) based on fair current risk-adjusted capital (moderate loss scenario) reflecting improvement over results in 1999. High quality investment portfolio (8.4) containing no exposure to mortgages, junk bonds, or unaffiliated stocks.
Principal Business: Medicare (88%), comp med (12%)
Mem Phys: 01: 493   **00:** 493   **01 MLR** 74%   **/ 01 Admin Exp** 24%
Enroll(000): Q1 02: 1   **01:** 1   **00:** 1   **Med Exp PMPM:** $321
Principal Investments: Cash and equiv (84%), other (16%)
Provider Compensation ($000): Contr fee ($3,743), FFS ($1,384)
Total Member Encounters: Phys (476), non-phys (761)
Group Affiliation: Family Health Care Clinic Inc
Licensed in: MS
Address: 4635 Highway 80 East, Pearl, MS 39208
Phone: (601) 825-7280   **Dom State:** MS   **Commenced Bus:** December 1996

Data Date	Weiss Safety Rating	RACR #1	RACR #2	Total Assets ($mil)	Capital ($mil)	Net Premium ($mil)	Net Income ($mil)
3-02	D	0.78	0.67	3.2	1.5	1.9	0.2
3-01	D	0.69	0.59	2.3	1.0	1.5	0.1
2001	D	0.78	0.67	3.8	1.4	6.9	0.1
2000	D	0.51	0.43	2.1	0.9	3.4	-0.3
1999	D	0.49	0.42	1.4	1.2	6.1	0.0
1998	D	0.61	0.52	3.0	1.0	6.2	0.3
1997	N/A	N/A	N/A	1.1	0.4	23.1	0.3

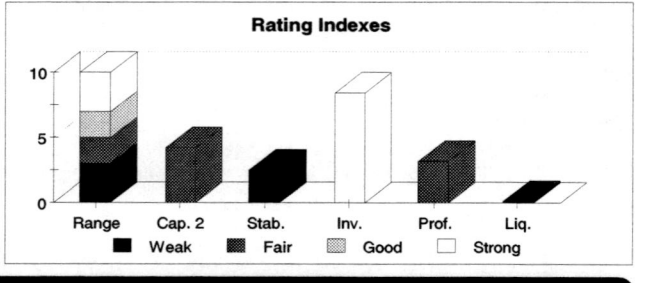

Rating Indexes chart: Range, Cap. 2, Stab., Inv., Prof., Liq. — Weak / Fair / Good / Strong

FAMILY HEALTH PLAN INC   E   Very Weak

Major Rating Factors: Weak profitability index (0.9 on a scale of 0 to 10) with $29.3 million in losses in the last five years. Poor capitalization index (0.0) based on weak current risk-adjusted capital (severe loss scenario). Fair overall results on stability tests (4.9) based on a steep decline in premium revenue in 2002.
Other Rating Factors: Good liquidity (5.6) with sufficient resources (cash flows and marketable investments) to handle a spike in claims. High quality investment portfolio (9.9) containing no exposure to mortgages, junk bonds, or unaffiliated stocks.
Principal Business: Comp med (54%), Medicaid (46%)
Mem Phys: 02: 923   **01:** 830   **02 MLR** 88%   **/ 02 Admin Exp** 15%
Enroll(000): Q1 03: 58   **02:** 45   **01:** 44   **Med Exp PMPM:** $141
Principal Investments: Cash and equiv (97%), other (3%)
Provider Compensation ($000): Contr fee ($52,431), FFS ($3,726), capitation ($1,138), other ($13,370)
Total Member Encounters: Phys (965,051), non-phys (228,085)
Group Affiliation: Catholic HealthCare Partners
Licensed in: OH
Address: 2200 Jefferson Ave., 6th Fl, Toledo, OH 43624-1120
Phone: (419) 241-6501   **Dom State:** OH   **Commenced Bus:** January 1986

Data Date	Weiss Safety Rating	RACR #1	RACR #2	Total Assets ($mil)	Capital ($mil)	Net Premium ($mil)	Net Income ($mil)
3-03	E	0.29	0.24	25.3	8.5	30.8	-2.4
3-02	E	0.18	0.16	29.4	5.9	20.0	-0.4
2002	E	0.34	0.29	26.9	9.8	85.7	-4.7
2001	E	0.19	0.17	17.1	6.5	108.4	-8.2
2000	E	0.00	0.00	15.7	1.6	115.5	-3.5
1999	E	0.03	0.03	15.4	1.9	101.4	-5.3
1998	D	0.09	0.08	14.5	3.0	76.2	-7.7

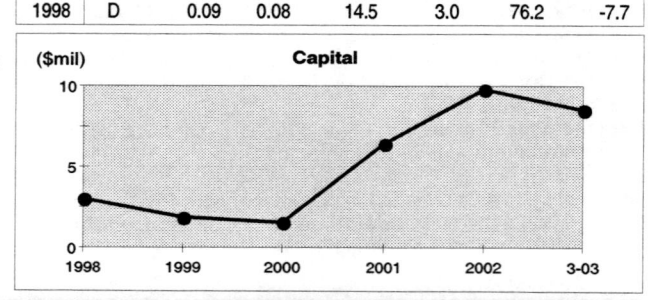

Capital chart ($mil) 1998–3-03

FEDERAL HOME LIFE INSURANCE COMPANY   B   Good

Major Rating Factors: Good overall results on stability tests (5.8 on a scale of 0 to 10) despite fair financial strength of affiliated General Electric Corp Group and negative cash flow from operations for 2002. Other stability subfactors include good operational trends, good risk adjusted capital for prior years and excellent risk diversification. Good quality investment portfolio (5.3) despite mixed results such as: no exposure to mortgages and substantial holdings of BBB bonds but small junk bond holdings. Strong capitalization (7.0) based on excellent risk adjusted capital (severe loss scenario).
Other Rating Factors: Excellent profitability (7.5) with operating gains in each of the last five years. Excellent liquidity (7.3).
Principal Business: Individual health insurance (48%), individual life insurance (44%), group health insurance (5%), individual annuities (1%), and reinsurance (1%).
Principal Investments: NonCMO investment grade bonds (39%), common & preferred stock (38%), CMOs and structured securities (9%), noninv. grade bonds (8%), and misc. investments (7%).
Investments in Affiliates: 38%
Group Affiliation: General Electric Corp Group
Licensed in: All states except NY, PR
Commenced Business: September 1906
Address: 700 Main St, Lynchburg, VA 24504
Phone: (804) 845-0911   **Domicile State:** VA   **NAIC Code:** 67695

Data Date	Weiss Safety Rating	RACR #1	RACR #2	Total Assets ($mil)	Capital ($mil)	Net Premium ($mil)	Net Income ($mil)
6-03	B	1.12	1.03	2,199.3	969.0	19.0	3.8
6-02	B	1.24	1.13	2,282.5	1,001.0	20.3	8.8
2002	B	1.11	1.03	2,195.5	956.5	38.4	12.7
2001	B	1.16	1.05	2,297.6	919.3	47.2	48.4
2000	B	1.14	1.01	2,310.1	798.0	49.2	29.4
1999	B	1.10	0.97	2,308.6	650.3	56.8	523.4
1998	B	1.11	0.85	1,990.1	250.4	49.7	35.6

General Electric Corp Group
Composite Group Rating: C+
Largest Group Members

Largest Group Members	Assets ($mil)	Weiss Safety Rating
GENERAL ELECTRIC CAPITAL ASR CO	30673	C+
GE LIFE ANNUITY ASR CO	18888	B
EMPLOYERS REINSURANCE CORP	15569	C+
FIRST COLONY LIFE INS CO	13330	B
EMPLOYERS REASSURANCE CORP	5653	C

Winter 2003 - 04   II. Analysis of Largest Companies

FEDERATED MUTUAL INS CO *   B+   Good

Major Rating Factors: Good overall results on stability tests (5.0 on a scale of 0 to 10) despite weak results on operational trends. Strengths include potential support from affiliation with Federated Mutual. Strong long-term capitalization index (8.0) based on excellent current risk adjusted capital (severe and moderate loss scenarios), despite some fluctuation in capital levels.

Other Rating Factors: Ample reserve history (7.0) that can protect against increases in claims costs. Excellent liquidity (7.0) with ample operational cash flow and liquid investments. Fair profitability index (4.3) with operating losses during 2001.

Principal Business: Group accident & health (26%), workers compensation (16%), other liability (16%), auto liability (15%), commercial multiple peril (7%), auto physical damage (6%), and other lines (14%).

Principal Investments: Investment grade bonds (77%), misc. investments (22%), non investment grade bonds (1%), and real estate (1%).

Investments in Affiliates: 10%
Group Affiliation: Federated Mutual
Licensed in: All states except AK, HI, NH, PR
Commenced Business: August 1904
Address: 121 E Park Square, Owatonna, MN 55060
Phone: (507) 455-5200   **Domicile State:** MN   **NAIC Code:** 13935

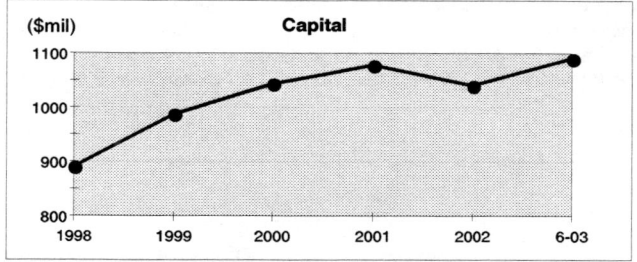

Data Date	Weiss Safety Rating	RACR #1	RACR #2	Loss Ratio %	Total Assets ($mil)	Capital ($mil)	Net Premium ($mil)	Net Income ($mil)
6-03	B+	2.33	1.69	N/A	3,013.6	1,091.3	570.7	20.5
6-02	B+	2.44	1.76	N/A	2,768.0	1,047.1	542.4	-2.7
2002	B+	2.31	1.69	86.9	2,840.6	1,039.4	1,041.7	13.3
2001	B+	2.57	1.87	94.3	2,671.6	1,079.7	965.0	-21.8
2000	A-	3.20	2.34	84.3	2,463.7	1,042.6	796.3	49.4
1999	A-	3.07	2.24	81.1	2,525.6	987.9	803.8	63.4
1998	A-	2.99	2.07	79.3	2,475.9	890.2	770.7	74.8

FIDELITY SECURITY LIFE INSURANCE COMPANY   B-   Good

Major Rating Factors: Good quality investment portfolio (5.1 on a scale of 0 to 10) despite mixed results such as: large holdings of BBB rated bonds but junk bond exposure equal to 73% of capital. Good overall profitability (6.3). Return on equity has been fair, averaging 8.9%. Good liquidity (5.5) with sufficient resources to handle a spike in claims.

Other Rating Factors: Good overall results on stability tests (5.2) excellent operational trends and excellent risk diversification. Strong capitalization (7.4) based on excellent risk adjusted capital (severe loss scenario).

Principal Business: Group health insurance (84%), group life insurance (7%), group retirement contracts (4%), individual life insurance (2%), and other lines (3%).

Principal Investments: NonCMO investment grade bonds (54%), CMOs and structured securities (31%), noninv. grade bonds (9%), policy loans (2%), and misc. investments (4%).

Investments in Affiliates: None
Group Affiliation: Fidelity Security Group
Licensed in: All states except NY, PR
Commenced Business: July 1969
Address: 3130 Broadway, Kansas City, MO 64111
Phone: (816) 750-1060   **Domicile State:** MO   **NAIC Code:** 71870

Data Date	Weiss Safety Rating	RACR #1	RACR #2	Total Assets ($mil)	Capital ($mil)	Net Premium ($mil)	Net Income ($mil)
6-03	B-	2.00	1.25	410.0	46.0	70.0	0.0
6-02	B-	1.85	1.18	403.2	43.3	55.9	-2.7
2002	B-	2.01	1.20	402.4	45.5	109.9	0.1
2001	B-	1.79	1.13	410.2	43.6	123.9	1.3
2000	B-	1.88	1.19	403.6	42.7	107.6	6.2
1999	B-	1.96	1.25	411.0	44.7	113.0	5.1
1998	B-	1.90	1.24	400.3	41.4	128.8	4.7

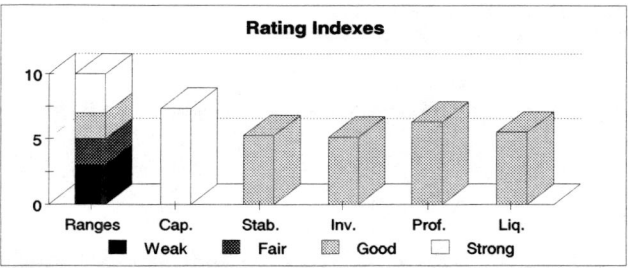

FIRST CENTRAL NATIONAL LIFE INSURANCE CO OF NY   B   Good

Major Rating Factors: Good quality investment portfolio (6.4 on a scale of 0 to 10) with no exposure to mortgages and small junk bond holdings. Fair overall results on stability tests (4.7) including fair financial strength of affiliated HSBC Holdings. Strong capitalization (10.0) based on excellent risk adjusted capital (severe loss scenario). Moreover, capital levels have been consistently high over the last five years.

Other Rating Factors: Excellent profitability (9.6) with operating gains in each of the last five years. Excellent liquidity (8.3).

Principal Business: Credit health insurance (49%), credit life insurance (48%), and individual life insurance (3%).

Principal Investments: NonCMO investment grade bonds (79%), noninv. grade bonds (9%), CMOs and structured securities (8%), common & preferred stock (2%), and cash (2%).

Investments in Affiliates: None
Group Affiliation: HSBC Holdings
Licensed in: DE, NY
Commenced Business: November 1971
Address: 225 W 34th St Suite 1708, New York, NY 10122-1798
Phone: (908) 781-4090   **Domicile State:** NY   **NAIC Code:** 79340

Data Date	Weiss Safety Rating	RACR #1	RACR #2	Total Assets ($mil)	Capital ($mil)	Net Premium ($mil)	Net Income ($mil)
6-03	B	5.02	4.52	48.4	32.4	3.3	0.8
6-02	B	4.79	4.31	49.9	32.1	2.6	1.6
2002	B	4.90	4.41	47.6	31.6	5.9	3.5
2001	B	4.56	4.10	50.2	30.4	6.6	3.7
2000	B	4.39	3.96	50.9	29.4	9.7	3.8
1999	B	4.30	3.87	49.1	28.2	11.1	3.9
1998	B	4.04	3.64	44.3	24.4	10.2	1.8

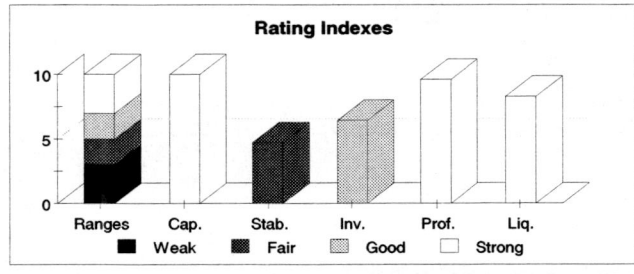

www.WeissRatings.com   * Denotes a Weiss Recommended Company

II. Analysis of Largest Companies

Winter 2003 - 04

FIRST CHOICE HEALTH PLAN INC — D — Weak

Major Rating Factors: Weak profitability index (0.9 on a scale of 0 to 10) with $10.9 million in losses in the last five years. Weak liquidity (0.0) as a spike in claims may stretch capacity. Fair capitalization (4.8) based on good current risk-adjusted capital (severe loss scenario).
Other Rating Factors: High quality investment portfolio (9.9) containing no exposure to mortgages, junk bonds, or unaffiliated stocks.
Principal Business: Comp med (98%), med supp (2%)
Mem Phys: 02: 16,000 **01:** 16,000 **02 MLR** 168% **/ 02 Admin Exp** 32%
Enroll(000): Q1 03: 17 **02:** 29 **01:** 48 **Med Exp PMPM:** $152
Principal Investments: Cash and equiv (20%), other (80%)
Provider Compensation ($000): Contr fee ($71,179), capitation ($1,704)
Total Member Encounters: Phys (223,204), non-phys (57,714)
Group Affiliation: First Choice Health Network
Licensed in: WA
Address: 601 Union St Suite 1100, Seattle, WA 98101
Phone: (206) 292-8255 **Dom State:** WA **Commenced Bus:** December 1995

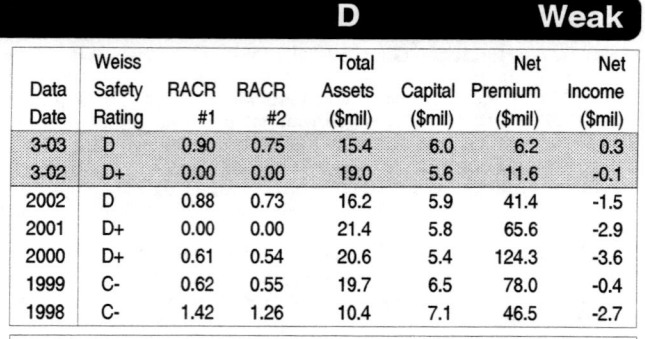

Data Date	Weiss Safety Rating	RACR #1	RACR #2	Total Assets ($mil)	Capital ($mil)	Net Premium ($mil)	Net Income ($mil)
3-03	D	0.90	0.75	15.4	6.0	6.2	0.3
3-02	D+	0.00	0.00	19.0	5.6	11.6	-0.1
2002	D	0.88	0.73	16.2	5.9	41.4	-1.5
2001	D+	0.00	0.00	21.4	5.8	65.6	-2.9
2000	D+	0.61	0.54	20.6	5.4	124.3	-3.6
1999	C-	0.62	0.55	19.7	6.5	78.0	-0.4
1998	C-	1.42	1.26	10.4	7.1	46.5	-2.7

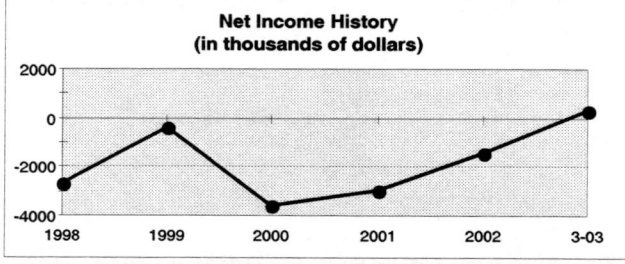

Net Income History (in thousands of dollars) — 1998: ~-2700; 1999: ~-300; 2000: ~-3600; 2001: ~-2900; 2002: ~-1500; 3-03: ~300

FIRST COMMUNITY HEALTH PLAN INC — C+ — Fair

Major Rating Factors: Fair profitability index (4.6 on a scale of 0 to 10) due to a decline in earnings during 2002. Strong overall capitalization (10.0) based on excellent current risk-adjusted capital (severe loss scenario) despite some fluctuation in capital levels. High quality investment portfolio (9.9) containing no exposure to mortgages, junk bonds, or unaffiliated stocks.
Other Rating Factors: Excellent liquidity (8.8) with ample operational cash flow and liquid investments.
Principal Business: Med supp (100%)
Mem Phys: 02: 10 **01:** 10 **02 MLR** 59% **/ 02 Admin Exp** 24%
Enroll(000): Q1 03: 4 **02:** 4 **01:** 4 **Med Exp PMPM:** $59
Principal Investments: Cash and equiv (100%)
Provider Compensation ($000): FFS ($2,886), contr fee ($6)
Total Member Encounters: N/A
Group Affiliation: First Community Health Plans Group
Licensed in: AL
Address: 188 Sparkman Dr, Huntsville, AL 35805
Phone: (256) 864-4100 **Dom State:** AL **Commenced Bus:** January 1996

Data Date	Weiss Safety Rating	RACR #1	RACR #2	Total Assets ($mil)	Capital ($mil)	Net Premium ($mil)	Net Income ($mil)
3-03	C+	8.77	7.31	5.9	4.5	1.2	0.0
3-02	D-	12.18	10.63	4.7	3.3	1.2	0.1
2002	C+	8.79	7.33	5.8	4.5	4.8	1.0
2001	D-	12.19	10.63	4.7	3.2	4.6	1.7
2000	N/A	N/A	N/A	6.5	1.6	13.0	N/A
1999	N/A	N/A	N/A	9.1	-3.0	34.7	N/A
1998	N/A	N/A	N/A	5.6	0.2	10.3	N/A

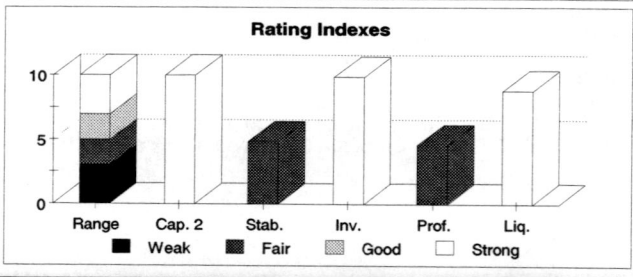

Rating Indexes: Range – Weak; Cap. 2 – Strong; Stab. – Weak; Inv. – Strong; Prof. – Weak; Liq. – Strong

FIRST FORTIS LIFE INSURANCE COMPANY — C+ — Fair

Major Rating Factors: Fair overall results on stability tests (4.7 on a scale of 0 to 10) including fair financial strength of affiliated Fortis Inc. Good quality investment portfolio (6.6) despite mixed results such as: no exposure to mortgages and substantial holdings of BBB bonds but small junk bond holdings. Good liquidity (6.9) with sufficient resources to handle a spike in claims.
Other Rating Factors: Strong capitalization (10.0) based on excellent risk adjusted capital (severe loss scenario). Excellent profitability (7.5) with operating gains in each of the last five years.
Principal Business: Group health insurance (42%), group life insurance (18%), credit health insurance (18%), credit life insurance (12%), and other lines (11%).
Principal Investments: NonCMO investment grade bonds (64%), CMOs and structured securities (27%), noninv. grade bonds (7%), and common & preferred stock (2%).
Investments in Affiliates: None
Group Affiliation: Fortis Inc
Licensed in: NY
Commenced Business: April 1974
Address: 220 Salina Meadows Pkwy #255, Syracuse, NY 13212
Phone: (315) 451-0066 **Domicile State:** NY **NAIC Code:** 81477

Data Date	Weiss Safety Rating	RACR #1	RACR #2	Total Assets ($mil)	Capital ($mil)	Net Premium ($mil)	Net Income ($mil)
6-03	C+	4.86	3.25	229.0	69.0	32.3	5.6
6-02	C+	3.99	2.69	237.3	58.0	36.3	2.7
2002	C+	4.39	2.94	226.7	64.0	71.7	8.8
2001	C+	3.43	2.31	252.4	55.8	80.7	12.5
2000	C+	2.78	1.87	222.9	37.4	79.5	5.7
1999	C+	2.38	1.65	213.7	30.4	73.9	1.8
1998	C+	2.52	1.74	179.8	28.8	83.8	1.2

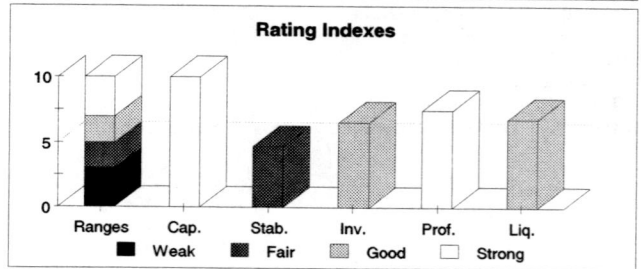

Rating Indexes: Ranges – Weak; Cap. – Strong; Stab. – Weak; Inv. – Good; Prof. – Good; Liq. – Good

FIRST GREAT WEST LIFE & ANNUITY INS   B   Good

Major Rating Factors: Good overall profitability (6.1 on a scale of 0 to 10). Excellent expense controls. Good liquidity (6.9) with sufficient resources to handle a spike in claims as well as a significant increase in policy surrenders. Fair overall results on stability tests (4.0).
Other Rating Factors: Strong capitalization (9.5) based on excellent risk adjusted capital (severe loss scenario). High quality investment portfolio (7.6).
Principal Business: Group health insurance (31%), individual annuities (29%), group retirement contracts (26%), group life insurance (10%), and individual life insurance (4%).
Principal Investments: CMOs and structured securities (50%), nonCMO investment grade bonds (43%), cash (5%), and noninv. grade bonds (2%).
Investments in Affiliates: None
Group Affiliation: Great West Life Asr
Licensed in: IA, NY
Commenced Business: April 1997
Address: 125 Wolf Rd Ste 110, Albany, NY 12205
Phone: (518) 437-1816 **Domicile State:** NY **NAIC Code:** 60214

Data Date	Weiss Safety Rating	RACR #1	RACR #2	Total Assets ($mil)	Capital ($mil)	Net Premium ($mil)	Net Income ($mil)
6-03	B	3.82	2.64	279.3	35.3	14.6	1.4
6-02	C+	3.46	2.25	242.0	30.9	10.9	-0.8
2002	C+	3.50	2.53	253.0	33.2	22.8	1.6
2001	C+	3.54	2.31	241.5	33.4	33.9	7.1
2000	C+	2.85	2.56	233.4	27.0	65.3	0.0
1999	C	N/A	N/A	169.0	29.3	30.6	1.2
1998	C	1.43	1.28	104.1	12.8	75.2	-2.2

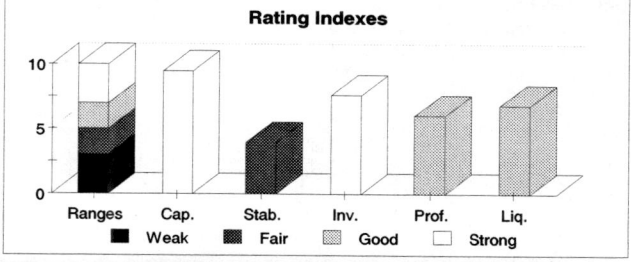

FIRST PLAN OF MINNESOTA *   B+   Good

Major Rating Factors: Good overall capitalization (6.4 on a scale of 0 to 10) based on good current risk-adjusted capital (severe loss scenario). Good overall results on stability tests (6.7). Rating is significantly influenced by the fair financial results of Aware Integrated Inc. Good liquidity (6.9) with sufficient resources (cash flows and marketable investments) to handle a spike in claims.
Other Rating Factors: Excellent profitability (8.0) despite a decline in earnings during 2002. High quality investment portfolio (9.9) containing no exposure to mortgages, junk bonds, or unaffiliated stocks.
Principal Business: Comp med (52%), Medicare (26%), Medicaid (22%).
Mem Phys: 02: 300 **01:** 300 **02 MLR** 92% **/ 02 Admin Exp** 5%
Enroll(000): 02: 13 **01:** 13 **Med Exp PMPM:** $312
Principal Investments: Cash and equiv (25%), real estate (7%), other (68%)
Provider Compensation ($000): Contr fee ($48,523), bonus arrang ($340), capitation ($41)
Total Member Encounters: N/A
Group Affiliation: Aware Integrated Inc
Licensed in: MN
Address: 525 S. Lake Ave., Suite 222, Duluth, MN 55802
Phone: (218) 834-7207 **Dom State:** MN **Commenced Bus:** November 1944

Data Date	Weiss Safety Rating	RACR #1	RACR #2	Total Assets ($mil)	Capital ($mil)	Net Premium ($mil)	Net Income ($mil)
2002	B+	1.14	0.95	19.3	6.9	52.9	1.6
2001	B+	1.19	1.00	17.8	5.5	47.1	1.8
2000	B	N/A	N/A	15.0	6.4	33.7	1.2
1999	B	1.33	1.09	11.5	4.8	30.1	0.3
1998	B	1.28	1.05	11.7	4.4	28.6	0.4

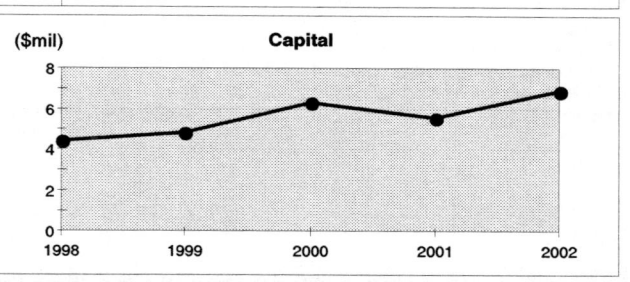

FIRST REHABILITATION INSURANCE COMPANY OF AMERICA   C+   Fair

Major Rating Factors: Fair overall results on stability tests (4.2 on a scale of 0 to 10). Strong capitalization (10.0) based on excellent risk adjusted capital (severe loss scenario). Moreover, capital has steadily grown over the last five years. High quality investment portfolio (8.8) with no exposure to mortgages and no exposure to junk bonds.
Other Rating Factors: Excellent profitability (7.9) with operating gains in each of the last five years. Excellent liquidity (7.4).
Principal Business: Group health insurance (99%) and group life insurance (1%).
Principal Investments: NonCMO investment grade bonds (77%), CMOs and structured securities (23%), and common & preferred stock (3%).
Investments in Affiliates: None
Group Affiliation: Rehab Services Corp
Licensed in: CO, CT, DC, DE, IL, MD, MA, MI, MN, NJ, NY, NC, PA, RI, SC, TN
Commenced Business: November 1972
Address: 600 Northern Blvd, Great Neck, NY 11021-5202
Phone: (516) 829-8100 **Domicile State:** NY **NAIC Code:** 81434

Data Date	Weiss Safety Rating	RACR #1	RACR #2	Total Assets ($mil)	Capital ($mil)	Net Premium ($mil)	Net Income ($mil)
6-03	C+	4.73	3.54	70.7	40.5	19.5	2.2
6-02	C+	4.77	3.52	62.0	34.5	17.7	2.1
2002	C+	4.04	3.09	77.3	38.3	48.1	5.4
2001	C+	4.43	3.44	65.9	32.9	30.5	4.7
2000	C+	3.99	3.42	58.8	28.2	22.7	4.5
1999	C+	3.57	3.21	52.6	24.4	19.6	4.0
1998	C+	3.42	3.03	44.5	21.0	18.4	3.1

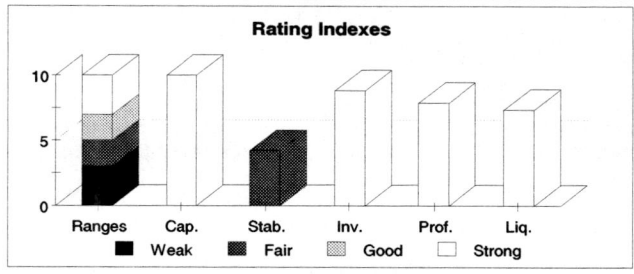

II. Analysis of Largest Companies

Winter 2003 - 04

FIRST RELIANCE STANDARD LIFE INSURANCE COMPANY   C   Fair

Major Rating Factors: Fair overall results on stability tests (3.8 on a scale of 0 to 10) including fair financial strength of affiliated Delphi Financial Group Inc. Strong capitalization (8.8) based on excellent risk adjusted capital (severe loss scenario). Capital levels have been relatively consistent over the last five years. High quality investment portfolio (8.4).
Other Rating Factors: Excellent profitability (7.8) with operating gains in each of the last five years. Excellent liquidity (7.0).
Principal Business: Group health insurance (50%), group life insurance (49%), and reinsurance (1%).
Principal Investments: NonCMO investment grade bonds (56%), CMOs and structured securities (42%), and common & preferred stock (3%).
Investments in Affiliates: None
Group Affiliation: Delphi Financial Group Inc
Licensed in: DC, NY
Commenced Business: October 1984
Address: 153 E 53rd St Suite 4950, New York, NY 10022
Phone: (215) 787-4000   **Domicile State:** NY   **NAIC Code:** 71005

Data Date	Weiss Safety Rating	RACR #1	RACR #2	Total Assets ($mil)	Capital ($mil)	Net Premium ($mil)	Net Income ($mil)
6-03	C	3.05	2.21	86.0	26.9	17.2	0.2
6-02	C	3.55	2.65	83.6	27.4	15.0	2.5
2002	C	3.12	2.28	82.8	26.9	30.9	4.4
2001	C	3.25	2.52	81.1	25.0	23.7	2.5
2000	C	3.29	2.58	78.0	24.9	24.5	5.6
1999	C	2.59	1.98	78.0	19.3	26.6	3.3
1998	C	2.24	1.69	72.3	15.9	26.0	3.0

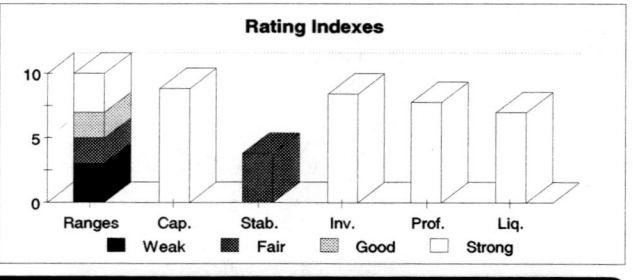

FIRST UNITED AMERICAN LIFE INSURANCE COMPANY   B   Good

Major Rating Factors: Good overall results on stability tests (6.2 on a scale of 0 to 10). Stability strengths include excellent operational trends and excellent risk diversification. Good quality investment portfolio (6.6) despite mixed results such as: no exposure to mortgages and large holdings of BBB rated bonds but small junk bond holdings. Good liquidity (6.5).
Other Rating Factors: Strong capitalization (7.4) based on excellent risk adjusted capital (severe loss scenario). Excellent profitability (9.1) with operating gains in each of the last five years.
Principal Business: Individual health insurance (73%), individual life insurance (22%), group health insurance (3%), and individual annuities (2%).
Principal Investments: NonCMO investment grade bonds (88%), noninv. grade bonds (7%), cash (2%), and policy loans (1%).
Investments in Affiliates: None
Group Affiliation: Torchmark Corp
Licensed in: NY
Commenced Business: December 1984
Address: 1020 7th North St, Liverpool, NY 13088
Phone: (315) 451-2544   **Domicile State:** NY   **NAIC Code:** 74101

Data Date	Weiss Safety Rating	RACR #1	RACR #2	Total Assets ($mil)	Capital ($mil)	Net Premium ($mil)	Net Income ($mil)
6-03	B	1.83	1.26	82.9	25.5	29.5	0.9
6-02	B	1.68	1.20	73.0	21.3	25.3	1.6
2002	B	1.89	1.28	79.8	25.0	49.2	3.0
2001	B	1.68	1.19	72.7	20.1	43.3	1.1
2000	B	1.68	1.21	66.3	18.4	39.5	1.4
1999	B	1.87	1.35	62.3	18.8	35.2	2.8
1998	B	1.96	1.44	58.1	18.1	33.6	1.8

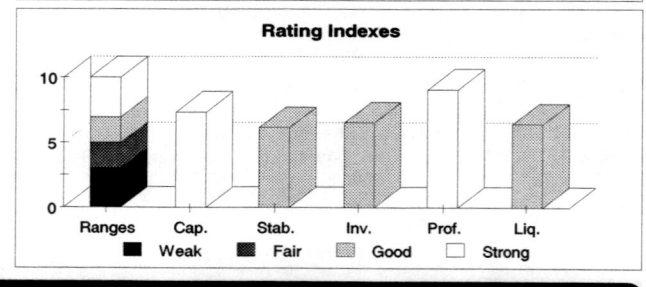

FIRST UNUM LIFE INSURANCE COMPANY   C-   Fair

Major Rating Factors: Fair overall results on stability tests (3.2 on a scale of 0 to 10) including fair financial strength of affiliated UnumProvident Corp and weak risk adjusted capital in prior years. Fair quality investment portfolio (3.7) with large holdings of BBB rated bonds in addition to significant exposure to junk bonds. Weak profitability (2.2) with operating losses during the first six months of 2003.
Other Rating Factors: Good capitalization (5.5) based on good risk adjusted capital (severe loss scenario). Good liquidity (6.8).
Principal Business: Group health insurance (57%), individual health insurance (25%), group life insurance (16%), reinsurance (1%), and individual life insurance (1%).
Principal Investments: NonCMO investment grade bonds (65%), CMOs and structured securities (18%), noninv. grade bonds (14%), mortgages in good standing (3%), and policy loans (1%).
Investments in Affiliates: None
Group Affiliation: UnumProvident Corp
Licensed in: NY
Commenced Business: January 1960
Address: Christiana Bldg Suite 100, Tarrytown, NY 10591
Phone: (914) 524-4056   **Domicile State:** NY   **NAIC Code:** 64297

Data Date	Weiss Safety Rating	RACR #1	RACR #2	Total Assets ($mil)	Capital ($mil)	Net Premium ($mil)	Net Income ($mil)
6-03	C-	1.35	0.81	1,172.9	107.1	206.5	-32.1
6-02	C+	1.76	1.08	1,045.3	136.2	179.6	1.0
2002	C-	1.80	1.06	1,096.7	141.0	365.6	13.6
2001	C+	1.63	1.00	1,042.3	130.1	360.1	-8.2
2000	C+	2.18	1.34	948.4	146.8	328.2	19.3
1999	C+	2.22	1.32	901.7	127.5	288.4	-40.4
1998	C+	0.40	0.38	740.1	111.5	233.0	2.1

UnumProvident Corp Composite Group Rating: C- Largest Group Members	Assets ($mil)	Weiss Safety Rating
UNUM LIFE INS CO OF AMERICA	10982	C-
PROVIDENT LIFE ACCIDENT INS CO	8557	C-
PAUL REVERE LIFE INS CO	4976	C-
COLONIAL LIFE ACCIDENT INS CO	1194	C-
FIRST UNUM LIFE INS CO	1097	C-

Winter 2003 - 04   II. Analysis of Largest Companies

FIRSTCAROLINACARE INC   C   Fair

Major Rating Factors: Weak profitability index (2.5 on a scale of 0 to 10) due to a decline in earnings during 2002. Average return on equity has been poor at -11%. Good overall results on stability tests (5.2) despite rapid premium growth over the last five years, rapid enrollment growth during the past five years. Strong capitalization index (8.5) based on excellent current risk-adjusted capital (severe loss scenario)
Other Rating Factors: High quality investment portfolio (9.9) containing no exposure to mortgages, junk bonds, or unaffiliated stocks. Excellent liquidity (7.5) with ample operational cash flow and liquid investments.
Principal Business: Comp med (100%)
Mem Phys: 02: 2,052   **01:** 1,923   **02 MLR** 85%   / **02 Admin Exp** 14%
Enroll(000): Q1 03: 8   **02:** 7   **01:** 6   **Med Exp PMPM:** $206
Principal Investments: Cash and equiv (90%), other (10%)
Provider Compensation ($000): Contr fee ($13,806), FFS ($2,594)
Total Member Encounters: Phys (57,888), non-phys (8,948)
Group Affiliation: FirstHealth of the Carolinas
Licensed in: NC, SC
Address: 315 N Page Rd, Commons II, #9, Pinehurst, NC 28374
Phone: (910) 215-5270   **Dom State:** NC   **Commenced Bus:** November 1996

Data Date	Weiss Safety Rating	RACR #1	RACR #2	Total Assets ($mil)	Capital ($mil)	Net Premium ($mil)	Net Income ($mil)
3-03	C	2.58	2.15	11.2	8.3	5.8	0.0
3-02	C	2.59	2.19	10.8	8.1	4.4	0.1
2002	C	2.56	2.14	11.0	8.2	19.2	0.2
2001	U	0.00	0.00	10.9	7.9	19.0	0.2
2000	U	N/A	N/A	7.9	7.6	0.5	0.1
1999	U	31.83	27.05	7.3	7.2	0.5	0.4
1998	B-	4.09	3.70	4.1	2.6	3.0	-2.0

Net Income History (in thousands of dollars)

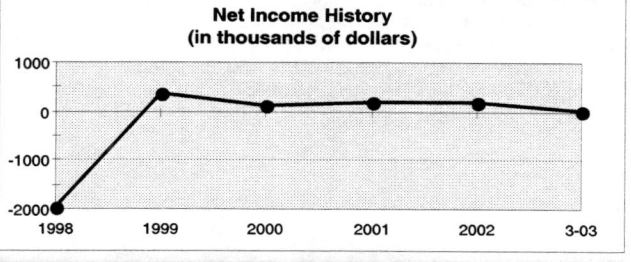

FIRSTCHOICE HEALTHPLANS OF CT INC   D-   Weak

Major Rating Factors: Weak profitability index (0.0 on a scale of 0 to 10) with operating losses during 1998, 1999, 2000 and 2001. Average return on equity has been extremely poor. Fair overall results on stability tests (4.2) based on rapid enrollment growth during the past five years, rapid premium growth over the last five years and a decline in the number of member physicians during 2002. Good capitalization index (6.1) based on good current risk-adjusted capital (severe loss scenario).
Other Rating Factors: Good liquidity (6.9) with sufficient resources (cash flows and marketable investments) to handle a spike in claims. High quality investment portfolio (9.9) containing no exposure to mortgages, junk bonds, or unaffiliated stocks.
Principal Business: Medicaid (98%), comp med (2%)
Mem Phys: 02: 3,608   **01:** 4,316   **02 MLR** 85%   / **02 Admin Exp** 14%
Enroll(000): Q1 03: 18   **02:** 17   **01:** 22   **Med Exp PMPM:** $136
Principal Investments: Cash and equiv (100%)
Provider Compensation ($000): FFS ($27,473), capitation ($7,014)
Total Member Encounters: Phys (18,259), non-phys (17,478)
Group Affiliation: WellCare Holdings LLC
Licensed in: CT
Address: 23 Maiden Lane, North Haven, CT 06473
Phone: (813) 290-6200   **Dom State:** CT   **Commenced Bus:** March 1995

Data Date	Weiss Safety Rating	RACR #1	RACR #2	Total Assets ($mil)	Capital ($mil)	Net Premium ($mil)	Net Income ($mil)
3-03	D-	1.09	0.91	11.2	5.6	8.7	0.4
3-02	E-	0.00	0.00	9.5	2.9	10.8	0.3
2002	E+	1.01	0.84	10.7	5.2	37.9	0.4
2001	E-	0.00	0.00	8.4	-0.1	41.4	-2.8
2000	E-	0.19	0.16	9.8	1.7	20.3	-3.3
1999	E-	0.09	0.08	6.9	0.7	29.4	-0.9
1998	F	0.25	0.21	4.4	0.6	9.7	-0.5

Net Income History (in thousands of dollars)

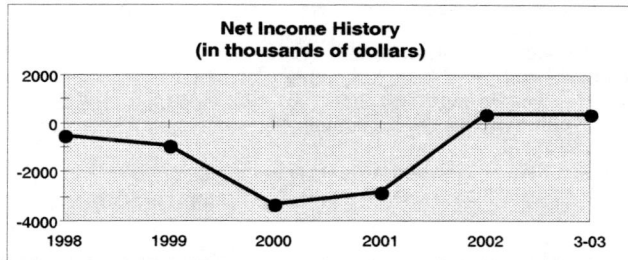

FIRSTGUARD HEALTH PLAN INC   C-   Fair

Major Rating Factors: Fair capitalization (3.1 on a scale of 0 to 10) based on weak current risk-adjusted capital (moderate loss scenario) reflecting improvement over results in 2001. Good profitability index (6.0) despite operating losses during 2001. Good overall results on stability tests (5.1) despite rapid enrollment growth during the past five years, rapid premium growth over the last five years and weak risk-adjusted capital in prior years.
Other Rating Factors: Good liquidity (6.3) with sufficient resources (cash flows and marketable investments) to handle a spike in claims. High quality investment portfolio (9.9) containing no exposure to mortgages, junk bonds, or unaffiliated stocks.
Principal Business: Medicaid (74%), comp med (26%)
Mem Phys: 02: 2,990   **01:** 2,225   **02 MLR** 82%   / **02 Admin Exp** 16%
Enroll(000): Q1 03: 48   **02:** 50   **01:** 44   **Med Exp PMPM:** $158
Principal Investments: Cash and equiv (36%), other (64%)
Provider Compensation ($000): Contr fee ($69,031), capitation ($11,064), FFS ($5,447)
Total Member Encounters: Phys (232,026), non-phys (26,001)
Group Affiliation: Swope Parkway Health Center
Licensed in: KS, MO
Address: 4001 Blue Parkway, Kansas City, MO 64130
Phone: (816) 922-7250   **Dom State:** MO   **Commenced Bus:** March 1995

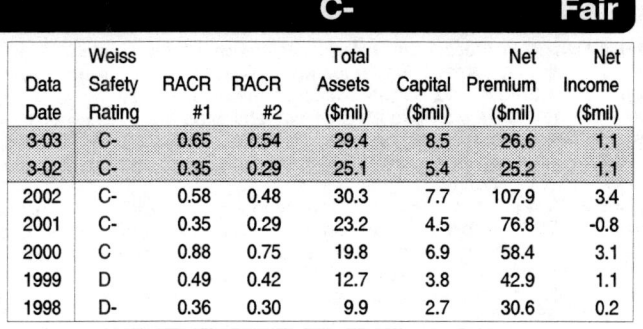

Data Date	Weiss Safety Rating	RACR #1	RACR #2	Total Assets ($mil)	Capital ($mil)	Net Premium ($mil)	Net Income ($mil)
3-03	C-	0.65	0.54	29.4	8.5	26.6	1.1
3-02	C-	0.35	0.29	25.1	5.4	25.2	1.1
2002	C-	0.58	0.48	30.3	7.7	107.9	3.4
2001	C-	0.35	0.29	23.2	4.5	76.8	-0.8
2000	C	0.88	0.75	19.8	6.9	58.4	3.1
1999	D	0.49	0.42	12.7	3.8	42.9	1.1
1998	D-	0.36	0.30	9.9	2.7	30.6	0.2

($mil) Capital

www.WeissRatings.com   * Denotes a Weiss Recommended Company

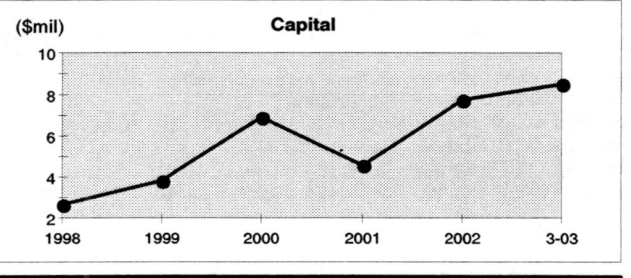

II. Analysis of Largest Companies   Winter 2003 - 04

FLORIDA COMBINED LIFE INSURANCE COMPANY INC   B   Good

Major Rating Factors: Good liquidity (6.8 on a scale of 0 to 10) with sufficient resources to handle a spike in claims. Good overall results on stability tests (5.4). Stability strengths include excellent operational trends and excellent risk diversification. Strong capitalization (8.2) based on excellent risk adjusted capital (severe loss scenario). Capital levels have been relatively consistent over the last five years.
Other Rating Factors: High quality investment portfolio (8.9). Excellent profitability (8.2) with operating gains in each of the last five years.
Principal Business: Group health insurance (48%), group life insurance (46%), reinsurance (4%), and individual life insurance (2%).
Principal Investments: NonCMO investment grade bonds (87%) and cash (12%).
Investments in Affiliates: None
Group Affiliation: Blue Cross Blue Shield Of Florida
Licensed in: AL, FL, GA, NC, SC
Commenced Business: May 1988
Address: 5011 Gate Pkwy Bld 200 Ste 400, Jacksonville, FL 32256
Phone: (800) 333-3256   **Domicile State:** FL   **NAIC Code:** 76031

Data Date	Weiss Safety Rating	RACR #1	RACR #2	Total Assets ($mil)	Capital ($mil)	Net Premium ($mil)	Net Income ($mil)
6-03	B	2.34	1.79	68.4	35.8	28.9	1.0
6-02	B	1.92	1.49	60.7	31.6	28.0	1.5
2002	B	2.32	1.80	65.5	34.5	56.5	2.9
2001	B	1.80	1.40	60.0	29.9	65.5	1.9
2000	B	1.93	1.51	56.0	30.0	56.4	2.1
1999	B	2.05	1.60	50.6	28.1	49.1	4.2
1998	B	1.57	1.21	31.8	16.1	31.5	1.4

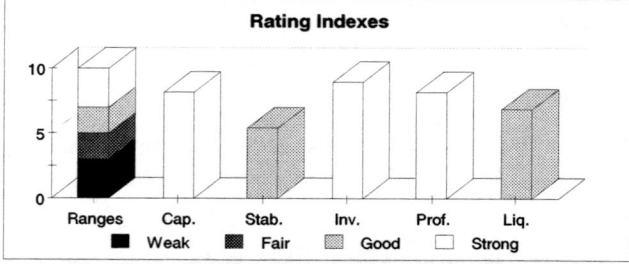

Rating Indexes (Ranges, Cap., Stab., Inv., Prof., Liq.) — Weak, Fair, Good, Strong

FLORIDA HEALTH CARE PLAN INC   B-   Good

Major Rating Factors: Fair profitability index (4.9 on a scale of 0 to 10) despite operating losses during 1998. Good capitalization (5.2) based on good current risk-adjusted capital (severe loss scenario) reflecting some improvement over results in 2000. Good overall results on stability tests (6.9) based on consistent premium and capital growth in the last five years.
Other Rating Factors: Good liquidity (7.0) with sufficient resources (cash flows and marketable investments) to handle a spike in claims. High quality investment portfolio (9.7) containing little or no exposure to mortgages, junk bonds, or unaffiliated stocks.
Principal Business: Medicare (56%), comp med (36%), other (7%).
Mem Phys: 01: 407   **00:** 386   **01 MLR** 89% / **01 Admin Exp** 9%
Enroll(000): Q2 02: 58   **01:** 56   **00:** 57   **Med Exp PMPM:** $324
Principal Investments: Cash and equiv (58%), real estate (42%), affiliate common stock (1%)
Provider Compensation ($000): Contr fee ($130,446), capitation ($28,263), salary ($24,404), FFS ($12,805), other ($22,518)
Total Member Encounters: Phys (401,988), non-phys (186,234)
Group Affiliation: Halifax Community Health System
Licensed in: FL
Address: 1340 Ridgewood Ave, Holly Hill, FL 32117
Phone: (386) 676-7100   **Dom State:** FL   **Commenced Bus:** July 1974

Data Date	Weiss Safety Rating	RACR #1	RACR #2	Total Assets ($mil)	Capital ($mil)	Net Premium ($mil)	Net Income ($mil)
6-02	B-	0.97	0.80	53.6	26.7	94.1	2.8
6-01	C+	0.86	0.69	49.0	18.7	77.1	1.2
2001	C+	0.97	0.80	56.1	23.7	245.5	6.2
2000	C+	0.85	0.69	48.2	18.5	146.7	1.6
1999	C	0.94	0.75	40.7	17.8	123.5	0.6
1998	N/A	N/A	N/A	37.0	17.4	116.1	-1.1
1997	B	1.63	1.03	41.5	20.1	106.5	3.9

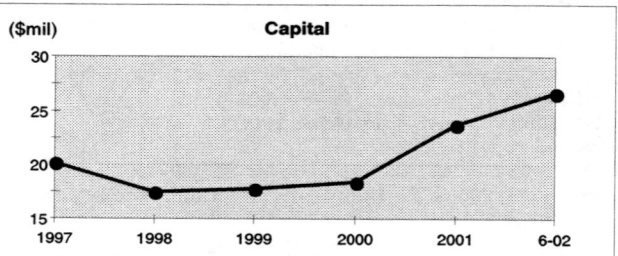

Capital ($mil) chart, 1997–6-02

FORT WAYNE HEALTH & CAS INS CO   C   Fair

Major Rating Factors: Fair overall results on stability tests (3.4 on a scale of 0 to 10) including weak risk adjusted capital in prior years, weak results on operational trends and negative cash flow from operations for 2002. Strengths include potentially strong support from affiliation with Swiss Reinsurance. The largest net exposure for one risk is conservative at 1.2% of capital. Fair long-term capitalization index (3.6) based on good current risk adjusted capital (moderate loss scenario).
Other Rating Factors: Fair profitability index (3.9) with operating losses during 1999 and 2000. Average return on equity over the last five years has been poor at -12.8%. A history of deficient reserves (1.6). Underreserving can have an adverse impact on capital and profits. In four of the last five years reserves (two year development) were between 33% and 249% deficient. Excellent liquidity (7.0) with ample operational cash flow and liquid investments.
Principal Business: Group accident & health (100%).
Principal Investments: Investment grade bonds (94%) and non investment grade bonds (6%).
Investments in Affiliates: None
Group Affiliation: Swiss Reinsurance
Licensed in: All states, the District of Columbia and Puerto Rico
Commenced Business: December 1980
Address: 1700 Magnavox Way, Ft Wayne, IN 46801
Phone: (219) 455-4535   **Domicile State:** IN   **NAIC Code:** 38830

Data Date	Weiss Safety Rating	RACR #1	RACR #2	Loss Ratio %	Total Assets ($mil)	Capital ($mil)	Net Premium ($mil)	Net Income ($mil)
6-03	C	1.64	1.13	N/A	474.3	172.2	48.5	18.9
6-02	C	0.37	0.29	N/A	516.2	121.0	116.0	11.6
2002	C	1.52	1.05	87.6	480.5	161.3	-93.0	39.1
2001	C	0.34	0.27	70.2	477.2	110.1	235.3	21.2
2000	C	0.26	0.20	90.1	468.4	93.1	229.3	-3.1
1999	C	0.14	0.10	117.5	490.1	67.8	238.6	-83.6
1998	C	0.34	0.25	92.9	365.2	74.9	141.5	1.5

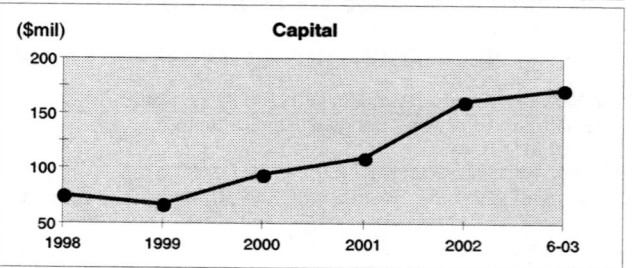

Capital ($mil) chart, 1998–6-03

166   www.WeissRatings.com

FORTIS BENEFITS INSURANCE COMPANY   B-   Good

Major Rating Factors: Good quality investment portfolio (6.5 on a scale of 0 to 10) despite mixed results such as: substantial holdings of BBB bonds but moderate junk bond exposure. Good liquidity (6.0) with sufficient resources to handle a spike in claims as well as a significant increase in policy surrenders. Fair profitability (4.8).
Other Rating Factors: Fair overall results on stability tests (3.5). Strong capitalization (7.3) based on excellent risk adjusted capital (severe loss scenario).
Principal Business: Group health insurance (45%), group life insurance (16%), individual life insurance (15%), reinsurance (12%), and other lines (11%).
Principal Investments: NonCMO investment grade bonds (60%), mortgages in good standing (15%), CMOs and structured securities (15%), noninv. grade bonds (6%), and misc. investments (4%).
Investments in Affiliates: None
Group Affiliation: Fortis Inc
Licensed in: All states except NY, PR
Commenced Business: September 1910
Address: 500 Bielenberg Dr, Woodbury, MN 55125
Phone: (612) 738-5063 **Domicile State:** MN **NAIC Code:** 70408

Data Date	Weiss Safety Rating	RACR #1	RACR #2	Total Assets ($mil)	Capital ($mil)	Net Premium ($mil)	Net Income ($mil)
6-03	B-	1.91	1.20	7,631.5	535.9	886.1	55.2
6-02	B-	1.53	0.98	7,764.6	525.5	872.4	56.7
2002	B-	1.78	1.13	7,321.5	503.3	1,750.4	111.4
2001	B-	1.81	1.12	8,487.6	485.0	856.2	-48.2
2000	B	1.73	1.01	9,115.9	434.0	2,422.1	88.9
1999	B	1.86	1.15	9,172.2	497.9	3,011.1	9.4
1998	B+	1.92	1.27	7,091.8	478.4	1,999.0	14.8

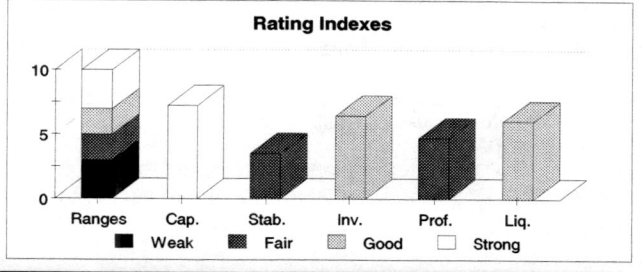

FORTIS INSURANCE COMPANY   B-   Good

Major Rating Factors: Good quality investment portfolio (6.7 on a scale of 0 to 10) despite mixed results such as: no exposure to mortgages and substantial holdings of BBB bonds but small junk bond holdings. Good overall profitability (5.4). Despite its volitility, return on equity has been excellent over the last five years averaging 27.3%. Good liquidity (6.8).
Other Rating Factors: Fair overall results on stability tests (3.5) including fair financial strength of affiliated Fortis Inc. Strong capitalization (7.7) based on excellent risk adjusted capital (severe loss scenario).
Principal Business: Individual health insurance (47%), group health insurance (45%), and individual life insurance (7%).
Principal Investments: NonCMO investment grade bonds (58%), CMOs and structured securities (28%), noninv. grade bonds (6%), real estate (4%), and mortgages in good standing (4%).
Investments in Affiliates: None
Group Affiliation: Fortis Inc
Licensed in: All states except HI, NY, PR
Commenced Business: March 1910
Address: 501 W Michigan, Milwaukee, WI 53201
Phone: (612) 738-4449 **Domicile State:** WI **NAIC Code:** 69477

Data Date	Weiss Safety Rating	RACR #1	RACR #2	Total Assets ($mil)	Capital ($mil)	Net Premium ($mil)	Net Income ($mil)
6-03	B-	2.06	1.45	687.7	166.4	268.1	40.1
6-02	B-	5.31	2.68	557.2	141.2	229.7	31.4
2002	B-	1.87	1.31	617.7	140.6	473.4	63.6
2001	C+	1.78	1.21	594.1	124.3	-224.4	48.4
2000	C+	2.94	1.53	1,098.2	125.0	179.4	71.3
1999	C+	1.60	0.99	1,433.1	141.1	478.1	1.5
1998	B-	1.12	1.02	1,908.4	743.6	788.1	59.4

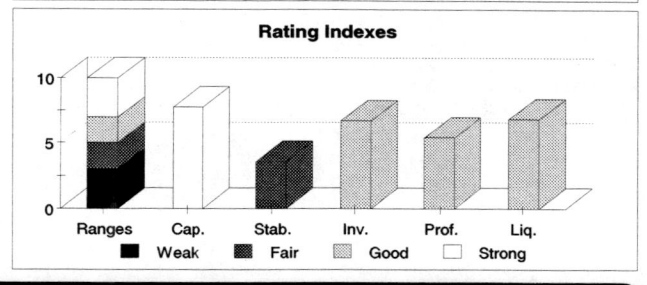

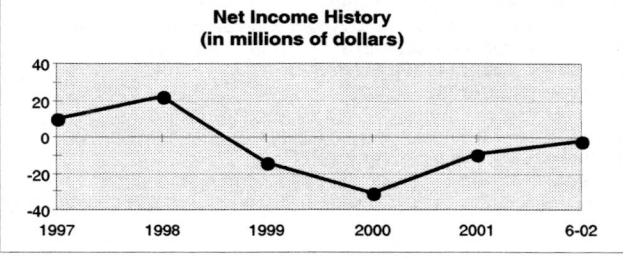

FREE STATE HEALTH PLAN INC   C+   Fair

Major Rating Factors: Good liquidity (5.6 on a scale of 0 to 10) with sufficient resources (cash flows and marketable investments) to handle a spike in claims. Weak profitability index (0.7) with $53.5 million in losses in the last three years. Average return on equity has been poor at -6%. Weak overall results on stability tests (1.3) based on a significant 61% decrease in enrollment during the period, a decline in the number of member physicians during 2001 and fair risk-adjusted capital in prior years. Potentially strong support from affiliation with CareFirst Inc.
Other Rating Factors: Strong capitalization (7.9) based on excellent current risk-adjusted capital (severe loss scenario) reflecting significant improvement over results in 2000. High quality investment portfolio (8.6) containing little or no exposure to mortgages, junk bonds, or unaffiliated stocks.
Principal Business: Comp med (75%), FEHB (16%), Medicaid (9%).
Mem Phys: 01: 1,692 00: 3,255 **01 MLR** 90% **/ 01 Admin Exp** 14%
Enroll(000): Q2 02: 27 01: 123 00: 318 **Med Exp PMPM:** $128
Principal Investments: Real estate (20%), cash and equiv (15%), affiliate common stock (12%), nonaffiliate common stock (6%), pref stock (1%), other (45%).
Provider Compensation ($000): Bonus arrang ($183,638), contr fee ($169,686), capitation ($49,217), salary ($35,206)
Total Member Encounters: N/A
Group Affiliation: CareFirst Inc
Licensed in: DC, MD
Address: 10455 Mill Run Circle, Owings Mill, MD 21117
Phone: (410) 581-3000 **Dom State:** MD **Commenced Bus:** August 1991

Data Date	Weiss Safety Rating	RACR #1	RACR #2	Total Assets ($mil)	Capital ($mil)	Net Premium ($mil)	Net Income ($mil)
6-02	C+	2.15	1.74	95.1	39.8	41.1	-1.6
6-01	C+	0.69	0.59	184.0	47.6	220.1	-4.6
2001	C+	2.14	1.74	136.4	50.6	374.1	-8.9
2000	C+	0.86	0.73	246.9	60.1	864.1	-30.4
1999	B	1.25	1.06	284.9	96.8	1,081.8	-14.2
1998	B-	1.94	1.63	283.5	113.0	937.5	22.0
1997	C+	2.22	1.41	256.3	90.4	709.1	10.6

*Denotes a Weiss Recommended Company

II. Analysis of Largest Companies — Winter 2003 - 04

GATEWAY HEALTH PLAN INC — C — Fair

Major Rating Factors: Fair capitalization (4.6 on a scale of 0 to 10) based on fair current risk-adjusted capital (moderate loss scenario) as results have slipped from the good range over the last year. Good overall profitability index (5.2) despite operating losses during 1999 and 2001. Good overall results on stability tests (5.8) despite rapid premium growth over the last five years, rapid enrollment growth during the past five years.

Other Rating Factors: Good liquidity (6.0) with sufficient resources (cash flows and marketable investments) to handle a spike in claims. High quality investment portfolio (9.8).
Principal Business: Medicaid (100%)
Mem Phys: 02: 7,752 01: 6,666 **02 MLR** 89% / **02 Admin Exp** 10%
Enroll(000): Q1 03: 231 02: 226 01: 167 **Med Exp PMPM:** $223
Principal Investments: Cash and equiv (21%), nonaffiliate common stock (14%), other (65%)
Provider Compensation ($000): Contr fee ($438,482), capitation ($68,882), other ($836)
Total Member Encounters: Phys (860,758), non-phys (334,697)
Group Affiliation: Gateway Health Plan LP
Licensed in: PA
Address: Two Chatham Ctr. Ste 500, Pittsburgh, PA 15219
Phone: (412) 255-4678 **Dom State:** PA **Commenced Bus:** August 1986

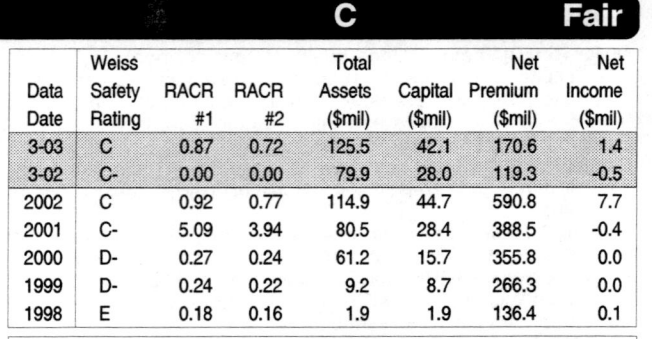

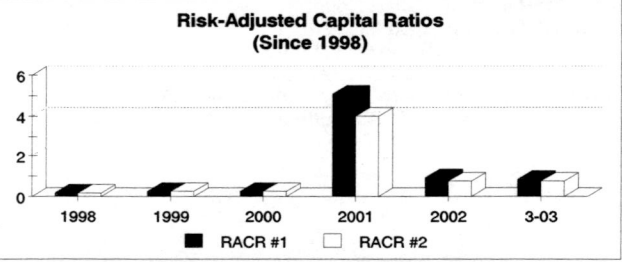

Data Date	Weiss Safety Rating	RACR #1	RACR #2	Total Assets ($mil)	Capital ($mil)	Net Premium ($mil)	Net Income ($mil)
3-03	C	0.87	0.72	125.5	42.1	170.6	1.4
3-02	C-	0.00	0.00	79.9	28.0	119.3	-0.5
2002	C	0.92	0.77	114.9	44.7	590.8	7.7
2001	C-	5.09	3.94	80.5	28.4	388.5	-0.4
2000	D-	0.27	0.24	61.2	15.7	355.8	0.0
1999	D-	0.24	0.22	9.2	8.7	266.3	0.0
1998	E	0.18	0.16	1.9	1.9	136.4	0.1

Risk-Adjusted Capital Ratios (Since 1998)

GE GROUP LIFE ASSURANCE COMPANY — B- — Good

Major Rating Factors: Good overall results on stability tests (5.3 on a scale of 0 to 10) despite fair financial strength of affiliated General Electric Corp Group. Other stability subfactors include excellent operational trends and excellent risk diversification. Good quality investment portfolio (6.8) despite mixed results such as: no exposure to mortgages and large holdings of BBB rated bonds but small junk bond holdings. Good liquidity (6.5).

Other Rating Factors: Strong capitalization (7.8) based on excellent risk adjusted capital (severe loss scenario). Excellent profitability (7.9) with operating gains in each of the last five years.
Principal Business: N/A
Principal Investments: NonCMO investment grade bonds (64%), CMOs and structured securities (31%), and noninv. grade bonds (5%).
Investments in Affiliates: None
Group Affiliation: General Electric Corp Group
Licensed in: All states, the District of Columbia and Puerto Rico
Commenced Business: January 1975
Address: 100 Bright Meadow Blvd, Enfield, CT 06083-1900
Phone: (860) 403-1179 **Domicile State:** CT **NAIC Code:** 80926

Data Date	Weiss Safety Rating	RACR #1	RACR #2	Total Assets ($mil)	Capital ($mil)	Net Premium ($mil)	Net Income ($mil)
6-03	B-	2.24	1.53	832.0	200.3	287.6	16.4
6-02	B-	2.38	1.69	834.0	185.7	276.8	16.7
2002	B-	2.25	1.53	845.1	202.5	570.1	29.0
2001	B-	2.49	1.76	836.5	202.7	490.0	35.0
2000	B-	2.26	1.57	762.8	159.8	399.7	23.9
1999	B-	2.43	1.71	624.0	146.9	389.7	13.3
1998	B-	2.23	1.55	646.9	150.1	444.6	17.7

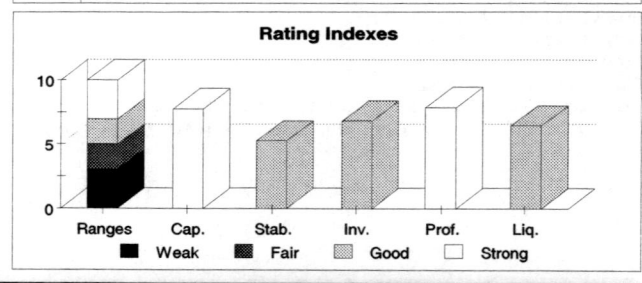

Rating Indexes: Ranges, Cap., Stab., Inv., Prof., Liq. — Weak / Fair / Good / Strong

GE REINSURANCE CORP — C — Fair

Major Rating Factors: Fair overall results on stability tests (4.0 on a scale of 0 to 10) including weak results on operational trends, weak risk adjusted capital in prior years and negative cash flow from operations for 2002. Strengths include potentially strong support from affiliation with General Electric Corp Group. The largest net exposure for one risk is conservative at 1.9% of capital. Poor long-term capitalization (2.2) based on weak current risk adjusted capital (moderate loss scenario), although results have slipped from the good range over the last two years.

Other Rating Factors: A history of deficient reserves (1.2) that places pressure on both capital and profits. The one year reserve development was deficient in three of the last five years by between 16% and 97%. Weak profitability index (1.4) with operating losses during 1998, 2001 and 2002. Average return on equity over the last five years has been poor at -10.4%. Excellent liquidity (7.0) with ample operational cash flow and liquid investments.
Principal Business: Group accident & health (100%).
Principal Investments: Investment grade bonds (94%), misc. investments (4%), and non investment grade bonds (2%).
Investments in Affiliates: 3%
Group Affiliation: General Electric Corp Group
Licensed in: All states except CO, HI, ME, MD, MA, NY, NC, SC, VT, VA, WY
Commenced Business: April 1969
Address: 540 Northwest Highway, Barrington, IL 60010
Phone: (847) 277-5300 **Domicile State:** IL **NAIC Code:** 22969

Data Date	Weiss Safety Rating	RACR #1	RACR #2	Loss Ratio %	Total Assets ($mil)	Capital ($mil)	Net Premium ($mil)	Net Income ($mil)
6-03	C	0.68	0.42	N/A	2,633.7	642.9	0.0	6.1
6-02	C	1.48	1.07	N/A	2,372.8	731.9	0.0	-9.6
2002	C	0.60	0.37	147.2	2,764.9	623.4	736.1	-306.7
2001	C	1.32	0.96	93.6	2,702.9	735.1	906.6	-71.0
2000	C	1.41	0.98	71.3	2,867.3	773.0	1,096.4	78.6
1999	C	1.19	0.81	83.6	2,950.5	754.7	1,081.1	40.1
1998	C	0.85	0.69	93.5	2,767.5	722.9	992.6	-105.3

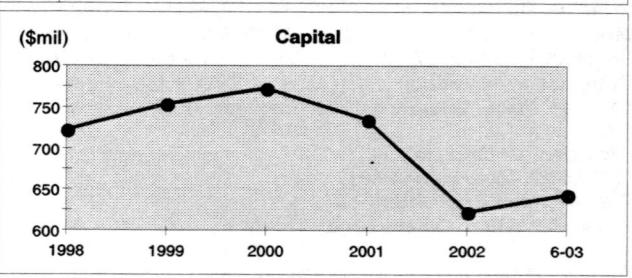

Capital ($mil) 1998–6-03

GEISINGER HEALTH PLAN   C   Fair

Major Rating Factors: Fair profitability index (4.1 on a scale of 0 to 10) with operating losses during 1999 and 2002. Fair capitalization (4.8) based on good current risk-adjusted capital (severe loss scenario) reflecting significant improvement over results in 1998. Good overall results on stability tests (6.2) despite inconsistent enrollment growth in the past five years due to declines in 2001 and 2002, a decline in the number of member physicians during 2002 but consistent premium and capital growth in the last five years.
Other Rating Factors: Good liquidity (6.8) with sufficient resources (cash flows and marketable investments) to handle a spike in claims. High quality investment portfolio (9.9).
Principal Business: Comp med (63%), Medicare (38%).
Mem Phys: 02: 3,979   **01:** 4,564   **02 MLR** 91%   / **02 Admin Exp** 10%
Enroll(000): Q1 03: 215   **02:** 227   **01:** 257   **Med Exp PMPM:** $198
Principal Investments: Cash and equiv (45%), nonaffiliate common stock (12%), other (43%).
Provider Compensation ($000): Contr fee ($283,255), FFS ($237,756), capitation ($64,309)
Total Member Encounters: Phys (1,260,347), non-phys (153,417)
Group Affiliation: Geisinger Health System Foundation
Licensed in: PA
Address: 100 N Academy Ave, Danville, PA 17822-3051
Phone: (570) 271-5254   **Dom State:** PA   **Commenced Bus:** March 1985

Data Date	Weiss Safety Rating	RACR #1	RACR #2	Total Assets ($mil)	Capital ($mil)	Net Premium ($mil)	Net Income ($mil)
3-03	C	0.90	0.75	133.4	60.2	160.0	11.5
3-02	C	0.83	0.66	123.7	53.1	158.2	3.5
2002	C	0.67	0.56	124.4	47.1	629.8	-8.4
2001	C	0.84	0.66	139.1	49.7	611.5	12.3
2000	D	N/A	N/A	125.3	46.0	587.2	16.7
1999	D	0.64	0.55	88.5	27.7	504.1	-2.8
1998	D	0.47	0.41	86.2	17.2	410.5	3.0

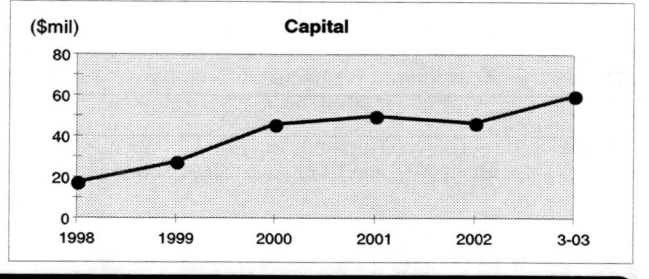

GERBER LIFE INSURANCE COMPANY   B-   Good

Major Rating Factors: Good liquidity (6.9 on a scale of 0 to 10) with sufficient resources to handle a spike in claims as well as a significant increase in policy surrenders. Good overall results on stability tests (5.2). Stability strengths include excellent operational trends and excellent risk diversification. Strong capitalization (8.3) based on excellent risk adjusted capital (severe loss scenario).
Other Rating Factors: High quality investment portfolio (7.3). Excellent profitability (9.0) with operating gains in each of the last five years.
Principal Business: Group health insurance (48%), individual life insurance (40%), reinsurance (5%), group life insurance (4%), and individual health insurance (3%).
Principal Investments: NonCMO investment grade bonds (78%), CMOs and structured securities (17%), policy loans (2%), common & preferred stock (2%), and cash (1%).
Investments in Affiliates: None
Group Affiliation: Novartis
Licensed in: All states, the District of Columbia and Puerto Rico
Commenced Business: September 1968
Address: 66 Church St, White Plains, NY 10601
Phone: (914) 761-4404   **Domicile State:** NY   **NAIC Code:** 70939

Data Date	Weiss Safety Rating	RACR #1	RACR #2	Total Assets ($mil)	Capital ($mil)	Net Premium ($mil)	Net Income ($mil)
6-03	B-	2.84	1.84	751.5	119.5	123.8	4.6
6-02	B-	2.62	1.69	632.5	97.7	117.1	10.2
2002	B-	2.55	1.63	687.2	108.1	211.9	18.7
2001	B-	2.45	1.56	580.1	91.6	187.0	13.2
2000	B-	2.39	1.51	482.1	80.9	167.8	18.5
1999	B-	2.33	1.47	416.5	70.6	156.9	14.2
1998	C+	2.11	1.37	349.6	56.8	152.7	7.8

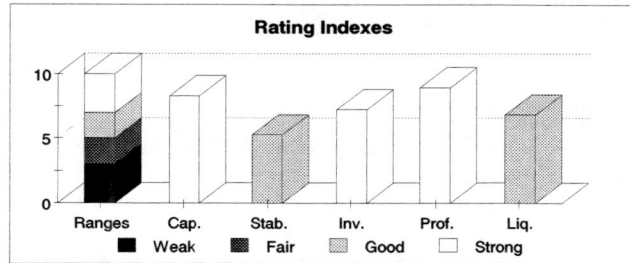

GHI HMO SELECT INC   C   Fair

Major Rating Factors: Weak profitability index (1.2 on a scale of 0 to 10). Poor capitalization index (0.4) based on weak current risk-adjusted capital (moderate loss scenario). Good overall results on stability tests (5.8). Rating is significantly influenced by the good financial results of GHI Services Group.
Other Rating Factors: Good liquidity (5.9) with sufficient resources (cash flows and marketable investments) to handle a spike in claims. High quality investment portfolio (9.9) containing no exposure to mortgages, junk bonds, or unaffiliated stocks.
Principal Business: Comp med (95%), FEHB (5%).
Mem Phys: 02: 17,790   **01:** 12,068   **02 MLR** 88%   / **02 Admin Exp** 16%
Enroll(000): Q1 03: 33   **02:** 33   **01:** 30   **Med Exp PMPM:** $169
Principal Investments: Cash and equiv (72%), other (28%).
Provider Compensation ($000): Contr fee ($46,722), FFS ($7,505), capitation ($4,801), bonus arrang ($1,957)
Total Member Encounters: Phys (83,290), non-phys (137,261)
Group Affiliation: GHI Services Group
Licensed in: NY
Address: 25 Barbarosa Lane, Kingston, NY 12401-1221
Phone: (845) 340-2200   **Dom State:** NY   **Commenced Bus:** June 1999

Data Date	Weiss Safety Rating	RACR #1	RACR #2	Total Assets ($mil)	Capital ($mil)	Net Premium ($mil)	Net Income ($mil)
3-03	C	0.34	0.28	20.2	5.6	21.1	-0.2
3-02	C	0.32	0.27	14.6	3.6	17.3	-0.5
2002	C	0.36	0.30	18.3	5.7	72.7	-2.4
2001	C	0.32	0.27	13.5	4.2	59.6	-4.8
2000	U	0.25	0.22	12.2	4.2	4.6	-7.3
1999	U	0.99	0.85	10.6	4.7	21.8	-4.4
1998	N/A	N/A	N/A	N/A	N/A	N/A	N/A

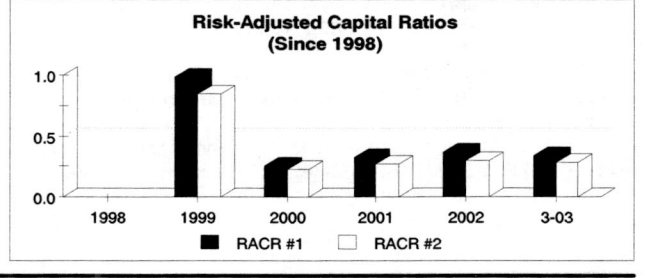

II. Analysis of Largest Companies

GHS HEALTH MAINTENANCE ORGANIZATION   B-   Good

Major Rating Factors: Fair overall results on stability tests (4.5 on a scale of 0 to 10) based on fair risk-adjusted capital in prior years, an overall decline in enrollment over the past five years. Strong capitalization (8.9) based on excellent current risk-adjusted capital (severe loss scenario) reflecting significant improvement over results in 2000. High quality investment portfolio (9.9) containing no exposure to mortgages, junk bonds, or unaffiliated stocks.
Other Rating Factors: Excellent liquidity (7.3) with ample operational cash flow and liquid investments. Weak profitability index (2.7) with operating losses during 1998, 1999 and 2000. Average return on equity has been poor at -6%.
Principal Business: Comp med (100%)
Mem Phys: 02: 3,299   **01:** 3,238   **02 MLR** 75%   / **02 Admin Exp** 19%
Enroll(000): Q1 03: 28   **02:** 31   **01:** 33   **Med Exp PMPM:** $128
Principal Investments: Cash and equiv (70%), other (30%)
Provider Compensation ($000): FFS ($37,746), capitation ($11,414), other ($439)
Total Member Encounters: Phys (30,496), non-phys (138,597)
Group Affiliation: Group Hospital Service of Oklahoma
Licensed in: OK
Address: 1400 S Boston, Tulsa, OK 74119
Phone: (918) 561-9900   **Dom State:** OK   **Commenced Bus:** August 1984

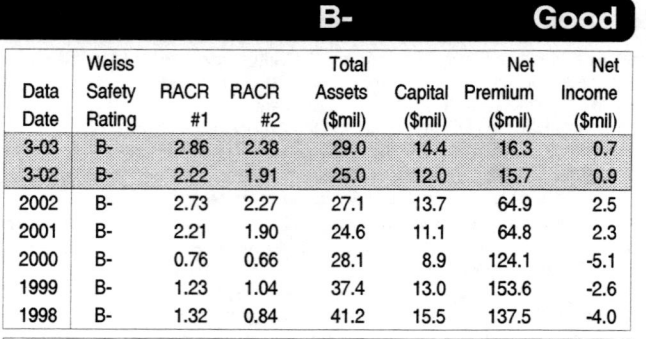

Data Date	Weiss Safety Rating	RACR #1	RACR #2	Total Assets ($mil)	Capital ($mil)	Net Premium ($mil)	Net Income ($mil)
3-03	B-	2.86	2.38	29.0	14.4	16.3	0.7
3-02	B-	2.22	1.91	25.0	12.0	15.7	0.9
2002	B-	2.73	2.27	27.1	13.7	64.9	2.5
2001	B-	2.21	1.90	24.6	11.1	64.8	2.3
2000	B-	0.76	0.66	28.1	8.9	124.1	-5.1
1999	B-	1.23	1.04	37.4	13.0	153.6	-2.6
1998	B-	1.32	0.84	41.2	15.5	137.5	-4.0

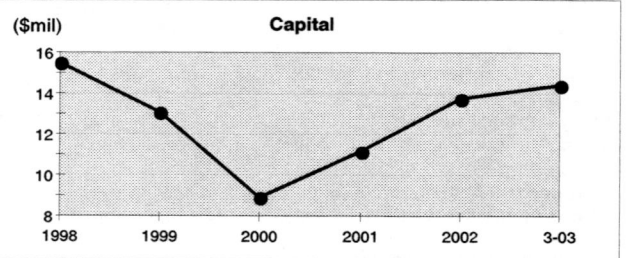

Capital chart (1998–3-03)

GOLDEN RULE INSURANCE COMPANY *   B+   Good

Major Rating Factors: Good capitalization (5.9 on a scale of 0 to 10) based on good risk adjusted capital (severe loss scenario). Good quality investment portfolio (5.1) despite mixed results such as: large holdings of BBB rated bonds but junk bond exposure equal to 69% of capital. Good liquidity (5.6) with sufficient resources to handle a spike in claims as well as a significant increase in policy surrenders.
Other Rating Factors: Good overall results on stability tests (5.0) excellent operational trends and excellent risk diversification. Excellent profitability (7.4) with operating gains in each of the last five years.
Principal Business: Group health insurance (62%), individual health insurance (17%), individual life insurance (12%), and individual annuities (8%).
Principal Investments: NonCMO investment grade bonds (59%), CMOs and structured securities (26%), noninv. grade bonds (8%), mortgages in good standing (4%), and misc. investments (2%).
Investments in Affiliates: 1%
Group Affiliation: Golden Rule Group
Licensed in: All states except NY, PR
Commenced Business: January 1941
Address: 712 Eleventh St, Lawrenceville, IL 62439-2395
Phone: (317) 290-8100   **Domicile State:** IL   **NAIC Code:** 62286

Data Date	Weiss Safety Rating	RACR #1	RACR #2	Total Assets ($mil)	Capital ($mil)	Net Premium ($mil)	Net Income ($mil)
6-03	B+	1.35	0.86	2,076.2	227.7	502.4	43.2
6-02	B	1.25	0.81	1,862.8	196.9	454.5	28.7
2002	B	1.27	0.82	1,975.4	207.1	946.5	37.9
2001	B	1.29	0.83	1,801.7	191.3	768.6	25.0
2000	B	1.56	0.99	1,678.8	208.0	643.1	32.4
1999	B	1.44	0.91	1,613.6	191.5	616.9	64.4
1998	B	1.90	1.15	1,579.5	219.1	631.2	26.0

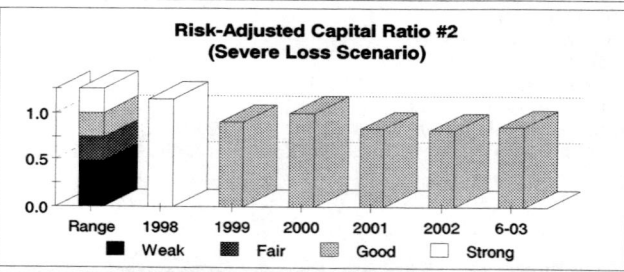

Risk-Adjusted Capital Ratio #2 (Severe Loss Scenario) chart

GOOD HEALTH HMO INC   B   Good

Major Rating Factors: Good overall profitability index (5.1 on a scale of 0 to 10) despite operating losses during 1999. Good overall results on stability tests (5.1). Potentially strong support from affiliation with RightCHOICE Managed Care Inc. Good liquidity (6.9) with sufficient resources (cash flows and marketable investments) to handle a spike in claims.
Other Rating Factors: Strong overall capitalization (8.0) based on excellent current risk-adjusted capital (severe loss scenario) despite some fluctuation in capital levels. High quality investment portfolio (9.9) containing no exposure to mortgages, junk bonds, or unaffiliated stocks.
Principal Business: Comp med (100%)
Mem Phys: 02: 2,829   **01:** 2,765   **02 MLR** 82%   / **02 Admin Exp** 11%
Enroll(000): Q1 03: 53   **02:** 50   **01:** 40   **Med Exp PMPM:** $198
Principal Investments: Cash and equiv (4%), other (96%)
Provider Compensation ($000): Contr fee ($65,225), FFS ($29,939), capitation ($12,247)
Total Member Encounters: Phys (308,686), non-phys (20,819)
Group Affiliation: RightCHOICE Managed Care Inc
Licensed in: KS, MO
Address: 2301 Main St One Pershing Sq, Kansas City, MO 64108
Phone: (816) 395-2222   **Dom State:** MO   **Commenced Bus:** January 1989

Data Date	Weiss Safety Rating	RACR #1	RACR #2	Total Assets ($mil)	Capital ($mil)	Net Premium ($mil)	Net Income ($mil)
3-03	B	2.16	1.80	36.4	22.8	36.8	0.2
3-02	B-	2.06	1.55	34.8	17.3	28.1	0.0
2002	B	2.13	1.78	35.8	22.6	129.8	6.6
2001	B-	2.09	1.56	31.4	17.3	93.7	1.4
2000	B	1.35	1.16	37.2	16.1	129.6	0.0
1999	B	1.68	1.45	40.5	17.5	113.3	-1.1
1998	B	2.71	2.36	35.6	20.6	78.9	1.4

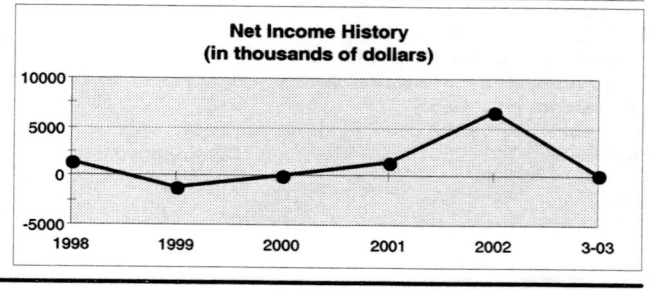

Net Income History (in thousands of dollars) chart

Winter 2003 - 04
II. Analysis of Largest Companies

GRAND VALLEY HEALTH PLAN INC — D- Weak

Major Rating Factors: Weak profitability index (1.1 on a scale of 0 to 10) with operating losses during 1998, 1999 and 2000. Average return on equity has been poor at -68%. Poor capitalization index (1.7) based on weak current risk-adjusted capital (moderate loss scenario). Weak liquidity (2.8) as a spike in claims may stretch capacity.
Other Rating Factors: Fair overall results on stability tests (4.8). High quality investment portfolio (9.9) containing no exposure to mortgages, junk bonds, or unaffiliated stocks.
Principal Business: Comp med (91%), FEHB (9%)
Mem Phys: 02: 299 **01:** 299 **02 MLR** 90% **/ 02 Admin Exp** 10%
Enroll(000): Q1 03: 19 **02:** 20 **01:** 21 **Med Exp PMPM:** $152
Principal Investments: Cash and equiv (51%), real estate (31%), other (18%)
Provider Compensation ($000): Contr fee ($19,290), salary ($16,274), FFS ($1,440), capitation ($350)
Total Member Encounters: Phys (19,974), non-phys (60,503)
Group Affiliation: Grand Valley Health Corp
Licensed in: MI
Address: 829 Forest Hill Ave SE, Grand Rapids, MI 49546
Phone: (616) 949-2410 **Dom State:** MI **Commenced Bus:** February 1982

Data Date	Weiss Safety Rating	RACR #1	RACR #2	Total Assets ($mil)	Capital ($mil)	Net Premium ($mil)	Net Income ($mil)
3-03	D-	0.47	0.39	8.0	2.6	11.1	0.3
3-02	E+	0.20	0.17	7.5	2.0	10.2	0.3
2002	E+	0.31	0.26	7.0	1.8	40.8	0.4
2001	E+	0.14	0.12	6.6	1.5	37.9	0.1
2000	E+	N/A	N/A	6.3	0.6	34.3	-0.4
1999	E+	0.20	0.17	7.5	0.8	32.7	-2.9
1998	D	0.70	0.59	9.7	2.0	35.3	-2.5

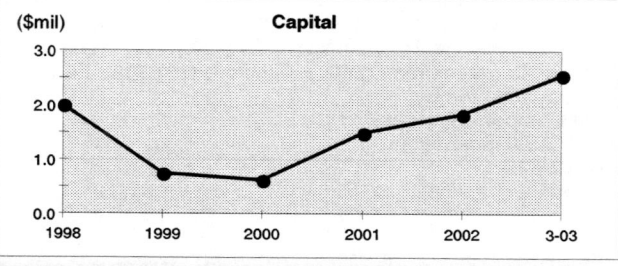

GRAPHIC ARTS BENEFIT CORP — C Fair

Major Rating Factors: Fair capitalization (4.6 on a scale of 0 to 10) based on fair current risk-adjusted capital (moderate loss scenario). Good overall profitability index (5.0). Good liquidity (6.8) with sufficient resources (cash flows and marketable investments) to handle a spike in claims.
Other Rating Factors: High quality investment portfolio (9.9) containing little or no exposure to mortgages, junk bonds, or unaffiliated stocks.
Principal Business: Comp med (100%)
Mem Phys: 02: N/A **01:** N/A **02 MLR** 86% **/ 02 Admin Exp** 11%
Enroll(000): Q1 03: 4 **02:** 4 **01:** 3 **Med Exp PMPM:** $258
Principal Investments: Cash and equiv (43%), nonaffiliate common stock (4%), other (53%)
Provider Compensation ($000): Contr fee ($10,249)
Total Member Encounters: N/A
Group Affiliation: None
Licensed in: DC, MD, VA
Address: 6411 Ivy Lane Suite 700, Greenbelt, MD 20770
Phone: (301) 474-7950 **Dom State:** MD **Commenced Bus:** August 1993

Data Date	Weiss Safety Rating	RACR #1	RACR #2	Total Assets ($mil)	Capital ($mil)	Net Premium ($mil)	Net Income ($mil)
3-03	C	0.87	0.73	4.1	2.0	2.3	0.2
3-02	N/A	N/A	N/A	N/A	N/A	N/A	N/A
2002	C	0.79	0.66	4.0	1.8	11.4	0.8
2001	N/A	N/A	N/A	3.7	1.0	11.7	N/A
2000	N/A	N/A	N/A	3.1	0.7	11.0	N/A
1999	N/A	N/A	N/A	3.4	1.2	9.5	N/A
1998	N/A	N/A	N/A	3.6	1.0	8.3	N/A

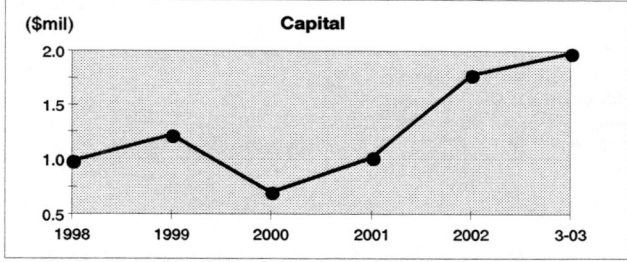

GREAT LAKES HEALTH PLAN INC — E- Very Weak

Major Rating Factors: Weak profitability index (0.9 on a scale of 0 to 10) with operating losses during 1999 and 2002. Poor capitalization index (0.0) based on weak current risk-adjusted capital (severe loss scenario). Low quality investment portfolio (0.0) containing no exposure to mortgages, junk bonds, or unaffiliated stocks.
Other Rating Factors: Weak overall results on stability tests (0.0). Weak liquidity (0.1) as a spike in claims may stretch capacity.
Principal Business: Medicaid (100%)
Mem Phys: 02: 4,073 **01:** 4,394 **02 MLR** 94% **/ 02 Admin Exp** 12%
Enroll(000): Q1 03: 97 **02:** 93 **01:** 82 **Med Exp PMPM:** $146
Principal Investments: Real estate (64%), other (19%), cash and equiv (17%)
Provider Compensation ($000): Contr fee ($132,959), capitation ($18,487)
Total Member Encounters: Phys (204,900), non-phys (142,811)
Group Affiliation: HealthCor Inc
Licensed in: MI
Address: 17117 W Nine Mile Suite 1600, Southfield, MI 48075
Phone: (248) 559-5656 **Dom State:** MI **Commenced Bus:** October 1994

Data Date	Weiss Safety Rating	RACR #1	RACR #2	Total Assets ($mil)	Capital ($mil)	Net Premium ($mil)	Net Income ($mil)
3-03	E-	0.00	0.00	14.4	-12.8	42.4	0.2
3-02	E	0.24	0.21	20.7	5.5	39.1	1.3
2002	E-	0.00	0.00	8.3	-12.4	163.2	-11.0
2001	E	0.24	0.21	26.1	6.1	143.7	5.8
2000	E-	0.06	0.05	22.7	4.1	127.0	7.5
1999	E-	0.00	0.00	17.6	-14.5	103.5	-12.3
1998	E	0.17	0.15	17.7	4.2	75.0	1.1

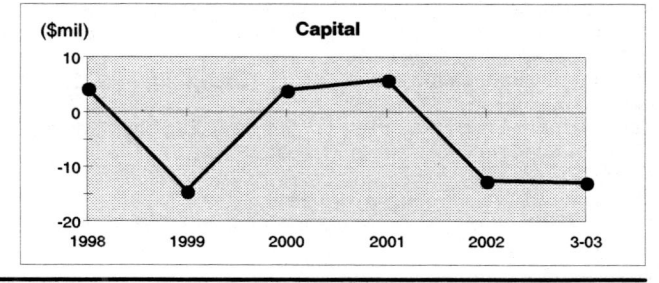

II. Analysis of Largest Companies

Winter 2003 - 04

GROUP HEALTH COOP OF EAU CLAIRE — D — Weak

Major Rating Factors: Poor capitalization (2.9 on a scale of 0 to 10) based on weak current risk-adjusted capital (moderate loss scenario) reflecting improvement over results in 2001. Fair profitability index (3.4) with operating losses during 2001. Good overall results on stability tests (6.4) despite rapid enrollment growth during the past five years but consistent premium and capital growth in the last five years.
Other Rating Factors: Good liquidity (6.8) with sufficient resources (cash flows and marketable investments) to handle a spike in claims. High quality investment portfolio (9.9) containing no exposure to mortgages, junk bonds, or unaffiliated stocks.
Principal Business: Comp med (35%), Medicaid (21%), FEHB (1%), dental (1%), other (41%)
Mem Phys: 02: 1,314   **01:** 1,449   **02 MLR** 89%   **/ 02 Admin Exp** 10%
Enroll(000): Q1 03: 24   **02:** 25   **01:** 25   **Med Exp PMPM:** $292
Principal Investments: Cash and equiv (55%), real estate (3%), other (43%)
Provider Compensation ($000): Contr fee ($81,928), FFS ($2,396), capitation ($2,032), other ($832)
Total Member Encounters: N/A
Group Affiliation: None
Licensed in: WI
Address: 2503 N Hillcrest Parkway, Altoona, WI 54720
Phone: (715) 552-4300   **Dom State:** WI   **Commenced Bus:** November 1976

Data Date	Weiss Safety Rating	RACR #1	RACR #2	Total Assets ($mil)	Capital ($mil)	Net Premium ($mil)	Net Income ($mil)
3-03	D	0.61	0.51	30.0	6.1	26.4	0.8
3-02	D-	0.37	0.31	26.0	5.1	25.7	0.3
2002	D	0.51	0.43	26.6	5.3	98.2	0.5
2001	D-	0.37	0.31	24.2	4.8	86.9	-0.4
2000	D+	0.53	0.45	20.8	5.2	62.6	0.6
1999	D+	0.60	0.50	14.0	4.6	45.6	0.1
1998	D+	0.68	0.57	12.9	4.5	42.1	0.9

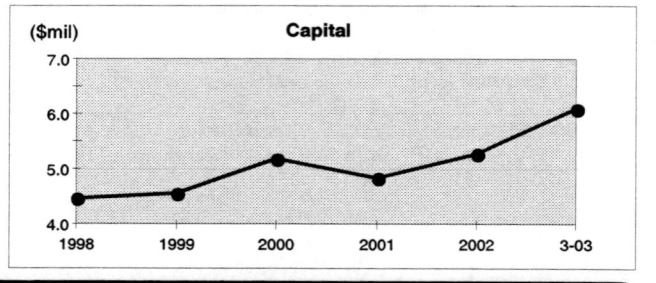

GROUP HEALTH COOP OF S CENTRAL WI * — A- — Excellent

Major Rating Factors: Strong overall capitalization (9.6 on a scale of 0 to 10) based on excellent current risk-adjusted capital (severe loss scenario) despite some fluctuation in capital levels. High quality investment portfolio (9.2). Excellent liquidity (7.1) with ample operational cash flow and liquid investments.
Other Rating Factors: Good overall profitability index (6.2) despite operating losses during 2000. Good overall results on stability tests (6.1).
Principal Business: Comp med (87%), FEHB (6%), Medicaid (5%), med supp (1%), other (1%)
Mem Phys: 02: N/A   **01:** N/A   **02 MLR** 82%   **/ 02 Admin Exp** 10%
Enroll(000): Q1 03: 52   **02:** 52   **01:** 52   **Med Exp PMPM:** $172
Principal Investments: Cash and equiv (30%), real estate (22%), nonaffiliate common stock (7%), other (40%)
Provider Compensation ($000): Capitation ($43,511), contr fee ($19,693), salary ($16,405), FFS ($3,862), other ($23,961)
Total Member Encounters: Phys (198,065), non-phys (60,599)
Group Affiliation: None
Licensed in: WI
Address: 8202 Excelsior Dr, Madison, WI 53717
Phone: (608) 251-4156   **Dom State:** WI   **Commenced Bus:** March 1976

Data Date	Weiss Safety Rating	RACR #1	RACR #2	Total Assets ($mil)	Capital ($mil)	Net Premium ($mil)	Net Income ($mil)
3-03	A-	3.47	2.89	49.9	30.5	36.3	3.6
3-02	B-	1.72	1.36	47.0	19.9	32.4	1.8
2002	A-	3.10	2.58	56.1	27.1	131.0	10.6
2001	B-	1.74	1.37	40.9	17.9	111.5	2.9
2000	C-	1.61	1.31	34.1	15.7	96.8	-0.5
1999	C-	2.13	1.73	36.1	14.0	84.8	1.7
1998	C+	1.92	1.54	30.5	19.9	73.8	3.0

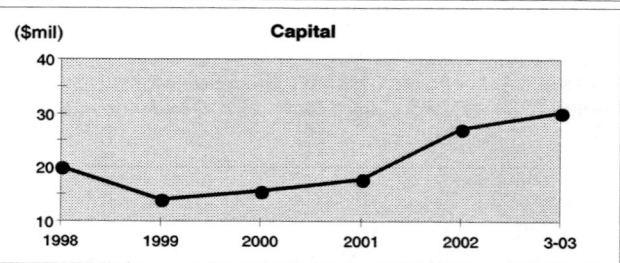

GROUP HEALTH COOPERATIVE PUGET SOUND — B — Good

Major Rating Factors: Good overall results on stability tests (5.5 on a scale of 0 to 10) based on consistent premium and capital growth in the last five years. Good liquidity (6.8) with sufficient resources (cash flows and marketable investments) to handle a spike in claims. Fair profitability index (4.9) despite operating losses during 1998, 1999 and 2002
Other Rating Factors: Strong capitalization (7.9) based on excellent current risk-adjusted capital (severe loss scenario) reflecting significant improvement over results in 1998. High quality investment portfolio (8.2) containing little or no exposure to mortgages, junk bonds, or unaffiliated stocks.
Principal Business: Comp med (62%), Medicare (25%), FEHB (10%), Medicaid (3%)
Mem Phys: 02: 7,749   **01:** 7,989   **02 MLR** 86%   **/ 02 Admin Exp** 11%
Enroll(000): Q1 03: 449   **02:** 444   **01:** 442   **Med Exp PMPM:** $261
Principal Investments: Real estate (44%), cash and equiv (12%), affiliate common stock (4%), other (40%)
Provider Compensation ($000): Salary ($569,172), FFS ($308,124), contr fee ($296,416), capitation ($208,064)
Total Member Encounters: Phys (1,590,169), non-phys (242,644)
Group Affiliation: Group Health Cooperative
Licensed in: WA
Address: 521 Wall St, Seattle, WA 98121
Phone: (206) 448-5528   **Dom State:** WA   **Commenced Bus:** November 1945

Data Date	Weiss Safety Rating	RACR #1	RACR #2	Total Assets ($mil)	Capital ($mil)	Net Premium ($mil)	Net Income ($mil)
3-03	B	2.07	1.73	683.3	208.9	444.0	31.6
3-02	B-	1.75	1.39	624.4	172.5	386.5	8.8
2002	B-	1.74	1.45	663.4	176.2	1,609.7	-7.0
2001	B-	1.75	1.40	649.1	172.1	1,419.7	20.8
2000	C	N/A	N/A	596.2	151.7	1,246.2	24.4
1999	C	1.08	0.88	591.2	126.3	1,164.6	-4.7
1998	C+	0.98	0.77	531.6	129.3	992.3	-12.1

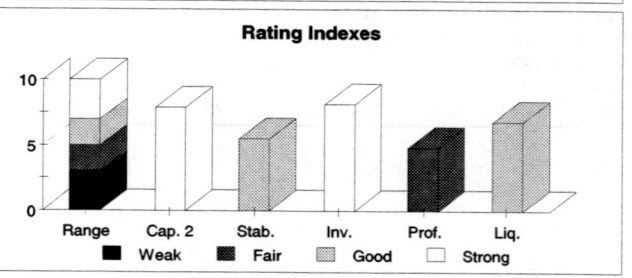

Winter 2003 - 04 — II. Analysis of Largest Companies

GROUP HEALTH INCORPORATED * B+ Good

Major Rating Factors: Good overall profitability index (6.5 on a scale of 0 to 10) despite a decline in earnings during 2002. Good capitalization (6.9) based on excellent current risk-adjusted capital (severe loss scenario) reflecting significant improvement over results in 1998. High quality investment portfolio (9.9) containing little or no exposure to mortgages, junk bonds, or unaffiliated stocks.
Other Rating Factors: Fair liquidity (5.0) as cash resources may not be adequate to cover a spike in claims.
Principal Business: Med only (55%), comp med (28%), FEHB (11%), dental (5%).
Mem Phys: 02: 63,161 **01:** 64,002   **02 MLR** 89% **/ 02 Admin Exp** 10%
Enroll(000): Q1 03: 1,664 **02:** 1,713 **01:** 1,650 **Med Exp PMPM:** $90
Principal Investments: Real estate (19%), other (6%), nonaffiliate common stock (4%), cash and equiv (71%).
Provider Compensation ($000): Contr fee ($1,813,945)
Total Member Encounters: N/A
Group Affiliation: GHI Services Group
Licensed in: NY
Address: 441 Ninth Ave, New York, NY 10001
Phone: (212) 615-0000 **Dom State:** NY **Commenced Bus:** December 1940

Data Date	Weiss Safety Rating	RACR #1	RACR #2	Total Assets ($mil)	Capital ($mil)	Net Premium ($mil)	Net Income ($mil)
3-03	B+	1.26	1.05	634.4	173.3	541.3	-0.8
3-02	B	1.54	1.21	600.9	179.3	480.0	2.8
2002	B+	1.27	1.06	610.9	173.9	2,045.1	14.0
2001	B	1.54	1.21	545.6	176.6	1,752.2	18.5
2000	C+	1.35	0.78	563.7	165.0	1,633.0	36.6
1999	C+	1.47	0.85	553.5	162.8	1,477.0	7.6
1998	C-	1.24	0.71	540.6	121.7	1,312.8	12.6

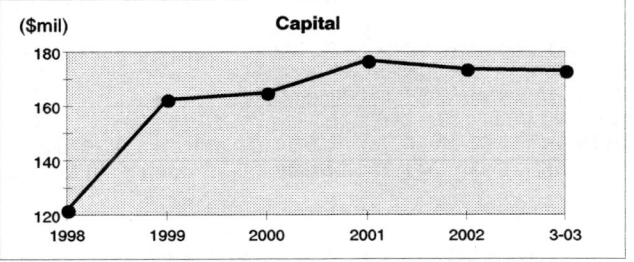

Capital chart (1998–3-03)

GROUP HEALTH OPTIONS INC B- Good

Major Rating Factors: Fair profitability index (3.5 on a scale of 0 to 10) with operating losses during 1998, 1999 and 2002. Good liquidity (6.9) with sufficient resources (cash flows and marketable investments) to handle a spike in claims. Strong capitalization (7.1) based on excellent current risk-adjusted capital (severe loss scenario) reflecting significant improvement over results in 1998.
Other Rating Factors: High quality investment portfolio (9.9) containing no exposure to mortgages, junk bonds, or unaffiliated stocks.
Principal Business: Comp med (100%).
Mem Phys: 02: 8,007 **01:** 7,368 **02 MLR** 89% **/ 02 Admin Exp** 11%
Enroll(000): Q1 03: 129 **02:** 139 **01:** 144 **Med Exp PMPM:** $183
Principal Investments: Cash and equiv (100%).
Provider Compensation ($000): Capitation ($236,866), FFS ($71,364)
Total Member Encounters: Phys (258,547), non-phys (35,652)
Group Affiliation: Group Health Cooperative
Licensed in: ID, WA
Address: 521 Wall St, Seattle, WA 98121
Phone: (206) 287-2100 **Dom State:** WA **Commenced Bus:** October 1990

Data Date	Weiss Safety Rating	RACR #1	RACR #2	Total Assets ($mil)	Capital ($mil)	Net Premium ($mil)	Net Income ($mil)
3-03	B-	1.44	1.20	62.2	24.2	88.3	0.7
3-02	B-	1.55	1.38	64.2	25.8	84.6	-0.7
2002	B-	1.36	1.13	64.9	22.8	347.1	-2.9
2001	B-	1.55	1.39	63.4	26.3	323.3	4.1
2000	C	0.87	0.77	71.1	20.9	297.8	1.3
1999	D+	0.68	0.61	54.8	19.4	280.5	-1.8
1998	D+	0.55	0.49	71.0	19.0	270.4	-0.9

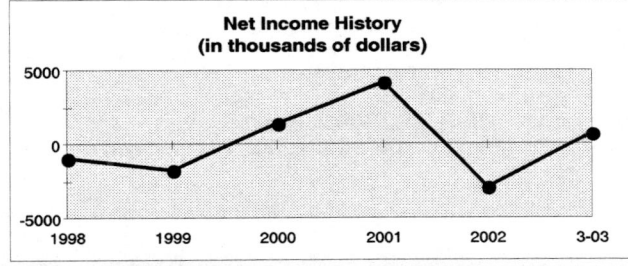

Net Income History (in thousands of dollars)

GROUP HEALTH PLAN INC B Good

Major Rating Factors: Good liquidity (7.0 on a scale of 0 to 10) with sufficient resources (cash flows and marketable investments) to handle a spike in claims. Fair profitability index (4.7) due to a decline in earnings during 2002. Fair overall results on stability tests (4.7).
Other Rating Factors: Strong capitalization index (9.7) based on excellent current risk-adjusted capital (severe loss scenario) despite some fluctuation in capital levels. High quality investment portfolio (9.0).
Principal Business: Comp med (51%), Medicare (32%), FEHB (14%), dental (3%).
Mem Phys: 02: 9,479 **01:** 8,202 **02 MLR** 96% **/ 02 Admin Exp** 3%
Enroll(000): Q1 03: 45 **02:** 44 **01:** 42 **Med Exp PMPM:** $817
Principal Investments: Real estate (29%), cash and equiv (8%), nonaffiliate common stock (4%), other (59%).
Provider Compensation ($000): Contr fee ($228,619), capitation ($5,564), bonus arrang ($4,504)
Total Member Encounters: N/A
Group Affiliation: HealthPartners Inc
Licensed in: MN
Address: 8100 34th Ave S, Minneapolis, MN 55440-1309
Phone: (952) 883-6584 **Dom State:** MN **Commenced Bus:** August 1957

Data Date	Weiss Safety Rating	RACR #1	RACR #2	Total Assets ($mil)	Capital ($mil)	Net Premium ($mil)	Net Income ($mil)
3-03	B	3.53	2.94	360.6	65.3	116.9	0.3
3-02	B-	1.86	1.29	354.9	63.7	103.3	0.3
2002	B	3.64	3.04	366.5	67.6	435.0	1.7
2001	B-	1.83	1.27	383.4	62.7	391.2	7.8
2000	C+	1.74	1.33	425.6	70.0	387.7	3.8
1999	C	1.64	1.26	459.0	54.3	398.3	4.0
1998	D+	1.51	1.16	385.6	60.2	375.7	-0.6

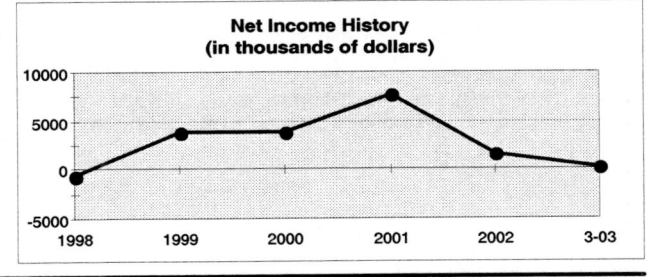

Net Income History (in thousands of dollars)

* Denotes a Weiss Recommended Company

II. Analysis of Largest Companies   Winter 2003 - 04

GROUP HEALTH PLAN INC   C+   Fair

Major Rating Factors: Fair profitability index (3.9 on a scale of 0 to 10) with operating losses during 1998 and 1999. Average return on equity has been poor at -3%. Good liquidity (6.2) with sufficient resources (cash flows and marketable investments) to handle a spike in claims. Weak overall results on stability tests (2.8) based on excessive capital growth during 2002. Potential support from affiliation with Coventry Health Care Inc.
Other Rating Factors: Strong capitalization index (7.4) based on excellent current risk-adjusted capital (severe loss scenario). High quality investment portfolio (9.8) containing little or no exposure to mortgages, junk bonds, or unaffiliated stocks.
Principal Business: Comp med (66%), Medicare (27%), FEHB (8%)
Mem Phys: 02: 7,339 **01:** 5,885   **02 MLR** 81% / **02 Admin Exp** 10%
Enroll(000): Q1 03: 189   **02:** 169   **01:** 192   **Med Exp PMPM:** $169
Principal Investments: Other (100%)
Provider Compensation ($000): Contr fee ($371,918), capitation ($15,931)
Total Member Encounters: Phys (739,581), non-phys (173,866)
Group Affiliation: Coventry Health Care Inc
Licensed in: IL, MO
Address: 111 Corporate Office Dr #400, Earth City, MO 63045
Phone: (314) 506-1700   **Dom State:** MO   **Commenced Bus:** November 1985

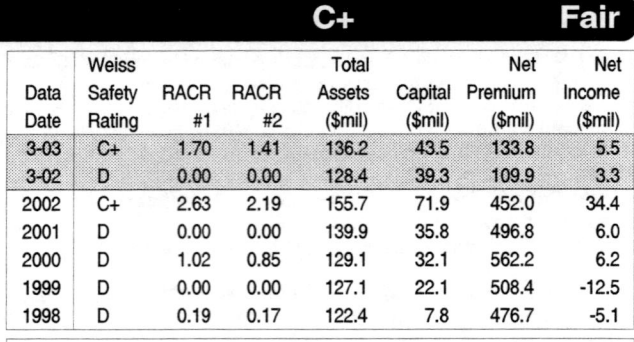

Data Date	Weiss Safety Rating	RACR #1	RACR #2	Total Assets ($mil)	Capital ($mil)	Net Premium ($mil)	Net Income ($mil)
3-03	C+	1.70	1.41	136.2	43.5	133.8	5.5
3-02	D	0.00	0.00	128.4	39.3	109.9	3.3
2002	C+	2.63	2.19	155.7	71.9	452.0	34.4
2001	D	0.00	0.00	139.9	35.8	496.8	6.0
2000	D	1.02	0.85	129.1	32.1	562.2	6.2
1999	D	0.00	0.00	127.1	22.1	508.4	-12.5
1998	D	0.19	0.17	122.4	7.8	476.7	-5.1

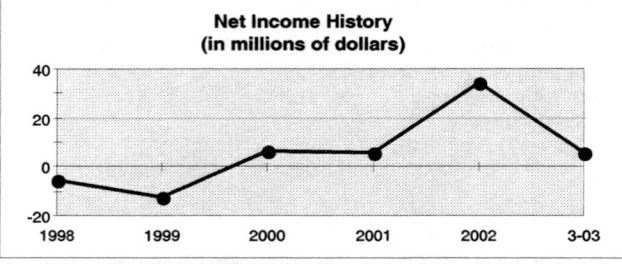

Net Income History (in millions of dollars) — chart showing values for 1998 through 3-03.

GROUP HOSP & MEDICAL SERVICES INC *   A   Excellent

Major Rating Factors: Excellent profitability (7.5 on a scale of 0 to 10) despite a decline in earnings during 2002. Strong capitalization (9.6) based on excellent current risk-adjusted capital (severe loss scenario). High quality investment portfolio (9.1) containing little or no exposure to mortgages, junk bonds, or unaffiliated stocks.
Other Rating Factors: Good liquidity (7.0) with sufficient resources (cash flows and marketable investments) to handle a spike in claims.
Principal Business: FEHB (57%), comp med (40%), dental (1%), med supp (1%)
Mem Phys: 02: 25,005 **01:** 21,918 **02 MLR** 89% / **02 Admin Exp** 8%
Enroll(000): Q1 03: 728 **02:** 748 **01:** 713 **Med Exp PMPM:** $176
Principal Investments: Affiliate common stock (14%), cash and equiv (12%), nonaffiliate common stock (6%), pref stock (1%), other (66%)
Provider Compensation ($000): Contr fee ($1,500,829), capitation ($8,250)
Total Member Encounters: Phys (5,839,522), non-phys (678,838)
Group Affiliation: CareFirst Inc
Licensed in: DC, MD, VA
Address: 550 12th St, SW, Washington, DC 20065
Phone: (202) 479-8000   **Dom State:** DC   **Commenced Bus:** March 1934

Data Date	Weiss Safety Rating	RACR #1	RACR #2	Total Assets ($mil)	Capital ($mil)	Net Premium ($mil)	Net Income ($mil)
3-03	A	3.42	2.85	1,141.0	300.9	479.6	11.2
3-02	B+	3.17	2.37	986.9	282.4	431.9	10.7
2002	A-	3.26	2.72	1,087.7	290.8	1,719.9	38.9
2001	B+	3.19	2.37	927.4	274.0	1,509.3	46.2
2000	B-	1.26	0.80	779.2	248.0	1,243.9	47.0
1999	C+	1.17	0.75	644.7	186.8	1,076.6	34.8
1998	C	1.15	0.72	611.3	158.7	954.3	39.0

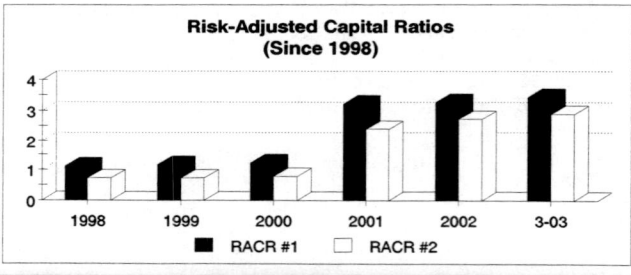

Risk-Adjusted Capital Ratios (Since 1998) — bar chart of RACR #1 and RACR #2.

GUARANTEE TRUST LIFE INSURANCE COMPANY   C+   Fair

Major Rating Factors: Fair overall results on stability tests (4.7 on a scale of 0 to 10). Strong current capitalization (7.0) based on excellent risk adjusted capital (severe loss scenario) reflecting improvement over results in 2002. High quality investment portfolio (7.0) despite no exposure to mortgages and substantial holdings of BBB bonds but small junk bond holdings.
Other Rating Factors: Excellent profitability (8.6) with operating gains in each of the last five years. Excellent liquidity (7.0).
Principal Business: Individual health insurance (56%), group health insurance (14%), individual life insurance (11%), credit health insurance (9%), and other lines (10%).
Principal Investments: CMOs and structured securities (37%), nonCMO investment grade bonds (30%), mortgages in good standing (13%), cash (6%), and misc. investments (14%).
Investments in Affiliates: 1%
Group Affiliation: Guarantee Trust
Licensed in: All states except NY
Commenced Business: June 1936
Address: 1275 Milwaukee Ave, Glenview, IL 60025
Phone: (847) 699-0600   **Domicile State:** IL   **NAIC Code:** 64211

Data Date	Weiss Safety Rating	RACR #1	RACR #2	Total Assets ($mil)	Capital ($mil)	Net Premium ($mil)	Net Income ($mil)
6-03	C+	1.33	1.00	233.1	54.7	100.2	1.6
6-02	B-	1.42	1.04	219.4	46.5	82.1	-2.3
2002	C+	1.28	0.96	246.5	53.3	210.9	0.5
2001	B-	1.50	1.08	253.3	50.1	170.3	3.1
2000	B-	1.85	1.28	213.5	48.8	149.0	4.9
1999	B-	1.75	1.20	194.6	45.3	137.6	3.3
1998	B-	1.65	1.13	189.0	42.9	136.8	4.1

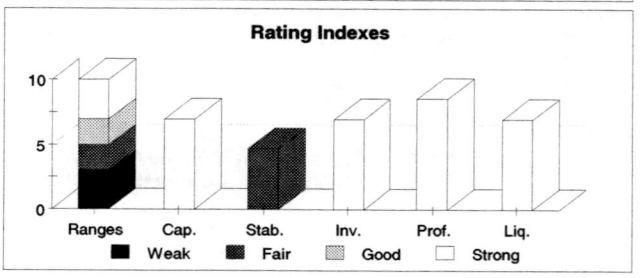

Rating Indexes — bar chart showing Ranges, Cap., Stab., Inv., Prof., Liq. with legend: Weak, Fair, Good, Strong.

www.WeissRatings.com

Winter 2003 - 04
II. Analysis of Largest Companies

GUARDIAN LIFE INSURANCE COMPANY OF AMERICA *   A   Excellent

Major Rating Factors: Good quality investment portfolio (5.7 on a scale of 0 to 10) despite mixed results such as: substantial holdings of BBB bonds but junk bond exposure equal to 53% of capital. Good overall profitability (5.9). Good liquidity (6.4) with sufficient resources to handle a spike in claims as well as a significant increase in policy surrenders.
Other Rating Factors: Good overall results on stability tests (6.1) good operational trends and excellent risk diversification. Strong capitalization (7.6) based on excellent risk adjusted capital (severe loss scenario).
Principal Business: Group health insurance (44%), individual life insurance (36%), reinsurance (11%), individual health insurance (5%), and group life insurance (4%).
Principal Investments: NonCMO investment grade bonds (49%), CMOs and structured securities (17%), common & preferred stock (11%), mortgages in good standing (9%), and misc. investments (15%).
Investments in Affiliates: 4%
Group Affiliation: Guardian Group
Licensed in: All states except PR
Commenced Business: July 1860
Address: 7 Hanover Square, New York, NY 10004-2616
Phone: (212) 598-8000   **Domicile State:** NY   **NAIC Code:** 64246

Data Date	Weiss Safety Rating	RACR #1	RACR #2	Total Assets ($mil)	Capital ($mil)	Net Premium ($mil)	Net Income ($mil)
6-03	A	2.07	1.43	20,577.2	2,082.3	2,664.3	111.4
6-02	A	1.81	1.20	20,281.3	1,302.9	2,678.8	-172.0
2002	A	2.05	1.44	19,545.3	1,913.3	5,248.9	-400.2
2001	A	2.01	1.33	19,493.4	1,527.5	4,336.5	-202.0
2000	A	1.96	1.29	17,989.3	1,653.9	5,140.5	386.8
1999	A	1.64	1.05	16,874.2	1,525.1	4,959.9	258.8
1998	A	1.70	1.11	15,786.3	1,555.4	5,825.9	109.4

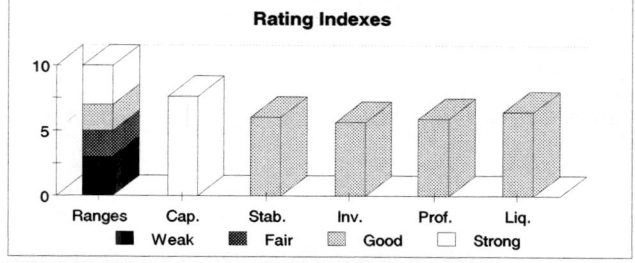

Rating Indexes (Ranges, Cap., Stab., Inv., Prof., Liq.) — Weak, Fair, Good, Strong

GUNDERSEN LUTHERAN HEALTH PLAN INC   C-   Fair

Major Rating Factors: Fair capitalization index (4.1 on a scale of 0 to 10) based on fair current risk-adjusted capital (moderate loss scenario). Excellent profitability (8.5) despite a decline in earnings during 2002. High quality investment portfolio (8.7) containing no exposure to mortgages, junk bonds, or unaffiliated stocks.
Other Rating Factors: Excellent overall results on stability tests (8.3) based on consistent premium and capital growth in the last five years but rapid enrollment growth during the past five years. Excellent liquidity (7.1) with ample operational cash flow and liquid investments.
Principal Business: Comp med (66%), Medicare (32%), other (2%)
Mem Phys: 02: 189   **01:** 131   **02 MLR** 88%   **/ 02 Admin Exp** 10%
Enroll(000): Q1 03: 31   **02:** 32   **01:** 32   **Med Exp PMPM:** $255
Principal Investments: Cash and equiv (100%)
Provider Compensation ($000): Capitation ($96,588)
Total Member Encounters: Phys (131,510), non-phys (126,903)
Group Affiliation: Gundersen Lutheran Inc
Licensed in: WI
Address: 1836 South Ave, La Crosse, WI 54601
Phone: (608) 782-7300   **Dom State:** WI   **Commenced Bus:** September 1995

Data Date	Weiss Safety Rating	RACR #1	RACR #2	Total Assets ($mil)	Capital ($mil)	Net Premium ($mil)	Net Income ($mil)
3-03	C-	0.79	0.66	20.9	7.0	30.0	0.5
3-02	D+	0.54	0.48	17.8	5.4	26.6	0.4
2002	C-	0.72	0.60	18.1	6.5	110.6	1.6
2001	D+	0.53	0.48	14.4	4.9	86.3	2.1
2000	E+	0.31	0.28	11.1	2.8	58.0	0.8
1999	E+	0.25	0.22	7.7	2.0	36.2	-0.3
1998	E+	0.24	0.21	6.5	1.4	28.5	0.1

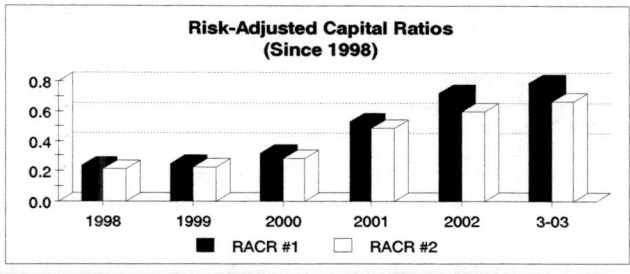

Risk-Adjusted Capital Ratios (Since 1998) — RACR #1, RACR #2

HARMONY HEALTH PLAN OF ILLINOIS INC   C+   Fair

Major Rating Factors: Fair capitalization (5.0 on a scale of 0 to 10) based on good current risk-adjusted capital (severe loss scenario) reflecting significant improvement over results in 2001. Fair overall results on stability tests (5.0) based on weak risk-adjusted capital in prior years, rapid premium growth over the last five years and rapid enrollment growth during the past five years. Good overall profitability index (6.3) despite a decline in earnings during 2002.
Other Rating Factors: High quality investment portfolio (9.9) containing no exposure to mortgages, junk bonds, or unaffiliated stocks. Excellent liquidity (7.1) with ample operational cash flow and liquid investments.
Principal Business: Medicaid (100%)
Mem Phys: 02: 3,144   **01:** 2,825   **02 MLR** 74%   **/ 02 Admin Exp** 19%
Enroll(000): Q1 03: 79   **02:** 77   **01:** 55   **Med Exp PMPM:** $92
Principal Investments: Cash and equiv (100%)
Provider Compensation ($000): Contr fee ($44,711), capitation ($18,773), bonus arrang ($3,555), salary ($1,181)
Total Member Encounters: N/A
Group Affiliation: Harmony Health Systems Inc
Licensed in: IL, IN
Address: 125 S Wacker Dr Ste 2600, Chicago, IL 60606
Phone: (312) 630-2025   **Dom State:** IL   **Commenced Bus:** July 1996

Data Date	Weiss Safety Rating	RACR #1	RACR #2	Total Assets ($mil)	Capital ($mil)	Net Premium ($mil)	Net Income ($mil)
3-03	C+	0.93	0.77	36.8	9.9	28.7	1.0
3-02	C-	0.50	0.43	31.2	7.3	20.8	0.9
2002	C	0.75	0.63	33.2	8.5	97.9	3.7
2001	C-	0.50	0.43	27.1	7.0	69.3	4.5
2000	D+	N/A	N/A	21.9	9.2	51.0	3.7
1999	D+	0.67	0.57	13.4	5.1	38.3	2.9
1998	N/A	N/A	N/A	8.3	1.9	25.4	-3.9

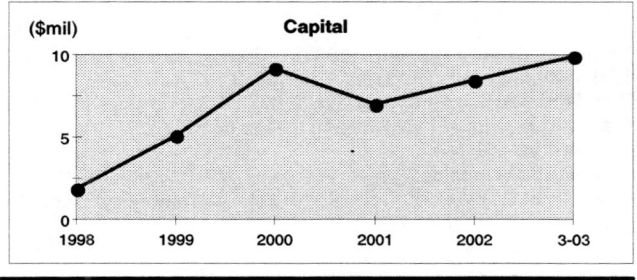

Capital ($mil) 1998–3-03

www.WeissRatings.com   175   * Denotes a Weiss Recommended Company

II. Analysis of Largest Companies

Winter 2003 - 04

HARTFORD LIFE & ACCIDENT INSURANCE COMPANY *   B+   Good

Major Rating Factors: Good overall results on stability tests (6.4 on a scale of 0 to 10). Stability strengths include excellent operational trends, good risk adjusted capital for prior years and excellent risk diversification. Good liquidity (6.9) with sufficient resources to handle a spike in claims as well as a significant increase in policy surrenders. Fair quality investment portfolio (4.4).
Other Rating Factors: Strong capitalization (7.0) based on excellent risk adjusted capital (severe loss scenario). Excellent profitability (8.5) with operating gains in each of the last five years.
Principal Business: Group health insurance (43%), reinsurance (28%), group life insurance (26%), and individual life insurance (3%).
Principal Investments: Common & preferred stock (41%), nonCMO investment grade bonds (37%), CMOs and structured securities (15%), noninv. grade bonds (3%), and misc. investments (5%).
Investments in Affiliates: 37%
Group Affiliation: Hartford Ins Group
Licensed in: All states except NY
Commenced Business: February 1967
Address: 200 Hopmeadow St, Simsbury, CT 06070
Phone: (860) 843-5867   **Domicile State:** CT   **NAIC Code:** 70815

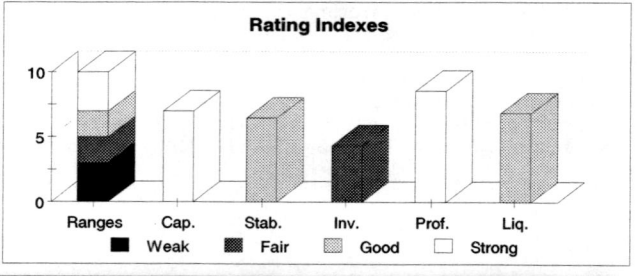

Data Date	Weiss Safety Rating	RACR #1	RACR #2	Total Assets ($mil)	Capital ($mil)	Net Premium ($mil)	Net Income ($mil)
6-03	B+	1.10	1.02	8,792.5	3,503.1	1,102.2	175.9
6-02	B+	1.05	0.98	7,797.6	2,810.9	1,127.3	127.4
2002	B+	1.06	0.98	8,053.9	3,018.9	2,213.8	166.7
2001	B+	1.06	0.99	7,992.9	2,992.2	2,279.2	121.9
2000	B+	1.04	0.97	6,875.0	2,406.7	1,970.7	299.7
1999	B+	1.00	0.94	6,312.8	2,214.5	2,450.4	71.7
1998	B+	1.06	0.99	5,165.5	2,010.2	1,624.9	57.3

Rating Indexes (Ranges, Cap., Stab., Inv., Prof., Liq.) — Weak / Fair / Good / Strong

HARVARD PILGRIM HC OF NEW ENGLAND   C-   Fair

Major Rating Factors: Weak profitability index (1.6 on a scale of 0 to 10) with modest operating losses during 1999 and 2002. Good capitalization index (6.6) based on good current risk-adjusted capital (severe loss scenario). Good overall results on stability tests (5.3) despite rapid premium growth over the last five years, rapid enrollment growth during the past five years. Rating is significantly influenced by the poor financial results of Harvard Pilgrim Health Care.
Other Rating Factors: Good liquidity (6.8) with sufficient resources (cash flows and marketable investments) to handle a spike in claims. High quality investment portfolio (9.8) containing no exposure to mortgages, junk bonds, or unaffiliated stocks.
Principal Business: Comp med (87%), Medicare (12%), other (1%).
Mem Phys: 02: 36,512   01: 35,767   **02 MLR** 87%   / **02 Admin Exp** 14%
Enroll(000): 02: 35   01: 23   **Med Exp PMPM:** $229
Principal Investments: Cash and equiv (4%), other (96%).
Provider Compensation ($000): None
Total Member Encounters: Phys (158,373), non-phys (36,777)
Group Affiliation: Harvard Pilgrim Health Care
Licensed in: NH, VT
Address: 93 Worcester Street, Wellesley, MA 02481
Phone: (781) 263-6000   **Dom State:** MA   **Commenced Bus:** October 1980

Data Date	Weiss Safety Rating	RACR #1	RACR #2	Total Assets ($mil)	Capital ($mil)	Net Premium ($mil)	Net Income ($mil)
2002	C-	1.18	0.98	14.3	10.5	92.3	-0.3
2001	E-	0.00	0.00	13.2	10.8	56.0	0.7
2000	E-	N/A	N/A	12.5	10.1	66.6	N/A
1999	F	1.73	1.45	12.0	10.1	47.5	-2.0
1998	C-	6.85	4.02	12.1	12.1	22.9	0.9

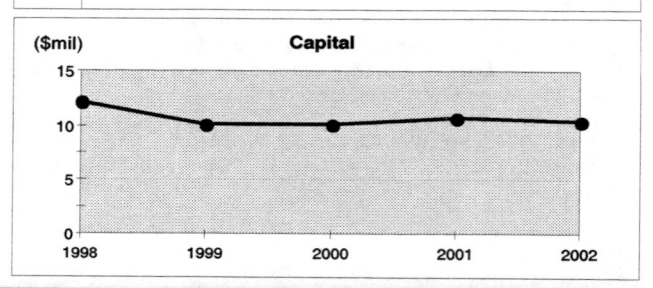

Capital ($mil) chart: 1998–2002

HARVARD PILGRIM HEALTH CARE INC   C-   Fair

Major Rating Factors: Fair overall results on stability tests (4.9 on a scale of 0 to 10) based on excessive capital growth during 2002. Weak profitability index (2.1) with operating losses during 1998, 1999 and 2000. Good liquidity (6.9) with sufficient resources (cash flows and marketable investments) to handle a spike in claims.
Other Rating Factors: Strong capitalization (7.3) based on excellent current risk-adjusted capital (severe loss scenario) reflecting significant improvement over results in 1998. High quality investment portfolio (9.9) containing little or no exposure to mortgages, junk bonds, or unaffiliated stocks.
Principal Business: Comp med (82%), Medicare (18%)
Mem Phys: 02: 36,512   01: 35,767   **02 MLR** 87%   / **02 Admin Exp** 10%
Enroll(000): Q1 03: 555   02: 561   01: 580   **Med Exp PMPM:** $216
Principal Investments: Cash and equiv (33%), real estate (8%), affiliate common stock (2%), other (57%).
Provider Compensation ($000): Bonus arrang ($857,593), capitation ($619,300), contr fee ($27,198), FFS ($6,100)
Total Member Encounters: Phys (2,872,366), non-phys (603,040)
Group Affiliation: Harvard Pilgrim Health Care
Licensed in: ME, MA
Address: 93 Worcester Street, Wellesley, MA 02481
Phone: (781) 263-6000   **Dom State:** MA   **Commenced Bus:** February 1969

Data Date	Weiss Safety Rating	RACR #1	RACR #2	Total Assets ($mil)	Capital ($mil)	Net Premium ($mil)	Net Income ($mil)
3-03	C-	1.59	1.32	439.8	176.7	453.7	9.3
3-02	D-	0.94	0.79	424.3	145.1	406.5	9.8
2002	C-	1.52	1.27	449.4	169.8	1,686.1	44.9
2001	D-	0.88	0.73	461.7	130.9	1,649.2	23.7
2000	E-	N/A	N/A	539.1	131.2	1,957.9	-13.3
1999	E-	0.57	0.47	777.4	133.6	2,515.7	-207.4
1998	D+	0.54	0.34	884.2	127.0	2,345.9	-14.9

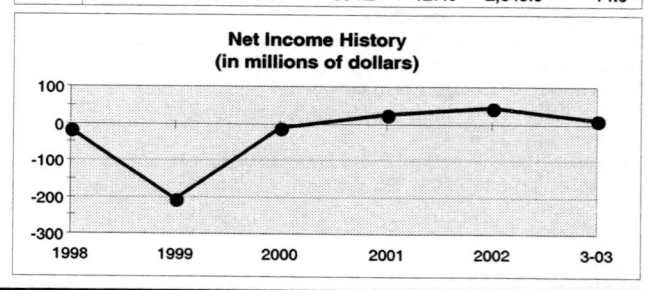

Net Income History (in millions of dollars): 1998–3-03

www.WeissRatings.com

HAWAII MANAGEMENT ALLIANCE ASSOC — D Weak

Major Rating Factors: Poor capitalization index (0.4 on a scale of 0 to 10) based on weak current risk-adjusted capital (moderate loss scenario). Fair profitability index (4.6). High quality investment portfolio (9.9) containing little or no exposure to mortgages, junk bonds, or unaffiliated stocks.
Other Rating Factors: Excellent liquidity (7.0) with ample operational cash flow and liquid investments.
Principal Business: Comp med (90%), dental (10%)
Mem Phys: 01: 3,591   **00:** 3,479   **01 MLR** 94%   **/ 01 Admin Exp** 27%
Enroll(000): Q2 02: 27   **01:** 26   **00:** 26   **Med Exp PMPM:** $121
Principal Investments: Cash and equiv (99%), nonaffiliate common stock (1%)
Provider Compensation ($000): Contr fee ($26,801)
Total Member Encounters: Phys (2,673)
Group Affiliation: GPF Life & Health Benefits Co
Licensed in: HI
Address: 737 Bishop St Ste 1200, Honolulu, HI 96813
Phone: (808) 591-0088   **Dom State:** HI   **Commenced Bus:** October 1990

Data Date	Weiss Safety Rating	RACR #1	RACR #2	Total Assets ($mil)	Capital ($mil)	Net Premium ($mil)	Net Income ($mil)
6-02	D	0.33	0.28	12.2	3.6	27.6	0.2
6-01	N/A	N/A	N/A	8.2	1.9	15.9	0.4
2001	D	0.33	0.28	16.5	3.4	40.0	0.3
2000	N/A	N/A	N/A	8.7	1.5	15.9	N/A
1999	N/A	N/A	N/A	5.2	1.5	10.8	N/A
1998	N/A	N/A	N/A	6.1	1.6	7.5	N/A
1997	N/A	N/A	N/A	7.6	1.8	29.3	N/A

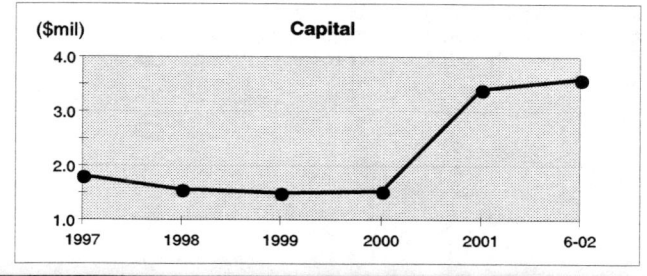

Capital ($mil) chart: 1997–6-02

HAWAII MEDICAL SERVICE ASSOCIATION — C Fair

Major Rating Factors: Weak profitability index (1.5 on a scale of 0 to 10) with operating losses during 2002. Good liquidity (6.8) with sufficient resources (cash flows and marketable investments) to handle a spike in claims. Strong capitalization (10.0) based on excellent current risk-adjusted capital (severe loss scenario) despite some fluctuation in capital levels.
Other Rating Factors: High quality investment portfolio (9.2).
Principal Business: Comp med (83%), FEHB (10%), dental (3%), other (3%)
Mem Phys: 02: 5,771   **01:** 5,642   **02 MLR** 93%   **/ 02 Admin Exp** 8%
Enroll(000): Q1 03: 670   **02:** 668   **01:** 629   **Med Exp PMPM:** $154
Principal Investments: Cash and equiv (22%), nonaffiliate common stock (20%), real estate (7%), other (51%)
Provider Compensation ($000): Contr fee ($1,113,968), capitation ($63,142), FFS ($3,624)
Total Member Encounters: Phys (4,168,798)
Group Affiliation: Hawaii Medical Service Assoc
Licensed in: HI
Address: 818 Keeaumoku St, Honolulu, HI 96814
Phone: (808) 948-5145   **Dom State:** HI   **Commenced Bus:** June 1938

Data Date	Weiss Safety Rating	RACR #1	RACR #2	Total Assets ($mil)	Capital ($mil)	Net Premium ($mil)	Net Income ($mil)
3-03	C	4.20	3.50	706.1	409.9	347.5	3.7
3-02	B	3.43	2.39	799.7	437.3	354.6	3.8
2002	C	4.17	3.48	718.4	407.6	1,283.6	-40.5
2001	B	3.43	2.39	798.0	430.6	965.3	19.1
2000	B	2.57	1.50	823.6	419.4	1,119.0	4.6
1999	B	2.77	1.62	653.3	474.0	1,037.5	35.9
1998	B	2.80	1.62	796.1	396.9	993.9	10.1

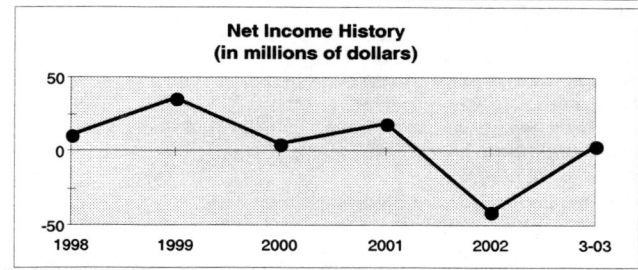

Net Income History (in millions of dollars): 1998–3-03

HCC LIFE INSURANCE COMPANY — B- Good

Major Rating Factors: Good overall profitability (6.3 on a scale of 0 to 10). Return on equity has been low, averaging 3.1%. Fair overall results on stability tests (4.0). Strong capitalization (8.6) based on excellent risk adjusted capital (severe loss scenario). Capital levels have been relatively consistent over the last five years.
Other Rating Factors: High quality investment portfolio (7.8). Excellent liquidity (8.1).
Principal Business: N/A
Principal Investments: NonCMO investment grade bonds (62%), CMOs and structured securities (19%), common & preferred stock (18%), noninv. grade bonds (1%), and cash (1%).
Investments in Affiliates: 16%
Group Affiliation: HCC Ins Holdings Inc
Licensed in: All states except AK, HI, ME, MA, MN, NH, NY, RI, VT, PR
Commenced Business: March 1981
Address: 300 N Meridian St Ste 2700, Indianapolis, IN 46204
Phone: (713) 996-1200   **Domicile State:** IN   **NAIC Code:** 92711

Data Date	Weiss Safety Rating	RACR #1	RACR #2	Total Assets ($mil)	Capital ($mil)	Net Premium ($mil)	Net Income ($mil)
6-03	B-	2.34	2.06	201.1	112.7	100.4	13.1
6-02	B-	2.21	1.94	147.9	84.8	74.2	12.7
2002	B-	2.36	2.09	188.3	109.2	169.9	27.2
2001	C	2.45	2.22	124.2	77.1	62.9	16.7
2000	C	1.45	1.36	110.3	63.3	38.5	1.8
1999	C	1.26	1.13	142.7	70.5	77.9	-4.5
1998	C	1.42	1.02	176.1	17.8	67.0	-5.8

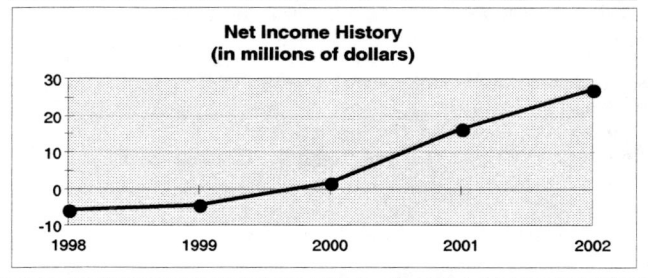

Net Income History (in millions of dollars): 1998–2002

II. Analysis of Largest Companies
Winter 2003 - 04

HEALTH ALLIANCE MEDICAL PLANS — C+ — Fair

Major Rating Factors: Fair overall results on stability tests (4.4 on a scale of 0 to 10). Good quality investment portfolio (5.9) with no exposure to mortgages and no exposure to junk bonds. Strong capitalization (7.9) based on excellent risk adjusted capital (severe loss scenario). Moreover, capital has steadily grown over the last five years.
Other Rating Factors: Excellent profitability (8.0) despite modest operating losses during 1998. Excellent liquidity (9.9).
Principal Business: Group health insurance (100%).
Principal Investments: Cash (60%), nonCMO investment grade bonds (22%), and common & preferred stock (16%).
Investments in Affiliates: 5%
Group Affiliation: Health Alliance Group
Licensed in: IL
Commenced Business: January 1980
Address: 102 E Main St Ste 200, Urbana, IL 61801
Phone: (217) 337-8134 **Domicile State:** IL **NAIC Code:** 77950

Data Date	Weiss Safety Rating	RACR #1	RACR #2	Total Assets ($mil)	Capital ($mil)	Net Premium ($mil)	Net Income ($mil)
6-03	C+	2.15	1.63	114.8	38.4	38.2	7.6
6-02	C	1.94	1.51	89.0	25.6	24.1	4.7
2002	C	2.19	1.73	95.1	29.6	52.1	9.4
2001	C	1.77	1.38	75.5	21.9	40.3	6.6
2000	D+	1.87	1.46	64.8	18.8	43.7	4.9
1999	D+	1.30	1.01	52.2	14.1	36.7	2.1
1998	D+	1.28	1.01	46.9	10.3	26.9	-0.7

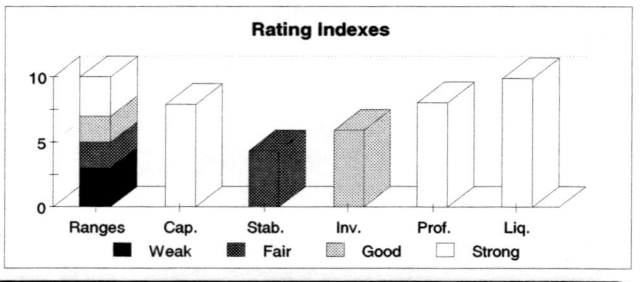

Rating Indexes chart: Ranges, Cap., Stab., Inv., Prof., Liq. (Weak, Fair, Good, Strong)

HEALTH ALLIANCE PLAN OF MICHIGAN * — A — Excellent

Major Rating Factors: Strong overall capitalization (7.6 on a scale of 0 to 10) based on excellent current risk-adjusted capital (severe loss scenario). Furthermore, this high level of risk-adjusted capital has been consistently maintained in previous years. Good overall profitability index (5.3) with operating gains in each of the last five years. Good quality investment portfolio (6.6) containing small junk bond exposure.
Other Rating Factors: Good liquidity (7.0) with sufficient resources (cash flows and marketable investments) to handle a spike in claims. Fair overall results on stability tests (4.9).
Principal Business: Comp med (78%), Medicare (11%), med supp (6%), FEHB (5%).
Mem Phys: 02: 6,408 **01:** 6,180 **02 MLR** 90% **/ 02 Admin Exp** 8%
Enroll(000): Q1 03: 474 **02:** 485 **01:** 462 **Med Exp PMPM:** $205
Principal Investments: Cash and equiv (51%), nonaffiliate common stock (22%), affiliate common stock (7%), real estate (2%), other (19%).
Provider Compensation ($000): Capitation ($821,301), contr fee ($119,605), bonus arrang ($92,254), other ($117,819)
Total Member Encounters: Phys (1,822,873), non-phys (918,785)
Group Affiliation: Henry Ford Health System
Licensed in: MI, OH
Address: 2850 W Grand Blvd, Detroit, MI 48202
Phone: (313) 872-8100 **Dom State:** MI **Commenced Bus:** February 1979

Data Date	Weiss Safety Rating	RACR #1	RACR #2	Total Assets ($mil)	Capital ($mil)	Net Premium ($mil)	Net Income ($mil)
3-03	A	1.82	1.52	316.7	153.8	333.4	7.0
3-02	A	2.08	1.62	345.9	183.5	323.2	4.7
2002	A	2.15	1.79	352.1	180.3	1,291.0	26.7
2001	A	2.08	1.62	330.9	177.8	1,133.5	26.2
2000	A	3.17	2.53	310.5	195.8	1,060.3	37.7
1999	A	2.89	2.51	263.7	159.8	981.7	19.1
1998	A-	1.68	1.39	254.4	144.6	992.4	9.2

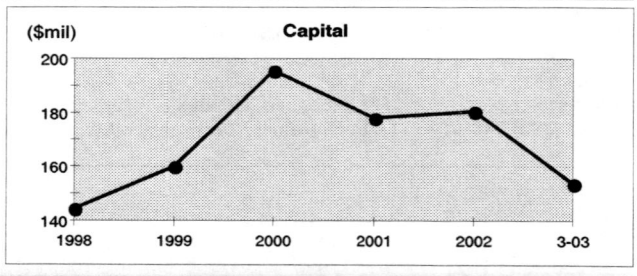

Capital chart ($mil), 1998–3-03

HEALTH ALLIANCE-MIDWEST INC — C+ — Fair

Major Rating Factors: Good overall capitalization (6.2 on a scale of 0 to 10) based on good current risk-adjusted capital (severe loss scenario). Good liquidity (5.6) with sufficient resources (cash flows and marketable investments) to handle a spike in claims. Excellent profitability (7.4).
Other Rating Factors: High quality investment portfolio (9.5) containing no exposure to mortgages, junk bonds, or unaffiliated stocks. Excellent overall results on stability tests (7.2) based on consistent premium and capital growth in the last five years. Fair financial strength from affiliates.
Principal Business: Comp med (98%), FEHB (2%).
Mem Phys: 02: 938 **01:** 844 **02 MLR** 86% **/ 02 Admin Exp** 13%
Enroll(000): Q1 03: 4 **02:** 9 **01:** 8 **Med Exp PMPM:** $163
Principal Investments: Cash and equiv (54%), other (46%).
Provider Compensation ($000): Contr fee ($14,575), capitation ($315), FFS ($279)
Total Member Encounters: Phys (45,741), non-phys (73,781)
Group Affiliation: Health Alliance Group
Licensed in: IL, IA
Address: 102 E Main St, Urbana, IL 61801
Phone: (217) 337-8000 **Dom State:** IL **Commenced Bus:** May 1997

Data Date	Weiss Safety Rating	RACR #1	RACR #2	Total Assets ($mil)	Capital ($mil)	Net Premium ($mil)	Net Income ($mil)
3-03	C+	1.12	0.93	7.4	3.6	2.0	0.0
3-02	C-	1.87	1.63	7.1	3.3	4.6	0.0
2002	C+	1.15	0.96	8.9	3.6	19.3	0.4
2001	C-	1.87	1.64	6.0	3.3	16.8	0.2
2000	C-	2.29	2.00	5.5	3.0	13.3	0.4
1999	D+	2.58	2.24	5.5	2.8	10.9	0.4
1998	N/A	N/A	N/A	3.8	2.5	6.6	N/A

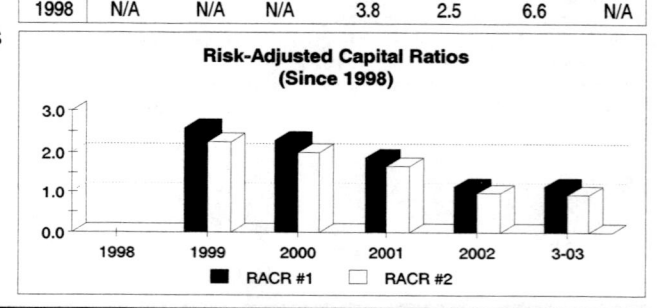

Risk-Adjusted Capital Ratios (Since 1998) chart — RACR #1, RACR #2

HEALTH CARE SERVICE CORP, A MUTUAL LEGAL RESERVE *   B+   Good

Major Rating Factors: Good quality investment portfolio (6.9 on a scale of 0 to 10) with no exposure to mortgages and no exposure to junk bonds. Good overall results on stability tests (5.0). Stability strengths include excellent operational trends, good risk adjusted capital for prior years and excellent risk diversification. Strong capitalization (7.6) based on excellent risk adjusted capital (severe loss scenario).
Other Rating Factors: Excellent profitability (8.1) with operating gains in each of the last five years. Excellent liquidity (7.1).
Principal Business: Group health insurance (76%) and individual health insurance (24%).
Principal Investments: NonCMO investment grade bonds (38%), common & preferred stock (27%), cash (20%), real estate (8%), and CMOs and structured securities (6%).
Investments in Affiliates: 23%
Group Affiliation: HCSC Group
Licensed in: IL, NM, TX
Commenced Business: January 1937
Address: 300 East Randolph Street, Chicago, IL 60601-5099
Phone: (312) 653-6000 **Domicile State:** IL **NAIC Code:** 70670

Data Date	Weiss Safety Rating	RACR #1	RACR #2	Total Assets ($mil)	Capital ($mil)	Net Premium ($mil)	Net Income ($mil)
6-03	B+	1.65	1.43	4,352.1	1,681.9	3,009.7	278.4
6-02	B+	1.09	0.95	3,776.3	1,376.9	2,630.0	164.6
2002	B+	1.39	1.20	4,161.0	1,460.8	5,556.4	245.9
2001	B+	0.96	0.83	3,593.2	1,180.9	4,631.5	387.1
2000	B+	1.09	0.95	3,282.0	1,306.0	3,836.8	173.8
1999	B+	1.66	1.36	2,650.3	1,238.8	3,287.7	110.8
1998	B+	1.70	1.38	2,508.5	1,142.2	2,909.6	49.7

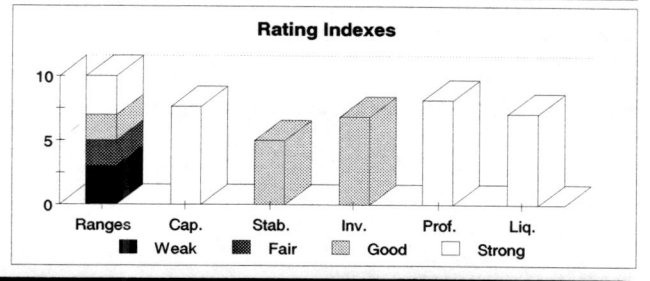

Rating Indexes (Ranges, Cap., Stab., Inv., Prof., Liq. — Weak, Fair, Good, Strong)

HEALTH FIRST HEALTH PLANS   C+   Fair

Major Rating Factors: Fair capitalization index (4.0 on a scale of 0 to 10) based on fair current risk-adjusted capital (moderate loss scenario). Fair overall results on stability tests (4.4). Good overall profitability index (5.6) despite a decline in earnings during 2002.
Other Rating Factors: Good liquidity (6.8) with sufficient resources (cash flows and marketable investments) to handle a spike in claims. High quality investment portfolio (9.9) containing no exposure to mortgages, junk bonds, or unaffiliated stocks.
Principal Business: Medicare (61%), comp med (39%)
Mem Phys: 02: 543 **01:** 485 **02 MLR** 88% / **02 Admin Exp** 10%
Enroll(000): Q1 03: 55 **02:** 60 **01:** 47 **Med Exp PMPM:** $246
Principal Investments: Cash and equiv (41%), real estate (12%), other (47%)
Provider Compensation ($000): Capitation ($76,997), FFS ($61,302), other ($17,447)
Total Member Encounters: N/A
Group Affiliation: Health First Inc
Licensed in: FL
Address: 8247 Devereux Dr Ste 103, Melbourne, FL 32940
Phone: (407) 953-5600 **Dom State:** FL **Commenced Bus:** January 1996

Data Date	Weiss Safety Rating	RACR #1	RACR #2	Total Assets ($mil)	Capital ($mil)	Net Premium ($mil)	Net Income ($mil)
3-03	C+	0.78	0.65	32.2	12.1	51.0	1.5
3-02	C-	0.00	0.00	37.9	13.8	43.0	1.7
2002	C+	0.71	0.59	40.4	10.9	179.5	0.3
2001	C-	0.00	0.00	36.6	12.7	205.0	3.0
2000	C-	1.26	1.07	29.0	14.9	143.9	5.0
1999	D-	0.00	0.00	30.1	11.5	84.4	2.2
1998	D-	1.03	0.89	26.5	8.9	77.5	-1.8

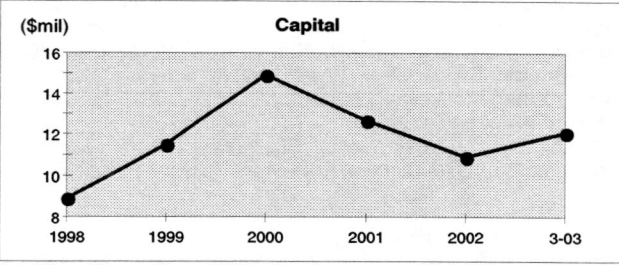

Capital ($mil) — 1998 through 3-03

HEALTH INSURANCE PLAN OF GREATER NY *   B+   Good

Major Rating Factors: Good liquidity (6.9 on a scale of 0 to 10) with sufficient resources (cash flows and marketable investments) to handle a spike in claims. Excellent profitability (9.3) with operating gains in each of the last five years. Strong capitalization (10.0) based on excellent current risk-adjusted capital (severe loss scenario).
Other Rating Factors: High quality investment portfolio (9.9) containing little or no exposure to mortgages, junk bonds, or unaffiliated stocks.
Principal Business: Comp med (54%), Medicare (36%), Medicaid (9%)
Mem Phys: 02: 18,693 **01:** 17,742 **02 MLR** 81% / **02 Admin Exp** 11%
Enroll(000): Q1 03: 868 **02:** 851 **01:** 773 **Med Exp PMPM:** $210
Principal Investments: Cash and equiv (23%), real estate (8%), affiliate common stock (2%), nonaffiliate common stock (1%), other (65%)
Provider Compensation ($000): Contr fee ($951,079), capitation ($918,656), FFS ($75,237), salary ($31,257)
Total Member Encounters: Phys (3,553,410), non-phys (2,366,997)
Group Affiliation: HIP Ins Group
Licensed in: NY
Address: 7 W 34th St, New York, NY 10001
Phone: (212) 630-5000 **Dom State:** NY **Commenced Bus:** March 1947

Data Date	Weiss Safety Rating	RACR #1	RACR #2	Total Assets ($mil)	Capital ($mil)	Net Premium ($mil)	Net Income ($mil)
3-03	B+	6.28	5.23	1,066.5	451.4	711.3	81.1
3-02	C	1.41	1.19	846.5	232.1	587.1	35.3
2002	B+	5.48	4.57	1,053.9	364.6	2,522.2	175.4
2001	C	1.41	1.19	840.0	192.4	2,166.2	84.1
2000	D-	0.64	0.37	832.5	137.8	1,977.4	67.1
1999	D-	0.55	0.32	726.8	114.4	1,771.5	25.2
1998	D	0.42	0.24	704.5	63.3	1,602.6	20.5

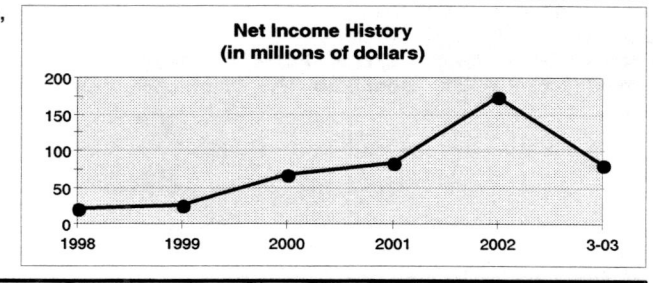

Net Income History (in millions of dollars) — 1998 through 3-03

www.WeissRatings.com   179   * Denotes a Weiss Recommended Company

II. Analysis of Largest Companies

HEALTH NET *   B+   Good

Major Rating Factors: Good capitalization index (6.2 on a scale of 0 to 10) based on good current risk-adjusted capital (severe loss scenario). Good overall results on stability tests (5.5) despite good risk-adjusted capital in prior years. Good liquidity (7.0) with sufficient resources (cash flows and marketable investments) to handle a spike in claims.
Other Rating Factors: Excellent profitability (7.1) with operating gains in each of the last five years.
Principal Business: Managed care (63%)
Mem Phys: 02: N/A   **01:** N/A   **02 MLR** 86%   / **02 Admin Exp** 10%
Enroll(000): Q1 03: 2,238   **02:** 2,393   **01:** 2,472   **Med Exp PMPM:** $153
Principal Investments ($000): Cash and equiv ($850,485)
Provider Compensation ($000): None
Total Member Encounters: N/A
Group Affiliation: Health Net Inc
Licensed in: CA
Address: 21281 Burbank Blvd, Woodland Hills, CA 91367
Phone: (818) 676-6775   **Dom State:** CA   **Commenced Bus:** March 1979

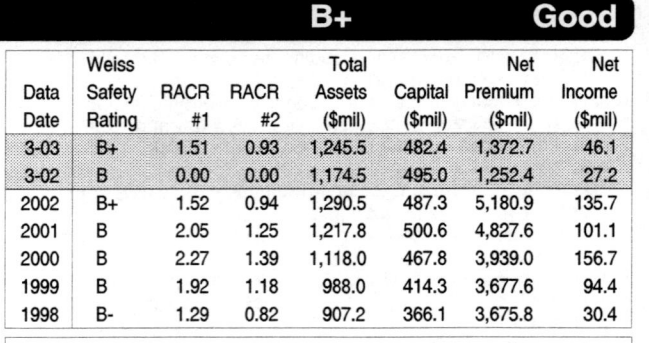

Data Date	Weiss Safety Rating	RACR #1	RACR #2	Total Assets ($mil)	Capital ($mil)	Net Premium ($mil)	Net Income ($mil)
3-03	B+	1.51	0.93	1,245.5	482.4	1,372.7	46.1
3-02	B	0.00	0.00	1,174.5	495.0	1,252.4	27.2
2002	B+	1.52	0.94	1,290.5	487.3	5,180.9	135.7
2001	B	2.05	1.25	1,217.8	500.6	4,827.6	101.1
2000	B	2.27	1.39	1,118.0	467.8	3,939.0	156.7
1999	B	1.92	1.18	988.0	414.3	3,677.6	94.4
1998	B-	1.29	0.82	907.2	366.1	3,675.8	30.4

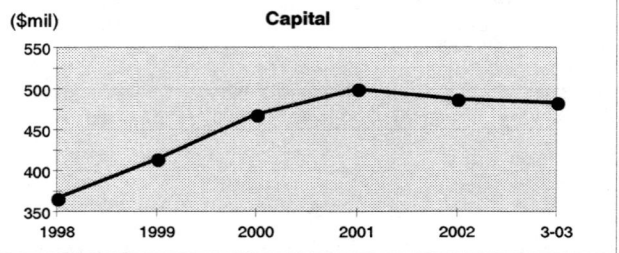

Capital ($mil) chart 1998–3-03

HEALTH NET HEALTH PLAN OF OREGON INC   C+   Fair

Major Rating Factors: Fair profitability index (3.6 on a scale of 0 to 10) with operating losses during 1999, 2000 and 2001. Return on equity has been low, averaging 1%. Good overall results on stability tests (5.2). Rating is significantly influenced by the fair financial results of Health Net Inc. Good liquidity (6.8) with sufficient resources (cash flows and marketable investments) to handle a spike in claims.
Other Rating Factors: Strong capitalization (8.3) based on excellent current risk-adjusted capital (severe loss scenario) reflecting improvement over results in 2000. High quality investment portfolio (9.9) containing no exposure to mortgages, junk bonds, or unaffiliated stocks.
Principal Business: Comp med (100%)
Mem Phys: 02: 5,369   **01:** 4,989   **02 MLR** 77%   / **02 Admin Exp** 17%
Enroll(000): Q1 03: 88   **02:** 81   **01:** 75   **Med Exp PMPM:** $140
Principal Investments: Cash and equiv (12%), other (88%)
Provider Compensation ($000): FFS ($107,914), capitation ($25,113)
Total Member Encounters: Phys (322,975), non-phys (82,638)
Group Affiliation: Health Net Inc
Licensed in: OR, WA
Address: 12901 SE 97th Avenue, Clackamsa, OR 97015-0286
Phone: (503) 802-7000   **Dom State:** OR   **Commenced Bus:** September 1989

Data Date	Weiss Safety Rating	RACR #1	RACR #2	Total Assets ($mil)	Capital ($mil)	Net Premium ($mil)	Net Income ($mil)
3-03	C+	2.38	1.98	55.6	26.9	50.6	2.1
3-02	C	1.58	1.28	46.1	19.1	40.1	1.4
2002	C+	2.18	1.82	47.9	24.7	171.2	8.5
2001	C	1.60	1.30	42.8	17.6	150.0	-0.6
2000	C	1.23	1.03	40.6	15.9	141.9	-5.3
1999	C	1.44	1.20	46.9	19.2	151.7	-0.6
1998	C	2.12	1.76	57.2	17.7	201.3	0.3

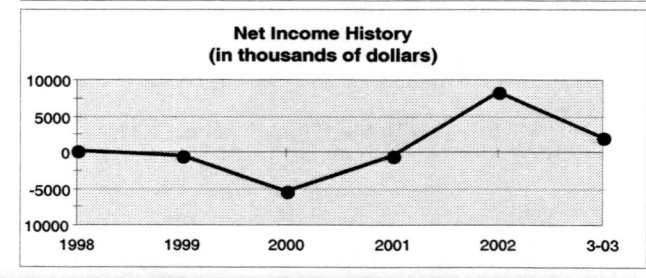

Net Income History (in thousands of dollars) chart 1998–3-03

HEALTH NET INS OF NEW YORK INC   B   Good

Major Rating Factors: Excellent profitability (10.0 on a scale of 0 to 10). Strong capitalization (9.3) based on excellent current risk-adjusted capital (severe loss scenario). High quality investment portfolio (9.9) containing no exposure to mortgages, junk bonds, or unaffiliated stocks.
Other Rating Factors: Excellent liquidity (7.4) with ample operational cash flow and liquid investments.
Principal Business: Comp med (98%), FEHB (2%)
Mem Phys: 02: N/A   **01:** N/A   **02 MLR** 77%   / **02 Admin Exp** 12%
Enroll(000): Q1 03: 60   **02:** 56   **01:** 55   **Med Exp PMPM:** $207
Principal Investments: Cash and equiv (92%), other (8%)
Provider Compensation ($000): Contr fee ($133,361), capitation ($6,922)
Total Member Encounters: Phys (530,379), non-phys (425,706)
Group Affiliation: Health Net Inc
Licensed in: NY
Address: 399 Knollwood Rd, White Plains, NY 10603-1900
Phone: (203) 402-4200   **Dom State:** NY   **Commenced Bus:** April 1991

Data Date	Weiss Safety Rating	RACR #1	RACR #2	Total Assets ($mil)	Capital ($mil)	Net Premium ($mil)	Net Income ($mil)
3-03	B	3.22	2.68	76.8	45.7	50.0	2.4
3-02	B	0.00	0.00	59.6	33.9	43.1	3.2
2002	B	2.97	2.47	67.2	42.5	178.2	12.9
2001	B	0.00	0.00	54.7	30.9	144.0	4.6
2000	N/A	N/A	N/A	45.9	27.0	115.3	N/A
1999	N/A	N/A	N/A	21.3	12.6	19.4	N/A
1998	N/A	N/A	N/A	4.3	4.1	0.3	N/A

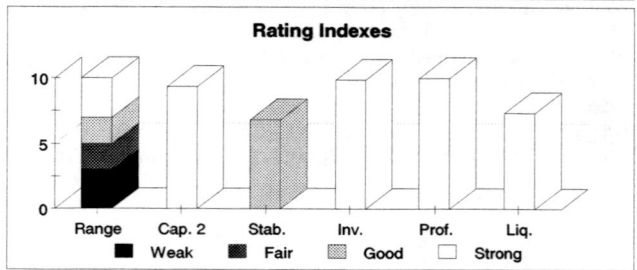

Rating Indexes chart: Range, Cap. 2, Stab., Inv., Prof., Liq. — Weak, Fair, Good, Strong

Winter 2003 - 04

II. Analysis of Largest Companies

HEALTH NET LIFE INSURANCE COMPANY   B-   Good

Major Rating Factors: Good current capitalization (6.4 on a scale of 0 to 10) based on excellent risk adjusted capital (severe loss scenario) reflecting significant improvement over results in 1999. Good overall profitability (5.1). Excellent expense controls. Good liquidity (6.8) with sufficient resources to handle a spike in claims.
Other Rating Factors: Fair overall results on stability tests (3.5) including fair financial strength of affiliated Health Net Inc and fair risk adjusted capital in prior years. High quality investment portfolio (9.4).
Principal Business: Group health insurance (74%), individual health insurance (22%), reinsurance (3%), and group life insurance (1%).
Principal Investments: NonCMO investment grade bonds (73%), CMOs and structured securities (20%), and cash (7%).
Investments in Affiliates: None
Group Affiliation: Health Net Inc
Licensed in: AL, AZ, AR, CA, CO, DC, DE, FL, GA, ID, IL, IN, IA, KS, LA, MS, MO, MT, NE, NV, NM, NC, ND, OK, OR, PA, SC, SD, TN, TX, UT, WA, WV, WY
Commenced Business: January 1987
Address: 225 N Main St, Pueblo, CO 81003
Phone: (719) 585-8017   **Domicile State:** CA   **NAIC Code:** 66141

Data Date	Weiss Safety Rating	RACR #1	RACR #2	Total Assets ($mil)	Capital ($mil)	Net Premium ($mil)	Net Income ($mil)
6-03	B-	2.14	1.77	284.1	146.7	290.7	7.4
6-02	C	1.85	1.51	169.7	85.4	206.6	0.2
2002	C	1.90	1.57	216.2	112.0	437.1	4.2
2001	C	1.93	1.58	146.5	72.1	275.3	1.7
2000	C	1.84	1.48	57.1	26.7	77.6	0.7
1999	C	0.82	0.67	58.7	18.3	113.0	-4.1
1998	C	N/A	N/A	22.4	8.2	49.2	-4.2

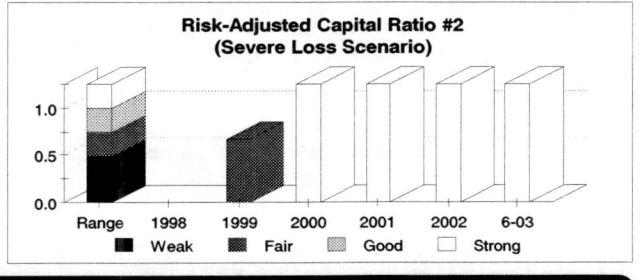

Risk-Adjusted Capital Ratio #2 (Severe Loss Scenario)

HEALTH NET OF ARIZONA INC   C-   Fair

Major Rating Factors: Fair overall results on stability tests (4.4 on a scale of 0 to 10) based on excessive capital growth during 2002, a significant 33% decrease in enrollment during the period. Weak profitability index (1.7) with $71.3 million in losses in the last four years. Average return on equity has been poor at -32%. Good liquidity (6.9) with sufficient resources (cash flows and marketable investments) to handle a spike in claims.
Other Rating Factors: Strong capitalization (8.2) based on excellent current risk-adjusted capital (severe loss scenario) reflecting significant improvement over results in 1999. High quality investment portfolio (9.4) containing no exposure to mortgages, junk bonds, or unaffiliated stocks.
Principal Business: Medicare (58%), comp med (31%), FEHB (10%)
Mem Phys: 02: 4,973   01: 3,697   **02 MLR** 86%   **/ 02 Admin Exp** 13%
Enroll(000): Q1 03: 105   02: 117   01: 173   **Med Exp PMPM:** $229
Principal Investments: Cash and equiv (58%), real estate (5%), other (36%)
Provider Compensation ($000): Contr fee ($337,812), capitation ($52,801), FFS ($33,206)
Total Member Encounters: Phys (1,474,285), non-phys (280,103)
Group Affiliation: Health Net Inc
Licensed in: AZ
Address: 2800 N 44th St Ste 900, Phoenix, AZ 85008-1553
Phone: (602) 224-5528   **Dom State:** AZ   **Commenced Bus:** November 1981

Data Date	Weiss Safety Rating	RACR #1	RACR #2	Total Assets ($mil)	Capital ($mil)	Net Premium ($mil)	Net Income ($mil)
3-03	C-	2.33	1.94	154.2	69.4	105.4	2.3
3-02	C-	1.13	0.92	131.0	57.9	125.5	0.0
2002	C-	2.23	1.86	156.4	66.8	462.6	-4.2
2001	C-	1.14	0.93	176.5	52.4	699.3	-25.1
2000	C-	1.11	0.92	233.6	63.9	783.8	-24.9
1999	C-	0.53	0.44	166.3	22.0	696.2	-17.2
1998	C+	0.69	0.58	130.4	23.1	634.9	6.1

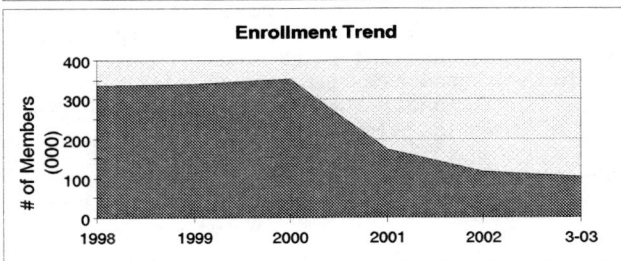

Enrollment Trend

HEALTH NET OF CONNECTICUT INC   B   Good

Major Rating Factors: Good liquidity (6.6 on a scale of 0 to 10) with sufficient resources (cash flows and marketable investments) to handle a spike in claims. Excellent profitability (9.0). Strong capitalization (7.3) based on excellent current risk-adjusted capital (severe loss scenario) reflecting significant improvement over results in 1998.
Other Rating Factors: High quality investment portfolio (9.9) containing no exposure to mortgages, junk bonds, or unaffiliated stocks. Excellent overall results on stability tests (7.9). Fair financial strength from affiliates.
Principal Business: Comp med (64%), Medicare (18%), Medicaid (16%)
Mem Phys: 02: 10,245   01: 9,509   **02 MLR** 93%   **/ 02 Admin Exp** 10%
Enroll(000): Q1 03: 476   02: 438   01: 457   **Med Exp PMPM:** $214
Principal Investments: Cash and equiv (17%), real estate (4%), other (79%)
Provider Compensation ($000): Contr fee ($730,436), capitation ($434,647)
Total Member Encounters: Phys (4,259,003), non-phys (4,920,890)
Group Affiliation: Health Net Inc
Licensed in: CT
Address: One Far Mill Crossing, Shelton, CT 06484-0944
Phone: (203) 402-4200   **Dom State:** CT   **Commenced Bus:** September 1977

Data Date	Weiss Safety Rating	RACR #1	RACR #2	Total Assets ($mil)	Capital ($mil)	Net Premium ($mil)	Net Income ($mil)
3-03	B	1.55	1.30	265.2	112.0	311.3	10.4
3-02	B-	1.19	0.97	244.6	89.0	307.7	1.4
2002	B	1.39	1.15	283.4	100.5	1,234.6	22.2
2001	B-	1.20	0.98	266.5	87.2	1,187.0	16.5
2000	C	1.03	0.88	271.2	71.7	1,048.0	15.3
1999	C-	0.81	0.68	250.9	58.2	996.1	27.0
1998	D+	0.45	0.37	N/A	N/A	N/A	1.3

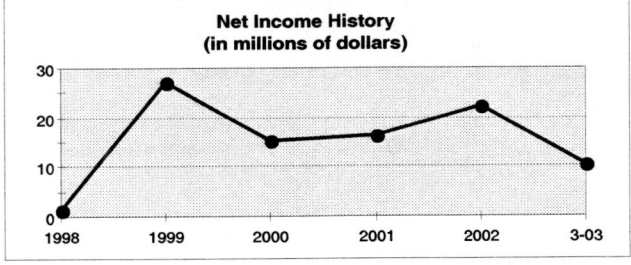

Net Income History (in millions of dollars)

www.WeissRatings.com   * Denotes a Weiss Recommended Company

II. Analysis of Largest Companies

Winter 2003 - 04

HEALTH NET OF NEW JERSEY INC — C   Fair

Major Rating Factors: Weak liquidity (2.1 on a scale of 0 to 10) as a spike in claims may stretch capacity. Good overall profitability index (6.7) despite modest operating losses during 1999. Good capitalization (6.8) based on excellent current risk-adjusted capital (severe loss scenario). Moreover, capital levels have been consistent over the last several years.
Other Rating Factors: High quality investment portfolio (9.9) containing little or no exposure to mortgages, junk bonds, or unaffiliated stocks. Excellent overall results on stability tests (7.7) despite good risk-adjusted capital in prior years but consistent premium and capital growth in the last five years.
Principal Business: Comp med (83%), Medicaid (17%)
Mem Phys: 02: 14,828   **01:** 15,569   **02 MLR** 115%   **/ 02 Admin Exp** 10%
Enroll(000): 02: 348   **01:** 316   **Med Exp PMPM:** $178
Principal Investments: Cash and equiv (43%), pref stock (1%), other (56%)
Provider Compensation ($000): Contr fee ($529,708), capitation ($32,272)
Total Member Encounters: Phys (2,500,886), non-phys (2,464,483)
Group Affiliation: Health Net Inc
Licensed in: NJ
Address: 3501 State Highway 66, Neptune, NJ 07754
Phone: (203) 381-6400   **Dom State:** NJ   **Commenced Bus:** May 1993

Data Date	Weiss Safety Rating	RACR #1	RACR #2	Total Assets ($mil)	Capital ($mil)	Net Premium ($mil)	Net Income ($mil)
2002	C	1.21	1.00	177.3	60.4	617.9	3.1
2001	C-	2.04	1.69	151.9	58.5	462.7	12.1
2000	C-	1.69	1.43	129.5	43.8	366.7	12.1
1999	C-	1.63	1.40	173.9	42.9	356.0	-0.1
1998	D+	1.42	1.21	157.9	39.7	385.0	7.3

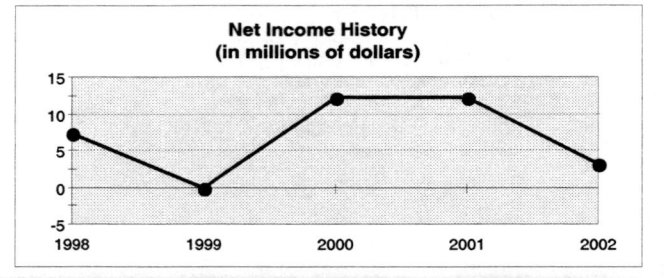

HEALTH NET OF NEW YORK INC — C-   Fair

Major Rating Factors: Weak profitability index (0.9 on a scale of 0 to 10) with operating losses during 1998, 2000 and 2001. Average return on equity has been poor at -34%. Good overall results on stability tests (5.4) despite weak risk-adjusted capital in prior years, inconsistent enrollment growth in the past five years due to declines in 2000, 2001 and 2002. Potentially strong support from affiliation with Health Net Inc. Good liquidity (6.5) with sufficient resources (cash flows and marketable investments) to handle a spike in claims.
Other Rating Factors: Strong capitalization (7.5) based on excellent current risk-adjusted capital (severe loss scenario) reflecting significant improvement over results in 1999. High quality investment portfolio (9.9) containing little or no exposure to mortgages, junk bonds, or unaffiliated stocks.
Principal Business: Comp med (87%), Medicare (13%)
Mem Phys: 02: 21,915   **01:** 21,544   **02 MLR** 105%   **/ 02 Admin Exp** 15%
Enroll(000): Q1 03: 201   **02:** 199   **01:** 213   **Med Exp PMPM:** $177
Principal Investments: Cash and equiv (62%), pref stock (1%), other (36%)
Provider Compensation ($000): Contr fee ($311,928), capitation ($26,441)
Total Member Encounters: Phys (1,843,081), non-phys (1,854,335)
Group Affiliation: Health Net Inc
Licensed in: NY
Address: 399 Knollwood Rd, White Plains, NY 10603
Phone: (203) 402-4200   **Dom State:** NY   **Commenced Bus:** September 1987

Data Date	Weiss Safety Rating	RACR #1	RACR #2	Total Assets ($mil)	Capital ($mil)	Net Premium ($mil)	Net Income ($mil)
3-03	C-	1.77	1.48	169.1	42.9	109.8	1.9
3-02	C-	1.23	0.98	126.9	34.2	103.1	5.9
2002	C-	1.59	1.32	174.9	38.3	416.2	22.6
2001	C-	1.24	0.99	122.0	29.5	356.9	-20.6
2000	C-	0.67	0.56	125.2	13.9	309.2	-10.7
1999	C-	0.63	0.52	186.4	17.5	358.5	0.8
1998	D+	0.92	0.78	135.1	16.5	294.0	-12.0

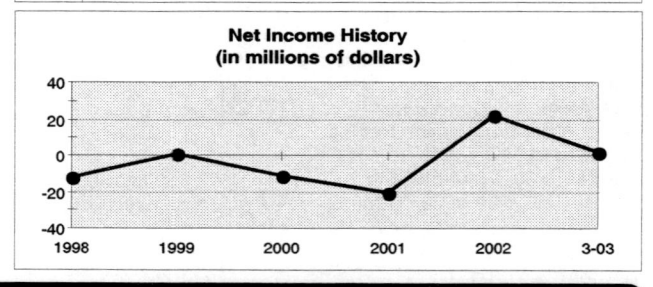

HEALTH NEW ENGLAND INC — D+   Weak

Major Rating Factors: Weak profitability index (1.7 on a scale of 0 to 10) due to a decline in earnings during 2002. Average return on equity has been poor at -40%. Poor capitalization index (2.4) based on weak current risk-adjusted capital (moderate loss scenario). Good overall results on stability tests (5.5).
Other Rating Factors: Good liquidity (5.8) with sufficient resources (cash flows and marketable investments) to handle a spike in claims. High quality investment portfolio (9.9) containing little or no exposure to mortgages, junk bonds, or unaffiliated stocks.
Principal Business: Comp med (99%), FEHB (1%)
Mem Phys: 02: 1,801   **01:** 1,917   **02 MLR** 87%   **/ 02 Admin Exp** 12%
Enroll(000): Q1 03: 71   **02:** 74   **01:** 77   **Med Exp PMPM:** $176
Principal Investments: Cash and equiv (28%), other (72%)
Provider Compensation ($000): Bonus arrang ($93,317), FFS ($32,486), contr fee ($29,453), capitation ($4,801)
Total Member Encounters: Phys (355,558), non-phys (175,182)
Group Affiliation: Baystate Health Systems Inc
Licensed in: MA
Address: 1 Monarch Pl, STe 1500, Springfield, MA 01144-1006
Phone: (413) 787-4000   **Dom State:** MA   **Commenced Bus:** January 1986

Data Date	Weiss Safety Rating	RACR #1	RACR #2	Total Assets ($mil)	Capital ($mil)	Net Premium ($mil)	Net Income ($mil)
3-03	D+	0.54	0.45	41.8	10.6	47.7	0.1
3-02	D+	0.52	0.44	40.1	8.6	44.3	0.3
2002	D+	0.53	0.44	42.4	10.4	184.7	0.8
2001	D+	0.52	0.44	42.2	7.9	168.4	1.9
2000	E+	0.33	0.28	43.7	5.7	163.2	1.6
1999	E	0.12	0.10	25.7	2.8	127.9	-2.9
1998	D	0.12	0.10	34.2	3.6	119.9	-6.2

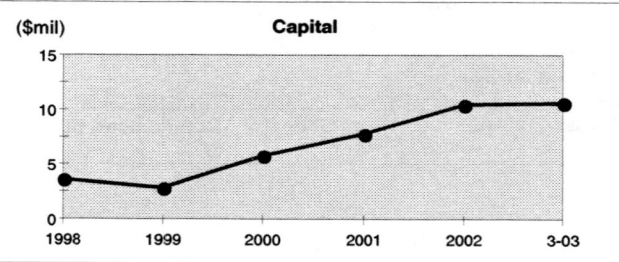

HEALTH OPTIONS INC *   B+   Good

Major Rating Factors: Good liquidity (6.1 on a scale of 0 to 10) with sufficient resources (cash flows and marketable investments) to handle a spike in claims. Strong overall capitalization (9.7) based on excellent current risk-adjusted capital (severe loss scenario) despite some fluctuation in capital levels. High quality investment portfolio (9.5).
Other Rating Factors: Excellent overall results on stability tests (7.6) based on consistent premium and capital growth in the last five years. Fair profitability index (5.0) despite operating losses during 1998. Return on equity has been fair, averaging 8% over the last five years.
Principal Business: Comp med (74%), Medicare (26%)
Mem Phys: 02: 15,792   **01:** 15,977   **02 MLR** 77%   / **02 Admin Exp** 17%
Enroll(000):   **02:** 748   **01:** 845   **Med Exp PMPM:** $181
Principal Investments: Nonaffiliate common stock (12%), cash and equiv (9%), other (78%)
Provider Compensation ($000): Contr fee ($1,454,610), capitation ($189,535), FFS ($118,554), bonus arrang ($1,365)
Total Member Encounters: Phys (5,655,286), non-phys (789,821)
Group Affiliation: Blue Cross Blue Shield Of Florida
Licensed in: AL, FL
Address: 4800 Deerwood Campus Pkwy, Jacksonville, FL 32246
Phone: (904) 791-6111   **Dom State:** FL   **Commenced Bus:** October 1984

Data Date	Weiss Safety Rating	RACR #1	RACR #2	Total Assets ($mil)	Capital ($mil)	Net Premium ($mil)	Net Income ($mil)
2002	B+	3.51	2.93	914.9	409.2	2,224.7	100.4
2001	B	2.27	1.75	824.4	323.5	2,259.8	4.2
2000	B	2.37	1.97	756.9	310.3	2,338.9	29.9
1999	B	2.67	2.23	742.8	315.1	1,861.2	23.9
1998	B	2.63	2.20	606.1	270.3	1,562.4	-15.1

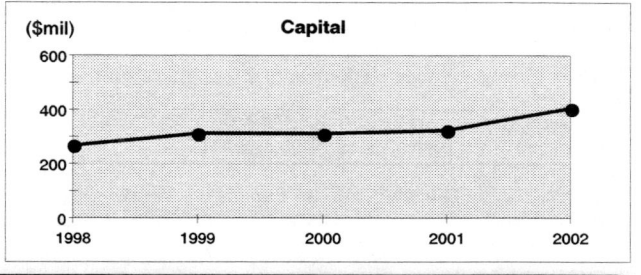

HEALTH PARTNERS OF PHILADELPHIA INC   C+   Fair

Major Rating Factors: Fair capitalization (4.5 on a scale of 0 to 10) based on fair current risk-adjusted capital (moderate loss scenario) reflecting improvement over results in 1998. Good overall profitability index (6.5) with operating gains in each of the last five years. Good liquidity (6.0) with sufficient resources (cash flows and marketable investments) to handle a spike in claims.
Other Rating Factors: High quality investment portfolio (9.9) containing no exposure to mortgages, junk bonds, or unaffiliated stocks. Excellent overall results on stability tests (7.9) based on consistent premium and capital growth in the last five years, steady enrollment growth, averaging 8% over the past five years.
Principal Business: Medicaid (73%), Medicare (27%)
Mem Phys: 02: 1,097   **01:** 1,119   **02 MLR** 89%   / **02 Admin Exp** 10%
Enroll(000): Q1 03: 146   **02:** 148   **01:** 136   **Med Exp PMPM:** $287
Principal Investments: Cash and equiv (34%), other (66%)
Provider Compensation ($000): Contr fee ($437,397), capitation ($47,049)
Total Member Encounters: Phys (1,095,673), non-phys (131,226)
Group Affiliation: None
Licensed in: PA
Address: 833 Chestnut St Suite 900, Philadelphia, PA 19107
Phone: (215) 849-9606   **Dom State:** PA   **Commenced Bus:** October 1988

Data Date	Weiss Safety Rating	RACR #1	RACR #2	Total Assets ($mil)	Capital ($mil)	Net Premium ($mil)	Net Income ($mil)
3-03	C+	0.86	0.71	138.7	40.2	156.7	1.9
3-02	C+	0.85	0.72	127.7	32.7	125.7	1.5
2002	C+	0.81	0.67	137.8	37.9	546.5	6.6
2001	C+	0.85	0.72	141.7	30.1	439.7	3.6
2000	C+	0.99	0.84	133.7	30.6	388.7	10.1
1999	C-	0.81	0.69	114.9	20.3	318.6	8.0
1998	D	0.57	0.49	76.2	12.5	271.3	2.4

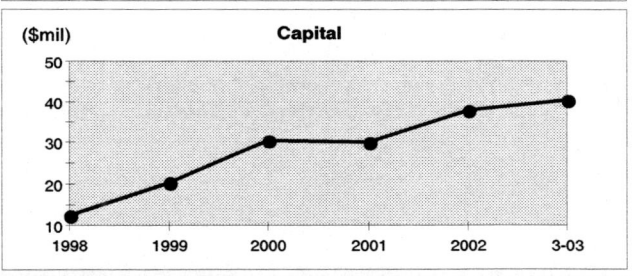

HEALTH PLAN OF MICHIGAN   B-   Good

Major Rating Factors: Good capitalization index (6.9 on a scale of 0 to 10) based on excellent current risk-adjusted capital (severe loss scenario). Good overall results on stability tests (6.9) based on consistent premium and capital growth in the last five years but rapid enrollment growth during the past five years. Excellent profitability (8.4).
Other Rating Factors: High quality investment portfolio (9.9) containing no exposure to mortgages, junk bonds, or unaffiliated stocks. Excellent liquidity (7.1) with ample operational cash flow and liquid investments.
Principal Business: Medicaid (100%)
Mem Phys: 02: 4,861   **01:** 4,532   **02 MLR** 80%   / **02 Admin Exp** 11%
Enroll(000): Q1 03: 51   **02:** 47   **01:** 33   **Med Exp PMPM:** $108
Principal Investments: Cash and equiv (100%)
Provider Compensation ($000): Contr fee ($46,956), capitation ($3,141), bonus arrang ($371)
Total Member Encounters: Phys (482,113), non-phys (339,194)
Group Affiliation: None
Licensed in: MI
Address: 17515 W Nine Mile Rd Ste 650, Southfield, MI 48075
Phone: (248) 557-3700   **Dom State:** MI   **Commenced Bus:** September 1995

Data Date	Weiss Safety Rating	RACR #1	RACR #2	Total Assets ($mil)	Capital ($mil)	Net Premium ($mil)	Net Income ($mil)
3-03	B-	1.26	1.05	19.2	9.0	19.2	0.5
3-02	C	0.77	0.65	14.4	5.6	14.1	0.8
2002	B-	1.18	0.99	18.0	8.5	64.7	3.7
2001	C	0.77	0.65	12.8	4.6	49.9	3.6
2000	E	0.20	0.17	7.6	1.1	34.0	1.4
1999	N/A	N/A	N/A	4.6	0.2	17.3	N/A
1998	N/A	N/A	N/A	0.9	0.1	1.7	N/A

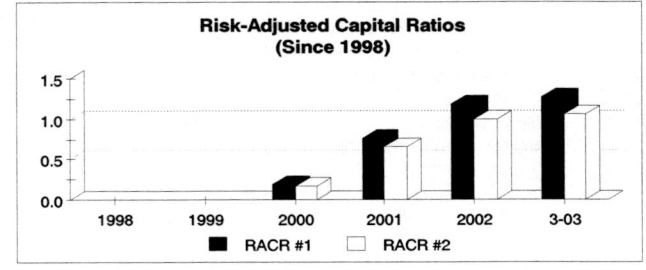

* Denotes a Weiss Recommended Company

II. Analysis of Largest Companies

Winter 2003 - 04

HEALTH PLAN OF NEVADA INC — C — Fair

Major Rating Factors: Good overall profitability index (6.5 on a scale of 0 to 10) with operating gains in each of the last five years. Good capitalization index (6.8) based on excellent current risk-adjusted capital (severe loss scenario). Good overall results on stability tests (6.0) despite excessive capital growth during 2002. Fair financial strength from affiliates.
Other Rating Factors: Good liquidity (6.9) with sufficient resources (cash flows and marketable investments) to handle a spike in claims. High quality investment portfolio (9.9) containing little or no exposure to mortgages, junk bonds, or unaffiliated stocks.
Principal Business: Comp med (47%), Medicare (45%), Medicaid (7%), FEHB (1%)
Mem Phys: 02: 2,514 **01:** 1,960 **02 MLR** 79% **/ 02 Admin Exp** 19%
Enroll(000): Q1 03: 275 **02:** 272 **01:** 259 **Med Exp PMPM:** $192
Principal Investments: Cash and equiv (56%), real estate (4%), pref stock (1%), other (39%)
Provider Compensation ($000): Contr fee ($343,758), capitation ($251,171), FFS ($3,122)
Total Member Encounters: Phys (589,522)
Group Affiliation: Sierra Health Services
Licensed in: AZ, NV
Address: 2720 N Tenaya Way, Las Vegas, NV 89128
Phone: (702) 242-7779 **Dom State:** NV **Commenced Bus:** August 1982

Data Date	Weiss Safety Rating	RACR #1	RACR #2	Total Assets ($mil)	Capital ($mil)	Net Premium ($mil)	Net Income ($mil)
3-03	C	1.19	1.00	145.8	52.5	210.6	2.5
3-02	C	0.00	0.00	113.7	33.4	183.0	1.2
2002	C	1.03	0.86	165.7	45.1	767.9	9.6
2001	C	0.00	0.00	124.0	32.6	620.8	2.3
2000	C-	0.75	0.64	103.3	25.8	520.0	1.0
1999	C-	0.57	0.49	91.9	19.9	486.9	2.1
1998	C+	1.12	0.95	87.6	29.9	416.9	8.1

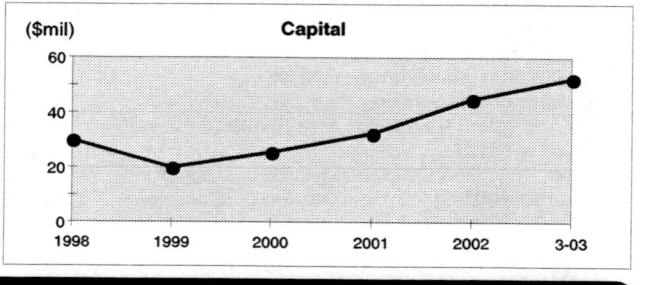

Capital ($mil) chart 1998–3-03

HEALTH PLAN OF SAN JOAQUIN * — B+ — Good

Major Rating Factors: Good overall results on stability tests (6.0 on a scale of 0 to 10). Excellent profitability (9.0) despite a decline in earnings during 2002. Strong overall capitalization (10.0) based on excellent current risk-adjusted capital (severe loss scenario). Moreover, capital has steadily grown over the last five years.
Other Rating Factors: Excellent liquidity (7.4) with ample operational cash flow and liquid investments.
Principal Business: Medicaid (90%), comp med (10%)
Mem Phys: 02: N/A **01:** N/A **02 MLR** 86% **/ 02 Admin Exp** 13%
Enroll(000): Q1 03: 63 **02:** 62 **01:** 56 **Med Exp PMPM:** $84
Principal Investments ($000): Cash and equiv ($45,539)
Provider Compensation ($000): None
Total Member Encounters: N/A
Group Affiliation: None
Licensed in: CA
Address: 1550 W Fremont St, Stockton, CA 95203-2643
Phone: (209) 939-3500 **Dom State:** CA **Commenced Bus:** February 1996

Data Date	Weiss Safety Rating	RACR #1	RACR #2	Total Assets ($mil)	Capital ($mil)	Net Premium ($mil)	Net Income ($mil)
3-03	B+	6.22	3.89	50.2	32.5	19.7	0.5
3-02	B	0.00	0.00	47.2	30.2	16.5	0.9
2002	B+	6.12	3.84	47.2	32.0	68.8	2.6
2001	B	5.56	3.47	42.9	29.3	61.9	4.7
2000	B	5.09	3.18	39.0	24.6	58.4	7.2
1999	D+	4.45	2.78	35.4	17.4	53.3	6.7
1998	D	2.80	1.76	26.7	10.7	48.7	7.5

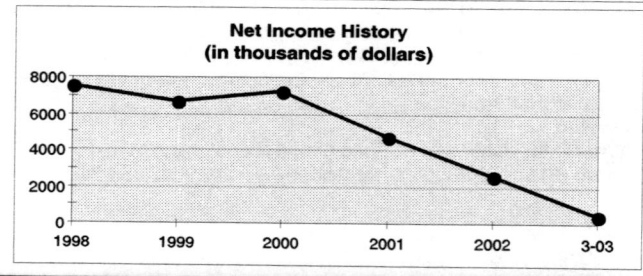

Net Income History (in thousands of dollars) chart 1998–3-03

HEALTH PLAN OF THE UPPER OHIO VALLEY — B- — Good

Major Rating Factors: Fair profitability index (3.9 on a scale of 0 to 10) with operating losses during 1998. Good capitalization (6.9) based on excellent current risk-adjusted capital (severe loss scenario) reflecting improvement over results in 2001. Good liquidity (6.8) with sufficient resources (cash flows and marketable investments) to handle a spike in claims.
Other Rating Factors: High quality investment portfolio (7.9). Excellent overall results on stability tests (7.3) despite good risk-adjusted capital in prior years, a decline in enrollment during 2002 but consistent premium and capital growth in the last five years.
Principal Business: Comp med (56%), Medicaid (20%), Medicare (19%), FEHB (4%)
Mem Phys: 02: 1,908 **01:** 1,567 **02 MLR** 93% **/ 02 Admin Exp** 5%
Enroll(000): Q1 03: 93 **02:** 95 **01:** 103 **Med Exp PMPM:** $173
Principal Investments: Cash and equiv (38%), nonaffiliate common stock (32%), affiliate common stock (4%), real estate (3%), other (23%)
Provider Compensation ($000): Contr fee ($142,784), capitation ($45,955), bonus arrang ($11,174), FFS ($5,875)
Total Member Encounters: Phys (750,358), non-phys (59,923)
Group Affiliation: Health Plan Group
Licensed in: OH, WV
Address: 52160 National Rd E, St Clairsville, OH 43950
Phone: (740) 695-3585 **Dom State:** WV **Commenced Bus:** November 1979

Data Date	Weiss Safety Rating	RACR #1	RACR #2	Total Assets ($mil)	Capital ($mil)	Net Premium ($mil)	Net Income ($mil)
3-03	B-	1.28	1.07	66.0	30.7	55.6	1.9
3-02	B-	1.15	0.87	61.0	29.5	55.2	-0.1
2002	B-	1.20	1.00	67.9	29.4	220.3	1.4
2001	B-	1.15	0.87	62.6	28.2	208.7	1.0
2000	B-	1.29	1.06	64.1	29.6	189.2	5.0
1999	B-	1.41	1.17	57.5	26.9	157.0	0.6
1998	B-	1.60	1.35	51.3	26.2	145.3	-4.3

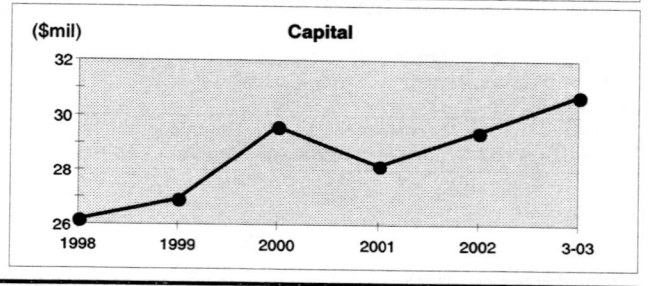

Capital ($mil) chart 1998–3-03

HEALTH PLUS OF LOUISIANA INC — E Very Weak

Major Rating Factors: Weak profitability index (0.9 on a scale of 0 to 10) with operating losses during 1998, 1999, 2001 and 2002. Average return on equity has been poor at -63%. Weak overall results on stability tests (0.5) based on a significant 15% decrease in enrollment during the period. Weak liquidity (2.6) as a spike in claims may stretch capacity.
Other Rating Factors: Fair capitalization index (3.4) based on weak current risk-adjusted capital (moderate loss scenario). High quality investment portfolio (9.9) containing no exposure to mortgages, junk bonds, or unaffiliated stocks.
Principal Business: Comp med (100%)
Mem Phys: 02: 886 **01:** 832 **02 MLR** 99% / **02 Admin Exp** 9%
Enroll(000): Q1 03: 21 **02:** 28 **01:** 33 **Med Exp PMPM:** $171
Principal Investments: Cash and equiv (100%)
Provider Compensation ($000): Contr fee ($48,327), capitation ($11,280)
Total Member Encounters: Phys (391,645), non-phys (55,719)
Group Affiliation: Willis-Knighton Health System
Licensed in: LA
Address: 2219 Line Avenue, Shreveport, LA 71104
Phone: (318) 212-8800 **Dom State:** LA **Commenced Bus:** January 1995

Data Date	Weiss Safety Rating	RACR #1	RACR #2	Total Assets ($mil)	Capital ($mil)	Net Premium ($mil)	Net Income ($mil)
3-03	E	0.70	0.58	20.3	5.5	12.7	-0.9
3-02	D+	0.57	0.49	16.9	4.5	17.7	-1.0
2002	E	0.25	0.21	14.2	1.6	62.0	-4.9
2001	D+	0.58	0.49	13.9	3.9	64.6	-2.1
2000	D+	1.16	0.99	11.9	6.0	43.6	0.3
1999	D+	1.33	1.13	9.8	5.5	29.9	-2.1
1998	D+	1.27	1.09	8.5	4.2	24.7	-2.3

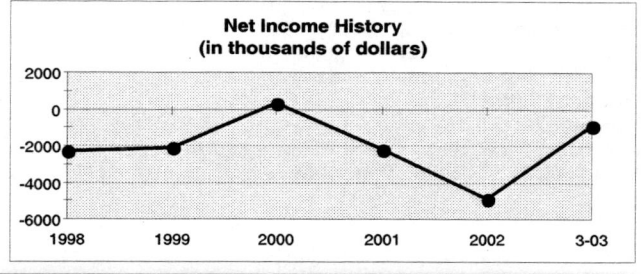

HEALTH RIGHT INC — C+ Fair

Major Rating Factors: Fair capitalization (5.0 on a scale of 0 to 10) based on good current risk-adjusted capital (severe loss scenario) reflecting significant improvement over results in 1998. Excellent profitability (9.4). High quality investment portfolio (9.9) containing no exposure to mortgages, junk bonds, or unaffiliated stocks.
Other Rating Factors: Excellent overall results on stability tests (7.3) based on consistent premium and capital growth in the last five years but rapid enrollment growth during the past five years. Excellent liquidity (7.2) with ample operational cash flow and liquid investments.
Principal Business: Medicaid (100%)
Mem Phys: 02: 834 **01:** 668 **02 MLR** 77% / **02 Admin Exp** 15%
Enroll(000): Q1 03: 11 **02:** 10 **01:** 9 **Med Exp PMPM:** $124
Principal Investments: Cash and equiv (100%)
Provider Compensation ($000): Contr fee ($13,721), capitation ($1,234)
Total Member Encounters: Phys (20,023), non-phys (44,522)
Group Affiliation: Unity Health Care Inc
Licensed in: DC
Address: 1101 14th St NW Ste 900, Washington, DC 20005
Phone: (202) 518-0373 **Dom State:** DC **Commenced Bus:** May 1998

Data Date	Weiss Safety Rating	RACR #1	RACR #2	Total Assets ($mil)	Capital ($mil)	Net Premium ($mil)	Net Income ($mil)
3-03	C+	0.92	0.77	6.1	3.2	5.9	0.4
3-02	C+	0.86	0.74	4.4	2.0	4.3	0.2
2002	C+	0.80	0.67	5.6	2.8	18.9	1.0
2001	C+	0.86	0.74	4.6	2.0	16.6	0.9
2000	C	1.11	0.95	2.5	1.0	7.8	0.4
1999	N/A	N/A	N/A	1.5	0.7	5.3	N/A
1998	U	0.58	0.50	1.0	0.3	1.8	0.1

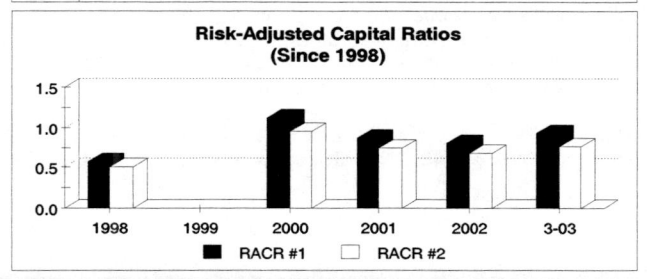

HEALTH TRADITION HEALTH PLAN — B- Good

Major Rating Factors: Good overall profitability index (6.3 on a scale of 0 to 10) despite a decline in earnings during 2002. Good capitalization (7.0) based on excellent current risk-adjusted capital (severe loss scenario) reflecting significant improvement over results in 1998. Good liquidity (7.0) with sufficient resources (cash flows and marketable investments) to handle a spike in claims.
Other Rating Factors: High quality investment portfolio (9.9) containing no exposure to mortgages, junk bonds, or unaffiliated stocks. Excellent overall results on stability tests (8.3) based on consistent premium and capital growth in the last five years.
Principal Business: Comp med (84%), Medicaid (12%), med supp (4%)
Mem Phys: 02: 797 **01:** 329 **02 MLR** 90% / **02 Admin Exp** 11%
Enroll(000): Q1 03: 28 **02:** 28 **01:** 28 **Med Exp PMPM:** $177
Principal Investments: Cash and equiv (60%), other (40%)
Provider Compensation ($000): Capitation ($39,005), FFS ($8,732), other ($12,202)
Total Member Encounters: Phys (47,857), non-phys (18,073)
Group Affiliation: Mayo Foundation
Licensed in: WI
Address: 4001 41st ST., NW, Rochester, WI 55901-8901
Phone: (507) 538-5209 **Dom State:** WI **Commenced Bus:** April 1986

Data Date	Weiss Safety Rating	RACR #1	RACR #2	Total Assets ($mil)	Capital ($mil)	Net Premium ($mil)	Net Income ($mil)
3-03	B-	1.32	1.10	13.7	6.2	18.7	0.0
3-02	C+	1.44	1.25	13.5	5.9	16.3	0.1
2002	B-	1.19	0.99	15.3	6.2	66.9	0.4
2001	C+	1.42	1.23	13.8	5.8	57.9	0.7
2000	C+	1.09	0.94	12.1	5.1	44.5	0.9
1999	C+	1.68	1.45	10.2	4.2	38.1	0.2
1998	D+	0.67	0.56	8.7	4.1	34.8	0.1

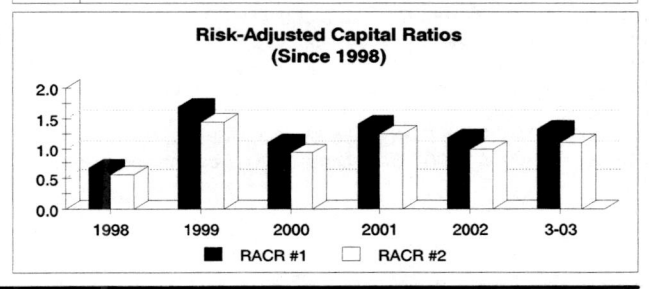

II. Analysis of Largest Companies

Winter 2003 - 04

HEALTHAMERICA PENNSYLVANIA INC — C+ — Fair

Major Rating Factors: Fair overall results on stability tests (3.6 on a scale of 0 to 10) based on good risk-adjusted capital in prior years, an excessive 36% enrollment growth during the period. Good capitalization (6.9) based on excellent current risk-adjusted capital (severe loss scenario). Good liquidity (5.7) with sufficient resources (cash flows and marketable investments) to handle a spike in claims.
Other Rating Factors: Excellent profitability (8.0) despite a decline in earnings during 2002. High quality investment portfolio (9.9) containing no exposure to mortgages, junk bonds, or unaffiliated stocks.
Principal Business: Comp med (50%), Medicare (32%), FEHB (18%)
Mem Phys: 02: 14,980 **01:** 14,222   **02 MLR** 90% / **02 Admin Exp** 8%
Enroll(000): Q1 03: 260 **02:** 268 **01:** 197   **Med Exp PMPM:** $187
Principal Investments: Cash and equiv (13%), other (87%)
Provider Compensation ($000): Contr fee ($434,571), capitation ($18,446), FFS ($11,802), salary ($7,091), other ($17,493)
Total Member Encounters: Phys (1,565,026), non-phys (139,392)
Group Affiliation: Coventry Health Care Inc
Licensed in: OH, PA
Address: Five Gateway Center, Pittsburgh, PA 15222
Phone: (800) 788-6445   **Dom State:** PA   **Commenced Bus:** January 1975

Data Date	Weiss Safety Rating	RACR #1	RACR #2	Total Assets ($mil)	Capital ($mil)	Net Premium ($mil)	Net Income ($mil)
3-03	C+	1.27	1.05	184.8	42.6	168.5	4.1
3-02	C+	1.90	1.54	173.6	59.9	129.2	8.1
2002	C+	1.14	0.95	192.7	38.6	577.3	14.1
2001	C+	1.90	1.54	175.2	49.6	448.5	16.3
2000	C	1.68	1.39	145.5	42.1	429.5	12.2
1999	C	1.23	1.02	136.2	27.6	420.1	6.3
1998	C-	1.30	1.13	112.2	21.6	454.1	17.3

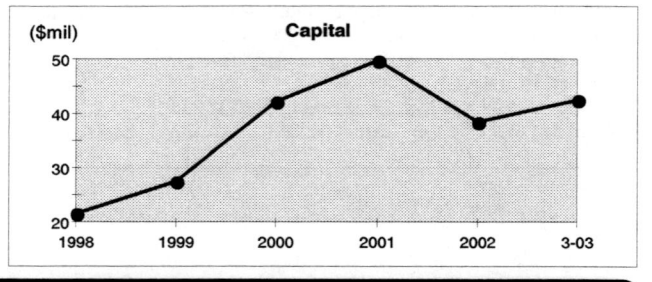

HEALTHASSURANCE PENNSYLVANIA INC — B- — Good

Major Rating Factors: Good capitalization index (6.6 on a scale of 0 to 10) based on good current risk-adjusted capital (severe loss scenario). Good liquidity (5.9) with sufficient resources (cash flows and marketable investments) to handle a spike in claims. Excellent profitability (8.4).
Other Rating Factors: High quality investment portfolio (9.4) containing no exposure to mortgages, junk bonds, or unaffiliated stocks. Excellent overall results on stability tests (7.9) based on healthy premium and capital growth during 2002. Fair financial strength from affiliates.
Principal Business: Comp med (85%), Medicaid (15%)
Mem Phys: 02: 14,295 **01:** 12,198   **02 MLR** 85% / **02 Admin Exp** 13%
Enroll(000): Q1 03: 291 **02:** 289 **01:** 233   **Med Exp PMPM:** $131
Principal Investments: Cash and equiv (24%), other (76%)
Provider Compensation ($000): Contr fee ($307,522), capitation ($61,590), FFS ($11,313), salary ($2,847), other ($6,097)
Total Member Encounters: Phys (771,642), non-phys (92,198)
Group Affiliation: Coventry Health Care Inc
Licensed in: PA
Address: 3721 Tecport Dr. PO Box 67103, Harrisburg, PA 17106-7103
Phone: (800) 788-6445   **Dom State:** PA   **Commenced Bus:** June 2001

Data Date	Weiss Safety Rating	RACR #1	RACR #2	Total Assets ($mil)	Capital ($mil)	Net Premium ($mil)	Net Income ($mil)
3-03	B-	1.16	0.97	134.9	35.7	140.0	4.3
3-02	B-	0.00	0.00	98.6	20.9	106.3	0.4
2002	B-	1.00	0.84	122.1	31.2	478.1	4.9
2001	B-	0.00	0.00	91.8	20.0	220.3	0.7
2000	N/A	N/A	N/A	N/A	N/A	N/A	N/A
1999	N/A	N/A	N/A	N/A	N/A	N/A	N/A
1998	N/A	N/A	N/A	N/A	N/A	N/A	N/A

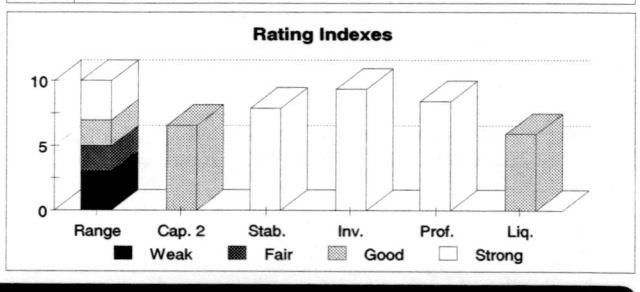

HEALTHCARE INC — C+ — Fair

Major Rating Factors: Fair profitability index (4.5 on a scale of 0 to 10) with operating losses during 2000 and 2001. Return on equity has been low, averaging 1%. Fair overall results on stability tests (3.8) based on rapid premium growth over the last five years, a decline in the number of member physicians during 2002. Strong capitalization index (7.5) based on excellent current risk-adjusted capital (severe loss scenario).
Other Rating Factors: High quality investment portfolio (9.9) containing no exposure to mortgages, junk bonds, or unaffiliated stocks. Excellent liquidity (7.2) with ample operational cash flow and liquid investments.
Principal Business: Comp med (99%)
Mem Phys: 02: 1,717 **01:** 3,501   **02 MLR** 84% / **02 Admin Exp** 14%
Enroll(000): Q1 03: 0 **02:** 23 **01:** 23   **Med Exp PMPM:** $136
Principal Investments: Cash and equiv (100%)
Provider Compensation ($000): Capitation ($41,435)
Total Member Encounters: Phys (17,564), non-phys (11,219)
Group Affiliation: Medical Resource Network LLC
Licensed in: GA
Address: 2000 South Park Place Ste 200, Atlanta, GA 30339
Phone: (770) 956-6930   **Dom State:** GA   **Commenced Bus:** April 1996

Data Date	Weiss Safety Rating	RACR #1	RACR #2	Total Assets ($mil)	Capital ($mil)	Net Premium ($mil)	Net Income ($mil)
3-03	C+	1.75	1.46	11.4	5.8	0.0	0.0
3-02	U	0.46	0.39	10.4	4.0	10.6	-0.1
2002	C+	1.72	1.43	16.1	5.7	44.7	1.1
2001	U	0.45	0.39	15.3	4.1	38.8	-0.6
2000	U	0.71	0.61	10.3	5.0	32.7	-0.4
1999	U	0.00	0.00	5.4	5.2	0.3	0.2
1998	N/A	N/A	N/A	5.3	5.2	0.3	N/A

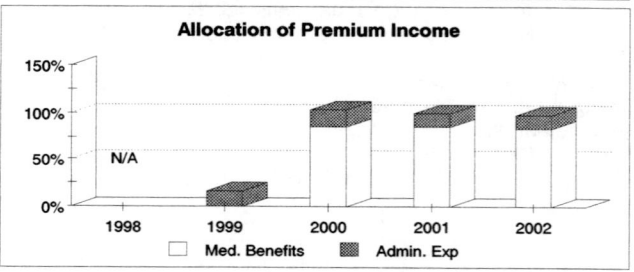

www.WeissRatings.com

HEALTHCARE USA OF MISSOURI LLC — B- Good

Major Rating Factors: Good liquidity (6.9 on a scale of 0 to 10) with sufficient resources (cash flows and marketable investments) to handle a spike in claims. Excellent profitability (9.3) with operating gains in each of the last five years. Strong capitalization (7.8) based on excellent current risk-adjusted capital (severe loss scenario) reflecting improvement over results in 1998.

Other Rating Factors: High quality investment portfolio (9.9) containing no exposure to mortgages, junk bonds, or unaffiliated stocks. Excellent overall results on stability tests (7.7) based on consistent premium and capital growth in the last five years but rapid enrollment growth during the past five years. Rating is significantly influenced by the fair financial results of Coventry Health Care Inc.

Principal Business: Medicaid (100%)
Mem Phys: 02: 5,496 **01:** 4,401 **02 MLR** 85% **/ 02 Admin Exp** 9%
Enroll(000): Q1 03: 185 **02:** 155 **01:** 141 **Med Exp PMPM:** $121
Principal Investments: Cash and equiv (29%), other (71%)
Provider Compensation ($000): Contr fee ($176,096), capitation ($29,509), FFS ($7,467)
Total Member Encounters: Phys (481,966), non-phys (60,516)
Group Affiliation: Coventry Health Care Inc
Licensed in: MO
Address: 10 S Broadway #1200, St Louis, MO 63102-1712
Phone: (314) 241-5300 **Dom State:** MO **Commenced Bus:** July 1995

Data Date	Weiss Safety Rating	RACR #1	RACR #2	Total Assets ($mil)	Capital ($mil)	Net Premium ($mil)	Net Income ($mil)
3-03	B-	2.03	1.69	60.4	32.9	79.4	2.4
3-02	C+	1.71	1.43	53.3	25.9	60.9	2.1
2002	B-	1.84	1.53	52.7	30.1	251.6	11.3
2001	C+	1.71	1.43	50.0	23.6	214.0	7.4
2000	C	1.65	1.40	38.4	17.5	163.2	5.6
1999	C	1.70	1.46	30.8	13.6	128.4	4.6
1998	D+	1.11	0.95	31.0	8.6	111.1	3.8

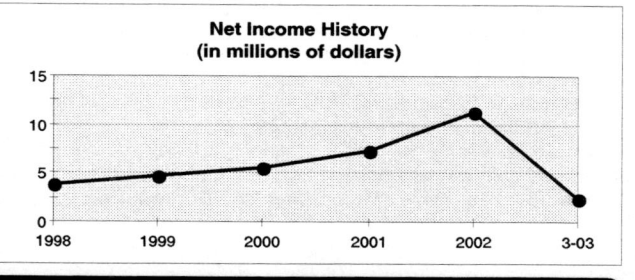

Net Income History (in millions of dollars)

HEALTHEASE OF FLORIDA INC — D- Weak

Major Rating Factors: Poor capitalization index (1.2 on a scale of 0 to 10) based on weak current risk-adjusted capital (moderate loss scenario). Good overall results on stability tests (5.5). Good liquidity (6.9) with sufficient resources (cash flows and marketable investments) to handle a spike in claims.

Other Rating Factors: Excellent profitability (8.2). High quality investment portfolio (9.9) containing no exposure to mortgages, junk bonds, or unaffiliated stocks.

Principal Business: Medicaid (100%)
Mem Phys: 02: 14,000 **01:** 12,329 **02 MLR** 84% **/ 02 Admin Exp** 15%
Enroll(000): Q1 03: 174 **02:** 166 **01:** 128 **Med Exp PMPM:** $115
Principal Investments: Cash and equiv (100%)
Provider Compensation ($000): Contr fee ($160,898), capitation ($43,733)
Total Member Encounters: Phys (64,037), non-phys (58,133)
Group Affiliation: WellCare Holdings LLC
Licensed in: FL
Address: 6800 Dale Mabry Hwy Ste 270, Tampa, FL 33614
Phone: (813) 290-6200 **Dom State:** FL **Commenced Bus:** May 2000

Data Date	Weiss Safety Rating	RACR #1	RACR #2	Total Assets ($mil)	Capital ($mil)	Net Premium ($mil)	Net Income ($mil)
3-03	D-	0.42	0.35	42.7	8.3	70.9	0.4
3-02	E	0.11	0.09	28.9	5.4	54.1	1.1
2002	D-	0.39	0.33	36.5	7.8	242.9	0.6
2001	E	0.11	0.09	28.1	4.5	185.3	5.6
2000	D-	N/A	N/A	29.2	5.3	83.8	5.2
1999	N/A	N/A	N/A	N/A	N/A	N/A	N/A
1998	N/A	N/A	N/A	N/A	N/A	N/A	N/A

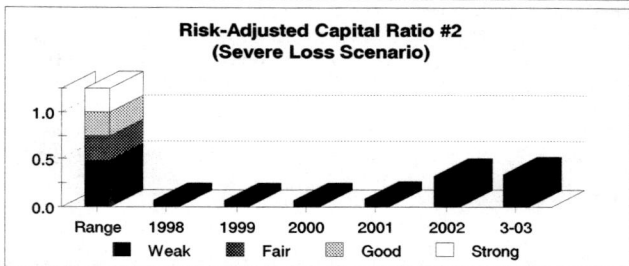

Risk-Adjusted Capital Ratio #2 (Severe Loss Scenario)
■ Weak ▨ Fair ▧ Good □ Strong

HEALTHGUARD OF LANCASTER INC — B Good

Major Rating Factors: Good liquidity (6.3 on a scale of 0 to 10) with sufficient resources (cash flows and marketable investments) to handle a spike in claims. Fair profitability index (4.5) due to a decline in earnings during 2002. Average return on equity has been poor at -5%. Strong capitalization (9.1) based on excellent current risk-adjusted capital (severe loss scenario) reflecting improvement over results in 1998.

Other Rating Factors: High quality investment portfolio (9.8) containing little or no exposure to mortgages, junk bonds, or unaffiliated stocks. Excellent overall results on stability tests (7.7) based on consistent premium and capital growth in the last five years. Rating is significantly influenced by the fair financial results of Highmark Inc.

Principal Business: Comp med (92%), FEHB (8%)
Mem Phys: 02: 984 **01:** 939 **02 MLR** 89% **/ 02 Admin Exp** 10%
Enroll(000): Q1 03: 62 **02:** 58 **01:** 59 **Med Exp PMPM:** $155
Principal Investments: Cash and equiv (26%), affiliate common stock (9%), other (65%)
Provider Compensation ($000): Bonus arrang ($86,430), capitation ($11,730), contr fee ($7,928)
Total Member Encounters: Phys (321,540), non-phys (136,249)
Group Affiliation: Highmark Inc
Licensed in: PA
Address: 280 Granite Run Dr 105, Lancaster, PA 17601-6820
Phone: (717) 560-9049 **Dom State:** PA **Commenced Bus:** July 1984

Data Date	Weiss Safety Rating	RACR #1	RACR #2	Total Assets ($mil)	Capital ($mil)	Net Premium ($mil)	Net Income ($mil)
3-03	B	3.03	2.52	48.5	18.5	37.9	1.4
3-02	B-	2.73	2.29	39.8	15.3	30.0	0.3
2002	B	2.91	2.43	43.7	17.6	122.4	1.9
2001	B-	2.18	1.83	37.0	15.4	112.8	3.6
2000	C+	1.55	1.29	32.9	10.9	118.8	1.8
1999	C+	1.49	1.24	31.4	9.6	104.7	0.7
1998	C+	1.29	1.07	29.4	8.8	81.9	-5.8

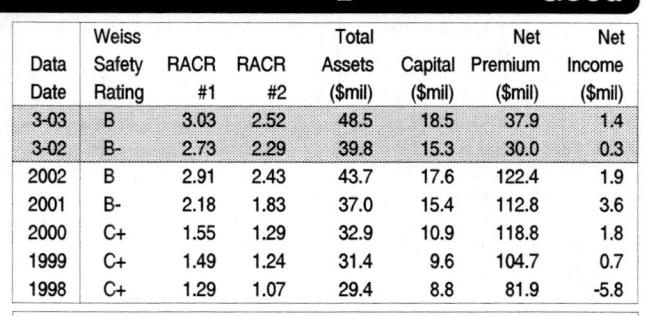

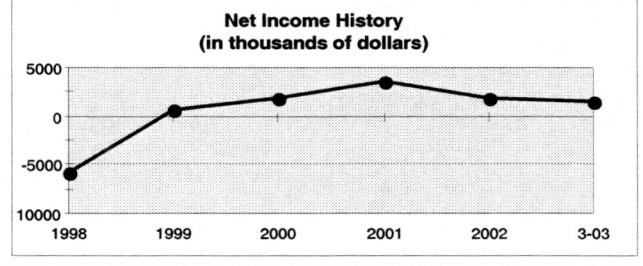

Net Income History (in thousands of dollars)

II. Analysis of Largest Companies

Winter 2003 - 04

HEALTHKEEPERS INC * — B+ — Good

Major Rating Factors: Good liquidity (6.8 on a scale of 0 to 10) with sufficient resources (cash flows and marketable investments) to handle a spike in claims. Excellent profitability (9.3) with operating gains in each of the last five years. Strong capitalization (10.0) based on excellent current risk-adjusted capital (severe loss scenario) reflecting improvement over results in 1999.
Other Rating Factors: High quality investment portfolio (9.9) containing no exposure to mortgages, junk bonds, or unaffiliated stocks. Excellent overall results on stability tests (8.4) based on consistent premium and capital growth in the last five years. Rating is significantly influenced by the good financial results of Anthem Ins Companies Inc.
Principal Business: Comp med (80%), Medicaid (15%), FEHB (6%).
Mem Phys: 02: 12,045 **01:** 10,355 **02 MLR** 80% **/ 02 Admin Exp** 13%
Enroll(000): Q1 03: 228 **02:** 238 **01:** 232 **Med Exp PMPM:** $135
Principal Investments: Cash and equiv (13%), other (87%).
Provider Compensation ($000): Contr fee ($187,814), FFS ($107,704), bonus arrang ($49,455), capitation ($30,825).
Total Member Encounters: Phys (1,089,634), non-phys (82,771).
Group Affiliation: Anthem Ins Companies Inc
Licensed in: VA
Address: 2220 Edward Holland Dr, Richmond, VA 23230
Phone: (804) 354-3479 **Dom State:** VA **Commenced Bus:** September 1986

Data Date	Weiss Safety Rating	RACR #1	RACR #2	Total Assets ($mil)	Capital ($mil)	Net Premium ($mil)	Net Income ($mil)
3-03	B+	3.83	3.19	178.7	93.0	121.6	6.2
3-02	B+	3.33	2.55	162.2	70.2	113.8	2.7
2002	B+	3.62	3.02	168.2	87.6	474.7	29.6
2001	B+	2.80	2.14	145.3	67.8	388.9	18.3
2000	B+	2.36	1.95	121.5	49.2	352.4	18.2
1999	B	1.20	0.99	90.1	27.0	315.3	4.7
1998	B	1.39	1.15	76.7	24.0	269.2	3.0

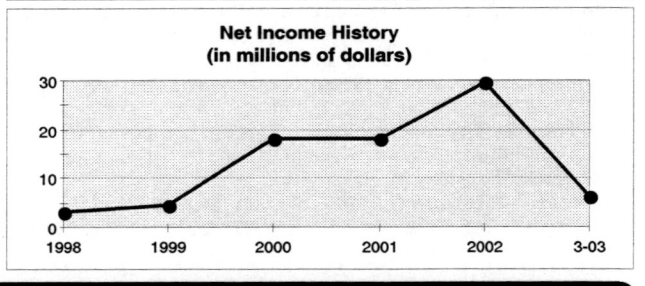

Net Income History (in millions of dollars)

HEALTHLINK HMO INC * — B+ — Good

Major Rating Factors: Good overall results on stability tests (5.2 on a scale of 0 to 10). Rating is significantly influenced by the good financial results of WellPoint Health Networks Inc. Excellent profitability (10.0) with operating gains in each of the last five years. Strong overall capitalization (10.0) based on excellent current risk-adjusted capital (severe loss scenario). Moreover, capital has steadily grown over the last five years.
Other Rating Factors: High quality investment portfolio (9.9) containing no exposure to mortgages, junk bonds, or unaffiliated stocks. Excellent liquidity (9.3) with ample operational cash flow and liquid investments.
Principal Business: Comp med (36%), other (64%).
Mem Phys: 02: 12,714 **01:** 11,369 **02 MLR** 15% **/ 02 Admin Exp** 23%
Enroll(000): Q1 03: 26 **02:** 14 **01:** 12 **Med Exp PMPM:** $13
Principal Investments: Cash and equiv (73%), other (27%).
Provider Compensation ($000): Capitation ($1,920), bonus arrang ($84).
Total Member Encounters: Phys (71,685), non-phys (3,583).
Group Affiliation: WellPoint Health Networks Inc
Licensed in: IL, MO
Address: 12443 Olive Blvd, St Louis, MO 63141
Phone: (314) 989-6028 **Dom State:** MO **Commenced Bus:** January 1993

Data Date	Weiss Safety Rating	RACR #1	RACR #2	Total Assets ($mil)	Capital ($mil)	Net Premium ($mil)	Net Income ($mil)
3-03	B+	18.82	15.69	26.3	24.7	5.3	2.1
3-02	B+	18.50	17.47	21.4	17.7	3.8	1.5
2002	B+	17.82	14.85	24.5	24.2	13.7	5.7
2001	B+	18.87	17.80	19.9	14.8	17.1	4.4
2000	B-	8.45	7.69	22.2	11.2	21.0	5.4
1999	B-	5.82	5.35	18.0	7.0	18.1	4.1
1998	B-	4.50	4.06	13.2	4.6	11.3	1.7

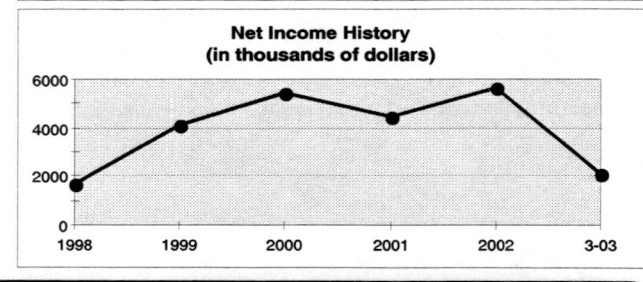

Net Income History (in thousands of dollars)

HEALTHNOW NY INC — B — Good

Major Rating Factors: Good capitalization (6.2 on a scale of 0 to 10) based on good current risk-adjusted capital (severe loss scenario) reflecting significant improvement over results in 1998. Good liquidity (6.9) with sufficient resources (cash flows and marketable investments) to handle a spike in claims. Excellent profitability (7.3) with operating gains in each of the last five years.
Other Rating Factors: High quality investment portfolio (9.9).
Principal Business: Comp med (78%), Medicare (10%), med supp (5%), Medicaid (3%), dental (1%), other (2%).
Mem Phys: 02: 6,525 **01:** 6,455 **02 MLR** 86% **/ 02 Admin Exp** 12%
Enroll(000): Q1 03: 648 **02:** 650 **01:** 623 **Med Exp PMPM:** $171
Principal Investments: Cash and equiv (38%), nonaffiliate common stock (19%), pref stock (1%), other (42%).
Provider Compensation ($000): Contr fee ($1,219,599), capitation ($42,574).
Total Member Encounters: Phys (3,990,811), non-phys (1,886,498).
Group Affiliation: None
Licensed in: NY
Address: 1901 Main St, Buffalo, NY 14208
Phone: (716) 887-6900 **Dom State:** NY **Commenced Bus:** March 1940

Data Date	Weiss Safety Rating	RACR #1	RACR #2	Total Assets ($mil)	Capital ($mil)	Net Premium ($mil)	Net Income ($mil)
3-03	B	1.10	0.92	463.3	137.2	429.8	8.7
3-02	B-	1.10	0.89	365.7	118.4	366.0	5.9
2002	B	1.03	0.86	432.8	128.9	1,520.1	35.5
2001	B-	1.10	0.89	327.0	115.6	1,289.7	15.3
2000	C	0.90	0.80	309.0	100.3	1,125.2	3.4
1999	C-	0.73	0.52	324.5	97.1	1,069.5	31.5
1998	D+	0.75	0.49	267.8	86.5	905.0	5.5

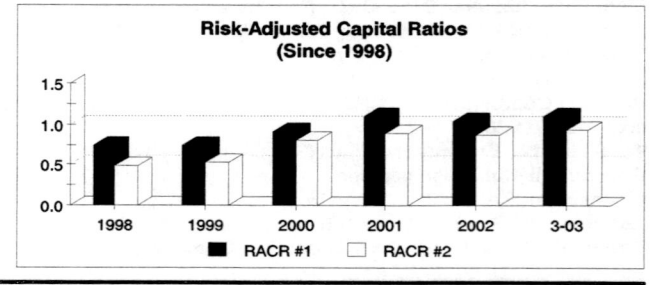

Risk-Adjusted Capital Ratios (Since 1998)

HEALTHPARTNERS *   B+   Good

Major Rating Factors: Good overall profitability index (6.6 on a scale of 0 to 10) despite a decline in earnings during 2002. Strong overall capitalization (7.5) based on excellent current risk-adjusted capital (severe loss scenario) despite some fluctuation in capital levels. High quality investment portfolio (8.7) containing little or no exposure to mortgages, junk bonds, or unaffiliated stocks.
Other Rating Factors: Excellent overall results on stability tests (7.8) based on consistent premium and capital growth in the last five years. Good financial strength from affiliates. Excellent liquidity (7.0) with ample operational cash flow and liquid investments.
Principal Business: Comp med (69%), Medicaid (14%), Medicare (10%), dental (4%), FEHB (1%).
Mem Phys: 02: 9,479   **01:** 8,202   **02 MLR** 89%   **/ 02 Admin Exp** 9%
Enroll(000): Q1 03: 355   **02:** 401   **01:** 397   **Med Exp PMPM:** $209
Principal Investments: Cash and equiv (47%), affiliate common stock (19%), other (34%).
Provider Compensation ($000): Bonus arrang ($452,224), capitation ($423,733), contr fee ($127,999)
Total Member Encounters: N/A
Group Affiliation: HealthPartners Inc
Licensed in: MN
Address: 8100 34th Ave S, Minneapolis, MN 55440-1309
Phone: (952) 883-6584   **Dom State:** MN   **Commenced Bus:** March 1984

Data Date	Weiss Safety Rating	RACR #1	RACR #2	Total Assets ($mil)	Capital ($mil)	Net Premium ($mil)	Net Income ($mil)
3-03	B+	1.76	1.47	237.4	136.6	272.4	1.5
3-02	B	1.86	1.58	174.5	120.2	270.5	0.7
2002	B+	1.74	1.45	232.5	135.3	1,120.1	15.1
2001	B	1.82	1.55	201.6	119.0	986.6	19.5
2000	B-	1.94	1.75	138.6	98.4	884.5	4.7
1999	C+	1.96	1.78	162.9	97.2	809.9	6.1
1998	C	1.92	1.74	139.2	87.6	731.2	-0.9

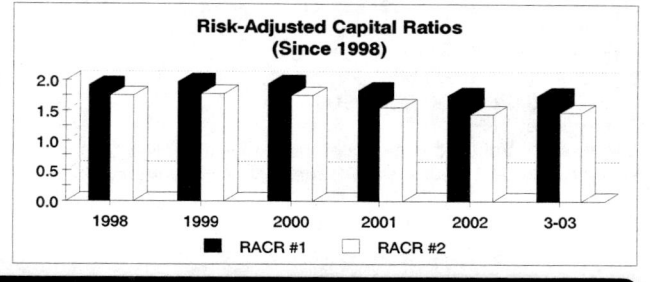

Risk-Adjusted Capital Ratios (Since 1998)

HEALTHPLAN OF TEXAS INC   C+   Fair

Major Rating Factors: Fair overall results on stability tests (4.1 on a scale of 0 to 10) based on an overall decline in enrollment over the past five years despite growth in 1999 and 2000. Excellent profitability (7.7) despite a decline in earnings during 2002. Strong capitalization index (7.2) based on excellent current risk-adjusted capital (severe loss scenario).
Other Rating Factors: High quality investment portfolio (9.8) containing no exposure to mortgages, junk bonds, or unaffiliated stocks. Excellent liquidity (7.1) with ample operational cash flow and liquid investments.
Principal Business: Comp med (100%)
Mem Phys: 02: 488   **01:** 503   **02 MLR** 82%   **/ 02 Admin Exp** 23%
Enroll(000): Q1 03: 2   **02:** 8   **01:** 8   **Med Exp PMPM:** $138
Principal Investments: Cash and equiv (87%), other (13%)
Provider Compensation ($000): Capitation ($5,423), FFS ($3,590), bonus arrang ($1,299), contr fee ($929)
Total Member Encounters: Phys (68,905), non-phys (56,584)
Group Affiliation: Trinity Mother Frances Group
Licensed in: TX
Address: 110 N College St Ste 900, Tyler, TX 75702
Phone: (903) 531-4447   **Dom State:** TX   **Commenced Bus:** September 1996

Data Date	Weiss Safety Rating	RACR #1	RACR #2	Total Assets ($mil)	Capital ($mil)	Net Premium ($mil)	Net Income ($mil)
3-03	C+	1.55	1.29	8.4	3.4	1.4	-0.1
3-02	D+	1.38	1.21	7.7	2.9	4.5	0.5
2002	C+	1.81	1.51	9.0	3.6	15.6	0.7
2001	D-	1.40	1.23	7.3	3.3	19.3	2.5
2000	D-	1.05	0.92	6.3	2.9	22.2	1.4
1999	E+	1.35	1.17	4.8	3.1	18.4	0.4
1998	E+	0.07	0.06	3.3	0.6	14.7	-2.1

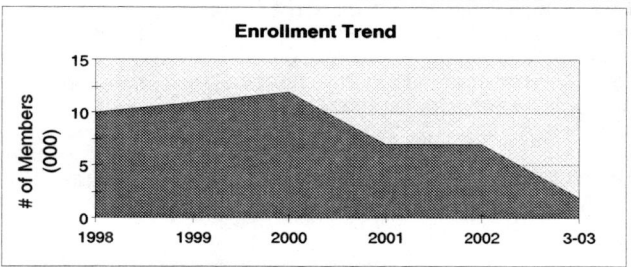

Enrollment Trend

HEALTHPLUS OF MICHIGAN   C+   Fair

Major Rating Factors: Fair profitability index (4.4 on a scale of 0 to 10) with modest operating losses during 1998. Fair capitalization (3.6) based on weak current risk-adjusted capital (moderate loss scenario). Good overall results on stability tests (6.6) based on consistent premium and capital growth in the last five years.
Other Rating Factors: Good liquidity (6.6) with sufficient resources (cash flows and marketable investments) to handle a spike in claims. High quality investment portfolio (8.6).
Principal Business: Comp med (58%), Medicaid (27%), Medicare (6%), FEHB (1%), other (7%).
Mem Phys: 02: 1,692   **01:** 1,585   **02 MLR** 92%   **/ 02 Admin Exp** 7%
Enroll(000): Q1 03: 107   **02:** 164   **01:** 159   **Med Exp PMPM:** $191
Principal Investments: Cash and equiv (72%), nonaffiliate common stock (15%), real estate (8%), other (5%).
Provider Compensation ($000): Capitation ($205,236), contr fee ($161,257)
Total Member Encounters: Phys (530,932), non-phys (628,671)
Group Affiliation: HealthPlus of Michigan
Licensed in: MI
Address: 2050 S Linden Rd, Flint, MI 48532
Phone: (810) 332-9161   **Dom State:** MI   **Commenced Bus:** October 1979

Data Date	Weiss Safety Rating	RACR #1	RACR #2	Total Assets ($mil)	Capital ($mil)	Net Premium ($mil)	Net Income ($mil)
3-03	C+	0.71	0.60	79.0	26.6	81.6	2.1
3-02	B-	0.85	0.70	74.5	27.3	98.0	1.6
2002	C+	0.66	0.55	82.4	24.9	401.9	0.8
2001	B-	0.85	0.70	77.1	25.0	344.1	0.4
2000	C+	1.03	0.88	80.3	27.7	306.9	1.0
1999	C+	1.07	0.92	84.8	27.0	288.5	3.3
1998	C	0.78	0.66	69.6	23.4	237.6	0.0

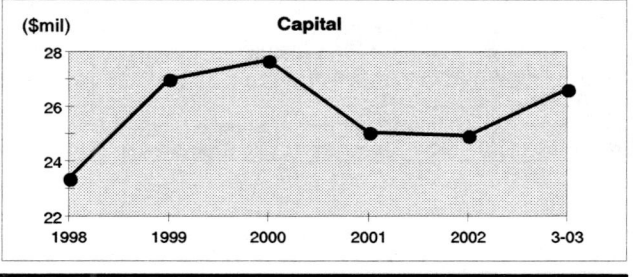

Capital

* Denotes a Weiss Recommended Company

II. Analysis of Largest Companies

Winter 2003 - 04

HEALTHSPRING INC

D-   **Weak**

Major Rating Factors: Weak profitability index (0.9 on a scale of 0 to 10) due to a decline in earnings during 2002. Average return on equity has been poor at -57%. Poor capitalization index (1.0) based on weak current risk-adjusted capital (moderate loss scenario). Weak overall results on stability tests (2.3) based on excessive premium growth during 2002, an excessive 59% enrollment growth during the period.
Other Rating Factors: Good liquidity (6.9) with sufficient resources (cash flows and marketable investments) to handle a spike in claims. High quality investment portfolio (9.9) containing no exposure to mortgages, junk bonds, or unaffiliated stocks.
Principal Business: Medicare (67%), comp med (31%), FEHB (2%)
Mem Phys: 02: 3,630   **01:** 2,331   **02 MLR** 83%   / **02 Admin Exp** 15%
Enroll(000): Q1 03: 69   **02:** 63   **01:** 40   **Med Exp PMPM:** $275
Principal Investments: Cash and equiv (96%), other (4%)
Provider Compensation ($000): Contr fee ($125,920), capitation ($29,577)
Total Member Encounters: Phys (202,631)
Group Affiliation: NewQuest LLC
Licensed in: TN, TX
Address: 44 Vantage Way Suite 300, Nashville, TN 37228
Phone: (615) 291-7000   **Dom State:** TN   **Commenced Bus:** July 1995

Data Date	Weiss Safety Rating	RACR #1	RACR #2	Total Assets ($mil)	Capital ($mil)	Net Premium ($mil)	Net Income ($mil)
3-03	D-	0.40	0.33	41.7	8.2	80.7	1.1
3-02	D+	0.69	0.59	26.3	8.5	45.5	1.5
2002	D-	0.33	0.28	51.1	7.0	204.0	0.6
2001	D+	0.69	0.59	32.6	10.8	137.5	8.7
2000	E+	0.41	0.35	22.7	3.8	92.3	-3.8
1999	E	0.21	0.18	9.8	2.0	76.8	-3.5
1998	E	0.29	0.25	11.0	3.1	59.2	-2.5

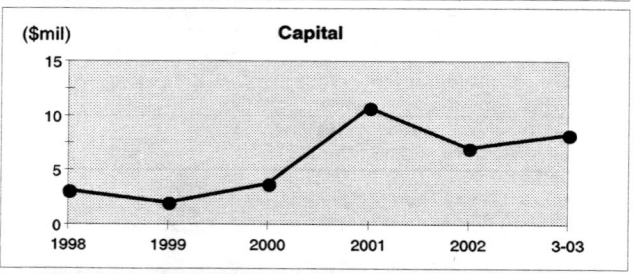

Capital chart 1998–3-03

HEALTHSPRING OF ALABAMA INC

E+   **Very Weak**

Major Rating Factors: Weak profitability index (0.9 on a scale of 0 to 10) with $45.2 million in losses in the last five years. Average return on equity over the last five years has been extremely poor. Poor capitalization index (2.2) based on weak current risk-adjusted capital (moderate loss scenario). Weak liquidity (1.2) as a spike in claims may stretch capacity.
Other Rating Factors: Fair overall results on stability tests (3.5) based on a significant 48% decrease in enrollment during the period, a steep decline in premium revenue in 2002. High quality investment portfolio (9.9) containing no exposure to mortgages, junk bonds, or unaffiliated stocks.
Principal Business: Comp med (59%), Medicare (28%), FEHB (11%), med supp (1%)
Mem Phys: 02: 4,545   **01:** 4,373   **02 MLR** 86%   / **02 Admin Exp** 21%
Enroll(000): Q1 03: 25   **02:** 26   **01:** 51   **Med Exp PMPM:** $166
Principal Investments: Cash and equiv (96%), other (4%)
Provider Compensation ($000): Contr fee ($86,778), capitation ($2,137)
Total Member Encounters: Phys (297,855), non-phys (159,454)
Group Affiliation: NewQuest LLC
Licensed in: AL
Address: Two Perimeter Park S., Ste200W, Birmingham, AL 35243
Phone: (205) 968-1000   **Dom State:** AL   **Commenced Bus:** May 1986

Data Date	Weiss Safety Rating	RACR #1	RACR #2	Total Assets ($mil)	Capital ($mil)	Net Premium ($mil)	Net Income ($mil)
3-03	E+	0.51	0.43	12.3	3.2	20.5	0.5
3-02	E	0.12	0.10	21.8	1.2	26.2	-0.5
2002	E	0.43	0.36	11.7	2.5	88.5	-1.5
2001	E	0.12	0.10	28.4	-0.6	211.9	-1.9
2000	E+	0.17	0.15	44.7	4.3	232.2	-19.2
1999	E+	0.19	0.17	43.5	4.0	229.7	-8.4
1998	E+	0.08	0.07	37.5	6.2	238.8	-14.2

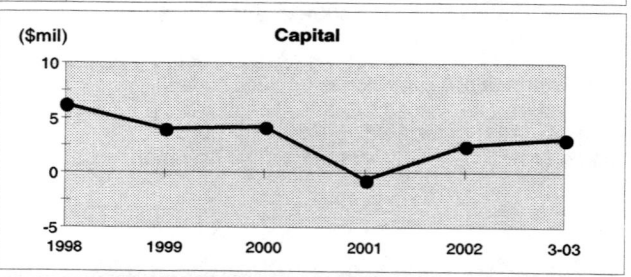

Capital chart 1998–3-03

HEALTHWISE

B   **Good**

Major Rating Factors: Fair overall results on stability tests (5.0 on a scale of 0 to 10) based on a significant 41% decrease in enrollment during the period. Rating is significantly influenced by the good financial results of Regence Group. Excellent profitability (8.7) despite a decline in earnings during 2002. Strong overall capitalization (10.0) based on excellent current risk-adjusted capital (severe loss scenario) despite some fluctuation in capital levels.
Other Rating Factors: High quality investment portfolio (9.0). Excellent liquidity (7.2) with ample operational cash flow and liquid investments.
Principal Business: Comp med (90%), med supp (5%), dental (5%)
Mem Phys: 02: 7,600   **01:** 7,500   **02 MLR** 71%   / **02 Admin Exp** 17%
Enroll(000): Q1 03: 12   **02:** 17   **01:** 29   **Med Exp PMPM:** $74
Principal Investments: Nonaffiliate common stock (15%), cash and equiv (14%), other (71%)
Provider Compensation ($000): Contr fee ($17,135), other ($4,271)
Total Member Encounters: Phys (203,353), non-phys (36,008)
Group Affiliation: Regence Group
Licensed in: UT
Address: 2890 E Cottonwood Pkwy, Salt Lake City, UT 84121
Phone: (801) 333-2000   **Dom State:** UT   **Commenced Bus:** September 1982

Data Date	Weiss Safety Rating	RACR #1	RACR #2	Total Assets ($mil)	Capital ($mil)	Net Premium ($mil)	Net Income ($mil)
3-03	B	12.96	10.80	39.5	32.0	4.9	1.1
3-02	B	7.29	5.07	39.2	31.0	7.4	0.9
2002	B	12.74	10.62	39.3	31.5	29.0	2.7
2001	B	7.30	5.08	37.6	30.0	32.3	4.2
2000	B	4.32	3.47	31.1	24.5	31.2	2.9
1999	B	2.86	2.28	21.4	15.0	31.4	2.6
1998	B	11.74	8.52	24.1	19.4	35.0	0.7

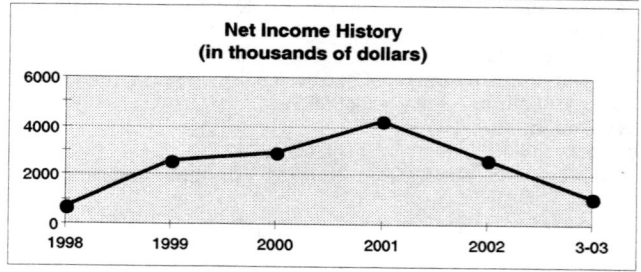

Net Income History (in thousands of dollars), 1998–3-03

Winter 2003 - 04   II. Analysis of Largest Companies

HEALTHY ALLIANCE LIFE INSURANCE COMPANY — B Good

Major Rating Factors: Good liquidity (5.4 on a scale of 0 to 10) with sufficient resources to handle a spike in claims. Good overall results on stability tests (5.2). Strengths include good financial support from affiliation with WellPoint Health Networks Inc, excellent operational trends, good risk adjusted capital for prior years and excellent risk diversification. Fair overall capitalization (4.8) based on mixed results -- excessive policy leverage mitigated by excellent risk adjusted capital (severe loss scenario).
Other Rating Factors: High quality investment portfolio (7.7). Excellent profitability (8.7) with operating gains in each of the last five years.
Principal Business: Group health insurance (78%) and individual health insurance (22%).
Principal Investments: NonCMO investment grade bonds (82%), CMOs and structured securities (15%), and , and , and misc. investments (2%).
Investments in Affiliates: None
Group Affiliation: WellPoint Health Networks Inc
Licensed in: AL, AZ, AR, CA, CO, DC, DE, HI, ID, IL, IN, IA, KS, LA, MD, MS, MO, MT, NE, NV, NM, NC, ND, OH, OK, OR, PA, SC, SD, TN, TX, UT, VA, WA, WV, WI
Commenced Business: June 1971
Address: 1831 Chestnut St, St Louis, MO 63103-2275
Phone: (877) 864-2273 **Domicile State:** MO **NAIC Code:** 78972

Data Date	Weiss Safety Rating	RACR #1	RACR #2	Total Assets ($mil)	Capital ($mil)	Net Premium ($mil)	Net Income ($mil)
6-03	B	1.43	1.15	578.8	171.5	550.7	27.7
6-02	C+	1.14	0.90	377.8	130.1	477.6	10.3
2002	B-	1.13	0.91	516.2	137.6	989.7	33.2
2001	C	1.09	0.87	302.1	113.7	825.2	26.7
2000	C	1.36	1.07	280.0	103.7	592.5	16.9
1999	C	1.29	1.01	245.0	83.8	505.9	0.1
1998	C	1.32	1.03	221.7	80.3	488.6	5.6

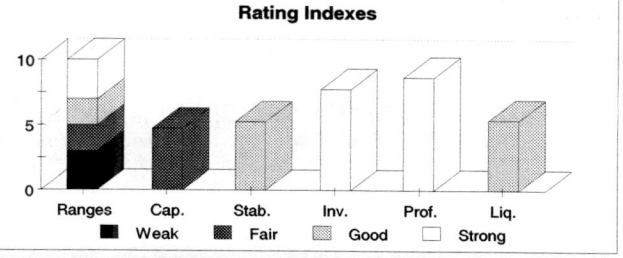

HEALTHY PALM BEACHES INC * — A- Excellent

Major Rating Factors: Strong overall capitalization (7.5 on a scale of 0 to 10) based on excellent current risk-adjusted capital (severe loss scenario) despite some fluctuation in capital levels. High quality investment portfolio (9.9) containing no exposure to mortgages, junk bonds, or unaffiliated stocks. Excellent liquidity (7.1) with ample operational cash flow and liquid investments.
Other Rating Factors: Good overall profitability index (6.2) despite a decline in earnings during 2002. Fair overall results on stability tests (4.7) based on rapid premium growth over the last five years, rapid enrollment growth during the past five years.
Principal Business: Medicaid (71%), other (29%)
Mem Phys: 02: 380 01: 406 **02 MLR** 78% / **02 Admin Exp** 21%
Enroll(000): Q1 03: 12 02: 10 01: 7 **Med Exp PMPM:** $78
Principal Investments: Cash and equiv (100%)
Provider Compensation ($000): Contr fee ($5,049), capitation ($2,190)
Total Member Encounters: Phys (55,093), non-phys (46,155)
Group Affiliation: None
Licensed in: FL
Address: 324 Datura St Suite 401, West Palm Beach, FL 33401
Phone: (561) 659-1270 **Dom State:** FL **Commenced Bus:** January 1998

Data Date	Weiss Safety Rating	RACR #1	RACR #2	Total Assets ($mil)	Capital ($mil)	Net Premium ($mil)	Net Income ($mil)
3-03	A-	1.76	1.47	3.7	2.0	2.7	-0.1
3-02	A-	1.62	1.41	2.8	2.0	1.9	0.0
2002	A-	1.88	1.57	3.9	2.2	10.4	0.1
2001	A-	1.63	1.41	2.4	1.8	7.7	0.5
2000	C-	2.49	2.18	2.8	1.5	4.0	0.1
1999	U	3.30	2.92	2.1	1.4	2.8	0.0
1998	N/A	N/A	N/A	1.7	1.4	2.3	0.1

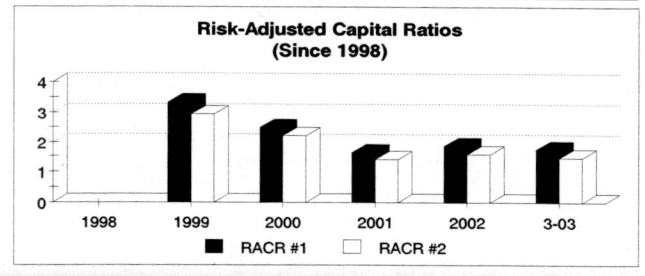

HEART OF AMERICA HMO — D Weak

Major Rating Factors: Weak profitability index (1.8 on a scale of 0 to 10) with operating losses during 1998 and 1999. Poor capitalization index (1.6) based on weak current risk-adjusted capital (moderate loss scenario). Good overall results on stability tests (6.0).
Other Rating Factors: Good liquidity (7.0) with sufficient resources (cash flows and marketable investments) to handle a spike in claims. High quality investment portfolio (9.2).
Principal Business: Comp med (61%), Medicare (36%), FEHB (3%)
Mem Phys: 02: 36 01: 36 **02 MLR** 90% / **02 Admin Exp** 8%
Enroll(000): Q1 03: 2 02: 2 01: 2 **Med Exp PMPM:** $162
Principal Investments: Cash and equiv (83%), nonaffiliate common stock (17%)
Provider Compensation ($000): FFS ($2,618), capitation ($1,785)
Total Member Encounters: Phys (9,486), non-phys (2,163)
Group Affiliation: None
Licensed in: ND
Address: 810 S Main Ave, Rugby, ND 58368
Phone: (701) 776-5848 **Dom State:** ND **Commenced Bus:** August 1982

Data Date	Weiss Safety Rating	RACR #1	RACR #2	Total Assets ($mil)	Capital ($mil)	Net Premium ($mil)	Net Income ($mil)
3-03	D	0.45	0.38	1.2	0.6	1.2	0.0
3-02	E	0.26	0.21	1.0	0.5	1.2	0.0
2002	D	0.49	0.41	1.1	0.6	4.9	0.1
2001	E	0.26	0.21	1.0	0.5	4.7	0.1
2000	U	0.28	0.23	1.0	0.4	4.7	0.1
1999	E	0.12	0.10	1.4	0.3	4.6	-0.4
1998	U	0.21	0.18	0.9	0.3	4.7	-0.1

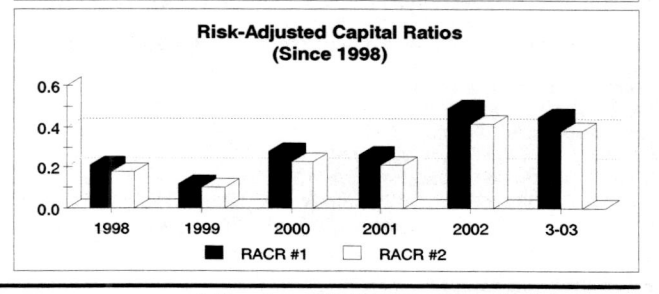

www.WeissRatings.com   * Denotes a Weiss Recommended Company

II. Analysis of Largest Companies

HEARTLAND HEALTH PLAN OF OKLAHOMA | E- Very Weak

Major Rating Factors: Weak profitability index (0.7 on a scale of 0 to 10) with $21.9 million in losses in the last five years. Poor capitalization index (0.0) based on weak current risk-adjusted capital (severe loss scenario). Weak overall results on stability tests (0.0) based on rapid premium growth over the last five years, a steep decline in capital during 2002 and a decline in the number of member physicians during 2002.
Other Rating Factors: Weak liquidity (0.1) as a spike in claims may stretch capacity. High quality investment portfolio (9.9) containing no exposure to mortgages, junk bonds, or unaffiliated stocks.
Principal Business: Medicaid (100%)
Mem Phys: 02: 1,286 **01:** 1,562 **02 MLR** 92% **/ 02 Admin Exp** 13%
Enroll(000): Q1 03: 91 **02:** 109 **01:** 100 **Med Exp PMPM:** $167
Principal Investments: Cash and equiv (100%)
Provider Compensation ($000): FFS ($174,031), capitation ($30,502)
Total Member Encounters: Phys (581,306), non-phys (203,357)
Group Affiliation: None
Licensed in: OK
Address: 100 N Broadway Ste 1400, Oklahoma City, OK 73102-8601
Phone: (405) 239-2234 **Dom State:** OK **Commenced Bus:** January 1995

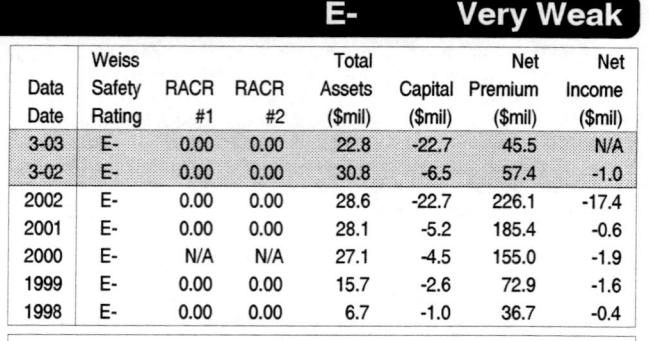

Data Date	Weiss Safety Rating	RACR #1	RACR #2	Total Assets ($mil)	Capital ($mil)	Net Premium ($mil)	Net Income ($mil)
3-03	E-	0.00	0.00	22.8	-22.7	45.5	N/A
3-02	E-	0.00	0.00	30.8	-6.5	57.4	-1.0
2002	E-	0.00	0.00	28.6	-22.7	226.1	-17.4
2001	E-	0.00	0.00	28.1	-5.2	185.4	-0.6
2000	E-	N/A	N/A	27.1	-4.5	155.0	-1.9
1999	E-	0.00	0.00	15.7	-2.6	72.9	-1.6
1998	E-	0.00	0.00	6.7	-1.0	36.7	-0.4

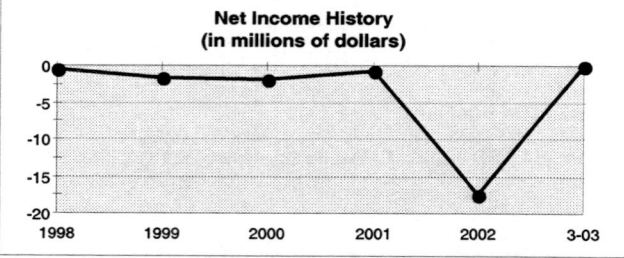

Net Income History (in millions of dollars)

HERITAGE PROVIDER NETWORK INC | D Weak

Major Rating Factors: Fair capitalization index (3.2 on a scale of 0 to 10) based on weak current risk-adjusted capital (moderate loss scenario). Good overall results on stability tests (5.9) despite fair risk diversification due to the company's size. Good liquidity (6.9) with sufficient resources (cash flows and marketable investments) to handle a spike in claims.
Other Rating Factors: Excellent profitability (7.4).
Principal Business: Managed care (100%)
Mem Phys: 02: N/A **01:** N/A **02 MLR** 99% **/ 02 Admin Exp** 1%
Enroll(000): Q1 03: 241 **02:** 195 **01:** 172 **Med Exp PMPM:** $171
Principal Investments ($000): Cash and equiv ($54,479), other ($35,066)
Provider Compensation ($000): None
Total Member Encounters: N/A
Group Affiliation: Heritage California Medical Groups
Licensed in: CA
Address: 18107 Sherman Way Ste 100, Reseda, CA 91335
Phone: (818) 654-3455 **Dom State:** CA **Commenced Bus:** May 1996

Data Date	Weiss Safety Rating	RACR #1	RACR #2	Total Assets ($mil)	Capital ($mil)	Net Premium ($mil)	Net Income ($mil)
3-03	D	0.55	0.33	119.2	18.4	125.2	0.6
3-02	E+	N/A	N/A	65.5	16.7	96.0	1.4
2002	D	0.00	0.00	65.4	14.4	380.5	0.3
2001	E+	0.52	0.32	53.4	11.1	287.0	0.1
2000	N/A	N/A	N/A	N/A	N/A	N/A	N/A
1999	N/A	N/A	N/A	N/A	N/A	N/A	N/A
1998	N/A	N/A	N/A	N/A	N/A	N/A	N/A

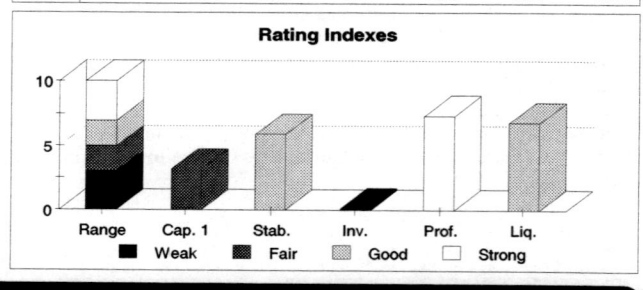

Rating Indexes (Range, Cap. 1, Stab., Inv., Prof., Liq.) — Weak, Fair, Good, Strong

HIGHMARK CASUALTY INS CO | C Fair

Major Rating Factors: Fair overall results on stability tests (3.4 on a scale of 0 to 10) including weak risk adjusted capital in prior years and weak results on operational trends. The largest net exposure for one risk is high at 3.2% of capital. Strengths include potentially strong support from affiliation with Highmark Inc. Fair profitability index (3.2). Fair expense controls. Return on equity has been fair, averaging 5.6% over the past five years.
Other Rating Factors: Poor long-term capitalization index (1.2) based on weak current risk adjusted capital (severe and moderate loss scenarios), although results have slipped from the good range over the last two years. Good liquidity (5.2) with sufficient resources (cash flows and marketable investments) to handle a spike in claims. Ample reserve history (7.0) that can protect against increases in claims costs.
Principal Business: Group accident & health (59%) and workers compensation (41%).
Principal Investments: Investment grade bonds (88%) and misc. investments (12%).
Investments in Affiliates: None
Group Affiliation: Highmark Inc
Licensed in: AL, FL, GA, ID, IL, IN, KS, KY, MD, MI, MS, MO, NV, NJ, NM, NC, OR, PA, SC, TX, UT, VA, WA, WV
Commenced Business: February 1978
Address: Fifth Avenue Pl 120 Fifth Ave, Pittsburgh, PA 15222-3099
Phone: (800) 328-5433 **Domicile State:** PA **NAIC Code:** 35599

Data Date	Weiss Safety Rating	RACR #1	RACR #2	Loss Ratio %	Total Assets ($mil)	Capital ($mil)	Net Premium ($mil)	Net Income ($mil)
6-03	C	0.42	0.28	N/A	80.2	30.3	36.5	2.6
6-02	B-	0.94	0.61	N/A	73.2	31.4	39.5	1.5
2002	C	0.40	0.26	71.7	74.8	28.3	50.7	0.3
2001	B-	1.31	0.85	69.8	67.3	33.0	32.7	0.1
2000	C+	7.72	3.85	60.5	55.5	39.7	18.1	3.5
1999	C+	4.81	2.64	56.3	52.5	36.4	16.8	2.2
1998	C+	4.56	2.63	56.8	50.7	34.6	18.0	2.1

Highmark Inc
Composite Group Rating: C+

Largest Group Members	Assets ($mil)	Weiss Safety Rating
HIGHMARK INC	3340	B-
KEYSTONE HEALTH PLAN WEST INC	588	B+
HIGHMARK LIFE INS CO	270	C+
UNITED CONCORDIA COMPANIES INC	214	D
MOUNTAIN STATE BL CROSS BL SHIELD	141	B+

Winter 2003 - 04
II. Analysis of Largest Companies

HIGHMARK INC   B-   Good

Major Rating Factors: Good liquidity (6.8 on a scale of 0 to 10) with sufficient resources (cash flows and marketable investments) to handle a spike in claims. Strong capitalization index (9.8) based on excellent current risk-adjusted capital (severe loss scenario). High quality investment portfolio (7.4) containing little or no exposure to mortgages, junk bonds, or unaffiliated stocks.
Other Rating Factors: Weak profitability index (2.3) with operating losses during 2002.
Principal Business: Comp med (70%), med supp (12%), med only (8%), FEHB (7%), vision (2%), other (2%).
Mem Phys: 02: 85,942   **01:** 83,712   **02 MLR** 88%   / **02 Admin Exp** 7%
Enroll(000): Q1 03: 3,435   **02:** 5,276   **01:** 5,713   **Med Exp PMPM:** $48
Principal Investments: Nonaffiliate common stock (19%), affiliate common stock (18%), cash and equiv (7%), real estate (1%), mortgs (1%), other (54%)
Provider Compensation ($000): Contr fee ($2,331,499), FFS ($746,515), capitation ($87,248), bonus arrang ($5,996)
Total Member Encounters: Phys (12,606,219), non-phys (3,523,381)
Group Affiliation: Highmark Inc
Licensed in: PA
Address: 1800 Center St, Camp Hill, PA 17011
Phone: (412) 544-7000   **Dom State:** PA   **Commenced Bus:** April 1940

Data Date	Weiss Safety Rating	RACR #1	RACR #2	Total Assets ($mil)	Capital ($mil)	Net Premium ($mil)	Net Income ($mil)
3-03	B-	3.56	2.97	3,377.7	1,862.7	976.2	-13.0
3-02	B	5.41	3.83	3,433.1	2,118.8	880.2	20.2
2002	B-	3.56	2.97	3,340.0	1,863.6	3,615.5	-130.0
2001	B	5.43	3.84	3,459.7	2,107.1	3,310.0	61.0
2000	B-	2.38	1.56	3,554.8	2,026.8	5,849.6	173.2
1999	B-	2.36	1.55	3,346.6	1,977.2	5,517.2	103.9
1998	B-	2.41	1.58	2,937.8	1,771.9	5,085.4	86.3

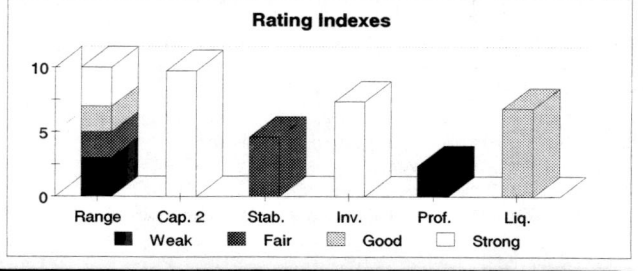

HIGHMARK LIFE INSURANCE COMPANY   C+   Fair

Major Rating Factors: Fair overall results on stability tests (4.4 on a scale of 0 to 10). Good overall profitability (6.3). Return on equity has been fair, averaging 6.8%. Strong capitalization (7.6) based on excellent risk adjusted capital (severe loss scenario).
Other Rating Factors: High quality investment portfolio (7.2). Excellent liquidity (7.0).
Principal Business: Group health insurance (66%), group life insurance (24%), and reinsurance (10%).
Principal Investments: NonCMO investment grade bonds (66%), CMOs and structured securities (27%), and common & preferred stock (7%).
Investments in Affiliates: None
Group Affiliation: Highmark Inc
Licensed in: All states except NY, PR
Commenced Business: May 1981
Address: 280 Trumbull St 15th Floor, Hartford, CT 06103
Phone: (800) 328-5433   **Domicile State:** CT   **NAIC Code:** 93440

Data Date	Weiss Safety Rating	RACR #1	RACR #2	Total Assets ($mil)	Capital ($mil)	Net Premium ($mil)	Net Income ($mil)
6-03	C+	1.88	1.40	281.0	70.1	102.5	4.1
6-02	C+	1.48	1.08	253.1	57.8	97.6	-1.9
2002	C+	1.68	1.25	269.5	64.2	198.7	-2.9
2001	C+	1.56	1.14	254.6	63.8	195.2	0.7
2000	C+	1.66	1.18	235.8	69.1	172.1	9.3
1999	C+	2.33	1.71	223.3	71.9	157.4	5.2
1998	C+	2.32	1.76	264.6	57.2	132.9	4.4

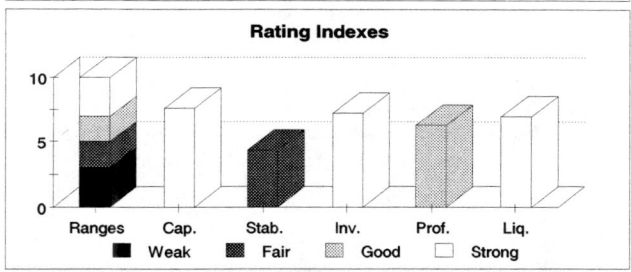

HIP INS CO OF NEW YORK   B   Good

Major Rating Factors: Good liquidity (6.8 on a scale of 0 to 10) with sufficient resources (cash flows and marketable investments) to handle a spike in claims. Excellent profitability (10.0). Strong capitalization index (10.0) based on excellent current risk-adjusted capital (severe loss scenario).
Other Rating Factors: High quality investment portfolio (9.9) containing no exposure to mortgages, junk bonds, or unaffiliated stocks.
Principal Business: Comp med (100%)
Mem Phys: 02: 19,426   **01:** 17,877   **02 MLR** 67%   / **02 Admin Exp** 20%
Enroll(000): Q1 03: 41   **02:** 37   **01:** 22   **Med Exp PMPM:** $39
Principal Investments: Cash and equiv (3%), other (97%)
Provider Compensation ($000): Contr fee ($13,997), FFS ($3,310)
Total Member Encounters: Phys (24,500), non-phys (20,347)
Group Affiliation: HIP Ins Group
Licensed in: NY
Address: 7 W 34th St, New York, NY 10001
Phone: (212) 630-5000   **Dom State:** NY   **Commenced Bus:** September 1994

Data Date	Weiss Safety Rating	RACR #1	RACR #2	Total Assets ($mil)	Capital ($mil)	Net Premium ($mil)	Net Income ($mil)
3-03	B	8.65	7.20	24.0	16.8	7.4	0.8
3-02	N/A	N/A	N/A	N/A	N/A	N/A	N/A
2002	N/A	N/A	N/A	23.3	16.0	20.5	2.3
2001	N/A	N/A	N/A	26.6	13.5	22.8	N/A
2000	U	2.77	2.37	17.6	9.0	16.8	4.1
1999	D+	2.08	1.87	9.5	4.9	8.5	0.7
1998	N/A	N/A	N/A	6.1	4.1	6.3	N/A

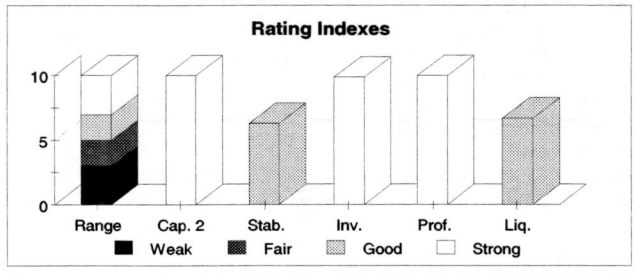

www.WeissRatings.com   * Denotes a Weiss Recommended Company

II. Analysis of Largest Companies

HMO COLORADO   C+   Fair

Major Rating Factors: Good overall results on stability tests (5.8 on a scale of 0 to 10) based on consistent premium and capital growth in the last five years but a decline in enrollment during 2002. Rating is significantly influenced by the good financial results of Anthem Ins Companies Inc. Good liquidity (6.9) with sufficient resources (cash flows and marketable investments) to handle a spike in claims. Weak profitability index (1.9) with operating losses during 1998, 1999, 2000 and 2001. Average return on equity has been poor at -46%.
Other Rating Factors: Strong capitalization (10.0) based on excellent current risk-adjusted capital (severe loss scenario) reflecting improvement over results in 1998. High quality investment portfolio (9.9) containing no exposure to mortgages, junk bonds, or unaffiliated stocks.
Principal Business: Comp med (100%)
Mem Phys: 02: 14,099 **01:** 14,613 **02 MLR** 77% **/ 02 Admin Exp** 15%
Enroll(000): Q1 03: 92 **02:** 102 **01:** 122 **Med Exp PMPM:** $155
Principal Investments: Cash and equiv (4%), other (96%)
Provider Compensation ($000): FFS ($142,455), contr fee ($63,128), capitation ($17,434), bonus arrang ($668)
Total Member Encounters: Phys (568,605), non-phys (357,737)
Group Affiliation: Anthem Ins Companies Inc
Licensed in: CO, NV, WI
Address: 700 Broadway, Denver, CO 80273
Phone: (303) 831-2131 **Dom State:** CO **Commenced Bus:** January 1980

Data Date	Weiss Safety Rating	RACR #1	RACR #2	Total Assets ($mil)	Capital ($mil)	Net Premium ($mil)	Net Income ($mil)
3-03	C+	4.31	3.59	122.4	61.2	64.1	8.5
3-02	C	2.87	2.05	128.6	46.5	64.9	3.9
2002	C	4.31	3.59	118.9	61.3	271.7	23.4
2001	C	2.85	2.05	129.6	42.8	268.7	-3.0
2000	C	2.51	2.07	108.4	32.2	227.0	-9.2
1999	C	2.53	2.16	98.5	26.7	163.1	-30.2
1998	C+	1.10	0.94	109.9	19.3	197.0	-20.6

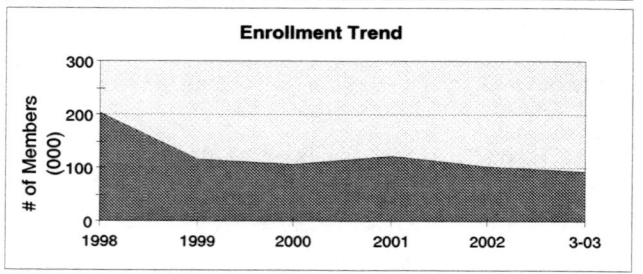

Enrollment Trend chart 1998–3-03

HMO HEALTH PLANS INC   C+   Fair

Major Rating Factors: Fair profitability index (4.0 on a scale of 0 to 10) due to a decline in earnings during 2002. Good capitalization (5.3) based on good current risk-adjusted capital (severe loss scenario) reflecting significant improvement over results in 2000. Good overall results on stability tests (5.6) despite weak risk-adjusted capital in prior years.
Other Rating Factors: High quality investment portfolio (9.9) containing no exposure to mortgages, junk bonds, or unaffiliated stocks. Excellent liquidity (7.2) with ample operational cash flow and liquid investments.
Principal Business: Comp med (88%), Medicare (12%)
Mem Phys: 02: 1,704 **01:** 1,700 **02 MLR** 82% **/ 02 Admin Exp** 19%
Enroll(000): Q1 03: 5 **02:** 5 **01:** 5 **Med Exp PMPM:** $158
Principal Investments: Cash and equiv (89%), other (11%)
Provider Compensation ($000): Contr fee ($9,567), FFS ($195)
Total Member Encounters: Phys (25,857), non-phys (19,036)
Group Affiliation: None
Licensed in: CO
Address: 700 Main Street, Suite 100, Alamosa, CO 81101
Phone: (719) 589-3696 **Dom State:** CO **Commenced Bus:** May 1975

Data Date	Weiss Safety Rating	RACR #1	RACR #2	Total Assets ($mil)	Capital ($mil)	Net Premium ($mil)	Net Income ($mil)
3-03	C+	0.98	0.81	5.3	2.7	3.4	0.4
3-02	C	0.71	0.61	3.9	1.7	2.9	0.0
2002	C	0.79	0.66	4.3	2.3	12.2	0.2
2001	C	0.72	0.61	3.5	1.7	10.4	0.8
2000	D	0.41	0.35	3.0	1.1	9.9	0.1
1999	N/A	N/A	N/A	2.3	0.3	7.6	N/A
1998	D	0.62	0.53	2.9	0.8	6.4	-0.2

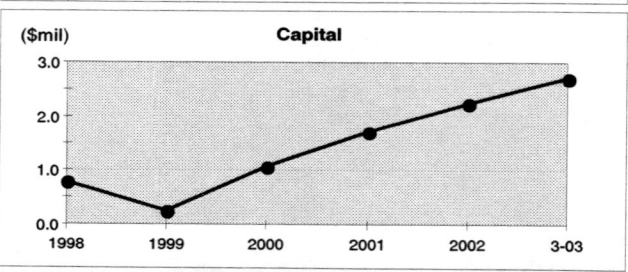

Capital chart ($mil) 1998–3-03

HMO LOUISIANA INC   B-   Good

Major Rating Factors: Fair overall results on stability tests (4.5 on a scale of 0 to 10) based on excessive capital growth during 2002, rapid premium growth over the last five years and rapid enrollment growth during the past five years. Potentially strong support from affiliation with Louisiana Health Services. Good liquidity (6.8) with sufficient resources (cash flows and marketable investments) to handle a spike in claims. Strong capitalization index (9.4) based on excellent current risk-adjusted capital (severe loss scenario).
Other Rating Factors: High quality investment portfolio (9.9) containing no exposure to mortgages, junk bonds, or unaffiliated stocks. Weak profitability index (0.9) with operating losses during 1998, 1999 and 2000. Average return on equity has been poor at -56%.
Principal Business: Comp med (100%)
Mem Phys: 02: 4,897 **01:** 4,722 **02 MLR** 78% **/ 02 Admin Exp** 15%
Enroll(000): Q1 03: 101 **02:** 106 **01:** 78 **Med Exp PMPM:** $152
Principal Investments: Cash and equiv (3%), other (97%)
Provider Compensation ($000): Contr fee ($160,815), capitation ($274)
Total Member Encounters: Phys (943,045), non-phys (179,650)
Group Affiliation: Louisiana Health Services
Licensed in: LA
Address: 5525 Reitz Ave, Baton Rouge, LA 70809-3802
Phone: (225) 295-3307 **Dom State:** LA **Commenced Bus:** July 1986

Data Date	Weiss Safety Rating	RACR #1	RACR #2	Total Assets ($mil)	Capital ($mil)	Net Premium ($mil)	Net Income ($mil)
3-03	B-	3.31	2.76	95.2	52.2	59.4	3.2
3-02	C+	2.94	2.19	74.8	37.1	45.2	3.0
2002	B-	3.08	2.56	87.2	48.6	213.4	12.5
2001	C+	3.00	2.22	63.9	33.0	139.2	6.4
2000	C-	0.27	0.22	41.6	3.9	178.7	-9.5
1999	C-	0.93	0.78	33.2	7.1	80.8	-7.7
1998	C-	1.65	1.40	12.3	4.6	22.9	-2.5

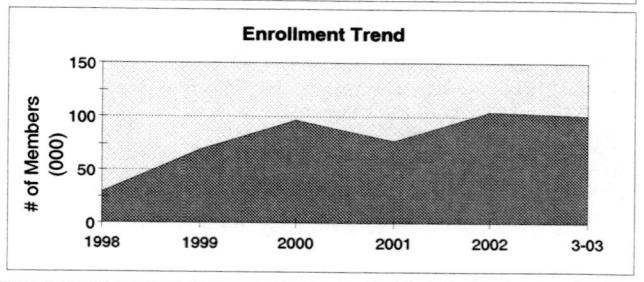

Enrollment Trend chart 1998–3-03

HMO MINNESOTA * B+ Good

Major Rating Factors: Good overall profitability index (5.7 on a scale of 0 to 10) despite a decline in earnings during 2002. Good overall results on stability tests (6.7) based on consistent premium and capital growth in the last five years. Good liquidity (6.1) with sufficient resources (cash flows and marketable investments) to handle a spike in claims.

Other Rating Factors: Strong capitalization (7.6) based on excellent current risk-adjusted capital (severe loss scenario) reflecting significant improvement over results in 1998. High quality investment portfolio (9.9).

Principal Business: Comp med (64%), Medicaid (33%), med supp (1%)
Mem Phys: 02: 6,234 **01:** 6,216 **02 MLR** 92% **/ 02 Admin Exp** 7%
Enroll(000): Q1 03: 197 **02:** 199 **01:** 190 **Med Exp PMPM:** $224
Principal Investments: Cash and equiv (15%), nonaffiliate common stock (5%), real estate (3%), other (77%)
Provider Compensation ($000): Contr fee ($266,851), bonus arrang ($178,559), FFS ($51,416), capitation ($15,540)
Total Member Encounters: Phys (980,470), non-phys (276,509)
Group Affiliation: Aware Integrated Inc
Licensed in: MN
Address: 3535 Blue Cross Rd, Eagan, MN 55122
Phone: (651) 662-1668 **Dom State:** MN **Commenced Bus:** November 1974

Data Date	Weiss Safety Rating	RACR #1	RACR #2	Total Assets ($mil)	Capital ($mil)	Net Premium ($mil)	Net Income ($mil)
3-03	B+	1.84	1.53	216.9	74.7	154.0	-3.5
3-02	N/A	N/A	N/A	N/A	N/A	N/A	N/A
2002	B+	1.89	1.57	218.7	77.1	570.3	4.5
2001	B+	1.90	1.41	193.8	66.2	469.4	24.8
2000	B	1.48	1.18	168.1	55.9	396.0	25.4
1999	B	1.03	0.83	141.0	36.6	327.2	8.2
1998	B	0.76	0.62	111.1	25.3	260.0	-9.9

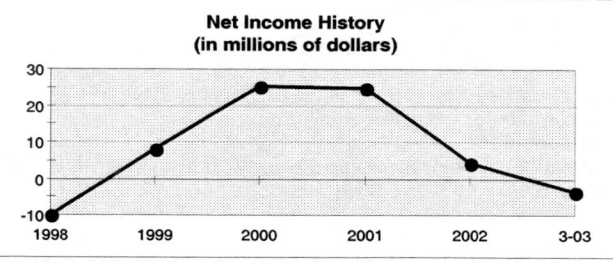

Net Income History (in millions of dollars)

HMO MISSOURI INC C+ Fair

Major Rating Factors: Fair overall results on stability tests (3.7 on a scale of 0 to 10) based on excessive capital growth during 2002. Rating is significantly influenced by the good financial results of WellPoint Health Networks Inc. Good overall profitability index (5.8) despite operating losses during 1998. Poor capitalization (2.9) based on good current risk-adjusted capital (moderate loss scenario) reflecting significant improvement over results in 1998.

Other Rating Factors: High quality investment portfolio (9.9) containing no exposure to mortgages, junk bonds, or unaffiliated stocks. Excellent liquidity (7.0) with ample operational cash flow and liquid investments.

Principal Business: Comp med (79%), FEHB (21%)
Mem Phys: 02: N/A **01:** 7,854 **02 MLR** 78% **/ 02 Admin Exp** 12%
Enroll(000): Q1 03: 103 **02:** 103 **01:** 89 **Med Exp PMPM:** $148
Principal Investments: Cash and equiv (32%), other (68%)
Provider Compensation ($000): Contr fee ($144,417), capitation ($19,155), bonus arrang ($1,433)
Total Member Encounters: Phys (541,541), non-phys (57,711)
Group Affiliation: WellPoint Health Networks Inc
Licensed in: IL, MO
Address: 1831 Chestnut, St Louis, MO 63103
Phone: (877) 864-2273 **Dom State:** MO **Commenced Bus:** December 1987

Data Date	Weiss Safety Rating	RACR #1	RACR #2	Total Assets ($mil)	Capital ($mil)	Net Premium ($mil)	Net Income ($mil)
3-03	C+	1.87	1.56	114.7	34.3	62.0	4.0
3-02	C	1.96	1.59	72.4	31.2	47.9	2.4
2002	C+	2.18	1.82	85.2	40.3	218.0	11.3
2001	C	1.96	1.59	67.8	28.3	158.9	9.5
2000	D+	0.59	0.49	61.6	19.0	219.6	4.8
1999	D+	0.51	0.43	79.1	17.6	210.8	8.9
1998	C-	0.31	0.26	87.3	15.3	206.2	-9.7

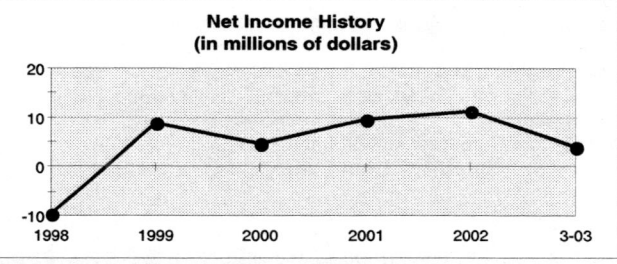

Net Income History (in millions of dollars)

HMO NEW MEXICO INC * B+ Good

Major Rating Factors: Good overall profitability index (5.6 on a scale of 0 to 10) despite operating losses during 1998. Good overall results on stability tests (5.9) despite weak risk-adjusted capital in prior years. Rating is significantly influenced by the good financial results of HCSC Group. Good liquidity (6.9) with sufficient resources (cash flows and marketable investments) to handle a spike in claims.

Other Rating Factors: Strong capitalization (9.1) based on excellent current risk-adjusted capital (severe loss scenario) reflecting significant improvement over results in 1998. High quality investment portfolio (9.9) containing no exposure to mortgages, junk bonds, or unaffiliated stocks.

Principal Business: Comp med (98%), stop loss (2%)
Mem Phys: 02: 3,362 **01:** 2,973 **02 MLR** 77% **/ 02 Admin Exp** 16%
Enroll(000): Q1 03: 34 **02:** 32 **01:** 25 **Med Exp PMPM:** $149
Principal Investments: Cash and equiv (20%), other (80%)
Provider Compensation ($000): Contr fee ($47,002), capitation ($1,445)
Total Member Encounters: Phys (181,700), non-phys (27,241)
Group Affiliation: HCSC Group
Licensed in: NM
Address: 12800 Indian School Rd NE, Albuquerque, NM 87112
Phone: (505) 291-3500 **Dom State:** NM **Commenced Bus:** September 1985

Data Date	Weiss Safety Rating	RACR #1	RACR #2	Total Assets ($mil)	Capital ($mil)	Net Premium ($mil)	Net Income ($mil)
3-03	B+	3.02	2.52	28.6	12.6	20.7	1.0
3-02	B-	2.93	2.39	18.9	9.7	14.5	1.3
2002	B+	2.83	2.36	23.7	11.7	65.2	3.7
2001	B-	2.93	2.39	17.5	8.4	42.4	2.9
2000	D+	N/A	N/A	12.0	4.6	39.1	0.4
1999	D	0.84	0.71	11.2	4.9	40.4	0.5
1998	C+	0.45	0.38	16.2	3.0	60.2	-9.7

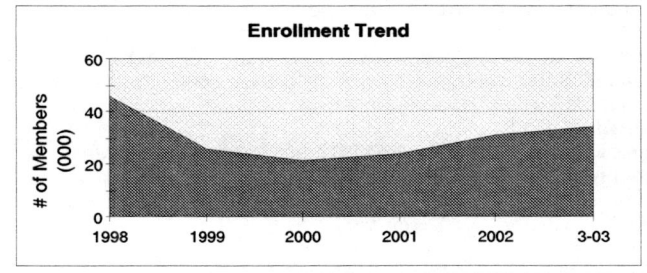

Enrollment Trend

II. Analysis of Largest Companies

Winter 2003 - 04

HMO OF NORTHEASTERN PENNSYLVANIA INC   B-   Good

Major Rating Factors: Good overall results on stability tests (5.2 on a scale of 0 to 10) despite weak risk-adjusted capital in prior years. Potentially strong support from affiliation with Hospital Svc Assoc of NE PA. Good liquidity (6.4) with sufficient resources (cash flows and marketable investments) to handle a spike in claims. High quality investment portfolio (8.6).
Other Rating Factors: Weak profitability index (0.9) with operating losses during 1998, 1999, 2000 and 2002. Average return on equity has been poor at -29%. Poor capitalization (2.9) based on good current risk-adjusted capital (moderate loss scenario) reflecting significant improvement over results in 1999.
Principal Business: Comp med (100%)
Mem Phys: 02: 2,827   01: 2,624   **02 MLR** 88% / **02 Admin Exp** 14%
Enroll(000): Q1 03: 129   02: 122   01: 100   **Med Exp PMPM:** $158
Principal Investments: Nonaffiliate common stock (18%), cash and equiv (11%), other (71%)
Provider Compensation ($000): FFS ($136,346), contr fee ($47,201), capitation ($18,143), bonus arrang ($2,080)
Total Member Encounters: Phys (613,849), non-phys (1,887)
Group Affiliation: Hospital Svc Assoc of NE PA
Licensed in: PA
Address: 19 N Main St, Wilkes Barre, PA 18711
Phone: (800) 432-8015   **Dom State:** PA   **Commenced Bus:** January 1987

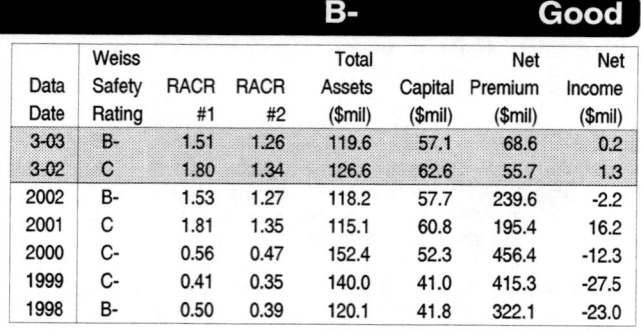

Data Date	Weiss Safety Rating	RACR #1	RACR #2	Total Assets ($mil)	Capital ($mil)	Net Premium ($mil)	Net Income ($mil)
3-03	B-	1.51	1.26	119.6	57.1	68.6	0.2
3-02	C	1.80	1.34	126.6	62.6	55.7	1.3
2002	B-	1.53	1.27	118.2	57.7	239.6	-2.2
2001	C	1.81	1.35	115.1	60.8	195.4	16.2
2000	C-	0.56	0.47	152.4	52.3	456.4	-12.3
1999	C-	0.41	0.35	140.0	41.0	415.3	-27.5
1998	B-	0.50	0.39	120.1	41.8	322.1	-23.0

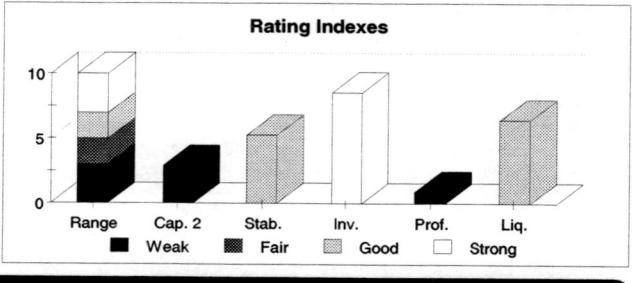

HMO PARTNERS INC   C   Fair

Major Rating Factors: Weak liquidity (2.1 on a scale of 0 to 10) as a spike in claims may stretch capacity. Good overall results on stability tests (6.9) based on consistent premium and capital growth in the last five years but a decline in enrollment during 2001. Excellent profitability (8.1) with operating gains in each of the last five years.
Other Rating Factors: Strong capitalization (7.4) based on excellent current risk-adjusted capital (severe loss scenario) reflecting significant improvement over results in 1997. High quality investment portfolio (7.5).
Principal Business: Comp med (100%)
Mem Phys: 01: 5,166   00: 4,943   **01 MLR** 195% / **01 Admin Exp** 9%
Enroll(000): Q2 02: 131   01: 157   00: 170   **Med Exp PMPM:** $157
Principal Investments: Cash and equiv (28%), nonaffiliate common stock (10%), other (62%)
Provider Compensation ($000): Bonus arrang ($276,993), FFS ($17,721), capitation ($4,604)
Total Member Encounters: Phys (77,474), non-phys (106,229)
Group Affiliation: Arkansas Bl Cross Bl Shield Group
Licensed in: AR
Address: 26 Corporate Hill Dr, Little Rock, AR 72205-4538
Phone: (501) 221-1800   **Dom State:** AR   **Commenced Bus:** January 1994

Data Date	Weiss Safety Rating	RACR #1	RACR #2	Total Assets ($mil)	Capital ($mil)	Net Premium ($mil)	Net Income ($mil)
6-02	C	1.73	1.37	63.8	28.6	53.1	2.7
6-01	C-	1.85	1.53	67.2	24.2	81.1	3.7
2001	C	1.90	1.49	62.6	27.3	158.3	7.1
2000	C-	1.65	1.37	70.2	21.8	124.7	6.3
1999	C-	1.05	0.88	68.0	14.8	125.8	4.7
1998	D+	0.88	0.75	54.0	10.6	104.9	3.1
1997	D+	0.69	0.43	34.0	7.3	122.3	0.8

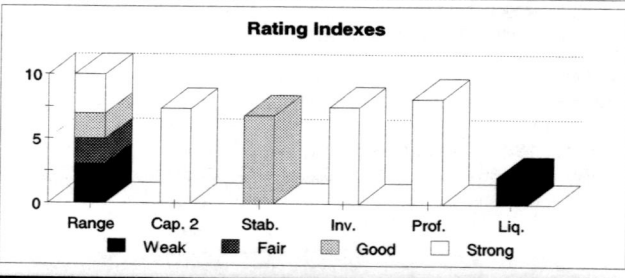

HOMETOWN HEALTH PLAN   C-   Fair

Major Rating Factors: Fair capitalization index (3.8 on a scale of 0 to 10) based on weak current risk-adjusted capital (moderate loss scenario). Weak profitability index (0.9) with operating losses during 1999, 2000 and 2002. Good liquidity (5.6) with sufficient resources (cash flows and marketable investments) to handle a spike in claims.
Other Rating Factors: High quality investment portfolio (8.9). Excellent overall results on stability tests (7.7) based on consistent premium and capital growth in the last five years. Potentially strong support from affiliation with Health Plan Group.
Principal Business: Medicare (52%), comp med (48%)
Mem Phys: 02: 2,004   01: 2,003   **02 MLR** 92% / **02 Admin Exp** 12%
Enroll(000): Q1 03: 30   02: 32   01: 36   **Med Exp PMPM:** $240
Principal Investments: Cash and equiv (46%), nonaffiliate common stock (15%), other (40%)
Provider Compensation ($000): Contr fee ($75,512), capitation ($21,463)
Total Member Encounters: Phys (240,569), non-phys (80,803)
Group Affiliation: Health Plan Group
Licensed in: OH
Address: 100 Lillian Gish Blvd, STe 301, Massillon, OH 44647
Phone: (877) 236-2289   **Dom State:** OH   **Commenced Bus:** January 1987

Data Date	Weiss Safety Rating	RACR #1	RACR #2	Total Assets ($mil)	Capital ($mil)	Net Premium ($mil)	Net Income ($mil)
3-03	C-	0.74	0.62	20.6	7.8	26.0	-0.5
3-02	D+	0.72	0.57	24.5	6.6	27.6	0.0
2002	C-	0.72	0.60	23.4	7.5	105.3	-3.1
2001	D+	0.72	0.58	22.3	7.7	89.1	2.2
2000	D-	0.31	0.25	19.4	3.2	68.4	-4.0
1999	D-	0.24	0.20	13.8	2.0	51.5	-2.0
1998	D-	0.31	0.26	11.3	2.0	39.2	0.3

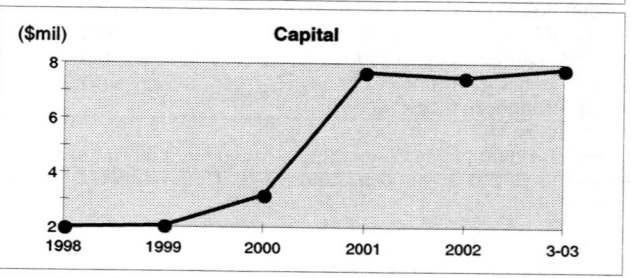

Winter 2003 - 04   II. Analysis of Largest Companies

HOMETOWN HEALTH PLAN INC   D+   Weak

Major Rating Factors: Weak profitability index (0.9 on a scale of 0 to 10) with modest operating losses during 1998, 1999, 2001 and 2002. Fair overall results on stability tests (5.0). Good overall capitalization (6.6) based on good current risk-adjusted capital (severe loss scenario).
Other Rating Factors: Good liquidity (5.7) with sufficient resources (cash flows and marketable investments) to handle a spike in claims. High quality investment portfolio (9.9) containing no exposure to mortgages, junk bonds, or unaffiliated stocks.
Principal Business: Comp med (65%), Medicare (35%).
Mem Phys: 02: 1,106   **01:** 1,129   **02 MLR** 87% / **02 Admin Exp** 14%
Enroll(000): Q1 03: 34   **02:** 33   **01:** 34   **Med Exp PMPM:** $240
Principal Investments: Cash and equiv (16%), real estate (1%), other (82%)
Provider Compensation ($000): FFS ($62,138), capitation ($38,457)
Total Member Encounters: Phys (70,500), non-phys (5,444)
Group Affiliation: Washoe Health System
Licensed in: NV
Address: 400 S Wells Ave, Reno, NV 89502
Phone: (775) 982-3000   **Dom State:** NV   **Commenced Bus:** February 1988

Data Date	Weiss Safety Rating	RACR #1	RACR #2	Total Assets ($mil)	Capital ($mil)	Net Premium ($mil)	Net Income ($mil)
3-03	D+	1.16	0.97	25.4	7.8	29.7	-0.2
3-02	D+	1.36	1.19	24.1	6.5	26.9	-0.2
2002	D+	1.13	0.94	25.7	7.4	111.5	-0.6
2001	D+	1.36	1.18	27.1	6.6	96.4	-0.6
2000	D+	1.10	0.94	25.9	8.0	99.2	0.2
1999	D+	0.92	0.79	26.5	7.7	103.9	-9.6
1998	D+	1.05	0.90	25.9	9.7	97.5	-12.3

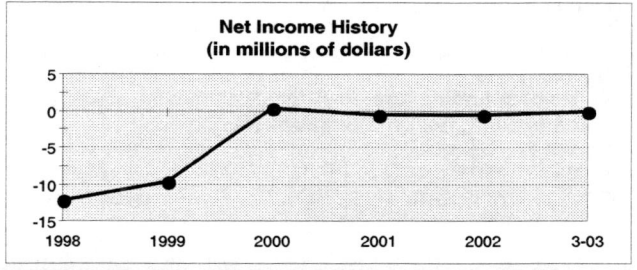

Net Income History (in millions of dollars)

HOMETOWN HEALTH PROVIDERS INS CO   C   Fair

Major Rating Factors: Fair profitability index (4.8 on a scale of 0 to 10). Good liquidity (6.1) with sufficient resources (cash flows and marketable investments) to handle a spike in claims. Strong capitalization (7.1) based on excellent current risk-adjusted capital (severe loss scenario).
Other Rating Factors: High quality investment portfolio (9.9) containing no exposure to mortgages, junk bonds, or unaffiliated stocks.
Principal Business: Comp med (92%), dental (8%).
Mem Phys: 02: 1,202   **01:** 1,158   **02 MLR** 88% / **02 Admin Exp** 14%
Enroll(000): Q1 03: 18   **02:** 21   **01:** 23   **Med Exp PMPM:** $107
Principal Investments: Cash and equiv (12%), real estate (2%), other (86%)
Provider Compensation ($000): FFS ($32,815)
Total Member Encounters: N/A
Group Affiliation: Washoe Health System
Licensed in: NV
Address: 400 S Wells Ave, Reno, NV 89502
Phone: (775) 982-3000   **Dom State:** NV   **Commenced Bus:** March 1982

Data Date	Weiss Safety Rating	RACR #1	RACR #2	Total Assets ($mil)	Capital ($mil)	Net Premium ($mil)	Net Income ($mil)
3-03	C	1.41	1.18	16.2	6.4	8.3	-3.9
3-02	N/A	N/A	N/A	N/A	N/A	N/A	N/A
2002	C	1.31	1.09	14.9	6.5	31.4	2.2
2001	N/A	N/A	N/A	16.2	3.7	31.1	N/A
2000	N/A	N/A	N/A	14.9	4.8	30.5	N/A
1999	N/A	N/A	N/A	10.2	3.4	31.5	N/A
1998	N/A	N/A	N/A	10.4	4.4	29.2	N/A

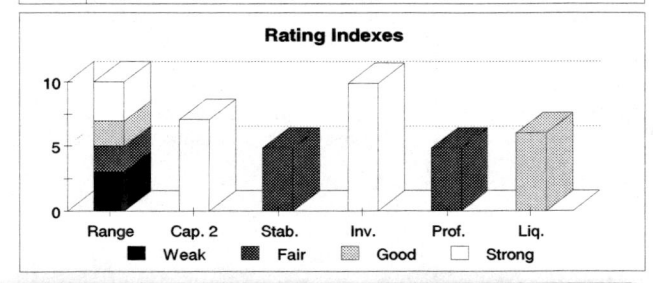

Rating Indexes (Range, Cap. 2, Stab., Inv., Prof., Liq.) — Weak, Fair, Good, Strong

HORIZON HEALTHCARE INS CO OF NY   C   Fair

Major Rating Factors: Weak profitability index (0.9 on a scale of 0 to 10). Good liquidity (5.2) with sufficient resources (cash flows and marketable investments) to handle a spike in claims. Strong capitalization index (8.6) based on excellent current risk-adjusted capital (severe loss scenario).
Other Rating Factors: High quality investment portfolio (9.9) containing no exposure to mortgages, junk bonds, or unaffiliated stocks.
Principal Business: Comp med (99%).
Mem Phys: 02: 21,254   **01:** 12,285   **02 MLR** 103% / **02 Admin Exp** 23%
Enroll(000): Q1 03: 54   **02:** 55   **01:** 59   **Med Exp PMPM:** $231
Principal Investments: Cash and equiv (33%), other (67%)
Provider Compensation ($000): Contr fee ($145,305), FFS ($12,623), capitation ($1,701)
Total Member Encounters: Phys (278,982), non-phys (202,685)
Group Affiliation: Horizon Healthcare Services Inc
Licensed in: NY
Address: 1180 Ave of the Americas Fl 8, New York, NY 10036-8401
Phone: (212) 626-2900   **Dom State:** NY   **Commenced Bus:** February 1999

Data Date	Weiss Safety Rating	RACR #1	RACR #2	Total Assets ($mil)	Capital ($mil)	Net Premium ($mil)	Net Income ($mil)
3-03	C	2.66	2.22	71.0	32.6	35.3	-3.6
3-02	N/A	N/A	N/A	N/A	N/A	N/A	N/A
2002	N/A	N/A	N/A	76.7	36.7	153.3	-26.8
2001	N/A	N/A	N/A	63.3	12.4	123.6	N/A
2000	N/A	N/A	N/A	36.5	12.9	58.5	N/A
1999	C	2.20	1.98	15.2	6.6	8.7	-3.7
1998	N/A	N/A	N/A	N/A	N/A	N/A	N/A

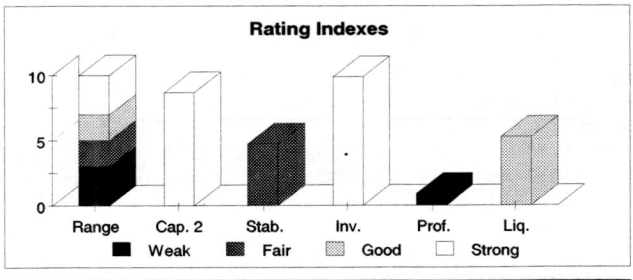

Rating Indexes (Range, Cap. 2, Stab., Inv., Prof., Liq.) — Weak, Fair, Good, Strong

www.WeissRatings.com   * Denotes a Weiss Recommended Company

II. Analysis of Largest Companies

Winter 2003 - 04

HORIZON HEALTHCARE OF NEW JERSEY INC * — B+ Good

Major Rating Factors: Good overall profitability index (5.5 on a scale of 0 to 10) despite operating losses during 1998. Good liquidity (6.5) with sufficient resources (cash flows and marketable investments) to handle a spike in claims. Strong capitalization (8.8) based on excellent current risk-adjusted capital (severe loss scenario) reflecting significant improvement over results in 1998.
Other Rating Factors: High quality investment portfolio (9.9) containing little or no exposure to mortgages, junk bonds, or unaffiliated stocks. Excellent overall results on stability tests (7.2) based on consistent premium and capital growth in the last five years.
Principal Business: Medicaid (40%), Medicare (33%), comp med (27%)
Mem Phys: 02: N/A **01:** 14,849 **02 MLR** 87% / **02 Admin Exp** 9%
Enroll(000): Q1 03: 467 **02:** 506 **01:** 479 **Med Exp PMPM:** $213
Principal Investments: Cash and equiv (16%), affiliate common stock (4%), other (79%)
Provider Compensation ($000): Contr fee ($1,040,664), capitation ($117,191), FFS ($85,632)
Total Member Encounters: Phys (2,943,138), non-phys (970,254)
Group Affiliation: Horizon Healthcare Services Inc
Licensed in: NJ
Address: 3 Penn Plaza East- PP-15E, Newark, NJ 07105-8100
Phone: (973) 466-8600 **Dom State:** NJ **Commenced Bus:** December 1973

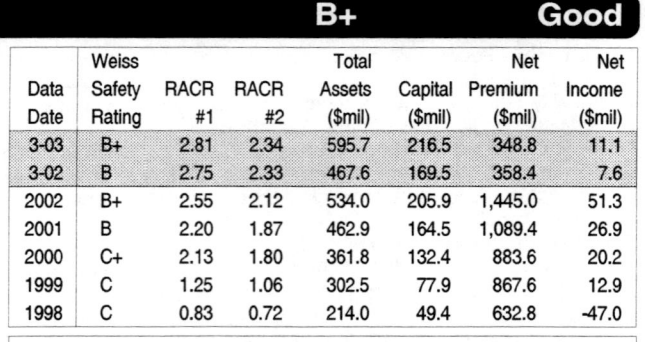

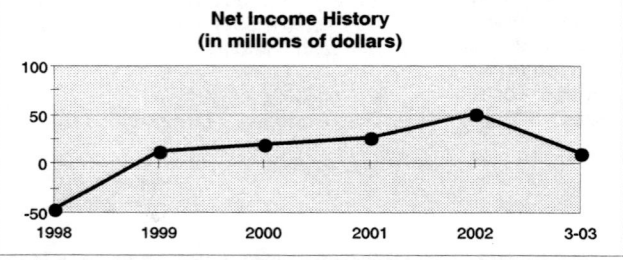

Data Date	Weiss Safety Rating	RACR #1	RACR #2	Total Assets ($mil)	Capital ($mil)	Net Premium ($mil)	Net Income ($mil)
3-03	B+	2.81	2.34	595.7	216.5	348.8	11.1
3-02	B	2.75	2.33	467.6	169.5	358.4	7.6
2002	B+	2.55	2.12	534.0	205.9	1,445.0	51.3
2001	B	2.20	1.87	462.9	164.5	1,089.4	26.9
2000	C+	2.13	1.80	361.8	132.4	883.6	20.2
1999	C	1.25	1.06	302.5	77.9	867.6	12.9
1998	C	0.83	0.72	214.0	49.4	632.8	-47.0

Net Income History (in millions of dollars)

HORIZON HEALTHCARE OF NEW YORK INC — C Fair

Major Rating Factors: Weak profitability index (0.0 on a scale of 0 to 10). Weak overall results on stability tests (0.0). Rating is significantly influenced by the strong financial results of Horizon Healthcare Services Inc. Weak liquidity (0.9) as a spike in claims may stretch capacity.
Other Rating Factors: Strong capitalization index (8.3) based on excellent current risk-adjusted capital (severe loss scenario). High quality investment portfolio (9.9) containing little or no exposure to mortgages, junk bonds, or unaffiliated stocks.
Principal Business: Comp med (100%)
Mem Phys: 02: N/A **01:** 12,285 **02 MLR** 83% / **02 Admin Exp** 198%
Enroll(000): Q1 03: 0 **02:** 0 **01:** 0 **Med Exp PMPM:** $216
Principal Investments: Affiliate common stock (2330%), cash and equiv (12%)
Provider Compensation ($000): Contr fee ($405), capitation ($26)
Total Member Encounters: Phys (2,216), non-phys (1,445)
Group Affiliation: Horizon Healthcare Services Inc
Licensed in: NY
Address: 1180 Avenue of Americas 8th Fl, New York, NY 10036
Phone: (212) 626-2900 **Dom State:** NY **Commenced Bus:** December 1999

Data Date	Weiss Safety Rating	RACR #1	RACR #2	Total Assets ($mil)	Capital ($mil)	Net Premium ($mil)	Net Income ($mil)
3-03	C	2.38	1.99	2.0	1.1	0.3	-0.1
3-02	U	4.79	4.06	3.7	2.6	0.2	-0.8
2002	U	1.65	1.38	1.6	0.8	1.1	-1.6
2001	U	0.00	0.00	9.4	8.1	0.3	-2.2
2000	U	4.67	3.69	11.4	N/A	N/A	-3.4
1999	N/A	N/A	N/A	7.4	6.1	N/A	N/A
1998	N/A	N/A	N/A	N/A	N/A	N/A	N/A

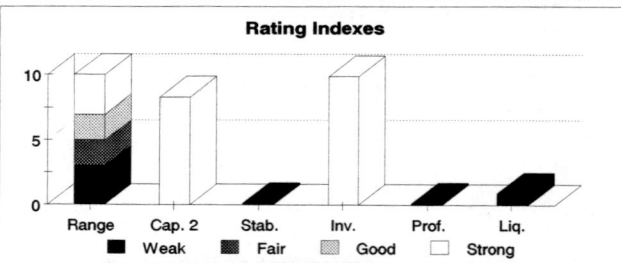

Rating Indexes

HORIZON HEALTHCARE SERVICES INC * — A Excellent

Major Rating Factors: Excellent profitability (8.6 on a scale of 0 to 10) with operating gains in each of the last five years. Strong capitalization (9.6) based on excellent current risk-adjusted capital (severe loss scenario) reflecting improvement over results in 1998. High quality investment portfolio (9.8) containing little or no exposure to mortgages, junk bonds, or unaffiliated stocks.
Other Rating Factors: Good liquidity (6.7) with sufficient resources (cash flows and marketable investments) to handle a spike in claims.
Principal Business: Comp med (82%), FEHB (8%), med supp (7%), dental (4%)
Mem Phys: 02: 24,296 **01:** 23,824 **02 MLR** 80% / **02 Admin Exp** 14%
Enroll(000): Q1 03: 1,406 **02:** 1,361 **01:** 1,348 **Med Exp PMPM:** $139
Principal Investments: Affiliate common stock (23%), nonaffiliate common stock (11%), other (69%)
Provider Compensation ($000): Contr fee ($2,023,878), FFS ($190,495), capitation ($58,935)
Total Member Encounters: Phys (8,764,205), non-phys (3,875,200)
Group Affiliation: Horizon Healthcare Services Inc
Licensed in: NJ
Address: 3 Penn Plaza East, Newark, NJ 07102-3194
Phone: (973) 466-4000 **Dom State:** NJ **Commenced Bus:** December 1932

Data Date	Weiss Safety Rating	RACR #1	RACR #2	Total Assets ($mil)	Capital ($mil)	Net Premium ($mil)	Net Income ($mil)
3-03	A	3.40	2.83	1,684.0	741.5	734.0	53.3
3-02	A-	2.90	2.23	1,481.8	592.2	672.5	30.0
2002	A	2.96	2.47	1,590.6	676.4	2,812.5	119.3
2001	A-	2.90	2.23	1,436.1	561.4	2,485.3	93.5
2000	B+	1.42	0.96	1,248.4	483.4	2,200.0	96.9
1999	B	1.43	0.93	1,147.0	405.6	1,937.8	78.2
1998	B-	1.30	0.83	1,049.1	320.5	1,574.7	18.3

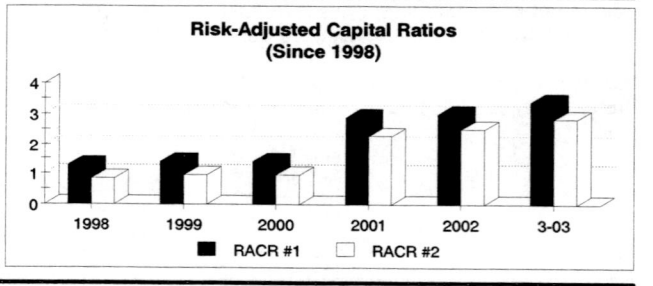

Risk-Adjusted Capital Ratios (Since 1998)

Winter 2003 - 04 — II. Analysis of Largest Companies

HOSPITAL SERV ASSN OF NORTH EAST PA *   B+   Good

Major Rating Factors: Good quality investment portfolio (5.3 on a scale of 0 to 10). Good liquidity (6.9) with sufficient resources (cash flows and marketable investments) to handle a spike in claims. Strong overall capitalization (10.0) based on excellent current risk-adjusted capital (severe loss scenario) despite some fluctuation in capital levels.
Other Rating Factors: Fair profitability index (4.7) due to a decline in earnings during 2002.
Principal Business: Comp med (79%), med supp (16%), FEHB (5%).
Mem Phys: 02: 110   **01:** 106   **02 MLR** 90%   **/ 02 Admin Exp** 11%
Enroll(000): Q1 03: 221   **02:** 228   **01:** 233   **Med Exp PMPM:** $97
Principal Investments: Nonaffiliate common stock (38%), cash and equiv (3%), real estate (3%), affiliate common stock (1%), other (51%)
Provider Compensation ($000): Contr fee ($174,281), FFS ($95,589)
Total Member Encounters: N/A
Group Affiliation: Hospital Svc Assoc of NE PA
Licensed in: PA
Address: 19 N Main St, Wilkes-Barre, PA 18711
Phone: (800) 829-8599   **Dom State:** PA   **Commenced Bus:** December 1938

Data Date	Weiss Safety Rating	RACR #1	RACR #2	Total Assets ($mil)	Capital ($mil)	Net Premium ($mil)	Net Income ($mil)
3-03	B+	5.08	4.23	588.5	367.7	72.8	8.2
3-02	B	5.21	3.20	599.2	412.0	72.5	8.9
2002	B+	5.13	4.27	588.7	370.9	298.0	1.6
2001	B	5.20	3.19	577.3	409.2	287.7	35.8
2000	B	4.00	2.37	612.5	451.9	358.4	27.7
1999	B	4.23	2.51	594.5	441.4	370.4	42.1
1998	B	3.72	2.21	580.8	409.8	361.2	40.9

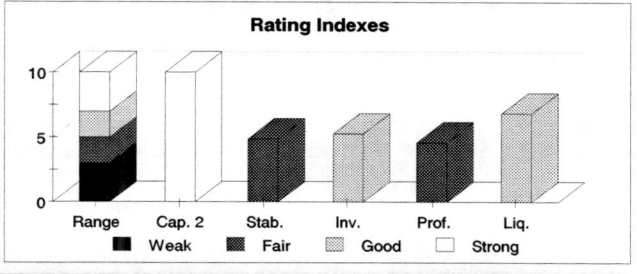

Rating Indexes (Range, Cap. 2, Stab., Inv., Prof., Liq.) — Weak / Fair / Good / Strong

HOUSEHOLD LIFE INSURANCE COMPANY   C   Fair

Major Rating Factors: Weak overall results on stability tests (2.4 on a scale of 0 to 10) including fair financial strength of affiliated HSBC Holdings, weak results on operational trends and negative cash flow from operations for 2002. Strong current capitalization (10.0) based on excellent risk adjusted capital (severe loss scenario) reflecting significant improvement over results in 1998. High quality investment portfolio (7.4).
Other Rating Factors: Excellent profitability (8.9) with operating gains in each of the last five years. Excellent liquidity (8.3).
Principal Business: Credit health insurance (47%), credit life insurance (36%), reinsurance (16%), and group health insurance (1%).
Principal Investments: NonCMO investment grade bonds (63%), CMOs and structured securities (20%), policy loans (11%), common & preferred stock (3%), and noninv. grade bonds (3%).
Investments in Affiliates: 3%
Group Affiliation: HSBC Holdings
Licensed in: All states except HI, NH, NY, VT, PR
Commenced Business: January 1981
Address: 33045 Hamilton Blvd, Farmington Hill, MI 48334
Phone: (810) 848-7811   **Domicile State:** MI   **NAIC Code:** 93777

Data Date	Weiss Safety Rating	RACR #1	RACR #2	Total Assets ($mil)	Capital ($mil)	Net Premium ($mil)	Net Income ($mil)
6-03	C	4.82	3.51	1,262.8	415.9	67.6	72.8
6-02	C	3.19	2.31	1,417.3	350.8	146.3	56.8
2002	C	3.50	2.47	1,285.5	332.1	218.6	129.5
2001	C	2.76	1.99	1,372.2	292.8	209.5	117.9
2000	C	1.54	1.09	1,510.5	258.7	690.9	76.3
1999	C	1.78	1.28	1,417.1	291.2	697.7	35.5
1998	C	1.12	0.64	1,217.8	67.2	164.2	25.7

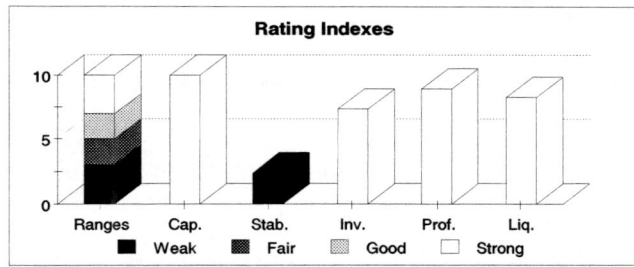

Rating Indexes (Ranges, Cap., Stab., Inv., Prof., Liq.) — Weak / Fair / Good / Strong

HUMANA EMPLOYERS HEALTH PLAN OF GA   C   Fair

Major Rating Factors: Weak profitability index (0.9 on a scale of 0 to 10) with $14.6 million in losses in the last four years. Average return on equity has been poor at -58%. Weak liquidity (0.0) as a spike in claims may stretch capacity. Good overall results on stability tests (5.0) despite rapid premium growth over the last five years, a decline in enrollment during 2002. Rating is significantly influenced by the fair financial results of Humana Inc.
Other Rating Factors: Strong capitalization index (10.0) based on excellent current risk-adjusted capital (severe loss scenario) despite some fluctuation in capital levels. High quality investment portfolio (9.9) containing no exposure to mortgages, junk bonds, or unaffiliated stocks.
Principal Business: Comp med (100%)
Mem Phys: 02: 730   **01:** 642   **02 MLR** 95%   **/ 02 Admin Exp** 15%
Enroll(000): Q1 03: 20   **02:** 18   **01:** 22   **Med Exp PMPM:** $169
Principal Investments: Cash and equiv (87%), other (13%)
Provider Compensation ($000): Contr fee ($25,150), FFS ($8,011), capitation ($6,573), salary ($790), other ($3)
Total Member Encounters: Phys (103,068), non-phys (36,850)
Group Affiliation: Humana Inc
Licensed in: GA
Address: 900 Ashwood Pkwy., Suite 400, Atlanta, GA 30338
Phone: (770) 393-9226   **Dom State:** GA   **Commenced Bus:** February 1997

Data Date	Weiss Safety Rating	RACR #1	RACR #2	Total Assets ($mil)	Capital ($mil)	Net Premium ($mil)	Net Income ($mil)
3-03	C	4.23	3.52	32.2	15.4	10.8	0.4
3-02	C	1.62	1.38	13.0	5.5	11.5	0.2
2002	C	1.38	1.15	21.7	5.0	43.5	-10.5
2001	C	1.65	1.41	12.6	5.3	34.8	-2.8
2000	C	1.88	1.58	6.0	3.4	20.0	0.0
1999	C	2.95	2.51	7.6	3.0	14.1	-1.4
1998	C	4.74	4.02	6.9	4.9	9.8	0.5

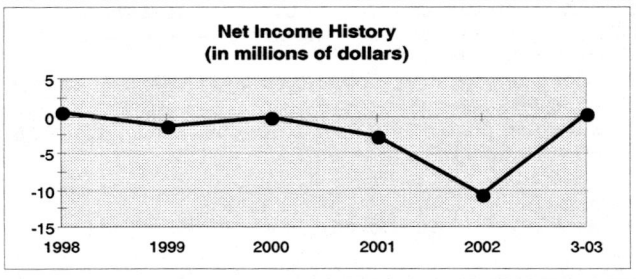

Net Income History (in millions of dollars), 1998 – 3-03

www.WeissRatings.com   199   * Denotes a Weiss Recommended Company

II. Analysis of Largest Companies

Winter 2003 - 04

HUMANA HEALTH INS CO OF FL INC — C- — Fair

Major Rating Factors: Weak profitability index (0.9 on a scale of 0 to 10) with operating losses during 1998, 1999, 2000 and 2001. Good quality investment portfolio (6.7) containing little or no exposure to mortgages, junk bonds, or unaffiliated stocks. Good liquidity (6.9) with sufficient resources (cash flows and marketable investments) to handle a spike in claims.
Other Rating Factors: Strong capitalization (10.0) based on excellent current risk-adjusted capital (severe loss scenario) reflecting improvement over results in 1998.
Principal Business: Comp med (99%)
Mem Phys: 02: N/A **01:** N/A **02 MLR** 70% **/ 02 Admin Exp** 26%
Enroll(000): Q1 03: 57 **02:** 59 **01:** N/A **Med Exp PMPM:** $477
Principal Investments: Cash and equiv (16%), pref stock (3%), other (82%)
Provider Compensation ($000): Contr fee ($156,146), FFS ($19,369), salary ($1,410), other ($13)
Total Member Encounters: Phys (476,013), non-phys (148,426)
Group Affiliation: Humana Inc
Licensed in: FL, KY
Address: 76 S Laura St, Jacksonville, FL 32202
Phone: (904) 296-7908 **Dom State:** FL **Commenced Bus:** May 1984

Data Date	Weiss Safety Rating	RACR #1	RACR #2	Total Assets ($mil)	Capital ($mil)	Net Premium ($mil)	Net Income ($mil)
3-03	C-	4.92	4.10	115.0	72.7	55.2	2.5
3-02	N/A	N/A	N/A	N/A	N/A	N/A	N/A
2002	C-	4.72	3.94	108.0	68.8	239.9	19.4
2001	C-	1.55	1.26	97.4	48.0	260.1	-9.9
2000	C-	1.47	1.19	114.3	48.8	304.7	-7.0
1999	C-	1.04	0.86	117.9	40.4	360.9	-51.7
1998	C-	0.98	0.81	98.7	43.4	384.2	-19.8

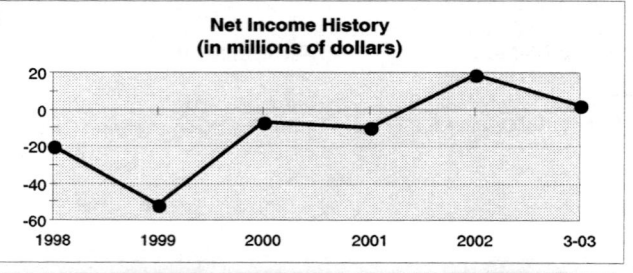

HUMANA HEALTH INSURANCE COMPANY OF FL INC — C- — Fair

Major Rating Factors: Weak profitability (1.8 on a scale of 0 to 10). Return on equity has been low, averaging -36.2%. Weak liquidity (0.4) as a spike in claims may stretch capacity. Weak overall results on stability tests (2.4) including negative cash flow from operations for 2001.
Other Rating Factors: Good overall capitalization (5.7) based on mixed results -- excessive policy leverage mitigated by excellent risk adjusted capital (severe loss scenario). High quality investment portfolio (8.5).
Principal Business: Group health insurance (98%) and individual health insurance (2%).
Principal Investments: NonCMO investment grade bonds (73%), cash (13%), CMOs and structured securities (11%), and common & preferred stock (3%).
Investments in Affiliates: None
Group Affiliation: Humana Inc
Licensed in: FL, KY
Commenced Business: May 1984
Address: 76 S Laura St, Jacksonville, FL 32202
Phone: (904) 296-7908 **Domicile State:** FL **NAIC Code:** 69671

Data Date	Weiss Safety Rating	RACR #1	RACR #2	Total Assets ($mil)	Capital ($mil)	Net Premium ($mil)	Net Income ($mil)
9-02	C-	1.98	1.59	99.1	57.9	153.6	9.4
9-01	C-	1.45	1.18	93.9	42.8	171.7	-11.0
2001	C-	1.55	1.26	97.4	48.0	225.7	-9.9
2000	C-	1.47	1.19	114.3	48.8	266.7	-7.0
1999	C-	1.04	0.86	117.9	40.4	318.5	-51.7
1998	C-	0.98	0.81	98.5	43.4	351.7	-19.8
1997	C	1.04	0.86	97.3	44.2	312.5	-7.9

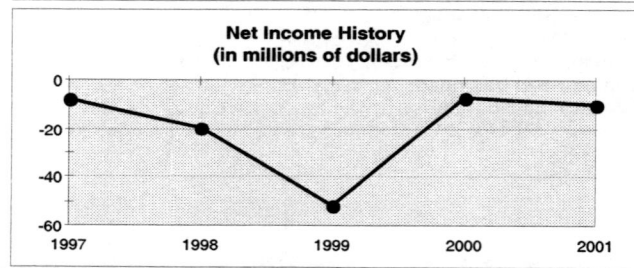

HUMANA HEALTH PLAN INC — C — Fair

Major Rating Factors: Weak profitability index (3.0 on a scale of 0 to 10) with $16.9 million in losses in the last two years. Return on equity has been low, averaging 0%. Good overall results on stability tests (6.3) based on consistent premium and capital growth in the last five years. Good liquidity (6.7) with sufficient resources (cash flows and marketable investments) to handle a spike in claims.
Other Rating Factors: Strong capitalization (7.6) based on excellent current risk-adjusted capital (severe loss scenario) reflecting significant improvement over results in 1998. High quality investment portfolio (9.0).
Principal Business: Comp med (62%), Medicare (32%), FEHB (5%), Medicaid (1%)
Mem Phys: 02: 10,262 **01:** 10,004 **02 MLR** 85% **/ 02 Admin Exp** 15%
Enroll(000): Q1 03: 765 **02:** 783 **01:** 803 **Med Exp PMPM:** $196
Principal Investments: Cash and equiv (26%), real estate (11%), mortgs (8%), pref stock (1%), other (54%)
Provider Compensation ($000): Contr fee ($1,250,346), capitation ($580,411), FFS ($58,485), salary ($13,135)
Total Member Encounters: Phys (3,505,656), non-phys (1,276,812)
Group Affiliation: Humana Inc
Licensed in: AZ, CO, IL, IN, KS, KY, MO, NV
Address: 201 W Main St, Louisville, KY 40202
Phone: (502) 580-8352 **Dom State:** KY **Commenced Bus:** September 1983

Data Date	Weiss Safety Rating	RACR #1	RACR #2	Total Assets ($mil)	Capital ($mil)	Net Premium ($mil)	Net Income ($mil)
3-03	C	1.83	1.53	412.5	177.8	569.4	4.8
3-02	C	1.64	1.37	376.3	150.8	548.7	-18.6
2002	C	1.77	1.47	432.0	169.0	2,199.7	-1.6
2001	C+	1.64	1.37	432.9	153.2	2,258.7	-15.3
2000	C+	0.86	0.72	528.2	169.6	2,171.4	27.0
1999	C+	1.16	0.95	493.1	157.1	2,061.4	8.1
1998	C+	0.76	0.64	487.9	131.6	1,942.7	-14.2

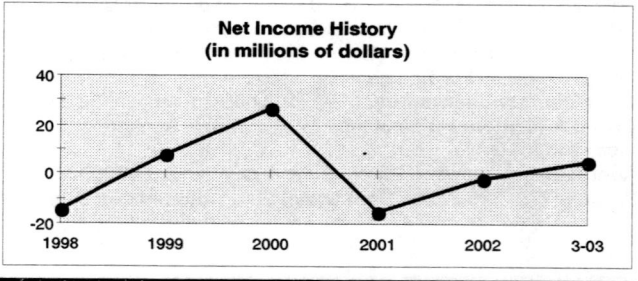

Winter 2003 - 04
II. Analysis of Largest Companies

HUMANA HEALTH PLAN OF OHIO INC   C+   Fair

Major Rating Factors: Fair profitability index (4.6 on a scale of 0 to 10) due to a decline in earnings during 2002. Fair overall results on stability tests (4.1). Rating is significantly influenced by the fair financial results of Humana Inc. Good liquidity (5.7) with sufficient resources (cash flows and marketable investments) to handle a spike in claims.

Other Rating Factors: Strong overall capitalization (7.6) based on excellent current risk-adjusted capital (severe loss scenario) despite some fluctuation in capital levels. High quality investment portfolio (9.3) containing little or no exposure to mortgages, junk bonds, or unaffiliated stocks.

Principal Business: Comp med (100%)
Mem Phys: 02: 1,932   **01:** 1,801   **02 MLR** 84% / **02 Admin Exp** 16%
Enroll(000): Q1 03: 179   **02:** 178   **01:** 191   **Med Exp PMPM:** $156
Principal Investments: Pref stock (5%), cash and equiv (3%), other (92%)
Provider Compensation ($000): Contr fee ($319,231), capitation ($9,622), FFS ($7,993), salary ($4,643)
Total Member Encounters: Phys (22,590), non-phys (8,295)
Group Affiliation: Humana Inc
Licensed in: IN, KY, OH
Address: 655 Eden Park Dr Ste 400, Cincinnati, OH 45202
Phone: (513) 784-5320   **Dom State:** OH   **Commenced Bus:** March 1979

Data Date	Weiss Safety Rating	RACR #1	RACR #2	Total Assets ($mil)	Capital ($mil)	Net Premium ($mil)	Net Income ($mil)
3-03	C+	1.82	1.52	112.2	41.2	110.9	3.7
3-02	C+	2.99	2.44	119.0	56.9	102.1	1.5
2002	C+	2.06	1.72	102.0	46.5	407.3	0.8
2001	C+	2.97	2.43	109.0	55.7	367.6	10.9
2000	C+	3.85	3.19	99.6	40.9	407.3	4.9
1999	B-	1.62	1.34	126.3	40.0	422.3	1.4
1998	B-	3.27	2.77	138.0	74.3	387.7	33.7

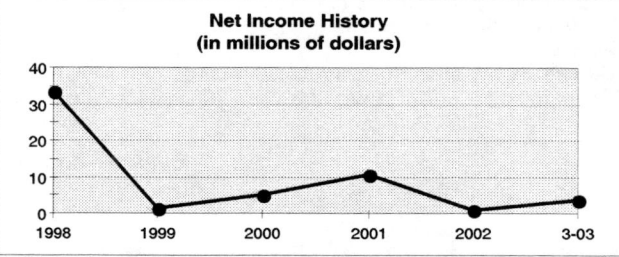

Net Income History (in millions of dollars)

HUMANA HEALTH PLAN OF TEXAS INC   D+   Weak

Major Rating Factors: Weak profitability index (0.9 on a scale of 0 to 10) with $178.2 million in losses in the last five years. Average return on equity over the last five years has been extremely poor. Weak overall results on stability tests (2.1) based on a decline in the number of member physicians during 2002, a steep decline in capital during 2002. Good capitalization index (6.9) based on excellent current risk-adjusted capital (severe loss scenario).

Other Rating Factors: Good liquidity (6.4) with sufficient resources (cash flows and marketable investments) to handle a spike in claims. High quality investment portfolio (9.9).

Principal Business: Comp med (64%), Medicare (28%), FEHB (8%)
Mem Phys: 02: 1,592   **01:** 1,957   **02 MLR** 89% / **02 Admin Exp** 16%
Enroll(000): Q1 03: 231   **02:** 239   **01:** 231   **Med Exp PMPM:** $204
Principal Investments: Cash and equiv (28%), real estate (7%), pref stock (7%), other (59%)
Provider Compensation ($000): Contr fee ($529,272), FFS ($34,657), capitation ($9,485), salary ($5,849), other ($65)
Total Member Encounters: Phys (1,382,297), non-phys (520,906)
Group Affiliation: Humana Inc
Licensed in: TX
Address: 1221 S. Mopac, Suite 200, Austin, TX 78746
Phone: (210) 617-1708   **Dom State:** TX   **Commenced Bus:** April 1982

Data Date	Weiss Safety Rating	RACR #1	RACR #2	Total Assets ($mil)	Capital ($mil)	Net Premium ($mil)	Net Income ($mil)
3-03	D+	1.29	1.07	173.5	44.3	177.2	2.5
3-02	D+	2.25	1.89	169.4	57.6	157.4	-7.5
2002	D+	1.22	1.01	172.8	41.1	646.2	-27.8
2001	D+	2.20	1.86	182.4	65.3	581.5	-1.4
2000	D+	0.46	0.39	259.1	33.2	1,037.8	-88.2
1999	D+	0.65	0.55	346.0	56.9	1,183.7	-50.7
1998	C-	0.22	0.19	149.6	1.9	472.7	-10.1

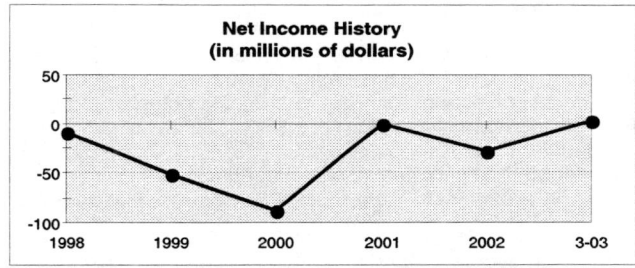

Net Income History (in millions of dollars)

HUMANA INS CO   C   Fair

Major Rating Factors: Fair overall results on stability tests (3.1 on a scale of 0 to 10) including fair financial strength of affiliated Humana Inc. Good current capitalization (5.3) based on mixed results -- excessive policy leverage mitigated by excellent risk adjusted capital (severe loss scenario) reflecting improvement over results in 2000. Good quality investment portfolio (6.7).

Other Rating Factors: Good overall profitability (5.7). Weak liquidity (1.1).

Principal Business: Group health insurance (97%), group life insurance (2%), and individual health insurance (1%).
Principal Investments: NonCMO investment grade bonds (59%), CMOs and structured securities (21%), common & preferred stock (7%), noninv. grade bonds (6%), and misc. investments (8%).
Investments in Affiliates: 1%
Group Affiliation: Humana Inc
Licensed in: All states except NH, NY, VT, PR
Commenced Business: December 1968
Address: 1100 Employers Blvd, De Pere, WI 54115
Phone: (920) 336-1100   **Domicile State:** WI   **NAIC Code:** 73288

Data Date	Weiss Safety Rating	RACR #1	RACR #2	Total Assets ($mil)	Capital ($mil)	Net Premium ($mil)	Net Income ($mil)
6-03	C	1.29	1.04	835.0	384.4	1,306.6	35.6
6-02	C	1.34	1.08	808.7	409.1	1,216.3	42.6
2002	C	1.42	1.13	864.6	416.5	2,442.5	45.5
2001	C	1.70	1.38	976.6	527.7	2,473.0	82.6
2000	C	1.06	0.86	884.9	348.0	2,557.3	55.8
1999	C	1.09	0.88	903.9	328.3	2,478.8	1.3
1998	C+	1.90	1.49	937.9	467.7	2,020.9	75.0

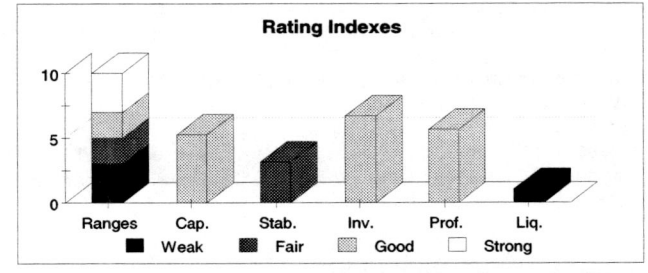

Rating Indexes (Ranges, Cap., Stab., Inv., Prof., Liq.) — Weak, Fair, Good, Strong

www.WeissRatings.com   201   * Denotes a Weiss Recommended Company

II. Analysis of Largest Companies
Winter 2003 - 04

HUMANA INS CO OF KENTUCKY   C   Fair

Major Rating Factors: Excellent profitability (10.0 on a scale of 0 to 10). Strong capitalization (8.2) based on excellent current risk-adjusted capital (severe loss scenario). Moreover, capital levels have been consistent in recent years. High quality investment portfolio (9.9) containing no exposure to mortgages, junk bonds, or unaffiliated stocks.
Other Rating Factors: Excellent liquidity (9.0) with ample operational cash flow and liquid investments.
Principal Business: Stop loss (88%), comp med (12%)
Mem Phys: 02: N/A   **01:** N/A   **02 MLR** 56% / **02 Admin Exp** 10%
Enroll(000): Q1 03: 0   **02:** 0   **01:** 0   **Med Exp PMPM:** $1,724
Principal Investments: Cash and equiv (77%), other (23%)
Provider Compensation ($000): Contr fee ($1,213), FFS ($135)
Total Member Encounters: Phys (47,240), non-phys (14,932)
Group Affiliation: Humana Inc
Licensed in: KY
Address: 500 W Main St, Louisville, KY 40202
Phone: (502) 580-1000   **Dom State:** KY   **Commenced Bus:** September 1996

Data Date	Weiss Safety Rating	RACR #1	RACR #2	Total Assets ($mil)	Capital ($mil)	Net Premium ($mil)	Net Income ($mil)
3-03	C	2.32	1.93	5.5	4.7	0.8	0.4
3-02	N/A	N/A	N/A	N/A	N/A	N/A	N/A
2002	U	2.14	1.78	5.1	4.3	3.0	0.9
2001	D+	2.72	2.45	4.0	0.3	0.3	0.0
2000	U	3.05	2.74	N/A	N/A	N/A	0.1
1999	U	3.02	2.71	N/A	N/A	N/A	0.1
1998	U	3.00	2.70	N/A	N/A	N/A	0.1

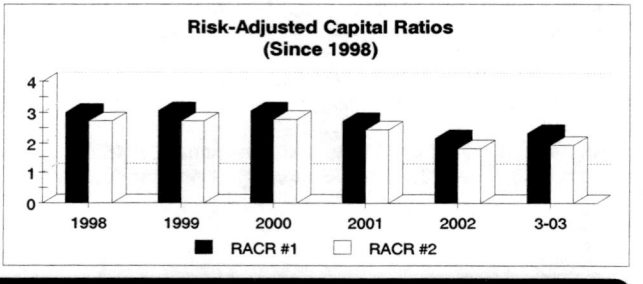

Risk-Adjusted Capital Ratios (Since 1998)

HUMANA MEDICAL PLAN INC   C+   Fair

Major Rating Factors: Fair overall results on stability tests (3.9 on a scale of 0 to 10) based on a decline in the number of member physicians during 2002. Good liquidity (6.9) with sufficient resources (cash flows and marketable investments) to handle a spike in claims. Excellent profitability (7.1) despite a decline in earnings during 2002
Other Rating Factors: Strong capitalization index (7.3) based on excellent current risk-adjusted capital (severe loss scenario). High quality investment portfolio (9.6) containing little or no exposure to mortgages, junk bonds, or unaffiliated stocks.
Principal Business: Medicare (78%), comp med (17%), Medicaid (4%)
Mem Phys: 02: 2,832   **01:** 5,519   **02 MLR** 84% / **02 Admin Exp** 13%
Enroll(000): Q1 03: 462   **02:** 454   **01:** 425   **Med Exp PMPM:** $353
Principal Investments: Cash and equiv (46%), real estate (7%), pref stock (1%), other (46%)
Provider Compensation ($000): Capitation ($1,353,437), contr fee ($495,560), salary ($10,887), FFS ($9,531), other ($5,368)
Total Member Encounters: Phys (3,639,243), non-phys (728,750)
Group Affiliation: Humana Inc
Licensed in: FL
Address: 3501 SW 160th Ave, Miramar, FL 33027
Phone: (305) 626-5616   **Dom State:** FL   **Commenced Bus:** January 1987

Data Date	Weiss Safety Rating	RACR #1	RACR #2	Total Assets ($mil)	Capital ($mil)	Net Premium ($mil)	Net Income ($mil)
3-03	C+	1.62	1.35	361.4	139.7	587.9	9.8
3-02	C	1.39	1.20	357.2	155.7	549.9	8.2
2002	C+	1.57	1.31	498.3	134.4	2,218.2	46.2
2001	C	1.38	1.19	482.5	140.2	2,137.8	51.0
2000	D+	0.01	0.01	408.2	48.5	2,359.7	-1.3
1999	C-	0.54	0.46	551.7	62.4	2,169.0	35.9
1998	C+	1.29	1.11	542.8	136.6	2,405.9	97.1

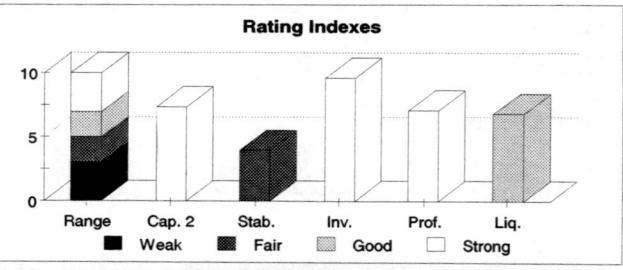

Rating Indexes

HUMANA WISCONSIN HEALTH ORGANIZATION   C   Fair

Major Rating Factors: Fair overall results on stability tests (3.1 on a scale of 0 to 10). Rating is significantly influenced by the fair financial results of Humana Inc. Weak profitability index (0.9) with $21.6 million in losses in the last two years. Average return on equity has been poor at -17%. Good quality investment portfolio (6.8) containing small junk bond exposure.
Other Rating Factors: Good liquidity (6.2) with sufficient resources (cash flows and marketable investments) to handle a spike in claims. Strong overall capitalization (7.3) based on excellent current risk-adjusted capital (severe loss scenario) despite some fluctuation in capital levels.
Principal Business: Comp med (100%)
Mem Phys: 02: 741   **01:** 531   **02 MLR** 90% / **02 Admin Exp** 12%
Enroll(000): Q1 03: 82   **02:** 86   **01:** 69   **Med Exp PMPM:** $241
Principal Investments: Cash and equiv (19%), pref stock (2%), other (79%)
Provider Compensation ($000): Contr fee ($206,117), FFS ($13,019), capitation ($3,029), salary ($2,747)
Total Member Encounters: Phys (571,190), non-phys (185,221)
Group Affiliation: Humana Inc
Licensed in: WI
Address: N19-W24133 Riverwood Dr., #300, Waukesha, WI 53188
Phone: (414) 223-3300   **Dom State:** WI   **Commenced Bus:** September 1985

Data Date	Weiss Safety Rating	RACR #1	RACR #2	Total Assets ($mil)	Capital ($mil)	Net Premium ($mil)	Net Income ($mil)
3-03	C	1.61	1.34	74.7	23.9	71.6	2.4
3-02	C	1.85	1.54	55.7	14.3	60.4	-0.5
2002	C	1.48	1.23	63.7	21.5	246.3	-6.4
2001	C	1.85	1.54	72.7	29.5	174.8	-15.2
2000	C+	2.33	1.93	60.9	20.9	168.3	5.4
1999	C	1.39	1.16	43.1	12.9	173.6	-3.4
1998	C	1.65	1.39	44.1	13.5	155.4	-0.4

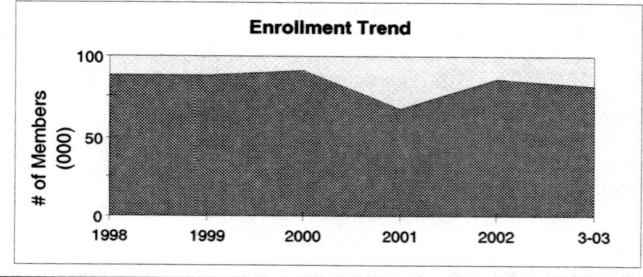

Enrollment Trend

Winter 2003 - 04 **II. Analysis of Largest Companies**

HUMANADENTAL INSURANCE COMPANY C+ Fair

Major Rating Factors: Fair overall results on stability tests (3.8 on a scale of 0 to 10) including fair financial strength of affiliated Humana Inc. Strong current capitalization (7.4) based on excellent risk adjusted capital (severe loss scenario) reflecting improvement over results in 2002. High quality investment portfolio (9.8).
Other Rating Factors: Excellent profitability (8.1) despite modest operating losses during 2001. Excellent liquidity (7.7).
Principal Business: Individual health insurance (87%), individual life insurance (10%), and individual annuities (4%).
Principal Investments: Cash (82%) and nonCMO investment grade bonds (18%).
Investments in Affiliates: None
Group Affiliation: Humana Inc
Licensed in: All states except ME, NY, PR
Commenced Business: October 1908
Address: 1100 Employers Blvd, De Pere, WI 54115
Phone: (920) 336-1100 **Domicile State:** WI **NAIC Code:** 70580

Data Date	Weiss Safety Rating	RACR #1	RACR #2	Total Assets ($mil)	Capital ($mil)	Net Premium ($mil)	Net Income ($mil)
6-03	C+	1.41	1.25	51.7	36.4	82.1	7.4
6-02	C+	2.28	2.03	29.6	13.5	30.4	0.2
2002	C+	1.08	0.91	37.2	24.9	90.9	6.1
2001	C+	4.93	2.89	10.4	8.4	3.8	0.0
2000	C+	5.68	2.84	9.2	8.9	0.0	0.2
1999	C+	6.33	3.62	9.0	8.7	93.1	11.8
1998	B-	2.95	1.57	733.0	61.8	308.5	14.9

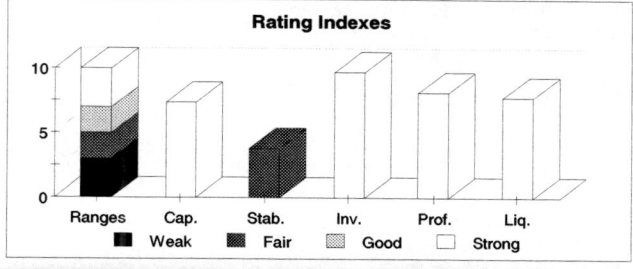

Rating Indexes (Ranges, Cap., Stab., Inv., Prof., Liq.) — Weak / Fair / Good / Strong

IHC BENEFIT ASR CO INC C Fair

Major Rating Factors: Fair profitability index (4.7 on a scale of 0 to 10) with modest operating losses during 1999. Good liquidity (6.8) with sufficient resources (cash flows and marketable investments) to handle a spike in claims. Strong capitalization (8.2) based on excellent current risk-adjusted capital (severe loss scenario) reflecting significant improvement over results in 1999.
Other Rating Factors: High quality investment portfolio (9.6) containing no exposure to mortgages, junk bonds, or unaffiliated stocks.
Principal Business: Comp med (91%), stop loss (9%)
Mem Phys: 02: N/A **01:** N/A **02 MLR** 81% / **02 Admin Exp** 16%
Enroll(000): Q1 03: 0 **02:** 0 **01:** 0 **Med Exp PMPM:** $203,039
Principal Investments: Cash and equiv (14%), other (86%)
Provider Compensation ($000): FFS ($8,914)
Total Member Encounters: Phys (30,424), non-phys (27,437)
Group Affiliation: Intermountain Health Care Inc
Licensed in: UT
Address: 4646 Lake Park Blvd, Salt Lake City, UT 84120-8212
Phone: (801) 442-5000 **Dom State:** UT **Commenced Bus:** July 1992

Data Date	Weiss Safety Rating	RACR #1	RACR #2	Total Assets ($mil)	Capital ($mil)	Net Premium ($mil)	Net Income ($mil)
3-03	C	2.32	1.94	8.0	4.7	2.4	0.1
3-02	C	0.00	0.00	10.6	6.8	3.0	0.1
2002	C	2.26	1.88	7.7	4.6	10.5	0.5
2001	N/A	N/A	N/A	9.9	6.6	12.0	N/A
2000	U	1.19	0.94	9.6	6.0	20.4	0.6
1999	C-	0.89	0.71	8.8	5.1	24.3	0.0
1998	C	0.96	0.76	9.1	5.7	25.3	0.6

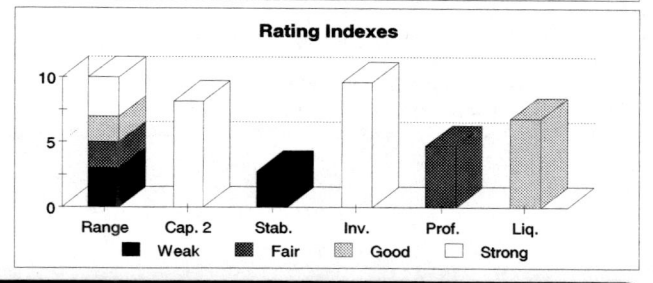

Rating Indexes (Range, Cap. 2, Stab., Inv., Prof., Liq.) — Weak / Fair / Good / Strong

IHC HEALTH PLANS INC B Good

Major Rating Factors: Good overall profitability index (5.3 on a scale of 0 to 10) despite operating losses during 1998 and 2001. Good capitalization (7.0) based on excellent current risk-adjusted capital (severe loss scenario) reflecting significant improvement over results in 1998. Good overall results on stability tests (6.4) based on consistent premium and capital growth in the last five years but a decline in enrollment during 2002.
Other Rating Factors: Good liquidity (6.6) with sufficient resources (cash flows and marketable investments) to handle a spike in claims. High quality investment portfolio (8.5).
Principal Business: Comp med (89%), Medicaid (11%)
Mem Phys: 02: 2,959 **01:** 2,964 **02 MLR** 87% / **02 Admin Exp** 8%
Enroll(000): Q1 03: 379 **02:** 378 **01:** 452 **Med Exp PMPM:** $119
Principal Investments: Nonaffiliate common stock (19%), cash and equiv (13%), affiliate common stock (3%), other (65%)
Provider Compensation ($000): Contr fee ($424,020), FFS ($163,750), bonus arrang ($17,908), capitation ($548)
Total Member Encounters: Phys (1,969,619), non-phys (1,132,351)
Group Affiliation: Intermountain Health Care Inc
Licensed in: ID, UT, WY
Address: 4646 Lake Park Blvd, Salt Lake City, UT 84120-8212
Phone: (801) 442-5000 **Dom State:** UT **Commenced Bus:** February 1984

Data Date	Weiss Safety Rating	RACR #1	RACR #2	Total Assets ($mil)	Capital ($mil)	Net Premium ($mil)	Net Income ($mil)
3-03	B	1.33	1.11	157.7	73.3	147.4	6.0
3-02	B-	1.03	0.77	189.9	65.4	180.9	7.9
2002	B	1.25	1.04	171.0	69.0	680.9	17.5
2001	B-	1.03	0.77	180.0	59.9	643.4	-1.3
2000	C+	1.53	1.23	165.0	66.2	579.9	13.8
1999	C	0.80	0.64	141.3	53.1	526.0	7.0
1998	D+	0.51	0.42	129.9	38.2	511.4	-5.2

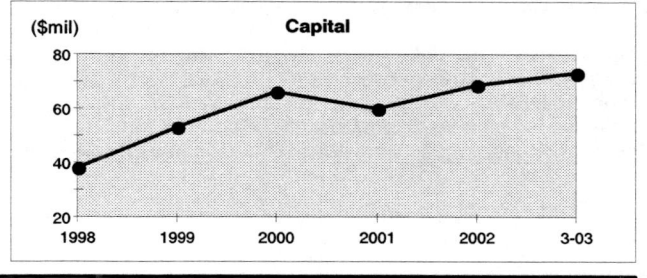

Capital ($mil) — 1998 through 3-03

www.WeissRatings.com * Denotes a Weiss Recommended Company

II. Analysis of Largest Companies
Winter 2003 - 04

ILLINOIS MUTUAL LIFE INSURANCE COMPANY — B — Good

Major Rating Factors: Good current capitalization (6.6 on a scale of 0 to 10) based on good risk adjusted capital (severe loss scenario), although results have slipped from the excellent range over the last two years. Good overall results on stability tests (5.1). Stability strengths include good operational trends and excellent risk diversification. Fair quality investment portfolio (4.8).
Other Rating Factors: Excellent profitability (7.2) with operating gains in each of the last five years. Excellent liquidity (7.0).
Principal Business: Individual annuities (52%), individual health insurance (31%), and individual life insurance (17%).
Principal Investments: NonCMO investment grade bonds (48%), common & preferred stock (19%), mortgages in good standing (9%), CMOs and structured securities (9%), and misc. investments (14%).
Investments in Affiliates: 1%
Group Affiliation: Illinois Mutual Group
Licensed in: All states except AK, DC, DE, HI, MT, NH, NY, PR
Commenced Business: July 1912
Address: 300 SW Adams, Peoria, IL 61634
Phone: (309) 674-8255   **Domicile State:** IL   **NAIC Code:** 64580

Data Date	Weiss Safety Rating	RACR #1	RACR #2	Total Assets ($mil)	Capital ($mil)	Net Premium ($mil)	Net Income ($mil)
6-03	B	1.65	0.95	1,011.4	104.0	64.2	1.6
6-02	B	1.92	1.13	918.9	102.4	103.6	3.0
2002	B	1.67	0.96	969.8	102.3	164.8	8.8
2001	B	2.25	1.34	850.9	105.9	177.5	0.2
2000	B	2.92	1.66	687.2	105.4	109.6	5.5
1999	B	3.09	1.77	637.5	102.8	79.3	9.8
1998	B	2.91	1.78	607.4	93.2	77.8	5.8

Risk-Adjusted Capital Ratio #2 (Severe Loss Scenario)

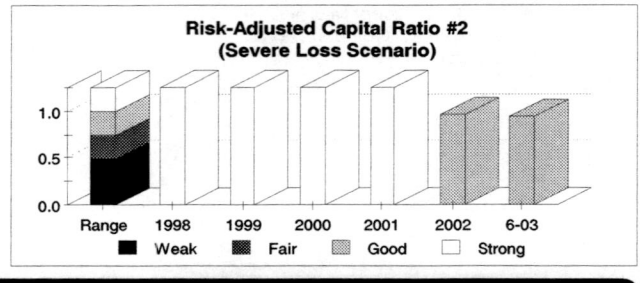

INDEPENDENCE AMERICAN INS CO — C — Fair

Major Rating Factors: Fair profitability index (4.9 on a scale of 0 to 10). Fair expense controls. Return on equity has been fair, averaging 29.4% over the past five years. Fair overall results on stability tests (3.5) including excessive premium growth and weak results on operational trends.
Other Rating Factors: History of adequate reserve strength (5.0) as reserves have been consistently at an acceptable level. Strong long-term capitalization index (7.4) based on excellent current risk adjusted capital (severe and moderate loss scenarios). Moreover, capital levels have been consistent in recent years. Excellent liquidity (8.6) with ample operational cash flow and liquid investments.
Principal Business: Group accident & health (100%).
Principal Investments: Misc. investments (69%), investment grade bonds (23%), cash (7%), and non investment grade bonds (1%).
Investments in Affiliates: None
Group Affiliation: Geneve Holdings Inc
Licensed in: AK, AR, CO, DE, ID, IL, IN, IA, KY, ME, MS, NV, NJ, NM, NY, OK, OR, PA, SC, TX, WA, WV
Commenced Business: March 1973
Address: 1013 Centre Rd, New Castle, DE 19805-1297
Phone: (212) 355-4141   **Domicile State:** DE   **NAIC Code:** 26581

Data Date	Weiss Safety Rating	RACR #1	RACR #2	Loss Ratio %	Total Assets ($mil)	Capital ($mil)	Net Premium ($mil)	Net Income ($mil)
6-03	C	1.40	1.11	N/A	42.9	25.6	1.0	1.8
6-02	C	6.92	5.02	N/A	13.6	11.8	0.0	0.1
2002	C	1.77	1.42	64.7	26.7	22.4	6.9	0.7
2001	C	8.66	6.99	40.1	8.9	7.8	0.4	0.5
2000	C	13.66	8.90	77.7	7.9	6.8	0.5	3.4
1999	C	9.08	6.61	169.0	7.4	5.8	1.1	3.0
1998	C	3.95	2.39	120.7	6.6	5.6	1.0	2.4

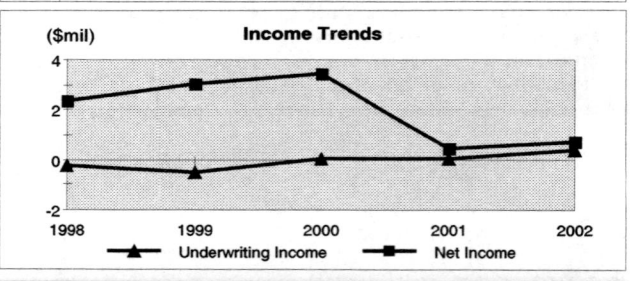

Income Trends

INDEPENDENCE BLUE CROSS — B- — Good

Major Rating Factors: Good overall profitability index (5.6 on a scale of 0 to 10) despite a decline in earnings during 2002. Good liquidity (6.8) with sufficient resources (cash flows and marketable investments) to handle a spike in claims. Strong capitalization (8.0) based on excellent current risk-adjusted capital (severe loss scenario) despite some fluctuation in capital levels.
Other Rating Factors: Low quality investment portfolio (2.9) containing little or no exposure to mortgages, junk bonds, or unaffiliated stocks.
Principal Business: Comp med (69%), med supp (22%), FEHB (10%)
Mem Phys: 02: 15,000   **01:** 15,000   **02 MLR** 79%   **/ 02 Admin Exp** 15%
Enroll(000): Q1 03: 144   **02:** 149   **01:** 173   **Med Exp PMPM:** $166
Principal Investments: Affiliate common stock (77%), nonaffiliate common stock (5%), mortgs (1%), other (17%).
Provider Compensation ($000): Contr fee ($300,192), FFS ($15,336), other ($3,703)
Total Member Encounters: Non-phys (296,844)
Group Affiliation: Independence Blue Cross Inc
Licensed in: PA
Address: 1901 Market St, Philadelphia, PA 19103-1480
Phone: (215) 241-2400   **Dom State:** PA   **Commenced Bus:** November 1938

Data Date	Weiss Safety Rating	RACR #1	RACR #2	Total Assets ($mil)	Capital ($mil)	Net Premium ($mil)	Net Income ($mil)
3-03	B-	2.13	1.78	1,202.2	722.6	109.1	18.1
3-02	B-	4.07	3.34	1,108.7	691.2	101.6	9.4
2002	B-	2.09	1.74	1,149.4	707.1	402.9	16.8
2001	B-	4.06	3.33	1,075.1	689.6	430.2	56.1
2000	B-	1.43	1.29	957.8	613.1	695.3	-10.8
1999	B-	1.36	1.23	948.8	553.2	648.5	18.2
1998	C+	1.26	1.14	845.2	464.6	666.1	-19.4

Net Income History (in millions of dollars)

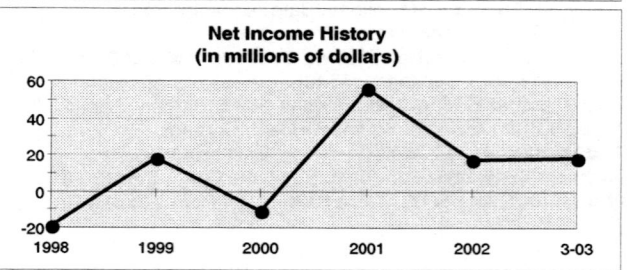

Winter 2003 - 04
II. Analysis of Largest Companies

INDEPENDENT HEALTH ASSOC INC — B — Good

Major Rating Factors: Good profitability index (5.0 on a scale of 0 to 10) despite operating losses during 2000. Good overall results on stability tests (5.3) despite excessive capital growth during 2002. Strong capitalization (9.1) based on excellent current risk-adjusted capital (severe loss scenario) reflecting significant improvement over results in 2000.
Other Rating Factors: High quality investment portfolio (9.9) containing little or no exposure to mortgages, junk bonds, or unaffiliated stocks. Excellent liquidity (7.1) with ample operational cash flow and liquid investments.
Principal Business: Comp med (69%), Medicare (20%), Medicaid (6%), FEHB (5%)
Mem Phys: 02: N/A   **01:** N/A   **02 MLR** 86%   **/ 02 Admin Exp** 10%
Enroll(000): Q1 03: 333   **02:** 334   **01:** 349   **Med Exp PMPM:** $158
Principal Investments: Cash and equiv (47%), real estate (4%), nonaffiliate common stock (3%), affiliate common stock (2%), other (44%)
Provider Compensation ($000): Capitation ($595,470), FFS ($2,048), other ($25,107)
Total Member Encounters: N/A
Group Affiliation: Independent Health Assoc Inc
Licensed in: NY
Address: 511 Farber Lakes Dr, Buffalo, NY 14221
Phone: (716) 635-3939   **Dom State:** NY   **Commenced Bus:** January 1980

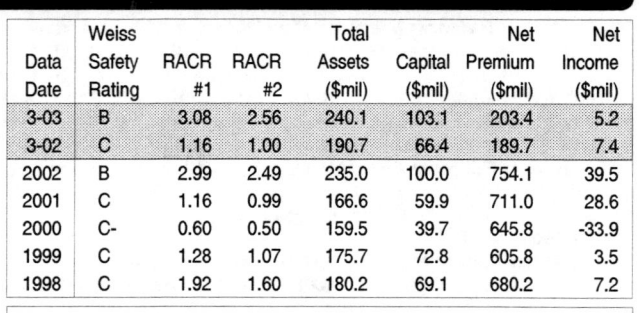

Data Date	Weiss Safety Rating	RACR #1	RACR #2	Total Assets ($mil)	Capital ($mil)	Net Premium ($mil)	Net Income ($mil)
3-03	B	3.08	2.56	240.1	103.1	203.4	5.2
3-02	C	1.16	1.00	190.7	66.4	189.7	7.4
2002	B	2.99	2.49	235.0	100.0	754.1	39.5
2001	C	1.16	0.99	166.6	59.9	711.0	28.6
2000	C-	0.60	0.50	159.5	39.7	645.8	-33.9
1999	C	1.28	1.07	175.7	72.8	605.8	3.5
1998	C	1.92	1.60	180.2	69.1	680.2	7.2

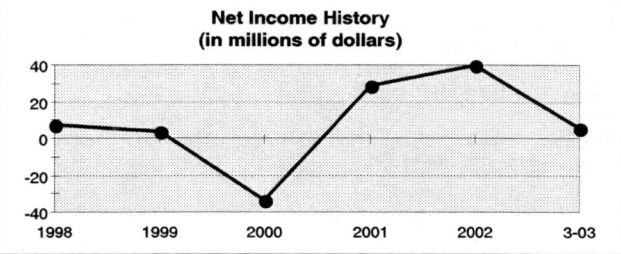

Net Income History (in millions of dollars)

INDEPENDENT HEALTH BENEFITS CORP — B- — Good

Major Rating Factors: Good overall profitability index (6.3 on a scale of 0 to 10) despite a decline in earnings during 2002. Strong capitalization (10.0) based on excellent current risk-adjusted capital (severe loss scenario) reflecting significant improvement over results in 2001. High quality investment portfolio (9.7) containing no exposure to mortgages, junk bonds, or unaffiliated stocks.
Other Rating Factors: Excellent liquidity (8.0) with ample operational cash flow and liquid investments.
Principal Business: Comp med (100%)
Mem Phys: 02: N/A   **01:** N/A   **02 MLR** 42%   **/ 02 Admin Exp** 60%
Enroll(000):   02: 21   **01:** 26   **Med Exp PMPM:** $4
Principal Investments: Cash and equiv (100%)
Provider Compensation ($000): FFS ($1,247)
Total Member Encounters: Phys (19,649), non-phys (7,311)
Group Affiliation: Independent Health Assoc Inc
Licensed in: NY
Address: 511 Farber Lakes Dr, Buffalo, NY 14221
Phone: (716) 631-3001   **Dom State:** NY   **Commenced Bus:** December 1995

Data Date	Weiss Safety Rating	RACR #1	RACR #2	Total Assets ($mil)	Capital ($mil)	Net Premium ($mil)	Net Income ($mil)
2002	B-	3.94	3.29	2.2	1.7	2.9	0.2
2001	C-	1.11	0.95	4.4	2.8	9.6	0.9
2000	N/A	N/A	N/A	4.2	2.8	7.7	N/A
1999	N/A	N/A	N/A	4.0	3.2	5.7	N/A
1998	N/A	N/A	N/A	2.8	1.2	7.5	N/A

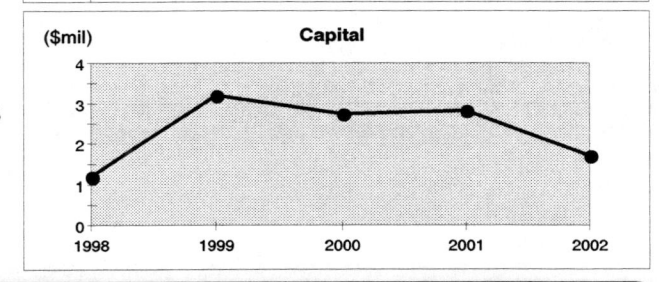

Capital ($mil)

INLAND EMPIRE HEALTH PLAN — C+ — Fair

Major Rating Factors: Good capitalization index (5.7 on a scale of 0 to 10) based on good current risk-adjusted capital (severe loss scenario). Good overall results on stability tests (6.0) despite rapid enrollment growth during the past five years. Good liquidity (7.0) with sufficient resources (cash flows and marketable investments) to handle a spike in claims.
Other Rating Factors: Excellent profitability (8.8) with operating gains in each of the last five years.
Principal Business: Managed care (7%)
Mem Phys: 02: N/A   **01:** N/A   **02 MLR** 89%   **/ 02 Admin Exp** 8%
Enroll(000): Q1 03: 246   **02:** 241   **01:** 208   **Med Exp PMPM:** $87
Principal Investments ($000): Cash and equiv ($32,318)
Provider Compensation ($000): None
Total Member Encounters: N/A
Group Affiliation: None
Licensed in: CA
Address: 303 E Vanderbilt Way Ste 400, San Bernardino, CA 92408
Phone: (909) 890-2000   **Dom State:** CA   **Commenced Bus:** September 1996

Data Date	Weiss Safety Rating	RACR #1	RACR #2	Total Assets ($mil)	Capital ($mil)	Net Premium ($mil)	Net Income ($mil)
3-03	C+	1.38	0.86	51.8	28.4	71.5	2.9
3-02	C	0.00	0.00	36.2	20.9	59.5	2.3
2002	C+	1.24	0.77	47.9	25.4	262.1	6.8
2001	C	0.00	0.00	33.8	18.6	214.6	4.2
2000	C	1.07	0.66	37.2	14.4	198.2	4.5
1999	D+	0.78	0.50	22.0	9.9	141.1	2.5
1998	N/A	N/A	N/A	17.1	7.4	128.0	4.4

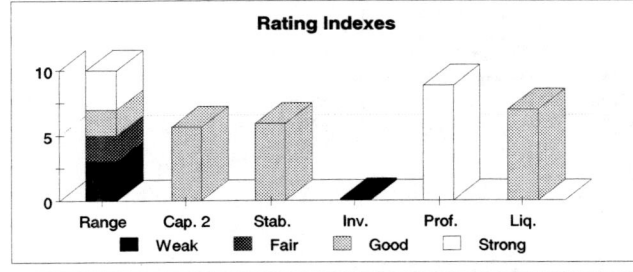

Rating Indexes: Range, Cap. 2, Stab., Inv., Prof., Liq. — Weak / Fair / Good / Strong

www.WeissRatings.com   * Denotes a Weiss Recommended Company

II. Analysis of Largest Companies

Winter 2003 - 04

IU HEALTH PLAN INC — E — Very Weak

Major Rating Factors: Weak profitability index (2.3 on a scale of 0 to 10) with modest operating losses during 1999, 2000, 2001 and 2002. Average return on equity has been poor at -8%. Poor capitalization index (0.0) based on weak current risk-adjusted capital (severe loss scenario). Good overall results on stability tests (6.4) based on consistent premium and capital growth in the last five years but rapid enrollment growth during the past five years.
Other Rating Factors: Good liquidity (6.8) with sufficient resources (cash flows and marketable investments) to handle a spike in claims. High quality investment portfolio (9.9) containing no exposure to mortgages, junk bonds, or unaffiliated stocks.
Principal Business: Medicaid (86%), comp med (14%)
Mem Phys: 02: 715   01: 690   **02 MLR** 90%   / **02 Admin Exp** 9%
Enroll(000): Q1 03: 98   02: 104   01: 64   **Med Exp PMPM:** $132
Principal Investments: Cash and equiv (57%), other (43%)
Provider Compensation ($000): Capitation ($133,526)
Total Member Encounters: Phys (174,587), non-phys (12,016)
Group Affiliation: IU Health Inc dba IU Medical Group
Licensed in: IN
Address: 3901 W 86th St Ste 230, Indianapolis, IN 46268-1797
Phone: (317) 871-8811   **Dom State:** IN   **Commenced Bus:** May 1989

Data Date	Weiss Safety Rating	RACR #1	RACR #2	Total Assets ($mil)	Capital ($mil)	Net Premium ($mil)	Net Income ($mil)
3-03	E	0.29	0.24	3.9	3.7	41.8	0.1
3-02	E	0.00	0.00	2.5	2.3	27.5	0.0
2002	E	0.00	0.00	3.6	3.4	147.0	-0.1
2001	E	0.22	0.20	3.2	2.3	93.4	-0.2
2000	D	0.72	0.63	1.8	1.8	19.2	-0.2
1999	D	0.53	0.46	1.4	1.3	16.9	-0.2
1998	D	0.43	0.37	1.5	1.4	15.2	0.0

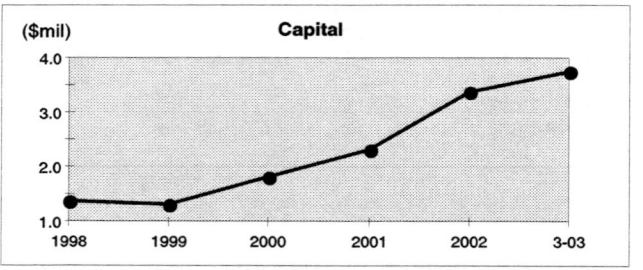

J M I C LIFE INSURANCE COMPANY — C — Fair

Major Rating Factors: Fair overall results on stability tests (3.7 on a scale of 0 to 10). Good quality investment portfolio (6.5) despite mixed results such as: no exposure to mortgages and substantial holdings of BBB bonds but minimal holdings in junk bonds. Strong capitalization (8.6) based on excellent risk adjusted capital (severe loss scenario). Moreover, capital levels have been consistently high over the last five years.
Other Rating Factors: Excellent profitability (8.7) with operating gains in each of the last five years. Excellent liquidity (8.1).
Principal Business: Credit health insurance (48%), credit life insurance (46%), and reinsurance (6%).
Principal Investments: NonCMO investment grade bonds (68%), CMOs and structured securities (21%), common & preferred stock (11%), and noninv. grade bonds (1%).
Investments in Affiliates: 3%
Group Affiliation: J M Family Enterprise Group
Licensed in: All states except CA, MI, NH, NY, RI, VT, PR
Commenced Business: June 1979
Address: 190 NW 12th Ave, Deerfield Beach, FL 33442
Phone: (954) 429-2007   **Domicile State:** FL   **NAIC Code:** 89958

Data Date	Weiss Safety Rating	RACR #1	RACR #2	Total Assets ($mil)	Capital ($mil)	Net Premium ($mil)	Net Income ($mil)
6-03	C	2.99	2.06	281.9	65.1	19.5	2.6
6-02	C	2.52	1.71	278.9	61.5	26.0	2.4
2002	C	3.10	2.26	226.5	62.5	51.7	3.2
2001	C	2.71	1.93	220.0	56.3	55.7	5.3
2000	C	2.45	1.70	211.6	51.3	51.0	7.8
1999	C	2.49	1.70	206.3	51.2	53.7	7.4
1998	C	2.36	1.62	194.0	43.2	54.9	2.8

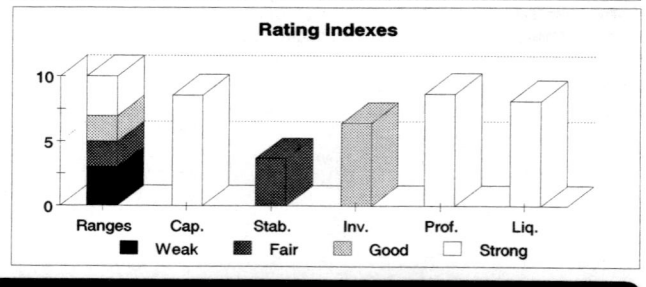

JEFFERSON PILOT FINANCIAL INS CO * — B+ — Good

Major Rating Factors: Good current capitalization (6.3 on a scale of 0 to 10) based on good risk adjusted capital (severe loss scenario), although results have slipped from the excellent range over the last two years. Good quality investment portfolio (5.4) despite mixed results such as: large holdings of BBB rated bonds but junk bond exposure equal to 84% of capital. Good overall profitability (6.9).
Other Rating Factors: Good overall results on stability tests (6.3) good operational trends and excellent risk diversification. Excellent liquidity (7.1).
Principal Business: Individual life insurance (56%), group health insurance (27%), group life insurance (14%), individual annuities (2%), and individual health insurance (1%).
Principal Investments: NonCMO investment grade bonds (49%), CMOs and structured securities (24%), mortgages in good standing (12%), noninv. grade bonds (7%), and misc. investments (7%).
Investments in Affiliates: 3%
Group Affiliation: Jefferson-Pilot Corp
Licensed in: All states except NY
Commenced Business: November 1903
Address: 8801 Indian Hills, Omaha, NE 68114
Phone: (336) 691-3000   **Domicile State:** NE   **NAIC Code:** 70254

Data Date	Weiss Safety Rating	RACR #1	RACR #2	Total Assets ($mil)	Capital ($mil)	Net Premium ($mil)	Net Income ($mil)
6-03	B+	1.57	0.91	11,630.2	829.8	732.3	129.7
6-02	B+	1.73	0.99	11,809.8	844.2	739.3	55.9
2002	B+	1.53	0.89	11,620.2	802.1	1,447.5	101.6
2001	B+	1.86	1.06	11,945.1	911.7	1,423.8	249.1
2000	B+	1.69	0.96	12,324.4	816.2	1,482.2	210.4
1999	B+	1.77	1.12	4,823.0	307.8	615.5	60.7
1998	B+	1.48	1.02	4,054.2	258.5	560.7	28.3

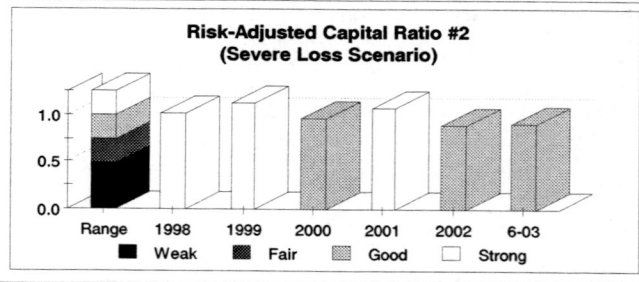

Winter 2003 - 04
II. Analysis of Largest Companies

JMH HEALTH PLAN — D — Weak

Major Rating Factors: Weak profitability index (2.5 on a scale of 0 to 10) with operating losses during 1999, 2000 and 2001. Weak liquidity (0.0) as a spike in claims may stretch capacity. Fair capitalization (3.4) based on weak current risk-adjusted capital (moderate loss scenario).
Other Rating Factors: Fair overall results on stability tests (3.8) based on a steep decline in capital during 2001, a steep decline in premium revenue in 2001. Good quality investment portfolio (5.5) containing no exposure to mortgages, junk bonds, or unaffiliated stocks.
Principal Business: Medicaid (29%), other (71%).
Mem Phys: 01: 3,576   00: 2,977   **01 MLR** 99%   / **01 Admin Exp** 6%
Enroll(000): Q2 02: 44   01: 43   00: 36   **Med Exp PMPM:** $67
Principal Investments: Cash and equiv (45%), other (55%)
Provider Compensation ($000): Contr fee ($16,707), capitation ($4,770)
Total Member Encounters: Phys (72,359), non-phys (35,295)
Group Affiliation: Public Health Trust of Dade County
Licensed in: FL
Address: 1801 NW 9th Ave Ste 700, Miami, FL 33136
Phone: (305) 575-3700   **Dom State:** FL   **Commenced Bus:** August 1985

Data Date	Weiss Safety Rating	RACR #1	RACR #2	Total Assets ($mil)	Capital ($mil)	Net Premium ($mil)	Net Income ($mil)
6-02	D	0.68	0.57	15.0	6.8	35.1	1.9
6-01	D	N/A	N/A	14.8	7.3	27.7	1.1
2001	D	0.00	0.00	16.3	4.9	32.3	-1.5
2000	D	0.80	0.67	11.8	6.2	45.6	-0.2
1999	U	1.07	0.91	10.5	6.4	35.9	-1.2
1998	N/A	N/A	N/A	10.9	7.6	31.2	N/A
1997	N/A	N/A	N/A	9.8	7.5	26.9	N/A

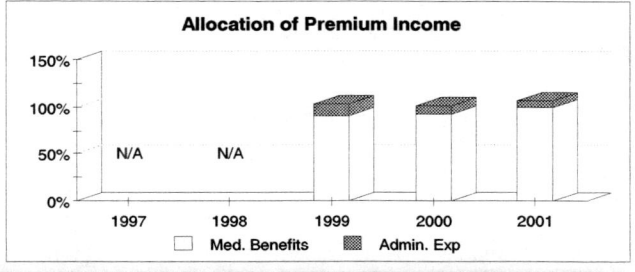

Allocation of Premium Income chart (1997-2001, Med. Benefits and Admin. Exp)

JOHN ALDEN LIFE INSURANCE COMPANY — C — Fair

Major Rating Factors: Fair profitability (4.4 on a scale of 0 to 10). Return on equity has been fair, averaging 6.9%. Fair overall results on stability tests (3.0). Good quality investment portfolio (6.8) despite mixed results such as: no exposure to mortgages and substantial holdings of BBB bonds but small junk bond holdings.
Other Rating Factors: Good liquidity (6.2). Strong capitalization (8.6) based on excellent risk adjusted capital (severe loss scenario).
Principal Business: Group health insurance (89%), individual health insurance (7%), individual life insurance (2%), and group life insurance (2%).
Principal Investments: NonCMO investment grade bonds (56%), CMOs and structured securities (29%), mortgages in good standing (6%), noninv. grade bonds (5%), and misc. investments (4%).
Investments in Affiliates: None
Group Affiliation: Fortis Inc
Licensed in: All states except NY, PR
Commenced Business: January 1974
Address: 7300 Corporate Center Dr, Miami, FL 33102-0270
Phone: (305) 715-3772   **Domicile State:** WI   **NAIC Code:** 65080

Data Date	Weiss Safety Rating	RACR #1	RACR #2	Total Assets ($mil)	Capital ($mil)	Net Premium ($mil)	Net Income ($mil)
6-03	C	3.07	2.07	672.3	142.5	163.5	25.1
6-02	C	1.46	1.07	691.3	144.9	160.5	14.7
2002	C	2.65	1.77	651.0	118.7	320.1	35.4
2001	C	2.29	1.56	696.2	129.7	106.1	8.2
2000	C	2.35	1.65	703.4	128.4	433.3	17.5
1999	C	1.90	1.27	744.5	109.7	492.6	22.1
1998	C	2.12	1.35	899.8	170.4	534.2	-84.1

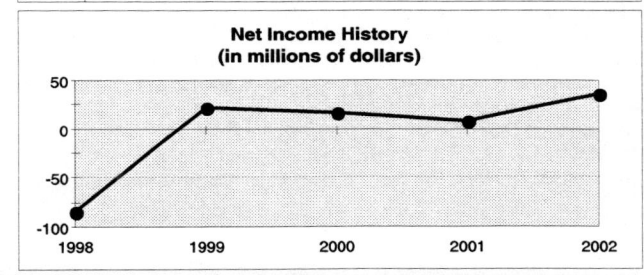

Net Income History (in millions of dollars), 1998-2002

JOHN DEERE HEALTH PLAN INC — B — Good

Major Rating Factors: Good overall profitability index (5.4 on a scale of 0 to 10) despite a decline in earnings during 2002. Good overall results on stability tests (5.7). Good liquidity (5.9) with sufficient resources (cash flows and marketable investments) to handle a spike in claims.
Other Rating Factors: Strong overall capitalization (7.0) based on excellent current risk-adjusted capital (severe loss scenario) despite some fluctuation in capital levels. High quality investment portfolio (9.9) containing little or no exposure to mortgages, junk bonds, or unaffiliated stocks.
Principal Business: Comp med (57%), Medicaid (22%), Medicare (18%), FEHB (1%), other (3%).
Mem Phys: 02: 11,189   01: 10,453   **02 MLR** 86%   / **02 Admin Exp** 13%
Enroll(000): Q1 03: 231   02: 207   01: 276   **Med Exp PMPM:** $174
Principal Investments: Cash and equiv (22%), nonaffiliate common stock (2%), other (76%).
Provider Compensation ($000): Contr fee ($260,805), bonus arrang ($231,779), capitation ($17,023), FFS ($3,501)
Total Member Encounters: Phys (1,373,898), non-phys (269,103)
Group Affiliation: Deere & Co
Licensed in: IL, IA, TN, VA
Address: 1300 River Drive, Moline, IL 61265
Phone: (309) 765-1200   **Dom State:** IL   **Commenced Bus:** July 1985

Data Date	Weiss Safety Rating	RACR #1	RACR #2	Total Assets ($mil)	Capital ($mil)	Net Premium ($mil)	Net Income ($mil)
3-03	B	1.38	1.15	178.8	73.1	153.3	0.7
3-02	B	1.50	1.17	193.9	74.9	158.7	0.2
2002	B	1.52	1.27	184.8	79.5	586.4	6.5
2001	B	1.51	1.18	188.4	74.3	572.2	7.9
2000	B	1.92	1.60	161.9	70.0	470.1	3.8
1999	B	2.29	1.90	134.0	71.0	424.9	6.0
1998	B	2.82	2.34	141.6	65.4	385.5	8.0

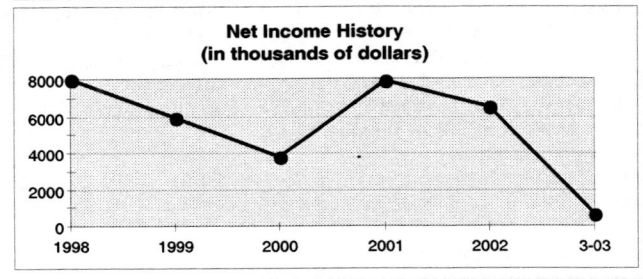

Net Income History (in thousands of dollars), 1998 through 3-03

www.WeissRatings.com   207   * Denotes a Weiss Recommended Company

II. Analysis of Largest Companies

Winter 2003 - 04

KAISER FOUNDATION HEALTH PLAN INC   B-   Good

Major Rating Factors: Good capitalization (6.1 on a scale of 0 to 10) based on fair current risk-adjusted capital (moderate loss scenario). Good liquidity (6.8) with sufficient resources (cash flows and marketable investments) to handle a spike in claims. Weak profitability index (2.2) with operating losses during 2002.
Other Rating Factors: Weak overall results on stability tests (2.7).
Principal Business: Managed care (76%)
Mem Phys: 02: N/A   01: N/A   **02 MLR** 103%   / **02 Admin Exp** 2%
Enroll(000): Q1 03: 6,581   02: 6,567   01: 6,433   **Med Exp PMPM:** $213
Principal Investments ($000): Cash and equiv ($40,415), other ($2,342,169)
Provider Compensation ($000): None
Total Member Encounters: N/A
Group Affiliation: Kaiser Foundation
Licensed in: CA, HI
Address: One Kaiser Plaza, Oakland, CA 94612
Phone: (510) 271-5910   **Dom State:** CA   **Commenced Bus:** N/A

Data Date	Weiss Safety Rating	RACR #1	RACR #2	Total Assets ($mil)	Capital ($mil)	Net Premium ($mil)	Net Income ($mil)
3-03	B-	0.91	0.61	5,132.0	920.1	4,571.4	37.4
3-02	B-	0.00	0.00	5,176.1	1,406.1	3,950.6	55.9
2002	B-	0.90	0.60	5,406.7	916.7	16,142.5	-117.6
2001	B-	1.14	0.77	5,368.3	1,336.1	14,129.9	120.3
2000	B	2.04	1.26	5,438.7	1,306.6	12,590.1	162.6
1999	B	1.83	1.14	5,975.3	1,177.0	11,214.1	25.7
1998	B	1.72	1.08	5,722.7	1,223.9	9,977.0	47.8

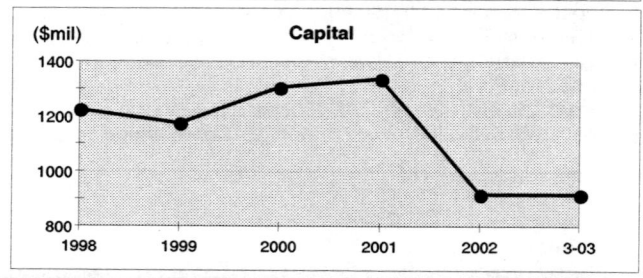

Capital ($mil) chart 1998–3-03: ~1225, ~1175, ~1305, ~1335, ~905, ~920

KAISER FOUNDATION HP MID-ATL STATES   C-   Fair

Major Rating Factors: Weak profitability index (0.9 on a scale of 0 to 10) with $90.5 million in losses in the last four years. Low quality investment portfolio (2.6) containing no exposure to mortgages, junk bonds, or unaffiliated stocks. Weak liquidity (0.7) as a spike in claims may stretch capacity.
Other Rating Factors: Good overall results on stability tests (5.3) despite fair risk-adjusted capital in prior years. Potentially strong support from affiliation with Kaiser Foundation. Strong capitalization (7.3) based on excellent current risk-adjusted capital (severe loss scenario) reflecting significant improvement over results in 1998.
Principal Business: Comp med (57%), FEHB (28%), Medicare (15%)
Mem Phys: 02: 8,406   01: 6,590   **02 MLR** 96%   / **02 Admin Exp** 6%
Enroll(000): Q1 03: 502   02: 508   01: 516   **Med Exp PMPM:** $201
Principal Investments: Real estate (53%), cash and equiv (1%), other (47%)
Provider Compensation ($000): Contr fee ($404,950), salary ($267,069), FFS ($125,719), capitation ($2,614), other ($391,646)
Total Member Encounters: Phys (1,805,057), non-phys (1,058,999)
Group Affiliation: Kaiser Foundation
Licensed in: DC, MD, VA
Address: 2101 E Jefferson St, Rockville, MD 20852
Phone: (301) 816-6470   **Dom State:** MD   **Commenced Bus:** November 1972

Data Date	Weiss Safety Rating	RACR #1	RACR #2	Total Assets ($mil)	Capital ($mil)	Net Premium ($mil)	Net Income ($mil)
3-03	C-	1.58	1.31	434.3	103.7	330.3	3.6
3-02	C-	1.98	1.56	442.2	99.9	334.7	1.0
2002	C-	1.46	1.22	427.1	97.1	1,291.5	-36.6
2001	C-	1.97	1.56	429.2	98.0	1,245.7	-16.7
2000	C+	1.40	1.11	465.7	126.3	1,177.5	-28.0
1999	C+	0.76	0.73	457.6	146.5	1,071.7	-9.2
1998	B	0.61	0.61	423.1	117.8	937.4	13.0

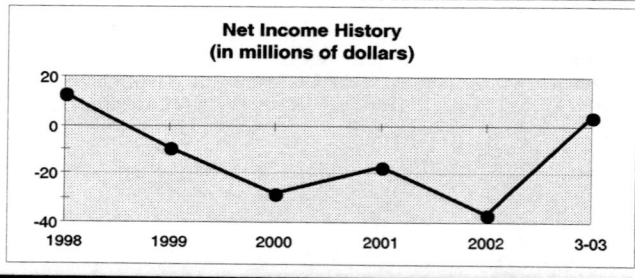

Net Income History (in millions of dollars) chart 1998–3-03

KAISER FOUNDATION HP NORTHWEST   B   Good

Major Rating Factors: Excellent profitability (8.4 on a scale of 0 to 10) despite a decline in earnings during 2002. Strong capitalization (10.0) based on excellent current risk-adjusted capital (severe loss scenario) reflecting significant improvement over results in 1998. Excellent overall results on stability tests (7.8) based on consistent premium and capital growth in the last five years.
Other Rating Factors: Excellent liquidity (7.1) with ample operational cash flow and liquid investments. Low quality investment portfolio (2.8) containing little or no exposure to mortgages, junk bonds, or unaffiliated stocks.
Principal Business: Comp med (60%), Medicare (25%), FEHB (7%), dental (4%), Medicaid (3%)
Mem Phys: 02: 891   01: 879   **02 MLR** 92%   / **02 Admin Exp** 1%
Enroll(000): Q1 03: 444   02: 446   01: 447   **Med Exp PMPM:** $230
Principal Investments: Real estate (88%), other (13%)
Provider Compensation ($000): Salary ($531,287), contr fee ($258,414), FFS ($45,432), capitation ($1,245), other ($386,616)
Total Member Encounters: Phys (1,527,156), non-phys (1,124,210)
Group Affiliation: Kaiser Foundation
Licensed in: OR, WA
Address: 500 NE Multnomah St, Suite 100, Portland, OR 97232-2099
Phone: (503) 813-2800   **Dom State:** OR   **Commenced Bus:** May 1942

Data Date	Weiss Safety Rating	RACR #1	RACR #2	Total Assets ($mil)	Capital ($mil)	Net Premium ($mil)	Net Income ($mil)
3-03	B	3.85	3.20	463.9	203.7	353.5	11.6
3-02	B	2.91	2.28	367.5	178.0	331.4	15.4
2002	B	3.51	2.93	468.2	189.5	1,338.3	9.2
2001	B	2.90	2.27	365.0	160.5	1,154.0	18.5
2000	B	1.78	1.38	345.0	145.6	1,035.2	26.6
1999	B-	1.31	1.05	302.1	119.5	943.4	16.2
1998	B-	0.86	0.75	298.9	98.3	854.7	12.9

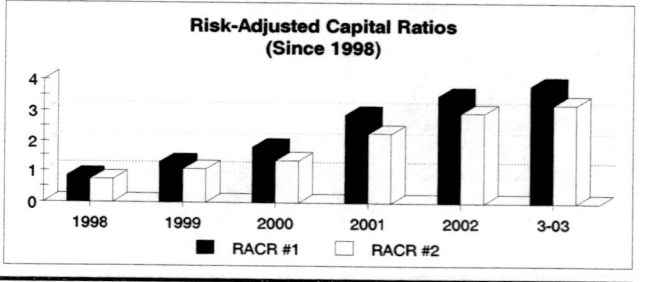

Risk-Adjusted Capital Ratios (Since 1998) bar chart — RACR #1 (black), RACR #2 (white)

Winter 2003 - 04 II. Analysis of Largest Companies

KAISER FOUNDATION HP OF CO — B Good

Major Rating Factors: Good overall profitability index (5.8 on a scale of 0 to 10) despite operating losses during 1998. Good liquidity (6.8) with sufficient resources (cash flows and marketable investments) to handle a spike in claims. Fair overall results on stability tests (3.1). Potential support from affiliation with Kaiser Foundation.

Other Rating Factors: Strong capitalization (8.7) based on excellent current risk-adjusted capital (severe loss scenario) reflecting significant improvement over results in 1998. High quality investment portfolio (7.5) containing no exposure to mortgages, junk bonds, or unaffiliated stocks.

Principal Business: Comp med (59%), Medicare (33%), FEHB (7%)
Mem Phys: 02: 628   **01:** 598   **02 MLR** 90%   **/ 02 Admin Exp** 6%
Enroll(000): Q1 03: 402   **02:** 402   **01:** 406   **Med Exp PMPM:** $215
Principal Investments: Real estate (53%), cash and equiv (8%), other (39%)
Provider Compensation ($000): Contr fee ($377,432), salary ($131,331), FFS ($35,439), capitation ($2,237), other ($505,189)
Total Member Encounters: Phys (1,357,164), non-phys (1,263,884)
Group Affiliation: Kaiser Foundation
Licensed in: CO
Address: 10350 E Dakota Ave, Denver, CO 80231
Phone: (303) 338-3454   **Dom State:** CO   **Commenced Bus:** July 1969

Data Date	Weiss Safety Rating	RACR #1	RACR #2	Total Assets ($mil)	Capital ($mil)	Net Premium ($mil)	Net Income ($mil)
3-03	B	2.72	2.26	384.6	125.8	319.9	24.8
3-02	B	2.94	2.34	340.0	136.0	300.8	14.6
2002	B	2.25	1.87	383.6	104.4	1,154.6	42.4
2001	B	2.83	2.27	372.3	142.3	980.2	38.2
2000	B-	0.88	0.71	373.5	123.1	854.9	38.1
1999	B-	0.80	0.64	281.6	53.5	757.2	21.0
1998	B-	0.66	0.52	287.4	55.7	698.8	-10.6

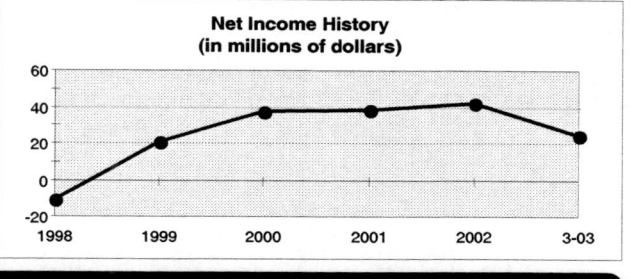

Net Income History (in millions of dollars)

KAISER FOUNDATION HP OF GA — B Good

Major Rating Factors: Good liquidity (6.9 on a scale of 0 to 10) with sufficient resources (cash flows and marketable investments) to handle a spike in claims. Excellent profitability (8.7) despite a decline in earnings during 2002. Strong capitalization (7.9) based on excellent current risk-adjusted capital (severe loss scenario) reflecting significant improvement over results in 1998.

Other Rating Factors: High quality investment portfolio (7.1) containing no exposure to mortgages, junk bonds, or unaffiliated stocks. Excellent overall results on stability tests (8.1) based on consistent premium and capital growth in the last five years. Rating is significantly influenced by the fair financial results of Kaiser Foundation.

Principal Business: Comp med (77%), Medicare (14%), FEHB (10%)
Mem Phys: 02: 235   **01:** 223   **02 MLR** 95%   **/ 02 Admin Exp** 4%
Enroll(000): Q1 03: 272   **02:** 275   **01:** 273   **Med Exp PMPM:** $195
Principal Investments: Real estate (59%), cash and equiv (41%)
Provider Compensation ($000): Contr fee ($268,309), FFS ($7,452), capitation ($1,184), other ($366,098)
Total Member Encounters: Phys (156,509), non-phys (115,733)
Group Affiliation: Kaiser Foundation
Licensed in: GA
Address: 3495 Piedmont Road NE, Atlanta, GA 30305-1736
Phone: (404) 364-7000   **Dom State:** GA   **Commenced Bus:** October 1985

Data Date	Weiss Safety Rating	RACR #1	RACR #2	Total Assets ($mil)	Capital ($mil)	Net Premium ($mil)	Net Income ($mil)
3-03	B	2.10	1.75	171.5	64.7	181.5	1.2
3-02	B-	1.93	1.54	165.0	53.8	165.4	5.2
2002	B	1.95	1.62	163.1	61.0	675.0	8.2
2001	B-	1.94	1.54	158.3	55.4	608.2	24.6
2000	C	1.23	0.97	140.6	52.1	493.1	9.3
1999	C	0.88	0.68	143.5	36.0	444.8	3.0
1998	B-	0.34	0.27	128.2	31.9	401.6	6.3

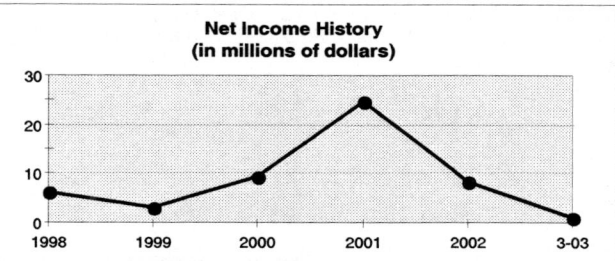

Net Income History (in millions of dollars)

KAISER FOUNDATION HP OF OH — B- Good

Major Rating Factors: Fair profitability index (4.4 on a scale of 0 to 10) with operating losses during 2002. Fair overall results on stability tests (4.9) based on excessive capital growth during 2002. Rating is significantly influenced by the fair financial results of Kaiser Foundation. Strong capitalization (9.3) based on excellent current risk-adjusted capital (severe loss scenario) reflecting significant improvement over results in 1998.

Other Rating Factors: High quality investment portfolio (9.1) containing no exposure to mortgages, junk bonds, or unaffiliated stocks. Excellent liquidity (7.2) with ample operational cash flow and liquid investments.

Principal Business: Comp med (59%), Medicare (35%), FEHB (5%)
Mem Phys: 02: 282   **01:** 281   **02 MLR** 95%   **/ 02 Admin Exp** 3%
Enroll(000): Q1 03: 153   **02:** 158   **01:** 167   **Med Exp PMPM:** $248
Principal Investments: Cash and equiv (72%), real estate (27%)
Provider Compensation ($000): Salary ($300,463), contr fee ($149,447), FFS ($28,302)
Total Member Encounters: Phys (550,748), non-phys (129,132)
Group Affiliation: Kaiser Foundation
Licensed in: OH
Address: 1001 Lakeside Ave Ste 1200, Cleveland, OH 44114
Phone: (510) 271-5910   **Dom State:** OH   **Commenced Bus:** October 1976

Data Date	Weiss Safety Rating	RACR #1	RACR #2	Total Assets ($mil)	Capital ($mil)	Net Premium ($mil)	Net Income ($mil)
3-03	B-	3.19	2.66	221.6	67.8	113.0	1.8
3-02	B-	2.42	1.96	217.4	54.8	125.9	-0.8
2002	B-	3.05	2.54	220.5	65.9	507.8	-4.7
2001	B-	2.43	1.96	214.6	54.1	484.6	8.7
2000	B-	1.70	1.46	241.2	81.9	454.7	14.4
1999	B-	1.12	0.94	194.3	54.7	440.7	14.2
1998	B-	0.66	0.56	195.0	43.4	420.0	21.4

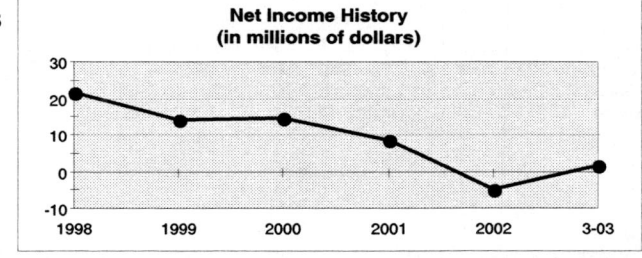

Net Income History (in millions of dollars)

www.WeissRatings.com   * Denotes a Weiss Recommended Company

II. Analysis of Largest Companies
Winter 2003 - 04

KAISER PERMANENTE HEALTH ALTERNATIVE — B — Good

Major Rating Factors: Fair profitability index (4.5 on a scale of 0 to 10) with operating losses during 2001. Strong capitalization (10.0) based on excellent current risk-adjusted capital (severe loss scenario). High quality investment portfolio (9.9) containing no exposure to mortgages, junk bonds, or unaffiliated stocks.
Other Rating Factors: Excellent liquidity (7.6) with ample operational cash flow and liquid investments.
Principal Business: Dental (73%), comp med (27%)
Mem Phys: 02: N/A **01:** N/A **02 MLR** 92% **/ 02 Admin Exp** 2%
Enroll(000): Q1 03: 16 **02:** 11 **01:** 15 **Med Exp PMPM:** $31
Principal Investments: Cash and equiv (46%), other (54%)
Provider Compensation ($000): Capitation ($4,518), FFS ($309)
Total Member Encounters: N/A
Group Affiliation: Kaiser Foundation
Licensed in: OR, WA
Address: 500 NE Multnomah St Ste 100, Portland, OR 97232-2099
Phone: (503) 813-2800 **Dom State:** OR **Commenced Bus:** August 1989

Data Date	Weiss Safety Rating	RACR #1	RACR #2	Total Assets ($mil)	Capital ($mil)	Net Premium ($mil)	Net Income ($mil)
3-03	B	5.65	4.71	4.0	3.7	1.9	0.3
3-02	B-	2.07	1.77	3.5	3.3	1.3	0.0
2002	B	5.08	4.23	3.8	3.5	5.2	0.3
2001	B-	2.07	1.77	3.5	3.4	5.0	-0.1
2000	B-	3.44	3.09	3.5	3.3	4.0	0.0
1999	B-	3.13	2.82	3.4	3.3	2.2	0.0
1998	B-	3.12	2.81	3.2	3.2	1.5	0.1

Risk-Adjusted Capital Ratios (Since 1998)

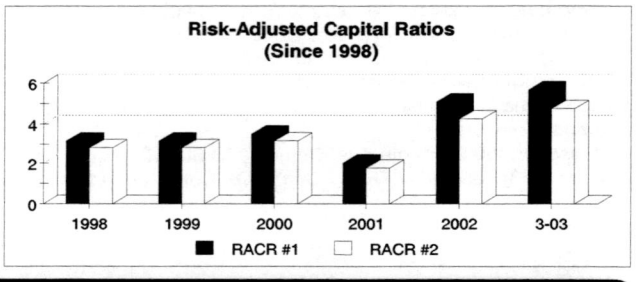

KAISER PERMANENTE INS CO — B- — Good

Major Rating Factors: Fair overall results on stability tests (3.7 on a scale of 0 to 10). Strong capitalization (8.4) based on excellent risk adjusted capital (severe loss scenario). Moreover, capital has steadily grown over the last five years. High quality investment portfolio (9.8) with no exposure to mortgages and no exposure to junk bonds.
Other Rating Factors: Excellent profitability (8.4) with operating gains in each of the last five years. Excellent liquidity (7.7).
Principal Business: Group health insurance (99%) and reinsurance (1%).
Principal Investments: NonCMO investment grade bonds (96%) and cash (4%).
Investments in Affiliates: None
Group Affiliation: Kaiser Foundation
Licensed in: CA, CO, DC, GA, HI, KS, MD, MO, OH, OR, SC, VA, WA
Commenced Business: January 1995
Address: One Kaiser Plaza Suite 25B, Oakland, CA 94612
Phone: (510) 271-6321 **Domicile State:** CA **NAIC Code:** 60053

Data Date	Weiss Safety Rating	RACR #1	RACR #2	Total Assets ($mil)	Capital ($mil)	Net Premium ($mil)	Net Income ($mil)
6-03	B-	2.29	1.91	57.4	31.1	39.7	1.6
6-02	B-	2.71	2.08	54.7	28.4	36.0	2.0
2002	B-	2.27	1.89	54.4	29.5	72.8	2.9
2001	B-	3.54	2.61	49.9	26.3	36.2	3.8
2000	B-	2.35	1.79	34.2	11.8	19.0	1.4
1999	B-	2.10	1.89	31.8	10.6	9.9	2.1
1998	B	1.90	1.65	28.9	8.5	9.3	0.8

Rating Indexes

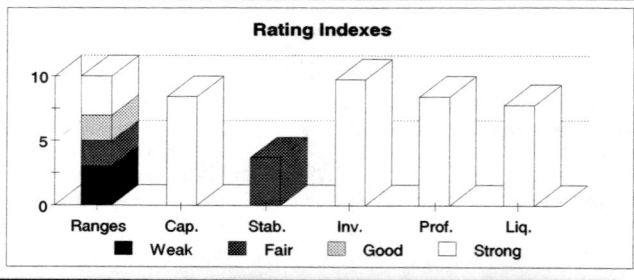

KANAWHA INSURANCE COMPANY — B- — Good

Major Rating Factors: Good quality investment portfolio (6.3 on a scale of 0 to 10) despite mixed results such as: substantial holdings of BBB bonds but moderate junk bond exposure. Good overall profitability (5.4) despite operating losses during the first six months of 2003. Return on equity has been low, averaging 4.5%. Good liquidity (6.4).
Other Rating Factors: Fair overall results on stability tests (4.6). Strong capitalization (7.3) based on excellent risk adjusted capital (severe loss scenario).
Principal Business: Individual health insurance (73%), individual life insurance (14%), reinsurance (7%), group health insurance (3%), and other lines (3%).
Principal Investments: NonCMO investment grade bonds (58%), mortgages in good standing (11%), common & preferred stock (8%), CMOs and structured securities (8%), and misc. investments (15%).
Investments in Affiliates: 1%
Group Affiliation: Kanawha Ins Group
Licensed in: All states except AK, DC, ME, NH, NY, VT, PR
Commenced Business: December 1958
Address: 210 S White St, Lancaster, SC 29721
Phone: (803) 283-5300 **Domicile State:** SC **NAIC Code:** 65110

Data Date	Weiss Safety Rating	RACR #1	RACR #2	Total Assets ($mil)	Capital ($mil)	Net Premium ($mil)	Net Income ($mil)
6-03	B-	1.75	1.17	499.8	65.4	53.2	-1.0
6-02	B-	1.91	1.27	479.6	69.9	49.3	1.5
2002	B-	1.69	1.12	494.5	67.2	98.5	-3.0
2001	B-	1.99	1.31	479.1	72.1	86.3	6.1
2000	B-	2.03	1.30	470.8	72.1	78.3	3.9
1999	B	2.04	1.27	474.9	76.2	80.3	6.4
1998	B	2.02	1.42	398.9	71.1	70.0	9.2

Rating Indexes

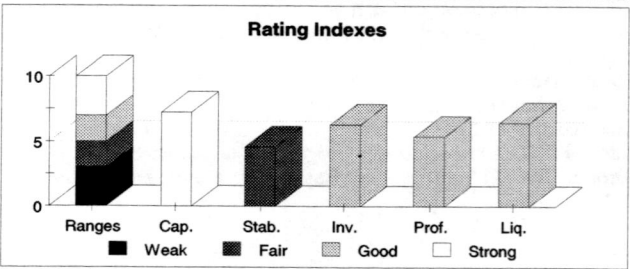

KANSAS CITY LIFE INSURANCE COMPANY — B — Good

Major Rating Factors: Good overall capitalization (6.0 on a scale of 0 to 10) based on good risk adjusted capital (severe loss scenario). However, capital levels have fluctuated somewhat during past years. Good overall profitability (6.4). Return on equity has been excellent over the last five years averaging 19.1%. Good liquidity (6.5).
Other Rating Factors: Fair quality investment portfolio (4.1). Fair overall results on stability tests (4.0).
Principal Business: Individual life insurance (50%), group health insurance (26%), reinsurance (10%), individual annuities (8%), and group life insurance (5%).
Principal Investments: NonCMO investment grade bonds (44%), CMOs and structured securities (19%), mortgages in good standing (15%), noninv. grade bonds (8%), and misc. investments (14%).
Investments in Affiliates: 5%
Group Affiliation: Kansas City Life Group
Licensed in: All states except NY, VT, PR
Commenced Business: May 1895
Address: 3520 Broadway, Kansas City, MO 64111-2565
Phone: (816) 753-7000 **Domicile State:** MO **NAIC Code:** 65129

Data Date	Weiss Safety Rating	RACR #1	RACR #2	Total Assets ($mil)	Capital ($mil)	Net Premium ($mil)	Net Income ($mil)
6-03	B	1.28	0.88	2,740.8	220.8	97.5	67.7
6-02	B	1.28	0.93	2,652.3	270.5	92.3	11.3
2002	B	1.36	0.92	2,649.3	241.9	180.0	14.8
2001	B	1.28	0.92	2,649.3	266.2	173.9	23.5
2000	B	1.50	1.01	2,621.0	248.0	290.0	42.3
1999	B	1.40	0.93	2,636.3	219.9	279.5	42.0
1998	B	1.41	0.94	2,488.1	209.2	292.9	36.2

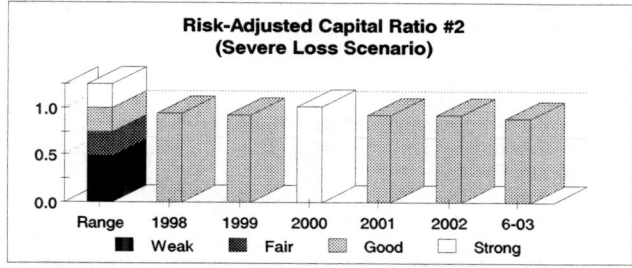

Risk-Adjusted Capital Ratio #2 (Severe Loss Scenario)

KERN HEALTH SYSTEMS — B — Good

Major Rating Factors: Good overall results on stability tests (6.1 on a scale of 0 to 10). Excellent profitability (10.0) with operating gains in each of the last five years. Strong capitalization index (10.0) based on excellent current risk-adjusted capital (severe loss scenario).
Other Rating Factors: Excellent liquidity (8.3) with ample operational cash flow and liquid investments.
Principal Business: Managed care (2%)
Mem Phys: 02: N/A **01:** N/A **02 MLR** 81% **/ 02 Admin Exp** 8%
Enroll(000): **02:** 75 **01:** 68 **Med Exp PMPM:** $80
Principal Investments ($000): Cash and equiv ($76,621), other ($69,506)
Provider Compensation ($000): None
Total Member Encounters: N/A
Group Affiliation: None
Licensed in: CA
Address: 1600 Norris Rd, Bakersfield, CA 93308-2234
Phone: (661) 391-4000 **Dom State:** CA **Commenced Bus:** June 1996

Data Date	Weiss Safety Rating	RACR #1	RACR #2	Total Assets ($mil)	Capital ($mil)	Net Premium ($mil)	Net Income ($mil)
2002	B	9.80	5.96	81.5	61.6	84.3	11.8
2001	B-	0.00	0.00	73.9	49.8	70.9	9.0
2000	B-	N/A	N/A	56.4	40.8	58.1	9.6
1999	C+	2.02	1.46	46.3	31.2	53.9	13.2
1998	C+	1.52	1.08	37.9	18.1	52.9	9.7

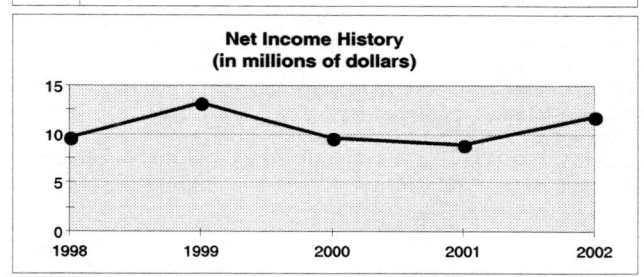

Net Income History (in millions of dollars)

KEYSTONE HEALTH PLAN CENTRAL INC * — B+ — Good

Major Rating Factors: Excellent profitability (7.5 on a scale of 0 to 10) despite a decline in earnings during 2002. Strong capitalization (7.7) based on excellent current risk-adjusted capital (severe loss scenario) reflecting significant improvement over results in 1998. High quality investment portfolio (9.9).
Other Rating Factors: Excellent overall results on stability tests (7.8) based on consistent premium and capital growth in the last five years but a decline in enrollment during 2002. Fair financial strength from affiliates. Excellent liquidity (7.1) with ample operational cash flow and liquid investments.
Principal Business: Comp med (52%), Medicare (38%), FEHB (2%), other (7%)
Mem Phys: 02: 1,927 **01:** 1,837 **02 MLR** 85% **/ 02 Admin Exp** 10%
Enroll(000): Q1 03: 144 **02:** 145 **01:** 158 **Med Exp PMPM:** $202
Principal Investments: Cash and equiv (64%), nonaffiliate common stock (4%), other (34%)
Provider Compensation ($000): Contr fee ($297,490), capitation ($39,045), FFS ($34,046)
Total Member Encounters: Phys (1,073,670), non-phys (63,349)
Group Affiliation: Capital Bl Cross/Highmark Inc
Licensed in: PA
Address: 300 Corporate Center Dr 602, Camp Hill, PA 17011
Phone: (717) 763-3458 **Dom State:** PA **Commenced Bus:** November 1988

Data Date	Weiss Safety Rating	RACR #1	RACR #2	Total Assets ($mil)	Capital ($mil)	Net Premium ($mil)	Net Income ($mil)
3-03	B+	1.89	1.58	166.0	54.9	112.5	3.5
3-02	B	1.84	1.53	155.9	46.0	108.0	1.4
2002	B+	2.03	1.69	186.4	51.3	429.6	8.7
2001	B	1.44	1.20	162.0	43.4	416.4	10.8
2000	B-	1.11	0.93	131.8	32.3	380.0	-0.3
1999	B-	1.11	0.93	123.4	24.4	332.6	1.2
1998	C+	0.91	0.76	108.2	22.7	335.2	1.6

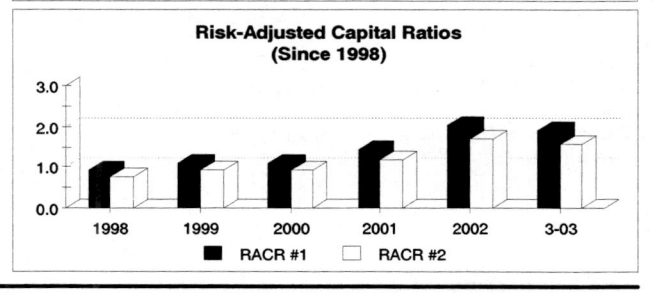

Risk-Adjusted Capital Ratios (Since 1998)

Denotes a Weiss Recommended Company

II. Analysis of Largest Companies

Winter 2003 - 04

KEYSTONE HEALTH PLAN EAST INC * — B+ Good

Major Rating Factors: Good liquidity (6.0 on a scale of 0 to 10) with sufficient resources (cash flows and marketable investments) to handle a spike in claims. Excellent profitability (8.1) despite a decline in earnings during 2002. Strong overall capitalization (8.7) based on excellent current risk-adjusted capital (severe loss scenario) despite some fluctuation in capital levels.
Other Rating Factors: High quality investment portfolio (8.9). Excellent overall results on stability tests (8.4) based on steady enrollment growth, averaging 8% over the past five years, consistent premium and capital growth in the last five years. Good financial strength from affiliates.
Principal Business: Comp med (38%), Medicare (34%), Medicaid (23%), FEHB (4%)
Mem Phys: 02: 18,501 **01:** 17,425 **02 MLR** 89% **/ 02 Admin Exp** 9%
Enroll(000): Q1 03: 1,220 **02:** 1,227 **01:** 1,059 **Med Exp PMPM:** $237
Principal Investments: Nonaffiliate common stock (9%), affiliate common stock (3%), cash and equiv (2%), pref stock (1%), other (85%)
Provider Compensation ($000): Contr fee ($1,688,603), capitation ($1,486,640), FFS ($54,355)
Total Member Encounters: Phys (10,064,835), non-phys (3,059,853)
Group Affiliation: Independence Bl Cross/Highmark Inc
Licensed in: PA
Address: 1901 Market St, Philadelphia, PA 19101
Phone: (215) 241-2001 **Dom State:** PA **Commenced Bus:** January 1987

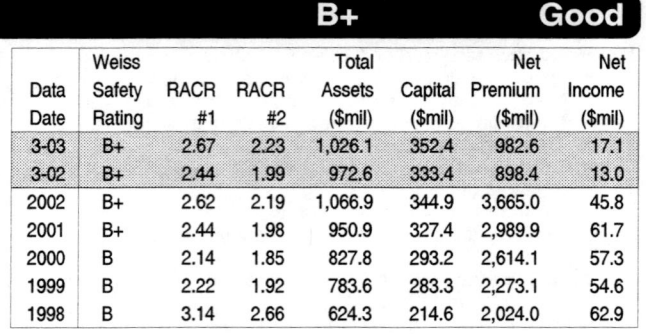

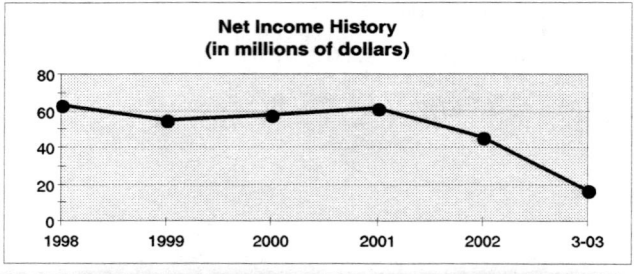

Data Date	Weiss Safety Rating	RACR #1	RACR #2	Total Assets ($mil)	Capital ($mil)	Net Premium ($mil)	Net Income ($mil)
3-03	B+	2.67	2.23	1,026.1	352.4	982.6	17.1
3-02	B+	2.44	1.99	972.6	333.4	898.4	13.0
2002	B+	2.62	2.19	1,066.9	344.9	3,665.0	45.8
2001	B+	2.44	1.98	950.9	327.4	2,989.9	61.7
2000	B	2.14	1.85	827.8	293.2	2,614.1	57.3
1999	B	2.22	1.92	783.6	283.3	2,273.1	54.6
1998	B	3.14	2.66	624.3	214.6	2,024.0	62.9

Net Income History (in millions of dollars)

KEYSTONE HEALTH PLAN WEST INC * — B+ Good

Major Rating Factors: Good overall profitability index (5.9 on a scale of 0 to 10) despite a decline in earnings during 2002. Good liquidity (6.9) with sufficient resources (cash flows and marketable investments) to handle a spike in claims. Strong capitalization (8.0) based on excellent current risk-adjusted capital (severe loss scenario) reflecting significant improvement over results in 1998.
Other Rating Factors: High quality investment portfolio (9.9) containing no exposure to mortgages, junk bonds, or unaffiliated stocks. Excellent overall results on stability tests (7.8) based on consistent premium and capital growth in the last five years. Fair financial strength from affiliates.
Principal Business: Medicare (76%), comp med (23%)
Mem Phys: 02: 11,099 **01:** 10,790 **02 MLR** 91% **/ 02 Admin Exp** 7%
Enroll(000): Q1 03: 386 **02:** 411 **01:** 373 **Med Exp PMPM:** $355
Principal Investments: Cash and equiv (42%), other (58%)
Provider Compensation ($000): Contr fee ($1,554,888), capitation ($76,809), bonus arrang ($3,946)
Total Member Encounters: Phys (3,496,707), non-phys (637,709)
Group Affiliation: Highmark Inc
Licensed in: PA
Address: Fifth Ave Pl, 120 Fifth Ave, Pittsburgh, PA 15222-3099
Phone: (412) 544-7000 **Dom State:** PA **Commenced Bus:** December 1986

Data Date	Weiss Safety Rating	RACR #1	RACR #2	Total Assets ($mil)	Capital ($mil)	Net Premium ($mil)	Net Income ($mil)
3-03	B+	2.12	1.77	498.2	224.8	486.3	14.3
3-02	B	2.38	1.88	482.6	202.8	439.8	11.7
2002	B+	2.01	1.68	588.5	212.6	1,822.8	17.1
2001	B	1.89	1.49	523.1	185.3	1,540.7	29.1
2000	B-	1.84	1.52	475.0	149.9	1,518.7	59.6
1999	C+	1.27	1.05	502.4	103.3	1,348.2	0.3
1998	C+	0.83	0.70	383.7	64.5	1,203.9	-10.6

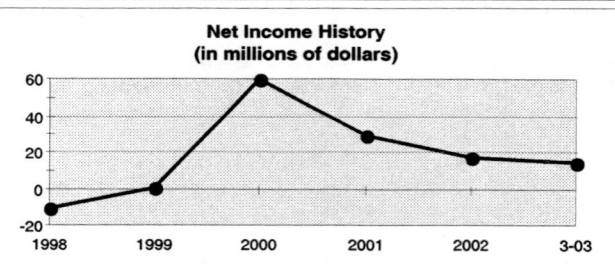

Net Income History (in millions of dollars)

LA HEALTH SERVICE & INDEMNITY CO — B Good

Major Rating Factors: Good liquidity (5.6 on a scale of 0 to 10) with sufficient resources (cash flows and marketable investments) to handle a spike in claims. Fair profitability index (4.2) with operating losses during 1999. Strong capitalization (8.2) based on excellent current risk-adjusted capital (severe loss scenario) despite some fluctuation in capital levels.
Other Rating Factors: High quality investment portfolio (9.3) containing little or no exposure to mortgages, junk bonds, or unaffiliated stocks.
Principal Business: Comp med (73%), FEHB (20%), med supp (7%)
Mem Phys: 02: 10,482 **01:** 10,458 **02 MLR** 80% **/ 02 Admin Exp** 21%
Enroll(000): Q1 03: 537 **02:** 496 **01:** 458 **Med Exp PMPM:** $134
Principal Investments: Affiliate common stock (16%), real estate (9%), nonaffiliate common stock (5%), other (76%)
Provider Compensation ($000): FFS ($296,574), contr fee ($283,507), other ($172,883)
Total Member Encounters: Phys (3,928,929), non-phys (813,004)
Group Affiliation: Louisiana Health Services
Licensed in: LA
Address: 5525 Reitz Ave, Baton Rouge, LA 70809-3802
Phone: (225) 295-3307 **Dom State:** LA **Commenced Bus:** January 1975

Data Date	Weiss Safety Rating	RACR #1	RACR #2	Total Assets ($mil)	Capital ($mil)	Net Premium ($mil)	Net Income ($mil)
3-03	B	2.34	1.95	409.6	182.0	259.1	9.2
3-02	B	0.00	0.00	369.9	159.2	221.6	10.5
2002	B	2.22	1.85	410.4	173.3	954.8	27.3
2001	N/A	N/A	N/A	339.9	141.5	817.5	N/A
2000	U	1.60	1.24	279.7	115.1	875.3	7.3
1999	C+	1.56	1.21	264.0	106.7	796.1	-15.7
1998	C+	1.70	1.32	250.4	118.5	688.3	10.3

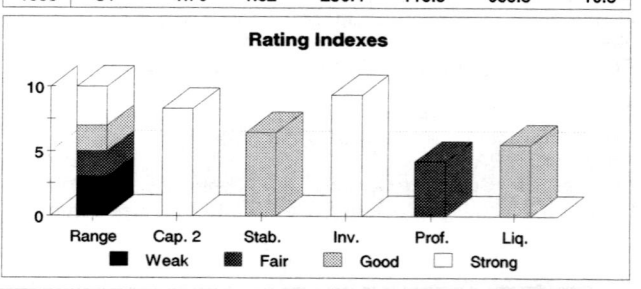

Rating Indexes (Range, Cap. 2, Stab., Inv., Prof., Liq.) — Weak, Fair, Good, Strong

Winter 2003 - 04   II. Analysis of Largest Companies

LIBERTY LIFE ASSURANCE COMPANY OF BOSTON — B- Good

Major Rating Factors: Good capitalization (5.1 on a scale of 0 to 10) based on good risk adjusted capital (moderate loss scenario). Fair overall results on stability tests (3.5) including fair risk adjusted capital in prior years. Low quality investment portfolio (2.6) containing substantial holdings of BBB bonds in addition to significant exposure to junk bonds.
Other Rating Factors: Weak profitability (2.1) with investment rated income below regulatory standards in relation to interest assumptions of reserves. Excellent liquidity (7.8).
Principal Business: Group health insurance (31%), individual annuities (29%), group life insurance (21%), and individual life insurance (19%).
Principal Investments: NonCMO investment grade bonds (57%), CMOs and structured securities (31%), noninv. grade bonds (8%), cash (2%), and policy loans (1%).
Investments in Affiliates: None
Group Affiliation: Liberty Mutual Group
Licensed in: All states except PR
Commenced Business: January 1964
Address: 175 Berkeley St, Boston, MA 02117
Phone: (617) 357-9500 **Domicile State:** MA **NAIC Code:** 65315

Data Date	Weiss Safety Rating	RACR #1	RACR #2	Total Assets ($mil)	Capital ($mil)	Net Premium ($mil)	Net Income ($mil)
6-03	B-	1.06	0.51	7,190.9	125.3	248.3	0.2
6-02	B-	1.35	0.65	7,407.5	147.1	239.9	-4.0
2002	B-	1.07	0.52	6,725.4	124.8	469.0	-30.7
2001	B-	1.14	0.55	6,659.2	131.0	411.2	-10.1
2000	B-	1.46	0.74	6,183.0	140.6	954.2	-0.1
1999	B-	1.57	0.88	5,308.4	141.9	864.6	12.9
1998	B-	1.64	0.96	4,508.3	115.4	668.1	9.7

Junk Bonds as a % of Capital

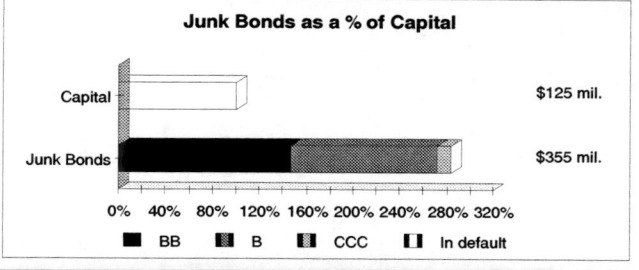

Capital: $125 mil.
Junk Bonds: $355 mil.

0% 40% 80% 120% 160% 200% 240% 280% 320%

■ BB ■ B ■ CCC □ In default

LIBERTY LIFE INSURANCE COMPANY — B- Good

Major Rating Factors: Good overall results on stability tests (5.2 on a scale of 0 to 10) despite fair financial strength of affiliated RBC Holdings (USA) Group and fair risk adjusted capital in prior years. Other stability subfactors include excellent operational trends and excellent risk diversification. Good current capitalization (6.5) based on good risk adjusted capital (severe loss scenario), although results have slipped from the excellent range during the last year. Good overall profitability (6.8).
Other Rating Factors: Good liquidity (6.8). Fair quality investment portfolio (4.6).
Principal Business: Individual life insurance (51%), group health insurance (32%), group life insurance (8%), individual health insurance (5%), and individual annuities (4%).
Principal Investments: CMOs and structured securities (36%), nonCMO investment grade bonds (32%), mortgages in good standing (17%), policy loans (5%), and misc. investments (10%).
Investments in Affiliates: None
Group Affiliation: RBC Holdings (USA) Group
Licensed in: All states except NY, PR
Commenced Business: January 1906
Address: 2000 Wade Hampton Blvd, Greenville, SC 29615
Phone: (864) 609-3645 **Domicile State:** SC **NAIC Code:** 65323

Data Date	Weiss Safety Rating	RACR #1	RACR #2	Total Assets ($mil)	Capital ($mil)	Net Premium ($mil)	Net Income ($mil)
6-03	B-	1.64	0.94	1,453.9	193.2	117.4	6.5
6-02	B-	1.88	1.03	1,358.8	123.5	117.0	6.2
2002	B-	1.82	1.01	1,399.1	131.7	231.8	11.2
2001	B-	1.71	0.95	1,346.4	114.5	242.3	20.0
2000	C+	1.31	0.70	1,302.0	81.3	248.8	33.4
1999	C+	1.72	0.97	1,366.6	140.2	244.5	17.5
1998	C+	1.83	1.03	1,353.5	146.3	249.9	25.0

RBC Holdings (USA) Group Composite Group Rating: C+ Largest Group Members	Assets ($mil)	Weiss Safety Rating
BUSINESS MEN'S ASSURANCE CO OF AMER	2633	C
LIBERTY LIFE INS CO	1399	B-

LIBERTY NATIONAL LIFE INSURANCE COMPANY — B Good

Major Rating Factors: Good quality investment portfolio (5.7 on a scale of 0 to 10) despite mixed results such as: large holdings of BBB rated bonds but junk bond exposure equal to 85% of capital. Good liquidity (6.3) with sufficient resources to handle a spike in claims as well as a significant increase in policy surrenders. Good overall results on stability tests (5.4) excellent operational trends and excellent risk diversification.
Other Rating Factors: Strong capitalization (7.0) based on excellent risk adjusted capital (severe loss scenario). Excellent profitability (8.5) with operating gains in each of the last five years.
Principal Business: Individual life insurance (68%), individual health insurance (26%), reinsurance (3%), group life insurance (1%), and individual annuities (1%).
Principal Investments: NonCMO investment grade bonds (73%), noninv. grade bonds (9%), common & preferred stock (6%), policy loans (5%), and misc. investments (7%).
Investments in Affiliates: 6%
Group Affiliation: Torchmark Corp
Licensed in: All states except NY, PR
Commenced Business: July 1929
Address: 2001 Third Ave S, Birmingham, AL 35233
Phone: (205) 325-4918 **Domicile State:** AL **NAIC Code:** 65331

Data Date	Weiss Safety Rating	RACR #1	RACR #2	Total Assets ($mil)	Capital ($mil)	Net Premium ($mil)	Net Income ($mil)
6-03	B	1.53	1.01	3,997.3	381.3	251.2	54.7
6-02	B	1.35	0.91	3,780.7	332.4	249.2	27.0
2002	B	1.66	1.10	3,890.9	422.9	510.0	82.2
2001	B	1.56	1.05	3,738.0	390.2	477.7	126.4
2000	B	1.70	1.17	3,562.0	376.2	453.3	105.9
1999	B	1.40	1.02	3,412.3	314.4	538.9	79.4
1998	B	1.52	1.10	3,363.3	339.0	519.5	140.3

Adverse Trends in Operations

Decrease in premium volume from 1999 to 2000 (16%)
Decrease in capital during 1999 (7%)

II. Analysis of Largest Companies

Winter 2003 - 04

LIFE INSURANCE COMPANY OF NORTH AMERICA — D — Weak

Major Rating Factors: Weak overall results on stability tests (2.2 on a scale of 0 to 10) including weak risk adjusted capital in prior years. Fair quality investment portfolio (4.2) with substantial holdings of BBB bonds in addition to moderate junk bond exposure. Good overall profitability (5.7). Excellent expense controls. Return on equity has been good over the last five years, averaging 12.1%.
Other Rating Factors: Good liquidity (6.4). Strong capitalization (7.1) based on excellent risk adjusted capital (severe loss scenario).
Principal Business: Group health insurance (44%), group life insurance (37%), individual life insurance (10%), and reinsurance (9%).
Principal Investments: NonCMO investment grade bonds (35%), common & preferred stock (29%), mortgages in good standing (21%), CMOs and structured securities (6%), and misc. investments (10%).
Investments in Affiliates: 21%
Group Affiliation: CIGNA Group
Licensed in: All states except NY
Commenced Business: September 1957
Address: 1601 Chestnut ST, 2 Liberty Pl, Philadelphia, PA 19192-2235
Phone: (860) 726-7234 **Domicile State:** PA **NAIC Code:** 65498

Data Date	Weiss Safety Rating	RACR #1	RACR #2	Total Assets ($mil)	Capital ($mil)	Net Premium ($mil)	Net Income ($mil)
6-03	D	1.52	1.04	4,978.3	506.8	781.8	113.1
6-02	D+	0.51	0.41	4,871.0	384.0	722.9	-15.0
2002	D	0.48	0.42	4,813.7	424.4	1,536.9	16.7
2001	C	0.53	0.43	5,124.2	410.4	1,649.4	10.8
2000	C+	0.84	0.62	5,260.7	417.8	1,628.9	56.9
1999	C+	1.77	1.09	5,084.7	520.8	2,345.5	186.2
1998	C+	1.94	1.25	3,857.2	541.4	1,141.5	116.0

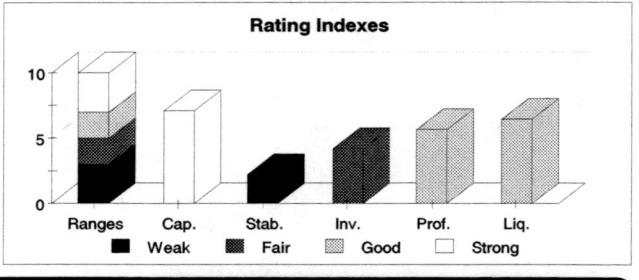

Rating Indexes (bar chart: Ranges—Weak/Fair; Cap.—Strong; Stab.—Weak; Inv.—Fair; Prof.—Good; Liq.—Good)

LIFE INVESTORS INSURANCE COMPANY OF AMERICA — B — Good

Major Rating Factors: Good overall results on stability tests (5.4 on a scale of 0 to 10) despite fair risk adjusted capital in prior years. Other stability subfactors include excellent operational trends and excellent risk diversification. Good capitalization (5.5) based on good risk adjusted capital (moderate loss scenario). Good liquidity (5.4).
Other Rating Factors: Fair quality investment portfolio (3.6). Excellent profitability (7.0).
Principal Business: Individual health insurance (22%), individual annuities (21%), group health insurance (17%), individual life insurance (15%), and other lines (26%).
Principal Investments: NonCMO investment grade bonds (44%), CMOs and structured securities (22%), mortgages in good standing (17%), noninv. grade bonds (8%), and misc. investments (9%).
Investments in Affiliates: None
Group Affiliation: AEGON USA Group
Licensed in: All states except NY, PR
Commenced Business: November 1931
Address: 4333 Edgewood Rd NE, Cedar Rapids, IA 52499
Phone: (319) 398-8511 **Domicile State:** IA **NAIC Code:** 64130

Data Date	Weiss Safety Rating	RACR #1	RACR #2	Total Assets ($mil)	Capital ($mil)	Net Premium ($mil)	Net Income ($mil)
6-03	B	1.36	0.70	11,110.0	742.8	557.4	20.8
6-02	B	1.04	0.55	10,442.9	602.6	577.2	-33.8
2002	B	1.34	0.69	10,641.5	718.6	1,117.2	-65.2
2001	B	1.11	0.59	10,187.7	606.3	1,055.0	-43.6
2000	B	1.31	0.73	7,605.9	578.9	853.6	58.1
1999	B	1.42	0.79	7,375.0	597.2	853.9	102.4
1998	B	1.29	0.76	7,392.9	525.1	1,029.1	140.8

Adverse Trends in Operations
Decrease in capital during 2000 (3%)
Decrease in premium volume from 1998 to 1999 (17%)

LIFEWISE HEALTH PLAN OF OREGON — B — Good

Major Rating Factors: Good overall profitability index (6.0 on a scale of 0 to 10) despite operating losses during 1998 and 1999. Good liquidity (6.4) with sufficient resources (cash flows and marketable investments) to handle a spike in claims. Strong capitalization (7.9) based on excellent current risk-adjusted capital (severe loss scenario).
Other Rating Factors: High quality investment portfolio (9.9) containing little or no exposure to mortgages, junk bonds, or unaffiliated stocks.
Principal Business: Comp med (99%), med supp (1%).
Mem Phys: 02: 8,547 **01:** 7,586 **02 MLR** 80% **/ 02 Admin Exp** 15%
Enroll(000): Q1 03: 155 **02:** 159 **01:** 146 **Med Exp PMPM:** $149
Principal Investments: Cash and equiv (12%), other (88%).
Provider Compensation ($000): Contr fee ($235,429), FFS ($26,975), bonus arrang ($172)
Total Member Encounters: Phys (1,606,080), non-phys (802)
Group Affiliation: PREMERA
Licensed in: ID, OR
Address: 2020 SW 4th St Suite 1000, Portland, OR 97201
Phone: (503) 295-6707 **Dom State:** OR **Commenced Bus:** January 1987

Data Date	Weiss Safety Rating	RACR #1	RACR #2	Total Assets ($mil)	Capital ($mil)	Net Premium ($mil)	Net Income ($mil)
3-03	B	2.08	1.73	127.4	49.1	89.3	5.5
3-02	N/A	N/A	N/A	N/A	N/A	N/A	N/A
2002	B	0.00	0.00	113.7	43.4	337.7	14.3
2001	N/A	N/A	N/A	83.3	29.5	268.9	N/A
2000	U	0.57	0.46	62.3	20.2	182.6	3.9
1999	C-	0.66	0.54	41.9	16.5	114.6	-0.4
1998	C-	0.84	0.69	38.5	16.7	92.4	-6.0

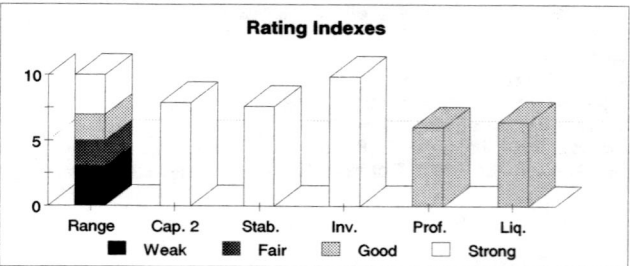

Rating Indexes (bar chart: Range—Weak/Fair; Cap. 2—Strong; Stab.—Strong; Inv.—Strong; Prof.—Good; Liq.—Good)

LOCAL INITIATIVE HEALTH AUTH LA   C   Fair

Major Rating Factors: Good overall results on stability tests (6.1 on a scale of 0 to 10). Excellent profitability (8.8). Strong capitalization (7.1) based on good current risk-adjusted capital (moderate loss scenario) reflecting improvement over results in 2001.
Other Rating Factors: Excellent liquidity (7.1) with ample operational cash flow and liquid investments.
Principal Business: None
Mem Phys: 02: N/A   **01:** N/A   **02 MLR** 94%   **/ 02 Admin Exp** 3%
Enroll(000): Q1 03: 830   **02:** 819   **01:** 727   **Med Exp PMPM:** $94
Principal Investments ($000): Cash and equiv ($60,178), other ($26,858)
Provider Compensation ($000): None
Total Member Encounters: N/A
Group Affiliation: None
Licensed in: CA
Address: 555 W Fifth St 29th Floor, Los Angeles, CA 90013-3036
Phone: (213) 694-1250   **Dom State:** CA   **Commenced Bus:** April 1997

Data Date	Weiss Safety Rating	RACR #1	RACR #2	Total Assets ($mil)	Capital ($mil)	Net Premium ($mil)	Net Income ($mil)
3-03	C	1.22	0.74	247.0	67.3	245.0	5.4
3-02	D+	N/A	N/A	140.0	43.5	217.2	3.9
2002	C	1.06	0.65	164.2	61.9	930.2	22.3
2001	D+	0.71	0.44	196.9	39.6	809.4	12.6
2000	N/A	N/A	N/A	101.1	15.9	648.8	4.4
1999	N/A	N/A	N/A	N/A	N/A	N/A	N/A
1998	N/A	N/A	N/A	N/A	N/A	N/A	N/A

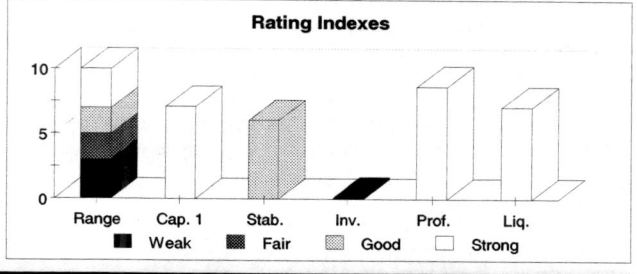

Rating Indexes bar chart: Range (Weak), Cap. 1 (Strong), Stab. (Good), Inv. (Fair), Prof. (Strong), Liq. (Strong)

LONDON LIFE REINSURANCE COMPANY   B   Good

Major Rating Factors: Fair current capitalization (4.0 on a scale of 0 to 10) based on mixed results -- excessive policy leverage mitigated by excellent risk adjusted capital (severe loss scenario) reflecting improvement over results in 2000. Fair profitability (4.4). Excellent expense controls. Return on equity has been low, averaging 0.4%. Fair overall results on stability tests (4.0) including weak results on operational trends and negative cash flow from operations for 2002.
Other Rating Factors: High quality investment portfolio (7.2). Excellent liquidity (8.2).
Principal Business: Reinsurance (100%).
Principal Investments: NonCMO investment grade bonds (80%), CMOs and structured securities (14%), noninv. grade bonds (2%), and cash (2%).
Investments in Affiliates: None
Group Affiliation: Great West Life Asr
Licensed in: All states except ME, NH, NY, VT, VA, PR
Commenced Business: December 1969
Address: 1787 Sentry Parkway, Ste 420, Blue Bell, PA 1942-22
Phone: (215) 542-7200   **Domicile State:** PA   **NAIC Code:** 76694

Data Date	Weiss Safety Rating	RACR #1	RACR #2	Total Assets ($mil)	Capital ($mil)	Net Premium ($mil)	Net Income ($mil)
6-03	B	3.98	2.53	730.4	65.7	26.4	1.5
6-02	C+	2.82	1.35	589.1	55.4	-60.7	3.3
2002	C+	2.28	1.30	830.0	64.1	-12.6	0.0
2001	C+	1.68	0.92	671.5	56.0	69.1	-4.7
2000	C+	1.59	0.89	748.8	53.8	456.6	-3.1
1999	C+	3.34	2.00	456.8	58.4	58.5	1.8
1998	C	2.69	1.68	330.2	46.9	33.9	3.2

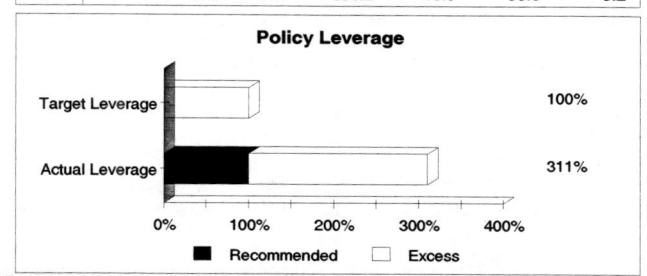

Policy Leverage chart: Target Leverage 100%, Actual Leverage 311%

LOVELACE HEALTH SYSTEMS INC   C   Fair

Major Rating Factors: Weak profitability index (2.5 on a scale of 0 to 10) with operating losses during 1999 and 2002. Return on equity has been low, averaging 1%. Good overall results on stability tests (5.5) despite excessive capital growth during 2002. Good liquidity (6.8) with sufficient resources (cash flows and marketable investments) to handle a spike in claims.
Other Rating Factors: Strong capitalization (7.5) based on excellent current risk-adjusted capital (severe loss scenario) reflecting improvement over results in 1999. High quality investment portfolio (7.6) containing no exposure to mortgages, junk bonds, or unaffiliated stocks.
Principal Business: Medicaid (39%), comp med (33%), Medicare (22%), FEHB (8%), med supp (2%).
Mem Phys: 02: 4,770   **01:** 3,692   **02 MLR** 82%   **/ 02 Admin Exp** 21%
Enroll(000): Q1 03: 227   **02:** 245   **01:** 238   **Med Exp PMPM:** $140
Principal Investments: Real estate (65%), cash and equiv (35%)
Provider Compensation ($000): Contr fee ($189,140), salary ($58,327), capitation ($10,894), other ($140,707)
Total Member Encounters: Phys (1,169,839), non-phys (464,496)
Group Affiliation: Ardent Health Services LLC
Licensed in: NM
Address: 5400 Gibson Blvd SE, Albuquerque, NM 87108
Phone: (505) 262-7075   **Dom State:** NM   **Commenced Bus:** March 1985

Data Date	Weiss Safety Rating	RACR #1	RACR #2	Total Assets ($mil)	Capital ($mil)	Net Premium ($mil)	Net Income ($mil)
3-03	C	1.74	1.45	153.6	60.6	133.3	0.8
3-02	C	1.74	1.44	155.1	35.4	122.5	-2.9
2002	C	1.60	1.33	166.7	55.8	497.4	-7.2
2001	C+	1.75	1.45	150.2	39.8	419.8	5.0
2000	C	1.16	0.94	152.7	35.2	504.0	0.7
1999	C	1.10	0.88	143.0	34.5	475.7	-6.9
1998	C+	1.71	1.40	154.8	47.1	431.5	8.1

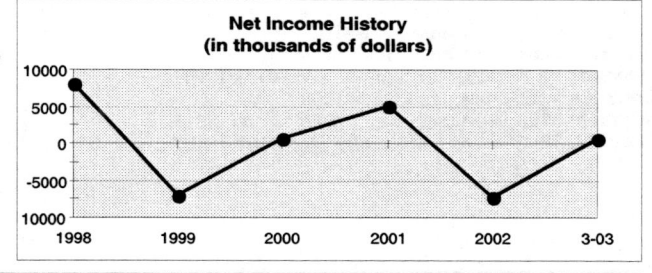

Net Income History (in thousands of dollars) line chart from 1998 to 3-03

II. Analysis of Largest Companies
Winter 2003 - 04

M PLAN — C- Fair

Major Rating Factors: Fair capitalization (3.1 on a scale of 0 to 10) based on weak current risk-adjusted capital (moderate loss scenario) reflecting improvement over results in 2001. Good liquidity (7.0) with sufficient resources (cash flows and marketable investments) to handle a spike in claims. Excellent profitability (8.3) with operating gains in each of the last five years.
Other Rating Factors: High quality investment portfolio (9.9) containing little or no exposure to mortgages, junk bonds, or unaffiliated stocks. Excellent overall results on stability tests (7.1) based on consistent premium and capital growth in the last five years.
Principal Business: Comp med (21%), FEHB (2%), Medicare (1%)
Mem Phys: 02: 4,687 **01:** 4,507 **02 MLR** 89% **/ 02 Admin Exp** 8%
Enroll(000): **02:** 181 **01:** 178 **Med Exp PMPM:** $201
Principal Investments: Cash and equiv (98%), other (1%)
Provider Compensation ($000): Capitation ($245,605), salary ($31,364)
Total Member Encounters: N/A
Group Affiliation: Clarian Health Partners Inc
Licensed in: IN
Address: 8802 N Meridian St Suite 100, Indianapolis, IN 46260
Phone: (317) 571-5300 **Dom State:** IN **Commenced Bus:** June 1989

Data Date	Weiss Safety Rating	RACR #1	RACR #2	Total Assets ($mil)	Capital ($mil)	Net Premium ($mil)	Net Income ($mil)
2002	C-	0.65	0.54	47.5	17.6	481.7	6.5
2001	D+	0.42	0.38	30.8	12.0	385.1	2.3
2000	D+	0.60	0.53	30.6	13.0	332.4	1.5
1999	D+	0.77	0.68	31.6	13.6	285.0	2.3
1998	D+	0.71	0.63	31.5	11.5	272.3	1.9

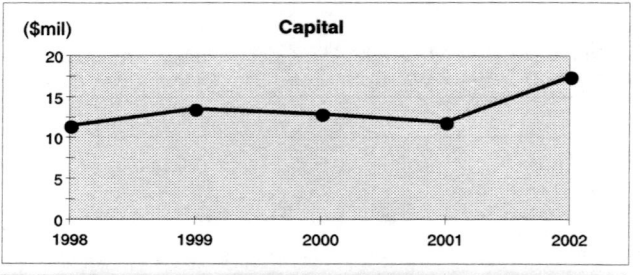

M-CARE — B- Good

Major Rating Factors: Good overall profitability index (5.2 on a scale of 0 to 10) despite a decline in earnings during 2002. Good capitalization (6.9) based on excellent current risk-adjusted capital (severe loss scenario) reflecting significant improvement over results in 1998. Good liquidity (6.9) with sufficient resources (cash flows and marketable investments) to handle a spike in claims.
Other Rating Factors: High quality investment portfolio (9.9). Excellent overall results on stability tests (7.7) based on consistent premium and capital growth in the last five years.
Principal Business: Comp med (74%), Medicare (17%), Medicaid (5%), FEHB (4%)
Mem Phys: 02: 5,866 **01:** 6,013 **02 MLR** 92% **/ 02 Admin Exp** 7%
Enroll(000): Q1 03: 190 **02:** 205 **01:** 198 **Med Exp PMPM:** $186
Principal Investments: Cash and equiv (73%), nonaffiliate common stock (8%), other (19%)
Provider Compensation ($000): Contr fee ($246,645), capitation ($188,331), FFS ($16,424)
Total Member Encounters: Phys (795,011), non-phys (252,900)
Group Affiliation: University of Michigan
Licensed in: MI
Address: 2301 Commonwealth Blvd, Ann Arbor, MI 48105
Phone: (734) 747-8700 **Dom State:** MI **Commenced Bus:** October 1986

Data Date	Weiss Safety Rating	RACR #1	RACR #2	Total Assets ($mil)	Capital ($mil)	Net Premium ($mil)	Net Income ($mil)
3-03	B-	1.23	1.03	123.2	43.3	113.2	2.2
3-02	C+	1.01	0.78	142.7	40.8	123.9	1.2
2002	B-	1.18	0.99	136.2	41.5	488.7	4.3
2001	C+	1.01	0.78	131.6	40.7	488.8	10.4
2000	C-	N/A	N/A	128.1	31.6	417.8	13.8
1999	C-	0.50	0.42	84.8	17.6	361.0	-3.6
1998	C	0.50	0.41	79.6	15.5	290.9	-14.1

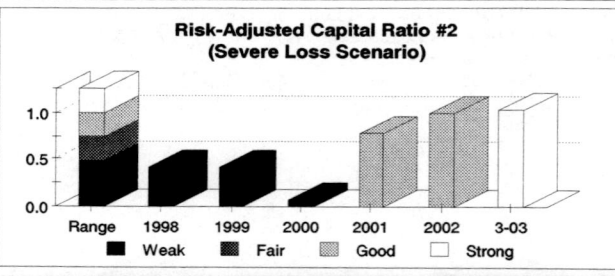

MADISON NATIONAL LIFE INSURANCE COMPANY INC — C Fair

Major Rating Factors: Fair overall results on stability tests (4.1 on a scale of 0 to 10) including fair risk adjusted capital in prior years. Good current capitalization (6.3) based on good risk adjusted capital (severe loss scenario) reflecting some improvement over results in 1999. Good quality investment portfolio (6.4) despite mixed results such as: no exposure to mortgages and substantial holdings of BBB bonds but small junk bond holdings.
Other Rating Factors: Good liquidity (6.4). Excellent profitability (7.5) with operating gains in each of the last five years.
Principal Business: Group health insurance (30%), individual life insurance (20%), group life insurance (16%), credit health insurance (11%), and other lines (24%).
Principal Investments: NonCMO investment grade bonds (55%), common & preferred stock (21%), CMOs and structured securities (9%), policy loans (4%), and noninv. grade bonds (3%).
Investments in Affiliates: 19%
Group Affiliation: Geneve Holdings Inc
Licensed in: All states except ME, NH, NY, VT, PR
Commenced Business: March 1962
Address: 6120 University Ave, Middleton, WI 53562
Phone: (608) 238-2691 **Domicile State:** WI **NAIC Code:** 65781

Data Date	Weiss Safety Rating	RACR #1	RACR #2	Total Assets ($mil)	Capital ($mil)	Net Premium ($mil)	Net Income ($mil)
6-03	C	1.05	0.91	468.0	100.1	32.3	12.0
6-02	C	0.80	0.68	475.3	81.0	27.4	0.7
2002	C	0.82	0.72	448.2	87.6	57.6	0.1
2001	C	0.79	0.68	444.3	79.1	53.4	4.5
2000	C-	0.68	0.58	418.2	62.4	50.4	10.8
1999	C-	0.60	0.53	396.7	54.7	43.7	10.4
1998	C	0.73	0.67	233.5	59.7	29.9	1.0

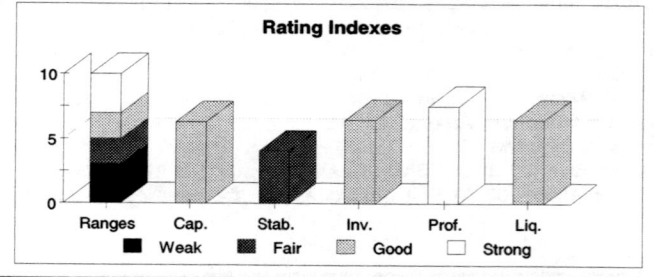

Winter 2003 - 04   II. Analysis of Largest Companies

MAGNAHEALTH OF NY INC   D+   Weak

Major Rating Factors: Weak profitability index (0.3 on a scale of 0 to 10) with modest operating losses during 1998, 1999, 2000 and 2001. Average return on equity has been poor at -8%. Fair overall results on stability tests (3.7) based on a decline in the number of member physicians during 2001, an overall decline in enrollment over the past five years despite growth in 2000 and 2001. Strong capitalization (10.0) based on excellent current risk-adjusted capital (severe loss scenario) reflecting improvement over results in 2000

Other Rating Factors: High quality investment portfolio (9.9) containing no exposure to mortgages, junk bonds, or unaffiliated stocks. Excellent liquidity (8.6) with ample operational cash flow and liquid investments.

Principal Business: Comp med (100%)
Mem Phys: 01: 6,822   **00:** 7,773   **01 MLR** 130%   **/ 01 Admin Exp** 48%
Enroll(000): Q2 02: 0   **01:** 0   **00:** 0   **Med Exp PMPM:** $317
Principal Investments: Cash and equiv (96%), other (4%)
Provider Compensation ($000): FFS ($788)
Total Member Encounters: N/A
Group Affiliation: None
Licensed in: NY
Address: 825 East Gate Blvd, Garden City, NY 11530
Phone: (516) 227-6900   **Dom State:** NY   **Commenced Bus:** August 1996

Data Date	Weiss Safety Rating	RACR #1	RACR #2	Total Assets ($mil)	Capital ($mil)	Net Premium ($mil)	Net Income ($mil)
6-02	D+	7.37	6.52	3.1	2.1	0.4	-0.1
6-01	D+	1.13	0.94	3.6	2.5	0.4	0.0
2001	D+	8.45	7.35	3.1	2.2	0.7	-0.3
2000	D+	1.15	0.96	3.5	2.5	0.8	-0.1
1999	D+	1.20	1.01	3.1	2.6	0.6	-0.2
1998	D+	3.72	3.15	4.4	2.7	4.0	-0.3
1997	N/A	N/A	N/A	4.5	3.0	5.0	N/A

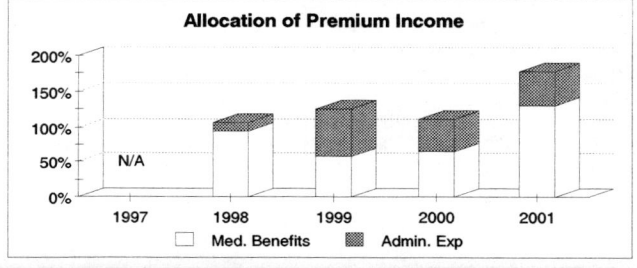

Allocation of Premium Income (bar chart 1997-2001, Med. Benefits / Admin. Exp)

MAINE PARTNERS HEALTH PLAN INC   C   Fair

Major Rating Factors: Weak profitability index (0.9 on a scale of 0 to 10) with operating losses during 1998, 1999, 2000 and 2001. Average return on equity has been poor at -29%. Good overall results on stability tests (5.2) despite rapid premium growth over the last five years, a decline in enrollment during 2002. Rating is significantly influenced by the good financial results of Anthem Ins Companies Inc. Good liquidity (6.6) with sufficient resources (cash flows and marketable investments) to handle a spike in claims.

Other Rating Factors: Strong capitalization (8.1) based on excellent current risk-adjusted capital (severe loss scenario) reflecting improvement over results in 1999. High quality investment portfolio (9.9) containing no exposure to mortgages, junk bonds, or unaffiliated stocks.

Principal Business: Comp med (100%)
Mem Phys: 02: 1,692   **01:** 1,476   **02 MLR** 81%   **/ 02 Admin Exp** 16%
Enroll(000): Q1 03: 36   **02:** 37   **01:** 48   **Med Exp PMPM:** $171
Principal Investments: Cash and equiv (21%), other (79%)
Provider Compensation ($000): Contr fee ($44,114), FFS ($27,393), capitation ($17,432)
Total Member Encounters: Phys (354,814), non-phys (170,275)
Group Affiliation: Anthem Ins Companies Inc
Licensed in: ME
Address: 2 Gannett Dr, South Portland, ME 04106-6911
Phone: (207) 822-7000   **Dom State:** ME   **Commenced Bus:** January 1998

Data Date	Weiss Safety Rating	RACR #1	RACR #2	Total Assets ($mil)	Capital ($mil)	Net Premium ($mil)	Net Income ($mil)
3-03	C	2.26	1.88	42.7	13.9	28.3	1.7
3-02	C-	1.40	1.20	33.6	9.4	26.4	0.0
2002	C	2.03	1.69	38.5	12.4	107.4	2.8
2001	C-	1.39	1.19	32.7	9.4	115.5	-6.8
2000	C	1.71	1.48	23.8	9.5	93.1	-1.8
1999	C	0.94	0.82	21.6	2.9	44.3	-1.9
1998	N/A	N/A	N/A	10.8	4.0	18.5	-0.6

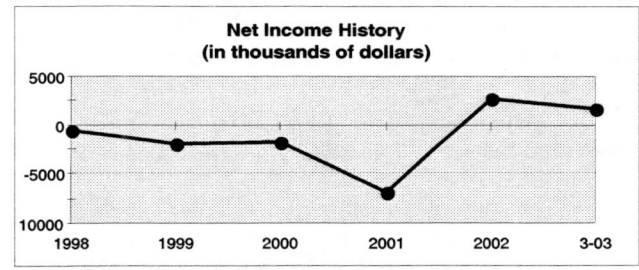

Net Income History (in thousands of dollars) (line chart 1998-3-03)

MAMSI LIFE & HEALTH INS CO   B   Good

Major Rating Factors: Excellent profitability (9.3 on a scale of 0 to 10). Strong capitalization (10.0) based on excellent current risk-adjusted capital (severe loss scenario) reflecting significant improvement over results in 1998. High quality investment portfolio (9.9) containing no exposure to mortgages, junk bonds, or unaffiliated stocks.

Other Rating Factors: Excellent liquidity (7.0) with ample operational cash flow and liquid investments.

Principal Business: Comp med (100%)
Mem Phys: 02: 47,232   **01:** 44,199   **02 MLR** 82%   **/ 02 Admin Exp** 8%
Enroll(000): Q1 03: 376   **02:** 376   **01:** 348   **Med Exp PMPM:** $125
Principal Investments: Cash and equiv (40%), other (60%)
Provider Compensation ($000): Contr fee ($529,262), capitation ($1,565)
Total Member Encounters: Phys (1,917,001), non-phys (184,327)
Group Affiliation: Mid Atlantic Medical Services
Licensed in: AL, AZ, AR, CA, CO, DC, DE, GA, HI, ID, IL, IN, KS, KY, LA, MD, MS, MO, NE, NV, NM, NC, ND, OK, PA, SC, SD, TN, TX, UT, VA, WV
Address: 4 Taft Court, Rockville, MD 20850
Phone: (301) 340-9346   **Dom State:** MD   **Commenced Bus:** November 1955

Data Date	Weiss Safety Rating	RACR #1	RACR #2	Total Assets ($mil)	Capital ($mil)	Net Premium ($mil)	Net Income ($mil)
3-03	B	3.94	3.28	337.7	187.9	180.3	13.4
3-02	B	0.00	0.00	227.7	113.8	151.7	6.3
2002	B	3.64	3.04	312.5	175.2	660.4	48.9
2001	N/A	N/A	N/A	220.9	108.3	520.0	N/A
2000	U	1.51	1.22	151.3	80.0	423.3	20.8
1999	C	1.26	1.02	108.5	51.4	319.6	7.6
1998	C-	0.76	0.63	74.3	34.5	252.1	9.0

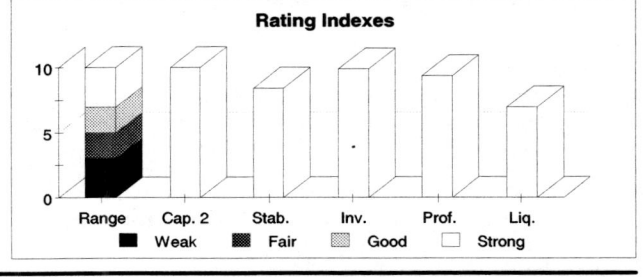

Rating Indexes (bar chart: Range, Cap. 2, Stab., Inv., Prof., Liq. — Weak / Fair / Good / Strong)

www.WeissRatings.com   217   * Denotes a Weiss Recommended Company

II. Analysis of Largest Companies

Winter 2003 - 04

MANAGED HEALTH INC — E+ — Very Weak

Major Rating Factors: Weak profitability index (1.9 on a scale of 0 to 10) with operating losses during 1997, 1998, 1999 and 2000. Weak liquidity (0.0) as a spike in claims may stretch capacity. Fair capitalization (3.4) based on weak current risk-adjusted capital (moderate loss scenario) as results have slipped from the good range over the last year.
Other Rating Factors: Good overall results on stability tests (5.6) despite rapid premium growth over the last five years, a decline in enrollment during 2001. High quality investment portfolio (9.9) containing no exposure to mortgages, junk bonds, or unaffiliated stocks.
Principal Business: Comp med (60%), Medicare (40%)
Mem Phys: 01: N/A **00:** N/A **01 MLR** 88% **/ 01 Admin Exp** 10%
Enroll(000): Q2 02: 22 **01:** 18 **00:** 89 **Med Exp PMPM:** $374
Principal Investments: Cash and equiv (100%)
Provider Compensation ($000): FFS ($170,520), other ($67,330)
Total Member Encounters: N/A
Group Affiliation: HealthFirst Inc
Licensed in: NY
Address: 25 Broadway, 9th Floor, New York, NY 10004
Phone: (212) 801-6000 **Dom State:** NY **Commenced Bus:** October 1990

Data Date	Weiss Safety Rating	RACR #1	RACR #2	Total Assets ($mil)	Capital ($mil)	Net Premium ($mil)	Net Income ($mil)
6-02	E+	0.69	0.58	71.2	33.7	82.5	-0.4
6-01	E+	1.86	1.59	91.4	27.2	134.6	5.8
2001	E+	0.00	0.00	85.6	28.1	272.2	9.1
2000	E	1.15	0.97	72.5	18.4	112.0	-1.1
1999	E	0.87	0.74	17.2	7.1	31.3	-1.9
1998	E	0.64	0.56	5.0	2.0	12.1	-2.9
1997	E	0.00	0.00	4.4	0.8	15.9	-1.5

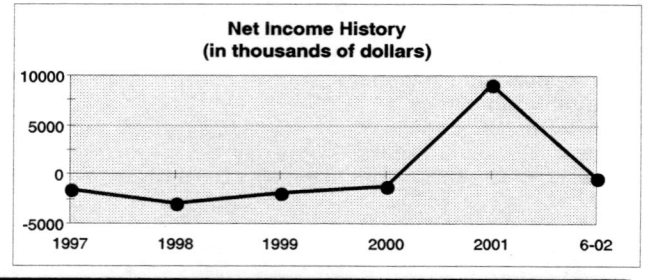

Net Income History (in thousands of dollars)

MANAGED HEALTH SERVICES INS CORP — C — Fair

Major Rating Factors: Fair capitalization index (4.6 on a scale of 0 to 10) based on fair current risk-adjusted capital (moderate loss scenario). Fair liquidity (4.8) as cash resources may not be adequate to cover a spike in claims. Good overall profitability index (6.0) despite operating losses during 1998 and 1999.
Other Rating Factors: Good overall results on stability tests (5.0) despite rapid enrollment growth during the past five years. High quality investment portfolio (9.4) containing no exposure to mortgages, junk bonds, or unaffiliated stocks.
Principal Business: Medicaid (100%)
Mem Phys: 02: 5,589 **01:** 4,722 **02 MLR** 83% **/ 02 Admin Exp** 13%
Enroll(000): Q1 03: 103 **02:** 99 **01:** 89 **Med Exp PMPM:** $147
Principal Investments: Cash and equiv (21%), other (79%)
Provider Compensation ($000): Contr fee ($119,520), capitation ($44,832), bonus arrang ($102)
Total Member Encounters: Phys (299,893), non-phys (352,891)
Group Affiliation: Centene Corp
Licensed in: WI
Address: 1205 S 70th St #500, Milwaukee, WI 53214-3167
Phone: (314) 345-4600 **Dom State:** WI **Commenced Bus:** December 1990

Data Date	Weiss Safety Rating	RACR #1	RACR #2	Total Assets ($mil)	Capital ($mil)	Net Premium ($mil)	Net Income ($mil)
3-03	C	0.87	0.72	44.6	14.4	58.5	2.0
3-02	D	0.44	0.37	37.7	7.1	45.8	0.7
2002	C	0.80	0.66	43.1	13.3	200.4	6.0
2001	D	0.44	0.37	32.7	6.3	152.8	3.6
2000	D	0.34	0.29	25.0	4.5	74.1	1.0
1999	D	0.16	0.13	20.4	2.7	71.4	-4.4
1998	D	0.31	0.26	20.2	5.3	75.6	-1.1

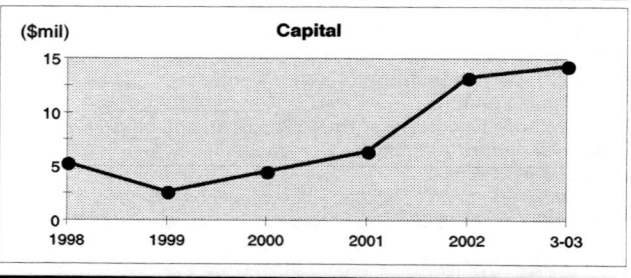

Capital ($mil)

MATTHEW THORNTON HEALTH PLAN * — B+ — Good

Major Rating Factors: Good overall results on stability tests (5.6 on a scale of 0 to 10) based on healthy premium and capital growth during 2002 but rapid enrollment growth during the past five years. Rating is significantly influenced by the good financial results of Anthem Ins Companies Inc. Good liquidity (6.7) with sufficient resources (cash flows and marketable investments) to handle a spike in claims. Excellent profitability (7.7) despite operating losses during 1998 and 1999.
Other Rating Factors: Strong capitalization (9.5) based on excellent current risk-adjusted capital (severe loss scenario) reflecting improvement over results in 1998. High quality investment portfolio (9.9) containing little or no exposure to mortgages, junk bonds, or unaffiliated stocks.
Principal Business: Comp med (97%), Medicaid (3%)
Mem Phys: 02: 6,159 **01:** 6,619 **02 MLR** 80% **/ 02 Admin Exp** 13%
Enroll(000): Q1 03: 216 **02:** 225 **01:** 194 **Med Exp PMPM:** $181
Principal Investments: Cash and equiv (10%), nonaffiliate common stock (1%), other (90%)
Provider Compensation ($000): Bonus arrang ($440,062), capitation ($15,569)
Total Member Encounters: Phys (1,331,383), non-phys (638,157)
Group Affiliation: Anthem Ins Companies Inc
Licensed in: NH
Address: 3000 Goffs Falls Rd, Manchester, NH 03111-0001
Phone: (603) 695-7000 **Dom State:** NH **Commenced Bus:** November 1971

Data Date	Weiss Safety Rating	RACR #1	RACR #2	Total Assets ($mil)	Capital ($mil)	Net Premium ($mil)	Net Income ($mil)
3-03	B+	3.33	2.78	210.3	99.7	160.7	5.4
3-02	B	2.33	1.76	182.4	76.1	124.0	7.5
2002	B+	3.14	2.62	198.3	93.8	570.6	30.5
2001	B	2.33	1.76	178.3	65.8	482.4	29.6
2000	C-	1.59	1.32	115.9	35.7	382.2	11.4
1999	C-	2.32	1.99	69.5	23.2	152.8	-1.0
1998	C-	1.33	1.12	53.7	17.6	204.1	-10.4

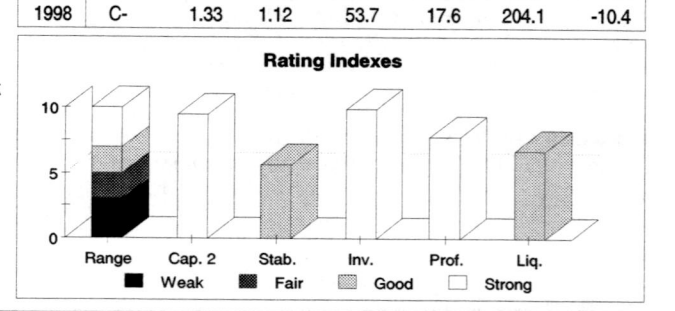

Rating Indexes: Range, Cap. 2, Stab., Inv., Prof., Liq. — Weak, Fair, Good, Strong

Winter 2003 - 04   II. Analysis of Largest Companies

MAYO HEALTH PLAN ARIZONA   C-   Fair

Major Rating Factors: Weak profitability index (0.9 on a scale of 0 to 10) with operating losses during 2001. Good liquidity (6.9) with sufficient resources (cash flows and marketable investments) to handle a spike in claims. Strong capitalization (7.1) based on excellent current risk-adjusted capital (severe loss scenario) reflecting improvement over results in 2001.
Other Rating Factors: High quality investment portfolio (9.9) containing no exposure to mortgages, junk bonds, or unaffiliated stocks. Excellent overall results on stability tests (7.3) based on consistent premium and capital growth in the last five years but a decline in enrollment during 2002.
Principal Business: Comp med (100%)
Mem Phys: 02: 3,696   **01:** 3,296   **02 MLR** 86% / **02 Admin Exp** 11%
Enroll(000): Q1 03: 16   **02:** 30   **01:** 37   **Med Exp PMPM:** $144
Principal Investments: Cash and equiv (36%), other (64%)
Provider Compensation ($000): Contr fee ($37,092), FFS ($15,565), capitation ($5,727)
Total Member Encounters: Phys (266,292), non-phys (8,639)
Group Affiliation: Mayo Foundation
Licensed in: AZ
Address: 13400 E Shea Blvd, Scottsdale, AZ 85259
Phone: (480) 301-6725   **Dom State:** AZ   **Commenced Bus:** June 1997

Data Date	Weiss Safety Rating	RACR #1	RACR #2	Total Assets ($mil)	Capital ($mil)	Net Premium ($mil)	Net Income ($mil)
3-03	C-	1.44	1.20	19.9	11.8	10.1	0.8
3-02	D+	0.94	0.79	20.0	8.1	16.9	0.4
2002	C-	1.35	1.12	18.1	11.0	67.0	2.4
2001	D+	0.94	0.79	16.6	7.7	67.3	-3.9
2000	N/A	N/A	N/A	11.5	3.6	48.2	N/A
1999	N/A	N/A	N/A	9.7	2.2	30.4	N/A
1998	N/A	N/A	N/A	3.9	1.9	8.3	N/A

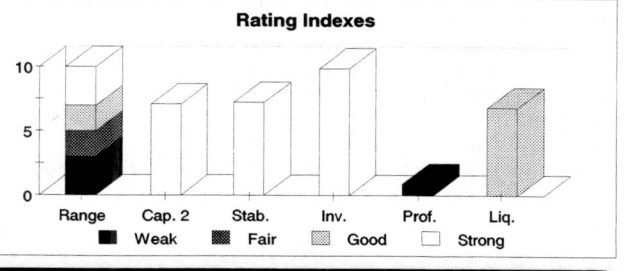

Rating Indexes (Range, Cap. 2, Stab., Inv., Prof., Liq.; Weak / Fair / Good / Strong)

MCLAREN HEALTH PLAN INC   C+   Fair

Major Rating Factors: Good capitalization (6.5 on a scale of 0 to 10) based on good current risk-adjusted capital (severe loss scenario) reflecting significant improvement over results in 2000. Good liquidity (7.0) with sufficient resources (cash flows and marketable investments) to handle a spike in claims. Excellent profitability (8.1).
Other Rating Factors: High quality investment portfolio (9.6). Excellent overall results on stability tests (7.2) based on consistent premium and capital growth in the last five years but rapid enrollment growth during the past five years.
Principal Business: Medicaid (100%)
Mem Phys: 02: 1,377   **01:** 797   **02 MLR** 85% / **02 Admin Exp** 8%
Enroll(000): Q1 03: 22   **02:** 21   **01:** 16   **Med Exp PMPM:** $138
Principal Investments: Cash and equiv (92%), nonaffiliate common stock (6%), other (1%)
Provider Compensation ($000): Contr fee ($28,385), capitation ($2,073)
Total Member Encounters: Phys (34,676), non-phys (4,283)
Group Affiliation: McLaren Health Care Corp
Licensed in: MI
Address: 401 S Ballenger Hwy, Flint, MI 48532-3685
Phone: (810) 342-1008   **Dom State:** MI   **Commenced Bus:** August 1998

Data Date	Weiss Safety Rating	RACR #1	RACR #2	Total Assets ($mil)	Capital ($mil)	Net Premium ($mil)	Net Income ($mil)
3-03	C+	1.15	0.96	16.7	6.9	10.0	0.6
3-02	C-	0.66	0.54	14.5	3.8	7.7	0.4
2002	C+	1.03	0.86	17.0	6.3	35.4	2.8
2001	C-	0.67	0.54	13.4	3.5	28.4	2.0
2000	D-	0.36	0.31	5.7	1.5	17.9	0.6
1999	N/A	N/A	N/A	3.7	0.9	8.5	N/A
1998	N/A	N/A	N/A	1.2	0.1	1.0	N/A

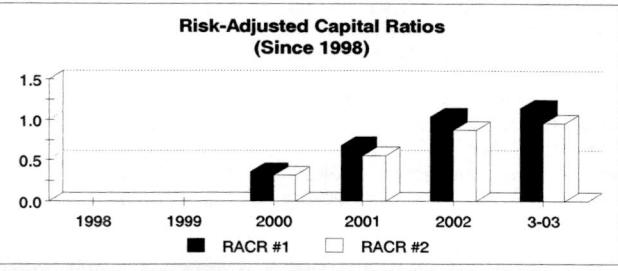

Risk-Adjusted Capital Ratios (Since 1998) — RACR #1, RACR #2

MCS HEALTH MANAGEMENT OPTIONS   C   Fair

Major Rating Factors: Good capitalization index (5.3 on a scale of 0 to 10) based on good current risk-adjusted capital (severe loss scenario). Good overall results on stability tests (5.7) based on consistent premium and capital growth in the last five years but a decline in the number of member physicians during 2002 and rapid enrollment growth during the past five years. Good liquidity (6.0) with sufficient resources (cash flows and marketable investments) to handle a spike in claims.
Other Rating Factors: Excellent profitability (8.1). High quality investment portfolio (9.9).
Principal Business: Medicaid (100%)
Mem Phys: 02: 3,700   **01:** 7,000   **02 MLR** 84% / **02 Admin Exp** 8%
Enroll(000): 02: 561   **01:** 439   **Med Exp PMPM:** $51
Principal Investments: Cash and equiv (38%), nonaffiliate common stock (14%), other (48%)
Provider Compensation ($000): Capitation ($168,387), FFS ($87,926), contr fee ($54,415)
Total Member Encounters: Phys (877,745)
Group Affiliation: Medical Card System/Wellpoint Health
Licensed in: PR
Address: 255 Ponce de Leon Ave Ste 203, Hato Rey, PR 00917
Phone: (787) 758-2500   **Dom State:** PR   **Commenced Bus:** April 1997

Data Date	Weiss Safety Rating	RACR #1	RACR #2	Total Assets ($mil)	Capital ($mil)	Net Premium ($mil)	Net Income ($mil)
2002	C	0.97	0.81	91.6	25.7	367.8	13.5
2001	D	0.54	0.42	77.5	12.7	237.3	10.6
2000	E	0.24	0.20	38.3	2.6	99.1	2.1
1999	N/A	N/A	N/A	6.7	0.7	30.3	N/A
1998	N/A	N/A	N/A	3.1	0.7	10.1	N/A

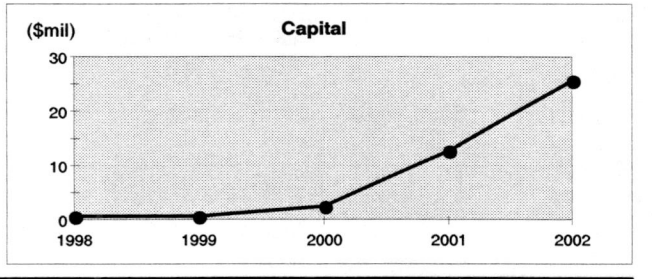

Capital ($mil) 1998–2002

www.WeissRatings.com   219   * Denotes a Weiss Recommended Company

II. Analysis of Largest Companies
Winter 2003 - 04

MD INDIVIDUAL PRACTICE ASSOC INC *   B+   Good

Major Rating Factors: Good overall results on stability tests (5.6 on a scale of 0 to 10) despite excessive capital growth during 2002. Potentially strong support from affiliation with Mid Atlantic Medical Services Inc. Good liquidity (7.0) with sufficient resources (cash flows and marketable investments) to handle a spike in claims. Excellent profitability (7.4) with operating gains in each of the last five years.
Other Rating Factors: Strong capitalization index (10.0) based on excellent current risk-adjusted capital (severe loss scenario) despite some fluctuation in capital levels. High quality investment portfolio (9.9) containing no exposure to mortgages, junk bonds, or unaffiliated stocks.
Principal Business: FEHB (82%), comp med (18%)
Mem Phys: 02: 39,352   **01:** 34,364   **02 MLR** 90%   **/ 02 Admin Exp** 7%
Enroll(000): Q1 03: 201   **02:** 176   **01:** 123   **Med Exp PMPM:** $191
Principal Investments: Cash and equiv (65%), other (35%)
Provider Compensation ($000): Capitation ($218,139), contr fee ($114,457)
Total Member Encounters: Phys (899,805), non-phys (86,519)
Group Affiliation: Mid Atlantic Medical Services Inc
Licensed in: DC, DE, MD, VA, WV
Address: 4 Taft Ct, Rockville, MD 20850
Phone: (301) 762-8205   **Dom State:** MD   **Commenced Bus:** December 1980

Data Date	Weiss Safety Rating	RACR #1	RACR #2	Total Assets ($mil)	Capital ($mil)	Net Premium ($mil)	Net Income ($mil)
3-03	B+	3.79	3.16	113.6	56.6	124.7	6.0
3-02	B-	3.01	2.73	85.9	44.6	92.6	4.2
2002	B+	3.37	2.81	93.3	50.8	379.3	5.0
2001	B-	2.91	2.64	75.3	40.5	236.2	1.5
2000	C+	3.29	2.89	58.5	42.6	241.3	2.3
1999	C+	3.29	2.85	80.4	57.4	234.4	13.6
1998	C+	2.93	2.48	62.9	42.0	223.1	12.2

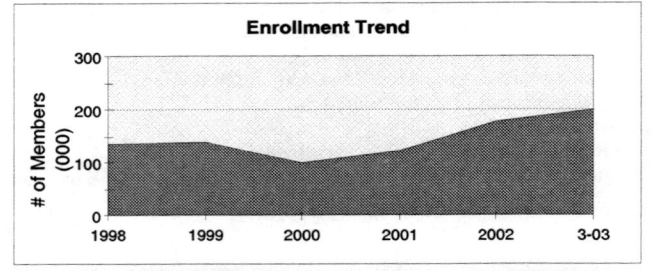

Enrollment Trend chart, 1998–3-03

MDNY HEALTHCARE INC   E   Very Weak

Major Rating Factors: Weak profitability index (2.1 on a scale of 0 to 10) with operating losses during 1997, 1998, 1999 and 2001. Average return on equity has been poor at -14%. Poor capitalization index (0.0) based on weak current risk-adjusted capital (severe loss scenario). Weak liquidity (0.0) as a spike in claims may stretch capacity.
Other Rating Factors: Fair overall results on stability tests (3.6) based on a steep decline in premium revenue in 2001, a steep decline in capital during 2001 and a significant 28% decrease in enrollment during the period. High quality investment portfolio (7.6) containing no exposure to mortgages, junk bonds, or unaffiliated stocks.
Principal Business: Comp med (100%)
Mem Phys: 01: N/A   **00:** N/A   **01 MLR** 83%   **/ 01 Admin Exp** 17%
Enroll(000): Q2 02: 59   **01:** 55   **00:** 77   **Med Exp PMPM:** $153
Principal Investments: Cash and equiv (70%), other (30%)
Provider Compensation ($000): Contr fee ($72,402), FFS ($30,683), capitation ($1,827)
Total Member Encounters: Phys (563,687), non-phys (30,219)
Group Affiliation: None
Licensed in: NY
Address: One Huntington Quadrangle 4C01, Melville, NY 11747
Phone: (516) 454-1900   **Dom State:** NY   **Commenced Bus:** January 1996

Data Date	Weiss Safety Rating	RACR #1	RACR #2	Total Assets ($mil)	Capital ($mil)	Net Premium ($mil)	Net Income ($mil)
6-02	E	0.20	0.17	42.8	6.7	77.1	0.3
6-01	E+	0.23	0.20	33.6	8.2	76.9	0.0
2001	E	0.20	0.17	45.2	6.4	146.6	-1.8
2000	E+	0.25	0.21	25.3	8.2	190.9	5.0
1999	E+	0.00	0.00	26.3	3.0	144.8	-0.9
1998	D	0.33	0.28	17.2	4.0	90.5	-1.3
1997	D+	0.80	0.52	11.7	4.2	50.0	-3.1

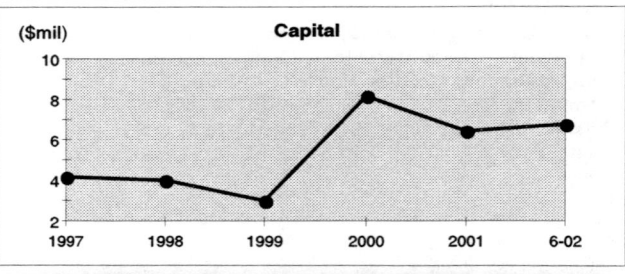

Capital chart, 1997–6-02

MEDCO CONTAINMENT LIFE INSURANCE COMPANY   C   Fair

Major Rating Factors: Fair overall results on stability tests (4.2 on a scale of 0 to 10) including negative cash flow from operations for 2002. Strong capitalization (10.0) based on excellent risk adjusted capital (severe loss scenario). Moreover, capital levels have been consistently high over the last five years. High quality investment portfolio (9.8).
Other Rating Factors: Excellent profitability (9.0) with operating gains in each of the last five years. Excellent liquidity (10.0).
Principal Business: Group health insurance (100%).
Principal Investments: NonCMO investment grade bonds (100%).
Investments in Affiliates: None
Group Affiliation: Merck & Co
Licensed in: All states except FL, NH, NJ, NY, PR
Commenced Business: July 1955
Address: 5073 Ritter Rd, Mechanicsburg, PA 17055
Phone: (717) 795-9133   **Domicile State:** PA   **NAIC Code:** 63762

Data Date	Weiss Safety Rating	RACR #1	RACR #2	Total Assets ($mil)	Capital ($mil)	Net Premium ($mil)	Net Income ($mil)
6-03	C	6.95	6.26	40.9	35.5	1.1	0.2
6-02	C	6.39	5.75	42.4	33.0	1.1	0.4
2002	C	6.92	6.23	39.5	35.3	2.3	2.4
2001	C	6.32	5.69	40.6	32.7	-4.3	7.7
2000	C	4.60	4.14	45.5	25.3	10.6	4.0
1999	C	4.72	4.25	36.1	21.2	7.0	4.2
1998	C-	3.60	3.24	40.6	17.1	10.2	6.7

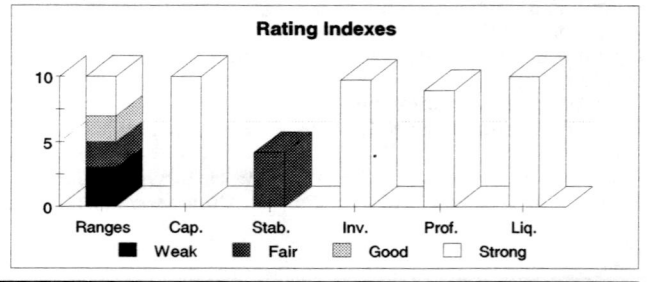

Rating Indexes chart: Ranges, Cap., Stab., Inv., Prof., Liq. — Weak, Fair, Good, Strong

Winter 2003 - 04
II. Analysis of Largest Companies

MEDICA * — A- Excellent

Major Rating Factors: Excellent profitability (7.6 on a scale of 0 to 10) despite a decline in earnings during 2002. Strong overall capitalization (8.2) based on excellent current risk-adjusted capital (severe loss scenario). Furthermore, this high level of risk-adjusted capital has been consistently maintained in previous years. High quality investment portfolio (8.2).
Other Rating Factors: Excellent overall results on stability tests (7.5) based on consistent premium and capital growth in the last five years. Good liquidity (6.6) with sufficient resources (cash flows and marketable investments) to handle a spike in claims.
Principal Business: Comp med (62%), Medicaid (28%), med only (5%), Medicare (3%), med supp (2%)
Mem Phys: 02: 17,174 **01:** 15,940   **02 MLR** 87% **/ 02 Admin Exp** 10%
Enroll(000): Q1 03: 489 **02:** 494 **01:** 458   **Med Exp PMPM:** $212
Principal Investments: Cash and equiv (21%), nonaffiliate common stock (14%), real estate (1%), other (65%)
Provider Compensation ($000): Contr fee ($715,612), bonus arrang ($393,017), FFS ($41,553), capitation ($21,639), other ($9,027)
Total Member Encounters: N/A
Group Affiliation: Medica Holding Co
Licensed in: MN, ND
Address: 5601 Smetana Dr, Minnetonka, MN 55343
Phone: (952) 992-3635   **Dom State:** MN   **Commenced Bus:** December 1974

Data Date	Weiss Safety Rating	RACR #1	RACR #2	Total Assets ($mil)	Capital ($mil)	Net Premium ($mil)	Net Income ($mil)
3-03	A-	2.33	1.94	599.3	254.5	367.9	13.0
3-02	B+	2.16	1.61	472.1	234.6	329.5	11.1
2002	B+	2.33	1.94	561.8	255.3	1,389.4	23.8
2001	B+	2.16	1.61	471.5	232.6	1,183.7	29.1
2000	B+	1.85	1.47	430.3	185.7	1,166.8	28.6
1999	B+	1.84	1.49	439.8	185.6	1,157.5	3.7
1998	B+	1.85	1.44	434.8	175.9	1,221.6	12.3

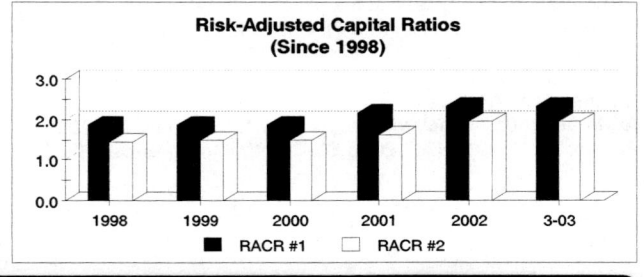

Risk-Adjusted Capital Ratios (Since 1998)

MEDICA HEALTH PLANS OF WI — C Fair

Major Rating Factors: Weak profitability index (1.4 on a scale of 0 to 10) with modest operating losses during 1998, 1999, 2000 and 2002. Poor capitalization (2.9) based on weak current risk-adjusted capital (moderate loss scenario) as results have slipped from the fair range over the last year. Good overall results on stability tests (6.1) based on consistent premium and capital growth in the last five years but rapid enrollment growth during the past five years. Rating is significantly influenced by the good financial results of Medica Holding Co.
Other Rating Factors: High quality investment portfolio (9.9) containing no exposure to mortgages, junk bonds, or unaffiliated stocks. Excellent liquidity (7.1) with ample operational cash flow and liquid investments.
Principal Business: Comp med (100%)
Mem Phys: 02: 17,174 **01:** 15,940   **02 MLR** 93% **/ 02 Admin Exp** 11%
Enroll(000): Q1 03: 4 **02:** 4 **01:** 4   **Med Exp PMPM:** $186
Principal Investments: Cash and equiv (99%), other (1%)
Provider Compensation ($000): Contr fee ($6,274), bonus arrang ($2,994), FFS ($221), capitation ($56)
Total Member Encounters: Phys (52,718), non-phys (54,636)
Group Affiliation: Medica Holding Co
Licensed in: WI
Address: 5601 Smetana Dr, Minnetonka, MN 55343
Phone: (952) 992-3635   **Dom State:** WI   **Commenced Bus:** February 1998

Data Date	Weiss Safety Rating	RACR #1	RACR #2	Total Assets ($mil)	Capital ($mil)	Net Premium ($mil)	Net Income ($mil)
3-03	C	0.62	0.51	3.6	2.1	2.6	0.3
3-02	C	0.98	0.83	3.4	2.0	2.6	0.1
2002	C	0.53	0.44	3.3	1.8	10.5	-0.4
2001	C	0.98	0.83	3.2	1.8	7.8	0.2
2000	C	0.52	0.43	2.4	1.5	5.0	-0.1
1999	C	0.56	0.47	2.2	1.7	2.4	-0.1
1998	C	0.60	0.51	2.0	1.8	0.9	-0.1

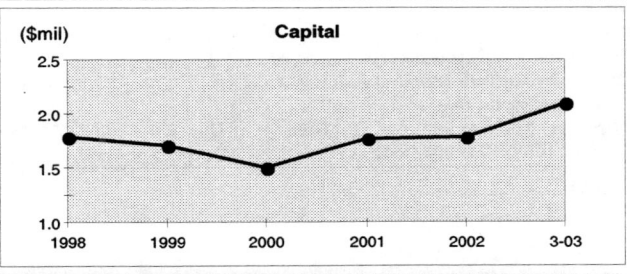

Capital ($mil)

MEDICA INS CO — B Good

Major Rating Factors: Good overall profitability index (5.5 on a scale of 0 to 10) despite operating losses during 1999. Good liquidity (6.9) with sufficient resources (cash flows and marketable investments) to handle a spike in claims. Strong capitalization index (8.4) based on excellent current risk-adjusted capital (severe loss scenario).
Other Rating Factors: High quality investment portfolio (9.7) containing no exposure to mortgages, junk bonds, or unaffiliated stocks.
Principal Business: Comp med (98%), stop loss (2%)
Mem Phys: 02: 17,174 **01:** 15,940   **02 MLR** 83% **/ 02 Admin Exp** 14%
Enroll(000): Q1 03: 330 **02:** 356 **01:** 372   **Med Exp PMPM:** $53
Principal Investments: Cash and equiv (51%), other (49%)
Provider Compensation ($000): Contr fee ($127,156), bonus arrang ($87,406), FFS ($4,814), capitation ($1,108), other ($10,058)
Total Member Encounters: Phys (1,687,191), non-phys (1,382,115)
Group Affiliation: Allina Health System
Licensed in: MN, ND, WI
Address: 5601 Smetana Dr, Minnetonka, MN 55343
Phone: (952) 992-2900   **Dom State:** MN   **Commenced Bus:** June 1984

Data Date	Weiss Safety Rating	RACR #1	RACR #2	Total Assets ($mil)	Capital ($mil)	Net Premium ($mil)	Net Income ($mil)
3-03	B	2.51	2.09	103.2	55.7	75.0	2.2
3-02	N/A	N/A	N/A	N/A	N/A	N/A	N/A
2002	N/A	N/A	N/A	101.5	56.6	279.9	7.4
2001	N/A	N/A	N/A	94.4	50.1	270.4	N/A
2000	D	0.29	0.20	88.1	36.5	255.6	8.6
1999	D	0.24	0.15	71.7	21.8	N/A	-3.3
1998	C-	0.41	0.26	56.3	25.0	N/A	1.2

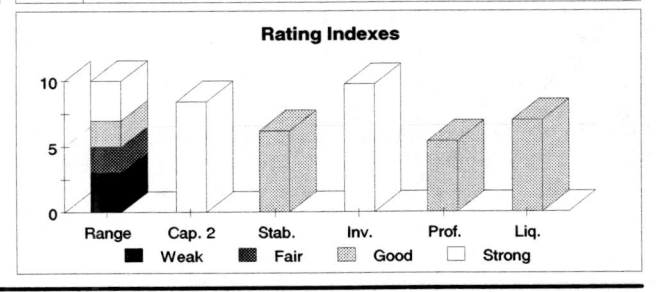

Rating Indexes

www.WeissRatings.com   221   * Denotes a Weiss Recommended Company

II. Analysis of Largest Companies

Winter 2003 - 04

MEDICAL ASSOC CLINIC HEALTH PLAN — C — Fair

Major Rating Factors: Fair profitability index (4.0 on a scale of 0 to 10) with operating losses during 1998. Fair capitalization index (4.5) based on fair current risk-adjusted capital (moderate loss scenario). Good liquidity (7.0) with sufficient resources (cash flows and marketable investments) to handle a spike in claims.
Other Rating Factors: High quality investment portfolio (9.8) containing no exposure to mortgages, junk bonds, or unaffiliated stocks. Excellent overall results on stability tests (7.2) based on consistent premium and capital growth in the last five years.
Principal Business: Comp med (71%), Medicare (17%), med supp (12%)
Mem Phys: 02: 264   **01:** 264   **02 MLR** 90%   **/ 02 Admin Exp** 9%
Enroll(000): Q1 03: 7   **02:** 7   **01:** 6   **Med Exp PMPM:** $202
Principal Investments: Cash and equiv (82%), other (18%)
Provider Compensation ($000): Capitation ($15,194)
Total Member Encounters: Phys (72,122)
Group Affiliation: None
Licensed in: WI
Address: 1605 Associates Dr., Suite 101, Dubuque, IA 52002-2270
Phone: (563) 556-8070   **Dom State:** WI   **Commenced Bus:** January 1985

Data Date	Weiss Safety Rating	RACR #1	RACR #2	Total Assets ($mil)	Capital ($mil)	Net Premium ($mil)	Net Income ($mil)
3-03	C	0.85	0.71	1.9	1.5	5.0	0.0
3-02	C	0.87	0.76	1.7	1.5	4.1	0.0
2002	C	0.84	0.70	2.6	1.5	17.2	0.0
2001	C	0.86	0.76	2.2	1.4	14.2	0.0
2000	C-	1.08	0.95	2.1	1.4	11.6	0.1
1999	C-	1.14	1.00	1.9	1.3	9.8	0.0
1998	N/A	N/A	N/A	1.8	1.2	8.3	N/A

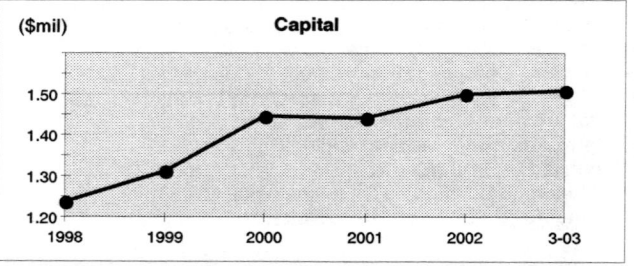

MEDICAL ASSOCIATES HEALTH PLAN INC — C+ — Fair

Major Rating Factors: Good capitalization (5.4 on a scale of 0 to 10) based on good current risk-adjusted capital (severe loss scenario) reflecting some improvement over results in 1998. Excellent profitability (7.7) with operating gains in each of the last five years. High quality investment portfolio (9.8) containing little or no exposure to mortgages, junk bonds, or unaffiliated stocks.
Other Rating Factors: Excellent overall results on stability tests (7.7) based on consistent premium and capital growth in the last five years. Excellent liquidity (7.0) with ample operational cash flow and liquid investments.
Principal Business: Comp med (73%), Medicare (17%), med supp (10%)
Mem Phys: 02: 264   **01:** 264   **02 MLR** 85%   **/ 02 Admin Exp** 10%
Enroll(000): Q1 03: 27   **02:** 26   **01:** 25   **Med Exp PMPM:** $180
Principal Investments: Cash and equiv (75%), nonaffiliate common stock (4%), other (20%)
Provider Compensation ($000): Contr fee ($28,449), capitation ($27,648)
Total Member Encounters: Phys (285,831)
Group Affiliation: Medical Associates Clinic
Licensed in: IL, IA
Address: 1605 Associates Dr., Suite 101, Dubuque, IA 52002-2270
Phone: (563) 556-8070   **Dom State:** IA   **Commenced Bus:** August 1987

Data Date	Weiss Safety Rating	RACR #1	RACR #2	Total Assets ($mil)	Capital ($mil)	Net Premium ($mil)	Net Income ($mil)
3-03	C+	0.99	0.83	12.8	6.1	18.2	0.9
3-02	C	0.78	0.66	11.2	5.7	15.5	1.1
2002	C	0.87	0.72	11.1	5.3	64.6	1.8
2001	C	0.78	0.66	11.7	4.7	56.8	0.8
2000	D	0.66	0.56	10.1	4.0	52.8	0.1
1999	D	0.65	0.55	10.4	3.7	51.3	0.6
1998	D+	0.63	0.54	9.5	3.4	48.3	1.0

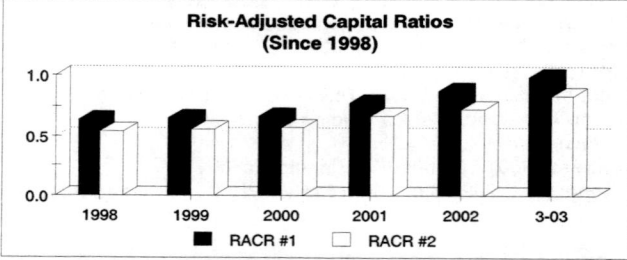

MEDICAL CENTER HEALTH PLAN — E+ — Very Weak

Major Rating Factors: Weak profitability index (0.9 on a scale of 0 to 10) with modest operating losses during 1999, 2000 and 2002. Average return on equity has been extremely poor. Poor capitalization index (0.6) based on weak current risk-adjusted capital (moderate loss scenario). Weak liquidity (2.2) as a spike in claims may stretch capacity.
Other Rating Factors: Fair overall results on stability tests (3.9) based on an overall decline in enrollment over the past five years despite growth in 1999. High quality investment portfolio (9.9) containing no exposure to mortgages, junk bonds, or unaffiliated stocks
Principal Business: Medicaid (100%)
Mem Phys: 02: N/A   **01:** 4,920   **02 MLR** 87%   **/ 02 Admin Exp** 15%
Enroll(000):   **02:** 45   **01:** 52   **Med Exp PMPM:** $130
Principal Investments: Cash and equiv (100%)
Provider Compensation ($000): FFS ($66,106), capitation ($11,600)
Total Member Encounters: Phys (164,261), non-phys (41,276)
Group Affiliation: None
Licensed in: IL, MO
Address: 200 Stevens Drive, Philadelphia, PA 19113
Phone: (314) 505-5000   **Dom State:** MO   **Commenced Bus:** February 1988

Data Date	Weiss Safety Rating	RACR #1	RACR #2	Total Assets ($mil)	Capital ($mil)	Net Premium ($mil)	Net Income ($mil)
2002	E+	0.36	0.30	19.5	5.0	87.5	-0.6
2001	E	0.18	0.15	21.3	2.9	82.1	1.1
2000	E-	0.00	0.00	32.5	-0.7	145.6	-13.9
1999	E+	0.26	0.22	43.0	5.4	164.5	-14.5
1998	D-	0.39	0.33	35.0	2.9	139.9	0.5

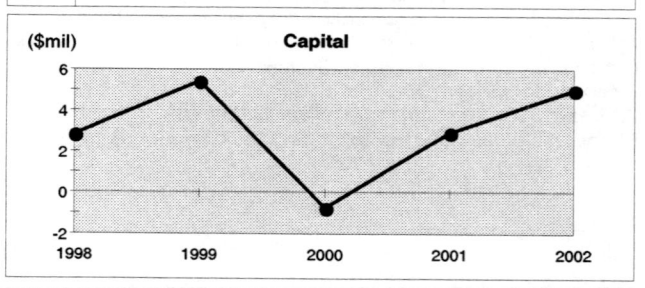

Winter 2003 - 04
II. Analysis of Largest Companies

MEDICAL HEALTH INS CORP OF OHIO C- Fair

Major Rating Factors: Weak profitability index (0.9 on a scale of 0 to 10) with operating losses during 1998, 1999, 2000 and 2001. Average return on equity has been poor at -43%. Good overall results on stability tests (5.1) despite a decline in enrollment during 2002, excessive capital growth during 2002. Potential support from affiliation with Mutual Holding Group. Strong capitalization (8.4) based on excellent current risk-adjusted capital (severe loss scenario) reflecting significant improvement over results in 1998.
Other Rating Factors: High quality investment portfolio (9.9) containing no exposure to mortgages, junk bonds, or unaffiliated stocks. Excellent liquidity (7.1) with ample operational cash flow and liquid investments.
Principal Business: Comp med (92%), FEHB (8%)
Mem Phys: 02: 20,256 **01:** 18,387 **02 MLR** 83% **/ 02 Admin Exp** 8%
Enroll(000): Q1 03: 100 **02:** 60 **01:** 101 **Med Exp PMPM:** $174
Principal Investments: Cash and equiv (63%), other (37%)
Provider Compensation ($000): Contr fee ($158,333), capitation ($8,729), bonus arrang ($4,691), FFS ($2,258), salary ($1,455), other ($23)
Total Member Encounters: Phys (524,143), non-phys (152,091)
Group Affiliation: Mutual Holding Group
Licensed in: OH
Address: 2060 E Ninth St, Cleveland, OH 44115-1355
Phone: (216) 687-7000 **Dom State:** OH **Commenced Bus:** January 1985

Data Date	Weiss Safety Rating	RACR #1	RACR #2	Total Assets ($mil)	Capital ($mil)	Net Premium ($mil)	Net Income ($mil)
3-03	C-	2.46	2.05	65.0	33.6	40.4	3.8
3-02	D+	0.84	0.71	54.5	17.5	53.8	3.2
2002	C-	2.17	1.81	58.5	29.7	201.0	14.7
2001	D+	0.84	0.71	51.2	16.4	273.7	-8.6
2000	D	0.73	0.63	56.9	16.0	289.1	-4.2
1999	D	0.64	0.55	46.9	15.0	266.8	-8.3
1998	D	0.64	0.54	40.7	11.9	234.5	-16.0

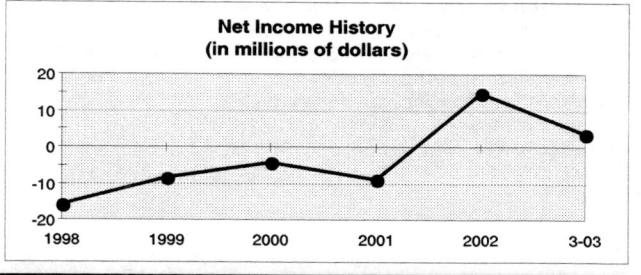

MEDICAL LIFE INSURANCE COMPANY B Good

Major Rating Factors: Good quality investment portfolio (6.8 on a scale of 0 to 10) despite mixed results such as: no exposure to mortgages and large holdings of BBB rated bonds but minimal holdings in junk bonds. Good liquidity (6.5) with sufficient resources to handle a spike in claims. Good overall results on stability tests (5.7) excellent operational trends and excellent risk diversification.
Other Rating Factors: Strong capitalization (10.0) based on excellent risk adjusted capital (severe loss scenario). Excellent profitability (9.2) with operating gains in each of the last five years.
Principal Business: Group life insurance (52%), group health insurance (28%), reinsurance (20%), and individual life insurance (1%).
Principal Investments: NonCMO investment grade bonds (90%), noninv. grade bonds (5%), common & preferred stock (2%), and cash (2%).
Investments in Affiliates: 1%
Group Affiliation: HCSC Group
Licensed in: All states except CA, NY, PR
Commenced Business: November 1975
Address: 1220 Huron Rd, Cleveland, OH 44115-1700
Phone: (216) 522-8713 **Domicile State:** OH **NAIC Code:** 86991

Data Date	Weiss Safety Rating	RACR #1	RACR #2	Total Assets ($mil)	Capital ($mil)	Net Premium ($mil)	Net Income ($mil)
6-03	B	3.99	3.02	232.6	135.4	103.4	5.8
6-02	B-	3.58	2.72	219.6	124.4	98.6	3.0
2002	B-	3.86	2.93	225.9	130.5	200.0	8.8
2001	B-	3.36	2.57	215.1	121.6	203.1	11.1
2000	B-	3.15	2.44	198.9	108.9	194.5	11.5
1999	B-	3.29	2.57	181.8	97.6	178.4	7.9
1998	B-	3.16	2.47	170.0	90.2	166.2	11.6

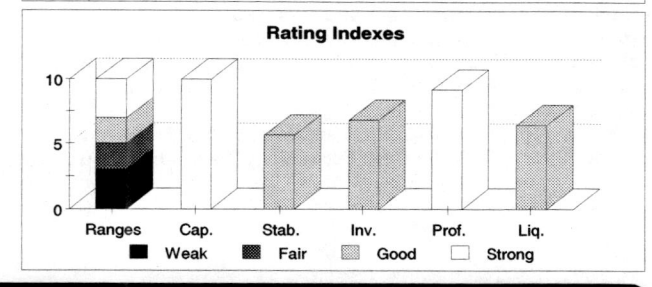

MEGA LIFE & HEALTH INSURANCE COMPANY C+ Fair

Major Rating Factors: Fair overall results on stability tests (4.8 on a scale of 0 to 10). Good current capitalization (5.9) based on mixed results -- excessive policy leverage mitigated by excellent risk adjusted capital (severe loss scenario) reflecting improvement over results in 2002. Good quality investment portfolio (6.5) despite mixed results such as: no exposure to mortgages and substantial holdings of BBB bonds but minimal holdings in junk bonds.
Other Rating Factors: Good overall profitability (6.3). Excellent liquidity (7.0).
Principal Business: Group health insurance (92%), individual health insurance (5%), reinsurance (2%), individual life insurance (1%), and group life insurance (1%).
Principal Investments: NonCMO investment grade bonds (57%), CMOs and structured securities (23%), common & preferred stock (7%), noninv. grade bonds (3%), and misc. investments (11%).
Investments in Affiliates: 4%
Group Affiliation: United Group Of Companies
Licensed in: All states except NY, PR
Commenced Business: June 1982
Address: 4001 McEwen Dr, Suite 200, Dallas, TX 75244
Phone: (972) 392-6700 **Domicile State:** OK **NAIC Code:** 97055

Data Date	Weiss Safety Rating	RACR #1	RACR #2	Total Assets ($mil)	Capital ($mil)	Net Premium ($mil)	Net Income ($mil)
6-03	C+	1.41	1.05	989.5	236.1	512.5	19.8
6-02	C+	1.74	1.30	832.6	212.1	359.1	5.0
2002	C+	1.29	0.98	927.5	204.3	873.0	0.2
2001	C+	1.86	1.38	819.9	208.4	570.8	18.6
2000	C+	1.88	1.42	766.2	216.7	464.0	28.0
1999	C+	2.51	1.74	755.3	206.6	467.2	40.5
1998	C+	1.83	1.30	717.1	149.8	497.0	-5.9

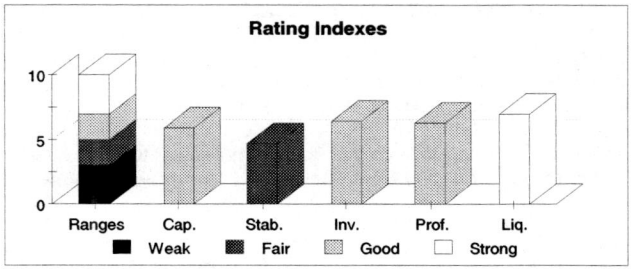

www.WeissRatings.com * Denotes a Weiss Recommended Company

II. Analysis of Largest Companies
Winter 2003 - 04

MEMORIAL PROHEALTH INC — D — Weak

Major Rating Factors: Weak profitability index (0.7 on a scale of 0 to 10). Poor capitalization index (1.7) based on weak current risk-adjusted capital (moderate loss scenario). Furthermore, this low level of risk-adjusted capital has been consistent in previous years. Fair overall results on stability tests (3.2) based on rapid premium growth over the last five years, an excessive 89% enrollment growth during the period.
Other Rating Factors: Good liquidity (5.5) with sufficient resources (cash flows and marketable investments) to handle a spike in claims. High quality investment portfolio (9.9) containing no exposure to mortgages, junk bonds, or unaffiliated stocks.
Principal Business: Comp med (100%)
Mem Phys: 01: 863 **00:** 835 **01 MLR** 109% / **01 Admin Exp** 20%
Enroll(000): Q2 02: 7 **01:** 8 **00:** 4 **Med Exp PMPM:** $213
Principal Investments: Cash and equiv (100%)
Provider Compensation ($000): Contr fee ($11,405), FFS ($3,317)
Total Member Encounters: N/A
Group Affiliation: Memorial Health System
Licensed in: GA
Address: 7135 Hodgson Memorial Dr #12, Savannah, GA 31406
Phone: (912) 350-6643 **Dom State:** GA **Commenced Bus:** July 1999

Data Date	Weiss Safety Rating	RACR #1	RACR #2	Total Assets ($mil)	Capital ($mil)	Net Premium ($mil)	Net Income ($mil)
6-02	D	0.45	0.39	10.3	3.4	7.9	-1.7
6-01	U	N/A	N/A	5.3	2.6	6.2	0.4
2001	D	0.49	0.41	8.0	1.6	13.7	-3.8
2000	U	N/A	N/A	3.8	2.2	4.6	0.4
1999	U	14.37	13.57	2.0	1.8	0.3	-0.6
1998	N/A	N/A	N/A	1.8	1.1	0.1	N/A
1997	N/A	N/A	N/A	1.6	N/A	N/A	N/A

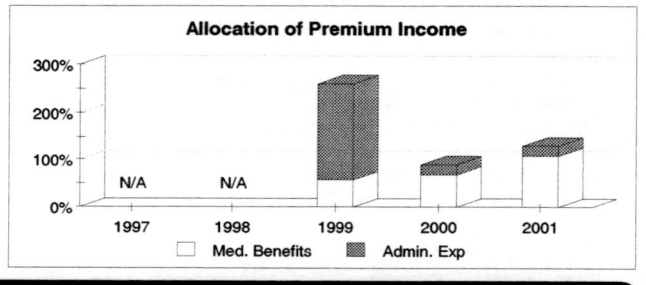

Allocation of Premium Income (bar chart, 1997–2001; Med. Benefits / Admin. Exp)

MEMPHIS MANAGED CARE CORP — E — Very Weak

Major Rating Factors: Weak profitability index (0.8 on a scale of 0 to 10) with operating losses during 1998, 1999 and 2002. Poor capitalization index (0.0) based on weak current risk-adjusted capital (severe loss scenario). Weak overall results on stability tests (0.4) based on a steep decline in premium revenue in 2002.
Other Rating Factors: Good liquidity (6.9) with sufficient resources (cash flows and marketable investments) to handle a spike in claims. High quality investment portfolio (9.9) containing no exposure to mortgages, junk bonds, or unaffiliated stocks.
Principal Business: Medicaid (100%)
Mem Phys: 02: N/A **01:** N/A **02 MLR** 99% / **02 Admin Exp** 3%
Enroll(000): Q1 03: 197 **02:** 191 **01:** 172 **Med Exp PMPM:** $53
Principal Investments: Cash and equiv (80%), other (20%)
Provider Compensation ($000): Contr fee ($143,050), capitation ($11,741)
Total Member Encounters: Phys (975,480), non-phys (162,961)
Group Affiliation: Regional Medical Ctr/UT Medical Grp
Licensed in: TN
Address: 1407 Union Ave, Suite 1100, Memphis, TN 38104
Phone: (901) 725-7100 **Dom State:** TN **Commenced Bus:** January 1994

Data Date	Weiss Safety Rating	RACR #1	RACR #2	Total Assets ($mil)	Capital ($mil)	Net Premium ($mil)	Net Income ($mil)
3-03	E	0.13	0.11	13.2	9.6	N/A	4.9
3-02	D-	0.43	0.36	51.4	1.5	84.9	-5.1
2002	E	0.05	0.04	13.6	5.1	117.0	-1.7
2001	D-	0.42	0.36	56.4	13.6	227.9	10.8
2000	D-	1.44	1.22	23.1	6.4	132.9	3.6
1999	E-	0.00	0.00	20.0	5.0	96.4	-0.7
1998	E-	0.00	0.00	10.7	-7.0	80.3	-7.2

Capital ($mil) chart, 1998–3-03

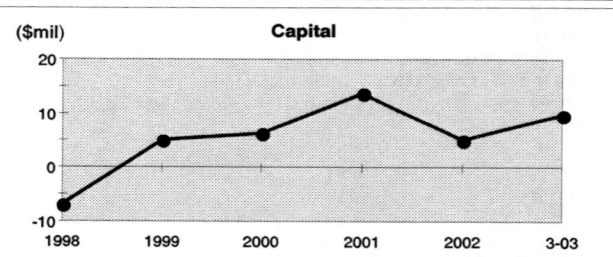

MERCY HEALTH PLANS OF MISSOURI INC — C- — Fair

Major Rating Factors: Weak profitability index (0.9 on a scale of 0 to 10) with operating losses during 1997, 1998, 1999 and 2001. Average return on equity has been extremely poor. Good capitalization index (5.0) based on good current risk-adjusted capital (severe loss scenario). Good overall results on stability tests (5.7) despite rapid premium growth over the last five years.
Other Rating Factors: Good liquidity (6.9) with sufficient resources (cash flows and marketable investments) to handle a spike in claims. High quality investment portfolio (9.9) containing no exposure to mortgages, junk bonds, or unaffiliated stocks.
Principal Business: Comp med (59%), Medicare (28%), Medicaid (8%), FEHB (3%), other (2%)
Mem Phys: 01: 8,575 **00:** 5,890 **01 MLR** 94% / **01 Admin Exp** 7%
Enroll(000): Q2 02: 203 **01:** 176 **00:** 152 **Med Exp PMPM:** $192
Principal Investments: Cash and equiv (97%), other (3%)
Provider Compensation ($000): Contr fee ($205,464), capitation ($154,514)
Total Member Encounters: Phys (1,534,552), non-phys (105,127)
Group Affiliation: Sisters of Mercy Health System
Licensed in: IL, MO, TX
Address: 425 South Woods Mill Rd, Chesterfield, MO 63017-3492
Phone: (314) 214-8100 **Dom State:** MO **Commenced Bus:** January 1995

Data Date	Weiss Safety Rating	RACR #1	RACR #2	Total Assets ($mil)	Capital ($mil)	Net Premium ($mil)	Net Income ($mil)
6-02	C-	0.91	0.78	70.3	18.2	266.9	2.7
6-01	C-	0.85	0.74	63.4	8.9	186.1	0.2
2001	C-	0.91	0.78	70.4	15.8	402.6	-2.6
2000	D	0.44	0.39	41.0	8.6	280.4	0.2
1999	D-	0.32	0.28	37.9	5.0	224.5	-13.3
1998	D-	0.74	0.65	35.4	7.7	173.5	-7.1
1997	E+	0.38	0.24	28.9	5.6	117.1	-20.7

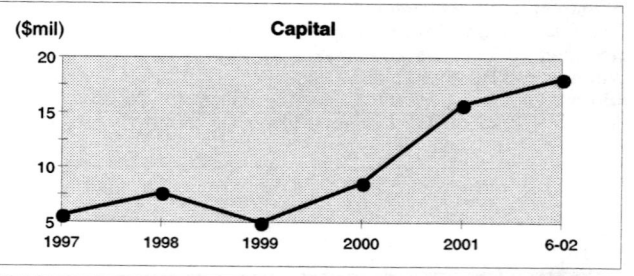

Capital ($mil) chart, 1997–6-02

Winter 2003 - 04 **II. Analysis of Largest Companies**

MERCYCARE INS CO   D   Weak

Major Rating Factors: Weak profitability index (2.4 on a scale of 0 to 10) with operating losses during 1999. Poor capitalization (1.8) based on weak current risk-adjusted capital (moderate loss scenario). Good liquidity (6.6) with sufficient resources (cash flows and marketable investments) to handle a spike in claims.
Other Rating Factors: High quality investment portfolio (8.3) containing little or no exposure to mortgages, junk bonds, or unaffiliated stocks.
Principal Business: Comp med (84%), Medicaid (16%)
Mem Phys: 02: 282   **01:** 321   **02 MLR** 92%   **/ 02 Admin Exp** 8%
Enroll(000): Q1 03: 30   **02:** 30   **01:** 29   **Med Exp PMPM:** $174
Principal Investments: Cash and equiv (52%), other (48%)
Provider Compensation ($000): FFS ($31,848), capitation ($17,877), other ($12,535)
Total Member Encounters: Phys (186,250), non-phys (33,861)
Group Affiliation: Southern Wisconsin Health Care Sys
Licensed in: IL, WI
Address: 3430 Palmer Dr, Janesville, WI 53546
Phone: (608) 752-3431   **Dom State:** WI   **Commenced Bus:** January 1994

Data Date	Weiss Safety Rating	RACR #1	RACR #2	Total Assets ($mil)	Capital ($mil)	Net Premium ($mil)	Net Income ($mil)
3-03	D	0.48	0.40	14.3	6.9	18.1	0.0
3-02	D	0.00	0.00	13.1	6.8	16.5	0.4
2002	D	0.00	0.00	14.4	6.9	67.2	0.4
2001	N/A	N/A	N/A	13.4	6.1	57.6	N/A
2000	U	0.41	0.36	8.7	4.2	49.0	0.0
1999	E+	0.35	0.31	9.1	3.7	42.2	-2.6
1998	D+	1.48	1.06	7.9	3.4	28.3	0.1

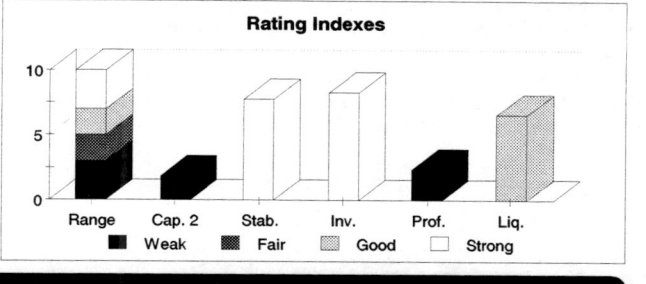

Rating Indexes (bar chart: Range, Cap. 2, Stab., Inv., Prof., Liq. — Weak / Fair / Good / Strong)

MERIT LIFE INSURANCE COMPANY *   B+   Good

Major Rating Factors: Good overall results on stability tests (6.4 on a scale of 0 to 10). Stability strengths include excellent operational trends and excellent risk diversification. Fair quality investment portfolio (3.8). Strong capitalization (10.0) based on excellent risk adjusted capital (severe loss scenario). Moreover, capital levels have been consistently high over the last five years.
Other Rating Factors: Excellent profitability (9.2) with operating gains in each of the last five years. Excellent liquidity (8.2).
Principal Business: Credit health insurance (36%), individual life insurance (34%), credit life insurance (23%), individual health insurance (7%), and reinsurance (1%).
Principal Investments: NonCMO investment grade bonds (58%), CMOs and structured securities (23%), noninv. grade bonds (14%), mortgages in good standing (5%), and real estate (1%).
Investments in Affiliates: None
Group Affiliation: American International Group
Licensed in: All states except AK, NH, NY, VT, PR
Commenced Business: October 1957
Address: 601 NW Second St, Evansville, IN 47708-1013
Phone: (812) 424-8031   **Domicile State:** IN   **NAIC Code:** 65951

Data Date	Weiss Safety Rating	RACR #1	RACR #2	Total Assets ($mil)	Capital ($mil)	Net Premium ($mil)	Net Income ($mil)
6-03	B+	11.21	5.82	1,020.5	521.8	49.5	24.0
6-02	A-	10.03	5.04	974.1	451.6	47.4	25.3
2002	A-	10.14	5.20	929.6	474.6	110.9	45.3
2001	A-	9.83	5.06	922.5	437.7	121.2	54.0
2000	A	11.08	5.77	943.3	434.8	156.8	30.1
1999	A	11.67	6.09	864.8	406.7	150.1	35.2
1998	A	11.76	6.20	802.8	372.9	127.0	44.3

Adverse Trends in Operations

Decrease in premium volume from 2001 to 2002 (9%)
Decrease in premium volume from 2000 to 2001 (23%)
Decrease in asset base during 2001 (2%)

METROPOLITAN HEALTH PLAN *   A-   Excellent

Major Rating Factors: Strong capitalization (7.8 on a scale of 0 to 10) based on excellent current risk-adjusted capital (severe loss scenario) reflecting significant improvement over results in 1998. High quality investment portfolio (9.9) containing no exposure to mortgages, junk bonds, or unaffiliated stocks. Excellent liquidity (7.3) with ample operational cash flow and liquid investments.
Other Rating Factors: Good overall profitability index (6.8) despite operating losses during 1998. Good overall results on stability tests (6.2) based on consistent premium and capital growth in the last five years but a decline in the number of member physicians during 2002.
Principal Business: Medicaid (84%), Medicare (10%), other (7%)
Mem Phys: 02: 278   **01:** 362   **02 MLR** 84%   **/ 02 Admin Exp** 10%
Enroll(000): Q1 03: 21   **02:** 21   **01:** 21   **Med Exp PMPM:** $332
Principal Investments: Cash and equiv (98%), other (2%)
Provider Compensation ($000): Contr fee ($71,752), FFS ($6,053), capitation ($659)
Total Member Encounters: Phys (71,664), non-phys (26,534)
Group Affiliation: None
Licensed in: MN
Address: 822 S Third St Ste 140, Minneapolis, MN 55415
Phone: (612) 347-7596   **Dom State:** MN   **Commenced Bus:** March 1984

Data Date	Weiss Safety Rating	RACR #1	RACR #2	Total Assets ($mil)	Capital ($mil)	Net Premium ($mil)	Net Income ($mil)
3-03	A-	1.98	1.65	40.9	23.5	24.3	1.2
3-02	B-	0.00	0.00	31.1	16.4	24.0	1.3
2002	A-	1.90	1.58	40.2	22.6	99.9	6.9
2001	B-	1.84	1.56	29.3	15.1	77.7	4.6
2000	D+	1.53	1.29	25.3	12.2	73.5	4.0
1999	D+	0.91	0.78	24.5	8.3	82.8	0.3
1998	D+	0.89	0.75	20.2	8.1	72.4	-6.4

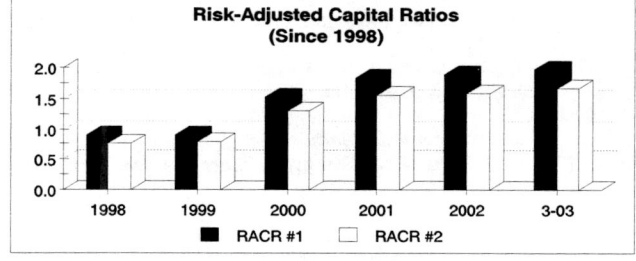

Risk-Adjusted Capital Ratios (Since 1998) (bar chart 1998–3-03, RACR #1 / RACR #2)

www.WeissRatings.com   225   * Denotes a Weiss Recommended Company

II. Analysis of Largest Companies
Winter 2003 - 04

METROWEST HEALTH PLAN INC — B — Good

Major Rating Factors: Good overall profitability index (6.2 on a scale of 0 to 10) despite a decline in earnings during 2002. Strong capitalization index (7.0) based on excellent current risk-adjusted capital (severe loss scenario) despite some fluctuation in capital levels. High quality investment portfolio (9.9) containing no exposure to mortgages, junk bonds, or unaffiliated stocks.
Other Rating Factors: Excellent overall results on stability tests (7.3). Excellent liquidity (7.3) with ample operational cash flow and liquid investments
Principal Business: Medicaid (100%)
Mem Phys: 02: 325   **01:** 310   **02 MLR** 84%   **/ 02 Admin Exp** 14%
Enroll(000): Q1 03: 8   **02:** 8   **01:** 5   **Med Exp PMPM:** $179
Principal Investments: Cash and equiv (100%)
Provider Compensation ($000): Capitation ($11,346)
Total Member Encounters: Phys (14,780), non-phys (3,695)
Group Affiliation: Tarrant County Hosp Dist dba JPSHN
Licensed in: TX
Address: 1500 S Main St 3rd Floor OPC, Fort Worth, TX 76104
Phone: (817) 665-5100   **Dom State:** TX   **Commenced Bus:** September 1997

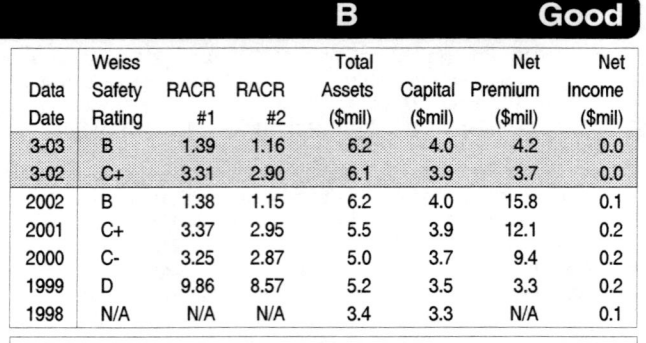

Data Date	Weiss Safety Rating	RACR #1	RACR #2	Total Assets ($mil)	Capital ($mil)	Net Premium ($mil)	Net Income ($mil)
3-03	B	1.39	1.16	6.2	4.0	4.2	0.0
3-02	C+	3.31	2.90	6.1	3.9	3.7	0.0
2002	B	1.38	1.15	6.2	4.0	15.8	0.1
2001	C+	3.37	2.95	5.5	3.9	12.1	0.2
2000	C-	3.25	2.87	5.0	3.7	9.4	0.2
1999	D	9.86	8.57	5.2	3.5	3.3	0.2
1998	N/A	N/A	N/A	3.4	3.3	N/A	0.1

Risk-Adjusted Capital Ratios (Since 1998)

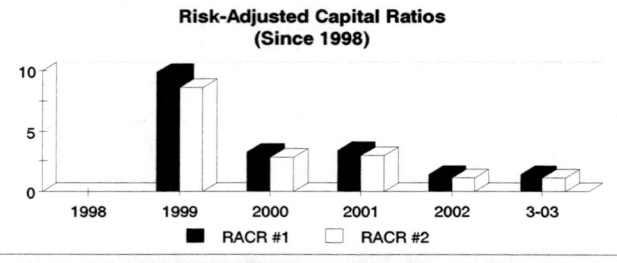

MID-WEST NATIONAL LIFE INSURANCE COMPANY OF TN — C — Fair

Major Rating Factors: Fair overall results on stability tests (4.3 on a scale of 0 to 10). Strong capitalization (6.5) based on excellent risk adjusted capital (severe loss scenario). Moreover, capital has steadily grown over the last five years. Good quality investment portfolio (6.8) despite mixed results such as: no exposure to mortgages and large holdings of BBB rated bonds but small junk bond holdings.
Other Rating Factors: Excellent profitability (8.3) with operating gains in each of the last five years. Excellent liquidity (7.4).
Principal Business: Group health insurance (81%), individual health insurance (9%), individual life insurance (7%), reinsurance (2%), and group life insurance (1%).
Principal Investments: NonCMO investment grade bonds (66%), CMOs and structured securities (27%), noninv. grade bonds (5%), common & preferred stock (1%), and policy loans (1%).
Investments in Affiliates: 1%
Group Affiliation: United Group Of Companies
Licensed in: All states except ME, NH, NY, VT
Commenced Business: May 1965
Address: 4001 McEwen Dr, Suite 200, Dallas, TX 75244
Phone: (972) 392-6700   **Domicile State:** TN   **NAIC Code:** 66087

Data Date	Weiss Safety Rating	RACR #1	RACR #2	Total Assets ($mil)	Capital ($mil)	Net Premium ($mil)	Net Income ($mil)
6-03	C	1.69	1.22	372.5	89.5	196.5	8.9
6-02	C	2.00	1.39	297.0	75.8	138.6	8.8
2002	C	1.63	1.18	327.7	77.6	311.3	14.9
2001	C	2.13	1.52	271.9	68.9	206.0	13.8
2000	C	2.42	1.74	217.5	62.9	165.5	15.3
1999	C	2.45	1.73	195.1	57.1	144.2	6.4
1998	C	2.43	1.72	182.5	53.0	134.9	6.6

Rating Indexes

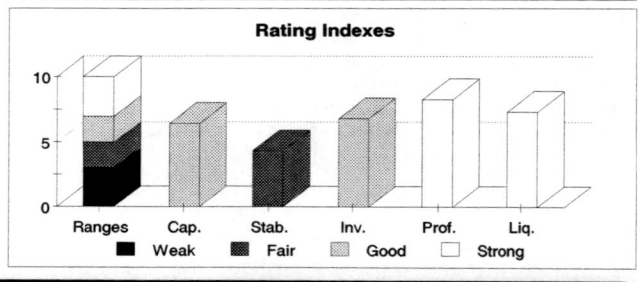

MIDWEST HEALTH PLAN INC — B — Good

Major Rating Factors: Good capitalization (6.8 on a scale of 0 to 10) based on excellent current risk-adjusted capital (severe loss scenario) reflecting significant improvement over results in 1999. Fair liquidity (4.5) as cash resources may not be adequate to cover a spike in claims. Excellent profitability (9.2) with operating gains in each of the last five years.
Other Rating Factors: High quality investment portfolio (9.9) containing no exposure to mortgages, junk bonds, or unaffiliated stocks. Excellent overall results on stability tests (7.3) based on consistent premium and capital growth in the last five years but rapid enrollment growth during the past five years.
Principal Business: Medicaid (100%)
Mem Phys: 02: 495   **01:** 459   **02 MLR** 84%   **/ 02 Admin Exp** 9%
Enroll(000): Q1 03: 42   **02:** 40   **01:** 35   **Med Exp PMPM:** $145
Principal Investments: Cash and equiv (96%), other (4%)
Provider Compensation ($000): Contr fee ($48,216), capitation ($14,144), bonus arrang ($1,682)
Total Member Encounters: Phys (186,504), non-phys (37,094)
Group Affiliation: Midwest-HC Inc
Licensed in: MI
Address: 5050 Schaefer Rd, Dearborn, MI 48126
Phone: (313) 581-3700   **Dom State:** MI   **Commenced Bus:** June 1993

Data Date	Weiss Safety Rating	RACR #1	RACR #2	Total Assets ($mil)	Capital ($mil)	Net Premium ($mil)	Net Income ($mil)
3-03	B	1.19	1.00	27.7	11.0	21.2	1.0
3-02	C	0.00	0.00	22.9	6.9	18.6	0.6
2002	B	1.10	0.92	27.4	10.1	78.6	3.5
2001	C	0.97	0.82	21.1	6.1	66.4	1.9
2000	C	0.87	0.74	15.1	4.0	42.9	2.0
1999	C	0.54	0.46	10.9	3.1	26.8	0.5
1998	C	2.58	2.25	6.6	2.3	18.2	1.9

Risk-Adjusted Capital Ratios (Since 1998)

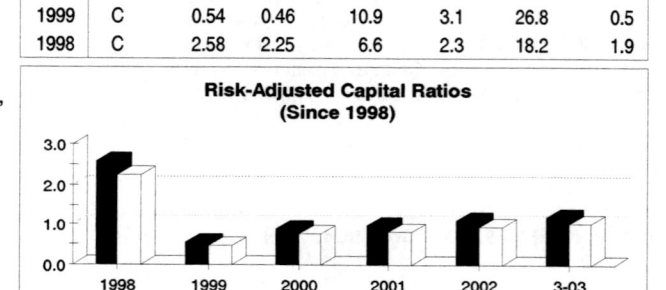

Winter 2003 - 04 II. Analysis of Largest Companies

MIDWEST SECURITY LIFE INSURANCE COMPANY *   B+   Good

Major Rating Factors: Good overall results on stability tests (5.2 on a scale of 0 to 10) despite fair financial strength of affiliated United HealthGroup Inc and fair risk adjusted capital in prior years. Other stability subfactors include excellent operational trends and excellent risk diversification. Good current capitalization (5.8) based on excellent risk adjusted capital (severe loss scenario) reflecting significant improvement over results in 1998. Good liquidity (6.3).
Other Rating Factors: High quality investment portfolio (7.5). Excellent profitability (9.2) with operating gains in each of the last five years.
Principal Business: Group health insurance (97%), individual annuities (2%), and group life insurance (1%).
Principal Investments: NonCMO investment grade bonds (48%), CMOs and structured securities (41%), real estate (5%), cash (3%), and misc. investments (2%).
Investments in Affiliates: None
Group Affiliation: United HealthGroup Inc
Licensed in: AK, AZ, AR, CO, DE, ID, IL, IN, IA, KS, KY, LA, MI, MN, MS, MO, NE, NV, NM, ND, OH, OK, OR, SC, SD, TX, UT, WA, WI
Commenced Business: March 1973
Address: 2700 Midwest Dr, Onalaska, WI 54650-8764
Phone: (608) 783-7130   **Domicile State:** WI   **NAIC Code:** 79480

Data Date	Weiss Safety Rating	RACR #1	RACR #2	Total Assets ($mil)	Capital ($mil)	Net Premium ($mil)	Net Income ($mil)
6-03	B+	1.88	1.42	132.8	51.9	107.6	7.5
6-02	C+	1.59	1.20	116.8	39.4	98.1	5.4
2002	B	1.66	1.25	122.9	44.4	203.2	16.0
2001	C	1.47	1.10	109.8	33.9	166.7	7.9
2000	C	1.29	0.94	85.0	25.8	118.2	4.3
1999	C	1.14	0.81	71.6	21.6	96.6	3.4
1998	C	1.01	0.72	70.4	18.4	91.4	2.2

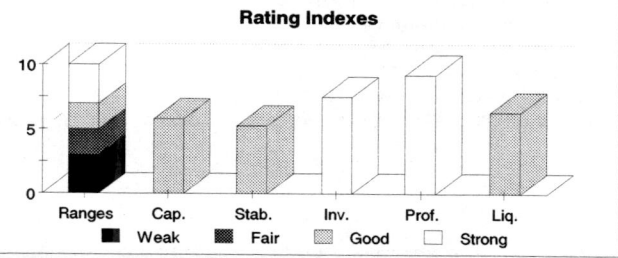

Rating Indexes (Ranges, Cap., Stab., Inv., Prof., Liq.; Weak / Fair / Good / Strong)

MII LIFE INCORPORATED   B   Good

Major Rating Factors: Good overall results on stability tests (5.9 on a scale of 0 to 10). Stability strengths include good operational trends and good risk diversification. Strong capitalization (9.2) based on excellent risk adjusted capital (severe loss scenario). Moreover, capital levels have been consistently high over the last five years. High quality investment portfolio (7.9).
Other Rating Factors: Excellent profitability (8.3) with operating gains in each of the last five years. Excellent liquidity (7.4).
Principal Business: Group life insurance (57%), group health insurance (23%), reinsurance (16%), and individual life insurance (4%).
Principal Investments: NonCMO investment grade bonds (76%), common & preferred stock (19%), and CMOs and structured securities (9%).
Investments in Affiliates: 14%
Group Affiliation: Aware Integrated Inc
Licensed in: AZ, MI, MN, ND, SD, WI
Commenced Business: September 1959
Address: 3535 Blue Cross Rd, St Paul, MN 55122
Phone: (800) 859-2144   **Domicile State:** MN   **NAIC Code:** 61522

Data Date	Weiss Safety Rating	RACR #1	RACR #2	Total Assets ($mil)	Capital ($mil)	Net Premium ($mil)	Net Income ($mil)
6-03	B	3.41	2.49	62.0	38.4	11.0	1.0
6-02	B	3.31	2.40	54.0	36.5	10.3	1.2
2002	B	3.23	2.38	63.6	36.7	21.0	1.7
2001	B	3.03	2.22	51.0	35.7	19.6	2.5
2000	B	3.13	2.29	43.9	32.0	17.1	2.1
1999	B	3.38	2.49	41.6	30.6	17.4	3.6
1998	B	3.08	2.27	37.8	27.4	16.7	3.1

Adverse Trends in Operations

Increase in policy surrenders from 2001 to 2002 (177%)
Decrease in premium volume from 1999 to 2000 (2%)
Increase in policy surrenders from 1998 to 1999 (2000%)

MISSOURI CARE HEALTH PLAN   D+   Weak

Major Rating Factors: Weak profitability index (1.4 on a scale of 0 to 10) with operating losses during 1998, 1999, 2000 and 2001. Poor capitalization index (2.6) based on weak current risk-adjusted capital (moderate loss scenario). Furthermore, this low level of risk-adjusted capital has been consistent in previous years. Fair overall results on stability tests (4.6) based on weak risk-adjusted capital in prior years, rapid premium growth over the last five years and rapid enrollment growth during the past five years.
Other Rating Factors: Good liquidity (6.9) with sufficient resources (cash flows and marketable investments) to handle a spike in claims. High quality investment portfolio (9.9) containing no exposure to mortgages, junk bonds, or unaffiliated stocks.
Principal Business: Medicaid (100%)
Mem Phys: 02: 692   **01:** 719   **02 MLR** 89%   **/ 02 Admin Exp** 13%
Enroll(000): Q1 03: 31   **02:** 30   **01:** 28   **Med Exp PMPM:** $135
Principal Investments: Cash and equiv (100%)
Provider Compensation ($000): FFS ($43,934), capitation ($4,622)
Total Member Encounters: Phys (155,929), non-phys (29,096)
Group Affiliation: Curators of University of Missouri
Licensed in: MO
Address: 2404 Forum Blvd, Columbia, MO 65203
Phone: (573) 441-2100   **Dom State:** MO   **Commenced Bus:** September 1997

Data Date	Weiss Safety Rating	RACR #1	RACR #2	Total Assets ($mil)	Capital ($mil)	Net Premium ($mil)	Net Income ($mil)
3-03	D+	0.57	0.47	12.3	4.6	15.7	0.4
3-02	D	0.60	0.51	10.8	3.8	12.9	-0.1
2002	D	0.52	0.43	9.7	4.2	53.1	0.2
2001	D	0.60	0.51	11.8	4.0	43.9	-0.4
2000	D	0.42	0.36	7.0	1.8	28.4	-2.3
1999	D+	0.97	0.83	10.4	4.1	22.1	-2.5
1998	D+	1.48	1.26	8.6	4.2	12.9	-3.8

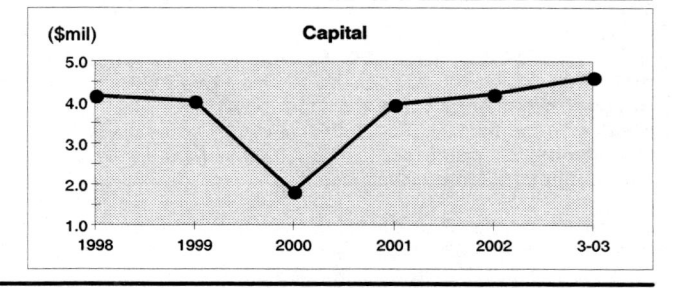

Capital ($mil) — 1998: ~4.2, 1999: ~4.1, 2000: ~1.8, 2001: ~4.0, 2002: ~4.2, 3-03: ~4.6

www.WeissRatings.com   * Denotes a Weiss Recommended Company

II. Analysis of Largest Companies — Winter 2003 - 04

MOLINA HEALTHCARE OF CALIFORNIA — C+ — Fair

Major Rating Factors: Good overall profitability index (6.7 on a scale of 0 to 10) despite a decline in earnings during 2002. Good capitalization (6.6) based on fair current risk-adjusted capital (moderate loss scenario). Good liquidity (7.0) with sufficient resources (cash flows and marketable investments) to handle a spike in claims.
Other Rating Factors: Weak overall results on stability tests (2.9) based on fair risk diversification due to the size of the company's affiliate group, rapid enrollment growth during the past five years.
Principal Business: None
Mem Phys: 02: N/A **01:** N/A **02 MLR** 85% **/ 02 Admin Exp** 10%
Enroll(000): Q1 03: 289 **02:** 286 **01:** 255 **Med Exp PMPM:** $82
Principal Investments ($000): Cash and equiv ($44,256)
Provider Compensation ($000): None
Total Member Encounters: N/A
Group Affiliation: Molina Healthcare Inc
Licensed in: CA, UT, WA
Address: One Golden Shore Dr, Long Beach, CA 90802
Phone: (562) 435-3666 **Dom State:** CA **Commenced Bus:** April 1989

Data Date	Weiss Safety Rating	RACR #1	RACR #2	Total Assets ($mil)	Capital ($mil)	Net Premium ($mil)	Net Income ($mil)
3-03	C+	0.98	0.62	85.7	30.0	82.8	3.6
3-02	B-	0.00	0.00	83.2	37.4	73.2	3.4
2002	C+	0.85	0.53	79.4	26.4	314.1	13.4
2001	B-	1.66	1.05	77.0	34.0	259.3	16.3
2000	B-	1.20	0.79	62.6	22.7	202.2	13.8
1999	C+	1.04	0.69	101.6	20.6	178.1	9.5
1998	C	0.92	0.60	38.3	11.2	132.1	2.6

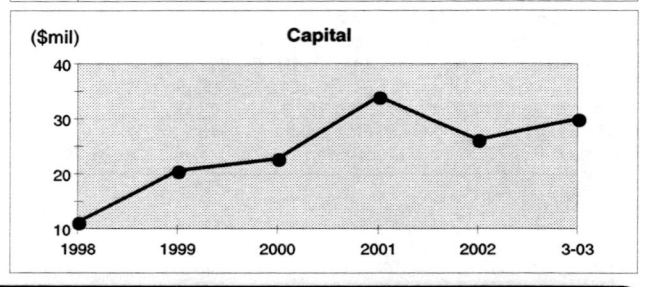

Capital ($mil) chart 1998–3-03

MOLINA HEALTHCARE OF MICHIGAN INC — B- — Good

Major Rating Factors: Fair capitalization (4.7 on a scale of 0 to 10) based on fair current risk-adjusted capital (moderate loss scenario) as results have slipped from the good range over the last year. Good overall profitability index (5.6). Good overall results on stability tests (6.8).
Other Rating Factors: Good liquidity (6.9) with sufficient resources (cash flows and marketable investments) to handle a spike in claims. High quality investment portfolio (9.9) containing no exposure to mortgages, junk bonds, or unaffiliated stocks.
Principal Business: Medicaid (100%)
Mem Phys: 02: 1,098 **01:** 901 **02 MLR** 85% **/ 02 Admin Exp** 15%
Enroll(000): Q1 03: 35 **02:** 33 **01:** 26 **Med Exp PMPM:** $126
Principal Investments: Cash and equiv (100%)
Provider Compensation ($000): Contr fee ($18,910), FFS ($18,748), capitation ($4,963), bonus arrang ($301)
Total Member Encounters: Phys (205,028), non-phys (14,488)
Group Affiliation: Molina Healthcare Inc
Licensed in: MI
Address: 100 W Big Beaver Ste 600, Troy, MI 48084-5209
Phone: (248) 925-1700 **Dom State:** MI **Commenced Bus:** January 1998

Data Date	Weiss Safety Rating	RACR #1	RACR #2	Total Assets ($mil)	Capital ($mil)	Net Premium ($mil)	Net Income ($mil)
3-03	B-	0.88	0.74	20.8	5.7	15.0	-0.1
3-02	B-	0.96	0.82	17.9	6.6	11.8	0.7
2002	B-	0.90	0.75	19.0	5.8	52.4	0.1
2001	B-	1.06	0.90	17.9	5.9	43.3	0.5
2000	N/A	N/A	N/A	12.3	2.9	32.2	N/A
1999	N/A	N/A	N/A	10.0	2.6	20.4	N/A
1998	N/A	N/A	N/A	N/A	N/A	N/A	N/A

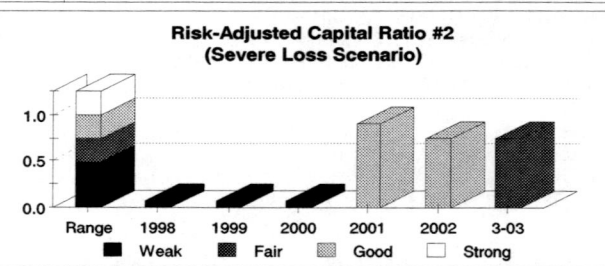

Risk-Adjusted Capital Ratio #2 (Severe Loss Scenario) chart — Weak / Fair / Good / Strong

MOLINA HEALTHCARE OF UTAH INC — C — Fair

Major Rating Factors: Weak profitability index (1.0 on a scale of 0 to 10) with modest operating losses during 2001 and 2002. Return on equity has been low, averaging 1%. Good capitalization (6.8) based on excellent current risk-adjusted capital (severe loss scenario) reflecting significant improvement over results in 2000. Good overall results on stability tests (5.6) based on consistent premium and capital growth in the last five years but a decline in the number of member physicians during 2002 and rapid enrollment growth during the past five years. Potentially strong support from affiliation with Molina Healthcare Inc.
Other Rating Factors: Good liquidity (6.1) with sufficient resources (cash flows and marketable investments) to handle a spike in claims. High quality investment portfolio (9.9) containing no exposure to mortgages, junk bonds, or unaffiliated stocks.
Principal Business: Medicaid (95%), other (5%)
Mem Phys: 02: 2,100 **01:** 2,400 **02 MLR** 95% **/ 02 Admin Exp** 7%
Enroll(000): Q1 03: 44 **02:** 42 **01:** 16 **Med Exp PMPM:** $170
Principal Investments: Cash and equiv (96%), other (4%)
Provider Compensation ($000): FFS ($43,995), capitation ($175)
Total Member Encounters: Phys (267,036), non-phys (181,372)
Group Affiliation: Molina Healthcare Inc
Licensed in: UT
Address: 7050 Union Park Ctr Ste 200, Midvale, UT 84047
Phone: (801) 858-0400 **Dom State:** UT **Commenced Bus:** May 1996

Data Date	Weiss Safety Rating	RACR #1	RACR #2	Total Assets ($mil)	Capital ($mil)	Net Premium ($mil)	Net Income ($mil)
3-03	C	1.21	1.01	29.1	4.9	26.0	0.2
3-02	C	0.82	0.69	10.5	3.6	8.0	-0.1
2002	C	1.20	1.00	28.6	4.9	63.3	0.0
2001	C	0.81	0.68	10.0	3.4	27.1	-1.4
2000	C	0.51	0.43	5.2	1.2	17.0	0.0
1999	C-	0.71	0.61	3.3	1.1	9.9	0.4
1998	C-	0.86	0.74	3.0	1.2	8.4	0.3

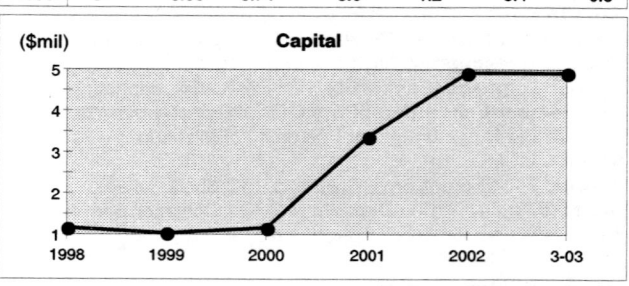

Capital ($mil) chart 1998–3-03

MOLINA HEALTHCARE OF WASHINGTON INC — B — Good

Major Rating Factors: Good overall profitability index (5.7 on a scale of 0 to 10) despite operating losses during 1998 and 1999. Good overall results on stability tests (5.4) despite excessive capital growth during 2002. Fair financial strength from affiliates. Strong capitalization (7.6) based on excellent current risk-adjusted capital (severe loss scenario) reflecting significant improvement over results in 1998.

Other Rating Factors: High quality investment portfolio (9.9) containing no exposure to mortgages, junk bonds, or unaffiliated stocks. Excellent liquidity (7.2) with ample operational cash flow and liquid investments.
Principal Business: Medicaid (97%), comp med (3%)
Mem Phys: 02: 7,996   01: 6,241   02 MLR 76% / 02 Admin Exp 12%
Enroll(000): Q1 03: 178   02: 161   01: 134   Med Exp PMPM: $111
Principal Investments: Cash and equiv (100%)
Provider Compensation ($000): Contr fee ($135,354), capitation ($50,956), FFS ($18,457)
Total Member Encounters: Phys (1,018,239), non-phys (233,706)
Group Affiliation: Molina Healthcare Inc
Licensed in: ID, WA
Address: 21540 30th Dr SE Ste 400, Bothell, WA 98021
Phone: (425) 424-1100   **Dom State:** WA   **Commenced Bus:** June 1985

Data Date	Weiss Safety Rating	RACR #1	RACR #2	Total Assets ($mil)	Capital ($mil)	Net Premium ($mil)	Net Income ($mil)
3-03	B	1.82	1.52	66.4	29.6	80.3	2.9
3-02	B-	1.36	1.17	60.9	24.1	60.4	7.2
2002	B	1.76	1.47	55.9	28.5	256.3	18.6
2001	B-	1.36	1.17	53.9	18.2	206.6	9.4
2000	C-	1.54	1.30	29.0	9.7	103.8	3.4
1999	C-	1.25	1.07	20.2	6.0	86.7	-0.2
1998	C	0.77	0.65	48.2	10.4	206.7	-8.5

Net Income History (in millions of dollars)

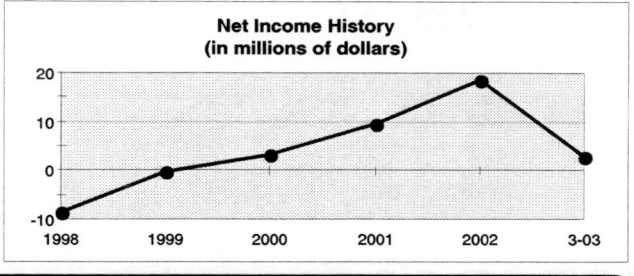

MOUNT CARMEL HEALTH PLAN INC — D+ — Weak

Major Rating Factors: Weak profitability index (1.2 on a scale of 0 to 10) with operating losses during 1998, 1999, 2000 and 2001. Average return on equity has been extremely poor. Good overall results on stability tests (5.5) despite excessive capital growth during 2002, rapid premium growth over the last five years. Strong capitalization index (7.9) based on excellent current risk-adjusted capital (severe loss scenario).

Other Rating Factors: High quality investment portfolio (9.9) containing no exposure to mortgages, junk bonds, or unaffiliated stocks. Excellent liquidity (7.4) with ample operational cash flow and liquid investments.
Principal Business: Med only (100%)
Mem Phys: 02: 2,327   01: N/A   02 MLR 85% / 02 Admin Exp 4%
Enroll(000): Q1 03: 15   02: 15   01: 18   Med Exp PMPM: $485
Principal Investments: Cash and equiv (95%), other (5%)
Provider Compensation ($000): Contr fee ($81,057), capitation ($3,851)
Total Member Encounters: N/A
Group Affiliation: Trinity Health
Licensed in: OH
Address: 495 Cooper Rd Ste 200, Westerville, OH 43081
Phone: (614) 898-8750   **Dom State:** OH   **Commenced Bus:** April 1997

Data Date	Weiss Safety Rating	RACR #1	RACR #2	Total Assets ($mil)	Capital ($mil)	Net Premium ($mil)	Net Income ($mil)
3-03	D+	2.11	1.76	35.7	24.0	27.9	3.3
3-02	D-	0.54	0.46	23.3	14.1	28.9	1.3
2002	D+	1.81	1.51	40.3	20.7	112.5	11.3
2001	D-	0.55	0.46	26.1	7.9	105.6	-6.7
2000	E+	0.15	0.13	19.5	1.6	75.5	-6.9
1999	E+	0.36	0.31	20.0	3.1	59.9	-8.5
1998	E	0.26	0.22	11.1	1.9	34.2	-3.5

Net Income History (in millions of dollars)

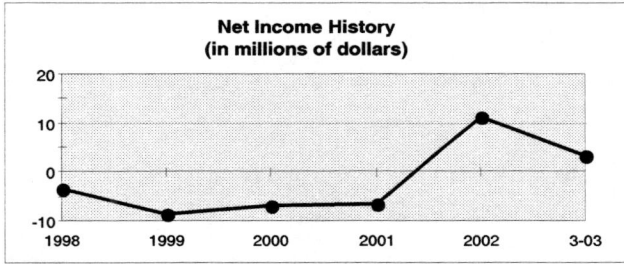

MOUNTAIN STATE BL CROSS BL SHIELD * — B+ — Good

Major Rating Factors: Good liquidity (6.8 on a scale of 0 to 10) with sufficient resources (cash flows and marketable investments) to handle a spike in claims. Excellent profitability (7.8) with operating gains in each of the last five years. Strong capitalization (7.9) based on excellent current risk-adjusted capital (severe loss scenario).

Other Rating Factors: High quality investment portfolio (9.9) containing little or no exposure to mortgages, junk bonds, or unaffiliated stocks.
Principal Business: Comp med (59%), FEHB (30%), med supp (8%), stop loss (2%)
Mem Phys: 02: 9,163   01: 9,662   02 MLR 85% / 02 Admin Exp 14%
Enroll(000): Q1 03: 159   02: 158   01: 154   Med Exp PMPM: $178
Principal Investments: Cash and equiv (12%), nonaffiliate common stock (4%), real estate (1%), affiliate common stock (1%), other (82%)
Provider Compensation ($000): FFS ($315,580), contr fee ($12,465)
Total Member Encounters: Phys (1,365,286), non-phys (251,704)
Group Affiliation: Highmark Inc
Licensed in: WV
Address: 700 Market Square, Parkersburg, WV 26101
Phone: (304) 424-7700   **Dom State:** WV   **Commenced Bus:** January 1983

Data Date	Weiss Safety Rating	RACR #1	RACR #2	Total Assets ($mil)	Capital ($mil)	Net Premium ($mil)	Net Income ($mil)
3-03	B+	2.07	1.72	156.0	44.7	106.7	4.1
3-02	B-	1.60	1.28	126.4	34.1	94.4	2.5
2002	B+	1.84	1.54	141.4	39.9	391.2	12.3
2001	B-	1.27	1.02	120.2	30.4	330.2	9.6
2000	C	0.81	0.50	129.5	24.7	259.6	6.3
1999	C-	0.72	0.44	113.5	18.6	222.6	3.7
1998	D	0.48	0.42	108.6	19.5	198.7	1.5

Net Income History (in millions of dollars)

---

* Denotes a Weiss Recommended Company

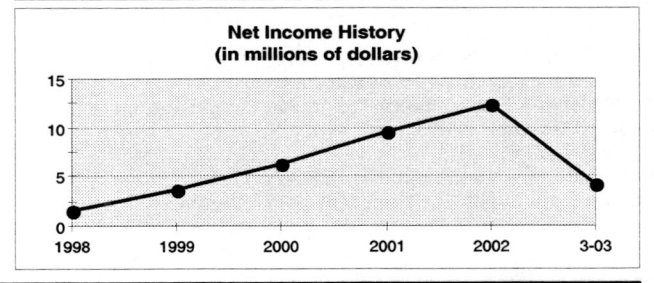

II. Analysis of Largest Companies
Winter 2003 - 04

MUTUAL OF OMAHA INSURANCE COMPANY * A-   Excellent

Major Rating Factors: Good overall results on stability tests (6.8 on a scale of 0 to 10) despite negative cash flow from operations for 2002. Strengths that enhance stability include excellent operational trends and excellent risk diversification. Good quality investment portfolio (6.1) despite mixed results such as: no exposure to mortgages and substantial holdings of BBB bonds but minimal holdings in junk bonds. Good liquidity (6.8).
Other Rating Factors: Strong capitalization (7.1) based on excellent risk adjusted capital (severe loss scenario). Excellent profitability (7.0).
Principal Business: Individual health insurance (43%), group health insurance (34%), and reinsurance (23%).
Principal Investments: Common & preferred stock (34%), nonCMO investment grade bonds (28%), CMOs and structured securities (27%), noninv. grade bonds (4%), and misc. investments (8%).
Investments in Affiliates: 36%
Group Affiliation: Mutual Of Omaha Group
Licensed in: All states, the District of Columbia and Puerto Rico
Commenced Business: January 1910
Address: Mutual Of Omaha Plaza, Omaha, NE 68175
Phone: (402) 342-7600 **Domicile State:** NE **NAIC Code:** 71412

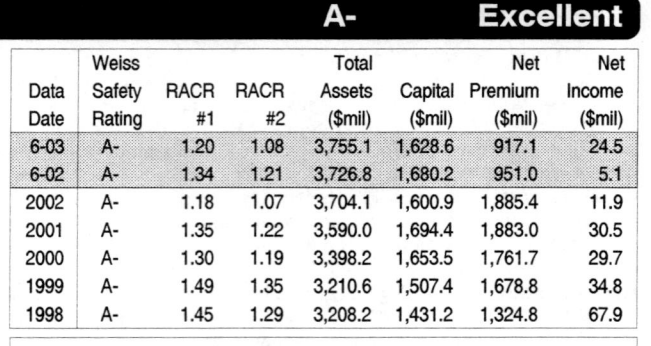

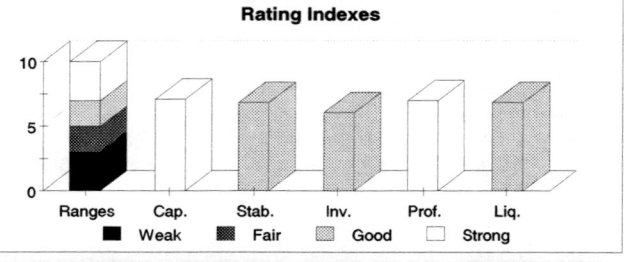

Data Date	Weiss Safety Rating	RACR #1	RACR #2	Total Assets ($mil)	Capital ($mil)	Net Premium ($mil)	Net Income ($mil)
6-03	A-	1.20	1.08	3,755.1	1,628.6	917.1	24.5
6-02	A-	1.34	1.21	3,726.8	1,680.2	951.0	5.1
2002	A-	1.18	1.07	3,704.1	1,600.9	1,885.4	11.9
2001	A-	1.35	1.22	3,590.0	1,694.4	1,883.0	30.5
2000	A-	1.30	1.19	3,398.2	1,653.5	1,761.7	29.7
1999	A-	1.49	1.35	3,210.6	1,507.4	1,678.8	34.8
1998	A-	1.45	1.29	3,208.2	1,431.2	1,324.8	67.9

MVP HEALTH INS CO B-   Good

Major Rating Factors: Fair profitability index (3.3 on a scale of 0 to 10). Strong capitalization index (8.7) based on excellent current risk-adjusted capital (severe loss scenario). High quality investment portfolio (9.9) containing no exposure to mortgages, junk bonds, or unaffiliated stocks.
Other Rating Factors: Excellent liquidity (7.6) with ample operational cash flow and liquid investments.
Principal Business: Comp med (100%)
Mem Phys: 02: 10,702 **01:** 8,638 **02 MLR** 80% **/ 02 Admin Exp** 16%
Enroll(000): Q1 03: 50 **02:** 40 **01:** 5 **Med Exp PMPM:** $37
Principal Investments: Cash and equiv (80%), other (20%)
Provider Compensation ($000): Contr fee ($7,531)
Total Member Encounters: Phys (23,712), non-phys (6,756)
Group Affiliation: MVP Group
Licensed in: NY
Address: 625 State St, Schenectady, NY 12305
Phone: (518) 388-2451 **Dom State:** NY **Commenced Bus:** July 2001

Data Date	Weiss Safety Rating	RACR #1	RACR #2	Total Assets ($mil)	Capital ($mil)	Net Premium ($mil)	Net Income ($mil)
3-03	B-	2.67	2.23	18.4	4.5	13.7	-0.9
3-02	B-	0.00	0.00	5.4	3.9	1.6	-0.1
2002	B-	3.20	2.67	10.9	5.4	12.5	0.0
2001	B-	0.00	0.00	4.3	4.0	0.2	0.0
2000	N/A	N/A	N/A	N/A	N/A	N/A	N/A
1999	N/A	N/A	N/A	N/A	N/A	N/A	N/A
1998	N/A	N/A	N/A	N/A	N/A	N/A	N/A

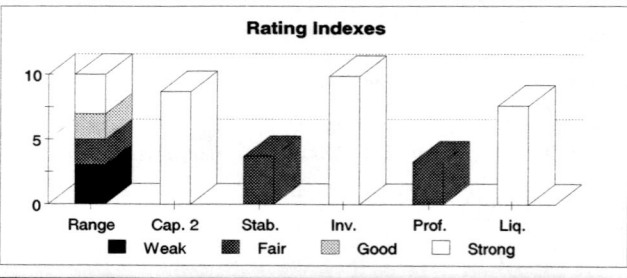

MVP HEALTH PLAN INC * B+   Good

Major Rating Factors: Good capitalization (6.9 on a scale of 0 to 10) based on excellent current risk-adjusted capital (severe loss scenario) reflecting significant improvement over results in 1998. Good liquidity (6.6) with sufficient resources (cash flows and marketable investments) to handle a spike in claims. Excellent profitability (9.1) with operating gains in each of the last five years.
Other Rating Factors: High quality investment portfolio (9.9) containing little or no exposure to mortgages, junk bonds, or unaffiliated stocks. Excellent overall results on stability tests (8.3) based on consistent premium and capital growth in the last five years.
Principal Business: Comp med (94%), FEHB (6%)
Mem Phys: 02: 16,840 **01:** 11,452 **02 MLR** 85% **/ 02 Admin Exp** 13%
Enroll(000): Q1 03: 356 **02:** 348 **01:** 369 **Med Exp PMPM:** $170
Principal Investments: Cash and equiv (28%), affiliate common stock (7%), other (65%)
Provider Compensation ($000): Contr fee ($462,450), capitation ($199,840), bonus arrang ($24,575), FFS ($20,709)
Total Member Encounters: Phys (2,926,955), non-phys (727,582)
Group Affiliation: MVP Group
Licensed in: NY, VT
Address: 625 State St, Schenectady, NY 12305
Phone: (518) 388-2451 **Dom State:** NY **Commenced Bus:** July 1983

Data Date	Weiss Safety Rating	RACR #1	RACR #2	Total Assets ($mil)	Capital ($mil)	Net Premium ($mil)	Net Income ($mil)
3-03	B+	1.26	1.05	264.0	76.2	236.4	4.4
3-02	B-	0.95	0.81	234.0	52.2	212.3	5.1
2002	B+	1.19	0.99	252.8	71.8	857.1	27.4
2001	C+	0.93	0.80	228.2	55.7	773.9	24.4
2000	C	0.91	0.79	173.5	40.9	611.7	20.9
1999	D+	0.70	0.61	106.0	20.0	425.1	9.1
1998	D	0.60	0.53	88.8	10.9	388.9	4.0

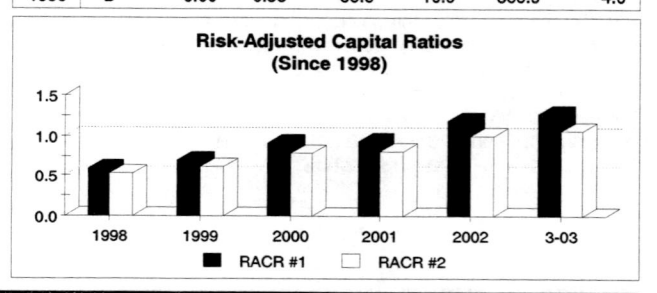

Winter 2003 - 04

II. Analysis of Largest Companies

MVP HEALTH SERVICES CORP — B Good

Major Rating Factors: Excellent profitability (8.9 on a scale of 0 to 10). Strong capitalization (10.0) based on excellent current risk-adjusted capital (severe loss scenario) despite some fluctuation in capital levels. High quality investment portfolio (9.9) containing no exposure to mortgages, junk bonds, or unaffiliated stocks.

Other Rating Factors: Excellent liquidity (8.9) with ample operational cash flow and liquid investments.

Principal Business: Dental (94%), comp med (6%)
Mem Phys: 02: 8,839 **01:** 4,995 **02 MLR** 71% **/ 02 Admin Exp** 10%
Enroll(000): Q1 03: 19 **02:** 14 **01:** 43 **Med Exp PMPM:** $7
Principal Investments: Cash and equiv (100%)
Provider Compensation ($000): Contr fee ($2,905)
Total Member Encounters: Phys (15,283), non-phys (2,527)
Group Affiliation: MVP Group
Licensed in: NY
Address: 625 State St, Schenectady, NY 12301
Phone: (518) 370-4793 **Dom State:** NY **Commenced Bus:** June 1993

Data Date	Weiss Safety Rating	RACR #1	RACR #2	Total Assets ($mil)	Capital ($mil)	Net Premium ($mil)	Net Income ($mil)
3-03	B	6.31	5.26	5.7	4.0	1.1	0.1
3-02	C+	3.99	3.53	4.5	3.4	0.9	0.1
2002	B	6.08	5.07	4.5	3.9	3.4	0.6
2001	C+	3.97	3.52	4.7	3.3	4.2	0.3
2000	B	N/A	N/A	3.9	2.9	2.4	0.3
1999	N/A	N/A	N/A	3.3	2.6	1.6	N/A
1998	N/A	N/A	N/A	2.8	2.5	1.3	N/A

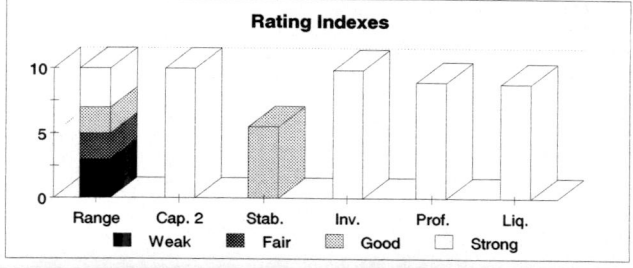

Rating Indexes (Range, Cap. 2, Stab., Inv., Prof., Liq.) — Weak, Fair, Good, Strong

NATIONAL BENEFIT LIFE INSURANCE COMPANY * — B+ Good

Major Rating Factors: Good overall results on stability tests (6.7 on a scale of 0 to 10). Stability strengths include good operational trends and excellent risk diversification. Good quality investment portfolio (6.5) despite mixed results such as: no exposure to mortgages and substantial holdings of BBB bonds but small junk bond holdings. Good overall profitability (6.6). Excellent expense controls.

Other Rating Factors: Strong capitalization (10.0) based on excellent risk adjusted capital (severe loss scenario). Excellent liquidity (7.2).

Principal Business: Reinsurance (52%), individual life insurance (33%), group health insurance (12%), and group life insurance (2%).
Principal Investments: NonCMO investment grade bonds (42%), CMOs and structured securities (33%), noninv. grade bonds (8%), policy loans (7%), and misc. investments (9%).
Investments in Affiliates: None
Group Affiliation: Citigroup Inc
Licensed in: All states except PR
Commenced Business: May 1963
Address: 333 West 34th Street, New York, NY 10001-2402
Phone: (212) 615-7500 **Domicile State:** NY **NAIC Code:** 61409

Data Date	Weiss Safety Rating	RACR #1	RACR #2	Total Assets ($mil)	Capital ($mil)	Net Premium ($mil)	Net Income ($mil)
6-03	B+	5.54	3.18	736.6	242.9	137.0	24.9
6-02	B+	5.08	3.09	644.2	205.9	137.6	17.8
2002	B+	5.07	2.93	693.6	215.4	261.1	22.6
2001	B+	5.13	3.10	618.8	189.6	104.9	-19.1
2000	B+	9.13	5.43	527.7	208.3	102.6	40.8
1999	B	8.58	5.04	485.9	173.5	93.1	39.9
1998	B-	7.72	4.50	465.5	152.3	95.2	36.8

Adverse Trends in Operations

Change in premium mix from 2001 to 2002 (5.3%)
Decrease in capital during 2001 (9%)
Decrease in premium volume from 1998 to 1999 (2%)

NATIONAL HERITAGE INSURANCE COMPANY — E Very Weak

Major Rating Factors: Weak profitability (2.9 on a scale of 0 to 10). Excellent expense controls. Return on equity has been fair, averaging 6.9%. Weak liquidity (0.5) as a spike in claims may stretch capacity. Weak overall results on stability tests (0.2) including weak risk adjusted capital in prior years and negative cash flow from operations for 2002.

Other Rating Factors: Fair overall capitalization (3.0) based on mixed results -- excessive policy leverage mitigated by good risk adjusted capital (severe loss scenario). High quality investment portfolio (9.7).

Principal Business: Group health insurance (100%).
Principal Investments: Cash (61%) and nonCMO investment grade bonds (39%).
Investments in Affiliates: None
Group Affiliation: None
Licensed in: TX
Commenced Business: December 1976
Address: 5400 Legacy Dr HI-4A-85, Plano, TX 75024
Phone: (972) 605-6275 **Domicile State:** TX **NAIC Code:** 86916

Data Date	Weiss Safety Rating	RACR #1	RACR #2	Total Assets ($mil)	Capital ($mil)	Net Premium ($mil)	Net Income ($mil)
6-03	E	0.95	0.79	373.2	158.0	68.6	3.9
6-02	E	0.40	0.33	920.7	175.5	1,966.6	3.9
2002	E	0.52	0.45	406.3	154.0	2,623.4	-1.9
2001	E	0.47	0.39	967.3	178.3	3,360.1	0.4
2000	E	0.45	0.37	916.9	166.3	3,238.8	-23.1
1999	E	0.58	0.47	853.1	199.3	2,909.7	2.2
1998	E	0.54	0.44	1,072.0	204.8	3,153.7	102.5

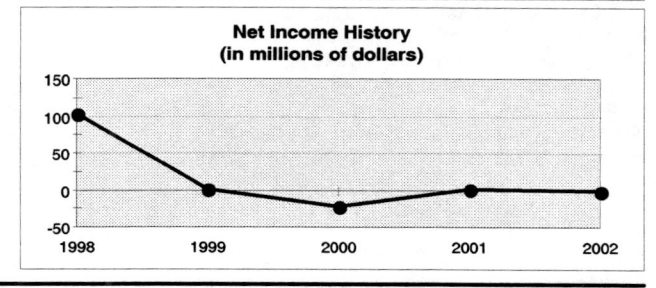

Net Income History (in millions of dollars)

www.WeissRatings.com   * Denotes a Weiss Recommended Company

II. Analysis of Largest Companies Winter 2003 - 04

NATIONALCARE INSURANCE COMPANY — B — Good

Major Rating Factors: Good overall results on stability tests (5.2 on a scale of 0 to 10). Strengths include good financial support from affiliation with Unitrin Inc, excellent operational trends and excellent risk diversification. Fair quality investment portfolio (4.6). Strong capitalization (7.6) based on excellent risk adjusted capital (severe loss scenario).
Other Rating Factors: Excellent profitability (8.7) with operating gains in each of the last five years. Excellent liquidity (9.5).
Principal Business: Individual health insurance (100%).
Principal Investments: Common & preferred stock (69%), nonCMO investment grade bonds (21%), cash (7%), and CMOs and structured securities (2%).
Investments in Affiliates: 69%
Group Affiliation: Unitrin Inc
Licensed in: OK
Commenced Business: October 1979
Address: 6100 NW Grand Blvd, Oklahoma City, OK 73118
Phone: (405) 848-7931 **Domicile State:** OK **NAIC Code:** 90522

Data Date	Weiss Safety Rating	RACR #1	RACR #2	Total Assets ($mil)	Capital ($mil)	Net Premium ($mil)	Net Income ($mil)
6-03	B	1.43	1.40	120.6	118.0	4.0	0.8
6-02	B	1.30	1.28	108.9	107.6	3.6	0.5
2002	B	1.41	1.39	114.2	113.8	7.4	9.4
2001	B	1.29	1.27	107.4	106.4	6.8	1.4
2000	B	1.31	1.29	96.9	94.7	6.3	1.3
1999	B	1.34	1.33	85.2	83.0	5.5	0.9
1998	B-	1.47	1.45	65.9	63.7	4.7	0.9

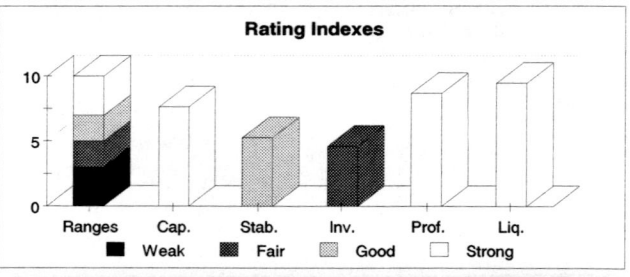

Rating Indexes (Ranges, Cap., Stab., Inv., Prof., Liq. — Weak, Fair, Good, Strong)

NEIGHBORHOOD HEALTH PARTNERSHIP INC — B- — Good

Major Rating Factors: Fair capitalization (4.2 on a scale of 0 to 10) based on fair current risk-adjusted capital (moderate loss scenario) as results have slipped from the good range over the last year. Good overall results on stability tests (5.6) despite weak risk-adjusted capital in prior years. Rating is significantly influenced by the fair financial results of Fortis Inc. Excellent profitability (8.2) with operating gains in each of the last five years.
Other Rating Factors: High quality investment portfolio (9.9) containing no exposure to mortgages, junk bonds, or unaffiliated stocks. Weak liquidity (2.5) as a spike in claims may stretch capacity.
Principal Business: Comp med (48%), Medicare (48%), Medicaid (4%)
Mem Phys: 02: 10,213 **01:** 8,215 **02 MLR** 88% **/ 02 Admin Exp** 11%
Enroll(000): Q1 03: 211 **02:** 209 **01:** 157 **Med Exp PMPM:** $271
Principal Investments: Cash and equiv (42%), other (58%)
Provider Compensation ($000): FFS ($482,266), capitation ($86,768), contr fee ($8,164)
Total Member Encounters: Phys (913,772), non-phys (180,001)
Group Affiliation: Fortis Inc
Licensed in: FL
Address: 7600 Corporate Center Dr, Miami, FL 33126
Phone: (305) 715-9635 **Dom State:** FL **Commenced Bus:** July 1993

Data Date	Weiss Safety Rating	RACR #1	RACR #2	Total Assets ($mil)	Capital ($mil)	Net Premium ($mil)	Net Income ($mil)
3-03	B-	0.80	0.67	120.1	20.6	189.0	4.7
3-02	C+	1.25	1.07	104.8	12.9	148.0	2.9
2002	B-	0.80	0.67	148.2	20.8	671.0	9.5
2001	C+	1.25	1.06	116.4	16.4	240.2	4.5
2000	C	0.67	0.57	99.1	13.3	409.2	2.0
1999	D-	0.37	0.32	85.4	16.0	353.5	3.4
1998	D-	0.49	0.30	56.4	8.8	321.9	5.1

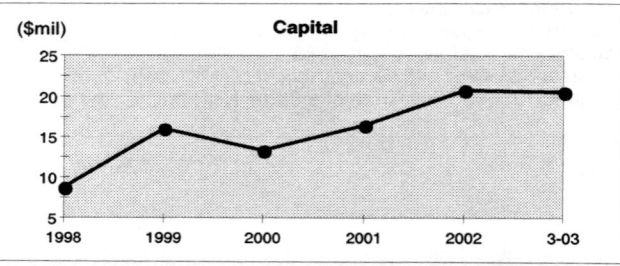

Capital ($mil), 1998–3-03

NEIGHBORHOOD HEALTH PLAN — D- — Weak

Major Rating Factors: Weak profitability index (0.8 on a scale of 0 to 10) with $15.4 million in losses in the last two years. Poor capitalization (2.2) based on weak current risk-adjusted capital (moderate loss scenario) as results have slipped from the good range over the last two years. Weak overall results on stability tests (1.5).
Other Rating Factors: Weak liquidity (0.7) as a spike in claims may stretch capacity. High quality investment portfolio (9.9) containing no exposure to mortgages, junk bonds, or unaffiliated stocks.
Principal Business: Medicaid (87%), comp med (13%)
Mem Phys: 02: 2,261 **01:** 1,710 **02 MLR** 96% **/ 02 Admin Exp** 7%
Enroll(000): Q1 03: 123 **02:** 125 **01:** 127 **Med Exp PMPM:** $251
Principal Investments: Cash and equiv (27%), other (73%)
Provider Compensation ($000): Contr fee ($210,076), FFS ($86,873), capitation ($79,786)
Total Member Encounters: Phys (911,985), non-phys (51,335)
Group Affiliation: None
Licensed in: MA
Address: 253 Summer St, Boston, MA 02210-1120
Phone: (617) 772-5500 **Dom State:** MA **Commenced Bus:** December 1987

Data Date	Weiss Safety Rating	RACR #1	RACR #2	Total Assets ($mil)	Capital ($mil)	Net Premium ($mil)	Net Income ($mil)
3-03	D-	0.51	0.43	52.4	16.7	88.0	1.2
3-02	D	1.09	0.92	68.1	20.7	90.3	-6.5
2002	D-	0.49	0.41	59.2	15.9	394.3	-14.1
2001	D	1.09	0.92	73.7	27.8	340.7	-1.3
2000	D	1.18	0.99	72.5	28.9	289.0	5.9
1999	D	1.05	0.88	67.9	19.8	193.5	3.4
1998	C	1.29	1.08	44.0	17.1	138.0	5.5

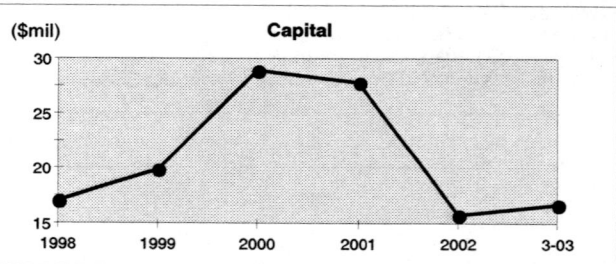

Capital ($mil), 1998–3-03

Winter 2003 - 04

II. Analysis of Largest Companies

NEIGHBORHOOD HEALTH PLAN OF RI INC   C-   Fair

Major Rating Factors: Fair overall results on stability tests (4.1 on a scale of 0 to 10) based on rapid premium growth over the last five years, rapid enrollment growth during the past five years. Poor capitalization (1.4) based on weak current risk-adjusted capital (moderate loss scenario) as results have slipped from the fair range over the last year. Good overall profitability index (6.0) despite operating losses during 2002.
Other Rating Factors: Good liquidity (6.2) with sufficient resources (cash flows and marketable investments) to handle a spike in claims. High quality investment portfolio (9.9) containing no exposure to mortgages, junk bonds, or unaffiliated stocks.
Principal Business: Medicaid (90%), comp med (10%)
Mem Phys: 02: 44,310 **01:** 44,002 **02 MLR** 92% **/ 02 Admin Exp** 10%
Enroll(000): Q1 03: 66 **02:** 71 **01:** 75 **Med Exp PMPM:** $138
Principal Investments: Cash and equiv (59%), other (41%)
Provider Compensation ($000): Contr fee ($110,200), capitation ($8,876), bonus arrang ($1,020)
Total Member Encounters: Phys (420,089), non-phys (72,732)
Group Affiliation: None
Licensed in: RI
Address: 50 Holden St., Ste. 200, Providence, RI 02908
Phone: (401) 459-6000 **Dom State:** RI **Commenced Bus:** December 1994

Data Date	Weiss Safety Rating	RACR #1	RACR #2	Total Assets ($mil)	Capital ($mil)	Net Premium ($mil)	Net Income ($mil)
3-03	C-	0.45	0.37	38.5	7.1	29.0	-0.7
3-02	C	0.75	0.63	37.9	10.0	36.1	0.7
2002	C-	0.49	0.41	29.1	7.7	130.3	-1.2
2001	C	0.75	0.64	27.9	9.3	120.5	7.3
2000	D-	0.32	0.27	27.0	2.4	85.5	1.1
1999	E+	0.38	0.32	9.1	1.3	42.3	0.3
1998	E	0.30	0.25	7.1	0.9	37.6	0.4

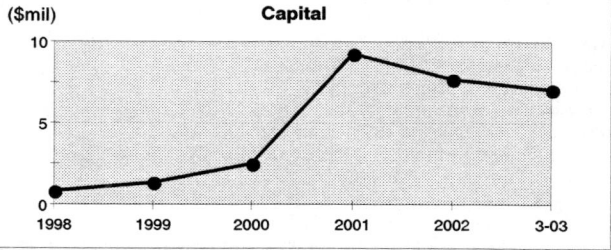

Capital chart ($mil) from 1998 to 3-03, rising from near 1 in 1998 to ~9 in 2001, declining slightly to ~7 by 3-03.

NETWORK HEALTH PLAN OF WISCONSIN INC   D+   Weak

Major Rating Factors: Weak profitability index (1.3 on a scale of 0 to 10) with operating losses during 1999, 2000 and 2001. Average return on equity has been poor at -12%. Fair capitalization (4.2) based on fair current risk-adjusted capital (moderate loss scenario) reflecting improvement over results in 2000. Good liquidity (6.9) with sufficient resources (cash flows and marketable investments) to handle a spike in claims.
Other Rating Factors: High quality investment portfolio (9.9) containing little or no exposure to mortgages, junk bonds, or unaffiliated stocks. Excellent overall results on stability tests (7.4) based on consistent premium and capital growth in the last five years.
Principal Business: Comp med (73%), Medicaid (20%), Medicare (6%)
Mem Phys: 02: 817 **01:** 550 **02 MLR** 88% **/ 02 Admin Exp** 10%
Enroll(000): Q1 03: 113 **02:** 112 **01:** 104 **Med Exp PMPM:** $158
Principal Investments: Cash and equiv (56%), real estate (10%), affiliate common stock (9%), other (25%)
Provider Compensation ($000): Contr fee ($153,365), capitation ($47,149)
Total Member Encounters: Phys (379,514), non-phys (207,531)
Group Affiliation: Affinity Health System
Licensed in: WI
Address: 1570 Midway Pl, Menasha, WI 54952
Phone: (920) 720-1200 **Dom State:** WI **Commenced Bus:** April 1983

Data Date	Weiss Safety Rating	RACR #1	RACR #2	Total Assets ($mil)	Capital ($mil)	Net Premium ($mil)	Net Income ($mil)
3-03	D+	0.81	0.68	49.3	22.2	67.0	2.6
3-02	D	0.46	0.39	41.1	20.7	55.4	1.4
2002	D+	0.73	0.60	45.2	19.9	232.1	5.9
2001	D	0.46	0.39	41.3	18.9	200.8	-2.2
2000	D+	0.42	0.35	39.2	17.0	202.7	-7.8
1999	C	0.51	0.43	38.2	16.9	189.2	-9.0
1998	B-	1.26	1.06	34.7	18.1	150.5	2.8

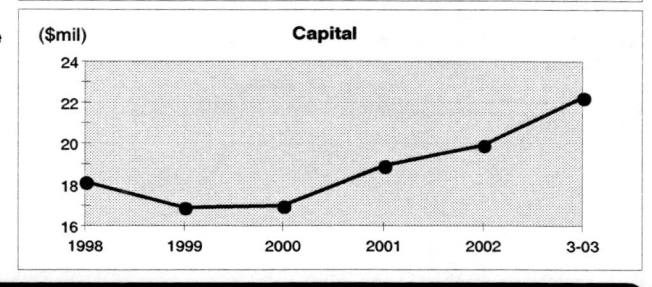

Capital chart ($mil) from 1998 to 3-03, dipping from ~18 to ~17 in 1999-2000, rising to ~22 by 3-03.

NEVADACARE INC   C   Fair

Major Rating Factors: Fair profitability index (3.5 on a scale of 0 to 10) due to a decline in earnings during 2002. Return on equity has been low, averaging 4%. Fair capitalization index (3.4) based on weak current risk-adjusted capital (moderate loss scenario). Good liquidity (6.4) with sufficient resources (cash flows and marketable investments) to handle a spike in claims.
Other Rating Factors: High quality investment portfolio (9.9) containing no exposure to mortgages, junk bonds, or unaffiliated stocks. Excellent overall results on stability tests (7.4) based on consistent premium and capital growth in the last five years but rapid enrollment growth during the past five years.
Principal Business: Medicaid (72%), comp med (28%)
Mem Phys: 02: 9,331 **01:** 8,070 **02 MLR** 90% **/ 02 Admin Exp** 10%
Enroll(000): Q1 03: 107 **02:** 107 **01:** 101 **Med Exp PMPM:** $130
Principal Investments: Cash and equiv (72%), real estate (16%), other (12%)
Provider Compensation ($000): Contr fee ($142,415), capitation ($10,542), FFS ($9,061)
Total Member Encounters: Phys (344,913), non-phys (1,241,423)
Group Affiliation: Health Management Solutions Inc
Licensed in: IL, IA, NV
Address: 10600 W Charleston Blvd, Las Vegas, NV 89102
Phone: (702) 304-5500 **Dom State:** NV **Commenced Bus:** April 1992

Data Date	Weiss Safety Rating	RACR #1	RACR #2	Total Assets ($mil)	Capital ($mil)	Net Premium ($mil)	Net Income ($mil)
3-03	C	0.69	0.58	47.8	14.4	47.2	-0.2
3-02	C-	0.61	0.51	41.6	10.0	43.7	0.0
2002	C	0.69	0.58	50.7	14.5	181.5	1.1
2001	C-	0.62	0.52	43.3	10.1	158.8	4.6
2000	D-	0.17	0.15	29.5	3.6	118.0	-3.1
1999	D-	0.09	0.07	27.5	2.2	92.3	1.0
1998	D	0.28	0.24	12.5	2.0	42.5	0.1

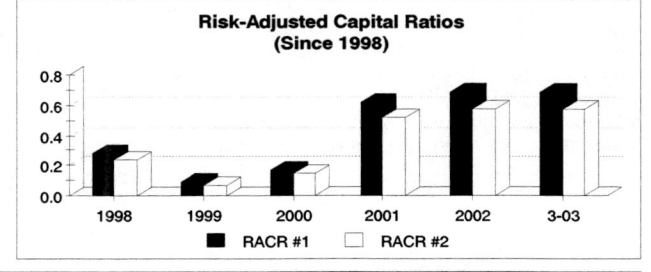

Risk-Adjusted Capital Ratios (Since 1998) bar chart showing RACR #1 (black) and RACR #2 (white) from 1998 to 3-03.

www.WeissRatings.com   233   * Denotes a Weiss Recommended Company

II. Analysis of Largest Companies

Winter 2003 - 04

NIAGARA FIRE INS CO — C- Fair

Major Rating Factors: Fair reserve development (3.6 on a scale of 0 to 10) as reserves have generally been sufficient to cover claims. In 1998, the two year reserve development was 18% deficient. Fair profitability index (3.8) with operating losses during 1998, 2000, 2001 and the first six months of 2002. Average return on equity over the last five years has been poor at -2.3%.
Other Rating Factors: Fair overall results on stability tests (3.3) including weak results on operational trends and negative cash flow from operations for 2002. The largest net exposure for one risk is conservative at 1.1% of capital. Strong long-term capitalization index (8.2) based on excellent current risk adjusted capital (severe and moderate loss scenarios), despite some fluctuation in capital levels. Excellent liquidity (7.0) with ample operational cash flow and liquid investments.
Principal Business: Other accident & health (100%).
Principal Investments: Investment grade bonds (98%) and misc. investments (2%).
Investments in Affiliates: None
Group Affiliation: CNA Financial Corp
Licensed in: All states except PR
Commenced Business: August 1855
Address: 1209 Orange St, Wilmington, DE 60685
Phone: (312) 822-5000 **Domicile State:** DE **NAIC Code:** 35106

Data Date	Weiss Safety Rating	RACR #1	RACR #2	Loss Ratio %	Total Assets ($mil)	Capital ($mil)	Net Premium ($mil)	Net Income ($mil)
6-03	C-	4.52	2.66	N/A	124.2	72.0	0.3	-0.1
6-02	C-	1.39	0.91	N/A	133.1	66.9	1,152.1	4.8
2002	C-	3.37	2.09	91.7	120.6	71.8	33.1	8.1
2001	C-	1.40	0.89	110.2	130.4	61.3	55.6	-9.1
2000	C-	3.26	1.99	86.1	107.7	72.6	19.4	-1.8
1999	C-	3.40	1.93	84.7	116.4	68.0	16.2	2.9
1998	C-	3.06	1.77	90.0	154.7	65.6	35.0	-7.1

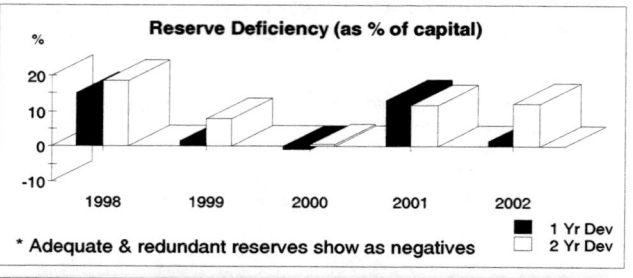

Reserve Deficiency (as % of capital)
* Adequate & redundant reserves show as negatives
■ 1 Yr Dev   □ 2 Yr Dev

NIPPON LIFE INSURANCE COMPANY OF AMERICA — B- Good

Major Rating Factors: Good overall profitability (5.2 on a scale of 0 to 10). Return on equity has been low, averaging 1.8%. Fair overall results on stability tests (3.6) including weak results on operational trends and negative cash flow from operations for 2002. Strong capitalization (9.5) based on excellent risk adjusted capital (severe loss scenario).
Other Rating Factors: High quality investment portfolio (7.4). Excellent liquidity (7.9).
Principal Business: Group health insurance (93%), group retirement contracts (4%), and group life insurance (4%).
Principal Investments: NonCMO investment grade bonds (64%), mortgages in good standing (18%), CMOs and structured securities (17%), and noninv. grade bonds (1%).
Investments in Affiliates: None
Group Affiliation: None
Licensed in: All states except ME, NH, NC, WY, PR
Commenced Business: July 1973
Address: 650 8th St, Des Moines, IA 50309
Phone: (212) 682-3992 **Domicile State:** IA **NAIC Code:** 81264

Data Date	Weiss Safety Rating	RACR #1	RACR #2	Total Assets ($mil)	Capital ($mil)	Net Premium ($mil)	Net Income ($mil)
6-03	B-	3.41	2.64	147.5	97.4	109.8	2.0
6-02	B-	4.40	3.12	173.3	95.3	106.9	0.0
2002	B-	3.43	2.66	145.2	95.8	208.9	1.9
2001	B-	4.39	2.94	324.4	95.2	175.8	-3.5
2000	B-	8.89	5.57	302.9	97.2	108.4	0.2
1999	B-	9.41	7.47	269.6	97.8	83.7	3.6
1998	C+	9.42	8.48	218.3	93.7	59.0	3.9

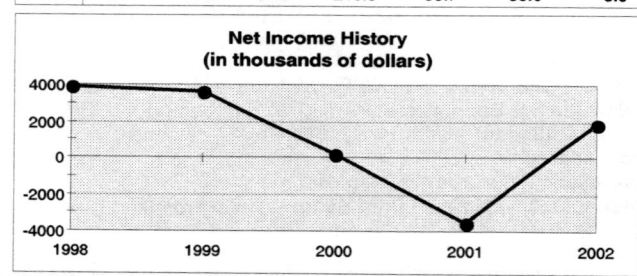

Net Income History (in thousands of dollars)

NORIDIAN MUTUAL INS CO * — B+ Good

Major Rating Factors: Good overall profitability index (5.9 on a scale of 0 to 10) despite a decline in earnings during 2002. Good liquidity (6.6) with sufficient resources (cash flows and marketable investments) to handle a spike in claims. Strong capitalization (8.3) based on excellent current risk-adjusted capital (severe loss scenario) despite some fluctuation in capital levels.
Other Rating Factors: High quality investment portfolio (7.4).
Principal Business: Comp med (78%), med supp (10%), FEHB (7%), stop loss (4%).
Mem Phys: 02: 1,523 **01:** 1,506 **02 MLR** 87% / **02 Admin Exp** 10%
Enroll(000): Q1 03: 291 **02:** 300 **01:** 307 **Med Exp PMPM:** $137
Principal Investments: Nonaffiliate common stock (19%), real estate (8%), cash and equiv (5%), affiliate common stock (4%), other (64%).
Provider Compensation ($000): Contr fee ($255,560), FFS ($237,009), capitation ($8,095).
Total Member Encounters: Phys (3,473,330), non-phys (1,693,278)
Group Affiliation: Bl Cross & Bl Shield of North Dakota
Licensed in: MN, ND, SD
Address: 4510 13th Ave SW, Fargo, ND 58121
Phone: (701) 282-1100 **Dom State:** ND **Commenced Bus:** April 1940

Data Date	Weiss Safety Rating	RACR #1	RACR #2	Total Assets ($mil)	Capital ($mil)	Net Premium ($mil)	Net Income ($mil)
3-03	B+	2.38	1.98	298.8	140.2	148.4	2.3
3-02	B-	2.37	1.80	268.2	138.0	140.1	2.7
2002	B+	2.33	1.94	283.4	137.2	574.1	17.7
2001	B-	2.37	1.79	267.1	137.3	525.3	23.8
2000	C+	1.90	1.12	241.9	125.9	484.0	24.9
1999	C+	1.73	1.02	220.4	111.0	456.4	1.8
1998	B-	1.76	1.03	219.7	105.4	412.5	-8.1

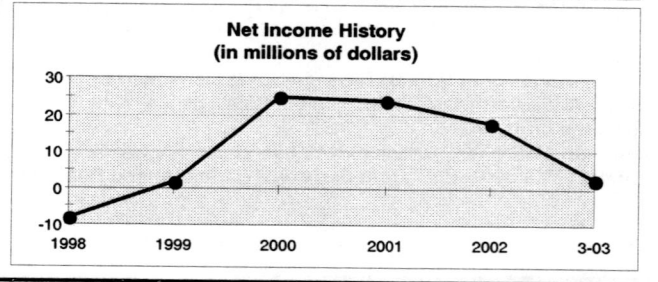

Net Income History (in millions of dollars)

Winter 2003 - 04 **II. Analysis of Largest Companies**

NORTHWESTERN LONG TERM CARE INSURANCE COMPANY   B   Good

Major Rating Factors: Good quality investment portfolio (6.0 on a scale of 0 to 10) despite mixed results such as: no exposure to mortgages and large holdings of BBB rated bonds but minimal holdings in junk bonds. Fair overall results on stability tests (4.9) including weak results on operational trends. Weak profitability (1.6) with operating losses during the first six months of 2003.
Other Rating Factors: Strong capitalization (9.9) based on excellent risk adjusted capital (severe loss scenario). Excellent liquidity (7.5).
Principal Business: Individual health insurance (100%).
Principal Investments: NonCMO investment grade bonds (68%), common & preferred stock (16%), CMOs and structured securities (11%), noninv. grade bonds (3%), and cash (2%).
Investments in Affiliates: None
Group Affiliation: Northwestern Mutual Group
Licensed in: All states except PR
Commenced Business: October 1953
Address: 720 E Wisconsin Ave, Milwaukee, WI 53202
Phone: (414) 299-3136   **Domicile State:** WI   **NAIC Code:** 69000

Data Date	Weiss Safety Rating	RACR #1	RACR #2	Total Assets ($mil)	Capital ($mil)	Net Premium ($mil)	Net Income ($mil)
6-03	B	4.65	2.95	81.7	54.5	11.9	-6.0
6-02	B	6.99	3.90	73.0	59.2	3.0	-8.2
2002	B	5.65	3.38	71.9	55.6	11.3	-17.6
2001	B	7.62	4.21	73.6	61.7	3.7	-12.0
2000	B	8.45	5.54	77.3	63.9	2.6	-10.1
1999	B	8.52	7.67	77.8	65.7	0.7	-6.8
1998	U	7.94	7.15	64.8	57.8	0.0	-5.3

Adverse Trends in Operations

Decrease in asset base during 2002 (2%)
Decrease in capital during 2002 (10%)
Decrease in asset base during 2001 (5%)
Decrease in capital during 2001 (3%)
Decrease in capital during 2000 (3%)

OCHSNER HEALTH PLAN   D   Weak

Major Rating Factors: Poor capitalization index (2.0 on a scale of 0 to 10) based on weak current risk-adjusted capital (moderate loss scenario). Good liquidity (5.7) with sufficient resources (cash flows and marketable investments) to handle a spike in claims. Excellent profitability (7.8) despite a decline in earnings during 2002.
Other Rating Factors: High quality investment portfolio (9.9) containing little or no exposure to mortgages, junk bonds, or unaffiliated stocks. Excellent overall results on stability tests (7.8) based on consistent premium and capital growth in the last five years.
Principal Business: Comp med (54%), Medicare (46%)
Mem Phys: 02: 3,751   01: 3,341   **02 MLR** 90%   / **02 Admin Exp** 8%
Enroll(000): 02: 204   01: 185   **Med Exp PMPM:** $263
Principal Investments: Cash and equiv (48%), other (52%)
Provider Compensation ($000): Contr fee ($364,618), capitation ($193,005), FFS ($48,095), bonus arrang ($2,394)
Total Member Encounters: N/A
Group Affiliation: Ochsner Clinic Foundation
Licensed in: LA
Address: 1 Galleria Blvd Suite 850, Metairie, LA 70001
Phone: (504) 836-6600   **Dom State:** LA   **Commenced Bus:** June 1985

Data Date	Weiss Safety Rating	RACR #1	RACR #2	Total Assets ($mil)	Capital ($mil)	Net Premium ($mil)	Net Income ($mil)
2002	D	0.50	0.42	154.3	33.7	683.9	8.4
2001	D-	0.41	0.35	136.0	26.9	557.6	11.0
2000	E+	0.35	0.30	103.5	22.7	534.2	13.7
1999	N/A	N/A	N/A	134.0	14.2	573.9	N/A
1998	E+	0.06	0.05	90.2	2.3	473.5	-8.4

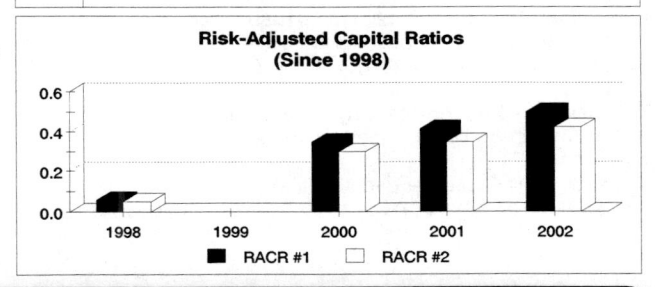

Risk-Adjusted Capital Ratios (Since 1998)

ODS HEALTH PLAN INC   C+   Fair

Major Rating Factors: Fair profitability index (3.4 on a scale of 0 to 10) with operating losses during 2000 and 2001. Fair quality investment portfolio (4.6) containing little or no exposure to mortgages, junk bonds, or unaffiliated stocks. Good liquidity (6.4) with sufficient resources (cash flows and marketable investments) to handle a spike in claims.
Other Rating Factors: Strong capitalization (7.3) based on excellent current risk-adjusted capital (severe loss scenario) reflecting significant improvement over results in 2001.
Principal Business: Comp med (95%), stop loss (3%), Medicaid (1%)
Mem Phys: 02: N/A   01: N/A   **02 MLR** 83%   / **02 Admin Exp** 13%
Enroll(000): Q1 03: 39   02: 42   01: 78   **Med Exp PMPM:** $124
Principal Investments: Affiliate common stock (31%), nonaffiliate common stock (15%), other (64%)
Provider Compensation ($000): FFS ($76,084), bonus arrang ($12,928), contr fee ($855), capitation ($26)
Total Member Encounters: N/A
Group Affiliation: Health Services Group
Licensed in: OR
Address: 601 SW Second Ave, Portland, OR 97204
Phone: (503) 228-6554   **Dom State:** OR   **Commenced Bus:** December 1988

Data Date	Weiss Safety Rating	RACR #1	RACR #2	Total Assets ($mil)	Capital ($mil)	Net Premium ($mil)	Net Income ($mil)
3-03	C+	1.63	1.36	77.3	27.9	26.6	1.9
3-02	D+	0.87	0.69	52.6	24.0	27.7	0.1
2002	C+	1.54	1.28	52.6	26.5	107.9	2.8
2001	D+	0.88	0.69	56.4	24.5	186.5	-1.8
2000	C+	N/A	N/A	55.2	20.1	209.3	-8.7
1999	N/A	N/A	N/A	71.9	24.4	224.7	N/A
1998	N/A	N/A	N/A	68.3	25.5	180.3	N/A

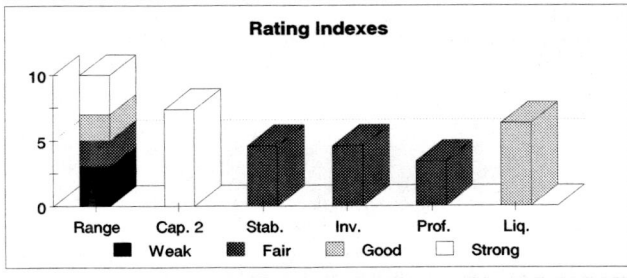

Rating Indexes

www.WeissRatings.com   * Denotes a Weiss Recommended Company

II. Analysis of Largest Companies
Winter 2003 - 04

OLD REPUBLIC LIFE INSURANCE COMPANY | B | Good

Major Rating Factors: Good liquidity (6.9 on a scale of 0 to 10) with sufficient resources to handle a spike in claims. Fair profitability (3.6) with operating losses during the first six months of 2003. Return on equity has been low, averaging 1.2%. Fair overall results on stability tests (4.6) including negative cash flow from operations for 2002.
Other Rating Factors: Strong capitalization (7.6) based on excellent risk adjusted capital (severe loss scenario). High quality investment portfolio (7.3).
Principal Business: Individual life insurance (49%), group health insurance (29%), individual health insurance (12%), reinsurance (8%), and individual annuities (8%).
Principal Investments: NonCMO investment grade bonds (84%), common & preferred stock (8%), noninv. grade bonds (4%), mortgages in good standing (3%), and misc. investments (1%).
Investments in Affiliates: 8%
Group Affiliation: Old Republic Group
Licensed in: All states except NY
Commenced Business: April 1923
Address: 307 N Michigan Ave, Chicago, IL 60601
Phone: (312) 346-8100 **Domicile State:** IL **NAIC Code:** 67261

Data Date	Weiss Safety Rating	RACR #1	RACR #2	Total Assets ($mil)	Capital ($mil)	Net Premium ($mil)	Net Income ($mil)
6-03	B	1.85	1.38	106.6	26.1	10.9	-1.6
6-02	B-	1.88	1.44	105.7	25.8	9.0	-1.3
2002	B-	1.79	1.34	107.0	24.4	22.8	-0.4
2001	B-	1.86	1.40	110.9	26.7	22.9	1.9
2000	B-	1.99	1.51	109.1	28.3	20.1	5.0
1999	B-	1.54	1.18	109.1	23.3	30.8	0.1
1998	B-	1.34	1.09	96.2	23.1	26.3	-2.6

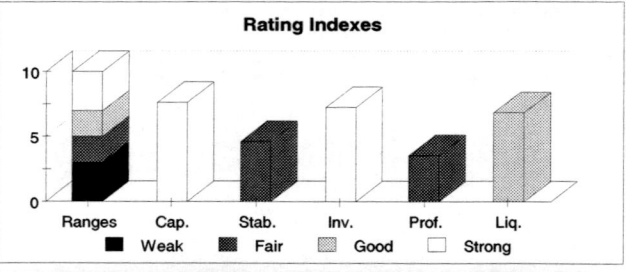

OMNICARE HEALTH PLAN INC | D | Weak

Major Rating Factors: Weak profitability index (2.6 on a scale of 0 to 10) with operating losses during 1998, 2000 and 2002. Poor capitalization index (1.4) based on weak current risk-adjusted capital (moderate loss scenario). Good overall results on stability tests (6.8) based on consistent premium and capital growth in the last five years but rapid enrollment growth during the past five years.
Other Rating Factors: Good liquidity (6.9) with sufficient resources (cash flows and marketable investments) to handle a spike in claims. High quality investment portfolio (9.9) containing no exposure to mortgages, junk bonds, or unaffiliated stocks.
Principal Business: Medicaid (100%)
Mem Phys: 02: 1,128 **01:** 1,067 **02 MLR** 84% **/ 02 Admin Exp** 16%
Enroll(000): Q1 03: 112 **02:** 115 **01:** 80 **Med Exp PMPM:** $80
Principal Investments: Cash and equiv (41%), other (59%)
Provider Compensation ($000): Contr fee ($96,985), FFS ($7,553), capitation ($6,135)
Total Member Encounters: Phys (938,418), non-phys (131,167)
Group Affiliation: United American HealthCare Corp
Licensed in: TN
Address: 1991 Corporate Ave 4th Fl, Memphis, TN 38132
Phone: (901) 346-0064 **Dom State:** TN **Commenced Bus:** January 1994

Data Date	Weiss Safety Rating	RACR #1	RACR #2	Total Assets ($mil)	Capital ($mil)	Net Premium ($mil)	Net Income ($mil)
3-03	D	0.44	0.37	9.3	7.1	3.9	0.1
3-02	D	0.56	0.47	25.4	7.7	42.1	0.4
2002	D	0.00	0.00	10.3	7.1	110.8	-1.9
2001	D	0.56	0.47	26.0	7.1	113.5	3.1
2000	D-	0.34	0.28	21.8	5.1	88.1	-0.4
1999	D	0.52	0.44	19.1	5.5	73.6	3.0
1998	E	0.09	0.08	17.5	2.9	0.1	-0.4

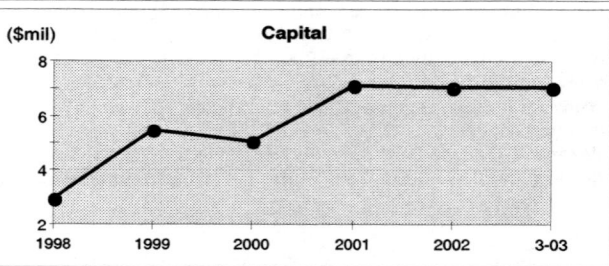

ON LOK SENIOR HEALTH SERVICES | B- | Good

Major Rating Factors: Fair overall results on stability tests (4.8 on a scale of 0 to 10). Excellent profitability (8.7). Strong capitalization index (10.0) based on excellent current risk-adjusted capital (severe loss scenario).
Other Rating Factors: Excellent liquidity (8.2) with ample operational cash flow and liquid investments.
Principal Business: Medicare (5%), Medicaid (3%), other (91%)
Mem Phys: 02: N/A **01:** N/A **02 MLR** 86% **/ 02 Admin Exp** 6%
Enroll(000): Q1 03: 1 **02:** 1 **01:** 1 **Med Exp PMPM:** $4,025
Principal Investments ($000): Cash and equiv ($24,646), stocks ($23)
Provider Compensation ($000): None
Total Member Encounters: N/A
Group Affiliation: None
Licensed in: CA
Address: 1333 Bush St, San Francisco, CA 94109-5611
Phone: (415) 292-8888 **Dom State:** CA **Commenced Bus:** September 1971

Data Date	Weiss Safety Rating	RACR #1	RACR #2	Total Assets ($mil)	Capital ($mil)	Net Premium ($mil)	Net Income ($mil)
3-03	B-	8.45	5.26	38.4	30.2	13.0	1.5
3-02	N/A	N/A	N/A	33.9	25.0	12.3	1.4
2002	B-	8.08	5.03	36.5	28.7	49.7	4.7
2001	N/A	N/A	N/A	32.9	23.6	47.0	4.8
2000	N/A	N/A	N/A	N/A	N/A	N/A	N/A
1999	N/A	N/A	N/A	N/A	N/A	N/A	N/A
1998	N/A	N/A	N/A	N/A	N/A	N/A	N/A

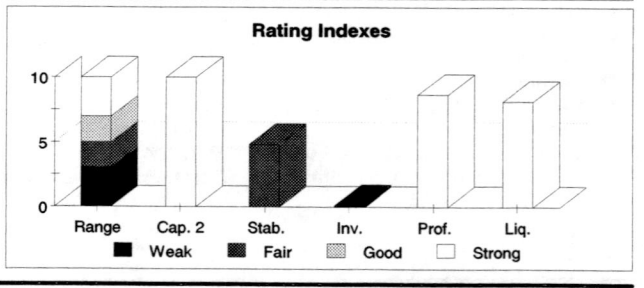

Winter 2003 - 04
II. Analysis of Largest Companies

ONE HEALTH PLAN OF AZ INC — B — Good

Major Rating Factors: Fair profitability index (3.8 on a scale of 0 to 10) with operating losses during 1998. Return on equity has been fair, averaging 8% over the last five years. Fair overall results on stability tests (3.8) based on rapid premium growth over the last five years, a significant 50% decrease in enrollment during the period and a decline in the number of member physicians during 2002. Rating is significantly influenced by the good financial results of Great West Life Asr. Strong capitalization index (10.0) based on excellent current risk-adjusted capital (severe loss scenario).

Other Rating Factors: High quality investment portfolio (9.9) containing no exposure to mortgages, junk bonds, or unaffiliated stocks. Weak liquidity (2.2) as a spike in claims may stretch capacity.

Principal Business: Comp med (100%)
Mem Phys: 02: 3,837 01: 6,099 **02 MLR** 328% / **02 Admin Exp** 66%
Enroll(000): Q1 03: 6 02: 7 01: 14 **Med Exp PMPM:** $150
Principal Investments: Cash and equiv (32%), other (68%)
Provider Compensation ($000): Bonus arrang ($21,497)
Total Member Encounters: Phys (40,167), non-phys (19,760)
Group Affiliation: Great West Life Asr
Licensed in: AZ
Address: 3131 E Camel Back Rd #240, Phoenix, AZ 85016
Phone: (602) 667-9537 **Dom State:** AZ **Commenced Bus:** March 1998

Data Date	Weiss Safety Rating	RACR #1	RACR #2	Total Assets ($mil)	Capital ($mil)	Net Premium ($mil)	Net Income ($mil)
3-03	B	13.85	11.54	9.1	5.1	0.9	0.1
3-02	B	0.00	0.00	11.2	4.8	1.7	0.0
2002	B	13.94	11.61	9.3	5.1	5.8	0.3
2001	B	0.00	0.00	20.7	4.8	7.8	0.1
2000	B	0.85	0.72	10.7	3.8	24.3	0.6
1999	B	2.09	1.77	5.6	2.3	9.2	0.4
1998	N/A	N/A	N/A	2.7	2.4	0.1	-0.1

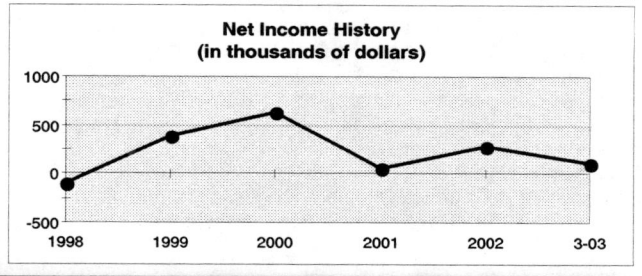

Net Income History (in thousands of dollars)

ONE HEALTH PLAN OF CALIFORNIA INC — B- — Good

Major Rating Factors: Fair profitability index (4.9 on a scale of 0 to 10) with operating losses during 2001. Fair overall results on stability tests (4.2) based on fair risk-adjusted capital in prior years. Rating is significantly influenced by the good financial results of Great West Life Asr. Good liquidity (6.6) with sufficient resources (cash flows and marketable investments) to handle a spike in claims.

Other Rating Factors: Strong capitalization (10.0) based on excellent current risk-adjusted capital (severe loss scenario) reflecting significant improvement over results in 2001.

Principal Business: Comp med (100%)
Mem Phys: 02: N/A 01: N/A **02 MLR** 124% / **02 Admin Exp** 19%
Enroll(000): Q1 03: 58 02: 59 01: 68 **Med Exp PMPM:** $178
Principal Investments ($000): Cash and equiv ($43,634), bonds ($38,682)
Provider Compensation ($000): None
Total Member Encounters: N/A
Group Affiliation: Great West Life Asr
Licensed in: CA
Address: 655 N Central Ave #1900, Glendale, CA 95110
Phone: (818) 539-9000 **Dom State:** CA **Commenced Bus:** March 1996

Data Date	Weiss Safety Rating	RACR #1	RACR #2	Total Assets ($mil)	Capital ($mil)	Net Premium ($mil)	Net Income ($mil)
3-03	B-	5.55	3.50	52.2	18.0	28.5	-0.9
3-02	B-	0.00	0.00	55.9	19.6	27.6	1.1
2002	B-	5.74	3.62	50.0	19.1	109.4	0.4
2001	B-	1.14	0.68	55.7	18.8	140.2	-1.5
2000	B-	2.79	1.64	75.1	34.7	144.5	18.9
1999	B-	5.17	2.97	62.9	30.1	118.4	25.0
1998	B-	3.73	2.22	49.8	21.1	93.7	11.2

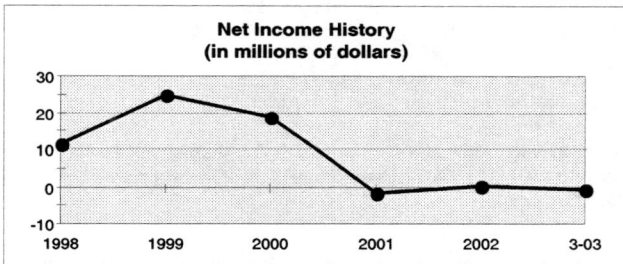

Net Income History (in millions of dollars)

ONE HEALTH PLAN OF COLORADO INC — B — Good

Major Rating Factors: Fair profitability index (3.1 on a scale of 0 to 10) with modest operating losses during 2000 and 2002. Strong capitalization (10.0) based on excellent current risk-adjusted capital (severe loss scenario) reflecting significant improvement over results in 1998. High quality investment portfolio (9.9) containing no exposure to mortgages, junk bonds, or unaffiliated stocks.

Other Rating Factors: Weak overall results on stability tests (2.2) based on a significant 33% decrease in enrollment during the period. Rating is significantly influenced by the good financial results of Great West Life Asr. Weak liquidity (2.0) as a spike in claims may stretch capacity.

Principal Business: Comp med (100%)
Mem Phys: 02: 4,811 01: 4,261 **02 MLR** 410% / **02 Admin Exp** 64%
Enroll(000): Q1 03: 21 02: 32 01: 47 **Med Exp PMPM:** $168
Principal Investments: Cash and equiv (9%), other (91%)
Provider Compensation ($000): Contr fee ($84,598)
Total Member Encounters: Phys (195,612), non-phys (61,635)
Group Affiliation: Great West Life Asr
Licensed in: CO
Address: 8525 E Orchard Rd 4T3, Greenwood Village, CO 80111
Phone: (303) 773-0046 **Dom State:** CO **Commenced Bus:** June 1996

Data Date	Weiss Safety Rating	RACR #1	RACR #2	Total Assets ($mil)	Capital ($mil)	Net Premium ($mil)	Net Income ($mil)
3-03	B	7.99	6.66	20.8	8.6	3.2	0.2
3-02	B	8.54	6.23	31.3	7.9	5.4	-0.3
2002	B	8.07	6.72	27.3	8.7	19.5	-0.3
2001	B	8.48	6.20	58.5	13.6	21.0	2.2
2000	B	1.33	1.12	31.3	9.0	64.5	-0.1
1999	B	1.32	1.11	16.1	5.2	49.5	1.9
1998	B	0.72	0.61	12.1	2.4	27.2	0.6

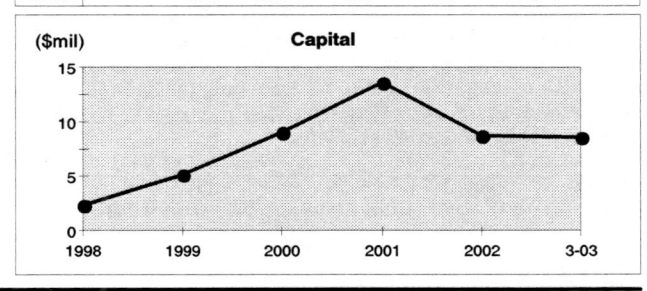

Capital ($mil)

II. Analysis of Largest Companies   Winter 2003 - 04

ONE HEALTH PLAN OF FLORDIA INC   B-   Good

Major Rating Factors: Fair liquidity (3.6 on a scale of 0 to 10) as cash resources may not be adequate to cover a spike in claims. Strong overall capitalization (9.3) based on excellent current risk-adjusted capital (severe loss scenario) despite some fluctuation in capital levels. High quality investment portfolio (9.6) containing no exposure to mortgages, junk bonds, or unaffiliated stocks.
Other Rating Factors: Weak profitability index (1.1) with operating losses during 2001 and 2002. Return on equity has been low, averaging 0%. Weak overall results on stability tests (2.2) based on a steep decline in capital during 2002, a steep decline in premium revenue in 2002 and a significant 30% decrease in enrollment during the period. Rating is significantly influenced by the good financial results of Great West Life Asr.
Principal Business: Comp med (100%)
Mem Phys: 02: 6,715   **01:** 2,902   **02 MLR** 133%   **/ 02 Admin Exp** 19%
Enroll(000): Q1 03: 4   **02:** 6   **01:** 9   **Med Exp PMPM:** $176
Principal Investments: Cash and equiv (7%), other (93%)
Provider Compensation ($000): FFS ($16,949), capitation ($323)
Total Member Encounters: Phys (30,168), non-phys (11,636)
Group Affiliation: Great West Life Asr
Licensed in: FL
Address: 7650 Courtney Campbell Cswy850, Tampa, FL 33607
Phone: (813) 207-0216   **Dom State:** FL   **Commenced Bus:** December 1996

Data Date	Weiss Safety Rating	RACR #1	RACR #2	Total Assets ($mil)	Capital ($mil)	Net Premium ($mil)	Net Income ($mil)
3-03	B-	3.17	2.64	8.9	4.6	1.9	0.1
3-02	B	2.82	1.97	11.5	6.4	3.3	0.4
2002	B-	3.02	2.52	8.5	4.4	12.5	-1.7
2001	B	2.82	1.97	12.4	6.8	22.3	-0.7
2000	B	2.50	2.08	12.2	6.7	18.6	1.5
1999	B	4.74	3.90	5.9	3.6	7.9	0.4
1998	B	8.34	6.67	5.2	4.9	1.5	0.1

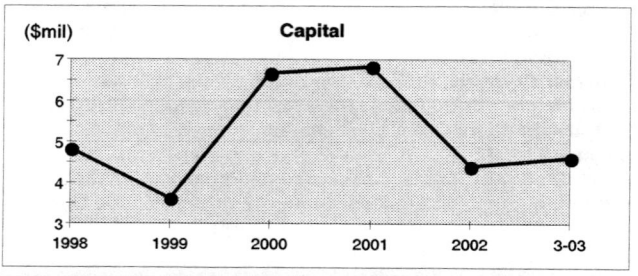

Capital chart 1998-3/03

ONE HEALTH PLAN OF GEORGIA INC   B   Good

Major Rating Factors: Fair overall results on stability tests (4.4 on a scale of 0 to 10) based on a significant 27% decrease in enrollment during the period. Rating is significantly influenced by the good financial results of Great West Life Asr. Excellent profitability (8.6) with operating gains in each of the last five years. Strong overall capitalization (10.0) based on excellent current risk-adjusted capital (severe loss scenario) despite some fluctuation in capital levels.
Other Rating Factors: High quality investment portfolio (9.9) containing no exposure to mortgages, junk bonds, or unaffiliated stocks. Excellent liquidity (7.1) with ample operational cash flow and liquid investments.
Principal Business: Comp med (100%)
Mem Phys: 02: 4,473   **01:** 4,010   **02 MLR** 139%   **/ 02 Admin Exp** 21%
Enroll(000): Q1 03: 5   **02:** 8   **01:** 10   **Med Exp PMPM:** $156
Principal Investments: Cash and equiv (42%), other (58%)
Provider Compensation ($000): FFS ($17,755)
Total Member Encounters: Phys (32,936), non-phys (8,903)
Group Affiliation: Great West Life Asr
Licensed in: GA
Address: 245 Perimeter Center Pl 7th Fl, Atlanta, GA 30346
Phone: (770) 901-9937   **Dom State:** GA   **Commenced Bus:** September 1996

Data Date	Weiss Safety Rating	RACR #1	RACR #2	Total Assets ($mil)	Capital ($mil)	Net Premium ($mil)	Net Income ($mil)
3-03	B	10.71	8.93	14.9	10.9	0.7	0.2
3-02	B	3.36	2.49	16.4	8.3	5.0	0.2
2002	B	10.91	9.09	14.4	11.1	12.1	1.0
2001	B	3.31	2.47	15.3	9.9	26.3	1.0
2000	B	1.51	1.28	16.7	6.9	33.2	1.5
1999	B	2.64	2.28	11.7	5.3	25.4	0.5
1998	B	2.84	2.47	9.9	4.7	19.2	1.6

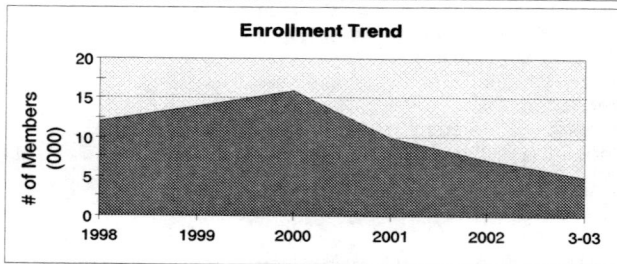

Enrollment Trend chart 1998-3/03

ONE HEALTH PLAN OF ILLINOIS INC   B-   Good

Major Rating Factors: Strong capitalization (10.0 on a scale of 0 to 10) based on excellent current risk-adjusted capital (severe loss scenario) reflecting significant improvement over results in 2000. High quality investment portfolio (9.7) containing no exposure to mortgages, junk bonds, or unaffiliated stocks. Weak profitability index (0.5) with modest operating losses during 2000 and 2002. Return on equity has been fair, averaging 9% over the last five years.
Other Rating Factors: Weak overall results on stability tests (1.5) based on a steep decline in capital during 2002, a significant 30% decrease in enrollment during the period. Rating is significantly influenced by the good financial results of Great West Life Asr. Weak liquidity (2.1) as a spike in claims may stretch capacity.
Principal Business: Comp med (100%)
Mem Phys: 02: 9,750   **01:** 10,120   **02 MLR** 375%   **/ 02 Admin Exp** 69%
Enroll(000): Q1 03: 15   **02:** 16   **01:** 23   **Med Exp PMPM:** $159
Principal Investments: Cash and equiv (31%), other (69%)
Provider Compensation ($000): Bonus arrang ($42,204)
Total Member Encounters: Phys (71,437), non-phys (14,152)
Group Affiliation: Great West Life Asr
Licensed in: IL
Address: 6250 River Rd #3030, Rosemont, IL 60018
Phone: (314) 543-8388   **Dom State:** IL   **Commenced Bus:** September 1995

Data Date	Weiss Safety Rating	RACR #1	RACR #2	Total Assets ($mil)	Capital ($mil)	Net Premium ($mil)	Net Income ($mil)
3-03	B-	5.36	4.47	13.3	3.5	2.2	0.0
3-02	B-	8.84	6.44	15.8	4.5	2.7	-0.1
2002	B-	7.48	6.23	14.6	5.3	10.2	-0.2
2001	B-	8.60	6.31	36.0	9.3	11.6	0.3
2000	C+	0.41	0.34	32.9	7.6	35.9	-3.7
1999	B	1.71	1.41	21.2	6.3	42.7	2.3
1998	B	0.96	0.81	14.6	3.4	28.7	1.3

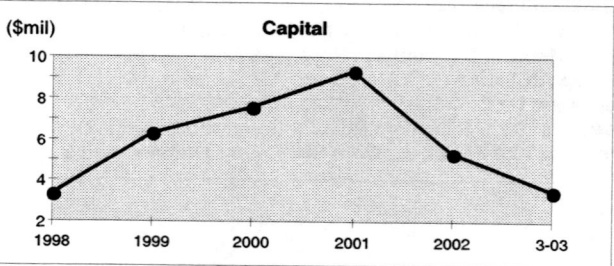

Capital chart 1998-3/03

Winter 2003 - 04   II. Analysis of Largest Companies

ONE HEALTH PLAN OF IN INC   B   Good

Major Rating Factors: Fair overall results on stability tests (3.4 on a scale of 0 to 10) based on a significant 39% decrease in enrollment during the period. Rating is significantly influenced by the good financial results of Great West Life Asr. Fair liquidity (3.2) as cash resources may not be adequate to cover a spike in claims. Strong capitalization index (10.0) based on excellent current risk-adjusted capital (severe loss scenario) despite some fluctuation in capital levels.
Other Rating Factors: High quality investment portfolio (9.9) containing no exposure to mortgages, junk bonds, or unaffiliated stocks. Weak profitability index (2.1) due to a decline in earnings during 2002. Average return on equity has been poor at 0%.
Principal Business: Comp med (100%)
Mem Phys: 02: 3,160   **01:** 3,329   **02 MLR** 318%   / **02 Admin Exp** 72%
Enroll(000): 02: 3   **01:** 5   **Med Exp PMPM:** $154
Principal Investments: Cash and equiv (60%), other (40%)
Provider Compensation ($000): Contr fee ($7,922), capitation ($170)
Total Member Encounters: Phys (14,138), non-phys (2,639)
Group Affiliation: Great West Life Asr
Licensed in: IN
Address: 9229 Delegates Row Ste 260, Indianapolis, IN 46240
Phone: (314) 543-8388   **Dom State:** IN   **Commenced Bus:** July 1997

Data Date	Weiss Safety Rating	RACR #1	RACR #2	Total Assets ($mil)	Capital ($mil)	Net Premium ($mil)	Net Income ($mil)
2002	B	11.07	9.23	6.3	4.5	2.3	0.1
2001	B	8.80	6.72	10.5	4.3	3.0	0.1
2000	B	1.86	1.56	6.4	3.3	9.9	-0.4
1999	B	6.95	5.71	5.0	3.7	4.2	0.2
1998	B	6.36	5.32	4.7	3.4	0.9	-0.1

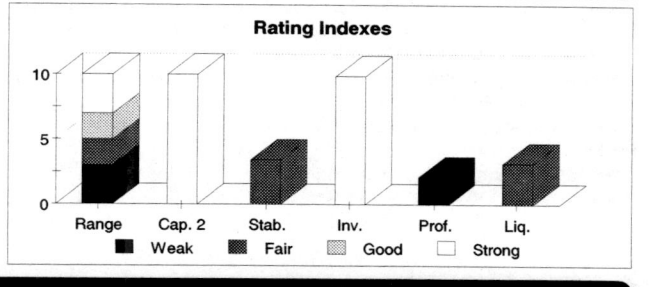

ONE HEALTH PLAN OF KANSAS/MISSOURI   B   Good

Major Rating Factors: Good overall profitability index (6.3 on a scale of 0 to 10). Strong overall capitalization (10.0) based on excellent current risk-adjusted capital (severe loss scenario). Moreover, capital levels have been consistent in recent years. High quality investment portfolio (9.9) containing no exposure to mortgages, junk bonds, or unaffiliated stocks.
Other Rating Factors: Excellent liquidity (7.4) with ample operational cash flow and liquid investments.
Principal Business: Comp med (100%)
Mem Phys: 02: 4,916   **01:** 4,763   **02 MLR** 61%   / **02 Admin Exp** 14%
Enroll(000): Q1 03: 1   **02:** 1   **01:** 1   **Med Exp PMPM:** $151
Principal Investments: Cash and equiv (11%), other (89%)
Provider Compensation ($000): FFS ($2,284)
Total Member Encounters: Phys (5,666), non-phys (2,068)
Group Affiliation: Great West Life Asr
Licensed in: MO
Address: 8575 W 110th Ste 225, Overland Park, KS 66210
Phone: (913) 451-0101   **Dom State:** KS   **Commenced Bus:** January 2001

Data Date	Weiss Safety Rating	RACR #1	RACR #2	Total Assets ($mil)	Capital ($mil)	Net Premium ($mil)	Net Income ($mil)
3-03	B	9.02	7.52	4.3	3.7	1.0	0.0
3-02	C+	6.05	3.91	4.1	2.9	0.9	0.0
2002	B	9.02	7.52	4.1	3.7	3.6	0.8
2001	C+	6.04	3.91	4.2	2.9	0.8	-0.1
2000	N/A	N/A	N/A	N/A	N/A	N/A	N/A
1999	N/A	N/A	N/A	N/A	N/A	N/A	N/A
1998	N/A	N/A	N/A	N/A	N/A	N/A	N/A

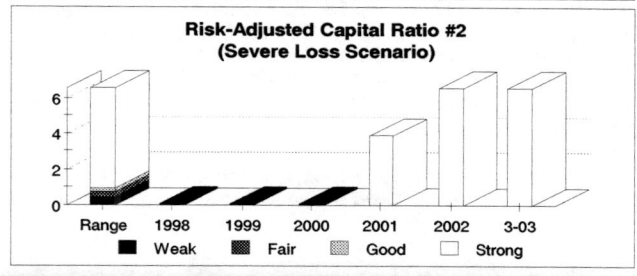

ONE HEALTH PLAN OF MA INC   B   Good

Major Rating Factors: Fair overall results on stability tests (4.1 on a scale of 0 to 10) based on a significant 49% decrease in enrollment during the period, a steep decline in premium revenue in 2002. Rating is significantly influenced by the good financial results of Great West Life Asr. Strong capitalization index (10.0) based on excellent current risk-adjusted capital (severe loss scenario). High quality investment portfolio (9.9) containing no exposure to mortgages, junk bonds, or unaffiliated stocks.
Other Rating Factors: Weak profitability index (0.5) with modest operating losses during 1999, 2000, 2001 and 2002. Average return on equity has been poor at -47%. Weak liquidity (2.4) as a spike in claims may stretch capacity.
Principal Business: Comp med (100%)
Mem Phys: 02: 16,873   **01:** 15,724   **02 MLR** 315%   / **02 Admin Exp** 63%
Enroll(000): Q1 03: 1   **02:** 2   **01:** 4   **Med Exp PMPM:** $174
Principal Investments: Cash and equiv (73%), other (27%)
Provider Compensation ($000): FFS ($5,583), contr fee ($1,395)
Total Member Encounters: N/A
Group Affiliation: Great West Life Asr
Licensed in: MA
Address: 375 Totten Pond Rd Suite 202, Waltham, MA 02541
Phone: (781) 622-2400   **Dom State:** MA   **Commenced Bus:** June 1997

Data Date	Weiss Safety Rating	RACR #1	RACR #2	Total Assets ($mil)	Capital ($mil)	Net Premium ($mil)	Net Income ($mil)
3-03	B	3.81	3.18	3.4	1.7	0.2	0.0
3-02	B	0.00	0.00	4.2	1.2	0.6	0.0
2002	B	3.54	2.95	4.0	1.5	1.9	-0.2
2001	B	0.00	0.00	6.5	1.3	2.6	-0.3
2000	B	0.84	0.71	10.5	1.5	7.9	-0.9
1999	B	1.05	0.90	5.9	1.2	7.3	-2.4
1998	B	2.71	2.33	3.8	2.3	7.5	0.1

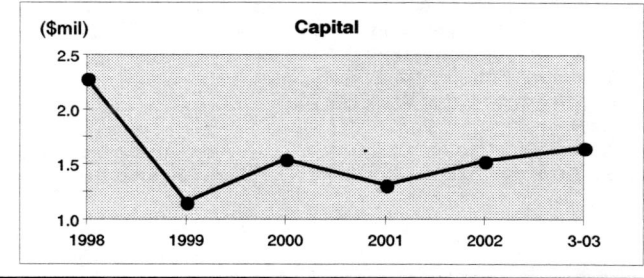

www.WeissRatings.com   239   * Denotes a Weiss Recommended Company

II. Analysis of Largest Companies

Winter 2003 - 04

ONE HEALTH PLAN OF NEW JERSEY INC — B- Good

Major Rating Factors: Fair overall results on stability tests (3.8 on a scale of 0 to 10) based on a decline in the number of member physicians during 2002, a steep decline in premium revenue in 2002 and a significant 60% decrease in enrollment during the period. Rating is significantly influenced by the good financial results of Great West Life Asr. Strong capitalization index (10.0) based on excellent current risk-adjusted capital (severe loss scenario). High quality investment portfolio (9.9) containing no exposure to mortgages, junk bonds, or unaffiliated stocks.

Other Rating Factors: Weak profitability index (1.9) with operating losses during 1998 and 2001. Average return on equity has been poor at -2%. Weak liquidity (2.9) as a spike in claims may stretch capacity.

Principal Business: Comp med (100%)
Mem Phys: 02: 11,166 01: 12,570 **02 MLR** 404% / **02 Admin Exp** 74%
Enroll(000): Q1 03: 1 02: 2 01: 6 **Med Exp PMPM:** $156
Principal Investments: Cash and equiv (28%), other (72%)
Provider Compensation ($000): FFS ($8,071), contr fee ($2,017)
Total Member Encounters: Phys (16,606), non-phys (5,492)
Group Affiliation: Great West Life Asr
Licensed in: NJ
Address: 1 Centennial Plaza, Piscataway, NJ 08855
Phone: (732) 980-4000 **Dom State:** NJ **Commenced Bus:** July 1998

Data Date	Weiss Safety Rating	RACR #1	RACR #2	Total Assets ($mil)	Capital ($mil)	Net Premium ($mil)	Net Income ($mil)
3-03	B-	12.97	10.81	5.6	4.7	0.2	0.1
3-02	B-	0.00	0.00	8.7	3.3	0.5	-0.1
2002	B-	12.07	10.06	5.7	4.3	1.9	0.1
2001	B-	0.00	0.00	11.9	3.5	3.7	-0.1
2000	B	0.91	0.77	8.0	3.1	18.1	0.2
1999	B	1.56	1.35	7.8	1.4	7.0	0.5
1998	N/A	N/A	N/A	4.3	2.3	0.1	-1.0

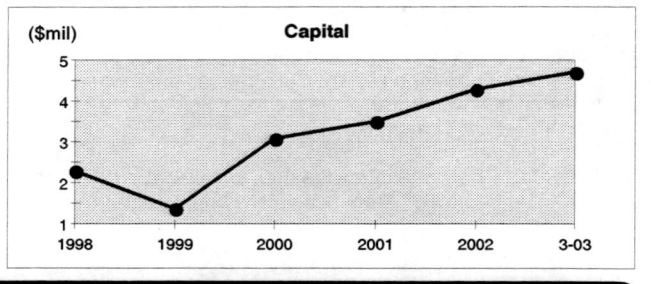

ONE HEALTH PLAN OF NORTH CAROLINA — B- Good

Major Rating Factors: Good liquidity (7.0 on a scale of 0 to 10) with sufficient resources (cash flows and marketable investments) to handle a spike in claims. Strong overall capitalization (10.0) based on excellent current risk-adjusted capital (severe loss scenario) despite some fluctuation in capital levels. High quality investment portfolio (9.9) containing no exposure to mortgages, junk bonds, or unaffiliated stocks.

Other Rating Factors: Weak profitability index (1.8). Weak overall results on stability tests (3.0) based on a steep decline in premium revenue in 2002, a decline in the number of member physicians during 2002 and a significant 20% decrease in enrollment during the period. Rating is significantly influenced by the good financial results of Great West Life Asr.

Principal Business: Comp med (100%)
Mem Phys: 02: 3,500 01: 6,158 **02 MLR** 245% / **02 Admin Exp** 59%
Enroll(000): Q1 03: 1 02: 1 01: 2 **Med Exp PMPM:** $116
Principal Investments: Cash and equiv (12%), other (88%)
Provider Compensation ($000): FFS ($2,962)
Total Member Encounters: N/A
Group Affiliation: Great West Life Asr
Licensed in: NC
Address: 6000 Fairview Road #500, Charlotte, NC 28210
Phone: (704) 552-9642 **Dom State:** NC **Commenced Bus:** March 1997

Data Date	Weiss Safety Rating	RACR #1	RACR #2	Total Assets ($mil)	Capital ($mil)	Net Premium ($mil)	Net Income ($mil)
3-03	B-	9.69	8.07	4.9	3.9	0.2	0.0
3-02	B-	4.25	2.78	6.6	3.4	0.2	0.1
2002	B-	9.66	8.05	5.0	3.9	0.9	0.4
2001	B-	4.25	2.78	5.7	3.3	5.4	-0.7
2000	B-	3.26	2.64	5.5	3.7	5.0	-0.5
1999	U	8.69	7.40	4.8	4.2	1.4	0.2
1998	N/A	N/A	N/A	N/A	N/A	N/A	N/A

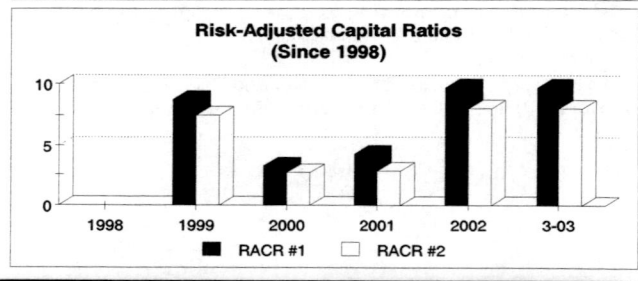

ONE HEALTH PLAN OF OHIO INC — B- Good

Major Rating Factors: Fair overall results on stability tests (4.1 on a scale of 0 to 10) based on a significant 50% decrease in enrollment during the period. Rating is significantly influenced by the good financial results of Great West Life Asr. Strong capitalization (10.0) based on excellent current risk-adjusted capital (severe loss scenario) reflecting improvement over results in 2000. High quality investment portfolio (9.9) containing no exposure to mortgages, junk bonds, or unaffiliated stocks.

Other Rating Factors: Weak profitability index (1.9) with operating losses during 1998, 1999, 2000 and 2001. Average return on equity has been poor at -38%. Weak liquidity (2.5) as a spike in claims may stretch capacity.

Principal Business: Comp med (100%)
Mem Phys: 02: 10,965 01: 11,920 **02 MLR** 357% / **02 Admin Exp** 61%
Enroll(000): Q1 03: 4 02: 4 01: 8 **Med Exp PMPM:** $150
Principal Investments: Cash and equiv (29%), other (71%)
Provider Compensation ($000): Contr fee ($13,158)
Total Member Encounters: N/A
Group Affiliation: Great West Life Asr
Licensed in: OH
Address: 25000 Country Club Blvd. #140, North Olmstead, OH 44070
Phone: (314) 543-8388 **Dom State:** OH **Commenced Bus:** May 1997

Data Date	Weiss Safety Rating	RACR #1	RACR #2	Total Assets ($mil)	Capital ($mil)	Net Premium ($mil)	Net Income ($mil)
3-03	B-	12.56	10.46	7.8	5.4	0.6	0.1
3-02	C+	7.22	4.89	8.8	4.9	0.9	0.0
2002	B-	12.38	10.32	7.7	5.3	3.1	0.3
2001	C+	7.22	4.88	14.1	5.0	5.0	-0.2
2000	C	1.33	1.11	13.8	4.6	19.3	-1.8
1999	C	1.34	1.14	7.6	2.4	14.7	-2.2
1998	C	1.70	1.45	4.0	1.5	6.8	-0.7

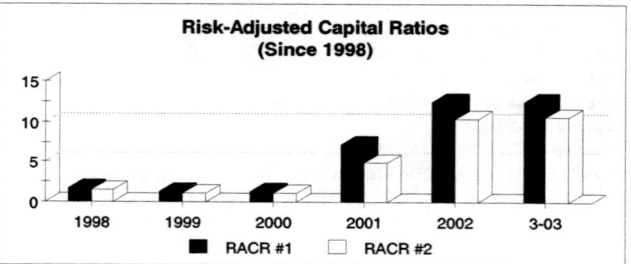

ONE HEALTH PLAN OF OREGON INC — B- Good

Major Rating Factors: Fair profitability index (4.0 on a scale of 0 to 10) with modest operating losses during 1999 and 2002. Strong capitalization index (10.0) based on excellent current risk-adjusted capital (severe loss scenario). High quality investment portfolio (9.9) containing no exposure to mortgages, junk bonds, or unaffiliated stocks.
Other Rating Factors: Weak liquidity (2.2) as a spike in claims may stretch capacity.
Principal Business: Comp med (100%)
Mem Phys: 02: 4,329   **01:** 5,232   **02 MLR** 343%   **/ 02 Admin Exp** 65%
Enroll(000): Q1 03: 8   **02:** 10   **01:** 15   **Med Exp PMPM:** $150
Principal Investments: Cash and equiv (50%), other (50%)
Provider Compensation ($000): Bonus arrang ($23,800)
Total Member Encounters: N/A
Group Affiliation: Great West Life Asr
Licensed in: OR
Address: 121 SW Morrison, Ste 475, Portland, OR 97204
Phone: (503) 222-3044   **Dom State:** OR   **Commenced Bus:** April 1997

Data Date	Weiss Safety Rating	RACR #1	RACR #2	Total Assets ($mil)	Capital ($mil)	Net Premium ($mil)	Net Income ($mil)
3-03	B-	11.58	9.65	10.1	4.7	1.2	0.0
3-02	D	0.00	0.00	11.8	4.7	1.9	0.1
2002	B-	11.65	9.71	10.1	4.7	6.5	0.0
2001	D	0.00	0.00	19.9	4.6	7.0	0.4
2000	D	0.82	0.49	8.1	3.1	19.8	0.1
1999	D-	1.13	1.02	4.1	1.1	6.2	-1.2
1998	N/A	N/A	N/A	3.5	1.7	1.6	N/A

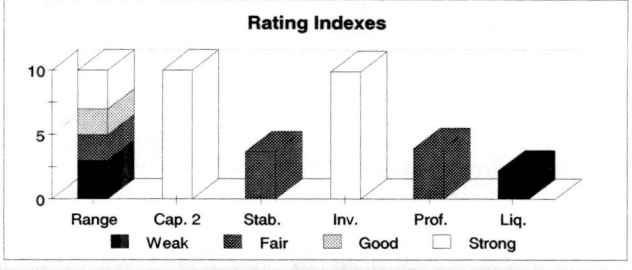

ONE HEALTH PLAN OF TENNESSEE — B Good

Major Rating Factors: Fair overall results on stability tests (3.4 on a scale of 0 to 10) based on a steep decline in premium revenue in 2002, a significant 63% decrease in enrollment during the period. Rating is significantly influenced by the good financial results of Great West Life Asr. Strong capitalization index (10.0) based on excellent current risk-adjusted capital (severe loss scenario). High quality investment portfolio (9.9) containing no exposure to mortgages, junk bonds, or unaffiliated stocks.
Other Rating Factors: Excellent liquidity (8.3) with ample operational cash flow and liquid investments. Weak profitability index (0.8) with operating losses during 1998, 1999, 2000 and 2001. Average return on equity has been poor at -45%.
Principal Business: Comp med (100%)
Mem Phys: 02: 3,931   **01:** 3,937   **02 MLR** 116%   **/ 02 Admin Exp** 19%
Enroll(000): Q1 03: 1   **02:** 1   **01:** 3   **Med Exp PMPM:** $147
Principal Investments: Cash and equiv (50%), other (50%)
Provider Compensation ($000): FFS ($5,296)
Total Member Encounters: Phys (7,002), non-phys (1,278)
Group Affiliation: Great West Life Asr
Licensed in: TN
Address: 3100 W End Ave #600, Nashville, TN 37203
Phone: (615) 269-6983   **Dom State:** TN   **Commenced Bus:** May 1997

Data Date	Weiss Safety Rating	RACR #1	RACR #2	Total Assets ($mil)	Capital ($mil)	Net Premium ($mil)	Net Income ($mil)
3-03	B	36.78	30.65	10.6	9.4	0.5	0.1
3-02	B	0.00	0.00	8.0	5.0	0.9	-0.1
2002	B	36.53	30.44	10.4	9.4	3.0	1.0
2001	B	0.00	0.00	10.0	4.5	6.0	-0.8
2000	B	1.43	1.18	11.1	4.4	12.5	-2.3
1999	B	0.84	0.70	3.8	0.8	5.4	-1.9
1998	B	4.18	3.50	2.8	2.3	1.5	-0.2

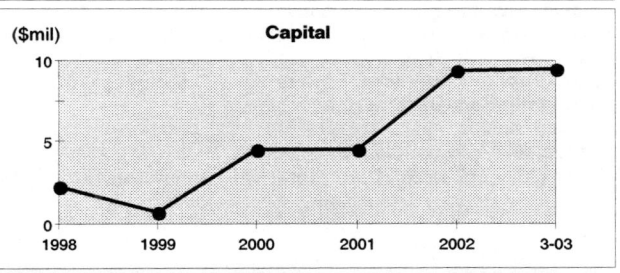

ONE HEALTH PLAN OF TEXAS INC — B Good

Major Rating Factors: Fair overall results on stability tests (4.4 on a scale of 0 to 10) based on a significant 39% decrease in enrollment during the period. Rating is significantly influenced by the good financial results of Great West Life Asr. Strong capitalization index (10.0) based on excellent current risk-adjusted capital (severe loss scenario). High quality investment portfolio (9.9) containing no exposure to mortgages, junk bonds, or unaffiliated stocks.
Other Rating Factors: Weak profitability index (2.2) with operating losses during 1999 and 2001. Return on equity has been low, averaging 4%. Weak liquidity (2.2) as a spike in claims may stretch capacity.
Principal Business: Comp med (100%)
Mem Phys: 02: 12,964   **01:** 14,139   **02 MLR** 343%   **/ 02 Admin Exp** 68%
Enroll(000): Q1 03: 17   **02:** 23   **01:** 39   **Med Exp PMPM:** $168
Principal Investments: Cash and equiv (34%), other (66%)
Provider Compensation ($000): FFS ($68,377), capitation ($66)
Total Member Encounters: Phys (125,809), non-phys (34,784)
Group Affiliation: Great West Life Asr
Licensed in: TX
Address: 8350 N Central Expway M1000, Dallas, TX 75206
Phone: (972) 813-7000   **Dom State:** TX   **Commenced Bus:** January 1996

Data Date	Weiss Safety Rating	RACR #1	RACR #2	Total Assets ($mil)	Capital ($mil)	Net Premium ($mil)	Net Income ($mil)
3-03	B	15.84	13.20	25.9	14.1	3.0	0.1
3-02	B	0.00	0.00	34.4	13.4	5.1	0.4
2002	B	16.62	13.85	31.7	14.9	18.3	0.1
2001	B	0.00	0.00	56.2	14.8	24.5	-0.1
2000	B	1.00	0.83	30.1	8.8	90.9	1.4
1999	B	1.41	1.18	23.1	6.5	56.6	-2.8
1998	B	0.94	0.80	12.5	2.9	33.7	1.0

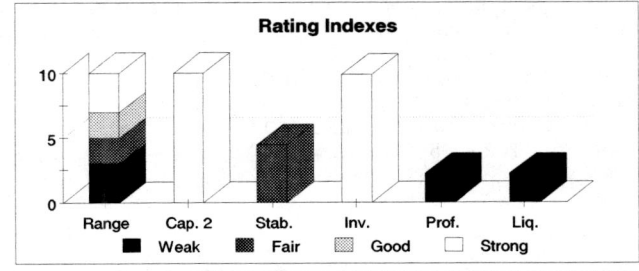

II. Analysis of Largest Companies

Winter 2003 - 04

ONE HEALTH PLAN OF WASHINGTON INC — B — Good

Major Rating Factors: Fair profitability index (3.7 on a scale of 0 to 10) with operating losses during 2001. Strong capitalization (10.0) based on excellent current risk-adjusted capital (severe loss scenario). Moreover, capital has steadily grown over the last five years. High quality investment portfolio (9.9) containing no exposure to mortgages, junk bonds, or unaffiliated stocks.
Other Rating Factors: Weak liquidity (2.9) as a spike in claims may stretch capacity.
Principal Business: Comp med (100%)
Mem Phys: 02: 7,689   **01:** 6,750   **02 MLR** 380%   **/ 02 Admin Exp** 69%
Enroll(000): Q1 03: 5   **02:** 6   **01:** 13   **Med Exp PMPM:** $138
Principal Investments: Cash and equiv (40%), other (60%)
Provider Compensation ($000): Bonus arrang ($16,618)
Total Member Encounters: Phys (34,383), non-phys (14,787)
Group Affiliation: Great West Life Asr
Licensed in: WA
Address: 3005 112th Ave NE Suite 220, Bellevue, WA 98004
Phone: (425) 827-2282   **Dom State:** WA   **Commenced Bus:** March 1997

Data Date	Weiss Safety Rating	RACR #1	RACR #2	Total Assets ($mil)	Capital ($mil)	Net Premium ($mil)	Net Income ($mil)
3-03	B	19.76	16.47	11.2	8.3	0.7	0.1
3-02	B	12.60	9.29	13.2	7.3	1.1	-0.3
2002	B	19.74	16.45	11.0	8.3	4.1	0.1
2001	B	12.74	9.36	20.3	7.7	5.9	-0.1
2000	C+	2.49	1.76	13.5	7.1	21.2	2.2
1999	C	2.19	1.97	7.9	4.4	8.4	0.6
1998	C	2.48	2.23	5.2	3.8	2.4	0.4

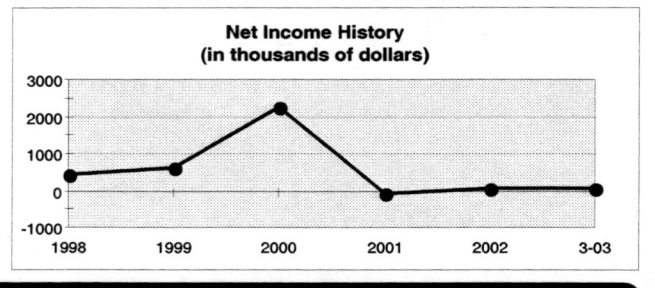

Net Income History (in thousands of dollars)

OPTIMA HEALTH PLAN — B — Good

Major Rating Factors: Good overall profitability index (6.5 on a scale of 0 to 10) despite operating losses during 1999 and 2001. Good liquidity (6.9) with sufficient resources (cash flows and marketable investments) to handle a spike in claims. Strong capitalization index (7.3) based on excellent current risk-adjusted capital (severe loss scenario).
Other Rating Factors: High quality investment portfolio (9.9) containing no exposure to mortgages, junk bonds, or unaffiliated stocks. Excellent overall results on stability tests (7.8) based on consistent premium and capital growth in the last five years.
Principal Business: Medicaid (50%), comp med (39%), FEHB (11%)
Mem Phys: 02: 2,618   **01:** 2,469   **02 MLR** 88%   **/ 02 Admin Exp** 8%
Enroll(000): Q1 03: 195   **02:** 200   **01:** 202   **Med Exp PMPM:** $178
Principal Investments: Cash and equiv (75%), other (25%)
Provider Compensation ($000): Contr fee ($374,386), capitation ($29,758), bonus arrang ($10,854)
Total Member Encounters: Phys (978,141), non-phys (702,115)
Group Affiliation: Sentara Health System
Licensed in: VA
Address: 4417 Corporation Lane, Virginia Beach, VA 23462
Phone: (757) 552-7220   **Dom State:** VA   **Commenced Bus:** December 1984

Data Date	Weiss Safety Rating	RACR #1	RACR #2	Total Assets ($mil)	Capital ($mil)	Net Premium ($mil)	Net Income ($mil)
3-03	B	1.59	1.32	122.4	53.3	128.1	6.1
3-02	B-	0.91	0.76	85.4	26.8	116.9	0.1
2002	B	1.33	1.11	113.5	46.0	489.7	19.8
2001	B-	1.12	0.94	73.9	26.7	391.4	-0.1
2000	C	0.81	0.69	54.4	18.3	325.8	2.3
1999	D-	0.25	0.21	54.2	12.1	361.2	-0.7
1998	D	0.20	0.18	41.6	9.3	298.9	0.4

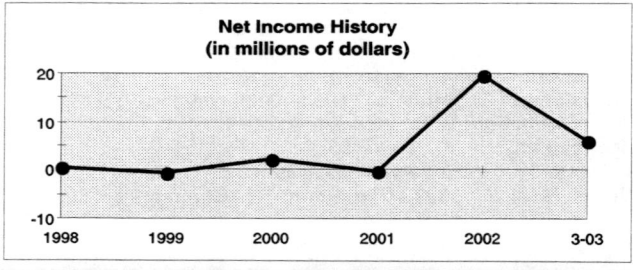

Net Income History (in millions of dollars)

OPTIMUM CHOICE INC — B — Good

Major Rating Factors: Good overall results on stability tests (6.7 on a scale of 0 to 10) based on healthy premium and capital growth during 2002. Good liquidity (6.8) with sufficient resources (cash flows and marketable investments) to handle a spike in claims. Excellent profitability (7.6) with operating gains in each of the last five years.
Other Rating Factors: Strong capitalization (7.7) based on excellent current risk-adjusted capital (severe loss scenario) reflecting improvement over results in 2001. High quality investment portfolio (9.9) containing no exposure to mortgages, junk bonds, or unaffiliated stocks.
Principal Business: Comp med (100%)
Mem Phys: 02: 39,352   **01:** 34,364   **02 MLR** 90%   **/ 02 Admin Exp** 7%
Enroll(000): Q1 03: 430   **02:** 444   **01:** 392   **Med Exp PMPM:** $171
Principal Investments: Cash and equiv (31%), other (69%)
Provider Compensation ($000): Capitation ($540,893), contr fee ($303,774)
Total Member Encounters: Phys (2,235,924), non-phys (214,992)
Group Affiliation: Mid Atlantic Medical Services Inc
Licensed in: DC, DE, MD, VA, WV
Address: 4 Taft Ct, Rockville, MD 20850
Phone: (301) 762-8205   **Dom State:** MD   **Commenced Bus:** September 1988

Data Date	Weiss Safety Rating	RACR #1	RACR #2	Total Assets ($mil)	Capital ($mil)	Net Premium ($mil)	Net Income ($mil)
3-03	B	1.91	1.59	251.2	107.4	261.5	13.6
3-02	B-	1.12	1.00	184.7	67.5	224.1	7.9
2002	B	1.66	1.38	219.4	94.0	948.7	14.9
2001	B-	1.14	1.01	165.9	59.8	740.9	6.5
2000	B-	1.52	1.31	144.9	67.7	722.0	3.5
1999	B-	1.30	1.15	138.9	64.1	669.7	6.9
1998	B-	1.35	1.17	123.9	56.0	630.1	12.5

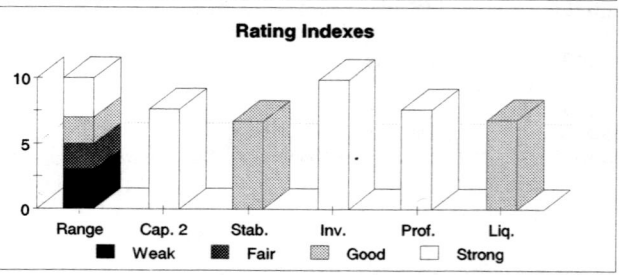

Rating Indexes: Range, Cap. 2, Stab., Inv., Prof., Liq. — Weak, Fair, Good, Strong

OPTIMUM CHOICE OF THE CAROLINAS INC   C   Fair

Major Rating Factors: Fair capitalization (4.8 on a scale of 0 to 10) based on good current risk-adjusted capital (severe loss scenario) as results have slipped from the excellent range over the last year. Weak profitability index (0.2) with $18.3 million in losses in the last five years. Average return on equity over the last five years has been extremely poor. Weak overall results on stability tests (0.7) based on an excessive 35% enrollment growth during the period. Rating is significantly influenced by the strong financial results of Mid Atlantic Medical Services Inc.
Other Rating Factors: Good liquidity (5.2) with sufficient resources (cash flows and marketable investments) to handle a spike in claims. High quality investment portfolio (9.9) containing no exposure to mortgages, junk bonds, or unaffiliated stocks.
Principal Business: Comp med (100%)
Mem Phys: 02: 8,477   **01:** 7,996   **02 MLR** 108%   / **02 Admin Exp** 14%
Enroll(000): Q1 03: 15   **02:** 14   **01:** 10   **Med Exp PMPM:** $212
Principal Investments: Cash and equiv (91%), other (9%)
Provider Compensation ($000): Contr fee ($28,045), capitation ($177)
Total Member Encounters: Phys (66,350), non-phys (6,380)
Group Affiliation: Mid Atlantic Medical Services Inc
Licensed in: NC, SC
Address: 4 Taft Court, Rockville, MD 20850
Phone: (301) 762-8205   **Dom State:** NC   **Commenced Bus:** July 1995

Data Date	Weiss Safety Rating	RACR #1	RACR #2	Total Assets ($mil)	Capital ($mil)	Net Premium ($mil)	Net Income ($mil)
3-03	C	0.89	0.75	13.1	4.2	9.5	0.2
3-02	C	2.49	2.10	12.7	6.2	6.3	-0.9
2002	C	0.69	0.58	13.0	3.4	28.4	-4.8
2001	C	2.49	2.11	12.0	7.1	19.2	-2.6
2000	D	1.01	0.86	8.5	3.6	18.1	-3.9
1999	D	0.43	0.37	13.5	2.5	20.9	-3.7
1998	D	0.89	0.76	14.5	2.9	14.2	-3.3

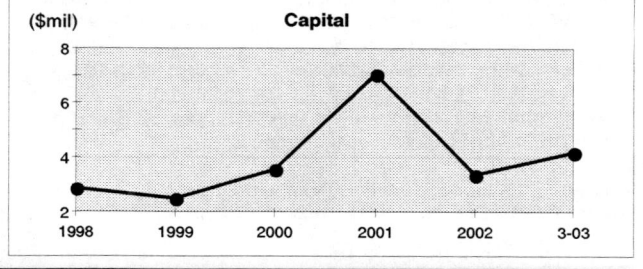

ORANGE PREVENTION & TREATMENT INTEGR   C   Fair

Major Rating Factors: Good overall results on stability tests (6.2 on a scale of 0 to 10). Good liquidity (6.9) with sufficient resources (cash flows and marketable investments) to handle a spike in claims. Excellent profitability (7.8).
Other Rating Factors: Strong overall capitalization (7.8) based on excellent current risk-adjusted capital (severe loss scenario) despite some fluctuation in capital levels.
Principal Business: None
Mem Phys: 02: N/A   **01:** N/A   **02 MLR** 93%   / **02 Admin Exp** 4%
Enroll(000): Q1 03: 300   **02:** 293   **01:** 258   **Med Exp PMPM:** $200
Principal Investments ($000): Bonds ($136,768), cash and equiv ($66,570)
Provider Compensation ($000): None
Total Member Encounters: N/A
Group Affiliation: None
Licensed in: CA
Address: 1120 W La Veta Ave, Orange, CA 92868
Phone: (714) 246-8400   **Dom State:** CA   **Commenced Bus:** June 2000

Data Date	Weiss Safety Rating	RACR #1	RACR #2	Total Assets ($mil)	Capital ($mil)	Net Premium ($mil)	Net Income ($mil)
3-03	C	2.54	1.67	267.6	148.4	180.6	1.0
3-02	N/A	N/A	N/A	N/A	N/A	N/A	N/A
2002	C	2.53	1.67	269.4	147.4	708.0	20.8
2001	C-	2.78	1.82	254.4	126.7	626.2	11.5
2000	N/A	N/A	N/A	N/A	N/A	N/A	N/A
1999	N/A	N/A	N/A	N/A	N/A	N/A	N/A
1998	N/A	N/A	N/A	N/A	N/A	N/A	N/A

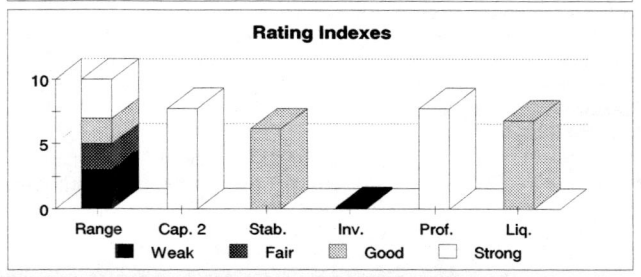

OXFORD HEALTH INS INC   B-   Good

Major Rating Factors: Fair profitability index (4.4 on a scale of 0 to 10) with operating losses during 1998. Good liquidity (6.8) with sufficient resources (cash flows and marketable investments) to handle a spike in claims. Strong capitalization index (9.4) based on excellent current risk-adjusted capital (severe loss scenario).
Other Rating Factors: High quality investment portfolio (9.9) containing no exposure to mortgages, junk bonds, or unaffiliated stocks.
Principal Business: Comp med (100%)
Mem Phys: 02: 53,000   **01:** 49,600   **02 MLR** 77%   / **02 Admin Exp** 14%
Enroll(000): Q1 03: 1,114   **02:** 1,086   **01:** 1,002   **Med Exp PMPM:** $55
Principal Investments: Cash and equiv (26%), other (74%)
Provider Compensation ($000): FFS ($410,820), contr fee ($245,915), capitation ($5,429), bonus arrang ($447)
Total Member Encounters: Phys (2,596,685), non-phys (666,967)
Group Affiliation: Oxford Group
Licensed in: CT, NH, NJ, NY, PA
Address: 1133 Avenue of the America, New York, NY 10036
Phone: (203) 459-6000   **Dom State:** NY   **Commenced Bus:** July 1987

Data Date	Weiss Safety Rating	RACR #1	RACR #2	Total Assets ($mil)	Capital ($mil)	Net Premium ($mil)	Net Income ($mil)
3-03	B-	3.32	2.76	391.7	181.9	276.7	17.7
3-02	N/A	N/A	N/A	N/A	N/A	N/A	N/A
2002	N/A	N/A	N/A	342.7	163.2	892.0	47.5
2001	N/A	N/A	N/A	325.2	201.2	589.8	N/A
2000	U	2.70	2.23	262.4	165.9	515.7	38.0
1999	N/A	N/A	N/A	146.7	63.5	470.7	N/A
1998	C-	0.91	0.75	261.9	72.3	464.0	-95.2

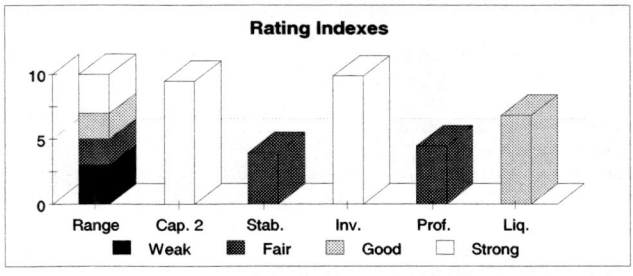

II. Analysis of Largest Companies

Winter 2003 - 04

OXFORD HEALTH PLANS (CT) INC — B — Good

Major Rating Factors: Good overall profitability index (6.1 on a scale of 0 to 10) despite a decline in earnings during 2002. Good overall results on stability tests (5.8) despite inconsistent enrollment growth in the past five years due to declines in 1999, 2000 and 2001, fair risk-adjusted capital in prior years. Rating is significantly influenced by the good financial results of Oxford Health Plans Inc. Good liquidity (6.9) with sufficient resources (cash flows and marketable investments) to handle a spike in claims.
Other Rating Factors: Strong capitalization (10.0) based on excellent current risk-adjusted capital (severe loss scenario) reflecting significant improvement over results in 1998. High quality investment portfolio (9.9) containing no exposure to mortgages, junk bonds, or unaffiliated stocks.
Principal Business: Comp med (96%), Medicare (4%)
Mem Phys: 02: 53,000 **01:** 49,600 **02 MLR** 79% / **02 Admin Exp** 15%
Enroll(000): Q1 03: 107 **02:** 82 **01:** 59 **Med Exp PMPM:** $191
Principal Investments: Cash and equiv (44%), other (56%)
Provider Compensation ($000): Contr fee ($134,232), FFS ($17,704), capitation ($2,015), bonus arrang ($216)
Total Member Encounters: Phys (420,432), non-phys (220,681)
Group Affiliation: Oxford Health Plans Inc
Licensed in: CT
Address: 48 Monroe Turnpike, Trumbull, CT 06611
Phone: (203) 459-6000 **Dom State:** CT **Commenced Bus:** October 1993

Data Date	Weiss Safety Rating	RACR #1	RACR #2	Total Assets ($mil)	Capital ($mil)	Net Premium ($mil)	Net Income ($mil)
3-03	B	4.28	3.57	109.1	49.4	79.7	2.8
3-02	C+	1.56	1.25	43.3	14.1	44.4	2.2
2002	B	1.78	1.48	61.9	20.1	203.7	8.5
2001	C+	1.66	1.33	43.8	12.3	148.0	10.7
2000	D+	2.04	1.72	41.2	14.2	139.8	8.3
1999	D	1.82	1.55	41.6	17.1	128.5	14.4
1998	D	0.64	0.54	43.0	7.3	163.7	-7.5

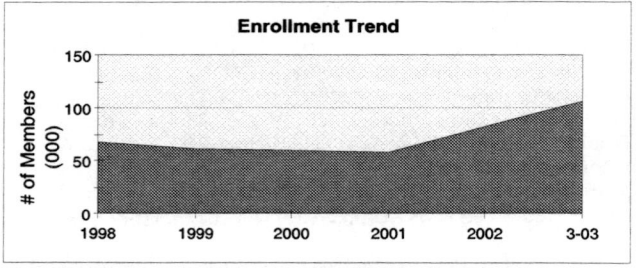

Enrollment Trend chart (1998–3-03)

OXFORD HEALTH PLANS (NJ) INC — B — Good

Major Rating Factors: Good overall profitability index (5.7 on a scale of 0 to 10) despite a decline in earnings during 2002. Good overall results on stability tests (5.1) despite a decline in enrollment during 2002, fair risk-adjusted capital in prior years. Good liquidity (5.9) with sufficient resources (cash flows and marketable investments) to handle a spike in claims.
Other Rating Factors: Strong capitalization (7.9) based on excellent current risk-adjusted capital (severe loss scenario) reflecting significant improvement over results in 1999. High quality investment portfolio (9.8) containing no exposure to mortgages, junk bonds, or unaffiliated stocks.
Principal Business: Comp med (98%), Medicare (2%)
Mem Phys: 02: 53,000 **01:** 49,600 **02 MLR** 87% / **02 Admin Exp** 12%
Enroll(000): Q1 03: 145 **02:** 158 **01:** 171 **Med Exp PMPM:** $178
Principal Investments: Cash and equiv (7%), other (93%)
Provider Compensation ($000): Contr fee ($277,882), FFS ($52,278), capitation ($7,151), bonus arrang ($673), other ($5,000)
Total Member Encounters: Phys (796,072), non-phys (389,051)
Group Affiliation: Oxford Health Plans Inc
Licensed in: NJ
Address: 111 Wood Ave S Ste 2, Iselin, NJ 08837
Phone: (203) 459-6000 **Dom State:** NJ **Commenced Bus:** April 1985

Data Date	Weiss Safety Rating	RACR #1	RACR #2	Total Assets ($mil)	Capital ($mil)	Net Premium ($mil)	Net Income ($mil)
3-03	B	2.11	1.76	107.5	48.7	100.2	6.1
3-02	C+	1.76	1.45	107.3	44.3	98.7	3.1
2002	B	1.73	1.44	105.7	44.0	404.1	12.1
2001	C+	1.88	1.55	109.0	41.4	387.2	21.6
2000	C-	2.17	1.83	122.1	48.0	388.5	24.5
1999	D+	0.64	0.55	114.8	22.3	388.3	11.6
1998	D+	1.01	0.85	173.3	41.7	497.4	-42.5

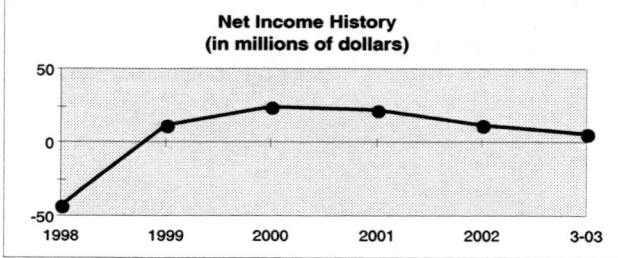

Net Income History (in millions of dollars) chart (1998–3-03)

OXFORD HEALTH PLANS (NY) INC * — B+ — Good

Major Rating Factors: Good liquidity (6.7 on a scale of 0 to 10) with sufficient resources (cash flows and marketable investments) to handle a spike in claims. Excellent profitability (7.8) despite a decline in earnings during 2002. Strong capitalization (8.7) based on excellent current risk-adjusted capital (severe loss scenario) reflecting significant improvement over results in 1998.
Other Rating Factors: High quality investment portfolio (9.4) containing little or no exposure to mortgages, junk bonds, or unaffiliated stocks. Excellent overall results on stability tests (7.3) based on consistent premium and capital growth in the last five years.
Principal Business: Comp med (83%), Medicare (17%)
Mem Phys: 02: 53,000 **01:** 49,600 **02 MLR** 80% / **02 Admin Exp** 11%
Enroll(000): Q1 03: 992 **02:** 1,031 **01:** 1,073 **Med Exp PMPM:** $206
Principal Investments: Affiliate common stock (17%), cash and equiv (15%), other (68%)
Provider Compensation ($000): Contr fee ($2,145,484), FFS ($286,104), capitation ($149,676), bonus arrang ($19,680)
Total Member Encounters: Phys (6,070,118), non-phys (2,793,340)
Group Affiliation: Oxford Health Plans Inc
Licensed in: NY
Address: 1133 Avenue of the Americas, New York, NY 06611
Phone: (203) 459-6000 **Dom State:** NY **Commenced Bus:** June 1986

Data Date	Weiss Safety Rating	RACR #1	RACR #2	Total Assets ($mil)	Capital ($mil)	Net Premium ($mil)	Net Income ($mil)
3-03	B+	2.72	2.26	1,066.7	535.3	853.2	67.8
3-02	B-	1.78	1.44	929.6	376.9	802.3	51.3
2002	B+	2.10	1.75	1,006.9	456.0	3,256.0	236.3
2001	B-	1.89	1.54	981.1	394.5	3,188.8	248.1
2000	C-	1.81	1.50	925.7	361.9	2,994.5	225.2
1999	D	1.36	1.14	875.2	312.3	3,148.8	277.3
1998	D	0.41	0.34	990.4	130.0	3,323.0	-256.0

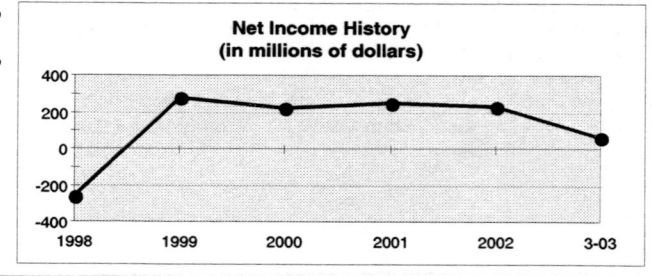

Net Income History (in millions of dollars) chart (1998–3-03)

Winter 2003 - 04 — II. Analysis of Largest Companies

PACIFIC GUARDIAN LIFE INSURANCE COMPANY LIMITED *   B+   Good

Major Rating Factors: Good quality investment portfolio (6.5 on a scale of 0 to 10) with no exposure to mortgages and minimal holdings in junk bonds. Good liquidity (6.2) with sufficient resources to handle a spike in claims as well as a significant increase in policy surrenders. Good overall results on stability tests (5.0) good operational trends and excellent risk diversification.
Other Rating Factors: Strong capitalization (8.4) based on excellent risk adjusted capital (severe loss scenario). Excellent profitability (7.7) with operating gains in each of the last five years.
Principal Business: Individual life insurance (38%), group health insurance (27%), individual annuities (19%), group life insurance (12%), and reinsurance (3%).
Principal Investments: NonCMO investment grade bonds (36%), CMOs and structured securities (27%), mortgages in good standing (26%), policy loans (6%), and misc. investments (5%).
Investments in Affiliates: None
Group Affiliation: Meiji Mutual Group
Licensed in: AK, AZ, CA, CO, HI, ID, IA, LA, MO, MT, NE, NV, NM, OK, OR, SD, TX, UT, WA, WY
Commenced Business: November 1947
Address: 1440 Kapiolani Blvd Ste 1700, Honolulu, HI 96814
Phone: (808) 955-2236   **Domicile State:** HI   **NAIC Code:** 64343

Data Date	Weiss Safety Rating	RACR #1	RACR #2	Total Assets ($mil)	Capital ($mil)	Net Premium ($mil)	Net Income ($mil)
6-03	B+	3.30	1.92	431.5	71.0	29.6	2.1
6-02	B	3.16	1.82	409.9	66.7	37.4	2.2
2002	B	3.14	1.82	420.5	67.5	68.2	5.5
2001	B	3.21	1.87	404.8	68.5	86.1	5.4
2000	B	3.44	1.84	352.1	63.5	73.3	5.0
1999	B	3.60	1.94	320.2	60.5	69.7	5.0
1998	B	3.55	2.12	288.2	57.8	53.6	5.6

Adverse Trends in Operations

Decrease in capital during 2002 (2%)
Increase in policy surrenders from 2001 to 2002 (43%)
Decrease in premium volume from 2001 to 2002 (21%)
Change in premium mix from 1998 to 1999 (4.1%)

PACIFIC HOSPITAL ASSOC *   A-   Excellent

Major Rating Factors: Excellent profitability (7.4 on a scale of 0 to 10). Strong capitalization (7.9) based on excellent current risk-adjusted capital (severe loss scenario) reflecting significant improvement over results in 2000. High quality investment portfolio (7.8).
Other Rating Factors: Good liquidity (6.9) with sufficient resources (cash flows and marketable investments) to handle a spike in claims.
Principal Business: Comp med (95%), dental (4%)
Mem Phys: 02: 13,731   01: 11,803   **02 MLR** 82%   **/ 02 Admin Exp** 9%
Enroll(000): Q1 03: 124   02: 116   01: 111   **Med Exp PMPM:** $149
Principal Investments: Nonaffiliate common stock (34%), cash and equiv (17%), real estate (9%), other (40%)
Provider Compensation ($000): Contr fee ($186,412), bonus arrang ($7,917), capitation ($972), other ($7,320)
Total Member Encounters: Phys (653,895), non-phys (88,877)
Group Affiliation: None
Licensed in: OR
Address: 250 Country Club Rd, Eugene, OR 97401
Phone: (541) 686-1242   **Dom State:** OR   **Commenced Bus:** July 1939

Data Date	Weiss Safety Rating	RACR #1	RACR #2	Total Assets ($mil)	Capital ($mil)	Net Premium ($mil)	Net Income ($mil)
3-03	A-	2.07	1.73	89.6	51.0	72.9	1.6
3-02	B-	1.37	1.01	76.8	41.3	58.7	2.5
2002	A-	2.09	1.74	88.5	51.3	246.0	13.6
2001	B-	1.36	1.01	75.7	38.8	211.3	12.3
2000	C+	0.84	0.66	58.5	29.1	163.0	3.8
1999	C	0.84	0.70	48.2	25.7	123.9	3.7
1998	N/A	N/A	N/A	43.7	22.3	94.1	N/A

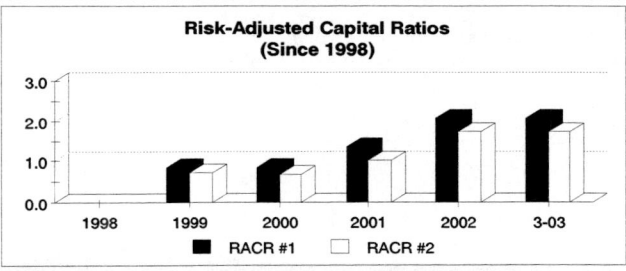

Risk-Adjusted Capital Ratios (Since 1998) — bar chart showing RACR #1 and RACR #2 for years 1998, 1999, 2000, 2001, 2002, 3-03.

PACIFIC LIFE & ANNUITY COMPANY   B   Good

Major Rating Factors: Good quality investment portfolio (5.3 on a scale of 0 to 10) despite mixed results such as: large holdings of BBB rated bonds but moderate junk bond exposure. Good overall results on stability tests (6.3). Stability strengths include excellent operational trends and excellent risk diversification. Strong capitalization (8.3) based on excellent risk adjusted capital (severe loss scenario).
Other Rating Factors: Excellent profitability (8.4) with operating gains in each of the last five years. Excellent liquidity (7.0).
Principal Business: Group health insurance (84%), individual annuities (13%), group life insurance (2%), and individual life insurance (1%).
Principal Investments: NonCMO investment grade bonds (76%), noninv. grade bonds (11%), CMOs and structured securities (3%), mortgages in good standing (2%), and common & preferred stock (1%).
Investments in Affiliates: None
Group Affiliation: Pacific Mutual
Licensed in: All states except VT, PR
Commenced Business: July 1983
Address: 100 W Clarendon Suite 2000, Phoenix, AZ 85013
Phone: (714) 640-3011   **Domicile State:** AZ   **NAIC Code:** 97268

Data Date	Weiss Safety Rating	RACR #1	RACR #2	Total Assets ($mil)	Capital ($mil)	Net Premium ($mil)	Net Income ($mil)
6-03	B	2.83	1.86	1,051.1	272.7	657.6	9.0
6-02	B	3.58	2.42	746.7	257.2	472.9	11.0
2002	B	3.24	2.13	853.8	267.0	1,010.5	22.5
2001	B	4.08	2.78	649.4	251.7	724.7	23.6
2000	B	4.94	3.33	461.7	225.7	434.6	28.2
1999	B	5.31	3.65	403.3	200.9	359.8	31.0
1998	B	1.60	1.17	337.9	76.7	499.2	5.1

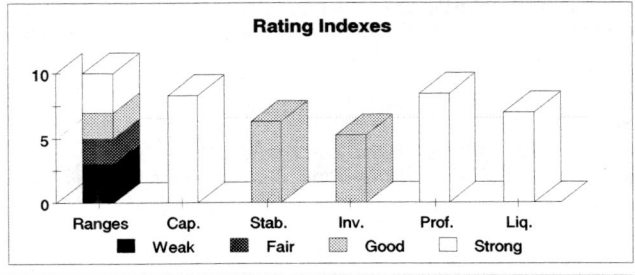

Rating Indexes — bar chart showing Ranges, Cap., Stab., Inv., Prof., Liq. with legend: Weak, Fair, Good, Strong.

* Denotes a Weiss Recommended Company

II. Analysis of Largest Companies

Winter 2003 - 04

PACIFICARE LIFE & HEALTH INSURANCE COMPANY — C- Fair

Major Rating Factors: Fair overall results on stability tests (3.2 on a scale of 0 to 10) including fair financial strength of affiliated PacifiCare Health Systems. Good overall profitability (6.1). Return on equity has been excellent over the last five years averaging 214.7%. Strong capitalization (7.2) based on excellent risk adjusted capital (severe loss scenario).
Other Rating Factors: High quality investment portfolio (8.7). Excellent liquidity (7.9).
Principal Business: Group health insurance (94%), group life insurance (5%), and individual health insurance (2%).
Principal Investments: NonCMO investment grade bonds (82%) and CMOs and structured securities (20%).
Investments in Affiliates: None
Group Affiliation: PacifiCare Health Systems
Licensed in: AL, AK, AZ, AR, CA, CO, DC, FL, GA, ID, IL, IN, IA, KS, KY, LA, MD, MA, MI, MS, MO, MT, NE, NV, NM, NC, ND, OH, OK, OR, PA, SC, SD, TN, TX, UT, VA, WA, WV, WY
Commenced Business: September 1967
Address: 23046 Avenida Dela Carlota 700, Laguna Hills, CA 92653-1519
Phone: (714) 206-5247 **Domicile State:** IN **NAIC Code:** 70785

Data Date	Weiss Safety Rating	RACR #1	RACR #2	Total Assets ($mil)	Capital ($mil)	Net Premium ($mil)	Net Income ($mil)
6-03	C-	1.44	1.16	96.2	40.6	102.6	53.7
6-02	C+	1.89	1.51	69.7	34.9	61.6	63.3
2002	C	1.58	1.27	78.4	35.5	130.9	124.8
2001	C+	2.82	2.24	78.3	44.8	88.8	146.4
2000	C+	4.04	3.19	98.0	59.5	92.3	134.6
1999	C+	9.51	7.33	187.8	141.2	98.1	120.9
1998	C+	2.30	1.81	83.6	42.8	105.5	26.0

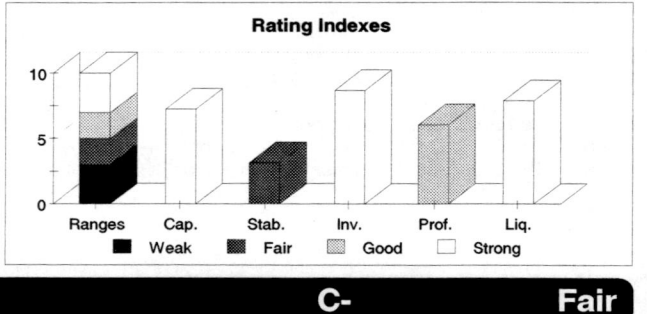

PACIFICARE LIFE ASSURANCE COMPANY — C- Fair

Major Rating Factors: Fair overall results on stability tests (3.2 on a scale of 0 to 10) including fair financial strength of affiliated PacifiCare Health Systems. Good overall capitalization (5.9) based on mixed results -- excessive policy leverage mitigated by excellent risk adjusted capital (severe loss scenario). However, capital levels have fluctuated somewhat during past years. Good liquidity (6.3).
Other Rating Factors: High quality investment portfolio (8.6). Excellent profitability (7.5) with operating gains in each of the last five years.
Principal Business: Group health insurance (94%), reinsurance (3%), group life insurance (2%), and individual health insurance (1%).
Principal Investments: NonCMO investment grade bonds (81%) and CMOs and structured securities (22%).
Investments in Affiliates: None
Group Affiliation: PacifiCare Health Systems
Licensed in: AZ, CA, CO, IL, IN, KY, NV, NM, OH, OK, OR, TX, UT, WA
Commenced Business: June 1973
Address: 3100 West Lake Ctr Dr LC03-381, Santa Ana, CA 92704
Phone: (714) 825-5379 **Domicile State:** CO **NAIC Code:** 84506

Data Date	Weiss Safety Rating	RACR #1	RACR #2	Total Assets ($mil)	Capital ($mil)	Net Premium ($mil)	Net Income ($mil)
6-03	C-	1.26	1.01	91.4	36.0	115.2	0.5
6-02	C+	1.58	1.27	83.2	32.0	71.0	3.7
2002	C	1.51	1.21	94.3	35.7	156.6	7.3
2001	C+	2.06	1.64	93.9	38.5	120.0	11.3
2000	C+	2.42	1.89	76.9	30.7	61.9	4.3
1999	C+	5.26	3.99	66.8	41.5	37.7	9.7
1998	C+	2.39	1.83	64.0	26.7	52.0	2.7

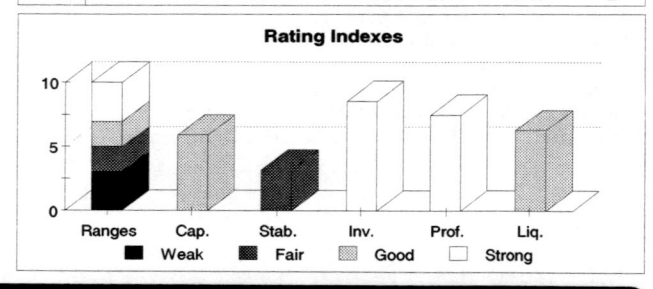

PACIFICARE OF ARIZONA INC — B- Good

Major Rating Factors: Good overall results on stability tests (6.1 on a scale of 0 to 10) despite excessive capital growth during 2002. Fair financial strength from affiliates. Good liquidity (7.0) with sufficient resources (cash flows and marketable investments) to handle a spike in claims. Excellent profitability (7.1) with operating gains in each of the last five years.
Other Rating Factors: Strong capitalization (8.0) based on excellent current risk-adjusted capital (severe loss scenario) reflecting significant improvement over results in 1998. High quality investment portfolio (9.9) containing little or no exposure to mortgages, junk bonds, or unaffiliated stocks.
Principal Business: Medicare (63%), comp med (33%), FEHB (5%)
Mem Phys: 02: 4,592 **01:** 4,085 **02 MLR** 78% **/ 02 Admin Exp** 12%
Enroll(000): Q1 03: 234 **02:** 230 **01:** 249 **Med Exp PMPM:** $248
Principal Investments: Cash and equiv (35%), pref stock (2%), other (64%)
Provider Compensation ($000): Contr fee ($479,047), capitation ($163,401), FFS ($67,187)
Total Member Encounters: Phys (1,322,894), non-phys (544,910)
Group Affiliation: PacifiCare Health Systems
Licensed in: AZ
Address: 410 N 44th St, 10th Floor, Phoenix, AZ 85008
Phone: (602) 244-8200 **Dom State:** AZ **Commenced Bus:** July 1997

Data Date	Weiss Safety Rating	RACR #1	RACR #2	Total Assets ($mil)	Capital ($mil)	Net Premium ($mil)	Net Income ($mil)
3-03	B-	2.12	1.77	207.5	103.3	240.0	13.0
3-02	B-	1.03	0.86	194.6	62.7	229.6	2.5
2002	B-	2.22	1.85	249.9	109.9	910.9	60.7
2001	C+	1.03	0.86	205.7	59.7	918.2	6.3
2000	C+	0.91	0.78	162.3	32.2	751.2	8.4
1999	C	1.29	1.12	182.5	46.0	630.5	21.0
1998	C-	0.59	0.51	129.9	20.1	629.4	23.1

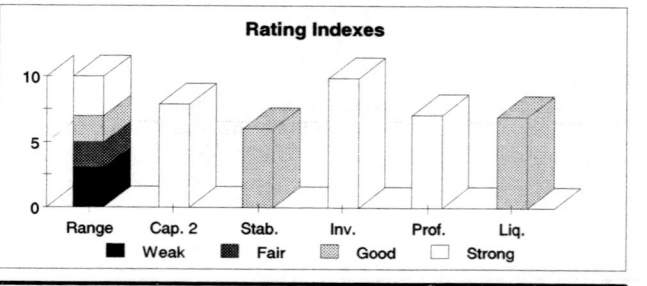

Winter 2003 - 04   II. Analysis of Largest Companies

PACIFICARE OF CALIFORNIA INC   C-   Fair

Major Rating Factors: Fair overall results on stability tests (4.4 on a scale of 0 to 10). Good capitalization (5.4) based on fair current risk-adjusted capital (moderate loss scenario) reflecting improvement over results in 1999. Good liquidity (6.9) with sufficient resources (cash flows and marketable investments) to handle a spike in claims.
Other Rating Factors: Excellent profitability (7.7) with operating gains in each of the last five years.
Principal Business: Managed care (43%)
Mem Phys: 02: N/A   **01:** N/A   **02 MLR** 88%   **/ 02 Admin Exp** 9%
Enroll(000): Q1 03: 1,704   **02:** 1,929   **01:** 2,066   **Med Exp PMPM:** $225
Principal Investments ($000): Cash and equiv ($924,202), bonds ($38,226)
Provider Compensation ($000): None
Total Member Encounters: N/A
Group Affiliation: PacifiCare Health Systems
Licensed in: CA
Address: 5995 Plaza Drive, Cypress, CA 90630
Phone: (714) 952-1121   **Dom State:** CA   **Commenced Bus:** March 1975

Data Date	Weiss Safety Rating	RACR #1	RACR #2	Total Assets ($mil)	Capital ($mil)	Net Premium ($mil)	Net Income ($mil)
3-03	C-	0.82	0.51	1,045.3	337.6	1,437.1	38.3
3-02	C-	0.00	0.00	950.6	251.8	1,566.1	-8.7
2002	C-	0.77	0.47	1,220.1	320.8	6,089.3	87.0
2001	C-	0.82	0.50	1,272.0	293.5	6,418.2	41.4
2000	C-	0.54	0.33	1,435.3	239.8	6,557.8	150.9
1999	C	0.49	0.32	1,130.9	243.4	6,208.2	259.7
1998	C+	0.89	0.55	1,039.8	309.7	5,741.9	242.5

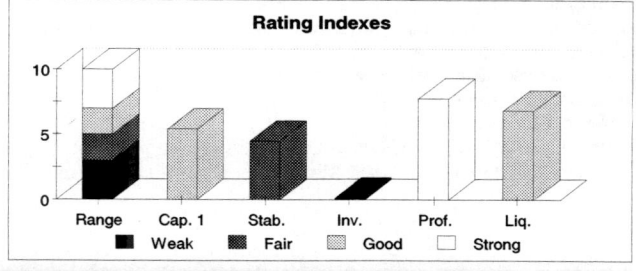

Rating Indexes (bar chart: Range, Cap.1, Stab., Inv., Prof., Liq.; legend: Weak, Fair, Good, Strong)

PACIFICARE OF COLORADO INC   B-   Good

Major Rating Factors: Good overall profitability index (5.4 on a scale of 0 to 10) despite operating losses during 1999 and 2000. Good overall results on stability tests (6.8) based on consistent premium and capital growth in the last five years but a decline in enrollment during 2002. Fair financial strength from affiliates. Good liquidity (6.9) with sufficient resources (cash flows and marketable investments) to handle a spike in claims.
Other Rating Factors: Strong capitalization (8.0) based on excellent current risk-adjusted capital (severe loss scenario) reflecting improvement over results in 1998. High quality investment portfolio (9.9).
Principal Business: Medicare (49%), comp med (38%), FEHB (13%)
Mem Phys: 02: 5,342   **01:** 4,863   **02 MLR** 84%   **/ 02 Admin Exp** 10%
Enroll(000): Q1 03: 226   **02:** 230   **01:** 256   **Med Exp PMPM:** $244
Principal Investments: Cash and equiv (34%), pref stock (9%), other (57%)
Provider Compensation ($000): Contr fee ($334,464), capitation ($263,556), FFS ($52,062), bonus arrang ($5,381), other ($60,020)
Total Member Encounters: Phys (1,559,545), non-phys (1,062,957)
Group Affiliation: PacifiCare Health Systems
Licensed in: CO
Address: 6455 S Yosemite St #100, Englewood, CO 80111-5109
Phone: (303) 220-5800   **Dom State:** CO   **Commenced Bus:** November 1987

Data Date	Weiss Safety Rating	RACR #1	RACR #2	Total Assets ($mil)	Capital ($mil)	Net Premium ($mil)	Net Income ($mil)
3-03	B-	2.14	1.78	207.7	102.7	223.9	10.7
3-02	C+	1.83	1.51	192.8	84.6	211.5	2.0
2002	B-	2.01	1.67	210.8	96.8	842.8	31.9
2001	C+	1.82	1.50	211.3	80.8	827.2	7.2
2000	C+	1.58	1.35	263.8	69.1	958.1	-24.2
1999	C+	1.14	1.00	196.1	44.7	816.1	-15.8
1998	B-	1.08	0.94	135.7	39.8	719.4	21.9

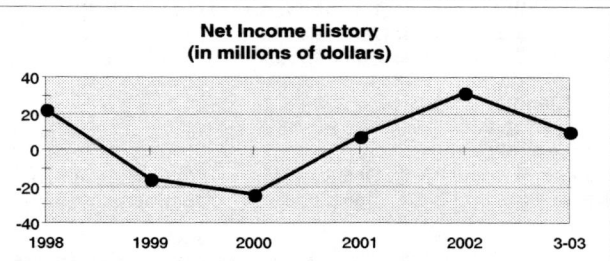

Net Income History (in millions of dollars) — line chart, 1998–3-03

PACIFICARE OF NEVADA INC   C-   Fair

Major Rating Factors: Fair overall results on stability tests (4.8 on a scale of 0 to 10) based on a significant 23% decrease in enrollment during the period, fair risk-adjusted capital in prior years and a decline in the number of member physicians during 2002. Rating is significantly influenced by the fair financial results of PacifiCare Health Systems. Weak profitability index (0.9) with operating losses during 1998. Average return on equity has been extremely poor. Strong capitalization (9.1) based on excellent current risk-adjusted capital (severe loss scenario) reflecting significant improvement over results in 1998.
Other Rating Factors: High quality investment portfolio (9.8) containing no exposure to mortgages, junk bonds, or unaffiliated stocks. Excellent liquidity (7.1) with ample operational cash flow and liquid investments.
Principal Business: Medicare (76%), comp med (20%), FEHB (4%)
Mem Phys: 02: 1,305   **01:** 1,530   **02 MLR** 82%   **/ 02 Admin Exp** 11%
Enroll(000): Q1 03: 49   **02:** 52   **01:** 67   **Med Exp PMPM:** $274
Principal Investments: Cash and equiv (40%), other (60%)
Provider Compensation ($000): Contr fee ($91,128), capitation ($73,511), FFS ($29,810)
Total Member Encounters: N/A
Group Affiliation: PacifiCare Health Systems
Licensed in: NV
Address: 700 E Warm Springs Rd, Las Vegas, NV 89119-4325
Phone: (702) 269-7500   **Dom State:** NV   **Commenced Bus:** July 1961

Data Date	Weiss Safety Rating	RACR #1	RACR #2	Total Assets ($mil)	Capital ($mil)	Net Premium ($mil)	Net Income ($mil)
3-03	C-	3.04	2.53	63.7	34.8	57.3	5.5
3-02	C-	1.37	1.15	55.9	25.0	63.6	3.2
2002	C-	2.62	2.18	73.4	29.2	238.0	18.9
2001	C-	1.37	1.15	66.4	22.5	256.9	1.1
2000	C-	1.14	0.96	51.7	7.6	233.3	2.4
1999	C-	1.94	1.64	62.0	15.8	192.7	7.5
1998	C-	0.67	0.58	85.1	6.8	194.7	-64.8

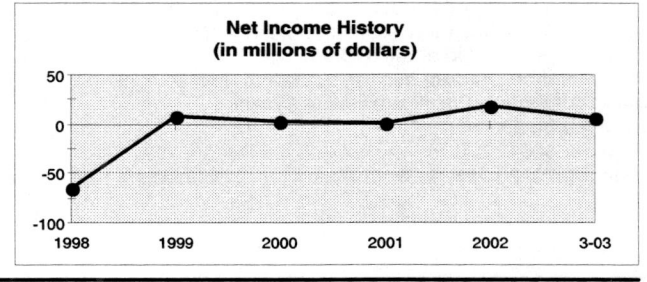

Net Income History (in millions of dollars) — line chart, 1998–3-03

www.WeissRatings.com   * Denotes a Weiss Recommended Company

II. Analysis of Largest Companies

Winter 2003 - 04

PACIFICARE OF OKLAHOMA INC — C- Fair

Major Rating Factors: Fair capitalization index (4.2 on a scale of 0 to 10) based on fair current risk-adjusted capital (moderate loss scenario). Weak profitability index (3.0) with operating losses during 2001 and 2002. Weak overall results on stability tests (1.5). Rating is significantly influenced by the fair financial results of PacifiCare Health Systems.
Other Rating Factors: Good liquidity (6.9) with sufficient resources (cash flows and marketable investments) to handle a spike in claims. High quality investment portfolio (9.9) containing no exposure to mortgages, junk bonds, or unaffiliated stocks.
Principal Business: Comp med (47%), Medicare (41%), FEHB (12%)
Mem Phys: 02: 1,986 **01:** 1,866 **02 MLR** 85% **/ 02 Admin Exp** 15%
Enroll(000): Q1 03: 115 **02:** 121 **01:** 122 **Med Exp PMPM:** $213
Principal Investments: Cash and equiv (98%), other (2%)
Provider Compensation ($000): Capitation ($218,866), contr fee ($73,736), FFS ($11,153), bonus arrang ($1,100)
Total Member Encounters: Phys (852), non-phys (216)
Group Affiliation: PacifiCare Health Systems
Licensed in: OK
Address: 7666 E 61st St, Tulsa, OK 74133
Phone: (918) 459-1100 **Dom State:** OK **Commenced Bus:** March 1985

Data Date	Weiss Safety Rating	RACR #1	RACR #2	Total Assets ($mil)	Capital ($mil)	Net Premium ($mil)	Net Income ($mil)
3-03	C-	0.80	0.67	43.1	11.2	98.9	2.5
3-02	B-	0.96	0.85	36.1	16.0	94.7	-0.2
2002	C-	0.71	0.59	43.5	9.6	362.4	-2.9
2001	B-	0.96	0.85	45.5	16.8	364.8	-0.8
2000	B-	1.79	1.58	46.9	24.9	309.9	5.6
1999	B-	1.84	1.62	42.3	23.8	277.8	11.3
1998	B-	1.24	1.09	50.8	13.1	278.7	11.6

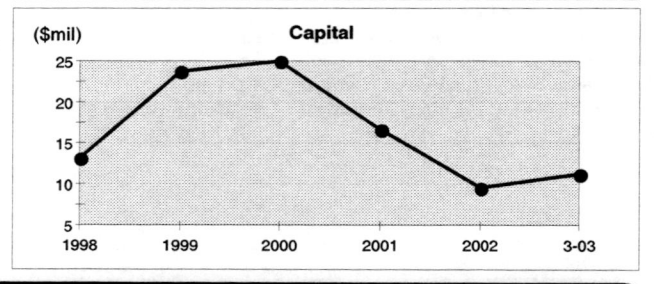

Capital chart (1998–3-03)

PACIFICARE OF OREGON — B- Good

Major Rating Factors: Fair profitability index (5.0 on a scale of 0 to 10) due to a decline in earnings during 2002. Good overall results on stability tests (5.4) despite a decline in enrollment during 2002. Rating is significantly influenced by the fair financial results of PacifiCare Health Systems. Good liquidity (6.8) with sufficient resources (cash flows and marketable investments) to handle a spike in claims.
Other Rating Factors: Strong capitalization index (8.2) based on excellent current risk-adjusted capital (severe loss scenario) despite some fluctuation in capital levels. High quality investment portfolio (9.9) containing no exposure to mortgages, junk bonds, or unaffiliated stocks.
Principal Business: Medicare (51%), comp med (44%), FEHB (5%)
Mem Phys: 02: 4,341 **01:** 4,077 **02 MLR** 86% **/ 02 Admin Exp** 12%
Enroll(000): Q1 03: 89 **02:** 93 **01:** 120 **Med Exp PMPM:** $251
Principal Investments: Cash and equiv (24%), other (76%)
Provider Compensation ($000): Contr fee ($178,512), capitation ($131,453), FFS ($7,143)
Total Member Encounters: Phys (128,735)
Group Affiliation: PacifiCare Health Systems
Licensed in: OR, WA
Address: 5 Centerpointe Dr Suite 600, Lake Oswego, OR 97035
Phone: (503) 603-7355 **Dom State:** OR **Commenced Bus:** February 1987

Data Date	Weiss Safety Rating	RACR #1	RACR #2	Total Assets ($mil)	Capital ($mil)	Net Premium ($mil)	Net Income ($mil)
3-03	B-	2.29	1.91	85.0	43.4	91.1	-3.1
3-02	B-	2.29	1.94	88.3	46.8	97.0	0.4
2002	B-	2.41	2.01	95.3	46.6	373.4	7.6
2001	B-	2.30	1.94	92.2	46.5	376.5	10.0
2000	B-	1.98	1.68	86.8	38.9	365.1	7.0
1999	B-	1.80	1.51	105.2	47.4	356.2	-2.0
1998	B-	1.43	1.22	87.7	35.4	330.1	3.5

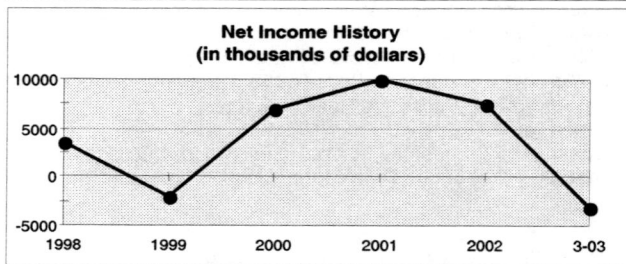

Net Income History (in thousands of dollars) chart (1998–3-03)

PACIFICARE OF TEXAS INC — D+ Weak

Major Rating Factors: Weak profitability index (0.9 on a scale of 0 to 10) with $182.3 million in losses in the last three years. Average return on equity has been poor at -58%. Poor capitalization index (2.2) based on weak current risk-adjusted capital (moderate loss scenario). Fair overall results on stability tests (4.2) based on a significant 39% decrease in enrollment during the period. Potentially strong support from affiliation with PacifiCare Health Systems.
Other Rating Factors: Fair liquidity (3.7) as cash resources may not be adequate to cover a spike in claims. High quality investment portfolio (9.9) containing no exposure to mortgages, junk bonds, or unaffiliated stocks.
Principal Business: Medicare (72%), comp med (22%), FEHB (5%)
Mem Phys: 02: 7,938 **01:** 8,813 **02 MLR** 95% **/ 02 Admin Exp** 10%
Enroll(000): Q1 03: 169 **02:** 201 **01:** 330 **Med Exp PMPM:** $299
Principal Investments: Cash and equiv (36%), other (64%)
Provider Compensation ($000): Contr fee ($676,157), capitation ($231,921), FFS ($77,817), bonus arrang ($3,937)
Total Member Encounters: Phys (21,680), non-phys (5,444)
Group Affiliation: PacifiCare Health Systems
Licensed in: TX
Address: 5001 LBJ Freeway Ste 600, Dallas, TX 75244
Phone: (972) 866-2693 **Dom State:** TX **Commenced Bus:** July 1986

Data Date	Weiss Safety Rating	RACR #1	RACR #2	Total Assets ($mil)	Capital ($mil)	Net Premium ($mil)	Net Income ($mil)
3-03	D+	0.51	0.43	171.4	69.8	197.0	28.4
3-02	D	0.27	0.23	189.2	45.8	273.0	-1.9
2002	D	0.30	0.25	238.7	40.0	1,004.4	-51.1
2001	D	0.26	0.22	297.4	47.5	1,412.1	-92.7
2000	D+	0.34	0.30	288.2	39.7	1,245.0	-38.6
1999	C	1.14	1.00	245.7	42.8	1,203.1	16.8
1998	C	0.46	0.41	102.3	15.7	560.3	10.9

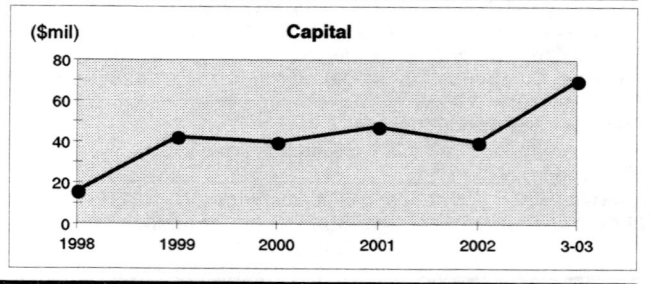

Capital chart (1998–3-03)

PACIFICARE OF WASHINGTON INC — C — Fair

Major Rating Factors: Fair profitability index (5.0 on a scale of 0 to 10) due to a decline in earnings during 2002. Poor capitalization index (2.9) based on weak current risk-adjusted capital (moderate loss scenario). Good liquidity (6.7) with sufficient resources (cash flows and marketable investments) to handle a spike in claims.
Other Rating Factors: High quality investment portfolio (9.9) containing little or no exposure to mortgages, junk bonds, or unaffiliated stocks.
Principal Business: FEHB (73%), comp med (25%), vision (2%)
Mem Phys: 02: 6,530   **01:** 5,803   **02 MLR** 89%   **/ 02 Admin Exp** 10%
Enroll(000): Q1 03: 123   **02:** 118   **01:** 136   **Med Exp PMPM:** $318
Principal Investments: Cash and equiv (43%), pref stock (3%), other (54%)
Provider Compensation ($000): Contr fee ($268,199), capitation ($199,587), FFS ($7,712)
Total Member Encounters: Phys (377,428)
Group Affiliation: PacifiCare Health Systems
Licensed in: OR, WA
Address: 7525 SE 24th, Mercer Island, WA 98040-9005
Phone: (206) 236-7400   **Dom State:** WA   **Commenced Bus:** December 1986

Data Date	Weiss Safety Rating	RACR #1	RACR #2	Total Assets ($mil)	Capital ($mil)	Net Premium ($mil)	Net Income ($mil)
3-03	C	0.61	0.51	116.3	41.9	146.6	-6.8
3-02	C-	0.61	0.53	101.4	40.5	137.4	-1.3
2002	C	0.69	0.58	139.4	47.5	544.5	4.0
2001	C-	0.61	0.53	129.5	43.0	541.3	11.4
2000	C	0.82	0.73	117.4	50.7	494.4	16.8
1999	C	0.81	0.68	125.4	72.1	414.4	6.8
1998	C-	0.71	0.63	125.2	61.2	395.0	1.4

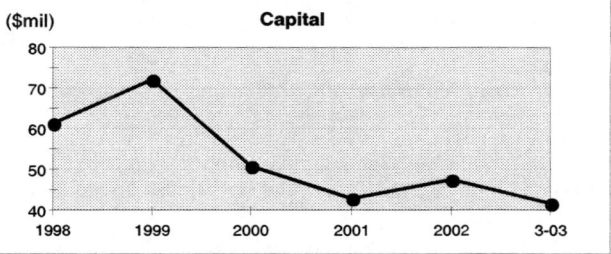

Capital ($mil) chart: 1998–3-03

PAN-AMERICAN LIFE INSURANCE COMPANY — C+ — Fair

Major Rating Factors: Fair quality investment portfolio (4.9 on a scale of 0 to 10) with large holdings of BBB rated bonds in addition to junk bond exposure equal to 62% of capital. Fair profitability (3.5). Fair overall results on stability tests (4.8).
Other Rating Factors: Strong capitalization (7.1) based on excellent risk adjusted capital (severe loss scenario). Excellent liquidity (7.3).
Principal Business: Reinsurance (35%), group health insurance (33%), individual life insurance (17%), individual health insurance (6%), and other lines (9%).
Principal Investments: NonCMO investment grade bonds (53%), CMOs and structured securities (18%), noninv. grade bonds (8%), policy loans (7%), and misc. investments (14%).
Investments in Affiliates: 4%
Group Affiliation: Pan-American Life
Licensed in: All states except AK, ME, MA, NH, NY, RI, SD, VT, WY
Commenced Business: March 1912
Address: Pan American Life Center, New Orleans, LA 70130
Phone: (504) 566-1300   **Domicile State:** LA   **NAIC Code:** 67539

Data Date	Weiss Safety Rating	RACR #1	RACR #2	Total Assets ($mil)	Capital ($mil)	Net Premium ($mil)	Net Income ($mil)
6-03	C+	1.89	1.09	2,449.0	195.7	95.1	1.1
6-02	C+	2.04	1.22	2,255.6	213.5	83.1	0.4
2002	C+	1.92	1.11	2,285.2	201.0	172.6	0.9
2001	C+	2.10	1.27	2,253.8	217.2	162.3	-6.5
2000	C+	2.27	1.36	2,192.6	216.8	145.6	6.1
1999	C+	2.23	1.35	2,141.8	213.1	135.3	8.5
1998	C+	2.10	1.28	2,015.3	200.1	193.5	-1.6

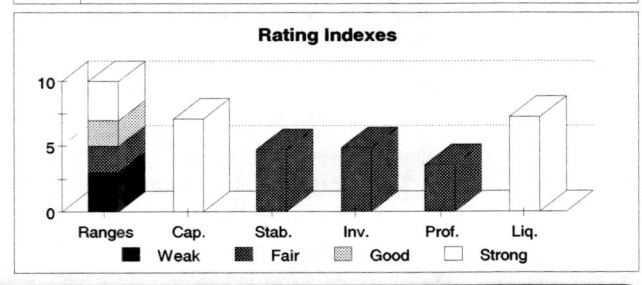

Rating Indexes chart — Ranges: Weak, Fair, Good, Strong; Cap., Stab., Inv., Prof., Liq.

PARAMOUNT CARE OF MI INC — C — Fair

Major Rating Factors: Fair overall results on stability tests (4.4 on a scale of 0 to 10) based on weak risk-adjusted capital in prior years, rapid premium growth over the last five years and an excessive 39% enrollment growth during the period. Rating is significantly influenced by the good financial results of ProMedica Health System Inc. Weak profitability index (0.9) with operating losses during 1998, 1999, 2000 and 2001. Average return on equity has been poor at -33%. Strong capitalization (7.0) based on excellent current risk-adjusted capital (severe loss scenario) reflecting significant improvement over results in 1998.
Other Rating Factors: High quality investment portfolio (9.9) containing no exposure to mortgages, junk bonds, or unaffiliated stocks. Excellent liquidity (7.0) with ample operational cash flow and liquid investments.
Principal Business: Medicare (53%), comp med (47%)
Mem Phys: 02: 1,896   **01:** 1,355   **02 MLR** 90%   **/ 02 Admin Exp** 10%
Enroll(000): Q1 03: 4   **02:** 5   **01:** 3   **Med Exp PMPM:** $259
Principal Investments: Cash and equiv (100%)
Provider Compensation ($000): Contr fee ($11,582), FFS ($201), capitation ($160)
Total Member Encounters: Phys (57,107), non-phys (30,484)
Group Affiliation: ProMedica Health System Inc
Licensed in: MI
Address: 106 Park Pl, Dundee, MI 48131
Phone: (734) 529-7800   **Dom State:** MI   **Commenced Bus:** June 1996

Data Date	Weiss Safety Rating	RACR #1	RACR #2	Total Assets ($mil)	Capital ($mil)	Net Premium ($mil)	Net Income ($mil)
3-03	C	1.37	1.14	4.7	2.3	3.9	-0.1
3-02	C-	0.70	0.59	2.7	0.9	3.0	0.1
2002	C-	0.99	0.82	4.4	2.4	13.3	0.0
2001	C-	0.70	0.59	2.6	0.9	10.0	-0.8
2000	C-	1.69	1.43	2.7	1.4	8.1	-0.2
1999	E+	0.55	0.47	1.6	0.5	4.5	-0.3
1998	U	0.39	0.33	0.8	0.5	0.3	-0.1

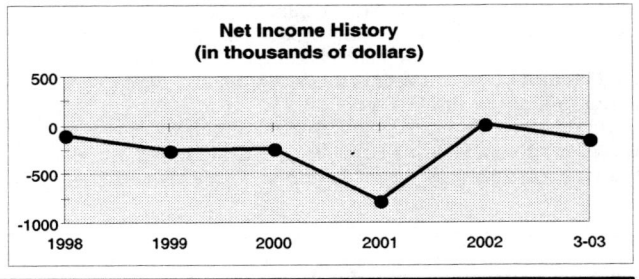

Net Income History (in thousands of dollars): 1998–3-03

II. Analysis of Largest Companies

Winter 2003 - 04

PARAMOUNT HEALTH CARE   B-   Good

Major Rating Factors: Fair profitability index (3.9 on a scale of 0 to 10) with operating losses during 1998 and 1999. Average return on equity has been poor at -10%. Good overall results on stability tests (5.8) based on healthy premium and capital growth during 2002. Good liquidity (6.8) with sufficient resources (cash flows and marketable investments) to handle a spike in claims.
Other Rating Factors: Strong capitalization index (7.0) based on excellent current risk-adjusted capital (severe loss scenario). High quality investment portfolio (9.1) containing little or no exposure to mortgages, junk bonds, or unaffiliated stocks.
Principal Business: Comp med (59%), Medicare (29%), Medicaid (11%), FEHB (1%)
Mem Phys: 02: 1,856   **01:** 1,926   **02 MLR** 90%   **/ 02 Admin Exp** 7%
Enroll(000): Q1 03: 152   **02:** 171   **01:** 164   **Med Exp PMPM:** $202
Principal Investments: Cash and equiv (32%), other (68%)
Provider Compensation ($000): Contr fee ($314,446), capitation ($77,966), FFS ($13,773)
Total Member Encounters: Phys (666,928), non-phys (247,028)
Group Affiliation: ProMedica Health System Inc
Licensed in: OH
Address: 1901 Indian Wood Cir, Maumee, OH 43537-4068
Phone: (419) 887-2500   **Dom State:** OH   **Commenced Bus:** April 1988

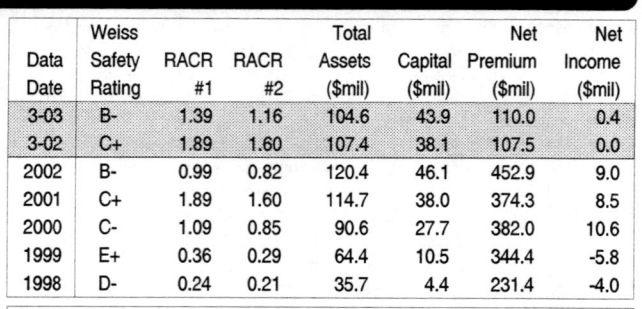

Data Date	Weiss Safety Rating	RACR #1	RACR #2	Total Assets ($mil)	Capital ($mil)	Net Premium ($mil)	Net Income ($mil)
3-03	B-	1.39	1.16	104.6	43.9	110.0	0.4
3-02	C+	1.89	1.60	107.4	38.1	107.5	0.0
2002	B-	0.99	0.82	120.4	46.1	452.9	9.0
2001	C+	1.89	1.60	114.7	38.0	374.3	8.5
2000	C-	1.09	0.85	90.6	27.7	382.0	10.6
1999	E+	0.36	0.29	64.4	10.5	344.4	-5.8
1998	D-	0.24	0.21	35.7	4.4	231.4	-4.0

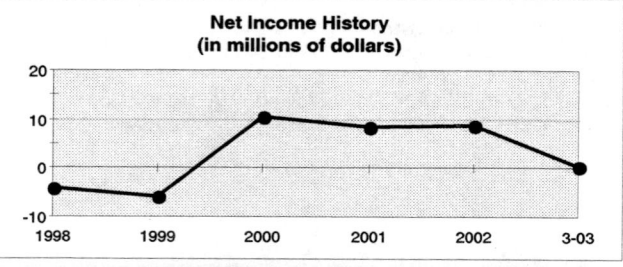

Net Income History (in millions of dollars)

PARKLAND COMMUNITY HEALTH PLAN INC   C-   Fair

Major Rating Factors: Fair overall results on stability tests (3.5 on a scale of 0 to 10) based on excessive premium growth during 2002, rapid enrollment growth during the past five years. Poor capitalization index (0.0) based on weak current risk-adjusted capital (severe loss scenario) as results have slipped from the fair range over the last year. Good overall profitability index (6.3) despite a decline in earnings during 2002.
Other Rating Factors: Good liquidity (6.8) with sufficient resources (cash flows and marketable investments) to handle a spike in claims. High quality investment portfolio (9.9) containing no exposure to mortgages, junk bonds, or unaffiliated stocks.
Principal Business: Medicaid (75%), other (25%)
Mem Phys: 02: 2,248   **01:** 1,988   **02 MLR** 85%   **/ 02 Admin Exp** 14%
Enroll(000): Q1 03: 106   **02:** 99   **01:** 75   **Med Exp PMPM:** $116
Principal Investments: Cash and equiv (100%)
Provider Compensation ($000): Contr fee ($109,646), capitation ($5,775)
Total Member Encounters: Phys (257,285), non-phys (7,413)
Group Affiliation: Dallas County Hospital District
Licensed in: TX
Address: 6300 Harry Hines Blvd, Dallas, TX 75245
Phone: (214) 590-0966   **Dom State:** TX   **Commenced Bus:** January 1998

Data Date	Weiss Safety Rating	RACR #1	RACR #2	Total Assets ($mil)	Capital ($mil)	Net Premium ($mil)	Net Income ($mil)
3-03	C-	0.28	0.23	29.5	3.5	39.4	-1.0
3-02	C-	0.69	0.59	22.7	6.2	31.5	1.4
2002	C-	0.00	0.00	29.7	4.3	142.1	1.1
2001	C-	0.69	0.59	22.5	3.5	102.2	2.2
2000	C-	0.56	0.47	17.0	2.2	67.6	0.8
1999	D+	1.44	1.23	14.7	2.4	21.2	0.6
1998	N/A	N/A	N/A	4.5	1.2	13.9	0.4

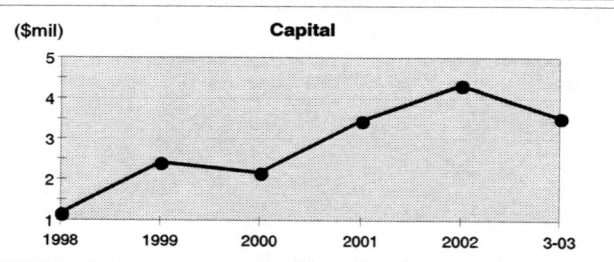

Capital ($mil)

PARTNERS NATIONAL HEALTH PLAN OF IN   E+   Very Weak

Major Rating Factors: Poor capitalization index (0.5 on a scale of 0 to 10) based on weak current risk-adjusted capital (moderate loss scenario). Good overall profitability index (6.8) with operating gains in each of the last five years. Good overall results on stability tests (6.8).
Other Rating Factors: Good liquidity (6.1) with sufficient resources (cash flows and marketable investments) to handle a spike in claims. High quality investment portfolio (9.9) containing little or no exposure to mortgages, junk bonds, or unaffiliated stocks.
Principal Business: Comp med (100%)
Mem Phys: 02: 2,271   **01:** 2,098   **02 MLR** 87%   **/ 02 Admin Exp** 10%
Enroll(000):   **02:** 67   **01:** 61   **Med Exp PMPM:** $167
Principal Investments: Cash and equiv (77%), nonaffiliate common stock (5%), affiliate common stock (2%), other (16%)
Provider Compensation ($000): Capitation ($50,058), FFS ($28,395), contr fee ($24,337), bonus arrang ($19,225)
Total Member Encounters: Phys (477,140), non-phys (54,350)
Group Affiliation: PNHP Corp
Licensed in: IN
Address: 100 East Wayne St, Suite 502, South Bend, IN 46601
Phone: (574) 233-4899   **Dom State:** IN   **Commenced Bus:** January 1987

Data Date	Weiss Safety Rating	RACR #1	RACR #2	Total Assets ($mil)	Capital ($mil)	Net Premium ($mil)	Net Income ($mil)
2002	E+	0.34	0.29	24.2	5.9	147.0	2.4
2001	E+	0.24	0.20	18.8	4.3	120.7	0.9
2000	E+	0.19	0.16	18.6	4.0	115.7	0.1
1999	E+	0.27	0.23	16.0	4.8	104.9	0.1
1998	D-	0.35	0.29	10.8	4.8	84.0	0.6

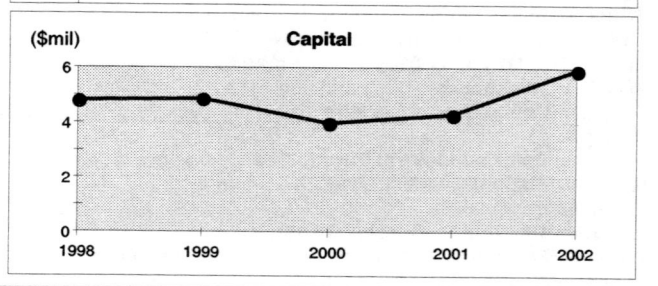

Capital ($mil)

Winter 2003 - 04
II. Analysis of Largest Companies

PARTNERS NATIONAL HEALTH PLANS OF NC — B — Good

Major Rating Factors: Good overall profitability index (6.0 on a scale of 0 to 10) despite operating losses during 2001. Strong capitalization (8.3) based on excellent current risk-adjusted capital (severe loss scenario) reflecting improvement over results in 2000. High quality investment portfolio (9.6) containing little or no exposure to mortgages, junk bonds, or unaffiliated stocks.

Other Rating Factors: Excellent overall results on stability tests (7.0) based on consistent premium and capital growth in the last five years but a decline in enrollment during 2002. Excellent liquidity (7.0) with ample operational cash flow and liquid investments.

Principal Business: Comp med (66%), Medicare (32%), dental (2%)
Mem Phys: 02: 13,624 **01:** 12,416 **02 MLR** 86% **/ 02 Admin Exp** 7%
Enroll(000): Q1 03: 92 **02:** 215 **01:** 296 **Med Exp PMPM:** $185
Principal Investments: Cash and equiv (61%), affiliate common stock (4%), other (36%)
Provider Compensation ($000): Contr fee ($409,200), capitation ($142,820), FFS ($30,313)
Total Member Encounters: Phys (1,739,638), non-phys (230,383)
Group Affiliation: Bl Cross & Bl Shield of N Carolina
Licensed in: NC, SC, VA
Address: 5635 Hanes Mill Rd, Winston-Salem, NC 27105
Phone: (336) 760-4822 **Dom State:** NC **Commenced Bus:** October 1986

Data Date	Weiss Safety Rating	RACR #1	RACR #2	Total Assets ($mil)	Capital ($mil)	Net Premium ($mil)	Net Income ($mil)
3-03	B	2.41	2.01	171.1	94.9	94.7	10.1
3-02	B	1.05	0.91	155.1	54.0	169.5	4.9
2002	B	2.08	1.73	193.4	83.0	653.4	29.3
2001	B	1.05	0.91	162.5	49.0	684.9	-9.6
2000	B+	1.06	0.89	137.0	48.8	627.4	0.0
1999	A-	1.18	1.02	115.8	47.8	488.6	8.1
1998	A-	1.32	1.16	92.1	44.7	363.6	9.6

Risk-Adjusted Capital Ratios (Since 1998)

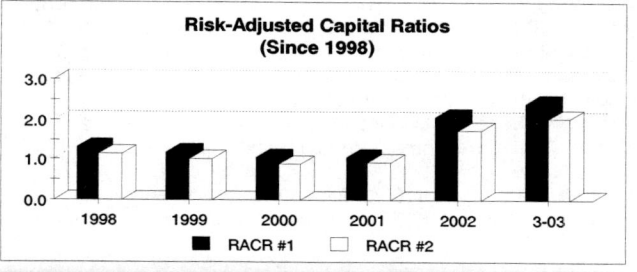

PAUL REVERE LIFE INSURANCE COMPANY — C- — Fair

Major Rating Factors: Fair overall results on stability tests (3.2 on a scale of 0 to 10) including fair financial strength of affiliated UnumProvident Corp and negative cash flow from operations for 2002. Fair quality investment portfolio (3.8) with large holdings of BBB rated bonds in addition to junk bond exposure equal to 61% of capital. Good liquidity (6.8).

Other Rating Factors: Strong capitalization (7.6) based on excellent risk adjusted capital (severe loss scenario). Excellent profitability (8.9) with operating gains in each of the last five years.

Principal Business: Individual health insurance (60%), reinsurance (27%), group health insurance (11%), group life insurance (2%), and individual life insurance (1%).
Principal Investments: NonCMO investment grade bonds (57%), CMOs and structured securities (21%), noninv. grade bonds (14%), and common & preferred stock (8%).
Investments in Affiliates: 5%
Group Affiliation: UnumProvident Corp
Licensed in: All states except PR
Commenced Business: July 1930
Address: 18 Chestnut St, Worcester, MA 01608
Phone: (508) 792-6377 **Domicile State:** MA **NAIC Code:** 67598

Data Date	Weiss Safety Rating	RACR #1	RACR #2	Total Assets ($mil)	Capital ($mil)	Net Premium ($mil)	Net Income ($mil)
6-03	C-	2.22	1.43	5,224.8	1,041.7	365.6	-3.3
6-02	C+	1.72	1.17	5,146.4	824.0	420.3	-47.0
2002	C-	1.98	1.30	4,976.4	911.4	810.2	26.3
2001	C+	1.91	1.31	5,162.6	881.8	903.4	89.5
2000	C+	1.26	0.98	4,829.5	747.6	1,106.5	20.6
1999	C+	1.48	1.04	5,295.8	670.1	1,073.5	42.0
1998	C	1.40	0.99	4,890.8	599.5	1,124.4	112.8

UnumProvident Corp Composite Group Rating: C- Largest Group Members	Assets ($mil)	Weiss Safety Rating
UNUM LIFE INS CO OF AMERICA	10982	C-
PROVIDENT LIFE ACCIDENT INS CO	8557	C-
PAUL REVERE LIFE INS CO	4976	C-
COLONIAL LIFE ACCIDENT INS CO	1194	C-
FIRST UNUM LIFE INS CO	1097	C-

PEKIN LIFE INSURANCE COMPANY * — B+ — Good

Major Rating Factors: Good quality investment portfolio (6.6 on a scale of 0 to 10) despite mixed results such as: substantial holdings of BBB bonds but moderate junk bond exposure. Good overall profitability (6.8). Excellent expense controls. Return on equity has been good over the last five years, averaging 12.1%. Good liquidity (6.5).

Other Rating Factors: Good overall results on stability tests (5.2) excellent operational trends and excellent risk diversification. Strong capitalization (7.4) based on excellent risk adjusted capital (severe loss scenario).

Principal Business: Group health insurance (27%), individual health insurance (24%), individual annuities (17%), individual life insurance (17%), and other lines (14%).
Principal Investments: NonCMO investment grade bonds (58%), CMOs and structured securities (30%), noninv. grade bonds (4%), cash (3%), and misc. investments (4%).
Investments in Affiliates: None
Group Affiliation: Pekin Ins Group
Licensed in: IL, IN, IA, KY, MI, MO, OH, WI
Commenced Business: September 1965
Address: 2505 Court St, Pekin, IL 61558
Phone: (309) 346-1161 **Domicile State:** IL **NAIC Code:** 67628

Data Date	Weiss Safety Rating	RACR #1	RACR #2	Total Assets ($mil)	Capital ($mil)	Net Premium ($mil)	Net Income ($mil)
6-03	B+	1.99	1.27	653.8	84.3	127.1	4.8
6-02	B+	2.00	1.24	561.3	82.3	92.0	-5.2
2002	B+	2.01	1.26	595.2	81.0	190.0	-9.8
2001	B+	2.06	1.26	550.2	87.8	176.4	12.0
2000	B+	1.94	1.20	520.6	86.0	176.0	3.6
1999	B+	2.36	1.41	526.1	93.8	174.6	8.6
1998	B+	2.72	1.71	485.0	91.2	147.7	10.0

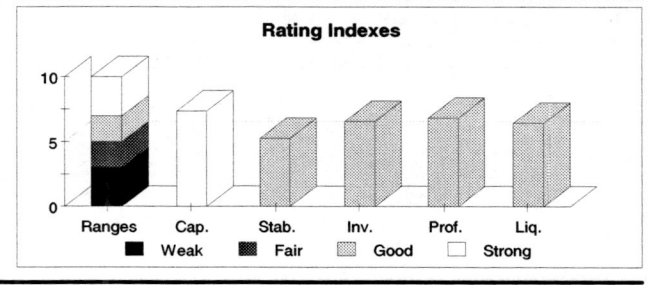

Rating Indexes (Ranges, Cap., Stab., Inv., Prof., Liq. — Weak, Fair, Good, Strong)

* Denotes a Weiss Recommended Company

II. Analysis of Largest Companies
Winter 2003 - 04

PENINSULA HEALTH CARE INC * B+ Good

Major Rating Factors: Excellent profitability (10.0 on a scale of 0 to 10) with operating gains in each of the last five years. Strong overall capitalization (10.0) based on excellent current risk-adjusted capital (severe loss scenario). Moreover, capital has steadily grown over the last five years. High quality investment portfolio (9.9) containing little or no exposure to mortgages, junk bonds, or unaffiliated stocks.

Other Rating Factors: Excellent overall results on stability tests (8.4) based on consistent premium and capital growth in the last five years. Rating is significantly influenced by the good financial results of Anthem Ins Companies Inc. Excellent liquidity (7.0) with ample operational cash flow and liquid investments.

Principal Business: Comp med (65%), Medicaid (35%)
Mem Phys: 02: 12,045 **01:** 10,355 **02 MLR** 72% **/ 02 Admin Exp** 10%
Enroll(000): Q1 03: 53 **02:** 52 **01:** 52 **Med Exp PMPM:** $124
Principal Investments: Cash and equiv (18%), other (82%)
Provider Compensation ($000): Contr fee ($54,650), FFS ($16,661), capitation ($5,645), bonus arrang ($5,518)
Total Member Encounters: Phys (244,612), non-phys (22,754)
Group Affiliation: Anthem Ins Companies Inc
Licensed in: VA
Address: 606 Denbigh Blvd Suite 500, Newport News, VA 23608
Phone: (757) 875-5760 **Dom State:** VA **Commenced Bus:** February 1994

Data Date	Weiss Safety Rating	RACR #1	RACR #2	Total Assets ($mil)	Capital ($mil)	Net Premium ($mil)	Net Income ($mil)
3-03	B+	6.59	5.49	56.2	35.6	29.7	2.0
3-02	B+	3.71	2.85	49.0	24.1	26.2	2.4
2002	B+	6.27	5.22	52.0	33.6	106.8	14.4
2001	B+	3.11	2.39	43.9	21.5	94.2	2.0
2000	B+	3.95	3.27	37.9	20.2	80.3	4.9
1999	B	2.84	2.32	26.2	13.8	68.6	3.8
1998	B	2.40	1.97	21.6	10.2	60.3	4.2

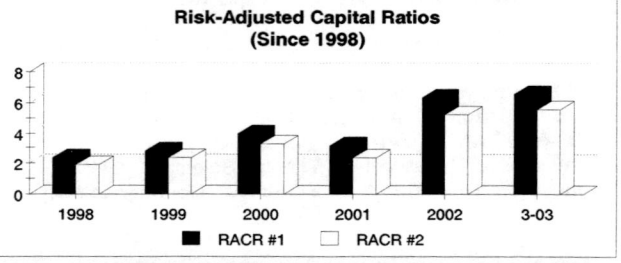

Risk-Adjusted Capital Ratios (Since 1998)

PENN TREATY NETWORK AMERICA LIFE INSURANCE COMPAN' D Weak

Major Rating Factors: Weak profitability (1.5 on a scale of 0 to 10) with operating losses during the first six months of 2003. Return on equity has been low, averaging -53.8%. Weak overall results on stability tests (1.1) including weak risk adjusted capital in prior years. Strong capitalization (8.0) based on excellent risk adjusted capital (severe loss scenario).

Other Rating Factors: High quality investment portfolio (7.3). Excellent liquidity (7.4).

Principal Business: Individual health insurance (98%), reinsurance (2%), and individual life insurance (1%).
Principal Investments: Cash (35%), nonCMO investment grade bonds (34%), common & preferred stock (21%), real estate (7%), and misc. investments (4%).
Investments in Affiliates: 21%
Group Affiliation: Penn Treaty Group
Licensed in: All states except KS, ME, MA, NJ, NY, WV, PR
Commenced Business: March 1954
Address: 3440 Lehigh St, Allentown, PA 18103
Phone: (610) 965-2222 **Domicile State:** PA **NAIC Code:** 63282

Data Date	Weiss Safety Rating	RACR #1	RACR #2	Total Assets ($mil)	Capital ($mil)	Net Premium ($mil)	Net Income ($mil)
6-03	D	1.93	1.64	124.1	27.8	8.2	-1.9
6-02	D-	0.88	0.77	105.3	15.2	2.9	0.1
2002	D	2.07	1.78	124.1	28.9	14.4	3.8
2001	D-	0.84	0.61	621.7	13.6	-57.8	-28.9
2000	D	0.74	0.49	485.8	15.0	99.1	-27.6
1999	C-	1.65	1.18	400.2	51.8	183.8	-7.1
1998	C-	2.29	1.63	314.0	60.1	122.9	5.3

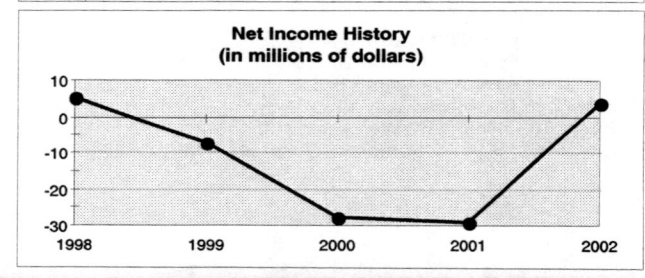

Net Income History (in millions of dollars)

PENNSYLVANIA LIFE INSURANCE COMPANY D+ Weak

Major Rating Factors: Weak overall results on stability tests (2.6 on a scale of 0 to 10) including weak risk adjusted capital in prior years. Good current capitalization (6.4) based on good risk adjusted capital (severe loss scenario), although results have slipped from the excellent range during the last year. Good quality investment portfolio (5.2).

Other Rating Factors: Good overall profitability (6.5). Good liquidity (6.9).
Principal Business: Individual health insurance (61%), individual annuities (27%), and individual life insurance (12%).
Principal Investments: NonCMO investment grade bonds (59%), CMOs and structured securities (33%), noninv. grade bonds (6%), and policy loans (1%).
Investments in Affiliates: 4%
Group Affiliation: Universal American Financial Corp
Licensed in: All states except NY
Commenced Business: January 1948
Address: 525 N Twelfth St, Leymone, PA 17043
Phone: (407) 628-1776 **Domicile State:** PA **NAIC Code:** 67660

Data Date	Weiss Safety Rating	RACR #1	RACR #2	Total Assets ($mil)	Capital ($mil)	Net Premium ($mil)	Net Income ($mil)
6-03	D+	1.52	0.93	455.9	51.3	68.2	3.1
6-02	D+	1.93	1.20	408.4	47.0	49.4	-0.2
2002	D+	2.00	1.21	429.3	48.8	110.2	-1.6
2001	D+	1.87	1.16	469.8	42.6	90.2	12.8
2000	D	1.63	0.99	437.8	36.1	80.7	9.9
1999	D	1.58	0.96	436.1	33.7	75.7	-1.1
1998	D	0.64	0.46	381.6	23.1	113.8	-25.4

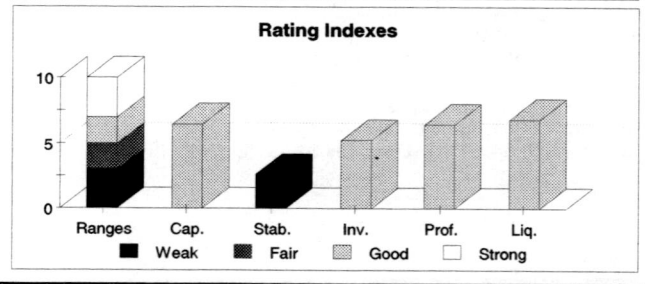

Rating Indexes

Winter 2003 - 04   II. Analysis of Largest Companies

PHN-HMO INC   C   Fair

Major Rating Factors: Weak profitability index (0.9 on a scale of 0 to 10) due to a decline in earnings during 2002. Average return on equity has been extremely poor. Poor capitalization index (2.9) based on good current risk-adjusted capital (moderate loss scenario). Weak overall results on stability tests (2.6) based on a significant 43% decrease in enrollment during the period. Rating is significantly influenced by the good financial results of CareFirst Inc.
Other Rating Factors: Good liquidity (6.8) with sufficient resources (cash flows and marketable investments) to handle a spike in claims. High quality investment portfolio (9.9) containing no exposure to mortgages, junk bonds, or unaffiliated stocks.
Principal Business: Comp med (100%)
Mem Phys: 02: 8,651   **01:** 7,349   **02 MLR** 76%   **/ 02 Admin Exp** 22%
Enroll(000): Q1 03: 20   **02:** 22   **01:** 38   **Med Exp PMPM:** $164
Principal Investments: Cash and equiv (57%), other (43%)
Provider Compensation ($000): Contr fee ($55,331), FFS ($5,405), capitation ($1,507)
Total Member Encounters: N/A
Group Affiliation: CareFirst Inc
Licensed in: MD
Address: 1099 Winterson Rd., Linthicum, MD 21090-2216
Phone: (410) 855-8817   **Dom State:** MD   **Commenced Bus:** January 1987

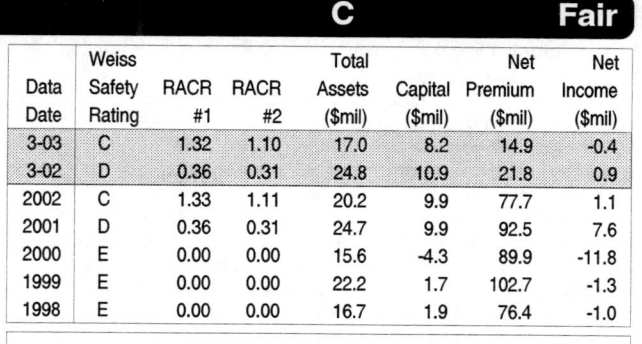

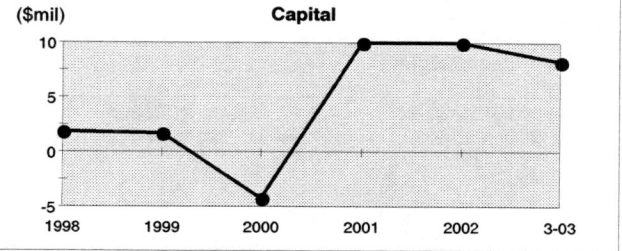

Data Date	Weiss Safety Rating	RACR #1	RACR #2	Total Assets ($mil)	Capital ($mil)	Net Premium ($mil)	Net Income ($mil)
3-03	C	1.32	1.10	17.0	8.2	14.9	-0.4
3-02	D	0.36	0.31	24.8	10.9	21.8	0.9
2002	C	1.33	1.11	20.2	9.9	77.7	1.1
2001	D	0.36	0.31	24.7	9.9	92.5	7.6
2000	E	0.00	0.00	15.6	-4.3	89.9	-11.8
1999	E	0.00	0.00	22.2	1.7	102.7	-1.3
1998	E	0.00	0.00	16.7	1.9	76.4	-1.0

PHP INS PLAN INC   D+   Weak

Major Rating Factors: Weak profitability index (0.9 on a scale of 0 to 10) with operating losses during 1999, 2000 and 2001. Average return on equity has been poor at -23%. Fair capitalization (4.2) based on fair current risk-adjusted capital (moderate loss scenario) reflecting improvement over results in 1998. Good liquidity (6.9) with sufficient resources (cash flows and marketable investments) to handle a spike in claims.
Other Rating Factors: High quality investment portfolio (9.9) containing no exposure to mortgages, junk bonds, or unaffiliated stocks. Excellent overall results on stability tests (7.5) based on consistent premium and capital growth in the last five years.
Principal Business: Comp med (98%), med supp (2%)
Mem Phys: 02: 1,566   **01:** 1,376   **02 MLR** 87%   **/ 02 Admin Exp** 11%
Enroll(000): Q1 03: 30   **02:** 26   **01:** 28   **Med Exp PMPM:** $172
Principal Investments: Cash and equiv (73%), other (27%)
Provider Compensation ($000): Capitation ($25,612), bonus arrang ($23,956), contr fee ($7,546)
Total Member Encounters: Phys (132,487), non-phys (20,494)
Group Affiliation: Prevea Health Services Inc
Licensed in: WI
Address: 301 N Broadway Suite 110, De Pere, WI 54115
Phone: (920) 490-6900   **Dom State:** WI   **Commenced Bus:** November 1996

Data Date	Weiss Safety Rating	RACR #1	RACR #2	Total Assets ($mil)	Capital ($mil)	Net Premium ($mil)	Net Income ($mil)
3-03	D+	0.80	0.67	16.9	4.3	19.3	0.6
3-02	E+	0.35	0.30	12.7	2.3	15.8	0.1
2002	D+	0.72	0.60	15.6	3.8	63.9	1.2
2001	E+	0.35	0.30	15.2	2.3	58.1	-1.1
2000	D	0.37	0.32	7.5	2.4	49.3	-2.5
1999	D	0.59	0.52	7.3	2.4	41.2	-0.2
1998	D-	0.31	0.27	4.2	1.2	31.1	0.1

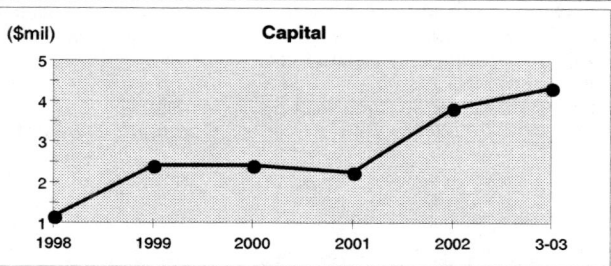

PHYSICIAN HEALTH PLAN OF SW MICHIGAN   C-   Fair

Major Rating Factors: Fair overall results on stability tests (4.8 on a scale of 0 to 10). Weak profitability index (1.9). Good capitalization index (6.8) based on excellent current risk-adjusted capital (severe loss scenario).
Other Rating Factors: Good liquidity (7.0) with sufficient resources (cash flows and marketable investments) to handle a spike in claims. High quality investment portfolio (9.9) containing no exposure to mortgages, junk bonds, or unaffiliated stocks.
Principal Business: Medicaid (69%), comp med (31%)
Mem Phys: 02: 1,156   **01:** 1,110   **02 MLR** 86%   **/ 02 Admin Exp** 13%
Enroll(000): Q1 03: 30   **02:** 32   **01:** 37   **Med Exp PMPM:** $130
Principal Investments: Cash and equiv (73%), other (27%)
Provider Compensation ($000): Contr fee ($52,285), capitation ($4,458)
Total Member Encounters: Phys (346,260), non-phys (875,917)
Group Affiliation: Bronson Healthcare Group Inc
Licensed in: MI
Address: 106 Farmers Alley Suite 300, Kalamazoo, MI 49005-1100
Phone: (269) 341-7200   **Dom State:** MI   **Commenced Bus:** June 2000

Data Date	Weiss Safety Rating	RACR #1	RACR #2	Total Assets ($mil)	Capital ($mil)	Net Premium ($mil)	Net Income ($mil)
3-03	C-	1.21	1.01	16.4	6.9	13.5	-0.6
3-02	D+	0.70	0.59	20.0	5.9	16.2	0.3
2002	C-	1.29	1.08	18.6	7.5	62.0	0.2
2001	D+	0.70	0.59	20.2	5.6	74.5	-0.6
2000	U	0.26	0.22	15.5	1.6	46.1	-2.6
1999	N/A	N/A	N/A	N/A	N/A	N/A	N/A
1998	N/A	N/A	N/A	N/A	N/A	N/A	N/A

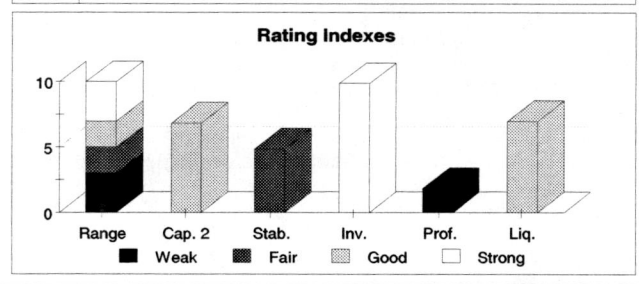

www.WeissRatings.com   * Denotes a Weiss Recommended Company

II. Analysis of Largest Companies Winter 2003 - 04

PHYSICIANS HEALTH PLAN OF NO IN — B Good

Major Rating Factors: Weak profitability index (1.2 on a scale of 0 to 10) with modest operating losses during 1999, 2000 and 2002. Good overall capitalization (5.7) based on good current risk-adjusted capital (severe loss scenario). Good overall results on stability tests (5.5).
Other Rating Factors: Good liquidity (5.7) with sufficient resources (cash flows and marketable investments) to handle a spike in claims. High quality investment portfolio (9.7).
Principal Business: Comp med (97%), FEHB (3%)
Mem Phys: 02: 1,143 **01:** 844 **02 MLR** 89% **/ 02 Admin Exp** 11%
Enroll(000): Q1 03: 60 **02:** 64 **01:** 66 **Med Exp PMPM:** $156
Principal Investments: Cash and equiv (14%), nonaffiliate common stock (7%), real estate (6%), other (72%).
Provider Compensation ($000): FFS ($59,463), contr fee ($35,081), bonus arrang ($28,504)
Total Member Encounters: Phys (297,007), non-phys (69,877)
Group Affiliation: None
Licensed in: IN
Address: 8101 W Jefferson Blvd, Ft Wayne, IN 46804
Phone: (260) 432-6690 **Dom State:** IN **Commenced Bus:** December 1983

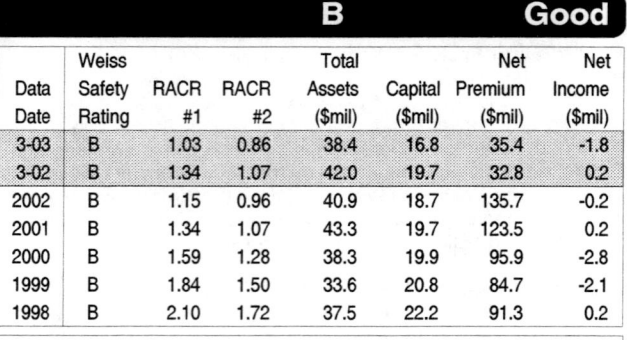

Data Date	Weiss Safety Rating	RACR #1	RACR #2	Total Assets ($mil)	Capital ($mil)	Net Premium ($mil)	Net Income ($mil)
3-03	B	1.03	0.86	38.4	16.8	35.4	-1.8
3-02	B	1.34	1.07	42.0	19.7	32.8	0.2
2002	B	1.15	0.96	40.9	18.7	135.7	-0.2
2001	B	1.34	1.07	43.3	19.7	123.5	0.2
2000	B	1.59	1.28	38.3	19.9	95.9	-2.8
1999	B	1.84	1.50	33.6	20.8	84.7	-2.1
1998	B	2.10	1.72	37.5	22.2	91.3	0.2

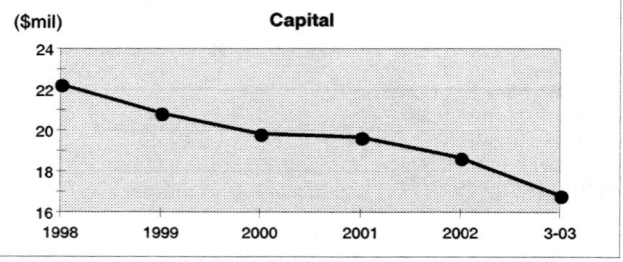

Capital chart 1998–3-03, declining from ~22 to ~17 ($mil).

PHYSICIANS HEALTH PLAN OF S MICHIGAN — C Fair

Major Rating Factors: Weak profitability index (2.5 on a scale of 0 to 10). Strong capitalization (7.1) based on excellent current risk-adjusted capital (severe loss scenario) reflecting significant improvement over results in 2000. High quality investment portfolio (9.9) containing no exposure to mortgages, junk bonds, or unaffiliated stocks.
Other Rating Factors: Excellent overall results on stability tests (7.6) despite a decline in enrollment during 2002. Excellent liquidity (7.0) with ample operational cash flow and liquid investments.
Principal Business: Comp med (100%)
Mem Phys: 02: 1,220 **01:** 1,127 **02 MLR** 86% **/ 02 Admin Exp** 12%
Enroll(000): Q1 03: 29 **02:** 28 **01:** 31 **Med Exp PMPM:** $163
Principal Investments: Cash and equiv (62%), other (38%)
Provider Compensation ($000): Contr fee ($59,523), capitation ($503)
Total Member Encounters: Phys (427,379), non-phys (656,443)
Group Affiliation: Foote Health System
Licensed in: MI
Address: One Jackson Square, Jackson, MI 49201
Phone: (517) 782-7154 **Dom State:** MI **Commenced Bus:** May 2000

Data Date	Weiss Safety Rating	RACR #1	RACR #2	Total Assets ($mil)	Capital ($mil)	Net Premium ($mil)	Net Income ($mil)
3-03	C	1.44	1.20	27.1	10.6	17.6	-0.5
3-02	C-	1.18	1.00	21.8	6.5	17.1	-0.5
2002	C	1.45	1.20	24.8	10.6	67.3	1.4
2001	C-	1.09	0.92	21.7	7.0	62.1	1.7
2000	U	0.69	0.58	18.1	4.4	40.5	-3.3
1999	N/A	N/A	N/A	N/A	N/A	N/A	N/A
1998	N/A	N/A	N/A	N/A	N/A	N/A	N/A

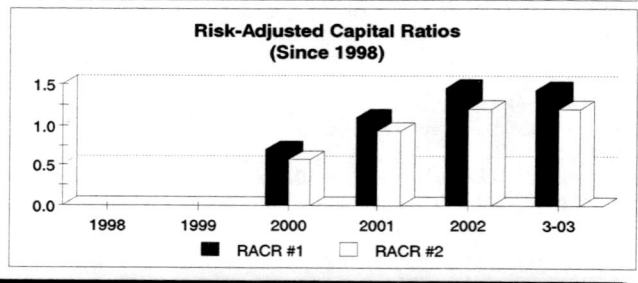

Risk-Adjusted Capital Ratios (Since 1998) bar chart, RACR #1 and RACR #2.

PHYSICIANS HP OF MID-MICHIGAN — C+ Fair

Major Rating Factors: Fair profitability index (4.1 on a scale of 0 to 10) with operating losses during 2001. Fair overall results on stability tests (4.5) based on a significant 21% decrease in enrollment during the period. Good capitalization index (5.2) based on good current risk-adjusted capital (severe loss scenario).
Other Rating Factors: Good liquidity (6.9) with sufficient resources (cash flows and marketable investments) to handle a spike in claims. High quality investment portfolio (9.9).
Principal Business: Comp med (81%), Medicaid (19%)
Mem Phys: 02: 1,305 **01:** 1,239 **02 MLR** 87% **/ 02 Admin Exp** 12%
Enroll(000): Q1 03: 72 **02:** 100 **01:** 126 **Med Exp PMPM:** $156
Principal Investments: Cash and equiv (77%), nonaffiliate common stock (10%), real estate (6%), other (7%).
Provider Compensation ($000): Contr fee ($214,906), capitation ($3,458)
Total Member Encounters: Phys (1,310,969), non-phys (2,439,277)
Group Affiliation: Sparrow Health System
Licensed in: MI
Address: 1400 E Michigan Ave, Lansing, MI 48912
Phone: (517) 349-2101 **Dom State:** MI **Commenced Bus:** October 1981

Data Date	Weiss Safety Rating	RACR #1	RACR #2	Total Assets ($mil)	Capital ($mil)	Net Premium ($mil)	Net Income ($mil)
3-03	C+	0.95	0.80	66.6	27.1	47.5	1.4
3-02	C	0.00	0.00	86.4	24.1	63.9	0.8
2002	C+	0.99	0.83	75.8	28.0	242.3	5.1
2001	C	0.00	0.00	93.3	25.2	261.8	-1.7
2000	C	1.16	0.96	100.3	33.9	310.0	3.7
1999	C	0.82	0.73	62.2	30.6	380.7	4.0
1998	C-	0.99	0.90	68.1	27.6	320.5	6.0

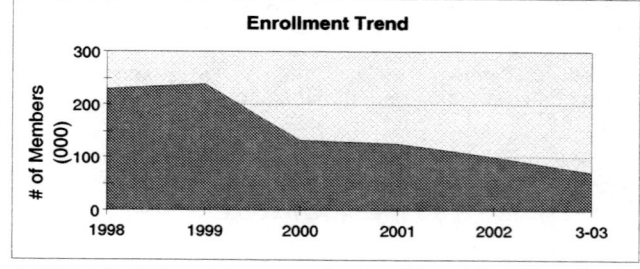

Enrollment Trend chart 1998–3-03, declining from ~240,000 to ~60,000 members.

Winter 2003 - 04   II. Analysis of Largest Companies

PHYSICIANS MUTUAL INSURANCE COMPANY *   A+   Excellent

Major Rating Factors: Good quality investment portfolio (6.8 on a scale of 0 to 10) with no exposure to mortgages and minimal holdings in junk bonds. Good liquidity (6.9) with sufficient resources to handle a spike in claims. Strong capitalization (9.9) based on excellent risk adjusted capital (severe loss scenario). Furthermore, this high level of risk adjusted capital has been consistently maintained over the last five years.
Other Rating Factors: Excellent profitability (9.3) with operating gains in each of the last five years. Excellent overall results on stability tests (7.4) excellent operational trends and excellent risk diversification.
Principal Business: Individual health insurance (98%), group health insurance (1%), and reinsurance (1%).
Principal Investments: CMOs and structured securities (42%), nonCMO investment grade bonds (35%), common & preferred stock (18%), noninv. grade bonds (2%), and misc. investments (3%).
Investments in Affiliates: 7%
Group Affiliation: Physicians Mutual Group
Licensed in: All states except PR
Commenced Business: December 1902
Address: 2600 Dodge St, Omaha, NE 68131
Phone: (402) 633-1000 **Domicile State:** NE **NAIC Code:** 80578

Data Date	Weiss Safety Rating	RACR #1	RACR #2	Total Assets ($mil)	Capital ($mil)	Net Premium ($mil)	Net Income ($mil)
6-03	A+	3.77	2.92	1,102.7	610.9	246.1	29.7
6-02	A	3.43	2.67	1,051.1	560.5	257.7	22.3
2002	A	3.61	2.84	1,069.5	582.7	501.5	49.7
2001	A	3.31	2.59	1,038.0	554.2	515.8	51.2
2000	A	3.10	2.36	1,021.4	526.9	513.4	50.9
1999	A	2.92	2.20	993.5	502.6	501.2	49.2
1998	A	2.97	2.24	949.5	479.4	492.5	50.2

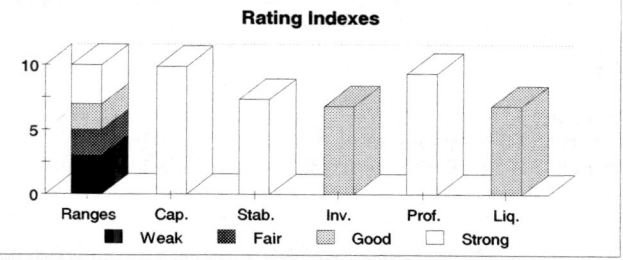

Rating Indexes (Ranges, Cap., Stab., Inv., Prof., Liq.; Weak, Fair, Good, Strong)

PHYSICIANS PLUS INS CORP   B-   Good

Major Rating Factors: Fair profitability index (4.9 on a scale of 0 to 10) despite operating losses during 1998, 1999 and 2000. Return on equity has been low, averaging 2%. Fair overall results on stability tests (5.0). Good liquidity (7.0) with sufficient resources (cash flows and marketable investments) to handle a spike in claims.
Other Rating Factors: Strong capitalization index (7.6) based on excellent current risk-adjusted capital (severe loss scenario). High quality investment portfolio (9.1) containing little or no exposure to mortgages, junk bonds, or unaffiliated stocks.
Principal Business: Comp med (99%), med supp (1%)
Mem Phys: 02: 1,100 01: 1,084 **02 MLR** 82% / **02 Admin Exp** 11%
Enroll(000): Q1 03: 89 02: 98 01: 102 **Med Exp PMPM:** $160
Principal Investments: Cash and equiv (22%), pref stock (7%), nonaffiliate common stock (7%), other (65%).
Provider Compensation ($000): Capitation ($130,718), FFS ($40,658), contr fee ($21,989)
Total Member Encounters: Phys (941,865), non-phys (135,061)
Group Affiliation: Meriter Health Services
Licensed in: WI
Address: 22 E Mifflin St #200, Madison, WI 53703-2821
Phone: (608) 282-8900 **Dom State:** WI **Commenced Bus:** October 1986

Data Date	Weiss Safety Rating	RACR #1	RACR #2	Total Assets ($mil)	Capital ($mil)	Net Premium ($mil)	Net Income ($mil)
3-03	B-	1.82	1.52	49.4	27.5	58.1	1.9
3-02	D+	0.69	0.59	35.2	18.0	57.4	2.6
2002	B-	1.43	1.19	46.4	26.1	233.7	9.2
2001	D+	0.66	0.56	39.7	16.2	217.3	6.8
2000	D-	0.45	0.38	29.1	13.7	239.3	-6.0
1999	D-	0.00	0.00	32.8	11.9	213.9	-4.0
1998	D+	0.88	0.75	36.3	17.3	181.6	-0.4

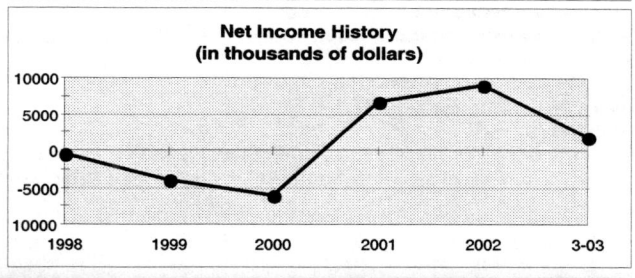

Net Income History (in thousands of dollars), 1998–3-03

PIEDMONT COMMUNITY HEALTHCARE   D   Weak

Major Rating Factors: Weak profitability index (0.9 on a scale of 0 to 10). Poor capitalization index (1.1) based on weak current risk-adjusted capital (moderate loss scenario). Good overall results on stability tests (6.8) based on healthy premium and capital growth during 2002.
Other Rating Factors: High quality investment portfolio (9.9) containing no exposure to mortgages, junk bonds, or unaffiliated stocks. Excellent liquidity (7.0) with ample operational cash flow and liquid investments.
Principal Business: Comp med (97%), FEHB (3%)
Mem Phys: 02: 363 01: 370 **02 MLR** 91% / **02 Admin Exp** 13%
Enroll(000): Q1 03: 15 02: 16 01: 11 **Med Exp PMPM:** $157
Principal Investments: Cash and equiv (100%)
Provider Compensation ($000): Contr fee ($21,341), bonus arrang ($4,086), capitation ($145)
Total Member Encounters: Phys (95,964), non-phys (44,446)
Group Affiliation: Centra Health/Integrated Healthcare
Licensed in: VA
Address: 2255 Langhorne Rd Ste 2, Lynchburg, VA 24501
Phone: (434) 947-4463 **Dom State:** VA **Commenced Bus:** January 1999

Data Date	Weiss Safety Rating	RACR #1	RACR #2	Total Assets ($mil)	Capital ($mil)	Net Premium ($mil)	Net Income ($mil)
3-03	D	0.41	0.34	11.2	3.2	8.6	0.1
3-02	D+	0.44	0.37	6.2	1.7	5.5	0.1
2002	D	0.00	0.00	8.9	3.1	27.2	-1.7
2001	D+	0.51	0.43	4.6	1.1	15.2	0.3
2000	D+	0.75	0.64	3.9	1.0	8.8	0.2
1999	D+	1.34	1.13	2.4	0.9	3.2	0.1
1998	N/A	N/A	N/A	N/A	N/A	N/A	N/A

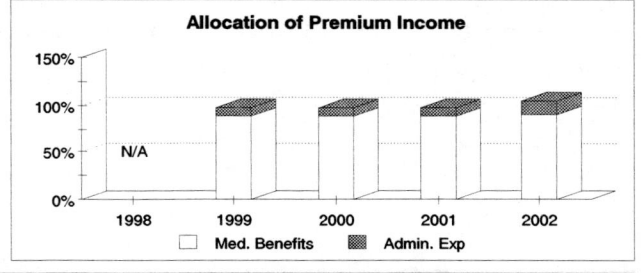

Allocation of Premium Income (1998–2002; Med. Benefits, Admin. Exp)

www.WeissRatings.com   255   * Denotes a Weiss Recommended Company

II. Analysis of Largest Companies   Winter 2003 - 04

PREFERRED HEALTH PARTNERSHIP TN   D+   Weak

Major Rating Factors: Weak profitability index (1.0 on a scale of 0 to 10) with operating losses during 1998, 1999, 2000 and 2001. Average return on equity has been extremely poor. Fair overall results on stability tests (3.3) based on weak risk-adjusted capital in prior years. Good capitalization (6.9) based on excellent current risk-adjusted capital (severe loss scenario) reflecting significant improvement over results in 1998.
Other Rating Factors: Good liquidity (6.9) with sufficient resources (cash flows and marketable investments) to handle a spike in claims. High quality investment portfolio (9.9) containing no exposure to mortgages, junk bonds, or unaffiliated stocks.
Principal Business: Medicaid (100%)
Mem Phys: 02: 4,257 **01:** 3,747 **02 MLR** 71% **/ 02 Admin Exp** 30%
Enroll(000): Q1 03: 136 **02:** 131 **01:** 118 **Med Exp PMPM:** $52
Principal Investments: Cash and equiv (5%), other (95%)
Provider Compensation ($000): FFS ($104,820), capitation ($1,966)
Total Member Encounters: Phys (851,920), non-phys (391,154)
Group Affiliation: PHP Companies Inc
Licensed in: TN
Address: 1420 Centerpoint Blvd, Knoxville, TN 37932
Phone: (865) 470-7470 **Dom State:** TN **Commenced Bus:** January 1994

Data Date	Weiss Safety Rating	RACR #1	RACR #2	Total Assets ($mil)	Capital ($mil)	Net Premium ($mil)	Net Income ($mil)
3-03	D+	1.27	1.06	72.5	12.8	0.1	0.9
3-02	D	1.03	0.87	93.8	18.9	54.2	0.7
2002	D+	1.89	1.58	82.4	20.9	110.0	2.6
2001	D	1.04	0.88	90.2	18.3	206.6	-2.1
2000	D	0.81	0.68	73.6	12.3	155.9	-2.3
1999	D-	1.08	0.95	48.4	9.6	129.0	-2.8
1998	D-	0.40	0.34	50.8	9.8	132.8	-31.0

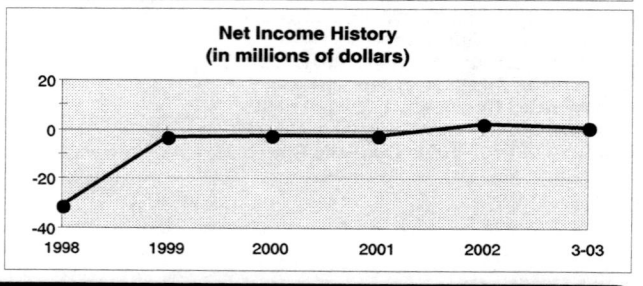

Net Income History (in millions of dollars)

PREFERRED MEDICAL PLAN INC   B   Good

Major Rating Factors: Good capitalization (6.8 on a scale of 0 to 10) based on excellent current risk-adjusted capital (severe loss scenario) reflecting significant improvement over results in 1999. Good overall results on stability tests (7.0) based on consistent premium and capital growth in the last five years. Excellent profitability (8.8) with operating gains in each of the last five years.
Other Rating Factors: High quality investment portfolio (9.7) containing no exposure to mortgages, junk bonds, or unaffiliated stocks. Excellent liquidity (7.1) with ample operational cash flow and liquid investments.
Principal Business: Comp med (63%), Medicaid (37%)
Mem Phys: 02: 2,267 **01:** 1,865 **02 MLR** 78% **/ 02 Admin Exp** 15%
Enroll(000): Q1 03: 46 **02:** 46 **01:** 41 **Med Exp PMPM:** $87
Principal Investments: Cash and equiv (91%), real estate (9%)
Provider Compensation ($000): Contr fee ($29,100), capitation ($12,067), FFS ($3,878)
Total Member Encounters: Phys (11,511)
Group Affiliation: None
Licensed in: FL
Address: 4950 SW 8th Street, Coral Gables, FL 33134
Phone: (305) 648-4000 **Dom State:** FL **Commenced Bus:** April 1975

Data Date	Weiss Safety Rating	RACR #1	RACR #2	Total Assets ($mil)	Capital ($mil)	Net Premium ($mil)	Net Income ($mil)
3-03	B	1.21	1.01	18.3	5.8	16.0	0.8
3-02	B-	1.38	1.17	16.4	4.9	13.4	0.8
2002	B	1.07	0.90	16.9	4.9	58.2	3.5
2001	B-	1.38	1.17	15.6	5.1	47.3	3.1
2000	C	1.26	1.06	15.0	4.7	40.8	2.1
1999	C	0.75	0.64	13.1	4.3	34.5	1.3
1998	C	1.50	1.28	13.0	4.8	27.2	1.5

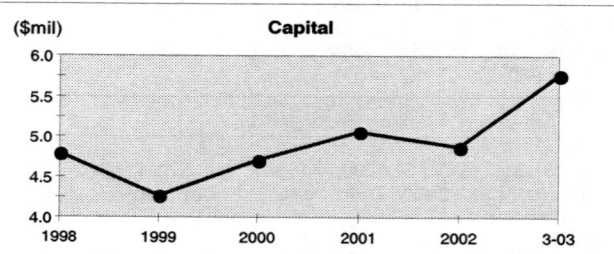

Capital ($mil)

PREFERRED PLUS OF KANSAS INC   B-   Good

Major Rating Factors: Fair profitability index (4.2 on a scale of 0 to 10) with modest operating losses during 2002. Return on equity has been fair, averaging 8% over the last five years. Fair capitalization index (4.6) based on fair current risk-adjusted capital (moderate loss scenario). Fair overall results on stability tests (4.4).
Other Rating Factors: Good liquidity (6.4) with sufficient resources (cash flows and marketable investments) to handle a spike in claims. High quality investment portfolio (8.9).
Principal Business: Comp med (100%)
Mem Phys: 02: 2,592 **01:** 1,956 **02 MLR** 91% **/ 02 Admin Exp** 9%
Enroll(000): Q1 03: 93 **02:** 96 **01:** 83 **Med Exp PMPM:** $176
Principal Investments: Cash and equiv (38%), nonaffiliate common stock (34%), other (29%)
Provider Compensation ($000): Contr fee ($103,259), capitation ($46,802), bonus arrang ($32,900), FFS ($3,955)
Total Member Encounters: Phys (767,381), non-phys (1,261,776)
Group Affiliation: Via Christi Health Systems
Licensed in: KS
Address: 8535 E 21st N, Wichita, KS 67206
Phone: (316) 609-2345 **Dom State:** KS **Commenced Bus:** January 1992

Data Date	Weiss Safety Rating	RACR #1	RACR #2	Total Assets ($mil)	Capital ($mil)	Net Premium ($mil)	Net Income ($mil)
3-03	B-	0.88	0.73	42.4	15.3	54.8	0.6
3-02	B-	0.90	0.69	44.4	18.3	51.5	0.7
2002	B-	0.87	0.72	42.5	15.1	206.9	-0.2
2001	B-	0.90	0.69	40.5	17.6	182.0	1.9
2000	B-	1.00	0.82	41.3	16.0	148.5	0.3
1999	C	0.82	0.68	43.0	16.9	137.7	0.4
1998	D+	0.81	0.62	37.4	16.0	124.1	3.5

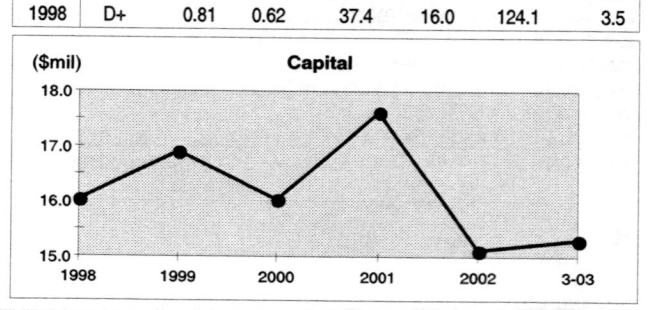

Capital ($mil)

www.WeissRatings.com

PREFERREDONE COMMUNITY HEALTH PLAN — B Good

Major Rating Factors: Good liquidity (7.0 on a scale of 0 to 10) with sufficient resources (cash flows and marketable investments) to handle a spike in claims. Excellent profitability (8.3) despite a decline in earnings during 2002. Strong capitalization (8.8) based on excellent current risk-adjusted capital (severe loss scenario) reflecting significant improvement over results in 1998.
Other Rating Factors: High quality investment portfolio (9.9). Excellent overall results on stability tests (7.8) based on consistent premium and capital growth in the last five years.
Principal Business: Comp med (100%)
Mem Phys: 02: 12,635 **01:** 9,689   **02 MLR** 81% / **02 Admin Exp** 12%
Enroll(000): Q1 03: 39 **02:** 33 **01:** 25   **Med Exp PMPM:** $157
Principal Investments: Cash and equiv (28%), nonaffiliate common stock (9%), other (63%)
Provider Compensation ($000): Contr fee ($24,547), FFS ($15,181), bonus arrang ($13,423)
Total Member Encounters: N/A
Group Affiliation: Fairview Hosp/North Memorial Health
Licensed in: MN
Address: 6105 Golden Hills Dr, Golden Valley, MN 55416
Phone: (763) 847-4000   **Dom State:** MN   **Commenced Bus:** January 1996

Data Date	Weiss Safety Rating	RACR #1	RACR #2	Total Assets ($mil)	Capital ($mil)	Net Premium ($mil)	Net Income ($mil)
3-03	B	2.79	2.33	37.1	21.9	22.9	2.2
3-02	C+	1.85	1.54	26.7	15.8	14.1	0.9
2002	B	2.53	2.11	33.2	19.8	67.4	5.2
2001	C+	1.85	1.54	19.5	9.4	48.9	9.1
2000	D+	0.88	0.73	17.2	6.0	43.4	1.9
1999	D+	0.73	0.61	12.4	5.2	29.6	-1.9
1998	D+	0.60	0.50	9.7	2.9	24.1	-0.5

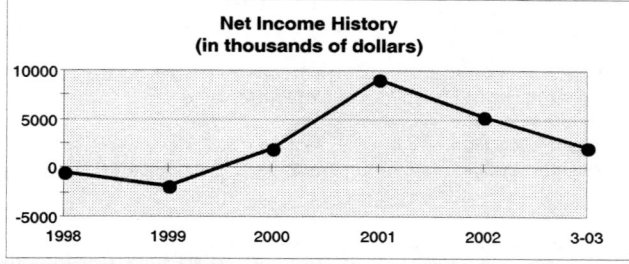

Net Income History (in thousands of dollars)

PREMERA BLUE CROSS — B Good

Major Rating Factors: Good overall profitability index (6.0 on a scale of 0 to 10) despite a decline in earnings during 2002. Good quality investment portfolio (6.6) containing small junk bond exposure. Good liquidity (6.0) with sufficient resources (cash flows and marketable investments) to handle a spike in claims.
Other Rating Factors: Strong capitalization (7.7) based on excellent current risk-adjusted capital (severe loss scenario) reflecting significant improvement over results in 2000.
Principal Business: Comp med (84%), FEHB (8%), med supp (4%), Medicaid (4%)
Mem Phys: 02: 19,457 **01:** 19,860   **02 MLR** 84% / **02 Admin Exp** 13%
Enroll(000): Q1 03: 899 **02:** 912 **01:** 975   **Med Exp PMPM:** $161
Principal Investments: Affiliate common stock (12%), nonaffiliate common stock (10%), real estate (7%), cash and equiv (2%), other (69%)
Provider Compensation ($000): Contr fee ($1,681,767), FFS ($156,610), capitation ($2,636), bonus arrang ($1,464)
Total Member Encounters: Phys (14,038,413), non-phys (981,267)
Group Affiliation: PREMERA
Licensed in: AK, WA
Address: 7001 220th St SW, Mountlake Terrace, WA 98043
Phone: (425) 918-4000   **Dom State:** WA   **Commenced Bus:** May 1945

Data Date	Weiss Safety Rating	RACR #1	RACR #2	Total Assets ($mil)	Capital ($mil)	Net Premium ($mil)	Net Income ($mil)
3-03	B	1.95	1.62	896.3	319.1	559.4	5.6
3-02	B	1.73	1.29	859.4	330.6	525.4	7.1
2002	B	1.86	1.55	819.8	311.6	2,147.8	7.5
2001	B	1.74	1.30	844.9	329.0	2,074.4	38.5
2000	C+	1.14	0.71	728.1	271.1	1,770.4	31.2
1999	C+	1.28	0.82	679.1	248.6	1,520.5	32.8
1998	C	1.40	0.90	616.6	209.8	1,376.8	5.5

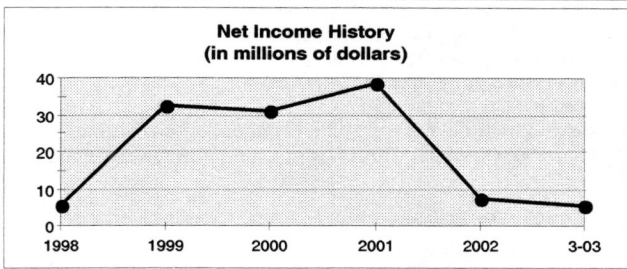

Net Income History (in millions of dollars)

PREMIER MEDICAL INS GROUP INC — C+ Fair

Major Rating Factors: Fair profitability index (3.2 on a scale of 0 to 10). Low quality investment portfolio (2.4) containing little or no exposure to mortgages, junk bonds, or unaffiliated stocks. Strong overall capitalization (7.0) based on excellent current risk-adjusted capital (severe loss scenario) despite some fluctuation in capital levels.
Other Rating Factors: Excellent liquidity (8.8) with ample operational cash flow and liquid investments.
Principal Business: Comp med (100%)
Mem Phys: 02: 1,802 **01:** 1,726   **02 MLR** 95% / **02 Admin Exp** 7%
Enroll(000): Q1 03: 0 **02:** 0 **01:** 1   **Med Exp PMPM:** $121
Principal Investments: Affiliate common stock (92%), cash and equiv (2%), other (6%)
Provider Compensation ($000): Capitation ($1,485)
Total Member Encounters: Phys (1,286), non-phys (181)
Group Affiliation: Dean Health Group
Licensed in: IL, WI
Address: 1277 Deming Way, Madison, WI 53717
Phone: (608) 836-1400   **Dom State:** WI   **Commenced Bus:** January 1997

Data Date	Weiss Safety Rating	RACR #1	RACR #2	Total Assets ($mil)	Capital ($mil)	Net Premium ($mil)	Net Income ($mil)
3-03	C+	1.39	1.16	42.0	40.9	0.2	0.0
3-02	C+	0.00	0.00	46.3	45.2	0.2	0.0
2002	C+	1.46	1.22	42.7	42.5	0.9	0.1
2001	N/A	N/A	N/A	44.9	44.0	1.6	N/A
2000	U	1.25	1.11	42.2	42.0	1.5	0.1
1999	C+	1.24	1.10	40.9	40.7	1.3	0.0
1998	U	1.25	1.11	40.3	40.2	N/A	0.1

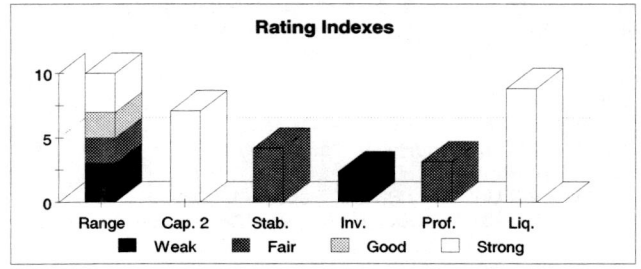

Rating Indexes — Range, Cap. 2, Stab., Inv., Prof., Liq. ■ Weak ▨ Fair ▦ Good □ Strong

II. Analysis of Largest Companies
Winter 2003 - 04

PRESBYTERIAN HEALTH PLAN INC — C+ — Fair

Major Rating Factors: Fair profitability index (3.5 on a scale of 0 to 10) with operating losses during 1998, 1999 and 2000. Average return on equity has been poor at -23%. Good capitalization index (6.9) based on excellent current risk-adjusted capital (severe loss scenario). Good overall results on stability tests (5.9) despite excessive capital growth during 2002.
Other Rating Factors: High quality investment portfolio (9.9) containing little or no exposure to mortgages, junk bonds, or unaffiliated stocks. Excellent liquidity (7.1) with ample operational cash flow and liquid investments.
Principal Business: Medicaid (57%), comp med (27%), Medicare (13%), FEHB (4%)
Mem Phys: 02: 5,244   **01:** 4,143   **02 MLR** 87%   **/ 02 Admin Exp** 9%
Enroll(000): Q1 03: 233   **02:** 229   **01:** 222   **Med Exp PMPM:** $217
Principal Investments: Cash and equiv (99%)
Provider Compensation ($000): Contr fee ($352,423), capitation ($182,602), FFS ($41,476)
Total Member Encounters: Phys (1,414,721), non-phys (1,069,711)
Group Affiliation: Presbyterian Health Services
Licensed in: NM
Address: 2301 Buena Vista SE, Albuquerque, NM 87106
Phone: (505) 923-5700   **Dom State:** NM   **Commenced Bus:** July 1987

Data Date	Weiss Safety Rating	RACR #1	RACR #2	Total Assets ($mil)	Capital ($mil)	Net Premium ($mil)	Net Income ($mil)
3-03	C+	1.28	1.06	147.4	72.1	183.5	2.3
3-02	D+	0.00	0.00	113.8	48.6	163.7	4.1
2002	C+	1.17	0.98	150.9	67.6	676.0	19.8
2001	D+	0.76	0.65	107.7	44.2	607.6	11.5
2000	D	0.27	0.23	81.8	18.2	612.3	-1.8
1999	C-	0.00	0.00	99.7	18.3	623.3	-26.0
1998	D+	0.42	0.37	113.4	25.0	518.4	-8.4

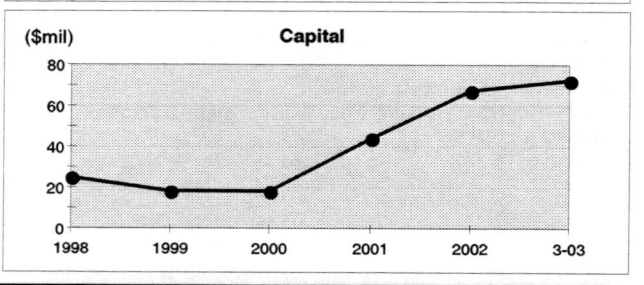

PRIMECARE MEDICAL NETWORK INC — D — Weak

Major Rating Factors: Fair capitalization index (4.8 on a scale of 0 to 10) based on fair current risk-adjusted capital (moderate loss scenario). Furthermore, this low level of risk-adjusted capital has been consistent in previous years. Good overall results on stability tests (5.9) despite fair risk diversification due to the size of the company's affiliate group. Good liquidity (6.9) with sufficient resources (cash flows and marketable investments) to handle a spike in claims.
Other Rating Factors: Excellent profitability (8.4) despite a decline in earnings during 2002.
Principal Business: Managed care (100%)
Mem Phys: 02: N/A   **01:** N/A   **02 MLR** 87%   **/ 02 Admin Exp** 12%
Enroll(000): **02:** 262   **01:** 245   **Med Exp PMPM:** $73
Principal Investments ($000): Cash and equiv ($29,133)
Provider Compensation ($000): None
Total Member Encounters: N/A
Group Affiliation: PhyCor Inc
Licensed in: CA
Address: 3281 E Guasti Rd 7th Fl, Ontario, CA 91761-7643
Phone: (909) 605-8000   **Dom State:** CA   **Commenced Bus:** October 1998

Data Date	Weiss Safety Rating	RACR #1	RACR #2	Total Assets ($mil)	Capital ($mil)	Net Premium ($mil)	Net Income ($mil)
2002	D	0.75	0.47	43.7	13.6	255.8	1.0
2001	D-	0.61	0.38	38.0	11.8	232.8	2.2
2000	E+	0.48	0.29	25.3	7.7	212.1	1.3
1999	N/A	N/A	N/A	N/A	N/A	N/A	N/A
1998	N/A	N/A	N/A	N/A	N/A	N/A	N/A

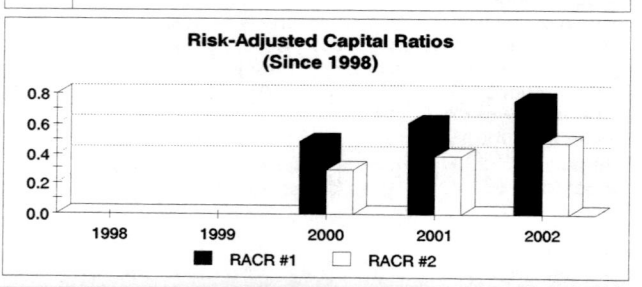

PRIMEHEALTH OF ALABAMA INC — E — Very Weak

Major Rating Factors: Weak profitability index (0.9 on a scale of 0 to 10) with $19.6 million in losses in the last five years. Average return on equity over the last five years has been extremely poor. Poor capitalization index (0.0) based on weak current risk-adjusted capital (severe loss scenario). Fair overall results on stability tests (3.3) based on an overall decline in enrollment over the past five years despite growth in 2002, a steep decline in capital during 2002. Potentially strong support from affiliation with PrimeHealth Companies.
Other Rating Factors: Good liquidity (5.6) with sufficient resources (cash flows and marketable investments) to handle a spike in claims. High quality investment portfolio (9.9) containing no exposure to mortgages, junk bonds, or unaffiliated stocks.
Principal Business: Comp med (86%), FEHB (14%)
Mem Phys: 02: 1,119   **01:** 975   **02 MLR** 88%   **/ 02 Admin Exp** 11%
Enroll(000): Q1 03: 8   **02:** 9   **01:** 8   **Med Exp PMPM:** $174
Principal Investments: Cash and equiv (85%), other (15%)
Provider Compensation ($000): Contr fee ($15,719), FFS ($1,968), capitation ($225)
Total Member Encounters: Phys (21,151)
Group Affiliation: PrimeHealth Companies
Licensed in: AL
Address: 1400 University Blvd S, Mobile, AL 36609
Phone: (251) 342-0022   **Dom State:** AL   **Commenced Bus:** January 1992

Data Date	Weiss Safety Rating	RACR #1	RACR #2	Total Assets ($mil)	Capital ($mil)	Net Premium ($mil)	Net Income ($mil)
3-03	E	0.29	0.24	3.7	1.2	4.4	0.0
3-02	E	0.18	0.16	6.5	1.6	4.6	-0.1
2002	E	0.30	0.25	3.7	1.2	19.9	-0.4
2001	E	0.19	0.16	6.5	1.7	16.9	-0.6
2000	E-	0.05	0.04	7.2	1.2	19.7	-2.0
1999	E-	0.00	0.00	10.3	1.0	26.9	-6.5
1998	E+	0.01	0.01	10.4	1.9	39.1	-10.2

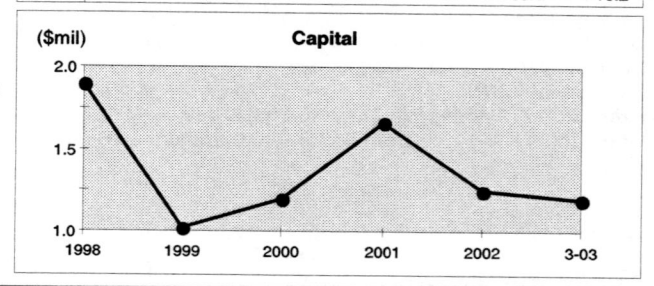

Winter 2003 - 04   II. Analysis of Largest Companies

PRINCIPAL LIFE INSURANCE COMPANY *   A-   Excellent

Major Rating Factors: Good quality investment portfolio (5.6 on a scale of 0 to 10) despite mixed results such as: large holdings of BBB rated bonds but junk bond exposure equal to 88% of capital. Good overall profitability (5.9) although investment income, in comparison to reserve requirements, is below regulatory standards. Good overall results on stability tests (5.5) good operational trends and excellent risk diversification.
Other Rating Factors: Strong capitalization (7.5) based on excellent risk adjusted capital (severe loss scenario). Excellent liquidity (7.0).
Principal Business: Group health insurance (41%), individual life insurance (20%), individual annuities (20%), group retirement contracts (11%), and other lines (9%).
Principal Investments: NonCMO investment grade bonds (53%), mortgages in good standing (18%), CMOs and structured securities (12%), noninv. grade bonds (8%), and misc. investments (10%).
Investments in Affiliates: 4%
Group Affiliation: Principal Financial Group
Licensed in: All states, the District of Columbia and Puerto Rico
Commenced Business: September 1879
Address: 711 High St, Des Moines, IA 50392-0001
Phone: (800) 986-3343   **Domicile State:** IA   **NAIC Code:** 61271

Data Date	Weiss Safety Rating	RACR #1	RACR #2	Total Assets ($mil)	Capital ($mil)	Net Premium ($mil)	Net Income ($mil)
6-03	A-	2.67	1.34	83,957.6	3,739.8	2,381.7	182.3
6-02	A-	2.84	1.40	78,491.3	3,287.0	2,663.2	28.6
2002	A-	2.85	1.39	78,002.4	3,339.2	5,065.9	402.1
2001	A-	3.12	1.54	77,162.4	3,483.8	4,743.9	415.0
2000	A-	2.70	1.36	75,573.4	3,356.4	15,653.3	912.6
1999	A-	2.45	1.28	76,017.7	3,152.0	15,709.8	713.7
1998	A-	2.27	1.25	70,096.1	3,031.5	14,120.3	511.4

Adverse Trends in Operations

Decrease in capital during 2002 (4%)
Change in premium mix from 2000 to 2001 (13%)
Decrease in premium volume from 2000 to 2001 (70%)
Increase in policy surrenders from 1999 to 2000 (32%)

PRIORITY HEALTH *   B+   Good

Major Rating Factors: Good liquidity (6.9 on a scale of 0 to 10) with sufficient resources (cash flows and marketable investments) to handle a spike in claims. Excellent profitability (7.0) despite operating losses during 1998. Strong capitalization (7.0) based on excellent current risk-adjusted capital (severe loss scenario) reflecting significant improvement over results in 1999.
Other Rating Factors: High quality investment portfolio (9.9) containing no exposure to mortgages, junk bonds, or unaffiliated stocks. Excellent overall results on stability tests (8.0) based on consistent premium and capital growth in the last five years.
Principal Business: Comp med (95%), Medicaid (5%)
Mem Phys: 02: 2,546   01: 2,368   **02 MLR** 88% / **02 Admin Exp** 9%
Enroll(000): Q1 03: 311   02: 289   01: 269   **Med Exp PMPM:** $161
Principal Investments: Cash and equiv (63%), real estate (1%), other (36%)
Provider Compensation ($000): Bonus arrang ($377,153), capitation ($123,847), FFS ($36,273)
Total Member Encounters: Phys (2,131,861), non-phys (57,807)
Group Affiliation: Spectrum Health Corp & Holland Hosp
Licensed in: MI
Address: 1231 E Beltline Ave NE, Grand Rapids, MI 49505-4501
Phone: (800) 942-0954   **Dom State:** MI   **Commenced Bus:** October 1986

Data Date	Weiss Safety Rating	RACR #1	RACR #2	Total Assets ($mil)	Capital ($mil)	Net Premium ($mil)	Net Income ($mil)
3-03	B+	1.37	1.14	177.9	67.7	183.5	6.4
3-02	B-	1.05	0.90	138.4	46.7	143.2	3.5
2002	B+	1.24	1.04	150.4	61.9	606.9	15.7
2001	B-	1.06	0.90	125.9	43.5	473.7	13.9
2000	C-	0.70	0.59	101.4	25.9	396.0	9.4
1999	D	0.61	0.51	81.1	18.3	319.4	4.6
1998	D-	0.66	0.56	48.1	14.0	234.4	-5.0

Net Income History (in millions of dollars)

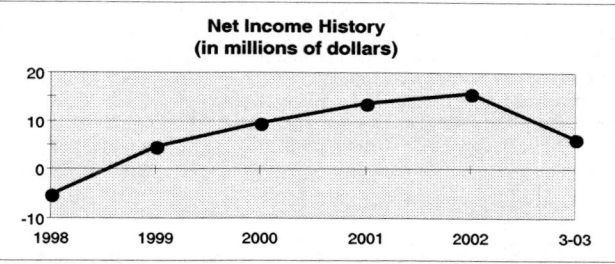

PRIORITY HEALTH CARE INC *   B+   Good

Major Rating Factors: Good liquidity (6.8 on a scale of 0 to 10) with sufficient resources (cash flows and marketable investments) to handle a spike in claims. Excellent profitability (9.4) with operating gains in each of the last five years. Strong capitalization (9.6) based on excellent current risk-adjusted capital (severe loss scenario) reflecting significant improvement over results in 1998.
Other Rating Factors: High quality investment portfolio (9.9) containing no exposure to mortgages, junk bonds, or unaffiliated stocks. Excellent overall results on stability tests (8.0) based on consistent premium and capital growth in the last five years. Rating is significantly influenced by the good financial results of Anthem Ins Companies Inc.
Principal Business: Comp med (68%), Medicaid (32%)
Mem Phys: 02: 12,045   01: 10,355   **02 MLR** 81% / **02 Admin Exp** 12%
Enroll(000): Q1 03: 72   02: 86   01: 79   **Med Exp PMPM:** $144
Principal Investments: Cash and equiv (11%), other (89%)
Provider Compensation ($000): Contr fee ($93,778), FFS ($26,919), bonus arrang ($11,521), capitation ($8,804)
Total Member Encounters: Phys (425,561), non-phys (34,030)
Group Affiliation: Anthem Ins Companies Inc
Licensed in: VA
Address: 621 Lynnhaven Parkway, Ste 450, Virginia Beach, VA 23452
Phone: (804) 354-3479   **Dom State:** VA   **Commenced Bus:** May 1984

Data Date	Weiss Safety Rating	RACR #1	RACR #2	Total Assets ($mil)	Capital ($mil)	Net Premium ($mil)	Net Income ($mil)
3-03	B+	3.47	2.89	70.7	38.7	43.0	1.9
3-02	B+	2.89	2.24	63.3	31.2	41.6	2.4
2002	B+	3.27	2.72	65.6	36.5	176.0	11.3
2001	B+	2.44	1.89	58.5	29.0	147.2	8.1
2000	B	2.01	1.65	47.7	20.8	132.3	9.4
1999	C+	0.72	0.58	32.9	11.0	122.7	3.3
1998	C+	0.37	0.30	29.0	6.5	120.1	2.2

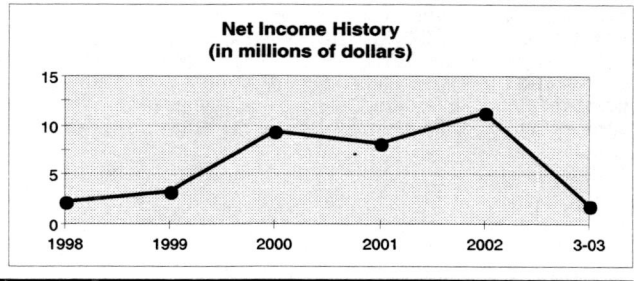

Net Income History (in millions of dollars)

PROVIDENCE HEALTH PLAN C+ Fair

Major Rating Factors: Fair profitability index (4.8 on a scale of 0 to 10) with operating losses during 1998 and 2000. Fair overall results on stability tests (4.8) based on weak risk-adjusted capital in prior years, a significant 29% decrease in enrollment during the period. Good liquidity (6.8) with sufficient resources (cash flows and marketable investments) to handle a spike in claims.
Other Rating Factors: Strong capitalization (7.8) based on excellent current risk-adjusted capital (severe loss scenario) reflecting significant improvement over results in 2000. High quality investment portfolio (9.9) containing no exposure to mortgages, junk bonds, or unaffiliated stocks.
Principal Business: Medicare (49%), comp mix (46%), Medicaid (4%)
Mem Phys: 02: 4,808 **01:** 4,335 **02 MLR** 83% **/ 02 Admin Exp** 10%
Enroll(000): Q1 03: 149 **02:** 149 **01:** 209 **Med Exp PMPM:** $202
Principal Investments: Cash and equiv (13%), other (87%)
Provider Compensation ($000): Contr fee ($293,296), bonus arrang ($90,236), FFS ($22,442), capitation ($20,893)
Total Member Encounters: Phys (1,988,941), non-phys (152,175)
Group Affiliation: Providence Health Plans
Licensed in: OR, WA
Address: 3601 SW Murray Blvd Ste 10, Beaverton, OR 97005
Phone: (503) 215-3215 **Dom State:** OR **Commenced Bus:** January 1985

Data Date	Weiss Safety Rating	RACR #1	RACR #2	Total Assets ($mil)	Capital ($mil)	Net Premium ($mil)	Net Income ($mil)
3-03	C+	1.99	1.66	157.8	86.4	136.5	6.6
3-02	C	0.85	0.64	138.6	75.3	129.1	3.1
2002	C+	1.85	1.54	163.4	81.3	520.9	29.1
2001	C	0.85	0.64	152.7	73.5	633.3	5.8
2000	C-	0.54	0.44	187.6	63.5	763.6	-8.8
1999	C	0.64	0.52	204.5	62.5	689.6	2.1
1998	C	0.66	0.54	187.9	54.1	708.7	-13.7

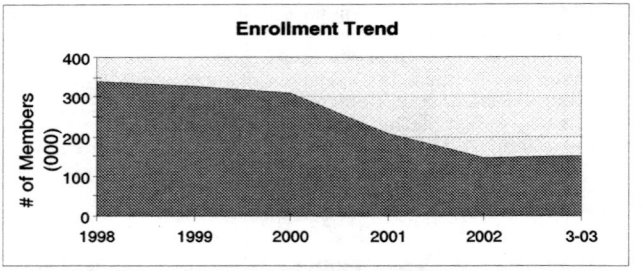

Enrollment Trend (chart: # of Members (000), declining from ~340 in 1998 to ~150 in 3-03)

PROVIDENT LIFE & ACCIDENT INSURANCE COMPANY C- Fair

Major Rating Factors: Fair overall results on stability tests (3.2 on a scale of 0 to 10) including fair financial strength of affiliated UnumProvident Corp, negative cash flow from operations for 2002 and fair risk adjusted capital in prior years. Fair quality investment portfolio (3.7) with large holdings of BBB rated bonds in addition to significant exposure to junk bonds. Good liquidity (6.8).
Other Rating Factors: Strong capitalization (7.3) based on excellent risk adjusted capital (severe loss scenario). Excellent profitability (7.7) despite modest operating losses during 2002.
Principal Business: Individual health insurance (47%), group health insurance (22%), individual life insurance (18%), group life insurance (11%), and reinsurance (1%).
Principal Investments: NonCMO investment grade bonds (62%), noninv. grade bonds (19%), CMOs and structured securities (16%), common & preferred stock (2%), and misc. investments (2%).
Investments in Affiliates: None
Group Affiliation: UnumProvident Corp
Licensed in: All states except NY
Commenced Business: December 1887
Address: 1 Fountain Square, Chattanooga, TN 37402
Phone: (423) 755-1373 **Domicile State:** TN **NAIC Code:** 68195

Data Date	Weiss Safety Rating	RACR #1	RACR #2	Total Assets ($mil)	Capital ($mil)	Net Premium ($mil)	Net Income ($mil)
6-03	C-	2.43	1.21	8,875.7	1,100.9	673.4	-34.9
6-02	C+	1.99	1.01	8,825.5	902.7	693.1	-126.7
2002	C-	1.91	0.93	8,556.8	927.3	1,387.4	-91.4
2001	C+	2.32	1.18	8,716.9	999.3	1,403.5	16.4
2000	C+	2.71	1.40	8,689.6	1,008.0	1,264.9	98.0
1999	C	1.15	0.60	10,199.4	488.6	1,357.5	45.7
1998	C	1.27	0.66	10,108.3	518.2	1,215.0	16.2

UnumProvident Corp
Composite Group Rating: C-
Largest Group Members

	Assets ($mil)	Weiss Safety Rating
UNUM LIFE INS CO OF AMERICA	10982	C-
PROVIDENT LIFE ACCIDENT INS CO	8557	C-
PAUL REVERE LIFE INS CO	4976	C-
COLONIAL LIFE ACCIDENT INS CO	1194	C-
FIRST UNUM LIFE INS CO	1097	C-

PROVIDENT LIFE & CASUALTY INSURANCE COMPANY C- Fair

Major Rating Factors: Fair overall results on stability tests (3.2 on a scale of 0 to 10) including fair financial strength of affiliated UnumProvident Corp. Fair quality investment portfolio (3.7) with large holdings of BBB rated bonds in addition to significant exposure to junk bonds. Fair profitability (4.2). Excellent expense controls. Return on equity has been low, averaging 3.8%.
Other Rating Factors: Strong capitalization (7.3) based on excellent risk adjusted capital (severe loss scenario). Excellent liquidity (7.1).
Principal Business: Individual health insurance (69%), group health insurance (13%), reinsurance (10%), group life insurance (5%), and individual life insurance (3%).
Principal Investments: NonCMO investment grade bonds (64%), CMOs and structured securities (21%), and noninv. grade bonds (15%).
Investments in Affiliates: None
Group Affiliation: UnumProvident Corp
Licensed in: AK, AR, CO, CT, DC, DE, GA, HI, ID, IL, IA, KY, LA, MA, MS, MO, NE, NH, NJ, NM, NY, NC, ND, OH, OK, PA, RI, SC, SD, TN, VA, WA
Commenced Business: December 1952
Address: 1 Fountain Square, Chattanooga, TN 37402
Phone: (423) 755-1373 **Domicile State:** TN **NAIC Code:** 68209

Data Date	Weiss Safety Rating	RACR #1	RACR #2	Total Assets ($mil)	Capital ($mil)	Net Premium ($mil)	Net Income ($mil)
6-03	C-	2.26	1.20	609.1	75.8	39.1	0.1
6-02	C+	1.92	1.05	588.2	65.3	38.5	-7.9
2002	C-	1.97	1.05	597.6	64.7	77.9	-2.8
2001	C+	2.22	1.22	592.3	73.3	80.2	0.4
2000	C+	2.31	1.37	570.2	67.1	90.9	-5.1
1999	C+	2.29	1.39	564.1	72.1	98.3	-3.6
1998	C+	2.70	1.63	518.9	77.7	85.6	-0.2

UnumProvident Corp
Composite Group Rating: C-
Largest Group Members

	Assets ($mil)	Weiss Safety Rating
UNUM LIFE INS CO OF AMERICA	10982	C-
PROVIDENT LIFE ACCIDENT INS CO	8557	C-
PAUL REVERE LIFE INS CO	4976	C-
COLONIAL LIFE ACCIDENT INS CO	1194	C-
FIRST UNUM LIFE INS CO	1097	C-

Winter 2003 - 04
II. Analysis of Largest Companies

QCA HEALTH PLAN INC — E — Very Weak

Major Rating Factors: Weak profitability index (1.6 on a scale of 0 to 10) with operating losses during 1998, 1999, 2000 and 2001. Average return on equity has been extremely poor. Poor capitalization index (0.0) based on weak current risk-adjusted capital (severe loss scenario). Good overall results on stability tests (5.6) despite rapid premium growth over the last five years.
Other Rating Factors: Good liquidity (6.9) with sufficient resources (cash flows and marketable investments) to handle a spike in claims. High quality investment portfolio (9.9) containing no exposure to mortgages, junk bonds, or unaffiliated stocks.
Principal Business: Comp med (100%)
Mem Phys: 02: 4,133 **01:** 3,362 **02 MLR** 86% / **02 Admin Exp** 12%
Enroll(000): Q1 03: 31 **02:** 34 **01:** 67 **Med Exp PMPM:** $115
Principal Investments: Cash and equiv (100%)
Provider Compensation ($000): Bonus arrang ($55,828), FFS ($16,046)
Total Member Encounters: Phys (616,999), non-phys (168,647)
Group Affiliation: None
Licensed in: AR
Address: 10800 Financial Ctr Pkwy 540, Little Rock, AR 72211-3570
Phone: (501) 228-7111 **Dom State:** AR **Commenced Bus:** July 1996

Data Date	Weiss Safety Rating	RACR #1	RACR #2	Total Assets ($mil)	Capital ($mil)	Net Premium ($mil)	Net Income ($mil)
3-03	E	0.26	0.22	25.4	5.3	18.1	0.7
3-02	E	0.09	0.07	19.9	2.8	21.3	0.4
2002	E	0.22	0.18	21.4	4.5	81.3	2.0
2001	E	0.09	0.07	21.5	2.3	111.3	-0.6
2000	E	0.11	0.09	15.3	2.1	68.4	-5.4
1999	E	0.08	0.07	17.2	1.1	68.4	-10.2
1998	E	0.08	0.07	10.2	3.8	23.8	-5.7

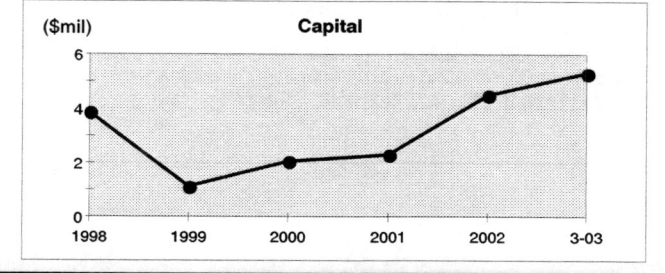

QCC INS CO — C+ — Fair

Major Rating Factors: Fair quality investment portfolio (3.8 on a scale of 0 to 10). Good liquidity (6.1) with sufficient resources (cash flows and marketable investments) to handle a spike in claims. Excellent profitability (7.5) despite a decline in earnings during 2002.
Other Rating Factors: Strong capitalization (8.9) based on excellent current risk-adjusted capital (severe loss scenario).
Principal Business: Comp med (90%), Medicare (8%)
Mem Phys: 02: 15,000 **01:** 15,000 **02 MLR** 83% / **02 Admin Exp** 11%
Enroll(000): Q1 03: 773 **02:** 782 **01:** N/A **Med Exp PMPM:** $398
Principal Investments: Cash and equiv (15%), nonaffiliate common stock (7%), other (78%)
Provider Compensation ($000): Contr fee ($1,729,463), FFS ($43,001), capitation ($211), other ($9,255)
Total Member Encounters: N/A
Group Affiliation: Independence Blue Cross Inc
Licensed in: AZ, CO, DC, DE, FL, GA, IN, KS, MA, MS, MT, NE, NV, NM, ND, OH, OK, PA, SC, SD, TN, TX, UT, WA, WV
Address: 1901 Market St 39th Floor, Philadelphia, PA 19103
Phone: (215) 241-2529 **Dom State:** PA **Commenced Bus:** December 1981

Data Date	Weiss Safety Rating	RACR #1	RACR #2	Total Assets ($mil)	Capital ($mil)	Net Premium ($mil)	Net Income ($mil)
3-03	C+	2.88	2.40	967.5	285.6	635.6	20.4
3-02	N/A	N/A	N/A	N/A	N/A	N/A	N/A
2002	C+	0.00	0.00	951.6	270.9	2,250.6	53.4
2001	C	0.88	0.70	742.8	231.5	2,071.5	71.6
2000	C	0.79	0.63	556.6	182.6	1,808.5	25.7
1999	C	0.94	0.77	531.2	177.7	1,612.6	7.2
1998	C	1.18	0.97	464.6	179.5	1,277.5	15.4

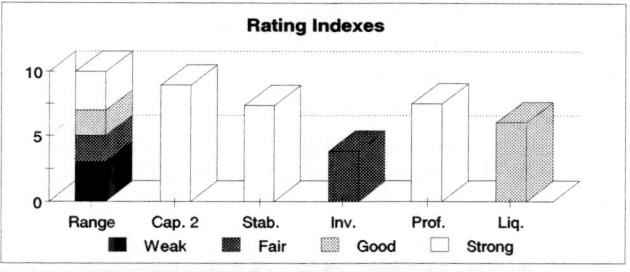

QCC INSURANCE COMPANY — C — Fair

Major Rating Factors: Fair overall capitalization (4.1 on a scale of 0 to 10) based on mixed results -- excessive policy leverage mitigated by fair risk adjusted capital (severe loss scenario). Fair quality investment portfolio (4.4). Fair overall results on stability tests (3.5) including fair risk adjusted capital in prior years.
Other Rating Factors: Weak liquidity (2.0). Excellent profitability (8.7) with operating gains in each of the last five years.
Principal Business: Group health insurance (89%), individual health insurance (10%), and reinsurance (1%).
Principal Investments: NonCMO investment grade bonds (61%), CMOs and structured securities (12%), noninv. grade bonds (12%), cash (8%), and common & preferred stock (7%).
Investments in Affiliates: 2%
Group Affiliation: Independence Blue Cross Inc
Licensed in: AZ, CO, DC, DE, FL, GA, IN, KS, MA, MS, MT, NE, NV, NM, ND, OH, OK, PA, SC, SD, TN, TX, UT, WA, WV
Commenced Business: December 1981
Address: 1901 Market St 39th Floor, Philadelphia, PA 19103
Phone: (215) 241-2529 **Domicile State:** PA **NAIC Code:** 93688

Data Date	Weiss Safety Rating	RACR #1	RACR #2	Total Assets ($mil)	Capital ($mil)	Net Premium ($mil)	Net Income ($mil)
9-02	C	0.92	0.72	940.4	264.3	1,721.9	58.6
9-01	C	0.85	0.68	705.4	214.4	1,533.1	41.9
2001	C	0.88	0.70	742.8	231.5	2,079.7	71.6
2000	C	0.79	0.63	556.6	182.6	1,808.5	25.7
1999	C	0.94	0.77	531.2	177.7	1,612.6	7.2
1998	C	1.18	0.97	464.6	179.5	1,277.5	15.4
1997	C+	2.14	1.77	360.7	155.3	621.6	11.2

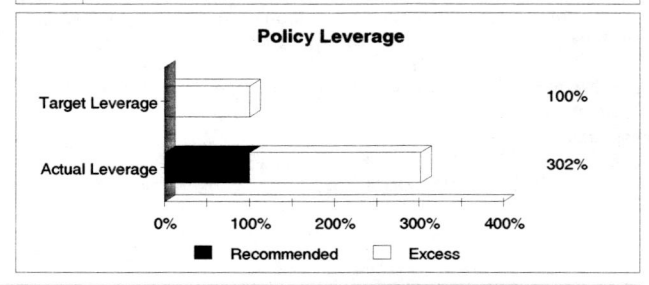

Policy Leverage: Target Leverage 100%; Actual Leverage 302%

II. Analysis of Largest Companies
Winter 2003 - 04

QUAL CHOICE HEALTH PLAN INC — D- Weak

Major Rating Factors: Poor long-term capitalization index (1.9 on a scale of 0 to 10) based on weak current risk adjusted capital (moderate loss scenario). Vulnerable liquidity (2.2) as a spike in claims may stretch capacity.
Other Rating Factors: Weak overall results on stability tests (1.3) including weak risk adjusted capital in prior years and weak results on operational trends. Fair profitability index (3.4) with operating losses during 1998, 1999, 2000, 2001 and the first three months of 2002. Average return on equity over the last five years has been poor at -39.8%. Ample reserve history (7.1) that can protect against increases in claims costs.
Principal Business: Group accident & health (100%).
Principal Investments: Investment grade bonds (70%), misc. investments (24%), and cash (6%).
Investments in Affiliates: None
Group Affiliation: University Hospitals Health System
Licensed in: OH
Commenced Business: September 1993
Address: 6000 Parkland Blvd, Cleveland, OH 44124
Phone: (440) 460-0093 **Domicile State:** OH **NAIC Code:** 10001

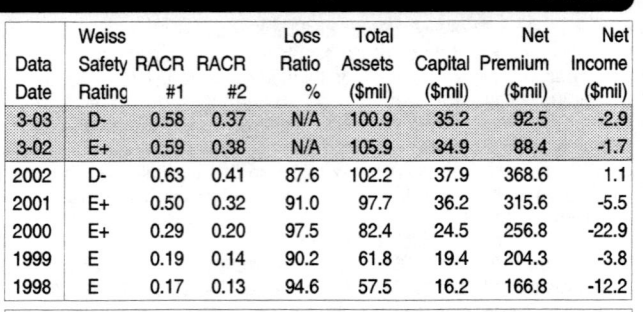

Data Date	Weiss Safety Rating	RACR #1	RACR #2	Loss Ratio %	Total Assets ($mil)	Capital ($mil)	Net Premium ($mil)	Net Income ($mil)
3-03	D-	0.58	0.37	N/A	100.9	35.2	92.5	-2.9
3-02	E+	0.59	0.38	N/A	105.9	34.9	88.4	-1.7
2002	D-	0.63	0.41	87.6	102.2	37.9	368.6	1.1
2001	E+	0.50	0.32	91.0	97.7	36.2	315.6	-5.5
2000	E+	0.29	0.20	97.5	82.4	24.5	256.8	-22.9
1999	E	0.19	0.14	90.2	61.8	19.4	204.3	-3.8
1998	E	0.17	0.13	94.6	57.5	16.2	166.8	-12.2

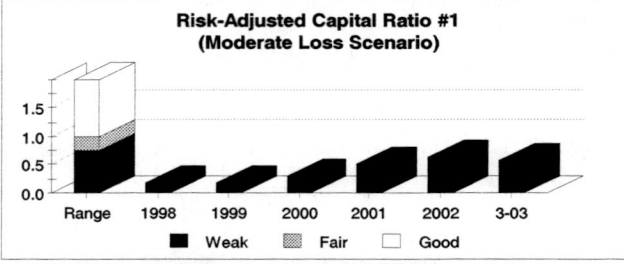

Risk-Adjusted Capital Ratio #1 (Moderate Loss Scenario)

QUALCHOICE OF NORTH CAROLINA INC — D+ Weak

Major Rating Factors: Weak profitability index (0.9 on a scale of 0 to 10) with operating losses during 1997, 1998, 1999 and 2000. Average return on equity has been extremely poor. Poor capitalization index (2.9) based on weak current risk-adjusted capital (moderate loss scenario). Fair overall results on stability tests (3.4) based on rapid premium growth over the last five years, a significant 43% decrease in enrollment during the period.
Other Rating Factors: High quality investment portfolio (9.9) containing no exposure to mortgages, junk bonds, or unaffiliated stocks. Excellent liquidity (7.1) with ample operational cash flow and liquid investments.
Principal Business: Medicare (55%), comp med (44%).
Mem Phys: 01: 2,224 **00:** 1,989 **01 MLR** 88% / **01 Admin Exp** 13%
Enroll(000): Q2 02: 12 **01:** 39 **00:** 68 **Med Exp PMPM:** $205
Principal Investments: Cash and equiv (100%)
Provider Compensation ($000): Contr fee ($71,760), bonus arrang ($43,261), FFS ($14,479), capitation ($1,195)
Total Member Encounters: N/A
Group Affiliation: North Carolina Baptist Hospital Inc
Licensed in: NC
Address: 100 Kimel Forest Dr, Winston-Salem, NC 27103
Phone: (336) 716-0900 **Dom State:** NC **Commenced Bus:** October 1994

Data Date	Weiss Safety Rating	RACR #1	RACR #2	Total Assets ($mil)	Capital ($mil)	Net Premium ($mil)	Net Income ($mil)
6-02	D+	0.74	0.62	26.0	10.8	55.8	-3.9
6-01	D	0.43	0.36	42.7	10.8	76.3	-1.4
2001	D+	0.73	0.62	49.9	14.7	149.1	0.3
2000	D	0.42	0.35	52.1	10.8	186.2	-11.0
1999	D-	0.19	0.16	44.1	7.1	172.0	-10.1
1998	D-	0.30	0.25	49.3	9.3	113.7	-16.9
1997	D-	0.28	0.19	26.5	-2.6	39.8	-14.1

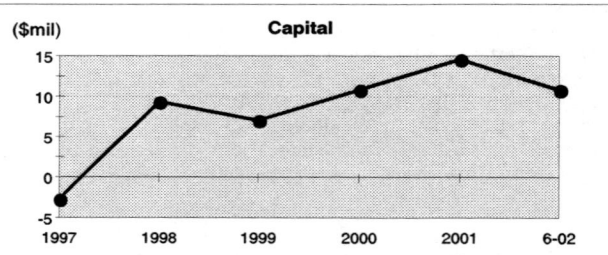

Capital ($mil)

REGENCE BL CROSS BL SHIELD OREGON — B- Good

Major Rating Factors: Fair profitability index (3.6 on a scale of 0 to 10) with operating losses during 2001. Fair quality investment portfolio (4.8). Good liquidity (7.0) with sufficient resources (cash flows and marketable investments) to handle a spike in claims.
Other Rating Factors: Strong capitalization (7.9) based on excellent current risk-adjusted capital (severe loss scenario) reflecting improvement over results in 2000.
Principal Business: Comp med (82%), FEHB (9%), dental (5%), med supp (3%).
Mem Phys: 02: N/A **01:** N/A **02 MLR** 77% / **02 Admin Exp** 13%
Enroll(000): Q1 03: 991 **02:** 1,018 **01:** 620 **Med Exp PMPM:** $105
Principal Investments: Nonaffiliate common stock (17%), cash and equiv (10%), real estate (7%), affiliate common stock (5%), other (61%)
Provider Compensation ($000): Contr fee ($900,660), bonus arrang ($81,990), capitation ($15,590), FFS ($14,498)
Total Member Encounters: Phys (3,941,351), non-phys (4,080,561)
Group Affiliation: Regence Group
Licensed in: OR, WA
Address: 100 SW Market St, Portland, OR 97201
Phone: (503) 225-5221 **Dom State:** OR **Commenced Bus:** June 1942

Data Date	Weiss Safety Rating	RACR #1	RACR #2	Total Assets ($mil)	Capital ($mil)	Net Premium ($mil)	Net Income ($mil)
3-03	B-	2.09	1.75	544.7	230.2	368.9	2.4
3-02	B-	2.83	2.15	559.8	272.6	325.8	3.7
2002	B-	2.14	1.78	561.6	235.6	1,343.8	10.4
2001	B-	2.84	2.15	557.4	266.3	1,086.8	-6.1
2000	B-	1.38	0.83	500.5	206.8	1,010.5	3.5
1999	B-	1.64	0.98	492.2	228.2	945.2	15.7
1998	B	1.86	1.11	495.6	234.7	849.3	18.9

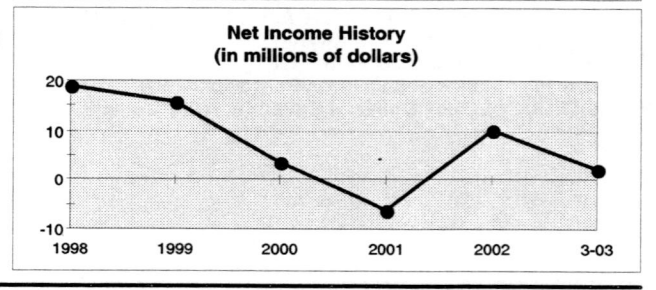

Net Income History (in millions of dollars)

Winter 2003 - 04   II. Analysis of Largest Companies

REGENCE BLUE CROSS BLUE SHIELD OF UT — B- Good

Major Rating Factors: Fair quality investment portfolio (4.9 on a scale of 0 to 10) containing little or no exposure to mortgages, junk bonds, or unaffiliated stocks. Good overall profitability index (5.6) despite a decline in earnings during 2002. Good liquidity (6.8) with sufficient resources (cash flows and marketable investments) to handle a spike in claims.
Other Rating Factors: Strong capitalization (8.6) based on excellent current risk-adjusted capital (severe loss scenario) reflecting significant improvement over results in 1999.
Principal Business: Comp med (61%), FEHB (26%), med supp (9%), stop loss (3%).
Mem Phys: 02: 7,600 **01:** 7,600 **02 MLR** 81% **/ 02 Admin Exp** 16%
Enroll(000): Q1 03: 322 **02:** 332 **01:** 251 **Med Exp PMPM:** $119
Principal Investments: Nonaffiliate common stock (25%), affiliate common stock (24%), cash and equiv (8%), real estate (6%), other (36%)
Provider Compensation ($000): Contr fee ($197,982), other ($209,270)
Total Member Encounters: Phys (1,799,435), non-phys (835,852)
Group Affiliation: Regence Group
Licensed in: UT
Address: 2980 E Cottonwood Pkwy, Salt Lake City, UT 84109
Phone: (801) 333-2000 **Dom State:** UT **Commenced Bus:** January 1945

Data Date	Weiss Safety Rating	RACR #1	RACR #2	Total Assets ($mil)	Capital ($mil)	Net Premium ($mil)	Net Income ($mil)
3-03	B-	2.63	2.19	252.7	84.8	135.7	2.8
3-02	B-	2.74	2.04	242.7	103.6	125.4	2.9
2002	B-	2.57	2.14	242.1	82.9	511.8	15.1
2001	B-	2.73	2.04	238.5	99.9	452.1	15.6
2000	C+	0.88	0.57	210.0	85.9	371.9	16.8
1999	C+	0.79	0.51	203.7	71.1	326.2	2.1
1998	B	0.89	0.58	169.7	71.1	283.5	-5.7

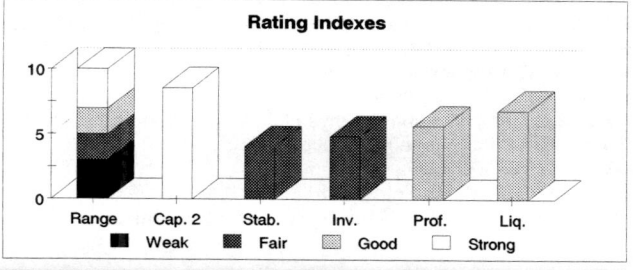

Rating Indexes chart: Range (Weak), Cap. 2 (Strong), Stab. (Fair), Inv. (Fair), Prof. (Good), Liq. (Good)

REGENCE BLUESHIELD — B Good

Major Rating Factors: Good liquidity (6.7 on a scale of 0 to 10) with sufficient resources (cash flows and marketable investments) to handle a spike in claims. Fair profitability index (4.5) due to a decline in earnings during 2002. Strong capitalization (10.0) based on excellent current risk-adjusted capital (severe loss scenario) despite some fluctuation in capital levels.
Other Rating Factors: High quality investment portfolio (7.4).
Principal Business: Comp med (79%), FEHB (7%), dental (6%), med supp (5%), Medicaid (3%).
Mem Phys: 02: 21,653 **01:** 21,577 **02 MLR** 82% **/ 02 Admin Exp** 17%
Enroll(000): Q1 03: 990 **02:** 1,018 **01:** 1,006 **Med Exp PMPM:** $102
Principal Investments: Nonaffiliate common stock (23%), cash and equiv (18%), affiliate common stock (8%), real estate (4%), other (47%)
Provider Compensation ($000): Contr fee ($1,254,471), capitation ($16,796)
Total Member Encounters: Phys (3,830,579), non-phys (3,360,833)
Group Affiliation: Regence Group
Licensed in: WA
Address: 1800 9th Ave, Seattle, WA 98101
Phone: (206) 464-3600 **Dom State:** WA **Commenced Bus:** April 1933

Data Date	Weiss Safety Rating	RACR #1	RACR #2	Total Assets ($mil)	Capital ($mil)	Net Premium ($mil)	Net Income ($mil)
3-03	B	3.71	3.10	796.9	349.7	405.8	4.6
3-02	B	3.47	2.51	798.5	422.1	359.1	6.6
2002	B	3.67	3.06	754.2	345.6	1,505.9	10.4
2001	B	3.46	2.50	779.7	411.6	1,452.7	39.9
2000	B	1.62	1.00	811.7	390.1	1,559.7	24.3
1999	B	1.74	1.05	768.7	390.9	1,329.6	21.9
1998	B	1.97	1.18	755.8	394.6	1,126.8	13.1

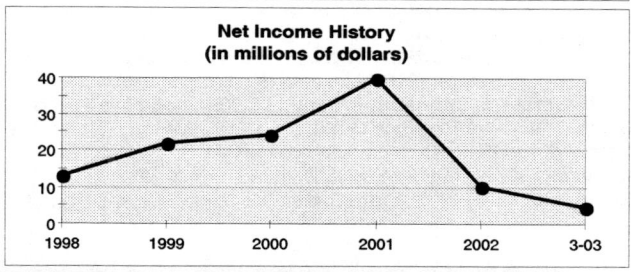

Net Income History (in millions of dollars): 1998 ~13, 1999 ~22, 2000 ~24, 2001 ~40, 2002 ~10, 3-03 ~5

REGENCE BLUESHIELD OF IDAHO INC — C Fair

Major Rating Factors: Poor current capitalization (2.6 on a scale of 0 to 10) based on excessive policy leverage and weak risk adjusted capital (moderate loss scenario), although results have slipped from the fair range during the last year. Weak profitability (2.0) with operating losses during the first six months of 2003. Weak liquidity (1.0).
Other Rating Factors: Weak overall results on stability tests (2.7). High quality investment portfolio (7.0).
Principal Business: Group health insurance (80%) and individual health insurance (20%).
Principal Investments: NonCMO investment grade bonds (51%), CMOs and structured securities (36%), real estate (5%), common & preferred stock (3%), and misc. investments (5%).
Investments in Affiliates: None
Group Affiliation: Regence Group
Licensed in: ID, WA
Commenced Business: April 1946
Address: 1602 21st Ave, Lewiston, ID 83501
Phone: (208) 798-2141 **Domicile State:** ID **NAIC Code:** 60131

Data Date	Weiss Safety Rating	RACR #1	RACR #2	Total Assets ($mil)	Capital ($mil)	Net Premium ($mil)	Net Income ($mil)
6-03	C	0.59	0.47	144.7	29.7	179.7	-5.3
6-02	C	0.84	0.67	141.4	46.7	225.6	-0.8
2002	C	0.76	0.61	165.3	36.7	451.3	-3.8
2001	C	1.04	0.83	146.7	48.2	405.9	2.1
2000	C	1.08	0.86	131.4	47.4	380.3	4.2
1999	C	1.26	0.99	125.2	45.4	310.1	3.8
1998	C	1.20	0.87	116.4	40.9	270.8	4.8

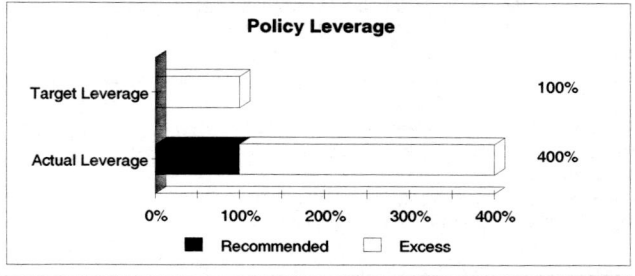

Policy Leverage chart: Target Leverage 100% (Recommended); Actual Leverage 400% (with Excess portion)

www.WeissRatings.com   * Denotes a Weiss Recommended Company

II. Analysis of Largest Companies — Winter 2003 - 04

REGENCE HEALTH MAINTENANCE OF OREGON — B — Good

Major Rating Factors: Good liquidity (7.0 on a scale of 0 to 10) with sufficient resources (cash flows and marketable investments) to handle a spike in claims. Fair profitability index (4.4) due to a decline in earnings during 2002. Return on equity has been low, averaging 3%. Strong overall capitalization (10.0) based on excellent current risk-adjusted capital (severe loss scenario) despite some fluctuation in capital levels.

Other Rating Factors: High quality investment portfolio (9.8) containing little or no exposure to mortgages, junk bonds, or unaffiliated stocks. Excellent overall results on stability tests (7.6) based on consistent premium and capital growth in the last five years. Rating is significantly influenced by the good financial results of Regence Group.

Principal Business: Comp med (85%), Medicare (15%).
Mem Phys: 02: 7,725 **01:** 7,462 **02 MLR** 84% **/ 02 Admin Exp** 16%
Enroll(000): Q1 03: 12 **02:** 13 **01:** 13 **Med Exp PMPM:** $153
Principal Investments: Cash and equiv (13%), other (87%).
Provider Compensation ($000): Bonus arrang ($19,118), contr fee ($3,795), capitation ($475), FFS ($379).
Total Member Encounters: Phys (114,331), non-phys (59,717)
Group Affiliation: Regence Group
Licensed in: OR, WA
Address: 100 SW Market St, Portland, OR 97201
Phone: (800) 452-7278 **Dom State:** OR **Commenced Bus:** March 1986

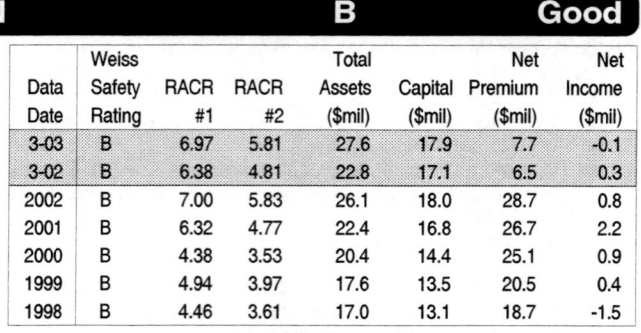

Data Date	Weiss Safety Rating	RACR #1	RACR #2	Total Assets ($mil)	Capital ($mil)	Net Premium ($mil)	Net Income ($mil)
3-03	B	6.97	5.81	27.6	17.9	7.7	-0.1
3-02	B	6.38	4.81	22.8	17.1	6.5	0.3
2002	B	7.00	5.83	26.1	18.0	28.7	0.8
2001	B	6.32	4.77	22.4	16.8	26.7	2.2
2000	B	4.38	3.53	20.4	14.4	25.1	0.9
1999	B	4.94	3.97	17.6	13.5	20.5	0.4
1998	B	4.46	3.61	17.0	13.1	18.7	-1.5

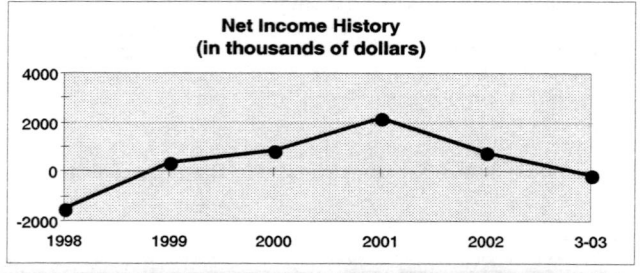

Net Income History (in thousands of dollars)

REGENCE HMO OREGON — B- — Good

Major Rating Factors: Fair profitability index (3.3 on a scale of 0 to 10) with operating losses during 1998, 1999 and 2002. Fair overall results on stability tests (4.6) based on weak risk-adjusted capital in prior years, an overall decline in enrollment over the past five years. Good liquidity (6.7) with sufficient resources (cash flows and marketable investments) to handle a spike in claims.

Other Rating Factors: Strong capitalization (8.5) based on excellent current risk-adjusted capital (severe loss scenario) reflecting significant improvement over results in 1999. High quality investment portfolio (9.7) containing little or no exposure to mortgages, junk bonds, or unaffiliated stocks.

Principal Business: Medicare (55%), comp med (45%).
Mem Phys: 02: 7,725 **01:** 7,462 **02 MLR** 88% **/ 02 Admin Exp** 12%
Enroll(000): Q1 03: 164 **02:** 181 **01:** 191 **Med Exp PMPM:** $218
Principal Investments: Cash and equiv (25%), affiliate common stock (10%), real estate (2%), other (62%).
Provider Compensation ($000): Bonus arrang ($347,627), contr fee ($110,231), capitation ($16,175), FFS ($9,233).
Total Member Encounters: Phys (2,702,839), non-phys (1,169,883)
Group Affiliation: Regence Group
Licensed in: OR
Address: 100 SW Market Street, Portland, OR 97201
Phone: (503) 225-5221 **Dom State:** OR **Commenced Bus:** March 1977

Data Date	Weiss Safety Rating	RACR #1	RACR #2	Total Assets ($mil)	Capital ($mil)	Net Premium ($mil)	Net Income ($mil)
3-03	B-	2.52	2.10	238.3	103.2	137.7	2.4
3-02	B-	2.05	1.64	224.7	116.7	136.6	1.0
2002	B-	2.44	2.04	238.1	101.1	549.6	-1.6
2001	B-	2.02	1.62	229.7	114.9	560.6	26.0
2000	B-	0.78	0.65	229.8	82.0	645.9	9.4
1999	B-	0.64	0.53	212.0	72.2	642.2	-13.9
1998	B	0.64	0.53	188.5	64.0	652.2	-16.1

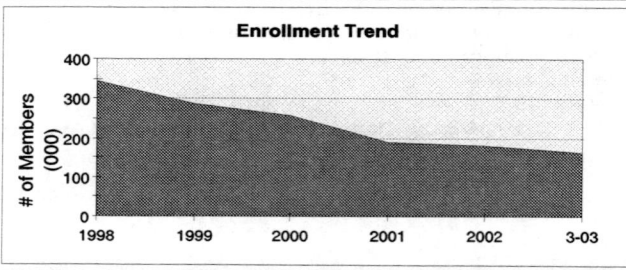

Enrollment Trend

REGENCECARE — C+ — Fair

Major Rating Factors: Fair overall results on stability tests (4.6 on a scale of 0 to 10) based on rapid premium growth over the last five years, rapid enrollment growth during the past five years. Rating is significantly influenced by the good financial results of Regence Group. Good liquidity (6.7) with sufficient resources (cash flows and marketable investments) to handle a spike in claims. Weak profitability index (0.9) with $17.4 million in losses in the last five years. Average return on equity over the last five years has been poor at -47%.

Other Rating Factors: Strong capitalization (9.4) based on excellent current risk-adjusted capital (severe loss scenario) reflecting improvement over results in 2000. High quality investment portfolio (9.9) containing little or no exposure to mortgages, junk bonds, or unaffiliated stocks.

Principal Business: Comp med (100%).
Mem Phys: 02: 12,872 **01:** 8,918 **02 MLR** 92% **/ 02 Admin Exp** 15%
Enroll(000): Q1 03: 34 **02:** 38 **01:** 42 **Med Exp PMPM:** $164
Principal Investments: Cash and equiv (43%), other (57%).
Provider Compensation ($000): Contr fee ($76,417), capitation ($1,534), bonus arrang ($1,149)
Total Member Encounters: Phys (196,217), non-phys (152,250)
Group Affiliation: Regence Group
Licensed in: WA
Address: 1800 Ninth Ave, Seattle, WA 98101
Phone: (206) 340-6600 **Dom State:** WA **Commenced Bus:** April 1986

Data Date	Weiss Safety Rating	RACR #1	RACR #2	Total Assets ($mil)	Capital ($mil)	Net Premium ($mil)	Net Income ($mil)
3-03	C+	3.32	2.76	32.1	20.9	22.6	0.3
3-02	B-	4.78	4.04	35.6	23.5	20.9	-0.1
2002	C+	3.24	2.70	32.3	20.5	85.5	-3.4
2001	B-	4.78	4.04	35.1	23.4	81.0	-1.1
2000	B-	1.09	0.93	41.0	12.7	147.9	-6.9
1999	B	1.21	1.02	21.1	7.1	72.8	-3.5
1998	B	1.35	1.17	11.2	3.3	24.0	-2.6

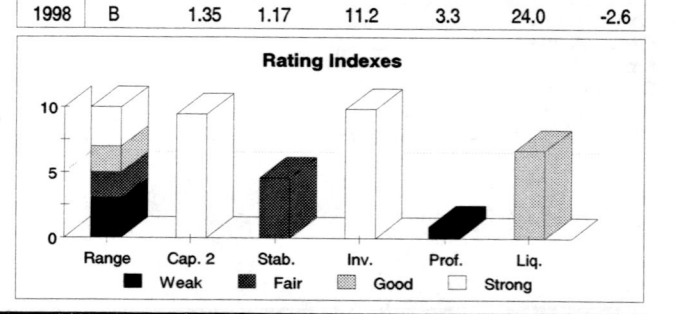

Rating Indexes: Range, Cap. 2, Stab., Inv., Prof., Liq. — Weak, Fair, Good, Strong

RELIANCE STANDARD LIFE INSURANCE COMPANY   C   Fair

Major Rating Factors: Good quality investment portfolio (5.1 on a scale of 0 to 10) despite mixed results such as: large holdings of BBB rated bonds but moderate junk bond exposure. Weak overall results on stability tests (2.0) including weak results on operational trends. Strong capitalization (7.1) based on excellent risk adjusted capital (severe loss scenario).
Other Rating Factors: Excellent profitability (7.7) with operating gains in each of the last five years. Excellent liquidity (7.4).
Principal Business: Group health insurance (43%), group life insurance (33%), individual annuities (13%), group retirement contracts (9%), and individual life insurance (2%).
Principal Investments: NonCMO investment grade bonds (56%), CMOs and structured securities (28%), common & preferred stock (6%), noninv. grade bonds (5%), and misc. investments (4%).
Investments in Affiliates: 2%
Group Affiliation: Delphi Financial Group Inc
Licensed in: All states except NY
Commenced Business: April 1907
Address: 115 S LaSalle St, Chicago, IL 60603
Phone: (215) 787-4000   **Domicile State:** IL   **NAIC Code:** 68381

Data Date	Weiss Safety Rating	RACR #1	RACR #2	Total Assets ($mil)	Capital ($mil)	Net Premium ($mil)	Net Income ($mil)
6-03	C	1.69	1.06	2,174.2	264.3	292.5	1.9
6-02	C	2.18	1.45	1,990.7	255.8	241.4	18.0
2002	C	1.69	1.11	2,117.2	252.1	561.3	27.4
2001	C	1.99	1.24	1,898.0	243.3	364.8	1.7
2000	C	1.93	1.19	1,835.7	248.5	502.9	55.6
1999	C	1.97	1.30	1,628.5	214.3	440.9	30.0
1998	C	1.85	1.21	1,558.5	191.4	359.0	19.6

Adverse Trends in Operations

Change in premium mix from 2001 to 2002 (5.4%)
Increase in policy surrenders from 2001 to 2002 (12312%)
Decrease in premium volume from 2000 to 2001 (27%)
Change in premium mix from 2000 to 2001 (7%)
Change in asset mix during 2000 (4.3%)

RESERVE NATIONAL INSURANCE COMPANY   B   Good

Major Rating Factors: Good overall results on stability tests (5.2 on a scale of 0 to 10). Strengths include good financial support from affiliation with Unitrin Inc, excellent operational trends and excellent risk diversification. Strong capitalization (9.9) based on excellent risk adjusted capital (severe loss scenario). Capital levels have been relatively consistent over the last five years. High quality investment portfolio (7.7).
Other Rating Factors: Excellent profitability (9.1) with operating gains in each of the last five years. Excellent liquidity (7.1).
Principal Business: Individual health insurance (72%), group health insurance (27%), and individual life insurance (1%).
Principal Investments: NonCMO investment grade bonds (84%), common & preferred stock (6%), cash (6%), real estate (2%), and noninv. grade bonds (1%).
Investments in Affiliates: None
Group Affiliation: Unitrin Inc
Licensed in: AL, AZ, AR, CO, FL, GA, ID, IL, IN, IA, KS, KY, LA, MS, MO, MT, NE, NV, NM, NC, OH, OK, OR, SC, SD, TN, TX, UT, VA, WA, WY
Commenced Business: September 1956
Address: 6100 NW Grand Blvd, Oklahoma City, OK 73118
Phone: (405) 848-7931   **Domicile State:** OK   **NAIC Code:** 68462

Data Date	Weiss Safety Rating	RACR #1	RACR #2	Total Assets ($mil)	Capital ($mil)	Net Premium ($mil)	Net Income ($mil)
6-03	B	3.91	2.95	143.4	81.9	58.5	3.6
6-02	B	3.96	2.97	138.7	81.1	56.4	1.4
2002	B	3.80	2.85	137.5	78.3	113.6	7.0
2001	B	4.00	3.00	137.6	80.4	108.3	8.2
2000	B	3.59	2.68	124.9	70.3	106.9	10.2
1999	B	3.08	2.31	114.1	60.0	107.8	8.7
1998	B-	2.17	1.64	107.4	41.7	110.2	7.4

Unitrin Inc
Composite Group Rating: B
Largest Group Members	Assets ($mil)	Weiss Safety Rating
TRINITY UNIVERSAL INS CO	2344	C
UNITED INS CO OF AMERICA	2069	B+
RELIABLE LIFE INS CO	636	B
UNION NATIONAL LIFE INS CO	366	A
RESERVE NATIONAL INS CO	137	B

RESOURCE LIFE INSURANCE COMPANY   C+   Fair

Major Rating Factors: Fair overall results on stability tests (3.3 on a scale of 0 to 10) including fair financial strength of affiliated Aon Corp. Strong capitalization (10.0) based on excellent risk adjusted capital (severe loss scenario). Capital levels have been relatively consistent over the last five years. High quality investment portfolio (8.2).
Other Rating Factors: Excellent profitability (7.8). Excellent liquidity (8.8).
Principal Business: Credit health insurance (54%), credit life insurance (42%), and reinsurance (4%).
Principal Investments: NonCMO investment grade bonds (132%), common & preferred stock (5%), CMOs and structured securities (4%), and noninv. grade bonds (2%).
Investments in Affiliates: 5%
Group Affiliation: Aon Corp
Licensed in: All states except NJ, PR
Commenced Business: December 1963
Address: 123 N Wacker Dr, Chicago, IL 60606
Phone: (312) 701-3700   **Domicile State:** IL   **NAIC Code:** 61506

Data Date	Weiss Safety Rating	RACR #1	RACR #2	Total Assets ($mil)	Capital ($mil)	Net Premium ($mil)	Net Income ($mil)
6-03	C+	4.54	3.34	113.5	32.7	1.4	1.5
6-02	B-	3.83	3.19	71.3	27.1	1.2	0.1
2002	C+	4.12	3.24	72.0	30.2	2.7	0.8
2001	B-	3.78	2.89	61.6	26.0	2.2	-0.6
2000	B-	4.01	3.12	48.9	25.4	1.4	3.1
1999	B-	3.83	3.14	61.8	26.7	6.0	0.7
1998	B-	4.49	4.04	44.5	26.7	3.0	2.7

Aon Corp
Composite Group Rating: C
Largest Group Members	Assets ($mil)	Weiss Safety Rating
COMBINED INS CO OF AMERICA	2261	C
VIRGINIA SURETY CO INC	1449	B-
COMBINED LIFE INS CO OF NEW YORK	273	C+
RESOURCE LIFE INS CO	72	C+
STERLING LIFE INS CO	61	C

II. Analysis of Largest Companies

Winter 2003 - 04

ROCHESTER AREA HEALTH MAINTENANCE OR — B — Good

Major Rating Factors: Good overall profitability index (7.0 on a scale of 0 to 10) despite operating losses during 1998. Good overall results on stability tests (5.8) despite excessive capital growth during 2002. Strong capitalization (7.9) based on excellent current risk-adjusted capital (severe loss scenario) reflecting significant improvement over results in 2000.
Other Rating Factors: High quality investment portfolio (9.9) containing no exposure to mortgages, junk bonds, or unaffiliated stocks. Excellent liquidity (7.2) with ample operational cash flow and liquid investments.
Principal Business: Medicare (56%), comp med (38%), Medicaid (6%)
Mem Phys: 02: 3,324 **01:** 3,075 **02 MLR** 86% **/ 02 Admin Exp** 9%
Enroll(000): 02: 149 **01:** 155 **Med Exp PMPM:** $236
Principal Investments: Cash and equiv (87%), other (13%)
Provider Compensation ($000): Capitation ($396,840), contr fee ($41,417)
Total Member Encounters: Phys (1,487,757), non-phys (706,448)
Group Affiliation: Preferred Care Inc
Licensed in: NY
Address: 259 Monroe Ave, Rochester, NY 14607
Phone: (585) 325-3920 **Dom State:** NY **Commenced Bus:** November 1979

Data Date	Weiss Safety Rating	RACR #1	RACR #2	Total Assets ($mil)	Capital ($mil)	Net Premium ($mil)	Net Income ($mil)
2002	B	2.05	1.71	120.7	55.7	499.0	24.4
2001	C+	0.92	0.81	87.4	26.9	442.2	17.5
2000	C	0.45	0.40	72.6	11.2	400.8	8.5
1999	C	0.77	0.67	75.6	18.2	341.7	3.0
1998	C	0.96	0.83	51.7	15.2	291.9	-11.1

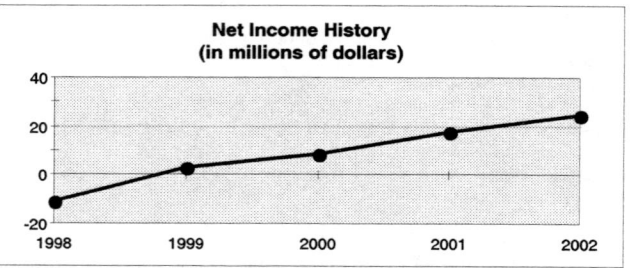

Net Income History (in millions of dollars)

ROCKY MOUNTAIN HEALTH MAINT ORG — D+ — Weak

Major Rating Factors: Poor capitalization index (2.2 on a scale of 0 to 10) based on weak current risk-adjusted capital (moderate loss scenario). Furthermore, this low level of risk-adjusted capital has been consistent in previous years. Fair profitability index (4.3) due to a decline in earnings during 2001. Good overall results on stability tests (5.6) despite inconsistent enrollment growth in the past five years due to declines in 1998 and 2001, weak risk-adjusted capital in prior years.
Other Rating Factors: Good liquidity (6.9) with sufficient resources (cash flows and marketable investments) to handle a spike in claims. High quality investment portfolio (9.9) containing no exposure to mortgages, junk bonds, or unaffiliated stocks.
Principal Business: Comp med (58%), Medicaid (24%), Medicare (14%), FEHB (4%)
Mem Phys: 01: 4,712 **00:** 4,490 **01 MLR** 88% **/ 01 Admin Exp** 12%
Enroll(000): Q2 02: 121 **01:** 119 **00:** 122 **Med Exp PMPM:** $180
Principal Investments: Cash and equiv (94%), other (6%)
Provider Compensation ($000): Capitation ($161,739), contr fee ($81,342), FFS ($17,687)
Total Member Encounters: N/A
Group Affiliation: Rocky Mountain Health Co
Licensed in: CO
Address: 2775 Crossroads Blvd, Grand Junction, CO 81506
Phone: (970) 244-7760 **Dom State:** CO **Commenced Bus:** January 1974

Data Date	Weiss Safety Rating	RACR #1	RACR #2	Total Assets ($mil)	Capital ($mil)	Net Premium ($mil)	Net Income ($mil)
6-02	D+	0.49	0.43	61.6	14.4	164.8	0.5
6-01	D+	0.62	0.55	68.7	14.9	147.4	3.3
2001	D+	0.50	0.44	65.1	12.9	296.7	1.8
2000	D	0.48	0.42	67.0	11.5	268.8	3.8
1999	D	0.39	0.34	56.6	7.5	N/A	1.0
1998	D+	0.68	0.57	47.7	10.7	N/A	2.4
1997	D+	0.50	0.33	39.0	8.4	N/A	-1.9

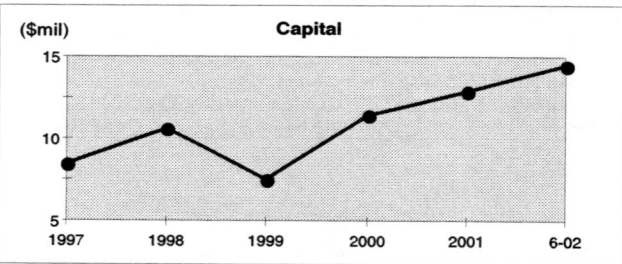

Capital ($mil)

ROCKY MOUNTAIN HOSPITAL & MEDICAL — C+ — Fair

Major Rating Factors: Good liquidity (6.9 on a scale of 0 to 10) with sufficient resources (cash flows and marketable investments) to handle a spike in claims. Weak profitability index (0.9) with operating losses during 1999 and 2000. Strong capitalization (10.0) based on excellent current risk-adjusted capital (severe loss scenario).
Other Rating Factors: High quality investment portfolio (8.3) containing little or no exposure to mortgages, junk bonds, or unaffiliated stocks.
Principal Business: Comp med (57%), FEHB (37%), med supp (5%), dental (2%)
Mem Phys: 02: 14,879 **01:** 16,869 **02 MLR** 77% **/ 02 Admin Exp** 12%
Enroll(000): Q1 03: 365 **02:** 293 **01:** 264 **Med Exp PMPM:** $135
Principal Investments: Affiliate common stock (32%), real estate (7%), cash and equiv (2%), other (59%)
Provider Compensation ($000): FFS ($302,053), contr fee ($134,189), bonus arrang ($1)
Total Member Encounters: Phys (947,207), non-phys (669,395)
Group Affiliation: Anthem Ins Companies Inc
Licensed in: CO, NV
Address: 700 Broadway, Denver, CO 80273
Phone: (303) 831-2131 **Dom State:** CO **Commenced Bus:** October 1938

Data Date	Weiss Safety Rating	RACR #1	RACR #2	Total Assets ($mil)	Capital ($mil)	Net Premium ($mil)	Net Income ($mil)
3-03	C+	3.71	3.09	335.5	154.5	170.2	22.3
3-02	C+	0.00	0.00	262.1	110.5	139.7	5.3
2002	C	3.30	2.75	306.3	136.2	581.3	46.1
2001	U	1.15	0.86	258.8	110.3	447.4	33.2
2000	C-	0.69	0.49	197.3	61.8	348.2	-0.2
1999	N/A	N/A	N/A	201.1	48.6	272.7	-229.8
1998	N/A	N/A	N/A	152.7	39.2	233.8	N/A

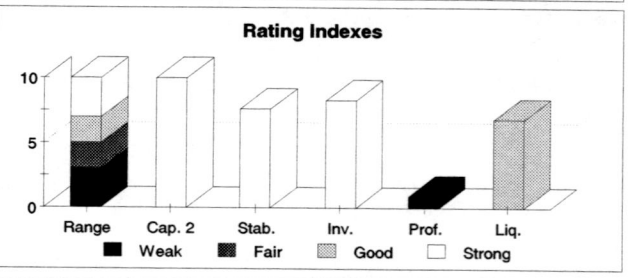

Rating Indexes — Range, Cap. 2, Stab., Inv., Prof., Liq. ■ Weak ▨ Fair ▦ Good □ Strong

www.WeissRatings.com

Winter 2003 - 04

II. Analysis of Largest Companies

ROYAL STATE NATIONAL INSURANCE COMPANY LIMITED C+ Fair

Major Rating Factors: Fair overall results on stability tests (4.3 on a scale of 0 to 10) including fair financial strength of affiliated Royal State Group. Strong capitalization (9.5) based on excellent risk adjusted capital (severe loss scenario). Moreover, capital levels have been consistently high over the last five years. High quality investment portfolio (9.0).
Other Rating Factors: Excellent profitability (9.0) with operating gains in each of the last five years. Excellent liquidity (7.1).
Principal Business: Reinsurance (41%), group health insurance (36%), group life insurance (21%), and individual life insurance (2%).
Principal Investments: NonCMO investment grade bonds (89%), cash (5%), and common & preferred stock (3%).
Investments in Affiliates: 3%
Group Affiliation: Royal State Group
Licensed in: HI
Commenced Business: August 1961
Address: 819 S Beretania St, Honolulu, HI 96813
Phone: (808) 539-1600   **Domicile State:** HI   **NAIC Code:** 68551

Data Date	Weiss Safety Rating	RACR #1	RACR #2	Total Assets ($mil)	Capital ($mil)	Net Premium ($mil)	Net Income ($mil)
6-03	C+	3.38	2.69	47.5	26.5	14.6	2.8
6-02	C-	2.99	2.32	45.3	23.3	14.0	3.6
2002	C-	3.36	2.65	46.0	25.5	28.8	6.7
2001	C-	3.08	2.39	41.9	22.5	27.0	6.2
2000	C-	3.04	2.30	38.1	18.9	20.2	3.7
1999	C-	3.02	2.23	32.5	16.0	14.9	3.7
1998	C-	3.53	2.71	29.4	14.2	13.1	3.6

Royal State Group Composite Group Rating: C- Largest Group Members	Assets ($mil)	Weiss Safety Rating
DTRIC INS CO LTD	49	C-
ROYAL STATE NATIONAL INS CO LTD	46	C+

SAINT MARYS HEALTHFIRST D- Weak

Major Rating Factors: Weak profitability index (0.7 on a scale of 0 to 10) with $37.7 million in losses in the last five years. Average return on equity over the last five years has been extremely poor. Weak overall results on stability tests (0.5) based on a steep decline in premium revenue in 2002. Good quality investment portfolio (5.5).
Other Rating Factors: Good liquidity (6.9) with sufficient resources (cash flows and marketable investments) to handle a spike in claims. Strong capitalization index (8.3) based on excellent current risk-adjusted capital (severe loss scenario).
Principal Business: Med only (84%), dental (2%), other (14%)
Mem Phys: 02: 1,027   01: 956   **02 MLR** 84%   / **02 Admin Exp** 19%
Enroll(000): Q1 03: 65   02: 30   01: 31   **Med Exp PMPM:** $168
Principal Investments: Cash and equiv (44%), nonaffiliate common stock (37%), real estate (19%)
Provider Compensation ($000): Contr fee ($56,340), capitation ($12,382)
Total Member Encounters: Phys (118,630), non-phys (96,744)
Group Affiliation: Saint Mary's Health Care Corp
Licensed in: NV
Address: 1510 Meadow Wood Lane, Reno, NV 89502
Phone: (775) 770-6000   **Dom State:** NV   **Commenced Bus:** June 1993

Data Date	Weiss Safety Rating	RACR #1	RACR #2	Total Assets ($mil)	Capital ($mil)	Net Premium ($mil)	Net Income ($mil)
3-03	D-	2.37	1.98	26.0	7.0	21.0	0.1
3-02	D-	0.94	0.73	33.8	12.1	16.3	-0.5
2002	D-	1.77	1.48	24.1	5.1	73.1	-0.5
2001	D-	0.94	0.73	39.8	12.4	107.7	-12.3
2000	E+	0.23	0.20	27.9	2.6	84.1	-3.5
1999	E+	0.22	0.19	14.5	2.4	51.8	-12.5
1998	D-	0.49	0.42	12.8	2.3	33.2	-9.0

Net Income History (in millions of dollars)

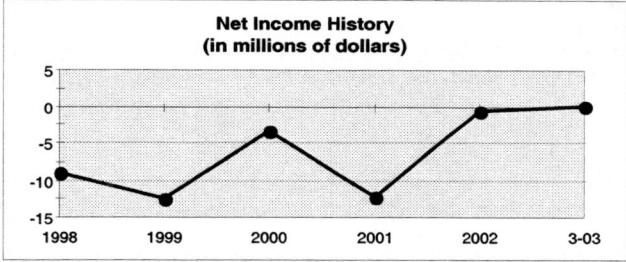

SAN FRANCISCO HEALTH PLAN B Good

Major Rating Factors: Good overall results on stability tests (5.9 on a scale of 0 to 10) despite rapid enrollment growth during the past five years. Excellent profitability (8.9) with operating gains in each of the last five years. Strong capitalization index (7.6) based on excellent current risk-adjusted capital (severe loss scenario).
Other Rating Factors: Excellent liquidity (7.5) with ample operational cash flow and liquid investments.
Principal Business: Medicaid (77%), comp med (23%)
Mem Phys: 02: N/A   01: N/A   **02 MLR** 87%   / **02 Admin Exp** 9%
Enroll(000): Q1 03: 40   02: 38   01: 34   **Med Exp PMPM:** $104
Principal Investments ($000): Cash and equiv ($20,850)
Provider Compensation ($000): None
Total Member Encounters: N/A
Group Affiliation: None
Licensed in: CA
Address: 568 Howard St 5th Floor, San Francisco, CA 94105
Phone: (415) 547-7800   **Dom State:** CA   **Commenced Bus:** March 1996

Data Date	Weiss Safety Rating	RACR #1	RACR #2	Total Assets ($mil)	Capital ($mil)	Net Premium ($mil)	Net Income ($mil)
3-03	B	2.52	1.56	25.1	12.1	14.9	0.7
3-02	B-	0.00	0.00	20.7	9.6	12.1	0.9
2002	B	2.36	1.46	22.6	11.4	51.7	2.7
2001	B-	0.00	0.00	18.7	8.7	44.4	2.5
2000	B-	1.43	0.91	16.4	6.2	36.7	1.1
1999	C-	1.32	0.84	17.8	5.1	31.1	1.8
1998	C-	1.16	0.74	10.8	3.4	26.7	2.6

Net Income History (in thousands of dollars)

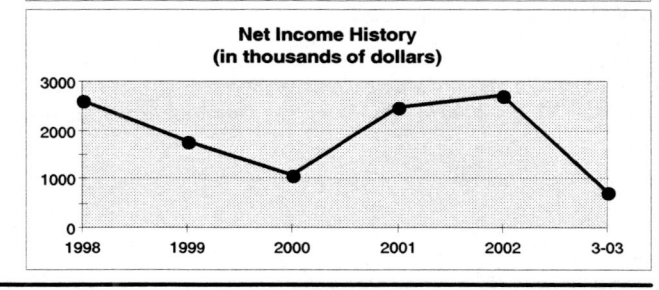

II. Analysis of Largest Companies
Winter 2003 - 04

SAN MATEO HEALTH COMMISSION — C- Fair

Major Rating Factors: Fair overall results on stability tests (3.1 on a scale of 0 to 10) based on good risk-adjusted capital in prior years. Weak profitability index (0.9) with operating losses during 1999, 2000 and 2001. Good capitalization (6.8) based on excellent current risk-adjusted capital (severe loss scenario). However, capital levels have fluctuated during prior years.
Other Rating Factors: Excellent liquidity (7.0) with ample operational cash flow and liquid investments.
Principal Business: None
Mem Phys: 02: N/A **01:** N/A **02 MLR** 94% **/ 02 Admin Exp** 9%
Enroll(000): Q1 03: 49 **02:** 47 **01:** 41 **Med Exp PMPM:** $194
Principal Investments ($000): Cash and equiv ($31,207), bonds ($5,991), other ($13,487)
Provider Compensation ($000): None
Total Member Encounters: N/A
Group Affiliation: None
Licensed in: CA
Address: 701 Gateway Blvd Ste 400, S San Francisco, CA 94080
Phone: (650) 616-0050 **Dom State:** CA **Commenced Bus:** December 1987

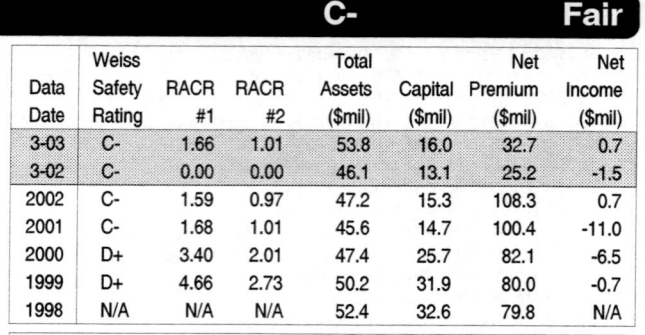

Data Date	Weiss Safety Rating	RACR #1	RACR #2	Total Assets ($mil)	Capital ($mil)	Net Premium ($mil)	Net Income ($mil)
3-03	C-	1.66	1.01	53.8	16.0	32.7	0.7
3-02	C-	0.00	0.00	46.1	13.1	25.2	-1.5
2002	C-	1.59	0.97	47.2	15.3	108.3	0.7
2001	C-	1.68	1.01	45.6	14.7	100.4	-11.0
2000	D+	3.40	2.01	47.4	25.7	82.1	-6.5
1999	D+	4.66	2.73	50.2	31.9	80.0	-0.7
1998	N/A	N/A	N/A	52.4	32.6	79.8	N/A

Net Income History (in millions of dollars) — chart spanning 1998 to 3-03.

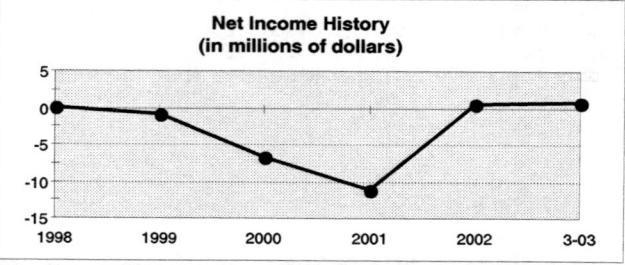

SANTA CLARA COUNTY — D+ Weak

Major Rating Factors: Fair capitalization index (4.2 on a scale of 0 to 10) based on weak current risk-adjusted capital (moderate loss scenario). Fair overall results on stability tests (4.9). Excellent profitability (8.2) despite a decline in earnings during 2002.
Other Rating Factors: Excellent liquidity (7.1) with ample operational cash flow and liquid investments.
Principal Business: Managed care (30%)
Mem Phys: 02: N/A **01:** N/A **02 MLR** 89% **/ 02 Admin Exp** 10%
Enroll(000): Q1 03: 49 **02:** 46 **01:** 47 **Med Exp PMPM:** $88
Principal Investments ($000): Cash and equiv ($12,229)
Provider Compensation ($000): None
Total Member Encounters: N/A
Group Affiliation: None
Licensed in: CA
Address: 2325 Enborg Lane Suite 290, San Jose, CA 95128
Phone: (408) 885-4760 **Dom State:** CA **Commenced Bus:** September 1985

Data Date	Weiss Safety Rating	RACR #1	RACR #2	Total Assets ($mil)	Capital ($mil)	Net Premium ($mil)	Net Income ($mil)
3-03	D+	0.68	0.42	13.8	3.8	15.3	0.1
3-02	D	0.00	0.00	10.5	3.4	12.4	0.2
2002	D+	0.67	0.41	13.7	3.7	54.9	0.5
2001	D	0.74	0.46	12.1	3.2	42.5	0.6
2000	N/A	N/A	N/A	N/A	N/A	N/A	N/A
1999	D-	0.40	0.25	7.7	1.7	37.5	0.2
1998	D-	0.39	0.24	2.4	1.5	31.7	0.2

Risk-Adjusted Capital Ratio #1 (Moderate Loss Scenario) — bar chart with Weak / Fair / Good ranges.

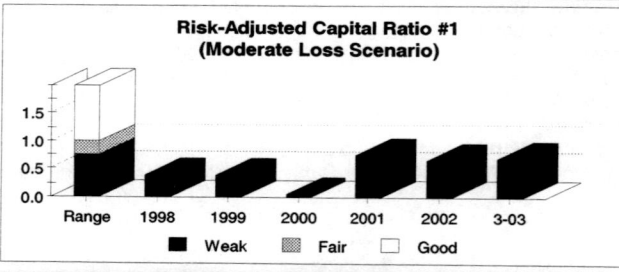

SANTA CLARA COUNTY HEALTH AUTHORITY — B Good

Major Rating Factors: Good overall results on stability tests (5.9 on a scale of 0 to 10) despite rapid enrollment growth during the past five years. Excellent profitability (9.1) with operating gains in each of the last five years. Strong capitalization index (7.8) based on excellent current risk-adjusted capital (severe loss scenario).
Other Rating Factors: Excellent liquidity (7.4) with ample operational cash flow and liquid investments.
Principal Business: Managed care (18%)
Mem Phys: 02: N/A **01:** N/A **02 MLR** 82% **/ 02 Admin Exp** 11%
Enroll(000): Q1 03: 79 **02:** 75 **01:** 53 **Med Exp PMPM:** $95
Principal Investments ($000): Cash and equiv ($18,581), other ($995)
Provider Compensation ($000): None
Total Member Encounters: N/A
Group Affiliation: None
Licensed in: CA
Address: 210 E Hacienda Ave, Campbell, CA 95008
Phone: (408) 376-2000 **Dom State:** CA **Commenced Bus:** February 1997

Data Date	Weiss Safety Rating	RACR #1	RACR #2	Total Assets ($mil)	Capital ($mil)	Net Premium ($mil)	Net Income ($mil)
3-03	B	2.68	1.66	33.9	18.5	26.6	0.7
3-02	C+	0.00	0.00	24.8	14.5	18.6	0.8
2002	B	2.58	1.60	28.9	17.9	88.1	4.2
2001	C+	0.00	0.00	23.0	13.7	61.0	2.6
2000	C+	2.31	1.51	19.5	11.1	54.7	5.0
1999	D	1.62	1.01	18.9	6.1	55.2	5.0
1998	E	0.22	0.14	11.4	1.1	47.1	4.1

Net Income History (in thousands of dollars) — chart spanning 1998 to 3-03.

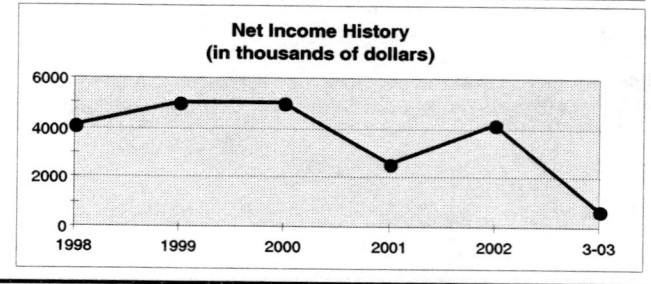

Winter 2003 - 04
II. Analysis of Largest Companies

SANTA CRUZ-MONTEREY MGD MED CARE — C — Fair

Major Rating Factors: Good overall results on stability tests (6.0 on a scale of 0 to 10). Excellent profitability (7.9). Strong overall capitalization (7.1) based on excellent current risk-adjusted capital (severe loss scenario).
Other Rating Factors: Excellent liquidity (7.1) with ample operational cash flow and liquid investments.
Principal Business: Managed care (2%)
Mem Phys: 02: N/A   **01:** N/A   **02 MLR** 93%   **/ 02 Admin Exp** 6%
Enroll(000): Q1 03: 87   **02:** 85   **01:** 288   **Med Exp PMPM:** $84
Principal Investments ($000): Cash and equiv ($58,622), other ($6,115)
Provider Compensation ($000): None
Total Member Encounters: N/A
Group Affiliation: None
Licensed in: CA
Address: 375 Encinal St Ste A, Santa Cruz, CA 95060
Phone: (831) 457-3850   **Dom State:** CA   **Commenced Bus:** N/A

Data Date	Weiss Safety Rating	RACR #1	RACR #2	Total Assets ($mil)	Capital ($mil)	Net Premium ($mil)	Net Income ($mil)
3-03	C	1.89	1.18	78.3	37.3	52.3	0.6
3-02	N/A	N/A	N/A	73.5	32.4	47.7	0.1
2002	U	1.86	1.16	79.2	36.7	203.5	4.4
2001	N/A	N/A	N/A	70.9	32.3	188.4	13.1
2000	N/A	N/A	N/A	54.0	19.2	143.2	6.3
1999	N/A	N/A	N/A	N/A	N/A	N/A	N/A
1998	N/A	N/A	N/A	N/A	N/A	N/A	N/A

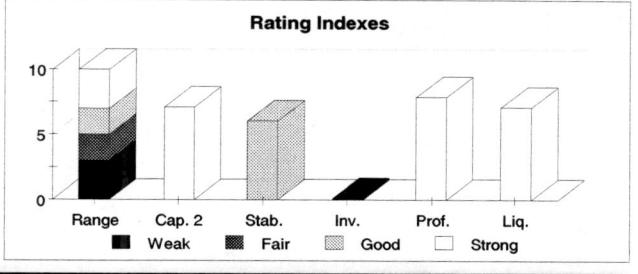

SCAN HEALTH PLAN — E — Very Weak

Major Rating Factors: Good overall results on stability tests (6.1 on a scale of 0 to 10) despite rapid enrollment growth during the past five years. Excellent profitability (8.9) with operating gains in each of the last five years. Strong capitalization (10.0) based on excellent current risk-adjusted capital (severe loss scenario) reflecting significant improvement over results in 1999.
Other Rating Factors: Excellent liquidity (7.7) with ample operational cash flow and liquid investments.
Principal Business: None
Mem Phys: 02: N/A   **01:** N/A   **02 MLR** 83%   **/ 02 Admin Exp** 7%
Enroll(000): Q1 03: 51   **02:** 54   **01:** 47   **Med Exp PMPM:** $415
Principal Investments ($000): Cash and equiv ($145,945), bonds ($5,120)
Provider Compensation ($000): None
Total Member Encounters: N/A
Group Affiliation: None
Licensed in: CA
Address: 3780 Kilroy Airport Way #600, Long Beach, CA 90806-2460
Phone: (562) 989-5100   **Dom State:** CA   **Commenced Bus:** March 1985

Data Date	Weiss Safety Rating	RACR #1	RACR #2	Total Assets ($mil)	Capital ($mil)	Net Premium ($mil)	Net Income ($mil)
3-03	E	5.11	3.16	181.1	82.8	153.1	29.5
3-02	C-	0.00	0.00	117.0	14.4	127.9	-5.5
2002	E-	3.27	2.02	162.7	53.3	302.9	35.0
2001	C-	0.75	0.46	115.2	19.9	438.4	1.1
2000	C-	1.21	0.76	100.5	18.8	340.4	6.9
1999	C-	0.63	0.40	44.1	11.9	279.7	5.1
1998	C-	0.72	0.46	21.3	6.8	170.2	1.8

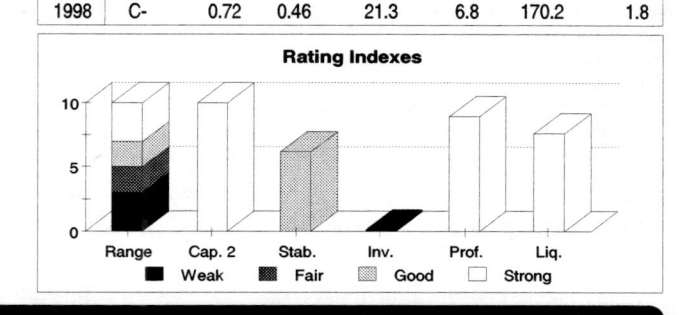

SCOTT & WHITE HEALTH PLAN — B — Good

Major Rating Factors: Good overall profitability index (5.3 on a scale of 0 to 10) despite operating losses during 1998. Strong capitalization (7.4) based on excellent current risk-adjusted capital (severe loss scenario) reflecting significant improvement over results in 1998. High quality investment portfolio (9.7) containing little or no exposure to mortgages, junk bonds, or unaffiliated stocks.
Other Rating Factors: Excellent overall results on stability tests (8.2) based on steady enrollment growth, averaging 4% over the past five years, consistent premium and capital growth in the last five years. Excellent liquidity (7.0) with ample operational cash flow and liquid investments.
Principal Business: Comp med (79%), Medicare (20%)
Mem Phys: 02: 641   **01:** 613   **02 MLR** 85%   **/ 02 Admin Exp** 11%
Enroll(000): Q1 03: 168   **02:** 168   **01:** 163   **Med Exp PMPM:** $176
Principal Investments: Cash and equiv (69%), nonaffiliate common stock (4%), other (26%)
Provider Compensation ($000): Capitation ($244,445), contr fee ($43,671), FFS ($21,006), bonus arrang ($10,576)
Total Member Encounters: Phys (958,118)
Group Affiliation: Scott & White Group
Licensed in: TX
Address: 2401 S 31st St, Temple, TX 76508
Phone: (254) 298-3000   **Dom State:** TX   **Commenced Bus:** January 1982

Data Date	Weiss Safety Rating	RACR #1	RACR #2	Total Assets ($mil)	Capital ($mil)	Net Premium ($mil)	Net Income ($mil)
3-03	B	1.68	1.40	79.5	33.3	110.6	3.1
3-02	C+	0.00	0.00	59.7	24.6	93.1	0.5
2002	B	1.46	1.22	79.7	29.0	409.6	4.0
2001	C+	0.89	0.76	60.7	24.8	344.5	0.6
2000	C+	0.83	0.72	53.2	19.5	285.0	0.5
1999	C	0.78	0.67	63.1	17.7	264.1	2.7
1998	C	0.70	0.61	58.3	13.2	221.6	-1.0

www.WeissRatings.com   * Denotes a Weiss Recommended Company

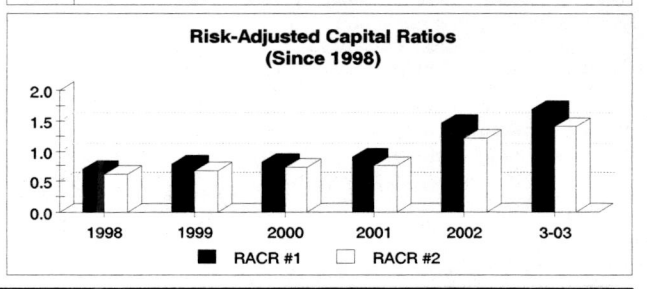

II. Analysis of Largest Companies

SCRIPPS CLINIC HEALTH PLAN SERVICES E   Very Weak

Major Rating Factors: Poor capitalization index (0.0 on a scale of 0 to 10) based on weak current risk-adjusted capital (severe loss scenario). Weak liquidity (0.1) as a spike in claims may stretch capacity. Fair overall results on stability tests (4.9) based on poor risk diversification due to the company's size.
Other Rating Factors: Good overall profitability index (6.2).
Principal Business: Managed care (100%)
Mem Phys: 02: N/A **01:** N/A **02 MLR** 100% / **02 Admin Exp** 4%
Enroll(000): Q1 03: 142 **02:** 152 **01:** 174 **Med Exp PMPM:** $136
Principal Investments ($000): Cash and equiv ($24,625)
Provider Compensation ($000): None
Total Member Encounters: N/A
Group Affiliation: Scripps Health
Licensed in: CA
Address: 10170 Sorrento Valley Rd, San Diego, CA 92121
Phone: (858) 784-5961 **Dom State:** CA **Commenced Bus:** October 1997

Data Date	Weiss Safety Rating	RACR #1	RACR #2	Total Assets ($mil)	Capital ($mil)	Net Premium ($mil)	Net Income ($mil)
3-03	E	0.16	0.09	24.3	3.7	61.4	0.0
3-02	E	0.00	0.00	25.3	3.6	69.1	0.0
2002	E	0.16	0.09	29.3	3.7	266.8	0.2
2001	E	0.11	0.06	24.0	3.6	266.9	-0.2
2000	U	0.03	0.02	16.8	1.7	177.5	0.6
1999	N/A	N/A	N/A	N/A	N/A	N/A	N/A
1998	N/A	N/A	N/A	N/A	N/A	N/A	N/A

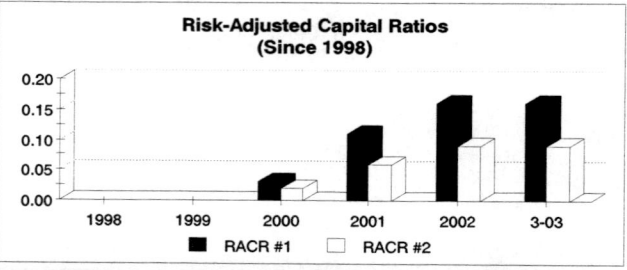

Risk-Adjusted Capital Ratios (Since 1998)

SD STATE MEDICAL HOLDING CO D+   Weak

Major Rating Factors: Weak profitability index (1.2 on a scale of 0 to 10) with operating losses during 1999, 2001 and 2002. Average return on equity has been poor at -1%. Poor capitalization (2.2) based on weak current risk-adjusted capital (moderate loss scenario) as results have slipped from the fair range over the last two years. Fair overall results on stability tests (4.5) based on weak risk-adjusted capital in prior years.
Other Rating Factors: Good liquidity (5.6) with sufficient resources (cash flows and marketable investments) to handle a spike in claims. High quality investment portfolio (9.4) containing little or no exposure to mortgages, junk bonds, or unaffiliated stocks.
Principal Business: Comp med (100%)
Mem Phys: 02: 1,350 **01:** 1,260 **02 MLR** 93% / **02 Admin Exp** 10%
Enroll(000): Q1 03: 38 **02:** 40 **01:** 35 **Med Exp PMPM:** $160
Principal Investments: Cash and equiv (62%), affiliate common stock (9%), nonaffiliate common stock (1%), other (28%).
Provider Compensation ($000): Contr fee ($71,199), other ($518)
Total Member Encounters: Phys (153,905), non-phys (35,268)
Group Affiliation: South Dakota State Medical Holding
Licensed in: SD
Address: 1323 S Minnesota Ave, Sioux Falls, SD 57105
Phone: (605) 334-4000 **Dom State:** SD **Commenced Bus:** April 1986

Data Date	Weiss Safety Rating	RACR #1	RACR #2	Total Assets ($mil)	Capital ($mil)	Net Premium ($mil)	Net Income ($mil)
3-03	D+	0.52	0.43	19.6	6.5	20.8	-0.5
3-02	C	0.76	0.64	19.0	7.5	18.3	-0.2
2002	D+	0.51	0.42	19.5	6.4	77.1	-1.9
2001	C	0.76	0.64	17.9	7.4	58.5	-0.9
2000	C	1.10	0.92	15.4	7.3	43.7	1.8
1999	C	0.86	0.72	11.5	5.6	34.2	-0.2
1998	C+	1.02	0.84	12.3	6.7	35.6	0.6

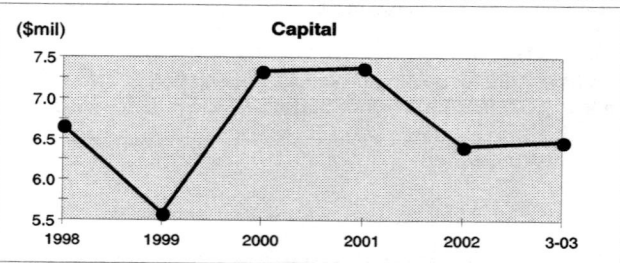

Capital

SEARS LIFE INSURANCE COMPANY C   Fair

Major Rating Factors: Fair overall results on stability tests (3.4 on a scale of 0 to 10). Good overall profitability (6.9). Return on equity has been excellent over the last five years averaging 24.4%. Strong capitalization (8.0) based on excellent risk adjusted capital (severe loss scenario). Moreover, capital has steadily grown over the last five years.
Other Rating Factors: High quality investment portfolio (8.2). Excellent liquidity (8.4).
Principal Business: Group health insurance (64%), group life insurance (29%), individual health insurance (6%), and individual life insurance (1%).
Principal Investments: NonCMO investment grade bonds (76%) and CMOs and structured securities (24%).
Investments in Affiliates: None
Group Affiliation: Sears Life Holding
Licensed in: All states except CT, GA, NH, NJ, NY, PR
Commenced Business: May 1956
Address: 10255 W Higgins Rd Ste 700, Rosemont, IL 60018
Phone: (847) 375-8001 **Domicile State:** IL **NAIC Code:** 69914

Data Date	Weiss Safety Rating	RACR #1	RACR #2	Total Assets ($mil)	Capital ($mil)	Net Premium ($mil)	Net Income ($mil)
6-03	C	7.15	6.43	56.2	47.6	0.0	4.7
6-02	C	6.89	6.20	46.1	40.4	0.0	2.6
2002	C	6.46	5.81	49.3	43.1	0.0	5.1
2001	C	6.44	5.80	42.0	37.9	0.0	0.9
2000	C	5.01	4.51	43.9	30.5	0.0	15.6
1999	C	4.32	3.88	33.3	21.3	0.0	6.2
1998	C	3.97	3.58	23.0	15.2	0.0	4.6

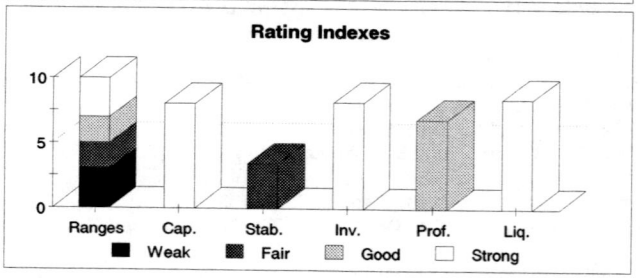

Rating Indexes
Ranges, Cap., Stab., Inv., Prof., Liq.
■ Weak ▨ Fair ▨ Good ☐ Strong

Winter 2003 - 04
II. Analysis of Largest Companies

SECURECARE OF IOWA INC — C — Fair

Major Rating Factors: Fair liquidity (3.3 on a scale of 0 to 10) as cash resources may not be adequate to cover a spike in claims. Good overall profitability index (5.4). Good capitalization (5.8) based on good current risk-adjusted capital (severe loss scenario) reflecting significant improvement over results in 2001.

Other Rating Factors: Good overall results on stability tests (5.5) based on consistent premium and capital growth in the last five years but a decline in enrollment during 2002. High quality investment portfolio (8.5).
Principal Business: Comp med (97%), FEHB (3%)
Mem Phys: 02: 1,925   **01:** 2,100   **02 MLR** 93%   **/ 02 Admin Exp** 9%
Enroll(000): Q1 03: 0   **02:** 13   **01:** 29   **Med Exp PMPM:** $195
Principal Investments: Cash and equiv (47%), nonaffiliate common stock (29%), affiliate common stock (7%), other (16%)
Provider Compensation ($000): Contr fee ($49,076), capitation ($143)
Total Member Encounters: Phys (93,782)
Group Affiliation: None
Licensed in: IA
Address: 11111 Aurora Ave, Des Moines, IA 50322
Phone: (515) 331-7878   **Dom State:** IA   **Commenced Bus:** October 1994

Data Date	Weiss Safety Rating	RACR #1	RACR #2	Total Assets ($mil)	Capital ($mil)	Net Premium ($mil)	Net Income ($mil)
3-03	C	1.04	0.87	18.9	7.7	0.0	0.5
3-02	C-	0.61	0.48	19.5	5.4	15.4	0.1
2002	C	0.93	0.77	21.4	6.9	53.1	1.5
2001	C-	0.61	0.48	19.5	5.2	56.5	0.4
2000	C-	0.62	0.52	18.2	4.4	54.6	0.6
1999	N/A	N/A	N/A	16.0	4.5	51.0	N/A
1998	N/A	N/A	N/A	11.8	3.9	39.2	N/A

Rating Indexes chart: Range, Cap. 2, Stab., Inv., Prof., Liq. (Weak, Fair, Good, Strong)

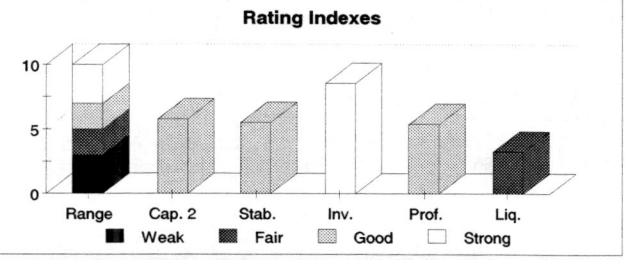

SECURITY HEALTH PLAN OF WI INC — B- — Good

Major Rating Factors: Fair profitability index (4.2 on a scale of 0 to 10) with operating losses during 1999. Good capitalization (5.0) based on good current risk-adjusted capital (severe loss scenario) reflecting significant improvement over results in 2000. Good overall results on stability tests (5.5) despite weak risk-adjusted capital in prior years.

Other Rating Factors: Good liquidity (6.9) with sufficient resources (cash flows and marketable investments) to handle a spike in claims. High quality investment portfolio (9.9) containing no exposure to mortgages, junk bonds, or unaffiliated stocks.
Principal Business: Comp med (77%), Medicaid (13%), med supp (9%)
Mem Phys: 02: 1,360   **01:** 1,271   **02 MLR** 89%   **/ 02 Admin Exp** 8%
Enroll(000): Q1 03: 116   **02:** 117   **01:** 118   **Med Exp PMPM:** $181
Principal Investments: Cash and equiv (22%), other (78%)
Provider Compensation ($000): Contr fee ($174,563), capitation ($76,847)
Total Member Encounters: N/A
Group Affiliation: Marshfield Clinic
Licensed in: WI
Address: 1515 Saint Joseph Ave, Marshfield, WI 54449
Phone: (715) 221-9555   **Dom State:** WI   **Commenced Bus:** September 1986

Data Date	Weiss Safety Rating	RACR #1	RACR #2	Total Assets ($mil)	Capital ($mil)	Net Premium ($mil)	Net Income ($mil)
3-03	B-	0.93	0.78	76.6	19.6	80.9	1.6
3-02	C	0.76	0.63	66.2	16.7	70.5	1.4
2002	B-	0.96	0.80	77.6	22.2	285.8	7.3
2001	C	0.76	0.63	63.0	15.6	256.2	2.3
2000	D+	0.49	0.42	55.9	10.9	233.1	0.9
1999	C	0.54	0.46	45.1	8.8	170.6	-2.7
1998	C	0.75	0.64	42.8	11.5	164.7	1.5

Capital ($mil) chart from 1998 to 3-03

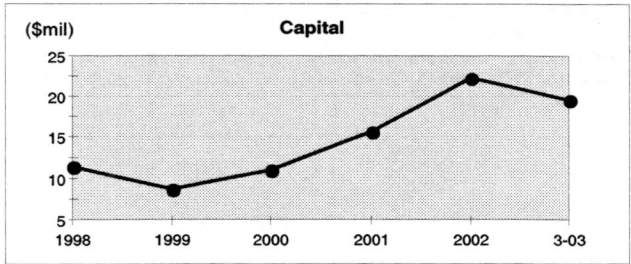

SELECT HEALTH OF SOUTH CAROLINA INC — D+ — Weak

Major Rating Factors: Weak profitability index (0.9 on a scale of 0 to 10) with operating losses during 1998, 1999 and 2000. Average return on equity has been poor at -47%. Fair capitalization (3.6) based on weak current risk-adjusted capital (moderate loss scenario). Good overall results on stability tests (5.2) despite rapid premium growth over the last five years, rapid enrollment growth during the past five years.

Other Rating Factors: Good liquidity (7.0) with sufficient resources (cash flows and marketable investments) to handle a spike in claims. High quality investment portfolio (9.9).
Principal Business: Medicaid (100%)
Mem Phys: 02: 1,632   **01:** 1,439   **02 MLR** 79%   **/ 02 Admin Exp** 19%
Enroll(000): Q1 03: 57   **02:** 55   **01:** 37   **Med Exp PMPM:** $71
Principal Investments: Cash and equiv (94%), nonaffiliate common stock (6%)
Provider Compensation ($000): Contr fee ($21,718), FFS ($10,289), capitation ($5,215)
Total Member Encounters: Phys (225,760), non-phys (21,573)
Group Affiliation: AmeriHealth Mercy Health Plan
Licensed in: SC
Address: 7410 Northside Dr Suite 208, Charleston, SC 29420
Phone: (843) 569-1759   **Dom State:** SC   **Commenced Bus:** December 1996

Data Date	Weiss Safety Rating	RACR #1	RACR #2	Total Assets ($mil)	Capital ($mil)	Net Premium ($mil)	Net Income ($mil)
3-03	D+	0.73	0.60	15.8	4.3	15.3	-0.1
3-02	D	0.92	0.79	13.5	3.9	10.1	0.0
2002	D+	0.76	0.64	16.9	4.5	49.7	0.4
2001	D	0.92	0.79	12.8	3.9	28.3	0.4
2000	D-	1.11	0.96	9.8	2.9	16.5	-1.2
1999	D-	1.80	1.56	4.7	2.5	7.3	-1.8
1998	D	0.94	0.81	3.3	1.2	5.3	-2.0

Risk-Adjusted Capital Ratios (Since 1998) chart: RACR #1, RACR #2

www.WeissRatings.com   * Denotes a Weiss Recommended Company

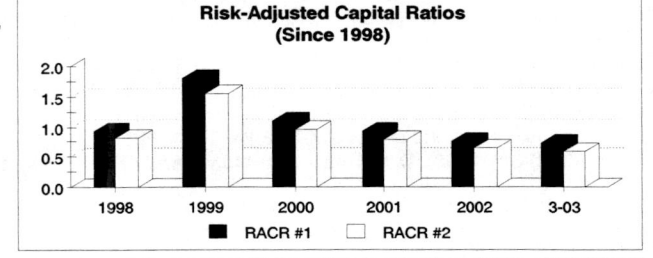

II. Analysis of Largest Companies

Winter 2003 - 04

SENTARA HEALTH PLANS INC — C+ Fair

Major Rating Factors: Fair overall results on stability tests (4.6 on a scale of 0 to 10) based on rapid premium growth over the last five years, rapid enrollment growth during the past five years. Potentially strong support from affiliation with Sentara Health System. Weak profitability index (2.8) with operating losses during 2000 and 2001. Strong overall capitalization (9.0) based on excellent current risk-adjusted capital (severe loss scenario) despite some fluctuation in capital levels.
Other Rating Factors: High quality investment portfolio (9.9) containing no exposure to mortgages, junk bonds, or unaffiliated stocks. Excellent liquidity (7.0) with ample operational cash flow and liquid investments.
Principal Business: Comp med (100%)
Mem Phys: 02: 2,632 **01:** 2,469 **02 MLR** 91% / **02 Admin Exp** 7%
Enroll(000): Q1 03: 17 **02:** 17 **01:** 17 **Med Exp PMPM:** $178
Principal Investments: Cash and equiv (52%), other (48%)
Provider Compensation ($000): Contr fee ($34,162), capitation ($1,083)
Total Member Encounters: Phys (115,347), non-phys (24,361)
Group Affiliation: Sentara Health System
Licensed in: VA
Address: 4417 Corporation Lane, Virginia Beach, VA 23462
Phone: (757) 552-7220 **Dom State:** VA **Commenced Bus:** September 1988

Data Date	Weiss Safety Rating	RACR #1	RACR #2	Total Assets ($mil)	Capital ($mil)	Net Premium ($mil)	Net Income ($mil)
3-03	C+	2.98	2.48	17.5	10.4	11.3	1.6
3-02	C	3.58	2.97	13.4	7.9	9.5	0.1
2002	C+	2.57	2.15	14.4	8.8	39.9	1.0
2001	C	3.57	2.96	11.9	7.6	34.3	-0.3
2000	C-	3.46	2.91	15.2	7.8	25.0	-5.1
1999	D	7.08	5.75	11.7	10.0	8.2	2.5
1998	D-	4.38	3.61	14.6	7.1	10.9	3.7

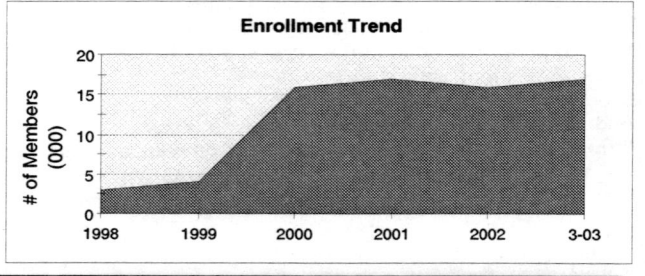

Enrollment Trend

SERVICE LIFE & CASUALTY INSURANCE COMPANY — C Fair

Major Rating Factors: Fair quality investment portfolio (3.1 on a scale of 0 to 10). Fair overall results on stability tests (3.9) including negative cash flow from operations for 2002. Good overall profitability (6.0). Return on equity has been fair, averaging 7.3%.
Other Rating Factors: Strong capitalization (7.3) based on excellent risk adjusted capital (severe loss scenario). Excellent liquidity (7.9).
Principal Business: Credit life insurance (41%), credit health insurance (33%), reinsurance (25%), and group health insurance (1%).
Principal Investments: CMOs and structured securities (36%), nonCMO investment grade bonds (29%), real estate (17%), mortgages in good standing (10%), and misc. investments (9%).
Investments in Affiliates: None
Group Affiliation: Service Ins Group
Licensed in: AZ, CO, LA, MS, NM, OK, SC, TX
Commenced Business: January 1970
Address: 6907 Capital of Texas Hwy, Austin, TX 78731
Phone: (512) 343-0600 **Domicile State:** TX **NAIC Code:** 77151

Data Date	Weiss Safety Rating	RACR #1	RACR #2	Total Assets ($mil)	Capital ($mil)	Net Premium ($mil)	Net Income ($mil)
6-03	C	2.21	1.17	194.3	30.6	19.4	1.1
6-02	C	1.99	1.15	186.5	31.0	28.6	4.1
2002	C	2.13	1.13	196.5	29.9	42.7	3.4
2001	C	1.95	1.11	190.2	27.3	32.5	4.2
2000	C	2.52	1.25	171.8	23.1	27.8	1.9
1999	C	2.90	1.51	162.2	28.5	38.9	0.5
1998	C	3.45	1.95	144.3	29.4	12.3	5.6

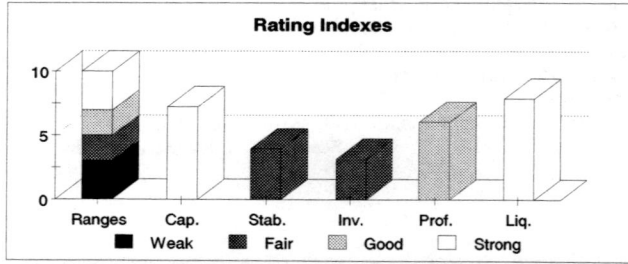

Rating Indexes — Ranges, Cap., Stab., Inv., Prof., Liq.; Weak, Fair, Good, Strong

SETON HEALTH PLAN INC — E Very Weak

Major Rating Factors: Weak profitability index (0.8 on a scale of 0 to 10) with $11.6 million in losses in the last four years. Average return on equity has been extremely poor. Poor capitalization index (0.0) based on weak current risk-adjusted capital (severe loss scenario). Weak liquidity (0.3) as a spike in claims may stretch capacity.
Other Rating Factors: Fair overall results on stability tests (4.5) based on rapid premium growth over the last five years, rapid enrollment growth during the past five years. High quality investment portfolio (9.9) containing no exposure to mortgages, junk bonds, or unaffiliated stocks.
Principal Business: Comp med (79%), Medicaid (21%)
Mem Phys: 02: 4,715 **01:** 4,271 **02 MLR** 98% / **02 Admin Exp** 18%
Enroll(000): Q1 03: 35 **02:** 33 **01:** 35 **Med Exp PMPM:** $116
Principal Investments: Cash and equiv (95%), other (5%)
Provider Compensation ($000): Contr fee ($33,415), capitation ($9,013), FFS ($2,301)
Total Member Encounters: Phys (290,371), non-phys (65,801)
Group Affiliation: Ascension Health System
Licensed in: TX
Address: 305 E Huntland Dr Ste 200, Austin, TX 78752
Phone: (512) 324-1953 **Dom State:** TX **Commenced Bus:** July 1995

Data Date	Weiss Safety Rating	RACR #1	RACR #2	Total Assets ($mil)	Capital ($mil)	Net Premium ($mil)	Net Income ($mil)
3-03	E	0.20	0.17	15.8	2.3	10.5	-0.2
3-02	E	0.00	0.00	12.1	1.7	12.5	-0.5
2002	E	0.21	0.17	15.2	2.3	48.6	-6.3
2001	E	0.00	0.00	12.2	2.2	38.9	-1.4
2000	E	N/A	N/A	9.7	-2.5	47.4	-3.9
1999	E	0.10	0.09	6.8	1.5	16.2	-0.1
1998	N/A	N/A	N/A	4.0	1.6	12.8	0.2

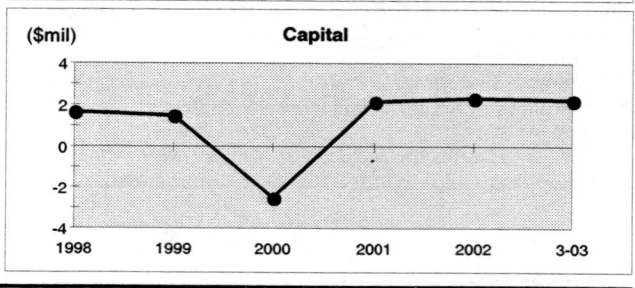

Capital ($mil)

SHA LLC — C- Fair

Major Rating Factors: Fair capitalization (3.1 on a scale of 0 to 10) based on weak current risk-adjusted capital (moderate loss scenario). Fair overall results on stability tests (3.8) based on a steep decline in capital during 2002. Weak profitability index (1.5) with operating losses during 1998, 1999 and 2000. Average return on equity has been extremely poor.

Other Rating Factors: Good liquidity (6.8) with sufficient resources (cash flows and marketable investments) to handle a spike in claims. High quality investment portfolio (9.9) containing little or no exposure to mortgages, junk bonds, or unaffiliated stocks.

Principal Business: Comp med (75%), Medicaid (12%), FEHB (9%), other (3%).

Mem Phys: 02: 2,656 **01:** 2,526 **02 MLR** 83% **/ 02 Admin Exp** 17%

Enroll(000): Q1 03: 92 **02:** 91 **01:** 78 **Med Exp PMPM:** $149

Principal Investments: Cash and equiv (25%), affiliate common stock (24%), real estate (8%), other (43%).

Provider Compensation ($000): Contr fee ($120,989), capitation ($18,798), FFS ($9,575)

Total Member Encounters: Phys (406,677), non-phys (158,720)

Group Affiliation: Covenant Health System

Licensed in: TX

Address: 12940 Research Blvd, Austin, TX 78750-3203

Phone: (512) 257-6001 **Dom State:** TX **Commenced Bus:** August 1994

Data Date	Weiss Safety Rating	RACR #1	RACR #2	Total Assets ($mil)	Capital ($mil)	Net Premium ($mil)	Net Income ($mil)
3-03	C-	0.64	0.54	31.9	7.0	53.2	1.7
3-02	C-	0.87	0.73	28.2	9.2	38.0	3.6
2002	C-	0.66	0.55	31.0	7.3	181.2	10.1
2001	C-	0.86	0.73	30.6	9.2	158.3	2.6
2000	D-	0.56	0.47	27.7	7.8	162.0	-2.8
1999	E+	0.35	0.29	34.4	6.0	175.2	-16.2
1998	D+	0.48	0.40	30.2	2.6	176.5	-17.6

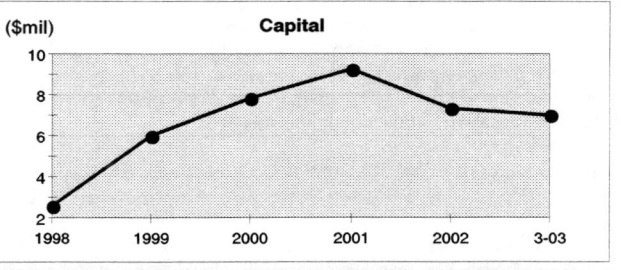

SHARP HEALTH PLAN — C- Fair

Major Rating Factors: Fair overall results on stability tests (3.8 on a scale of 0 to 10) based on poor risk diversification due to the size of the company's affiliate group, rapid enrollment growth during the past five years. Weak profitability index (0.9) with operating losses during 1999, 2000, 2001 and 2002. Good liquidity (6.8) with sufficient resources (cash flows and marketable investments) to handle a spike in claims.

Other Rating Factors: Strong capitalization index (10.0) based on excellent current risk-adjusted capital (severe loss scenario).

Principal Business: Managed care (62%)

Mem Phys: 02: N/A **01:** N/A **02 MLR** 95% **/ 02 Admin Exp** 8%

Enroll(000): Q1 03: 124 **02:** 119 **01:** 101 **Med Exp PMPM:** $105

Principal Investments ($000): Cash and equiv ($14,236), bonds ($2,725), stocks ($2,488)

Provider Compensation ($000): None

Total Member Encounters: N/A

Group Affiliation: San Diego Hospital Assoc

Licensed in: CA

Address: 4305 University Ave Suite 200, San Diego, CA 92105

Phone: (619) 637-6530 **Dom State:** CA **Commenced Bus:** November 1992

Data Date	Weiss Safety Rating	RACR #1	RACR #2	Total Assets ($mil)	Capital ($mil)	Net Premium ($mil)	Net Income ($mil)
3-03	C-	18.38	11.24	26.2	5.0	43.0	-0.1
3-02	D-	0.00	0.00	19.2	3.7	32.7	-0.7
2002	D-	0.00	0.00	26.7	4.6	146.5	-4.6
2001	D-	0.40	0.25	21.9	4.3	115.0	-4.1
2000	D	0.37	0.23	15.4	3.1	95.9	-0.4
1999	D+	0.54	0.33	17.7	3.5	80.3	-0.6
1998	D+	0.83	0.52	13.1	4.2	61.0	0.9

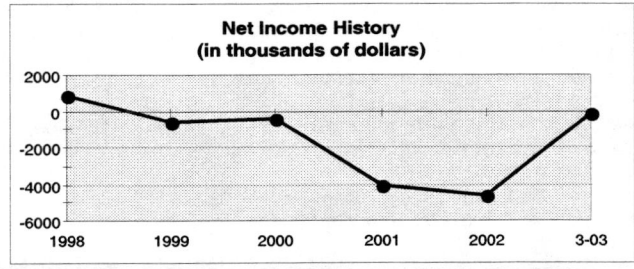

SIOUX VALLEY HEALTH PLAN — E+ Very Weak

Major Rating Factors: Weak profitability index (1.4 on a scale of 0 to 10) with operating losses during each of the last five years. Poor capitalization index (0.7) based on weak current risk-adjusted capital (moderate loss scenario). Good overall results on stability tests (6.4) despite rapid premium growth over the last five years.

Other Rating Factors: Good liquidity (5.6) with sufficient resources (cash flows and marketable investments) to handle a spike in claims. High quality investment portfolio (9.9) containing no exposure to mortgages, junk bonds, or unaffiliated stocks.

Principal Business: Comp med (84%), Medicare (15%).

Mem Phys: 02: 5,853 **01:** 4,447 **02 MLR** 93% **/ 02 Admin Exp** 9%

Enroll(000): Q1 03: 22 **02:** 23 **01:** 32 **Med Exp PMPM:** $182

Principal Investments: Cash and equiv (51%), other (49%).

Provider Compensation ($000): Contr fee ($60,620)

Total Member Encounters: Phys (91,624), non-phys (45,144)

Group Affiliation: Sioux Valley Group

Licensed in: IA, SD

Address: 1100 East 21st St., STe 600, Sioux Falls, SD 57105

Phone: (605) 328-6868 **Dom State:** SD **Commenced Bus:** January 1998

Data Date	Weiss Safety Rating	RACR #1	RACR #2	Total Assets ($mil)	Capital ($mil)	Net Premium ($mil)	Net Income ($mil)
3-03	E+	0.37	0.31	15.6	6.0	12.9	0.1
3-02	E	0.20	0.17	15.4	3.9	19.2	0.1
2002	E	0.24	0.20	13.4	4.9	64.1	-1.3
2001	E	0.20	0.17	13.3	3.8	60.1	-0.9
2000	E	0.04	0.03	9.2	1.4	41.0	-2.5
1999	E	0.05	0.04	4.9	1.1	24.4	-2.3
1998	N/A	N/A	N/A	4.0	1.5	12.7	-2.5

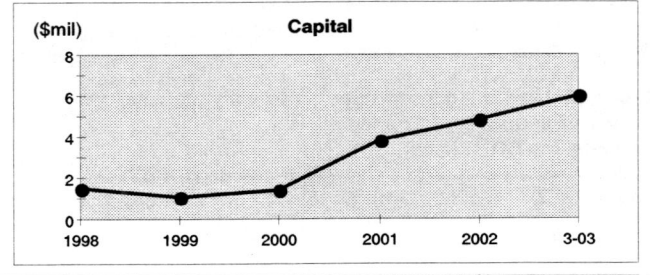

II. Analysis of Largest Companies

Winter 2003 - 04

SIOUX VALLEY HEALTH PLAN MINNESOTA   D-   Weak

Major Rating Factors: Weak profitability index (1.0 on a scale of 0 to 10) with modest operating losses during 1998, 1999, 2000 and 2002. Fair capitalization (4.5) based on fair current risk-adjusted capital (moderate loss scenario) as results have slipped from the good range over the last year. Good overall results on stability tests (5.4) despite fair risk-adjusted capital in prior years, rapid premium growth over the last five years. Poor financial strength from affiliates.
Other Rating Factors: Good liquidity (6.8) with sufficient resources (cash flows and marketable investments) to handle a spike in claims. High quality investment portfolio (9.9) containing no exposure to mortgages, junk bonds, or unaffiliated stocks.
Principal Business: Comp med (77%), Medicare (23%)
Mem Phys: 02: 4,845   **01:** 3,623   **02 MLR** 91%   / **02 Admin Exp** 10%
Enroll(000): Q1 03: 2   **02:** 3   **01:** 2   **Med Exp PMPM:** $225
Principal Investments: Cash and equiv (76%), other (24%)
Provider Compensation ($000): Contr fee ($6,518)
Total Member Encounters: Phys (9,172), non-phys (4,578)
Group Affiliation: Sioux Valley Group
Licensed in: MN
Address: 1100 E. 21st St., Suite 600, Sioux Falls, SD 57105
Phone: (605) 357-6868   **Dom State:** MN   **Commenced Bus:** January 1998

Data Date	Weiss Safety Rating	RACR #1	RACR #2	Total Assets ($mil)	Capital ($mil)	Net Premium ($mil)	Net Income ($mil)
3-03	D-	0.85	0.71	2.3	1.2	1.6	0.1
3-02	D-	1.51	1.27	2.2	1.3	1.7	0.0
2002	D-	0.79	0.66	2.4	1.2	7.5	-0.1
2001	D-	1.52	1.28	2.2	1.3	5.1	0.2
2000	D-	1.39	1.18	1.8	1.0	3.8	-0.3
1999	D	2.18	1.83	1.6	1.2	2.4	-0.4
1998	D+	2.72	2.31	1.8	1.6	0.3	-0.4

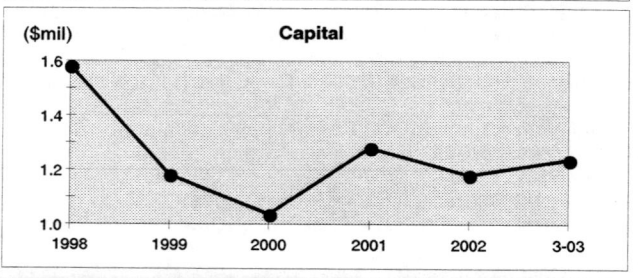

Capital chart 1998–3-03

SOUTHERN HEALTH SERVICES INC   C-   Fair

Major Rating Factors: Weak profitability index (0.9 on a scale of 0 to 10) with operating losses during 2000 and 2001. Average return on equity has been poor at -16%. Good overall results on stability tests (6.7) based on consistent premium and capital growth in the last five years but a decline in enrollment during 2002. Potentially strong support from affiliation with Coventry Health Care Inc. Good liquidity (6.1) with sufficient resources (cash flows and marketable investments) to handle a spike in claims.
Other Rating Factors: Strong capitalization (8.0) based on excellent current risk-adjusted capital (severe loss scenario) reflecting significant improvement over results in 2000. High quality investment portfolio (9.9) containing little or no exposure to mortgages, junk bonds, or unaffiliated stocks.
Principal Business: Comp med (85%), Medicaid (15%)
Mem Phys: 02: 7,754   **01:** 7,565   **02 MLR** 85%   / **02 Admin Exp** 13%
Enroll(000): Q1 03: 103   **02:** 98   **01:** 122   **Med Exp PMPM:** $150
Principal Investments: Cash and equiv (11%), real estate (4%), other (85%)
Provider Compensation ($000): Contr fee ($176,812), FFS ($10,789), capitation ($8,776)
Total Member Encounters: Phys (844,753), non-phys (186,569)
Group Affiliation: Coventry Health Care Inc
Licensed in: VA
Address: 9881 Mayland Dr, Richmond, VA 23233
Phone: (804) 747-3700   **Dom State:** VA   **Commenced Bus:** April 1991

Data Date	Weiss Safety Rating	RACR #1	RACR #2	Total Assets ($mil)	Capital ($mil)	Net Premium ($mil)	Net Income ($mil)
3-03	C-	2.16	1.80	79.9	34.2	65.2	0.8
3-02	D+	1.84	1.55	70.8	25.4	59.8	0.5
2002	C-	2.01	1.68	69.9	32.2	233.6	7.3
2001	D+	1.84	1.56	69.1	20.6	245.3	-20.0
2000	C-	0.70	0.55	61.2	14.0	214.7	-2.6
1999	C	1.11	0.93	22.6	7.2	84.9	0.7
1998	C-	0.89	0.75	21.1	6.4	89.2	1.2

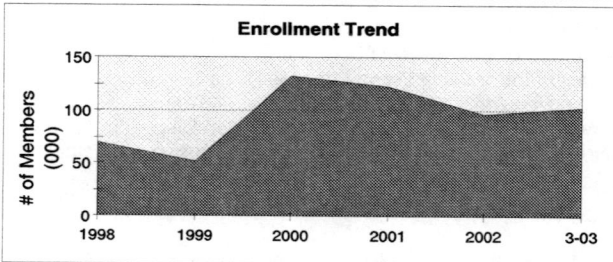

Enrollment Trend chart 1998–3-03

SOUTHWEST TEXAS HMO INC   C+   Fair

Major Rating Factors: Good overall results on stability tests (5.1 on a scale of 0 to 10) despite excessive capital growth during 2002, a decline in enrollment during 2002. Potentially strong support from affiliation with HCSC Group. Good liquidity (6.9) with sufficient resources (cash flows and marketable investments) to handle a spike in claims. Weak profitability index (0.9) with operating losses during 1999, 2000 and 2001. Average return on equity has been poor at -44%.
Other Rating Factors: Strong capitalization (9.3) based on excellent current risk-adjusted capital (severe loss scenario) reflecting significant improvement over results in 1999. High quality investment portfolio (9.9) containing no exposure to mortgages, junk bonds, or unaffiliated stocks.
Principal Business: Comp med (66%), Medicaid (20%), FEHB (14%)
Mem Phys: 02: 29,277   **01:** 20,703   **02 MLR** 90%   / **02 Admin Exp** 12%
Enroll(000): Q1 03: 381   **02:** 548   **01:** 696   **Med Exp PMPM:** $164
Principal Investments: Cash and equiv (55%), other (45%)
Provider Compensation ($000): Contr fee ($1,032,985), capitation ($214,681), FFS ($35,643)
Total Member Encounters: Phys (2,565,926), non-phys (737,107)
Group Affiliation: HCSC Group
Licensed in: TX
Address: 901 S Central Expressway, Richardson, TX 75080
Phone: (972) 766-6900   **Dom State:** TX   **Commenced Bus:** February 1984

Data Date	Weiss Safety Rating	RACR #1	RACR #2	Total Assets ($mil)	Capital ($mil)	Net Premium ($mil)	Net Income ($mil)
3-03	C+	3.20	2.67	292.9	154.4	207.5	1.1
3-02	C	2.63	2.21	462.6	116.4	332.0	-3.3
2002	C+	3.21	2.67	357.3	155.1	1,351.1	55.2
2001	C	2.60	2.19	446.9	116.4	1,248.4	-222.2
2000	C	7.23	6.17	384.4	100.3	847.5	-38.9
1999	C	0.67	0.57	426.0	89.5	1,784.5	-13.4
1998	C+	1.43	1.24	353.9	92.8	1,575.7	0.2

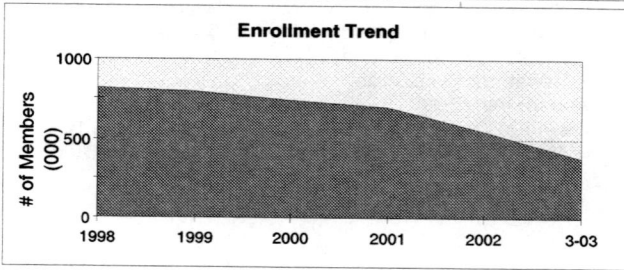

Enrollment Trend chart 1998–3-03

Winter 2003 - 04
II. Analysis of Largest Companies

STANDARD INSURANCE COMPANY — B- Good

Major Rating Factors: Good quality investment portfolio (6.1 on a scale of 0 to 10) despite mixed results such as: no exposure to mortgages and substantial holdings of BBB bonds but small junk bond holdings. Good liquidity (6.8) with sufficient resources to cover a large increase in policy surrenders despite significant exposure to policies that are subject to withdrawal with minimal or no penalty. Good overall results on stability tests (5.1) good operational trends and excellent risk diversification.
Other Rating Factors: Strong capitalization (7.8) based on excellent risk adjusted capital (severe loss scenario). Excellent profitability (7.6) with operating gains in each of the last five years.
Principal Business: Group health insurance (48%), group life insurance (28%), reinsurance (10%), individual annuities (7%), and other lines (7%).
Principal Investments: NonCMO investment grade bonds (64%), mortgages in good standing (32%), noninv. grade bonds (2%), and real estate (1%).
Investments in Affiliates: None
Group Affiliation: Stancorp Financial Group
Licensed in: All states except NY, PR
Commenced Business: April 1906
Address: 1100 SW Sixth Ave, Portland, OR 97204
Phone: (503) 321-7000 **Domicile State:** OR **NAIC Code:** 69019

Data Date	Weiss Safety Rating	RACR #1	RACR #2	Total Assets ($mil)	Capital ($mil)	Net Premium ($mil)	Net Income ($mil)
6-03	B-	2.45	1.51	7,873.7	793.5	1,159.8	53.3
6-02	B-	2.30	1.45	6,239.5	607.5	694.1	28.3
2002	B-	2.75	1.67	7,344.6	808.2	1,470.1	20.0
2001	B-	2.49	1.58	6,109.4	631.7	1,292.1	128.3
2000	B-	2.62	1.36	6,539.6	507.6	1,601.5	44.9
1999	B-	2.90	1.48	5,721.2	506.7	1,290.2	116.8
1998	B-	2.22	1.30	4,973.6	392.9	1,127.4	95.7

Adverse Trends in Operations

Change in premium mix from 2000 to 2001 (7%)
Decrease in asset base during 2001 (7%)
Decrease in premium volume from 2000 to 2001 (19%)
Increase in policy surrenders from 1998 to 1999 (38%)

STANDARD LIFE & ACCIDENT INSURANCE COMPANY — B Good

Major Rating Factors: Good overall results on stability tests (5.8 on a scale of 0 to 10). Stability strengths include excellent operational trends and excellent risk diversification. Good quality investment portfolio (5.2) despite mixed results such as: no exposure to mortgages and large holdings of BBB rated bonds but small junk bond holdings. Good liquidity (6.8).
Other Rating Factors: Strong capitalization (8.7) based on excellent risk adjusted capital (severe loss scenario). Excellent profitability (7.7) despite modest operating losses during 2001.
Principal Business: Individual health insurance (66%), reinsurance (19%), individual life insurance (9%), individual annuities (4%), and group health insurance (1%).
Principal Investments: NonCMO investment grade bonds (69%), common & preferred stock (11%), mortgages in good standing (10%), noninv. grade bonds (7%), and misc. investments (4%).
Investments in Affiliates: 2%
Group Affiliation: American National Group Inc
Licensed in: All states except ME, MA, MN, NH, NJ, NY, WI, PR
Commenced Business: June 1976
Address: 201 Robert S Kerr Ave Ste 600, Oklahoma City, OK 73102
Phone: (409) 763-4661 **Domicile State:** OK **NAIC Code:** 86355

Data Date	Weiss Safety Rating	RACR #1	RACR #2	Total Assets ($mil)	Capital ($mil)	Net Premium ($mil)	Net Income ($mil)
6-03	B	3.06	2.10	462.0	156.3	111.3	8.6
6-02	B	3.41	2.20	453.9	153.2	104.0	4.5
2002	B	2.81	1.92	443.4	149.4	212.5	13.4
2001	B	3.72	2.42	438.0	152.2	186.7	-1.3
2000	B	4.78	3.12	404.9	153.4	157.6	15.3
1999	B	4.58	2.99	380.7	138.2	152.6	9.2
1998	B	4.09	2.76	364.5	128.4	160.8	11.0

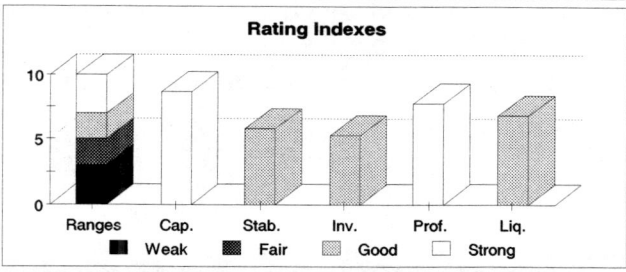

Rating Indexes (Ranges, Cap., Stab., Inv., Prof., Liq. — Weak, Fair, Good, Strong)

STANDARD SECURITY LIFE INSURANCE CO OF NEW YORK — B Good

Major Rating Factors: Good overall results on stability tests (5.1 on a scale of 0 to 10) despite fair financial strength of affiliated Geneve Holdings Inc. Other stability subfactors include excellent operational trends and excellent risk diversification. Good quality investment portfolio (6.7) despite mixed results such as: no exposure to mortgages and substantial holdings of BBB bonds but small junk bond holdings. Strong capitalization (9.9) based on excellent risk adjusted capital (severe loss scenario).
Other Rating Factors: Excellent profitability (7.9) with operating gains in each of the last five years. Excellent liquidity (7.4).
Principal Business: Group health insurance (88%), reinsurance (11%), and group life insurance (1%).
Principal Investments: NonCMO investment grade bonds (56%), CMOs and structured securities (11%), common & preferred stock (9%), noninv. grade bonds (4%), and misc. investments (12%).
Investments in Affiliates: 7%
Group Affiliation: Geneve Holdings Inc
Licensed in: All states, the District of Columbia and Puerto Rico
Commenced Business: December 1958
Address: 485 Madison Ave, New York, NY 10022-5872
Phone: (212) 355-4141 **Domicile State:** NY **NAIC Code:** 69078

Data Date	Weiss Safety Rating	RACR #1	RACR #2	Total Assets ($mil)	Capital ($mil)	Net Premium ($mil)	Net Income ($mil)
6-03	B	3.77	2.91	227.9	77.7	44.7	3.6
6-02	B-	4.36	3.18	228.0	73.7	39.9	3.2
2002	B	4.05	3.18	212.6	80.7	77.2	8.5
2001	B-	4.81	3.64	192.8	71.2	64.1	7.5
2000	B-	5.48	4.13	183.2	63.1	52.0	7.1
1999	B-	4.84	3.96	158.0	57.0	47.1	3.9
1998	B-	4.68	3.84	141.8	53.3	44.2	4.9

Geneve Holdings Inc
Composite Group Rating: C
Largest Group Members

	Assets ($mil)	Weiss Safety Rating
MADISON NATIONAL LIFE INS CO INC	448	C
STANDARD SECURITY LIFE INS CO OF NY	213	B
SOUTHERN LIFE HEALTH INS CO	147	C-
INDEPENDENCE AMERICAN INS CO	27	C

II. Analysis of Largest Companies
Winter 2003 - 04

STATE MUTUAL INSURANCE COMPANY — C Fair

Major Rating Factors: Fair current capitalization (4.0 on a scale of 0 to 10) based on mixed results -- excessive policy leverage mitigated by excellent risk adjusted capital (severe loss scenario) reflecting improvement over results in 1998. Fair quality investment portfolio (4.6) with large holdings of BBB rated bonds in addition to junk bond exposure equal to 87% of capital. Fair overall results on stability tests (3.8).
Other Rating Factors: Good overall profitability (5.2) although investment income, in comparison to reserve requirements, is below regulatory standards. Good liquidity (5.8).
Principal Business: Individual health insurance (72%) and individual life insurance (27%).
Principal Investments: NonCMO investment grade bonds (55%), policy loans (11%), mortgages in good standing (10%), noninv. grade bonds (8%), and misc. investments (16%).
Investments in Affiliates: 4%
Group Affiliation: State Mutual Ins Group
Licensed in: AL, AZ, AR, CO, DC, DE, FL, GA, HI, ID, IL, IN, IA, KS, KY, LA, MD, MN, MS, MO, MT, NE, NV, NM, NC, ND, OH, OK, OR, SC, SD, TN, TX, UT, VT, VA, WA, WV, WI, WY
Commenced Business: April 1936
Address: One State Mutual Dr, Rome, GA 30162
Phone: (800) 241-7598 **Domicile State:** GA **NAIC Code:** 69132

Data Date	Weiss Safety Rating	RACR #1	RACR #2	Total Assets ($mil)	Capital ($mil)	Net Premium ($mil)	Net Income ($mil)
6-03	C	1.83	1.04	341.7	26.0	10.1	0.7
6-02	C	1.91	1.10	323.5	28.4	-70.3	0.9
2002	C	2.03	1.10	324.1	28.2	-60.5	5.0
2001	C	1.62	0.95	302.9	24.0	31.3	5.6
2000	C	1.94	1.04	286.3	20.0	32.9	4.0
1999	C	1.61	0.87	276.8	17.1	34.6	3.6
1998	C	1.53	0.81	265.2	15.2	36.9	2.9

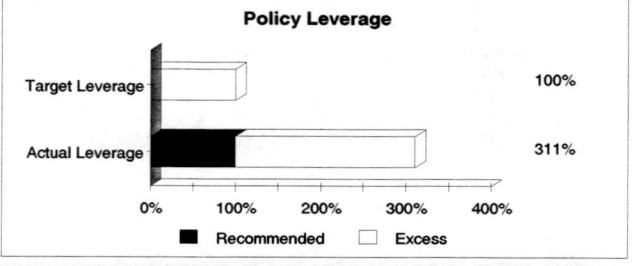

Policy Leverage
Target Leverage: 100%
Actual Leverage: 311%

STATES WEST LIFE INSURANCE COMPANY — B- Good

Major Rating Factors: Fair overall results on stability tests (4.7 on a scale of 0 to 10). Strong capitalization (8.5) based on excellent risk adjusted capital (severe loss scenario). Moreover, capital levels have been consistently high over the last five years. High quality investment portfolio (8.8) with no exposure to mortgages and minimal holdings in junk bonds.
Other Rating Factors: Excellent profitability (8.5) with operating gains in each of the last five years. Excellent liquidity (7.0).
Principal Business: Group life insurance (48%), group health insurance (46%), and reinsurance (5%).
Principal Investments: NonCMO investment grade bonds (58%) and CMOs and structured securities (44%).
Investments in Affiliates: None
Group Affiliation: PREMERA
Licensed in: AK, AZ, CA, ID, MT, NM, ND, OR, UT, WA, WY
Commenced Business: November 1981
Address: 7007 220th SW, Mountlake Terrace, WA 98043
Phone: (206) 670-4584 **Domicile State:** WA **NAIC Code:** 94188

Data Date	Weiss Safety Rating	RACR #1	RACR #2	Total Assets ($mil)	Capital ($mil)	Net Premium ($mil)	Net Income ($mil)
6-03	B-	2.67	2.00	55.3	27.7	15.2	0.1
6-02	C	2.89	2.16	49.1	27.9	14.5	1.3
2002	C+	2.63	1.98	50.9	27.7	29.6	1.1
2001	C	2.78	2.07	45.9	26.6	24.8	3.7
2000	C	2.04	1.43	40.0	21.8	19.2	2.1
1999	C	2.19	1.52	37.5	19.6	16.1	3.7
1998	C	2.01	1.43	31.5	15.4	15.8	1.6

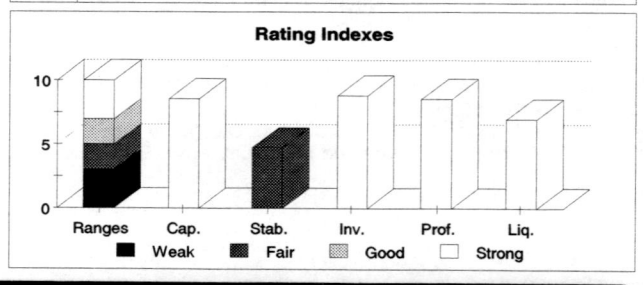

Rating Indexes
Ranges — Cap. (Weak), Stab. (Fair), Inv. (Good), Prof., Liq. (Strong)

STONEBRIDGE LIFE INSURANCE COMPANY — B- Good

Major Rating Factors: Good overall results on stability tests (5.2 on a scale of 0 to 10) despite fair risk adjusted capital in prior years. Other stability subfactors include good operational trends and excellent risk diversification. Good quality investment portfolio (6.3) despite mixed results such as: no exposure to mortgages and large holdings of BBB rated bonds but small junk bond holdings. Good overall profitability (6.4).
Other Rating Factors: Strong capitalization (8.1) based on excellent risk adjusted capital (severe loss scenario). Excellent liquidity (7.4).
Principal Business: Group health insurance (65%), group life insurance (17%), individual life insurance (8%), individual health insurance (5%), and other lines (5%).
Principal Investments: NonCMO investment grade bonds (66%), CMOs and structured securities (18%), noninv. grade bonds (5%), cash (4%), and misc. investments (8%).
Investments in Affiliates: None
Group Affiliation: AEGON USA Group
Licensed in: All states except PR
Commenced Business: May 1906
Address: 29 S Main St, Rutland, VT 05701-5014
Phone: (410) 685-5500 **Domicile State:** VT **NAIC Code:** 65021

Data Date	Weiss Safety Rating	RACR #1	RACR #2	Total Assets ($mil)	Capital ($mil)	Net Premium ($mil)	Net Income ($mil)
6-03	B-	2.81	1.70	1,990.7	315.9	319.3	80.1
6-02	B-	1.58	1.01	1,922.5	208.0	356.1	44.8
2002	B-	1.79	1.09	1,869.3	196.5	688.3	115.9
2001	B-	1.15	0.73	1,776.4	145.1	770.6	75.4
2000	B	1.60	1.06	1,713.4	232.9	843.5	105.2
1999	B	1.67	1.09	1,691.3	243.4	847.4	95.4
1998	B	1.44	0.98	1,523.7	190.5	811.2	50.3

Adverse Trends in Operations
Decrease in premium volume from 2001 to 2002 (11%)
Decrease in capital during 2001 (38%)
Decrease in premium volume from 2000 to 2001 (9%)
Decrease in capital during 2000 (4%)

Winter 2003 - 04
II. Analysis of Largest Companies

SUMMA INS CO | B- | Good

Major Rating Factors: Good overall profitability index (5.7 on a scale of 0 to 10) despite a decline in earnings during 2002. Strong capitalization index (7.6) based on excellent current risk-adjusted capital (severe loss scenario). High quality investment portfolio (8.5) containing little or no exposure to mortgages, junk bonds, or unaffiliated stocks.
Other Rating Factors: Excellent liquidity (7.0) with ample operational cash flow and liquid investments.
Principal Business: Comp med (100%)
Mem Phys: 02: 6,200 **01:** 6,197 **02 MLR** 74% **/ 02 Admin Exp** 17%
Enroll(000): Q1 03: 11 **02:** 10 **01:** 7 **Med Exp PMPM:** $151
Principal Investments: Affiliate common stock (55%), cash and equiv (10%), other (36%)
Provider Compensation ($000): Contr fee ($14,527)
Total Member Encounters: Phys (10,239), non-phys (7,949)
Group Affiliation: Summa Health Systems
Licensed in: OH
Address: 10 N Main St, Akron, OH 44308
Phone: (330) 996-8410 **Dom State:** OH **Commenced Bus:** February 1996

Data Date	Weiss Safety Rating	RACR #1	RACR #2	Total Assets ($mil)	Capital ($mil)	Net Premium ($mil)	Net Income ($mil)
3-03	B-	1.80	1.50	29.3	22.3	6.4	0.4
3-02	N/A	N/A	N/A	N/A	N/A	N/A	N/A
2002	C+	1.87	1.55	29.4	23.3	21.0	2.0
2001	D	1.22	1.08	29.4	25.5	11.6	3.3
2000	D	0.00	0.00	19.5	16.8	6.8	N/A
1999	D	0.79	0.67	6.1	4.5	N/A	0.7
1998	D	1.46	0.97	5.3	3.7	N/A	0.4

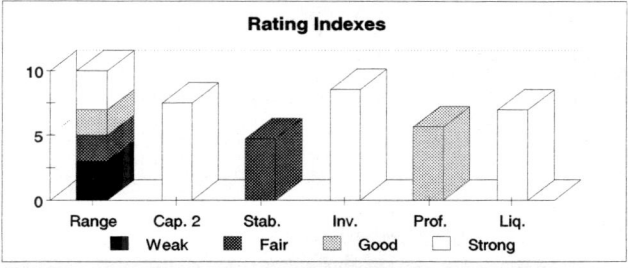

Rating Indexes

SUMMACARE INC | B- | Good

Major Rating Factors: Fair profitability index (4.5 on a scale of 0 to 10) due to a decline in earnings during 2002. Fair overall results on stability tests (4.5). Good capitalization index (5.5) based on good current risk-adjusted capital (severe loss scenario).
Other Rating Factors: Good liquidity (7.0) with sufficient resources (cash flows and marketable investments) to handle a spike in claims. High quality investment portfolio (9.9) containing no exposure to mortgages, junk bonds, or unaffiliated stocks.
Principal Business: Comp med (38%), Medicare (32%), Medicaid (24%), FEHB (4%), other (2%)
Mem Phys: 02: 6,200 **01:** 6,197 **02 MLR** 86% **/ 02 Admin Exp** 12%
Enroll(000): Q1 03: 98 **02:** 102 **01:** 86 **Med Exp PMPM:** $198
Principal Investments: Cash and equiv (61%), other (39%)
Provider Compensation ($000): Capitation ($197,550), contr fee ($24,604)
Total Member Encounters: Phys (180,496), non-phys (116,424)
Group Affiliation: Summa Health Systems
Licensed in: OH
Address: 10 N Main St, Akron, OH 44309
Phone: (330) 996-8410 **Dom State:** OH **Commenced Bus:** March 1993

Data Date	Weiss Safety Rating	RACR #1	RACR #2	Total Assets ($mil)	Capital ($mil)	Net Premium ($mil)	Net Income ($mil)
3-03	B-	1.01	0.84	43.6	18.2	71.7	-0.5
3-02	C+	0.84	0.76	37.9	17.2	62.2	1.8
2002	C+	0.78	0.65	46.1	14.2	257.6	0.5
2001	C+	0.88	0.80	43.6	16.3	207.7	2.8
2000	E+	0.70	0.64	32.3	11.6	184.4	7.4
1999	E	0.29	0.26	19.8	19.8	151.8	1.9
1998	E	0.13	0.12	14.9	14.9	107.5	-2.6

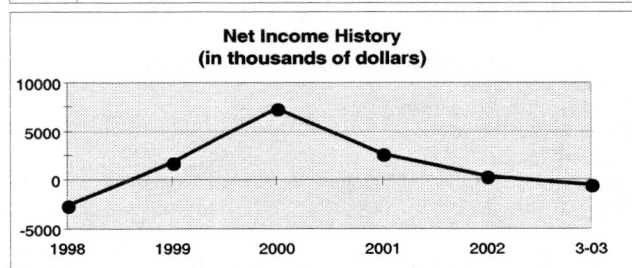

Net Income History (in thousands of dollars)

SUN HEALTH MEDISUN INC | B- | Good

Major Rating Factors: Good overall profitability index (5.1 on a scale of 0 to 10) despite operating losses during 1998 and 1999. Good capitalization (5.3) based on good current risk-adjusted capital (severe loss scenario) reflecting some improvement over results in 2001. Good overall results on stability tests (6.9) based on consistent premium and capital growth in the last five years.
Other Rating Factors: High quality investment portfolio (9.9) containing no exposure to mortgages, junk bonds, or unaffiliated stocks. Excellent liquidity (7.1) with ample operational cash flow and liquid investments.
Principal Business: Medicare (99%)
Mem Phys: 02: 402 **01:** 319 **02 MLR** 91% **/ 02 Admin Exp** 7%
Enroll(000): Q1 03: 16 **02:** 16 **01:** 10 **Med Exp PMPM:** $526
Principal Investments: Cash and equiv (100%)
Provider Compensation ($000): Capitation ($79,169), contr fee ($37,778)
Total Member Encounters: Phys (213,845), non-phys (13,467)
Group Affiliation: Sun Health Corp Inc
Licensed in: AZ
Address: 13632 N 99th Ave Suite B, Sun City, AZ 85351
Phone: (623) 974-7434 **Dom State:** AZ **Commenced Bus:** May 1985

Data Date	Weiss Safety Rating	RACR #1	RACR #2	Total Assets ($mil)	Capital ($mil)	Net Premium ($mil)	Net Income ($mil)
3-03	B-	0.97	0.81	10.4	4.8	26.6	0.5
3-02	C-	0.00	0.00	7.1	4.0	20.3	0.5
2002	B-	0.87	0.72	16.3	4.3	91.6	1.2
2001	C-	0.73	0.64	11.0	3.5	44.9	0.8
2000	D	0.75	0.65	7.1	2.6	32.4	0.5
1999	D	4.58	4.02	4.5	2.2	2.7	-1.1
1998	D	7.27	6.09	1.6	1.3	1.0	-0.2

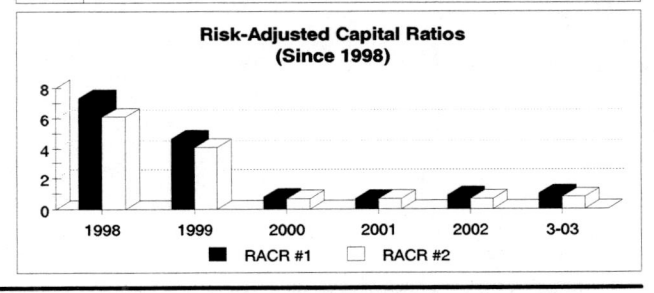

Risk-Adjusted Capital Ratios (Since 1998)

www.WeissRatings.com | 277 | * Denotes a Weiss Recommended Company

II. Analysis of Largest Companies

Winter 2003 - 04

SUN LIFE ASR CO OF CANADA — C+ — Fair

Major Rating Factors: Fair capitalization for the current period (4.7 on a scale of 0 to 10) based on fair risk adjusted capital (moderate loss scenario) reflecting some improvement over results in 2001. Fair quality investment portfolio (3.1) with substantial holdings of BBB bonds in addition to junk bond exposure equal to 96% of capital. Fair profitability (3.9).
Other Rating Factors: Fair overall results on stability tests (4.4) including weak risk adjusted capital in prior years. Good liquidity (5.5).
Principal Business: Individual life insurance (58%), group health insurance (24%), group life insurance (13%), and reinsurance (4%).
Principal Investments: NonCMO investment grade bonds (47%), mortgages in good standing (21%), CMOs and structured securities (9%), common & preferred stock (7%), and misc. investments (17%).
Investments in Affiliates: 3%
Group Affiliation: Sun Life Assurance Group
Licensed in: All states except NY
Commenced Business: May 1871
Address: One Sun Life Executive Park, Wellesley Hills, MA 02481
Phone: (781) 237-6030 **Domicile State:** MI **NAIC Code:** 80802

Data Date	Weiss Safety Rating	RACR #1	RACR #2	Total Assets ($mil)	Capital ($mil)	Net Premium ($mil)	Net Income ($mil)
6-03	C+	0.96	0.61	9,562.8	436.5	846.4	75.8
6-02	B-	0.62	0.45	8,121.0	343.6	709.2	-4.4
2002	C+	0.71	0.45	8,284.2	357.8	1,447.0	-51.9
2001	B-	0.61	0.44	7,969.3	459.5	1,398.1	83.2
2000	B-	0.66	0.49	7,884.6	412.9	1,384.0	145.0
1999	U	0.75	0.54	7,753.4	442.2	1,741.3	-105.3
1998	N/A	N/A	N/A	6,970.7	519.6	1,471.3	-82.0

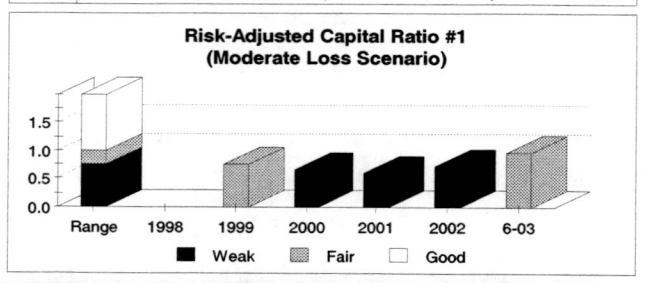

Risk-Adjusted Capital Ratio #1 (Moderate Loss Scenario)

SUPERIOR HEALTHPLAN INC — D- — Weak

Major Rating Factors: Weak profitability index (1.4 on a scale of 0 to 10) with operating losses during 1998, 1999, 2000 and 2001. Average return on equity has been poor at -33%. Poor capitalization index (0.7) based on weak current risk-adjusted capital (moderate loss scenario). Fair overall results on stability tests (4.5) in spite of healthy premium and capital growth during 2002 but an excessive 115% enrollment growth during the period. Potentially strong support from affiliation with Centene Corp.
Other Rating Factors: Fair liquidity (3.6) as cash resources may not be adequate to cover a spike in claims. High quality investment portfolio (9.7) containing no exposure to mortgages, junk bonds, or unaffiliated stocks.
Principal Business: Medicaid (96%), comp med (4%)
Mem Phys: 02: 3,355 **01:** 2,294 **02 MLR** 87% **/ 02 Admin Exp** 13%
Enroll(000): Q1 03: 123 **02:** 118 **01:** 55 **Med Exp PMPM:** $93
Principal Investments: Cash and equiv (65%), other (35%)
Provider Compensation ($000): Contr fee ($78,308), capitation ($11,459), bonus arrang ($28)
Total Member Encounters: N/A
Group Affiliation: Centene Corp
Licensed in: TX
Address: 2100 South Ih 35 Suite 202, Austin, TX 78704
Phone: (512) 692-1454 **Dom State:** TX **Commenced Bus:** February 1997

Data Date	Weiss Safety Rating	RACR #1	RACR #2	Total Assets ($mil)	Capital ($mil)	Net Premium ($mil)	Net Income ($mil)
3-03	D-	0.38	0.31	29.0	5.3	44.8	1.0
3-02	E	0.16	0.14	15.0	2.4	23.7	-0.2
2002	D-	0.28	0.23	25.2	4.2	111.4	0.5
2001	E	0.16	0.13	20.3	2.6	85.8	-1.6
2000	E	0.18	0.15	7.1	1.7	33.7	-1.3
1999	U	1.84	1.57	1.8	1.5	0.3	-0.5
1998	N/A	N/A	N/A	2.5	2.5	N/A	-0.1

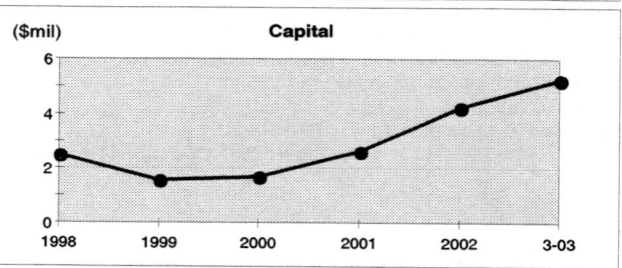

Capital

SWISS RE LIFE & HEALTH AMERICA INCORPORATED — C — Fair

Major Rating Factors: Fair overall results on stability tests (3.4 on a scale of 0 to 10) including fair financial strength of affiliated Swiss Reinsurance Group and fair risk adjusted capital in prior years. Good quality investment portfolio (6.4) despite mixed results such as: no exposure to mortgages and substantial holdings of BBB bonds but small junk bond holdings. Good liquidity (6.9).
Other Rating Factors: Weak profitability (1.7). Strong capitalization (7.1) based on excellent risk adjusted capital (severe loss scenario).
Principal Business: Reinsurance (100%).
Principal Investments: NonCMO investment grade bonds (57%), CMOs and structured securities (28%), common & preferred stock (10%), noninv. grade bonds (4%), and policy loans (1%).
Investments in Affiliates: 10%
Group Affiliation: Swiss Reinsurance Group
Licensed in: All states except ME, NH, WY
Commenced Business: September 1967
Address: 969 High Ridge Rd, Stamford, CT 06904-2060
Phone: (203) 321-3141 **Domicile State:** CT **NAIC Code:** 82627

Data Date	Weiss Safety Rating	RACR #1	RACR #2	Total Assets ($mil)	Capital ($mil)	Net Premium ($mil)	Net Income ($mil)
6-03	C	1.34	1.06	10,038.8	1,809.7	1,127.2	19.5
6-02	C-	1.10	0.87	8,626.1	1,373.2	1,152.0	-62.4
2002	C	1.39	1.12	9,214.6	1,888.1	2,333.7	340.5
2001	C-	1.27	1.01	8,248.8	1,588.5	1,753.5	-1,631.4
2000	C	1.22	0.94	6,890.0	1,009.8	1,738.7	-650.9
1999	C	0.97	0.76	3,690.2	419.5	768.0	36.4
1998	C	0.89	0.65	2,457.8	246.7	675.4	-150.7

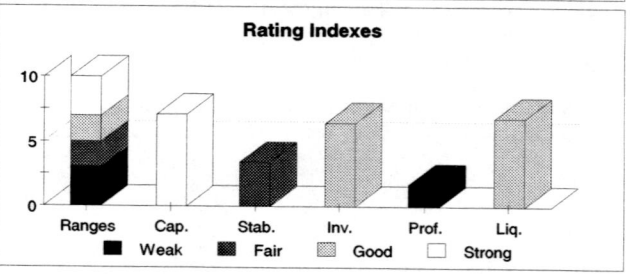

Rating Indexes

Winter 2003 - 04

II. Analysis of Largest Companies

TENET CHOICES INC — D- — Weak

Major Rating Factors: Poor capitalization index (0.0 on a scale of 0 to 10) based on weak current risk-adjusted capital (severe loss scenario). Fair profitability index (4.8). Good overall results on stability tests (6.9) based on consistent premium and capital growth in the last five years but rapid enrollment growth during the past five years.

Other Rating Factors: High quality investment portfolio (9.9) containing no exposure to mortgages, junk bonds, or unaffiliated stocks. Excellent liquidity (7.0) with ample operational cash flow and liquid investments.

Principal Business: Medicare (95%), comp med (5%)
Mem Phys: 02: 1,195   **01:** 1,007   **02 MLR** 84%   **/ 02 Admin Exp** 15%
Enroll(000): Q1 03: 34   **02:** 33   **01:** 27   **Med Exp PMPM:** $487
Principal Investments: Cash and equiv (100%)
Provider Compensation ($000): Capitation ($172,784)
Total Member Encounters: Phys (290,604), non-phys (215,603)
Group Affiliation: Tenet Healthcare Corp
Licensed in: LA
Address: 200 W Esplanade Ave Ste 600, Kenner, LA 70065
Phone: (504) 461-9800   **Dom State:** LA   **Commenced Bus:** January 1997

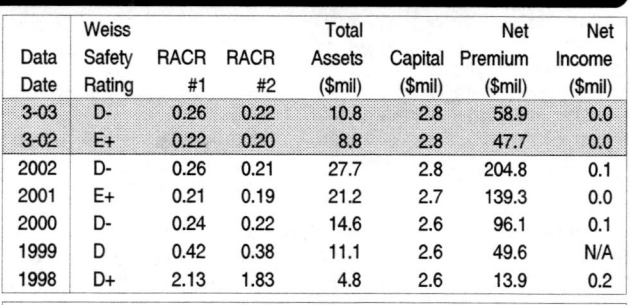

Data Date	Weiss Safety Rating	RACR #1	RACR #2	Total Assets ($mil)	Capital ($mil)	Net Premium ($mil)	Net Income ($mil)
3-03	D-	0.26	0.22	10.8	2.8	58.9	0.0
3-02	E+	0.22	0.20	8.8	2.8	47.7	0.0
2002	D-	0.26	0.21	27.7	2.8	204.8	0.1
2001	E+	0.21	0.19	21.2	2.7	139.3	0.0
2000	D-	0.24	0.22	14.6	2.6	96.1	0.1
1999	D	0.42	0.38	11.1	2.6	49.6	N/A
1998	D+	2.13	1.83	4.8	2.6	13.9	0.2

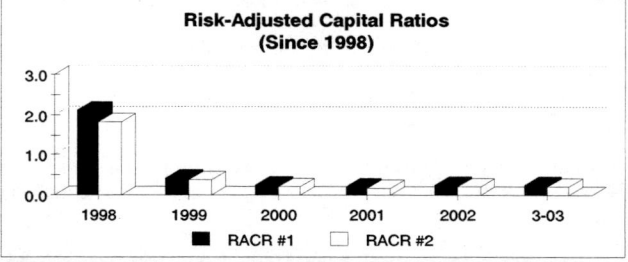

Risk-Adjusted Capital Ratios (Since 1998)

TEXAS CHILDRENS HEALTH PLAN INC — D+ — Weak

Major Rating Factors: Weak profitability index (0.9 on a scale of 0 to 10) with operating losses during 1998, 1999 and 2000. Fair overall results on stability tests (4.9) based on rapid premium growth over the last five years, rapid enrollment growth during the past five years. Strong capitalization index (7.8) based on excellent current risk-adjusted capital (severe loss scenario).

Other Rating Factors: High quality investment portfolio (9.3) containing little or no exposure to mortgages, junk bonds, or unaffiliated stocks. Excellent liquidity (7.2) with ample operational cash flow and liquid investments.

Principal Business: Comp med (80%), Medicaid (4%), other (16%)
Mem Phys: 02: N/A   **01:** N/A   **02 MLR** 77%   **/ 02 Admin Exp** 14%
Enroll(000): Q1 03: 98   **02:** 92   **01:** 68   **Med Exp PMPM:** $77
Principal Investments: Cash and equiv (86%), nonaffiliate common stock (2%), other (12%)
Provider Compensation ($000): Contr fee ($60,178), capitation ($4,852), FFS ($4,445)
Total Member Encounters: Phys (61,652), non-phys (3,282)
Group Affiliation: None
Licensed in: TX
Address: 1919 S Braeswood 6th Fl, Houston, TX 77030
Phone: (832) 824-2090   **Dom State:** TX   **Commenced Bus:** April 1997

Data Date	Weiss Safety Rating	RACR #1	RACR #2	Total Assets ($mil)	Capital ($mil)	Net Premium ($mil)	Net Income ($mil)
3-03	D+	1.98	1.65	52.3	19.6	33.3	1.9
3-02	D	1.37	1.16	29.8	13.3	22.7	4.1
2002	D+	1.81	1.51	44.2	17.9	95.8	9.6
2001	D	1.32	1.13	28.3	9.3	68.8	4.3
2000	E	0.38	0.32	14.1	1.9	30.7	-5.1
1999	E	0.04	0.04	8.3	0.5	30.4	-2.5
1998	N/A	N/A	N/A	10.4	1.1	29.1	-3.4

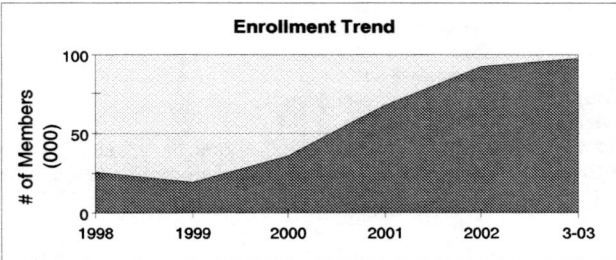

Enrollment Trend

THREE RIVERS HEALTH PLANS INC * — B+ — Good

Major Rating Factors: Good capitalization (6.8 on a scale of 0 to 10) based on excellent current risk-adjusted capital (severe loss scenario) reflecting significant improvement over results in 1998. Excellent profitability (10.0) with operating gains in each of the last five years. High quality investment portfolio (9.9) containing little or no exposure to mortgages, junk bonds, or unaffiliated stocks.

Other Rating Factors: Excellent overall results on stability tests (7.5) based on consistent premium and capital growth in the last five years but rapid enrollment growth during the past five years. Excellent liquidity (7.1) with ample operational cash flow and liquid investments.

Principal Business: Medicaid (98%), comp med (2%)
Mem Phys: 02: 9,439   **01:** 7,300   **02 MLR** 80%   **/ 02 Admin Exp** 10%
Enroll(000): Q1 03: 195   **02:** 191   **01:** 143   **Med Exp PMPM:** $183
Principal Investments: Cash and equiv (95%), pref stock (5%)
Provider Compensation ($000): Contr fee ($325,526), capitation ($32,598)
Total Member Encounters: Phys (1,308,146), non-phys (801,251)
Group Affiliation: Three Rivers Holdings Inc
Licensed in: PA
Address: 1789 S Braddock Ave Suite 370, Swissvale, PA 15218
Phone: (412) 858-4000   **Dom State:** PA   **Commenced Bus:** April 1996

Data Date	Weiss Safety Rating	RACR #1	RACR #2	Total Assets ($mil)	Capital ($mil)	Net Premium ($mil)	Net Income ($mil)
3-03	B+	1.20	1.00	93.5	42.4	128.4	5.5
3-02	B+	1.80	1.53	75.1	41.9	91.9	5.1
2002	B+	1.10	0.92	85.7	38.8	456.9	24.6
2001	B+	1.79	1.52	72.8	37.5	303.6	24.0
2000	B-	1.26	1.06	61.1	26.0	271.4	16.6
1999	C-	0.93	0.79	49.3	13.2	192.5	8.3
1998	D	0.60	0.51	28.1	5.9	120.2	5.5

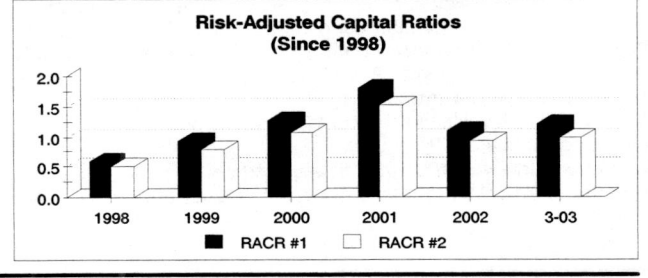

Risk-Adjusted Capital Ratios (Since 1998)

www.WeissRatings.com   * Denotes a Weiss Recommended Company

II. Analysis of Largest Companies

Winter 2003 - 04

TOTAL HEALTH CARE INC — D+ — Weak

Major Rating Factors: Weak profitability index (0.9 on a scale of 0 to 10) with operating losses during 1998, 1999 and 2001. Fair capitalization (4.0) based on fair current risk-adjusted capital (moderate loss scenario) reflecting improvement over results in 2001. Good overall results on stability tests (5.3) despite weak risk-adjusted capital in prior years.
Other Rating Factors: Good liquidity (6.9) with sufficient resources (cash flows and marketable investments) to handle a spike in claims. High quality investment portfolio (9.3) containing little or no exposure to mortgages, junk bonds, or unaffiliated stocks.
Principal Business: Medicaid (92%), comp med (7%).
Mem Phys: 02: 382   **01:** 369   **02 MLR** 83%   **/ 02 Admin Exp** 14%
Enroll(000): Q1 03: 56   **02:** 53   **01:** 55   **Med Exp PMPM:** $133
Principal Investments: Cash and equiv (87%), affiliate common stock (22%), other (2%).
Provider Compensation ($000): Contr fee ($56,598), capitation ($24,634), bonus arrang ($415)
Total Member Encounters: Phys (243,532), non-phys (84,901)
Group Affiliation: Total Health Care Inc
Licensed in: MI
Address: 3011 W. Grand Blvd., Ste 1600, Detroit, MI 48202
Phone: (313) 871-2000   **Dom State:** MI   **Commenced Bus:** May 1976

Data Date	Weiss Safety Rating	RACR #1	RACR #2	Total Assets ($mil)	Capital ($mil)	Net Premium ($mil)	Net Income ($mil)
3-03	D+	0.78	0.65	31.9	9.3	26.9	1.1
3-02	D	0.52	0.44	24.2	4.8	26.8	0.0
2002	D+	0.67	0.56	29.2	7.9	102.8	2.4
2001	D	0.51	0.44	22.5	4.5	104.2	-4.0
2000	D+	N/A	N/A	25.5	5.5	97.7	0.3
1999	D+	0.60	0.51	20.9	4.3	84.2	-3.1
1998	B-	0.96	0.79	35.3	13.7	80.2	-18.8

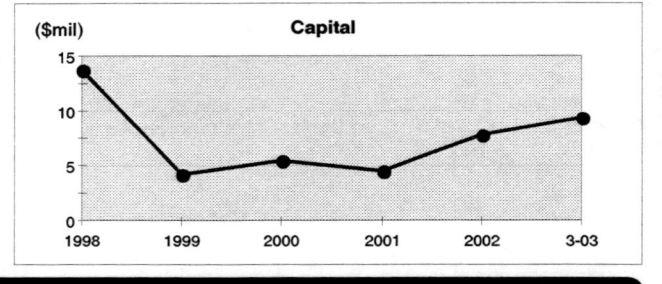

TOTAL HEALTH CHOICE — D+ — Weak

Major Rating Factors: Weak profitability index (0.9 on a scale of 0 to 10) with modest operating losses during 1998, 1999, 2000 and 2002. Fair capitalization index (3.8) based on fair current risk-adjusted capital (moderate loss scenario). Good liquidity (7.0) with sufficient resources (cash flows and marketable investments) to handle a spike in claims.
Other Rating Factors: High quality investment portfolio (9.9) containing no exposure to mortgages, junk bonds, or unaffiliated stocks. Excellent overall results on stability tests (7.1) based on consistent premium and capital growth in the last five years.
Principal Business: Comp med (99%)
Mem Phys: 02: 355   **01:** 293   **02 MLR** 80%   **/ 02 Admin Exp** 21%
Enroll(000): Q1 03: 19   **02:** 20   **01:** 18   **Med Exp PMPM:** $132
Principal Investments: Cash and equiv (96%), other (4%).
Provider Compensation ($000): Contr fee ($18,496), capitation ($11,553), bonus arrang ($22)
Total Member Encounters: Phys (26,842), non-phys (1,210)
Group Affiliation: Total Health Care Inc
Licensed in: FL
Address: 8701 SW 137th Ave Ste 200, Miami, FL 33183
Phone: (305) 408-5700   **Dom State:** FL   **Commenced Bus:** February 1997

Data Date	Weiss Safety Rating	RACR #1	RACR #2	Total Assets ($mil)	Capital ($mil)	Net Premium ($mil)	Net Income ($mil)
3-03	D+	0.75	0.63	11.5	3.1	12.0	0.2
3-02	D	0.69	0.59	8.5	2.5	9.6	0.0
2002	D+	0.68	0.57	8.7	2.8	37.9	-0.2
2001	D	0.66	0.57	7.9	2.4	35.9	0.0
2000	D	0.55	0.47	6.9	1.7	30.6	-0.8
1999	D	0.60	0.51	7.2	1.9	25.2	-0.7
1998	C	0.00	0.00	5.0	-1.2	26.6	-5.9

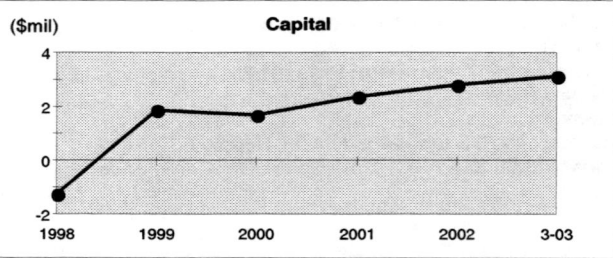

TOUCHPOINT HEALTH PLAN INC — D- — Weak

Major Rating Factors: Poor capitalization index (0.6 on a scale of 0 to 10) based on weak current risk-adjusted capital (moderate loss scenario). Fair profitability index (4.6) with operating losses during 1999. Return on equity has been fair, averaging 8% over the last five years. Good liquidity (5.2) with sufficient resources (cash flows and marketable investments) to handle a spike in claims.
Other Rating Factors: High quality investment portfolio (8.0). Excellent overall results on stability tests (7.8) based on consistent premium and capital growth in the last five years.
Principal Business: Comp med (92%), Medicaid (8%).
Mem Phys: 02: 1,027   **01:** 939   **02 MLR** 90%   **/ 02 Admin Exp** 8%
Enroll(000): Q1 03: 139   **02:** 153   **01:** 140   **Med Exp PMPM:** $155
Principal Investments: Cash and equiv (44%), nonaffiliate common stock (15%), real estate (13%), affiliate common stock (7%), other (21%).
Provider Compensation ($000): Bonus arrang ($154,051), capitation ($112,078), contr fee ($12,128), FFS ($4,764)
Total Member Encounters: N/A
Group Affiliation: United Health Wisconsin Group
Licensed in: WI
Address: 5 Innovation Court, Appleton, WI 54914
Phone: (920) 735-6300   **Dom State:** WI   **Commenced Bus:** April 1988

Data Date	Weiss Safety Rating	RACR #1	RACR #2	Total Assets ($mil)	Capital ($mil)	Net Premium ($mil)	Net Income ($mil)
3-03	D-	0.36	0.30	65.8	16.6	78.9	2.3
3-02	D-	0.32	0.25	73.2	13.5	74.2	-0.2
2002	D-	0.34	0.28	63.5	16.2	303.1	3.3
2001	D-	0.31	0.25	73.6	14.2	244.6	2.1
2000	D+	0.49	0.41	54.8	14.2	214.1	1.7
1999	D+	0.52	0.42	40.9	14.3	192.6	-1.9
1998	C-	0.59	0.49	38.9	12.9	161.9	0.8

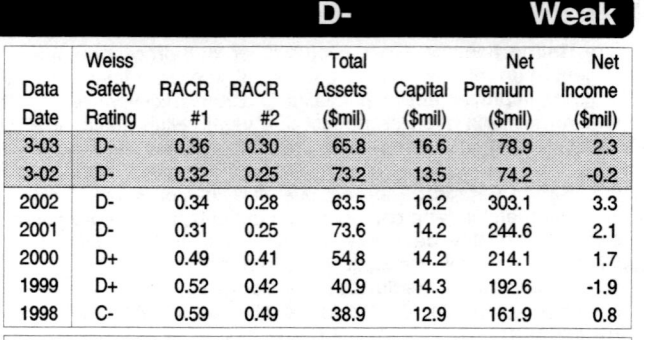

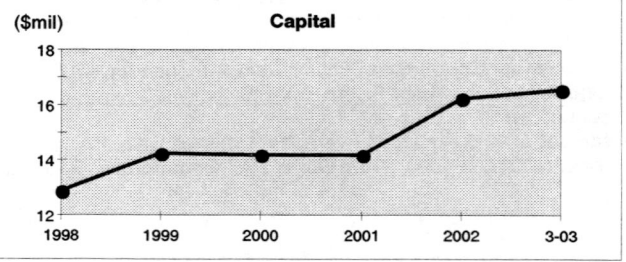

TOUCHPOINT INS CO INC   D+   Weak

Major Rating Factors: Fair profitability index (3.9 on a scale of 0 to 10). Strong capitalization (10.0) based on excellent current risk-adjusted capital (severe loss scenario). High quality investment portfolio (9.8).
Other Rating Factors: Excellent liquidity (8.0) with ample operational cash flow and liquid investments.
Principal Business: Comp med (94%), dental (3%), other (3%)
Mem Phys: 02: 1,027   **01:** 939   **02 MLR** 75%   **/ 02 Admin Exp** 25%
Enroll(000): Q1 03: 31   **02:** 38   **01:** 36   **Med Exp PMPM:** $7
Principal Investments: Cash and equiv (83%), nonaffiliate common stock (6%), other (10%)
Provider Compensation ($000): Capitation ($1,634), bonus arrang ($1,577), FFS ($360)
Total Member Encounters: N/A
Group Affiliation: United Health WI Group
Licensed in: WI
Address: 5 Innovation Ct, Appleton, WI 54912
Phone: (920) 735-6300   **Dom State:** WI   **Commenced Bus:** January 1999

Data Date	Weiss Safety Rating	RACR #1	RACR #2	Total Assets ($mil)	Capital ($mil)	Net Premium ($mil)	Net Income ($mil)
3-03	D+	4.53	3.77	4.1	3.3	1.1	0.1
3-02	N/A	N/A	N/A	N/A	N/A	N/A	N/A
2002	D+	0.00	0.00	4.9	3.4	4.4	0.1
2001	N/A	N/A	N/A	5.4	3.3	5.6	N/A
2000	U	2.12	1.75	3.9	2.4	3.9	-0.1
1999	C-	1.45	0.98	6.4	3.1	5.7	0.1
1998	U	3.03	2.73	N/A	N/A	N/A	0.0

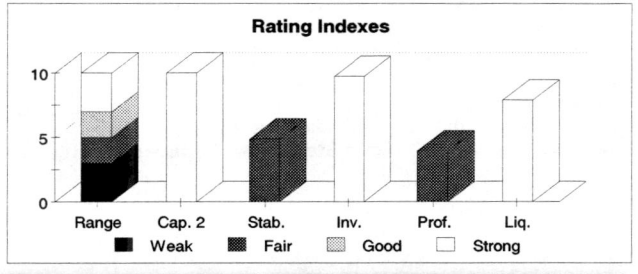

TRUSTMARK INSURANCE COMPANY   B   Good

Major Rating Factors: Good quality investment portfolio (5.9 on a scale of 0 to 10) with no exposure to mortgages and minimal holdings in junk bonds. Good overall profitability (6.1). Return on equity has been fair, averaging 5.0%. Good liquidity (5.9) with sufficient resources to handle a spike in claims.
Other Rating Factors: Good overall results on stability tests (5.2) good operational trends and excellent risk diversification. Strong capitalization (7.0) based on excellent risk adjusted capital (severe loss scenario).
Principal Business: Group health insurance (73%), reinsurance (12%), group life insurance (7%), individual health insurance (6%), and individual life insurance (2%).
Principal Investments: NonCMO investment grade bonds (45%), CMOs and structured securities (31%), common & preferred stock (18%), real estate (3%), and misc. investments (3%).
Investments in Affiliates: 10%
Group Affiliation: Trustmark Group
Licensed in: All states, the District of Columbia and Puerto Rico
Commenced Business: January 1913
Address: 400 Field Dr, Lake Forest, IL 60045-2581
Phone: (847) 615-1500   **Domicile State:** IL   **NAIC Code:** 61425

Data Date	Weiss Safety Rating	RACR #1	RACR #2	Total Assets ($mil)	Capital ($mil)	Net Premium ($mil)	Net Income ($mil)
6-03	B	1.32	1.03	981.0	184.7	439.7	18.7
6-02	B	1.45	1.10	1,062.9	224.1	512.4	9.2
2002	B	1.54	1.20	1,107.5	234.2	994.9	21.9
2001	B	1.47	1.12	1,123.5	219.3	989.2	27.2
2000	B	1.45	1.08	1,115.1	207.0	927.3	6.1
1999	B	1.64	1.23	1,051.4	247.1	911.4	-12.2
1998	B	1.80	1.37	979.0	256.6	823.5	18.1

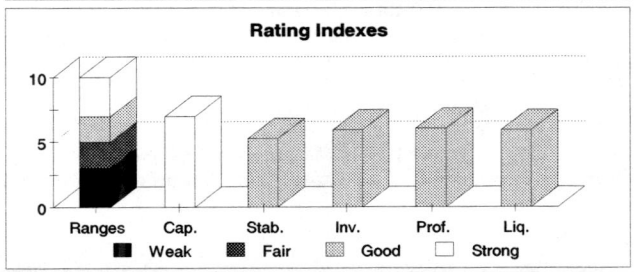

TRUSTMARK LIFE INSURANCE COMPANY   B-   Good

Major Rating Factors: Good current capitalization (6.1 on a scale of 0 to 10) based on good risk adjusted capital (severe loss scenario), although results have slipped from the excellent range during the last year. Good quality investment portfolio (6.8) despite mixed results such as: substantial holdings of BBB bonds but moderate junk bond exposure. Good overall profitability (5.8).
Other Rating Factors: Good liquidity (6.4). Fair overall results on stability tests (3.5) including negative cash flow from operations for 2002.
Principal Business: Reinsurance (82%) and group health insurance (18%).
Principal Investments: NonCMO investment grade bonds (59%), CMOs and structured securities (33%), noninv. grade bonds (4%), common & preferred stock (2%), and misc. investments (2%).
Investments in Affiliates: None
Group Affiliation: Trustmark Group
Licensed in: All states except AL, AK, NJ, VA, PR
Commenced Business: February 1925
Address: 400 Field Dr, Lake Forest, IL 60045-2581
Phone: (847) 615-1500   **Domicile State:** IL   **NAIC Code:** 62863

Data Date	Weiss Safety Rating	RACR #1	RACR #2	Total Assets ($mil)	Capital ($mil)	Net Premium ($mil)	Net Income ($mil)
6-03	B-	1.32	0.89	667.0	67.2	52.6	2.2
6-02	B-	1.50	0.90	763.8	49.5	68.6	2.3
2002	B-	2.16	1.24	653.7	62.0	12.6	16.0
2001	B-	1.40	0.85	747.6	47.7	148.1	2.7
2000	B-	1.30	0.84	700.4	43.6	163.3	-2.2
1999	B-	1.37	0.89	684.3	45.5	166.6	-5.1
1998	B-	1.85	1.18	603.1	52.8	135.8	4.7

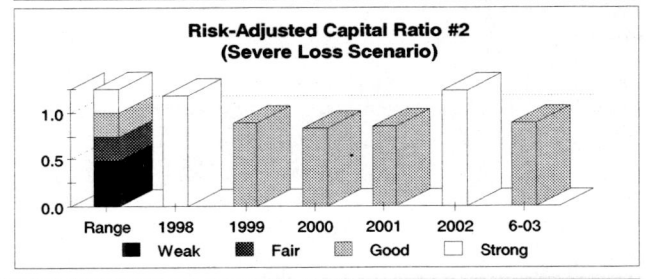

II. Analysis of Largest Companies

Winter 2003 - 04

TUFTS ASSOCIATED HEALTH MAINT ORG — B Good

Major Rating Factors: Good capitalization index (6.7 on a scale of 0 to 10) based on good current risk-adjusted capital (severe loss scenario). Good quality investment portfolio (5.8) containing large exposure to common stock. Good overall results on stability tests (6.0).
Other Rating Factors: Good liquidity (6.9) with sufficient resources (cash flows and marketable investments) to handle a spike in claims. Excellent profitability (8.2) despite a decline in earnings during 2002.
Principal Business: Comp med (68%), Medicare (32%).
Mem Phys: 02: 19,654 **01:** 18,671 **02 Admin Exp** 9%
Enroll(000): Q1 03: 677 **02:** 729 **01:** 701 **Med Exp PMPM:** $241
Principal Investments: Nonaffiliate common stock (43%), cash and equiv (29%), affiliate common stock (3%), pref stock (1%), other (25%).
Provider Compensation ($000): Contr fee ($623,788), capitation ($622,419), bonus arrang ($486,016), FFS ($312,094), salary ($22,006)
Total Member Encounters: Phys (3,286,950), non-phys (554,349)
Group Affiliation: Tufts Associated Health Plans Inc
Licensed in: MA
Address: 333 Wyman St, Waltham, MA 02254
Phone: (781) 466-9400 **Dom State:** MA **Commenced Bus:** December 1981

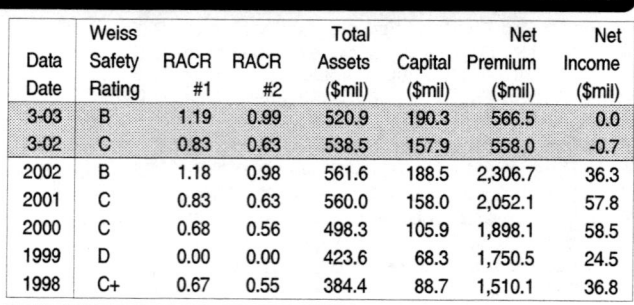

Data Date	Weiss Safety Rating	RACR #1	RACR #2	Total Assets ($mil)	Capital ($mil)	Net Premium ($mil)	Net Income ($mil)
3-03	B	1.19	0.99	520.9	190.3	566.5	0.0
3-02	C	0.83	0.63	538.5	157.9	558.0	-0.7
2002	B	1.18	0.98	561.6	188.5	2,306.7	36.3
2001	C	0.83	0.63	560.0	158.0	2,052.1	57.8
2000	C	0.68	0.56	498.3	105.9	1,898.1	58.5
1999	D	0.00	0.00	423.6	68.3	1,750.5	24.5
1998	C+	0.67	0.55	384.4	88.7	1,510.1	36.8

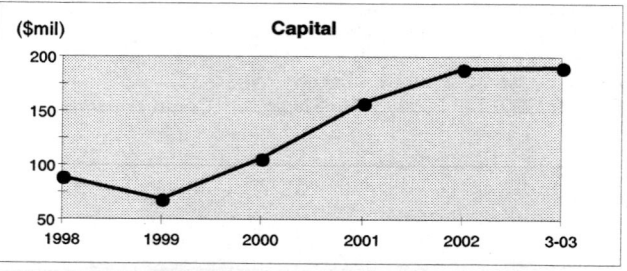

($mil) Capital

UCARE MINNESOTA * — B+ Good

Major Rating Factors: Good overall profitability index (6.7 on a scale of 0 to 10) despite a decline in earnings during 2002. Good capitalization index (5.4) based on good current risk-adjusted capital (severe loss scenario). Good liquidity (6.8) with sufficient resources (cash flows and marketable investments) to handle a spike in claims.
Other Rating Factors: High quality investment portfolio (9.9) containing no exposure to mortgages, junk bonds, or unaffiliated stocks. Excellent overall results on stability tests (8.0) based on consistent premium and capital growth in the last five years.
Principal Business: Medicaid (59%), Medicare (41%).
Mem Phys: 02: 23,047 **01:** 21,185 **02 MLR** 92% **/ 02 Admin Exp** 7%
Enroll(000): Q1 03: 107 **02:** 105 **01:** 99 **Med Exp PMPM:** $361
Principal Investments: Cash and equiv (54%), other (46%).
Provider Compensation ($000): Contr fee ($385,953), capitation ($31,224), FFS ($27,691), bonus arrang ($958)
Total Member Encounters: Phys (84,503), non-phys (35,288)
Group Affiliation: Dept of Family Practice U of MN
Licensed in: MN
Address: 2000 Summer St NE, Minneapolis, MN 55413
Phone: (612) 676-6500 **Dom State:** MN **Commenced Bus:** March 1988

Data Date	Weiss Safety Rating	RACR #1	RACR #2	Total Assets ($mil)	Capital ($mil)	Net Premium ($mil)	Net Income ($mil)
3-03	B+	0.98	0.82	149.5	42.8	131.5	2.8
3-02	B+	1.10	0.93	134.0	36.5	113.9	2.7
2002	B+	0.00	0.00	150.7	40.2	478.4	6.9
2001	B+	1.10	0.92	144.5	33.8	398.0	7.4
2000	B+	1.20	1.00	103.7	26.5	290.9	5.7
1999	B+	1.66	1.39	78.8	22.4	185.2	1.3
1998	B+	2.13	1.78	57.5	19.8	122.4	0.3

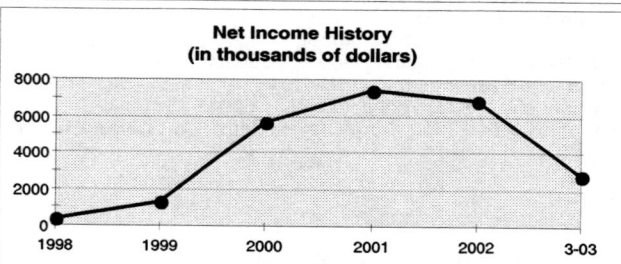

Net Income History (in thousands of dollars)

UCSD HEALTH PLAN — D- Weak

Major Rating Factors: Weak profitability index (0.9 on a scale of 0 to 10) with modest operating losses during each of the last five years. Poor capitalization index (2.6) based on weak current risk-adjusted capital (moderate loss scenario). Furthermore, this low level of risk-adjusted capital has been consistent in previous years. Weak overall results on stability tests (2.1).
Other Rating Factors: Good liquidity (6.8) with sufficient resources (cash flows and marketable investments) to handle a spike in claims.
Principal Business: Medicaid (100%).
Mem Phys: 02: N/A **01:** N/A **02 MLR** 90% **/ 02 Admin Exp** 16%
Enroll(000): Q1 03: 13 **02:** 12 **01:** 12 **Med Exp PMPM:** $92
Principal Investments ($000): Cash and equiv ($1,338)
Provider Compensation ($000): None
Total Member Encounters: N/A
Group Affiliation: None
Licensed in: CA
Address: 1899 McKee St, San Diego, CA 92110
Phone: (619) 471-9042 **Dom State:** CA **Commenced Bus:** September 1997

Data Date	Weiss Safety Rating	RACR #1	RACR #2	Total Assets ($mil)	Capital ($mil)	Net Premium ($mil)	Net Income ($mil)
3-03	D-	0.73	0.47	4.1	1.5	3.9	-0.7
3-02	D-	0.00	0.00	5.6	1.9	3.6	-0.4
2002	D-	0.88	0.57	4.6	1.8	14.9	-0.9
2001	D-	0.65	0.41	6.2	1.9	23.3	-0.2
2000	D-	0.87	0.56	6.9	2.1	29.3	-1.9
1999	D-	1.00	0.70	6.2	2.0	11.8	-3.8
1998	N/A	N/A	N/A	2.6	2.2	N/A	-1.4

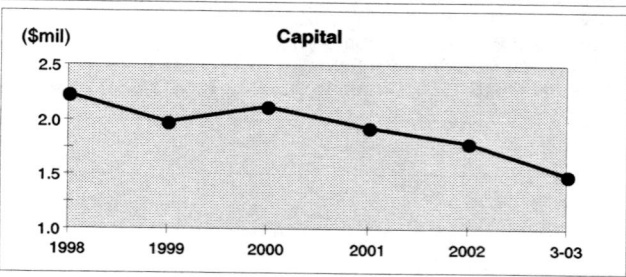

($mil) Capital

Winter 2003 - 04   II. Analysis of Largest Companies

ULTIMED HMO OF MICHIGAN INC   C-   Fair

Major Rating Factors: Weak profitability index (0.9 on a scale of 0 to 10) with modest operating losses during 2001 and 2002. Return on equity has been low, averaging 3%. Weak overall results on stability tests (2.4) based on a steep decline in capital during 2002. Weak liquidity (2.5) as a spike in claims may stretch capacity.
Other Rating Factors: Strong capitalization (8.7) based on excellent current risk-adjusted capital (severe loss scenario) reflecting significant improvement over results in 1998. High quality investment portfolio (9.1) containing no exposure to mortgages, junk bonds, or unaffiliated stocks.
Principal Business: Comp med (3%), other (97%)
Mem Phys: 02: N/A 01: 700 02 MLR 78% / 02 Admin Exp 27%
Enroll(000): Q1 03: 13 02: 14 01: 15 Med Exp PMPM: $88
Principal Investments: Cash and equiv (100%)
Provider Compensation ($000): Contr fee ($9,735), capitation ($1,978), bonus arrang ($741), FFS ($16), other ($1,084)
Total Member Encounters: Phys (23,681), non-phys (24,063)
Group Affiliation: Advance Medical Security Inc
Licensed in: MI
Address: 2401 20th St, Detroit, MI 48216
Phone: (313) 961-1717 **Dom State:** MI **Commenced Bus:** August 1994

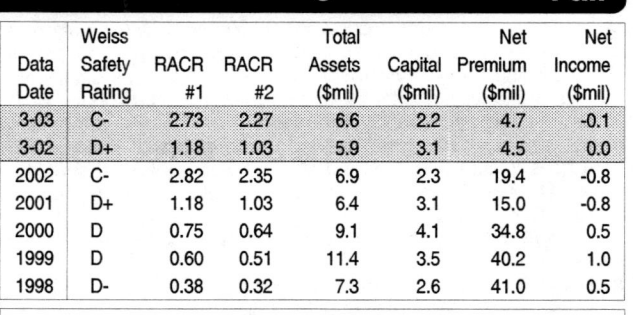

Data Date	Weiss Safety Rating	RACR #1	RACR #2	Total Assets ($mil)	Capital ($mil)	Net Premium ($mil)	Net Income ($mil)
3-03	C-	2.73	2.27	6.6	2.2	4.7	-0.1
3-02	D+	1.18	1.03	5.9	3.1	4.5	0.0
2002	C-	2.82	2.35	6.9	2.3	19.4	-0.8
2001	D+	1.18	1.03	6.4	3.1	15.0	-0.8
2000	D	0.75	0.64	9.1	4.1	34.8	0.5
1999	D	0.60	0.51	11.4	3.5	40.2	1.0
1998	D-	0.38	0.32	7.3	2.6	41.0	0.5

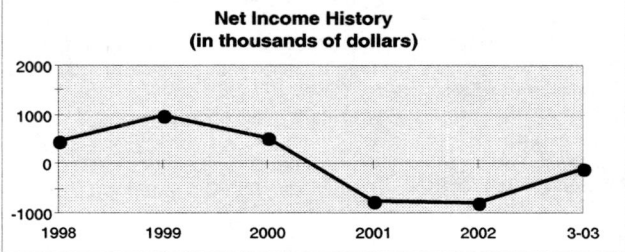

Net Income History (in thousands of dollars)

UNICARE HEALTH PLAN OF OKLAHOMA   B   Good

Major Rating Factors: Good overall profitability index (6.4 on a scale of 0 to 10). Good capitalization index (6.9) based on excellent current risk-adjusted capital (severe loss scenario) despite some fluctuation in capital levels. Good liquidity (6.9) with sufficient resources (cash flows and marketable investments) to handle a spike in claims.
Other Rating Factors: Fair overall results on stability tests (4.0) based on an excessive 68% enrollment growth during the period. Rating is significantly influenced by the good financial results of WellPoint Health Networks Inc. High quality investment portfolio (9.9) containing no exposure to mortgages, junk bonds, or unaffiliated stocks.
Principal Business: Medicaid (100%)
Mem Phys: 02: 877 01: 664 02 MLR 86% / 02 Admin Exp 12%
Enroll(000): Q1 03: 52 02: 41 01: 25 Med Exp PMPM: $152
Principal Investments: Cash and equiv (74%), other (26%)
Provider Compensation ($000): Contr fee ($47,575), capitation ($9,480)
Total Member Encounters: Phys (64,817), non-phys (9,482)
Group Affiliation: WellPoint Health Networks Inc
Licensed in: OK
Address: 120 N Robinson Ave Ste 73, Oklahoma City, OK 73102-7400
Phone: (877) 864-2273 **Dom State:** OK **Commenced Bus:** July 2000

Data Date	Weiss Safety Rating	RACR #1	RACR #2	Total Assets ($mil)	Capital ($mil)	Net Premium ($mil)	Net Income ($mil)
3-03	B	1.29	1.07	21.8	4.5	22.2	-0.9
3-02	B	2.04	1.73	15.7	4.9	14.6	0.1
2002	B	1.49	1.24	20.1	5.5	69.6	0.7
2001	U	2.02	1.72	14.6	4.8	38.9	1.7
2000	B	N/A	N/A	6.5	2.6	9.7	-0.1
1999	N/A	N/A	N/A	N/A	N/A	N/A	N/A
1998	N/A	N/A	N/A	N/A	N/A	N/A	N/A

Risk-Adjusted Capital Ratio #2 (Severe Loss Scenario)
Range / 1998 / 1999 / 2000 / 2001 / 2002 / 3-03
■ Weak   ▨ Fair   ░ Good   □ Strong

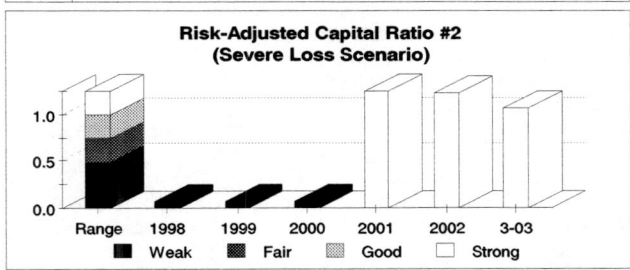

UNICARE HEALTH PLAN OF VIRGINIA INC   B   Good

Major Rating Factors: Good overall profitability index (5.8 on a scale of 0 to 10). Strong overall capitalization (7.5) based on excellent current risk-adjusted capital (severe loss scenario) despite some fluctuation in capital levels. High quality investment portfolio (9.9) containing no exposure to mortgages, junk bonds, or unaffiliated stocks.
Other Rating Factors: Excellent liquidity (7.0) with ample operational cash flow and liquid investments.
Principal Business: Medicaid (86%), comp med (14%)
Mem Phys: 02: 1,431 01: 1,393 02 MLR 86% / 02 Admin Exp 6%
Enroll(000): Q1 03: 42 02: 39 01: 42 Med Exp PMPM: $143
Principal Investments: Cash and equiv (79%), other (21%)
Provider Compensation ($000): Contr fee ($55,214), capitation ($9,687)
Total Member Encounters: Phys (260,048), non-phys (39,132)
Group Affiliation: WellPoint Health Networks Inc
Licensed in: VA
Address: 4701 Cox Rd Ste 301, Glen Ellen, VA 23060-6802
Phone: (805) 864-2273 **Dom State:** VA **Commenced Bus:** December 2001

Data Date	Weiss Safety Rating	RACR #1	RACR #2	Total Assets ($mil)	Capital ($mil)	Net Premium ($mil)	Net Income ($mil)
3-03	B	1.72	1.43	18.7	8.4	22.2	-0.4
3-02	U	4.08	3.46	16.7	6.1	19.7	1.0
2002	B	1.79	1.49	19.5	8.8	80.1	3.8
2001	U	4.15	3.50	10.7	5.0	7.6	-1.0
2000	N/A	N/A	N/A	N/A	N/A	N/A	N/A
1999	N/A	N/A	N/A	N/A	N/A	N/A	N/A
1998	N/A	N/A	N/A	N/A	N/A	N/A	N/A

Rating Indexes
Range / Cap. 2 / Stab. / Inv. / Prof. / Liq.
■ Weak   ▨ Fair   ░ Good   □ Strong

www.WeissRatings.com   283   * Denotes a Weiss Recommended Company

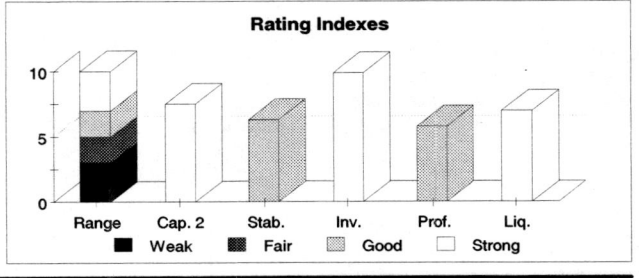

II. Analysis of Largest Companies

Winter 2003 - 04

UNICARE HEALTH PLANS OF TEXAS INC   C   Fair

Major Rating Factors: Fair overall results on stability tests (4.4 on a scale of 0 to 10) based on a significant 42% decrease in enrollment during the period, a steep decline in premium revenue in 2002. Rating is significantly influenced by the good financial results of WellPoint Health Networks Inc. Weak profitability index (0.4) with operating losses during 1998, 1999, 2000 and 2002. Average return on equity has been extremely poor. Good liquidity (6.8) with sufficient resources (cash flows and marketable investments) to handle a spike in claims.

Other Rating Factors: Strong capitalization index (9.2) based on excellent current risk-adjusted capital (severe loss scenario). High quality investment portfolio (9.9) containing no exposure to mortgages, junk bonds, or unaffiliated stocks.

Principal Business: Comp med (100%)
Mem Phys: 02: 4,887   **01:** 4,245   **02 MLR** 92%   / **02 Admin Exp** 14%
Enroll(000): Q1 03: 40   **02:** 48   **01:** 82   **Med Exp PMPM:** $149
Principal Investments: Cash and equiv (55%), other (45%)
Provider Compensation ($000): Contr fee ($117,300), capitation ($9,704)
Total Member Encounters: Phys (200,652), non-phys (67,078)
Group Affiliation: WellPoint Health Networks Inc
Licensed in: TX
Address: Two Greenway Plaza Suite 500, Houston, TX 77046
Phone: (713) 479-4100   **Dom State:** TX   **Commenced Bus:** January 1997

Data Date	Weiss Safety Rating	RACR #1	RACR #2	Total Assets ($mil)	Capital ($mil)	Net Premium ($mil)	Net Income ($mil)
3-03	C	3.08	2.57	45.4	26.4	26.0	-1.3
3-02	C-	1.26	0.94	52.3	26.7	33.7	-2.0
2002	C	3.20	2.67	47.6	27.4	125.1	-4.1
2001	D+	1.26	0.94	50.7	20.8	161.8	19.4
2000	E+	0.12	0.10	45.2	-9.3	181.8	-36.0
1999	D-	0.36	0.30	32.8	3.6	74.1	-32.8
1998	D+	1.07	0.90	22.1	9.1	48.3	-12.6

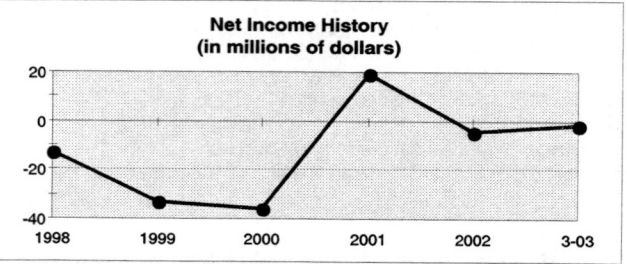

Net Income History (in millions of dollars)

UNICARE HEALTH PLANS OF THE MIDWEST *   B+   Good

Major Rating Factors: Good overall profitability index (6.2 on a scale of 0 to 10) with operating gains in each of the last five years. Good overall results on stability tests (6.9) based on consistent premium and capital growth in the last five years but a decline in enrollment during 2002. Rating is significantly influenced by the good financial results of WellPoint Health Networks Inc. Good liquidity (5.9) with sufficient resources (cash flows and marketable investments) to handle a spike in claims.

Other Rating Factors: Strong capitalization (8.7) based on excellent current risk-adjusted capital (severe loss scenario) reflecting improvement over results in 1999. High quality investment portfolio (9.9) containing no exposure to mortgages, junk bonds, or unaffiliated stocks.

Principal Business: Comp med (89%), FEHB (11%)
Mem Phys: 02: 9,780   **01:** 8,454   **02 MLR** 88%   / **02 Admin Exp** 11%
Enroll(000): Q1 03: 162   **02:** 163   **01:** 173   **Med Exp PMPM:** $145
Principal Investments: Cash and equiv (16%), other (84%)
Provider Compensation ($000): Contr fee ($201,515), capitation ($81,107), bonus arrang ($473)
Total Member Encounters: Phys (186,327), non-phys (35,499)
Group Affiliation: WellPoint Health Networks Inc
Licensed in: IL, IN
Address: 233 South Wacker Dr, Ste 3900, Chicago, IL 60606
Phone: (877) 864-2273   **Dom State:** IL   **Commenced Bus:** August 1993

Data Date	Weiss Safety Rating	RACR #1	RACR #2	Total Assets ($mil)	Capital ($mil)	Net Premium ($mil)	Net Income ($mil)
3-03	B+	2.71	2.26	151.4	36.6	91.9	2.0
3-02	B	2.37	2.06	118.8	36.0	83.9	3.4
2002	B+	2.67	2.23	118.8	36.0	333.5	2.4
2001	B	2.31	2.01	118.6	32.6	333.3	0.6
2000	B	1.49	1.27	98.6	29.9	361.5	0.5
1999	B-	0.95	0.82	66.6	17.2	388.0	3.9
1998	C+	1.63	1.42	89.9	15.3	332.8	2.0

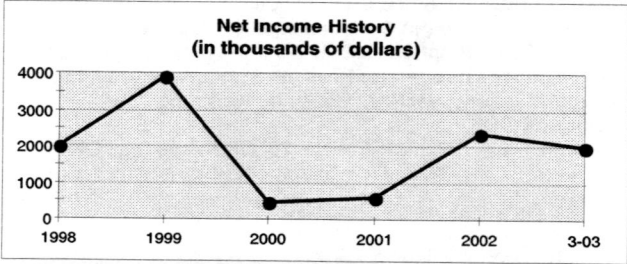

Net Income History (in thousands of dollars)

UNICARE LIFE & HEALTH INSURANCE COMPANY   B   Good

Major Rating Factors: Good overall capitalization (5.7 on a scale of 0 to 10) based on mixed results -- excessive policy leverage mitigated by excellent risk adjusted capital (severe loss scenario). Moreover, capital levels have been consistently high over the last five years. Good quality investment portfolio (6.5) despite mixed results such as: substantial holdings of BBB bonds but moderate junk bond exposure. Good liquidity (6.4).

Other Rating Factors: Good overall results on stability tests (5.1) excellent operational trends, excellent risk adjusted capital for prior years and excellent risk diversification. Fair profitability (3.9).

Principal Business: Group health insurance (62%), individual health insurance (19%), and group life insurance (18%).
Principal Investments: NonCMO investment grade bonds (70%), CMOs and structured securities (11%), cash (11%), and noninv. grade bonds (8%).
Investments in Affiliates: None
Group Affiliation: WellPoint Health Networks Inc
Licensed in: All states, the District of Columbia and Puerto Rico
Commenced Business: December 1980
Address: 1209 Orange St, Wilmington, DE 19801
Phone: (877) 864-2273   **Domicile State:** DE   **NAIC Code:** 80314

Data Date	Weiss Safety Rating	RACR #1	RACR #2	Total Assets ($mil)	Capital ($mil)	Net Premium ($mil)	Net Income ($mil)
6-03	B	1.75	1.32	1,463.5	283.0	740.5	30.1
6-02	B	1.73	1.26	1,324.5	256.7	672.9	-2.7
2002	B	1.62	1.21	1,381.4	259.5	1,381.0	-10.7
2001	C	1.69	1.25	1,217.7	255.6	1,214.1	20.2
2000	B-	1.40	1.04	1,260.1	226.0	1,234.3	-70.2
1999	B-	1.99	1.46	1,237.4	225.4	1,109.1	-22.0
1998	B-	1.59	1.19	1,227.6	226.7	1,139.8	32.0

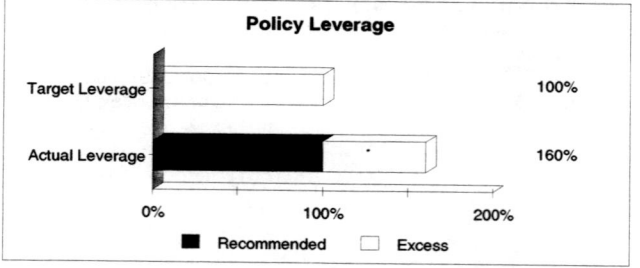

Policy Leverage
Target Leverage: 100%
Actual Leverage: 160%
(Recommended / Excess)

Winter 2003 - 04
II. Analysis of Largest Companies

UNION FIDELITY LIFE INSURANCE COMPANY — C+ — Fair

Major Rating Factors: Fair overall results on stability tests (4.8 on a scale of 0 to 10) including fair financial strength of affiliated General Electric Corp Group. Good quality investment portfolio (6.6) despite mixed results such as: no exposure to mortgages and large holdings of BBB rated bonds but small junk bond holdings. Strong capitalization (10.0) based on excellent risk adjusted capital (severe loss scenario).
Other Rating Factors: Excellent profitability (7.9). Excellent liquidity (8.0).
Principal Business: Reinsurance (38%), group health insurance (34%), group life insurance (20%), individual health insurance (8%), and individual life insurance (7%).
Principal Investments: NonCMO investment grade bonds (72%), CMOs and structured securities (13%), noninv. grade bonds (6%), common & preferred stock (6%), and misc. investments (3%).
Investments in Affiliates: 2%
Group Affiliation: General Electric Corp Group
Licensed in: All states, the District of Columbia and Puerto Rico
Commenced Business: February 1926
Address: 123 N Wacker Dr, Chicago, IL 60606
Phone: (215) 953-3427 **Domicile State:** IL **NAIC Code:** 62596

Data Date	Weiss Safety Rating	RACR #1	RACR #2	Total Assets ($mil)	Capital ($mil)	Net Premium ($mil)	Net Income ($mil)
6-03	C+	10.62	6.02	1,288.3	630.5	107.6	26.2
6-02	C+	8.47	5.00	1,404.0	582.1	123.7	38.3
2002	C+	10.77	6.02	1,328.7	603.7	230.6	45.7
2001	C+	7.57	4.51	1,369.9	546.9	323.5	74.0
2000	C+	5.32	3.29	1,273.6	410.4	365.6	99.7
1999	C+	N/A	N/A	1,313.7	350.4	533.9	47.6
1998	C+	3.51	2.42	880.4	198.1	335.7	30.9

General Electric Corp Group Composite Group Rating: C+ Largest Group Members	Assets ($mil)	Weiss Safety Rating
GENERAL ELECTRIC CAPITAL ASR CO	30673	C+
GE LIFE ANNUITY ASR CO	18888	B
EMPLOYERS REINSURANCE CORP	15569	C+
FIRST COLONY LIFE INS CO	13330	B
EMPLOYERS REASSURANCE CORP	5653	C

UNION HEALTH SERVICE INC — C — Fair

Major Rating Factors: Weak profitability index (2.3 on a scale of 0 to 10) with modest operating losses during 2000 and 2002. Good capitalization index (6.0) based on good current risk-adjusted capital (severe loss scenario). Good overall results on stability tests (5.3).
Other Rating Factors: Good liquidity (6.6) with sufficient resources (cash flows and marketable investments) to handle a spike in claims. High quality investment portfolio (7.9).
Principal Business: Med only (76%), Medicare (10%), FEHB (4%), dental (4%), other (6%).
Mem Phys: 02: 188 01: 175 **02 MLR** 83% / **02 Admin Exp** 19%
Enroll(000): Q1 03: 31 02: 30 01: 25 **Med Exp PMPM:** $82
Principal Investments: Nonaffiliate common stock (19%), cash and equiv (16%), other (66%).
Provider Compensation ($000): Contr fee ($9,004), other ($17,946)
Total Member Encounters: Phys (126,646)
Group Affiliation: None
Licensed in: IL
Address: 1634 W Polk St, Chicago, IL 60612
Phone: (312) 829-4224 **Dom State:** IL **Commenced Bus:** April 1955

Data Date	Weiss Safety Rating	RACR #1	RACR #2	Total Assets ($mil)	Capital ($mil)	Net Premium ($mil)	Net Income ($mil)
3-03	C	1.08	0.90	11.5	6.8	8.9	0.3
3-02	C+	1.37	1.10	11.9	7.1	7.7	-0.1
2002	C	1.01	0.84	11.6	6.4	32.5	-1.0
2001	C+	1.37	1.10	11.7	7.0	28.2	0.2
2000	C	2.13	1.73	10.5	6.3	24.5	-0.7
1999	C	2.48	2.02	10.4	5.8	22.6	0.6
1998	C-	2.49	2.04	9.9	6.0	23.1	1.7

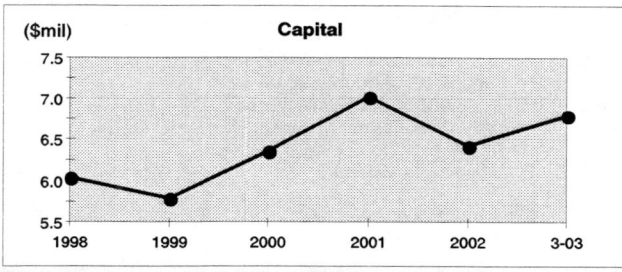

Capital chart ($mil), 1998–3-03: values approximately 6.0, 5.7, 6.3, 7.0, 6.4, 6.8

UNION LABOR LIFE INSURANCE COMPANY — D+ — Weak

Major Rating Factors: Weak profitability (1.3 on a scale of 0 to 10). Excellent expense controls. Weak overall results on stability tests (2.8). Fair overall capitalization (3.6) based on mixed results -- excessive policy leverage mitigated by fair risk adjusted capital (moderate loss scenario).
Other Rating Factors: Fair quality investment portfolio (4.2). Good liquidity (5.0).
Principal Business: Group health insurance (68%), group life insurance (20%), individual health insurance (5%), reinsurance (5%), and group retirement contracts (1%).
Principal Investments: NonCMO investment grade bonds (29%), CMOs and structured securities (24%), real estate (18%), mortgages in good standing (10%), and misc. investments (19%).
Investments in Affiliates: 3%
Group Affiliation: Union Labor Group
Licensed in: All states except PR
Commenced Business: May 1927
Address: 111 Massachusetts Ave NW, Washington, DC 20001
Phone: (202) 682-6690 **Domicile State:** MD **NAIC Code:** 69744

Data Date	Weiss Safety Rating	RACR #1	RACR #2	Total Assets ($mil)	Capital ($mil)	Net Premium ($mil)	Net Income ($mil)
3-03	D+	0.82	0.51	3,022.6	51.6	101.8	-5.1
3-02	C-	0.80	0.53	2,983.5	43.0	97.5	-3.4
2002	D+	0.86	0.54	3,063.7	51.1	412.0	14.5
2001	C-	0.85	0.58	2,925.9	51.8	382.1	-45.7
2000	C	1.58	1.02	2,948.2	112.4	345.0	8.0
1999	C-	1.83	1.32	2,701.7	119.5	320.8	-12.9
1998	C-	1.95	1.35	2,693.4	111.8	298.0	-4.1

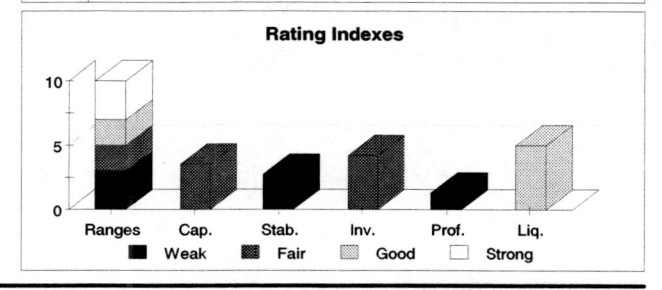

Rating Indexes bar chart: Ranges, Cap. (Fair), Stab. (Weak), Inv. (Fair), Prof. (Weak), Liq. (Good). Legend: Weak, Fair, Good, Strong.

www.WeissRatings.com   285   * Denotes a Weiss Recommended Company

II. Analysis of Largest Companies
Winter 2003 - 04

UNION SECURITY LIFE INSURANCE COMPANY B Good

Major Rating Factors: Good quality investment portfolio (6.6 on a scale of 0 to 10) despite mixed results such as: no exposure to mortgages and substantial holdings of BBB bonds but small junk bond holdings. Good overall profitability (6.3). Return on equity has been good over the last five years, averaging 12.0%. Fair overall results on stability tests (4.4) including fair financial strength of affiliated Fortis Inc and negative cash flow from operations for 2002.
Other Rating Factors: Strong capitalization (8.9) based on excellent risk adjusted capital (severe loss scenario). Excellent liquidity (7.1).
Principal Business: Credit health insurance (46%), credit life insurance (38%), reinsurance (15%), and group life insurance (1%).
Principal Investments: NonCMO investment grade bonds (56%), CMOs and structured securities (28%), cash (8%), and noninv. grade bonds (7%).
Investments in Affiliates: None
Group Affiliation: Fortis Inc
Licensed in: All states except ME, NY
Commenced Business: May 1955
Address: 260 Interstate N Cir SE, Atlanta, GA 30339-2210
Phone: (404) 264-6976 **Domicile State:** DE **NAIC Code:** 98884

Data Date	Weiss Safety Rating	RACR #1	RACR #2	Total Assets ($mil)	Capital ($mil)	Net Premium ($mil)	Net Income ($mil)
6-03	B	3.66	2.24	166.3	52.9	28.7	5.1
6-02	B	2.48	1.54	175.9	49.9	39.8	2.4
2002	B	3.20	1.98	184.2	51.7	81.8	3.1
2001	B	2.35	1.46	196.7	50.5	101.1	2.0
2000	B	2.66	1.65	222.5	60.1	107.5	5.0
1999	B	3.18	2.03	206.7	68.0	96.2	14.4
1998	B	3.21	2.03	222.3	61.4	99.1	8.1

Rating Indexes

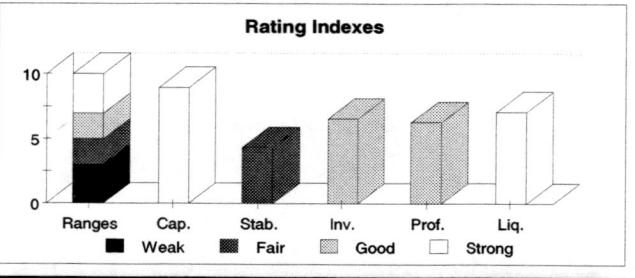

UNITED AMERICAN INSURANCE COMPANY B Good

Major Rating Factors: Good overall capitalization (5.1 on a scale of 0 to 10) based on good risk adjusted capital (moderate loss scenario). However, capital levels have fluctuated somewhat during past years. Good quality investment portfolio (5.7) despite mixed results such as: large holdings of BBB rated bonds but junk bond exposure equal to 63% of capital. Good liquidity (6.9).
Other Rating Factors: Good overall results on stability tests (5.1) excellent operational trends and excellent risk diversification. Excellent profitability (8.3) with operating gains in each of the last five years.
Principal Business: Individual health insurance (87%), individual life insurance (8%), group health insurance (3%), and individual annuities (2%).
Principal Investments: NonCMO investment grade bonds (74%), noninv. grade bonds (10%), common & preferred stock (8%), cash (2%), and misc. investments (5%).
Investments in Affiliates: 5%
Group Affiliation: Torchmark Corp
Licensed in: All states except NY, PR
Commenced Business: August 1981
Address: 3700 S Stonebridge Dr, McKinney, TX 75070
Phone: (972) 529-5085 **Domicile State:** DE **NAIC Code:** 92916

Data Date	Weiss Safety Rating	RACR #1	RACR #2	Total Assets ($mil)	Capital ($mil)	Net Premium ($mil)	Net Income ($mil)
6-03	B	1.06	0.75	969.0	136.2	375.3	39.9
6-02	B+	1.26	0.90	895.0	146.0	369.2	19.9
2002	B	1.45	1.04	910.9	176.5	732.7	69.8
2001	B+	1.37	0.98	923.1	159.1	722.4	51.0
2000	B+	1.17	0.83	839.5	106.3	635.4	31.1
1999	A-	1.99	1.41	823.6	145.4	544.7	41.8
1998	A-	1.82	1.36	775.0	144.2	479.7	39.3

Risk-Adjusted Capital Ratio #1 (Moderate Loss Scenario)

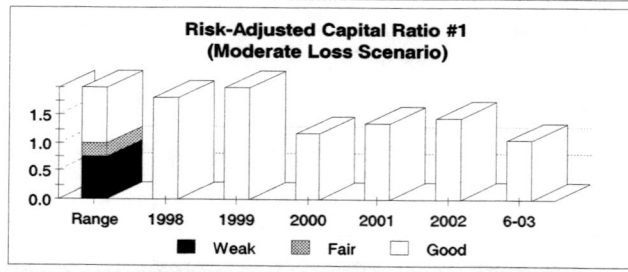

UNITED CONCORDIA COMPANIES INC D Weak

Major Rating Factors: Poor overall capitalization (1.6 on a scale of 0 to 10) based on excessive policy leverage and weak risk adjusted capital (moderate loss scenario). Weak profitability (1.3) with operating losses during the first six months of 2003. Weak liquidity (0.8) as a spike in claims may stretch capacity.
Other Rating Factors: Weak overall results on stability tests (1.6) including weak risk adjusted capital in prior years, negative cash flow from operations for 2002 and lack of operational experience. Good quality investment portfolio (5.6).
Principal Business: Group health insurance (100%).
Principal Investments: NonCMO investment grade bonds (53%) and common & preferred stock (43%).
Investments in Affiliates: 43%
Group Affiliation: Highmark Inc
Licensed in: PA
Commenced Business: January 2001
Address: 4401 Deer Path Rd, Harrisburg, PA 17110
Phone: (800) 972-4191 **Domicile State:** PA **NAIC Code:** 89070

Data Date	Weiss Safety Rating	RACR #1	RACR #2	Total Assets ($mil)	Capital ($mil)	Net Premium ($mil)	Net Income ($mil)
6-03	D	0.42	0.38	210.2	76.5	162.4	-8.9
6-02	D-	0.43	0.38	110.8	37.2	153.0	-4.9
2002	D-	0.35	0.33	0.0	0.0	0.0	0.0
2001	D-	0.53	0.47	0.0	0.0	0.0	0.0
2000	N/A	N/A	N/A	0.0	0.0	0.0	0.0
1999	N/A	N/A	N/A	0.0	0.0	0.0	0.0
1998	N/A	N/A	N/A	0.0	0.0	0.0	0.0

Policy Leverage

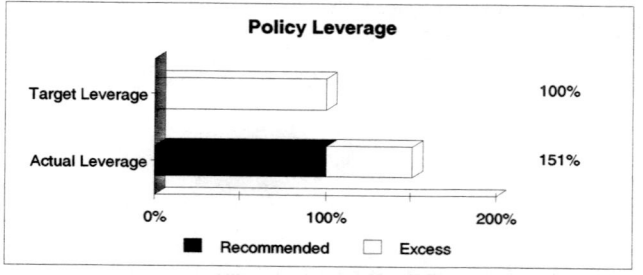

Target Leverage 100%
Actual Leverage 151%

Winter 2003 - 04
II. Analysis of Largest Companies

UNITED CONCORDIA INSURANCE COMPANY — C+ Fair

Major Rating Factors: Fair overall results on stability tests (4.5 on a scale of 0 to 10) including negative cash flow from operations for 2002. Good overall profitability (6.7). Good liquidity (6.8) with sufficient resources to handle a spike in claims.
Other Rating Factors: Strong capitalization (7.6) based on excellent risk adjusted capital (severe loss scenario). High quality investment portfolio (9.2).
Principal Business: Group health insurance (99%) and reinsurance (1%).
Principal Investments: NonCMO investment grade bonds (81%).
Investments in Affiliates: None
Group Affiliation: Highmark Inc
Licensed in: AK, AZ, AR, CA, CO, CT, FL, GA, ID, IN, IA, KS, LA, ME, MD, MI, MN, MS, MT, NE, NV, NM, ND, OH, OK, OR, SC, SD, TN, TX, UT, VT, VA, WA, WV, WY
Commenced Business: December 1975
Address: 2198 E Camelback Rd Ste 260, Phoenix, AZ 85016
Phone: (717) 763-6627 **Domicile State:** AZ **NAIC Code:** 85766

Data Date	Weiss Safety Rating	RACR #1	RACR #2	Total Assets ($mil)	Capital ($mil)	Net Premium ($mil)	Net Income ($mil)
6-03	C+	1.91	1.40	50.6	29.9	36.5	1.4
6-02	C+	1.46	1.20	59.5	29.8	53.6	2.5
2002	C+	1.49	1.12	53.4	28.5	90.1	3.9
2001	C+	1.03	0.85	51.8	27.3	128.3	12.9
2000	C+	N/A	N/A	24.6	10.3	64.1	2.1
1999	C+	1.02	0.85	15.6	8.3	38.2	-0.5
1998	C+	1.59	1.33	12.7	7.3	23.6	-1.2

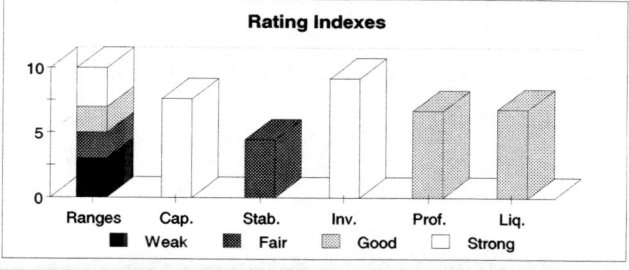

UNITED CONCORDIA LIFE & HEALTH INSURANCE — C+ Fair

Major Rating Factors: Fair overall results on stability tests (4.4 on a scale of 0 to 10) including weak risk adjusted capital in prior years. Good current capitalization (5.4) based on mixed results -- excessive policy leverage mitigated by good risk adjusted capital (severe loss scenario) reflecting significant improvement over results in 2000. Good liquidity (6.4) with sufficient resources to handle a spike in claims.
Other Rating Factors: High quality investment portfolio (7.1). Excellent profitability (8.4) despite modest operating losses during 1998 and 1999.
Principal Business: Group health insurance (52%) and reinsurance (48%).
Principal Investments: NonCMO investment grade bonds (41%), common & preferred stock (26%), and CMOs and structured securities (17%).
Investments in Affiliates: 26%
Group Affiliation: Highmark Inc
Licensed in: DC, DE, IL, KY, MD, MO, NJ, PA
Commenced Business: December 1965
Address: 4401 Deer Path Rd, Harrisburg, PA 17110
Phone: (717) 763-3151 **Domicile State:** PA **NAIC Code:** 62294

Data Date	Weiss Safety Rating	RACR #1	RACR #2	Total Assets ($mil)	Capital ($mil)	Net Premium ($mil)	Net Income ($mil)
6-03	C+	1.02	0.89	134.2	79.3	193.6	12.7
6-02	C+	0.71	0.63	101.4	47.2	167.2	3.9
2002	C+	0.81	0.71	126.0	65.5	359.9	21.5
2001	C	0.66	0.59	95.6	50.5	307.5	21.9
2000	C	0.50	0.43	61.2	23.4	211.4	11.9
1999	C	0.48	0.43	33.7	11.8	87.7	-0.6
1998	C	1.14	1.09	17.0	11.5	13.2	-0.3

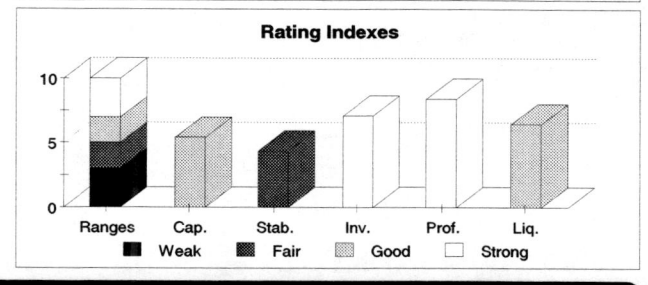

UNITED HEALTHCARE INS CO OF NY — B- Good

Major Rating Factors: Fair profitability index (4.9 on a scale of 0 to 10). Strong capitalization (10.0) based on excellent current risk-adjusted capital (severe loss scenario) reflecting improvement over results in 2000. High quality investment portfolio (9.6) containing little or no exposure to mortgages, junk bonds, or unaffiliated stocks.
Other Rating Factors: Weak liquidity (2.1) as a spike in claims may stretch capacity.
Principal Business: Comp med (66%), med supp (32%), other (2%)
Mem Phys: 02: N/A 01: N/A **02 MLR** 302% **/ 02 Admin Exp** 14%
Enroll(000): Q1 03: 1,595 02: 1,573 01: 1,489 **Med Exp PMPM:** $95
Principal Investments: Cash and equiv (9%), other (91%)
Provider Compensation ($000): Contr fee ($1,695,987), FFS ($38,547)
Total Member Encounters: Phys (11,923,429), non-phys (2,679,391)
Group Affiliation: United HealthGroup Inc
Licensed in: DC, NY
Address: 2950 Expressway Dr S Suite 240, Islandia, NY 11749-1412
Phone: (877) 832-7734 **Dom State:** NY **Commenced Bus:** December 1995

Data Date	Weiss Safety Rating	RACR #1	RACR #2	Total Assets ($mil)	Capital ($mil)	Net Premium ($mil)	Net Income ($mil)
3-03	B-	12.86	10.72	902.3	150.9	169.3	8.3
3-02	B-	0.00	0.00	807.7	114.6	131.4	7.4
2002	B-	8.02	6.69	828.8	94.0	580.7	27.1
2001	N/A	N/A	N/A	760.4	108.5	447.9	N/A
2000	U	1.25	0.75	640.7	91.2	374.7	21.7
1999	B-	1.71	1.19	321.2	71.6	269.0	14.3
1998	C+	1.44	0.99	286.6	54.1	211.2	1.6

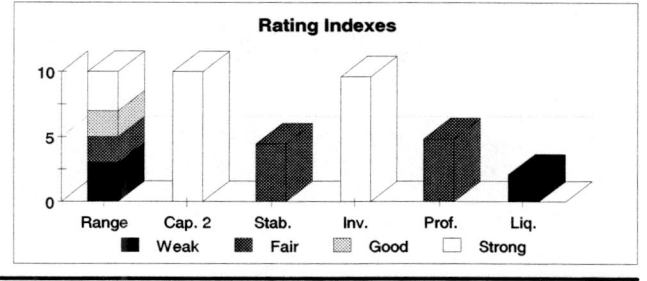

II. Analysis of Largest Companies

UNITED HEALTHCARE INSURANCE COMPANY — B- Good

Major Rating Factors: Fair overall capitalization (4.7 on a scale of 0 to 10) based on mixed results -- excessive policy leverage mitigated by good risk adjusted capital (severe loss scenario). However, capital levels have fluctuated somewhat during past years. Fair overall results on stability tests (4.9). Good liquidity (6.6).
Other Rating Factors: High quality investment portfolio (7.7). Excellent profitability (8.7) with operating gains in each of the last five years.
Principal Business: Group health insurance (91%) and reinsurance (8%).
Principal Investments: NonCMO investment grade bonds (76%), CMOs and structured securities (14%), common & preferred stock (9%), and , and misc. investments (1%).
Investments in Affiliates: 12%
Group Affiliation: United HealthGroup Inc
Licensed in: All states except NY
Commenced Business: April 1972
Address: 450 Columbus Blvd, Hartford, CT 06115
Phone: (860) 702-5000 **Domicile State:** CT **NAIC Code:** 79413

Data Date	Weiss Safety Rating	RACR #1	RACR #2	Total Assets ($mil)	Capital ($mil)	Net Premium ($mil)	Net Income ($mil)
6-03	B-	1.15	0.97	4,775.7	870.6	5,110.6	443.4
6-02	B-	1.28	1.08	4,193.0	792.9	3,855.8	310.0
2002	B-	0.90	0.77	4,723.5	1,078.0	8,166.6	662.2
2001	B-	0.97	0.83	4,202.8	989.8	6,610.8	503.0
2000	B-	1.04	0.89	3,862.6	1,011.9	6,212.9	417.8
1999	B-	1.00	0.85	3,395.4	875.2	5,975.4	275.7
1998	B-	1.14	0.96	3,264.5	919.4	5,737.0	272.1

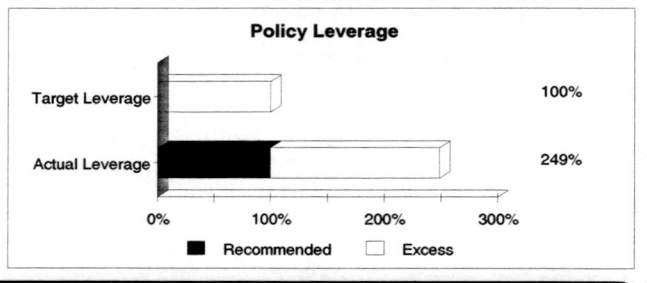

Policy Leverage
Target Leverage: 100%
Actual Leverage: 249%

UNITED HEALTHCARE INSURANCE COMPANY OF IL — C+ Fair

Major Rating Factors: Fair liquidity (3.8 on a scale of 0 to 10) as cash from operations and sale of marketable assets may not be adequate to cover a spike in claims. Fair overall results on stability tests (4.4) including fair risk adjusted capital in prior years. Good overall capitalization (5.0) based on mixed results -- excessive policy leverage mitigated by excellent risk adjusted capital (severe loss scenario).
Other Rating Factors: High quality investment portfolio (8.8). Excellent profitability (8.9) with operating gains in each of the last five years.
Principal Business: Group health insurance (100%).
Principal Investments: NonCMO investment grade bonds (87%), CMOs and structured securities (7%), and cash (6%).
Investments in Affiliates: None
Group Affiliation: United HealthGroup Inc
Licensed in: FL, IL
Commenced Business: December 1991
Address: 233 N Michigan Ave, Chicago, IL 60601
Phone: (312) 424-4460 **Domicile State:** IL **NAIC Code:** 60318

Data Date	Weiss Safety Rating	RACR #1	RACR #2	Total Assets ($mil)	Capital ($mil)	Net Premium ($mil)	Net Income ($mil)
6-03	C+	1.60	1.31	117.0	66.0	168.5	18.0
6-02	C	1.22	1.00	110.1	51.9	164.5	2.0
2002	C	1.21	0.99	103.8	48.6	325.5	12.7
2001	C	1.08	0.89	109.4	47.8	351.2	11.6
2000	C	0.89	0.74	96.5	36.9	291.3	13.0
1999	C	0.73	0.60	77.3	28.6	242.1	4.5
1998	C	0.77	0.63	85.4	29.8	246.9	9.6

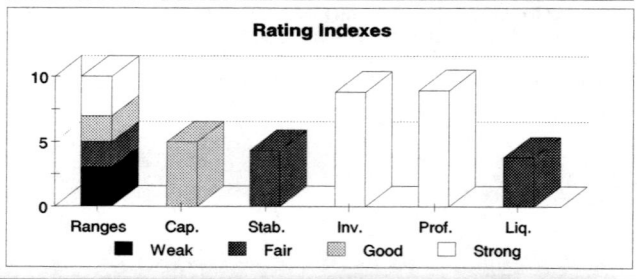

Rating Indexes
Ranges, Cap., Stab., Inv., Prof., Liq.
Weak / Fair / Good / Strong

UNITED HEALTHCARE INSURANCE COMPANY OF OH — C Fair

Major Rating Factors: Fair current capitalization (3.2 on a scale of 0 to 10) based on mixed results -- excessive policy leverage mitigated by fair risk adjusted capital (severe loss scenario), although results have slipped from the good range over the last two years. Fair overall results on stability tests (3.2) including fair risk adjusted capital in prior years. Good overall profitability (6.8).
Other Rating Factors: Good liquidity (6.5). High quality investment portfolio (8.7).
Principal Business: Group health insurance (100%).
Principal Investments: NonCMO investment grade bonds (100%) and CMOs and structured securities (7%).
Investments in Affiliates: None
Group Affiliation: United HealthGroup Inc
Licensed in: OH
Commenced Business: July 1991
Address: 9200 Worthington Rd, Columbus, OH 43082
Phone: (614) 410-7000 **Domicile State:** OH **NAIC Code:** 73518

Data Date	Weiss Safety Rating	RACR #1	RACR #2	Total Assets ($mil)	Capital ($mil)	Net Premium ($mil)	Net Income ($mil)
6-03	C	0.64	0.53	90.3	36.2	198.0	17.6
6-02	C+	0.73	0.60	71.9	33.0	147.2	16.4
2002	C	0.75	0.61	87.2	37.9	324.1	36.2
2001	B-	1.17	0.97	76.3	42.6	199.9	25.9
2000	B-	1.85	1.52	75.5	50.2	160.0	34.1
1999	B-	2.44	1.98	59.2	44.5	98.3	27.9
1998	C+	2.57	2.06	47.5	33.4	69.5	16.8

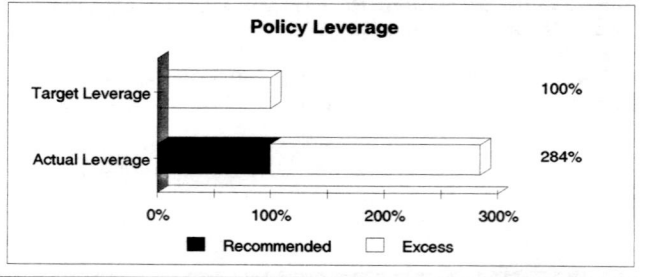

Policy Leverage
Target Leverage: 100%
Actual Leverage: 284%

Winter 2003 - 04   II. Analysis of Largest Companies

UNITED HEALTHCARE OF ALABAMA INC *   B+   Good

Major Rating Factors: Good overall results on stability tests (6.3 on a scale of 0 to 10) based on consistent premium and capital growth in the last five years but a decline in enrollment during 2002. Rating is significantly influenced by the good financial results of UnitedHealth Group Inc. Good liquidity (6.8) with sufficient resources (cash flows and marketable investments) to handle a spike in claims. Excellent profitability (9.0) with operating gains in each of the last five years.
Other Rating Factors: Strong capitalization index (10.0) based on excellent current risk-adjusted capital (severe loss scenario). High quality investment portfolio (9.6) containing no exposure to mortgages, junk bonds, or unaffiliated stocks.
Principal Business: Medicare (56%), comp med (41%), med supp (3%)
Mem Phys: 02: 7,352   01: 6,450   **02 MLR** 77%   **/ 02 Admin Exp** 10%
Enroll(000): Q1 03: 81   02: 87   01: 114   **Med Exp PMPM:** $231
Principal Investments: Cash and equiv (8%), other (92%)
Provider Compensation ($000): Contr fee ($227,501), FFS ($30,710), capitation ($30,456)
Total Member Encounters: Phys (2,313,031), non-phys (1,564,993)
Group Affiliation: UnitedHealth Group Inc
Licensed in: AL
Address: 3700 Colonnade Parkway, Birmingham, AL 35243
Phone: (205) 977-6300   **Dom State:** AL   **Commenced Bus:** March 1986

Data Date	Weiss Safety Rating	RACR #1	RACR #2	Total Assets ($mil)	Capital ($mil)	Net Premium ($mil)	Net Income ($mil)
3-03	B+	4.11	3.42	122.0	72.1	83.5	10.9
3-02	C+	0.00	0.00	127.5	67.3	95.5	8.9
2002	B+	3.59	2.99	123.5	62.5	361.3	36.5
2001	C+	0.00	0.00	133.4	58.9	394.8	32.8
2000	C	1.28	1.07	115.7	30.2	407.7	6.9
1999	C-	0.61	0.51	93.6	13.5	382.4	5.8
1998	C-	0.35	0.29	93.8	2.9	347.9	0.2

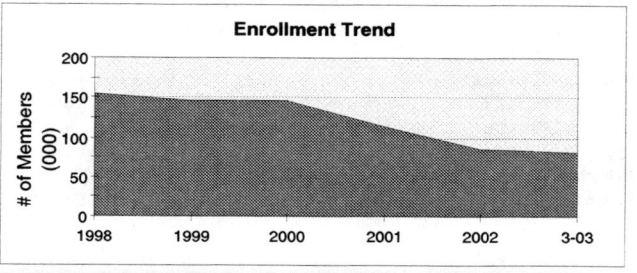

Enrollment Trend (chart: # of Members (000), 1998–3-03)

UNITED HEALTHCARE OF ARIZONA INC   C   Fair

Major Rating Factors: Fair overall results on stability tests (4.5 on a scale of 0 to 10) based on fair risk-adjusted capital in prior years, a significant 23% decrease in enrollment during the period. Rating is significantly influenced by the good financial results of UnitedHealth Group Inc. Weak profitability index (2.3) with operating losses during 1998, 1999 and 2000. Average return on equity has been poor at -18%. Good quality investment portfolio (6.2) containing little or no exposure to mortgages, junk bonds, or unaffiliated stocks.
Other Rating Factors: Good liquidity (6.7) with sufficient resources (cash flows and marketable investments) to handle a spike in claims. Strong capitalization (10.0) based on excellent current risk-adjusted capital (severe loss scenario) reflecting significant improvement over results in 1999.
Principal Business: Comp med (100%)
Mem Phys: 02: 6,749   01: 5,703   **02 MLR** 70%   **/ 02 Admin Exp** 18%
Enroll(000): Q1 03: 114   02: 138   01: 179   **Med Exp PMPM:** $122
Principal Investments: Affiliate common stock (50%), other (50%)
Provider Compensation ($000): Contr fee ($237,515), capitation ($10,676), FFS ($95)
Total Member Encounters: Phys (1,777,531), non-phys (2,439,258)
Group Affiliation: UnitedHealth Group Inc
Licensed in: AZ
Address: 3141 N Third Ave, Phoenix, AZ 85013
Phone: (602) 664-2600   **Dom State:** AZ   **Commenced Bus:** July 1985

Data Date	Weiss Safety Rating	RACR #1	RACR #2	Total Assets ($mil)	Capital ($mil)	Net Premium ($mil)	Net Income ($mil)
3-03	C	4.13	3.44	136.4	92.6	69.3	2.5
3-02	C	2.64	2.17	160.0	93.7	84.5	6.2
2002	C	4.01	3.34	131.7	89.8	328.6	30.6
2001	C	2.64	2.17	160.6	88.5	416.9	5.8
2000	C	1.32	1.08	189.7	62.0	583.9	-34.9
1999	C	0.68	0.57	146.8	31.1	598.9	-13.7
1998	C	0.89	0.75	130.7	28.0	512.0	-1.5

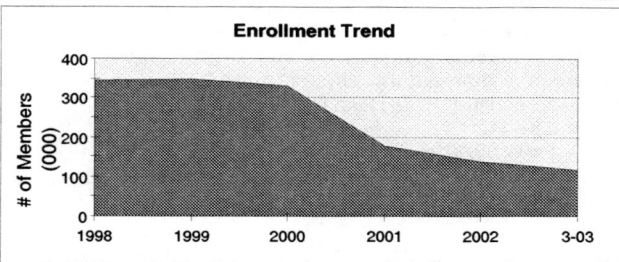

Enrollment Trend (chart: # of Members (000), 1998–3-03)

UNITED HEALTHCARE OF ARKANSAS INC *   B+   Good

Major Rating Factors: Good liquidity (6.7 on a scale of 0 to 10) with sufficient resources (cash flows and marketable investments) to handle a spike in claims. Excellent profitability (7.5) despite operating losses during 1998. Strong capitalization (10.0) based on excellent current risk-adjusted capital (severe loss scenario) reflecting significant improvement over results in 1998.
Other Rating Factors: High quality investment portfolio (9.1) containing no exposure to mortgages, junk bonds, or unaffiliated stocks. Excellent overall results on stability tests (7.2) despite a decline in enrollment during 2002 but consistent premium and capital growth in the last five years. Rating is significantly influenced by the good financial results of UnitedHealth Group Inc.
Principal Business: Comp med (100%)
Mem Phys: 02: 2,744   01: 2,809   **02 MLR** 70%   **/ 02 Admin Exp** 19%
Enroll(000): Q1 03: 49   02: 57   01: 60   **Med Exp PMPM:** $144
Principal Investments: Cash and equiv (2%), other (98%)
Provider Compensation ($000): Contr fee ($84,661), FFS ($13,957), capitation ($3,443)
Total Member Encounters: Phys (880,877), non-phys (395,386)
Group Affiliation: UnitedHealth Group Inc
Licensed in: AR
Address: 415 N McKinley St, Ste 820, Little Rock, AR 72205
Phone: (501) 664-7700   **Dom State:** AR   **Commenced Bus:** April 1992

Data Date	Weiss Safety Rating	RACR #1	RACR #2	Total Assets ($mil)	Capital ($mil)	Net Premium ($mil)	Net Income ($mil)
3-03	B+	4.04	3.36	46.4	28.6	33.7	4.5
3-02	B	2.30	1.85	40.1	19.8	35.4	2.1
2002	B+	3.44	2.87	39.5	24.1	145.3	13.0
2001	B	2.30	1.85	33.6	17.9	149.0	6.0
2000	B	1.61	1.35	27.4	10.4	120.3	2.2
1999	B	1.50	1.28	24.9	8.4	100.5	1.1
1998	B-	0.57	0.48	24.2	3.2	80.6	-1.5

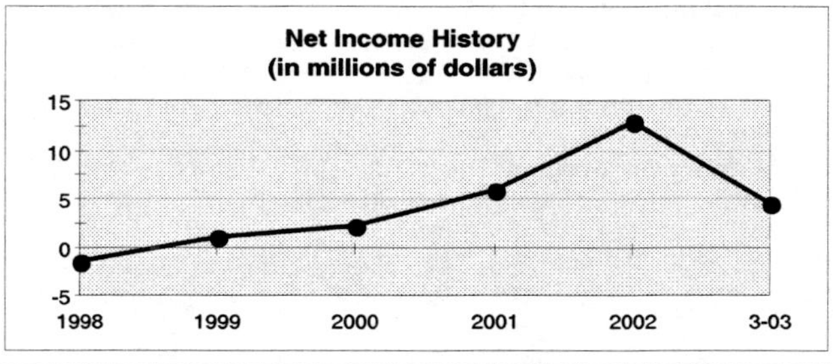

Net Income History (in millions of dollars) (chart, 1998–3-03)

www.WeissRatings.com   * Denotes a Weiss Recommended Company

II. Analysis of Largest Companies

UNITED HEALTHCARE OF COLORADO INC | C- | Fair

Major Rating Factors: Fair liquidity (4.8 on a scale of 0 to 10) as cash resources may not be adequate to cover a spike in claims. Weak profitability index (0.9) with $44.0 million in losses in the last five years. Average return on equity over the last five years has been poor at -71%. Strong capitalization index (7.0) based on excellent current risk-adjusted capital (severe loss scenario).
Other Rating Factors: High quality investment portfolio (9.9) containing no exposure to mortgages, junk bonds, or unaffiliated stocks. Excellent overall results on stability tests (7.3) despite a decline in enrollment during 2002 but consistent premium and capital growth in the last five years. Rating is significantly influenced by the good financial results of UnitedHealth Group Inc.
Principal Business: Comp med (88%), Medicaid (12%)
Mem Phys: 02: 6,886 **01:** 7,482   **02 MLR** 94% / **02 Admin Exp** 16%
Enroll(000): Q1 03: 64   **02:** 71   **01:** 102   **Med Exp PMPM:** $210
Principal Investments: Cash and equiv (17%), other (83%)
Provider Compensation ($000): Contr fee ($210,443), capitation ($8,492)
Total Member Encounters: Phys (1,095,333), non-phys (229,849)
Group Affiliation: UnitedHealth Group Inc
Licensed in: CO
Address: 8051 E Maplewood Ave Ste 300, Greenwood Village, CO 80111
Phone: (303) 267-4500   **Dom State:** CO   **Commenced Bus:** March 1986

Data Date	Weiss Safety Rating	RACR #1	RACR #2	Total Assets ($mil)	Capital ($mil)	Net Premium ($mil)	Net Income ($mil)
3-03	C-	1.37	1.14	64.7	28.3	46.8	1.6
3-02	C	1.65	1.36	59.5	24.6	60.8	-2.0
2002	C-	1.28	1.07	64.8	26.8	233.6	-17.5
2001	C	1.65	1.36	54.9	25.7	214.3	-4.6
2000	C	1.25	1.05	43.9	17.6	171.3	-7.4
1999	C	1.65	1.38	34.6	16.9	119.5	-2.4
1998	C	0.22	0.19	30.9	4.1	118.9	-12.1

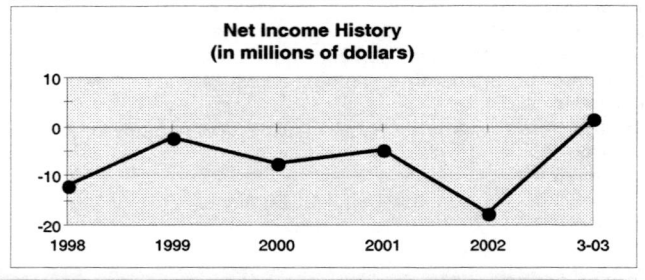

Net Income History (in millions of dollars)

UNITED HEALTHCARE OF FLORIDA INC | C- | Fair

Major Rating Factors: Fair capitalization (4.6 on a scale of 0 to 10) based on fair current risk-adjusted capital (moderate loss scenario) reflecting improvement over results in 2001. Weak profitability index (2.1) with operating losses during 1998, 1999 and 2001. Average return on equity has been poor at -6%. Weak liquidity (2.3) as a spike in claims may stretch capacity.
Other Rating Factors: Good overall results on stability tests (5.2) despite weak risk-adjusted capital in prior years. Rating is significantly influenced by the good financial results of UnitedHealth Group Inc. High quality investment portfolio (9.4) containing no exposure to mortgages, junk bonds, or unaffiliated stocks.
Principal Business: Comp med (75%), Medicare (18%), Medicaid (7%)
Mem Phys: 02: 24,129   **01:** 21,518   **02 MLR** 84% / **02 Admin Exp** 15%
Enroll(000): Q1 03: 733   **02:** 688   **01:** 872   **Med Exp PMPM:** $195
Principal Investments: Cash and equiv (13%), other (87%)
Provider Compensation ($000): Contr fee ($1,820,835), capitation ($52,243)
Total Member Encounters: Phys (12,362,685), non-phys (7,785,103)
Group Affiliation: UnitedHealth Group Inc
Licensed in: FL
Address: 495 N. Keller Road, Ste 200, Maitlanc, FL 32751
Phone: (407) 428-2302   **Dom State:** FL   **Commenced Bus:** March 1973

Data Date	Weiss Safety Rating	RACR #1	RACR #2	Total Assets ($mil)	Capital ($mil)	Net Premium ($mil)	Net Income ($mil)
3-03	C-	0.88	0.73	483.2	93.0	616.0	8.5
3-02	D+	0.55	0.45	394.2	68.3	547.5	2.3
2002	C-	0.84	0.70	448.4	88.2	2,168.3	20.9
2001	D+	0.55	0.45	504.1	74.5	2,571.4	-29.7
2000	C	0.88	0.72	525.1	96.6	2,156.7	7.7
1999	C	0.77	0.62	512.2	82.5	1,910.1	-9.2
1998	C+	1.07	0.90	527.4	97.1	1,706.3	-20.7

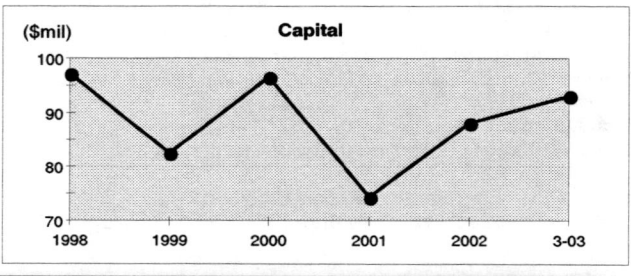

Capital ($mil)

UNITED HEALTHCARE OF GEORGIA INC | C+ | Fair

Major Rating Factors: Fair profitability index (4.0 on a scale of 0 to 10) with operating losses during 1998, 1999 and 2001. Average return on equity has been poor at -15%. Fair overall results on stability tests (4.7) based on weak risk-adjusted capital in prior years, a significant 34% decrease in enrollment during the period. Rating is significantly influenced by the good financial results of UnitedHealth Group Inc. Good liquidity (6.1) with sufficient resources (cash flows and marketable investments) to handle a spike in claims.
Other Rating Factors: Strong capitalization (9.3) based on excellent current risk-adjusted capital (severe loss scenario) reflecting significant improvement over results in 1998. High quality investment portfolio (8.6) containing no exposure to mortgages, junk bonds, or unaffiliated stocks.
Principal Business: Comp med (100%)
Mem Phys: 02: 7,501   **01:** 5,555   **02 MLR** 81% / **02 Admin Exp** 15%
Enroll(000): Q1 03: 67   **02:** 79   **01:** 120   **Med Exp PMPM:** $135
Principal Investments: Other (3%), cash and equiv (97%)
Provider Compensation ($000): Contr fee ($141,161), FFS ($25,864), capitation ($9,284)
Total Member Encounters: Phys (1,225,876), non-phys (713,097)
Group Affiliation: UnitedHealth Group Inc
Licensed in: GA
Address: 2970 Clairmont Rd, Suite 300, Atlanta, GA 30329-1634
Phone: (404) 982-8800   **Dom State:** GA   **Commenced Bus:** April 1986

Data Date	Weiss Safety Rating	RACR #1	RACR #2	Total Assets ($mil)	Capital ($mil)	Net Premium ($mil)	Net Income ($mil)
3-03	C+	3.18	2.65	61.4	35.1	43.0	1.5
3-02	C-	1.86	1.50	61.0	26.7	52.4	0.7
2002	C+	3.06	2.55	59.9	33.7	199.4	7.6
2001	C-	1.85	1.49	66.3	26.6	252.0	-2.8
2000	D+	1.17	0.98	55.3	15.9	255.2	4.3
1999	D+	0.70	0.59	62.3	11.7	303.3	-2.7
1998	C	0.41	0.34	77.8	8.7	333.9	-13.8

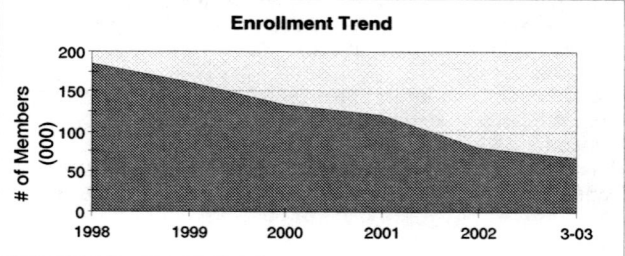

Enrollment Trend

UNITED HEALTHCARE OF ILLINOIS INC — C+ Fair

Major Rating Factors: Fair profitability index (4.2 on a scale of 0 to 10) with operating losses during 1998, 1999 and 2000. Average return on equity has been poor at -13%. Fair overall results on stability tests (3.9) based on excessive capital growth during 2002, a significant 50% decrease in enrollment during the period. Rating is significantly influenced by the good financial results of UnitedHealth Group Inc. Good liquidity (6.8) with sufficient resources (cash flows and marketable investments) to handle a spike in claims.

Other Rating Factors: Strong capitalization (10.0) based on excellent current risk-adjusted capital (severe loss scenario) reflecting significant improvement over results in 1998. High quality investment portfolio (8.5) containing no exposure to mortgages, junk bonds, or unaffiliated stocks.

Principal Business: Comp med (77%), Medicaid (23%)
Mem Phys: 02: 15,090 01: 15,130 **02 MLR** 70% **/ 02 Admin Exp** 18%
Enroll(000): Q1 03: 64 02: 69 01: 139 **Med Exp PMPM:** $86
Principal Investments: Other (10%), cash and equiv (90%)
Provider Compensation ($000): Contr fee ($90,011), bonus arrang ($40,392), FFS ($20,699), capitation ($9,124)
Total Member Encounters: Phys (412,373), non-phys (29,876)
Group Affiliation: UnitedHealth Group Inc
Licensed in: IL, IN
Address: 233 N Michigan Ave, Chicago, IL 60601
Phone: (312) 424-4600 **Dom State:** IL **Commenced Bus:** March 1976

Data Date	Weiss Safety Rating	RACR #1	RACR #2	Total Assets ($mil)	Capital ($mil)	Net Premium ($mil)	Net Income ($mil)
3-03	C+	8.75	7.29	108.3	74.4	34.0	2.0
3-02	C	2.28	1.80	115.7	63.6	44.2	3.2
2002	C+	8.59	7.16	105.7	72.9	153.7	22.6
2001	C	2.28	1.80	152.5	60.1	463.5	6.1
2000	C	1.22	0.99	195.1	39.6	541.9	-1.6
1999	C	0.82	0.68	178.4	30.6	585.4	-15.4
1998	C	0.69	0.58	178.7	27.6	748.4	-20.2

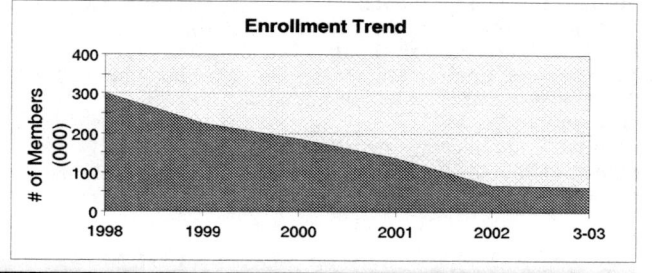

Enrollment Trend chart

UNITED HEALTHCARE OF KENTUCKY — C+ Fair

Major Rating Factors: Fair liquidity (4.5 on a scale of 0 to 10) as cash resources may not be adequate to cover a spike in claims. Good overall results on stability tests (5.1) despite inconsistent enrollment growth in the past five years due to declines in 2001 and 2002. Rating is significantly influenced by the good financial results of UnitedHealth Group Inc. Weak profitability index (0.9) with $19.2 million in losses in the last three years.

Other Rating Factors: Strong capitalization (8.3) based on excellent current risk-adjusted capital (severe loss scenario) reflecting improvement over results in 2000. High quality investment portfolio (8.2) containing little or no exposure to mortgages, junk bonds, or unaffiliated stocks.

Principal Business: Comp med (100%)
Mem Phys: 02: 6,500 01: 6,005 **02 MLR** 88% **/ 02 Admin Exp** 17%
Enroll(000): Q1 03: 64 02: 83 01: 148 **Med Exp PMPM:** $141
Principal Investments: Other (10%), cash and equiv (90%)
Provider Compensation ($000): Contr fee ($201,880), capitation ($7,130)
Total Member Encounters: Phys (1,589,844), non-phys (991,041)
Group Affiliation: UnitedHealth Group Inc
Licensed in: IN, KY
Address: 2424 Harrodsburg Road, Lexington, KY 40504
Phone: (859) 260-3600 **Dom State:** KY **Commenced Bus:** May 1986

Data Date	Weiss Safety Rating	RACR #1	RACR #2	Total Assets ($mil)	Capital ($mil)	Net Premium ($mil)	Net Income ($mil)
3-03	C+	2.43	2.02	65.6	29.9	42.1	3.6
3-02	C+	1.72	1.42	69.4	25.6	60.4	-4.1
2002	C+	2.17	1.81	59.2	26.4	221.1	-3.8
2001	C+	1.72	1.42	73.7	27.1	304.1	-8.6
2000	B-	1.11	0.92	68.8	15.9	288.8	-6.9
1999	B	2.25	1.87	53.8	22.0	195.2	3.3
1998	B	3.10	2.61	43.7	18.6	111.9	3.0

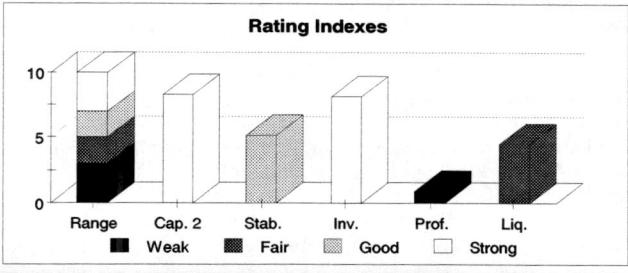

Rating Indexes chart (Range, Cap. 2, Stab., Inv., Prof., Liq.; Weak / Fair / Good / Strong)

UNITED HEALTHCARE OF LOUISIANA INC — C Fair

Major Rating Factors: Fair liquidity (4.6 on a scale of 0 to 10) as cash resources may not be adequate to cover a spike in claims. Weak profitability index (1.9) with operating losses during 1998, 1999 and 2000. Average return on equity has been poor at -75%. Good overall results on stability tests (5.0). Rating is significantly influenced by the good financial results of UnitedHealth Group Inc.

Other Rating Factors: Strong capitalization index (8.1) based on excellent current risk-adjusted capital (severe loss scenario). High quality investment portfolio (9.4) containing no exposure to mortgages, junk bonds, or unaffiliated stocks.

Principal Business: Comp med (100%)
Mem Phys: 02: 7,000 01: 6,800 **02 MLR** 81% **/ 02 Admin Exp** 18%
Enroll(000): Q1 03: 88 02: 92 01: 87 **Med Exp PMPM:** $173
Principal Investments: Other (3%), cash and equiv (97%)
Provider Compensation ($000): Contr fee ($149,893), FFS ($27,519), capitation ($7,442)
Total Member Encounters: Phys (1,441,897), non-phys (836,421)
Group Affiliation: UnitedHealth Group Inc
Licensed in: LA
Address: 3838 N Causeway Blvd Ste 2100, Metairie, LA 70002
Phone: (504) 849-3510 **Dom State:** LA **Commenced Bus:** November 1986

Data Date	Weiss Safety Rating	RACR #1	RACR #2	Total Assets ($mil)	Capital ($mil)	Net Premium ($mil)	Net Income ($mil)
3-03	C	2.21	1.84	70.7	29.4	60.2	-0.2
3-02	C-	1.86	1.48	62.9	26.7	48.2	0.4
2002	C	2.25	1.87	69.9	29.9	230.4	2.9
2001	C-	1.86	1.48	63.7	26.6	196.2	1.5
2000	D+	0.81	0.67	57.6	14.6	191.3	-5.8
1999	D+	0.69	0.58	58.2	17.7	282.7	-1.5
1998	C	0.00	0.00	80.2	4.1	296.6	-21.0

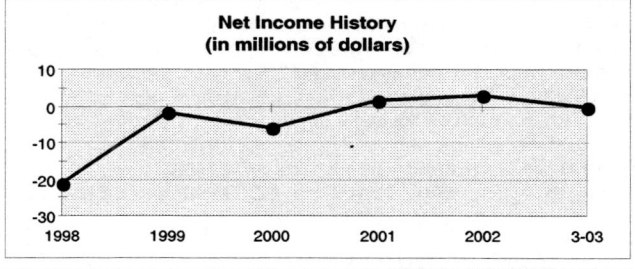

Net Income History (in millions of dollars) chart

II. Analysis of Largest Companies

UNITED HEALTHCARE OF MID-ATLANTIC — C Fair

Major Rating Factors: Weak profitability index (1.9 on a scale of 0 to 10) with operating losses during 1998, 2000 and 2001. Average return on equity has been poor at -28%. Good overall results on stability tests (5.6) despite weak risk-adjusted capital in prior years. Rating is significantly influenced by the good financial results of UnitedHealth Group Inc. Good liquidity (6.0) with sufficient resources (cash flows and marketable investments) to handle a spike in claims.
Other Rating Factors: Strong capitalization (7.9) based on excellent current risk-adjusted capital (severe loss scenario) reflecting significant improvement over results in 1998. High quality investment portfolio (9.9) containing little or no exposure to mortgages, junk bonds, or unaffiliated stocks.
Principal Business: Medicaid (52%), comp med (48%)
Mem Phys: 02: 21,569 **01:** 20,919 **02 MLR** 87% / **02 Admin Exp** 14%
Enroll(000): Q1 03: 171 **02:** 187 **01:** 180 **Med Exp PMPM:** $166
Principal Investments: Cash and equiv (24%), other (76%)
Provider Compensation ($000): Contr fee ($342,577), capitation ($20,281)
Total Member Encounters: Phys (2,563,091), non-phys (3,075,926)
Group Affiliation: UnitedHealth Group Inc
Licensed in: DC, MD, VA
Address: 6300 Security Blvd., Baltimore, MD 21207-5102
Phone: (410) 277-6000 **Dom State:** MD **Commenced Bus:** December 1978

Data Date	Weiss Safety Rating	RACR #1	RACR #2	Total Assets ($mil)	Capital ($mil)	Net Premium ($mil)	Net Income ($mil)
3-03	C	2.05	1.71	145.4	59.2	109.6	2.4
3-02	C	2.16	1.80	137.0	57.5	101.9	3.5
2002	C	1.96	1.63	139.1	56.5	421.1	3.3
2001	C	2.16	1.79	136.9	55.6	425.9	-16.1
2000	C	0.77	0.64	135.4	25.0	521.2	-17.1
1999	C	0.71	0.60	109.9	21.3	518.2	4.3
1998	C	0.52	0.43	135.7	17.4	409.9	-6.9

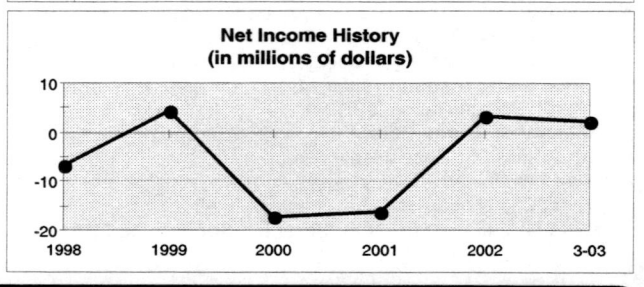

Net Income History (in millions of dollars)

UNITED HEALTHCARE OF MISSISSIPPI INC — C Fair

Major Rating Factors: Fair overall results on stability tests (4.3 on a scale of 0 to 10) based on a significant 23% decrease in enrollment during the period, a decline in the number of member physicians during 2002. Rating is significantly influenced by the good financial results of UnitedHealth Group Inc. Weak profitability index (1.1) with operating losses during 1998, 1999 and 2001. Average return on equity has been poor at -63%. Good liquidity (6.2) with sufficient resources (cash flows and marketable investments) to handle a spike in claims.
Other Rating Factors: Strong capitalization (9.1) based on excellent current risk-adjusted capital (severe loss scenario) reflecting significant improvement over results in 1998. High quality investment portfolio (9.9) containing no exposure to mortgages, junk bonds, or unaffiliated stocks.
Principal Business: Comp med (100%)
Mem Phys: 02: 2,100 **01:** 2,627 **02 MLR** 76% / **02 Admin Exp** 19%
Enroll(000): Q1 03: 20 **02:** 23 **01:** 30 **Med Exp PMPM:** $154
Principal Investments: Cash and equiv (6%), other (94%)
Provider Compensation ($000): Contr fee ($38,638), FFS ($10,117), capitation ($2,195)
Total Member Encounters: Phys (368,375), non-phys (175,008)
Group Affiliation: UnitedHealth Group Inc
Licensed in: MS
Address: 795 Woodlands Pkwy Ste 101, Ridgeland, MS 39157
Phone: (504) 849-3510 **Dom State:** MS **Commenced Bus:** January 1993

Data Date	Weiss Safety Rating	RACR #1	RACR #2	Total Assets ($mil)	Capital ($mil)	Net Premium ($mil)	Net Income ($mil)
3-03	C	3.05	2.54	22.9	11.1	14.6	1.4
3-02	C	1.53	1.30	21.3	7.5	17.2	0.8
2002	C	2.77	2.31	21.0	10.0	64.6	3.4
2001	C	1.53	1.29	21.4	6.8	65.9	-1.9
2000	C	2.45	2.05	21.5	8.1	59.0	3.9
1999	C	1.39	1.17	19.4	4.4	56.7	-0.8
1998	C	0.54	0.46	19.8	2.6	59.4	-8.6

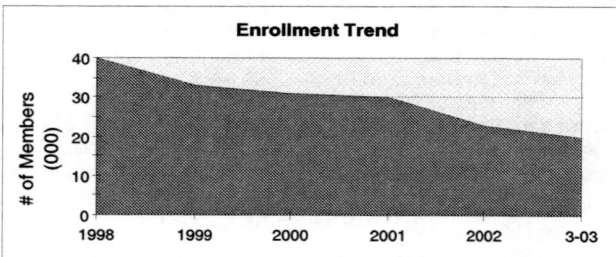

Enrollment Trend

UNITED HEALTHCARE OF NC INC * — B+ Good

Major Rating Factors: Good liquidity (6.8 on a scale of 0 to 10) with sufficient resources (cash flows and marketable investments) to handle a spike in claims. Excellent profitability (9.1) with operating gains in each of the last five years. Strong overall capitalization (8.5) based on excellent current risk-adjusted capital (severe loss scenario) despite some fluctuation in capital levels.
Other Rating Factors: High quality investment portfolio (9.6) containing little or no exposure to mortgages, junk bonds, or unaffiliated stocks. Excellent overall results on stability tests (7.8) based on consistent premium and capital growth in the last five years. Rating is significantly influenced by the good financial results of UnitedHealth Group Inc.
Principal Business: Comp med (90%), Medicare (7%), Medicaid (3%)
Mem Phys: 02: 13,989 **01:** 13,806 **02 MLR** 78% / **02 Admin Exp** 15%
Enroll(000): Q1 03: 261 **02:** 273 **01:** 320 **Med Exp PMPM:** $157
Principal Investments: Cash and equiv (28%), other (72%)
Provider Compensation ($000): Contr fee ($482,983), FFS ($49,978), capitation ($17,594), bonus arrang ($710)
Total Member Encounters: Phys (4,125,670), non-phys (2,715,662)
Group Affiliation: UnitedHealth Group Inc
Licensed in: NC
Address: 3803 N Elm St, Greensboro, NC 27455
Phone: (336) 282-0900 **Dom State:** NC **Commenced Bus:** May 1985

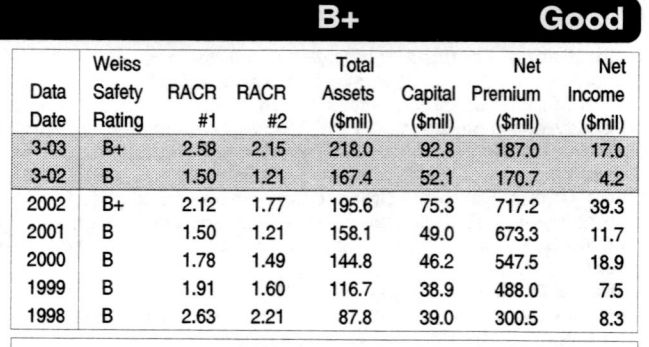

Data Date	Weiss Safety Rating	RACR #1	RACR #2	Total Assets ($mil)	Capital ($mil)	Net Premium ($mil)	Net Income ($mil)
3-03	B+	2.58	2.15	218.0	92.8	187.0	17.0
3-02	B	1.50	1.21	167.4	52.1	170.7	4.2
2002	B+	2.12	1.77	195.6	75.3	717.2	39.3
2001	B	1.50	1.21	158.1	49.0	673.3	11.7
2000	B	1.78	1.49	144.8	46.2	547.5	18.9
1999	B	1.91	1.60	116.7	38.9	488.0	7.5
1998	B	2.63	2.21	87.8	39.0	300.5	8.3

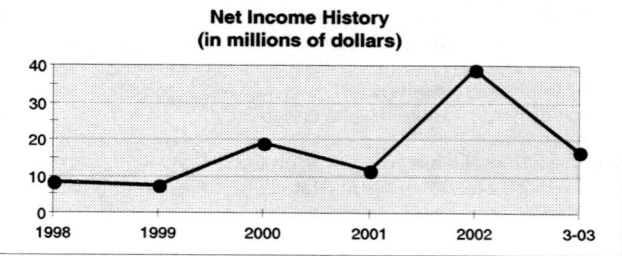

Net Income History (in millions of dollars)

Winter 2003 - 04
II. Analysis of Largest Companies

UNITED HEALTHCARE OF NEW ENGLAND INC — B — Good

Major Rating Factors: Good overall results on stability tests (5.3 on a scale of 0 to 10) despite excessive capital growth during 2002, a decline in enrollment during 2002. Rating is significantly influenced by the good financial results of UnitedHealth Group Inc. Good liquidity (6.2) with sufficient resources (cash flows and marketable investments) to handle a spike in claims. Excellent profitability (7.1) despite operating losses during 1998 and 1999.

Other Rating Factors: Strong capitalization index (10.0) based on excellent current risk-adjusted capital (severe loss scenario). High quality investment portfolio (7.4).

Principal Business: Comp med (59%), Medicare (24%), Medicaid (17%)
Mem Phys: 02: 13,390 **01:** 12,453 **02 MLR** 80% **/ 02 Admin Exp** 12%
Enroll(000): Q1 03: 153 **02:** 155 **01:** 168 **Med Exp PMPM:** $180
Principal Investments: Nonaffiliate common stock (24%), other (80%)
Provider Compensation ($000): Contr fee ($340,525), capitation ($19,444)
Total Member Encounters: Phys (2,188,500), non-phys (4,165,343)
Group Affiliation: UnitedHealth Group Inc
Licensed in: MA, RI
Address: 475 Kilvert St Suite 310, Warwick, RI 02886
Phone: (401) 737-6900 **Dom State:** RI **Commenced Bus:** December 1984

Data Date	Weiss Safety Rating	RACR #1	RACR #2	Total Assets ($mil)	Capital ($mil)	Net Premium ($mil)	Net Income ($mil)
3-03	B	3.64	3.03	157.4	87.3	111.8	4.3
3-02	C+	2.08	1.58	133.1	65.8	106.9	4.9
2002	B	3.47	2.89	152.3	83.3	435.9	24.2
2001	C+	2.08	1.58	140.9	60.9	448.5	22.0
2000	C-	1.08	0.90	141.4	35.5	557.9	16.0
1999	D+	0.32	0.27	120.2	12.4	512.4	-0.9
1998	C-	0.20	0.17	123.5	11.0	500.1	-22.5

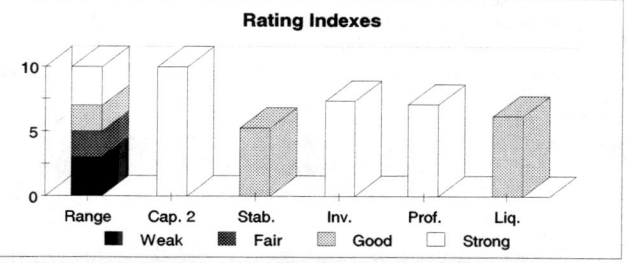

UNITED HEALTHCARE OF NEW JERSEY INC — C+ — Fair

Major Rating Factors: Good overall results on stability tests (5.3 on a scale of 0 to 10) despite inconsistent enrollment growth in the past five years due to declines in 2001 and 2002. Rating is significantly influenced by the good financial results of UnitedHealth Group Inc. Good liquidity (5.0) with sufficient resources (cash flows and marketable investments) to handle a spike in claims. Weak profitability index (1.0) with modest operating losses during each of the last five years. Average return on equity over the last five years has been poor at -20%.

Other Rating Factors: Strong capitalization (7.2) based on excellent current risk-adjusted capital (severe loss scenario) reflecting improvement over results in 2000. High quality investment portfolio (9.9) containing no exposure to mortgages, junk bonds, or unaffiliated stocks.

Principal Business: Comp med (100%)
Mem Phys: 02: 12,532 **01:** 11,830 **02 MLR** 83% **/ 02 Admin Exp** 18%
Enroll(000): Q1 03: 66 **02:** 70 **01:** 81 **Med Exp PMPM:** $177
Principal Investments: Cash and equiv (18%), other (82%)
Provider Compensation ($000): Contr fee ($154,898), capitation ($5,453)
Total Member Encounters: Phys (390,711), non-phys (106,178)
Group Affiliation: UnitedHealth Group Inc
Licensed in: NJ
Address: 695 Route 46 W Ste 100, Fairfield, NJ 07004
Phone: (212) 216-6400 **Dom State:** NJ **Commenced Bus:** May 1987

Data Date	Weiss Safety Rating	RACR #1	RACR #2	Total Assets ($mil)	Capital ($mil)	Net Premium ($mil)	Net Income ($mil)
3-03	C+	1.53	1.27	51.1	18.2	45.2	-1.9
3-02	C+	1.79	1.49	49.2	18.6	48.5	-0.3
2002	C+	1.75	1.46	50.0	20.8	192.2	-0.6
2001	C+	1.79	1.49	51.4	19.9	187.0	-0.3
2000	C+	1.01	0.85	43.5	11.9	158.2	-1.5
1999	C+	1.53	1.28	43.3	14.0	127.8	-1.0
1998	B-	1.30	1.09	39.4	11.5	106.4	-6.6

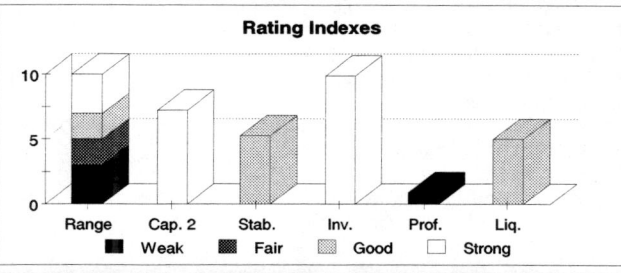

UNITED HEALTHCARE OF NY INC — B — Good

Major Rating Factors: Good overall profitability index (6.0 on a scale of 0 to 10) despite operating losses during 1998. Good liquidity (6.2) with sufficient resources (cash flows and marketable investments) to handle a spike in claims. Strong capitalization (8.3) based on excellent current risk-adjusted capital (severe loss scenario) reflecting improvement over results in 2001.

Other Rating Factors: High quality investment portfolio (9.9) containing no exposure to mortgages, junk bonds, or unaffiliated stocks. Excellent overall results on stability tests (8.1) based on consistent premium and capital growth in the last five years. Rating is significantly influenced by the good financial results of UnitedHealth Group Inc.

Principal Business: Comp med (39%), Medicare (31%), Medicaid (23%), other (7%)
Mem Phys: 02: 33,181 **01:** 29,282 **02 MLR** 87% **/ 02 Admin Exp** 12%
Enroll(000): Q1 03: 127 **02:** 128 **01:** 120 **Med Exp PMPM:** $196
Principal Investments: Cash and equiv (29%), other (71%)
Provider Compensation ($000): Contr fee ($218,483), FFS ($48,104), capitation ($18,647)
Total Member Encounters: Phys (869,608), non-phys (131,829)
Group Affiliation: UnitedHealth Group Inc
Licensed in: NY
Address: 2 Penn Plaza Ste 700, New York, NY 10121
Phone: (212) 216-6400 **Dom State:** NY **Commenced Bus:** January 1987

Data Date	Weiss Safety Rating	RACR #1	RACR #2	Total Assets ($mil)	Capital ($mil)	Net Premium ($mil)	Net Income ($mil)
3-03	B	2.42	2.01	131.6	51.5	94.3	7.6
3-02	B-	1.37	1.12	89.0	19.1	66.8	-2.1
2002	B	2.04	1.70	135.5	43.4	334.7	3.9
2001	B-	1.35	1.11	119.9	37.8	343.7	2.0
2000	B-	1.42	1.19	96.0	21.6	254.5	7.1
1999	C	1.75	1.49	74.5	20.4	209.9	3.8
1998	C+	1.41	1.18	65.6	15.6	175.1	-2.0

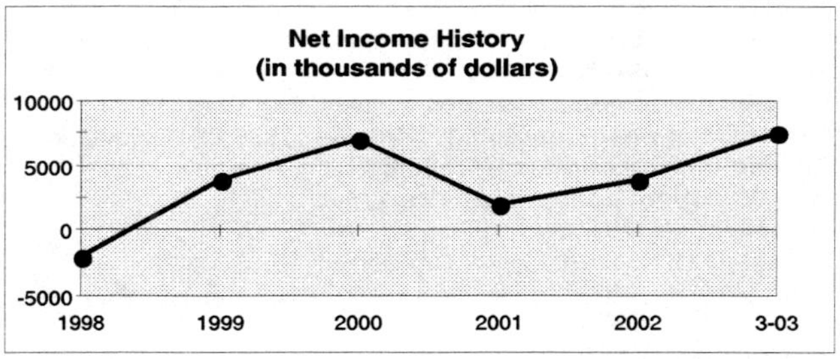

www.WeissRatings.com   * Denotes a Weiss Recommended Company

II. Analysis of Largest Companies
Winter 2003 - 04

UNITED HEALTHCARE OF OHIO INC — B- Good

Major Rating Factors: Good overall profitability index (5.1 on a scale of 0 to 10) despite operating losses during 2000. Good overall results on stability tests (5.1) despite a decline in enrollment during 2002, excessive capital growth during 2002. Rating is significantly influenced by the good financial results of UnitedHealth Group Inc. Good liquidity (5.9) with sufficient resources (cash flows and marketable investments) to handle a spike in claims.

Other Rating Factors: Strong capitalization (8.2) based on excellent current risk-adjusted capital (severe loss scenario) reflecting significant improvement over results in 2000. High quality investment portfolio (9.3) containing little or no exposure to mortgages, junk bonds, or unaffiliated stocks.

Principal Business: Comp med (81%), Medicare (16%), FEHB (3%)
Mem Phys: 02: 19,800 **01:** 19,000 **02 MLR** 81% **/ 02 Admin Exp** 15%
Enroll(000): Q1 03: 476 **02:** 523 **01:** 665 **Med Exp PMPM:** $171
Principal Investments: Cash and equiv (3%), other (97%)
Provider Compensation ($000): Contr fee ($1,186,333), capitation ($62,128)
Total Member Encounters: Phys (7,941,743), non-phys (6,024,905)
Group Affiliation: UnitedHealth Group Inc
Licensed in: KY, OH
Address: 9200 Worthington Rd, Westerville, OH 43082-8823
Phone: (614) 410-7000 **Dom State:** OH **Commenced Bus:** August 1985

Data Date	Weiss Safety Rating	RACR #1	RACR #2	Total Assets ($mil)	Capital ($mil)	Net Premium ($mil)	Net Income ($mil)
3-03	B-	2.32	1.93	358.3	169.9	361.4	23.1
3-02	C+	1.25	1.00	338.0	118.1	391.5	6.0
2002	B-	2.01	1.68	346.0	146.2	1,501.4	51.9
2001	C+	1.25	1.00	363.0	113.8	1,668.4	33.4
2000	C+	0.61	0.51	315.0	45.2	1,510.0	-19.3
1999	B-	1.17	0.92	291.3	71.0	1,271.4	15.6
1998	B-	1.09	0.91	293.9	53.5	1,118.6	6.0

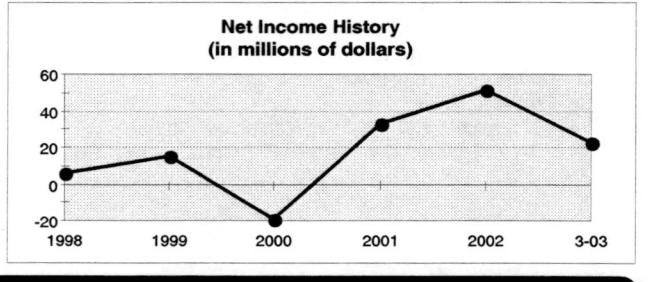

Net Income History (in millions of dollars)

UNITED HEALTHCARE OF TENNESSEE INC — C+ Fair

Major Rating Factors: Fair overall results on stability tests (4.6 on a scale of 0 to 10) based on a significant 33% decrease in enrollment during the period. Rating is significantly influenced by the good financial results of UnitedHealth Group Inc. Good liquidity (5.1) with sufficient resources (cash flows and marketable investments) to handle a spike in claims. Weak profitability index (1.7) with operating losses during 1998 and 1999. Average return on equity has been poor at -27%.

Other Rating Factors: Strong capitalization (8.0) based on excellent current risk-adjusted capital (severe loss scenario) reflecting significant improvement over results in 1998. High quality investment portfolio (9.3) containing no exposure to mortgages, junk bonds, or unaffiliated stocks.

Principal Business: Comp med (100%)
Mem Phys: 02: 9,596 **01:** 10,011 **02 MLR** 80% **/ 02 Admin Exp** 19%
Enroll(000): Q1 03: 55 **02:** 60 **01:** 90 **Med Exp PMPM:** $147
Principal Investments: Other (2%), cash and equiv (98%)
Provider Compensation ($000): Contr fee ($116,007), FFS ($16,412), capitation ($4,228)
Total Member Encounters: Phys (1,096,686), non-phys (507,436)
Group Affiliation: UnitedHealth Group Inc
Licensed in: TN
Address: 10 Cadillac Dr Ste 200, Brentwood, TN 37027
Phone: (615) 297-9500 **Dom State:** TN **Commenced Bus:** January 1992

Data Date	Weiss Safety Rating	RACR #1	RACR #2	Total Assets ($mil)	Capital ($mil)	Net Premium ($mil)	Net Income ($mil)
3-03	C+	2.18	1.82	42.7	19.5	36.9	1.7
3-02	C+	1.32	1.09	43.2	17.7	43.9	1.6
2002	C+	2.02	1.68	40.8	17.9	165.1	2.1
2001	C+	1.32	1.09	43.5	15.9	195.7	0.9
2000	C	1.19	0.99	44.9	12.6	194.2	1.8
1999	C	1.00	0.83	42.4	11.2	188.2	-3.3
1998	C	0.56	0.47	45.7	6.8	183.4	-9.1

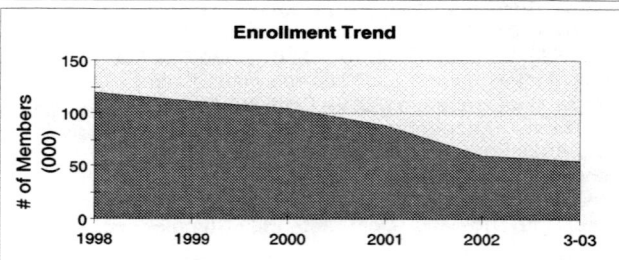

Enrollment Trend

UNITED HEALTHCARE OF THE MIDLANDS * — B+ Good

Major Rating Factors: Good liquidity (6.6 on a scale of 0 to 10) with sufficient resources (cash flows and marketable investments) to handle a spike in claims. Excellent profitability (8.2) with operating gains in each of the last five years. Strong overall capitalization (8.6) based on excellent current risk-adjusted capital (severe loss scenario). Moreover, capital has steadily grown over the last five years.

Other Rating Factors: High quality investment portfolio (9.5) containing little or no exposure to mortgages, junk bonds, or unaffiliated stocks. Excellent overall results on stability tests (7.3) based on consistent premium and capital growth in the last five years but a decline in the number of member physicians during 2002. Rating is significantly influenced by the good financial results of UnitedHealth Group Inc.

Principal Business: Medicaid (36%), Medicare (35%), comp med (28%)
Mem Phys: 02: 920 **01:** 1,178 **02 MLR** 82% **/ 02 Admin Exp** 13%
Enroll(000): Q1 03: 60 **02:** 61 **01:** 67 **Med Exp PMPM:** $179
Principal Investments: Cash and equiv (12%), other (88%)
Provider Compensation ($000): Contr fee ($135,822), capitation ($4,345)
Total Member Encounters: Phys (163,588), non-phys (1,978,913)
Group Affiliation: UnitedHealth Group Inc
Licensed in: IA, NE
Address: 2717 N. 118th Circle, Omaha, NE 68164-9672
Phone: (402) 445-5000 **Dom State:** NE **Commenced Bus:** October 1984

Data Date	Weiss Safety Rating	RACR #1	RACR #2	Total Assets ($mil)	Capital ($mil)	Net Premium ($mil)	Net Income ($mil)
3-03	B+	2.66	2.22	69.7	24.3	43.3	0.5
3-02	B	1.74	1.38	72.6	16.9	40.8	0.2
2002	B+	2.64	2.20	80.9	24.0	166.6	9.9
2001	B	1.74	1.38	73.0	15.0	164.2	1.9
2000	B	1.58	1.30	61.6	12.8	146.9	3.6
1999	B	1.53	1.28	37.2	9.1	131.9	2.7
1998	B	1.51	1.26	31.2	6.9	106.1	2.7

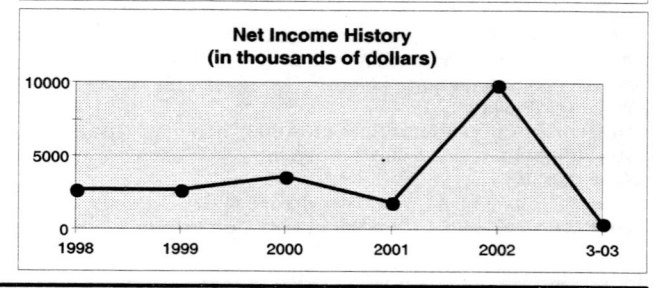

Net Income History (in thousands of dollars)

UNITED HEALTHCARE OF THE MIDWEST INC *   B+   Good

Major Rating Factors: Good liquidity (6.4 on a scale of 0 to 10) with sufficient resources (cash flows and marketable investments) to handle a spike in claims. Excellent profitability (8.1) with operating gains in each of the last five years. Strong overall capitalization (7.9) based on excellent current risk-adjusted capital (severe loss scenario). Moreover, capital has steadily grown over the last five years.

Other Rating Factors: High quality investment portfolio (9.5) containing little or no exposure to mortgages, junk bonds, or unaffiliated stocks. Excellent overall results on stability tests (7.1) based on consistent premium and capital growth in the last five years but a decline in enrollment during 2002. Rating is significantly influenced by the good financial results of UnitedHealth Group Inc.

Principal Business: Comp med (72%), Medicare (28%)
Mem Phys: 02: 12,077   **01:** 11,386   **02 MLR** 80% / **02 Admin Exp** 15%
Enroll(000): Q1 03: 351   **02:** 436   **01:** 533   **Med Exp PMPM:** $188
Principal Investments: Cash and equiv (15%), other (85%)
Provider Compensation ($000): Contr fee ($968,229), capitation ($104,030), bonus arrang ($31,825)
Total Member Encounters: N/A
Group Affiliation: UnitedHealth Group Inc
Licensed in: IL, KS, MO
Address: 13655 Riverport Dr, Maryland Heights, MO 63043-8560
Phone: (314) 592-7000   **Dom State:** MO   **Commenced Bus:** August 1985

Data Date	Weiss Safety Rating	RACR #1	RACR #2	Total Assets ($mil)	Capital ($mil)	Net Premium ($mil)	Net Income ($mil)
3-03	B+	2.09	1.74	332.1	143.4	302.2	11.5
3-02	B+	1.73	1.41	317.9	129.6	342.2	12.5
2002	B+	1.95	1.63	353.8	133.6	1,367.2	48.6
2001	B+	1.73	1.41	341.7	117.9	1,418.5	29.1
2000	B	1.46	1.21	288.8	81.4	1,130.7	9.0
1999	B	1.41	1.19	253.2	76.6	1,074.7	10.3
1998	B	1.48	1.24	223.8	63.4	884.7	4.6

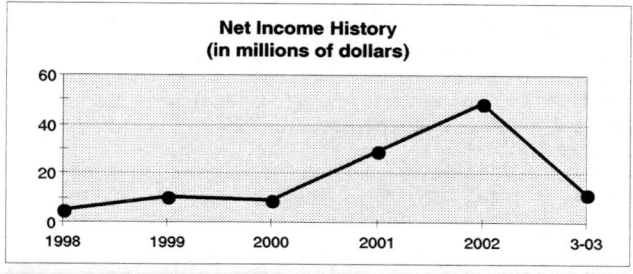

Net Income History (in millions of dollars)

UNITED HEALTHCARE OF TX INC   D+   Weak

Major Rating Factors: Weak profitability index (0.9 on a scale of 0 to 10) with $29.0 million in losses in the last three years. Average return on equity has been poor at -85%. Poor capitalization index (2.6) based on weak current risk-adjusted capital (moderate loss scenario). Weak liquidity (1.0) as a spike in claims may stretch capacity.

Other Rating Factors: Fair overall results on stability tests (4.6) based on a significant 20% decrease in enrollment during the period. Rating is significantly influenced by the good financial results of UnitedHealth Group Inc. High quality investment portfolio (9.6) containing no exposure to mortgages, junk bonds, or unaffiliated stocks.

Principal Business: Comp med (100%)
Mem Phys: 02: 21,276   **01:** 19,183   **02 MLR** 85% / **02 Admin Exp** 19%
Enroll(000): Q1 03: 156   **02:** 195   **01:** 244   **Med Exp PMPM:** $174
Principal Investments: Cash and equiv (7%), other (93%)
Provider Compensation ($000): Contr fee ($452,424), capitation ($16,409)
Total Member Encounters: Phys (1,366,376), non-phys (96,237)
Group Affiliation: UnitedHealth Group Inc
Licensed in: TX
Address: 1250 Capital of Texas Hwy 400, Austin, TX 78746
Phone: (512) 347-2600   **Dom State:** TX   **Commenced Bus:** August 1985

Data Date	Weiss Safety Rating	RACR #1	RACR #2	Total Assets ($mil)	Capital ($mil)	Net Premium ($mil)	Net Income ($mil)
3-03	D+	0.56	0.47	85.9	23.2	110.6	-1.3
3-02	D+	0.00	0.00	89.3	16.8	140.0	0.4
2002	D+	0.44	0.37	81.7	19.5	538.4	-7.4
2001	D+	0.27	0.23	87.1	16.1	551.2	-15.2
2000	C	0.56	0.47	112.7	28.0	594.0	-6.5
1999	C	1.00	0.83	102.3	35.0	465.6	1.5
1998	C	0.45	0.38	93.9	22.2	464.1	-34.4

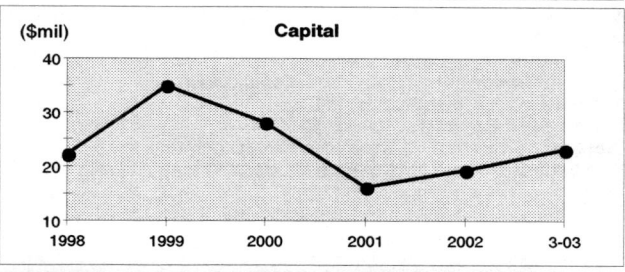

Capital ($mil)

UNITED HEALTHCARE OF UTAH   C   Fair

Major Rating Factors: Fair overall results on stability tests (4.4 on a scale of 0 to 10) based on weak risk-adjusted capital in prior years, a significant 54% decrease in enrollment during the period. Rating is significantly influenced by the good financial results of UnitedHealth Group Inc. Weak profitability index (1.8) with operating losses during 1998, 1999, 2000 and 2001. Average return on equity has been poor at -23%. Good liquidity (6.2) with sufficient resources (cash flows and marketable investments) to handle a spike in claims.

Other Rating Factors: Strong capitalization (9.3) based on excellent current risk-adjusted capital (severe loss scenario) reflecting significant improvement over results in 2000. High quality investment portfolio (9.4) containing no exposure to mortgages, junk bonds, or unaffiliated stocks.

Principal Business: Comp med (80%), Medicaid (20%)
Mem Phys: 02: 3,342   **01:** 2,945   **02 MLR** 84% / **02 Admin Exp** 18%
Enroll(000): Q1 03: 48   **02:** 55   **01:** 120   **Med Exp PMPM:** $111
Principal Investments: Cash and equiv (1%), other (99%)
Provider Compensation ($000): Contr fee ($126,321), capitation ($5,981)
Total Member Encounters: Phys (1,178,730), non-phys (720,064)
Group Affiliation: UnitedHealth Group Inc
Licensed in: UT
Address: 2795 E Cottonwood Pkwy Ste 300, Salt Lake City, UT 84121-0409
Phone: (801) 942-6200   **Dom State:** UT   **Commenced Bus:** March 1984

Data Date	Weiss Safety Rating	RACR #1	RACR #2	Total Assets ($mil)	Capital ($mil)	Net Premium ($mil)	Net Income ($mil)
3-03	C	3.17	2.64	41.1	24.8	22.6	-0.9
3-02	C	1.87	1.51	58.0	22.2	46.4	-1.9
2002	C	3.37	2.81	40.6	26.5	138.6	3.4
2001	C	1.86	1.51	61.5	24.4	231.1	-7.0
2000	C+	0.59	0.50	48.5	7.7	250.9	-5.2
1999	C+	0.73	0.62	46.0	9.1	223.6	-1.6
1998	C+	0.82	0.70	32.7	6.9	167.1	-0.3

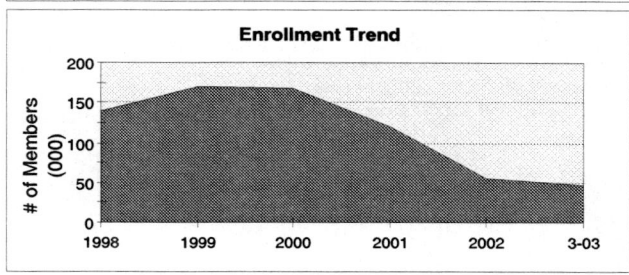

Enrollment Trend

* Denotes a Weiss Recommended Company

II. Analysis of Largest Companies
Winter 2003 - 04

UNITED HEALTHCARE OF WISCONSIN INC * — B+ Good

Major Rating Factors: Good liquidity (5.9 on a scale of 0 to 10) with sufficient resources (cash flows and marketable investments) to handle a spike in claims. Excellent profitability (9.1) despite a decline in earnings during 2002. Strong capitalization (7.1) based on excellent current risk-adjusted capital (severe loss scenario). Moreover, capital has steadily grown over the last five years.
Other Rating Factors: High quality investment portfolio (9.4) containing little or no exposure to mortgages, junk bonds, or unaffiliated stocks. Excellent overall results on stability tests (8.0) based on consistent premium and capital growth in the last five years. Rating is significantly influenced by the good financial results of UnitedHealth Group Inc.
Principal Business: Comp med (77%), Medicaid (18%), Medicare (5%)
Mem Phys: 02: 4,757 **01:** 4,826 **02 MLR** 86% **/ 02 Admin Exp** 12%
Enroll(000): Q1 03: 259 **02:** 277 **01:** 285 **Med Exp PMPM:** $182
Principal Investments: Cash and equiv (14%), real estate (6%), other (79%)
Provider Compensation ($000): Contr fee ($5,255,274), FFS ($45,967), capitation ($35,420)
Total Member Encounters: Phys (1,204,891), non-phys (803,808)
Group Affiliation: UnitedHealth Group Inc
Licensed in: WI
Address: 10701 West Research Dr, Wauwatosa, WI 53226
Phone: (414) 443-4000 **Dom State:** WI **Commenced Bus:** June 1986

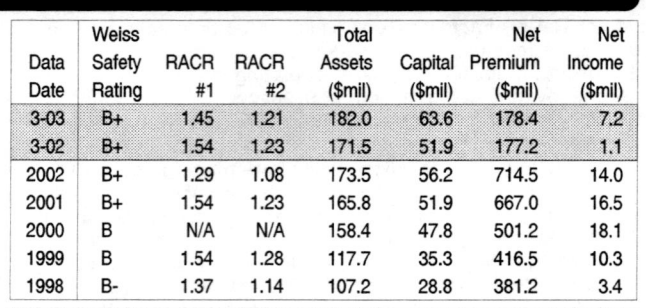

Data Date	Weiss Safety Rating	RACR #1	RACR #2	Total Assets ($mil)	Capital ($mil)	Net Premium ($mil)	Net Income ($mil)
3-03	B+	1.45	1.21	182.0	63.6	178.4	7.2
3-02	B+	1.54	1.23	171.5	51.9	177.2	1.1
2002	B+	1.29	1.08	173.5	56.2	714.5	14.0
2001	B+	1.54	1.23	165.8	51.9	667.0	16.5
2000	B	N/A	N/A	158.4	47.8	501.2	18.1
1999	B	1.54	1.28	117.7	35.3	416.5	10.3
1998	B-	1.37	1.14	107.2	28.8	381.2	3.4

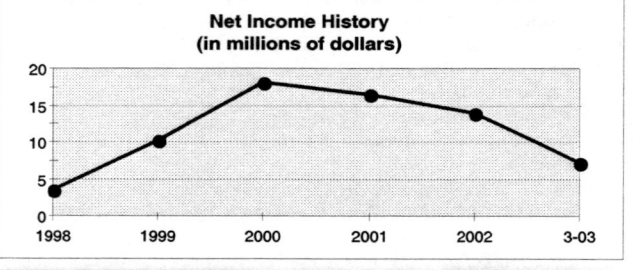

UNITED STATES LIFE INSURANCE COMPANY IN NYC — B Good

Major Rating Factors: Good overall results on stability tests (5.8 on a scale of 0 to 10). Stability strengths include good operational trends and excellent risk diversification. Good liquidity (6.3) with sufficient resources to cover a large increase in policy surrenders despite significant exposure to policies that are subject to withdrawal with minimal or no penalty. Fair quality investment portfolio (4.4).
Other Rating Factors: Strong capitalization (7.3) based on excellent risk adjusted capital (severe loss scenario). Excellent profitability (7.4) with operating gains in each of the last five years.
Principal Business: Group health insurance (41%), individual life insurance (33%), group life insurance (20%), individual annuities (3%), and other lines (2%).
Principal Investments: NonCMO investment grade bonds (61%), CMOs and structured securities (16%), noninv. grade bonds (12%), policy loans (6%), and mortgages in good standing (4%).
Investments in Affiliates: 4%
Group Affiliation: American International Group
Licensed in: All states except PR
Commenced Business: March 1850
Address: 390 Park Ave, New York, NY 10022-4684
Phone: (212) 709-6000 **Domicile State:** NY **NAIC Code:** 70106

Data Date	Weiss Safety Rating	RACR #1	RACR #2	Total Assets ($mil)	Capital ($mil)	Net Premium ($mil)	Net Income ($mil)
6-03	B	2.43	1.20	3,422.9	313.5	157.2	16.7
6-02	B	2.70	1.37	2,370.9	223.5	144.4	12.6
2002	B	2.42	1.20	3,250.1	297.1	353.3	57.9
2001	B	2.70	1.41	2,268.9	223.2	281.0	15.2
2000	B	2.91	1.54	2,210.8	226.4	277.2	54.6
1999	B	2.05	1.08	2,206.8	146.8	254.8	48.0
1998	B	2.08	1.24	2,183.8	212.1	620.2	31.2

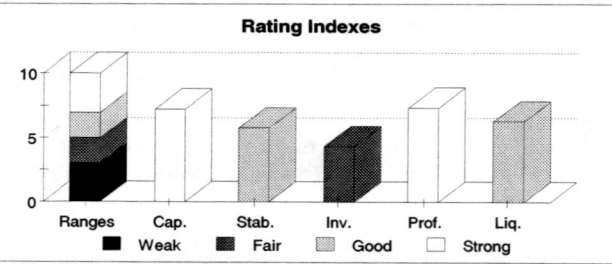

UNITED TEACHER ASSOCIATES INSURANCE COMPANY — C+ Fair

Major Rating Factors: Fair overall results on stability tests (4.4 on a scale of 0 to 10) including fair financial strength of affiliated American Financial Corp. Fair profitability (4.6). Excellent expense controls. Return on equity has been low, averaging -1.7%. Good quality investment portfolio (6.5).
Other Rating Factors: Strong capitalization (7.1) based on excellent risk adjusted capital (severe loss scenario). Excellent liquidity (7.0).
Principal Business: Individual health insurance (38%), reinsurance (33%), group retirement contracts (14%), individual annuities (8%), and group health insurance (7%).
Principal Investments: NonCMO investment grade bonds (59%), CMOs and structured securities (33%), noninv. grade bonds (4%), policy loans (2%), and real estate (1%).
Investments in Affiliates: None
Group Affiliation: American Financial Corp
Licensed in: All states except NH, NY, RI, VT
Commenced Business: January 1959
Address: 5508 Parkcrest Dr, Austin, TX 78731
Phone: (512) 451-2224 **Domicile State:** TX **NAIC Code:** 63479

Data Date	Weiss Safety Rating	RACR #1	RACR #2	Total Assets ($mil)	Capital ($mil)	Net Premium ($mil)	Net Income ($mil)
6-03	C+	1.59	1.04	396.3	47.1	113.4	3.3
6-02	C	1.83	1.22	329.7	46.3	83.8	1.1
2002	C+	1.71	1.10	353.0	45.9	175.6	0.9
2001	C	1.39	0.93	298.9	36.9	156.7	0.0
2000	C	1.55	1.05	274.2	32.8	110.2	-2.4
1999	C	1.66	1.11	208.1	21.0	64.2	-8.0
1998	C	1.65	1.10	217.6	32.6	83.1	8.0

American Financial Corp
Composite Group Rating: C
Largest Group Members

	Assets ($mil)	Weiss Safety Rating
GREAT AMERICAN LIFE INS CO	6389	C
GREAT AMERICAN INS CO	4515	C
ANNUITY INVESTORS LIFE INS CO	969	C
REPUBLIC INDEMNITY CO OF AMERICA	630	C+
INFINITY INS CO	480	C+

UNITED WISCONSIN INS CO   C   Fair

Major Rating Factors: Fair overall results on stability tests (3.7 on a scale of 0 to 10) including weak results on operational trends and excessive premium growth. History of adequate reserve strength (6.9) as reserves have been consistently at an acceptable level.

Other Rating Factors: Good overall profitability index (5.6) despite operating losses during 1999 and 2000. Return on equity has been low, averaging 4.0% over the past five years. Strong long-term capitalization index (7.2) based on excellent current risk adjusted capital (severe and moderate loss scenarios), despite some fluctuation in capital levels. Excellent liquidity (7.9) with ample operational cash flow and liquid investments.

Principal Business: Group accident & health (48%), workers compensation (46%), and other accident & health (6%).

Principal Investments: Investment grade bonds (92%) and misc. investments (9%).

Investments in Affiliates: None
Group Affiliation: Cobalt Corp
Licensed in: AZ, CO, DC, DE, FL, GA, ID, IL, IN, IA, KS, KY, LA, MD, MI, MN, MS, MO, MT, NE, NM, NC, ND, OH, OK, OR, PA, SC, SD, TN, TX, UT, VA, WA, WI, WY
Commenced Business: July 1958
Address: 401 W. Michigan St, Milwaukee, WI 53203
Phone: (262) 787-7400   **Domicile State:** WI   **NAIC Code:** 29157

Data Date	Weiss Safety Rating	RACR #1	RACR #2	Loss Ratio %	Total Assets ($mil)	Capital ($mil)	Net Premium ($mil)	Net Income ($mil)
6-03	C	1.88	1.07	N/A	104.8	51.9	51.4	2.4
6-02	C	2.53	1.25	N/A	85.6	44.4	51.7	-0.8
2002	C	2.03	1.15	60.8	94.7	48.7	40.4	2.7
2001	C	1.83	1.01	71.7	76.7	40.7	79.1	2.3
2000	C	2.10	1.21	80.1	86.1	38.2	71.5	-2.0
1999	C	2.93	1.64	83.3	73.2	39.4	51.5	-1.1
1998	C	3.36	1.89	69.3	71.4	41.9	53.6	6.0

UNITED WISCONSIN LIFE INSURANCE COMPANY   C   Fair

Major Rating Factors: Fair profitability (4.8 on a scale of 0 to 10). Return on equity has been fair, averaging 5.6%. Fair overall results on stability tests (4.2). Good liquidity (6.3) with sufficient resources to handle a spike in claims.

Other Rating Factors: Strong capitalization (7.8) based on excellent risk adjusted capital (severe loss scenario). High quality investment portfolio (7.9).

Principal Business: Group health insurance (94%), group life insurance (4%), and individual health insurance (2%).

Principal Investments: NonCMO investment grade bonds (56%), CMOs and structured securities (31%), noninv. grade bonds (2%), common & preferred stock (2%), and cash (2%).

Investments in Affiliates: 9%
Group Affiliation: American Medical Security Group Inc
Licensed in: All states except AK, CT, HI, ME, MA, NH, NJ, NY, RI, VT, PR
Commenced Business: March 1966
Address: 3100 AMS Blvd, Green Bay, WI 54313
Phone: (800) 232-5432   **Domicile State:** WI   **NAIC Code:** 97179

Data Date	Weiss Safety Rating	RACR #1	RACR #2	Total Assets ($mil)	Capital ($mil)	Net Premium ($mil)	Net Income ($mil)
6-03	C	1.89	1.52	329.7	167.6	358.9	13.0
6-02	C	1.53	1.24	309.0	144.0	387.0	7.0
2002	C	1.77	1.42	322.3	157.5	757.4	13.0
2001	C	1.62	1.31	316.0	155.6	840.4	17.8
2000	C	1.40	1.12	315.1	147.2	931.2	7.0
1999	C	1.35	1.08	346.6	150.0	1,009.7	-20.9
1998	C	1.64	1.30	350.9	183.3	890.7	22.5

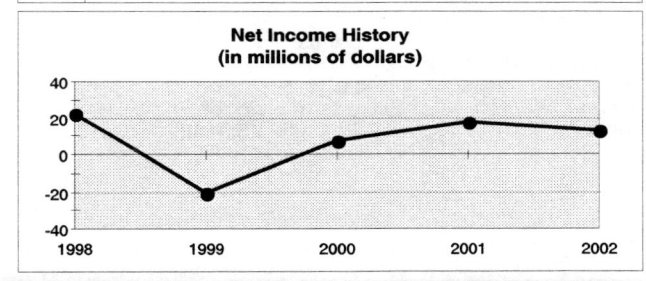

UNITY HEALTH PLANS INS CORP   B   Good

Major Rating Factors: Good overall profitability index (5.1 on a scale of 0 to 10) despite a decline in earnings during 2002. Good overall results on stability tests (5.9). Fair financial strength from affiliates. Good liquidity (5.7) with sufficient resources (cash flows and marketable investments) to handle a spike in claims.

Other Rating Factors: Strong capitalization (7.2) based on excellent current risk-adjusted capital (severe loss scenario) reflecting improvement over results in 2000. High quality investment portfolio (9.9) containing little or no exposure to mortgages, junk bonds, or unaffiliated stocks.

Principal Business: Comp med (93%), FEHB (4%), Medicaid (3%).
Mem Phys: 02: 2,462   01: 2,234   **02 MLR** 88%   / **02 Admin Exp** 9%
Enroll(000): Q1 03: 81   02: 77   01: 74   **Med Exp PMPM:** $191
Principal Investments: Cash and equiv (6%), real estate (6%), other (88%).
Provider Compensation ($000): Contr fee ($84,786), capitation ($55,877), FFS ($32,222)
Total Member Encounters: Phys (164,685), non-phys (261,076)
Group Affiliation: Cobalt Corp
Licensed in: WI
Address: 840 Carolina St, Sauk City, WI 53583
Phone: (608) 643-2491   **Dom State:** WI   **Commenced Bus:** January 1984

Data Date	Weiss Safety Rating	RACR #1	RACR #2	Total Assets ($mil)	Capital ($mil)	Net Premium ($mil)	Net Income ($mil)
3-03	B	1.50	1.25	53.4	19.4	56.9	2.5
3-02	C+	1.33	1.10	42.5	14.5	47.9	0.6
2002	B	1.39	1.16	46.9	17.9	197.0	4.4
2001	C+	1.33	1.10	43.1	14.0	168.3	5.5
2000	C+	1.04	0.89	38.5	10.9	158.8	-2.6
1999	B-	1.37	1.19	25.0	10.0	143.3	-0.8
1998	B	1.88	1.61	28.6	14.1	136.8	1.3

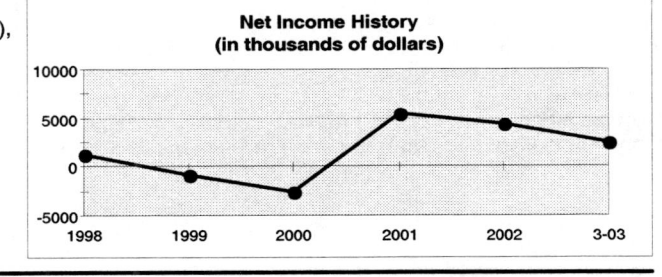

II. Analysis of Largest Companies

UNIVERSAL CARE — D- Weak

Major Rating Factors: Weak profitability index (1.8 on a scale of 0 to 10) with operating losses during 2001 and 2002. Average return on equity has been poor at -1%. Poor capitalization index (0.0) based on weak current risk-adjusted capital (severe loss scenario). Weak overall results on stability tests (2.8) based on rapid enrollment growth during the past five years.
Other Rating Factors: Weak liquidity (0.0) as a spike in claims may stretch capacity.
Principal Business: Comp med (48%), Medicaid (44%), dental (4%), other (5%).
Mem Phys: 02: N/A **01:** N/A **02 MLR** 92% **/ 02 Admin Exp** 8%
Enroll(000): Q1 03: 348 **02:** 355 **01:** 317 **Med Exp PMPM:** $98
Principal Investments ($000): Cash and equiv ($20,168), stocks ($322)
Provider Compensation ($000): None
Total Member Encounters: N/A
Group Affiliation: None
Licensed in: CA
Address: 1600 E Hill St, Signal Hill, CA 90806-3682
Phone: (562) 424-6200 **Dom State:** CA **Commenced Bus:** November 1985

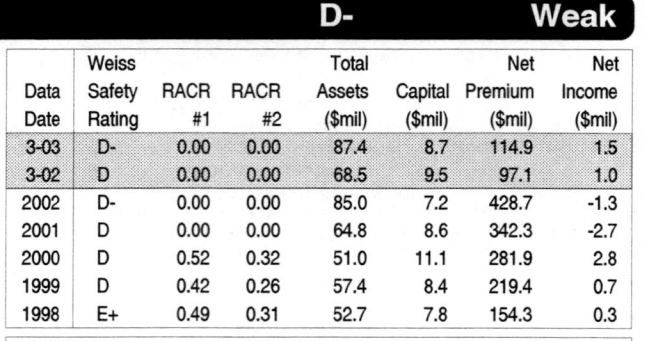

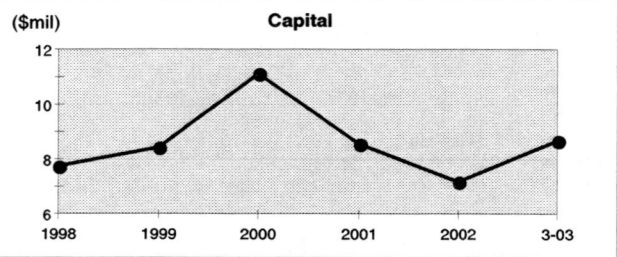

Data Date	Weiss Safety Rating	RACR #1	RACR #2	Total Assets ($mil)	Capital ($mil)	Net Premium ($mil)	Net Income ($mil)
3-03	D-	0.00	0.00	87.4	8.7	114.9	1.5
3-02	D	0.00	0.00	68.5	9.5	97.1	1.0
2002	D-	0.00	0.00	85.0	7.2	428.7	-1.3
2001	D	0.00	0.00	64.8	8.6	342.3	-2.7
2000	D	0.52	0.32	51.0	11.1	281.9	2.8
1999	D	0.42	0.26	57.4	8.4	219.4	0.7
1998	E+	0.49	0.31	52.7	7.8	154.3	0.3

UNIVERSAL UNDERWRITERS LIFE INSURANCE COMPANY — B Good

Major Rating Factors: Good overall results on stability tests (5.6 on a scale of 0 to 10) despite fair financial strength of affiliated Zurich Financial Services Group. Other stability subfactors include good operational trends and excellent risk diversification. Strong capitalization (10.0) based on excellent risk adjusted capital (severe loss scenario). Capital levels have been relatively consistent over the last five years. High quality investment portfolio (8.1).
Other Rating Factors: Excellent profitability (8.0) with operating gains in each of the last five years. Excellent liquidity (7.4).
Principal Business: Credit life insurance (41%), credit health insurance (39%), and individual life insurance (20%).
Principal Investments: NonCMO investment grade bonds (57%), CMOs and structured securities (36%), cash (2%), common & preferred stock (2%), and misc. investments (3%).
Investments in Affiliates: 5%
Group Affiliation: Zurich Financial Services Group
Licensed in: All states except NY, PR
Commenced Business: October 1965
Address: 1600 McConnor Parkway, Schaumburg, IL 60196-6801
Phone: (847) 874-7400 **Domicile State:** KS **NAIC Code:** 70173

Data Date	Weiss Safety Rating	RACR #1	RACR #2	Total Assets ($mil)	Capital ($mil)	Net Premium ($mil)	Net Income ($mil)
6-03	B	11.42	7.21	358.7	160.9	31.1	5.9
6-02	B+	7.73	4.86	355.1	114.7	30.9	6.6
2002	B+	8.99	5.72	369.3	123.2	61.5	8.4
2001	B+	6.59	3.97	350.6	108.9	65.2	11.1
2000	B	6.99	4.20	315.3	114.6	63.0	24.3
1999	B	7.70	4.97	313.3	112.1	69.1	19.0
1998	B	6.74	4.47	297.3	96.3	69.0	20.4

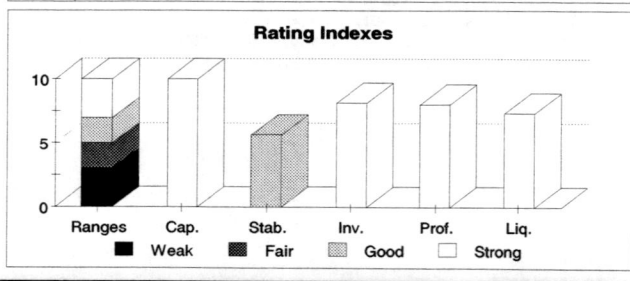

UNIVERSITY HEALTH CARE INC — C Fair

Major Rating Factors: Fair capitalization (3.8 on a scale of 0 to 10) based on fair current risk-adjusted capital (moderate loss scenario) reflecting improvement over results in 2001. Good overall profitability index (6.5). Good liquidity (6.9) with sufficient resources (cash flows and marketable investments) to handle a spike in claims.
Other Rating Factors: High quality investment portfolio (9.9). Excellent overall results on stability tests (7.4).
Principal Business: Medicaid (100%).
Mem Phys: 02: 3,204 **01:** 3,112 **02 MLR** 90% **/ 02 Admin Exp** 7%
Enroll(000): Q1 03: 127 **02:** 129 **01:** 120 **Med Exp PMPM:** $239
Principal Investments: Cash and equiv (70%), nonaffiliate common stock (7%), other (23%).
Provider Compensation ($000): Contr fee ($162,076), bonus arrang ($139,290), capitation ($59,838), FFS ($9,977)
Total Member Encounters: Phys (1,286,768), non-phys (346,821)
Group Affiliation: UHC Group
Licensed in: KY
Address: 305 W Broadway Ave 3rd Floor, Louisville, KY 40202
Phone: (502) 852-5872 **Dom State:** KY **Commenced Bus:** October 2000

Data Date	Weiss Safety Rating	RACR #1	RACR #2	Total Assets ($mil)	Capital ($mil)	Net Premium ($mil)	Net Income ($mil)
3-03	C	0.76	0.63	81.8	23.0	103.3	-0.3
3-02	D+	0.51	0.42	85.5	14.6	94.1	-3.4
2002	C	0.77	0.64	90.5	23.4	395.7	6.4
2001	D+	0.51	0.42	90.4	18.0	368.2	6.4
2000	U	0.55	0.45	79.9	11.0	82.1	0.9
1999	N/A	N/A	N/A	N/A	N/A	N/A	N/A
1998	N/A	N/A	N/A	N/A	N/A	N/A	N/A

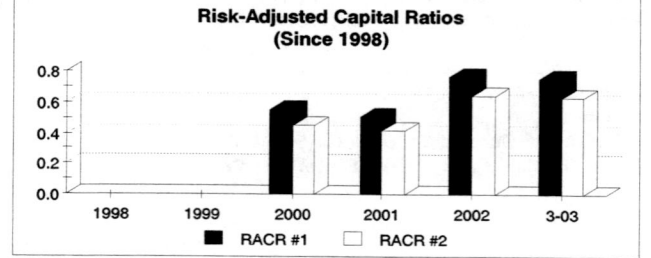

Winter 2003 - 04

II. Analysis of Largest Companies

UNIVERSITY HEALTH PLANS INC   D+   Weak

Major Rating Factors: Weak profitability index (0.9 on a scale of 0 to 10) with operating losses during 1998, 1999, 2001 and 2002. Average return on equity has been poor at -64%. Poor capitalization index (2.8) based on weak current risk-adjusted capital (moderate loss scenario). Furthermore, this low level of risk-adjusted capital has been consistent in previous years. Good liquidity (6.8) with sufficient resources (cash flows and marketable investments) to handle a spike in claims.

Other Rating Factors: High quality investment portfolio (9.9) containing no exposure to mortgages, junk bonds, or unaffiliated stocks. Excellent overall results on stability tests (7.4) based on consistent premium and capital growth in the last five years but a decline in enrollment during 2002. Potentially strong support from affiliation with Centene Corp.

Principal Business: Medicaid (89%), comp med (11%)
Mem Phys: 02: 8,887 **01:** 7,016 **02 MLR** 93% **/ 02 Admin Exp** 13%
Enroll(000): Q1 03: 53 **02:** 53 **01:** 57 **Med Exp PMPM:** $187
Principal Investments: Cash and equiv (100%)
Provider Compensation ($000): Contr fee ($112,841), capitation ($11,835)
Total Member Encounters: N/A
Group Affiliation: Centene Corp
Licensed in: NJ
Address: 550 Broad St 17th Floor, Newark, NJ 07102
Phone: (973) 623-8700 **Dom State:** NJ **Commenced Bus:** October 1994

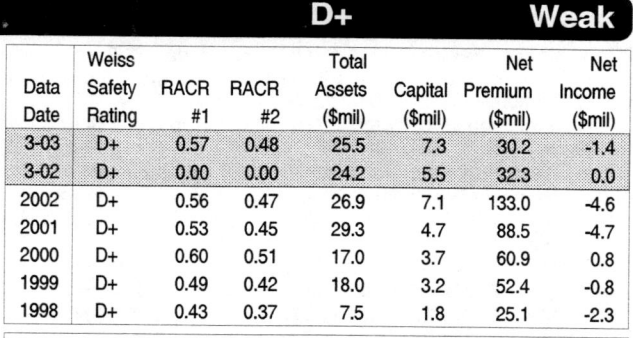

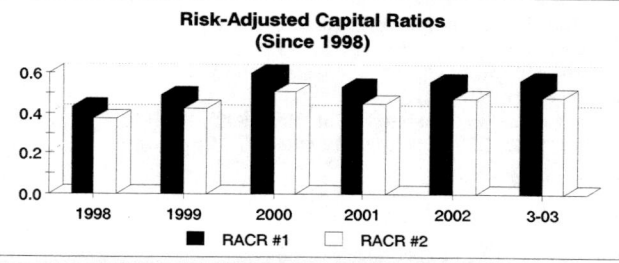

Data Date	Weiss Safety Rating	RACR #1	RACR #2	Total Assets ($mil)	Capital ($mil)	Net Premium ($mil)	Net Income ($mil)
3-03	D+	0.57	0.48	25.5	7.3	30.2	-1.4
3-02	D+	0.00	0.00	24.2	5.5	32.3	0.0
2002	D+	0.56	0.47	26.9	7.1	133.0	-4.6
2001	D+	0.53	0.45	29.3	4.7	88.5	-4.7
2000	D+	0.60	0.51	17.0	3.7	60.9	0.8
1999	D+	0.49	0.42	18.0	3.2	52.4	-0.8
1998	D+	0.43	0.37	7.5	1.8	25.1	-2.3

Risk-Adjusted Capital Ratios (Since 1998)

UNUM LIFE INSURANCE COMPANY OF AMERICA   C-   Fair

Major Rating Factors: Fair overall results on stability tests (3.2 on a scale of 0 to 10) including fair financial strength of affiliated UnumProvident Corp and fair risk adjusted capital in prior years. Fair quality investment portfolio (4.9) with large holdings of BBB rated bonds in addition to junk bond exposure equal to 87% of capital. Weak profitability (2.7) with operating losses during the first six months of 2003.

Other Rating Factors: Good liquidity (6.7). Strong capitalization (7.2) based on excellent risk adjusted capital (severe loss scenario).

Principal Business: Group health insurance (53%), group life insurance (28%), individual health insurance (11%), reinsurance (6%), and individual life insurance (1%).

Principal Investments: NonCMO investment grade bonds (59%), CMOs and structured securities (23%), noninv. grade bonds (11%), mortgages in good standing (5%), and policy loans (1%).

Investments in Affiliates: None
Group Affiliation: UnumProvident Corp
Licensed in: All states except NY
Commenced Business: September 1966
Address: 2211 Congress St, Portland, ME 04122
Phone: (207) 770-9306 **Domicile State:** ME **NAIC Code:** 62235

Data Date	Weiss Safety Rating	RACR #1	RACR #2	Total Assets ($mil)	Capital ($mil)	Net Premium ($mil)	Net Income ($mil)
6-03	C-	1.94	1.12	11,383.4	1,241.1	1,366.2	-41.2
6-02	C+	1.82	1.07	9,651.8	1,065.5	1,419.9	-123.0
2002	C-	1.87	1.06	10,982.4	1,130.5	2,758.5	-192.6
2001	C+	2.26	1.34	8,433.4	1,218.0	2,738.5	46.7
2000	C+	2.60	1.51	8,152.7	1,239.1	2,820.5	122.9
1999	C+	2.39	1.38	8,221.5	1,160.9	2,804.1	-353.5
1998	B-	0.84	0.70	7,296.0	1,087.0	2,443.6	22.3

UnumProvident Corp Composite Group Rating: C- Largest Group Members	Assets ($mil)	Weiss Safety Rating
UNUM LIFE INS CO OF AMERICA	10982	C-
PROVIDENT LIFE ACCIDENT INS CO	8557	C-
PAUL REVERE LIFE INS CO	4976	C-
COLONIAL LIFE ACCIDENT INS CO	1194	C-
FIRST UNUM LIFE INS CO	1097	C-

UPMC HEALTH PLAN INC   C-   Fair

Major Rating Factors: Weak profitability index (0.9 on a scale of 0 to 10) with operating losses during 1998, 1999, 2001 and 2002. Average return on equity has been extremely poor. Good capitalization (5.2) based on good current risk-adjusted capital (severe loss scenario) reflecting significant improvement over results in 1998. Good liquidity (7.0) with sufficient resources (cash flows and marketable investments) to handle a spike in claims.

Other Rating Factors: High quality investment portfolio (9.5) containing no exposure to mortgages, junk bonds, or unaffiliated stocks. Excellent overall results on stability tests (7.4) based on consistent premium and capital growth in the last five years but rapid enrollment growth during the past five years.

Principal Business: Comp med (62%), Medicaid (33%), Medicare (5%).
Mem Phys: 02: N/A **01:** N/A **02 MLR** 90% **/ 02 Admin Exp** 10%
Enroll(000): Q1 03: 329 **02:** 346 **01:** 324 **Med Exp PMPM:** $159
Principal Investments: Cash and equiv (98%), other (2%)
Provider Compensation ($000): Contr fee ($627,980), capitation ($11,246)
Total Member Encounters: Phys (2,152,654), non-phys (399,965)
Group Affiliation: UPMC Health System
Licensed in: PA
Address: 112 Washington Pl, Pittsburgh, PA 15219
Phone: (412) 434-1200 **Dom State:** PA **Commenced Bus:** March 1996

Data Date	Weiss Safety Rating	RACR #1	RACR #2	Total Assets ($mil)	Capital ($mil)	Net Premium ($mil)	Net Income ($mil)
3-03	C-	0.96	0.80	163.5	63.1	190.8	7.3
3-02	C-	0.00	0.00	145.8	39.6	172.1	0.1
2002	C-	0.83	0.69	166.8	55.7	708.4	-5.2
2001	C-	0.72	0.61	141.5	38.1	530.2	-1.3
2000	D	0.65	0.55	92.7	22.1	351.1	0.1
1999	D-	0.60	0.51	58.9	12.4	186.7	-17.9
1998	D-	0.31	0.27	27.3	4.0	87.8	-16.2

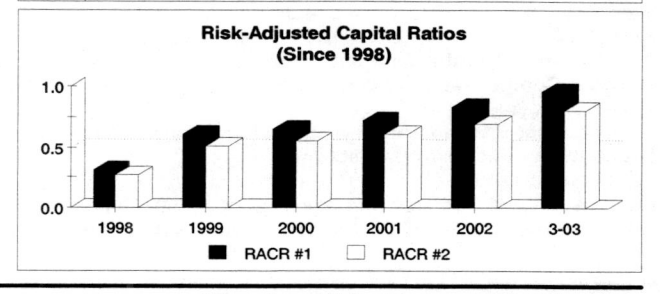

Risk-Adjusted Capital Ratios (Since 1998)

II. Analysis of Largest Companies

Winter 2003 - 04

UPPER PENINSULA HEALTH PLAN INC — C- Fair

Major Rating Factors: Fair capitalization index (3.0 on a scale of 0 to 10) based on weak current risk-adjusted capital (moderate loss scenario). Good overall profitability index (6.0) despite a decline in earnings during 2002. Good overall results on stability tests (5.6) despite rapid premium growth over the last five years.
Other Rating Factors: Good liquidity (6.9) with sufficient resources (cash flows and marketable investments) to handle a spike in claims. High quality investment portfolio (9.9) containing no exposure to mortgages, junk bonds, or unaffiliated stocks.
Principal Business: Medicaid (99%)
Mem Phys: 02: 702 **01:** 605 **02 MLR** 91% **/ 02 Admin Exp** 8%
Enroll(000): Q1 03: 26 **02:** 19 **01:** 18 **Med Exp PMPM:** $132
Principal Investments: Cash and equiv (91%), other (9%)
Provider Compensation ($000): Contr fee ($30,107)
Total Member Encounters: Phys (115,374), non-phys (249,588)
Group Affiliation: Upper Peninsula Managed Care LLC
Licensed in: MI
Address: 228 W Washington St, Marquette, MI 49855
Phone: (906) 225-7500 **Dom State:** MI **Commenced Bus:** August 1998

Data Date	Weiss Safety Rating	RACR #1	RACR #2	Total Assets ($mil)	Capital ($mil)	Net Premium ($mil)	Net Income ($mil)
3-03	C-	0.63	0.53	9.8	2.8	10.2	-0.2
3-02	E	0.00	0.00	9.1	2.5	8.0	0.4
2002	C-	0.66	0.55	8.6	3.0	32.4	0.0
2001	E	0.00	0.00	8.2	2.1	30.9	1.5
2000	U	0.00	0.00	6.5	0.1	29.9	0.2
1999	N/A	N/A	N/A	3.9	0.2	27.9	N/A
1998	N/A	N/A	N/A	1.2	-0.5	3.8	N/A

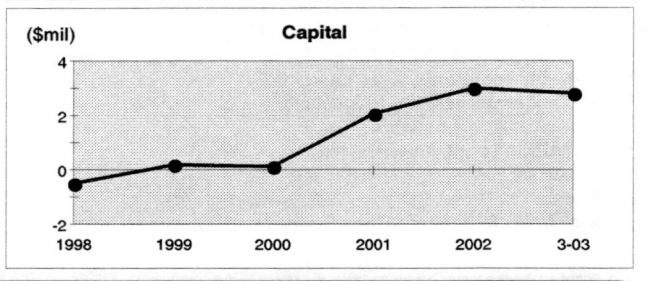

USABLE LIFE — C+ Fair

Major Rating Factors: Fair overall results on stability tests (4.6 on a scale of 0 to 10). Good quality investment portfolio (6.1) despite mixed results such as: no exposure to mortgages and substantial holdings of BBB bonds but minimal holdings in junk bonds. Strong capitalization (8.9) based on excellent risk adjusted capital (severe loss scenario). Moreover, capital levels have been consistently high over the last five years.
Other Rating Factors: Excellent profitability (8.6) with operating gains in each of the last five years. Excellent liquidity (7.6).
Principal Business: Group life insurance (38%), group health insurance (34%), individual health insurance (23%), individual life insurance (4%), and reinsurance (1%).
Principal Investments: NonCMO investment grade bonds (82%), common & preferred stock (13%), noninv. grade bonds (3%), and policy loans (2%).
Investments in Affiliates: 2%
Group Affiliation: Arkansas Bl Cross Bl Shield Group
Licensed in: All states except AK, CT, FL, KY, NY, PR
Commenced Business: December 1980
Address: 320 W Capitol Suite 700, Little Rock, AR 72201
Phone: (501) 375-7200 **Domicile State:** AR **NAIC Code:** 94358

Data Date	Weiss Safety Rating	RACR #1	RACR #2	Total Assets ($mil)	Capital ($mil)	Net Premium ($mil)	Net Income ($mil)
6-03	C+	3.26	2.28	125.5	60.1	35.9	3.8
6-02	C+	3.41	2.39	112.4	55.1	29.8	2.9
2002	C+	3.23	2.26	117.6	54.9	62.1	5.1
2001	C+	3.34	2.33	107.6	52.6	58.1	3.3
2000	C+	3.28	2.33	95.2	49.1	48.3	4.5
1999	C+	3.33	2.39	84.4	44.8	40.2	3.8
1998	C+	3.33	2.42	73.8	41.1	34.8	4.4

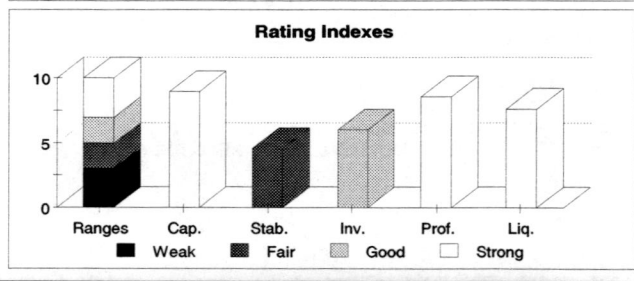

VALLEY BAPTIST HEALTH PLAN INC — C- Fair

Major Rating Factors: Fair capitalization (4.9 on a scale of 0 to 10) based on good current risk-adjusted capital (severe loss scenario) reflecting some improvement over results in 2001. Weak profitability index (1.9) with operating losses during 1998 and 2000. Average return on equity has been poor at -6%. Good overall results on stability tests (5.3) despite fair risk-adjusted capital in prior years, rapid premium growth over the last five years and rapid enrollment growth during the past five years.
Other Rating Factors: Good liquidity (7.0) with sufficient resources (cash flows and marketable investments) to handle a spike in claims. High quality investment portfolio (9.9) containing no exposure to mortgages, junk bonds, or unaffiliated stocks.
Principal Business: Comp med (100%)
Mem Phys: 02: N/A **01:** N/A **02 MLR** 78% **/ 02 Admin Exp** 20%
Enroll(000): Q1 03: 11 **02:** 11 **01:** 11 **Med Exp PMPM:** $172
Principal Investments: Cash and equiv (81%), other (19%)
Provider Compensation ($000): Contr fee ($11,130), FFS ($6,778), capitation ($542), other ($4,724)
Total Member Encounters: Phys (59,851), non-phys (22,600)
Group Affiliation: Valley Baptist Group
Licensed in: TX
Address: 2005 N Ed Carey Dr, Harlingen, TX 78550-8257
Phone: (956) 389-2273 **Dom State:** TX **Commenced Bus:** September 1998

Data Date	Weiss Safety Rating	RACR #1	RACR #2	Total Assets ($mil)	Capital ($mil)	Net Premium ($mil)	Net Income ($mil)
3-03	C-	0.92	0.76	9.5	4.9	8.4	0.5
3-02	D+	0.78	0.66	10.8	3.5	7.9	-0.2
2002	C-	0.81	0.68	11.5	4.3	30.0	0.7
2001	D+	0.78	0.67	8.1	3.8	27.7	0.3
2000	D	0.78	0.67	5.0	1.6	15.7	-1.3
1999	U	1.46	1.26	5.7	2.6	10.6	0.2
1998	N/A	N/A	N/A	4.0	2.0	3.2	-0.1

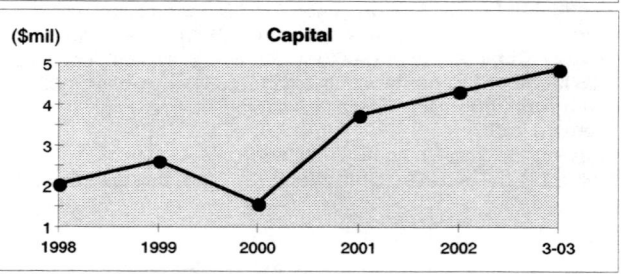

Winter 2003 - 04   II. Analysis of Largest Companies

VALLEY HEALTH PLAN   B-   Good

Major Rating Factors: Fair profitability index (3.7 on a scale of 0 to 10) with operating losses during 1999 and 2000. Return on equity has been low, averaging 4%. Good capitalization (5.4) based on good current risk-adjusted capital (severe loss scenario) reflecting some improvement over results in 1999. Good overall results on stability tests (6.3) based on consistent premium and capital growth in the last five years. Rating is significantly influenced by the fair financial results of Cobalt Corp.
Other Rating Factors: Good liquidity (5.7) with sufficient resources (cash flows and marketable investments) to handle a spike in claims. High quality investment portfolio (9.6) containing little or no exposure to mortgages, junk bonds, or unaffiliated stocks.
Principal Business: Comp med (96%), med supp (3%), Medicaid (1%)
Mem Phys: 02: 365   **01:** 379   **02 MLR** 92% / **02 Admin Exp** 7%
Enroll(000): Q1 03: 25   **02:** 30   **01:** 31   **Med Exp PMPM:** $221
Principal Investments: Other (100%)
Provider Compensation ($000): FFS ($59,385), capitation ($20,181)
Total Member Encounters: N/A
Group Affiliation: Cobalt Corp
Licensed in: WI
Address: 401 W Michigan St., Milwaukee, WI 53202
Phone: (414) 226-5882   **Dom State:** WI   **Commenced Bus:** August 1988

Data Date	Weiss Safety Rating	RACR #1	RACR #2	Total Assets ($mil)	Capital ($mil)	Net Premium ($mil)	Net Income ($mil)
3-03	B-	0.98	0.82	24.9	8.3	20.1	-0.1
3-02	C	1.08	0.88	19.5	8.2	21.4	0.4
2002	B-	0.98	0.82	18.6	8.4	88.1	1.1
2001	C	1.08	0.88	18.8	7.8	80.7	0.6
2000	C	1.00	0.83	19.2	7.2	77.9	-0.6
1999	C	0.88	0.73	16.9	6.5	76.2	-0.1
1998	B	1.05	0.87	15.3	6.6	70.2	0.9

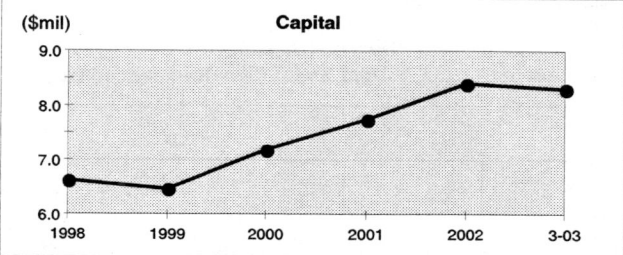

Capital chart 1998–3-03

VANTAGE HEALTH PLAN INC   D-   Weak

Major Rating Factors: Weak profitability index (0.9 on a scale of 0 to 10) with operating losses during 1998, 1999, 2000 and 2002. Average return on equity has been poor at -22%. Poor capitalization index (0.0) based on weak current risk-adjusted capital (severe loss scenario) as results have slipped from the good range over the last four years. Weak overall results on stability tests (0.5) based on rapid premium growth over the last five years.
Other Rating Factors: Weak liquidity (0.5) as a spike in claims may stretch capacity. Fair quality investment portfolio (3.9).
Principal Business: Comp med (100%)
Mem Phys: 02: 3,976   **01:** 3,261   **02 MLR** 94% / **02 Admin Exp** 16%
Enroll(000): Q1 03: 5   **02:** 5   **01:** 5   **Med Exp PMPM:** $199
Principal Investments: Cash and equiv (51%), other (49%)
Provider Compensation ($000): Bonus arrang ($11,669)
Total Member Encounters: Phys (23,105), non-phys (14,687)
Group Affiliation: None
Licensed in: OH
Address: 4602 Timber Commons Dr, Sandusky, OH 44870
Phone: (419) 621-9858   **Dom State:** OH   **Commenced Bus:** January 1996

Data Date	Weiss Safety Rating	RACR #1	RACR #2	Total Assets ($mil)	Capital ($mil)	Net Premium ($mil)	Net Income ($mil)
3-03	D-	0.29	0.24	4.1	0.8	3.5	0.0
3-02	D+	1.09	0.91	3.8	1.9	3.1	-0.1
2002	D-	0.29	0.24	3.4	0.8	13.3	-1.2
2001	D+	1.09	0.91	3.9	2.0	8.8	0.1
2000	D	1.29	1.09	3.0	1.8	6.8	-0.1
1999	D	1.61	1.35	3.4	1.9	5.7	-0.2
1998	D+	2.73	2.30	2.9	2.0	3.6	-0.2

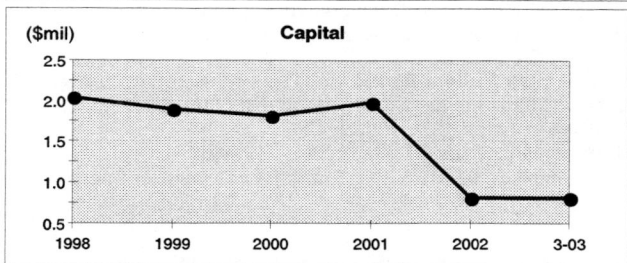

Capital chart 1998–3-03

VANTAGE HEALTH PLAN INC   B-   Good

Major Rating Factors: Good overall profitability index (6.3 on a scale of 0 to 10) despite operating losses during 1998. Good capitalization (5.8) based on good current risk-adjusted capital (severe loss scenario) reflecting significant improvement over results in 1998. High quality investment portfolio (9.9) containing no exposure to mortgages, junk bonds, or unaffiliated stocks.
Other Rating Factors: Excellent overall results on stability tests (7.9) based on consistent premium and capital growth in the last five years. Excellent liquidity (7.1) with ample operational cash flow and liquid investments.
Principal Business: Comp med (100%)
Mem Phys: 02: 1,293   **01:** 1,184   **02 MLR** 83% / **02 Admin Exp** 13%
Enroll(000): Q1 03: 14   **02:** 14   **01:** 10   **Med Exp PMPM:** $179
Principal Investments: Cash and equiv (94%), other (6%)
Provider Compensation ($000): Contr fee ($24,463)
Total Member Encounters: Phys (84,811), non-phys (12,499)
Group Affiliation: None
Licensed in: IL
Address: 909 N 18th St Ste 201, Monroe, LA 71201
Phone: (318) 361-0900   **Dom State:** LA   **Commenced Bus:** December 1994

Data Date	Weiss Safety Rating	RACR #1	RACR #2	Total Assets ($mil)	Capital ($mil)	Net Premium ($mil)	Net Income ($mil)
3-03	B-	1.04	0.87	11.7	5.3	9.1	0.4
3-02	C-	0.95	0.80	7.6	3.3	6.7	0.2
2002	B-	1.02	0.85	9.8	5.2	30.1	1.4
2001	C-	0.96	0.81	7.4	3.2	20.3	1.0
2000	D	0.71	0.60	4.4	2.2	16.8	0.4
1999	D	0.59	0.50	3.6	1.7	15.1	0.3
1998	D	0.56	0.47	4.1	1.3	14.4	-1.8

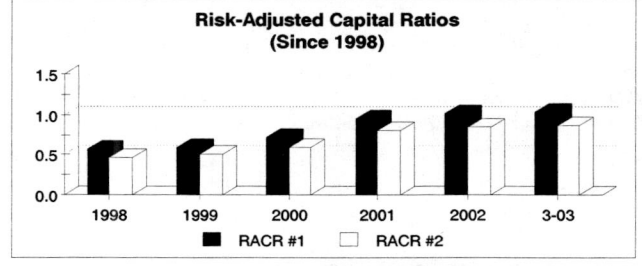

Risk-Adjusted Capital Ratios (Since 1998) — RACR #1, RACR #2

www.WeissRatings.com   * Denotes a Weiss Recommended Company

II. Analysis of Largest Companies

Winter 2003 - 04

VENTURA COUNTY HEALTH CARE PLAN — D+ — Weak

Major Rating Factors: Weak profitability index (0.9 on a scale of 0 to 10). Poor capitalization index (1.6) based on weak current risk-adjusted capital (moderate loss scenario). Furthermore, this low level of risk-adjusted capital has been consistent in previous years. Fair overall results on stability tests (3.2).
Other Rating Factors: Fair liquidity (4.6) as cash resources may not be adequate to cover a spike in claims.
Principal Business: Comp med (82%), other (18%)
Mem Phys: 02: N/A **01:** N/A **02 MLR** 93% / **02 Admin Exp** 10%
Enroll(000): Q1 03: 11 **02:** 11 **01:** N/A **Med Exp PMPM:** $198
Principal Investments ($000): Cash and equiv ($575), other ($1,500)
Provider Compensation ($000): None
Total Member Encounters: N/A
Group Affiliation: None
Licensed in: CA
Address: 233 Knoll Dr, Ventura, CA 93003
Phone: (805) 677-5157 **Dom State:** CA **Commenced Bus:** June 1996

Data Date	Weiss Safety Rating	RACR #1	RACR #2	Total Assets ($mil)	Capital ($mil)	Net Premium ($mil)	Net Income ($mil)
3-03	D+	0.59	0.38	3.8	1.1	3.5	0.0
3-02	C-	0.00	0.00	4.0	1.6	3.0	0.0
2002	D+	0.59	0.38	3.7	1.1	13.5	-0.4
2001	N/A	N/A	N/A	N/A	N/A	N/A	N/A
2000	C-	N/A	N/A	3.9	1.2	10.0	N/A
1999	C-	1.80	1.14	2.9	1.2	7.8	0.0
1998	C-	1.57	0.99	2.6	1.2	6.7	0.0

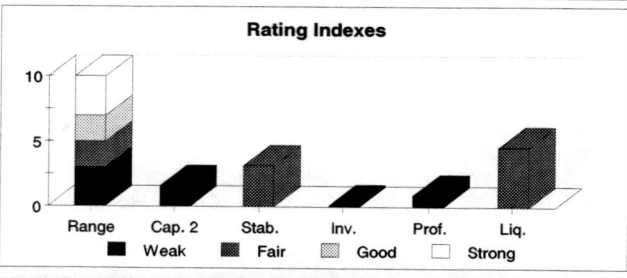

Rating Indexes (bar chart: Range, Cap. 2, Stab., Inv., Prof., Liq.; legend: Weak, Fair, Good, Strong)

VERMONT HEALTH PLAN LLC — B- — Good

Major Rating Factors: Fair profitability index (4.7 on a scale of 0 to 10) with operating losses during 1998 and 1999. Good overall results on stability tests (6.9) based on consistent premium and capital growth in the last five years. Good liquidity (6.8) with sufficient resources (cash flows and marketable investments) to handle a spike in claims
Other Rating Factors: Strong capitalization (7.4) based on excellent current risk-adjusted capital (severe loss scenario) reflecting significant improvement over results in 1999. High quality investment portfolio (9.9) containing no exposure to mortgages, junk bonds, or unaffiliated stocks.
Principal Business: Comp med (100%)
Mem Phys: 02: 4,391 **01:** 4,286 **02 MLR** 81% / **02 Admin Exp** 15%
Enroll(000): Q1 03: 27 **02:** 28 **01:** 29 **Med Exp PMPM:** $183
Principal Investments: Cash and equiv (32%), other (68%)
Provider Compensation ($000): Bonus arrang ($43,257), contr fee ($12,869), capitation ($4,243)
Total Member Encounters: Phys (132,521), non-phys (84,695)
Group Affiliation: Blue Cross Blue Shield of Vermont
Licensed in: VT
Address: 445 Industrial Lane, Berlin, VT 05602
Phone: (802) 223-6131 **Dom State:** VT **Commenced Bus:** January 1997

Data Date	Weiss Safety Rating	RACR #1	RACR #2	Total Assets ($mil)	Capital ($mil)	Net Premium ($mil)	Net Income ($mil)
3-03	B-	1.69	1.41	36.6	12.5	21.2	1.1
3-02	C	0.98	0.84	33.5	8.3	17.8	0.5
2002	B-	1.53	1.27	34.1	11.3	76.0	3.5
2001	C	1.01	0.86	28.2	7.9	62.6	2.2
2000	D+	0.76	0.65	20.9	5.6	59.1	1.6
1999	D	0.56	0.48	16.8	4.0	43.9	-3.5
1998	C-	0.86	0.72	11.6	4.4	21.9	-0.9

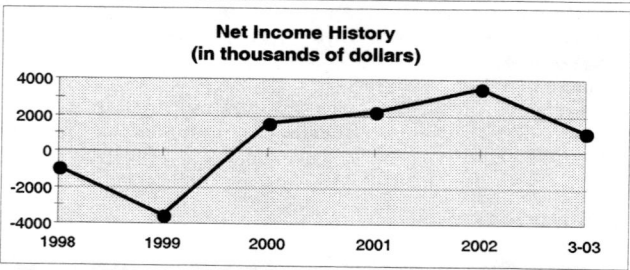

Net Income History (in thousands of dollars) — line chart 1998 through 3-03

VICTORY HEALTH PLAN INC — D+ — Weak

Major Rating Factors: Weak profitability index (0.9 on a scale of 0 to 10) with operating losses during 1997, 1998, 1999 and 2000. Average return on equity has been extremely poor. Fair overall results on stability tests (5.0) based on rapid enrollment growth during the past five years. Good overall capitalization (6.4) based on good current risk-adjusted capital (severe loss scenario).
Other Rating Factors: High quality investment portfolio (9.9) containing no exposure to mortgages, junk bonds, or unaffiliated stocks. Excellent liquidity (7.0) with ample operational cash flow and liquid investments.
Principal Business: Medicaid (100%)
Mem Phys: 01: 1,138 **00:** 844 **01 MLR** 85% / **01 Admin Exp** 13%
Enroll(000): Q2 02: 33 **01:** 36 **00:** 14 **Med Exp PMPM:** $132
Principal Investments: Cash and equiv (91%), other (9%)
Provider Compensation ($000): Capitation ($35,758), FFS ($229)
Total Member Encounters: Phys (160,906), non-phys (41,642)
Group Affiliation: Windsor Health Group Inc
Licensed in: TN
Address: 215 Centerview Dr Ste 300, Brentwood, TN 37027
Phone: (615) 782-7800 **Dom State:** TN **Commenced Bus:** January 1994

Data Date	Weiss Safety Rating	RACR #1	RACR #2	Total Assets ($mil)	Capital ($mil)	Net Premium ($mil)	Net Income ($mil)
6-02	D+	1.08	0.95	9.7	6.5	32.2	0.1
6-01	D	1.72	1.48	7.7	6.4	13.7	0.3
2001	D+	1.07	0.95	11.2	6.4	45.4	0.3
2000	D	1.66	1.43	12.2	5.9	23.1	-12.5
1999	D	1.14	0.93	11.7	7.4	22.0	-11.5
1998	D	2.15	1.83	10.3	5.6	17.9	-25.7
1997	D	1.60	1.02	6.5	2.7	17.5	-8.3

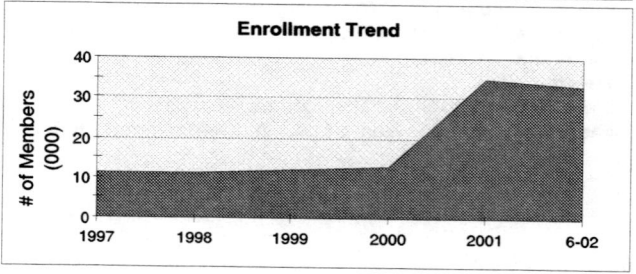

Enrollment Trend — area chart # of Members (000) from 1997 through 6-02

VIRGINIA PREMIER HEALTH PLAN INC   D   Weak

Major Rating Factors: Poor capitalization index (2.2 on a scale of 0 to 10) based on weak current risk-adjusted capital (moderate loss scenario). Fair profitability index (3.8) with operating losses during 1998 and 1999. Average return on equity has been poor at -35%. Good overall results on stability tests (6.9) based on consistent premium and capital growth in the last five years but rapid enrollment growth during the past five years.
Other Rating Factors: Good liquidity (6.2) with sufficient resources (cash flows and marketable investments) to handle a spike in claims. High quality investment portfolio (9.9) containing no exposure to mortgages, junk bonds, or unaffiliated stocks.
Principal Business: Medicaid (100%)
Mem Phys: 02: 6,025   **01:** 5,964   **02 MLR** 90%   **/ 02 Admin Exp** 6%
Enroll(000): Q1 03: 71   **02:** 68   **01:** 66   **Med Exp PMPM:** $198
Principal Investments: Cash and equiv (39%), other (61%)
Provider Compensation ($000): Contr fee ($105,138), capitation ($43,765), FFS ($9,876)
Total Member Encounters: Phys (769,685), non-phys (17,352)
Group Affiliation: UHS Managed Care Inc
Licensed in: VA
Address: 600 E Broad St, Ste 400, Richmond, VA 23219
Phone: (804) 819-5151   **Dom State:** VA   **Commenced Bus:** November 1995

Data Date	Weiss Safety Rating	RACR #1	RACR #2	Total Assets ($mil)	Capital ($mil)	Net Premium ($mil)	Net Income ($mil)
3-03	D	0.51	0.43	34.1	12.0	48.1	0.1
3-02	E+	0.34	0.29	27.4	7.5	40.9	1.0
2002	D	0.50	0.42	36.4	11.8	175.8	5.2
2001	E+	0.34	0.29	20.6	6.8	77.1	1.2
2000	E	0.26	0.22	12.2	4.2	55.0	0.1
1999	E	0.17	0.14	9.0	2.6	42.8	-1.7
1998	E	0.23	0.20	6.4	0.7	26.5	-2.4

Risk-Adjusted Capital Ratios (Since 1998)

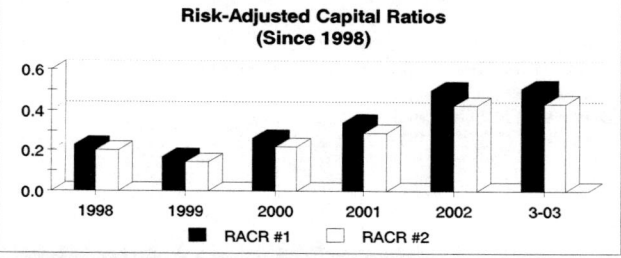

VISION SERVICE PLAN INS CO   C   Fair

Major Rating Factors: Fair overall results on stability tests (3.2 on a scale of 0 to 10) including fair financial strength of affiliated Vision Service Plan Group and weak results on operational trends. Strong long-term capitalization index (9.1) based on excellent current risk adjusted capital (severe and moderate loss scenarios). Moreover, capital levels have been consistent in recent years.
Other Rating Factors: Ample reserve history (9.4) that helps to protect the company against sharp claims increases. Excellent profitability (9.6) with operating gains in each of the last five years. Excellent expense controls. Return on equity has been excellent over the last five years averaging 20.9%. Excellent liquidity (7.6) with ample operational cash flow and liquid investments.
Principal Business: Group accident & health (100%).
Principal Investments: Investment grade bonds (89%) and cash (17%).
Investments in Affiliates: None
Group Affiliation: Vision Service Plan Group
Licensed in: FL, GA, ID, MD, MO, NM
Commenced Business: June 1987
Address: 3333 Quality Drive, Rancho Cordova, CA 95670
Phone: (916) 851-5000   **Domicile State:** MO   **NAIC Code:** 32395

Data Date	Weiss Safety Rating	RACR #1	RACR #2	Loss Ratio %	Total Assets ($mil)	Capital ($mil)	Net Premium ($mil)	Net Income ($mil)
6-03	C	6.65	3.56	N/A	38.7	32.8	23.7	2.4
6-02	C	3.66	2.12	N/A	32.8	27.0	21.9	1.8
2002	C	6.37	3.41	83.7	37.8	30.1	43.8	5.0
2001	C	2.19	1.34	80.9	29.2	23.8	40.4	7.2
2000	C	1.67	1.01	87.5	22.0	17.4	39.7	3.3
1999	C	1.86	1.10	79.2	24.0	12.7	32.3	4.9
1998	C	2.09	1.23	92.7	19.3	7.7	17.3	0.3

Rating Indexes

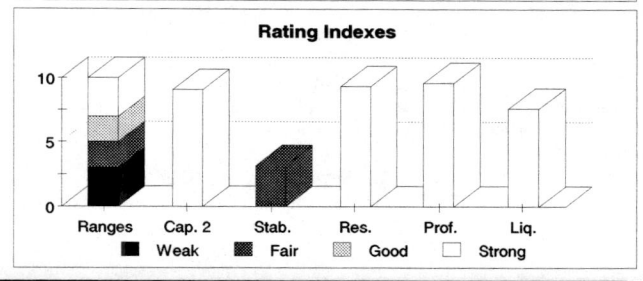

VISTA HEALTHPLAN   E   Very Weak

Major Rating Factors: Weak profitability index (0.9 on a scale of 0 to 10). Poor capitalization index (0.0) based on weak current risk-adjusted capital (severe loss scenario). Fair liquidity (3.6) as cash resources may not be adequate to cover a spike in claims.
Other Rating Factors: Good overall results on stability tests (5.5) despite a decline in enrollment during 2002, a decline in the number of member physicians during 2002. High quality investment portfolio (9.9) containing no exposure to mortgages, junk bonds, or unaffiliated stocks.
Principal Business: Comp med (73%), Medicare (18%), Medicaid (9%)
Mem Phys: 02: 7,993   **01:** 12,569   **02 MLR** 91%   **/ 02 Admin Exp** 13%
Enroll(000): Q1 03: 261   **02:** 273   **01:** 307   **Med Exp PMPM:** $153
Principal Investments: Cash and equiv (68%), other (32%)
Provider Compensation ($000): FFS ($424,161), capitation ($111,279)
Total Member Encounters: Phys (397,616), non-phys (23,735)
Group Affiliation: Florida Health Plan Holdings LLC
Licensed in: FL
Address: 300 S Park Rd, Hollywood, FL 33021
Phone: (954) 962-3008   **Dom State:** FL   **Commenced Bus:** September 1985

Data Date	Weiss Safety Rating	RACR #1	RACR #2	Total Assets ($mil)	Capital ($mil)	Net Premium ($mil)	Net Income ($mil)
3-03	E	0.12	0.10	70.8	9.3	148.5	0.9
3-02	E	0.02	0.02	47.3	3.7	98.1	-4.6
2002	E	0.10	0.09	88.6	7.2	587.2	-23.8
2001	E	0.02	0.02	99.9	4.8	653.8	-17.8
2000	E-	N/A	N/A	N/A	N/A	N/A	-15.0
1999	F	0.05	0.04	N/A	N/A	N/A	-18.0
1998	D+	3.61	2.57	N/A	N/A	N/A	0.1

Risk-Adjusted Capital Ratio #2 (Severe Loss Scenario)

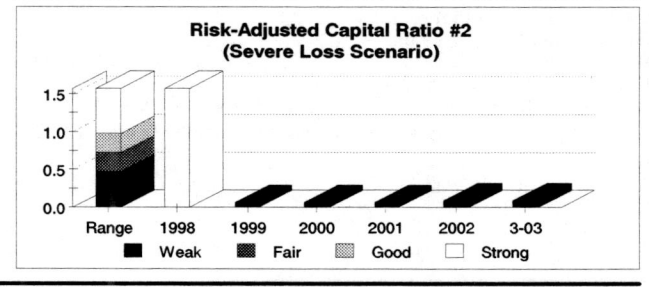

II. Analysis of Largest Companies
Winter 2003 - 04

VISTA HEALTHPLAN OF SOUTH FLORIDA — E — Very Weak

Major Rating Factors: Weak profitability index (0.7 on a scale of 0 to 10) with operating losses during 1999, 2000 and 2002. Average return on equity has been extremely poor. Poor capitalization index (0.0) based on weak current risk-adjusted capital (severe loss scenario). Weak overall results on stability tests (1.0) based on excessive premium growth during 2002, a significant 27% decrease in enrollment during the period.
Other Rating Factors: Fair liquidity (3.4) as cash resources may not be adequate to cover a spike in claims. High quality investment portfolio (9.9) containing no exposure to mortgages, junk bonds, or unaffiliated stocks.
Principal Business: Medicare (58%), comp med (36%), Medicaid (6%)
Mem Phys: 02: 9,837   01: 10,025   **02 MLR** 90%   / **02 Admin Exp** 12%
Enroll(000): Q1 03: 100   02: 106   01: 146   **Med Exp PMPM:** $245
Principal Investments: Cash and equiv (54%), other (46%)
Provider Compensation ($000): FFS ($313,434), capitation ($58,572)
Total Member Encounters: Phys (26,654)
Group Affiliation: Florida Health Plan Holdings LLC
Licensed in: FL
Address: 1340 Concord Terrace, Sunrise, FL 33323
Phone: (954) 858-3000   **Dom State:** FL   **Commenced Bus:** November 1994

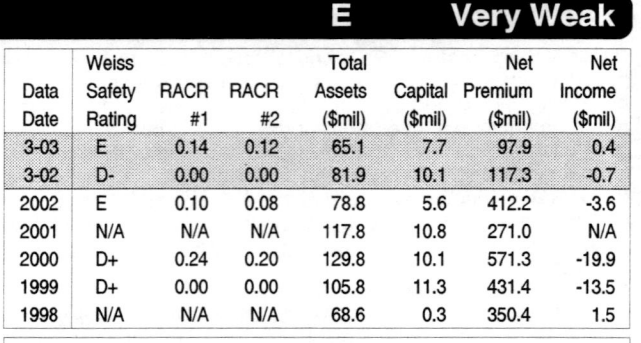

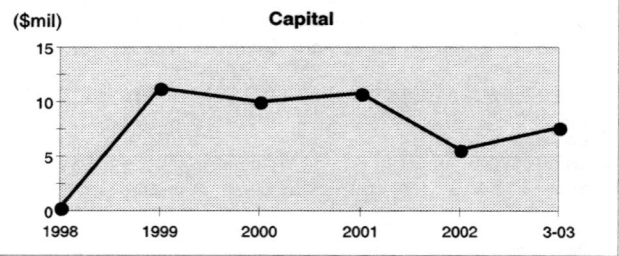

Data Date	Weiss Safety Rating	RACR #1	RACR #2	Total Assets ($mil)	Capital ($mil)	Net Premium ($mil)	Net Income ($mil)
3-03	E	0.14	0.12	65.1	7.7	97.9	0.4
3-02	D-	0.00	0.00	81.9	10.1	117.3	-0.7
2002	E	0.10	0.08	78.8	5.6	412.2	-3.6
2001	N/A	N/A	N/A	117.8	10.8	271.0	N/A
2000	D+	0.24	0.20	129.8	10.1	571.3	-19.9
1999	D+	0.00	0.00	105.8	11.3	431.4	-13.5
1998	N/A	N/A	N/A	68.6	0.3	350.4	1.5

VIVA HEALTH INC — C — Fair

Major Rating Factors: Fair capitalization (4.1 on a scale of 0 to 10) based on fair current risk-adjusted capital (moderate loss scenario) reflecting improvement over results in 1998. Weak profitability index (2.3) with operating losses during 1998 and 1999. Average return on equity has been poor at -49%. Good liquidity (7.0) with sufficient resources (cash flows and marketable investments) to handle a spike in claims.
Other Rating Factors: High quality investment portfolio (9.9) containing no exposure to mortgages, junk bonds, or unaffiliated stocks. Excellent overall results on stability tests (7.5) based on consistent premium and capital growth in the last five years.
Principal Business: Medicare (64%), comp med (36%)
Mem Phys: 02: 4,280   01: 3,759   **02 MLR** 83%   / **02 Admin Exp** 15%
Enroll(000):   02: 39   01: N/A   **Med Exp PMPM:** $491
Principal Investments: Cash and equiv (65%), other (35%)
Provider Compensation ($000): Contr fee ($110,703), capitation ($64,280), FFS ($12,311), bonus arrang ($96)
Total Member Encounters: Phys (409,342), non-phys (376,779)
Group Affiliation: U of AL at Birmingham
Licensed in: AL
Address: 1400 21st Place S, Birmingham, AL 35205
Phone: (205) 939-1718   **Dom State:** AL   **Commenced Bus:** February 1996

Data Date	Weiss Safety Rating	RACR #1	RACR #2	Total Assets ($mil)	Capital ($mil)	Net Premium ($mil)	Net Income ($mil)
2002	C	0.79	0.66	29.1	10.1	138.0	2.9
2001	C-	0.99	0.86	26.6	7.9	95.8	1.9
2000	D	0.54	0.47	19.0	2.3	59.2	0.7
1999	D	0.38	0.32	14.4	2.3	58.5	-2.1
1998	D	0.35	0.30	9.0	2.1	34.6	-5.6

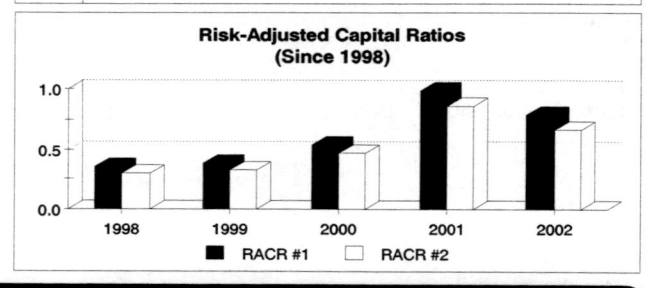

VOYAGER LIFE INSURANCE COMPANY — C+ — Fair

Major Rating Factors: Fair overall results on stability tests (4.7 on a scale of 0 to 10) including fair financial strength of affiliated Fortis Inc. Good quality investment portfolio (6.7) despite mixed results such as: no exposure to mortgages and substantial holdings of BBB bonds but small junk bond holdings. Good overall profitability (6.2). Excellent expense controls. Return on equity has been excellent over the last five years averaging 16.4%.
Other Rating Factors: Strong capitalization (8.8) based on excellent risk adjusted capital (severe loss scenario). Excellent liquidity (7.5).
Principal Business: Reinsurance (64%), credit health insurance (20%), credit life insurance (13%), and group health insurance (3%).
Principal Investments: NonCMO investment grade bonds (67%), CMOs and structured securities (18%), noninv. grade bonds (6%), common & preferred stock (4%), and cash (2%).
Investments in Affiliates: None
Group Affiliation: Fortis Inc
Licensed in: All states except ME, MA, MN, NH, NJ, NY, RI, VT, PR
Commenced Business: May 1965
Address: 3237 Satellite Blvd #400, Duluth, GA 30096-4640
Phone: (817) 347-3850   **Domicile State:** GA   **NAIC Code:** 66699

Data Date	Weiss Safety Rating	RACR #1	RACR #2	Total Assets ($mil)	Capital ($mil)	Net Premium ($mil)	Net Income ($mil)
6-03	C+	3.42	2.22	129.2	31.2	28.2	3.3
6-02	C+	3.90	2.52	152.1	42.3	41.9	-1.1
2002	C+	3.05	2.01	146.8	28.2	71.5	6.9
2001	C+	2.76	1.69	144.5	34.7	79.2	2.8
2000	C+	2.68	1.74	146.3	37.2	92.7	8.8
1999	C+	2.39	1.57	135.5	34.9	86.1	-1.6
1998	C+	1.38	1.12	127.4	37.4	67.8	2.6

Fortis Inc
Composite Group Rating: C+
Largest Group Members

	Assets ($mil)	Weiss Safety Rating
FORTIS BENEFITS INS CO	7322	B-
AMERICAN BANKERS INS CO OF FL	1082	C
AMERICAN MEMORIAL LIFE INS CO	1075	C
UNITED FAMILY LIFE INS CO	997	C+
AMERICAN BANKERS LIFE ASR CO OF FL	925	B-

Winter 2003 - 04
II. Analysis of Largest Companies

VYTRA HEALTH PLANS LONG ISLAND INC — B Good

Major Rating Factors: Good overall profitability index (6.6 on a scale of 0 to 10) despite operating losses during 1998. Good overall results on stability tests (5.4). Good liquidity (6.6) with sufficient resources (cash flows and marketable investments) to handle a spike in claims.
Other Rating Factors: Strong capitalization index (7.6) based on excellent current risk-adjusted capital (severe loss scenario). High quality investment portfolio (9.9) containing no exposure to mortgages, junk bonds, or unaffiliated stocks.
Principal Business: Comp med (92%), Medicaid (6%), other (1%)
Mem Phys: 02: 9,698 **01:** 8,496 **02 MLR** 80% **/ 02 Admin Exp** 16%
Enroll(000): Q1 03: 107 **02:** 103 **01:** 90 **Med Exp PMPM:** $163
Principal Investments: Cash and equiv (47%), other (53%)
Provider Compensation ($000): Contr fee ($182,092), capitation ($7,529), FFS ($838)
Total Member Encounters: Phys (14,467), non-phys (8,328)
Group Affiliation: HIP Ins Group
Licensed in: NY
Address: 395 N Service Rd Corporate Ctr, Melville, NY 11747-3127
Phone: (631) 694-4000 **Dom State:** NY **Commenced Bus:** January 1986

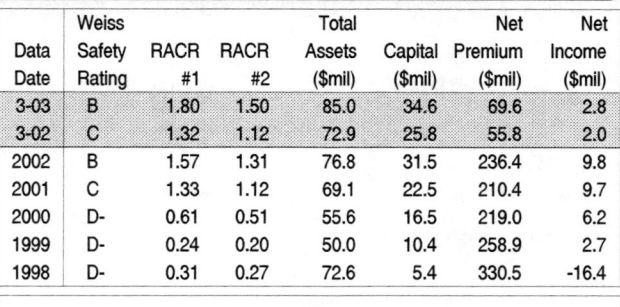

Data Date	Weiss Safety Rating	RACR #1	RACR #2	Total Assets ($mil)	Capital ($mil)	Net Premium ($mil)	Net Income ($mil)
3-03	B	1.80	1.50	85.0	34.6	69.6	2.8
3-02	C	1.32	1.12	72.9	25.8	55.8	2.0
2002	B	1.57	1.31	76.8	31.5	236.4	9.8
2001	C	1.33	1.12	69.1	22.5	210.4	9.7
2000	D-	0.61	0.51	55.6	16.5	219.0	6.2
1999	D-	0.24	0.20	50.0	10.4	258.9	2.7
1998	D-	0.31	0.27	72.6	5.4	330.5	-16.4

Net Income History (in millions of dollars)

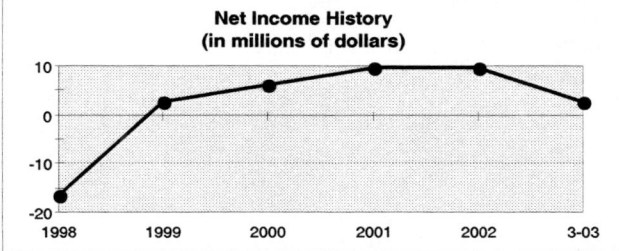

VYTRA HEALTH SERVICES INC — C Fair

Major Rating Factors: Weak profitability index (0.8 on a scale of 0 to 10) with operating losses during 2000, 2001 and 2002. Poor capitalization (0.0) based on weak current risk-adjusted capital (severe loss scenario). Weak liquidity (0.0) as a spike in claims may stretch capacity.
Other Rating Factors: High quality investment portfolio (9.9) containing no exposure to mortgages, junk bonds, or unaffiliated stocks.
Principal Business: Comp med (100%)
Mem Phys: 02: 10,136 **01:** 9,198 **02 MLR** 91% **/ 02 Admin Exp** 12%
Enroll(000): Q1 03: 52 **02:** 57 **01:** 54 **Med Exp PMPM:** $104
Principal Investments: Cash and equiv (20%), other (80%)
Provider Compensation ($000): Contr fee ($54,865), FFS ($16,660), capitation ($626)
Total Member Encounters: Phys (7,877), non-phys (2,054)
Group Affiliation: HIP Ins Group
Licensed in: NY
Address: 395 Service Rd Corporate Ctr, Melville, NY 11747
Phone: (631) 694-4000 **Dom State:** NY **Commenced Bus:** October 1995

Data Date	Weiss Safety Rating	RACR #1	RACR #2	Total Assets ($mil)	Capital ($mil)	Net Premium ($mil)	Net Income ($mil)
3-03	C	0.14	0.12	16.3	2.3	15.3	0.1
3-02	D-	0.17	0.15	20.3	5.6	19.6	1.6
2002	C	0.12	0.10	15.7	2.0	76.0	-1.5
2001	D-	0.17	0.15	20.1	3.9	92.0	-1.0
2000	C	N/A	N/A	16.6	1.8	83.1	-0.3
1999	N/A	N/A	N/A	10.4	1.9	60.4	N/A
1998	N/A	N/A	N/A	122.2	1.5	46.9	N/A

Capital ($mil)

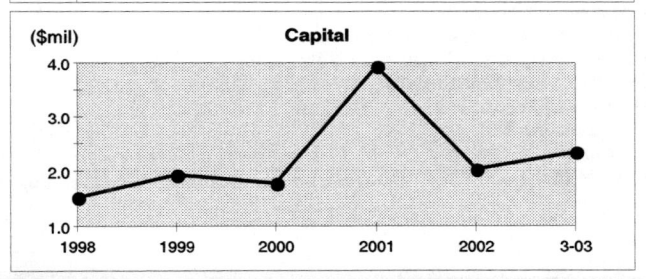

WASHINGTON NATIONAL INSURANCE COMPANY — E Very Weak

Major Rating Factors: Weak overall results on stability tests (0.2 on a scale of 0 to 10) including weak financial strength of affiliated Conseco Group, weak risk adjusted capital in prior years and negative cash flow from operations for 2002. Fair quality investment portfolio (4.3) with substantial holdings of BBB bonds in addition to moderate junk bond exposure. Good capitalization (5.5) based on good risk adjusted capital (severe loss scenario).
Other Rating Factors: Good overall profitability (5.9). Good liquidity (6.6).
Principal Business: Group health insurance (58%), individual health insurance (25%), reinsurance (8%), individual life insurance (5%), and other lines (4%).
Principal Investments: NonCMO investment grade bonds (31%), common & preferred stock (28%), CMOs and structured securities (28%), noninv. grade bonds (6%), and misc. investments (6%).
Investments in Affiliates: 21%
Group Affiliation: Conseco Group
Licensed in: All states except NY, PR
Commenced Business: September 1923
Address: 300 Tower Parkway, Lincolnshire, IL 60069
Phone: (847) 793-3379 **Domicile State:** IL **NAIC Code:** 70319

Data Date	Weiss Safety Rating	RACR #1	RACR #2	Total Assets ($mil)	Capital ($mil)	Net Premium ($mil)	Net Income ($mil)
6-03	E	0.92	0.81	872.7	178.5	32.7	7.1
6-02	E	0.39	0.34	1,038.0	185.1	44.8	7.3
2002	E	0.92	0.80	911.4	181.9	83.9	-1.0
2001	E+	0.54	0.47	1,131.4	253.4	86.2	28.7
2000	C	1.32	1.02	891.2	154.7	81.4	31.7
1999	C	1.55	1.21	1,092.9	209.3	78.9	42.9
1998	C	1.11	0.82	1,075.3	120.0	95.7	27.2

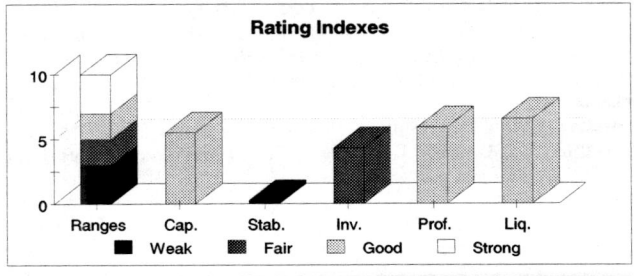

Rating Indexes: Ranges, Cap., Stab., Inv., Prof., Liq. — Weak, Fair, Good, Strong

---

www.WeissRatings.com   305   * Denotes a Weiss Recommended Company

II. Analysis of Largest Companies

Winter 2003 - 04

WEA INSURANCE CORPORATION — C- — Fair

Major Rating Factors: Fair overall results on stability tests (3.1 on a scale of 0 to 10). Weak profitability (2.5). Excellent expense controls. Return on equity has been low, averaging -1.7%. Good current capitalization (5.2) based on mixed results -- excessive policy leverage mitigated by excellent risk adjusted capital (severe loss scenario) reflecting improvement over results in 2001.
Other Rating Factors: Good quality investment portfolio (6.2). Good liquidity (5.4).
Principal Business: Group health insurance (100%).
Principal Investments: NonCMO investment grade bonds (71%), common & preferred stock (14%), and CMOs and structured securities (13%).
Investments in Affiliates: None
Group Affiliation: WEA Inc
Licensed in: WI
Commenced Business: July 1985
Address: 45 Nob Hill Rd, Madison, WI 53713
Phone: (608) 276-4000 **Domicile State:** WI **NAIC Code:** 72273

Data Date	Weiss Safety Rating	RACR #1	RACR #2	Total Assets ($mil)	Capital ($mil)	Net Premium ($mil)	Net Income ($mil)
6-03	C-	1.52	1.18	347.2	134.6	362.5	25.9
6-02	C-	0.97	0.72	261.2	74.6	292.4	-14.2
2002	C-	1.28	1.00	307.7	105.6	648.1	20.0
2001	C	1.33	0.99	285.3	94.7	525.7	-22.4
2000	C	1.84	1.31	303.6	127.8	434.2	-10.2
1999	C	2.28	1.58	310.3	157.0	368.3	-4.4
1998	C	2.47	1.72	287.2	151.0	326.3	10.8

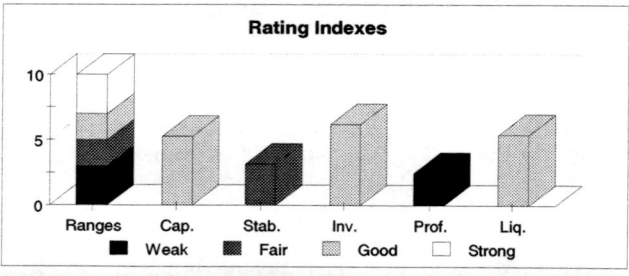

Rating Indexes (Ranges, Cap., Stab., Inv., Prof., Liq.) — Weak, Fair, Good, Strong

WELBORN CLINIC/WELBORN HEALTH PLANS — E — Very Weak

Major Rating Factors: Weak profitability index (0.9 on a scale of 0 to 10) with modest operating losses during 1998, 1999, 2000 and 2002. Average return on equity has been poor at -58%. Poor capitalization index (0.0) based on weak current risk-adjusted capital (severe loss scenario). Good overall results on stability tests (6.2).
Other Rating Factors: Good liquidity (6.9) with sufficient resources (cash flows and marketable investments) to handle a spike in claims. High quality investment portfolio (9.9) containing no exposure to mortgages, junk bonds, or unaffiliated stocks.
Principal Business: Comp med (78%), Medicare (16%), med only (6%)
Mem Phys: 02: N/A **01:** N/A **02 MLR** 92% **/ 02 Admin Exp** 8%
Enroll(000): 02: 39 **01:** 38 **Med Exp PMPM:** $213
Principal Investments: Cash and equiv (95%), real estate (5%)
Provider Compensation ($000): Contr fee ($45,012), capitation ($34,202), FFS ($6,601), bonus arrang ($1,296), other ($12,206)
Total Member Encounters: Phys (334,972), non-phys (22,254)
Group Affiliation: None
Licensed in: IN
Address: 421 Chestnut Street, Evansville, IN 47713
Phone: (812) 426-9884 **Dom State:** IN **Commenced Bus:** July 1986

Data Date	Weiss Safety Rating	RACR #1	RACR #2	Total Assets ($mil)	Capital ($mil)	Net Premium ($mil)	Net Income ($mil)
2002	E	0.24	0.20	23.5	4.8	107.1	0.0
2001	E+	0.21	0.18	21.7	4.1	121.2	0.4
2000	E+	0.19	0.16	20.2	3.4	122.5	-3.7
1999	D-	0.00	0.00	13.5	2.7	104.0	-4.4
1998	C-	0.61	0.53	13.9	5.5	97.9	-4.6

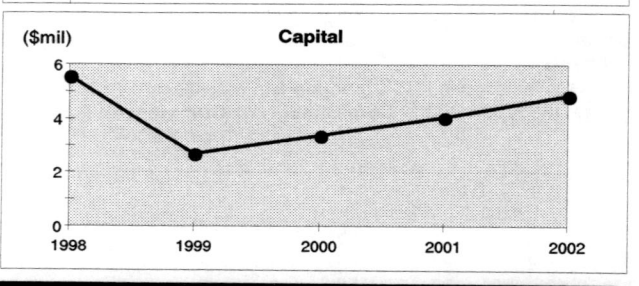

Capital chart 1998–2002

WELL CARE HMO INC — D+ — Weak

Major Rating Factors: Poor capitalization index (2.9 on a scale of 0 to 10) based on good current risk-adjusted capital (moderate loss scenario). Fair profitability index (4.2) due to a decline in earnings during 2002. Fair overall results on stability tests (4.9) based on rapid premium growth over the last five years, rapid enrollment growth during the past five years.
Other Rating Factors: Good liquidity (6.9) with sufficient resources (cash flows and marketable investments) to handle a spike in claims. High quality investment portfolio (9.9) containing no exposure to mortgages, junk bonds, or unaffiliated stocks.
Principal Business: Medicare (49%), Medicaid (43%), comp med (8%)
Mem Phys: 02: 14,000 **01:** 15,000 **02 MLR** 86% **/ 02 Admin Exp** 14%
Enroll(000): 02: 238 **01:** 188 **Med Exp PMPM:** $190
Principal Investments: Cash and equiv (100%)
Provider Compensation ($000): Contr fee ($421,564), capitation ($50,813)
Total Member Encounters: Phys (630,966), non-phys (423,620)
Group Affiliation: WellCare Holdings LLC
Licensed in: FL
Address: 6800 N Dale Mabry Hwy Ste 209, Tampa, FL 33614
Phone: (813) 290-6200 **Dom State:** FL **Commenced Bus:** March 1986

Data Date	Weiss Safety Rating	RACR #1	RACR #2	Total Assets ($mil)	Capital ($mil)	Net Premium ($mil)	Net Income ($mil)
2002	D+	20.08	16.73	131.3	20.4	566.4	2.3
2001	E	0.17	0.14	106.3	15.4	455.1	2.5
2000	D-	0.01	0.01	64.9	1.1	263.9	1.1
1999	D-	0.19	0.16	52.0	8.6	156.3	0.6
1998	D-	0.15	0.13	44.4	6.7	120.2	2.4

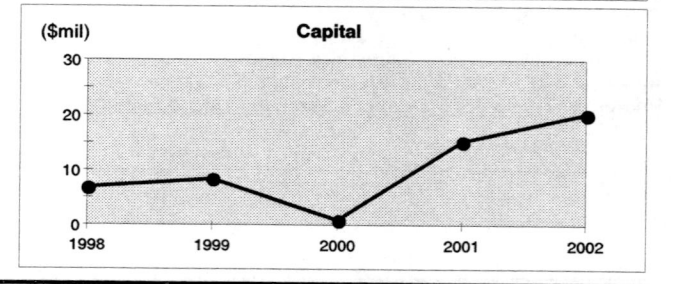

Capital chart 1998–2002

WELLCARE OF NEW YORK INC — E+ Very Weak

Major Rating Factors: Weak profitability index (0.8 on a scale of 0 to 10) with operating losses during 1998, 2000 and 2002. Average return on equity has been poor at -22%. Fair capitalization index (3.4) based on weak current risk-adjusted capital (moderate loss scenario). Good overall results on stability tests (5.1).
Other Rating Factors: Good liquidity (6.9) with sufficient resources (cash flows and marketable investments) to handle a spike in claims. High quality investment portfolio (8.2) containing no exposure to mortgages, junk bonds, or unaffiliated stocks.
Principal Business: Medicaid (59%), comp med (23%), Medicare (18%)
Mem Phys: 02: 8,910 **01:** 8,600 **02 MLR** 81% / **02 Admin Exp** 21%
Enroll(000): Q1 03: 45 **02:** 43 **01:** 33 **Med Exp PMPM:** $119
Principal Investments: Cash and equiv (62%), other (38%)
Provider Compensation ($000): Contr fee ($38,366), capitation ($12,244)
Total Member Encounters: Phys (78,881), non-phys (20,748)
Group Affiliation: WellCare Holdings LLC
Licensed in: NY
Address: 280 Broadway 3rd Floor, Newburgh, NY 12550
Phone: (813) 290-6200 **Dom State:** NY **Commenced Bus:** January 1987

Data Date	Weiss Safety Rating	RACR #1	RACR #2	Total Assets ($mil)	Capital ($mil)	Net Premium ($mil)	Net Income ($mil)
3-03	E+	0.69	0.57	27.0	5.4	21.5	1.1
3-02	E-	0.03	0.03	13.2	2.2	15.0	0.5
2002	E+	0.53	0.44	23.1	4.2	67.1	-1.3
2001	E-	0.03	0.03	14.7	0.7	55.4	1.8
2000	E-	0.00	0.00	12.7	0.1	56.1	-3.2
1999	E-	0.07	0.06	18.0	2.0	81.3	5.3
1998	E-	0.00	0.00	17.8	-14.6	133.4	-18.7

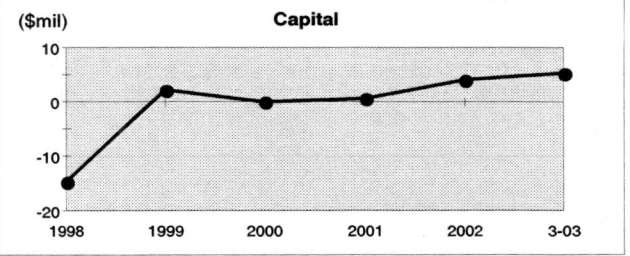

WELLMARK HEALTH PLAN OF IOWA — B- Good

Major Rating Factors: Good overall results on stability tests (5.2 on a scale of 0 to 10). Rating is significantly influenced by the good financial results of IASD Health Group. Good liquidity (6.6) with sufficient resources (cash flows and marketable investments) to handle a spike in claims. Strong capitalization index (8.0) based on excellent current risk-adjusted capital (severe loss scenario) despite some fluctuation in capital levels.
Other Rating Factors: High quality investment portfolio (9.2). Weak profitability index (2.5) with operating losses during 1998, 1999, 2000 and 2001. Average return on equity has been poor at -2%.
Principal Business: Comp med (100%)
Mem Phys: 02: 4,242 **01:** 4,688 **02 MLR** 85% / **02 Admin Exp** 11%
Enroll(000): Q1 03: 73 **02:** 67 **01:** 70 **Med Exp PMPM:** $134
Principal Investments: Nonaffiliate common stock (21%), cash and equiv (20%), other (60%)
Provider Compensation ($000): Contr fee ($90,060), FFS ($11,596), capitation ($9,688)
Total Member Encounters: Phys (291,913), non-phys (120,837)
Group Affiliation: IASD Health Group
Licensed in: IA
Address: 636 Grand Ave, Des Moines, IA 50309-2565
Phone: (515) 245-4500 **Dom State:** IA **Commenced Bus:** January 1997

Data Date	Weiss Safety Rating	RACR #1	RACR #2	Total Assets ($mil)	Capital ($mil)	Net Premium ($mil)	Net Income ($mil)
3-03	B-	2.17	1.81	49.8	21.5	40.4	0.8
3-02	B-	1.59	1.23	43.6	17.6	31.2	0.4
2002	B-	2.13	1.78	46.2	21.1	130.7	3.2
2001	B-	1.59	1.23	39.8	17.3	122.8	-1.0
2000	B	1.48	1.23	42.4	18.8	139.3	-2.4
1999	B	2.61	2.15	36.0	22.5	91.2	-1.1
1998	B-	2.95	2.40	35.9	24.5	65.2	-0.9

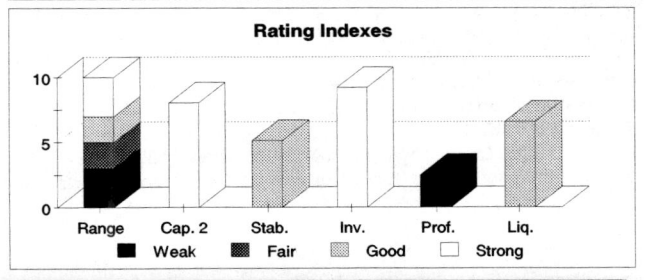

WELLMARK INC — B- Good

Major Rating Factors: Good capitalization (6.7 on a scale of 0 to 10) based on good risk adjusted capital (severe loss scenario). Good overall profitability (5.3). Excellent expense controls. Good overall results on stability tests (5.0). Stability strengths include excellent operational trends and excellent risk diversification.
Other Rating Factors: Fair liquidity (4.7). Low quality investment portfolio (2.9).
Principal Business: Group health insurance (74%) and individual health insurance (26%).
Principal Investments: Common & preferred stock (57%), nonCMO investment grade bonds (38%), CMOs and structured securities (6%), mortgages in good standing (2%), and noninv. grade bonds (1%).
Investments in Affiliates: 10%
Group Affiliation: IASD Health Group
Licensed in: IA, SD
Commenced Business: October 1939
Address: 636 Grand Ave, Des Moines, IA 50309
Phone: (515) 245-4500 **Domicile State:** IA **NAIC Code:** 88848

Data Date	Weiss Safety Rating	RACR #1	RACR #2	Total Assets ($mil)	Capital ($mil)	Net Premium ($mil)	Net Income ($mil)
6-03	B-	1.30	0.97	1,015.0	447.8	808.3	14.6
6-02	B-	1.16	0.90	830.1	393.1	737.1	15.3
2002	B-	1.13	0.86	901.1	394.4	1,504.0	-20.5
2001	B-	1.22	0.93	891.7	392.2	1,394.9	21.7
2000	B-	1.46	1.16	863.3	375.8	1,227.5	28.1
1999	B-	1.67	1.34	828.4	407.1	1,125.7	-6.1
1998	B	1.73	1.37	794.4	404.7	1,014.2	17.3

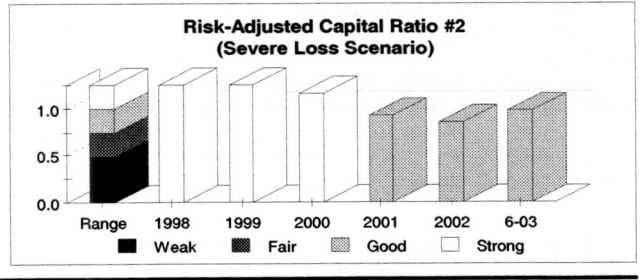

II. Analysis of Largest Companies

WELLMARK OF SOUTH DAKOTA INC   B-   Good

Major Rating Factors: Good current capitalization (5.1 on a scale of 0 to 10) based on mixed results -- excessive policy leverage mitigated by good risk adjusted capital (severe loss scenario) reflecting some improvement over results in 2001. Fair quality investment portfolio (3.6). Fair liquidity (3.3).
Other Rating Factors: Fair overall results on stability tests (4.9) including fair risk adjusted capital in prior years. Excellent profitability (8.8) with operating gains in each of the last five years.
Principal Business: Group health insurance (69%) and individual health insurance (31%).
Principal Investments: NonCMO investment grade bonds (53%), common & preferred stock (31%), CMOs and structured securities (11%), cash (2%), and real estate (2%).
Investments in Affiliates: None
Group Affiliation: IASD Health Group
Licensed in: SD
Commenced Business: August 1996
Address: 1601 W Madison St, Sioux Falls, SD 57104
Phone: (605) 361-5819 **Domicile State:** SD **NAIC Code:** 60128

Data Date	Weiss Safety Rating	RACR #1	RACR #2	Total Assets ($mil)	Capital ($mil)	Net Premium ($mil)	Net Income ($mil)
6-03	B-	1.03	0.77	138.4	48.6	156.8	5.1
6-02	C+	0.83	0.61	112.2	40.3	137.5	2.3
2002	C+	0.93	0.70	123.0	44.6	286.0	3.3
2001	C+	0.87	0.64	118.8	40.7	253.9	2.2
2000	B-	0.92	0.69	89.5	37.9	197.6	5.2
1999	B-	0.94	0.72	82.8	34.3	181.6	3.6
1998	B-	0.88	0.66	75.3	30.9	158.0	2.9

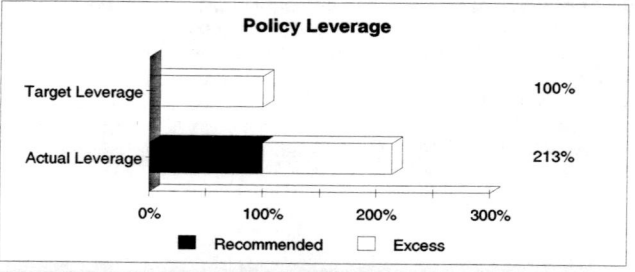

Policy Leverage: Target Leverage 100%, Actual Leverage 213%

WELLPATH SELECT INC   C-   Fair

Major Rating Factors: Fair overall results on stability tests (4.7 on a scale of 0 to 10). Rating is significantly influenced by the fair financial results of Coventry Health Care Inc. Weak profitability index (0.9) with operating losses during 1998, 1999 and 2000. Average return on equity has been extremely poor. Good liquidity (6.5) with sufficient resources (cash flows and marketable investments) to handle a spike in claims.
Other Rating Factors: Strong capitalization index (8.6) based on excellent current risk-adjusted capital (severe loss scenario). High quality investment portfolio (9.6) containing no exposure to mortgages, junk bonds, or unaffiliated stocks.
Principal Business: Comp med (91%), Medicaid (8%), other (1%)
Mem Phys: 02: 11,037 **01:** 11,280 **02 MLR** 84% **/ 02 Admin Exp** 16%
Enroll(000): Q1 03: 74 **02:** 75 **01:** 65 **Med Exp PMPM:** $143
Principal Investments: Cash and equiv (16%), other (84%)
Provider Compensation ($000): Contr fee ($115,732), capitation ($9,335)
Total Member Encounters: N/A
Group Affiliation: Coventry Health Care Inc
Licensed in: NC, SC
Address: 6330 Quadrangle Dr Suite 500, Chapel Hill, NC 27514
Phone: (919) 493-1210 **Dom State:** NC **Commenced Bus:** January 1996

Data Date	Weiss Safety Rating	RACR #1	RACR #2	Total Assets ($mil)	Capital ($mil)	Net Premium ($mil)	Net Income ($mil)
3-03	C-	2.62	2.19	60.8	27.3	42.8	0.4
3-02	D+	1.28	1.03	32.3	15.1	16.5	0.9
2002	C-	2.56	2.13	55.7	27.1	143.0	3.6
2001	D+	1.27	1.02	53.1	22.1	198.7	2.7
2000	D	0.27	0.22	49.1	7.3	215.4	-22.2
1999	D	0.19	0.17	34.9	5.0	185.4	-12.5
1998	C+	1.06	0.91	31.4	6.9	81.3	-8.5

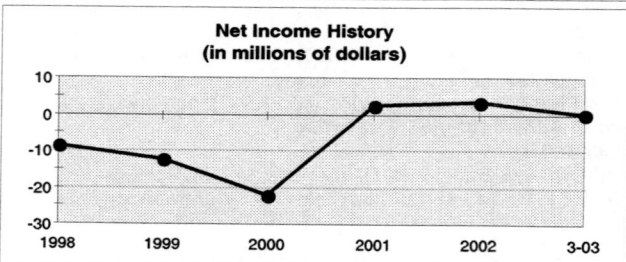

Net Income History (in millions of dollars) 1998 through 3-03

WESTERN HEALTH ADVANTAGE   E+   Very Weak

Major Rating Factors: Poor capitalization index (0.0 on a scale of 0 to 10) based on weak current risk-adjusted capital (severe loss scenario). Weak overall results on stability tests (1.8) based on rapid enrollment growth during the past five years. Good overall profitability index (5.3).
Other Rating Factors: Good liquidity (7.0) with sufficient resources (cash flows and marketable investments) to handle a spike in claims.
Principal Business: Comp med (62%), Medicaid (19%), Medicare (19%)
Mem Phys: 02: N/A **01:** N/A **02 MLR** 88% **/ 02 Admin Exp** 11%
Enroll(000): Q1 03: 61 **02:** 60 **01:** 55 **Med Exp PMPM:** $132
Principal Investments ($000): Cash and equiv ($3,996), bonds ($718), other ($437)
Provider Compensation ($000): None
Total Member Encounters: N/A
Group Affiliation: None
Licensed in: CA
Address: 1331 Garden Hwy Ste 100, Sacramento, CA 95833
Phone: (916) 563-3180 **Dom State:** CA **Commenced Bus:** May 1997

Data Date	Weiss Safety Rating	RACR #1	RACR #2	Total Assets ($mil)	Capital ($mil)	Net Premium ($mil)	Net Income ($mil)
3-03	E+	0.06	0.04	15.9	1.2	29.1	-0.4
3-02	E+	0.00	0.00	13.8	1.4	23.5	0.0
2002	E+	0.09	0.06	16.0	1.6	103.3	0.2
2001	E+	0.19	0.12	13.1	1.4	81.3	-0.1
2000	E+	0.29	0.19	12.1	1.4	58.4	-0.5
1999	E+	0.21	0.14	9.1	1.0	37.0	-1.9
1998	N/A	N/A	N/A	5.9	N/A	19.4	-2.4

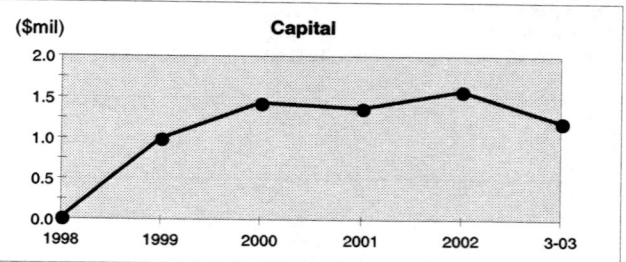

Capital ($mil) chart, 1998 through 3-03

Winter 2003 - 04 — II. Analysis of Largest Companies

WESTWARD LIFE INSURANCE COMPANY — C — Fair

Major Rating Factors: Fair overall results on stability tests (3.9 on a scale of 0 to 10). Strong capitalization (10.0) based on excellent risk adjusted capital (severe loss scenario). Moreover, capital levels have been consistently high over the last five years. High quality investment portfolio (7.1) with no exposure to mortgages and minimal holdings in junk bonds.
Other Rating Factors: Excellent profitability (8.4) with operating gains in each of the last five years. Excellent liquidity (9.2).
Principal Business: N/A
Principal Investments: NonCMO investment grade bonds (39%), CMOs and structured securities (34%), common & preferred stock (24%), and noninv. grade bonds (2%).
Investments in Affiliates: 9%
Group Affiliation: Westward Group
Licensed in: AK, AZ, AR, CA, HI, ID, IL, IN, IA, KY, MD, MI, MS, MO, MT, NE, NV, NM, NC, ND, OH, OR, SC, SD, TN, TX, UT, WA, WI
Commenced Business: December 1965
Address: 4040 Paramount Blvd, Lakewood, CA 90712
Phone: (562) 420-6103 **Domicile State:** AZ **NAIC Code:** 78301

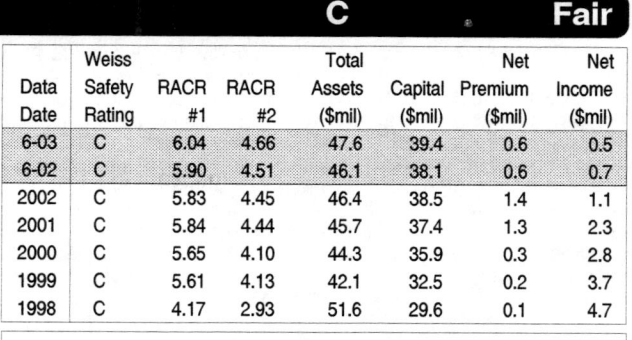

Data Date	Weiss Safety Rating	RACR #1	RACR #2	Total Assets ($mil)	Capital ($mil)	Net Premium ($mil)	Net Income ($mil)
6-03	C	6.04	4.66	47.6	39.4	0.6	0.5
6-02	C	5.90	4.51	46.1	38.1	0.6	0.7
2002	C	5.83	4.45	46.4	38.5	1.4	1.1
2001	C	5.84	4.44	45.7	37.4	1.3	2.3
2000	C	5.65	4.10	44.3	35.9	0.3	2.8
1999	C	5.61	4.13	42.1	32.5	0.2	3.7
1998	C	4.17	2.93	51.6	29.6	0.1	4.7

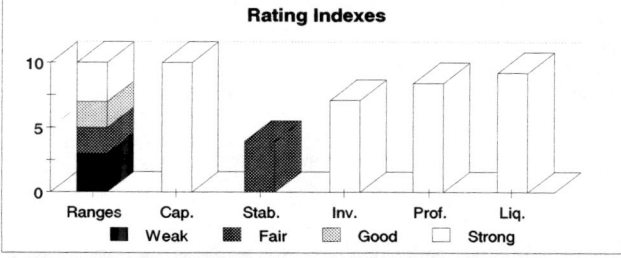

Rating Indexes (Ranges, Cap., Stab., Inv., Prof., Liq. — Weak, Fair, Good, Strong)

WINHEALTH PARTNERS — D+ — Weak

Major Rating Factors: Poor capitalization index (2.0 on a scale of 0 to 10) based on weak current risk-adjusted capital (moderate loss scenario). Furthermore, this low level of risk-adjusted capital has been consistent in previous years. Fair profitability index (3.9) with operating losses during 1998 and 2000. Good overall results on stability tests (6.5) based on consistent premium and capital growth in the last five years but rapid enrollment growth during the past five years.
Other Rating Factors: High quality investment portfolio (9.9) containing no exposure to mortgages, junk bonds, or unaffiliated stocks. Excellent liquidity (7.1) with ample operational cash flow and liquid investments.
Principal Business: Comp med (85%), FEHB (3%), other (12%)
Mem Phys: 02: 241 01: 208 **02 MLR** 88% / **02 Admin Exp** 11%
Enroll(000): Q1 03: 12 02: 11 01: 10 **Med Exp PMPM:** $160
Principal Investments: Cash and equiv (96%), other (4%)
Provider Compensation ($000): Bonus arrang ($10,724), contr fee ($6,437), FFS ($1,678)
Total Member Encounters: Phys (62,872), non-phys (18,225)
Group Affiliation: None
Licensed in: WY
Address: 2515 Warren Ave Ste 504, Cheyenne, WY 82001
Phone: (307) 638-7700 **Dom State:** WY **Commenced Bus:** May 1996

Data Date	Weiss Safety Rating	RACR #1	RACR #2	Total Assets ($mil)	Capital ($mil)	Net Premium ($mil)	Net Income ($mil)
3-03	D+	0.51	0.42	7.7	2.8	7.0	0.0
3-02	D+	0.51	0.43	6.0	2.3	5.4	0.0
2002	D+	0.53	0.44	7.5	2.9	22.7	0.5
2001	D+	0.51	0.43	5.2	2.3	17.6	0.1
2000	D+	0.60	0.50	4.3	2.0	12.5	-0.2
1999	D+	0.76	0.64	3.8	2.0	9.0	0.2
1998	D+	0.98	0.83	2.8	1.7	5.3	-0.2

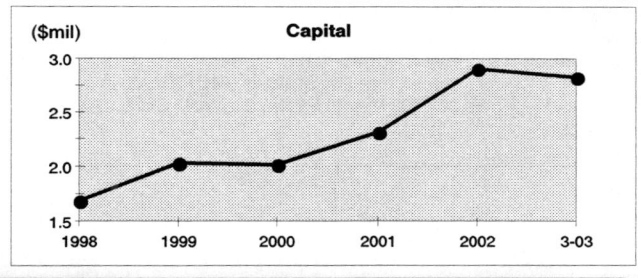

Capital ($mil) — 1998 through 3-03

WISCONSIN PHYSICIANS SERVICE INS — C+ — Fair

Major Rating Factors: Good overall profitability index (6.5 on a scale of 0 to 10) despite operating losses during 1998. Good quality investment portfolio (6.6) containing little or no exposure to mortgages, junk bonds, or unaffiliated stocks. Good liquidity (6.7) with sufficient resources (cash flows and marketable investments) to handle a spike in claims.
Other Rating Factors: Strong capitalization (8.9) based on excellent current risk-adjusted capital (severe loss scenario) reflecting significant improvement over results in 1998.
Principal Business: Comp med (83%), med supp (13%), stop loss (3%), dental (2%)
Mem Phys: 02: N/A 01: N/A **02 MLR** 79% / **02 Admin Exp** 15%
Enroll(000): Q1 03: 94 02: 99 01: 113 **Med Exp PMPM:** $183
Principal Investments: Real estate (27%), affiliate common stock (16%), nonaffiliate common stock (13%), cash and equiv (9%), other (36%)
Provider Compensation ($000): Contr fee ($150,468), FFS ($79,112), capitation ($395)
Total Member Encounters: Phys (601,510), non-phys (177,194)
Group Affiliation: Wisconsin Physicians Ins Group
Licensed in: OH, WI
Address: 1717 West Broadway, Madison, WI 53713
Phone: (608) 221-4711 **Dom State:** WI **Commenced Bus:** April 1977

Data Date	Weiss Safety Rating	RACR #1	RACR #2	Total Assets ($mil)	Capital ($mil)	Net Premium ($mil)	Net Income ($mil)
3-03	C+	2.86	2.39	177.1	82.8	70.6	11.7
3-02	C-	1.58	1.22	153.8	60.7	74.3	3.5
2002	C+	2.54	2.12	165.4	74.4	294.9	20.5
2001	D+	1.59	1.23	150.8	59.1	274.8	5.6
2000	D	1.15	0.73	142.1	60.8	217.5	3.7
1999	D+	1.31	0.83	141.4	66.4	197.8	6.5
1998	D+	1.00	0.63	146.8	58.2	245.4	-4.7

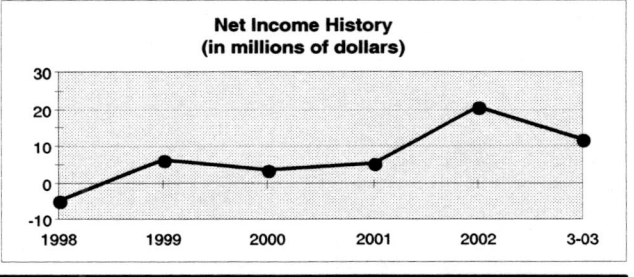

Net Income History (in millions of dollars) — 1998 through 3-03

www.WeissRatings.com   309   * Denotes a Weiss Recommended Company

II. Analysis of Largest Companies
Winter 2003 - 04

WORLD INSURANCE COMPANY   C   Fair

Major Rating Factors: Fair overall results on stability tests (3.9 on a scale of 0 to 10) including negative cash flow from operations for 2002. Good quality investment portfolio (5.7) despite mixed results such as: no exposure to mortgages and substantial holdings of BBB bonds but small junk bond holdings. Good overall profitability (5.7). Excellent expense controls.
Other Rating Factors: Good liquidity (6.1). Strong capitalization (7.1) based on excellent risk adjusted capital (severe loss scenario).
Principal Business: Individual health insurance (88%), reinsurance (5%), group health insurance (3%), and individual life insurance (3%).
Principal Investments: CMOs and structured securities (47%), nonCMO investment grade bonds (29%), common & preferred stock (15%), noninv. grade bonds (4%), and misc. investments (5%).
Investments in Affiliates: 11%
Group Affiliation: World Ins Group
Licensed in: All states except AK, MA, NJ, NY, PR
Commenced Business: November 1903
Address: 11808 Grant St, Omaha, NE 68164
Phone: (402) 496-8000   **Domicile State:** NE   **NAIC Code:** 70629

Data Date	Weiss Safety Rating	RACR #1	RACR #2	Total Assets ($mil)	Capital ($mil)	Net Premium ($mil)	Net Income ($mil)
6-03	C	1.29	1.04	215.9	73.7	84.3	4.1
6-02	C	1.02	0.82	210.6	57.8	102.3	2.4
2002	C	1.14	0.93	212.6	65.9	193.3	7.1
2001	C	0.98	0.79	221.5	56.2	211.0	-3.1
2000	C	1.09	0.88	198.0	53.6	179.1	-1.3
1999	C	1.54	1.18	177.8	50.1	137.9	4.5
1998	C	1.53	1.17	174.3	45.5	102.9	5.3

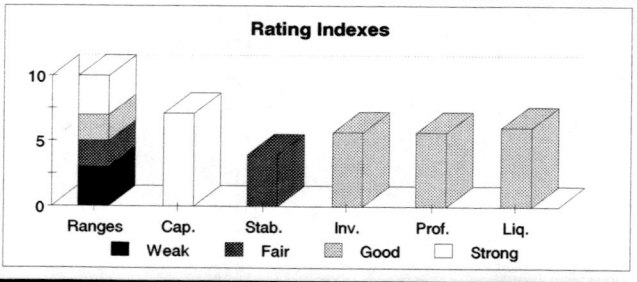

XL LIFE INSURANCE & ANNUITY COMPANY   C-   Fair

Major Rating Factors: Fair overall results on stability tests (3.2 on a scale of 0 to 10) including fair financial strength of affiliated XL Capital Ltd and negative cash flow from operations for 2002. Fair overall capitalization (4.0) based on mixed results -- excessive policy leverage mitigated by excellent risk adjusted capital (severe loss scenario). Nevertheless, capital levels have fluctuated during prior years. Fair profitability (3.6) with operating losses during the first six months of 2003.
Other Rating Factors: High quality investment portfolio (9.8). Excellent liquidity (7.0).
Principal Business: N/A
Principal Investments: NonCMO investment grade bonds (81%) and cash (19%).
Investments in Affiliates: None
Group Affiliation: XL Capital Ltd
Licensed in: All states except PR
Commenced Business: August 1978
Address: 645 Maryville Centre Dr, St Louis, MO 63141
Phone: (314) 275-5295   **Domicile State:** IL   **NAIC Code:** 88080

Data Date	Weiss Safety Rating	RACR #1	RACR #2	Total Assets ($mil)	Capital ($mil)	Net Premium ($mil)	Net Income ($mil)
6-03	C-	11.54	7.00	333.6	31.0	0.0	-1.8
6-02	C	0.72	0.71	10.5	7.6	-12.3	1.7
2002	C	9.98	8.98	26.1	24.5	-12.3	2.2
2001	C	2.87	2.64	161.6	84.8	-0.8	6.0
2000	C	3.20	2.93	158.7	84.7	-29.6	9.7
1999	C	2.49	2.28	127.4	58.2	27.4	2.3
1998	C	2.85	2.61	111.5	56.0	9.6	8.5

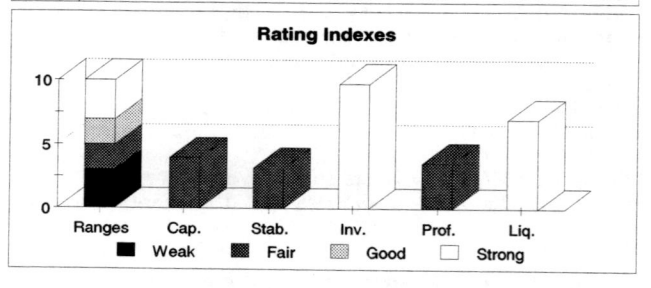

Section III

Weiss Recommended Companies

A compilation of those

U.S. HMOs and Health Insurers

receiving a Weiss Safety Rating of A+, A, A-, or B+.

Companies are listed in alphabetical order.

Section III Contents

This section provides contact addresses and phone numbers for all recommended carriers analyzed by Weiss. It contains all insurers receiving a Weiss Safety Rating of A+, A, A-, or B+. If an insurer is not on this list, it should not automatically be assumed that the firm is weak. Indeed, there are many firms that have not achieved a B+ or better rating but are in relatively good condition with adequate resources to cover their risk during an average recession. Not being included in this list should not be construed as a recommendation to cancel policies.

1. **Weiss Safety Rating** — Our rating is measured on a scale from A to F and considers a wide range of factors. Highly-rated companies are, in our opinion, less likely to experience financial difficulties than lower-rated firms. See *About the Weiss Safety Ratings* on page 11 for more information.

2. **Insurance Company Name** — The legally-registered name, which can sometimes differ from the name that the company uses for advertising. An insurer's name can be very similar to the name of other companies, so make sure you note the exact name before contacting your agent.

3. **Address** — The address of the main office where you can contact the firm for additional financial data or for the location of local branches and/or registered agents.

4. **Telephone Number** — The number to call for additional financial data or for the phone numbers of local branches and/or registered agents.

The Weiss Safety Ratings are not deemed to be a recommendation concerning the purchase or sale of the securities of any insurance company that is publicly owned.

III. Weiss Recommended Companies Addresses and Phone Numbers

Winter 2003 - 04

WEISS SAFETY RATING	INSURANCE COMPANY NAME	ADDRESS	CITY	STATE	ZIP	PHONE
A-	ALFA LIFE INS CORP	2108 EAST SOUTH BLVD	MONTGOMERY	AL	36116	(334) 288-3900
A	ALFA MUTUAL INS CO	2108 EAST SOUTH BLVD	MONTGOMERY	AL	36116	(334) 288-3900
A-	ALLSTATE INS CO	3075 SANDERS RD, STE G2H	NORTHBROOK	IL	60062	(847) 402-5000
A-	ALLSTATE LIFE INS CO	3100 SANDERS RD	NORTHBROOK	IL	60062	(847) 402-5000
B+	ALLSTATE LIFE INS CO OF NEW YORK	ONE ALLSTATE DR	FARMINGVILLE	NY	11738	(516) 451-5300
B+	ALOHACARE	1357 KAPIOLANI BLVD #1250	HONOLULU	HI	96814	(808) 973-1650
A	AMERICAN FIDELITY ASR CO	2000 N CLASSEN BLVD 7 EAST	OKLAHOMA CITY	OK	73106	(405) 523-2000
B+	AMERICAN GENERAL LIFE INS CO	2727-A ALLEN PARKWAY	HOUSTON	TX	77019	(713) 522-1111
B+	AMERICAN HEALTH & LIFE INS CO	307 WEST 7TH STREET, STE 400	FORT WORTH	TX	76102	(817) 348-7500
B+	AMERICHOICE OF NEW YORK INC	7 HANOVER SQUARE	NEW YORK	NY	10004	(212) 509-5999
B+	AMERITAS LIFE INS CORP	5900 O STREET	LINCOLN	NE	68510	(402) 467-1122
B+	ANTHEM HEALTH PLANS OF KENTUCKY INC	9901 LINN STATION RD	LOUISVILLE	KY	40223	(502) 423-2011
B+	ANTHEM HEALTH PLANS OF VIRGINIA	2015 STAPLES MILL RD	RICHMOND	VA	23230	(804) 354-7000
B+	ARKANSAS BLUE CROSS AND BLUE SHIELD	601 S GAINES	LITTLE ROCK	AR	72201	(501) 378-2000
B+	ATRIUM HEALTH PLAN INC	400 2ND ST., STE 270	HUDSON	WI	54106	(715) 386-6886
A	AUTO-OWNERS INS CO	6101 ANACAPRI BLVD	LANSING	MI	48917	(517) 323-1200
A-	AUTO-OWNERS LIFE INS CO	6101 ANACAPRI BLVD	LANSING	MI	48917	(517) 323-1200
B+	AVEMCO INS CO	411 AVIATION WAY	FREDERICK	MD	21701	(301) 694-5700
B+	BALBOA LIFE INS CO	18581 TELLER AVENUE	IRVINE	CA	92612	(949) 553-0700
B+	BCI HMO INC	300 EAST RANDOLPH STREET	CHICAGO	IL	60601	(312) 653-6600
A	BLUE CROSS BLUE SHIELD HEALTHCARE GA	3350 PEACHTREE RD NE	ATLANTA	GA	30326	(404) 842-8400
A	BLUE CROSS BLUE SHIELD OF ARIZONA	2444 W LAS PALMARITAS DR	PHOENIX	AZ	85021	(602) 864-4100
B+	BLUE CROSS BLUE SHIELD OF DELAWARE	ONE BRANDYWINE GATEWAY	WILMINGTON	DE	19801	(302) 421-3000
B+	BLUE CROSS BLUE SHIELD OF FLORIDA	4800 DEERWOOD CAMPUS PKWY	JACKSONVILLE	FL	32246	(800) 477-3736
A	BLUE CROSS BLUE SHIELD OF GEORGIA	3350 PEACHTREE RD NE	ATLANTA	GA	30326	(404) 842-8000
B+	BLUE CROSS BLUE SHIELD OF KC	2301 MAIN ST	KANSAS CITY	MO	64108	(816) 395-2222
A	BLUE CROSS BLUE SHIELD OF MA	401 PARK DR LANDMARK CENTER	BOSTON	MA	02215	(617) 246-5000
B+	BLUE CROSS BLUE SHIELD OF MINNESOTA	3535 BLUE CROSS RD	ST PAUL	MN	55164	(651) 662-8000
B+	BLUE CROSS BLUE SHIELD OF RI	444 WESTMINSTER ST	PROVIDENCE	RI	02903	(401) 459-1000
B+	BLUE CROSS BLUE SHIELD OF SC INC	2501 FARAWAY DR	COLUMBIA	SC	29219	(803) 788-3860
B+	BLUE CROSS BLUE SHIELD OF WYOMING	4000 HOUSE AVE	CHEYENNE	WY	82001	(307) 634-1393
A	BLUE CROSS OF CALIFORNIA	4553 LA TIENDA DR., T1-2C5	THOUSAND OAKS	CA	91362	(818) 234-2345
B+	BLUE CROSS OF IDAHO HEALTH SERVICE	3000 E PINE AVE	MERIDIAN	ID	83642	(208) 345-4550
B+	BLUECROSS BLUESHIELD OF TENNESSEE	801 PINE ST	CHATTANOOGA	TN	37402	(423) 755-5600
B+	BLUEGRASS FAMILY HEALTH INC	651 PERIMETER PARK, STE 300	LEXINGTON	KY	40517	(859) 269-4475
A-	CALIFORNIA PHYSICIANS SERVICE	FIFTY BEALE ST	SAN FRANCISCO	CA	94105	(415) 229-5821
A-	CALIFORNIA STATE AUTO ASN INTER-INS	100 VAN NESS AVE	SAN FRANCISCO	CA	94102	(415) 565-2012
B+	CAPITAL BLUE CROSS OF PENNSYLVANIA	2500 ELMERTON AVE	HARRISBURG	PA	17110	(717) 541-7000
B+	CAPITAL DISTRICT PHYSICIANS HEALTH P	1223 WASHINGTON AVE	ALBANY	NY	12206	(518) 641-3000
A-	CAREFIRST BLUECHOICE INC	550 12TH ST SW	WASHINGTON	DC	20065	(202) 479-8000
B+	CAREFIRST OF MARYLAND INC	10455 MILL RUN CIRCLE	OWINGS MILLS	MD	21117	(410) 581-3000
B+	CARIBBEAN AMERICAN LIFE ASR CO	273 PONCE DE LEON AVE STE 350	HATO REY	PR	00918	(787) 250-6470
A-	CENTRAL STATES INDEMNITY CO OF OMAHA	1212 N 96TH ST	OMAHA	NE	68114	(402) 397-1111
A	CENTURION LIFE INS CO	206 EIGHTH STREET	DES MOINES	IA	50309	(515) 243-2131

III. Weiss Recommended Companies Addresses and Phone Numbers

WEISS SAFETY RATING	INSURANCE COMPANY NAME	ADDRESS	CITY	STATE	ZIP	PHONE
A-	CINCINNATI INS CO	6200 S GILMORE RD	FAIRFIELD	OH	45014	(513) 870-2000
B+	CITICORP LIFE INS CO	3225 NORTH CENTRAL AVENUE	PHOENIX	AZ	85012	(860) 308-1000
B+	COLORADO BANKERS LIFE INS CO	5990 GREENWOOD PLAZA BLVD	ENGLEWOOD	CO	80111	(303) 220-8500
B+	COLUMBIA UNITED PROVIDERS INC	19120 SE 34TH STREET #201	VANCOUVER	WA	98683	(360) 896-7093
B+	COLUMBUS LIFE INS CO	400 E 4TH ST	CINCINNATI	OH	45202	(513) 361-6700
A	COMMUNITY HEALTH PLAN OF WASHINGTON	720 OLIVE WAY STE 300	SEATTLE	WA	98101	(206) 521-8833
A-	COMPANION HEALTH CARE CORP	4101 PERCIVAL RD	COLUMBIA	SC	29219	(803) 786-8466
B+	COMPANION LIFE INS CO	2501 FARAWAY DR	COLUMBIA	SC	29219	(803) 735-1251
B+	CONNECTICARE INC	30 BATTERSON PARK RD	FARMINGTON	CT	06032	(860) 674-5700
A+	COUNTRY LIFE INS CO	1701 TOWANDA AVE	BLOOMINGTON	IL	61701	(309) 821-3000
B+	CUMIS INS SOCIETY INC	5910 MINERAL POINT RD	MADISON	WI	53705	(608) 238-5851
B+	DEAN HEALTH PLAN INC	1277 DEMING WAY	MADISON	WI	53562	(608) 836-1400
A-	EMPIRE HEALTHCHOICE ASSURANCE INC	11 W 42ND ST	NEW YORK	NY	10036	(212) 476-7470
B+	EXCELLUS HEALTH PLAN INC	165 COURT ST	ROCHESTER	NY	14647	(716) 238-4506
A-	FARM BUREAU LIFE INS CO	5400 UNIVERSITY AVE	WEST DES MOINES	IA	50266	(515) 225-5400
A-	FARM BUREAU LIFE INS CO OF MISSOURI	701 S COUNTRY CLUB DR	JEFFERSON CITY	MO	65109	(573) 893-1400
B+	FARM FAMILY LIFE INS CO	344 ROUTE 9W	GLENMONT	NY	12077	(518) 431-5000
B+	FEDERAL INS CO	251 N ILLINOIS STE 1100	INDIANAPOLIS	IN	46204	(908) 903-2000
A-	FEDERATED LIFE INS CO	121 E PARK SQUARE	OWATONNA	MN	55060	(800) 533-0472
B+	FEDERATED MUTUAL INS CO	121 E PARK SQUARE	OWATONNA	MN	55060	(507) 455-5200
B+	FIRST PLAN OF MINNESOTA	525 S. LAKE AVE., SUITE 222	DULUTH	MN	55802	(218) 834-7207
A	GEORGIA FARM BUREAU MUTUAL INS CO	1620 BASS RD	MACON	GA	31210	(912) 474-8411
B+	GOLDEN RULE INS CO	712 ELEVENTH ST	LAWRENCEVILLE	IL	62439	(618) 943-8000
A+	GOVERNMENT EMPLOYEES INS CO	ONE GEICO PLAZA	WASHINGTON	DC	20076	(800) 841-3000
B+	GRANGE LIFE INS CO	650 S FRONT ST	COLUMBUS	OH	43216	(614) 445-2820
A-	GRANGE MUTUAL CAS CO	650 S FRONT ST	COLUMBUS	OH	43206	(614) 445-2900
B+	GREAT NORTHERN INS CO	1000 PILLSBURY CENTER	MINNEAPOLIS	MN	55402	(908) 903-2000
B+	GREAT-WEST LIFE & ANNUITY INS CO	8515 E ORCHARD RD	ENGLEWOOD	CO	80111	(303) 737-3000
A-	GROUP HEALTH COOP OF S CENTRAL WI	8202 EXCELSIOR DR	MADISON	WI	53717	(608) 251-4156
B+	GROUP HEALTH INCORPORATED	441 NINTH AVE	NEW YORK	NY	10001	(212) 615-0000
A	GROUP HOSP & MEDICAL SERVICES INC	550 12TH ST, SW	WASHINGTON	DC	20065	(202) 479-8000
A	GUARDIAN LIFE INS CO OF AMERICA	7 HANOVER SQUARE	NEW YORK	NY	10004	(212) 598-1800
B+	HARTFORD FIRE INS CO	HARTFORD PLAZA	HARTFORD	CT	06115	(860) 547-5000
B+	HARTFORD LIFE & ACCIDENT INS CO	200 HOPMEADOW ST	SIMSBURY	CT	06070	(860) 843-5867
B+	HARTFORD LIFE & ANNUITY INS CO	200 HOPMEADOW ST	SIMSBURY	CT	06070	(860) 843-5867
B+	HARTFORD LIFE INS CO	200 HOPMEADOW ST	SIMSBURY	CT	06070	(860) 843-5867
A	HEALTH ALLIANCE PLAN OF MICHIGAN	2850 W GRAND BLVD	DETROIT	MI	48202	(313) 872-8100
B+	HEALTH CARE SVC CORP A MUT LEG RES	300 EAST RANDOLPH STREET	CHICAGO	IL	60601	(312) 653-6000
B+	HEALTH INSURANCE PLAN OF GREATER NY	7 W 34TH ST	NEW YORK	NY	10001	(212) 630-5000
B+	HEALTH NET	21281 BURBANK BLVD	WOODLAND HILLS	CA	91367	(818) 676-6775
B+	HEALTH OPTIONS INC	4800 DEERWOOD CAMPUS PKWY	JACKSONVILLE	FL	32246	(904) 791-6111
B+	HEALTH PLAN OF SAN JOAQUIN	1550 W FREMONT ST	STOCKTON	CA	95203	(209) 939-3500
B+	HEALTHKEEPERS INC	2220 EDWARD HOLLAND DR	RICHMOND	VA	23230	(804) 354-3479
B+	HEALTHLINK HMO INC	12443 OLIVE BLVD	ST LOUIS	MO	63141	(314) 989-6028

III. Weiss Recommended Companies Addresses and Phone Numbers

Winter 2003 - 04

WEISS SAFETY RATING	INSURANCE COMPANY NAME	ADDRESS	CITY	STATE	ZIP	PHONE
B+	HEALTHPARTNERS	8100 34TH AVE S, PO BOX 1309	MINNEAPOLIS	MN	55440	(952) 883-6584
A-	HEALTHY PALM BEACHES INC	324 DATURA ST SUITE 401	WEST PALM BEACH	FL	33401	(561) 659-1270
B+	HMO MINNESOTA	3535 BLUE CROSS RD	EAGAN	MN	55122	(651) 662-1668
B+	HMO NEW MEXICO INC	12800 INDIAN SCHOOL RD NE	ALBUQUERQUE	NM	87112	(505) 291-3500
B+	HORIZON HEALTHCARE OF NEW JERSEY INC	3 PENN PLAZA EAST- PP-15E	NEWARK	NJ	07105	(973) 466-8600
A	HORIZON HEALTHCARE SERVICES INC	3 PENN PLAZA EAST	NEWARK	NJ	07102	(973) 466-4000
B+	HOSPITAL SERV ASSN OF NORTH EAST PA	19 N MAIN ST	WILKES-BARRE	PA	18711	(800) 829-8599
B+	IDS LIFE INS CO OF NEW YORK	20 MADISON AVENUE EXTENSION	ALBANY	NY	12203	(518) 869-8613
B+	JEFFERSON PILOT FINANCIAL INS CO	8801 INDIAN HILLS	OMAHA	NE	68114	(603) 226-5000
A	JEFFERSON-PILOT LIFE INS CO	100 N GREENE ST	GREENSBORO	NC	27401	(336) 691-3000
A-	JOHN HANCOCK LIFE INS CO	JOHN HANCOCK PLACE	BOSTON	MA	02117	(617) 572-6000
A	KENTUCKY FARM BUREAU MUTUAL INS CO	9201 BUNSEN PARKWAY	LOUISVILLE	KY	40220	(502) 495-5000
B+	KEYSTONE HEALTH PLAN CENTRAL INC	300 CORPORATE CENTER DR 602	CAMP HILL	PA	17011	(717) 763-3458
B+	KEYSTONE HEALTH PLAN EAST INC	1901 MARKET ST	PHILADELPHIA	PA	19101	(215) 241-2001
B+	KEYSTONE HEALTH PLAN WEST INC	FIFTH AVE PL, 120 FIFTH AVE	PITTSBURGH	PA	15222	(412) 544-7000
B+	LINCOLN BENEFIT LIFE CO	206 S 13TH ST, SUITE 200	LINCOLN	NE	68508	(800) 525-9287
B+	MANUFACTURERS LIFE INS CO USA	38500 WOODWARD AVE	BLOOMFIELD HILLS	MI	48304	(416) 926-0100
A	MASSACHUSETTS MUTUAL LIFE INS CO	1295 STATE ST	SPRINGFIELD	MA	01111	(413) 788-8411
B+	MATTHEW THORNTON HEALTH PLAN	3000 GOFFS FALLS RD	MANCHESTER	NH	03111	(603) 695-7000
B+	MD INDIVIDUAL PRACTICE ASSOC INC	4 TAFT CT	ROCKVILLE	MD	20850	(301) 762-8205
A-	MEDICA	5601 SMETANA DR	MINNETONKA	MN	55343	(952) 992-3635
B+	MERIT LIFE INS CO	601 NW SECOND ST	EVANSVILLE	IN	47708	(812) 424-8031
A-	METROPOLITAN HEALTH PLAN	822 S THIRD ST STE 140	MINNEAPOLIS	MN	55415	(612) 347-7596
B+	METROPOLITAN LIFE INS CO	1 MADISON AVE	NEW YORK	NY	10010	(212) 578-2211
B+	METROPOLITAN PROPERTY & CAS INS CO	700 QUAKER LANE	WARWICK	RI	02886	(401) 827-2400
A-	MIDLAND NATIONAL LIFE INS CO	ONE MIDLAND PLAZA	SIOUX FALLS	SD	57193	(312) 648-7600
B+	MIDWEST SECURITY LIFE INS CO	2700 MIDWEST DR	ONALASKA	WI	54650	(608) 783-7130
A-	MINNESOTA LIFE INS CO	400 N ROBERT ST	ST PAUL	MN	55101	(651) 665-3500
B+	MOUNTAIN STATE BL CROSS BL SHIELD	700 MARKET SQUARE	PARKERSBURG	WV	26101	(304) 424-7700
A-	MUTUAL OF OMAHA INS CO	MUTUAL OF OMAHA PLAZA	OMAHA	NE	68175	(402) 342-7600
B+	MVP HEALTH PLAN INC	625 STATE ST	SCHENECTADY	NY	12305	(518) 388-2451
B+	NATIONAL BENEFIT LIFE INS CO	333 WEST 34TH STREET	NEW YORK	NY	10001	(212) 615-7500
B+	NATIONAL CASUALTY CO	8877 N GAINEY CENTER DR	SCOTTSDALE	AZ	85258	(602) 948-0505
A-	NATIONAL GUARDIAN LIFE INS CO	2 E GILMAN ST	MADISON	WI	53703	(608) 257-5611
B+	NATIONAL UNION FIRE INS CO OF PITTSB	70 PINE STREET 22 FL	NEW YORK	NY	10270	(212) 770-8596
B+	NATIONWIDE LIFE INS CO	ONE NATIONWIDE PLAZA	COLUMBUS	OH	43215	(800) 882-2822
B+	NATIONWIDE MUTUAL FIRE INS CO	ONE NATIONWIDE PLAZA	COLUMBUS	OH	43216	(614) 249-3004
A	NEW YORK LIFE INS CO	51 MADISON AVE	NEW YORK	NY	10010	(212) 576-7000
B+	NORIDIAN MUTUAL INS CO	4510 13TH AVE SW	FARGO	ND	58121	(701) 282-1100
A-	NORTH CAROLINA FARM BU MUTUAL INS CO	5301 GLENWOOD AVE	RALEIGH	NC	27612	(919) 782-1705
A	NORTHWESTERN MUTUAL LIFE INS CO	720 E WISCONSIN AVE	MILWAUKEE	WI	53202	(414) 271-1444
A-	OLD REPUBLIC INS CO	414 W PITTSBURGH ST	GREENSBURG	PA	15601	(412) 834-5000
B+	OXFORD HEALTH PLANS (NY) INC	1133 AVENUE OF THE AMERICAS	NEW YORK	NY	06611	(203) 459-6000
B+	PACIFIC GUARDIAN LIFE INS CO LTD	1440 KAPIOLANI BLVD STE 1700	HONOLULU	HI	96814	(808) 955-2236

III. Weiss Recommended Companies Addresses and Phone Numbers

WEISS SAFETY RATING	INSURANCE COMPANY NAME	ADDRESS	CITY	STATE	ZIP	PHONE
A-	PACIFIC HOSPITAL ASSOC	250 COUNTRY CLUB RD	EUGENE	OR	97401	(541) 686-1242
A-	PACIFIC LIFE INS CO	700 NEWPORT CENTER DR	NEWPORT BEACH	CA	92660	(949) 640-3011
B+	PEKIN LIFE INS CO	2505 COURT ST	PEKIN	IL	61558	(309) 346-1161
B+	PENINSULA HEALTH CARE INC	606 DENBIGH BLVD SUITE 500	NEWPORT NEWS	VA	23608	(757) 875-5760
B+	PHYSICIANS LIFE INS CO	2600 DODGE ST	OMAHA	NE	68131	(402) 633-1000
A+	PHYSICIANS MUTUAL INS CO	2600 DODGE ST	OMAHA	NE	68131	(402) 633-1000
B+	PRIMERICA LIFE INS CO	3120 BRECKINRIDGE BLVD	DULUTH	GA	30199	(770) 381-1000
A-	PRINCIPAL LIFE INS CO	711 HIGH ST	DES MOINES	IA	50392	(515) 247-5111
B+	PRIORITY HEALTH	1231 E BELTLINE AVE NE	GRAND RAPIDS	MI	49505	(800) 942-0954
B+	PRIORITY HEALTH CARE INC	621 LYNNHAVEN PARKWAY, STE 450	VIRGINIA BEACH	VA	23452	(804) 354-3479
A+	PROTECTIVE INS CO	1099 N MERIDIAN ST	INDIANAPOLIS	IN	46204	(317) 636-9800
B+	SAVINGS BANK LIFE INS CO OF MA	ONE LINSCOTT RD	WOBURN	MA	01801	(781) 938-3500
A	SENTRY INS A MUTUAL CO	1800 N POINT DR	STEVENS POINT	WI	54481	(715) 346-6000
A-	SENTRY LIFE INS CO	1800 NORTH POINT DR	STEVENS POINT	WI	54481	(715) 346-6000
B+	SHELTER LIFE INS CO	1817 W BROADWAY	COLUMBIA	MO	65218	(573) 445-8441
B+	SIRIUS AMERICA INS CO	32 LOOCKERMAN SQ STE L100	DOVER	DE	19901	(212) 702-3700
A-	SOUTHERN FARM BUREAU LIFE INS CO	1401 LIVINGSTON LANE	JACKSON	MS	39213	(601) 981-7422
B+	SOUTHERN NATL LIFE INS CO INC	5525 REITZ AVE	BATON ROUGE	LA	70809	(225) 295-2583
B+	STATE AUTOMOBILE MUTUAL INS CO	518 E BROAD ST	COLUMBUS	OH	43215	(614) 464-5000
B+	STATE FARM MUTUAL AUTOMOBILE INS CO	ONE STATE FARM PLAZA	BLOOMINGTON	IL	61710	(309) 735-8480
B+	SURETY LIFE INS CO	206 S 13TH ST SUITE 300	LINCOLN	NE	68508	(800) 525-9287
A+	TEACHERS INS & ANNUITY ASN OF AM	730 THIRD AVE 7TH FLOOR	NEW YORK	NY	10017	(212) 490-9000
B+	THREE RIVERS HEALTH PLANS INC	1789 S BRADDOCK AVE SUITE 370	SWISSVALE	PA	15218	(412) 858-4000
B+	TRAVELERS INS CO LIFE DEPT	ONE CITYPLACE	HARTFORD	CT	06103	(860) 308-7397
B+	UCARE MINNESOTA	2000 SUMMER ST NE	MINNEAPOLIS	MN	55413	(612) 676-6500
B+	UNICARE HEALTH PLANS OF THE MIDWEST	233 SOUTH WACKER DR, STE 3900	CHICAGO	IL	60606	(877) 864-2273
A	UNION NATIONAL LIFE INS CO	8282 GOODWOOD BLVD	BATON ROUGE	LA	70806	(225) 927-3430
A	UNITED FARM FAMILY LIFE INS CO	225 S EAST ST	INDIANAPOLIS	IN	46202	(317) 692-7200
B+	UNITED HEALTHCARE OF ALABAMA INC	3700 COLONNADE PARKWAY	BIRMINGHAM	AL	35243	(205) 977-6300
B+	UNITED HEALTHCARE OF ARKANSAS INC	415 N MCKINLEY ST, STE 820	LITTLE ROCK	AR	72205	(501) 664-7700
B+	UNITED HEALTHCARE OF NC INC	3803 N ELM ST	GREENSBORO	NC	27455	(336) 282-0900
B+	UNITED HEALTHCARE OF THE MIDLANDS	2717 N. 118TH CIRCLE	OMAHA	NE	68164	(402) 445-5000
B+	UNITED HEALTHCARE OF THE MIDWEST INC	13655 RIVERPORT DR	MARYLAND HEIGHTS	MO	63043	(314) 592-7000
B+	UNITED HEALTHCARE OF WISCONSIN INC	10701 WEST RESEARCH DR	WAUWATOSA	WI	53226	(414) 443-4000
B+	UNITED INS CO OF AMERICA	ONE E WACKER DR	CHICAGO	IL	60601	(312) 661-4681
B+	UNITED OF OMAHA LIFE INS CO	MUTUAL OF OMAHA PLAZA	OMAHA	NE	68175	(402) 342-7600
A-	USAA LIFE INS CO	9800 FREDERICKSBURG RD	SAN ANTONIO	TX	78288	(210) 498-8000
B+	WESTERN & SOUTHERN LIFE INS CO	400 BROADWAY	CINCINNATI	OH	45202	(513) 629-1800

Section IV

Weiss Recommended Companies by State

A summary analysis of those

U.S. HMOs and Health Insurers

receiving a Weiss Safety Rating of A+, A, A-, or B+.

Companies are ranked by Weiss Safety Rating
in each state where they are licensed to do business.

Section IV Contents

This section provides a list of the recommended carriers licensed to do business in each state. It contains all insurers receiving a Weiss Safety Rating of A+, A, A-, or B+. If an insurer is not on this list, it should not automatically be assumed that the firm is weak. Indeed, there are many firms that have not achieved a B+ or better rating but are in relatively good condition with adequate resources to cover their risk during an average recession. Not being included in this list should not be construed as a recommendation to cancel policies.

Companies are ranked within each state by their Weiss Safety Rating, and are listed alphabetically within each rating category. Companies with the same rating should be viewed as having the same relative safety regardless of their ranking in this table.

1. **Insurance Company Name** The legally-registered name, which can sometimes differ from the name that the company uses for advertising. An insurer's name can be very similar to the name of other companies which may not be on our Recommended List, so make sure you note the exact name before contacting your agent.

2. **Domicile State** The state which has primary regulatory responsibility for the company. It may differ from the location of the company's corporate headquarters. You do not have to be living in the domicile state to purchase insurance from this firm, provided it is licensed to do business in your state.

3. **Total Assets** All assets admitted by state insurance regulators in millions of dollars as of the most recent year end. This includes investments and current business assets such as receivables from agents, reinsurers and subscribers.

The Weiss Safety Ratings are not deemed to be a recommendation concerning the purchase or sale of the securities of any insurance company that is publicly owned.

IV. Weiss Recommended Companies by State

Alabama

Weiss Safety Rating: A+

INSURANCE COMPANY NAME	DOM. STATE	TOTAL ASSETS ($MIL)
GOVERNMENT EMPLOYEES INS CO	MD	8,737.7
PHYSICIANS MUTUAL INS CO	NE	1,102.7
PROTECTIVE INS CO	IN	443.4
TEACHERS INS & ANNUITY ASN OF AM	NY	147,114.8

Weiss Safety Rating: A

INSURANCE COMPANY NAME	DOM. STATE	TOTAL ASSETS ($MIL)
ALFA MUTUAL INS CO	AL	1,151.8
AMERICAN FIDELITY ASR CO	OK	2,382.6
AUTO-OWNERS INS CO	MI	6,582.7
CENTURION LIFE INS CO	MO	1,024.0
GUARDIAN LIFE INS CO OF AMERICA	NY	20,577.2
JEFFERSON-PILOT LIFE INS CO	NC	13,405.5
MASSACHUSETTS MUTUAL LIFE INS CO	MA	80,322.1
NEW YORK LIFE INS CO	NY	87,505.8
NORTHWESTERN MUTUAL LIFE INS CO	WI	114,436.3
SENTRY INS A MUTUAL CO	WI	4,177.1
UNION NATIONAL LIFE INS CO	LA	377.5

Weiss Safety Rating: A-

INSURANCE COMPANY NAME	DOM. STATE	TOTAL ASSETS ($MIL)
ALFA LIFE INS CORP	AL	821.5
ALLSTATE INS CO	IL	40,978.7
ALLSTATE LIFE INS CO	IL	60,033.7
AUTO-OWNERS LIFE INS CO	MI	1,251.5
CENTRAL STATES INDEMNITY CO OF OMAHA	NE	243.1
CINCINNATI INS CO	OH	7,143.1
FEDERATED LIFE INS CO	MN	864.3
GRANGE MUTUAL CAS CO	OH	1,116.1
JOHN HANCOCK LIFE INS CO	MA	73,183.9
MIDLAND NATIONAL LIFE INS CO	IA	10,748.6
MINNESOTA LIFE INS CO	MN	17,352.3
MUTUAL OF OMAHA INS CO	NE	3,755.1
NATIONAL GUARDIAN LIFE INS CO	WI	947.4
OLD REPUBLIC INS CO	PA	1,644.5
PACIFIC LIFE INS CO	CA	54,639.9
PRINCIPAL LIFE INS CO	IA	83,957.6
SENTRY LIFE INS CO	WI	2,101.2
SOUTHERN FARM BUREAU LIFE INS CO	MS	7,776.4
USAA LIFE INS CO	TX	9,167.0

Weiss Safety Rating: B+

INSURANCE COMPANY NAME	DOM. STATE	TOTAL ASSETS ($MIL)
AMERICAN GENERAL LIFE INS CO	TX	24,549.9
AMERICAN HEALTH & LIFE INS CO	TX	1,236.5
AMERITAS LIFE INS CORP	NE	2,417.9
AVEMCO INS CO	MD	191.7
BALBOA LIFE INS CO	CA	124.5
CITICORP LIFE INS CO	AZ	1,058.7
COLORADO BANKERS LIFE INS CO	CO	113.3
COLUMBUS LIFE INS CO	OH	2,187.1
COMPANION LIFE INS CO	SC	75.6
CUMIS INS SOCIETY INC	WI	826.9
FEDERAL INS CO	IN	18,983.3
FEDERATED MUTUAL INS CO	MN	3,013.6
GOLDEN RULE INS CO	IL	2,076.2
GREAT NORTHERN INS CO	MN	1,088.5
GREAT-WEST LIFE & ANNUITY INS CO	CO	27,323.0
HARTFORD FIRE INS CO	CT	15,857.7
HARTFORD LIFE & ACCIDENT INS CO	CT	8,792.5
HARTFORD LIFE & ANNUITY INS CO	CT	49,622.7
HARTFORD LIFE INS CO	CT	97,564.5
HEALTH OPTIONS INC	FL	914.9
JEFFERSON PILOT FINANCIAL INS CO	NE	11,630.2
LINCOLN BENEFIT LIFE CO	NE	1,823.4
MANUFACTURERS LIFE INS CO USA	MI	53,737.8
MERIT LIFE INS CO	IN	1,020.5
METROPOLITAN LIFE INS CO	NY	220,093.6
METROPOLITAN PROPERTY & CAS INS CO	RI	4,789.1
NATIONAL BENEFIT LIFE INS CO	NY	736.6
NATIONAL CASUALTY CO	WI	92.6
NATIONAL UNION FIRE INS CO OF PITTSB	PA	18,196.9
NATIONWIDE LIFE INS CO	OH	80,569.1
NATIONWIDE MUTUAL FIRE INS CO	OH	3,610.4
PHYSICIANS LIFE INS CO	NE	1,195.8
PRIMERICA LIFE INS CO	MA	5,073.8
SIRIUS AMERICA INS CO	DE	216.5
STATE AUTOMOBILE MUTUAL INS CO	OH	1,299.8
STATE FARM MUTUAL AUTOMOBILE INS CO	IL	70,070.4
SURETY LIFE INS CO	NE	50.3
TRAVELERS INS CO LIFE DEPT	CT	58,317.0
UNITED HEALTHCARE OF ALABAMA INC	AL	122.0
UNITED INS CO OF AMERICA	IL	2,064.3
UNITED OF OMAHA LIFE INS CO	NE	12,298.3
WESTERN & SOUTHERN LIFE INS CO	OH	7,850.2

Alaska

INSURANCE COMPANY NAME	DOM. STATE	TOTAL ASSETS ($MIL)
Weiss Safety Rating: A+		
COUNTRY LIFE INS CO	IL	4,387.5
GOVERNMENT EMPLOYEES INS CO	MD	8,737.7
PHYSICIANS MUTUAL INS CO	NE	1,102.7
PROTECTIVE INS CO	IN	443.4
TEACHERS INS & ANNUITY ASN OF AM	NY	147,114.8
Weiss Safety Rating: A		
AMERICAN FIDELITY ASR CO	OK	2,382.6
CENTURION LIFE INS CO	MO	1,024.0
GUARDIAN LIFE INS CO OF AMERICA	NY	20,577.2
JEFFERSON-PILOT LIFE INS CO	NC	13,405.5
MASSACHUSETTS MUTUAL LIFE INS CO	MA	80,322.1
NEW YORK LIFE INS CO	NY	87,505.8
NORTHWESTERN MUTUAL LIFE INS CO	WI	114,436.3
SENTRY INS A MUTUAL CO	WI	4,177.1
Weiss Safety Rating: A-		
ALLSTATE INS CO	IL	40,978.7
ALLSTATE LIFE INS CO	IL	60,033.7
CENTRAL STATES INDEMNITY CO OF OMAHA	NE	243.1
CINCINNATI INS CO	OH	7,143.1
JOHN HANCOCK LIFE INS CO	MA	73,183.9
MIDLAND NATIONAL LIFE INS CO	IA	10,748.6
MINNESOTA LIFE INS CO	MN	17,352.3
MUTUAL OF OMAHA INS CO	NE	3,755.1
NATIONAL GUARDIAN LIFE INS CO	WI	947.4
OLD REPUBLIC INS CO	PA	1,644.5
PACIFIC LIFE INS CO	CA	54,639.9
PRINCIPAL LIFE INS CO	IA	83,957.6
SENTRY LIFE INS CO	WI	2,101.2
USAA LIFE INS CO	TX	9,167.0
Weiss Safety Rating: B+		
AMERICAN GENERAL LIFE INS CO	TX	24,549.9
AMERICAN HEALTH & LIFE INS CO	TX	1,236.5
AMERITAS LIFE INS CORP	NE	2,417.9
AVEMCO INS CO	MD	191.7
BALBOA LIFE INS CO	CA	124.5
CITICORP LIFE INS CO	AZ	1,058.7
COLORADO BANKERS LIFE INS CO	CO	113.3
COMPANION LIFE INS CO	SC	75.6
CUMIS INS SOCIETY INC	WI	826.9
FEDERAL INS CO	IN	18,983.3
GOLDEN RULE INS CO	IL	2,076.2
GREAT NORTHERN INS CO	MN	1,088.5
GREAT-WEST LIFE & ANNUITY INS CO	CO	27,323.0
HARTFORD FIRE INS CO	CT	15,857.7
HARTFORD LIFE & ACCIDENT INS CO	CT	8,792.5
HARTFORD LIFE & ANNUITY INS CO	CT	49,622.7
HARTFORD LIFE INS CO	CT	97,564.5
JEFFERSON PILOT FINANCIAL INS CO	NE	11,630.2
LINCOLN BENEFIT LIFE CO	NE	1,823.4
MANUFACTURERS LIFE INS CO USA	MI	53,737.8
METROPOLITAN LIFE INS CO	NY	220,093.6
MIDWEST SECURITY LIFE INS CO	WI	132.8
NATIONAL BENEFIT LIFE INS CO	NY	736.6
NATIONAL CASUALTY CO	WI	92.6
NATIONAL UNION FIRE INS CO OF PITTSB	PA	18,196.9
NATIONWIDE LIFE INS CO	OH	80,569.1
NATIONWIDE MUTUAL FIRE INS CO	OH	3,610.4
PACIFIC GUARDIAN LIFE INS CO LTD	HI	431.5
PHYSICIANS LIFE INS CO	NE	1,195.8
PRIMERICA LIFE INS CO	MA	5,073.8
SIRIUS AMERICA INS CO	DE	216.8
STATE FARM MUTUAL AUTOMOBILE INS CO	IL	70,070.4
SURETY LIFE INS CO	NE	50.3
TRAVELERS INS CO LIFE DEPT	CT	58,317.0
UNITED OF OMAHA LIFE INS CO	NE	12,298.3

IV. Weiss Recommended Companies by State

Arizona

Winter 2003 - 04

Weiss Safety Rating: A+

INSURANCE COMPANY NAME	DOM. STATE	TOTAL ASSETS ($MIL)
COUNTRY LIFE INS CO	IL	4,387.5
GOVERNMENT EMPLOYEES INS CO	MD	8,737.7
PHYSICIANS MUTUAL INS CO	NE	1,102.7
PROTECTIVE INS CO	IN	443.4
TEACHERS INS & ANNUITY ASN OF AM	NY	147,114.8

Weiss Safety Rating: A

INSURANCE COMPANY NAME	DOM. STATE	TOTAL ASSETS ($MIL)
AMERICAN FIDELITY ASR CO	OK	2,382.6
AUTO-OWNERS INS CO	MI	6,582.7
BLUE CROSS BLUE SHIELD OF ARIZONA	AZ	409.0
CENTURION LIFE INS CO	MO	1,024.0
GUARDIAN LIFE INS CO OF AMERICA	NY	20,577.2
JEFFERSON-PILOT LIFE INS CO	NC	13,405.5
MASSACHUSETTS MUTUAL LIFE INS CO	MA	80,322.1
NEW YORK LIFE INS CO	NY	87,505.8
NORTHWESTERN MUTUAL LIFE INS CO	WI	114,436.3
SENTRY INS A MUTUAL CO	WI	4,177.1

Weiss Safety Rating: A-

INSURANCE COMPANY NAME	DOM. STATE	TOTAL ASSETS ($MIL)
ALLSTATE INS CO	IL	40,978.7
ALLSTATE LIFE INS CO	IL	60,033.7
AUTO-OWNERS LIFE INS CO	MI	1,251.5
CENTRAL STATES INDEMNITY CO OF OMAHA	NE	243.1
CINCINNATI INS CO	OH	7,143.1
FARM BUREAU LIFE INS CO	IA	4,695.3
FEDERATED LIFE INS CO	MN	864.3
JOHN HANCOCK LIFE INS CO	MA	73,183.9
MIDLAND NATIONAL LIFE INS CO	IA	10,748.6
MINNESOTA LIFE INS CO	MN	17,352.3
MUTUAL OF OMAHA INS CO	NE	3,755.1
NATIONAL GUARDIAN LIFE INS CO	WI	947.4
OLD REPUBLIC INS CO	PA	1,644.5
PACIFIC LIFE INS CO	CA	54,639.9
PRINCIPAL LIFE INS CO	IA	83,957.6
SENTRY LIFE INS CO	WI	2,101.2
USAA LIFE INS CO	TX	9,167.0

Weiss Safety Rating: B+

INSURANCE COMPANY NAME	DOM. STATE	TOTAL ASSETS ($MIL)
AMERICAN GENERAL LIFE INS CO	TX	24,549.9
AMERICAN HEALTH & LIFE INS CO	TX	1,236.5
AMERITAS LIFE INS CORP	NE	2,417.9
AVEMCO INS CO	MD	191.7
BALBOA LIFE INS CO	CA	124.5
CITICORP LIFE INS CO	AZ	1,058.7
COLORADO BANKERS LIFE INS CO	CO	113.3
COLUMBUS LIFE INS CO	OH	2,187.1
COMPANION LIFE INS CO	SC	75.6
CUMIS INS SOCIETY INC	WI	826.9
FEDERAL INS CO	IN	18,983.3
FEDERATED MUTUAL INS CO	MN	3,013.6
GOLDEN RULE INS CO	IL	2,076.2
GREAT NORTHERN INS CO	MN	1,088.5
GREAT-WEST LIFE & ANNUITY INS CO	CO	27,323.0
HARTFORD FIRE INS CO	CT	15,857.7
HARTFORD LIFE & ACCIDENT INS CO	CT	8,792.5
HARTFORD LIFE & ANNUITY INS CO	CT	49,622.7
HARTFORD LIFE INS CO	CT	97,564.5
JEFFERSON PILOT FINANCIAL INS CO	NE	11,630.2
LINCOLN BENEFIT LIFE CO	NE	1,823.4
MANUFACTURERS LIFE INS CO USA	MI	53,737.8
MERIT LIFE INS CO	IN	1,020.5
METROPOLITAN LIFE INS CO	NY	220,093.6
METROPOLITAN PROPERTY & CAS INS CO	RI	4,789.1
MIDWEST SECURITY LIFE INS CO	WI	132.8
NATIONAL BENEFIT LIFE INS CO	NY	736.6
NATIONAL CASUALTY CO	WI	92.6
NATIONAL UNION FIRE INS CO OF PITTSB	PA	18,196.9
NATIONWIDE LIFE INS CO	OH	80,569.1
NATIONWIDE MUTUAL FIRE INS CO	OH	3,610.4
PACIFIC GUARDIAN LIFE INS CO LTD	HI	431.5
PHYSICIANS LIFE INS CO	NE	1,195.8
PRIMERICA LIFE INS CO	MA	5,073.8
SIRIUS AMERICA INS CO	DE	216.8
STATE AUTOMOBILE MUTUAL INS CO	OH	1,299.8
STATE FARM MUTUAL AUTOMOBILE INS CO	IL	70,070.4
SURETY LIFE INS CO	NE	50.3
TRAVELERS INS CO LIFE DEPT	CT	58,317.0
UNITED INS CO OF AMERICA	IL	2,064.3
UNITED OF OMAHA LIFE INS CO	NE	12,298.3
WESTERN & SOUTHERN LIFE INS CO	OH	7,850.2

Arkansas

INSURANCE COMPANY NAME	DOM. STATE	TOTAL ASSETS ($MIL)
Weiss Safety Rating: A+		
COUNTRY LIFE INS CO	IL	4,387.5
GOVERNMENT EMPLOYEES INS CO	MD	8,737.7
PHYSICIANS MUTUAL INS CO	NE	1,102.7
PROTECTIVE INS CO	IN	443.4
TEACHERS INS & ANNUITY ASN OF AM	NY	147,114.8
Weiss Safety Rating: A		
AMERICAN FIDELITY ASR CO	OK	2,382.6
CENTURION LIFE INS CO	MO	1,024.0
GUARDIAN LIFE INS CO OF AMERICA	NY	20,577.2
JEFFERSON-PILOT LIFE INS CO	NC	13,405.5
MASSACHUSETTS MUTUAL LIFE INS CO	MA	80,322.1
NEW YORK LIFE INS CO	NY	87,505.8
NORTHWESTERN MUTUAL LIFE INS CO	WI	114,436.3
SENTRY INS A MUTUAL CO	WI	4,177.1
UNION NATIONAL LIFE INS CO	LA	377.5
Weiss Safety Rating: A-		
ALFA LIFE INS CORP	AL	821.5
ALLSTATE INS CO	IL	40,978.7
ALLSTATE LIFE INS CO	IL	60,033.7
CENTRAL STATES INDEMNITY CO OF OMAHA	NE	243.1
CINCINNATI INS CO	OH	7,143.1
FEDERATED LIFE INS CO	MN	864.3
JOHN HANCOCK LIFE INS CO	MA	73,183.9
MIDLAND NATIONAL LIFE INS CO	IA	10,748.6
MINNESOTA LIFE INS CO	MN	17,352.3
MUTUAL OF OMAHA INS CO	NE	3,755.1
NATIONAL GUARDIAN LIFE INS CO	WI	947.4
OLD REPUBLIC INS CO	PA	1,644.5
PACIFIC LIFE INS CO	CA	54,639.9
PRINCIPAL LIFE INS CO	IA	83,957.6
SENTRY LIFE INS CO	WI	2,101.2
SOUTHERN FARM BUREAU LIFE INS CO	MS	7,776.4
USAA LIFE INS CO	TX	9,167.0
Weiss Safety Rating: B+		
AMERICAN GENERAL LIFE INS CO	TX	24,549.9
AMERICAN HEALTH & LIFE INS CO	TX	1,236.5
AMERITAS LIFE INS CORP	NE	2,417.9
ARKANSAS BLUE CROSS AND BLUE SHIELD	AR	508.1
AVEMCO INS CO	MD	191.7
BALBOA LIFE INS CO	CA	124.5
CITICORP LIFE INS CO	AZ	1,058.7
COLORADO BANKERS LIFE INS CO	CO	113.3
COLUMBUS LIFE INS CO	OH	2,187.1
COMPANION LIFE INS CO	SC	75.6
CUMIS INS SOCIETY INC	WI	826.9
FEDERAL INS CO	IN	18,983.3
FEDERATED MUTUAL INS CO	MN	3,013.6
GOLDEN RULE INS CO	IL	2,076.2
GREAT NORTHERN INS CO	MN	1,088.5
GREAT-WEST LIFE & ANNUITY INS CO	CO	27,323.0
HARTFORD FIRE INS CO	CT	15,857.7
HARTFORD LIFE & ACCIDENT INS CO	CT	8,792.5
HARTFORD LIFE & ANNUITY INS CO	CT	49,622.7
HARTFORD LIFE INS CO	CT	97,564.5
JEFFERSON PILOT FINANCIAL INS CO	NE	11,630.2
LINCOLN BENEFIT LIFE CO	NE	1,823.4
MANUFACTURERS LIFE INS CO USA	MI	53,737.8
MERIT LIFE INS CO	IN	1,020.5
METROPOLITAN LIFE INS CO	NY	220,093.6
METROPOLITAN PROPERTY & CAS INS CO	RI	4,789.1
MIDWEST SECURITY LIFE INS CO	WI	132.8
NATIONAL BENEFIT LIFE INS CO	NY	736.6
NATIONAL CASUALTY CO	WI	92.6
NATIONAL UNION FIRE INS CO OF PITTSB	PA	18,196.9
NATIONWIDE LIFE INS CO	OH	80,569.1
NATIONWIDE MUTUAL FIRE INS CO	OH	3,610.4
PHYSICIANS LIFE INS CO	NE	1,195.8
PRIMERICA LIFE INS CO	MA	5,073.8
SHELTER LIFE INS CO	MO	811.0
SIRIUS AMERICA INS CO	DE	216.8
STATE AUTOMOBILE MUTUAL INS CO	OH	1,299.8
STATE FARM MUTUAL AUTOMOBILE INS CO	IL	70,070.4
SURETY LIFE INS CO	NE	50.3
TRAVELERS INS CO LIFE DEPT	CT	58,317.0
UNITED HEALTHCARE OF ARKANSAS INC	AR	46.4
UNITED INS CO OF AMERICA	IL	2,064.3
UNITED OF OMAHA LIFE INS CO	NE	12,298.3
WESTERN & SOUTHERN LIFE INS CO	OH	7,850.2

IV. Weiss Recommended Companies by State

California

Weiss Safety Rating: A+

INSURANCE COMPANY NAME	DOM. STATE	TOTAL ASSETS ($MIL)
GOVERNMENT EMPLOYEES INS CO	MD	8,737.7
PHYSICIANS MUTUAL INS CO	NE	1,102.7
PROTECTIVE INS CO	IN	443.4
TEACHERS INS & ANNUITY ASN OF AM	NY	147,114.8

Weiss Safety Rating: A

INSURANCE COMPANY NAME	DOM. STATE	TOTAL ASSETS ($MIL)
AMERICAN FIDELITY ASR CO	OK	2,382.6
BLUE CROSS OF CALIFORNIA	CA	4,397.8
CENTURION LIFE INS CO	MO	1,024.0
GUARDIAN LIFE INS CO OF AMERICA	NY	20,577.2
JEFFERSON-PILOT LIFE INS CO	NC	13,405.5
MASSACHUSETTS MUTUAL LIFE INS CO	MA	80,322.1
NEW YORK LIFE INS CO	NY	87,505.8
NORTHWESTERN MUTUAL LIFE INS CO	WI	114,436.3
SENTRY INS A MUTUAL CO	WI	4,177.1

Weiss Safety Rating: A-

INSURANCE COMPANY NAME	DOM. STATE	TOTAL ASSETS ($MIL)
ALLSTATE INS CO	IL	40,978.7
ALLSTATE LIFE INS CO	IL	60,033.7
CALIFORNIA PHYSICIANS SERVICE	CA	2,083.3
CALIFORNIA STATE AUTO ASN INTER-INS	CA	4,180.2
CENTRAL STATES INDEMNITY CO OF OMAHA	NE	243.1
CINCINNATI INS CO	OH	7,143.1
FEDERATED LIFE INS CO	MN	864.3
JOHN HANCOCK LIFE INS CO	MA	73,183.9
MIDLAND NATIONAL LIFE INS CO	IA	10,748.6
MINNESOTA LIFE INS CO	MN	17,352.3
MUTUAL OF OMAHA INS CO	NE	3,755.1
NATIONAL GUARDIAN LIFE INS CO	WI	947.4
OLD REPUBLIC INS CO	PA	1,644.5
PACIFIC LIFE INS CO	CA	54,639.9
PRINCIPAL LIFE INS CO	IA	83,957.6
SENTRY LIFE INS CO	WI	2,101.2
USAA LIFE INS CO	TX	9,167.0

Weiss Safety Rating: B+

INSURANCE COMPANY NAME	DOM. STATE	TOTAL ASSETS ($MIL)
ALLSTATE LIFE INS CO OF NEW YORK	NY	4,816.0
AMERICAN GENERAL LIFE INS CO	TX	24,549.9
AMERICAN HEALTH & LIFE INS CO	TX	1,236.5
AMERITAS LIFE INS CORP	NE	2,417.9
AVEMCO INS CO	MD	191.7
BALBOA LIFE INS CO	CA	124.5
CITICORP LIFE INS CO	AZ	1,058.7
COLORADO BANKERS LIFE INS CO	CO	113.3
COLUMBUS LIFE INS CO	OH	2,187.1
CUMIS INS SOCIETY INC	WI	826.9
FEDERAL INS CO	IN	18,983.3
FEDERATED MUTUAL INS CO	MN	3,013.6
GOLDEN RULE INS CO	IL	2,076.2
GREAT NORTHERN INS CO	MN	1,088.5
GREAT-WEST LIFE & ANNUITY INS CO	CO	27,323.0
HARTFORD FIRE INS CO	CT	15,857.7
HARTFORD LIFE & ACCIDENT INS CO	CT	8,792.5
HARTFORD LIFE & ANNUITY INS CO	CT	49,622.7
HARTFORD LIFE INS CO	CT	97,564.5
HEALTH NET	CA	1,245.5
HEALTH PLAN OF SAN JOAQUIN	CA	50.2
JEFFERSON PILOT FINANCIAL INS CO	NE	11,630.2
LINCOLN BENEFIT LIFE CO	NE	1,823.4
MANUFACTURERS LIFE INS CO USA	MI	53,737.8
MERIT LIFE INS CO	IN	1,020.5
METROPOLITAN LIFE INS CO	NY	220,093.6
NATIONAL BENEFIT LIFE INS CO	NY	736.6
NATIONAL CASUALTY CO	WI	92.6
NATIONAL UNION FIRE INS CO OF PITTSB	PA	18,196.9
NATIONWIDE LIFE INS CO	OH	80,569.1
NATIONWIDE MUTUAL FIRE INS CO	OH	3,610.4
PACIFIC GUARDIAN LIFE INS CO LTD	HI	431.5
PHYSICIANS LIFE INS CO	NE	1,195.8
PRIMERICA LIFE INS CO	MA	5,073.8
SIRIUS AMERICA INS CO	DE	216.8
STATE FARM MUTUAL AUTOMOBILE INS CO	IL	70,070.4
SURETY LIFE INS CO	NE	50.3
TRAVELERS INS CO LIFE DEPT	CT	58,317.0
UNITED INS CO OF AMERICA	IL	2,064.3
UNITED OF OMAHA LIFE INS CO	NE	12,298.3
WESTERN & SOUTHERN LIFE INS CO	OH	7,850.2

Colorado

INSURANCE COMPANY NAME	DOM. STATE	TOTAL ASSETS ($MIL)
Weiss Safety Rating: A+		
COUNTRY LIFE INS CO	IL	4,387.5
GOVERNMENT EMPLOYEES INS CO	MD	8,737.7
PHYSICIANS MUTUAL INS CO	NE	1,102.7
PROTECTIVE INS CO	IN	443.4
TEACHERS INS & ANNUITY ASN OF AM	NY	147,114.8
Weiss Safety Rating: A		
AMERICAN FIDELITY ASR CO	OK	2,382.6
AUTO-OWNERS INS CO	MI	6,582.7
CENTURION LIFE INS CO	MO	1,024.0
GUARDIAN LIFE INS CO OF AMERICA	NY	20,577.2
JEFFERSON-PILOT LIFE INS CO	NC	13,405.5
MASSACHUSETTS MUTUAL LIFE INS CO	MA	80,322.1
NEW YORK LIFE INS CO	NY	87,505.8
NORTHWESTERN MUTUAL LIFE INS CO	WI	114,436.3
SENTRY INS A MUTUAL CO	WI	4,177.1
Weiss Safety Rating: A-		
ALLSTATE INS CO	IL	40,978.7
ALLSTATE LIFE INS CO	IL	60,033.7
AUTO-OWNERS LIFE INS CO	MI	1,251.5
CENTRAL STATES INDEMNITY CO OF OMAHA	NE	243.1
CINCINNATI INS CO	OH	7,143.1
FARM BUREAU LIFE INS CO	IA	4,695.3
FEDERATED LIFE INS CO	MN	864.3
JOHN HANCOCK LIFE INS CO	MA	73,183.9
MIDLAND NATIONAL LIFE INS CO	IA	10,748.6
MINNESOTA LIFE INS CO	MN	17,352.3
MUTUAL OF OMAHA INS CO	NE	3,755.1
NATIONAL GUARDIAN LIFE INS CO	WI	947.4
OLD REPUBLIC INS CO	PA	1,644.5
PACIFIC LIFE INS CO	CA	54,639.9
PRINCIPAL LIFE INS CO	IA	83,957.6
SENTRY LIFE INS CO	WI	2,101.2
USAA LIFE INS CO	TX	9,167.0
Weiss Safety Rating: B+		
AMERICAN GENERAL LIFE INS CO	TX	24,549.9
AMERICAN HEALTH & LIFE INS CO	TX	1,236.5
AMERITAS LIFE INS CORP	NE	2,417.9
AVEMCO INS CO	MD	191.7
BALBOA LIFE INS CO	CA	124.5
CITICORP LIFE INS CO	AZ	1,058.7
COLORADO BANKERS LIFE INS CO	CO	113.3
COLUMBUS LIFE INS CO	OH	2,187.1
COMPANION LIFE INS CO	SC	75.6
CUMIS INS SOCIETY INC	WI	826.9
FEDERAL INS CO	IN	18,983.3
FEDERATED MUTUAL INS CO	MN	3,013.6
GOLDEN RULE INS CO	IL	2,076.2
GREAT NORTHERN INS CO	MN	1,088.5
GREAT-WEST LIFE & ANNUITY INS CO	CO	27,323.0

INSURANCE COMPANY NAME	DOM. STATE	TOTAL ASSETS ($MIL)
HARTFORD FIRE INS CO	CT	15,857.7
HARTFORD LIFE & ACCIDENT INS CO	CT	8,792.5
HARTFORD LIFE & ANNUITY INS CO	CT	49,622.7
HARTFORD LIFE INS CO	CT	97,564.5
JEFFERSON PILOT FINANCIAL INS CO	NE	11,630.2
LINCOLN BENEFIT LIFE CO	NE	1,823.4
MANUFACTURERS LIFE INS CO USA	MI	53,737.8
MERIT LIFE INS CO	IN	1,020.5
METROPOLITAN LIFE INS CO	NY	220,093.6
METROPOLITAN PROPERTY & CAS INS CO	RI	4,789.1
MIDWEST SECURITY LIFE INS CO	WI	132.8
NATIONAL BENEFIT LIFE INS CO	NY	736.6
NATIONAL CASUALTY CO	WI	92.6
NATIONAL UNION FIRE INS CO OF PITTSB	PA	18,196.9
NATIONWIDE LIFE INS CO	OH	80,569.1
NATIONWIDE MUTUAL FIRE INS CO	OH	3,610.4
PACIFIC GUARDIAN LIFE INS CO LTD	HI	431.5
PHYSICIANS LIFE INS CO	NE	1,195.8
PRIMERICA LIFE INS CO	MA	5,073.8
SHELTER LIFE INS CO	MO	811.0
SIRIUS AMERICA INS CO	DE	216.8
STATE AUTOMOBILE MUTUAL INS CO	OH	1,299.8
STATE FARM MUTUAL AUTOMOBILE INS CO	IL	70,070.4
SURETY LIFE INS CO	NE	50.3
TRAVELERS INS CO LIFE DEPT	CT	58,317.0
UNITED INS CO OF AMERICA	IL	2,064.3
UNITED OF OMAHA LIFE INS CO	NE	12,298.3
WESTERN & SOUTHERN LIFE INS CO	OH	7,850.2

Connecticut

Weiss Safety Rating: A+

INSURANCE COMPANY NAME	DOM. STATE	TOTAL ASSETS ($MIL)
COUNTRY LIFE INS CO	IL	4,387.5
GOVERNMENT EMPLOYEES INS CO	MD	8,737.7
PHYSICIANS MUTUAL INS CO	NE	1,102.7
PROTECTIVE INS CO	IN	443.4
TEACHERS INS & ANNUITY ASN OF AM	NY	147,114.8

Weiss Safety Rating: A

INSURANCE COMPANY NAME	DOM. STATE	TOTAL ASSETS ($MIL)
ALFA MUTUAL INS CO	AL	1,151.8
AMERICAN FIDELITY ASR CO	OK	2,382.6
CENTURION LIFE INS CO	MO	1,024.0
GUARDIAN LIFE INS CO OF AMERICA	NY	20,577.2
JEFFERSON-PILOT LIFE INS CO	NC	13,405.5
MASSACHUSETTS MUTUAL LIFE INS CO	MA	80,322.1
NEW YORK LIFE INS CO	NY	87,505.8
NORTHWESTERN MUTUAL LIFE INS CO	WI	114,436.3
SENTRY INS A MUTUAL CO	WI	4,177.1

Weiss Safety Rating: A-

INSURANCE COMPANY NAME	DOM. STATE	TOTAL ASSETS ($MIL)
ALLSTATE INS CO	IL	40,978.7
ALLSTATE LIFE INS CO	IL	60,033.7
CENTRAL STATES INDEMNITY CO OF OMAHA	NE	243.1
CINCINNATI INS CO	OH	7,143.1
FEDERATED LIFE INS CO	MN	864.3
JOHN HANCOCK LIFE INS CO	MA	73,183.9
MIDLAND NATIONAL LIFE INS CO	IA	10,748.6
MINNESOTA LIFE INS CO	MN	17,352.3
MUTUAL OF OMAHA INS CO	NE	3,755.1
NATIONAL GUARDIAN LIFE INS CO	WI	947.4
OLD REPUBLIC INS CO	PA	1,644.5
PACIFIC LIFE INS CO	CA	54,639.9
PRINCIPAL LIFE INS CO	IA	83,957.6
SENTRY LIFE INS CO	WI	2,101.2
USAA LIFE INS CO	TX	9,167.0

Weiss Safety Rating: B+

INSURANCE COMPANY NAME	DOM. STATE	TOTAL ASSETS ($MIL)
AMERICAN GENERAL LIFE INS CO	TX	24,549.9
AMERICAN HEALTH & LIFE INS CO	TX	1,236.5
AMERITAS LIFE INS CORP	NE	2,417.9
AVEMCO INS CO	MD	191.7
BALBOA LIFE INS CO	CA	124.5
CITICORP LIFE INS CO	AZ	1,058.7
COLORADO BANKERS LIFE INS CO	CO	113.3
COLUMBUS LIFE INS CO	OH	2,187.1
CONNECTICARE INC	CT	156.2
CUMIS INS SOCIETY INC	WI	826.9
FARM FAMILY LIFE INS CO	NY	889.2
FEDERAL INS CO	IN	18,983.3
FEDERATED MUTUAL INS CO	MN	3,013.6
GOLDEN RULE INS CO	IL	2,076.2
GREAT NORTHERN INS CO	MN	1,088.5
GREAT-WEST LIFE & ANNUITY INS CO	CO	27,323.0
HARTFORD FIRE INS CO	CT	15,857.7
HARTFORD LIFE & ACCIDENT INS CO	CT	8,792.5
HARTFORD LIFE & ANNUITY INS CO	CT	49,622.7
HARTFORD LIFE INS CO	CT	97,564.5
JEFFERSON PILOT FINANCIAL INS CO	NE	11,630.2
LINCOLN BENEFIT LIFE CO	NE	1,823.4
MANUFACTURERS LIFE INS CO USA	MI	53,737.8
MERIT LIFE INS CO	IN	1,020.5
METROPOLITAN LIFE INS CO	NY	220,093.6
METROPOLITAN PROPERTY & CAS INS CO	RI	4,789.1
NATIONAL BENEFIT LIFE INS CO	NY	736.6
NATIONAL CASUALTY CO	WI	92.6
NATIONAL UNION FIRE INS CO OF PITTSB	PA	18,196.9
NATIONWIDE LIFE INS CO	OH	80,569.1
NATIONWIDE MUTUAL FIRE INS CO	OH	3,610.4
PHYSICIANS LIFE INS CO	NE	1,195.8
PRIMERICA LIFE INS CO	MA	5,073.8
SAVINGS BANK LIFE INS CO OF MA	MA	1,548.3
SIRIUS AMERICA INS CO	DE	216.8
STATE FARM MUTUAL AUTOMOBILE INS CO	IL	70,070.4
SURETY LIFE INS CO	NE	50.3
TRAVELERS INS CO LIFE DEPT	CT	58,317.0
UNITED INS CO OF AMERICA	IL	2,064.3
UNITED OF OMAHA LIFE INS CO	NE	12,298.3

Delaware

INSURANCE COMPANY NAME	DOM. STATE	TOTAL ASSETS ($MIL)
Weiss Safety Rating: A+		
COUNTRY LIFE INS CO	IL	4,387.5
GOVERNMENT EMPLOYEES INS CO	MD	8,737.7
PHYSICIANS MUTUAL INS CO	NE	1,102.7
PROTECTIVE INS CO	IN	443.4
TEACHERS INS & ANNUITY ASN OF AM	NY	147,114.8
Weiss Safety Rating: A		
AMERICAN FIDELITY ASR CO	OK	2,382.6
CENTURION LIFE INS CO	MO	1,024.0
GUARDIAN LIFE INS CO OF AMERICA	NY	20,577.2
JEFFERSON-PILOT LIFE INS CO	NC	13,405.5
MASSACHUSETTS MUTUAL LIFE INS CO	MA	80,322.1
NEW YORK LIFE INS CO	NY	87,505.8
NORTHWESTERN MUTUAL LIFE INS CO	WI	114,436.3
SENTRY INS A MUTUAL CO	WI	4,177.1
Weiss Safety Rating: A-		
ALLSTATE INS CO	IL	40,978.7
ALLSTATE LIFE INS CO	IL	60,033.7
CENTRAL STATES INDEMNITY CO OF OMAHA	NE	243.1
CINCINNATI INS CO	OH	7,143.1
FEDERATED LIFE INS CO	MN	864.3
JOHN HANCOCK LIFE INS CO	MA	73,183.9
MIDLAND NATIONAL LIFE INS CO	IA	10,748.6
MINNESOTA LIFE INS CO	MN	17,352.3
MUTUAL OF OMAHA INS CO	NE	3,755.1
NATIONAL GUARDIAN LIFE INS CO	WI	947.4
OLD REPUBLIC INS CO	PA	1,644.5
PACIFIC LIFE INS CO	CA	54,639.9
PRINCIPAL LIFE INS CO	IA	83,957.6
SENTRY LIFE INS CO	WI	2,101.2
USAA LIFE INS CO	TX	9,167.0
Weiss Safety Rating: B+		
ALLSTATE LIFE INS CO OF NEW YORK	NY	4,816.0
AMERICAN GENERAL LIFE INS CO	TX	24,549.9
AMERICAN HEALTH & LIFE INS CO	TX	1,236.5
AMERITAS LIFE INS CORP	NE	2,417.9
AVEMCO INS CO	MD	191.7
BALBOA LIFE INS CO	CA	124.5
BLUE CROSS BLUE SHIELD OF DELAWARE	DE	206.6
CITICORP LIFE INS CO	AZ	1,058.7
COLORADO BANKERS LIFE INS CO	CO	113.3
COLUMBUS LIFE INS CO	OH	2,187.1
COMPANION LIFE INS CO	SC	75.6
CUMIS INS SOCIETY INC	WI	826.9
FARM FAMILY LIFE INS CO	NY	889.2
FEDERAL INS CO	IN	18,983.3
FEDERATED MUTUAL INS CO	MN	3,013.6
GOLDEN RULE INS CO	IL	2,076.2
GREAT NORTHERN INS CO	MN	1,088.5
GREAT-WEST LIFE & ANNUITY INS CO	CO	27,323.0
HARTFORD FIRE INS CO	CT	15,857.7
HARTFORD LIFE & ACCIDENT INS CO	CT	8,792.5
HARTFORD LIFE & ANNUITY INS CO	CT	49,622.7
HARTFORD LIFE INS CO	CT	97,564.5
JEFFERSON PILOT FINANCIAL INS CO	NE	11,630.2
LINCOLN BENEFIT LIFE CO	NE	1,823.4
MANUFACTURERS LIFE INS CO USA	MI	53,737.8
MD INDIVIDUAL PRACTICE ASSOC INC	MD	113.6
MERIT LIFE INS CO	IN	1,020.5
METROPOLITAN LIFE INS CO	NY	220,093.6
METROPOLITAN PROPERTY & CAS INS CO	RI	4,789.1
MIDWEST SECURITY LIFE INS CO	WI	132.8
NATIONAL BENEFIT LIFE INS CO	NY	736.6
NATIONAL CASUALTY CO	WI	92.6
NATIONAL UNION FIRE INS CO OF PITTSB	PA	18,196.9
NATIONWIDE LIFE INS CO	OH	80,569.1
NATIONWIDE MUTUAL FIRE INS CO	OH	3,610.4
PHYSICIANS LIFE INS CO	NE	1,195.8
PRIMERICA LIFE INS CO	MA	5,073.8
SIRIUS AMERICA INS CO	DE	216.8
STATE FARM MUTUAL AUTOMOBILE INS CO	IL	70,070.4
SURETY LIFE INS CO	NE	50.3
TRAVELERS INS CO LIFE DEPT	CT	58,317.0
UNITED INS CO OF AMERICA	IL	2,064.3
UNITED OF OMAHA LIFE INS CO	NE	12,298.3
WESTERN & SOUTHERN LIFE INS CO	OH	7,850.2

IV. Weiss Recommended Companies by State

District of Columbia

Weiss Safety Rating: A+

INSURANCE COMPANY NAME	DOM. STATE	TOTAL ASSETS ($MIL)
GOVERNMENT EMPLOYEES INS CO	MD	8,737.7
PHYSICIANS MUTUAL INS CO	NE	1,102.7
PROTECTIVE INS CO	IN	443.4
TEACHERS INS & ANNUITY ASN OF AM	NY	147,114.8

Weiss Safety Rating: A

INSURANCE COMPANY NAME	DOM. STATE	TOTAL ASSETS ($MIL)
AMERICAN FIDELITY ASR CO	OK	2,382.6
CENTURION LIFE INS CO	MO	1,024.0
GROUP HOSP & MEDICAL SERVICES INC	DC	1,141.0
GUARDIAN LIFE INS CO OF AMERICA	NY	20,577.2
JEFFERSON-PILOT LIFE INS CO	NC	13,405.5
MASSACHUSETTS MUTUAL LIFE INS CO	MA	80,322.1
NEW YORK LIFE INS CO	NY	87,505.8
NORTHWESTERN MUTUAL LIFE INS CO	WI	114,436.3
SENTRY INS A MUTUAL CO	WI	4,177.1

Weiss Safety Rating: A-

INSURANCE COMPANY NAME	DOM. STATE	TOTAL ASSETS ($MIL)
ALLSTATE INS CO	IL	40,978.7
ALLSTATE LIFE INS CO	IL	60,033.7
CAREFIRST BLUECHOICE INC	DC	261.2
CENTRAL STATES INDEMNITY CO OF OMAHA	NE	243.1
CINCINNATI INS CO	OH	7,143.1
JOHN HANCOCK LIFE INS CO	MA	73,183.9
MIDLAND NATIONAL LIFE INS CO	IA	10,748.6
MINNESOTA LIFE INS CO	MN	17,352.3
MUTUAL OF OMAHA INS CO	NE	3,755.1
NATIONAL GUARDIAN LIFE INS CO	WI	947.4
OLD REPUBLIC INS CO	PA	1,644.5
PACIFIC LIFE INS CO	CA	54,639.9
PRINCIPAL LIFE INS CO	IA	83,957.6
SENTRY LIFE INS CO	WI	2,101.2
USAA LIFE INS CO	TX	9,167.0

Weiss Safety Rating: B+

INSURANCE COMPANY NAME	DOM. STATE	TOTAL ASSETS ($MIL)
ALLSTATE LIFE INS CO OF NEW YORK	NY	4,816.0
AMERICAN GENERAL LIFE INS CO	TX	24,549.9
AMERICAN HEALTH & LIFE INS CO	TX	1,236.5
AMERITAS LIFE INS CORP	NE	2,417.9
AVEMCO INS CO	MD	191.7
BALBOA LIFE INS CO	CA	124.5
CITICORP LIFE INS CO	AZ	1,058.7
COLORADO BANKERS LIFE INS CO	CO	113.3
COLUMBUS LIFE INS CO	OH	2,187.1
COMPANION LIFE INS CO	SC	75.6
CUMIS INS SOCIETY INC	WI	826.9
FEDERAL INS CO	IN	18,983.3
FEDERATED MUTUAL INS CO	MN	3,013.6
GOLDEN RULE INS CO	IL	2,076.2
GREAT NORTHERN INS CO	MN	1,088.5
GREAT-WEST LIFE & ANNUITY INS CO	CO	27,323.0
HARTFORD FIRE INS CO	CT	15,857.7
HARTFORD LIFE & ACCIDENT INS CO	CT	8,792.5
HARTFORD LIFE & ANNUITY INS CO	CT	49,622.7
HARTFORD LIFE INS CO	CT	97,564.5
JEFFERSON PILOT FINANCIAL INS CO	NE	11,630.2
LINCOLN BENEFIT LIFE CO	NE	1,823.4
MANUFACTURERS LIFE INS CO USA	MI	53,737.8
MD INDIVIDUAL PRACTICE ASSOC INC	MD	113.6
MERIT LIFE INS CO	IN	1,020.5
METROPOLITAN LIFE INS CO	NY	220,093.6
METROPOLITAN PROPERTY & CAS INS CO	RI	4,789.1
NATIONAL BENEFIT LIFE INS CO	NY	736.6
NATIONAL CASUALTY CO	WI	92.6
NATIONAL UNION FIRE INS CO OF PITTSB	PA	18,196.9
NATIONWIDE LIFE INS CO	OH	80,569.1
NATIONWIDE MUTUAL FIRE INS CO	OH	3,610.4
PHYSICIANS LIFE INS CO	NE	1,195.8
PRIMERICA LIFE INS CO	MA	5,073.8
SAVINGS BANK LIFE INS CO OF MA	MA	1,548.3
SIRIUS AMERICA INS CO	DE	216.8
STATE AUTOMOBILE MUTUAL INS CO	OH	1,299.8
STATE FARM MUTUAL AUTOMOBILE INS CO	IL	70,070.4
SURETY LIFE INS CO	NE	50.3
TRAVELERS INS CO LIFE DEPT	CT	58,317.0
UNITED INS CO OF AMERICA	IL	2,064.3
UNITED OF OMAHA LIFE INS CO	NE	12,298.3
WESTERN & SOUTHERN LIFE INS CO	OH	7,850.2

Florida

INSURANCE COMPANY NAME	DOM. STATE	TOTAL ASSETS ($MIL)
Weiss Safety Rating: A+		
GOVERNMENT EMPLOYEES INS CO	MD	8,737.7
PHYSICIANS MUTUAL INS CO	NE	1,102.7
PROTECTIVE INS CO	IN	443.4
TEACHERS INS & ANNUITY ASN OF AM	NY	147,114.8
Weiss Safety Rating: A		
ALFA MUTUAL INS CO	AL	1,151.8
AMERICAN FIDELITY ASR CO	OK	2,382.6
AUTO-OWNERS INS CO	MI	6,582.7
CENTURION LIFE INS CO	MO	1,024.0
GUARDIAN LIFE INS CO OF AMERICA	NY	20,577.2
JEFFERSON-PILOT LIFE INS CO	NC	13,405.5
MASSACHUSETTS MUTUAL LIFE INS CO	MA	80,322.1
NEW YORK LIFE INS CO	NY	87,505.8
NORTHWESTERN MUTUAL LIFE INS CO	WI	114,436.3
SENTRY INS A MUTUAL CO	WI	4,177.1
UNION NATIONAL LIFE INS CO	LA	377.5
Weiss Safety Rating: A-		
ALFA LIFE INS CORP	AL	821.5
ALLSTATE INS CO	IL	40,978.7
ALLSTATE LIFE INS CO	IL	60,033.7
AUTO-OWNERS LIFE INS CO	MI	1,251.5
CENTRAL STATES INDEMNITY CO OF OMAHA	NE	243.1
CINCINNATI INS CO	OH	7,143.1
FEDERATED LIFE INS CO	MN	864.3
HEALTHY PALM BEACHES INC	FL	3.7
JOHN HANCOCK LIFE INS CO	MA	73,183.9
MIDLAND NATIONAL LIFE INS CO	IA	10,748.6
MINNESOTA LIFE INS CO	MN	17,352.3
MUTUAL OF OMAHA INS CO	NE	3,755.1
NATIONAL GUARDIAN LIFE INS CO	WI	947.4
OLD REPUBLIC INS CO	PA	1,644.5
PACIFIC LIFE INS CO	CA	54,639.9
PRINCIPAL LIFE INS CO	IA	83,957.6
SENTRY LIFE INS CO	WI	2,101.2
SOUTHERN FARM BUREAU LIFE INS CO	MS	7,776.4
USAA LIFE INS CO	TX	9,167.0
Weiss Safety Rating: B+		
AMERICAN GENERAL LIFE INS CO	TX	24,549.9
AMERICAN HEALTH & LIFE INS CO	TX	1,236.5
AMERITAS LIFE INS CORP	NE	2,417.9
AVEMCO INS CO	MD	191.7
BALBOA LIFE INS CO	CA	124.5
BLUE CROSS BLUE SHIELD OF FLORIDA	FL	2,530.3
CITICORP LIFE INS CO	AZ	1,058.7
COLORADO BANKERS LIFE INS CO	CO	113.3
COLUMBUS LIFE INS CO	OH	2,187.1
COMPANION LIFE INS CO	SC	75.6
CUMIS INS SOCIETY INC	WI	826.9
FEDERAL INS CO	IN	18,983.3
FEDERATED MUTUAL INS CO	MN	3,013.6
GOLDEN RULE INS CO	IL	2,076.2
GREAT NORTHERN INS CO	MN	1,088.5
GREAT-WEST LIFE & ANNUITY INS CO	CO	27,323.0
HARTFORD FIRE INS CO	CT	15,857.7
HARTFORD LIFE & ACCIDENT INS CO	CT	8,792.5
HARTFORD LIFE & ANNUITY INS CO	CT	49,622.7
HARTFORD LIFE INS CO	CT	97,564.5
HEALTH OPTIONS INC	FL	914.9
JEFFERSON PILOT FINANCIAL INS CO	NE	11,630.2
LINCOLN BENEFIT LIFE CO	NE	1,823.4
MANUFACTURERS LIFE INS CO USA	MI	53,737.8
MERIT LIFE INS CO	IN	1,020.5
METROPOLITAN LIFE INS CO	NY	220,093.6
METROPOLITAN PROPERTY & CAS INS CO	RI	4,789.1
NATIONAL BENEFIT LIFE INS CO	NY	736.6
NATIONAL CASUALTY CO	WI	92.6
NATIONAL UNION FIRE INS CO OF PITTSB	PA	18,196.9
NATIONWIDE LIFE INS CO	OH	80,569.1
NATIONWIDE MUTUAL FIRE INS CO	OH	3,610.4
PHYSICIANS LIFE INS CO	NE	1,195.8
PRIMERICA LIFE INS CO	MA	5,073.8
SIRIUS AMERICA INS CO	DE	216.8
STATE AUTOMOBILE MUTUAL INS CO	OH	1,299.8
STATE FARM MUTUAL AUTOMOBILE INS CO	IL	70,070.4
SURETY LIFE INS CO	NE	50.3
TRAVELERS INS CO LIFE DEPT	CT	58,317.0
UNITED INS CO OF AMERICA	IL	2,064.3
UNITED OF OMAHA LIFE INS CO	NE	12,298.3
WESTERN & SOUTHERN LIFE INS CO	OH	7,850.2

Georgia

INSURANCE COMPANY NAME	DOM. STATE	TOTAL ASSETS ($MIL)
Weiss Safety Rating: A+		
GOVERNMENT EMPLOYEES INS CO	MD	8,737.7
PHYSICIANS MUTUAL INS CO	NE	1,102.7
PROTECTIVE INS CO	IN	443.4
TEACHERS INS & ANNUITY ASN OF AM	NY	147,114.8
Weiss Safety Rating: A		
ALFA MUTUAL INS CO	AL	1,151.8
AMERICAN FIDELITY ASR CO	OK	2,382.6
AUTO-OWNERS INS CO	MI	6,582.7
BLUE CROSS BLUE SHIELD HEALTHCARE GA	GA	255.4
BLUE CROSS BLUE SHIELD OF GEORGIA	GA	798.7
CENTURION LIFE INS CO	MO	1,024.0
GEORGIA FARM BUREAU MUTUAL INS CO	GA	642.5
GUARDIAN LIFE INS CO OF AMERICA	NY	20,577.2
JEFFERSON-PILOT LIFE INS CO	NC	13,405.5
MASSACHUSETTS MUTUAL LIFE INS CO	MA	80,322.1
NEW YORK LIFE INS CO	NY	87,505.8
NORTHWESTERN MUTUAL LIFE INS CO	WI	114,436.3
SENTRY INS A MUTUAL CO	WI	4,177.1
UNION NATIONAL LIFE INS CO	LA	377.5
Weiss Safety Rating: A-		
ALFA LIFE INS CORP	AL	821.5
ALLSTATE INS CO	IL	40,978.7
ALLSTATE LIFE INS CO	IL	60,033.7
AUTO-OWNERS LIFE INS CO	MI	1,251.5
CENTRAL STATES INDEMNITY CO OF OMAHA	NE	243.1
CINCINNATI INS CO	OH	7,143.1
FEDERATED LIFE INS CO	MN	864.3
GRANGE MUTUAL CAS CO	OH	1,116.1
JOHN HANCOCK LIFE INS CO	MA	73,183.9
MIDLAND NATIONAL LIFE INS CO	IA	10,748.6
MINNESOTA LIFE INS CO	MN	17,352.3
MUTUAL OF OMAHA INS CO	NE	3,755.1
NATIONAL GUARDIAN LIFE INS CO	WI	947.4
OLD REPUBLIC INS CO	PA	1,644.5
PACIFIC LIFE INS CO	CA	54,639.9
PRINCIPAL LIFE INS CO	IA	83,957.6
SENTRY LIFE INS CO	WI	2,101.2
SOUTHERN FARM BUREAU LIFE INS CO	MS	7,776.4
USAA LIFE INS CO	TX	9,167.0
Weiss Safety Rating: B+		
AMERICAN GENERAL LIFE INS CO	TX	24,549.9
AMERICAN HEALTH & LIFE INS CO	TX	1,236.5
AMERITAS LIFE INS CORP	NE	2,417.9
AVEMCO INS CO	MD	191.7
BALBOA LIFE INS CO	CA	124.5
CITICORP LIFE INS CO	AZ	1,058.7
COLORADO BANKERS LIFE INS CO	CO	113.3
COLUMBUS LIFE INS CO	OH	2,187.1
COMPANION LIFE INS CO	SC	75.6

INSURANCE COMPANY NAME	DOM. STATE	TOTAL ASSETS ($MIL)
CUMIS INS SOCIETY INC	WI	826.9
FEDERAL INS CO	IN	18,983.3
FEDERATED MUTUAL INS CO	MN	3,013.6
GOLDEN RULE INS CO	IL	2,076.2
GRANGE LIFE INS CO	OH	159.8
GREAT NORTHERN INS CO	MN	1,088.5
GREAT-WEST LIFE & ANNUITY INS CO	CO	27,323.0
HARTFORD FIRE INS CO	CT	15,857.7
HARTFORD LIFE & ACCIDENT INS CO	CT	8,792.5
HARTFORD LIFE & ANNUITY INS CO	CT	49,622.7
HARTFORD LIFE INS CO	CT	97,564.5
JEFFERSON PILOT FINANCIAL INS CO	NE	11,630.2
LINCOLN BENEFIT LIFE CO	NE	1,823.4
MANUFACTURERS LIFE INS CO USA	MI	53,737.8
MERIT LIFE INS CO	IN	1,020.5
METROPOLITAN LIFE INS CO	NY	220,093.6
METROPOLITAN PROPERTY & CAS INS CO	RI	4,789.1
NATIONAL BENEFIT LIFE INS CO	NY	736.6
NATIONAL CASUALTY CO	WI	92.6
NATIONAL UNION FIRE INS CO OF PITTSB	PA	18,196.9
NATIONWIDE LIFE INS CO	OH	80,569.1
NATIONWIDE MUTUAL FIRE INS CO	OH	3,610.4
PHYSICIANS LIFE INS CO	NE	1,195.8
PRIMERICA LIFE INS CO	MA	5,073.8
SIRIUS AMERICA INS CO	DE	216.8
STATE AUTOMOBILE MUTUAL INS CO	OH	1,299.8
STATE FARM MUTUAL AUTOMOBILE INS CO	IL	70,070.4
SURETY LIFE INS CO	NE	50.3
TRAVELERS INS CO LIFE DEPT	CT	58,317.0
UNITED INS CO OF AMERICA	IL	2,064.3
UNITED OF OMAHA LIFE INS CO	NE	12,298.3
WESTERN & SOUTHERN LIFE INS CO	OH	7,850.2

Hawaii

INSURANCE COMPANY NAME	DOM. STATE	TOTAL ASSETS ($MIL)
Weiss Safety Rating: A+		
GOVERNMENT EMPLOYEES INS CO	MD	8,737.7
PHYSICIANS MUTUAL INS CO	NE	1,102.7
PROTECTIVE INS CO	IN	443.4
TEACHERS INS & ANNUITY ASN OF AM	NY	147,114.8
Weiss Safety Rating: A		
AMERICAN FIDELITY ASR CO	OK	2,382.6
CENTURION LIFE INS CO	MO	1,024.0
GUARDIAN LIFE INS CO OF AMERICA	NY	20,577.2
JEFFERSON-PILOT LIFE INS CO	NC	13,405.5
MASSACHUSETTS MUTUAL LIFE INS CO	MA	80,322.1
NEW YORK LIFE INS CO	NY	87,505.8
NORTHWESTERN MUTUAL LIFE INS CO	WI	114,436.3
SENTRY INS A MUTUAL CO	WI	4,177.1
Weiss Safety Rating: A-		
ALLSTATE INS CO	IL	40,978.7
ALLSTATE LIFE INS CO	IL	60,033.7
CENTRAL STATES INDEMNITY CO OF OMAHA	NE	243.1
CINCINNATI INS CO	OH	7,143.1
JOHN HANCOCK LIFE INS CO	MA	73,183.9
MIDLAND NATIONAL LIFE INS CO	IA	10,748.6
MINNESOTA LIFE INS CO	MN	17,352.3
MUTUAL OF OMAHA INS CO	NE	3,755.1
NATIONAL GUARDIAN LIFE INS CO	WI	947.4
OLD REPUBLIC INS CO	PA	1,644.5
PACIFIC LIFE INS CO	CA	54,639.9
PRINCIPAL LIFE INS CO	IA	83,957.6
SENTRY LIFE INS CO	WI	2,101.2
USAA LIFE INS CO	TX	9,167.0
Weiss Safety Rating: B+		
ALOHACARE	HI	33.5
AMERICAN GENERAL LIFE INS CO	TX	24,549.9
AMERICAN HEALTH & LIFE INS CO	TX	1,236.5
AMERITAS LIFE INS CORP	NE	2,417.9
AVEMCO INS CO	MD	191.7
BALBOA LIFE INS CO	CA	124.5
CITICORP LIFE INS CO	AZ	1,058.7
COLORADO BANKERS LIFE INS CO	CO	113.3
CUMIS INS SOCIETY INC	WI	826.9
FEDERAL INS CO	IN	18,983.3
GOLDEN RULE INS CO	IL	2,076.2
GREAT NORTHERN INS CO	MN	1,088.5
GREAT-WEST LIFE & ANNUITY INS CO	CO	27,323.0
HARTFORD FIRE INS CO	CT	15,857.7
HARTFORD LIFE & ACCIDENT INS CO	CT	8,792.5
HARTFORD LIFE & ANNUITY INS CO	CT	49,622.7
HARTFORD LIFE INS CO	CT	97,564.5
JEFFERSON PILOT FINANCIAL INS CO	NE	11,630.2
LINCOLN BENEFIT LIFE CO	NE	1,823.4
MANUFACTURERS LIFE INS CO USA	MI	53,737.8
MERIT LIFE INS CO	IN	1,020.5
METROPOLITAN LIFE INS CO	NY	220,093.6
METROPOLITAN PROPERTY & CAS INS CO	RI	4,789.1
NATIONAL BENEFIT LIFE INS CO	NY	736.6
NATIONAL CASUALTY CO	WI	92.6
NATIONAL UNION FIRE INS CO OF PITTSB	PA	18,196.9
NATIONWIDE LIFE INS CO	OH	80,569.1
NATIONWIDE MUTUAL FIRE INS CO	OH	3,610.4
PACIFIC GUARDIAN LIFE INS CO LTD	HI	431.5
PHYSICIANS LIFE INS CO	NE	1,195.8
PRIMERICA LIFE INS CO	MA	5,073.8
SIRIUS AMERICA INS CO	DE	216.8
STATE FARM MUTUAL AUTOMOBILE INS CO	IL	70,070.4
SURETY LIFE INS CO	NE	50.3
TRAVELERS INS CO LIFE DEPT	CT	58,317.0
UNITED INS CO OF AMERICA	IL	2,064.3
UNITED OF OMAHA LIFE INS CO	NE	12,298.3
WESTERN & SOUTHERN LIFE INS CO	OH	7,850.2

IV. Weiss Recommended Companies by State

Winter 2003 - 04

Idaho

INSURANCE COMPANY NAME	DOM. STATE	TOTAL ASSETS ($MIL)
Weiss Safety Rating: A+		
COUNTRY LIFE INS CO	IL	4,387.5
GOVERNMENT EMPLOYEES INS CO	MD	8,737.7
PHYSICIANS MUTUAL INS CO	NE	1,102.7
PROTECTIVE INS CO	IN	443.4
TEACHERS INS & ANNUITY ASN OF AM	NY	147,114.8
Weiss Safety Rating: A		
AMERICAN FIDELITY ASR CO	OK	2,382.6
CENTURION LIFE INS CO	MO	1,024.0
GUARDIAN LIFE INS CO OF AMERICA	NY	20,577.2
JEFFERSON-PILOT LIFE INS CO	NC	13,405.5
MASSACHUSETTS MUTUAL LIFE INS CO	MA	80,322.1
NEW YORK LIFE INS CO	NY	87,505.8
NORTHWESTERN MUTUAL LIFE INS CO	WI	114,436.3
SENTRY INS A MUTUAL CO	WI	4,177.1
Weiss Safety Rating: A-		
ALLSTATE INS CO	IL	40,978.7
ALLSTATE LIFE INS CO	IL	60,033.7
CENTRAL STATES INDEMNITY CO OF OMAHA	NE	243.1
CINCINNATI INS CO	OH	7,143.1
FARM BUREAU LIFE INS CO	IA	4,695.3
FEDERATED LIFE INS CO	MN	864.3
JOHN HANCOCK LIFE INS CO	MA	73,183.9
MIDLAND NATIONAL LIFE INS CO	IA	10,748.6
MINNESOTA LIFE INS CO	MN	17,352.3
MUTUAL OF OMAHA INS CO	NE	3,755.1
NATIONAL GUARDIAN LIFE INS CO	WI	947.4
OLD REPUBLIC INS CO	PA	1,644.5
PACIFIC LIFE INS CO	CA	54,639.9
PRINCIPAL LIFE INS CO	IA	83,957.6
SENTRY LIFE INS CO	WI	2,101.2
USAA LIFE INS CO	TX	9,167.0
Weiss Safety Rating: B+		
AMERICAN GENERAL LIFE INS CO	TX	24,549.9
AMERICAN HEALTH & LIFE INS CO	TX	1,236.5
AMERITAS LIFE INS CORP	NE	2,417.9
AVEMCO INS CO	MD	191.7
BALBOA LIFE INS CO	CA	124.5
BLUE CROSS OF IDAHO HEALTH SERVICE	ID	177.2
CITICORP LIFE INS CO	AZ	1,058.7
COLORADO BANKERS LIFE INS CO	CO	113.3
COLUMBUS LIFE INS CO	OH	2,187.1
COMPANION LIFE INS CO	SC	75.6
CUMIS INS SOCIETY INC	WI	826.9
FEDERAL INS CO	IN	18,983.3
FEDERATED MUTUAL INS CO	MN	3,013.6
GOLDEN RULE INS CO	IL	2,076.2
GREAT NORTHERN INS CO	MN	1,088.5
GREAT-WEST LIFE & ANNUITY INS CO	CO	27,323.0
HARTFORD FIRE INS CO	CT	15,857.7

INSURANCE COMPANY NAME	DOM. STATE	TOTAL ASSETS ($MIL)
HARTFORD LIFE & ACCIDENT INS CO	CT	8,792.5
HARTFORD LIFE & ANNUITY INS CO	CT	49,622.7
HARTFORD LIFE INS CO	CT	97,564.5
JEFFERSON PILOT FINANCIAL INS CO	NE	11,630.2
LINCOLN BENEFIT LIFE CO	NE	1,823.4
MANUFACTURERS LIFE INS CO USA	MI	53,737.8
MERIT LIFE INS CO	IN	1,020.5
METROPOLITAN LIFE INS CO	NY	220,093.6
METROPOLITAN PROPERTY & CAS INS CO	RI	4,789.1
MIDWEST SECURITY LIFE INS CO	WI	132.8
NATIONAL BENEFIT LIFE INS CO	NY	736.6
NATIONAL CASUALTY CO	WI	92.6
NATIONAL UNION FIRE INS CO OF PITTSB	PA	18,196.9
NATIONWIDE LIFE INS CO	OH	80,569.1
NATIONWIDE MUTUAL FIRE INS CO	OH	3,610.4
PACIFIC GUARDIAN LIFE INS CO LTD	HI	431.5
PHYSICIANS LIFE INS CO	NE	1,195.8
PRIMERICA LIFE INS CO	MA	5,073.8
SIRIUS AMERICA INS CO	DE	216.8
STATE FARM MUTUAL AUTOMOBILE INS CO	IL	70,070.4
SURETY LIFE INS CO	NE	50.3
TRAVELERS INS CO LIFE DEPT	CT	58,317.0
UNITED INS CO OF AMERICA	IL	2,064.3
UNITED OF OMAHA LIFE INS CO	NE	12,298.3
WESTERN & SOUTHERN LIFE INS CO	OH	7,850.2

Illinois

INSURANCE COMPANY NAME	DOM. STATE	TOTAL ASSETS ($MIL)
Weiss Safety Rating: A+		
COUNTRY LIFE INS CO	IL	4,387.5
GOVERNMENT EMPLOYEES INS CO	MD	8,737.7
PHYSICIANS MUTUAL INS CO	NE	1,102.7
PROTECTIVE INS CO	IN	443.4
TEACHERS INS & ANNUITY ASN OF AM	NY	147,114.8
Weiss Safety Rating: A		
AMERICAN FIDELITY ASR CO	OK	2,382.6
AUTO-OWNERS INS CO	MI	6,582.7
CENTURION LIFE INS CO	MO	1,024.0
GUARDIAN LIFE INS CO OF AMERICA	NY	20,577.2
JEFFERSON-PILOT LIFE INS CO	NC	13,405.5
MASSACHUSETTS MUTUAL LIFE INS CO	MA	80,322.1
NEW YORK LIFE INS CO	NY	87,505.8
NORTHWESTERN MUTUAL LIFE INS CO	WI	114,436.3
SENTRY INS A MUTUAL CO	WI	4,177.1
Weiss Safety Rating: A-		
ALLSTATE INS CO	IL	40,978.7
ALLSTATE LIFE INS CO	IL	60,033.7
AUTO-OWNERS LIFE INS CO	MI	1,251.5
CENTRAL STATES INDEMNITY CO OF OMAHA	NE	243.1
CINCINNATI INS CO	OH	7,143.1
FEDERATED LIFE INS CO	MN	864.3
GRANGE MUTUAL CAS CO	OH	1,116.1
JOHN HANCOCK LIFE INS CO	MA	73,183.9
MIDLAND NATIONAL LIFE INS CO	IA	10,748.6
MINNESOTA LIFE INS CO	MN	17,352.3
MUTUAL OF OMAHA INS CO	NE	3,755.1
NATIONAL GUARDIAN LIFE INS CO	WI	947.4
OLD REPUBLIC INS CO	PA	1,644.5
PACIFIC LIFE INS CO	CA	54,639.9
PRINCIPAL LIFE INS CO	IA	83,957.6
SENTRY LIFE INS CO	WI	2,101.2
USAA LIFE INS CO	TX	9,167.0
Weiss Safety Rating: B+		
ALLSTATE LIFE INS CO OF NEW YORK	NY	4,816.0
AMERICAN GENERAL LIFE INS CO	TX	24,549.9
AMERICAN HEALTH & LIFE INS CO	TX	1,236.5
AMERITAS LIFE INS CORP	NE	2,417.9
AVEMCO INS CO	MD	191.7
BALBOA LIFE INS CO	CA	124.5
BCI HMO INC	IL	10.4
CITICORP LIFE INS CO	AZ	1,058.7
COLORADO BANKERS LIFE INS CO	CO	113.3
COLUMBUS LIFE INS CO	OH	2,187.1
COMPANION LIFE INS CO	SC	75.6
CUMIS INS SOCIETY INC	WI	826.9
FEDERAL INS CO	IN	18,983.3
FEDERATED MUTUAL INS CO	MN	3,013.6
GOLDEN RULE INS CO	IL	2,076.2
GRANGE LIFE INS CO	OH	159.8
GREAT NORTHERN INS CO	MN	1,088.5
GREAT-WEST LIFE & ANNUITY INS CO	CO	27,323.0
HARTFORD FIRE INS CO	CT	15,857.7
HARTFORD LIFE & ACCIDENT INS CO	CT	8,792.5
HARTFORD LIFE & ANNUITY INS CO	CT	49,622.7
HARTFORD LIFE INS CO	CT	97,564.5
HEALTH CARE SVC CORP A MUT LEG RES	IL	4,352.1
HEALTHLINK HMO INC	MO	26.3
JEFFERSON PILOT FINANCIAL INS CO	NE	11,630.2
LINCOLN BENEFIT LIFE CO	NE	1,823.4
MANUFACTURERS LIFE INS CO USA	MI	53,737.8
MERIT LIFE INS CO	IN	1,020.5
METROPOLITAN LIFE INS CO	NY	220,093.6
METROPOLITAN PROPERTY & CAS INS CO	RI	4,789.1
MIDWEST SECURITY LIFE INS CO	WI	132.8
NATIONAL BENEFIT LIFE INS CO	NY	736.6
NATIONAL CASUALTY CO	WI	92.6
NATIONAL UNION FIRE INS CO OF PITTSB	PA	18,196.9
NATIONWIDE LIFE INS CO	OH	80,569.1
NATIONWIDE MUTUAL FIRE INS CO	OH	3,610.4
PEKIN LIFE INS CO	IL	653.8
PHYSICIANS LIFE INS CO	NE	1,195.8
PRIMERICA LIFE INS CO	MA	5,073.8
SHELTER LIFE INS CO	MO	811.0
SIRIUS AMERICA INS CO	DE	216.8
STATE AUTOMOBILE MUTUAL INS CO	OH	1,299.8
STATE FARM MUTUAL AUTOMOBILE INS CO	IL	70,070.4
SURETY LIFE INS CO	NE	50.3
TRAVELERS INS CO LIFE DEPT	CT	58,317.0
UNICARE HEALTH PLANS OF THE MIDWEST	IL	151.4
UNITED HEALTHCARE OF THE MIDWEST INC	MO	332.1
UNITED INS CO OF AMERICA	IL	2,064.3
UNITED OF OMAHA LIFE INS CO	NE	12,298.3
WESTERN & SOUTHERN LIFE INS CO	OH	7,850.2

IV. Weiss Recommended Companies by State

Indiana

Weiss Safety Rating: A+

INSURANCE COMPANY NAME	DOM. STATE	TOTAL ASSETS ($MIL)
COUNTRY LIFE INS CO	IL	4,387.5
GOVERNMENT EMPLOYEES INS CO	MD	8,737.7
PHYSICIANS MUTUAL INS CO	NE	1,102.7
PROTECTIVE INS CO	IN	443.4
TEACHERS INS & ANNUITY ASN OF AM	NY	147,114.8

Weiss Safety Rating: A

INSURANCE COMPANY NAME	DOM. STATE	TOTAL ASSETS ($MIL)
ALFA MUTUAL INS CO	AL	1,151.8
AMERICAN FIDELITY ASR CO	OK	2,382.6
AUTO-OWNERS INS CO	MI	6,582.7
CENTURION LIFE INS CO	MO	1,024.0
GUARDIAN LIFE INS CO OF AMERICA	NY	20,577.2
JEFFERSON-PILOT LIFE INS CO	NC	13,405.5
MASSACHUSETTS MUTUAL LIFE INS CO	MA	80,322.1
NEW YORK LIFE INS CO	NY	87,505.8
NORTHWESTERN MUTUAL LIFE INS CO	WI	114,436.3
SENTRY INS A MUTUAL CO	WI	4,177.1
UNITED FARM FAMILY LIFE INS CO	IN	1,466.7

Weiss Safety Rating: A-

INSURANCE COMPANY NAME	DOM. STATE	TOTAL ASSETS ($MIL)
ALLSTATE INS CO	IL	40,978.7
ALLSTATE LIFE INS CO	IL	60,033.7
AUTO-OWNERS LIFE INS CO	MI	1,251.5
CENTRAL STATES INDEMNITY CO OF OMAHA	NE	243.1
CINCINNATI INS CO	OH	7,143.1
FEDERATED LIFE INS CO	MN	864.3
GRANGE MUTUAL CAS CO	OH	1,116.1
JOHN HANCOCK LIFE INS CO	MA	73,183.9
MIDLAND NATIONAL LIFE INS CO	IA	10,748.6
MINNESOTA LIFE INS CO	MN	17,352.3
MUTUAL OF OMAHA INS CO	NE	3,755.1
NATIONAL GUARDIAN LIFE INS CO	WI	947.4
OLD REPUBLIC INS CO	PA	1,644.5
PACIFIC LIFE INS CO	CA	54,639.9
PRINCIPAL LIFE INS CO	IA	83,957.6
SENTRY LIFE INS CO	WI	2,101.2
USAA LIFE INS CO	TX	9,167.0

Weiss Safety Rating: B+

INSURANCE COMPANY NAME	DOM. STATE	TOTAL ASSETS ($MIL)
AMERICAN GENERAL LIFE INS CO	TX	24,549.9
AMERICAN HEALTH & LIFE INS CO	TX	1,236.5
AMERITAS LIFE INS CORP	NE	2,417.9
AVEMCO INS CO	MD	191.7
BALBOA LIFE INS CO	CA	124.5
BCI HMO INC	IL	10.4
CITICORP LIFE INS CO	AZ	1,058.7
COLORADO BANKERS LIFE INS CO	CO	113.3
COLUMBUS LIFE INS CO	OH	2,187.1
COMPANION LIFE INS CO	SC	75.6
CUMIS INS SOCIETY INC	WI	826.9
FEDERAL INS CO	IN	18,983.3
FEDERATED MUTUAL INS CO	MN	3,013.6
GOLDEN RULE INS CO	IL	2,076.2
GRANGE LIFE INS CO	OH	159.8
GREAT NORTHERN INS CO	MN	1,088.5
GREAT-WEST LIFE & ANNUITY INS CO	CO	27,323.0
HARTFORD FIRE INS CO	CT	15,857.7
HARTFORD LIFE & ACCIDENT INS CO	CT	8,792.5
HARTFORD LIFE & ANNUITY INS CO	CT	49,622.7
HARTFORD LIFE INS CO	CT	97,564.5
JEFFERSON PILOT FINANCIAL INS CO	NE	11,630.2
LINCOLN BENEFIT LIFE CO	NE	1,823.4
MANUFACTURERS LIFE INS CO USA	MI	53,737.8
MERIT LIFE INS CO	IN	1,020.5
METROPOLITAN LIFE INS CO	NY	220,093.6
METROPOLITAN PROPERTY & CAS INS CO	RI	4,789.1
MIDWEST SECURITY LIFE INS CO	WI	132.8
NATIONAL BENEFIT LIFE INS CO	NY	736.6
NATIONAL CASUALTY CO	WI	92.6
NATIONAL UNION FIRE INS CO OF PITTSB	PA	18,196.9
NATIONWIDE LIFE INS CO	OH	80,569.1
NATIONWIDE MUTUAL FIRE INS CO	OH	3,610.4
PEKIN LIFE INS CO	IL	653.8
PHYSICIANS LIFE INS CO	NE	1,195.8
PRIMERICA LIFE INS CO	MA	5,073.8
SHELTER LIFE INS CO	MO	811.0
SIRIUS AMERICA INS CO	DE	216.8
STATE AUTOMOBILE MUTUAL INS CO	OH	1,299.8
STATE FARM MUTUAL AUTOMOBILE INS CO	IL	70,070.4
SURETY LIFE INS CO	NE	50.3
TRAVELERS INS CO LIFE DEPT	CT	58,317.0
UNICARE HEALTH PLANS OF THE MIDWEST	IL	151.4
UNITED INS CO OF AMERICA	IL	2,064.3
UNITED OF OMAHA LIFE INS CO	NE	12,298.3
WESTERN & SOUTHERN LIFE INS CO	OH	7,850.2

Iowa

INSURANCE COMPANY NAME	DOM. STATE	TOTAL ASSETS ($MIL)
Weiss Safety Rating: A+		
COUNTRY LIFE INS CO	IL	4,387.5
GOVERNMENT EMPLOYEES INS CO	MD	8,737.7
PHYSICIANS MUTUAL INS CO	NE	1,102.7
PROTECTIVE INS CO	IN	443.4
TEACHERS INS & ANNUITY ASN OF AM	NY	147,114.8
Weiss Safety Rating: A		
AMERICAN FIDELITY ASR CO	OK	2,382.6
AUTO-OWNERS INS CO	MI	6,582.7
CENTURION LIFE INS CO	MO	1,024.0
GUARDIAN LIFE INS CO OF AMERICA	NY	20,577.2
JEFFERSON-PILOT LIFE INS CO	NC	13,405.5
MASSACHUSETTS MUTUAL LIFE INS CO	MA	80,322.1
NEW YORK LIFE INS CO	NY	87,505.8
NORTHWESTERN MUTUAL LIFE INS CO	WI	114,436.3
SENTRY INS A MUTUAL CO	WI	4,177.1
Weiss Safety Rating: A-		
ALLSTATE INS CO	IL	40,978.7
ALLSTATE LIFE INS CO	IL	60,033.7
AUTO-OWNERS LIFE INS CO	MI	1,251.5
CENTRAL STATES INDEMNITY CO OF OMAHA	NE	243.1
CINCINNATI INS CO	OH	7,143.1
FARM BUREAU LIFE INS CO	IA	4,695.3
FEDERATED LIFE INS CO	MN	864.3
GRANGE MUTUAL CAS CO	OH	1,116.1
JOHN HANCOCK LIFE INS CO	MA	73,183.9
MIDLAND NATIONAL LIFE INS CO	IA	10,748.6
MINNESOTA LIFE INS CO	MN	17,352.3
MUTUAL OF OMAHA INS CO	NE	3,755.1
NATIONAL GUARDIAN LIFE INS CO	WI	947.4
OLD REPUBLIC INS CO	PA	1,644.5
PACIFIC LIFE INS CO	CA	54,639.9
PRINCIPAL LIFE INS CO	IA	83,957.6
SENTRY LIFE INS CO	WI	2,101.2
USAA LIFE INS CO	TX	9,167.0
Weiss Safety Rating: B+		
AMERICAN GENERAL LIFE INS CO	TX	24,549.9
AMERICAN HEALTH & LIFE INS CO	TX	1,236.5
AMERITAS LIFE INS CORP	NE	2,417.9
AVEMCO INS CO	MD	191.7
BALBOA LIFE INS CO	CA	124.5
CITICORP LIFE INS CO	AZ	1,058.7
COLORADO BANKERS LIFE INS CO	CO	113.3
COLUMBUS LIFE INS CO	OH	2,187.1
COMPANION LIFE INS CO	SC	75.6
CUMIS INS SOCIETY INC	WI	826.9
FEDERAL INS CO	IN	18,983.3
FEDERATED MUTUAL INS CO	MN	3,013.6
GOLDEN RULE INS CO	IL	2,076.2
GRANGE LIFE INS CO	OH	159.8
GREAT NORTHERN INS CO	MN	1,088.5
GREAT-WEST LIFE & ANNUITY INS CO	CO	27,323.0
HARTFORD FIRE INS CO	CT	15,857.7
HARTFORD LIFE & ACCIDENT INS CO	CT	8,792.5
HARTFORD LIFE & ANNUITY INS CO	CT	49,622.7
HARTFORD LIFE INS CO	CT	97,564.5
JEFFERSON PILOT FINANCIAL INS CO	NE	11,630.2
LINCOLN BENEFIT LIFE CO	NE	1,823.4
MANUFACTURERS LIFE INS CO USA	MI	53,737.8
MERIT LIFE INS CO	IN	1,020.5
METROPOLITAN LIFE INS CO	NY	220,093.6
METROPOLITAN PROPERTY & CAS INS CO	RI	4,789.1
MIDWEST SECURITY LIFE INS CO	WI	132.8
NATIONAL BENEFIT LIFE INS CO	NY	736.6
NATIONAL CASUALTY CO	WI	92.6
NATIONAL UNION FIRE INS CO OF PITTSB	PA	18,196.9
NATIONWIDE LIFE INS CO	OH	80,569.1
NATIONWIDE MUTUAL FIRE INS CO	OH	3,610.4
PACIFIC GUARDIAN LIFE INS CO LTD	HI	431.5
PEKIN LIFE INS CO	IL	653.8
PHYSICIANS LIFE INS CO	NE	1,195.8
PRIMERICA LIFE INS CO	MA	5,073.8
SHELTER LIFE INS CO	MO	811.0
SIRIUS AMERICA INS CO	DE	216.8
STATE AUTOMOBILE MUTUAL INS CO	OH	1,299.8
STATE FARM MUTUAL AUTOMOBILE INS CO	IL	70,070.4
SURETY LIFE INS CO	NE	50.3
TRAVELERS INS CO LIFE DEPT	CT	58,317.0
UNITED HEALTHCARE OF THE MIDLANDS	NE	69.7
UNITED INS CO OF AMERICA	IL	2,064.3
UNITED OF OMAHA LIFE INS CO	NE	12,298.3
WESTERN & SOUTHERN LIFE INS CO	OH	7,850.2

Kansas

Weiss Safety Rating: A+

INSURANCE COMPANY NAME	DOM. STATE	TOTAL ASSETS ($MIL)
COUNTRY LIFE INS CO	IL	4,387.5
GOVERNMENT EMPLOYEES INS CO	MD	8,737.7
PHYSICIANS MUTUAL INS CO	NE	1,102.7
PROTECTIVE INS CO	IN	443.4
TEACHERS INS & ANNUITY ASN OF AM	NY	147,114.8

Weiss Safety Rating: A

INSURANCE COMPANY NAME	DOM. STATE	TOTAL ASSETS ($MIL)
AMERICAN FIDELITY ASR CO	OK	2,382.6
AUTO-OWNERS INS CO	MI	6,582.7
CENTURION LIFE INS CO	MO	1,024.0
GUARDIAN LIFE INS CO OF AMERICA	NY	20,577.2
JEFFERSON-PILOT LIFE INS CO	NC	13,405.5
MASSACHUSETTS MUTUAL LIFE INS CO	MA	80,322.1
NEW YORK LIFE INS CO	NY	87,505.8
NORTHWESTERN MUTUAL LIFE INS CO	WI	114,436.3
SENTRY INS A MUTUAL CO	WI	4,177.1

Weiss Safety Rating: A-

INSURANCE COMPANY NAME	DOM. STATE	TOTAL ASSETS ($MIL)
ALLSTATE INS CO	IL	40,978.7
ALLSTATE LIFE INS CO	IL	60,033.7
AUTO-OWNERS LIFE INS CO	MI	1,251.5
CENTRAL STATES INDEMNITY CO OF OMAHA	NE	243.1
CINCINNATI INS CO	OH	7,143.1
FARM BUREAU LIFE INS CO	IA	4,695.3
FEDERATED LIFE INS CO	MN	864.3
GRANGE MUTUAL CAS CO	OH	1,116.1
JOHN HANCOCK LIFE INS CO	MA	73,183.9
MIDLAND NATIONAL LIFE INS CO	IA	10,748.6
MINNESOTA LIFE INS CO	MN	17,352.3
MUTUAL OF OMAHA INS CO	NE	3,755.1
NATIONAL GUARDIAN LIFE INS CO	WI	947.4
OLD REPUBLIC INS CO	PA	1,644.5
PACIFIC LIFE INS CO	CA	54,639.9
PRINCIPAL LIFE INS CO	IA	83,957.6
SENTRY LIFE INS CO	WI	2,101.2
USAA LIFE INS CO	TX	9,167.0

Weiss Safety Rating: B+

INSURANCE COMPANY NAME	DOM. STATE	TOTAL ASSETS ($MIL)
AMERICAN GENERAL LIFE INS CO	TX	24,549.9
AMERICAN HEALTH & LIFE INS CO	TX	1,236.5
AMERITAS LIFE INS CORP	NE	2,417.9
AVEMCO INS CO	MD	191.7
BALBOA LIFE INS CO	CA	124.5
BLUE CROSS BLUE SHIELD OF KC	MO	399.8
CITICORP LIFE INS CO	AZ	1,058.7
COLORADO BANKERS LIFE INS CO	CO	113.3
COLUMBUS LIFE INS CO	OH	2,187.1
COMPANION LIFE INS CO	SC	75.6
CUMIS INS SOCIETY INC	WI	826.9
FEDERAL INS CO	IN	18,983.3
FEDERATED MUTUAL INS CO	MN	3,013.6
GOLDEN RULE INS CO	IL	2,076.2
GRANGE LIFE INS CO	OH	159.8
GREAT NORTHERN INS CO	MN	1,088.5
GREAT-WEST LIFE & ANNUITY INS CO	CO	27,323.0
HARTFORD FIRE INS CO	CT	15,857.7
HARTFORD LIFE & ACCIDENT INS CO	CT	8,792.5
HARTFORD LIFE & ANNUITY INS CO	CT	49,622.7
HARTFORD LIFE INS CO	CT	97,564.5
JEFFERSON PILOT FINANCIAL INS CO	NE	11,630.2
LINCOLN BENEFIT LIFE CO	NE	1,823.4
MANUFACTURERS LIFE INS CO USA	MI	53,737.8
MERIT LIFE INS CO	IN	1,020.5
METROPOLITAN LIFE INS CO	NY	220,093.6
METROPOLITAN PROPERTY & CAS INS CO	RI	4,789.1
MIDWEST SECURITY LIFE INS CO	WI	132.8
NATIONAL BENEFIT LIFE INS CO	NY	736.6
NATIONAL CASUALTY CO	WI	92.6
NATIONAL UNION FIRE INS CO OF PITTSB	PA	18,196.9
NATIONWIDE LIFE INS CO	OH	80,569.1
NATIONWIDE MUTUAL FIRE INS CO	OH	3,610.4
PHYSICIANS LIFE INS CO	NE	1,195.8
PRIMERICA LIFE INS CO	MA	5,073.8
SHELTER LIFE INS CO	MO	811.0
SIRIUS AMERICA INS CO	DE	216.8
STATE AUTOMOBILE MUTUAL INS CO	OH	1,299.8
STATE FARM MUTUAL AUTOMOBILE INS CO	IL	70,070.4
SURETY LIFE INS CO	NE	50.3
TRAVELERS INS CO LIFE DEPT	CT	58,317.0
UNITED HEALTHCARE OF THE MIDWEST INC	MO	332.1
UNITED INS CO OF AMERICA	IL	2,064.3
UNITED OF OMAHA LIFE INS CO	NE	12,298.3
WESTERN & SOUTHERN LIFE INS CO	OH	7,850.2

Winter 2003 - 04

IV. Weiss Recommended Companies by State

Kentucky

INSURANCE COMPANY NAME	DOM. STATE	TOTAL ASSETS ($MIL)
Weiss Safety Rating: A+		
COUNTRY LIFE INS CO	IL	4,387.5
GOVERNMENT EMPLOYEES INS CO	MD	8,737.7
PHYSICIANS MUTUAL INS CO	NE	1,102.7
PROTECTIVE INS CO	IN	443.4
TEACHERS INS & ANNUITY ASN OF AM	NY	147,114.8
Weiss Safety Rating: A		
AMERICAN FIDELITY ASR CO	OK	2,382.6
AUTO-OWNERS INS CO	MI	6,582.7
CENTURION LIFE INS CO	MO	1,024.0
GUARDIAN LIFE INS CO OF AMERICA	NY	20,577.2
JEFFERSON-PILOT LIFE INS CO	NC	13,405.5
KENTUCKY FARM BUREAU MUTUAL INS CO	KY	1,142.6
MASSACHUSETTS MUTUAL LIFE INS CO	MA	80,322.1
NEW YORK LIFE INS CO	NY	87,505.8
NORTHWESTERN MUTUAL LIFE INS CO	WI	114,436.3
SENTRY INS A MUTUAL CO	WI	4,177.1
Weiss Safety Rating: A-		
ALLSTATE INS CO	IL	40,978.7
ALLSTATE LIFE INS CO	IL	60,033.7
AUTO-OWNERS LIFE INS CO	MI	1,251.5
CENTRAL STATES INDEMNITY CO OF OMAHA	NE	243.1
CINCINNATI INS CO	OH	7,143.1
FEDERATED LIFE INS CO	MN	864.3
GRANGE MUTUAL CAS CO	OH	1,116.1
JOHN HANCOCK LIFE INS CO	MA	73,183.9
MIDLAND NATIONAL LIFE INS CO	IA	10,748.6
MINNESOTA LIFE INS CO	MN	17,352.3
MUTUAL OF OMAHA INS CO	NE	3,755.1
NATIONAL GUARDIAN LIFE INS CO	WI	947.4
OLD REPUBLIC INS CO	PA	1,644.5
PACIFIC LIFE INS CO	CA	54,639.9
PRINCIPAL LIFE INS CO	IA	83,957.6
SENTRY LIFE INS CO	WI	2,101.2
SOUTHERN FARM BUREAU LIFE INS CO	MS	7,776.4
USAA LIFE INS CO	TX	9,167.0
Weiss Safety Rating: B+		
AMERICAN GENERAL LIFE INS CO	TX	24,549.9
AMERICAN HEALTH & LIFE INS CO	TX	1,236.5
AMERITAS LIFE INS CORP	NE	2,417.9
ANTHEM HEALTH PLANS OF KENTUCKY INC	KY	659.5
AVEMCO INS CO	MD	191.7
BALBOA LIFE INS CO	CA	124.5
BLUEGRASS FAMILY HEALTH INC	KY	82.2
CITICORP LIFE INS CO	AZ	1,058.7
COLORADO BANKERS LIFE INS CO	CO	113.3
COLUMBUS LIFE INS CO	OH	2,187.1
COMPANION LIFE INS CO	SC	75.6
CUMIS INS SOCIETY INC	WI	826.9
FEDERAL INS CO	IN	18,983.3
FEDERATED MUTUAL INS CO	MN	3,013.6
GOLDEN RULE INS CO	IL	2,076.2
GRANGE LIFE INS CO	OH	159.8
GREAT NORTHERN INS CO	MN	1,088.5
GREAT-WEST LIFE & ANNUITY INS CO	CO	27,323.0
HARTFORD FIRE INS CO	CT	15,857.7
HARTFORD LIFE & ACCIDENT INS CO	CT	8,792.5
HARTFORD LIFE & ANNUITY INS CO	CT	49,622.7
HARTFORD LIFE INS CO	CT	97,564.5
JEFFERSON PILOT FINANCIAL INS CO	NE	11,630.2
LINCOLN BENEFIT LIFE CO	NE	1,823.4
MANUFACTURERS LIFE INS CO USA	MI	53,737.8
MERIT LIFE INS CO	IN	1,020.5
METROPOLITAN LIFE INS CO	NY	220,093.6
METROPOLITAN PROPERTY & CAS INS CO	RI	4,789.1
MIDWEST SECURITY LIFE INS CO	WI	132.8
NATIONAL BENEFIT LIFE INS CO	NY	736.6
NATIONAL CASUALTY CO	WI	92.6
NATIONAL UNION FIRE INS CO OF PITTSB	PA	18,196.9
NATIONWIDE LIFE INS CO	OH	80,569.1
NATIONWIDE MUTUAL FIRE INS CO	OH	3,610.4
PEKIN LIFE INS CO	IL	653.8
PHYSICIANS LIFE INS CO	NE	1,195.8
PRIMERICA LIFE INS CO	MA	5,073.8
SHELTER LIFE INS CO	MO	811.0
SIRIUS AMERICA INS CO	DE	216.8
STATE AUTOMOBILE MUTUAL INS CO	OH	1,299.8
STATE FARM MUTUAL AUTOMOBILE INS CO	IL	70,070.4
SURETY LIFE INS CO	NE	50.3
TRAVELERS INS CO LIFE DEPT	CT	58,317.0
UNITED INS CO OF AMERICA	IL	2,064.3
UNITED OF OMAHA LIFE INS CO	NE	12,298.3
WESTERN & SOUTHERN LIFE INS CO	OH	7,850.2

www.WeissRatings.com

IV. Weiss Recommended Companies by State

Winter 2003 - 04

Louisiana

INSURANCE COMPANY NAME	DOM. STATE	TOTAL ASSETS ($MIL)
Weiss Safety Rating: A+		
GOVERNMENT EMPLOYEES INS CO	MD	8,737.7
PHYSICIANS MUTUAL INS CO	NE	1,102.7
PROTECTIVE INS CO	IN	443.4
Weiss Safety Rating: A		
AMERICAN FIDELITY ASR CO	OK	2,382.6
CENTURION LIFE INS CO	MO	1,024.0
GUARDIAN LIFE INS CO OF AMERICA	NY	20,577.2
JEFFERSON-PILOT LIFE INS CO	NC	13,405.5
MASSACHUSETTS MUTUAL LIFE INS CO	MA	80,322.1
NEW YORK LIFE INS CO	NY	87,505.8
NORTHWESTERN MUTUAL LIFE INS CO	WI	114,436.3
SENTRY INS A MUTUAL CO	WI	4,177.1
UNION NATIONAL LIFE INS CO	LA	377.5
Weiss Safety Rating: A-		
ALFA LIFE INS CORP	AL	821.5
ALLSTATE INS CO	IL	40,978.7
ALLSTATE LIFE INS CO	IL	60,033.7
CENTRAL STATES INDEMNITY CO OF OMAHA	NE	243.1
CINCINNATI INS CO	OH	7,143.1
FEDERATED LIFE INS CO	MN	864.3
JOHN HANCOCK LIFE INS CO	MA	73,183.9
MIDLAND NATIONAL LIFE INS CO	IA	10,748.6
MINNESOTA LIFE INS CO	MN	17,352.3
MUTUAL OF OMAHA INS CO	NE	3,755.1
NATIONAL GUARDIAN LIFE INS CO	WI	947.4
OLD REPUBLIC INS CO	PA	1,644.5
PACIFIC LIFE INS CO	CA	54,639.9
PRINCIPAL LIFE INS CO	IA	83,957.6
SENTRY LIFE INS CO	WI	2,101.2
SOUTHERN FARM BUREAU LIFE INS CO	MS	7,776.4
USAA LIFE INS CO	TX	9,167.0
Weiss Safety Rating: B+		
AMERICAN GENERAL LIFE INS CO	TX	24,549.9
AMERICAN HEALTH & LIFE INS CO	TX	1,236.5
AMERITAS LIFE INS CORP	NE	2,417.9
AVEMCO INS CO	MD	191.7
BALBOA LIFE INS CO	CA	124.5
CITICORP LIFE INS CO	AZ	1,058.7
COLORADO BANKERS LIFE INS CO	CO	113.3
COLUMBUS LIFE INS CO	OH	2,187.1
COMPANION LIFE INS CO	SC	75.6
CUMIS INS SOCIETY INC	WI	826.9
FEDERAL INS CO	IN	18,983.3
FEDERATED MUTUAL INS CO	MN	3,013.6
GOLDEN RULE INS CO	IL	2,076.2
GREAT NORTHERN INS CO	MN	1,088.5
GREAT-WEST LIFE & ANNUITY INS CO	CO	27,323.0
HARTFORD FIRE INS CO	CT	15,857.7
HARTFORD LIFE & ACCIDENT INS CO	CT	8,792.5

INSURANCE COMPANY NAME	DOM. STATE	TOTAL ASSETS ($MIL)
HARTFORD LIFE & ANNUITY INS CO	CT	49,622.7
HARTFORD LIFE INS CO	CT	97,564.5
JEFFERSON PILOT FINANCIAL INS CO	NE	11,630.2
LINCOLN BENEFIT LIFE CO	NE	1,823.4
MANUFACTURERS LIFE INS CO USA	MI	53,737.8
MERIT LIFE INS CO	IN	1,020.5
METROPOLITAN LIFE INS CO	NY	220,093.6
METROPOLITAN PROPERTY & CAS INS CO	RI	4,789.1
MIDWEST SECURITY LIFE INS CO	WI	132.8
NATIONAL BENEFIT LIFE INS CO	NY	736.6
NATIONAL CASUALTY CO	WI	92.6
NATIONAL UNION FIRE INS CO OF PITTSB	PA	18,196.9
NATIONWIDE LIFE INS CO	OH	80,569.1
NATIONWIDE MUTUAL FIRE INS CO	OH	3,610.4
PACIFIC GUARDIAN LIFE INS CO LTD	HI	431.5
PHYSICIANS LIFE INS CO	NE	1,195.8
PRIMERICA LIFE INS CO	MA	5,073.8
SHELTER LIFE INS CO	MO	811.0
SIRIUS AMERICA INS CO	DE	216.8
SOUTHERN NATL LIFE INS CO INC	LA	11.9
STATE FARM MUTUAL AUTOMOBILE INS CO	IL	70,070.4
SURETY LIFE INS CO	NE	50.3
TRAVELERS INS CO LIFE DEPT	CT	58,317.0
UNITED INS CO OF AMERICA	IL	2,064.3
UNITED OF OMAHA LIFE INS CO	NE	12,298.3
WESTERN & SOUTHERN LIFE INS CO	OH	7,850.2

Maine

INSURANCE COMPANY NAME	DOM. STATE	TOTAL ASSETS ($MIL)
Weiss Safety Rating: A+		
COUNTRY LIFE INS CO	IL	4,387.5
GOVERNMENT EMPLOYEES INS CO	MD	8,737.7
PHYSICIANS MUTUAL INS CO	NE	1,102.7
PROTECTIVE INS CO	IN	443.4
TEACHERS INS & ANNUITY ASN OF AM	NY	147,114.8
Weiss Safety Rating: A		
AMERICAN FIDELITY ASR CO	OK	2,382.6
GUARDIAN LIFE INS CO OF AMERICA	NY	20,577.2
JEFFERSON-PILOT LIFE INS CO	NC	13,405.5
MASSACHUSETTS MUTUAL LIFE INS CO	MA	80,322.1
NEW YORK LIFE INS CO	NY	87,505.8
NORTHWESTERN MUTUAL LIFE INS CO	WI	114,436.3
SENTRY INS A MUTUAL CO	WI	4,177.1
Weiss Safety Rating: A-		
ALLSTATE INS CO	IL	40,978.7
ALLSTATE LIFE INS CO	IL	60,033.7
CENTRAL STATES INDEMNITY CO OF OMAHA	NE	243.1
CINCINNATI INS CO	OH	7,143.1
FEDERATED LIFE INS CO	MN	864.3
JOHN HANCOCK LIFE INS CO	MA	73,183.9
MIDLAND NATIONAL LIFE INS CO	IA	10,748.6
MINNESOTA LIFE INS CO	MN	17,352.3
MUTUAL OF OMAHA INS CO	NE	3,755.1
NATIONAL GUARDIAN LIFE INS CO	WI	947.4
OLD REPUBLIC INS CO	PA	1,644.5
PACIFIC LIFE INS CO	CA	54,639.9
PRINCIPAL LIFE INS CO	IA	83,957.6
SENTRY LIFE INS CO	WI	2,101.2
USAA LIFE INS CO	TX	9,167.0
Weiss Safety Rating: B+		
AMERICAN GENERAL LIFE INS CO	TX	24,549.9
AMERICAN HEALTH & LIFE INS CO	TX	1,236.5
AMERITAS LIFE INS CORP	NE	2,417.9
AVEMCO INS CO	MD	191.7
BALBOA LIFE INS CO	CA	124.5
CITICORP LIFE INS CO	AZ	1,058.7
COLORADO BANKERS LIFE INS CO	CO	113.3
COLUMBUS LIFE INS CO	OH	2,187.1
COMPANION LIFE INS CO	SC	75.6
CUMIS INS SOCIETY INC	WI	826.9
FARM FAMILY LIFE INS CO	NY	889.2
FEDERAL INS CO	IN	18,983.3
FEDERATED MUTUAL INS CO	MN	3,013.6
GOLDEN RULE INS CO	IL	2,076.2
GREAT NORTHERN INS CO	MN	1,088.5
GREAT-WEST LIFE & ANNUITY INS CO	CO	27,323.0
HARTFORD FIRE INS CO	CT	15,857.7
HARTFORD LIFE & ACCIDENT INS CO	CT	8,792.5
HARTFORD LIFE & ANNUITY INS CO	CT	49,622.7
HARTFORD LIFE INS CO	CT	97,564.5
JEFFERSON PILOT FINANCIAL INS CO	NE	11,630.2
LINCOLN BENEFIT LIFE CO	NE	1,823.4
MANUFACTURERS LIFE INS CO USA	MI	53,737.8
MERIT LIFE INS CO	IN	1,020.5
METROPOLITAN LIFE INS CO	NY	220,093.6
METROPOLITAN PROPERTY & CAS INS CO	RI	4,789.1
NATIONAL BENEFIT LIFE INS CO	NY	736.6
NATIONAL CASUALTY CO	WI	92.6
NATIONAL UNION FIRE INS CO OF PITTSB	PA	18,196.9
NATIONWIDE LIFE INS CO	OH	80,569.1
NATIONWIDE MUTUAL FIRE INS CO	OH	3,610.4
PHYSICIANS LIFE INS CO	NE	1,195.8
PRIMERICA LIFE INS CO	MA	5,073.8
SAVINGS BANK LIFE INS CO OF MA	MA	1,548.3
SIRIUS AMERICA INS CO	DE	216.8
STATE FARM MUTUAL AUTOMOBILE INS CO	IL	70,070.4
SURETY LIFE INS CO	NE	50.3
TRAVELERS INS CO LIFE DEPT	CT	58,317.0
UNITED INS CO OF AMERICA	IL	2,064.3
UNITED OF OMAHA LIFE INS CO	NE	12,298.3

IV. Weiss Recommended Companies by State

Maryland

INSURANCE COMPANY NAME	DOM. STATE	TOTAL ASSETS ($MIL)
Weiss Safety Rating: A+		
COUNTRY LIFE INS CO	IL	4,387.5
GOVERNMENT EMPLOYEES INS CO	MD	8,737.7
PHYSICIANS MUTUAL INS CO	NE	1,102.7
PROTECTIVE INS CO	IN	443.4
TEACHERS INS & ANNUITY ASN OF AM	NY	147,114.8
Weiss Safety Rating: A		
AMERICAN FIDELITY ASR CO	OK	2,382.6
CENTURION LIFE INS CO	MO	1,024.0
GROUP HOSP & MEDICAL SERVICES INC	DC	1,141.0
GUARDIAN LIFE INS CO OF AMERICA	NY	20,577.2
JEFFERSON-PILOT LIFE INS CO	NC	13,405.5
MASSACHUSETTS MUTUAL LIFE INS CO	MA	80,322.1
NEW YORK LIFE INS CO	NY	87,505.8
NORTHWESTERN MUTUAL LIFE INS CO	WI	114,436.3
SENTRY INS A MUTUAL CO	WI	4,177.1
Weiss Safety Rating: A-		
ALLSTATE INS CO	IL	40,978.7
ALLSTATE LIFE INS CO	IL	60,033.7
CAREFIRST BLUECHOICE INC	DC	261.2
CENTRAL STATES INDEMNITY CO OF OMAHA	NE	243.1
CINCINNATI INS CO	OH	7,143.1
FEDERATED LIFE INS CO	MN	864.3
JOHN HANCOCK LIFE INS CO	MA	73,183.9
MIDLAND NATIONAL LIFE INS CO	IA	10,748.6
MINNESOTA LIFE INS CO	MN	17,352.3
MUTUAL OF OMAHA INS CO	NE	3,755.1
NATIONAL GUARDIAN LIFE INS CO	WI	947.4
OLD REPUBLIC INS CO	PA	1,644.5
PACIFIC LIFE INS CO	CA	54,639.9
PRINCIPAL LIFE INS CO	IA	83,957.6
SENTRY LIFE INS CO	WI	2,101.2
USAA LIFE INS CO	TX	9,167.0
Weiss Safety Rating: B+		
AMERICAN GENERAL LIFE INS CO	TX	24,549.9
AMERICAN HEALTH & LIFE INS CO	TX	1,236.5
AMERITAS LIFE INS CORP	NE	2,417.9
AVEMCO INS CO	MD	191.7
BALBOA LIFE INS CO	CA	124.5
CAREFIRST OF MARYLAND INC	MD	822.5
CITICORP LIFE INS CO	AZ	1,058.7
COLORADO BANKERS LIFE INS CO	CO	113.3
COLUMBUS LIFE INS CO	OH	2,187.1
COMPANION LIFE INS CO	SC	75.6
CUMIS INS SOCIETY INC	WI	826.9
FARM FAMILY LIFE INS CO	NY	889.2
FEDERAL INS CO	IN	18,983.3
FEDERATED MUTUAL INS CO	MN	3,013.6
GOLDEN RULE INS CO	IL	2,076.2
GREAT NORTHERN INS CO	MN	1,088.5
GREAT-WEST LIFE & ANNUITY INS CO	CO	27,323.0
HARTFORD FIRE INS CO	CT	15,857.7
HARTFORD LIFE & ACCIDENT INS CO	CT	8,792.5
HARTFORD LIFE & ANNUITY INS CO	CT	49,622.7
HARTFORD LIFE INS CO	CT	97,564.5
JEFFERSON PILOT FINANCIAL INS CO	NE	11,630.2
LINCOLN BENEFIT LIFE CO	NE	1,823.4
MANUFACTURERS LIFE INS CO USA	MI	53,737.8
MD INDIVIDUAL PRACTICE ASSOC INC	MD	113.6
MERIT LIFE INS CO	IN	1,020.5
METROPOLITAN LIFE INS CO	NY	220,093.6
METROPOLITAN PROPERTY & CAS INS CO	RI	4,789.1
NATIONAL BENEFIT LIFE INS CO	NY	736.6
NATIONAL CASUALTY CO	WI	92.6
NATIONAL UNION FIRE INS CO OF PITTSB	PA	18,196.9
NATIONWIDE LIFE INS CO	OH	80,569.1
NATIONWIDE MUTUAL FIRE INS CO	OH	3,610.4
PHYSICIANS LIFE INS CO	NE	1,195.8
PRIMERICA LIFE INS CO	MA	5,073.8
SIRIUS AMERICA INS CO	DE	216.8
STATE AUTOMOBILE MUTUAL INS CO	OH	1,299.8
STATE FARM MUTUAL AUTOMOBILE INS CO	IL	70,070.4
SURETY LIFE INS CO	NE	50.3
TRAVELERS INS CO LIFE DEPT	CT	58,317.0
UNITED INS CO OF AMERICA	IL	2,064.3
UNITED OF OMAHA LIFE INS CO	NE	12,298.3
WESTERN & SOUTHERN LIFE INS CO	OH	7,850.2

Massachusetts

INSURANCE COMPANY NAME	DOM. STATE	TOTAL ASSETS ($MIL)
Weiss Safety Rating: A+		
COUNTRY LIFE INS CO	IL	4,387.5
GOVERNMENT EMPLOYEES INS CO	MD	8,737.7
PHYSICIANS MUTUAL INS CO	NE	1,102.7
PROTECTIVE INS CO	IN	443.4
TEACHERS INS & ANNUITY ASN OF AM	NY	147,114.8
Weiss Safety Rating: A		
ALFA MUTUAL INS CO	AL	1,151.8
AMERICAN FIDELITY ASR CO	OK	2,382.6
BLUE CROSS BLUE SHIELD OF MA	MA	2,033.0
CENTURION LIFE INS CO	MO	1,024.0
GUARDIAN LIFE INS CO OF AMERICA	NY	20,577.2
JEFFERSON-PILOT LIFE INS CO	NC	13,405.5
MASSACHUSETTS MUTUAL LIFE INS CO	MA	80,322.1
NEW YORK LIFE INS CO	NY	87,505.8
NORTHWESTERN MUTUAL LIFE INS CO	WI	114,436.3
SENTRY INS A MUTUAL CO	WI	4,177.1
Weiss Safety Rating: A-		
ALLSTATE INS CO	IL	40,978.7
ALLSTATE LIFE INS CO	IL	60,033.7
CENTRAL STATES INDEMNITY CO OF OMAHA	NE	243.1
CINCINNATI INS CO	OH	7,143.1
FEDERATED LIFE INS CO	MN	864.3
JOHN HANCOCK LIFE INS CO	MA	73,183.9
MIDLAND NATIONAL LIFE INS CO	IA	10,748.6
MINNESOTA LIFE INS CO	MN	17,352.3
MUTUAL OF OMAHA INS CO	NE	3,755.1
OLD REPUBLIC INS CO	PA	1,644.5
PACIFIC LIFE INS CO	CA	54,639.9
PRINCIPAL LIFE INS CO	IA	83,957.6
SENTRY LIFE INS CO	WI	2,101.2
USAA LIFE INS CO	TX	9,167.0
Weiss Safety Rating: B+		
AMERICAN GENERAL LIFE INS CO	TX	24,549.9
AMERICAN HEALTH & LIFE INS CO	TX	1,236.5
AMERITAS LIFE INS CORP	NE	2,417.9
AVEMCO INS CO	MD	191.7
BALBOA LIFE INS CO	CA	124.5
CITICORP LIFE INS CO	AZ	1,058.7
COLORADO BANKERS LIFE INS CO	CO	113.3
COLUMBUS LIFE INS CO	OH	2,187.1
COMPANION LIFE INS CO	SC	75.6
CUMIS INS SOCIETY INC	WI	826.9
FARM FAMILY LIFE INS CO	NY	889.2
FEDERAL INS CO	IN	18,983.3
FEDERATED MUTUAL INS CO	MN	3,013.6
GOLDEN RULE INS CO	IL	2,076.2
GREAT NORTHERN INS CO	MN	1,088.5
GREAT-WEST LIFE & ANNUITY INS CO	CO	27,323.0
HARTFORD FIRE INS CO	CT	15,857.7
HARTFORD LIFE & ACCIDENT INS CO	CT	8,792.5
HARTFORD LIFE & ANNUITY INS CO	CT	49,622.7
HARTFORD LIFE INS CO	CT	97,564.5
JEFFERSON PILOT FINANCIAL INS CO	NE	11,630.2
LINCOLN BENEFIT LIFE CO	NE	1,823.4
MANUFACTURERS LIFE INS CO USA	MI	53,737.8
MERIT LIFE INS CO	IN	1,020.5
METROPOLITAN LIFE INS CO	NY	220,093.6
METROPOLITAN PROPERTY & CAS INS CO	RI	4,789.1
NATIONAL BENEFIT LIFE INS CO	NY	736.6
NATIONAL CASUALTY CO	WI	92.6
NATIONAL UNION FIRE INS CO OF PITTSB	PA	18,196.9
NATIONWIDE LIFE INS CO	OH	80,569.1
NATIONWIDE MUTUAL FIRE INS CO	OH	3,610.4
PHYSICIANS LIFE INS CO	NE	1,195.8
PRIMERICA LIFE INS CO	MA	5,073.8
SAVINGS BANK LIFE INS CO OF MA	MA	1,548.3
SIRIUS AMERICA INS CO	DE	216.8
STATE FARM MUTUAL AUTOMOBILE INS CO	IL	70,070.4
SURETY LIFE INS CO	NE	50.3
TRAVELERS INS CO LIFE DEPT	CT	58,317.0
UNITED INS CO OF AMERICA	IL	2,064.3
UNITED OF OMAHA LIFE INS CO	NE	12,298.3

IV. Weiss Recommended Companies by State

Michigan

Weiss Safety Rating: A+

INSURANCE COMPANY NAME	DOM. STATE	TOTAL ASSETS ($MIL)
COUNTRY LIFE INS CO	IL	4,387.5
GOVERNMENT EMPLOYEES INS CO	MD	8,737.7
PHYSICIANS MUTUAL INS CO	NE	1,102.7
PROTECTIVE INS CO	IN	443.4
TEACHERS INS & ANNUITY ASN OF AM	NY	147,114.8

Weiss Safety Rating: A

INSURANCE COMPANY NAME	DOM. STATE	TOTAL ASSETS ($MIL)
ALFA MUTUAL INS CO	AL	1,151.8
AMERICAN FIDELITY ASR CO	OK	2,382.6
AUTO-OWNERS INS CO	MI	6,582.7
CENTURION LIFE INS CO	MO	1,024.0
GUARDIAN LIFE INS CO OF AMERICA	NY	20,577.2
HEALTH ALLIANCE PLAN OF MICHIGAN	MI	316.7
JEFFERSON-PILOT LIFE INS CO	NC	13,405.5
MASSACHUSETTS MUTUAL LIFE INS CO	MA	80,322.1
NEW YORK LIFE INS CO	NY	87,505.8
NORTHWESTERN MUTUAL LIFE INS CO	WI	114,436.3
SENTRY INS A MUTUAL CO	WI	4,177.1

Weiss Safety Rating: A-

INSURANCE COMPANY NAME	DOM. STATE	TOTAL ASSETS ($MIL)
ALLSTATE INS CO	IL	40,978.7
ALLSTATE LIFE INS CO	IL	60,033.7
AUTO-OWNERS LIFE INS CO	MI	1,251.5
CENTRAL STATES INDEMNITY CO OF OMAHA	NE	243.1
CINCINNATI INS CO	OH	7,143.1
FEDERATED LIFE INS CO	MN	864.3
JOHN HANCOCK LIFE INS CO	MA	73,183.9
MIDLAND NATIONAL LIFE INS CO	IA	10,748.6
MINNESOTA LIFE INS CO	MN	17,352.3
MUTUAL OF OMAHA INS CO	NE	3,755.1
NATIONAL GUARDIAN LIFE INS CO	WI	947.4
OLD REPUBLIC INS CO	PA	1,644.5
PACIFIC LIFE INS CO	CA	54,639.9
PRINCIPAL LIFE INS CO	IA	83,957.6
SENTRY LIFE INS CO	WI	2,101.2
USAA LIFE INS CO	TX	9,167.0

Weiss Safety Rating: B+

INSURANCE COMPANY NAME	DOM. STATE	TOTAL ASSETS ($MIL)
AMERICAN GENERAL LIFE INS CO	TX	24,549.9
AMERICAN HEALTH & LIFE INS CO	TX	1,236.5
AMERITAS LIFE INS CORP	NE	2,417.9
AVEMCO INS CO	MD	191.7
BALBOA LIFE INS CO	CA	124.5
CITICORP LIFE INS CO	AZ	1,058.7
COLORADO BANKERS LIFE INS CO	CO	113.3
COLUMBUS LIFE INS CO	OH	2,187.1
COMPANION LIFE INS CO	SC	75.6
CUMIS INS SOCIETY INC	WI	826.9
FEDERAL INS CO	IN	18,983.3
FEDERATED MUTUAL INS CO	MN	3,013.6
GOLDEN RULE INS CO	IL	2,076.2
GRANGE LIFE INS CO	OH	159.8
GREAT NORTHERN INS CO	MN	1,088.5
GREAT-WEST LIFE & ANNUITY INS CO	CO	27,323.0
HARTFORD FIRE INS CO	CT	15,857.7
HARTFORD LIFE & ACCIDENT INS CO	CT	8,792.5
HARTFORD LIFE & ANNUITY INS CO	CT	49,622.7
HARTFORD LIFE INS CO	CT	97,564.5
JEFFERSON PILOT FINANCIAL INS CO	NE	11,630.2
LINCOLN BENEFIT LIFE CO	NE	1,823.4
MANUFACTURERS LIFE INS CO USA	MI	53,737.8
MERIT LIFE INS CO	IN	1,020.5
METROPOLITAN LIFE INS CO	NY	220,093.6
METROPOLITAN PROPERTY & CAS INS CO	RI	4,789.1
MIDWEST SECURITY LIFE INS CO	WI	132.8
NATIONAL BENEFIT LIFE INS CO	NY	736.6
NATIONAL CASUALTY CO	WI	92.6
NATIONAL UNION FIRE INS CO OF PITTSB	PA	18,196.9
NATIONWIDE LIFE INS CO	OH	80,569.1
NATIONWIDE MUTUAL FIRE INS CO	OH	3,610.4
PEKIN LIFE INS CO	IL	653.8
PHYSICIANS LIFE INS CO	NE	1,195.8
PRIMERICA LIFE INS CO	MA	5,073.4
PRIORITY HEALTH	MI	177.9
SIRIUS AMERICA INS CO	DE	216.8
STATE AUTOMOBILE MUTUAL INS CO	OH	1,299.8
STATE FARM MUTUAL AUTOMOBILE INS CO	IL	70,070.4
SURETY LIFE INS CO	NE	50.3
TRAVELERS INS CO LIFE DEPT	CT	58,317.0
UNITED INS CO OF AMERICA	IL	2,064.3
UNITED OF OMAHA LIFE INS CO	NE	12,298.3
WESTERN & SOUTHERN LIFE INS CO	OH	7,850.2

Minnesota

INSURANCE COMPANY NAME	DOM. STATE	TOTAL ASSETS ($MIL)
Weiss Safety Rating: A+		
COUNTRY LIFE INS CO	IL	4,387.5
GOVERNMENT EMPLOYEES INS CO	MD	8,737.7
PHYSICIANS MUTUAL INS CO	NE	1,102.7
PROTECTIVE INS CO	IN	443.4
TEACHERS INS & ANNUITY ASN OF AM	NY	147,114.8
Weiss Safety Rating: A		
AMERICAN FIDELITY ASR CO	OK	2,382.6
AUTO-OWNERS INS CO	MI	6,582.7
CENTURION LIFE INS CO	MO	1,024.0
GUARDIAN LIFE INS CO OF AMERICA	NY	20,577.2
JEFFERSON-PILOT LIFE INS CO	NC	13,405.5
MASSACHUSETTS MUTUAL LIFE INS CO	MA	80,322.1
NEW YORK LIFE INS CO	NY	87,505.8
NORTHWESTERN MUTUAL LIFE INS CO	WI	114,436.3
SENTRY INS A MUTUAL CO	WI	4,177.1
Weiss Safety Rating: A-		
ALLSTATE INS CO	IL	40,978.7
ALLSTATE LIFE INS CO	IL	60,033.7
AUTO-OWNERS LIFE INS CO	MI	1,251.5
CENTRAL STATES INDEMNITY CO OF OMAHA	NE	243.1
CINCINNATI INS CO	OH	7,143.1
FARM BUREAU LIFE INS CO	IA	4,695.3
FEDERATED LIFE INS CO	MN	864.3
GRANGE MUTUAL CAS CO	OH	1,116.1
JOHN HANCOCK LIFE INS CO	MA	73,183.9
MEDICA	MN	599.3
METROPOLITAN HEALTH PLAN	MN	40.9
MIDLAND NATIONAL LIFE INS CO	IA	10,748.6
MINNESOTA LIFE INS CO	MN	17,352.3
MUTUAL OF OMAHA INS CO	NE	3,755.1
NATIONAL GUARDIAN LIFE INS CO	WI	947.4
OLD REPUBLIC INS CO	PA	1,644.5
PACIFIC LIFE INS CO	CA	54,639.9
PRINCIPAL LIFE INS CO	IA	83,957.6
SENTRY LIFE INS CO	WI	2,101.2
USAA LIFE INS CO	TX	9,167.0
Weiss Safety Rating: B+		
AMERICAN GENERAL LIFE INS CO	TX	24,549.9
AMERICAN HEALTH & LIFE INS CO	TX	1,236.5
AMERITAS LIFE INS CORP	NE	2,417.9
AVEMCO INS CO	MD	191.7
BALBOA LIFE INS CO	CA	124.5
BLUE CROSS BLUE SHIELD OF MINNESOTA	MN	1,346.9
CITICORP LIFE INS CO	AZ	1,058.7
COLORADO BANKERS LIFE INS CO	CO	113.3
COLUMBUS LIFE INS CO	OH	2,187.1
COMPANION LIFE INS CO	SC	75.6
CUMIS INS SOCIETY INC	WI	826.9
FEDERAL INS CO	IN	18,983.3
FEDERATED MUTUAL INS CO	MN	3,013.6
FIRST PLAN OF MINNESOTA	MN	19.3
GOLDEN RULE INS CO	IL	2,076.2
GREAT NORTHERN INS CO	MN	1,088.5
GREAT-WEST LIFE & ANNUITY INS CO	CO	27,323.0
HARTFORD FIRE INS CO	CT	15,857.7
HARTFORD LIFE & ACCIDENT INS CO	CT	8,792.5
HARTFORD LIFE & ANNUITY INS CO	CT	49,622.7
HARTFORD LIFE INS CO	CT	97,564.5
HEALTHPARTNERS	MN	237.4
HMO MINNESOTA	MN	216.9
JEFFERSON PILOT FINANCIAL INS CO	NE	11,630.2
LINCOLN BENEFIT LIFE CO	NE	1,823.4
MANUFACTURERS LIFE INS CO USA	MI	53,737.8
MERIT LIFE INS CO	IN	1,020.5
METROPOLITAN LIFE INS CO	NY	220,093.6
METROPOLITAN PROPERTY & CAS INS CO	RI	4,789.1
MIDWEST SECURITY LIFE INS CO	WI	132.8
NATIONAL BENEFIT LIFE INS CO	NY	736.6
NATIONAL CASUALTY CO	WI	92.6
NATIONAL UNION FIRE INS CO OF PITTSB	PA	18,196.9
NATIONWIDE LIFE INS CO	OH	80,569.1
NATIONWIDE MUTUAL FIRE INS CO	OH	3,610.4
NORIDIAN MUTUAL INS CO	ND	298.8
PHYSICIANS LIFE INS CO	NE	1,195.8
PRIMERICA LIFE INS CO	MA	5,073.8
SIRIUS AMERICA INS CO	DE	216.8
STATE AUTOMOBILE MUTUAL INS CO	OH	1,299.8
STATE FARM MUTUAL AUTOMOBILE INS CO	IL	70,070.4
SURETY LIFE INS CO	NE	50.3
TRAVELERS INS CO LIFE DEPT	CT	58,317.0
UCARE MINNESOTA	MN	149.5
UNITED INS CO OF AMERICA	IL	2,064.3
UNITED OF OMAHA LIFE INS CO	NE	12,298.3
WESTERN & SOUTHERN LIFE INS CO	OH	7,850.2

IV. Weiss Recommended Companies by State

Mississippi

INSURANCE COMPANY NAME	DOM. STATE	TOTAL ASSETS ($MIL)
Weiss Safety Rating: A+		
GOVERNMENT EMPLOYEES INS CO	MD	8,737.7
PHYSICIANS MUTUAL INS CO	NE	1,102.7
PROTECTIVE INS CO	IN	443.4
TEACHERS INS & ANNUITY ASN OF AM	NY	147,114.8
Weiss Safety Rating: A		
AMERICAN FIDELITY ASR CO	OK	2,382.6
AUTO-OWNERS INS CO	MI	6,582.7
CENTURION LIFE INS CO	MO	1,024.0
GUARDIAN LIFE INS CO OF AMERICA	NY	20,577.2
JEFFERSON-PILOT LIFE INS CO	NC	13,405.5
MASSACHUSETTS MUTUAL LIFE INS CO	MA	80,322.1
NEW YORK LIFE INS CO	NY	87,505.8
NORTHWESTERN MUTUAL LIFE INS CO	WI	114,436.3
SENTRY INS A MUTUAL CO	WI	4,177.1
UNION NATIONAL LIFE INS CO	LA	377.5
Weiss Safety Rating: A-		
ALFA LIFE INS CORP	AL	821.5
ALLSTATE INS CO	IL	40,978.7
ALLSTATE LIFE INS CO	IL	60,033.7
AUTO-OWNERS LIFE INS CO	MI	1,251.5
CENTRAL STATES INDEMNITY CO OF OMAHA	NE	243.1
CINCINNATI INS CO	OH	7,143.1
FEDERATED LIFE INS CO	MN	864.3
JOHN HANCOCK LIFE INS CO	MA	73,183.9
MIDLAND NATIONAL LIFE INS CO	IA	10,748.6
MINNESOTA LIFE INS CO	MN	17,352.3
MUTUAL OF OMAHA INS CO	NE	3,755.1
NATIONAL GUARDIAN LIFE INS CO	WI	947.4
OLD REPUBLIC INS CO	PA	1,644.5
PACIFIC LIFE INS CO	CA	54,639.9
PRINCIPAL LIFE INS CO	IA	83,957.6
SENTRY LIFE INS CO	WI	2,101.2
SOUTHERN FARM BUREAU LIFE INS CO	MS	7,776.4
USAA LIFE INS CO	TX	9,167.0
Weiss Safety Rating: B+		
AMERICAN GENERAL LIFE INS CO	TX	24,549.9
AMERICAN HEALTH & LIFE INS CO	TX	1,236.5
AMERITAS LIFE INS CORP	NE	2,417.9
AVEMCO INS CO	MD	191.7
BALBOA LIFE INS CO	CA	124.5
CITICORP LIFE INS CO	AZ	1,058.7
COLORADO BANKERS LIFE INS CO	CO	113.3
COLUMBUS LIFE INS CO	OH	2,187.1
COMPANION LIFE INS CO	SC	75.6
CUMIS INS SOCIETY INC	WI	826.9
FEDERAL INS CO	IN	18,983.3
FEDERATED MUTUAL INS CO	MN	3,013.6
GOLDEN RULE INS CO	IL	2,076.2
GREAT NORTHERN INS CO	MN	1,088.5
GREAT-WEST LIFE & ANNUITY INS CO	CO	27,323.0
HARTFORD FIRE INS CO	CT	15,857.7
HARTFORD LIFE & ACCIDENT INS CO	CT	8,792.5
HARTFORD LIFE & ANNUITY INS CO	CT	49,622.7
HARTFORD LIFE INS CO	CT	97,564.5
JEFFERSON PILOT FINANCIAL INS CO	NE	11,630.2
LINCOLN BENEFIT LIFE CO	NE	1,823.4
MANUFACTURERS LIFE INS CO USA	MI	53,737.8
MERIT LIFE INS CO	IN	1,020.5
METROPOLITAN LIFE INS CO	NY	220,093.6
METROPOLITAN PROPERTY & CAS INS CO	RI	4,789.1
MIDWEST SECURITY LIFE INS CO	WI	132.8
NATIONAL BENEFIT LIFE INS CO	NY	736.6
NATIONAL CASUALTY CO	WI	92.6
NATIONAL UNION FIRE INS CO OF PITTSB	PA	18,196.9
NATIONWIDE LIFE INS CO	OH	80,569.1
NATIONWIDE MUTUAL FIRE INS CO	OH	3,610.4
PHYSICIANS LIFE INS CO	NE	1,195.8
PRIMERICA LIFE INS CO	MA	5,073.8
SHELTER LIFE INS CO	MO	811.0
SIRIUS AMERICA INS CO	DE	216.8
STATE AUTOMOBILE MUTUAL INS CO	OH	1,299.8
STATE FARM MUTUAL AUTOMOBILE INS CO	IL	70,070.4
SURETY LIFE INS CO	NE	50.3
TRAVELERS INS CO LIFE DEPT	CT	58,317.0
UNITED INS CO OF AMERICA	IL	2,064.3
UNITED OF OMAHA LIFE INS CO	NE	12,298.3
WESTERN & SOUTHERN LIFE INS CO	OH	7,850.2

Missouri

INSURANCE COMPANY NAME	DOM. STATE	TOTAL ASSETS ($MIL)
Weiss Safety Rating: A+		
COUNTRY LIFE INS CO	IL	4,387.5
GOVERNMENT EMPLOYEES INS CO	MD	8,737.7
PHYSICIANS MUTUAL INS CO	NE	1,102.7
PROTECTIVE INS CO	IN	443.4
TEACHERS INS & ANNUITY ASN OF AM	NY	147,114.8
Weiss Safety Rating: A		
AMERICAN FIDELITY ASR CO	OK	2,382.6
ALTO-OWNERS INS CO	MI	6,582.7
CENTURION LIFE INS CO	MO	1,024.0
GUARDIAN LIFE INS CO OF AMERICA	NY	20,577.2
JEFFERSON-PILOT LIFE INS CO	NC	13,405.5
MASSACHUSETTS MUTUAL LIFE INS CO	MA	80,322.1
NEW YORK LIFE INS CO	NY	87,505.8
NORTHWESTERN MUTUAL LIFE INS CO	WI	114,436.3
SENTRY INS A MUTUAL CO	WI	4,177.1
Weiss Safety Rating: A-		
ALFA LIFE INS CORP	AL	821.5
ALLSTATE INS CO	IL	40,978.7
ALLSTATE LIFE INS CO	IL	60,033.7
AUTO-OWNERS LIFE INS CO	MI	1,251.5
CENTRAL STATES INDEMNITY CO OF OMAHA	NE	243.1
CINCINNATI INS CO	OH	7,143.1
FARM BUREAU LIFE INS CO OF MISSOURI	MO	293.5
FEDERATED LIFE INS CO	MN	864.3
GRANGE MUTUAL CAS CO	OH	1,116.1
JOHN HANCOCK LIFE INS CO	MA	73,183.9
MIDLAND NATIONAL LIFE INS CO	IA	10,748.6
MINNESOTA LIFE INS CO	MN	17,352.3
MUTUAL OF OMAHA INS CO	NE	3,755.1
NATIONAL GUARDIAN LIFE INS CO	WI	947.4
OLD REPUBLIC INS CO	PA	1,644.5
PACIFIC LIFE INS CO	CA	54,639.9
PRINCIPAL LIFE INS CO	IA	83,957.6
SENTRY LIFE INS CO	WI	2,101.2
USAA LIFE INS CO	TX	9,167.0
Weiss Safety Rating: B+		
ALLSTATE LIFE INS CO OF NEW YORK	NY	4,816.0
AMERICAN GENERAL LIFE INS CO	TX	24,549.9
AMERICAN HEALTH & LIFE INS CO	TX	1,236.5
AMERITAS LIFE INS CORP	NE	2,417.9
AVEMCO INS CO	MD	191.7
BALBOA LIFE INS CO	CA	124.5
BLUE CROSS BLUE SHIELD OF KC	MO	399.8
CITICORP LIFE INS CO	AZ	1,058.7
COLORADO BANKERS LIFE INS CO	CO	113.3
COLUMBUS LIFE INS CO	OH	2,187.1
COMPANION LIFE INS CO	SC	75.6
CUMIS INS SOCIETY INC	WI	826.9
FEDERAL INS CO	IN	18,983.3
FEDERATED MUTUAL INS CO	MN	3,013.6
GOLDEN RULE INS CO	IL	2,076.2
GRANGE LIFE INS CO	OH	159.8
GREAT NORTHERN INS CO	MN	1,088.5
GREAT-WEST LIFE & ANNUITY INS CO	CO	27,323.0
HARTFORD FIRE INS CO	CT	15,857.7
HARTFORD LIFE & ACCIDENT INS CO	CT	8,792.5
HARTFORD LIFE & ANNUITY INS CO	CT	49,622.7
HARTFORD LIFE INS CO	CT	97,564.5
HEALTHLINK HMO INC	MO	26.3
JEFFERSON PILOT FINANCIAL INS CO	NE	11,630.2
LINCOLN BENEFIT LIFE CO	NE	1,823.4
MANUFACTURERS LIFE INS CO USA	MI	53,737.8
MERIT LIFE INS CO	IN	1,020.5
METROPOLITAN LIFE INS CO	NY	220,093.6
METROPOLITAN PROPERTY & CAS INS CO	RI	4,789.1
MIDWEST SECURITY LIFE INS CO	WI	132.8
NATIONAL BENEFIT LIFE INS CO	NY	736.6
NATIONAL CASUALTY CO	WI	92.6
NATIONAL UNION FIRE INS CO OF PITTSB	PA	18,196.9
NATIONWIDE LIFE INS CO	OH	80,569.1
NATIONWIDE MUTUAL FIRE INS CO	OH	3,610.4
PACIFIC GUARDIAN LIFE INS CO LTD	HI	431.5
PEKIN LIFE INS CO	IL	653.8
PHYSICIANS LIFE INS CO	NE	1,195.8
PRIMERICA LIFE INS CO	MA	5,073.8
SHELTER LIFE INS CO	MO	811.0
SIRIUS AMERICA INS CO	DE	216.8
STATE AUTOMOBILE MUTUAL INS CO	OH	1,299.8
STATE FARM MUTUAL AUTOMOBILE INS CO	IL	70,070.4
SURETY LIFE INS CO	NE	50.3
TRAVELERS INS CO LIFE DEPT	CT	58,317.0
UNITED HEALTHCARE OF THE MIDWEST INC	MO	332.1
UNITED INS CO OF AMERICA	IL	2,064.3
UNITED OF OMAHA LIFE INS CO	NE	12,298.3
WESTERN & SOUTHERN LIFE INS CO	OH	7,850.2

IV. Weiss Recommended Companies by State

Winter 2003 - 04

Montana

INSURANCE COMPANY NAME	DOM. STATE	TOTAL ASSETS ($MIL)
Weiss Safety Rating: A+		
COUNTRY LIFE INS CO	IL	4,387.5
GOVERNMENT EMPLOYEES INS CO	MD	8,737.7
PHYSICIANS MUTUAL INS CO	NE	1,102.7
PROTECTIVE INS CO	IN	443.4
TEACHERS INS & ANNUITY ASN OF AM	NY	147,114.8
Weiss Safety Rating: A		
AMERICAN FIDELITY ASR CO	OK	2,382.6
CENTURION LIFE INS CO	MO	1,024.0
GUARDIAN LIFE INS CO OF AMERICA	NY	20,577.2
JEFFERSON-PILOT LIFE INS CO	NC	13,405.5
MASSACHUSETTS MUTUAL LIFE INS CO	MA	80,322.1
NEW YORK LIFE INS CO	NY	87,505.8
NORTHWESTERN MUTUAL LIFE INS CO	WI	114,436.3
SENTRY INS A MUTUAL CO	WI	4,177.1
Weiss Safety Rating: A-		
ALLSTATE INS CO	IL	40,978.7
ALLSTATE LIFE INS CO	IL	60,033.7
CENTRAL STATES INDEMNITY CO OF OMAHA	NE	243.1
CINCINNATI INS CO	OH	7,143.1
FARM BUREAU LIFE INS CO	IA	4,695.3
FEDERATED LIFE INS CO	MN	864.3
JOHN HANCOCK LIFE INS CO	MA	73,183.9
MIDLAND NATIONAL LIFE INS CO	IA	10,748.6
MINNESOTA LIFE INS CO	MN	17,352.3
MUTUAL OF OMAHA INS CO	NE	3,755.1
NATIONAL GUARDIAN LIFE INS CO	WI	947.4
OLD REPUBLIC INS CO	PA	1,644.5
PACIFIC LIFE INS CO	CA	54,639.9
PRINCIPAL LIFE INS CO	IA	83,957.6
SENTRY LIFE INS CO	WI	2,101.2
USAA LIFE INS CO	TX	9,167.0
Weiss Safety Rating: B+		
AMERICAN GENERAL LIFE INS CO	TX	24,549.9
AMERICAN HEALTH & LIFE INS CO	TX	1,236.5
AMERITAS LIFE INS CORP	NE	2,417.9
AVEMCO INS CO	MD	191.7
BALBOA LIFE INS CO	CA	124.5
CITICORP LIFE INS CO	AZ	1,058.7
COLORADO BANKERS LIFE INS CO	CO	113.3
COLUMBUS LIFE INS CO	OH	2,187.1
COMPANION LIFE INS CO	SC	75.6
CUMIS INS SOCIETY INC	WI	826.9
FEDERAL INS CO	IN	18,983.3
FEDERATED MUTUAL INS CO	MN	3,013.6
GOLDEN RULE INS CO	IL	2,076.2
GREAT NORTHERN INS CO	MN	1,088.5
GREAT-WEST LIFE & ANNUITY INS CO	CO	27,323.0
HARTFORD FIRE INS CO	CT	15,857.7
HARTFORD LIFE & ACCIDENT INS CO	CT	8,792.5

INSURANCE COMPANY NAME	DOM. STATE	TOTAL ASSETS ($MIL)
HARTFORD LIFE & ANNUITY INS CO	CT	49,622.7
HARTFORD LIFE INS CO	CT	97,564.5
JEFFERSON PILOT FINANCIAL INS CO	NE	11,630.2
LINCOLN BENEFIT LIFE CO	NE	1,823.4
MANUFACTURERS LIFE INS CO USA	MI	53,737.8
MERIT LIFE INS CO	IN	1,020.5
METROPOLITAN LIFE INS CO	NY	220,093.6
METROPOLITAN PROPERTY & CAS INS CO	RI	4,789.1
NATIONAL BENEFIT LIFE INS CO	NY	736.6
NATIONAL CASUALTY CO	WI	92.6
NATIONAL UNION FIRE INS CO OF PITTSB	PA	18,196.9
NATIONWIDE LIFE INS CO	OH	80,569.1
NATIONWIDE MUTUAL FIRE INS CO	OH	3,610.4
PACIFIC GUARDIAN LIFE INS CO LTD	HI	431.5
PHYSICIANS LIFE INS CO	NE	1,195.8
PRIMERICA LIFE INS CO	MA	5,073.8
SIRIUS AMERICA INS CO	DE	216.8
STATE AUTOMOBILE MUTUAL INS CO	OH	1,299.8
STATE FARM MUTUAL AUTOMOBILE INS CO	IL	70,070.4
SURETY LIFE INS CO	NE	50.3
TRAVELERS INS CO LIFE DEPT	CT	58,317.0
UNITED INS CO OF AMERICA	IL	2,064.3
UNITED OF OMAHA LIFE INS CO	NE	12,298.3
WESTERN & SOUTHERN LIFE INS CO	OH	7,850.2

Nebraska

INSURANCE COMPANY NAME	DOM. STATE	TOTAL ASSETS ($MIL)
Weiss Safety Rating: A+		
COUNTRY LIFE INS CO	IL	4,387.5
GOVERNMENT EMPLOYEES INS CO	MD	8,737.7
PHYSICIANS MUTUAL INS CO	NE	1,102.7
PROTECTIVE INS CO	IN	443.4
TEACHERS INS & ANNUITY ASN OF AM	NY	147,114.8
Weiss Safety Rating: A		
AMERICAN FIDELITY ASR CO	OK	2,382.6
AUTO-OWNERS INS CO	MI	6,582.7
CENTURION LIFE INS CO	MO	1,024.0
GUARDIAN LIFE INS CO OF AMERICA	NY	20,577.2
JEFFERSON-PILOT LIFE INS CO	NC	13,405.5
MASSACHUSETTS MUTUAL LIFE INS CO	MA	80,322.1
NEW YORK LIFE INS CO	NY	87,505.8
NORTHWESTERN MUTUAL LIFE INS CO	WI	114,436.3
SENTRY INS A MUTUAL CO	WI	4,177.1
Weiss Safety Rating: A-		
ALLSTATE INS CO	IL	40,978.7
ALLSTATE LIFE INS CO	IL	60,033.7
AUTO-OWNERS LIFE INS CO	MI	1,251.5
CENTRAL STATES INDEMNITY CO OF OMAHA	NE	243.1
CINCINNATI INS CO	OH	7,143.1
FARM BUREAU LIFE INS CO	IA	4,695.3
FEDERATED LIFE INS CO	MN	864.3
JOHN HANCOCK LIFE INS CO	MA	73,183.9
MIDLAND NATIONAL LIFE INS CO	IA	10,748.6
MINNESOTA LIFE INS CO	MN	17,352.3
MUTUAL OF OMAHA INS CO	NE	3,755.1
NATIONAL GUARDIAN LIFE INS CO	WI	947.4
OLD REPUBLIC INS CO	PA	1,644.5
PACIFIC LIFE INS CO	CA	54,639.9
PRINCIPAL LIFE INS CO	IA	83,957.6
SENTRY LIFE INS CO	WI	2,101.2
USAA LIFE INS CO	TX	9,167.0
Weiss Safety Rating: B+		
ALLSTATE LIFE INS CO OF NEW YORK	NY	4,816.0
AMERICAN GENERAL LIFE INS CO	TX	24,549.9
AMERICAN HEALTH & LIFE INS CO	TX	1,236.5
AMERITAS LIFE INS CORP	NE	2,417.9
AVEMCO INS CO	MD	191.7
BALBOA LIFE INS CO	CA	124.5
CITICORP LIFE INS CO	AZ	1,058.7
COLORADO BANKERS LIFE INS CO	CO	113.3
COLUMBUS LIFE INS CO	OH	2,187.1
COMPANION LIFE INS CO	SC	75.6
CUMIS INS SOCIETY INC	WI	826.9
FEDERAL INS CO	IN	18,983.3
FEDERATED MUTUAL INS CO	MN	3,013.6
GOLDEN RULE INS CO	IL	2,076.2
GREAT NORTHERN INS CO	MN	1,088.5
GREAT-WEST LIFE & ANNUITY INS CO	CO	27,323.0
HARTFORD FIRE INS CO	CT	15,857.7
HARTFORD LIFE & ACCIDENT INS CO	CT	8,792.5
HARTFORD LIFE & ANNUITY INS CO	CT	49,622.7
HARTFORD LIFE INS CO	CT	97,564.5
JEFFERSON PILOT FINANCIAL INS CO	NE	11,630.2
LINCOLN BENEFIT LIFE CO	NE	1,823.4
MANUFACTURERS LIFE INS CO USA	MI	53,737.8
MERIT LIFE INS CO	IN	1,020.5
METROPOLITAN LIFE INS CO	NY	220,093.6
METROPOLITAN PROPERTY & CAS INS CO	RI	4,789.1
MIDWEST SECURITY LIFE INS CO	WI	132.8
NATIONAL BENEFIT LIFE INS CO	NY	736.6
NATIONAL CASUALTY CO	WI	92.6
NATIONAL UNION FIRE INS CO OF PITTSB	PA	18,196.9
NATIONWIDE LIFE INS CO	OH	80,569.1
NATIONWIDE MUTUAL FIRE INS CO	OH	3,610.4
PACIFIC GUARDIAN LIFE INS CO LTD	HI	431.5
PHYSICIANS LIFE INS CO	NE	1,195.8
PRIMERICA LIFE INS CO	MA	5,073.8
SHELTER LIFE INS CO	MO	811.0
SIRIUS AMERICA INS CO	DE	216.8
STATE AUTOMOBILE MUTUAL INS CO	OH	1,299.8
STATE FARM MUTUAL AUTOMOBILE INS CO	IL	70,070.4
SURETY LIFE INS CO	NE	50.3
TRAVELERS INS CO LIFE DEPT	CT	58,317.0
UNITED HEALTHCARE OF THE MIDLANDS	NE	69.7
UNITED INS CO OF AMERICA	IL	2,064.3
UNITED OF OMAHA LIFE INS CO	NE	12,298.3
WESTERN & SOUTHERN LIFE INS CO	OH	7,850.2

IV. Weiss Recommended Companies by State
Winter 2003 - 04

Nevada

INSURANCE COMPANY NAME	DOM. STATE	TOTAL ASSETS ($MIL)
Weiss Safety Rating: A+		
COUNTRY LIFE INS CO	IL	4,387.5
GOVERNMENT EMPLOYEES INS CO	MD	8,737.7
PHYSICIANS MUTUAL INS CO	NE	1,102.7
PROTECTIVE INS CO	IN	443.4
TEACHERS INS & ANNUITY ASN OF AM	NY	147,114.8
Weiss Safety Rating: A		
AMERICAN FIDELITY ASR CO	OK	2,382.6
AUTO-OWNERS INS CO	MI	6,582.7
CENTURION LIFE INS CO	MO	1,024.0
GUARDIAN LIFE INS CO OF AMERICA	NY	20,577.2
JEFFERSON-PILOT LIFE INS CO	NC	13,405.5
MASSACHUSETTS MUTUAL LIFE INS CO	MA	80,322.1
NEW YORK LIFE INS CO	NY	87,505.8
NORTHWESTERN MUTUAL LIFE INS CO	WI	114,436.3
SENTRY INS A MUTUAL CO	WI	4,177.1
Weiss Safety Rating: A-		
ALLSTATE INS CO	IL	40,978.7
ALLSTATE LIFE INS CO	IL	60,033.7
AUTO-OWNERS LIFE INS CO	MI	1,251.5
CALIFORNIA STATE AUTO ASN INTER-INS	CA	4,180.2
CENTRAL STATES INDEMNITY CO OF OMAHA	NE	243.1
CINCINNATI INS CO	OH	7,143.1
FARM BUREAU LIFE INS CO	IA	4,695.3
FEDERATED LIFE INS CO	MN	864.3
JOHN HANCOCK LIFE INS CO	MA	73,183.9
MIDLAND NATIONAL LIFE INS CO	IA	10,748.6
MINNESOTA LIFE INS CO	MN	17,352.3
MUTUAL OF OMAHA INS CO	NE	3,755.1
NATIONAL GUARDIAN LIFE INS CO	WI	947.4
OLD REPUBLIC INS CO	PA	1,644.5
PACIFIC LIFE INS CO	CA	54,639.9
PRINCIPAL LIFE INS CO	IA	83,957.6
SENTRY LIFE INS CO	WI	2,101.2
USAA LIFE INS CO	TX	9,167.0
Weiss Safety Rating: B+		
AMERICAN GENERAL LIFE INS CO	TX	24,549.9
AMERICAN HEALTH & LIFE INS CO	TX	1,236.5
AMERITAS LIFE INS CORP	NE	2,417.9
AVEMCO INS CO	MD	191.7
BALBOA LIFE INS CO	CA	124.5
CITICORP LIFE INS CO	AZ	1,058.7
COLORADO BANKERS LIFE INS CO	CO	113.3
COLUMBUS LIFE INS CO	OH	2,187.1
COMPANION LIFE INS CO	SC	75.6
CUMIS INS SOCIETY INC	WI	826.9
FEDERAL INS CO	IN	18,983.3
FEDERATED MUTUAL INS CO	MN	3,013.6
GOLDEN RULE INS CO	IL	2,076.2
GREAT NORTHERN INS CO	MN	1,088.5

INSURANCE COMPANY NAME	DOM. STATE	TOTAL ASSETS ($MIL)
GREAT-WEST LIFE & ANNUITY INS CO	CO	27,323.0
HARTFORD FIRE INS CO	CT	15,857.7
HARTFORD LIFE & ACCIDENT INS CO	CT	8,792.5
HARTFORD LIFE & ANNUITY INS CO	CT	49,622.7
HARTFORD LIFE INS CO	CT	97,564.5
JEFFERSON PILOT FINANCIAL INS CO	NE	11,630.2
LINCOLN BENEFIT LIFE CO	NE	1,823.4
MANUFACTURERS LIFE INS CO USA	MI	53,737.8
MERIT LIFE INS CO	IN	1,020.5
METROPOLITAN LIFE INS CO	NY	220,093.6
METROPOLITAN PROPERTY & CAS INS CO	RI	4,789.1
MIDWEST SECURITY LIFE INS CO	WI	132.8
NATIONAL BENEFIT LIFE INS CO	NY	736.6
NATIONAL CASUALTY CO	WI	92.6
NATIONAL UNION FIRE INS CO OF PITTSB	PA	18,196.9
NATIONWIDE LIFE INS CO	OH	80,569.1
NATIONWIDE MUTUAL FIRE INS CO	OH	3,610.4
PACIFIC GUARDIAN LIFE INS CO LTD	HI	431.5
PHYSICIANS LIFE INS CO	NE	1,195.8
PRIMERICA LIFE INS CO	MA	5,073.8
SIRIUS AMERICA INS CO	DE	216.8
STATE FARM MUTUAL AUTOMOBILE INS CO	IL	70,070.4
SURETY LIFE INS CO	NE	50.3
TRAVELERS INS CO LIFE DEPT	CT	58,317.0
UNITED INS CO OF AMERICA	IL	2,064.3
UNITED OF OMAHA LIFE INS CO	NE	12,298.3
WESTERN & SOUTHERN LIFE INS CO	OH	7,850.2

New Hampshire

Weiss Safety Rating: A+

INSURANCE COMPANY NAME	DOM. STATE	TOTAL ASSETS ($MIL)
GOVERNMENT EMPLOYEES INS CO	MD	8,737.7
PHYSICIANS MUTUAL INS CO	NE	1,102.7
PROTECTIVE INS CO	IN	443.4
TEACHERS INS & ANNUITY ASN OF AM	NY	147,114.8

Weiss Safety Rating: A

INSURANCE COMPANY NAME	DOM. STATE	TOTAL ASSETS ($MIL)
AMERICAN FIDELITY ASR CO	OK	2,382.6
CENTURION LIFE INS CO	MO	1,024.0
GUARDIAN LIFE INS CO OF AMERICA	NY	20,577.2
JEFFERSON-PILOT LIFE INS CO	NC	13,405.5
MASSACHUSETTS MUTUAL LIFE INS CO	MA	80,322.1
NEW YORK LIFE INS CO	NY	87,505.8
NORTHWESTERN MUTUAL LIFE INS CO	WI	114,436.3
SENTRY INS A MUTUAL CO	WI	4,177.1

Weiss Safety Rating: A-

INSURANCE COMPANY NAME	DOM. STATE	TOTAL ASSETS ($MIL)
ALLSTATE INS CO	IL	40,978.7
ALLSTATE LIFE INS CO	IL	60,033.7
CENTRAL STATES INDEMNITY CO OF OMAHA	NE	243.1
CINCINNATI INS CO	OH	7,143.1
FEDERATED LIFE INS CO	MN	864.3
JOHN HANCOCK LIFE INS CO	MA	73,183.9
MIDLAND NATIONAL LIFE INS CO	IA	10,748.6
MINNESOTA LIFE INS CO	MN	17,352.3
MUTUAL OF OMAHA INS CO	NE	3,755.1
OLD REPUBLIC INS CO	PA	1,644.5
PACIFIC LIFE INS CO	CA	54,639.9
PRINCIPAL LIFE INS CO	IA	83,957.6
SENTRY LIFE INS CO	WI	2,101.2
USAA LIFE INS CO	TX	9,167.0

Weiss Safety Rating: B+

INSURANCE COMPANY NAME	DOM. STATE	TOTAL ASSETS ($MIL)
AMERICAN GENERAL LIFE INS CO	TX	24,549.9
AMERICAN HEALTH & LIFE INS CO	TX	1,236.5
AMERITAS LIFE INS CORP	NE	2,417.9
AVEMCO INS CO	MD	191.7
BALBOA LIFE INS CO	CA	124.5
CITICORP LIFE INS CO	AZ	1,058.7
COLORADO BANKERS LIFE INS CO	CO	113.3
COLUMBUS LIFE INS CO	OH	2,187.1
COMPANION LIFE INS CO	SC	75.6
CUMIS INS SOCIETY INC	WI	826.9
FARM FAMILY LIFE INS CO	NY	889.2
FEDERAL INS CO	IN	18,983.3
GOLDEN RULE INS CO	IL	2,076.2
GREAT NORTHERN INS CO	MN	1,088.5
GREAT-WEST LIFE & ANNUITY INS CO	CO	27,323.0
HARTFORD FIRE INS CO	CT	15,857.7
HARTFORD LIFE & ACCIDENT INS CO	CT	8,792.5
HARTFORD LIFE & ANNUITY INS CO	CT	49,622.7
HARTFORD LIFE INS CO	CT	97,564.5
JEFFERSON PILOT FINANCIAL INS CO	NE	11,630.2
LINCOLN BENEFIT LIFE CO	NE	1,823.4
MANUFACTURERS LIFE INS CO USA	MI	53,737.8
MATTHEW THORNTON HEALTH PLAN	NH	210.3
METROPOLITAN LIFE INS CO	NY	220,093.6
METROPOLITAN PROPERTY & CAS INS CO	RI	4,789.1
NATIONAL BENEFIT LIFE INS CO	NY	736.6
NATIONAL CASUALTY CO	WI	92.6
NATIONAL UNION FIRE INS CO OF PITTSB	PA	18,196.9
NATIONWIDE LIFE INS CO	OH	80,569.1
NATIONWIDE MUTUAL FIRE INS CO	OH	3,610.4
PHYSICIANS LIFE INS CO	NE	1,195.8
PRIMERICA LIFE INS CO	MA	5,073.8
SAVINGS BANK LIFE INS CO OF MA	MA	1,548.3
SIRIUS AMERICA INS CO	DE	216.8
STATE FARM MUTUAL AUTOMOBILE INS CO	IL	70,070.4
SURETY LIFE INS CO	NE	50.3
TRAVELERS INS CO LIFE DEPT	CT	58,317.0
UNITED INS CO OF AMERICA	IL	2,064.3
UNITED OF OMAHA LIFE INS CO	NE	12,298.3

IV. Weiss Recommended Companies by State

New Jersey

INSURANCE COMPANY NAME	DOM. STATE	TOTAL ASSETS ($MIL)
Weiss Safety Rating: A+		
PHYSICIANS MUTUAL INS CO	NE	1,102.7
PROTECTIVE INS CO	IN	443.4
TEACHERS INS & ANNUITY ASN OF AM	NY	147,114.8
Weiss Safety Rating: A		
AMERICAN FIDELITY ASR CO	OK	2,382.6
CENTURION LIFE INS CO	MO	1,024.0
GUARDIAN LIFE INS CO OF AMERICA	NY	20,577.2
HORIZON HEALTHCARE SERVICES INC	NJ	1,684.0
JEFFERSON-PILOT LIFE INS CO	NC	13,405.5
MASSACHUSETTS MUTUAL LIFE INS CO	MA	80,322.1
NEW YORK LIFE INS CO	NY	87,505.8
NORTHWESTERN MUTUAL LIFE INS CO	WI	114,436.3
SENTRY INS A MUTUAL CO	WI	4,177.1
Weiss Safety Rating: A-		
ALLSTATE LIFE INS CO	IL	60,033.7
CENTRAL STATES INDEMNITY CO OF OMAHA	NE	243.1
CINCINNATI INS CO	OH	7,143.1
FEDERATED LIFE INS CO	MN	864.3
JOHN HANCOCK LIFE INS CO	MA	73,183.9
MIDLAND NATIONAL LIFE INS CO	IA	10,748.6
MINNESOTA LIFE INS CO	MN	17,352.3
MUTUAL OF OMAHA INS CO	NE	3,755.1
NATIONAL GUARDIAN LIFE INS CO	WI	947.4
OLD REPUBLIC INS CO	PA	1,644.5
PACIFIC LIFE INS CO	CA	54,639.9
PRINCIPAL LIFE INS CO	IA	83,957.6
SENTRY LIFE INS CO	WI	2,101.2
USAA LIFE INS CO	TX	9,167.0
Weiss Safety Rating: B+		
ALLSTATE LIFE INS CO OF NEW YORK	NY	4,816.0
AMERICAN GENERAL LIFE INS CO	TX	24,549.9
AMERICAN HEALTH & LIFE INS CO	TX	1,236.5
AMERITAS LIFE INS CORP	NE	2,417.9
AVEMCO INS CO	MD	191.7
BALBOA LIFE INS CO	CA	124.5
CITICORP LIFE INS CO	AZ	1,058.7
COLORADO BANKERS LIFE INS CO	CO	113.3
COLUMBUS LIFE INS CO	OH	2,187.1
CUMIS INS SOCIETY INC	WI	826.9
FARM FAMILY LIFE INS CO	NY	889.2
FEDERAL INS CO	IN	18,983.3
FEDERATED MUTUAL INS CO	MN	3,013.6
GOLDEN RULE INS CO	IL	2,076.2
GREAT NORTHERN INS CO	MN	1,088.5
GREAT-WEST LIFE & ANNUITY INS CO	CO	27,323.0
HARTFORD FIRE INS CO	CT	15,857.7
HARTFORD LIFE & ACCIDENT INS CO	CT	8,792.5
HARTFORD LIFE & ANNUITY INS CO	CT	49,622.7
HARTFORD LIFE INS CO	CT	97,564.5
HORIZON HEALTHCARE OF NEW JERSEY INC	NJ	595.7
JEFFERSON PILOT FINANCIAL INS CO	NE	11,630.2
LINCOLN BENEFIT LIFE CO	NE	1,823.4
MANUFACTURERS LIFE INS CO USA	MI	53,737.8
MERIT LIFE INS CO	IN	1,020.5
METROPOLITAN LIFE INS CO	NY	220,093.6
METROPOLITAN PROPERTY & CAS INS CO	RI	4,789.1
NATIONAL BENEFIT LIFE INS CO	NY	736.6
NATIONAL CASUALTY CO	WI	92.6
NATIONAL UNION FIRE INS CO OF PITTSB	PA	18,196.9
NATIONWIDE LIFE INS CO	OH	80,569.1
NATIONWIDE MUTUAL FIRE INS CO	OH	3,610.4
PHYSICIANS LIFE INS CO	NE	1,195.8
PRIMERICA LIFE INS CO	MA	5,073.8
SAVINGS BANK LIFE INS CO OF MA	MA	1,548.3
SIRIUS AMERICA INS CO	DE	216.8
STATE FARM MUTUAL AUTOMOBILE INS CO	IL	70,070.4
SURETY LIFE INS CO	NE	50.3
TRAVELERS INS CO LIFE DEPT	CT	58,317.0
UNITED INS CO OF AMERICA	IL	2,064.3
UNITED OF OMAHA LIFE INS CO	NE	12,298.3
WESTERN & SOUTHERN LIFE INS CO	OH	7,850.2

New Mexico

INSURANCE COMPANY NAME	DOM. STATE	TOTAL ASSETS ($MIL)
Weiss Safety Rating: A+		
COUNTRY LIFE INS CO	IL	4,387.5
GOVERNMENT EMPLOYEES INS CO	MD	8,737.7
PHYSICIANS MUTUAL INS CO	NE	1,102.7
PROTECTIVE INS CO	IN	443.4
TEACHERS INS & ANNUITY ASN OF AM	NY	147,114.8
Weiss Safety Rating: A		
AMERICAN FIDELITY ASR CO	OK	2,382.6
AUTO-OWNERS INS CO	MI	6,582.7
CENTURION LIFE INS CO	MO	1,024.0
GUARDIAN LIFE INS CO OF AMERICA	NY	20,577.2
JEFFERSON-PILOT LIFE INS CO	NC	13,405.5
MASSACHUSETTS MUTUAL LIFE INS CO	MA	80,322.1
NEW YORK LIFE INS CO	NY	87,505.8
NORTHWESTERN MUTUAL LIFE INS CO	WI	114,436.3
SENTRY INS A MUTUAL CO	WI	4,177.1
Weiss Safety Rating: A-		
ALLSTATE INS CO	IL	40,978.7
ALLSTATE LIFE INS CO	IL	60,033.7
AUTO-OWNERS LIFE INS CO	MI	1,251.5
CENTRAL STATES INDEMNITY CO OF OMAHA	NE	243.1
CINCINNATI INS CO	OH	7,143.1
FARM BUREAU LIFE INS CO	IA	4,695.3
FEDERATED LIFE INS CO	MN	864.3
JOHN HANCOCK LIFE INS CO	MA	73,183.9
MIDLAND NATIONAL LIFE INS CO	IA	10,748.6
MINNESOTA LIFE INS CO	MN	17,352.3
MUTUAL OF OMAHA INS CO	NE	3,755.1
NATIONAL GUARDIAN LIFE INS CO	WI	947.4
OLD REPUBLIC INS CO	PA	1,644.5
PACIFIC LIFE INS CO	CA	54,639.9
PRINCIPAL LIFE INS CO	IA	83,957.6
SENTRY LIFE INS CO	WI	2,101.2
USAA LIFE INS CO	TX	9,167.0
Weiss Safety Rating: B+		
AMERICAN GENERAL LIFE INS CO	TX	24,549.9
AMERICAN HEALTH & LIFE INS CO	TX	1,236.5
AMERITAS LIFE INS CORP	NE	2,417.9
AVEMCO INS CO	MD	191.7
BALBOA LIFE INS CO	CA	124.5
CITICORP LIFE INS CO	AZ	1,058.7
COLORADO BANKERS LIFE INS CO	CO	113.3
COLUMBUS LIFE INS CO	OH	2,187.1
COMPANION LIFE INS CO	SC	75.6
CUMIS INS SOCIETY INC	WI	826.9
FEDERAL INS CO	IN	18,983.3
FEDERATED MUTUAL INS CO	MN	3,013.6
GOLDEN RULE INS CO	IL	2,076.2
GREAT NORTHERN INS CO	MN	1,088.5
GREAT-WEST LIFE & ANNUITY INS CO	CO	27,323.0
HARTFORD FIRE INS CO	CT	15,857.7
HARTFORD LIFE & ACCIDENT INS CO	CT	8,792.5
HARTFORD LIFE & ANNUITY INS CO	CT	49,622.7
HARTFORD LIFE INS CO	CT	97,564.5
HEALTH CARE SVC CORP A MUT LEG RES	IL	4,352.1
HMO NEW MEXICO INC	NM	28.6
JEFFERSON PILOT FINANCIAL INS CO	NE	11,630.2
LINCOLN BENEFIT LIFE CO	NE	1,823.4
MANUFACTURERS LIFE INS CO USA	MI	53,737.8
MERIT LIFE INS CO	IN	1,020.5
METROPOLITAN LIFE INS CO	NY	220,093.6
METROPOLITAN PROPERTY & CAS INS CO	RI	4,789.1
MIDWEST SECURITY LIFE INS CO	WI	132.8
NATIONAL BENEFIT LIFE INS CO	NY	736.6
NATIONAL CASUALTY CO	WI	92.6
NATIONAL UNION FIRE INS CO OF PITTSB	PA	18,196.9
NATIONWIDE LIFE INS CO	OH	80,569.1
NATIONWIDE MUTUAL FIRE INS CO	OH	3,610.4
PACIFIC GUARDIAN LIFE INS CO LTD	HI	431.5
PHYSICIANS LIFE INS CO	NE	1,195.8
PRIMERICA LIFE INS CO	MA	5,073.8
SIRIUS AMERICA INS CO	DE	216.8
STATE FARM MUTUAL AUTOMOBILE INS CO	IL	70,070.4
SURETY LIFE INS CO	NE	50.3
TRAVELERS INS CO LIFE DEPT	CT	58,317.0
UNITED INS CO OF AMERICA	IL	2,064.3
UNITED OF OMAHA LIFE INS CO	NE	12,298.3
WESTERN & SOUTHERN LIFE INS CO	OH	7,850.2

IV. Weiss Recommended Companies by State

New York

INSURANCE COMPANY NAME	DOM. STATE	TOTAL ASSETS ($MIL)

Weiss Safety Rating: A+

INSURANCE COMPANY NAME	DOM. STATE	TOTAL ASSETS ($MIL)
GOVERNMENT EMPLOYEES INS CO	MD	8,737.7
PHYSICIANS MUTUAL INS CO	NE	1,102.7
PROTECTIVE INS CO	IN	443.4
TEACHERS INS & ANNUITY ASN OF AM	NY	147,114.8

Weiss Safety Rating: A

INSURANCE COMPANY NAME	DOM. STATE	TOTAL ASSETS ($MIL)
ALFA MUTUAL INS CO	AL	1,151.8
CENTURION LIFE INS CO	MO	1,024.0
GUARDIAN LIFE INS CO OF AMERICA	NY	20,577.2
MASSACHUSETTS MUTUAL LIFE INS CO	MA	80,322.1
NEW YORK LIFE INS CO	NY	87,505.8
NORTHWESTERN MUTUAL LIFE INS CO	WI	114,436.3
SENTRY INS A MUTUAL CO	WI	4,177.1

Weiss Safety Rating: A-

INSURANCE COMPANY NAME	DOM. STATE	TOTAL ASSETS ($MIL)
ALLSTATE INS CO	IL	40,978.7
CENTRAL STATES INDEMNITY CO OF OMAHA	NE	243.1
CINCINNATI INS CO	OH	7,143.1
EMPIRE HEALTHCHOICE ASSURANCE INC	NY	1,762.8
FEDERATED LIFE INS CO	MN	864.3
JOHN HANCOCK LIFE INS CO	MA	73,183.9
MUTUAL OF OMAHA INS CO	NE	3,755.1
OLD REPUBLIC INS CO	PA	1,644.5
PRINCIPAL LIFE INS CO	IA	83,957.6

Weiss Safety Rating: B+

INSURANCE COMPANY NAME	DOM. STATE	TOTAL ASSETS ($MIL)
ALLSTATE LIFE INS CO OF NEW YORK	NY	4,816.0
AMERICHOICE OF NEW YORK INC	NY	83.0
AVEMCO INS CO	MD	191.7
BALBOA LIFE INS CO	CA	124.5
CAPITAL DISTRICT PHYSICIANS HEALTH P	NY	246.1
CUMIS INS SOCIETY INC	WI	826.9
EXCELLUS HEALTH PLAN INC	NY	1,475.7
FARM FAMILY LIFE INS CO	NY	889.2
FEDERAL INS CO	IN	18,983.3
FEDERATED MUTUAL INS CO	MN	3,013.6
GREAT NORTHERN INS CO	MN	1,088.5
GROUP HEALTH INCORPORATED	NY	634.4
HARTFORD FIRE INS CO	CT	15,857.7
HARTFORD LIFE INS CO	CT	97,564.5
HEALTH INSURANCE PLAN OF GREATER NY	NY	1,066.5
IDS LIFE INS CO OF NEW YORK	NY	2,757.9
METROPOLITAN LIFE INS CO	NY	220,093.6
METROPOLITAN PROPERTY & CAS INS CO	RI	4,789.1
MVP HEALTH PLAN INC	NY	264.0
NATIONAL BENEFIT LIFE INS CO	NY	736.6
NATIONAL CASUALTY CO	WI	92.6
NATIONAL UNION FIRE INS CO OF PITTSB	PA	18,196.9
NATIONWIDE LIFE INS CO	OH	80,569.1
NATIONWIDE MUTUAL FIRE INS CO	OH	3,610.4
OXFORD HEALTH PLANS (NY) INC	NY	1,066.7
SIRIUS AMERICA INS CO	DE	216.8
STATE FARM MUTUAL AUTOMOBILE INS CO	IL	70,070.4
TRAVELERS INS CO LIFE DEPT	CT	58,317.0

North Carolina

INSURANCE COMPANY NAME	DOM. STATE	TOTAL ASSETS ($MIL)
Weiss Safety Rating: A+		
GOVERNMENT EMPLOYEES INS CO	MD	8,737.7
PHYSICIANS MUTUAL INS CO	NE	1,102.7
PROTECTIVE INS CO	IN	443.4
TEACHERS INS & ANNUITY ASN OF AM	NY	147,114.8
Weiss Safety Rating: A		
ALFA MUTUAL INS CO	AL	1,151.8
AMERICAN FIDELITY ASR CO	OK	2,382.6
AUTO-OWNERS INS CO	MI	6,582.7
CENTURION LIFE INS CO	MO	1,024.0
GUARDIAN LIFE INS CO OF AMERICA	NY	20,577.2
JEFFERSON-PILOT LIFE INS CO	NC	13,405.5
MASSACHUSETTS MUTUAL LIFE INS CO	MA	80,322.1
NEW YORK LIFE INS CO	NY	87,505.8
NORTHWESTERN MUTUAL LIFE INS CO	WI	114,436.3
SENTRY INS A MUTUAL CO	WI	4,177.1
Weiss Safety Rating: A-		
ALFA LIFE INS CORP	AL	821.5
ALLSTATE INS CO	IL	40,978.7
ALLSTATE LIFE INS CO	IL	60,033.7
AUTO-OWNERS LIFE INS CO	MI	1,251.5
CENTRAL STATES INDEMNITY CO OF OMAHA	NE	243.1
CINCINNATI INS CO	OH	7,143.1
FEDERATED LIFE INS CO	MN	864.3
JOHN HANCOCK LIFE INS CO	MA	73,183.9
MIDLAND NATIONAL LIFE INS CO	IA	10,748.6
MINNESOTA LIFE INS CO	MN	17,352.3
MUTUAL OF OMAHA INS CO	NE	3,755.1
NATIONAL GUARDIAN LIFE INS CO	WI	947.4
NORTH CAROLINA FARM BU MUTUAL INS CO	NC	1,007.2
OLD REPUBLIC INS CO	PA	1,644.5
PACIFIC LIFE INS CO	CA	54,639.9
PRINCIPAL LIFE INS CO	IA	83,957.6
SENTRY LIFE INS CO	WI	2,101.2
SOUTHERN FARM BUREAU LIFE INS CO	MS	7,776.4
USAA LIFE INS CO	TX	9,167.0
Weiss Safety Rating: B+		
ALLSTATE LIFE INS CO OF NEW YORK	NY	4,816.0
AMERICAN GENERAL LIFE INS CO	TX	24,549.9
AMERICAN HEALTH & LIFE INS CO	TX	1,236.5
AMERITAS LIFE INS CORP	NE	2,417.9
AVEMCO INS CO	MD	191.7
BALBOA LIFE INS CO	CA	124.5
CITICORP LIFE INS CO	AZ	1,058.7
COLORADO BANKERS LIFE INS CO	CO	113.3
COLUMBUS LIFE INS CO	OH	2,187.1
COMPANION LIFE INS CO	SC	75.6
CUMIS INS SOCIETY INC	WI	826.9
FEDERAL INS CO	IN	18,983.3
FEDERATED MUTUAL INS CO	MN	3,013.6
GOLDEN RULE INS CO	IL	2,076.2
GREAT NORTHERN INS CO	MN	1,088.5
GREAT-WEST LIFE & ANNUITY INS CO	CO	27,323.0
HARTFORD FIRE INS CO	CT	15,857.7
HARTFORD LIFE & ACCIDENT INS CO	CT	8,792.5
HARTFORD LIFE & ANNUITY INS CO	CT	49,622.7
HARTFORD LIFE INS CO	CT	97,564.5
JEFFERSON PILOT FINANCIAL INS CO	NE	11,630.2
LINCOLN BENEFIT LIFE CO	NE	1,823.4
MANUFACTURERS LIFE INS CO USA	MI	53,737.8
MERIT LIFE INS CO	IN	1,020.5
METROPOLITAN LIFE INS CO	NY	220,093.6
METROPOLITAN PROPERTY & CAS INS CO	RI	4,789.1
NATIONAL BENEFIT LIFE INS CO	NY	736.6
NATIONAL CASUALTY CO	WI	92.6
NATIONAL UNION FIRE INS CO OF PITTSB	PA	18,196.9
NATIONWIDE LIFE INS CO	OH	80,569.1
NATIONWIDE MUTUAL FIRE INS CO	OH	3,610.4
PHYSICIANS LIFE INS CO	NE	1,195.8
PRIMERICA LIFE INS CO	MA	5,073.8
SAVINGS BANK LIFE INS CO OF MA	MA	1,548.3
SIRIUS AMERICA INS CO	DE	216.8
STATE AUTOMOBILE MUTUAL INS CO	OH	1,299.8
STATE FARM MUTUAL AUTOMOBILE INS CO	IL	70,070.4
SURETY LIFE INS CO	NE	50.3
TRAVELERS INS CO LIFE DEPT	CT	58,317.0
UNITED HEALTHCARE OF NC INC	NC	218.0
UNITED INS CO OF AMERICA	IL	2,064.3
UNITED OF OMAHA LIFE INS CO	NE	12,298.3
WESTERN & SOUTHERN LIFE INS CO	OH	7,850.2

IV. Weiss Recommended Companies by State — Winter 2003 - 04

North Dakota

Weiss Safety Rating: A+

INSURANCE COMPANY NAME	DOM. STATE	TOTAL ASSETS ($MIL)
COUNTRY LIFE INS CO	IL	4,387.5
GOVERNMENT EMPLOYEES INS CO	MD	8,737.7
PHYSICIANS MUTUAL INS CO	NE	1,102.7
PROTECTIVE INS CO	IN	443.4
TEACHERS INS & ANNUITY ASN OF AM	NY	147,114.8

Weiss Safety Rating: A

INSURANCE COMPANY NAME	DOM. STATE	TOTAL ASSETS ($MIL)
AMERICAN FIDELITY ASR CO	OK	2,382.6
AUTO-OWNERS INS CO	MI	6,582.7
CENTURION LIFE INS CO	MO	1,024.0
GUARDIAN LIFE INS CO OF AMERICA	NY	20,577.2
JEFFERSON-PILOT LIFE INS CO	NC	13,405.5
MASSACHUSETTS MUTUAL LIFE INS CO	MA	80,322.1
NEW YORK LIFE INS CO	NY	87,505.8
NORTHWESTERN MUTUAL LIFE INS CO	WI	114,436.3
SENTRY INS A MUTUAL CO	WI	4,177.1

Weiss Safety Rating: A-

INSURANCE COMPANY NAME	DOM. STATE	TOTAL ASSETS ($MIL)
ALLSTATE INS CO	IL	40,978.7
ALLSTATE LIFE INS CO	IL	60,033.7
AUTO-OWNERS LIFE INS CO	MI	1,251.5
CENTRAL STATES INDEMNITY CO OF OMAHA	NE	243.1
CINCINNATI INS CO	OH	7,143.1
FARM BUREAU LIFE INS CO	IA	4,695.3
FEDERATED LIFE INS CO	MN	864.3
JOHN HANCOCK LIFE INS CO	MA	73,183.9
MEDICA	MN	599.3
MIDLAND NATIONAL LIFE INS CO	IA	10,748.6
MINNESOTA LIFE INS CO	MN	17,352.3
MUTUAL OF OMAHA INS CO	NE	3,755.1
NATIONAL GUARDIAN LIFE INS CO	WI	947.4
OLD REPUBLIC INS CO	PA	1,644.5
PACIFIC LIFE INS CO	CA	54,639.9
PRINCIPAL LIFE INS CO	IA	83,957.6
SENTRY LIFE INS CO	WI	2,101.2
USAA LIFE INS CO	TX	9,167.0

Weiss Safety Rating: B+

INSURANCE COMPANY NAME	DOM. STATE	TOTAL ASSETS ($MIL)
AMERICAN GENERAL LIFE INS CO	TX	24,549.9
AMERICAN HEALTH & LIFE INS CO	TX	1,236.5
AMERITAS LIFE INS CORP	NE	2,417.9
AVEMCO INS CO	MD	191.7
BALBOA LIFE INS CO	CA	124.5
CITICORP LIFE INS CO	AZ	1,058.7
COLORADO BANKERS LIFE INS CO	CO	113.3
COMPANION LIFE INS CO	SC	75.6
CUMIS INS SOCIETY INC	WI	826.9
FEDERAL INS CO	IN	18,983.3
FEDERATED MUTUAL INS CO	MN	3,013.6
GOLDEN RULE INS CO	IL	2,076.2
GREAT NORTHERN INS CO	MN	1,088.5
GREAT-WEST LIFE & ANNUITY INS CO	CO	27,323.0
HARTFORD FIRE INS CO	CT	15,857.7
HARTFORD LIFE & ACCIDENT INS CO	CT	8,792.5
HARTFORD LIFE & ANNUITY INS CO	CT	49,622.7
HARTFORD LIFE INS CO	CT	97,564.5
IDS LIFE INS CO OF NEW YORK	NY	2,757.9
JEFFERSON PILOT FINANCIAL INS CO	NE	11,630.2
LINCOLN BENEFIT LIFE CO	NE	1,823.4
MANUFACTURERS LIFE INS CO USA	MI	53,737.8
MERIT LIFE INS CO	IN	1,020.5
METROPOLITAN LIFE INS CO	NY	220,093.6
METROPOLITAN PROPERTY & CAS INS CO	RI	4,789.1
MIDWEST SECURITY LIFE INS CO	WI	132.8
NATIONAL BENEFIT LIFE INS CO	NY	736.6
NATIONAL CASUALTY CO	WI	92.6
NATIONAL UNION FIRE INS CO OF PITTSB	PA	18,196.9
NATIONWIDE LIFE INS CO	OH	80,569.1
NATIONWIDE MUTUAL FIRE INS CO	OH	3,610.4
NORIDIAN MUTUAL INS CO	ND	298.8
PHYSICIANS LIFE INS CO	NE	1,195.8
PRIMERICA LIFE INS CO	MA	5,073.8
SIRIUS AMERICA INS CO	DE	216.8
STATE AUTOMOBILE MUTUAL INS CO	OH	1,299.6
STATE FARM MUTUAL AUTOMOBILE INS CO	IL	70,070.4
SURETY LIFE INS CO	NE	50.3
TRAVELERS INS CO LIFE DEPT	CT	58,317.0
UNITED INS CO OF AMERICA	IL	2,064.3
UNITED OF OMAHA LIFE INS CO	NE	12,298.3
WESTERN & SOUTHERN LIFE INS CO	OH	7,850.2

Ohio

INSURANCE COMPANY NAME	DOM. STATE	TOTAL ASSETS ($MIL)
Weiss Safety Rating: A+		
COUNTRY LIFE INS CO	IL	4,387.5
GOVERNMENT EMPLOYEES INS CO	MD	8,737.7
PHYSICIANS MUTUAL INS CO	NE	1,102.7
PROTECTIVE INS CO	IN	443.4
TEACHERS INS & ANNUITY ASN OF AM	NY	147,114.8
Weiss Safety Rating: A		
ALFA MUTUAL INS CO	AL	1,151.8
AMERICAN FIDELITY ASR CO	OK	2,382.6
AUTO-OWNERS INS CO	MI	6,582.7
CENTURION LIFE INS CO	MO	1,024.0
GUARDIAN LIFE INS CO OF AMERICA	NY	20,577.2
HEALTH ALLIANCE PLAN OF MICHIGAN	MI	316.7
JEFFERSON-PILOT LIFE INS CO	NC	13,405.5
MASSACHUSETTS MUTUAL LIFE INS CO	MA	80,322.1
NEW YORK LIFE INS CO	NY	87,505.8
NORTHWESTERN MUTUAL LIFE INS CO	WI	114,436.3
SENTRY INS A MUTUAL CO	WI	4,177.1
UNITED FARM FAMILY LIFE INS CO	IN	1,466.7
Weiss Safety Rating: A-		
ALLSTATE INS CO	IL	40,978.7
ALLSTATE LIFE INS CO	IL	60,033.7
AUTO-OWNERS LIFE INS CO	MI	1,251.5
CENTRAL STATES INDEMNITY CO OF OMAHA	NE	243.1
CINCINNATI INS CO	OH	7,143.1
FEDERATED LIFE INS CO	MN	864.3
GRANGE MUTUAL CAS CO	OH	1,116.1
JOHN HANCOCK LIFE INS CO	MA	73,183.9
MIDLAND NATIONAL LIFE INS CO	IA	10,748.6
MINNESOTA LIFE INS CO	MN	17,352.3
MUTUAL OF OMAHA INS CO	NE	3,755.1
NATIONAL GUARDIAN LIFE INS CO	WI	947.4
OLD REPUBLIC INS CO	PA	1,644.5
PACIFIC LIFE INS CO	CA	54,639.9
PRINCIPAL LIFE INS CO	IA	83,957.6
SENTRY LIFE INS CO	WI	2,101.2
USAA LIFE INS CO	TX	9,167.0
Weiss Safety Rating: B+		
AMERICAN GENERAL LIFE INS CO	TX	24,549.9
AMERICAN HEALTH & LIFE INS CO	TX	1,236.5
AMERITAS LIFE INS CORP	NE	2,417.9
AVEMCO INS CO	MD	191.7
BALBOA LIFE INS CO	CA	124.5
CITICORP LIFE INS CO	AZ	1,058.7
COLORADO BANKERS LIFE INS CO	CO	113.3
COLUMBUS LIFE INS CO	OH	2,187.1
COMPANION LIFE INS CO	SC	75.6
CUMIS INS SOCIETY INC	WI	826.9
FEDERAL INS CO	IN	18,983.3
FEDERATED MUTUAL INS CO	MN	3,013.6
GOLDEN RULE INS CO	IL	2,076.2
GRANGE LIFE INS CO	OH	159.8
GREAT NORTHERN INS CO	MN	1,088.5
GREAT-WEST LIFE & ANNUITY INS CO	CO	27,323.0
HARTFORD FIRE INS CO	CT	15,857.7
HARTFORD LIFE & ACCIDENT INS CO	CT	8,792.5
HARTFORD LIFE & ANNUITY INS CO	CT	49,622.7
HARTFORD LIFE INS CO	CT	97,564.5
JEFFERSON PILOT FINANCIAL INS CO	NE	11,630.2
LINCOLN BENEFIT LIFE CO	NE	1,823.4
MANUFACTURERS LIFE INS CO USA	MI	53,737.8
MERIT LIFE INS CO	IN	1,020.5
METROPOLITAN LIFE INS CO	NY	220,093.6
METROPOLITAN PROPERTY & CAS INS CO	RI	4,789.1
MIDWEST SECURITY LIFE INS CO	WI	132.8
NATIONAL BENEFIT LIFE INS CO	NY	736.6
NATIONAL CASUALTY CO	WI	92.6
NATIONAL UNION FIRE INS CO OF PITTSB	PA	18,196.9
NATIONWIDE LIFE INS CO	OH	80,569.1
NATIONWIDE MUTUAL FIRE INS CO	OH	3,610.4
PEKIN LIFE INS CO	IL	653.8
PHYSICIANS LIFE INS CO	NE	1,195.8
PRIMERICA LIFE INS CO	MA	5,073.8
SIRIUS AMERICA INS CO	DE	216.8
STATE AUTOMOBILE MUTUAL INS CO	OH	1,299.8
STATE FARM MUTUAL AUTOMOBILE INS CO	IL	70,070.4
SURETY LIFE INS CO	NE	50.3
TRAVELERS INS CO LIFE DEPT	CT	58,317.0
UNITED INS CO OF AMERICA	IL	2,064.3
UNITED OF OMAHA LIFE INS CO	NE	12,298.3
WESTERN & SOUTHERN LIFE INS CO	OH	7,850.2

Oklahoma

INSURANCE COMPANY NAME	DOM. STATE	TOTAL ASSETS ($MIL)
Weiss Safety Rating: A+		
COUNTRY LIFE INS CO	IL	4,387.5
GOVERNMENT EMPLOYEES INS CO	MD	8,737.7
PHYSICIANS MUTUAL INS CO	NE	1,102.7
PROTECTIVE INS CO	IN	443.4
TEACHERS INS & ANNUITY ASN OF AM	NY	147,114.8
Weiss Safety Rating: A		
AMERICAN FIDELITY ASR CO	OK	2,382.6
CENTURION LIFE INS CO	MO	1,024.0
GUARDIAN LIFE INS CO OF AMERICA	NY	20,577.2
JEFFERSON-PILOT LIFE INS CO	NC	13,405.5
MASSACHUSETTS MUTUAL LIFE INS CO	MA	80,322.1
NEW YORK LIFE INS CO	NY	87,505.8
NORTHWESTERN MUTUAL LIFE INS CO	WI	114,436.3
SENTRY INS A MUTUAL CO	WI	4,177.1
UNION NATIONAL LIFE INS CO	LA	377.5
Weiss Safety Rating: A-		
ALLSTATE INS CO	IL	40,978.7
ALLSTATE LIFE INS CO	IL	60,033.7
CENTRAL STATES INDEMNITY CO OF OMAHA	NE	243.1
CINCINNATI INS CO	OH	7,143.1
FARM BUREAU LIFE INS CO	IA	4,695.3
FEDERATED LIFE INS CO	MN	864.3
JOHN HANCOCK LIFE INS CO	MA	73,183.9
MIDLAND NATIONAL LIFE INS CO	IA	10,748.6
MINNESOTA LIFE INS CO	MN	17,352.3
MUTUAL OF OMAHA INS CO	NE	3,755.1
NATIONAL GUARDIAN LIFE INS CO	WI	947.4
OLD REPUBLIC INS CO	PA	1,644.5
PACIFIC LIFE INS CO	CA	54,639.9
PRINCIPAL LIFE INS CO	IA	83,957.6
SENTRY LIFE INS CO	WI	2,101.2
USAA LIFE INS CO	TX	9,167.0
Weiss Safety Rating: B+		
AMERICAN GENERAL LIFE INS CO	TX	24,549.9
AMERICAN HEALTH & LIFE INS CO	TX	1,236.5
AMERITAS LIFE INS CORP	NE	2,417.9
AVEMCO INS CO	MD	191.7
BALBOA LIFE INS CO	CA	124.5
CITICORP LIFE INS CO	AZ	1,058.7
COLORADO BANKERS LIFE INS CO	CO	113.3
COLUMBUS LIFE INS CO	OH	2,187.1
COMPANION LIFE INS CO	SC	75.6
CUMIS INS SOCIETY INC	WI	826.9
FEDERAL INS CO	IN	18,983.3
FEDERATED MUTUAL INS CO	MN	3,013.6
GOLDEN RULE INS CO	IL	2,076.2
GREAT NORTHERN INS CO	MN	1,088.5
GREAT-WEST LIFE & ANNUITY INS CO	CO	27,323.0
HARTFORD FIRE INS CO	CT	15,857.7
HARTFORD LIFE & ACCIDENT INS CO	CT	8,792.5
HARTFORD LIFE & ANNUITY INS CO	CT	49,622.7
HARTFORD LIFE INS CO	CT	97,564.5
JEFFERSON PILOT FINANCIAL INS CO	NE	11,630.2
LINCOLN BENEFIT LIFE CO	NE	1,823.4
MANUFACTURERS LIFE INS CO USA	MI	53,737.8
MERIT LIFE INS CO	IN	1,020.5
METROPOLITAN LIFE INS CO	NY	220,093.6
METROPOLITAN PROPERTY & CAS INS CO	RI	4,789.1
MIDWEST SECURITY LIFE INS CO	WI	132.8
NATIONAL BENEFIT LIFE INS CO	NY	736.6
NATIONAL CASUALTY CO	WI	92.6
NATIONAL UNION FIRE INS CO OF PITTSB	PA	18,196.9
NATIONWIDE LIFE INS CO	OH	80,569.1
NATIONWIDE MUTUAL FIRE INS CO	OH	3,610.4
PACIFIC GUARDIAN LIFE INS CO LTD	HI	431.5
PHYSICIANS LIFE INS CO	NE	1,195.8
PRIMERICA LIFE INS CO	MA	5,073.8
SHELTER LIFE INS CO	MO	811.0
SIRIUS AMERICA INS CO	DE	216.8
STATE AUTOMOBILE MUTUAL INS CO	OH	1,299.8
STATE FARM MUTUAL AUTOMOBILE INS CO	IL	70,070.4
SURETY LIFE INS CO	NE	50.3
TRAVELERS INS CO LIFE DEPT	CT	58,317.0
UNITED INS CO OF AMERICA	IL	2,064.3
UNITED OF OMAHA LIFE INS CO	NE	12,298.3
WESTERN & SOUTHERN LIFE INS CO	OH	7,850.2

Oregon

INSURANCE COMPANY NAME	DOM. STATE	TOTAL ASSETS ($MIL)

Weiss Safety Rating: A+

INSURANCE COMPANY NAME	DOM. STATE	TOTAL ASSETS ($MIL)
COUNTRY LIFE INS CO	IL	4,387.5
GOVERNMENT EMPLOYEES INS CO	MD	8,737.7
PHYSICIANS MUTUAL INS CO	NE	1,102.7
PROTECTIVE INS CO	IN	443.4
TEACHERS INS & ANNUITY ASN OF AM	NY	147,114.8

Weiss Safety Rating: A

INSURANCE COMPANY NAME	DOM. STATE	TOTAL ASSETS ($MIL)
AMERICAN FIDELITY ASR CO	OK	2,382.6
AUTO-OWNERS INS CO	MI	6,582.7
CENTURION LIFE INS CO	MO	1,024.0
GUARDIAN LIFE INS CO OF AMERICA	NY	20,577.2
JEFFERSON-PILOT LIFE INS CO	NC	13,405.5
MASSACHUSETTS MUTUAL LIFE INS CO	MA	80,322.1
NEW YORK LIFE INS CO	NY	87,505.8
NORTHWESTERN MUTUAL LIFE INS CO	WI	114,436.3
SENTRY INS A MUTUAL CO	WI	4,177.1

Weiss Safety Rating: A-

INSURANCE COMPANY NAME	DOM. STATE	TOTAL ASSETS ($MIL)
ALLSTATE INS CO	IL	40,978.7
ALLSTATE LIFE INS CO	IL	60,033.7
AUTO-OWNERS LIFE INS CO	MI	1,251.5
CENTRAL STATES INDEMNITY CO OF OMAHA	NE	243.1
CINCINNATI INS CO	OH	7,143.1
FARM BUREAU LIFE INS CO	IA	4,695.3
FEDERATED LIFE INS CO	MN	864.3
JOHN HANCOCK LIFE INS CO	MA	73,183.9
MIDLAND NATIONAL LIFE INS CO	IA	10,748.6
MINNESOTA LIFE INS CO	MN	17,352.3
MUTUAL OF OMAHA INS CO	NE	3,755.1
NATIONAL GUARDIAN LIFE INS CO	WI	947.4
OLD REPUBLIC INS CO	PA	1,644.5
PACIFIC HOSPITAL ASSOC	OR	89.6
PACIFIC LIFE INS CO	CA	54,639.9
PRINCIPAL LIFE INS CO	IA	83,957.6
SENTRY LIFE INS CO	WI	2,101.2
USAA LIFE INS CO	TX	9,167.0

Weiss Safety Rating: B+

INSURANCE COMPANY NAME	DOM. STATE	TOTAL ASSETS ($MIL)
AMERICAN GENERAL LIFE INS CO	TX	24,549.9
AMERICAN HEALTH & LIFE INS CO	TX	1,236.5
AMERITAS LIFE INS CORP	NE	2,417.9
AVEMCO INS CO	MD	191.7
BALBOA LIFE INS CO	CA	124.5
CITICORP LIFE INS CO	AZ	1,058.7
COLORADO BANKERS LIFE INS CO	CO	113.3
COLUMBUS LIFE INS CO	OH	2,187.1
COMPANION LIFE INS CO	SC	75.6
CUMIS INS SOCIETY INC	WI	826.9
FEDERAL INS CO	IN	18,983.3
FEDERATED MUTUAL INS CO	MN	3,013.6
GOLDEN RULE INS CO	IL	2,076.2
GREAT NORTHERN INS CO	MN	1,088.5
GREAT-WEST LIFE & ANNUITY INS CO	CO	27,323.0
HARTFORD FIRE INS CO	CT	15,857.7
HARTFORD LIFE & ACCIDENT INS CO	CT	8,792.5
HARTFORD LIFE & ANNUITY INS CO	CT	49,622.7
HARTFORD LIFE INS CO	CT	97,564.5
JEFFERSON PILOT FINANCIAL INS CO	NE	11,630.2
LINCOLN BENEFIT LIFE CO	NE	1,823.4
MANUFACTURERS LIFE INS CO USA	MI	53,737.8
MERIT LIFE INS CO	IN	1,020.5
METROPOLITAN LIFE INS CO	NY	220,093.6
METROPOLITAN PROPERTY & CAS INS CO	RI	4,789.1
MIDWEST SECURITY LIFE INS CO	WI	132.8
NATIONAL BENEFIT LIFE INS CO	NY	736.6
NATIONAL CASUALTY CO	WI	92.6
NATIONAL UNION FIRE INS CO OF PITTSB	PA	18,196.9
NATIONWIDE LIFE INS CO	OH	80,569.1
NATIONWIDE MUTUAL FIRE INS CO	OH	3,610.4
PACIFIC GUARDIAN LIFE INS CO LTD	HI	431.5
PHYSICIANS LIFE INS CO	NE	1,195.8
PRIMERICA LIFE INS CO	MA	5,073.8
SIRIUS AMERICA INS CO	DE	216.8
STATE FARM MUTUAL AUTOMOBILE INS CO	IL	70,070.4
SURETY LIFE INS CO	NE	50.3
TRAVELERS INS CO LIFE DEPT	CT	58,317.0
UNITED INS CO OF AMERICA	IL	2,064.3
UNITED OF OMAHA LIFE INS CO	NE	12,298.3
WESTERN & SOUTHERN LIFE INS CO	OH	7,850.2

IV. Weiss Recommended Companies by State

Pennsylvania

Weiss Safety Rating: A+

INSURANCE COMPANY NAME	DOM. STATE	TOTAL ASSETS ($MIL)
COUNTRY LIFE INS CO	IL	4,387.5
GOVERNMENT EMPLOYEES INS CO	MD	8,737.7
PHYSICIANS MUTUAL INS CO	NE	1,102.7
PROTECTIVE INS CO	IN	443.4
TEACHERS INS & ANNUITY ASN OF AM	NY	147,114.8

Weiss Safety Rating: A

INSURANCE COMPANY NAME	DOM. STATE	TOTAL ASSETS ($MIL)
ALFA MUTUAL INS CO	AL	1,151.8
AMERICAN FIDELITY ASR CO	OK	2,382.6
AUTO-OWNERS INS CO	MI	6,582.7
CENTURION LIFE INS CO	MO	1,024.0
GUARDIAN LIFE INS CO OF AMERICA	NY	20,577.2
JEFFERSON-PILOT LIFE INS CO	NC	13,405.5
MASSACHUSETTS MUTUAL LIFE INS CO	MA	80,322.1
NEW YORK LIFE INS CO	NY	87,505.8
NORTHWESTERN MUTUAL LIFE INS CO	WI	114,436.3
SENTRY INS A MUTUAL CO	WI	4,177.1

Weiss Safety Rating: A-

INSURANCE COMPANY NAME	DOM. STATE	TOTAL ASSETS ($MIL)
ALLSTATE INS CO	IL	40,978.7
ALLSTATE LIFE INS CO	IL	60,033.7
AUTO-OWNERS LIFE INS CO	MI	1,251.5
CENTRAL STATES INDEMNITY CO OF OMAHA	NE	243.1
CINCINNATI INS CO	OH	7,143.1
FEDERATED LIFE INS CO	MN	864.3
GRANGE MUTUAL CAS CO	OH	1,116.1
JOHN HANCOCK LIFE INS CO	MA	73,183.9
MIDLAND NATIONAL LIFE INS CO	IA	10,748.6
MINNESOTA LIFE INS CO	MN	17,352.3
MUTUAL OF OMAHA INS CO	NE	3,755.1
NATIONAL GUARDIAN LIFE INS CO	WI	947.4
OLD REPUBLIC INS CO	PA	1,644.5
PACIFIC LIFE INS CO	CA	54,639.9
PRINCIPAL LIFE INS CO	IA	83,957.6
SENTRY LIFE INS CO	WI	2,101.2
USAA LIFE INS CO	TX	9,167.0

Weiss Safety Rating: B+

INSURANCE COMPANY NAME	DOM. STATE	TOTAL ASSETS ($MIL)
ALLSTATE LIFE INS CO OF NEW YORK	NY	4,816.0
AMERICAN GENERAL LIFE INS CO	TX	24,549.9
AMERICAN HEALTH & LIFE INS CO	TX	1,236.5
AMERITAS LIFE INS CORP	NE	2,417.9
AVEMCO INS CO	MD	191.7
BALBOA LIFE INS CO	CA	124.5
CAPITAL BLUE CROSS OF PENNSYLVANIA	PA	982.4
CITICORP LIFE INS CO	AZ	1,058.7
COLORADO BANKERS LIFE INS CO	CO	113.3
COLUMBUS LIFE INS CO	OH	2,187.1
COMPANION LIFE INS CO	SC	75.6
CUMIS INS SOCIETY INC	WI	826.9
FARM FAMILY LIFE INS CO	NY	889.2
FEDERAL INS CO	IN	18,983.3
FEDERATED MUTUAL INS CO	MN	3,013.6
GOLDEN RULE INS CO	IL	2,076.2
GRANGE LIFE INS CO	OH	159.8
GREAT NORTHERN INS CO	MN	1,088.5
GREAT-WEST LIFE & ANNUITY INS CO	CO	27,323.0
HARTFORD FIRE INS CO	CT	15,857.7
HARTFORD LIFE & ACCIDENT INS CO	CT	8,792.5
HARTFORD LIFE & ANNUITY INS CO	CT	49,622.7
HARTFORD LIFE INS CO	CT	97,564.5
HOSPITAL SERV ASSN OF NORTH EAST PA	PA	588.5
JEFFERSON PILOT FINANCIAL INS CO	NE	11,630.2
KEYSTONE HEALTH PLAN CENTRAL INC	PA	166.0
KEYSTONE HEALTH PLAN EAST INC	PA	1,026.1
KEYSTONE HEALTH PLAN WEST INC	PA	498.2
LINCOLN BENEFIT LIFE CO	NE	1,823.4
MANUFACTURERS LIFE INS CO USA	MI	53,737.8
MERIT LIFE INS CO	IN	1,020.5
METROPOLITAN LIFE INS CO	NY	220,093.6
METROPOLITAN PROPERTY & CAS INS CO	RI	4,789.1
NATIONAL BENEFIT LIFE INS CO	NY	736.6
NATIONAL CASUALTY CO	WI	92.6
NATIONAL UNION FIRE INS CO OF PITTSB	PA	18,196.9
NATIONWIDE LIFE INS CO	OH	80,569.1
NATIONWIDE MUTUAL FIRE INS CO	OH	3,610.4
PHYSICIANS LIFE INS CO	NE	1,195.8
PRIMERICA LIFE INS CO	MA	5,073.8
SAVINGS BANK LIFE INS CO OF MA	MA	1,548.3
SIRIUS AMERICA INS CO	DE	216.8
STATE AUTOMOBILE MUTUAL INS CO	OH	1,299.8
STATE FARM MUTUAL AUTOMOBILE INS CO	IL	70,070.4
SURETY LIFE INS CO	NE	50.3
THREE RIVERS HEALTH PLANS INC	PA	93.5
TRAVELERS INS CO LIFE DEPT	CT	58,317.0
UNITED INS CO OF AMERICA	IL	2,064.3
UNITED OF OMAHA LIFE INS CO	NE	12,298.3
WESTERN & SOUTHERN LIFE INS CO	OH	7,850.2

Puerto Rico

INSURANCE COMPANY NAME	DOM. STATE	TOTAL ASSETS ($MIL)
Weiss Safety Rating: A+		
TEACHERS INS & ANNUITY ASN OF AM	NY	147,114.8
Weiss Safety Rating: A		
JEFFERSON-PILOT LIFE INS CO	NC	13,405.5
MASSACHUSETTS MUTUAL LIFE INS CO	MA	80,322.1
NEW YORK LIFE INS CO	NY	87,505.8
SENTRY INS A MUTUAL CO	WI	4,177.1
Weiss Safety Rating: A-		
ALLSTATE INS CO	IL	40,978.7
ALLSTATE LIFE INS CO	IL	60,033.7
CINCINNATI INS CO	OH	7,143.1
JOHN HANCOCK LIFE INS CO	MA	73,183.9
MIDLAND NATIONAL LIFE INS CO	IA	10,748.6
MINNESOTA LIFE INS CO	MN	17,352.3
MUTUAL OF OMAHA INS CO	NE	3,755.1
OLD REPUBLIC INS CO	PA	1,644.5
PRINCIPAL LIFE INS CO	IA	83,957.6
SOUTHERN FARM BUREAU LIFE INS CO	MS	7,776.4
Weiss Safety Rating: B+		
AMERICAN GENERAL LIFE INS CO	TX	24,549.9
CARIBBEAN AMERICAN LIFE ASR CO	PR	189.0
CUMIS INS SOCIETY INC	WI	826.9
FEDERAL INS CO	IN	18,983.3
GREAT-WEST LIFE & ANNUITY INS CO	CO	27,323.0
HARTFORD FIRE INS CO	CT	15,857.7
HARTFORD LIFE & ACCIDENT INS CO	CT	8,792.5
HARTFORD LIFE & ANNUITY INS CO	CT	49,622.7
JEFFERSON PILOT FINANCIAL INS CO	NE	11,630.2
METROPOLITAN LIFE INS CO	NY	220,093.6
NATIONAL UNION FIRE INS CO OF PITTSB	PA	18,196.9
NATIONWIDE LIFE INS CO	OH	80,569.1
PRIMERICA LIFE INS CO	MA	5,073.8
TRAVELERS INS CO LIFE DEPT	CT	58,317.0
UNITED OF OMAHA LIFE INS CO	NE	12,298.3

IV. Weiss Recommended Companies by State

Winter 2003 - 04

Rhode Island

INSURANCE COMPANY NAME	DOM. STATE	TOTAL ASSETS ($MIL)
Weiss Safety Rating: A+		
COUNTRY LIFE INS CO	IL	4,387.5
GOVERNMENT EMPLOYEES INS CO	MD	8,737.7
PHYSICIANS MUTUAL INS CO	NE	1,102.7
PROTECTIVE INS CO	IN	443.4
Weiss Safety Rating: A		
AMERICAN FIDELITY ASR CO	OK	2,382.6
CENTURION LIFE INS CO	MO	1,024.0
GUARDIAN LIFE INS CO OF AMERICA	NY	20,577.2
JEFFERSON-PILOT LIFE INS CO	NC	13,405.5
MASSACHUSETTS MUTUAL LIFE INS CO	MA	80,322.1
NEW YORK LIFE INS CO	NY	87,505.8
NORTHWESTERN MUTUAL LIFE INS CO	WI	114,436.3
SENTRY INS A MUTUAL CO	WI	4,177.1
Weiss Safety Rating: A-		
ALLSTATE INS CO	IL	40,978.7
ALLSTATE LIFE INS CO	IL	60,033.7
CENTRAL STATES INDEMNITY CO OF OMAHA	NE	243.1
CINCINNATI INS CO	OH	7,143.1
FEDERATED LIFE INS CO	MN	864.3
JOHN HANCOCK LIFE INS CO	MA	73,183.9
MIDLAND NATIONAL LIFE INS CO	IA	10,748.6
MINNESOTA LIFE INS CO	MN	17,352.3
MUTUAL OF OMAHA INS CO	NE	3,755.1
NATIONAL GUARDIAN LIFE INS CO	WI	947.4
OLD REPUBLIC INS CO	PA	1,644.5
PACIFIC LIFE INS CO	CA	54,639.9
PRINCIPAL LIFE INS CO	IA	83,957.6
SENTRY LIFE INS CO	WI	2,101.2
USAA LIFE INS CO	TX	9,167.0
Weiss Safety Rating: B+		
AMERICAN GENERAL LIFE INS CO	TX	24,549.9
AMERICAN HEALTH & LIFE INS CO	TX	1,236.5
AMERITAS LIFE INS CORP	NE	2,417.9
AVEMCO INS CO	MD	191.7
BALBOA LIFE INS CO	CA	124.5
BLUE CROSS BLUE SHIELD OF RI	RI	458.3
CITICORP LIFE INS CO	AZ	1,058.7
COLORADO BANKERS LIFE INS CO	CO	113.3
COLUMBUS LIFE INS CO	OH	2,187.1
COMPANION LIFE INS CO	SC	75.6
CUMIS INS SOCIETY INC	WI	826.9
FARM FAMILY LIFE INS CO	NY	889.2
FEDERAL INS CO	IN	18,983.3
FEDERATED MUTUAL INS CO	MN	3,013.6
GOLDEN RULE INS CO	IL	2,076.2
GREAT NORTHERN INS CO	MN	1,088.5
GREAT-WEST LIFE & ANNUITY INS CO	CO	27,323.0
HARTFORD FIRE INS CO	CT	15,857.7
HARTFORD LIFE & ACCIDENT INS CO	CT	8,792.5
HARTFORD LIFE & ANNUITY INS CO	CT	49,622.7
HARTFORD LIFE INS CO	CT	97,564.5
JEFFERSON PILOT FINANCIAL INS CO	NE	11,630.2
LINCOLN BENEFIT LIFE CO	NE	1,823.4
MANUFACTURERS LIFE INS CO USA	MI	53,737.8
MERIT LIFE INS CO	IN	1,020.5
METROPOLITAN LIFE INS CO	NY	220,093.6
METROPOLITAN PROPERTY & CAS INS CO	RI	4,789.1
NATIONAL BENEFIT LIFE INS CO	NY	736.6
NATIONAL CASUALTY CO	WI	92.6
NATIONAL UNION FIRE INS CO OF PITTSB	PA	18,196.9
NATIONWIDE LIFE INS CO	OH	80,569.1
NATIONWIDE MUTUAL FIRE INS CO	OH	3,610.4
PHYSICIANS LIFE INS CO	NE	1,195.8
PRIMERICA LIFE INS CO	MA	5,073.8
SAVINGS BANK LIFE INS CO OF MA	MA	1,548.3
SIRIUS AMERICA INS CO	DE	216.8
STATE FARM MUTUAL AUTOMOBILE INS CO	IL	70,070.4
SURETY LIFE INS CO	NE	50.3
TRAVELERS INS CO LIFE DEPT	CT	58,317.0
UNITED INS CO OF AMERICA	IL	2,064.3
UNITED OF OMAHA LIFE INS CO	NE	12,298.3
WESTERN & SOUTHERN LIFE INS CO	OH	7,850.2

South Carolina

INSURANCE COMPANY NAME	DOM. STATE	TOTAL ASSETS ($MIL)
Weiss Safety Rating: A+		
GOVERNMENT EMPLOYEES INS CO	MD	8,737.7
PHYSICIANS MUTUAL INS CO	NE	1,102.7
PROTECTIVE INS CO	IN	443.4
TEACHERS INS & ANNUITY ASN OF AM	NY	147,114.8
Weiss Safety Rating: A		
ALFA MUTUAL INS CO	AL	1,151.8
AMERICAN FIDELITY ASR CO	OK	2,382.6
AUTO-OWNERS INS CO	MI	6,582.7
CENTURION LIFE INS CO	MO	1,024.0
GUARDIAN LIFE INS CO OF AMERICA	NY	20,577.2
JEFFERSON-PILOT LIFE INS CO	NC	13,405.5
MASSACHUSETTS MUTUAL LIFE INS CO	MA	80,322.1
NEW YORK LIFE INS CO	NY	87,505.8
NORTHWESTERN MUTUAL LIFE INS CO	WI	114,436.3
SENTRY INS A MUTUAL CO	WI	4,177.1
Weiss Safety Rating: A-		
ALFA LIFE INS CORP	AL	821.5
ALLSTATE INS CO	IL	40,978.7
ALLSTATE LIFE INS CO	IL	60,033.7
AUTO-OWNERS LIFE INS CO	MI	1,251.5
CENTRAL STATES INDEMNITY CO OF OMAHA	NE	243.1
CINCINNATI INS CO	OH	7,143.1
COMPANION HEALTH CARE CORP	SC	73.7
FEDERATED LIFE INS CO	MN	864.3
JOHN HANCOCK LIFE INS CO	MA	73,183.9
MIDLAND NATIONAL LIFE INS CO	IA	10,748.6
MINNESOTA LIFE INS CO	MN	17,352.3
MUTUAL OF OMAHA INS CO	NE	3,755.1
NATIONAL GUARDIAN LIFE INS CO	WI	947.4
OLD REPUBLIC INS CO	PA	1,644.5
PACIFIC LIFE INS CO	CA	54,639.9
PRINCIPAL LIFE INS CO	IA	83,957.6
SENTRY LIFE INS CO	WI	2,101.2
SOUTHERN FARM BUREAU LIFE INS CO	MS	7,776.4
USAA LIFE INS CO	TX	9,167.0
Weiss Safety Rating: B+		
AMERICAN GENERAL LIFE INS CO	TX	24,549.9
AMERICAN HEALTH & LIFE INS CO	TX	1,236.5
AMERITAS LIFE INS CORP	NE	2,417.9
AVEMCO INS CO	MD	191.7
BALBOA LIFE INS CO	CA	124.5
BLUE CROSS BLUE SHIELD OF SC INC	SC	1,045.1
CITICORP LIFE INS CO	AZ	1,058.7
COLORADO BANKERS LIFE INS CO	CO	113.3
COLUMBUS LIFE INS CO	OH	2,187.1
COMPANION LIFE INS CO	SC	75.6
CUMIS INS SOCIETY INC	WI	826.9
FEDERAL INS CO	IN	18,983.3
FEDERATED MUTUAL INS CO	MN	3,013.6
GOLDEN RULE INS CO	IL	2,076.2
GREAT NORTHERN INS CO	MN	1,088.5
GREAT-WEST LIFE & ANNUITY INS CO	CO	27,323.0
HARTFORD FIRE INS CO	CT	15,857.7
HARTFORD LIFE & ACCIDENT INS CO	CT	8,792.5
HARTFORD LIFE & ANNUITY INS CO	CT	49,622.7
HARTFORD LIFE INS CO	CT	97,564.5
JEFFERSON PILOT FINANCIAL INS CO	NE	11,630.2
LINCOLN BENEFIT LIFE CO	NE	1,823.4
MANUFACTURERS LIFE INS CO USA	MI	53,737.8
MERIT LIFE INS CO	IN	1,020.5
METROPOLITAN LIFE INS CO	NY	220,093.6
METROPOLITAN PROPERTY & CAS INS CO	RI	4,789.1
MIDWEST SECURITY LIFE INS CO	WI	132.8
NATIONAL BENEFIT LIFE INS CO	NY	736.6
NATIONAL CASUALTY CO	WI	92.6
NATIONAL UNION FIRE INS CO OF PITTSB	PA	18,196.9
NATIONWIDE LIFE INS CO	OH	80,569.1
NATIONWIDE MUTUAL FIRE INS CO	OH	3,610.4
PHYSICIANS LIFE INS CO	NE	1,195.8
PRIMERICA LIFE INS CO	MA	5,073.8
SIRIUS AMERICA INS CO	DE	216.8
STATE AUTOMOBILE MUTUAL INS CO	OH	1,299.8
STATE FARM MUTUAL AUTOMOBILE INS CO	IL	70,070.4
SURETY LIFE INS CO	NE	50.3
TRAVELERS INS CO LIFE DEPT	CT	58,317.0
UNITED INS CO OF AMERICA	IL	2,064.3
UNITED OF OMAHA LIFE INS CO	NE	12,298.3
WESTERN & SOUTHERN LIFE INS CO	OH	7,850.2

IV. Weiss Recommended Companies by State

South Dakota

INSURANCE COMPANY NAME	DOM. STATE	TOTAL ASSETS ($MIL)
Weiss Safety Rating: A+		
COUNTRY LIFE INS CO	IL	4,387.5
GOVERNMENT EMPLOYEES INS CO	MD	8,737.7
PHYSICIANS MUTUAL INS CO	NE	1,102.7
PROTECTIVE INS CO	IN	443.4
TEACHERS INS & ANNUITY ASN OF AM	NY	147,114.8
Weiss Safety Rating: A		
AMERICAN FIDELITY ASR CO	OK	2,382.6
AUTO-OWNERS INS CO	MI	6,582.7
CENTURION LIFE INS CO	MO	1,024.0
GUARDIAN LIFE INS CO OF AMERICA	NY	20,577.2
JEFFERSON-PILOT LIFE INS CO	NC	13,405.5
MASSACHUSETTS MUTUAL LIFE INS CO	MA	80,322.1
NEW YORK LIFE INS CO	NY	87,505.8
NORTHWESTERN MUTUAL LIFE INS CO	WI	114,436.3
SENTRY INS A MUTUAL CO	WI	4,177.1
Weiss Safety Rating: A-		
ALLSTATE INS CO	IL	40,978.7
ALLSTATE LIFE INS CO	IL	60,033.7
AUTO-OWNERS LIFE INS CO	MI	1,251.5
CENTRAL STATES INDEMNITY CO OF OMAHA	NE	243.1
CINCINNATI INS CO	OH	7,143.1
FARM BUREAU LIFE INS CO	IA	4,695.3
FEDERATED LIFE INS CO	MN	864.3
JOHN HANCOCK LIFE INS CO	MA	73,183.9
MIDLAND NATIONAL LIFE INS CO	IA	10,748.6
MINNESOTA LIFE INS CO	MN	17,352.3
MUTUAL OF OMAHA INS CO	NE	3,755.1
NATIONAL GUARDIAN LIFE INS CO	WI	947.4
OLD REPUBLIC INS CO	PA	1,644.5
PACIFIC LIFE INS CO	CA	54,639.9
PRINCIPAL LIFE INS CO	IA	83,957.6
SENTRY LIFE INS CO	WI	2,101.2
USAA LIFE INS CO	TX	9,167.0
Weiss Safety Rating: B+		
AMERICAN GENERAL LIFE INS CO	TX	24,549.9
AMERICAN HEALTH & LIFE INS CO	TX	1,236.5
AMERITAS LIFE INS CORP	NE	2,417.9
AVEMCO INS CO	MD	191.7
BALBOA LIFE INS CO	CA	124.5
CITICORP LIFE INS CO	AZ	1,058.7
COLORADO BANKERS LIFE INS CO	CO	113.3
COLUMBUS LIFE INS CO	OH	2,187.1
COMPANION LIFE INS CO	SC	75.6
CUMIS INS SOCIETY INC	WI	826.9
FEDERAL INS CO	IN	18,983.3
FEDERATED MUTUAL INS CO	MN	3,013.6
GOLDEN RULE INS CO	IL	2,076.2
GREAT NORTHERN INS CO	MN	1,088.5
GREAT-WEST LIFE & ANNUITY INS CO	CO	27,323.0

INSURANCE COMPANY NAME	DOM. STATE	TOTAL ASSETS ($MIL)
HARTFORD FIRE INS CO	CT	15,857.7
HARTFORD LIFE & ACCIDENT INS CO	CT	8,792.5
HARTFORD LIFE & ANNUITY INS CO	CT	49,622.7
HARTFORD LIFE INS CO	CT	97,564.5
JEFFERSON PILOT FINANCIAL INS CO	NE	11,630.2
LINCOLN BENEFIT LIFE CO	NE	1,823.4
MANUFACTURERS LIFE INS CO USA	MI	53,737.8
MERIT LIFE INS CO	IN	1,020.5
METROPOLITAN LIFE INS CO	NY	220,093.6
METROPOLITAN PROPERTY & CAS INS CO	RI	4,789.1
MIDWEST SECURITY LIFE INS CO	WI	132.8
NATIONAL BENEFIT LIFE INS CO	NY	736.6
NATIONAL CASUALTY CO	WI	92.6
NATIONAL UNION FIRE INS CO OF PITTSB	PA	18,196.9
NATIONWIDE LIFE INS CO	OH	80,569.1
NATIONWIDE MUTUAL FIRE INS CO	OH	3,610.4
NORIDIAN MUTUAL INS CO	ND	298.8
PACIFIC GUARDIAN LIFE INS CO LTD	HI	431.5
PHYSICIANS LIFE INS CO	NE	1,195.8
PRIMERICA LIFE INS CO	MA	5,073.8
SIRIUS AMERICA INS CO	DE	216.8
STATE AUTOMOBILE MUTUAL INS CO	OH	1,299.5
STATE FARM MUTUAL AUTOMOBILE INS CO	IL	70,070.4
SURETY LIFE INS CO	NE	50.3
TRAVELERS INS CO LIFE DEPT	CT	58,317.0
UNITED INS CO OF AMERICA	IL	2,064.3
UNITED OF OMAHA LIFE INS CO	NE	12,298.3
WESTERN & SOUTHERN LIFE INS CO	OH	7,850.2

Tennessee

INSURANCE COMPANY NAME	DOM. STATE	TOTAL ASSETS ($MIL)
Weiss Safety Rating: A+		
COUNTRY LIFE INS CO	IL	4,387.5
GOVERNMENT EMPLOYEES INS CO	MD	8,737.7
PHYSICIANS MUTUAL INS CO	NE	1,102.7
PROTECTIVE INS CO	IN	443.4
TEACHERS INS & ANNUITY ASN OF AM	NY	147,114.8
Weiss Safety Rating: A		
AMERICAN FIDELITY ASR CO	OK	2,382.6
AUTO-OWNERS INS CO	MI	6,582.7
CENTURION LIFE INS CO	MO	1,024.0
GUARDIAN LIFE INS CO OF AMERICA	NY	20,577.2
JEFFERSON-PILOT LIFE INS CO	NC	13,405.5
MASSACHUSETTS MUTUAL LIFE INS CO	MA	80,322.1
NEW YORK LIFE INS CO	NY	87,505.8
NORTHWESTERN MUTUAL LIFE INS CO	WI	114,436.3
SENTRY INS A MUTUAL CO	WI	4,177.1
UNION NATIONAL LIFE INS CO	LA	377.5
Weiss Safety Rating: A-		
ALFA LIFE INS CORP	AL	821.5
ALLSTATE INS CO	IL	40,978.7
ALLSTATE LIFE INS CO	IL	60,033.7
AUTO-OWNERS LIFE INS CO	MI	1,251.5
CENTRAL STATES INDEMNITY CO OF OMAHA	NE	243.1
CINCINNATI INS CO	OH	7,143.1
FEDERATED LIFE INS CO	MN	864.3
GRANGE MUTUAL CAS CO	OH	1,116.1
JOHN HANCOCK LIFE INS CO	MA	73,183.9
MIDLAND NATIONAL LIFE INS CO	IA	10,748.6
MINNESOTA LIFE INS CO	MN	17,352.3
MUTUAL OF OMAHA INS CO	NE	3,755.1
NATIONAL GUARDIAN LIFE INS CO	WI	947.4
OLD REPUBLIC INS CO	PA	1,644.5
PACIFIC LIFE INS CO	CA	54,639.9
PRINCIPAL LIFE INS CO	IA	83,957.6
SENTRY LIFE INS CO	WI	2,101.2
SOUTHERN FARM BUREAU LIFE INS CO	MS	7,776.4
USAA LIFE INS CO	TX	9,167.0
Weiss Safety Rating: B+		
AMERICAN GENERAL LIFE INS CO	TX	24,549.9
AMERICAN HEALTH & LIFE INS CO	TX	1,236.5
AMERITAS LIFE INS CORP	NE	2,417.9
AVEMCO INS CO	MD	191.7
BALBOA LIFE INS CO	CA	124.5
BLUECROSS BLUESHIELD OF TENNESSEE	TN	1,093.8
CITICORP LIFE INS CO	AZ	1,058.7
COLORADO BANKERS LIFE INS CO	CO	113.3
COLUMBUS LIFE INS CO	OH	2,187.1
COMPANION LIFE INS CO	SC	75.6
CUMIS INS SOCIETY INC	WI	826.9
FEDERAL INS CO	IN	18,983.3
FEDERATED MUTUAL INS CO	MN	3,013.6
GOLDEN RULE INS CO	IL	2,076.2
GRANGE LIFE INS CO	OH	159.8
GREAT NORTHERN INS CO	MN	1,088.5
GREAT-WEST LIFE & ANNUITY INS CO	CO	27,323.0
HARTFORD FIRE INS CO	CT	15,857.7
HARTFORD LIFE & ACCIDENT INS CO	CT	8,792.5
HARTFORD LIFE & ANNUITY INS CO	CT	49,622.7
HARTFORD LIFE INS CO	CT	97,564.5
JEFFERSON PILOT FINANCIAL INS CO	NE	11,630.2
LINCOLN BENEFIT LIFE CO	NE	1,823.4
MANUFACTURERS LIFE INS CO USA	MI	53,737.8
MERIT LIFE INS CO	IN	1,020.5
METROPOLITAN LIFE INS CO	NY	220,093.6
METROPOLITAN PROPERTY & CAS INS CO	RI	4,789.1
NATIONAL BENEFIT LIFE INS CO	NY	736.6
NATIONAL CASUALTY CO	WI	92.6
NATIONAL UNION FIRE INS CO OF PITTSB	PA	18,196.9
NATIONWIDE LIFE INS CO	OH	80,569.1
NATIONWIDE MUTUAL FIRE INS CO	OH	3,610.4
PHYSICIANS LIFE INS CO	NE	1,195.8
PRIMERICA LIFE INS CO	MA	5,073.8
SHELTER LIFE INS CO	MO	811.0
SIRIUS AMERICA INS CO	DE	216.8
STATE AUTOMOBILE MUTUAL INS CO	OH	1,299.8
STATE FARM MUTUAL AUTOMOBILE INS CO	IL	70,070.4
SURETY LIFE INS CO	NE	50.3
TRAVELERS INS CO LIFE DEPT	CT	58,317.0
UNITED INS CO OF AMERICA	IL	2,064.3
UNITED OF OMAHA LIFE INS CO	NE	12,298.3
WESTERN & SOUTHERN LIFE INS CO	OH	7,850.2

Texas

Weiss Safety Rating: A+

INSURANCE COMPANY NAME	DOM. STATE	TOTAL ASSETS ($MIL)
COUNTRY LIFE INS CO	IL	4,387.5
GOVERNMENT EMPLOYEES INS CO	MD	8,737.7
PHYSICIANS MUTUAL INS CO	NE	1,102.7
PROTECTIVE INS CO	IN	443.4
TEACHERS INS & ANNUITY ASN OF AM	NY	147,114.8

Weiss Safety Rating: A

INSURANCE COMPANY NAME	DOM. STATE	TOTAL ASSETS ($MIL)
AMERICAN FIDELITY ASR CO	OK	2,382.6
AUTO-OWNERS INS CO	MI	6,582.7
CENTURION LIFE INS CO	MO	1,024.0
GUARDIAN LIFE INS CO OF AMERICA	NY	20,577.2
JEFFERSON-PILOT LIFE INS CO	NC	13,405.5
MASSACHUSETTS MUTUAL LIFE INS CO	MA	80,322.1
NEW YORK LIFE INS CO	NY	87,505.8
NORTHWESTERN MUTUAL LIFE INS CO	WI	114,436.3
SENTRY INS A MUTUAL CO	WI	4,177.1
UNION NATIONAL LIFE INS CO	LA	377.5

Weiss Safety Rating: A-

INSURANCE COMPANY NAME	DOM. STATE	TOTAL ASSETS ($MIL)
ALLSTATE INS CO	IL	40,978.7
ALLSTATE LIFE INS CO	IL	60,033.7
AUTO-OWNERS LIFE INS CO	MI	1,251.5
CENTRAL STATES INDEMNITY CO OF OMAHA	NE	243.1
CINCINNATI INS CO	OH	7,143.1
FEDERATED LIFE INS CO	MN	864.3
JOHN HANCOCK LIFE INS CO	MA	73,183.9
MIDLAND NATIONAL LIFE INS CO	IA	10,748.6
MINNESOTA LIFE INS CO	MN	17,352.3
MUTUAL OF OMAHA INS CO	NE	3,755.1
NATIONAL GUARDIAN LIFE INS CO	WI	947.4
OLD REPUBLIC INS CO	PA	1,644.5
PACIFIC LIFE INS CO	CA	54,639.9
PRINCIPAL LIFE INS CO	IA	83,957.6
SENTRY LIFE INS CO	WI	2,101.2
SOUTHERN FARM BUREAU LIFE INS CO	MS	7,776.4
USAA LIFE INS CO	TX	9,167.0

Weiss Safety Rating: B+

INSURANCE COMPANY NAME	DOM. STATE	TOTAL ASSETS ($MIL)
ALLSTATE LIFE INS CO OF NEW YORK	NY	4,816.0
AMERICAN GENERAL LIFE INS CO	TX	24,549.9
AMERICAN HEALTH & LIFE INS CO	TX	1,236.5
AMERITAS LIFE INS CORP	NE	2,417.9
AVEMCO INS CO	MD	191.7
BALBOA LIFE INS CO	CA	124.5
CITICORP LIFE INS CO	AZ	1,058.7
COLORADO BANKERS LIFE INS CO	CO	113.3
COLUMBUS LIFE INS CO	OH	2,187.1
COMPANION LIFE INS CO	SC	75.6
CUMIS INS SOCIETY INC	WI	826.9
FEDERAL INS CO	IN	18,983.3
FEDERATED MUTUAL INS CO	MN	3,013.6
GOLDEN RULE INS CO	IL	2,076.2
GREAT NORTHERN INS CO	MN	1,088.5
GREAT-WEST LIFE & ANNUITY INS CO	CO	27,323.0
HARTFORD FIRE INS CO	CT	15,857.7
HARTFORD LIFE & ACCIDENT INS CO	CT	8,792.5
HARTFORD LIFE & ANNUITY INS CO	CT	49,622.7
HARTFORD LIFE INS CO	CT	97,564.5
HEALTH CARE SVC CORP A MUT LEG RES	IL	4,352.1
JEFFERSON PILOT FINANCIAL INS CO	NE	11,630.2
LINCOLN BENEFIT LIFE CO	NE	1,823.4
MANUFACTURERS LIFE INS CO USA	MI	53,737.8
MERIT LIFE INS CO	IN	1,020.5
METROPOLITAN LIFE INS CO	NY	220,093.6
METROPOLITAN PROPERTY & CAS INS CO	RI	4,789.1
MIDWEST SECURITY LIFE INS CO	WI	132.8
NATIONAL BENEFIT LIFE INS CO	NY	736.6
NATIONAL CASUALTY CO	WI	92.6
NATIONAL UNION FIRE INS CO OF PITTSB	PA	18,196.9
NATIONWIDE LIFE INS CO	OH	80,569.1
NATIONWIDE MUTUAL FIRE INS CO	OH	3,610.4
PACIFIC GUARDIAN LIFE INS CO LTD	HI	431.5
PHYSICIANS LIFE INS CO	NE	1,195.8
PRIMERICA LIFE INS CO	MA	5,073.4
SIRIUS AMERICA INS CO	DE	216.8
STATE FARM MUTUAL AUTOMOBILE INS CO	IL	70,070.4
SURETY LIFE INS CO	NE	50.3
TRAVELERS INS CO LIFE DEPT	CT	58,317.0
UNITED INS CO OF AMERICA	IL	2,064.3
UNITED OF OMAHA LIFE INS CO	NE	12,298.3
WESTERN & SOUTHERN LIFE INS CO	OH	7,850.2

Utah

INSURANCE COMPANY NAME	DOM. STATE	TOTAL ASSETS ($MIL)
Weiss Safety Rating: A+		
COUNTRY LIFE INS CO	IL	4,387.5
GOVERNMENT EMPLOYEES INS CO	MD	8,737.7
PHYSICIANS MUTUAL INS CO	NE	1,102.7
PROTECTIVE INS CO	IN	443.4
TEACHERS INS & ANNUITY ASN OF AM	NY	147,114.8
Weiss Safety Rating: A		
AMERICAN FIDELITY ASR CO	OK	2,382.6
AUTO-OWNERS INS CO	MI	6,582.7
CENTURION LIFE INS CO	MO	1,024.0
GUARDIAN LIFE INS CO OF AMERICA	NY	20,577.2
JEFFERSON-PILOT LIFE INS CO	NC	13,405.5
MASSACHUSETTS MUTUAL LIFE INS CO	MA	80,322.1
NEW YORK LIFE INS CO	NY	87,505.8
NORTHWESTERN MUTUAL LIFE INS CO	WI	114,436.3
SENTRY INS A MUTUAL CO	WI	4,177.1
Weiss Safety Rating: A-		
ALLSTATE INS CO	IL	40,978.7
ALLSTATE LIFE INS CO	IL	60,033.7
AUTO-OWNERS LIFE INS CO	MI	1,251.5
CALIFORNIA STATE AUTO ASN INTER-INS	CA	4,180.2
CENTRAL STATES INDEMNITY CO OF OMAHA	NE	243.1
CINCINNATI INS CO	OH	7,143.1
FARM BUREAU LIFE INS CO	IA	4,695.3
FEDERATED LIFE INS CO	MN	864.3
JOHN HANCOCK LIFE INS CO	MA	73,183.9
MIDLAND NATIONAL LIFE INS CO	IA	10,748.6
MINNESOTA LIFE INS CO	MN	17,352.3
MUTUAL OF OMAHA INS CO	NE	3,755.1
NATIONAL GUARDIAN LIFE INS CO	WI	947.4
OLD REPUBLIC INS CO	PA	1,644.5
PACIFIC LIFE INS CO	CA	54,639.9
PRINCIPAL LIFE INS CO	IA	83,957.6
SENTRY LIFE INS CO	WI	2,101.2
USAA LIFE INS CO	TX	9,167.0
Weiss Safety Rating: B+		
AMERICAN GENERAL LIFE INS CO	TX	24,549.9
AMERICAN HEALTH & LIFE INS CO	TX	1,236.5
AMERITAS LIFE INS CORP	NE	2,417.9
AVEMCO INS CO	MD	191.7
BALBOA LIFE INS CO	CA	124.5
CITICORP LIFE INS CO	AZ	1,058.7
COLORADO BANKERS LIFE INS CO	CO	113.3
COLUMBUS LIFE INS CO	OH	2,187.1
COMPANION LIFE INS CO	SC	75.6
CUMIS INS SOCIETY INC	WI	826.9
FEDERAL INS CO	IN	18,983.3
FEDERATED MUTUAL INS CO	MN	3,013.6
GOLDEN RULE INS CO	IL	2,076.2
GREAT NORTHERN INS CO	MN	1,088.5
GREAT-WEST LIFE & ANNUITY INS CO	CO	27,323.0
HARTFORD FIRE INS CO	CT	15,857.7
HARTFORD LIFE & ACCIDENT INS CO	CT	8,792.5
HARTFORD LIFE & ANNUITY INS CO	CT	49,622.7
HARTFORD LIFE INS CO	CT	97,564.5
JEFFERSON PILOT FINANCIAL INS CO	NE	11,630.2
LINCOLN BENEFIT LIFE CO	NE	1,823.4
MANUFACTURERS LIFE INS CO USA	MI	53,737.8
MERIT LIFE INS CO	IN	1,020.5
METROPOLITAN LIFE INS CO	NY	220,093.6
METROPOLITAN PROPERTY & CAS INS CO	RI	4,789.1
MIDWEST SECURITY LIFE INS CO	WI	132.8
NATIONAL BENEFIT LIFE INS CO	NY	736.6
NATIONAL CASUALTY CO	WI	92.6
NATIONAL UNION FIRE INS CO OF PITTSB	PA	18,196.9
NATIONWIDE LIFE INS CO	OH	80,569.1
NATIONWIDE MUTUAL FIRE INS CO	OH	3,610.4
PACIFIC GUARDIAN LIFE INS CO LTD	HI	431.5
PHYSICIANS LIFE INS CO	NE	1,195.8
PRIMERICA LIFE INS CO	MA	5,073.8
SIRIUS AMERICA INS CO	DE	216.8
STATE AUTOMOBILE MUTUAL INS CO	OH	1,299.8
STATE FARM MUTUAL AUTOMOBILE INS CO	IL	70,070.4
SURETY LIFE INS CO	NE	50.3
TRAVELERS INS CO LIFE DEPT	CT	58,317.0
UNITED INS CO OF AMERICA	IL	2,064.3
UNITED OF OMAHA LIFE INS CO	NE	12,298.3
WESTERN & SOUTHERN LIFE INS CO	OH	7,850.2

Vermont

INSURANCE COMPANY NAME	DOM. STATE	TOTAL ASSETS ($MIL)
Weiss Safety Rating: A+		
GOVERNMENT EMPLOYEES INS CO	MD	8,737.7
PHYSICIANS MUTUAL INS CO	NE	1,102.7
PROTECTIVE INS CO	IN	443.4
TEACHERS INS & ANNUITY ASN OF AM	NY	147,114.8
Weiss Safety Rating: A		
AMERICAN FIDELITY ASR CO	OK	2,382.6
GUARDIAN LIFE INS CO OF AMERICA	NY	20,577.2
JEFFERSON-PILOT LIFE INS CO	NC	13,405.5
MASSACHUSETTS MUTUAL LIFE INS CO	MA	80,322.1
NEW YORK LIFE INS CO	NY	87,505.8
NORTHWESTERN MUTUAL LIFE INS CO	WI	114,436.3
SENTRY INS A MUTUAL CO	WI	4,177.1
Weiss Safety Rating: A-		
ALLSTATE INS CO	IL	40,978.7
ALLSTATE LIFE INS CO	IL	60,033.7
CENTRAL STATES INDEMNITY CO OF OMAHA	NE	243.1
CINCINNATI INS CO	OH	7,143.1
FEDERATED LIFE INS CO	MN	864.3
JOHN HANCOCK LIFE INS CO	MA	73,183.9
MIDLAND NATIONAL LIFE INS CO	IA	10,748.6
MINNESOTA LIFE INS CO	MN	17,352.3
MUTUAL OF OMAHA INS CO	NE	3,755.1
NATIONAL GUARDIAN LIFE INS CO	WI	947.4
OLD REPUBLIC INS CO	PA	1,644.5
PACIFIC LIFE INS CO	CA	54,639.9
PRINCIPAL LIFE INS CO	IA	83,957.6
SENTRY LIFE INS CO	WI	2,101.2
USAA LIFE INS CO	TX	9,167.0
Weiss Safety Rating: B+		
AMERICAN GENERAL LIFE INS CO	TX	24,549.9
AMERICAN HEALTH & LIFE INS CO	TX	1,236.5
AMERITAS LIFE INS CORP	NE	2,417.9
AVEMCO INS CO	MD	191.7
BALBOA LIFE INS CO	CA	124.5
CAPITAL DISTRICT PHYSICIANS HEALTH P	NY	246.1
CITICORP LIFE INS CO	AZ	1,058.7
COLUMBUS LIFE INS CO	OH	2,187.1
COMPANION LIFE INS CO	SC	75.6
CUMIS INS SOCIETY INC	WI	826.9
FARM FAMILY LIFE INS CO	NY	889.2
FEDERAL INS CO	IN	18,983.3
FEDERATED MUTUAL INS CO	MN	3,013.6
GOLDEN RULE INS CO	IL	2,076.2
GREAT NORTHERN INS CO	MN	1,088.5
GREAT-WEST LIFE & ANNUITY INS CO	CO	27,323.0
HARTFORD FIRE INS CO	CT	15,857.7
HARTFORD LIFE & ACCIDENT INS CO	CT	8,792.5
HARTFORD LIFE & ANNUITY INS CO	CT	49,622.7
HARTFORD LIFE INS CO	CT	97,564.5
JEFFERSON PILOT FINANCIAL INS CO	NE	11,630.2
LINCOLN BENEFIT LIFE CO	NE	1,823.4
MANUFACTURERS LIFE INS CO USA	MI	53,737.8
METROPOLITAN LIFE INS CO	NY	220,093.6
METROPOLITAN PROPERTY & CAS INS CO	RI	4,789.1
MVP HEALTH PLAN INC	NY	264.0
NATIONAL BENEFIT LIFE INS CO	NY	736.6
NATIONAL CASUALTY CO	WI	92.6
NATIONAL UNION FIRE INS CO OF PITTSB	PA	18,196.9
NATIONWIDE LIFE INS CO	OH	80,569.1
NATIONWIDE MUTUAL FIRE INS CO	OH	3,610.4
PHYSICIANS LIFE INS CO	NE	1,195.8
PRIMERICA LIFE INS CO	MA	5,073.8
SAVINGS BANK LIFE INS CO OF MA	MA	1,548.3
SIRIUS AMERICA INS CO	DE	216.8
STATE FARM MUTUAL AUTOMOBILE INS CO	IL	70,070.4
SURETY LIFE INS CO	NE	50.3
TRAVELERS INS CO LIFE DEPT	CT	58,317.0
UNITED INS CO OF AMERICA	IL	2,064.3
UNITED OF OMAHA LIFE INS CO	NE	12,298.3

Virginia

INSURANCE COMPANY NAME	DOM. STATE	TOTAL ASSETS ($MIL)
Weiss Safety Rating: A+		
GOVERNMENT EMPLOYEES INS CO	MD	8,737.7
PHYSICIANS MUTUAL INS CO	NE	1,102.7
PROTECTIVE INS CO	IN	443.4
TEACHERS INS & ANNUITY ASN OF AM	NY	147,114.8
Weiss Safety Rating: A		
ALFA MUTUAL INS CO	AL	1,151.8
AMERICAN FIDELITY ASR CO	OK	2,382.6
AUTO-OWNERS INS CO	MI	6,582.7
CENTURION LIFE INS CO	MO	1,024.0
GROUP HOSP & MEDICAL SERVICES INC	DC	1,141.0
GUARDIAN LIFE INS CO OF AMERICA	NY	20,577.2
JEFFERSON-PILOT LIFE INS CO	NC	13,405.5
MASSACHUSETTS MUTUAL LIFE INS CO	MA	80,322.1
NEW YORK LIFE INS CO	NY	87,505.8
NORTHWESTERN MUTUAL LIFE INS CO	WI	114,436.3
SENTRY INS A MUTUAL CO	WI	4,177.1
Weiss Safety Rating: A-		
ALFA LIFE INS CORP	AL	821.5
ALLSTATE INS CO	IL	40,978.7
ALLSTATE LIFE INS CO	IL	60,033.7
AUTO-OWNERS LIFE INS CO	MI	1,251.5
CAREFIRST BLUECHOICE INC	DC	261.2
CENTRAL STATES INDEMNITY CO OF OMAHA	NE	243.1
CINCINNATI INS CO	OH	7,143.1
FEDERATED LIFE INS CO	MN	864.3
JOHN HANCOCK LIFE INS CO	MA	73,183.9
MIDLAND NATIONAL LIFE INS CO	IA	10,748.6
MINNESOTA LIFE INS CO	MN	17,352.3
MUTUAL OF OMAHA INS CO	NE	3,755.1
NATIONAL GUARDIAN LIFE INS CO	WI	947.4
OLD REPUBLIC INS CO	PA	1,644.5
PACIFIC LIFE INS CO	CA	54,639.9
PRINCIPAL LIFE INS CO	IA	83,957.6
SENTRY LIFE INS CO	WI	2,101.2
SOUTHERN FARM BUREAU LIFE INS CO	MS	7,776.4
USAA LIFE INS CO	TX	9,167.0
Weiss Safety Rating: B+		
AMERICAN GENERAL LIFE INS CO	TX	24,549.9
AMERICAN HEALTH & LIFE INS CO	TX	1,236.5
AMERITAS LIFE INS CORP	NE	2,417.9
ANTHEM HEALTH PLANS OF VIRGINIA	VA	1,621.3
AVEMCO INS CO	MD	191.7
BALBOA LIFE INS CO	CA	124.5
CITICORP LIFE INS CO	AZ	1,058.7
COLORADO BANKERS LIFE INS CO	CO	113.3
COLUMBUS LIFE INS CO	OH	2,187.1
COMPANION LIFE INS CO	SC	75.6
CUMIS INS SOCIETY INC	WI	826.9
FEDERAL INS CO	IN	18,983.3
FEDERATED MUTUAL INS CO	MN	3,013.6
GOLDEN RULE INS CO	IL	2,076.2
GREAT NORTHERN INS CO	MN	1,088.5
GREAT-WEST LIFE & ANNUITY INS CO	CO	27,323.0
HARTFORD FIRE INS CO	CT	15,857.7
HARTFORD LIFE & ACCIDENT INS CO	CT	8,792.5
HARTFORD LIFE & ANNUITY INS CO	CT	49,622.7
HARTFORD LIFE INS CO	CT	97,564.5
HEALTHKEEPERS INC	VA	178.7
JEFFERSON PILOT FINANCIAL INS CO	NE	11,630.2
LINCOLN BENEFIT LIFE CO	NE	1,823.4
MANUFACTURERS LIFE INS CO USA	MI	53,737.8
MD INDIVIDUAL PRACTICE ASSOC INC	MD	113.6
MERIT LIFE INS CO	IN	1,020.5
METROPOLITAN LIFE INS CO	NY	220,093.6
METROPOLITAN PROPERTY & CAS INS CO	RI	4,789.1
NATIONAL BENEFIT LIFE INS CO	NY	736.6
NATIONAL CASUALTY CO	WI	92.6
NATIONAL UNION FIRE INS CO OF PITTSB	PA	18,196.9
NATIONWIDE LIFE INS CO	OH	80,569.1
NATIONWIDE MUTUAL FIRE INS CO	OH	3,610.4
PENINSULA HEALTH CARE INC	VA	56.2
PHYSICIANS LIFE INS CO	NE	1,195.8
PRIMERICA LIFE INS CO	MA	5,073.8
PRIORITY HEALTH CARE INC	VA	70.7
SAVINGS BANK LIFE INS CO OF MA	MA	1,548.3
SIRIUS AMERICA INS CO	DE	216.8
STATE AUTOMOBILE MUTUAL INS CO	OH	1,299.8
STATE FARM MUTUAL AUTOMOBILE INS CO	IL	70,070.4
SURETY LIFE INS CO	NE	50.3
TRAVELERS INS CO LIFE DEPT	CT	58,317.0
UNITED INS CO OF AMERICA	IL	2,064.3
UNITED OF OMAHA LIFE INS CO	NE	12,298.3
WESTERN & SOUTHERN LIFE INS CO	OH	7,850.2

IV. Weiss Recommended Companies by State   Winter 2003 - 04

Washington

INSURANCE COMPANY NAME	DOM. STATE	TOTAL ASSETS ($MIL)
Weiss Safety Rating: A+		
COUNTRY LIFE INS CO	IL	4,387.5
GOVERNMENT EMPLOYEES INS CO	MD	8,737.7
PHYSICIANS MUTUAL INS CO	NE	1,102.7
PROTECTIVE INS CO	IN	443.4
TEACHERS INS & ANNUITY ASN OF AM	NY	147,114.8
Weiss Safety Rating: A		
AMERICAN FIDELITY ASR CO	OK	2,382.6
AUTO-OWNERS INS CO	MI	6,582.7
CENTURION LIFE INS CO	MO	1,024.0
COMMUNITY HEALTH PLAN OF WASHINGTON	WA	106.9
GUARDIAN LIFE INS CO OF AMERICA	NY	20,577.2
JEFFERSON-PILOT LIFE INS CO	NC	13,405.5
MASSACHUSETTS MUTUAL LIFE INS CO	MA	80,322.1
NEW YORK LIFE INS CO	NY	87,505.8
NORTHWESTERN MUTUAL LIFE INS CO	WI	114,436.3
SENTRY INS A MUTUAL CO	WI	4,177.1
Weiss Safety Rating: A-		
ALLSTATE INS CO	IL	40,978.7
ALLSTATE LIFE INS CO	IL	60,033.7
AUTO-OWNERS LIFE INS CO	MI	1,251.5
CENTRAL STATES INDEMNITY CO OF OMAHA	NE	243.1
CINCINNATI INS CO	OH	7,143.1
FARM BUREAU LIFE INS CO	IA	4,695.3
FEDERATED LIFE INS CO	MN	864.3
JOHN HANCOCK LIFE INS CO	MA	73,183.9
MIDLAND NATIONAL LIFE INS CO	IA	10,748.6
MINNESOTA LIFE INS CO	MN	17,352.3
MUTUAL OF OMAHA INS CO	NE	3,755.1
NATIONAL GUARDIAN LIFE INS CO	WI	947.4
OLD REPUBLIC INS CO	PA	1,644.5
PACIFIC LIFE INS CO	CA	54,639.9
PRINCIPAL LIFE INS CO	IA	83,957.6
SENTRY LIFE INS CO	WI	2,101.2
USAA LIFE INS CO	TX	9,167.0
Weiss Safety Rating: B+		
AMERICAN GENERAL LIFE INS CO	TX	24,549.9
AMERICAN HEALTH & LIFE INS CO	TX	1,236.5
AMERITAS LIFE INS CORP	NE	2,417.9
AVEMCO INS CO	MD	191.7
BALBOA LIFE INS CO	CA	124.5
CITICORP LIFE INS CO	AZ	1,058.7
COLORADO BANKERS LIFE INS CO	CO	113.3
COLUMBIA UNITED PROVIDERS INC	WA	13.4
COLUMBUS LIFE INS CO	OH	2,187.1
COMPANION LIFE INS CO	SC	75.6
CUMIS INS SOCIETY INC	WI	826.9
FEDERAL INS CO	IN	18,983.3
FEDERATED MUTUAL INS CO	MN	3,013.6
GOLDEN RULE INS CO	IL	2,076.2

INSURANCE COMPANY NAME	DOM. STATE	TOTAL ASSETS ($MIL)
GREAT NORTHERN INS CO	MN	1,088.5
GREAT-WEST LIFE & ANNUITY INS CO	CO	27,323.0
HARTFORD FIRE INS CO	CT	15,857.7
HARTFORD LIFE & ACCIDENT INS CO	CT	8,792.5
HARTFORD LIFE & ANNUITY INS CO	CT	49,622.7
HARTFORD LIFE INS CO	CT	97,564.5
JEFFERSON PILOT FINANCIAL INS CO	NE	11,630.2
LINCOLN BENEFIT LIFE CO	NE	1,823.4
MANUFACTURERS LIFE INS CO USA	MI	53,737.8
MERIT LIFE INS CO	IN	1,020.5
METROPOLITAN LIFE INS CO	NY	220,093.6
METROPOLITAN PROPERTY & CAS INS CO	RI	4,789.1
MIDWEST SECURITY LIFE INS CO	WI	132.8
NATIONAL BENEFIT LIFE INS CO	NY	736.6
NATIONAL CASUALTY CO	WI	92.6
NATIONAL UNION FIRE INS CO OF PITTSB	PA	18,196.9
NATIONWIDE LIFE INS CO	OH	80,569.1
NATIONWIDE MUTUAL FIRE INS CO	OH	3,610.4
PACIFIC GUARDIAN LIFE INS CO LTD	HI	431.5
PHYSICIANS LIFE INS CO	NE	1,195.8
PRIMERICA LIFE INS CO	MA	5,073.8
SIRIUS AMERICA INS CO	DE	216.8
STATE FARM MUTUAL AUTOMOBILE INS CO	IL	70,070.4
SURETY LIFE INS CO	NE	50.3
TRAVELERS INS CO LIFE DEPT	CT	58,317.0
UNITED INS CO OF AMERICA	IL	2,064.3
UNITED OF OMAHA LIFE INS CO	NE	12,298.3
WESTERN & SOUTHERN LIFE INS CO	OH	7,850.2

West Virginia

INSURANCE COMPANY NAME	DOM. STATE	TOTAL ASSETS ($MIL)
Weiss Safety Rating: A+		
COUNTRY LIFE INS CO	IL	4,387.5
GOVERNMENT EMPLOYEES INS CO	MD	8,737.7
PHYSICIANS MUTUAL INS CO	NE	1,102.7
PROTECTIVE INS CO	IN	443.4
TEACHERS INS & ANNUITY ASN OF AM	NY	147,114.8
Weiss Safety Rating: A		
AMERICAN FIDELITY ASR CO	OK	2,382.6
CENTURION LIFE INS CO	MO	1,024.0
GUARDIAN LIFE INS CO OF AMERICA	NY	20,577.2
JEFFERSON-PILOT LIFE INS CO	NC	13,405.5
MASSACHUSETTS MUTUAL LIFE INS CO	MA	80,322.1
NEW YORK LIFE INS CO	NY	87,505.8
NORTHWESTERN MUTUAL LIFE INS CO	WI	114,436.3
SENTRY INS A MUTUAL CO	WI	4,177.1
Weiss Safety Rating: A-		
ALLSTATE INS CO	IL	40,978.7
ALLSTATE LIFE INS CO	IL	60,033.7
CENTRAL STATES INDEMNITY CO OF OMAHA	NE	243.1
CINCINNATI INS CO	OH	7,143.1
FEDERATED LIFE INS CO	MN	864.3
JOHN HANCOCK LIFE INS CO	MA	73,183.9
MIDLAND NATIONAL LIFE INS CO	IA	10,748.6
MINNESOTA LIFE INS CO	MN	17,352.3
MUTUAL OF OMAHA INS CO	NE	3,755.1
NATIONAL GUARDIAN LIFE INS CO	WI	947.4
OLD REPUBLIC INS CO	PA	1,644.5
PACIFIC LIFE INS CO	CA	54,639.9
PRINCIPAL LIFE INS CO	IA	83,957.6
SENTRY LIFE INS CO	WI	2,101.2
USAA LIFE INS CO	TX	9,167.0
Weiss Safety Rating: B+		
AMERICAN GENERAL LIFE INS CO	TX	24,549.9
AMERICAN HEALTH & LIFE INS CO	TX	1,236.5
AMERITAS LIFE INS CORP	NE	2,417.9
AVEMCO INS CO	MD	191.7
BALBOA LIFE INS CO	CA	124.5
CITICORP LIFE INS CO	AZ	1,058.7
COLORADO BANKERS LIFE INS CO	CO	113.3
COLUMBUS LIFE INS CO	OH	2,187.1
COMPANION LIFE INS CO	SC	75.6
CUMIS INS SOCIETY INC	WI	826.9
FARM FAMILY LIFE INS CO	NY	889.2
FEDERAL INS CO	IN	18,983.3
FEDERATED MUTUAL INS CO	MN	3,013.6
GOLDEN RULE INS CO	IL	2,076.2
GREAT NORTHERN INS CO	MN	1,088.5
GREAT-WEST LIFE & ANNUITY INS CO	CO	27,323.0
HARTFORD FIRE INS CO	CT	15,857.7
HARTFORD LIFE & ACCIDENT INS CO	CT	8,792.5
HARTFORD LIFE & ANNUITY INS CO	CT	49,622.7
HARTFORD LIFE INS CO	CT	97,564.5
JEFFERSON PILOT FINANCIAL INS CO	NE	11,630.2
LINCOLN BENEFIT LIFE CO	NE	1,823.4
MANUFACTURERS LIFE INS CO USA	MI	53,737.8
MD INDIVIDUAL PRACTICE ASSOC INC	MD	113.6
MERIT LIFE INS CO	IN	1,020.5
METROPOLITAN LIFE INS CO	NY	220,093.6
METROPOLITAN PROPERTY & CAS INS CO	RI	4,789.1
MOUNTAIN STATE BL CROSS BL SHIELD	WV	156.0
NATIONAL BENEFIT LIFE INS CO	NY	736.6
NATIONAL CASUALTY CO	WI	92.6
NATIONAL UNION FIRE INS CO OF PITTSB	PA	18,196.9
NATIONWIDE LIFE INS CO	OH	80,569.1
NATIONWIDE MUTUAL FIRE INS CO	OH	3,610.4
PHYSICIANS LIFE INS CO	NE	1,195.8
PRIMERICA LIFE INS CO	MA	5,073.8
SIRIUS AMERICA INS CO	DE	216.8
STATE AUTOMOBILE MUTUAL INS CO	OH	1,299.8
STATE FARM MUTUAL AUTOMOBILE INS CO	IL	70,070.4
SURETY LIFE INS CO	NE	50.3
TRAVELERS INS CO LIFE DEPT	CT	58,317.0
UNITED INS CO OF AMERICA	IL	2,064.3
UNITED OF OMAHA LIFE INS CO	NE	12,298.3
WESTERN & SOUTHERN LIFE INS CO	OH	7,850.2

Wisconsin

Weiss Safety Rating: A+

INSURANCE COMPANY NAME	DOM. STATE	TOTAL ASSETS ($MIL)
COUNTRY LIFE INS CO	IL	4,387.5
GOVERNMENT EMPLOYEES INS CO	MD	8,737.7
PHYSICIANS MUTUAL INS CO	NE	1,102.7
PROTECTIVE INS CO	IN	443.4
TEACHERS INS & ANNUITY ASN OF AM	NY	147,114.8

Weiss Safety Rating: A

INSURANCE COMPANY NAME	DOM. STATE	TOTAL ASSETS ($MIL)
ALFA MUTUAL INS CO	AL	1,151.8
AMERICAN FIDELITY ASR CO	OK	2,382.6
AUTO-OWNERS INS CO	MI	6,582.7
CENTURION LIFE INS CO	MO	1,024.0
GUARDIAN LIFE INS CO OF AMERICA	NY	20,577.2
JEFFERSON-PILOT LIFE INS CO	NC	13,405.5
MASSACHUSETTS MUTUAL LIFE INS CO	MA	80,322.1
NEW YORK LIFE INS CO	NY	87,505.8
NORTHWESTERN MUTUAL LIFE INS CO	WI	114,436.3
SENTRY INS A MUTUAL CO	WI	4,177.1

Weiss Safety Rating: A-

INSURANCE COMPANY NAME	DOM. STATE	TOTAL ASSETS ($MIL)
ALLSTATE INS CO	IL	40,978.7
ALLSTATE LIFE INS CO	IL	60,033.7
AUTO-OWNERS LIFE INS CO	MI	1,251.5
CENTRAL STATES INDEMNITY CO OF OMAHA	NE	243.1
CINCINNATI INS CO	OH	7,143.1
FARM BUREAU LIFE INS CO	IA	4,695.3
FEDERATED LIFE INS CO	MN	864.3
GRANGE MUTUAL CAS CO	OH	1,116.1
GROUP HEALTH COOP OF S CENTRAL WI	WI	49.9
JOHN HANCOCK LIFE INS CO	MA	73,183.9
MIDLAND NATIONAL LIFE INS CO	IA	10,748.6
MINNESOTA LIFE INS CO	MN	17,352.3
MUTUAL OF OMAHA INS CO	NE	3,755.1
NATIONAL GUARDIAN LIFE INS CO	WI	947.4
OLD REPUBLIC INS CO	PA	1,644.5
PACIFIC LIFE INS CO	CA	54,639.9
PRINCIPAL LIFE INS CO	IA	83,957.6
SENTRY LIFE INS CO	WI	2,101.2
USAA LIFE INS CO	TX	9,167.0

Weiss Safety Rating: B+

INSURANCE COMPANY NAME	DOM. STATE	TOTAL ASSETS ($MIL)
AMERICAN GENERAL LIFE INS CO	TX	24,549.9
AMERICAN HEALTH & LIFE INS CO	TX	1,236.5
AMERITAS LIFE INS CORP	NE	2,417.9
ATRIUM HEALTH PLAN INC	WI	14.3
AVEMCO INS CO	MD	191.7
BALBOA LIFE INS CO	CA	124.5
CITICORP LIFE INS CO	AZ	1,058.7
COLORADO BANKERS LIFE INS CO	CO	113.3
COLUMBUS LIFE INS CO	OH	2,187.1
COMPANION LIFE INS CO	SC	75.6
CUMIS INS SOCIETY INC	WI	826.9
DEAN HEALTH PLAN INC	WI	123.0
FEDERAL INS CO	IN	18,983.3
FEDERATED MUTUAL INS CO	MN	3,013.6
GOLDEN RULE INS CO	IL	2,076.2
GRANGE LIFE INS CO	OH	159.8
GREAT NORTHERN INS CO	MN	1,088.5
GREAT-WEST LIFE & ANNUITY INS CO	CO	27,323.0
HARTFORD FIRE INS CO	CT	15,857.7
HARTFORD LIFE & ACCIDENT INS CO	CT	8,792.5
HARTFORD LIFE & ANNUITY INS CO	CT	49,622.7
HARTFORD LIFE INS CO	CT	97,564.5
JEFFERSON PILOT FINANCIAL INS CO	NE	11,630.2
LINCOLN BENEFIT LIFE CO	NE	1,823.4
MANUFACTURERS LIFE INS CO USA	MI	53,737.8
MERIT LIFE INS CO	IN	1,020.5
METROPOLITAN LIFE INS CO	NY	220,093.6
METROPOLITAN PROPERTY & CAS INS CO	RI	4,789.1
MIDWEST SECURITY LIFE INS CO	WI	132.8
NATIONAL BENEFIT LIFE INS CO	NY	736.6
NATIONAL CASUALTY CO	WI	92.6
NATIONAL UNION FIRE INS CO OF PITTSB	PA	18,196.9
NATIONWIDE LIFE INS CO	OH	80,569.1
NATIONWIDE MUTUAL FIRE INS CO	OH	3,610.4
PEKIN LIFE INS CO	IL	653.8
PHYSICIANS LIFE INS CO	NE	1,195.8
PRIMERICA LIFE INS CO	MA	5,073.8
SIRIUS AMERICA INS CO	DE	216.8
STATE AUTOMOBILE MUTUAL INS CO	OH	1,299.8
STATE FARM MUTUAL AUTOMOBILE INS CO	IL	70,070.4
SURETY LIFE INS CO	NE	50.3
TRAVELERS INS CO LIFE DEPT	CT	58,317.0
UNITED HEALTHCARE OF WISCONSIN INC	WI	182.0
UNITED INS CO OF AMERICA	IL	2,064.3
UNITED OF OMAHA LIFE INS CO	NE	12,298.3
WESTERN & SOUTHERN LIFE INS CO	OH	7,850.2

Wyoming

INSURANCE COMPANY NAME	DOM. STATE	TOTAL ASSETS ($MIL)
Weiss Safety Rating: A+		
COUNTRY LIFE INS CO	IL	4,387.5
GOVERNMENT EMPLOYEES INS CO	MD	8,737.7
PHYSICIANS MUTUAL INS CO	NE	1,102.7
PROTECTIVE INS CO	IN	443.4
TEACHERS INS & ANNUITY ASN OF AM	NY	147,114.8
Weiss Safety Rating: A		
AMERICAN FIDELITY ASR CO	OK	2,382.6
CENTURION LIFE INS CO	MO	1,024.0
GUARDIAN LIFE INS CO OF AMERICA	NY	20,577.2
JEFFERSON-PILOT LIFE INS CO	NC	13,405.5
MASSACHUSETTS MUTUAL LIFE INS CO	MA	80,322.1
NEW YORK LIFE INS CO	NY	87,505.8
NORTHWESTERN MUTUAL LIFE INS CO	WI	114,436.3
SENTRY INS A MUTUAL CO	WI	4,177.1
Weiss Safety Rating: A-		
ALLSTATE INS CO	IL	40,978.7
ALLSTATE LIFE INS CO	IL	60,033.7
CALIFORNIA STATE AUTO ASN INTER-INS	CA	4,180.2
CENTRAL STATES INDEMNITY CO OF OMAHA	NE	243.1
CINCINNATI INS CO	OH	7,143.1
FARM BUREAU LIFE INS CO	IA	4,695.3
FEDERATED LIFE INS CO	MN	864.3
JOHN HANCOCK LIFE INS CO	MA	73,183.9
MIDLAND NATIONAL LIFE INS CO	IA	10,748.6
MINNESOTA LIFE INS CO	MN	17,352.3
MUTUAL OF OMAHA INS CO	NE	3,755.1
NATIONAL GUARDIAN LIFE INS CO	WI	947.4
OLD REPUBLIC INS CO	PA	1,644.5
PACIFIC LIFE INS CO	CA	54,639.9
PRINCIPAL LIFE INS CO	IA	83,957.6
SENTRY LIFE INS CO	WI	2,101.2
USAA LIFE INS CO	TX	9,167.0
Weiss Safety Rating: B+		
AMERICAN GENERAL LIFE INS CO	TX	24,549.9
AMERICAN HEALTH & LIFE INS CO	TX	1,236.5
AMERITAS LIFE INS CORP	NE	2,417.9
AVEMCO INS CO	MD	191.7
BALBOA LIFE INS CO	CA	124.5
BLUE CROSS BLUE SHIELD OF WYOMING	WY	106.3
CITICORP LIFE INS CO	AZ	1,058.7
COLORADO BANKERS LIFE INS CO	CO	113.3
COLUMBUS LIFE INS CO	OH	2,187.1
COMPANION LIFE INS CO	SC	75.6
CUMIS INS SOCIETY INC	WI	826.9
FEDERAL INS CO	IN	18,983.3
FEDERATED MUTUAL INS CO	MN	3,013.6
GOLDEN RULE INS CO	IL	2,076.2
GREAT NORTHERN INS CO	MN	1,088.5
GREAT-WEST LIFE & ANNUITY INS CO	CO	27,323.0

INSURANCE COMPANY NAME	DOM. STATE	TOTAL ASSETS ($MIL)
HARTFORD FIRE INS CO	CT	15,857.7
HARTFORD LIFE & ACCIDENT INS CO	CT	8,792.5
HARTFORD LIFE & ANNUITY INS CO	CT	49,622.7
HARTFORD LIFE INS CO	CT	97,564.5
JEFFERSON PILOT FINANCIAL INS CO	NE	11,630.2
LINCOLN BENEFIT LIFE CO	NE	1,823.4
MANUFACTURERS LIFE INS CO USA	MI	53,737.8
MERIT LIFE INS CO	IN	1,020.5
METROPOLITAN LIFE INS CO	NY	220,093.6
METROPOLITAN PROPERTY & CAS INS CO	RI	4,789.1
NATIONAL BENEFIT LIFE INS CO	NY	736.6
NATIONAL CASUALTY CO	WI	92.6
NATIONAL UNION FIRE INS CO OF PITTSB	PA	18,196.9
NATIONWIDE LIFE INS CO	OH	80,569.1
NATIONWIDE MUTUAL FIRE INS CO	OH	3,610.4
PACIFIC GUARDIAN LIFE INS CO LTD	HI	431.5
PHYSICIANS LIFE INS CO	NE	1,195.8
PRIMERICA LIFE INS CO	MA	5,073.8
SIRIUS AMERICA INS CO	DE	216.8
STATE AUTOMOBILE MUTUAL INS CO	OH	1,299.8
STATE FARM MUTUAL AUTOMOBILE INS CO	IL	70,070.4
SURETY LIFE INS CO	NE	50.3
TRAVELERS INS CO LIFE DEPT	CT	58,317.0
UNITED INS CO OF AMERICA	IL	2,064.3
UNITED OF OMAHA LIFE INS CO	NE	12,298.3
WESTERN & SOUTHERN LIFE INS CO	OH	7,850.2

Section V

Long-Term Care Insurers

A list of rated companies providing

Long-Term Care Insurance.

Companies are listed in alphabetical order.

Section V Contents

This section provides contact addresses and phone numbers for all companies who sell long-term care insurance. The long-term care insurers in this section are listed in alphabetical order.

1. **Weiss Safety Rating** — Our rating is measured on a scale from A to F and considers a wide range of factors. Highly-rated companies are, in our opinion, less likely to experience financial difficulties than lower-rated firms. See *About the Weiss Safety Rating* on page 11 for more information.

2. **Insurance Company Name** — The legally registered name, which can sometimes differ from the name that the company uses for advertising. An insurer's name can be very similar to the name of other companies, so make sure you note the exact name before contacting your agent.

3. **Address** — The address of the main office where you can contact the firm for additional financial data or for the location of local branches and/or registered agents.

4. **Telephone Number** — The number to call for additional financial data or for the phone numbers of local branches and/or registered agents.

To compare long-term care insurance policies and to walk through the maze of options, prices, and insurers, see the Long-Term Care Insurance Planner on page 419. It helps narrow down the choices available by addressing questions such as:

- What can you afford to pay for insurance?
- What type of care and living arrangement will suit your needs?
- When will you most likely need to utilize the insurance benefits?
- How much can you afford to pay from your own savings?
- Do you want a tax-qualified or non-qualified policy?
- What kind of insurance agent are you working with?

The planner offers an easy-to-use analysis tool to help identify the policy that best meets your needs. Based on information provided by insurance agents and literature from the provider, it addresses questions such as:

- How safe is the insurer?
- How are the coverage and facility options defined?
- What are the terms of coverage and reimbursement?
- How will the benefits be triggered?
- What other features are included in the policy?

V. Long-Term Care Insurers

Winter 2003 - 04

WEISS SAFETY RATING	INSURANCE COMPANY NAME	ADDRESS	CITY	STATE	ZIP	PHONE
D	AF&L INS CO	Highlands Corporate Ctr	Coatesville	PA	19320	(610) 380-1851
B-	ALLIANZ LIFE INS CO OF NORTH AMERICA	5701 Golden Hills Dr	Minneapolis	MN	55416	(612) 347-6500
B-	AMERICAN FAMILY LIFE ASR CO OF COLUM	1932 Wynnton Rd	Columbus	GA	31999	(706) 323-3431
C	AMERICAN FAMILY LIFE ASR CO OF NY	.NULL.	.NULL.	.NU	.NULL.	(706) 660-7208
D	AMERICAN INDEPENDENT NETWORK INS CO	110A Walnut St	Elmira	NY	14905	(800) 222-3469
D	AMERICAN NETWORK INS CO	3440 Lehigh St	Allentown	PA	18103	(802) 655-5500
C-	AMERICAN PIONEER LIFE INS CO	600 Courtland St	Orlando	FL	32804	(407) 628-1776
D+	AMERICAN PROGRESSIVE L&H I C OF NY	6 International Dr Suite 190	Rye Brook	NY	10573	(914) 934-8300
C+	AMERUS LIFE INS CO	611 Fifth Ave	Des Moines	IA	50309	(515) 283-2371
E	BANKERS LIFE & CAS CO	222 Merchandise Mart Plaza	Chicago	IL	60654	(312) 396-6000
B	BC LIFE & HEALTH INS CO	21555 Oxnard St	Woodland Hills	CA	91367	(818) 703-2345
C	BCS LIFE INS CO	676 North St Clair St	Chicago	IL	60611	(312) 951-7700
B+	BLUE CROSS BLUE SHIELD OF FLORIDA	4800 Deerwood Campus Pkwy	Jacksonville	FL	32246	(800) 477-3736
B+	BLUE CROSS BLUE SHIELD OF MINNESOTA	3535 Blue Cross Rd	St Paul	MN	55164	(651) 662-8000
C-	CHRISTIAN FIDELITY LIFE INS CO	2721 N Central Ave	Phoenix	AZ	85004	(972) 937-4420
C-	CINCINNATI EQUITABLE LIFE INS CO	525 Vine St, Suite 2100	Cincinnati	OH	45202	(513) 621-1826
C	CNA GROUP LIFE ASR CO	CNA Plaza	Chicago	IL	60685	(312) 822-5000
C	COLONIAL AMERICAN LIFE INS CO	673 Cherry Lane	Souderton	PA	18964	(215) 723-3044
C-	COLONIAL LIFE & ACCIDENT INS CO	6335 S. East Street, Suite A	Indianapolis	IN	46227	(803) 798-7000
C	COMBINED INS CO OF AMERICA	123 N Wacker Dr	Chicago	IL	60606	(312) 701-3000
D	CONSTITUTION LIFE INS CO	4211 Norbourne Blvd	Louisville	KY	40207	(214) 954-7111
C+	CONTINENTAL ASSURANCE CO	CNA Plaza	Chicago	IL	60685	(312) 822-5000
C	CONTINENTAL CASUALTY CO	CNA Plaza	Chicago	IL	60685	(312) 822-5000
D	CONTINENTAL GENERAL INS CO	8901 Indian Hills Dr	Omaha	NE	68114	(402) 397-3200
A+	COUNTRY LIFE INS CO	1701 Towanda Ave	Bloomington	IL	61701	(309) 821-3000
C	EQUITABLE LIFE & CASUALTY INS CO	3 Triad Center Suite 200	Salt Lake City	UT	84180	(801) 579-3400
B+	EXCELLUS HEALTH PLAN INC	165 Court St	Rochester	NY	14647	(716) 238-4506
B	FEDERAL HOME LIFE INS CO	700 Main St	Lynchburg	VA	24504	(804) 845-0911
C-	FIRST UNUM LIFE INS CO	Christiana Bldg Suite 100	Tarrytown	NY	10591	(914) 524-4056
B	FLORIDA COMBINED LIFE INS CO INC	5011 Gate Pkwy Bld 200 Ste 400	Jacksonville	FL	32256	(904) 828-7800
B-	GE CAPITAL LIFE ASR CO OF NEW YORK	125 Park Ave 6th Floor	New York	NY	10017	(212) 672-4299
C+	GENERAL ELECTRIC CAPITAL ASR CO	6604 West Broad St	Richmond	VA	23230	(804) 662-2400
B-	GERBER LIFE INS CO	66 Church St	White Plains	NY	10601	(914) 761-4404
B+	GOLDEN RULE INS CO	712 Eleventh St	Lawrenceville	IL	62439	(618) 943-8000
C	GREAT AMERICAN LIFE INS CO	250 E Fifth St	Cincinnati	OH	45202	(513) 357-3300
D-	GREAT REPUBLIC LIFE INS CO	226 Second Ave W	Seattle	WA	98119	(206) 285-1422
C+	GUARANTEE TRUST LIFE INS CO	1275 Milwaukee Ave	Glenview	IL	60025	(847) 699-0600
C-	GUARANTY INCOME LIFE INS CO	929 Government St	Baton Rouge	LA	70802	(225) 383-0355
B-	HEALTH NET LIFE INS CO	225 N Main St	Pueblo	CO	81003	(719) 585-8017
A-	JOHN HANCOCK LIFE INS CO	John Hancock Place	Boston	MA	02117	(617) 572-6000
B-	KANAWHA INS CO	210 S White St	Lancaster	SC	29721	(803) 283-5300
B	LA HEALTH SERVICE & INDEMNITY CO	5525 Reitz Ave	Baton Rouge	LA	70809	(225) 295-3307
B	LIFE INVESTORS INS CO OF AMERICA	4333 Edgewood Rd NE	Cedar Rapids	IA	52499	(319) 398-8511
B+	LINCOLN BENEFIT LIFE CO	206 S 13th St, Suite 200	Lincoln	NE	68508	(800) 525-9287

Winter 2003 - 04 — V. Long-Term Care Insurers

WEISS SAFETY RATING	INSURANCE COMPANY NAME	ADDRESS	CITY	STATE	ZIP	PHONE
A	MASSACHUSETTS MUTUAL LIFE INS CO	1295 State St	Springfield	MA	01111	(413) 788-8411
C-	MEDAMERICA INS CO	Foster Plaza VIII 730 Holiday	Pittsburgh	PA	15220	(410) 684-3200
D+	MEDAMERICA INS CO OF NEW YORK	150 E Main Street	Rochester	NY	14647	(716) 238-4456
D+	MEDICO LIFE INS CO	.NULL.	.NULL.	.NU	.NULL.	(402) 391-6900
C+	MEGA LIFE & HEALTH INS CO	4001 McEwen Dr, Suite 200	Dallas	TX	75244	(972) 392-6700
B+	METROPOLITAN LIFE INS CO	1 Madison Ave	New York	NY	10010	(212) 578-2211
C	MID-WEST NATIONAL LIFE INS CO OF TN	4001 McEwen Dr, Suite 200	Dallas	TX	75244	(972) 392-6700
B-	MONUMENTAL LIFE INS CO	Two East Chase St	Baltimore	MD	21202	(410) 685-2900
A-	MUTUAL OF OMAHA INS CO	Mutual Of Omaha Plaza	Omaha	NE	68175	(402) 342-7600
D+	MUTUAL PROTECTIVE INS CO	.NULL.	.NULL.	.NU	.NULL.	(402) 391-6900
D	NATIONAL STATES INS CO	.NULL.	.NULL.	.NU	.NULL.	(314) 878-0101
A	NEW YORK LIFE INS CO	51 Madison Ave	New York	NY	10010	(212) 576-7000
B	NORTHWESTERN LONG TERM CARE INS CO	720 E Wisconsin Ave	Milwaukee	WI	53202	(414) 299-3136
C-	PACIFICARE LIFE & HEALTH INS CO	23046 Avenida Dela Carlota 700	Laguna Hills	CA	92653	(714) 206-5247
D	PENN TREATY NETWORK AMERICA INS CO	3440 Lehigh St	Allentown	PA	18103	(610) 965-2222
D+	PENNSYLVANIA LIFE INS CO	525 N Twelfth St	Leymone	PA	17043	(407) 628-1776
C+	PEOPLES BENEFIT LIFE INS CO	4333 Edgewood Road NE	Cedar Rapids	IA	52499	(319) 398-8511
A+	PHYSICIANS MUTUAL INS CO	2600 Dodge St	Omaha	NE	68131	(402) 633-1000
B	PREMERA BLUE CROSS	7001 220th St SW	Mountlake Terrace	WA	98043	(425) 918-4000
C-	PROVIDENT LIFE & ACCIDENT INS CO	1 Fountain Square	Chattanooga	TN	37402	(423) 755-1373
B-	PRUDENTIAL INS CO OF AMERICA	Prudential Plaza	Newark	NJ	07102	(877) 301-1212
C	PYRAMID LIFE INS CO	6201 Johnson Dr	Shawnee Mission	KS	66202	(913) 722-1110
D	SENIOR AMERICAN LIFE INS CO	1800 Street Rd	Warrington	PA	18976	(215) 918-0515
A-	SOUTHERN FARM BUREAU LIFE INS CO	1401 Livingston Lane	Jackson	MS	39213	(601) 981-7422
B+	STATE FARM MUTUAL AUTOMOBILE INS CO	One State Farm Plaza	Bloomington	IL	61710	(309) 735-8480
B	STATE LIFE INS CO	141 E Washington St	Indianapolis	IN	46204	(317) 285-1877
C	SWISS RE LIFE & HEALTH AMER INC	969 High Ridge Rd	Stamford	CT	06904	(203) 321-3141
A+	TEACHERS INS & ANNUITY ASN OF AM	730 Third Ave 7th Floor	New York	NY	10017	(212) 490-9000
D+	TEACHERS PROTV MUTUAL LIFE INS CO	116-118 N Prince St	Lancaster	PA	17603	(717) 394-7156
B-	TRANSAMERICA FINANCIAL LIFE INS CO	4 Manhattanville Rd	Purchase	NY	10577	(914) 697-8000
B-	TRANSAMERICA LIFE INS CO	4333 Edgewood Rd NE	Cedar Rapids	IA	52499	(319) 398-8511
B	TRANSAMERICA OCCIDENTAL L I C	4333 Edgewood Road NE	Cedar Rapids	IA	52499	(213) 742-2111
B	TRUSTMARK INS CO	400 Field Dr	Lake Forest	IL	60045	(847) 615-1500
D+	UNION BANKERS INS CO	1700 Redbud Blvd Suite 333	McKinney	TX	75069	(407) 628-1776
D+	UNION LABOR LIFE INS CO	111 Massachusetts Ave NW	Washington	DC	20001	(202) 682-6690
C-	UNION STANDARD OF AMERICA L I C	111 Massachusetts Ave NW	Washington	DC	20001	(202) 682-6639
B	UNITED AMERICAN INS CO	3700 S Stonebridge Dr	McKinney	TX	75070	(972) 529-5085
C	UNITED SECURITY ASSURANCE CO OF PA	673 Cherry Lane	Souderton	PA	18964	(215) 723-3044
C+	UNITED TEACHER ASSOCIATES INS CO	5508 Parkcrest Dr	Austin	TX	78731	(512) 451-2224
C	VALLEY FORGE LIFE INS CO	401 Penn St	Reading	PA	19601	(312) 822-5000

Section VI

Medicare Supplement Insurers

A list of all

Indemnity Insurers

providing Medicare supplement insurance,
with their addresses and phone numbers.

Section VI Contents

This section provides contact addresses and phone numbers for all companies who sell Medicare supplement (Medigap) insurance. These traditional indemnity insurers should not be confused with HMOs offering Medicare benefits, which can be found in Section VII, beginning on page 389. The Medigap insurers in this section are listed in alphabetical order. A price comparison of the companies' annual premiums customized for your age, gender, and zip code is available in Weiss Ratings' *Shopper's Guide to Medicare Supplement Insurance* listed on page 442.

1. **Weiss Safety Rating**   Our rating is measured on a scale from A to F and considers a wide range of factors. Highly-rated companies are, in our opinion, less likely to experience financial difficulties than lower-rated firms. See *About the Weiss Safety Rating* on page 11 for more information.

2. **Insurance Company Name**   The legally registered name, which can sometimes differ from the name that the company uses for advertising. An insurer's name can be very similar to the name of other companies, so make sure you note the exact name before contacting your agent.

3. **Address**   The address of the main office where you can contact the firm for additional financial data or for the location of local branches and/or registered agents.

4. **Telephone Number**   The number to call for additional financial data or for the phone numbers of local branches and/or registered agents.

VI. Medicare Supplement Insurers

Winter 2003 - 04

WEISS SAFETY RATING	INSURANCE COMPANY NAME	ADDRESS	CITY	STATE	ZIP	PHONE
B-	ALLIANZ LIFE INS CO OF NORTH AMERICA	5701 Golden Hills Dr	Minneapolis	MN	55416	(612) 347-6500
B	ALTA HEALTH & LIFE INS CO	10401 N Meridian St Ste 350	Indianapolis	IN	46290	(303) 737-3000
D+	AMALGAMATED LIFE & HEALTH INS CO	333 South Ashland Avenue	Chicago	IL	60607	(312) 738-6113
E+	AMERICAN CAPITOL INS CO	10555 Richmond Ave, 2nd Fl	Houston	TX	77042	(713) 974-2242
C+	AMERICAN COMMUNITY MUT INS CO	39201 W Seven Mile Rd	Livonia	MI	48152	(800) 233-3444
D+	AMERICAN EXCHANGE LIFE INS CO	80 E Campbell Rd Ste 345	Richardson	TX	75081	(214) 520-1450
B	AMERICAN FAMILY INS CO	6000 American Parkway	Madison	WI	53783	(608) 249-2111
B-	AMERICAN FAMILY LIFE ASR CO OF COLUM	1932 Wynnton Rd	Columbus	GA	31999	(706) 323-3431
C	AMERICAN FAMILY LIFE ASR CO OF NY	.NULL.	.NULL.	.NU	.NULL.	(706) 660-7208
B	AMERICAN FAMILY MUT INS CO	6000 American Pkwy	Madison	WI	53783	(608) 249-2111
B-	AMERICAN GENERAL LIFE & ACC INS CO	MC 2450 American General Ctr	Nashville	TN	37250	(615) 749-1000
B	AMERICAN INCOME LIFE INS CO	6435 Castleway West Dr Ste 201	Indianapolis	IN	46250	(254) 761-6400
C-	AMERICAN LIFE & HEALTH INS CO	237 E High Street	Jefferson City	MO	65102	(949) 380-0233
D	AMERICAN NETWORK INS CO	3440 Lehigh St	Allentown	PA	18103	(802) 655-5500
C-	AMERICAN PIONEER LIFE INS CO	600 Courtland St	Orlando	FL	32804	(407) 628-1776
D+	AMERICAN PROGRESSIVE L&H I C OF NY	6 International Dr Suite 190	Rye Brook	NY	10573	(914) 934-8300
B	AMERICAN REPUBLIC INS CO	601 Sixth Ave	Des Moines	IA	50309	(515) 245-2000
C+	ANTHEM HEALTH PLANS INC	370 Bassett Rd	North Haven	CT	06473	(203) 239-4911
B	ANTHEM HEALTH PLANS OF MAINE INC	2 Gannett Cr	S Portland	ME	04106	(207) 822-7000
B	ANTHEM HEALTH PLANS OF NEW HAMPSHIRE	3000 Goffs Falls Rd	Manchester	NH	03111	(207) 822-7000
B+	ANTHEM HEALTH PLANS OF VIRGINIA	2015 Staples Mill Rd	Richmond	VA	23230	(804) 354-7000
B-	ANTHEM INS COMPANIES INC	120 Monument Circle	Indianapolis	IN	46204	(317) 488-6484
B-	ANTHEM LIFE INS CO	6740 N High St Suite 200	Worthington	OH	43085	(614) 438-3959
B+	ARKANSAS BLUE CROSS AND BLUE SHIELD	601 S Gaines	Little Rock	AR	72201	(501) 378-2000
C+	ASURIS NORTHWEST HEALTH	106 N 2nd	Walla Walla	WA	99362	(509) 525-5220
B+	ATRIUM HEALTH PLAN INC	400 2nd St., Ste 270	Hudson	WI	54106	(715) 386-6886
A-	AUTO-OWNERS LIFE INS CO	6101 Anacapri Blvd	Lansing	MI	48917	(517) 323-1200
D+	AVERA HEALTH PLANS INC	3900 W Avera Dr Suite 200	Sioux Falls	SD	57108	(605) 322-4500
C	BANKERS FIDELITY LIFE INS CO	4370 Peachtree Rd NE	Atlanta	GA	30319	(404) 266-5500
E	BANKERS LIFE & CAS CO	222 Merchandise Mart Plaza	Chicago	IL	60654	(312) 396-6000
C+	BLUE CARE NETWORK OF MICHIGAN	25925 Telegraph	Southfield	MI	48086	(248) 354-7450
B	BLUE CROSS BLUE SHIELD OF ALABAMA	450 Riverchase Parkway E	Birmingham	AL	35298	(205) 988-2100
A	BLUE CROSS BLUE SHIELD OF ARIZONA	2444 W Las Palmaritas Dr	Phoenix	AZ	85021	(602) 864-4100
B+	BLUE CROSS BLUE SHIELD OF DELAWARE	One Brandywine Gateway	Wilmington	DE	19801	(302) 421-3000
B+	BLUE CROSS BLUE SHIELD OF FLORIDA	4800 Deerwood Campus Pkwy	Jacksonville	FL	32246	(800) 477-3736
A	BLUE CROSS BLUE SHIELD OF GEORGIA	3350 Peachtree Rd NE	Atlanta	GA	30326	(404) 842-8000
C+	BLUE CROSS BLUE SHIELD OF KANSAS INC	1133 SW Topeka Blvd	Topeka	KS	66629	(785) 291-7000
B+	BLUE CROSS BLUE SHIELD OF KC	2301 Main St	Kansas City	MO	64108	(816) 395-2222
A	BLUE CROSS BLUE SHIELD OF MA	401 Park Dr Landmark Center	Boston	MA	02215	(617) 246-5000
B	BLUE CROSS BLUE SHIELD OF MICHIGAN	600 Lafayette East	Detroit	MI	48226	(313) 225-9000
B+	BLUE CROSS BLUE SHIELD OF MINNESOTA	3535 Blue Cross Rd	St Paul	MN	55164	(651) 662-8000
C+	BLUE CROSS BLUE SHIELD OF MONTANA	560 N Park Ave	Helena	MT	59601	(406) 444-8200
B-	BLUE CROSS BLUE SHIELD OF MS, MUTUAL	3545 Lakeland Dr	Flowood	MS	39208	(601) 932-3704
B	BLUE CROSS BLUE SHIELD OF NC	1830 US 15-501 North	Chapel Hill	NC	27514	(919) 489-7431

VI. Medicare Supplement Insurers

WEISS SAFETY RATING	INSURANCE COMPANY NAME	ADDRESS	CITY	STATE	ZIP	PHONE
B	BLUE CROSS BLUE SHIELD OF NEBRASKA	7261 Mercy Rd	Omaha	NE	68124	(402) 390-1800
B	BLUE CROSS BLUE SHIELD OF OKLAHOMA	1215 S Boulder	Tulsa	OK	74119	(918) 560-3500
B+	BLUE CROSS BLUE SHIELD OF RI	444 Westminster St	Providence	RI	02903	(401) 459-1000
B+	BLUE CROSS BLUE SHIELD OF SC INC	2501 Faraway Dr	Columbia	SC	29219	(803) 788-3860
B	BLUE CROSS BLUE SHIELD OF VERMONT	445 Industrial Ln	Berlin	VT	05602	(802) 223-6131
B+	BLUE CROSS BLUE SHIELD OF WYOMING	4000 House Ave	Cheyenne	WY	82001	(307) 634-1393
B-	BLUE CROSS BLUE SHIELD UNITED OF WI	401 W Michigan St	Milwaukee	WI	53203	(414) 226-5823
B+	BLUE CROSS OF IDAHO HEALTH SERVICE	3000 Pine Ave	Meridian	ID	83642	(208) 345-4550
B+	BLUECROSS BLUESHIELD OF TENNESSEE	801 Pine St	Chattanooga	TN	37402	(423) 755-5600
B	CALFARM INS CO	1601 Exposition Blvd	Sacramento	CA	95815	(916) 924-4405
C-	CAPITAL ADVANTAGE INS CO	2500 Elmerton Avenue	Harrisburg	PA	17110	(717) 541-7219
B+	CAPITAL BLUE CROSS OF PENNSYLVANIA	2500 Elmerton Ave	Harrisburg	PA	17110	(717) 541-7000
B+	CAREFIRST OF MARYLAND INC	10455 Mill Run Circle	Owings Mills	MD	21117	(410) 581-3000
B	CELTIC INS CO	233 S Wacker Dr Suite 700	Chicago	IL	60606	(312) 332-5401
D+	CENTRAL BENEFITS MUTUAL INS CO	255 E Main St	Columbus	OH	43215	(614) 464-5711
D+	CENTRAL BENEFITS NATL LIFE INS CO	255 East Main St	Columbus	OH	43215	(614) 464-5711
B-	CENTRAL STATES H & L CO OF OMAHA	1212 N 96th St	Omaha	NE	68114	(402) 397-1111
C-	CHRISTIAN FIDELITY LIFE INS CO	2721 N Central Ave	Phoenix	AZ	85004	(972) 937-4420
E	COLONIAL PENN LIFE INS CO	399 Market St	Philadelphia	PA	19181	(215) 928-8000
C	COMBINED INS CO OF AMERICA	123 N Wacker Dr	Chicago	IL	60606	(312) 701-3000
D+	COMBINED UNDERWRITERS LIFE INS CO	307 N Glenwood	Tyler	TX	75702	(903) 597-3761
C	COMMUNITY INS CO	4361 Irwin Simpson Rd	Mason	OH	45040	(513) 872-8100
B+	COMPANION LIFE INS CO	2501 Faraway Dr	Columbia	SC	29219	(803) 735-1251
C-	CONNECTICUT GENERAL LIFE INS CO	900 Cottage Grove Rd, S-330	Bloomfield	CT	06002	(860) 726-7234
E	CONSECO HEALTH INS CO	11815 N Pennsylvania St	Carmel	IN	46032	(317) 817-3700
E	CONSECO SENIOR HEALTH INS CO	11815 N Pennsylvania St	Carmel	IN	46032	(317) 817-3700
D	CONSTITUTION LIFE INS CO	4211 Norbourne Blvd	Louisville	KY	40207	(214) 954-7111
D	CONTINENTAL GENERAL INS CO	8901 Indian Hills Dr	Omaha	NE	68114	(402) 397-3200
A+	COUNTRY LIFE INS CO	1701 Towanda Ave	Bloomington	IL	61701	(309) 821-3000
E-	DALLAS GENERAL LIFE INS CO	.NULL.	.NULL.	.NU	.NULL.	(214) 880-0808
B+	DEAN HEALTH PLAN INC	1277 Deming Way	Madison	WI	53562	(608) 836-1400
D	EDUCATORS MUTUAL INS ASN	852 E Arrowhead Ln	Murray	UT	84107	(801) 262-7476
A-	EMPIRE HEALTHCHOICE ASSURANCE INC	11 W 42nd St	New York	NY	10036	(212) 476-7470
C	EQUITABLE LIFE & CASUALTY INS CO	3 Triad Center Suite 200	Salt Lake City	UT	84180	(801) 579-3400
F	FAMILY HEALTH PLAN COOPERATIVE	300 N Executive Dr	Brookfield	WI	53005	(262) 787-2000
B	FEDERAL HOME LIFE INS CO	700 Main St	Lynchburg	VA	24504	(804) 845-0911
C+	FIRST COMMUNITY HEALTH PLAN INC	188 Sparkman Dr	Huntsville	AL	35805	(256) 864-4100
B+	FIRST PLAN OF MINNESOTA	525 S. Lake Ave., Suite 222	Duluth	MN	55802	(218) 834-7207
B	FIRST UNITED AMERICAN LIFE INS CO	1020 7th North St	Liverpool	NY	13088	(315) 451-2544
B-	FORTIS INS CO	501 W Michigan	Milwaukee	WI	53201	(612) 738-4449
B	GE CASUALTY INS CO	500 Virginia Drive	Ft. Washington	PA	19034	(267) 468-2000
B	GE LIFE & ANNUITY ASR CO	6610 W Broad St	Richmond	VA	23230	(804) 662-2400
B-	GERBER LIFE INS CO	66 Church St	White Plains	NY	10601	(914) 761-4404
B	GLOBE LIFE & ACCIDENT INS CO	1209 Orange St	Wilmington	DE	19801	(972) 569-4081

VI. Medicare Supplement Insurers

Winter 2003 - 04

WEISS SAFETY RATING	INSURANCE COMPANY NAME	ADDRESS	CITY	STATE	ZIP	PHONE
B+	GOLDEN RULE INS CO	712 Eleventh St	Lawrenceville	IL	62439	(618) 943-8000
B+	GROUP HEALTH INCORPORATED	441 Ninth Ave	New York	NY	10001	(212) 615-0000
A	GROUP HOSP & MEDICAL SERVICES INC	550 12th St, SW	Washington	DC	20065	(202) 479-8000
C+	GUARANTEE TRUST LIFE INS CO	1275 Milwaukee Ave	Glenview	IL	60025	(847) 699-0600
B+	HARTFORD LIFE & ACCIDENT INS CO	200 Hopmeadow St	Simsbury	CT	06070	(860) 843-5867
B+	HARTFORD LIFE INS CO	200 Hopmeadow St	Simsbury	CT	06070	(860) 843-5867
C	HAWAII MEDICAL SERVICE ASSOCIATION	818 Keeaumoku St	Honolulu	HI	96814	(808) 948-5145
B-	HCC LIFE INS CO	300 N Meridian St Ste 2700	Indianapolis	IN	46204	(713) 996-1200
A	HEALTH ALLIANCE PLAN OF MICHIGAN	2850 W Grand Blvd	Detroit	MI	48202	(313) 872-8100
B+	HEALTH CARE SVC CORP A MUT LEG RES	300 East Randolph Street	Chicago	IL	60601	(312) 653-6000
D	HEALTH INSURANCE CORPORATION OF AL	301 Brown Springs Rd	Montgomery	AL	36117	(205) 286-2809
B+	HEALTH INSURANCE PLAN OF GREATER NY	7 W 34th St	New York	NY	10001	(212) 630-5000
B-	HEALTH NET LIFE INS CO	225 N Main St	Pueblo	CO	81003	(719) 585-8017
B-	HEALTH TRADITION HEALTH PLAN	4001 41st ST., NW	Rochester	WI	55901	(507) 538-5209
B	HEALTHNOW NY INC	1901 Main St	Buffalo	NY	14208	(716) 887-6900
E+	HEALTHSPRING OF ALABAMA INC	Two Perimeter Park S., Ste200W	Birmingham	AL	35243	(205) 968-1000
B	HEALTHWISE	2890 E Cottonwood Pkwy	Salt Lake City	UT	84121	(801) 333-2000
B	HEALTHY ALLIANCE LIFE INS CO	1831 Chestnut St	St Louis	MO	63103	(877) 864-2273
B-	HIGHMARK INC	1800 Center St	Camp Hill	PA	17011	(412) 544-7000
B+	HMO MINNESOTA	3535 Blue Cross Rd	Eagan	MN	55122	(651) 662-1668
A	HORIZON HEALTHCARE SERVICES INC	3 Penn Plaza East	Newark	NJ	07102	(973) 466-4000
B+	HOSPITAL SERV ASSN OF NORTH EAST PA	19 N Main St	Wilkes-Barre	PA	18711	(800) 829-8599
C-	HUMANA HEALTH INS CO OF FL INC	76 S Laura St	Jacksonville	FL	32202	(904) 296-7908
C	HUMANA HEALTH PLAN INC	201 W Main St	Louisville	KY	40202	(502) 580-8352
C	HUMANA INS CO	1100 Employers Blvd	De Pere	WI	54115	(920) 336-1100
B	IDEALIFE INS CO	695 East Main Street	Stamford	CT	06904	(203) 352-3000
B-	INDEPENDENCE BLUE CROSS	1901 Market St	Philadelphia	PA	19103	(215) 241-2400
U	INTER-COUNTY HEALTH PLAN INC	720 Blair Mill Rd	Horsham	PA	19044	(215) 657-8900
U	INTER-COUNTY HOSPITALIZATION PLAN	720 Blair Mill Rd	Horsham	PA	19044	(215) 657-8900
B-	KANAWHA INS CO	210 S White St	Lancaster	SC	29721	(803) 283-5300
F	KPS HEALTH PLANS	400 Warren Ave	Bremerton	WA	98310	(360) 377-5576
B	LA HEALTH SERVICE & INDEMNITY CO	5525 Reitz Ave	Baton Rouge	LA	70809	(225) 295-3307
B-	LIFE INS CO OF GEORGIA	5780 Powers Ferry Rd NW	Atlanta	GA	30327	(770) 980-5100
B	LIFE INVESTORS INS CO OF AMERICA	4333 Edgewood Rd NE	Cedar Rapids	IA	52499	(319) 398-8511
B	LIFEWISE HEALTH PLAN OF OREGON	2020 SW 4th St Suite 1000	Portland	OR	97201	(503) 295-6707
U	LIFEWISE HEALTH PLAN OF OREGON	1133 NW Wall St	Bend	OR	97701	(503) 388-3307
C	LINCOLN HERITAGE LIFE INS CO	Government Ctr 200 Pleasant St	Malden	MA	02148	(602) 957-1650
C	LINCOLN MUTUAL LIFE & CAS INS CO	203 N 10th St	Fargo	ND	58102	(701) 282-1437
C	LOVELACE HEALTH SYSTEMS INC	5400 Gibson Blvd SE	Albuquerque	NM	87108	(505) 262-7075
A-	MEDICA	5601 Smetana Dr	Minnetonka	MN	55343	(952) 992-3635
C	MEDICAL ASSOC CLINIC HEALTH PLAN	1605 Associates Dr., Suite 101	Dubuque	IA	52002	(563) 556-8070
C-	MEDICAL MUTUAL OF OHIO	2060 E Ninth St	Cleveland	OH	44115	(216) 687-7000
D+	MEDICO LIFE INS CO	.NULL.	.NULL.	.NU	.NULL.	(402) 391-6900
B-	MISSOURI VALLEY LIFE AND HLTH INS CO	2301 Main St	Kansas City	MO	64108	(816) 395-2750

Winter 2003 - 04 — VI. Medicare Supplement Insurers

WEISS SAFETY RATING	INSURANCE COMPANY NAME	ADDRESS	CITY	STATE	ZIP	PHONE
B-	MONUMENTAL LIFE INS CO	Two East Chase St	Baltimore	MD	21202	(410) 685-2900
B+	MOUNTAIN STATE BL CROSS BL SHIELD	700 Market Square	Parkersburg	WV	26101	(304) 424-7700
A-	MUTUAL OF OMAHA INS CO	Mutual Of Omaha Plaza	Omaha	NE	68175	(402) 342-7600
D+	MUTUAL PROTECTIVE INS CO	.NULL.	.NULL.	.NU	.NULL.	(402) 391-6900
D-	NATIONAL FINANCIAL INS CO	110 W 7th St Suite 300	Fort Worth	TX	76102	(817) 878-3300
C+	NATIONAL FOUNDATION LIFE INS CO	110 W 7th St Suite 300	Fort Worth	TX	76102	(817) 878-3300
D	NATIONAL STATES INS CO	.NULL.	.NULL.	.NU	.NULL.	(314) 878-0101
B	NATIONALCARE INS CO	6100 NW Grand Blvd	Oklahoma City	OK	73118	(405) 848-7931
B+	NATIONWIDE LIFE INS CO	One Nationwide Plaza	Columbus	OH	43215	(800) 882-2822
D	NEW ERA LIFE INS CO	200 Westlake Park Blvd	Houston	TX	77079	(713) 368-7200
D	NEW ERA LIFE INS CO OF THE MIDWEST	200 Westlake Park Blvd	Houston	TX	77079	(713) 368-7200
A	NEW YORK LIFE INS CO	51 Madison Ave	New York	NY	10010	(212) 576-7000
B+	NORIDIAN MUTUAL INS CO	4510 13th Ave SW	Fargo	ND	58121	(701) 282-1100
C-	NORTH AMERICAN INS CO	1232 Fourier Drive	Madison	WI	53717	(608) 662-1232
D	OLD SURETY LIFE INS CO	5235 N Lincoln	Oklahoma City	OK	73105	(405) 523-2112
C-	OXFORD LIFE INS CO	2721 N Central Ave	Phoenix	AZ	85004	(602) 263-6666
C-	PACIFICARE LIFE & HEALTH INS CO	23046 Avenida Dela Carlota 700	Laguna Hills	CA	92653	(714) 206-5247
C-	PACIFICARE LIFE ASR CO	3100 West Lake Ctr Dr LC03-381	Santa Ana	CA	92704	(714) 825-5379
B+	PEKIN LIFE INS CO	2505 Court St	Pekin	IL	61558	(309) 346-1161
D	PENN TREATY NETWORK AMERICA INS CO	3440 Lehigh St	Allentown	PA	18103	(610) 965-2222
C+	PEOPLES BENEFIT LIFE INS CO	4333 Edgewood Road NE	Cedar Rapids	IA	52499	(319) 398-8511
D	PHILADELPHIA AMERICAN LIFE INS CO	3121 Buffalo Speedway	Houston	TX	77098	(281) 368-7247
D+	PHP INS PLAN INC	301 N Broadway Suite 110	De Pere	WI	54115	(920) 490-6900
C-	PHYSICIANS BENEFITS TRUST LIFE INS	20 N Michigan Ave Ste 700	Chicago	IL	60602	(816) 395-2750
E+	PHYSICIANS LIABILITY INS CO	5005 N Lincoln	Oklahoma City	OK	73105	(405) 290-5660
B+	PHYSICIANS LIFE INS CO	2600 Dodge St	Omaha	NE	68131	(402) 633-1000
A+	PHYSICIANS MUTUAL INS CO	2600 Dodge St	Omaha	NE	68131	(402) 633-1000
B-	PHYSICIANS PLUS INS CORP	22 E Mifflin St #200	Madison	WI	53703	(608) 282-8900
C-	PREFERRED HEALTH SYSTEMS INS CO	8535 E 21st St N	Wichita	KS	67206	(316) 609-2345
B	PREMERA BLUE CROSS	7001 220th St SW	Mountlake Terrace	WA	98043	(425) 918-4000
A-	PRINCIPAL LIFE INS CO	711 High St	Des Moines	IA	50392	(515) 247-5111
C	PYRAMID LIFE INS CO	6201 Johnson Dr	Shawnee Mission	KS	66202	(913) 722-1110
B-	REGENCE BL CROSS BL SHIELD OREGON	100 SW Market St	Portland	OR	97201	(503) 225-5221
B-	REGENCE BLUE CROSS BLUE SHIELD OF UT	2980 E Cottonwood Pkwy	Salt Lake City	UT	84109	(801) 333-2000
B	REGENCE BLUESHIELD	1800 9th Ave	Seattle	WA	98101	(206) 464-3600
C	REGENCE BLUESHIELD OF IDAHO INC	1602 21st Ave	Lewiston	ID	83501	(208) 798-2141
B	RESERVE NATIONAL INS CO	6100 NW Grand Blvd	Oklahoma City	OK	73118	(405) 848-7931
C+	ROCKY MOUNTAIN HOSPITAL & MEDICAL	700 Broadway	Denver	CO	80273	(303) 831-2131
B-	SECURITY HEALTH PLAN OF WI INC	1515 Saint Joseph Ave	Marshfield	WI	54449	(715) 221-9555
B+	SHELTER LIFE INS CO	1817 W Broadway	Columbia	MO	65218	(573) 445-8441
C-	SIERRA HEALTH AND LIFE INS CO INC	300 S Grand 22nd Floor	Los Angeles	CA	90071	(702) 242-7779
A-	SOUTHERN FARM BUREAU LIFE INS CO	1401 Livingston Lane	Jackson	MS	39213	(601) 981-7422
E+	SOUTHWEST SERVICE LIFE INS CO	.NULL.	.NULL.	.NU	.NULL.	(817) 284-4888
B	STANDARD LIFE & ACCIDENT INS CO	201 Robert S Kerr Ave Ste 600	Oklahoma City	OK	73102	(409) 763-4661

www.WeissRatings.com

VI. Medicare Supplement Insurers

WEISS SAFETY RATING	INSURANCE COMPANY NAME	ADDRESS	CITY	STATE	ZIP	PHONE
B+	STATE FARM MUTUAL AUTOMOBILE INS CO	One State Farm Plaza	Bloomington	IL	61710	(309) 735-8480
C	STATE MUTUAL INS CO	One State Mutual Dr	Rome	GA	30162	(800) 241-7598
C	STERLING LIFE INS CO	1000 N Milwaukee Ave 6th Floor	Glenview	IL	60025	(847) 953-8706
B-	SUN HEALTH MEDISUN INC	13632 N 99th Ave Suite B	Sun City	AZ	85351	(623) 974-7434
D-	TEXAS IMPERIAL LIFE INS CO	10555 Richmond Avenue,2nd Fl	Houston	TX	77042	(713) 974-2242
B-	TRANSAMERICA FINANCIAL LIFE INS CO	4 Manhattanville Rd	Purchase	NY	10577	(914) 697-8000
U	TRIPLE S INC	F D Roosevelt Ave 1441	San Juan	PR	00920	(787) 749-4949
B	TRUSTMARK INS CO	400 Field Dr	Lake Forest	IL	60045	(847) 615-1500
B+	UCARE MINNESOTA	2000 Summer St NE	Minneapolis	MN	55413	(612) 676-6500
B	UNICARE HEALTH INS OF THE MIDWEST	233 S Wacker Dr	Chicago	IL	60606	(877) 864-2273
B	UNICARE LIFE & HEALTH INS CO	1209 Orange St	Wilmington	DE	19801	(877) 864-2273
C-	UNIFIED LIFE INS CO	7201 W 129th St Suite 300	Overland Park	KS	66213	(913) 685-2233
D+	UNION BANKERS INS CO	1700 Redbud Blvd Suite 333	McKinney	TX	75069	(407) 628-1776
C+	UNION FIDELITY LIFE INS CO	123 N Wacker Dr	Chicago	IL	60606	(215) 953-3427
D+	UNION LABOR LIFE INS CO	111 Massachusetts Ave NW	Washington	DC	20001	(202) 682-6690
C-	UNION STANDARD OF AMERICA L I C	111 Massachusetts Ave NW	Washington	DC	20001	(202) 682-6639
B	UNITED AMERICAN INS CO	3700 S Stonebridge Dr	McKinney	TX	75070	(972) 529-5085
B-	UNITED HEALTHCARE INS CO	450 Columbus Blvd	Hartford	CT	06115	(860) 702-5000
B-	UNITED HEALTHCARE INS CO OF NY	2950 Expressway Dr S Suite 240	Islandia	NY	11749	(877) 832-7734
B+	UNITED HEALTHCARE OF ALABAMA INC	3700 Colonnade Parkway	Birmingham	AL	35243	(205) 977-6300
C+	UNITED TEACHER ASSOCIATES INS CO	5508 Parkcrest Dr	Austin	TX	78731	(512) 451-2224
C	UNITED WISCONSIN INS CO	401 W. Michigan St	Milwaukee	WI	53203	(262) 787-7400
D-	UNIVERSAL FIDELITY LIFE INS CO	2211 North Highway 81	Duncan	OK	73533	(580) 255-8530
A-	USAA LIFE INS CO	9800 Fredericksburg Rd	San Antonio	TX	78288	(210) 498-8000
C+	USABLE LIFE	320 W Capitol Suite 700	Little Rock	AR	72201	(501) 375-7200
B-	VALLEY HEALTH PLAN	401 W Michigan St.	Milwaukee	WI	53202	(414) 226-5882
B-	WELLMARK INC	636 Grand Ave	Des Moines	IA	50309	(515) 245-4500
B-	WELLMARK OF SOUTH DAKOTA INC	1601 W Madison St	Sioux Falls	SD	57104	(605) 361-5819
C+	WISCONSIN PHYSICIANS SERVICE INS	1717 West Broadway	Madison	WI	53713	(608) 221-4711
C	WORLD INS CO	11808 Grant St	Omaha	NE	68164	(402) 496-8000

Section VII

Analysis of Medicare HMO Complaints

An analysis of complaints filed against

U.S. Medicare HMOs.

Companies are listed in alphabetical order.

Section VII Contents

As discussed in the previous section, no single measure is an end-all indicator of the quality of service provided by an HMO or other health insurer. However, if you are a Medicare beneficiary, complaint information can give you a preliminary basis for informed shopping – especially for Medicare HMOs. It will answer questions such as: Does the company have a high rate of enrollee complaints against it? Are most complaints upheld or overturned? Are many withdrawn before a decision is rendered?

The complaint information on the following pages will give you an indication of what beneficiaries, like yourself, have experienced with various Medicare insurers. This section is based on "reconsideration" data, reprinted from the Centers for Medicare and Medicaid Services (formerly known as Health Care Financing Administration) for HMOs with Medicare contracts.

"Reconsiderations" are complaints by members of Medicare HMOs that have reached a federal review. Once they reach that stage, the complaints have already gone through at least two levels of internal HMO appeals. Consequently, they are relatively serious and involve anywhere from several hundred dollars to many thousands of dollars of unpaid medical bills. In this section, all complaints cited are reconsiderations.

Complaints that were settled within the HMO's internal appeal process are not reflected. It is difficult to say what types of complaints these might be, but, in general, they are more likely to pertain to services of a lower dollar value.

We have made no attempt to render an opinion on the data contained in this section. Rather, we are reprinting the information strictly to help provide you with valuable information when shopping for Medicare HMOs.

The Drawbacks of Complaint Data

One problem with the data are the time lag due to the lengthy reconsideration process. A company that has a high complaint rate in this section may have already begun to make improvements in its system to handle the types of issues that were raised in the complaints. Therefore, because it takes so long for a complaint to make it through the federal process, the company may appear to have worse service quality than it currently has.

Conversely, numerous companies that have obtained Medicare contracts very recently (within the past year), may show few or no complaints. But this may reflect merely the fact that the complaints filed against these companies have not yet reached the federal level. So before you make a final decision to select a company with a low level of complaints, find out how long it has had its Medicare contract. We estimate that the contract should be in force for about two years before these data reflect the complaints.

If you are interested in a company with a seemingly high complaint level, do take the time to ask the company what improvements, if any, it has made to correct the problems reflected in the complaint data. If a high rate of complaints against it have been upheld at the federal level, it will be far more difficult to explain away.

The plans included here are those from whom reconsiderations were received during 2002 or companies that had members enrolled in a specific Medicare contract as of July of that year. Not included are: 1) updates for later appeals of cases that have been decided and 2) companies whose contracts are so new that they don't have any current enrollment.

The plan name in this table represents one or more contracts with the Centers for Medicare and Medicaid Services (CMS). You may find some plans listed more than once; this is because they have contracts in different CMS-designated regions (see Column 3). If a plan has more than one contract in a particular region, the reconsideration data have been combined so that the company is only listed once for each region.

Three types of Medicare contracts are included here: risk, cost, and Health Care Prepayment Plans (HCPPs). A Medicare risk contract is one in which the CMS pays the HMO a capitalization rate equal to a percentage of the average fee-for-service expense, in a given geographic area. A Medicare cost contract is one in which the CMS reimburses the HMO for retroactively determined Part A and B costs. And an HCPP contract is similar to a cost contract but only Part B costs are paid by the CMS.

The following **BOLD** headings are the column reference guides for the tables beginning on page 395.

1. **Insurance Company Name**

    The legally-registered name, which sometimes can differ from the name that the plan uses for advertising. If you cannot find the plan you are interested in, or if you have any doubts regarding the precise name, verify the information before looking it up in this Guide. Also, determine the domicile state for confirmation.

2. **Domicile State**

    The state which has primary regulatory responsibility for the company. It may differ from the location of the company's corporate headquarters. You do not have to be living in the domicile state to purchase insurance from this firm, provided it is licensed to do business in your state.

    Also use this column to confirm that you have located the correct company. It is possible for two unrelated companies to have the same name if they are domiciled in different states.

3. **Weiss Safety Rating**

    Our rating is measured on a scale from A to F and considers a wide range of factors. Highly-rated companies are, in our opinion, less likely to experience financial difficulties than lower rated firms. See *About the Weiss Safety Ratings* on page 11 for more information.

4. **Region**

    The CMS region in which the HMO complaint data apply for a particular company. The regions are as follows:

    Boston: 1 (Connecticut, Maine, Massachusetts, New Hampshire, Rhode Island, Vermont), **New York: 2** (New Jersey, New York, Puerto Rico, Virgin Islands), **Philadelphia: 3** (Delaware, District of Columbia, Maryland, Pennsylvania, Virginia, West Virginia), **Atlanta: 4** (Alabama, Florida, Georgia, Kentucky, Mississippi, North Carolina, South Carolina, Tennessee), **Chicago: 5** (Illinois, Indiana, Michigan, Minnesota, Ohio, Wisconsin), **Dallas: 6** (Arkansas, Louisiana, Oklahoma, New Mexico, Texas), **Kansas: 7** (Iowa, Kansas, Missouri, Nebraska), **Denver: 8**

(Colorado, Montana, North Dakota, South Dakota, Utah, Wyoming), **San Francisco: 9** (Arizona, California, Guam, Hawaii, Nevada, Samoa), **Seattle: 10** (Alaska, Idaho, Oregon, Washington).

5. **Rate**
The number of reconsiderations per 1,000 members per year. It is calculated by dividing the sum of reconsiderations received over the two-year period into the sum of mid-year enrollments.

"N/R" means that there were "no reconsiderations" for that particular plan's contract in that particular region. "N/E" means there was "no enrollment" during 2002. This happens when the complaints reflect prior enrollments in specific contracts, demonstrate the lag time between enrollment, and the complaint being represented in the reconsideration system.

6. **Reconsiderations Received 2002**
The number of reconsiderations received by the CMS from the health plan for the Medicare contract(s) only. Regardless of the number of complaints upheld or overturned (See columns 8 and 9), if this number is high relative to other HMOs, it signals that the plan has trouble satisfying its policyholders.

The health plan may have other business besides treating Medicare beneficiaries but this figure only pertains to enrollees that are served under a Medicare contract.

7. **Reconsiderations Not Yet Decided**
The number of reconsiderations received during 2002 that have not yet been settled.

8. **Reconsiderations Upheld**
The number of cases in which the CMS upheld the decision of the HMO. This is the number of times CMS ruled against the policyholder in favor of the HMO. If the number is high relative to the total number of reconsiderations received (Column 6), it is a sign that the HMO's complaint process is somewhat ironclad and appeals beyond it are often futile. This, however, does not necessarily mean that the HMO was not at fault.

9. **Reconsiderations Overturned**
The number of cases in which the CMS completely overturned the decision of the HMO. This is the number of times the CMS ruled against the HMO in favor of the policyholder. If the number of complaints overturned is high, relative to the total number of reconsiderations received (Column 6), it is a sign that either the HMO is falling short in meeting the needs of its policyholders; or, its complaint process is not streamlined enough to carry complaints to the appropriate conclusion.

10. **Reconsiderations Partially Overturned**
The number of cases in which the CMS partially overturned the decision of the HMO. Individual complaints can encompass more than one service or several steps in a treatment program. This is the number of times that the CMS overturned one component of the HMO's ruling but upheld the rest.

11. Reconsiderations Retroactively Disenrolled

The number of cases in which the CMS Regional Office decided to retroactively disenroll the beneficiary for the period during which the contested services were incurred. For example, a beneficiary may be retroactively disenrolled if it is determined that he or she did not understand the restrictions of the HMO.

12. Reconsiderations Withdrawn

The number of reconsiderations that were withdrawn from review.

The Regional CMS office will investigate the case and determine if the enrolee should revert back to fee-for-service (disenroll). If the CMS does not grant disenrollment, the case re-enters the reconsideration process and follows the same course as other complaints.

A high number of disenrollments may indicate that the HMO has failed to clearly identify its coverage limitations at the time the policy is sold.

VII. Analysis of Medicare HMO Complaints

Winter 2003 - 04

INSURANCE COMPANY NAME	DOM. STATE	WEISS SAFETY RATING	REGION	RATE	RECONS REC'VD	RECONS NOT YET DECIDED	RECONS UPHELD	RECONS OVER-TURNED	RECONS PARTIALLY OVER-TURNED	RECONS RETRO DIS-ENROLLED	RECONS WITH-DRAWN
ADVANTAGE HEALTH SOLUTIONS INC	IN	U	5	1.81	3	0	3	0	0	0	0
AET HEALTH CARE PLAN INC	TX	C	4	N/E	--	--	--	--	--	--	--
AETNA HEALTH INC (A CT CORP)	CT	C	3	2.10	74	0	50	10	4	5	5
AETNA HEALTH INC (A NEW JERSEY CORP)	NJ	B-	2	7.74	224	0	172	23	5	13	11
AETNA HEALTH OF CALIFORNIA INC	CA	C	9	4.32	167	0	128	21	2	4	12
AETNA US HEALTHCARE INC (A MA CORP)	MA	C-	1	N/E	--	--	--	--	--	--	--
AMCARE HEALTH PLANS OF TEXAS INC	TX	F	6	1.21	11	0	6	2	0	3	0
AMERICAS HEALTH CHOICE MEDICAL PLANS	FL	D	4	N/E	--	--	--	--	--	--	--
AMERICHOICE OF NEW YORK INC	NY	B+	2	0.78	1	0	1	0	0	0	0
AMERICHOICE OF PENNSYLVANIA INC	PA	B	3	2.22	13	0	8	3	0	1	1
AMERIGROUP FLORIDA INC	FL	D+	4	0.58	20	0	12	5	1	0	2
AMERIHEALTH HMO INC	PA	B	2	4.36	14	0	11	0	2	1	0
ANTHEM HEALTH PLANS OF KENTUCKY INC	KY	B+	5	0.57	6	0	6	0	0	0	0
ARNETT HMO INC	IN	C	5	2.24	10	0	8	2	0	0	0
AVMED INC	FL	E	4	4.25	115	0	97	7	3	4	4
BLUE CARE NETWORK OF MICHIGAN	MI	C+	5	N/E	--	--	--	--	--	--	--
BLUE CROSS BLUE SHIELD HEALTHCARE GA	GA	A	4	4.32	84	0	59	15	2	8	0
BLUE CROSS BLUE SHIELD OF MA	MA	A	1	2.44	93	0	58	23	10	1	1
BLUE CROSS BLUE SHIELD UNITED OF WI	WI	B-	5	N/E	--	--	--	--	--	--	--
BLUE CROSS OF CALIFORNIA	CA	A	9	21.65	1245	0	1200	16	4	19	6
BLUE CROSS OF IDAHO HEALTH SERVICE	ID	B+	10	7.80	55	0	46	7	2	0	0
CALIFORNIA PHYSICIANS SERVICE	CA	A-	9	7.77	529	0	422	52	6	12	37
CAPITAL DISTRICT PHYSICIANS HEALTH P	NY	B+	2	7.58	57	0	36	10	6	5	0
CAPITAL HEALTH PLAN INC	FL	B-	4	2.16	10	0	10	0	0	0	0
CARELINK HEALTH PLANS INC	WV	C	3	N/E	--	--	--	--	--	--	--
CARITEN HEALTH PLAN INC	TN	C-	4	9.61	106	0	93	10	0	2	1
CENTRAL OREGON INDEPENDENT HEALTH SV	OR	C+	10	4.87	38	0	29	7	0	1	1
CHINESE COMMUNITY HEALTH PLAN	CA	C+	9	1.62	7	0	7	0	0	0	0
CIGNA HEALTHCARE OF ARIZONA INC	AZ	C+	9	3.99	168	0	149	10	2	2	5
COMMUNITY HEALTH PLAN OF OHIO	OH	E	5	N/E	--	--	--	--	--	--	--
COMMUNITY INS CO	OH	C	5	0.99	65	0	48	10	3	3	1
COMMUNITYCARE HMO INC	OK	C	6	3.51	69	0	44	12	1	8	4
CONNECTICARE INC	CT	B+	1	N/E	--	--	--	--	--	--	--
CONTRA COSTA HEALTH PLAN	CA	C	9	N/E	--	--	--	--	--	--	--
COORDINATED HEALTH PARTNERS INC	RI	C	1	4.24	179	0	145	17	4	9	4
COVENTRY HEALTH CARE OF DELAWARE INC	DE	B-	3	N/E	--	--	--	--	--	--	--
COVENTRY HEALTH CARE OF KANSAS INC	KS	D+	7	1.20	18	0	12	4	0	1	1
DEAN HEALTH PLAN INC	WI	B+	5	N/E	--	--	--	--	--	--	--
ELDER HEALTH MARYLAND HMO INC	MD	C-	3	0.44	1	0	0	1	0	0	0
ELDERPLAN INC	NY	E-	2	8.36	89	0	58	16	3	4	8
EMPIRE HEALTHCHOICE ASSURANCE INC	NY	A-	2	5.80	329	0	201	94	15	9	10
EVERCARE OF TEXAS LLC	TX	B-	9	0.68	1	0	1	0	0	0	0
EXCELLUS HEALTH PLAN INC	NY	B+	2	13.97	213	0	173	21	5	9	5
FALLON COMMUNITY HEALTH PLAN	MA	B	1	4.58	161	0	101	20	9	20	11
FAMILY HEALTH CARE PLUS INC	MS	D	4	101.53	106	0	1	0	0	86	19
FAMILY HEALTH PLAN INC	OH	E	5	N/E	--	--	--	--	--	--	--
FIRST PLAN OF MINNESOTA	MN	B+	5	N/E	--	--	--	--	--	--	--
FLORIDA HEALTH CARE PLAN INC	FL	B-	4	1.48	24	0	21	1	0	0	2
FREE STATE HEALTH PLAN INC	MD	C+	3	N/E	--	--	--	--	--	--	--
GEISINGER HEALTH PLAN	PA	C	3	3.96	137	0	122	12	1	0	2
GOOD HEALTH HMO INC	MO	B	7	N/E	--	--	--	--	--	--	--
GROUP HEALTH COOPERATIVE PUGET SOUND	WA	B	10	3.85	231	0	184	22	9	10	6

VII. Analysis of Medicare HMO Complaints

Winter 2003 - 04

INSURANCE COMPANY NAME	DOM. STATE	WEISS SAFETY RATING	REGION	RATE	RECONS REC'VD	RECONS NOT YET DECIDED	RECONS UPHELD	RECONS OVER-TURNED	RECONS PARTIALLY OVER-TURNED	RECONS RETRO DIS-ENROLLED	RECONS WITH-DRAWN
GROUP HEALTH PLAN INC	MN	B	5	1.42	24	0	21	0	0	1	2
GROUP HEALTH PLAN INC	MO	C+	7	5.67	97	1	82	8	0	5	1
GUNDERSEN LUTHERAN HEALTH PLAN INC	WI	C-	5	2.64	16	0	13	1	0	2	0
HARVARD PILGRIM HEALTH CARE INC	MA	C-	1	1.14	45	0	40	4	0	0	1
HAWAII MEDICAL SERVICE ASSOCIATION	HI	C	9	0.18	7	0	5	2	0	0	0
HEALTH ALLIANCE MEDICAL PLANS	IL	C+	5	3.64	24	0	17	6	0	0	1
HEALTH ALLIANCE PLAN OF MICHIGAN	MI	A	5	1.19	21	0	11	5	2	3	0
HEALTH FIRST HEALTH PLANS	FL	C+	4	4.88	79	0	65	9	1	2	2
HEALTH INSURANCE PLAN OF GREATER NY	NY	B+	2	7.25	309	0	137	118	28	18	8
HEALTH NET	CA	B+	9	11.53	1200	1	736	128	22	83	230
HEALTH NET OF ARIZONA INC	AZ	C-	9	9.94	406	0	332	34	5	27	8
HEALTH NET OF CONNECTICUT INC	CT	B	1	5.29	157	0	125	21	9	0	2
HEALTH NET OF NEW YORK INC	NY	C-	2	3.36	22	0	17	3	1	0	1
HEALTH NET OF PENNSYLVANIA INC	PA	U	3	1.57	6	0	4	1	0	0	1
HEALTH OPTIONS INC	FL	B+	4	1.55	198	0	125	35	5	22	11
HEALTH PARTNERS OF PHILADELPHIA INC	PA	C+	3	2.34	41	0	23	17	0	0	1
HEALTH PLAN OF NEVADA INC	NV	C	9	13.60	245	0	181	47	5	1	11
HEALTH PLAN OF THE REDWOODS	CA	F	9	3.38	38	0	30	6	1	0	1
HEALTH PLAN OF THE UPPER OHIO VALLEY	WV	B-	3	3.58	15	0	10	4	0	1	0
HEALTH PLAN OF THE UPPER OHIO VALLEY	WV	B-	5	2.38	3	0	3	0	0	0	0
HEALTHAMERICA PENNSYLVANIA INC	PA	C+	3	4.90	119	0	98	10	4	1	6
HEALTHNOW NY INC	NY	B	2	4.78	128	0	93	28	5	1	1
HEALTHPARTNERS	MN	B+	5	0.70	12	0	11	0	0	0	1
HEALTHPLUS OF MICHIGAN	MI	C+	5	0.72	2	0	2	0	0	0	0
HEALTHSPRING INC	TN	D-	4	1.36	28	0	19	6	1	0	2
HEALTHSPRING OF ALABAMA INC	AL	E+	4	7.51	26	0	12	12	1	0	1
HEART OF AMERICA HMO	ND	D	8	1.54	1	0	1	0	0	0	0
HMO BLUE	MA	U	1	N/E	--	--	--	--	--	--	--
HMO COLORADO	CO	C+	8	N/E	--	--	--	--	--	--	--
HMO HEALTH PLANS INC	CO	C+	8	N/E	--	--	--	--	--	--	--
HOMETOWN HEALTH PLAN INC	NV	D+	5	2.92	25	0	13	10	1	0	1
HOMETOWN HEALTH PLAN INC	NV	D+	9	3.71	23	0	11	10	0	1	1
HORIZON HEALTHCARE OF NEW JERSEY INC	NJ	B+	2	3.08	196	0	141	30	5	13	7
HUMANA HEALTH PLAN OF TEXAS INC	TX	D+	6	3.25	89	0	43	4	1	36	5
HUMANA HEALTH PLAN OF TEXAS INC	TX	D+	9	6.17	111	0	63	13	1	29	5
HUMANA INS CO	WI	C	5	4.64	259	0	168	30	13	44	4
INDEPENDENCE BLUE CROSS	PA	B-	3	3.12	79	0	59	8	1	8	3
INDEPENDENT HEALTH ASSOC INC	NY	B	2	3.34	72	0	56	6	2	6	2
INTERVALLEY HEALTH PLAN	CA	U	9	3.22	54	0	48	1	2	0	3
JOHN DEERE HEALTH PLAN INC	IL	B	4	1.10	19	0	15	4	0	0	0
KAISER FOUNDATION HEALTH PLAN INC	CA	B-	9	6.84	1277	0	946	145	17	131	38
KAISER FOUNDATION HP MID-ATL STATES	MD	C-	3	6.44	121	0	86	13	1	17	4
KAISER FOUNDATION HP NORTHWEST	OR	B	10	3.92	88	0	68	12	1	3	4
KAISER FOUNDATION HP OF CO	CO	B	8	2.43	138	0	114	14	4	4	2
KAISER FOUNDATION HP OF GA	GA	B	4	1.83	25	0	22	3	0	0	0
KAISER FOUNDATION HP OF OH	OH	B-	5	2.35	62	0	49	13	0	0	0
KEYSTONE HEALTH PLAN CENTRAL INC	PA	B+	3	7.27	158	0	95	44	10	6	3
KEYSTONE HEALTH PLAN EAST INC	PA	B+	3	2.28	328	0	238	35	11	31	13
KEYSTONE HEALTH PLAN WEST INC	PA	B+	3	4.47	840	0	734	62	7	21	16
LOVELACE HEALTH SYSTEMS INC	NM	C	6	1.07	19	0	16	3	0	0	0
M PLAN	IN	C-	5	1.07	8	0	5	3	0	0	0
M-CARE	MI	B-	5	4.28	24	0	21	3	0	0	0

VII. Analysis of Medicare HMO Complaints

INSURANCE COMPANY NAME	DOM. STATE	WEISS SAFETY RATING	REGION	RATE	RECONS REC'VD	RECONS NOT YET DECIDED	RECONS UPHELD	RECONS OVER-TURNED	RECONS PARTIALLY OVER-TURNED	RECONS RETRO DIS-ENROLLED	RECONS WITH-DRAWN
MANAGED HEALTH INC	NY	E+	2	2.55	54	0	25	22	5	0	2
MDNY HEALTHCARE INC	NY	E	2	N/E	--	--	--	--	--	--	--
MEDICA	MN	A-	5	0.45	9	0	9	0	0	0	0
MEDICAL ASSOC CLINIC HEALTH PLAN	WI	C	7	N/E	--	--	--	--	--	--	--
MEDICAL ASSOCIATES HEALTH PLAN INC	IA	C+	7	0.43	3	0	3	0	0	0	0
MERCY HEALTH PLANS OF MISSOURI INC	MO	C-	7	2.36	61	0	44	10	2	2	3
METROPOLITAN HEALTH PLAN	MN	A-	5	N/E	--	--	--	--	--	--	--
MOUNT CARMEL HEALTH PLAN INC	OH	D+	5	0.63	10	0	5	3	0	2	0
NATIONAL MED INC	CA	U	9	N/E	--	--	--	--	--	--	--
NEIGHBORHOOD HEALTH PARTNERSHIP INC	FL	B-	4	11.33	394	0	313	25	1	45	10
NETWORK HEALTH PLAN OF WISCONSIN INC	WI	D+	5	2.31	9	0	7	1	0	1	0
OCHSNER HEALTH PLAN	LA	D	6	4.28	181	0	118	22	2	27	12
OSF HEALTH PLANS INC	IL	E+	5	4.53	17	0	14	2	0	0	1
OXFORD HEALTH PLANS (CT) INC	CT	B	1	8.79	12	0	8	2	2	0	0
OXFORD HEALTH PLANS (NJ) INC	NJ	B	2	16.47	22	0	20	1	0	1	0
OXFORD HEALTH PLANS (NY) INC	NY	B+	2	4.03	267	0	222	33	6	2	4
PACIFICARE OF ARIZONA INC	AZ	B-	9	5.61	502	1	406	45	4	30	16
PACIFICARE OF CALIFORNIA INC	CA	C-	9	8.27	3352	0	2570	347	49	272	114
PACIFICARE OF COLORADO INC	CO	B-	8	7.26	321	0	193	25	2	75	26
PACIFICARE OF NEVADA INC	NV	C-	9	10.77	312	0	235	57	2	14	4
PACIFICARE OF OKLAHOMA INC	OK	C-	6	6.75	145	0	57	52	5	26	5
PACIFICARE OF OREGON	OR	B-	10	3.58	109	0	70	30	2	2	5
PACIFICARE OF TEXAS INC	TX	D+	6	9.38	1029	1	425	137	10	338	68
PACIFICARE OF WASHINGTON INC	WA	C	10	3.91	222	0	124	52	13	23	10
PARAMOUNT HEALTH CARE	OH	B-	5	2.10	39	0	29	4	0	5	1
PARTNERS NATIONAL HEALTH PLANS OF NC	NC	B	4	2.16	64	0	40	16	3	2	3
PREFERRED PLUS OF KANSAS INC	KS	B-	7	N/E	--	--	--	--	--	--	--
PRIMETIME MEDICAL INS CO	OH	D+	5	2.38	35	0	29	5	0	0	1
PROVIDENCE HEALTH PLAN	OR	C+	10	3.18	115	0	98	10	0	4	3
QUALCHOICE OF NORTH CAROLINA INC	NC	D+	4	3.67	44	0	21	17	1	4	1
REGENCE BLUESHIELD OF IDAHO INC	ID	C	10	2.61	16	0	14	2	0	0	0
REGENCE HMO OREGON	OR	B-	10	9.65	75	0	53	14	2	1	5
ROCHESTER AREA HEALTH MAINTENANCE OR	NY	B	2	1.69	69	0	47	14	6	1	1
ROCKY MOUNTAIN HEALTH MAINT ORG	CO	D+	8	1.25	23	0	21	0	0	1	1
SCAN HEALTH PLAN	CA	E	9	8.22	431	0	327	60	7	16	21
SCOTT & WHITE HEALTH PLAN	TX	B	6	0.08	2	0	1	1	0	0	0
SELECTCARE OF TEXAS LLC	TX	U	6	1.31	14	0	11	1	0	1	1
SIOUX VALLEY HEALTH PLAN	SD	E+	8	1.25	2	0	0	2	0	0	0
SIOUX VALLEY HEALTH PLAN MINNESOTA	MN	D-	8	N/E	--	--	--	--	--	--	--
STERLING LIFE INS CO	IL	C	10	0.61	13	0	13	0	0	0	0
SUMMACARE INC	OH	B-	5	8.22	93	0	38	46	4	1	4
SUN HEALTH MEDISUN INC	AZ	B-	9	12.06	184	0	160	8	1	3	12
TENET CHOICES INC	LA	D-	6	0.96	25	0	17	6	0	0	2
TEXAS HEALTH CHOICE LC	TX	U	6	N/E	--	--	--	--	--	--	--
THE OATH	LA	F	6	N/E	--	--	--	--	--	--	--
TUFTS ASSOCIATED HEALTH MAINT ORG	MA	B	1	1.95	185	0	156	16	5	7	1
UCARE MINNESOTA	MN	B+	5	1.52	38	2	31	4	1	0	0
UNION HEALTH SERVICE INC	IL	C	5	N/E	--	--	--	--	--	--	--
UNITED HEALTHCARE INS CO	CT	B-	5	N/E	--	--	--	--	--	--	--
UNITED HEALTHCARE INS CO OF IL	IL	C+	4	N/E	--	--	--	--	--	--	--
UNITED HEALTHCARE OF ALABAMA INC	AL	B+	4	0.21	6	0	5	0	0	1	0
UNITED HEALTHCARE OF ARKANSAS INC	AR	B+	6	N/E	--	--	--	--	--	--	--

VII. Analysis of Medicare HMO Complaints

Winter 2003 - 04

INSURANCE COMPANY NAME	DOM. STATE	WEISS SAFETY RATING	REGION	RATE	RECONS REC'VD	RECONS NOT YET DECIDED	RECONS UPHELD	RECONS OVER-TURNED	RECONS PARTIALLY OVER-TURNED	RECONS RETRO DIS-ENROLLED	RECONS WITH-DRAWN
UNITED HEALTHCARE OF FLORIDA INC	FL	C-	4	3.76	97	0	77	10	2	6	2
UNITED HEALTHCARE OF ILLINOIS INC	IL	C+	5	N/E	--	--	--	--	--	--	--
UNITED HEALTHCARE OF NC INC	NC	B+	4	0.62	5	0	3	1	0	1	0
UNITED HEALTHCARE OF NEW ENGLAND INC	RI	B	1	1.08	17	0	11	3	3	0	0
UNITED HEALTHCARE OF NY INC	NY	B	2	1.58	16	0	12	4	0	0	0
UNITED HEALTHCARE OF OHIO INC	OH	B-	5	0.92	33	0	23	2	3	2	3
UNITED HEALTHCARE OF THE MIDLANDS	NE	B+	7	1.63	15	0	12	2	1	0	0
UNITED HEALTHCARE OF THE MIDWEST INC	MO	B+	7	0.68	41	0	25	11	0	2	3
UNITED HEALTHCARE OF WISCONSIN INC	WI	B+	5	0.80	4	0	3	0	0	0	1
UNIVERSAL CARE	CA	D-	9	2.56	1	0	1	0	0	0	0
UPMC HEALTH PLAN INC	PA	C-	3	0.65	4	0	4	0	0	0	0
VISTA HEALTHPLAN	FL	E	4	3.26	37	0	25	6	1	5	0
VIVA HEALTH INC	AL	C	4	1.16	15	0	11	4	0	0	0
WELBORN CLINIC/WELBORN HEALTH PLANS	IN	E	5	2.65	13	0	10	1	0	2	0
WELL CARE HMO INC	FL	D+	4	2.32	99	0	71	15	3	3	7
WELLCARE OF NEW YORK INC	NY	E+	2	0.60	1	0	0	1	0	0	0
WESTERN HEALTH ADVANTAGE	CA	E+	9	4.28	12	0	8	4	0	0	0

Section VIII

Rating Upgrades and Downgrades

A list of all

U.S. HMOs and Health Insurers

receiving a rating upgrade or downgrade during the current quarter.

Section VIII Contents

This section identifies those companies receiving a rating change since the previous edition of this publication, whether it is a new rating to this guide, withdrawn rating, rating upgrade, rating downgrade or a, newly rated company. A rating may be withdrawn due to a merger, dissolution, or liquidation. A rating upgrade or downgrade may entail a change from one letter grade to another, or it may mean the addition or deletion of a plus or minus sign within the same letter grade previously assigned to the company. Ratings are normally updated once each quarter of the year. In some instances, however, a company's rating may be downgraded outside of the normal updates due to overriding circumstances.

1. **Insurance Company Name** — The legally-registered name, which can sometimes differ from the name that the company uses for advertising. An insurer's name can be very similar to that of another, so verify the company's exact name and state of domicile to make sure you are looking at the correct company.

2. **Domicile State** — The state which has primary regulatory responsibility for the company. It may differ from the location of the company's corporate headquarters. You do not have to be living in the domicile state to purchase insurance from this firm, provided it is licensed to do business in your state.

3. **New or Current Weiss Safety Rating** — The rating assigned to the company as of the date of this Guide's publication. Our rating is measured on a scale from A to F and considers a wide range of factors. Highly-rated companies are, in our opinion, less likely to experience financial difficulties than lower-rated firms. See *About the Weiss Safety Ratings* on page 11 for more information.

4. **Previous Weiss Safety Rating** — The rating assigned to the company prior to its most recent change.

5. **Date of Change** — The date on which the rating upgrade or downgrade officially occurred. Normally, all rating changes are put into effect on a single day each quarter of the year. In some instances, however, a rating may have been changed outside of this normal update.

VIII. Rating Upgrades and Downgrades

Rating Upgrades

ANTHEM HEALTH PLANS OF KENTUCKY INC. was upgraded to B+ from B in January 2004 based on strong capitalization and good profitability.

ANTHEM HEALTH PLANS OF MAINE INC (ME) was upgraded to B from B- in January 2004 based on an increase in the capitalization index.

BLUE CROSS BLUE SHIELD OF KC was upgraded to B+ from B in January 2004 based on strong capitalization, good profitability, liquidity and stability indexes.

BLUE CROSS BLUE SHIELD UNITED OF WI was upgraded to B- from C+ in January 2004 based on excellent capitalization and liquidity combined with good profitability.

BLUEGRASS FAMILY HEALTH INC was upgraded to B+ from B in January 2004 as a result of excellent results on the capitalization, profitability, liquidity and stability indexes.

CARE CHOICES HMO (MI) was upgraded to C from C- in January 2004 based on an increase in the capitalization index.

CARELINK HEALTH PLANS INC was upgraded to C from C- in January 2004 due to strong capitalization and relationship to Coventry Health Care Inc.

CAROLINA CARE PLAN INC was upgraded to B- from C+ in January 2004 due to the company's continued improvement in capitalization and profitability.

COMMUNITY HEALTH CHOICE INC (TX) was upgraded to E+ from E in January 2004 based on an increase in the capitalization index.

DAYTON AREA HEALTH PLAN (OH) was upgraded to B from B- in January 2004 based on an increase in the capitalization index.

FALLON COMMUNITY HEALTH PLAN was upgraded from B- to a B in January 2004 based on the entities continued strength in capitalization.

FIRSTCHOICE HEALTHPLANS OF CT INC was upgraded to D- from E+ in January 2004 based on the improvement in capitalization.

GRAND VALLEY HEALTH PLAN INC (MI) was upgraded to D- from E+ in January 2004 based on a substantial increase in the capitalization index and progress in the liquidity index.

GROUP HEALTH COOPERATIVE PUGET SOUND (WA) was upgraded to B from B- in January 2004 based on development in the stability index and an increase in the capitalization index.

GROUP HOSP & MEDICAL SERVICES INC was upgraded to A from A- in January 2004 as a result of the company's excellent results on the capitalization, profitability, liquidity, stability and investment safety indexes.

HARMONY HEALTH PLAN OF ILLINOIS INC (IL) was upgraded to C+ from C in January 2004 based on an increase in the capitalization index.

HEALTHSPRING OF ALABAMA INC (AL) was upgraded to E+ from E in January 2004 based on an increase in the capitalization index and progress in the liquidity index.

HMO COLORADO was upgraded to C+ from C in January 2004 due to strong capitalization and relationship with Anthem Insurance Companies Inc.

HMO HEALTH PLANS INC (CO) was upgraded to C+ from C in January 2004 based on a substantial increase in the capitalization index.

MEDICA was upgraded to A- from B+ in January 2004 due to the company's continued strength across each of the indexes.

MEDICAL ASSOCIATES HEALTH PLAN INC (IA) was upgraded to C+ from C in January 2004 based on an increase in the capitalization index.

MISSOURI CARE HEALTH PLAN (MO) was upgraded to D+ from D in January 2004 based on an increase in the capitalization index.

Rating Upgrades (Continued)

PACIFICARE OF TEXAS INC (TX) was upgraded to D+ from D in January 2004 based on substantial progress in the liquidity index and a substantial increase in the capitalization index.

PARAMOUNT CARE OF MI INC (MI) was upgraded to C from C- in January 2004 based on an increase in the capitalization index.

QCC INS CO was upgraded to C+ from C in January 2004 based on excellent capitalization and profitability index results and relationship to Independence Blue Cross Inc.

ROCKY MOUNTAIN HOSPITAL & MEDICAL was upgraded to C+ from C in January 2004 due to strong capitalization and affiliation with Anthem Insurance Companies Inc.

SCAN HEALTH PLAN was upgraded from E- to E in January 2004 due to the company's substantial improvement in all indexes since its capitalization deficiencies in 2002.

SHARP HEALTH PLAN (CA) was upgraded to C- from D- in January 2004 based on a substantial increase in the capitalization index.

SIOUX VALLEY HEALTH PLAN (SD) was upgraded to E+ from E in January 2004 based on an increase in the capitalization index and development in the stability index.

SUMMA INS CO was upgraded to B- from C+ in January 2004 based on the company's continued strength in capitalization and good profitability.

SUMMACARE INC (OH) was upgraded to B- from C+ in January 2004 based on a substantial increase in the capitalization index.

VIII. Rating Upgrades and Downgrades

Rating Downgrades

CAPITAL ADVANTAGE INS CO (PA) was downgraded to C- from C in January 2004 based on a substantial drop in the stability index.

Winter 2003 - 04 — VIII. Rating Upgrades and Downgrades

Appearing in this Edition for the First Time

INSURANCE COMPANY NAME	DOM. STATE	TOTAL ASSETS ($MIL)	CURRENT WEISS SAFETY RATING	DATE OF CHANGE
HIP INS CO OF NEW YORK	NY	24.0	B	01/09/2004
LIFEWISE HEALTH PLAN OF OREGON	OR	127.4	B	01/09/2004
MEDICA INS CO	MN	103.2	B	12/29/2003
OXFORD HEALTH INS INC	NY	391.7	B-	01/09/2004
CIGNA INS SERVICES CO	SC	11.7	C+	01/09/2004
QCC INS CO	PA	967.5	C+	01/09/2004
HORIZON HEALTHCARE INS CO OF NY	NY	71.0	C	01/09/2004
HORIZON HEALTHCARE OF NEW YORK INC	NY	2.0	C	12/23/2003
HUMANA INS CO OF KENTUCKY	KY	5.5	C	01/09/2004
SANTA CRUZ-MONTEREY MGD MED CARE	CA	78.3	C	12/23/2003
ALTUS DENTAL INS CO INC	RI	6.2	C-	12/29/2003
CIGNA INSURANCE GROUP INC	NH	2.1	C-	01/09/2004
TOUCHPOINT INS CO INC	WI	4.1	D+	01/09/2004
MERCYCARE INS CO	WI	14.3	D	01/09/2004
PROVIDERS DIRECT HEALTH PLAN OF GA	GA	4.9	F	12/18/2003

VIII. Rating Upgrades and Downgrades

Withdrawn Ratings

INSURANCE COMPANY NAME	DOM. STATE	TOTAL ASSETS ($MIL)	CURRENT WEISS SAFETY RATING	PREVIOUS WEISS SAFETY RATING	DATE OF CHANGE
EDUCATORS HEALTH CARE	UT	2.5	U	C-	12/29/2003

Appendix

Risk-Adjusted Capital in The Weiss Rating Models

There are three distinct rating models used to generate the ratings in this Guide. The first model is for companies that register with state insurance departments under the official classification of Life and Health Insurers. The second is for Blue Cross/ Blue Shield plans, Health Maintenance Organizations (HMOs), and other similar health plans, that register as Health plans with the state insurance departments. The third model is for companies that register under the official classification of Property and Casualty Insurers.

A key aspect of both models is the risk-adjusted capital calculations. Therefore, these are discussed in greater detail.

Risk-Adjusted Capital for Life and Health Insurers

Among the most important indicators used in the analyses of an individual company are our two risk-adjusted capital ratios, which are useful tools in determining exposure to investment, liquidity, and insurance risk in relation to the capital the company has to cover those risks.

The first risk-adjusted capital ratio evaluates the company's ability to withstand a moderate loss scenario. The second ratio evaluates the company's ability to withstand a severe loss scenario. (See Glossary for definitions.)

In order to calculate these risk-adjusted capital ratios, we follow these steps:

1. Capital Resources	First, we add up all of the company's resources which could be used to cover losses. These include capital, surplus, the Asset Valuation Reserve (AVR), and a portion of the provision for future policyholders' dividends, where appropriate. Additional credit may also be given for the use of conservative reserving assumptions and other "hidden capital" when applicable.
2. Target Capital	Next, we determine the company's target capital. This answers the question: Based upon the company's level of risk in both its insurance business and its investment portfolio, how much capital would it need to cover potential losses during a moderate loss scenario? In other words, we determine how much capital we believe this company *should* have.
3. Risk-Adjusted Capital Ratio #1	We compare the results of step 1 with those of step 2. Specifically, we divide the "capital resources" by the "target capital" and express it in terms of a ratio. This ratio is called RACR #1. (See next page for more detail on methodology.)
	If a company has a Risk-Adjusted Capital Ratio of 1.0 or more, it means the company has all of the capital we believe it requires to withstand potential losses which could be inflicted by a moderate loss scenario. If the company has less than 1.0, it does not currently have all of the basic capital resources we think it needs. During times of financial distress, companies often have access to additional capital through contributions from a parent company, current profits, or reductions in policyholder dividends. Therefore, an allowance is made in our rating system for firms with somewhat less than 1.0 Risk-Adjusted Capital Ratios.

4. Risk-Adjusted Capital Ratio #2	We repeat steps 2 and 3, but now assuming a severe loss scenario. This ratio is called RACR #2.
5. Capitalization Index	We convert RACR #1 and #2 into an index. It is measured on a scale of zero to ten, with ten being the best and seven or better considered strong. A company whose capital, surplus and AVR equal its target capital will have a Risk-Adjusted Capital Ratio of 1.0 and a Risk-Adjusted Capital Index of 7.0.

How We Determine Target Capital

The basic procedure for determining target capital is to ask these questions:

1. What is the breakdown of the company's investment portfolio and types of business?

2. For each category, what are the potential losses which could be incurred in the loss scenario?

3. In order to cover those potential losses, how much in capital resources does the company need? It stands to reason that more capital is needed as a cushion for losses on high-risk investments, such as junk bonds, than would be necessary for low-risk investments, such as AAA-rated utility bonds.

    Unfortunately, the same questions we have raised about Wall Street rating systems with respect to how they rate insurance companies, can be asked about the way they rate bonds. However, we do not rate bonds ourselves. Therefore, we must rely upon the bond ratings of other rating agencies. This is another reason why we have stricter capital requirements for the insurance companies. It accounts for the fact that they may need some extra protection in case an AAA-rated bond may not be quite as good as it appears to be.

4. Finally, target capital is adjusted for the company's spread of risk in the diversification of its investment portfolio, the size and number of the policies it writes and the diversification of its business.

Table 1 on the next page shows target capital percentages used by Moody's Investment Services in relation to Weiss Risk-Adjusted Capital Ratios #1 and #2 (RACR #1 and RACR #2), and reserve rates used by the National Association of Insurance Commissioners (NAIC).

The percentages shown in the table answer the question: How much should the firm hold in capital resources for every $100 it has committed to each category? Several of the items in Table 1 are expressed as ranges. The actual percentages used in the calculation of target capital for an individual company may vary due to the levels of risks in the operations, investments, or policy obligations of that specific company.

Table 1. Target Capital Percentages

Asset Risk	Weiss RACR#1 (%)	Weiss RACR#2 (%)	Moody's	NAIC
Bonds				
Government guaranteed bonds	0	0	0	0-1
Class 1	.5-.75	1-1.5	1	.3
Class 2	2	5	2	1
Class 3	5	15	5	4
Class 4	10	30	10	9
Class 5	20	60	20	20
Class 6	20	60	20	30
Collateralized Mortgage Obligations	0-1.75	0-4.75	0-1	0-1
Mortgages				
Class 1	.5	1	5	.1
Class 2				
Farm purchase money	2.2-20	5.5-25	5	3
Residential purchase money	1.7-20	3.8-25	1	.5
Commercial purchase money	2.2-20	5.5-25	5	3
Class 3	25-33	33-50	20	.2-20 ***
Real Estate				
Class 1	20	50	10	15
Class 2	10	33	12	10
Preferred Stock				
Class 1	3	5	3	3
Class 2	4	6	4	4
Class 3	7	9	7	7
Class 4	12	15	12	12
Class 5	22	29	22	22
Class 6	30	39	22	22
Class 7	3-30	5-39	3-22	RBC x % owned
Common Stock				
Class 1	25	33	20	30
Class 2	25-100	33-100	75	RBC x % owned
Short-term investment	.5	1	.5	.3
Premium notes	2	5	10	5
Collateral loans	2	5	10	5
Separate account equity	25	33		.3 **
Other invested assets	5	10	10	5
Insurance Risk				
Individual life reserves*	.06-.15	.08-.21	.075	.06-.15
Group life reserves*	.05-.12	.06-.16	.075	.05-.12
Individual Health Premiums				
Class 1	12-20	15-25	25	15-25
Class 2	9.6	12	25	12
Class 3	6.4	8	25	8
Class 4	12-28	15-35	25	15-35
Class 5	12-20	15-25	25	15-25
Group Health Premiums				
Class 1	5.6-12	7-15	10	7-15
Class 2	20	25	10	25
Class 3	9.6	12	10	25
Class 4	6.4	8	10	8
Class 5	12-20	15-25	10	15-25
Managed care credit	5-40	6-50	N/A	N/A
Premiums subject to rate guarantees	100-209	120-250	N/A	N/A
Individual claim reserves	4	5	6.25	5
Group claim reserves	4	5	6.25	5
Reinsurance	0-2	0-5	1	.5
Interest Rate Risk				
Policy loans	0-2	0-5	0	0
Life reserves	1-2	1-3	2	.75
Individual annuity reserves	1-3	1-5	3	.75-3
Group annuity reserves	1-2	1-3	1	.75-3
Guaranteed interest contract reserves	1-2	1-3		.75

All numbers are shown for illustrative purposes. Figures actually used in the formula vary annually based on industry experience.

*Based on net amount at risk.

**Risk-based capital for separate account assets that are not tied to an index = 100% of the risk-based capital of assets in the accounts.

***Based on average industry delinquency rate.

Appendix   *Risk-Adjusted Capital*

Investment Class   Descriptions

Investment Class		Descriptions
Government guaranteed bonds		Guaranteed bonds issued by U.S. and other governments which receive the top rating of state insurance commissioners.
Bonds -	Class 1	Investment grade bonds rated AAA, AA or A by Moody's or Standard & Poor's or deemed AAA - An equivalent by state insurance commissioners.
	Class 2	Investment grade bonds with some speculative elements, rated BBB or equivalent.
	Class 3	Noninvestment grade bonds, rated BB or equivalent.
	Class 4	Noninvestment grade bonds, rated B or equivalent.
	Class 5	Noninvestment grade bonds, rated CCC, CC or C or equivalent.
	Class 6	Noninvestment grade bonds, in or near default.
Collateralized Mortgage Obligations - (see glossary for definition)		Additional target capital assessment based on variability of prepayment schedules.
Mortgages -	Class 1	Mortgages guaranteed by VA, FHA or other government agencies.
	Class 2	Other mortgages in good standing: - Purchase money farm mortgages - Other farm mortgages - Purchase money residential mortgages - Other residential mortgages - Purchase money commercial mortgages - Other commercial mortgages
	Class 3	Mortgages 90 days past due or in process of foreclosure.
Real Estate -	Class 1	Properties acquired in satisfaction of debt.
	Class 2	Company occupied and other investment properties.
Preferred stock -	Class 1	Highest quality unaffiliated preferred stock.
	Class 2	High quality unaffiliated preferred stock.
	Class 3	Medium quality unaffiliated preferred stock.
	Class 4	Low quality unaffiliated preferred stock.
	Class 5	Lowest quality unaffiliated preferred stock.
	Class 6	Unaffiliated preferred stock, in or near default.
	Class 7	Affiliated preferred stock.
Common stock -	Class 1	Unaffiliated common stock
	Class 2	Affiliated common stock
Short-term investments		All investments whose maturities at the time of acquisition were one year or less.
Premium Notes		Loans for payment of premiums.
Collateral loans		Loans made to a company or individual where the underlying security is in the form of bonds, stocks, or other marketable securities.
Separate account assets		Investments held in an account segregated from the general assets of the company, generally used to provide variable annuity benefits.
Other invested assets		Any invested assets that do not fit under the main categories above.
Individual life reserves		Funds set aside for payment of life insurance benefits under an individual contract rather than a company or group; underwriting based on individual profile.
Group life reserves		Funds set aside for payment of life insurance benefits under a contract with at least 10 people whereby all members have a common interest and are joined for a reason other than to obtain insurance.
Individual health premiums	Class 1	Usual and customary hospital and medical premiums, which include traditional medical reimbursement plans, that are subject to annual rate increases based on the company's claims experience.
	Class 2	Medicare supplements, dental, and other limited benefits anticipating rate increases.
	Class 3	Hospital indemnity plans, accidental death and dismemberment policies, and other limited benefits not anticipating rate increases.
	Class 4	Noncancellable disability income.

	Class 5	Guaranteed renewable disability income.
Group health premiums	Class 1	Usual and customary hospital and medical premiums, which include traditional medical reimbursement plans, that are subject to annual rate increases based on the company's claims experience.
	Class 2	Stop loss and minimum premium where a known claims liability is minimal or nonexistent.
	Class 3	Medicare supplements, dental, and other limited benefits anticipating rate increases.
	Class 4	Hospital indemnity plans, accidental death and dismemberment policies, and other limited benefits not anticipating rate increases.
	Class 5	Disability Income.
Managed care credit		Premiums for HMO and PPO business which carry less risk than traditional indemnity business. Included in this credit are provider compensation arrangements such as salary, capitation and fixed payment per service.
Premiums subject to rate guarantees		Health insurance premiums from policies where the rate paid by the policyholder are guaranteed for a period of time, such as one year, 15 months, 27 months or 37 months.
Individual claim reserves		Accident and health reserves for claims on individual policies.
Group claim reserves		Accident and health reserves for claims on group policies.
Reinsurance		Amounts recoverable on paid and unpaid losses for all reinsurance ceded; unearned premiums on accident and health reinsurance ceded; and funds held with unauthorized reinsurers.
Policy loans		Loans against the cash value of a life insurance policy.
Life reserves		Reserves for life insurance claims net of reinsurance and policy loans.
Individual annuity reserves		Reserves held in order to pay off maturing individual annuities or those surrendered before maturity.
Group annuity reserves		Reserves held in order to pay off maturing group annuities or those surrendered before maturity.
GIC reserves		Reserves held to pay off maturing guaranteed interest contracts.

Table 2. Bond Default Rates - potential losses as a percent of bond portfolio

Bond Rating	(1) Moody's 15 Yr Rate (%)	(2) Moody's 12 Yr Rate (%)	(3) Worst Year (%)	(4) 3 Cum. Recession Years (%)	(5) Weiss 15 Year Rate (%)	(6) Assumed Loss Rate (%)	(7) Losses as % of Holdings (%)	(8) RACR #2 Rate (%)
Aaa	2.80	1.60	0.10	0.30	1.89	50	0.95	1.00
Aa	2.00	1.60	0.20	0.60	2.19	50	1.09	1.00
A	3.30	2.50	0.40	1.20	3.67	55	2.02	1.00
Baa	7.20	5.50	1.10	3.26	8.58	60	5.15	5.00
Ba	20.10	17.90	8.40	23.08	36.47	65	23.71	15.00
B	33.70	32.50	21.60	50.80	62.24	70	43.57	30.00

Comments On Target Capital Percentages

The factors that are chiefly responsible for the conservative results of our Risk-Adjusted Capital Ratios are the investment risks of bond Classes 2 - 6, mortgages, real estate and affiliate common stock as well as the interest rate risk for annuities and GICs. Comments on the basis of these figures are found below. Additional comments address factors that vary based on particular performance or risk characteristics of the individual company.

Bonds Target capital percentages for bonds are derived from a model that factors in historical cumulative bond default rates from the last 20 years and the additional loss potential during a prolonged economic decline. The continuance of post-World War II prosperity is by no means certain. Realistic analyses of potential losses must factor in the possibility of severe economic reversal. Table 2 shows how this was done for each bond rating classification. A 15-year cumulative default rate is used (column 1), due to the 15-year average maturity at issue of bonds held by life insurance companies. These are historical default rates for 1970-1990 for each bond class, taken from *Moody's Studies Loss Potential of Life Insurance Assets*.

To factor in the additional loss potential of a severe three-year-long economic decline, we reduced the base to Moody's 12-year rate (column 2), determined the worst single year experience (column 3), spread that experience over three years (column 4), and added the historical 12-year rate to the 3-year projection to derive the Weiss 15-year default rate (column 5). Note: Due to the shrinking base of nondefaulted bonds in each year, column 4 may be somewhat less than three times column 3, and column 5 may be somewhat less than the sum of column 2 and column 4.

The next step was to determine the losses that could be expected from these defaults. This would be equivalent to the capital a company should have to cover those losses. Loss rates were assigned for each bond class (column 6), based on the fact that higher-rated issues generally carry less debt and the fact that the debt is also better secured, leading to higher recovery rates upon default. Column 7 shows losses as a percent of holdings for each bond class. Column 8 shows the target capital percentages that are used in RACR #2 (Table 1, RACR #2 column, Bonds – classes 1 to 6).

Regulations limiting junk bond holdings of insurers to a set percent of assets are a tacit acknowledgement that the 10% and 20% maximum reserve requirements used by State Insurance Commissioners (Table 1, NAIC column, Bonds-classes 4, 5, and 6) are inadequate. If the figure adequately represented full loss potential, there would be no need to limit holdings through legislation since an adequate loss reserve would provide sufficient capital to absorb potential losses.

Mortgages Mortgage default rates for the Risk-Adjusted Capital Ratios are derived from historical studies of mortgage and real estate losses in selected depressed markets. The rate for RACR #2 (Table 1, RACR #2 column, Mortgages - class 2) will vary between 3.8% and 25%, based on the performance of the company's mortgage portfolio in terms of mortgage loans 90 days or more past due, in process of foreclosure and foreclosed during the previous year.

Real Estate The 33% rate (Table 1, RACR #2 column, Real Estate - Class 2) used for potential real estate losses in the Weiss ratios is based on historical losses in depressed markets. It avoids the commonly made assumption that the continuous appreciation of property values experienced since World War II must inevitably continue.

Affiliate Common Stock The target capital rate on affiliate common stock for RACR #2 can vary between 33% and 100% (Table 1, RACR #2 column, Common stock - Class 2), depending on the financial strength of the affiliate and the prospects for obtaining capital from the affiliate should the need arise.

Insurance Risk Calculations of target capital for insurance risk vary according to categories. For individual and group life insurance, target capital is a percentage of net amount at risk (total amount of insurance in force less reserves). Individual and group health insurance risk is calculated as a percentage of premium. Categories vary from "usual and customary hospital and medical premiums" where risk is relatively low because losses from one year are recouped by annual rate increases, to "noncancellable disability income" where the risk of loss is greater because disability benefits are paid in future years without the possibility of recovery.

Reinsurance This factor varies with the quality of the reinsuring companies and the type of reinsurance being used (e.g., co-insurance, modified co-insurance, yearly renewable term, etc.).

Interest Rate Risk On Annuities	The 1 - 5% rate on individual annuities as a percentage of reserves (Table 1, RACR #2 column 3, Individual annuity reserves), and the 1 - 3% rate for group annuities as a percentage of reserves (Table 1, RACR #2 column 3, Group annuity reserves and GICs), are derived from studies of potential losses that can occur when assets and liabilities are not properly matched. (See Glossary under "Asset/Liability Matching.")
	Companies are especially prone to losses in this area for one of two reasons: (1) They promise high interest rates on their annuities and have not locked in corresponding yields on their investments. If interest rates fall, the company will have difficulties earning the promised rate. (2) They lock in high returns on their investments but allow policy surrenders without market value adjustments. If market values decline and surrenders increase, liquidity problems can result in substantial losses.
	The target capital figure used for each company is based on the surrender characteristics of its policies, the interest rate used in calculating reserves and the actuarial analyses found in New York Regulation 126 filing, or similar studies where applicable.

Risk-Adjusted Capital for Property and Casualty Insurers

Over 100 companies that are registered with state insurance departments as property and casualty insurers offer health insurance policies. Included in this number are four Blue Cross/Blue Shield plans. Our ratings on these companies make use of the data in the Property and Casualty Statutory Statements that are required by state insurance departments. These financial statements employ a system of accounting that differs from that used by companies filing Life and Health Statutory Statements. Some of the chief distinguishing features of the Property and Casualty Statutory Accounting include:

- Life and health companies must hold reserves to protect specifically against investment losses. Property and casualty insurers keep no equivalent protection. One of the consequences of the lack of an investment loss reserve is that property and casualty companies, on the average, hold more nonaffiliated common stock than do life insurers. This factor is considered in our evaluation of capital adequacy.

- Policy reserves for life insurers are reduced to reflect investment income to be earned between the time premiums are received by the company, and the time when claims are to be paid. Property and casualty companies generally do not reduce or discount their reserves for the time value of money.

- Underwriting profits and losses for property and casualty insurers are calculated without reference to investment income.

Despite these factors, it is our goal to provide ratings that consumers can easily understand and to make technical differences as transparent to consumers as possible. The final ratings are intended to give the same message about our opinion of insurers financial safety.

As with the life and health companies, there are two risk-adjusted capital ratios, which measure whether the company has enough capital to cover unexpected losses.

However, unlike the life and health companies, the risks related to pricing and claims are more important, while the risks associated with investments are reduced because there is little exposure to risky investments such as junk bonds or mortgages.

Pricing Risk The risk that premium levels are not sufficient to establish adequate reserves and/or pay claims and related expenses. Individual target capital percentages are used for each line of business based on the riskiness of the line and the company's own experience with underwriting losses and reserve shortfalls. Target capital requirements are reduced to account for the time value of money.

Risky Lines of Business and Catastrophic Losses These include fire, earthquake, multiple peril (including storm damage), and similar personal and commercial property coverage. Even excluding Hurricane Andrew, the insured losses from natural disasters since 1989 have been far greater than in previous decades. Yet, too many insurance companies are basing their risk calculations on the assumption that losses will return to more normal levels. They are not ready for the possibility that the pattern of increasing disasters might be a real, continuing trend.

Also considered high-risk lines are medical malpractice, general liability, product liability, and other similar liability coverage. Court awards for damages often run into the millions. These settlement amounts can be very difficult to predict. This uncertainty hinders an insurer's ability to accurately assess how much to charge policyholders and how much to set aside to pay claims. Of special concern are large, unexpected liabilities related to environmental damages such as asbestos. Similar risk may lie hidden in coverage for medical equipment and procedures, industrial wastes, carcinogens, and other substances found in products previously viewed as benign. Companies that offer a variety of types of insurance in addition to health coverage can get into financial difficulties due to any of their lines of business. Accordingly, it is essential that the company's whole operation be strong. If the company is overrun with claims from an earthquake of hurricane, its ability to pay health claims will also be affected.

Risk-Adjusted Capital for Health Maintenance Organizations

As with the other rating systems, the HMO system includes two risk-adjusted capital ratios to measure a company's ability to withstand unexpected losses during moderate and severe loss scenarios. HMOs are more likely exposed to risk from pricing and claims than from investments. They have no interest rate risk, in terms of potential policy surrenders, the way life insurance companies do.

Capital resources include the company's net worth adjusted for surplus notes; credit or penalty for overstating or understating reserves; and credit or penalty for the company's ability to spread risk based on overall net worth of the company's affiliate group.

These health plans file yet another type of statutory statement, different from life and health or property and casualty insurers. The Weiss Rating System for HMOs addresses the unique business and accounting factors relevant to these firms. Among the many differences are the following:

- Rather than setting up reserves as a liability the way life insurance companies do, HMO claims reserves are part of net worth.

- Investments are carried at book value, but market value is shown on Schedule B of the statutory statement. Market values are considered in the capitalization and liquidity indexes.

- HMOs do not hold reserves to protect specifically against investment losses. This factor is considered in our evaluation of capital adequacy.

- HMOs do not have long-term obligations like life insurance and annuities. Accordingly, reserves are not discounted for the time value of money. Our analysis examines reserve adequacy by comparing one year's reserve estimates with claims and medical expenses actually paid during the subsequent year, without factoring in investment income.

LONG-TERM CARE INSURANCE PLANNER

This planner is designed to help you decide what kind of long-term care insurance is best for you and help you shop for the policy that meets your needs. Many insurers charge a lot more – or less – for very similar policies. So there's a great benefit to shopping around. No policy is exactly alike. However, if you follow these steps, it will be easier to compare policies side by side:

Step 1. Try to determine, ahead of time, what type of care you think you will need from others beyond the assistance your own family members may be able to provide:

	Yes	No
Custodial Care	[ ]	[ ]
Intermediate Care	[ ]	[ ]
Skilled Care	[ ]	[ ]

This isn't easy, because it's often hard to anticipate your future needs, but try your best to decide if you're going to want access to one of the following. Custodial care is provided by someone without medical training who helps you with daily activities. Intermediate care includes occasional nursing and rehabilitative care supervised by skilled medical personnel. Skilled care includes 24-hour care provided by a skilled nurse or therapist.

Step 2. Decide where you would most likely be receiving the care?

	Yes	No
In-Home Care*	[ ]	[ ]
Nursing Home*	[ ]	[ ]
Adult Day Care	[ ]	[ ]
Assisted Living Facility	[ ]	[ ]
Other _____	[ ]	[ ]

*Typically available with all three levels of care – custodial, intermediate, and skilled.

Most people prefer in-home care. However, if you have no family members to help you at home, in-home care could be prohibitively expensive, especially if it requires skilled care. Nursing homes are designed for 24-hour care and are best utilized for short-term stays. Adult day care is an option, but will probably require someone, such as a family member, who can drop you off and pick you up daily. Assisted living facilities are increasingly popular, offering a good balance between independence and assistance. Other types of care could include hospice care (for the terminally ill) or respite care (temporary assistance to help relieve family members).

Step 3. Check out the facilities in the area in which you plan to live, make sure you're comfortable with them, and find out much how they cost:

	Estimated Costs
In-Home Care	_____
Nursing Home	_____
Assisted Living Facility	_____
Adult Day Care	_____
Other	_____

The insurance company is going to pay you a daily benefit that will be applied toward the cost of your care. Most of the costs above that daily benefit will have to come out of your own pocket. Therefore, find a facility that you'd be comfortable with, and then try to get a general idea of how much it would cost. Each facility may offer a different rate schedule for each level of care it provides, so make sure you understand the differences. For care within your home, contact a home care agency and ask them about the going rates for home nurses and therapists. Also consider costs associated with any modifications that may be needed for your home, such as wheelchair accessibility, handicap rails, etc.

Step 4. Try to estimate how much of the long-term care expenses you will be able to pay on your own: $_____ per month.

Your financial planner may be able to give you an estimate of your retirement income available for health care. However, even a good estimate can be off the mark, so make sure your policy covers enough to avoid being financially strapped by long-term care expenses. Later, make sure your agent takes this information into consideration when he works out the terms of your policy. He should limit your out-of-pocket expenses to what you have indicated here.

Step 5. Try to arrive at a reasonable guess regarding when you might start using the benefits.
_____

Again, it's hard to predict. But if you're in reasonably good health and you have a family history of longevity, that's something to consider. If you're already suffering from chronic health problems, you may need the benefits sooner rather than later. If it's more than 10 years from now, you can buy a long-term care policy with an optional inflation protection feature to help protect against the rising cost of health care. This can add significantly to the cost, but you get what you pay for. Typically, the insurance company will add an extra five percent to your daily benefit, compounded annually. Thus, if the policy provides a $100 daily benefit now, it would rise to $163 in 10 years.

Step 6. Determine whether you prefer a "tax-qualified" policy or a "non-qualified" policy:

	Yes	No
Tax-Qualified Policy	[ ]	[ ]
Non-Qualified Policy	[ ]	[ ]

If you buy a <u>tax-qualified</u> policy, you will be able to claim the policy premiums as itemized medical expenses on your tax return. Furthermore, the benefits you receive will <u>not</u> be subject to federal income taxation, up to a dollar cap. If you purchase a <u>non-qualified</u> policy, you will not be able to itemize the premiums. As to the benefits, the IRS has yet to clarify whether or not they will be subject to federal income taxation. Do not assume that a tax-qualified policy will automatically be more beneficial. Reason: Typically, a tax-qualified policy will have stricter guidelines as to when you can access the policy benefits. You also may not be able to take advantage of the tax benefits. You may want to consult with a tax advisor on this subject.

Step 7. Find insurance agents in your area that <u>specialize</u> in long-term care policies:

Agent Name	Phone Number	Specialization in LTC?	Name of insurance company
_____	_____	(Y / N)	_____
_____	_____	(Y / N)	_____
_____	_____	(Y / N)	_____
_____	_____	(Y / N)	_____

Long-term care insurance is very complex. Therefore, make sure you work with an agent who specializes in long-term care policies, and don't limit your choices to someone you know or who is associated with your broker. The agent should be able to help educate you and clarify any questions you have – not only on policies he or she sells, but on others as well. Try to avoid agents that work strictly with one insurance company. Complete the remaining steps with the direct assistance of the agent you choose.

Step 8. Ask your agent for the names of at least three different policies, from different insurers, that you can compare.

	Policy A	Policy B	Policy C
Insurance Company Name	_____	_____	_____
Policy Name/Number	_____	_____	_____

Step 9. Have your agent check the safety rating for each company.

Safety Rating
Policy A: _____
Policy B: _____
Policy C: _____

It may be a long time before you begin to submit claims. Therefore, you will want to make sure your insurance company will still be viable at that time. If you use the Weiss Safety Ratings, we recommend you favor companies with a rating of B+ (good) or higher, and we suggest you avoid companies with a rating of D+ (weak) or lower.

Step 10. Favor companies that have more experience with long-term care insurance.

	Years of experience with long-term care	Have they ever raised rates for existing policyholders?
Policy A:	_____	(Y / N)
Policy B:	_____	(Y / N)
Policy C:	_____	(Y / N)

This should not be a deal breaker. But you're better off with a company that has been offering long-term care policies for a while and has never raised rates for existing policyholders. In contrast, companies that are new in long-term care – or have a history of raising rates on existing policies – are more likely to raise your rates in the future.

Step 11. If you're considering buying a policy with your spouse, check how you qualify for a spousal discount.

Policy A: _____
Policy B: _____
Policy C: _____

In some cases, you may need to be married to qualify; in others you don't have to be formally married. Some insurers require that the policies be exactly the same, while others do not.

Step 12. Ask your agent for quotes on the monthly premiums. Make sure the quotes are based on the preferences and needs that you outlined in steps 1-6.

	Single Policy Premium	Combined Policy Premium	% Savings
Policy A:	_____	_____	_____
Policy B:	_____	_____	_____
Policy C:	_____	_____	_____

If you can buy your long-term care policy with a spouse or significant other, make sure you take advantage of spousal discounts, which can save you up to 20% on the combined premium.

Step 13. Find out exactly what each policy covers in addition to the basics that you require:

	Policy A	Policy B	Policy C
Custodial	(Y / N)	(Y / N)	(Y / N)
Intermediate	(Y / N)	(Y / N)	(Y / N)
Skilled	(Y / N)	(Y / N)	(Y / N)

The actual policies that your agent has suggested may differ somewhat from your wish list of benefits, including some that you did not ask for, or excluding others that you wanted. This may help explain some, but not all, of the price differences.

Step 14. Ask your agent to give you a list of the types of facilities that are included and how they are defined. Facilities may include nursing home care, in-home care, adult day care, hospice care, assisted living facilities, and other options.

Policy A
_____
_____
_____

Policy B
_____
_____
_____

Policy C
_____
_____
_____

Step 15. Find out the basic terms of coverage and reimbursement, as follows:

Policy A: How the company calculates elimination period: _____

Facility of Care	Elimination Periods	Benefit Periods	Daily Benefit
In-home care:	_____	_____	_____
Nursing home	_____	_____	_____
Assisted living:	_____	_____	_____
Adult day care:	_____	_____	_____

Policy B: How the company calculates elimination period: _____

Facility of Care	Elimination Periods	Benefit Periods	Daily Benefit
In-home care:	_____	_____	_____
Nursing home	_____	_____	_____
Assisted living:	_____	_____	_____
Adult day care:	_____	_____	_____

Policy C: How the company calculates elimination period: _____

Facility of Care	Elimination Periods	Benefit Periods	Daily Benefit
In-home care:	_____	_____	_____
Nursing home	_____	_____	_____
Assisted living:	_____	_____	_____
Adult day care:	_____	_____	_____

Elimination Period: This is similar to a deductible. It is the amount of time you pay for services out of your own pocket before the insurance policy takes over. Typically, you can select elimination periods of 0, 30, 60, 90, or 180 days, depending on the policy and insurance company. But you must find out exactly how the elimination period is satisfied. Let's say, for example, you need care on days 1, 4 and 10. With some policies, that would be counted as only THREE days toward your elimination period. With other policies, it would be counted as TEN days, which would mean you'd start collecting the benefits much sooner.

Benefit Period (or maximum): Some companies tell you the length of time the policy will be paid; others just tell you the maximum value of benefits to be paid. The benefit period can typically range from 2 to 5 years, and some may even have an unlimited lifetime period.

Daily Benefit: The amount the policy will pay for each day of covered services. Some plans offer a daily benefit reimbursable on a weekly or monthly basis giving you more flexibility. For example, if you selected a daily benefit of $100 reimbursable on a weekly basis you would be reimbursed for up to $700 dollars per week in expenses no matter how much you incurred on any one day.

Step 16. Determine if the policy is "a pool of money" contract.

Pool of money?
Policy A: (Y / N)
Policy B: (Y / N)
Policy C: (Y / N)

Most current policies will actually give you more time to collect the benefits than indicated by the benefit period. For example, in a four-year policy, if you need care on and off, you may not use up all your benefits in that four-year period. So you could continue to collect those unused benefits in subsequent years as well. These are called "pool of money" contracts. (To calculate your pool, just multiple the total number of days by the daily benefit.) Other policies will actually end at the end of the four years, no matter what.

Step 17. Check into the requirements needed to activate the policy.

Policy A: _____
_____

Policy B: _____
_____

Policy C: _____
_____

You will need to meet what is referred to as "benefit triggers" before the policy can begin covering expenses, and these can vary from policy to policy. Under most policies, you will be qualified for benefits when you meet certain conditions, such as: 1) The inability to perform activities of daily living ("ADLs"), which typically include bathing, dressing, transferring, toileting, eating, continence, and taking medication on your own; and 2) cognitive impairment. Some plans require you to satisfy either condition (1) or (2); some require that you satisfy both conditions. Still others also allow for a third trigger, often referred to as "medical necessity." This means that a doctor determines if you need care due to an injury or sickness. Make sure you find out the precise requirements of each policy.

Step 18. Find out what other features are included (or can be added by a "rider") to the policy.
Your agent should explain any additional features that may be included in the policies you are comparing including the following:

	Policy A	Policy B	Policy C
Waiver of Premium	(Y / N)	(Y / N)	(Y / N)
Nonforfeiture	(Y / N)	(Y / N)	(Y / N)
Restoration of Benefits	(Y / N)	(Y / N)	(Y / N)
Alternate Care Plan	(Y / N)	(Y / N)	(Y / N)
Bed Reservation	(Y / N)	(Y / N)	(Y / N)
Guaranteed Renewable	(Y / N)	(Y / N)	(Y / N)
Inflation Protection	(Y / N)	(Y / N)	(Y / N)

Your agent will explain the details. Just make sure that you actually need these additional benefits, because they can add substantially to your total costs.

RECENT INDUSTRY FAILURES

2004

Institution	Headquarters	Industry	Date of Failure	Total Assets ($Mil)	Weiss Safety Rating
Statewide Insurance Co	Illinois	P&C	01/06/04	33.1	D- (Weak)

2003

Institution	Headquarters	Industry	Date of Failure	Total Assets ($Mil)	Weiss Safety Rating
American Natl Lawyers Ins	Tennessee	P&C	01/31/03	14.9	D+ (Weak)
Commercial Casualty Insurance Co	N Carolina	P&C	11/17/03	65.7	E (Very Weak)
Community Choice Michigan	Michigan	HMO	05/12/03	24.6	C- (Fair)
Doctors Ins Reciprocal RRG	Tennessee	P&C	01/31/03	26.6	C- (Fair)
Farmers Mutual Ins Co	W Virginia	P&C	04/15/03	10.4	D- (Weak)
Good Samaritan Life Insurance Co	Texas	L&H	07/15/03	n/a	U
Millers Ins Co	Texas	P&C	03/24/03	30.6	E+ (Very Weak)
Narragansett Bay Ins Co	Rhode Island	P&C	05/01/03	19.6	C- (Fair)
Old Standard Life Ins Co	Idaho	L&H	12/24/03	425.3	D (Weak)
Old West Annuity & Life	Arizona	L&H	12/24/03	224.4	D (Weak)
Pacific National Ins Co	California	P&C	08/05/03	35.7	D (Weak)
Patterson Insurance	Louisiana	P&C	03/17/03	18.4	E- (Very Weak)
Pawtucket Mutual Ins Co	Rhode Island	P&C	05/01/03	111.9	D+ (Weak)
Providers Direct Health Plan of Georgia	Georgia	HMO	03/28/03	4.9	U
Reciprocal Alliance RRG	Tennessee	P&C	01/31/03	31.6	C- (Fair)
Reciprocal of America	Virginia	P&C	01/29/03	478.8	C (Fair)
Republic Western Ins Co	Arizona	P&C	05/20/03	576.6	C- (Fair)
Security Indemnity Ins Co	New Jersey	P&C	06/27/03	39.6	D (Weak)
Superior Insurance Co	Florida	P&C	08/29/03	90.6	E (Very Weak)

2003 cont'd

Institution	Headquarters	Industry	Date of Failure	Total Assets ($Mil)	Weiss Safety Rating
Wasatch Crest Mutual Ins	Utah	P&C	07/31/03	12.4	E+ (Very Weak)
Washington Casualty Co	Washington	P&C	03/06/03	41.5	E (Very Weak)
Wellness Plan	Michigan	HMO	07/01/03	56.9	D (Weak)
Western United Life Ins	Washington	L&H	12/24/03	1559.8	C- (Fair)
Western Growers Ins Co	California	P&C	01/17/03	17.1	E (Very Weak)
White Hall Mutual Ins Co	Pennsylvania	P&C	04/10/03	7.8	D (Weak)

2002

Institution	Headquarters	Industry	Date of Failure	Total Assets ($Mil)	Weiss Safety Rating
Aberdeen Insurance Co	Texas	P&C	02/01/02	7.7	D (Weak)
Acceptance Ins Co	Nebraska	P&C	12/20/02	224.5	D+ (Weak)
Alistar Ins Co	California	P&C	04/11/02	19.9	E (Very Weak)
Amcare Health Plans of Louisiana	Louisiana	HMO	09/27/02	12.0	D+ (Weak)
Amcare Health Plans of Oklahoma	Oklahoma	HMO	09/18/02	16.9	E+ (Very Weak)
Amcare Health Plans of Texas Inc	Texas	HMO	04/05/02	35.8	D (Weak)
American Growers Ins Co	Nebraska	P&C	11/25/02	114.8	D+ (Weak)
American Horizon Ins Co	California	P&C	07/11/02	22.4	E (Very Weak)
Aries Insurance Company	Florida	P&C	05/10/02	10.6	U
Casualty Reciprocal Exch	Missouri	P&C	12/19/02	155.9	D- (Weak)
Catawba Ins Co	So Carolina	P&C	08/20/02	15.8	D (Weak)
Community Health Plan of the Rockies	Colorado	HMO	12/16/02	15.6	D- (Weak)
Consolidated Am Ins Co	So Carolina	P&C	08/20/02	5.6	U
Empire Lloyds Ins Co	Texas	P&C	12/30/02	1.6	E (Very Weak)
Equity Mutual Ins Co	Missouri	P&C	12/19/02	46.2	D (Weak)
Gallant Ins Co	Illinois	P&C	02/25/02	66.0	D- (Weak)
Grange Mutual Ins Co	Oregon	P&C	07/02/02	12.8	D+ (Weak)
Group Council Mutual Ins	New York	P&C	03/19/02	20.1	E- (Very Weak)
HealthPlan of the Redwoods	California	HMO	10/01/02	42.8	C- (Fair)
Legion Indemnity Co	Illinois	P&C	04/03/02	103.3	C (Fair)
Legion Ins Co	Pennsylvania	P&C	04/01/02	1295.2	C (Fair)
Lifeguard Inc	California	HMO	09/13/02	120.2	C- (Fair)
Lifeguard Life Ins Co	California	L&H	09/27/02	32.3	C+ (Fair)
London Pacific Life & Annuity Company	No Carolina	L&H	07/03/02	2147.9	C- (Fair)
National Auto & Casualty	California	P&C	03/15/02	26.2	D- (Weak)
Nodak Mutual Ins Co	No Dakota	P&C	09/23/02	68.0	C (Fair)

2002 cont'd

Institution	Headquarters	Industry	Date of Failure	Total Assets ($Mil)	Weiss Safety Rating
Oak Casualty Ins Co	Illinois	P&C	11/20/02	22.1	E (Very Weak)
Paula Ins Co	California	P&C	04/26/02	128.4	E+ (Very Weak)
Peoples Health Plan of Oh	Ohio	HMO	11/25/02	n/a	U
Piedmont Insurance Co	So. Carolina	L&H	11/27/02	2.7	E (Very Weak)
Renaissance Health Plan	Ohio	HMO	08/22/02	21.2	E (Very Weak)
South Carolina Ins Co	So Carolina	P&C	08/20/02	51.5	E+ (Very Weak)
The Oath for LA Inc	Louisiana	HMO	04/10/02	79.5	E+ (Very Weak)
Universal Care of TN	Tennessee	HMO	09/13/02	n/a	U
Valor Ins Co	Illinois	P&C	02/25/02	64.2	E+ (Very Weak)
Villanova Ins Co	Pennsylvania	P&C	04/01/02	152.5	C (Fair)
Western Specialty Ins Co	Illinois	P&C	05/06/02	13.1	E+ (Very Weak)

2001

Institution	Headquarters	Industry	Date of Failure	Total Assets ($Mil)	Weiss Safety Rating
American Agents Ins Co	New York	P&C	02/05/01	16.7	E (Very Weak)
American Vehicle Ins Co	Florida	P&C	03/06/01	6.2	U
Amwest Ins Co	Nebraska	P&C	05/05/01	0	U
Assoc. Physicians Ins Co	Illinois	P&C	08/16/01	N/A	U
Connecticut Surety Co	Connecticut	P&C	06/26/01	15.5	D (Weak)
Cumberland Surety Ins	Kentucky	P&C	02/27/01	N/A	U
Delta Casualty Co	Illinois	P&C	12/04/01	16.6	D- (Weak)
Far West Ins Co	Nebraska	P&C	11/09/01	42.5	U
First Nevada Ins Co	Nevada	P&C	02/20/01	4.4	D- (Weak)
Fortune Ins Co	Florida	P&C	05/19/01	26.2	E (Very Weak)
Frontier Ins Co	New York	P&C	08/24/01	469.1	E (Very Weak)
Frontier Pacific Ins Co	California	P&C	09/07/01	78.8	D- (Very Weak)
Great States Ins Co	California	P&C	03/30/01	93.0	C+ (Fair)
Gulf South Health Plans	Louisiana	HMO	06/19/01	33.6	D- (Weak)
Heritage Natl Ins Co	Oklahoma	L&H	06/22/01	N/A	U
HIH America C & L Co	California	P&C	03/30/01	167.1	C (Fair)
HIH America of Hawaii	Hawaii	P&C	03/30/01	35.6	C (Fair)
HRM Health Plans Inc	Pennsylvania	HMO	08/01/01	30.7	D (Weak)
IGF Insurance Co	Indiana	P&C	06/29/01	175.7	E+ (Very Weak)
Indep Indemnity Ins Co	Kansas	P&C	11/11/01	3.3	E (Very Weak)
Maxicare	California	HMO	05/25/01	61.6	E+ (Very Weak)
Maxicare Indiana	Indiana	HMO	05/04/01	26.6	D- (Weak)
Maxicare L&H Ins Co	Missouri	L&H	05/29/01	15.0	D- (Weak)
Medical One Inc	Puerto Rico	HMO	11/21/01	4.5	E- (Very Weak)
Montana Benefits & Life Co	Montana	L&H	06/20/01	4.8	D (Weak)
N.A.P.T.	Florida	L&H	08/10/01	N/A	U
Omnicare Health Plan	Michigan	HMO	07/30/01	25.8	E- (Very Weak)
Pennsylvania Casualty	Pennsylvania	P&C	11/19/01	38.8	D- (Weak)
Petrosurance Casualty	Oklahoma	P&C	05/29/01	32.8	D (Weak)

2001 cont'd

Institution	Headquarters	Industry	Date of Failure	Total Assets ($Mil)	Weiss Safety Rating
PHICO Insurance Co	Pennsylvania	P&C	08/16/01	727.3	D- (Weak)
PhysiciansChoice Ltd	Florida	L&H	08/10/01	N/A	U
Reliance Direct Ins Co	Pennsylvania	P&C	01/29/01	55.5	E (Very Weak)
Reliance Ins Co of IL	Illinois	P&C	01/29/01	91.5	E (Very Weak)
Reliance Ins Co	Pennsylvania	P&C	01/29/01	6068.8	E (Very Weak)
Reliance Lloyds	Texas	P&C	01/29/01	1.9	E (Very Weak)
RelianceNational Indemnity Co	Wisconsin	P&C	01/29/01	311.1	E (Very Weak)
Reliance National Inc Co	Delaware	P&C	01/29/01	130.4	E (Very Weak)
Reliance Surety Co	Delaware	P&C	01/29/01	24.6	U
Reliance Universal Ins Co	California	P&C	01/29/01	53.7	E (Very Weak)
Reliant Ins Co	Michigan	P&C	01/29/01	31.5	E (Very Weak)
Republic Casualty Co	Oklahoma	P&C	06/22/01	N/A	U
Sable Ins Co	California	P&C	01/29/01	19.4	D (Weak)
Savant Ins Co	Louisiana	P&C	06/20/01	N/A	U
Statewide Ins Co	Delaware	P&C	02/08/01	1.1	E+ (Very Weak)
Tennessee Coordinated Care Network	Tennessee	HMO	11/02/01	88.5	D- (Weak)
Tower Health (Cohen Medical Corp)	California	HMO	09/13/01	N/A	U
UPH Healthcare/Watts Health Foundation	California	HMO	08/08/01	71.2	D- (Weak)
Underwriters Guarantee Ins Co	Florida	P&C	11/06/01	20.0	D- (Weak)
Unisource Ins Co	Florida	P&C	09/24/01	5.1	D- (Weak)
United Capitol	Illinois	P&C	09/12/01	196.9	D (Weak)
United Pacific Ins Co	Pennsylvania	P&C	01/29/01	145.9	E (Very Weak)
United Pacific Ins Co of New York	New York	P&C	01/29/01	34.6	E (Very Weak)
UniversityHealth Alliance	Hawaii	L&H	07/05/01	7.4	E+ (Very Weak)
UniversityHealth Alliance	Hawaii	HMDI	07/05/01	7.4	E+ (Very Weak)
Villanova Ins Co	Pennsylvania	P&C	04/01/01	152.5	C (Fair)

2000

Institution	Headquarters	Industry	Date of Failure	Total Assets ($Mil)	Weiss Safety Rating
Acceleration National Ins	Ohio	P&C	05/01/00	28.0	D (Weak)
Advantage Care Inc.	Kentucky	HMO	11/08/00	12.5	D- (Weak)
Agora Syndicate Inc.	Illinois	P&C	09/14/00	N/A	U
Alliance General Ins Co	Illinois	P&C	01/07/00	26.9	E (Very Weak)
American Chambers Life	Ohio	L&H	02/29/00	35.1	E+ (Very Weak)
AmericanHealthcare Providers	Illinois	HMO	02/02/00	23.2	E+ (Very Weak)
American HMO Inc.	Illinois	HMO	05/11/00	14.8	D (Weak)
AmericanHealthcare Trust Inc.	Tennessee	HMO	05/11/00	14.8	D (Weak)
American Investors	Arkansas	L&H	07/11/00	8.5	E (Very Weak)
American Preferred Provider Plan – Mid Atlantic Inc	DC	HMO	04/26/00	N/A	U
American Unified L&H Ins Co	Illinois	L&H	07/27/00	3.8	D (Weak)
Bankers Commercial Life Ins Co	Texas	L&H	05/03/00	8.3	E- (Very Weak)
Beacon Health Plans Inc	Florida	HMO	01/20/00	8.5	E- (Very Weak)
Benefits Life Ins Co	Texas	L&H	08/16/00	5.7	E (Very Weak)
CA Compensation Ins Co	California	P&C	03/03/00	506.4	C (Fair)
Combined Benefit Life Ins	California	P&C	03/03/00	15.0	C (Fair)
Commercial Compensation Ins Co	New York	P&C	03/03/00	15.1	D (Weak)
Credit General Indem Co	Ohio	P&C	11/06/00	7.0	D (Weak)
Credit General Ins Co	Ohio	P&C	11/06/00	101.3	D (Weak)
Directcare Inc	Alabama	HMO	06/15/00	4.3	E- (Very Weak)
Family Health Plan Coop	Wisconsin	HMO	10/16/00	61.7	D (Weak)
First Mutual Ins Co	Kentucky	P&C	12/01/00	N/A	U
Forest Products Ins Exch	Minnesota	P&C	11/02/00	8.7	C (Fair)
Fremont Casualty Ins Co	Illinoi	P&C	11/27/00	557.5	C- (Fair)
Fremont Comp Ins Co	California	P&C	11/27/00	223.3	U

2000 cont'd

Institution	Headquarters	Industry	Date of Failure	Total Assets ($Mil)	Weiss Safety Rating
Fremont Indemnity Co	California	P&C	11/27/00	1314.3	C- (Fair)
Fremont Industrial Indemnity Co	California	P&C	11/27/00	594.9	C- (Fair)
Fremont Pacific Ins Co	California	P&C	11/27/00	37.4	C- (Fair)
Hamilton Ins Co	Pennsylvania	P&C	08/03/00	21.3	D (Weak)
Harvard Pilgrim Health Care Inc	Massachusetts	HMO	01/04/00	701.9	D+ (Weak)
Harvard Pilgrim Healthcare of New England	Massachusetts	HMO	01/04/00	12.3	C- (Fair)
Harvard Univ Group Health Plan	Massachusetts	HMO	01/04/00	N/A	U
Health Network of Colorado Springs	Colorado	HMO	08/14/00	2.6	D- (Weak)
HIP Health Plan of FL	Florida	HMO	07/19/00	64.3	D- (Weak)
Illinois Healthcare Ins Co	Illinois	L&H	06/30/00	13.0	D- (Weak)
International Indem Co	Georgia	P&C	11/07/00	61.9	D+ (Weak)
LMI Commercial Ins Co	Ohio	P&C	03/20/00	50.4	E+ (Very Weak)
Lumber Mutual Ins Co	Massachusetts	P&C	11/01/00	222.0	C (Fair)
Medical Comm Ins Co	Texas	L&H	08/30/00	2.2	E+ (Very Weak)
Mississippi Managed Care Network, Inc	Mississippi	HMO	01/28/00	5.5	D- (Weak)
New England Fidelity Ins Co	Massachusetts	P&C	11/15/00	17.8	D (Weak)
No Am Lumber Ins Co	Massachusetts	P&C	11/01/00	30.9	C- (Fair)
No Am Comm Health Plan	New York	HMO	10/20/00	N/A	U
Pilgrim Health Care Inc	Massachusetts	HMO	01/04/00	152.7	D+ (Weak)
Premiere Auto Ins Co	Pennsylvania	P&C	08/31/00	5.1	D- (Weak)
Proliance Ins Co	Ohio	P&C	12/28/00	6.8	E (Very Weak)
Queensway Casualty Ins Co	Florida	P&C	06/30/00	6.5	E (Very Weak)
SEACO Ins Co	Massachusetts	P&C	11/01/00	37.7	C- (Fair)
Sunstar Health Plan	Florida	HMO	02/01/00	17.9	E (Very Weak)

2000 cont'd

Institution	Headquarters	Industry	Date of Failure	Total Assets ($Mil)	Weiss Safety Rating
Superior National Ins Co	California	P&C	03/03/00	222.1	D (Weak)
Superior Pacific Casualty Co	California	P&C	03/03/00	93.4	D (Weak)
Total Health Care Inc	Ohio	HMO	07/26/00	18.0	C- (Fair)
Trust Assurance Co	Massachusetts	P&C	02/10/00	20.8	D+ (Weak)
Trust Ins Co	Massachusetts	P&C	02/10/00	151.2	C- (Fair)
Union American Ins Co	Florida	P&C	03/10/00	37.7	D (Weak)
Unistar Ins Co	Texas	P&C	05/22/00	7.2	D- (Weak)

State Insurance Commissioners' Departmental Contact Information

State	Official's Title	Website Address	Phone Number
Alabama	Insurance Commissioner	www.aldoi.org/	(334) 269-3550
Alaska	Director of Insurance	www.dced.state.ak.us/insurance/	(907) 465-2515
Arizona	Director of Insurance	www.state.az.us/id/	(800) 325-2548
Arkansas	Insurance Commissioner	www.state.ar.us/insurance/	(800) 282-9134
California	Bureau Chief	www.insurance.ca.gov/docs/index.html	(800) 927-4357
Colorado	Insurance Commissioner	www.dora.state.co.us/insurance/	(303) 894-7499
Connecticut	Insurance Commissioner	www.state.ct.us/cid/	(860) 297-3800
Delaware	Insurance Commissioner	www.state.de.us/inscom/	(302) 739-4251
Dist. of Columbia	Superintendent of Insurance	disr.washingtondc.gov/main.shtm	(202) 727-8000
Florida	Insurance Commissioner	www.fldfs.com	(800) 342-2762
Georgia	Insurance Commissioner	www.gainsurance.org/	(800) 656-2298
Hawaii	Insurance Commissioner	www.state.hi.us/dcca/ins/	(808) 586-2790
Idaho	Acting Director	www.doi.state.id.us/	(208) 334-4250
Illinois	Director of Insurance	www.ins.state.il.us/	(217) 782-4515
Indiana	Insurance Commissioner	www.ai.org/idoi/index.html	(317) 232-2385
Iowa	Insurance Commissioner	www.iid.state.ia.us/	(515) 281-5705
Kansas	Insurance Commissioner	www.ksinsurance.org/	(785) 296-3071
Kentucky	Insurance Commissioner	www.doi.state.ky.us/kentucky/	(800) 595-6053
Louisiana	Insurance Commissioner	www.ldi.la.gov/	(225) 342-0895
Maine	Superintendent of Insurance	www.state.me.us/pfr/ins/ins_index.htm	(207) 624-8475
Maryland	Insurance Commissioner	www.mdinsurance.state.md.us/	(800) 492-6116
Massachusetts	Insurance Commissioner	www.state.ma.us/doi/	(617) 521-7777
Michigan	Commissioner of Insurance	www.michigan.gov/cis	(517) 373-9273
Minnesota	Commissioner of Commerce	www.commerce.state.mn.us/	(651) 296-2488
Mississippi	Insurance Commissioner	www.doi.state.ms.us/	(601) 359-3569
Missouri	Director of Insurance	www.insurance.state.mo.us/	(573) 751-4126
Montana	Insurance Commissioner	sao.state.mt.us/	(406) 444-2040
Nebraska	Director of Insurance	www.nol.org/home/NDOI/	(402) 471-2201
Nevada	Insurance Commissioner	doi.state.nv.us/	(775) 687-4270
New Hampshire	Insurance Commissioner	www.state.nh.us/insurance/	(603) 271-2261
New Jersey	Commissioner of Insurance	www.state.nj.us/dobi/index.shtml	(609) 292-5360
New Mexico	Superintendent of Insurance	www.nmprc.state.nm.us/insurance/inshm.htm	(505) 827-4601
New York	Superintendent of Insurance	www.ins.state.ny.us/	(212) 480-6400
North Carolina	Insurance Commissioner	www.ncdoi.com/	(919) 733-2032
North Dakota	Insurance Commissioner	www.state.nd.us/ndins/	(701) 328-2440
Ohio	Insurance Commissioner	www.ohioinsurance.gov/	(800) 686-1526
Oklahoma	Insurance Commissioner	www.oid.state.ok.us/	(405) 521-2828
Oregon	Insurance Commissioner	www.cbs.state.or.us/external/ins/index.html	(503) 947-7980
Pennsylvania	Insurance Commissioner	www.insurance.state.pa.us/	(717) 783-0442
Puerto Rico	Commissioner of Insurance	www.ocs.gobierno.pr/	(787) 722-8686
Rhode Island	Insurance Commissioner	www.dbr.state.ri.us/	(401) 222-2223
South Carolina	Division Director	www.doi.state.sc.us/	(803) 737-6160
South Dakota	Director of Insurance	www.state.sd.us/dcr/insurance/	(605) 773-3563
Tennessee	Insurance Commissioner	www.state.tn.us/commerce/	(615) 741-6007
Texas	Insurance Commissioner	www.tdi.state.tx.us/	(512) 463-6169
Utah	Insurance Commissioner	www.insurance.utah.gov/	(801) 538-3800
Vermont	Insurance Commissioner	www.bishca.state.vt.us/	(802) 828-3301
Virgin Islands	Insurance Commissioner	www.usvi.org/	(340) 773-3130
Virginia	Insurance Commissioner	www.state.va.us/scc/division/boi/index.htm	(804) 371-9741
Washington	Insurance Commissioner	www.insurance.wa.gov/	(800) 562-6900
West Virginia	Insurance Commissioner	www.state.wv.us/insurance/	(304) 558-3354
Wisconsin	Insurance Commissioner	oci.wi.gov/oci_home.htm	(608) 266-3585
Wyoming	Insurance Commissioner	insurance.state.wy.us/	(307) 777-7401

Glossary

This glossary contains the most important terms used in this publication.

Admitted Assets The total of all investments and business interests that are acceptable under statutory accounting rules.

Asset/Liability Matching The designation of particular investments (assets) to particular policy obligations (liabilities) so that investments mature at the appropriate times and with appropriate yields to meet policy obligations as they come due.

Asset Valuation Reserve (AVR) A liability established under statutory accounting rules whose purpose is to protect the company's surplus from the effects of defaults and market value fluctuation on stocks, bonds, mortgages, and real estate. This replaces the Mandatory Securities Valuation Reserve (MSVR) and is more comprehensive in that it includes a mortgage loss reserve, whereas the MSVR did not.

Average Recession A recession involving a decline in real GDP which is approximately equivalent to the average of the postwar recessions of 1957-58, 1960, 1970, 1974-75, 1980, and 1981-82. It is assumed, however, that in today's market, the financial losses suffered from a recession of that magnitude would be greater than those experienced in previous decades. (See also "Severe Recession.")

Capital Strictly speaking, capital refers to funds raised through the sale of common and preferred stock. Mutual companies have capital in the form of retained earnings. In a more general sense, the term capital is commonly used to refer to a company's equity or net worth, that is, the difference between assets and liabilities (i.e., capital and surplus as shown on the balance sheet).

Capital Resources The sum of various resources which serve as a capital cushion to losses, including capital, surplus, and Asset Valuation Reserve (AVR).

Capitalization Index An index, expressed on a scale of zero to ten, with seven or higher considered excellent, that measures the adequacy of the company's capital resources to deal with a variety of business and economic scenarios. It combines Risk-Adjusted Capital Ratios #1 and #2 as well as a leverage test that examines pricing risk.

Cash and Demand Deposits Includes cash on hand and on deposit. A negative figure indicates that the company has more checks outstanding than current funds to cover those checks. This is not an unusual situation for an insurance company.

Collateralized Mortgage Obligation (CMO)	Mortgage-backed bond that splits the payments from mortgage pools into different classes, called tranches. The investor may purchase a bond or tranche that passes through to him or her the principal and interest payments made by the mortgage holders in that specific maturity class (usually two, five, 10, or 20 years). The risk associated with a CMO is in the variation of the payment speed on the mortgage pool which, if different than originally assumed, can cause the total return to vary greatly.
Common and Preferred Stocks	See "Stocks".
Deposit Funds	Accumulated contributions of a group out of which immediate annuities are purchased as the individual members of the group retire.
Direct Premiums Written	Total gross premiums derived from policies issued directly by the company. This figure excludes the impact of reinsurance.
Five-Year Profitability Index	See "Profitability Index."
Government Securities	Securities issued and/or guaranteed by U.S. and foreign governments which are rated as highest quality (Class 1) by state insurance commissioners. Included in this category are bonds issued by governmental agencies and guaranteed with the full faith and credit of the government. Regardless of the issuing entity, they are viewed as being relatively safer than the other investment categories. See "Investment Grade Bonds" to determine which items are excluded from this category.
Health Claims Reserve	Funds set aside from premiums for the eventual payment of health benefits after the end of the statement year.
Insurance Risk	The risk that the level of claims and related expenses will exceed current premiums plus reserves allocated for their payment.
Interest Rate Risk	The risk that, due to changes in interest rates, investment income will not meet the needs of policy commitments. This risk can be reduced by effective asset/liability matching.
Invested Assets	The total size of the firm's investment portfolio.
Investment Grade Bonds	This covers all investment grade bonds other than those listed in "Government Securities" (above). Specifically, this includes: (1) nonguaranteed obligations of governments, (2) obligations of governments rated as Class 2 by state insurance commissioners, (3) state and municipal bonds, plus (4) investment grade corporate bonds.
Investment Safety Index	Measured on a scale of zero to ten, with ten being the best and seven or better considered strong. Each investment area is rated as to quality and vulnerability during an unfavorable economic environment (updated using quarterly data when available).

Glossary

Investments in Affiliates	Includes bonds, preferred stocks, and common stocks, as well as other vehicles which many insurance companies use to invest in—and establish a corporate link with—affiliated companies.
Life and Annuity Claims Reserve	Funds set aside from premiums for the eventual payment of life and annuity claims.
Liquidity Index	An index, expressed on a scale from zero to ten, with seven or higher considered excellent, which measures the company's ability to raise the necessary cash to meet policyholder obligations. This index includes a stress test which considers the consequences of a spike in claims or a run on policy surrenders. Sometimes a company may appear to have the necessary resources, but may be unable to sell its investments at the prices at which they are valued in the company's financial statements.
Mandatory Security Valuation Reserve (MSVR)	Reserve for investment losses and asset value fluctuation mandated by the state insurance commissioners for companies registered as life and health insurers. As of December 31, 1992, this was replaced by the Asset Valuation Reserve. HMDI companies are not required to establish such a reserve.
Moderate Loss Scenario	An economic decline from current levels approximately equivalent to that of the average postwar recession.
Mortgages in Good Standing	Mortgages which are current in their payments (excludes mortgage-backed securities).
Net Premiums Written	The total dollar volume of premiums retained by the company. This figure is equal to direct premiums written, plus reinsurance assumed less reinsurance ceded.
Noninvestment Grade Bonds	Low-rated issues, commonly known as "junk bonds," which carry a high risk as defined by the state insurance commissioners. These include bond Classes 3 - 6.
Nonperforming Mortgages	Mortgages which are (a) 90 days or more past due or (b) in process of foreclosure.
Other Investments	Items not included in any of the other categories such as premium notes, collateral loans, short-term investments and other miscellaneous items.
Other Structured Securities	Nonresidential-mortgage-related and other securitized loan-backed or asset-backed securities. This category also includes CMOs with noninvestment grade ratings.
Policy Leverage	A measure of insurance risk based on the relationship of net premiums to capital resources.
Policy Loans	Loans to policyholders under insurance contracts.

Profitability Index	Measured on a scale of zero to ten, with ten being the best and seven or better considered strong. A composite of five factors: (1) gain or loss on operations, (2) consistency of operating results, (3) impact of operating results on surplus, (4) adequacy of investment income as compared to the needs of policy reserves, and (5) expenses in relation to industry averages. Thus, the overall index is an indicator of the health of a company's current and past operations.
Purchase Money Mortgages	Mortgages written by an insurance company to facilitate the sale of property owned by the company.
Real Estate	Direct real estate investments including property (a) occupied by the company, (b) acquired through foreclosure and (c) purchased as an investment.
Reinsurance Assumed	Insurance risk acquired by taking on partial or full responsibility for claims on policies written by other companies. (See "Reinsurance Ceded.")
Reinsurance Ceded	Insurance risk sold to another company.
Risk-Adjusted Capital	The capital resources that would be needed in a worsening economic environment (same as "Target Capital").
Risk-Adjusted Capital Ratio #1	The capital resources which a company currently has, in relation to the resources that would be needed to deal with a moderate loss scenario. This scenario is based on historical experience during an average recession and adjusted to reflect current conditions and vulnerabilities (updated using quarterly data when available).
Risk-Adjusted Capital Ratio #2	The capital resources which a company currently has, in relation to the resources that would be needed to deal with a severe loss scenario. This scenario is based on historical experience of the postwar period and adjusted to reflect current conditions and the potential impact of a severe recession (updated using quarterly data when available).
Safety Rating	Weiss Safety Ratings grade insurers on a scale from A (Excellent) to F (Failed). Ratings are based on five major factors: investment safety, policy leverage, capitalization, profitability, and stability of operations.
Separate Accounts	Funds segregated from the general account and valued at market. Used to fund indexed products, such as variable life and variable annuity products.
Severe Loss Scenario	An economic decline from current levels in which the loss experience of the single worst year of the postwar period is extended for a period of three years. (See also "Moderate Loss Scenario" above.)
Severe Recession	A prolonged economic slowdown in which the single worst year of the postwar period is extended for a period of three years. (See also "Average Recession" above.)
Stability Index	Measured on a scale of zero to ten. This integrates a wide variety of factors that reflects the company's financial stability and diversification of risk.

Glossary

State of Domicile Although most insurance companies are licensed to do business in many states, they have only one state of domicile. This is the state that has primary regulatory responsibility for the company. Use the state of domicile to make absolutely sure that you have the correct company. Bear in mind, however, that this need not be the state where the company's main offices are located.

State Guaranty Funds Funds that are designed to raise cash from existing insurance carriers to cover policy claims of bankrupt insurance companies.

Stocks Common and preferred equities, including ownership in affiliates.

Surplus The difference between assets and liabilities, including paid-in contributed surplus, plus the statutory equivalent of "retained earnings" in noninsurance business corporations.

Target Capital See "Risk-Adjusted Capital."

Total Assets Total admitted assets, including investments and other business assets. See "Admitted Assets."

Other Weiss Ratings Products

FOR UPDATES AND FURTHER INFORMATION: Fill out the order form on the next page, call us toll free at (800) 289-9222 or vist www.WeissRatings.com. Weiss Ratings offers the following products and services to choose from:

- **Ratings Online.** An on-line summary covering an individual company's Weiss rating and the factors contributing to the rating; available 24-hours a day by visiting www.WeissRatings.com. Price: $7.95

- **Ratings Over the Phone.** Call (800) 289-9222 to receive a company's rating over the telephone. Price: $15

- **Rating Analysis Report.** A detailed report on an individual company including the company's rating and an in-depth analysis of each of the factors contributing to the rating. Price: $45 plus $4.95 S/H.

- **Weiss Watchdog Service.** An immediate notification service announcing any changes in a company's rating, plus a quarterly rating update. Price: from $12 per company

- **Shopper's Guide to Long-Term Care Insurance.** Price comparisons for long-term care insurance based on your age, gender, and location. Long-term care policies are grouped based on comparable benefit features, followed by a complete list of each policy's benefits. Price: $45 plus $4.95 S/H.

- **Shopper's Guide to Medicare Supplement Insurance.** Price comparisons for Medigap insurance based on your age, gender, and zip code. Insurance companies are listed by Weiss rating to provide price and safety comparisons. Price: $45 plus $4.95 S/H.

- **Insurance Monitor Report.** A detailed, customized report containing insurance companies and/or HMOs you select. Included is a comprehensive financial analysis of each company and its Weiss Safety Rating, along with a list of Weiss Recommended Companies licensed to do business in your state. Price: starting at $75

- **Guide to Medical Malpractice Insurers.** Comprehensive ratings and analyses on the nation's medical malpractice insurers, making it easy to compare companies or shop for coverage. Includes a list of recommended insurers by state. Price: $85 plus $7.95 S/H.

- **Guide to Workers' Compensation Insurers.** Comprehensive ratings and analyses on the nation's workers' compensation insurers, making it easy to compare companies or shop for coverage. Includes a list of recommended insurers by state. Price: $85 plus $7.95 S/H.

- **Guide to Reinsurance Companies.** A comprehensive compilation of ratings and analysis providing insight into the financial safety of the nation's reinsurance companies. Also included are lists showing how much premium is assumed by line of business for each company. Price: $85 plus $7.95 S/H.

- **Guide to S&P 500 Stocks.** An in-depth review and analysis of the risk and performance of every S&P 500 stock. Includes rating commentary, charts and graphs. Price: $85 plus $7.95 S/H.

- **Top-Rated Stocks.** This monthly service highlights the cream of the investment crop with a complete list of those stocks receiving our highest Weiss Investment Ratings. Weiss' top-rated stocks averaged a positive 8.63% return in 2002, beating the broad market loss of -22.15. Price: $159 (plus $14.95 S/H) for a monthly subscription (12 issues) or $55 (plus $4.95 S/H) per single issue.

- **Weiss Ratings' Guides.** Issued quarterly, these Guides include ratings for all companies covered by Weiss, plus detailed explanations of the factors and ratios contributing to the ratings. Also included are lists of companies receiving Weiss' highest and lowest ratings. Price: $438 (plus $19.95 S/H) for a quarterly subscription to any one guide, or $219 (plus $8.95 S/H) for a single edition.

  - **Guide to Life, Health, and Annuity Insurers** covering more than 1,500 U.S. life, health and annuity insurers.

  - **Guide to Property and Casualty Insurers** covering more than 2,500 property and casualty insurers in the U.S.

  - **Guide to HMOs and Health Insurers** is the only source covering more than 1,200 U.S. health insurers including all Blue Cross/Blue Shield plans and over 500 HMOs.

  - **Guide to Banks and Thrifts** covering more than 9,000 banks and thrifts in the U.S.

  - **Guide to Brokerage Firms** is the only source covering the 600 largest U.S. stock brokers and dealers, including full service, discount, and online firms.

  - **Guide to Stock Mutual Funds** covering more than 7,000 equity mutual funds, including balanced funds, international funds, and individual sector funds

  - **Guide to Bond and Money Market Mutual Funds** covering more than 4,200 fixed income mutual funds, including government bond funds, municipal bond funds, and corporate bond funds.

  - **Guide to Closed-End Mutual Funds** covering more than 600 closed-end mutual funds, including growth funds, sector funds, international funds, municipal bond funds and other closed-end funds.

  - **Guide to Common Stocks** covering every single stock on the American Stock Exchange, New York Stock Exchange, and the NASDAQ, plus more.

Weiss Ratings Product Order Form

☐ **Weiss Ratings' Guides:**

____ Guide to Life, Health & Annuity Insurers	____ Guide to Brokerage Firms
____ Guide to Property & Casualty Insurers	____ Guide to Stock Mutual Funds
____ Guide to HMOs and Health Insurers	____ Guide to Bond & Money Market Mutual Funds
____ Guide to Banks and Thrifts	____ Guide to Common Stocks
____ Guide to Closed-End Mutual Funds	

Pricing for above Guides is $438 (plus $19.95 S/H) for a quarterly subscription (4 editions), or $219 (plus $8.95 S/H) per single edition

____ **Top-Rated Stocks**

Pricing for Service is $159 (plus $14.95 S/H) for a monthly subscription (12 issues), or $55 (plus $4.95 S/H) per single issue.

Guide to Medical Malpractice Insurers	____ $85 per edition plus $7.95 S/H
Guide to Workers' Compensation Insurers	____ $85 per edition plus $7.95 S/H
Guide to Reinsurance Companies	____ $85 per edition plus $7.95 S/H
Guide to S&P 500 Stocks	____ $85 per edition plus $7.95 S/H

☐ **Ratings Analysis Report:** $45 plus $4.95 S/H

Please specify the full name, city and state for each bank or S&L desired. For insurance companies, only the name and state of domicile are needed. For brokerage firms and stocks the full name is sufficient.

Company:_____ City:_____ State:____

☐ **Weiss Watchdog Service:** $12 per quarter for first company, $10 per quarter for each additional company.

Please specify the full name, city and state for each bank or S&L desired. For insurance companies, only the name and state of domicile are needed. For brokerage firms, stocks, and mutual funds the full name is sufficient.

Company:_____ City:_____ State:____

☐ **Shopper's Guide to Long-Term Care Insurance:** $45 plus $4.95 S/H

    Date of Birth: _____ State: _____

☐ **Shopper's Guide to Medicare Supplement Insurance:** $45 plus $4.95 S/H

    Date of Birth: _____ Gender: ____ Zip:_____ County:_____

☐ My check is enclosed in the amount of $ _____.

Florida residents, please add 6% sales tax. Non U.S. residents add an additional $20 for postage and handling.

☐ **MC**   ☐ **VISA**   ☐ **AMEX**   ☐ **DISC**   ☐☐☐☐☐☐☐☐☐☐☐☐☐☐☐☐ Exp. Date _____

Signature: _____

   Mr.   Mrs.   Ms.   Name:_____

Address: _____

City, State, Zip: _____

Phone: _____ E-Mail address: _____

For faster service, call our Customer Hotline at (800) 289-9222
www.WeissRatings.com

Return this form to: **Weiss Ratings, Inc., P.O. Box 109665, Palm Beach Gardens, FL 33410**